Fodor's 2003

Mexico

The Guide for All Budgets

Completely Updated

Where to Stay, Eat, and Explore

On and Off the Beaten Path

When to Go, What to Pack

Maps, Travel Tips, and Web Sites

Fodor's Travel Publications • New York, Toronto, London, Sydney, Auckland
www.fodors.com

Fodor's Mexico

EDITOR: Tania Inowlocki

Editorial Contributors: Rob Aikins, Patricia Alisau, Nuha Ansari, Paige Bierma, Paul Davidson, Satu Hummasti, Barbara Kastelein, Denise M. Leto, Amy Mansell, Shelagh McNally, Maribeth Mellin, Jane Onstott, Jennifer Paull, Kate Rice, Michael de Zayas
Editorial Production: Kristin Milavec
Maps: David Lindroth, *cartographer;* Rebecca Baer and Robert Blake, *map editors*
Design: Fabrizio La Rocca, *creative director;* Guido Caroti, *art director;* Jolie Novak, *senior picture editor;* Melanie Marin, *photo editor*
Cover Design: Pentagram
Production/Manufacturing: Yexenia (Jessie) Markland
Cover Photo (abandoned amusement park, Cancun): Joan Iaconetti

Copyright

ISBN 1-4000-1034-9

ISSN 0196-5999

Important Tip

Although all prices, opening times, and other details in this book are based on information supplied to us at press time, changes occur all the time in the travel world, and Fodor's cannot accept responsibility for facts that become outdated or for inadvertent errors or omissions. So **always confirm information when it matters,** especially if you're making a detour to visit a specific place.

Special Sales

Fodor's Travel Publications are available at special discounts for bulk purchases for sales promotions or premiums. Special editions, including personalized covers, excerpts of existing guides, and corporate imprints, can be created in large quantities for special needs. For more information, contact your local bookseller or write to Special Markets, Fodor's Travel Publications, 280 Park Avenue, New York, NY 10017. Inquiries from Canada should be directed to your local Canadian bookseller or sent to Random House of Canada, Ltd., Marketing Department, 2775 Matheson Boulevard East, Mississauga, Ontario L4W 4P7. Inquiries from the United Kingdom should be sent to Fodor's Travel Publications, 20 Vauxhall Bridge Road, London SW1V 2SA, England.

PRINTED IN THE UNITED STATES OF AMERICA

10 9 8 7 6 5 4 3 2 1

CONTENTS

Maps

ON THE ROAD WITH FODOR'S

A TRIP TAKES YOU OUT OF YOURSELF. Concerns of life at home completely disappear, driven away by more immediate thoughts—about, say, what marvels will beguile the next day, or where you'll have dinner. That's where Fodor's comes in. We make sure that you know all your options, so that you don't miss something that's around the next bend just because you didn't know it was there. Mindful that the best memories of your trip might have nothing to do with what you came to Mexico to see, we guide you to sights large and small all over the country. You might set out to hit the beach, but back at home you find yourself unable to forget spotting a gray whale or getting caught up in a marimba at a village *zócalo*. With Fodor's at your side, serendipitous discoveries are never far away.

About Our Writers

Our success in showing you every corner of Mexico is a credit to our extraordinary writers. Although there's no substitute for travel advice from a good friend who knows your style, our contributors are the next best thing—the kind of people you *would* poll for travel advice if you knew them.

San Diego writer **Rob Aikins,** who updated the Pacific Coast Resorts chapter, developed a love for the people and culture of Mexico while traveling the Baja and Pacific coasts looking for surfing spots. He later complemented those experiences by attending the Universidad Nacional Autónoma de México (UNAM) in Mexico City and conducting research in various parts of the country. He recently filmed a documentary in Northern Baja California. He has been an editorial contributor to Fodor's *San Diego* and *Brazil* titles.

So drawn to the surrealism of Mexico that she turned a one-week vacation into a 20-year sojourn, **Patricia Alisau** has traveled just about every inch of the country on assignment for Mexican and U.S. journals. She has written for Mexico's *Vogue* magazine and, as a foreign correspondent, for the *New York Times,* the *Chicago Tribune,* and the Associated Press. This year, she updated our Acapulco chapter and sections of the Yucatán Peninsula chapter.

Journalist **Paige Bierma,** who updated this edition's Smart Travel Tips and Background and Essentials, lived in Mexico City for four years while reporting on Mexican politics and social issues for the Associated Press and various Texas- and California-based newspapers. She's now freelancing in San Francisco, though she left her heart in Mexico City.

Writer and teacher **Paul Davidson** has traveled all over Mexico; for this edition, he covered Guadalajara. He has also contributed to Fodor's *China.*

Barbara Kastelein made her way to Latin America from Holland via Great Britain, under whose gray skies she obtained a doctorate in literary studies. A freelance writer with special interests in travel, environment, politics, and gastronomy, she has been living in Mexico's smoggy and sinful capital for seven years. She enjoys her colorful country of choice with her partner and two children. For this edition, Barbara updated the Mexico City, Side Trips from Mexico City, and Veracruz and the Northeast chapters.

Berkeley-based **Denise M. Leto,** who edited parts of this book, longs to leave the rains of Northern California behind for a spin through the tropics of Mexico. In the meantime, she seeks consolation at her favorite Mexican restaurant. Her own work has appeared on-line, in the *San Francisco Bay Guardian,* and in many a Fodor's guidebook.

A decade after her first trip to Morelia, **Amy Mansell** plunged into the heart of Mexico and found a life of writing, travel, and adventure in colorful San Miguel de Allende. She's currently working on a collection of short stories that include a famous street dog named Lupita. Amy updated the Heartland chapter for this edition.

Recipient of the prestigious Pluma de Plata award for writing on Mexico, **Maribeth Mellin** lives in San Diego near the Tijuana border in a home filled with folk art and photos from Latin America—including a snapshot of the 140-pound marlin she caught in the Sea of Cortez. She has authored travel books on Mexico, Costa Rica, Argentina, and Peru and is currently creating a fictional account of her adventures. Maribeth updated this year's Baja California chapter.

Since earning a B.A. in Spanish language and literature, **Jane Onstott** has lived and traveled extensively in Latin America. She worked as director of communications and information for the Darwin Research Station in the Galapagos Islands, and studied painting in Oaxaca between 1995 and 1998. Since 1986 Jane has contributed to Fodor's guides to Mexico and South America; this year, she updated the Sonora, Copper Canyon, and Oaxaca chapters.

Michael de Zayas, a Cuban-American writer who lives in New York, covered Chiapas and Tabasco for this edition. Since earning his M.F.A. in poetry from Sarah Lawrence College, he has lived in Mexico City, Berlin, Barcelona, Madrid, Miami Beach, and Weaverville, North Carolina. Michael has written first edition Fodor's guides to Spain, Chile, and Central America, and contributed to several other Fodor's titles, including *Cuba, Caribbean, Bahamas, South America, Argentina, New York City,* and *Florida.*

We'd also like to acknowledge Mexicana for its considerable assistance with travel arrangements.

You can rest assured that you're in good hands—and that no property mentioned in the book has paid to be included. Each has been selected strictly on its merits, as the best of its type in its price range.

How to Use This Book

Up front is Smart Travel Tips A to Z, arranged alphabetically by topic and loaded with tips, Web sites, and contact information. Destination: Mexico helps get you in the mood for your trip. All city chapters begin with exploring information, with a section for each neighborhood (each recommending a good tour and listing sights alphabetically). All regional chapters are divided geographically; within each area, towns are covered in logical geographical order, and attractive stretches of road between them are indicated by the designation *En Route.* To help you decide what you'll have time to visit, all chapters begin with our writers' favorite itineraries. (Mix itineraries from several chapters, and you can put together a really exceptional trip.) The A to Z section that ends every chapter lists additional resources. At the end of the book you'll find Background and Essentials, including Portraits, with an essay on Mexico's political and social transitions, followed by a chronology and suggested further reading.

Icons and Symbols

- ★ Our special recommendations
- ✕ Restaurant
- 🏨 Lodging establishment
- ✕🏨 Lodging establishment whose restaurant warrants a special trip
- ⛰ Archaeological site
- 🦆 Good for kids (rubber duck)
- ☞ Sends you to another section of the guide for more information
- ✉ Address
- ☎ Telephone number
- ⏲ Opening and closing times
- 🎟 Admission prices (those we give apply to adults; substantially reduced fees are almost always available for children, students, and senior citizens)

Numbers in white and black circles ③ ❸ that appear on the maps, in the margins, and within the tours correspond to one another.

For hotels, you can assume that all rooms have private baths, phones, TVs, and air-conditioning unless otherwise noted and that all hotels operate on the European Plan (with no meals) if we don't specify another meal plan. We always list a property's facilities but not whether you'll be charged extra to use them, so when pricing accommodations, do ask what's included. For restaurants, it's always a good idea to book ahead; we mention reservations only when they're essential or are not accepted. All restaurants we list are open daily for lunch and dinner unless stated otherwise; dress is mentioned only when men are required to wear a jacket or a jacket and tie. Look for an overview of local dining-out habits in Smart Travel Tips A to Z and in the Pleasures and Pastimes section that follows each chapter introduction.

Don't Forget to Write

Your experiences—positive and negative—matter to us. If we have missed or misstated something, we want to hear about it. We follow up on all suggestions. Contact the Mexico editor at editors@fodors.com or c/o Fodor's at 280 Park Avenue, New York, New York 10017. And have a fabulous trip!

Karen Cure

Karen Cure
Editorial Director

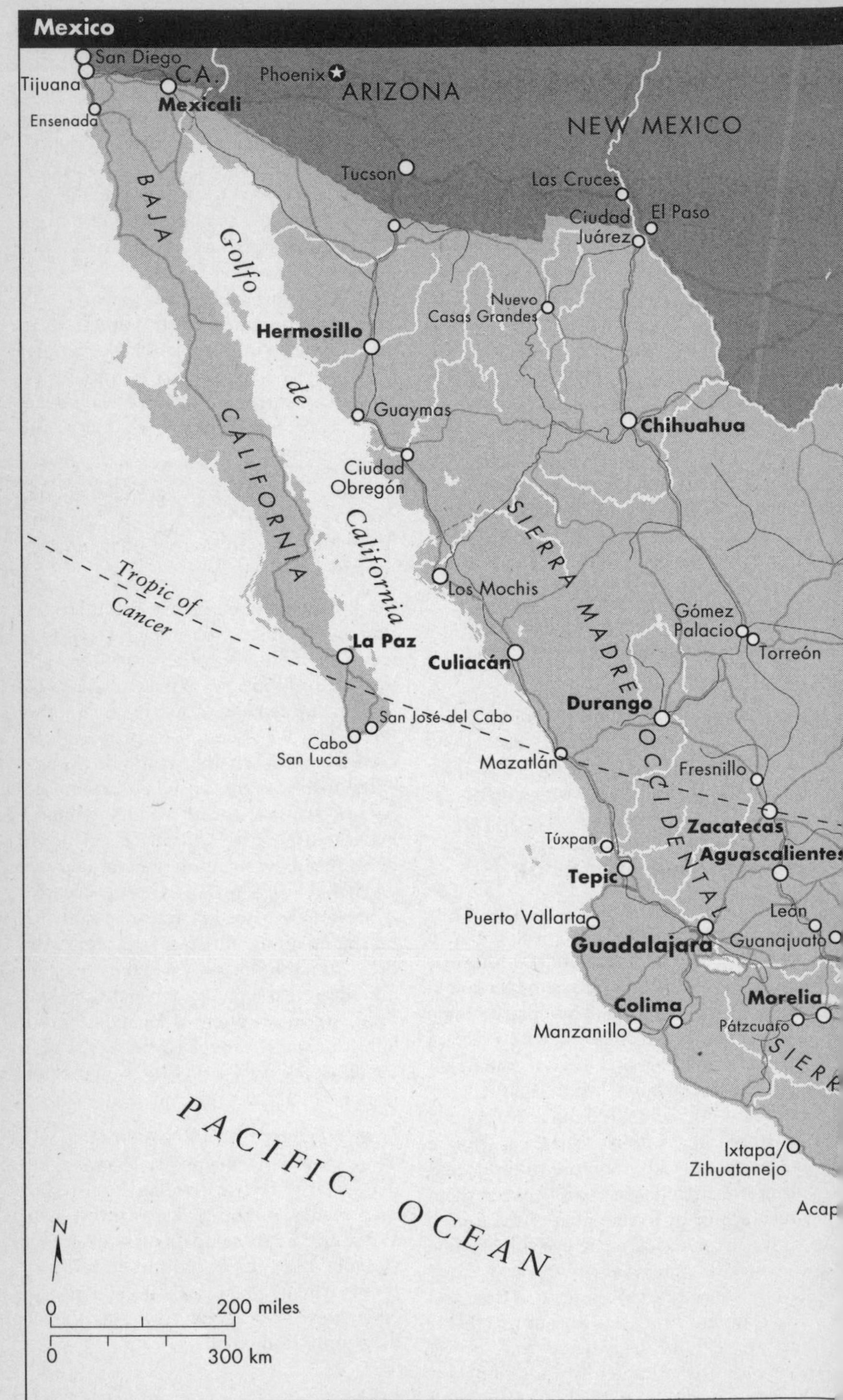
Mexico
San Diego
Tijuana
CA.
Mexicali
Ensenada
Phoenix
ARIZONA
NEW MEXICO
Tucson
Las Cruces
El Paso
Ciudad Juárez
BAJA CALIFORNIA
Golfo de California
Nuevo Casas Grandes
Hermosillo
Guaymas
Chihuahua
Ciudad Obregón
SIERRA MADRE OCCIDENTAL
Tropic of Cancer
Los Mochis
Gómez Palacio
Torreón
La Paz
Culiacán
Durango
San José del Cabo
Cabo San Lucas
Mazatlán
Fresnillo
Zacatecas
Túxpan
Aguascalientes
Tepic
León
Puerto Vallarta
Guadalajara
Guanajuato
Colima
Morelia
Manzanillo
Pátzcuaro
PACIFIC OCEAN
Ixtapa/ Zihuatanejo
N
0
200 miles
0
300 km

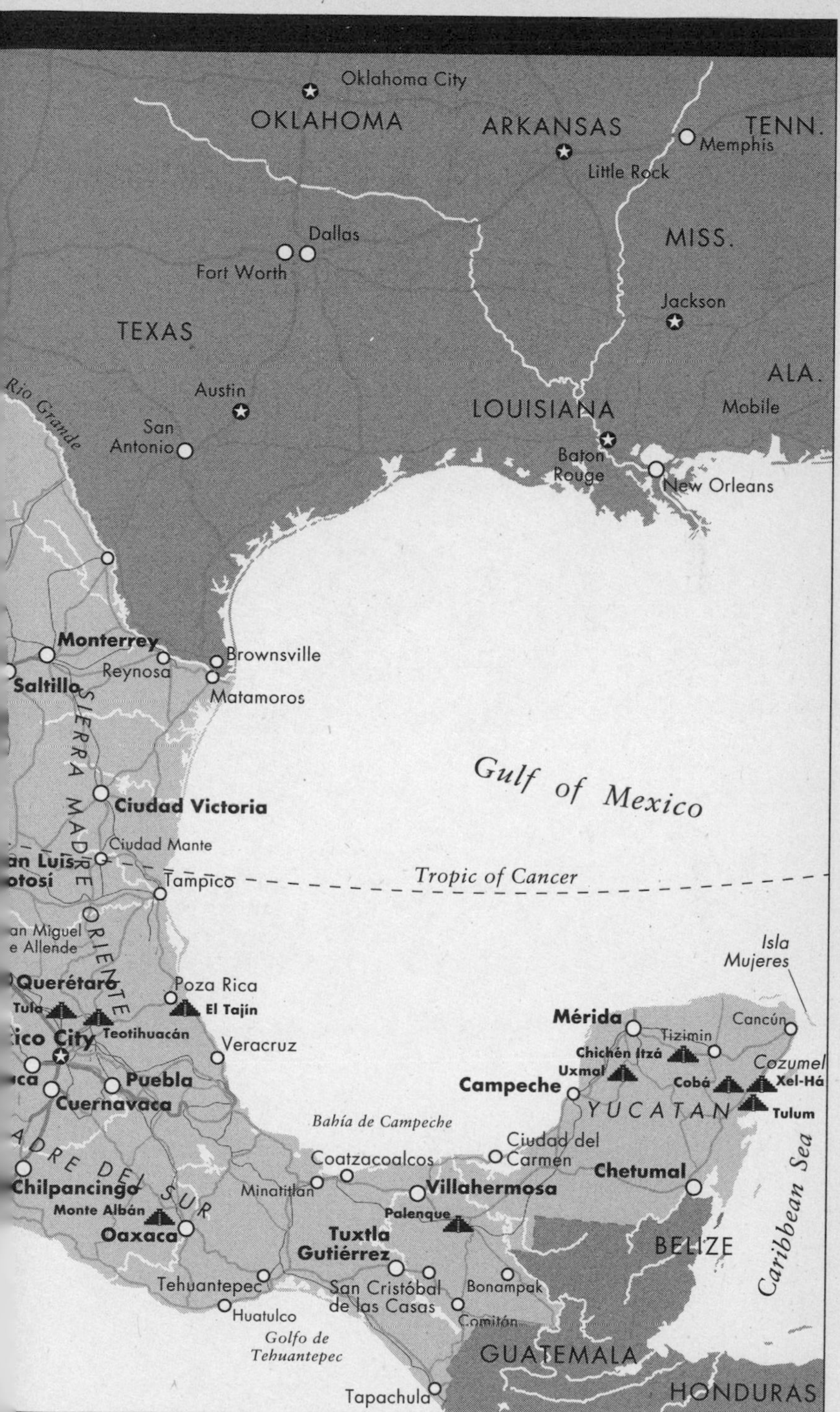
Oklahoma City
OKLAHOMA
ARKANSAS
TENN.
Memphis
Little Rock
Dallas
MISS.
Fort Worth
Jackson
TEXAS
ALA.
Rio Grande
Austin
LOUISIANA
Mobile
San Antonio
Baton Rouge
New Orleans
Monterrey
Brownsville
Reynosa
Saltillo
Matamoros
SIERRA MADRE ORIENTE
Gulf of Mexico
Ciudad Victoria
Ciudad Mante
Tampico
Tropic of Cancer
Isla Mujeres
Querétaro
Poza Rica
Tula
El Tajín
Teotihuacán
Mérida
Cancún
Tizimin
Veracruz
Chichén Itzá
Uxmal
Cozumel
Puebla
Campeche
Cobá
Xel-Há
Cuernavaca
YUCATAN
Tulum
Bahía de Campeche
Ciudad del Carmen
Coatzacoalcos
Chetumal
Chilpancingo
Minatitlan
Villahermosa
Monte Albán
Palenque
Oaxaca
Tuxtla Gutiérrez
BELIZE
Caribbean Sea
Tehuantepec
San Cristóbal de las Casas
Bonampak
Huatulco
Comitán
Golfo de Tehuantepec
GUATEMALA
Tapachula
HONDURAS

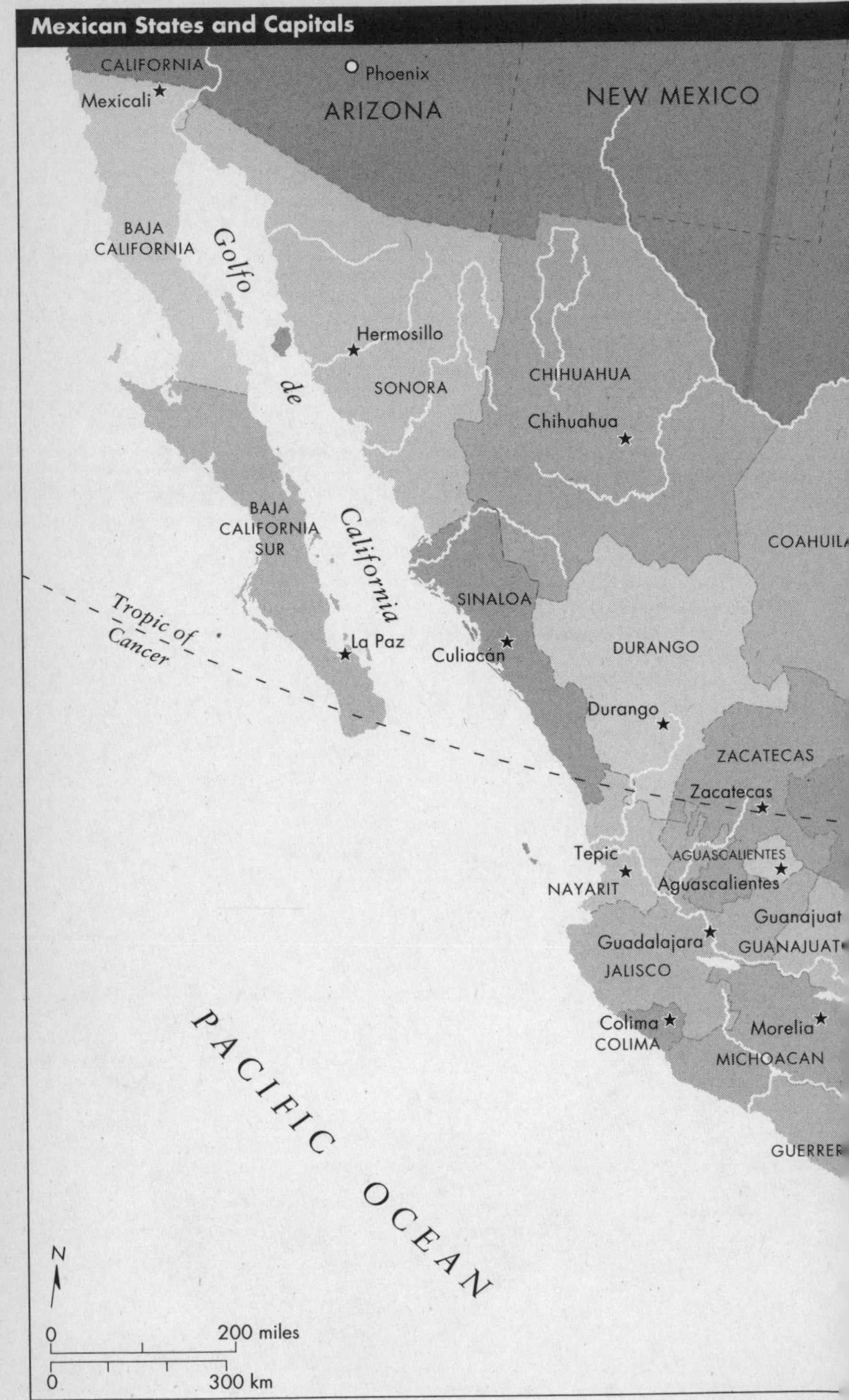
Mexican States and Capitals
CALIFORNIA
Mexicali
Phoenix
ARIZONA
NEW MEXICO
BAJA
CALIFORNIA
Golfo
de
California
Hermosillo
SONORA
CHIHUAHUA
Chihuahua
BAJA
CALIFORNIA
SUR
COAHUIL
SINALOA
Tropic of
Cancer
La Paz
Culiacán
DURANGO
Durango
ZACATECAS
Zacatecas
Tepic
AGUASCALIENTES
NAYARIT
Aguascalientes
Guanajuat
Guadalajara
GUANAJUAT
JALISCO
Colima
COLIMA
Morelia
MICHOACAN
PACIFIC OCEAN
GUERRER
N
0
200 miles
0
300 km

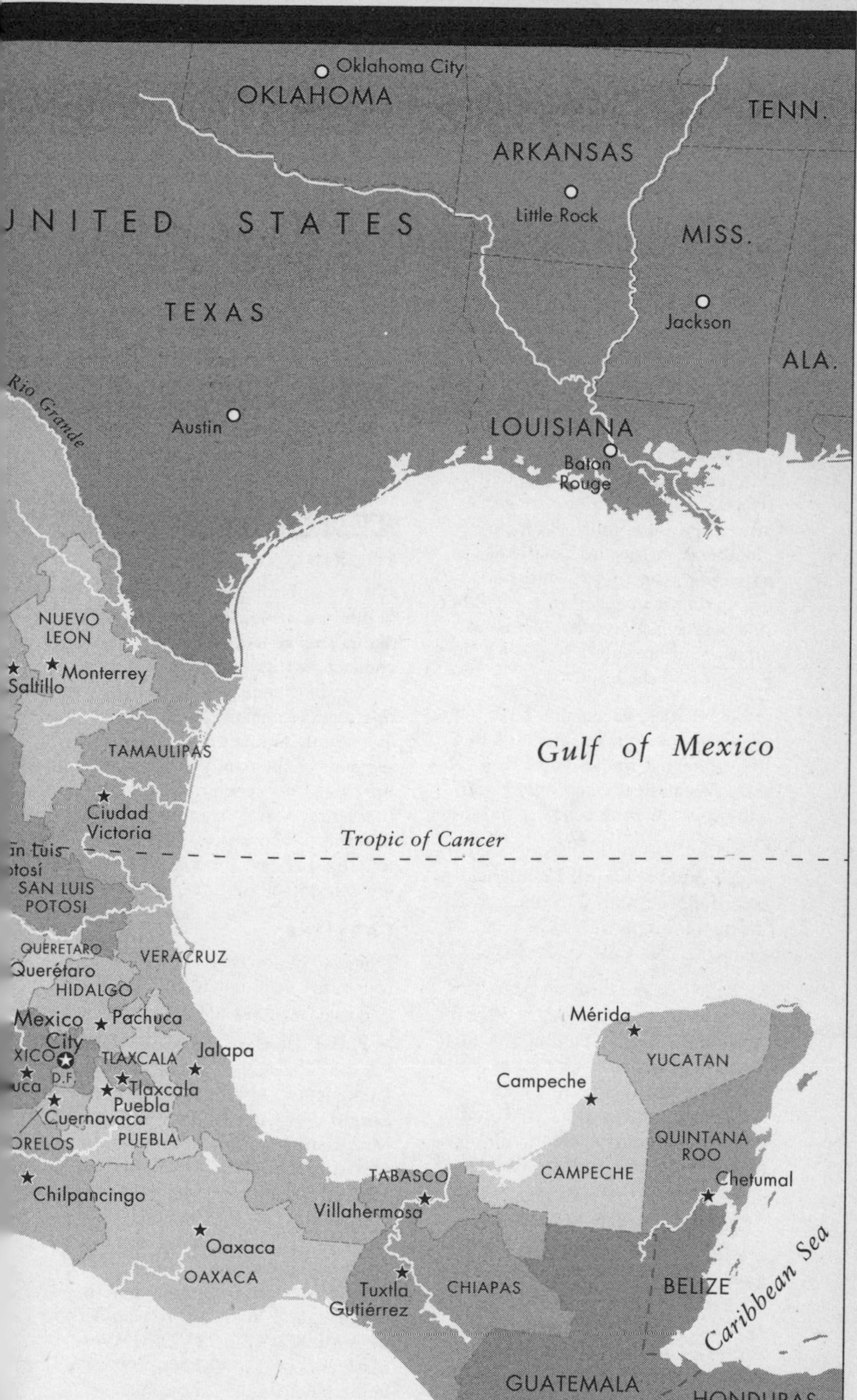
Oklahoma City
OKLAHOMA
TENN.
ARKANSAS
Little Rock
UNITED STATES
MISS.
TEXAS
Jackson
ALA.
Rio Grande
Austin
LOUISIANA
Baton Rouge
NUEVO LEON
Monterrey
Saltillo
TAMAULIPAS
Gulf of Mexico
Ciudad Victoria
Tropic of Cancer
SAN LUIS POTOSI
QUERETARO
Querétaro
VERACRUZ
HIDALGO
Mexico City
Pachuca
Mérida
TLAXCALA
Jalapa
YUCATAN
D.F.
Tlaxcala
Campeche
Puebla
Cuernavaca
PUEBLA
QUINTANA ROO
CAMPECHE
TABASCO
Chetumal
Chilpancingo
Villahermosa
Oaxaca
OAXACA
Tuxtla Gutiérrez
CHIAPAS
BELIZE
Caribbean Sea
GUATEMALA
HONDURAS

ESSENTIAL INFORMATION

ADDRESSES

The Mexican method of naming streets can be exasperatingly arbitrary, so **be patient when searching for street addresses.** Streets in the centers of many colonial cities (those built by the Spanish) are laid out in a grid surrounding the *zócalo* (main square) and often change names on different sides of the square. Other streets simply acquire a new name after a certain number of blocks. Numbered streets are usually designated *norte/sur* (north/south) or *oriente/poniente* (east/west) on either side of a central avenue. (Three of these are abbreviated: Nte., Ote., and Pte. Sur is spelled out.)

In many cities, streets that have proper names, such as Avenida Benito Juárez, change names when they cross some other street—and only a map will show where one begins and the other ends.

Blocks are often labeled numerically, according to distance from a chosen starting point, as in "la Calle de Pachuca," "2a Calle de Pachuca," etc.

Many Mexican addresses have "s/n" for *sin número* (no number) after the street name. This is common in small towns where there aren't many buildings on a block. Similarly, many hotels give their address as "Km 30 Carr. a Querétaro," which indicates that the property is at the 30th kilometer on the *carretera* (main highway) to Querétaro.

In Mexico City (and other cities), most addresses include their *colonia* (neighborhood), which is abbreviated as Col. Other abbreviations used in addresses include: Av. (*avenida,* or avenue); Calz. (*calzada,* or road); Fracc. (*fraccionamiento,* or housing estate); and Int. (interior).

Addresses in Mexico are written with the street name first, followed by the street number. A five-digit *código postal* (postal code) precedes, rather than follows, the name of the city. (Note that in this book, however, cities precede postal codes for the sake of clarity.) Apdo. (*apartado*) means box; Apdo. Postal, or A.P., means post-office box number. Here is a sample address: *Hacienda Paraíso, Calle Allende 211, 68000 Oaxaca, Oax.*

AIR TRAVEL

BOOKING

When you book **look for nonstop flights** and **remember that "direct" flights stop at least once.** Try to avoid connecting flights, which require a change of plane. Two airlines may operate a connecting flight jointly, so ask if your airline operates every segment of the trip; you may find that the carrier you prefer flies you only part of the way. For more booking tips and to check prices and make online flight reservations, log on to www.fodors.com.

CARRIERS

Domestic plane travel costs about four times as much as the bus, but it will save you considerable travel time.

➤ FROM THE U.S.: **AeroCalifornia** (☎ 800/237–6225) to Mexico City, Guadalajara, Hermosillo, La Paz, Loreto, Los Cabos, Manzanillo, Mazatlán, Monterrey, Tijuana. **Aeroméxico** (☎ 800/237–6639, WEB www.aeromexico.com) to Mexico City, Acapulco, Cancún, Cozumel, Guadalajara, Guaymas/San Carlos, Ixtapa/Zihuatanejo, León/El Bajío, Los Cabos, Mérida, Monterrey, Puerto Vallarta, and Veracruz. **Alaska Airlines** (☎ 800/426–0333, WEB www.alaskaair.com) to Cancún, Ixtapa/Zihuatanejo, Los Cabos, Puerto Vallarta. **America West** (☎ 800/235–9292, WEB www.americawest.com) to Mexico City, Acapulco, Guadalajara, Guaymas, Ixtapa/Zihuatanejo, Los

Cabos, Manzanillo, Mazatlán, Puerto Vallarta. **American** (☏ 800/433–7300, WEB www.aa.com) to Mexico City, Acapulco, Cancún, Guadalajara, León/El Bajío, Los Cabos, Monterrey, Puerto Vallarta. **Continental** (☏ 800/231–0856, WEB www.continental.com) to Acapulco, Mexico City, Cancún, Chihuahua City, Cozumel, Guadalajara, Ixtapa/Zihuatanejo, León/El Bajío, Los Cabos, Mazatlán, Mérida, Monterrey, Puerto Vallarta, Veracruz, Tampico. **Delta** (☏ 800/241–4141, WEB www.delta.com) to Mexico City, Acapulco, Cancún, Guadalajara, Guaymas, Ixtapa/Zihuatanejo, León/El Bajío, Los Cabos, La Paz, Mérida, Monterrey, Puerto Vallarta. **Mexicana** (☏ 800/531–7921, WEB www.mexicana.com) to Mexico City, Acapulco, Cancún, Guadalajara, Ixtapa/Zihuatanejo, León/El Bajío, Los Cabos, Mazatlán, Mérida, Puerto Vallarta, Zacatecas. **Northwest** (☏ 800/225–2525, WEB www.nwa.com) to Mexico City, Acapulco, Cancún, Cozumel, Ixtapa/Zihuatanejo, Los Cabos, and Puerto Vallarta. **United** (☏ 800/241–6522, WEB www.united.com) to Mexico City, Acapulco, Cancún, Guadalajara, León, Los Cabos, Puerto Vallarta. **US Airways** (☏ 800/428–4322, WEB www.usairways.com) to Cancún, Cozumel.

➤ FROM THE U.K.: **British Airways** (☏ 0845/773–3377, WEB www.britishairways.com) has nonstop flights from London to Mexico City and Cancún. **Air France** (☏ 0181/742–6600, WEB www.airfrance.com), via Paris. **American** (☏ 020/8572–5555; 0845/778–4789 outside London, WEB www.aa.com), from London via Chicago, Dallas, or Miami. **Continental** (☏ 01293/776–464, WEB www.continental.com), from London via Houston and Newark, and from Birmingham and Manchester via Newark. **Delta** (☏ 800/414–767, WEB www.delta.com), via Atlanta. **Iberia** (☏ 0845/601–2854, WEB www.iberia.com), via Madrid. **KLM** (☏ 08705/074–074, WEB www.klm.com), via Amsterdam. **Lufthansa** (☏ 0845/7737–747, WEB www.lufthansa.com), via Frankfurt. **United** (☏ 0845/8444–777, WEB www.united.com), via Chicago or Washington, D.C.

➤ DOMESTIC AIRLINES: **AeroCalifornia** (☏ 55/5207–1392, WEB www.aerocalifornia.com) serves Guadalajara, Loreto, Mérida, Oaxaca, Puebla, Tepic, Tijuana, Veracruz, Villahermosa, and several other gateways. **Aerocaribe** (reserve through Mexicana) serves the Yucatán and the South. **Aerolitoral** (reserve through Aeroméxico or Mexicana) serves northeastern Mexico. **Aeromar** (reserve through Mexicana or Aeroméxico) serves central Mexico. **Aeroméxico** (☏ 55/5625–2622 or 800/021–2622, WEB www.aeromexico.com) serves most major cities. **Aviacsa** (☏ 961/612–8081 in Chiapas; 55/5448–8900 in Mexico City) serves Cancún, Chetumal, Guadalajara, Mérida, and Tijuana. **Mexicana** (☏ 55/5448–0990 or 800/502–2000, WEB www.mexicana.com) serves most major cities.

CHECK-IN AND BOARDING

Always **ask your carrier about its check-in policy.** Plan to arrive at the airport about two hours before your scheduled departure time for domestic flights and 2½ to 3 hours before international flights.

Assuming that not everyone with a ticket will show up, airlines routinely overbook planes. When everyone does, airlines ask for volunteers to give up their seats. In return, these volunteers usually get a certificate for a free flight and are rebooked on the next flight out. If there are not enough volunteers, the airline must choose who will be denied boarding. The first to get bumped are passengers who checked in late and those flying on discounted tickets, so **get to the gate and check in as early as possible,** especially during peak periods.

Always **bring a government-issued photo I.D. to the airport;** even when it's not required, a passport is best.

CUTTING COSTS

The least expensive airfares to Mexico are priced for round-trip travel and must usually be purchased in advance. Airlines generally allow you to change your return date for a fee; most low-fare tickets, however, are nonrefundable. It's smart to **call a number of airlines,** and when you are quoted a good price, **book it on the spot**—the same fare may not be available the next day. Always **check different routings** and look into using alternate airports. Also, price off-peak flights, which may be significantly less expensive than others. Travel agents, especially low-fare specialists (☞ Discounts and Deals), are helpful.

Consolidators are another good source. They buy tickets for scheduled international flights at reduced rates from the airlines, then sell them at prices that beat the best fare available directly from the airlines. Sometimes you can even get your money back if you need to return the ticket. Carefully read the fine print detailing penalties for changes and cancellations, purchase the ticket with a credit card, and **confirm your consolidator reservation with the airline.**

When you **fly as a courier,** you trade your checked-luggage space for a ticket deeply subsidized by a courier service. There are restrictions on when you can book and how long you can stay. Some courier companies list with membership organizations, such as the Air Courier Association and the International Association of Air Travel Couriers; these require you to become a member before you can book a flight.

Many airlines, singly or in collaboration, offer discount air passes that allow foreigners to travel economically in a particular country or region. These visitor passes usually must be reserved and purchased before you leave home. Information about passes can be difficult to track down on airline Web sites, which tend to be geared to travelers departing from a given carrier's country rather than to those intending to visit that country. Try typing the name of the pass into a search engine, or search for "pass" within the carrier's Web site.

➤ CHEAP TICKETS: (☎ 800/377–1000, WEB www.cheaptickets.com). **Discount Airline Ticket Service** (☎ 800/576–1600, WEB www.bestfares.com). **Unitravel** (☎ 800/325–2222, WEB www.unitravel.com). **Up & Away Travel** (☎ 212/889–2345, WEB www.upandaway.com). **World Travel Network** (☎ 800/409–6753).

➤ COURIER RESOURCES: **Air Courier Association** (☎ 800/282–1202, WEB www.aircourier.org). **International Association of Air Travel Couriers** (☎ 352/475–1584, WEB www.courier.org). **Now Voyager Travel** (☎ 212/431–1616).

➤ DISCOUNT PASSES: **All Asia Pass,** Cathay Pacific (☎ 800/233–2742, WEB www.cathay-usa.com). **Boomerang Pass,** Qantas (☎ 800/227–4500; 0845/774–7767 in the U.K.; 131–313 in Australia; 0800/808–767 in New Zealand; WEB www.qantas.com). **Brazil Air Pass** (☎ 888/251–6844, WEB www.brtravel.com). **FlightPass,** EuropebyAir (☎ 888/387–2479, WEB www.europebyair.com). **Pacific Explorer Airpass** (☎ 2/9743–0253, in Australia, WEB www.hideawayholidays.com.au/explorer.htm). **Polypass,** Polynesian Airlines (☎ 800/264–0823 or 808/842–7659; 020/8846–0519 in the U.K.; 1300/653737 in Australia; 0800/800–993 in New Zealand; WEB www.polynesianairlines.co.nz). **SAS Air Passes,** Scandinavian Airlines (☎ 800/221–2350; 0845/6072–7727 in the U.K.; 1300/727707 in Australia; WEB www.scandinavian.net).

ENJOYING THE FLIGHT

State your seat preference when purchasing your ticket, and then repeat it when you confirm and when you check in. For more legroom, you can request one of the few emergency-aisle seats at check-in, if you are capable of lifting at least 50 pounds—a Federal Aviation Administration requirement of passengers in these seats. Seats behind a bulkhead also offer more legroom, but they don't have underseat storage. Don't sit in the row in front of the emergency aisle or in front of a bulkhead, where seats may not recline.

Ask the airline whether a snack or meal is served on the flight. If you have dietary concerns, **request special meals when booking.** These can be vegetarian, low-cholesterol, or kosher, for example. It's a good idea to pack some healthful snacks and a small (plastic) bottle of water in your carry-on bag. On long flights, try to maintain a normal routine, to help fight jet lag. At night, **get some sleep.** By day, **eat light meals, drink water** (not alcohol), and **move around the cabin** to stretch your legs. For additional jet-lag tips consult *Fodor's FYI: Travel Fit & Healthy* (available at bookstores everywhere).

Smoking policies vary from carrier to carrier. Many airlines prohibit smoking on all of their international flights; others allow smoking only on certain routes or certain departures. Ask your carrier about its policy.

FLYING TIMES

Mexico City is 4½ hours from New York, 4 hours from Chicago, and 3½ hours from Los Angeles. Cancún is 3½ hours from New York and from Chicago, 4½ hours from Los Angeles. Acapulco is 6 hours from New York, 4 hours from Chicago, and 3½ hours from Los Angeles.

From London, Mexico City is a 12½-hour flight, Cancún 11¾ hours.

HOW TO COMPLAIN

If your baggage goes astray or your flight goes awry, complain right away. Most carriers require that you **file a claim immediately.** The Aviation Consumer Protection Division of the Department of Transportation publishes *Fly-Rights,* which discusses airlines and consumer issues and is available on-line. At PassengerRights.com, a Web site, you can compose a letter of complaint and distribute it electronically.

➤ AIRLINE COMPLAINTS: **Aviation Consumer Protection Division** (✉ U.S. Department of Transportation, Room 4107, C-75, Washington, DC 20590, ☎ 202/366–2220, WEB www.dot.gov/airconsumer). **Federal Aviation Administration Consumer Hotline** (☎ 800/322–7873).

RECONFIRMING

Check the status of your flight before you leave for the airport. You can do this on your carrier's Web site, by linking to a flight-status checker (many Web booking services offer these), or by calling your carrier or travel agent. Always confirm international flights at least 72 hours ahead of the scheduled departure time.

AIRPORTS

The main gateway to Mexico is **Aeropuerto Internacional Benito Juárez** in Mexico City.

➤ AIRPORT INFORMATION: **Mexico City** (Aeropuerto Internacional Benito Juárez, ☎ 55/5571–3600). **Acapulco** (General Juan Alvarez airport, ☎ 744/466–9434). **Cancún** (Cancún airport, ☎ 998/886–0049). **Cozumel** (Cozumel airport, ☎ 987/872–0485). **Guadalajara** (Ramón F. Quintanilla García airport, ☎ 33/3688–5120). **Ixtapa/Zihuatenejo** (Manuel Zúrita Gallegos airport, ☎ 755/554–2070). **Los Cabos** (Licenciado Alberto de la Mora airport, ☎ 624/146–5112). **Manzanillo** (Playa de Oro airport, ☎ 314/333–2525). **Mazatlán** (Juan Buelna airport, ☎ 669/982–2399). **Mérida** (Hector José Navarrete Muñoz airport, ☎ 999/946–1340). **Puerto Vallarta** (Gustavo Díaz Ordaz airport, ☎ 322/221–1298).

BIKE TRAVEL

Bike travel in Mexico is a rough-and-ready proposition. Some roads have never seen a bicycle, and drivers are not accustomed to cyclists. In addition, most Mexican roads lack shoulders and are often pitted. Despite these drawbacks, cycling in Mexico can be fun if you plan ahead, and bikes are especially useful for travel to places where there are only dirt roads or tracks, or where public transportation is scant. In the Yucatán, for example, bikes are a primary form of transportation for locals, and bike-repair shops are common even in smaller towns. When planning your trip, consult an up-to-date AAA, Pemex, or Guía Roji map. You can find Pemex and Guía Roji maps in Mexico at most Sanborns restaurant/shops and major supermarket chains—such as Superama, Aurrera, and Commercial Mexicana—for less than $10. Be sure to carry plenty of water and everything you might need to repair your bike. Pack extra patch kits, as shards of glass often litter the roads. If you can take your bike apart and fold it up, buses will allow you to store it in the cargo space; likewise on trains in the Copper Canyon.

Bicycling Mexico (Hunter Publishing Inc.), by Ericka Weisbroth and Eric Ellman, is the bicyclist's bible, complete with maps, color photos, historical information, and a kilometer-by-kilometer breakdown of every route possible. For a list of companies that run organized bike tours of Mexico, *see* Tours and Packages.

BIKES IN FLIGHT

Most airlines accommodate bikes as luggage, provided they are dismantled and boxed; check with individual airlines about packing requirements. Airlines sell bike boxes, which are often free at bike shops, for about $15 (bike bags start at $100). International travelers often can substitute a bike for a piece of checked luggage at no charge; otherwise, the cost is about $100. Domestic and Canadian airlines charge $40–$80 each way.

BUSINESS HOURS

BANKS AND OFFICES

Banks are generally open weekdays 9–3. In larger cities, most are open until 5 or 7. Many of the larger banks keep a few branches open Saturday from 9 or 10 to 2:30 and Sunday 10–1:30; however, the extended hours are often for deposits or check cashing only. Banks will give you cash advances in pesos (for a fee) if you have a major credit card. Government offices are usually open to the public 8–3; along with banks and most private offices, they're closed on national holidays.

GAS STATIONS

Gas stations are normally open 7 AM–10 PM. Those near major thoroughfares in big cities stay open 24 hours, including most holidays.

MUSEUMS AND SIGHTS

Along with theaters and most archaeological sights, museums are closed on Monday, with few exceptions. Museums across the country have free admission on Sunday. Hours are normally 9 to 5 or 6.

SHOPS

Stores are generally open weekdays and Saturday from 9 or 10 AM to 7 or 8 PM; in resort areas, shops may also be open on Sunday. In some resort areas and small towns, shops may close for a two-hour lunch break—about 2–4. Airport shops are open seven days a week.

BUS TRAVEL

Getting to Mexico by bus is no longer for just the adventurous or budget-conscious. In the past, bus travelers were required to change to Mexican vehicles at the border, and vice versa. Now, however, in an effort to bring more American visitors and their tourist dollars to off-the-beaten-track markets and attractions, the Mexican government has removed this obstacle, and a growing number of trans-border bus tours are available.

Gateway cities in Texas, such as El Paso, Del Rio, Laredo, McAllen, Brownsville, and San Antonio, along with Tijuana, are served by several small private bus lines as well as by Greyhound. If you'll be leaving Mexico by bus, you can buy tickets from the Greyhound representative in Mexico City.

The Mexican bus network is extensive, far more so than that of the railroads. Buses go where trains do not, service is more frequent, tickets can be purchased on the spot (except during holidays and on long weekends, when advance purchase is crucial), and first-class buses are punctual, faster, and much more comfortable than trains. On all overnight bus rides, **bring something to eat** in case you don't like the restaurant where the bus stops, and **carry toilet paper,** as rest rooms might not have any.

In large cities, bus stations are a good distance from the center of town. Though there's a trend toward consolidation, some towns have different stations for each bus line. Bus service in Mexico City is well organized, operating out of four terminals.

CLASSES

For travel within Mexico, buses run the gamut from comfortable air-conditioned coaches with bathrooms, movies, reclining seats with seat belts, and refreshments (premier or deluxe) to dilapidated "vintage" buses (second and third class) on which pigs and chickens travel and frequent stops are made. A lower-class bus ride can be interesting if you're not in a hurry and want to see the sights and experience the local culture—and the fares are generally up to 30% cheaper than those in the premium categories. Still, you should be prepared for cracked windows and litter in the aisles. But for comfort's sake alone, if you're planning a long-distance haul, **buy tickets for first-class or better when traveling by bus within Mexico.** Smoking is prohibited on all first-class and deluxe buses.

There are several first-class bus lines. ADO serves Cancún, Oaxaca, Tampico, Veracruz, Villahermosa, and Yucatán from Mexico City; ADO GL offers deluxe service to the same destinations. Cristóbal Colón goes to Chiapas, Oaxaca, Puebla, and the Guatemala border from Mexico City. Estrella Blanca goes from Mexico City to Manzanillo, Mazatlán, Monterrey, and Nuevo Laredo. ETN goes to Mexico City, Manzanillo, Morelia, Puerto Vallarta, and Toluca. Estrella Blanca has first-class and deluxe service to all states but Yucatán, Quintana Roo, and Chiapas. You can take Estrella de Oro from Mexico City to Acapulco, Cuernavaca, Ixtapa, and Taxco.

PAYING

For the most part, you should plan to pay in pesos, although some of the deluxe bus services have started accepting credit cards such as Visa and MasterCard.

RESERVATIONS

Tickets for first-class or better—unlike tickets for the other classes—can and should be reserved in advance.

➤ BUS INFORMATION: **ADO** (☎ 55/5785–9659 or 01-800/702–8000). **ADO GL** (☎ 55/5785–9659). **Cristóbal Colón** (☎ 55/5133–2444). **Estrella Blanca** (☎ 55/5729–0707). **ETN** (☎ 55/5273–0251 or 01-800/715–5519). **Estrella de Oro** (☎ 55/5549–8520). **Greyhound** (☎ 800/231–2222, WEB www.greyhound.com; ✉ Amores 707-102, Col. del Valle, Mexico City, ☎ 55/5669–0986 or 01-800/010–0600).

CAMERAS AND PHOTOGRAPHY

You should **always ask permission before taking photos of people.** They may ask you for a *propina,* or tip, in which case a few pesos is customary. Some churches in Chiapas and elsewhere forbid cameras.

The *Kodak Guide to Shooting Great Travel Pictures* (available at bookstores everywhere) is loaded with tips.

➤ PHOTO HELP: **Kodak Information Center** (☎ 800/242–2424, WEB www.kodak.com).

EQUIPMENT PRECAUTIONS

Don't pack film and equipment in checked luggage, where it is much more susceptible to damage. X-ray machines used to view checked luggage are becoming much more powerful and therefore are much more likely to ruin your film. Try to **ask for hand inspection of film,** which becomes clouded after repeated exposure to airport X-ray machines, and **keep videotapes and computer disks away from metal detectors.** Always **keep film, tape, and computer disks out of the sun.** Carry an extra supply of batteries, and **be prepared to turn on your camera, camcorder, or laptop** to prove to airport security personnel that the device is real.

FILM AND DEVELOPING

Film—especially Kodak and Fuji brands—is fairly easy to find in many parts of Mexico. If purchased in a major city, a roll of 36-exposure print film costs about the same as in the United States; the price is slightly higher in tourist spots and in more remote places, where finding film might not be as easy. Advantix is now available in Mexico, although developing may take one or two days. It's a good idea to **pack more film than you think you'll need** on your trip. One-hour and overnight film developing is fairly common in Mexico.

VIDEOS

Videotapes are good quality and are easy to find in urban areas. A 120-minute tape costs about $3.

CAR RENTAL

When you think about renting a car, bear in mind that you may be sharing the road with bad local drivers—sometimes acquiring a driver's license in Mexico is more a question of paying someone off than of having tested skill. In addition, the highway system is very uneven from state to state: in some regions, modern, well-paved superhighways prevail; in others—particularly the mountains—potholes, untethered livestock, and dangerous, unrailed curves are the rule. Check on local road conditions before you rent.

Mexico manufactures Chrysler, Ford, General Motors, Honda, Nissan, and Volkswagen vehicles. With the exception of Volkswagen, you can get the same kind of midsize and luxury cars in Mexico that you can rent in the United States and Canada. Economy usually refers to a Volkswagen Beetle, which may or may not come with air-conditioning.

Rates begin at $45 a day and $260 a week in Mexico City and $35 a day and $230 a week in Acapulco for a compact car with air-conditioning, manual transmission, and unlimited mileage. This doesn't include tax on car rentals, which is 15%, or insurance, which runs about $100 a week. Avoid local car-rental agencies; **stick with the major companies** because they tend to be more reliable.

You can also hire a car with a driver; they're normally available through hotels and charge around $20 an hour within town, with a three-hour minimum requirement. Limousine service runs about $50 an hour within town, with a five-hour minimum. Rates for out-of-town trips are higher. **Negotiate a price beforehand** if you'll need the service for more than one day. If your hotel can't arrange limousine or car service, ask the concierge to refer you to a reliable *sitio* (cab stand); the rate will be lower.

➤ MAJOR AGENCIES: **Alamo** (☏ 800/522–9696, WEB www.alamo.com). **Avis** (☏ 800/331–1084; 800/272–5871 in Canada; 02/9353–9000, local number 136–333, in Australia; 0800/655–111 in New Zealand; 0870/606–0100 in the U.K., WEB www.avis.com). **Budget** (☏ 800/527–0700; 800/268–8900 in Canada; local number 1442/276–266 in the U.K., WEB www.budget.com). **Dollar** (☏ 800/800–4000; 0124/622–0111 in the U.K., through affiliate Sixt Kenning; 02/9223–1444 in Australia, WEB www.dollar.com). **Hertz** (☏ 800/654–3001; 800/263–0600 in Canada; 020/7026–0077 in the U.K.; local number 613/9698–2555 in Australia; 0800-654-321 in New Zealand, WEB www.hertz.com) **National Car Rental** (☏ 800/227–7368; 020/8750–2800 in the U.K., WEB www.nationalcar.com).

CUTTING COSTS

For a good deal, **book through a travel agent who will shop around.**

Do **look into wholesalers,** companies that do not own fleets but rent in bulk from those that do and often offer better rates than traditional car-rental operations. Prices are best during off-peak periods. Rentals booked through wholesalers often must be paid for before you leave home.

➤ WHOLESALERS: **Auto Europe** (☏ 207/842–2000 or 800/223–5555, FAX 207/842–2222, WEB www.autoeurope.com). **Kemwel** (☏ 800/678–0678 or 800/576–1590, FAX 207/842–2124, WEB www.kemwel.com).

INSURANCE

When driving a rented car you are generally responsible for any damage to or loss of the vehicle. You may also be liable for any property damage or personal injury that you may cause while driving. Before you rent, see what coverage you already have under the terms of your personal auto-insurance policy and credit cards.

REQUIREMENTS AND RESTRICTIONS

In Mexico your own driver's license is acceptable. An International Driver's Permit is a good idea; it's available from the U.S. and Canadian automobile associations, and, in the United Kingdom, from the Automobile Association or Royal Automobile Club. These international permits are universally recognized, and having one in your wallet may save you a problem with the local authorities.

SURCHARGES

Before you pick up a car in one city and leave it in another, **ask about drop-off charges or one-way service fees,** which can be substantial. Note, too, that some rental agencies charge extra if you return the car before the time specified in your contract. To avoid a hefty refueling fee, **fill the tank just before you turn in the car,** but be aware that gas stations near the rental outlet may overcharge. It's almost never a deal to buy the tank of gas in the car when you rent it; the understanding is that you'll return it empty, but some fuel usually remains.

CAR TRAVEL

There are two absolutely essential points to remember about driving in Mexico. First and foremost is to **carry Mexican auto insurance.**

Point No. 2: **if you enter Mexico with a car, you must leave with it.** In recent years, the high rate of U.S. vehicles being sold illegally in Mexico has caused the Mexican government to enact stringent regulations for bringing a car into the country—at great inconvenience to motoring American tourists. In order to drive into the country, **you must cross the border with the following documents:** title or registration for your vehicle; a birth certificate or passport; a credit card (AE, DC, MC, or V); a valid driver's license with a photo. The title holder, driver, and credit-card owner must be one and the same—that is, if your spouse's name is on the title of the car and yours isn't, you cannot be the one to bring the car into the country. For financed, leased, rental, or company cars, you must **bring a notarized letter of permission** from the bank, lien holder, rental agency, or company.

When you submit your paperwork at the border and pay a $20 charge on your credit card, you'll receive a car permit and a sticker to put on your vehicle, all valid for up to six months. Be sure to **turn in the permit and the sticker** at the border prior to their expiration date; otherwise you could incur high fines.

One alternative to going through this hassle when you cross is to **have your paperwork done in advance** at a branch of Sanborn's Mexican Insurance; look in the Yellow Pages for an office in almost every town on the U.S.–Mexico border. You'll still have to go through some of the procedures at the border, but all your paperwork will be in order, and Sanborn's express window will ensure that you get through relatively quickly. There's a $10 charge for this service. The fact that you drove in with a car is stamped on your tourist card, which you must give to immigration authorities at departure. If an emergency arises and you must fly home, there are complicated customs procedures to face.

If you bring the car into the country you must **be in the vehicle at all times when it is driven.** You cannot lend it to another person.

For day trips and local sightseeing, **consider engaging a car and driver** (who often acts as a guide) for a day; this can be a hassle-free, more economical way to travel than renting a car and driving yourself. Hotel desks will know which taxi companies to call, and you can negotiate a price with the driver.

Your driver's license may not be recognized outside your home country. International driving permits (IDPs) are available from the American and Canadian automobile associations and, in the United Kingdom, from the Automobile Association and Royal Automobile Club. These international permits, valid only in conjunction with your regular driver's license, are universally recognized; having one may save you a problem with local authorities.

EMERGENCY SERVICES

To help motorists on major highways, the Mexican Tourism Ministry operates a fleet of more than 350 pickup trucks, known as the Angeles Verdes, or Green Angels. The bilingual drivers provide mechanical help, first aid, radio-telephone communication, basic supplies and small parts, towing, tourist information, and protection. Services are free, and spare parts, fuel, and lubricants are provided at cost. Tips are always appreciated (figure $5–$10 for big jobs, $2–$3 for minor repairs). The Green Angels patrol fixed sections of the major highways twice daily 8–8 (later on holiday weekends). If you break down, **pull off the road as far as possible,** lift the hood of your car, hail a passing vehicle, and ask the driver to **notify the patrol.** Most bus and truck drivers will be quite helpful. If you witness an accident, do not stop to help—inform the nearest official.

➤ CONTACTS: **Green Angels, Mexico City** (☎ 55/5250–8555 or 55/5545–3008).

GASOLINE

Pemex franchises all gas stations in Mexico. Stations are located at most road junctions and in cities and towns; gas is measured in liters instead of gallons. Gas stations usually do not accept U.S. or Canadian credit cards or dollars. Fuel prices vary from region to region. They tend to be on the lower end in Mexico City and surroundings and near the U.S. border, increasing the farther you get from these areas. Overall, prices run slightly to moderately higher than in the United States. Premium unleaded gas (called Magna Premio) and regular unleaded gas (Magna Sin) are available nationwide, but it's still a good idea to **fill up whenever you can.** Fuel quality is generally lower than that in the United States and Europe. Vehicles with fuel-injected engines are likely to have problems after driving extended distances.

Gas-station attendants pump the gas for you and may also wash your windshield and check your oil and tire air pressure. A 5- or 10-peso tip is customary, depending on the number of services rendered. **Keep a close eye on the gas meter** to make sure the attendant is starting it at "0" and that you're charged the correct price.

INSURANCE

You must **carry Mexican auto insurance,** which you can purchase near border crossings on either the U.S. or Mexican side. If you injure anyone in an accident, you could well be jailed—whether it was your fault or not—unless you have insurance. Guilty until proven innocent is part of the country's Code Napoléon. Purchase enough Mexican automobile insurance at the border to cover your estimated trip. It's sold by the day, and if your trip is shorter than your original estimate, some companies might issue a prorated refund for the unused time upon application after you exit the country.

➤ CONTACTS: **Instant Mexico Auto Insurance** (✉ 223 Via de San Ysidro, San Ysidro, CA 92173, ☎ 619/428–3583). **Oscar Padilla** (✉ 120 Willow Rd., San Ysidro, CA 92173, ☎ 800/258–8600). **Sanborn's Mexican Insurance** (✉ 2009 S. 10th St., McAllen, TX 78503, ☎ 800/222–0158 or 956/686–0711).

ROAD CONDITIONS

There are several well-kept toll roads in Mexico—most of them four lanes wide. However, these *carreteras* (major highways) don't go too far out of the capital into the countryside. (*Cuota* means toll road; *libre* means no toll, and such roads are two lanes and usually not as smooth.) Some excellent new roads have opened in the past decade or so, making car travel safer and faster. These include highways connecting Acapulco and Mexico City; Cancún and Mérida; Nogales and Mazatlán; León and Aguascalientes; Guadalajara and Tepic; Mexico City, Morelia, and Guadalajara; Mexico City, Puebla, Teotihuacán, and Oaxaca; Mexico City and Veracruz; and Nuevo Laredo and Monterrey. However, tolls as high as $40 one way can make using these thoroughfares prohibitively expensive. Approaches to most of the large cities are also in good condition.

In rural areas, roads are quite poor: **use caution, especially during the rainy season,** when rock slides and potholes are a problem, and watch out for animals. Driving in Mexico's central highlands may also necessitate adjustments to your carburetor. Generally, driving times are longer than for comparable distances in the United States. *Topes* (speed bumps) are also common; it's best to slow down when approaching a village.

Common sense goes a long way: if you have a long distance to cover, **start early and fill up on gas**; don't let your tank get below half full. Allow extra time for unforeseen occurrences as well as for the trucks that seem to be everywhere. By day, **be alert to animals,** especially cattle and dogs.

Traffic can be horrendous in cities, particularly in Mexico City. As you would in metropolitan areas anywhere, **avoid rush hour** (7–9 AM and 6–8 PM) and when schools let out (2–3 PM). Signage is not always adequate in Mexico, so **travel with a companion and a good map.** Always lock your car, and never leave valuable items in the body of the car (the trunk will suffice for daytime outings, but don't pack it in front of prying eyes).

ROAD MAPS

The Mexican Tourism Ministry distributes free road maps from its tourism offices located in Mexican consulates and embassies abroad. The Mexican Secretariat of Tourism (☎ 800/482–9832 from the U.S. or Canada) will also mail maps on request, though it may take up to three months to receive them. Guía Roji and Pemex (the government petroleum monopoly) publish current city, regional, and national road maps, which are available in bookstores and big supermarket chains for under $10; gas stations generally do not carry maps.

RULES OF THE ROAD

When you sign up for Mexican car insurance, you should receive a booklet on Mexican rules of the road. Read this booklet in order to avoid breaking laws that differ from those of your country.

Illegally parked cars are either towed or have wheel blocks placed on the tires, which can require a trip to the traffic-police headquarters for payment of a fine. When in doubt, **park in a lot instead of on the street**; your car will probably be safer there anyway.

If an oncoming vehicle flicks its lights at you in daytime, slow down: it could mean trouble ahead. When approaching a narrow bridge, the first vehicle to flash its lights has right of way. One-way streets are common. One-way traffic is indicated by an arrow; two-way, by a double-pointed arrow. A circle with a diagonal line superimposed on the letter *E* (for *estacionamiento*) means "no parking." Other road signs follow the now-widespread system of international symbols, a copy of which will usually be provided when you rent a car in Mexico.

In Mexico City, **watch out for *"Hoy no Circula"* notices.** Because of pollution, all cars in the city without a Verification "0" rating (usually those built before 1994) are prohibited from driving one day a week (two days a week during high-alert periods). Posted signs show certain letters or numbers paired with each day of the week, indicating that vehicles with those letters or numbers in their license plates are not allowed to drive on the corresponding day. Foreigners are not exempt. Cars with license plate numbers ending in 5 or 6 are prohibited on Monday; 7 or 8 on Tuesday; 3 or 4 on Wednesday; 1 or 2 on Thursday; and 9 or 0 on Friday.

Mileage and speed limits are given in kilometers: 100 kph and 80 kph (62 and 50 mph, respectively) are the most common maximums. A few of the newer toll roads allow 110 kph (68 mph). In cities and small towns, **observe the posted speed limits,** which can be as low as 20 kph (12 mph).

Seat belts are now required by law throughout Mexico.

SAFETY ON THE ROAD

Never drive at night in remote and rural areas. *Banditos* are one concern, but so are potholes, free-roaming animals, cars with no working lights, road-hogging trucks, and difficulty in getting assistance. It's best to use toll roads whenever possible; although costly, they are much safer.

If you're driving from Manzanillo to Ixtapa/Zihuatanejo—about 8–10 hours with a meal stop—make the trip only during daylight hours, due to reports of carjackings around the area of Playa Azul. Military and police patrols have been increased on Highway 200 and the number of incidents has dramatically decreased; still, exercise caution.

Some of the biggest hassles on the road might be from police who pull you over for supposedly breaking the law, or for being a good prospect for a scam. Remember to **be polite**—displays of anger will only make matters worse—and be aware that a police officer might be pulling you over for something you didn't do. Although efforts are being made to fight corruption, it's still a fact of life in Mexico, and the $5 it costs to get your license back is definitely supplementary income for the officer who pulled you over with no intention of taking you down to police headquarters.

If you are stopped for speeding, the officer is supposed to take your license and hold it until you pay the fine at the local police station. But the officer will always prefer a *mordida* (small bribe) to wasting his time at the police station. If you decide to dispute a charge that seems preposterous, do so with a smile, and tell the officer that you would like to talk to the police captain when you get to the station. The officer usually will let you go rather than go to the station.

When crossing the streets by foot, **look both ways for oncoming traffic,** even with the light. Although pedestrians have the right of way by law, drivers disregard it. And more often than not, if a driver hits a pedestrian, he'll drive away as fast as he can without stopping, to avoid jail. Many Mexican drivers do not carry auto insurance, so you'll have to shoulder your own medical expenses.

CHILDREN IN MEXICO

Mexico has one of the strictest policies about children entering the country. All children, including infants, must have proof of citizenship (a birth certificate) for travel to Mexico. All children up to age 18 traveling with a single parent must also have a notarized letter from the other parent stating that the child has his or her permission to leave their home country. If the other parent is deceased or the child has only one legal parent, a notarized statement saying so must be obtained as proof. In addition, parents must now fill out a tourist card for each child over the age of 10 traveling with them.

If you are renting a car, don't forget to **arrange for a car seat** when you reserve. For general advice about traveling with children, consult *Fodor's FYI: Travel with Your Baby* (available in bookstores everywhere).

FLYING

If your children are two or older, **ask about children's airfares.** As a general rule, infants under two not occupying a seat fly at greatly reduced fares or even for free.When booking, **confirm carry-on allowances** if you're traveling with infants. In general, for babies charged 10% of the adult fare you are allowed one carry-on bag and a collapsible stroller; if the flight is full, the stroller may have to be checked or you may be limited to less.

Experts agree that it's a good idea to use safety seats aloft for children weighing less than 40 pounds. Airlines set their own policies: U.S. carriers usually require that the child be ticketed, even if he or she is young enough to ride free, since the seats must be strapped into regular seats. Do **check your airline's policy about using safety seats during takeoff and landing.** Safety seats are not allowed everywhere in the plane, so get your seat assignments as early as possible.

When reserving, **request children's meals or a freestanding bassinet** (not available at all airlines) if you need them. But note that bulkhead seats, where you must sit to use the bassinet, may lack an overhead bin or storage space on the floor.

FOOD AND SUPPLIES

Fresh milk isn't always readily available, though necessities such as disposable diapers can be found in almost every town.

LODGING

Most hotels in Mexico allow children under a certain age to stay in their parents' room at no extra charge, but others charge for them as extra adults; be sure to **find out the cutoff age for children's discounts.**

Many hotel chains in Mexico offer services that make it easier to travel with children. They include connecting family rooms, play areas such as kiddie pools and playgrounds, and kids' clubs with special activities and outings. Check with your hotel before booking to see if the services are included in the price or if there is an extra charge.

SIGHTS AND ATTRACTIONS

The larger tourist areas have plenty of activities for children. Places that are especially appealing to children are indicated by a rubber-duckie icon ( ) in the margin.

COMPUTERS ON THE ROAD

Internet cafés have sprung up all over Mexico, making e-mail by far the easiest way to get in touch with people back home.

If you have a Toshiba or Macintosh laptop, bear in mind that having it serviced might be hopeless. Parts for these machines are hard to come by in Mexico.

Carry a spare battery because replacement batteries are expensive and difficult to find. Always check with your hotel about surge protection, especially if the property isn't part of a major chain and/or is in an out-of-the-way place. Extreme electrical fluctuations and surges can damage or destroy your computer. Check with IBM for its pen-size modem tester that plugs into a telephone and jack to test if the line is safe.

CONSUMER PROTECTION

Whether you're shopping for gifts or purchasing travel services, **pay with a major credit card** whenever possible, so you can cancel payment or get reimbursed if there's a problem (and you can provide documentation). If you're doing business with a particular company for the first time, **contact your local Better Business Bureau and the attorney general's offices** in your state and (for U.S. businesses) the company's home state as well. Have any complaints been filed? Finally, if you're buying a package or tour, always **consider travel insurance** that includes default coverage (☞ Insurance).

➤ BBBs: **Council of Better Business Bureaus** (✉ 4200 Wilson Blvd., Suite 800, Arlington, VA 22203, ☎ 703/276–0100, FAX 703/525–8277, WEB www.bbb.org).

CRUISE TRAVEL

To learn how to plan, choose, and book a cruise-ship voyage, consult *Fodor's FYI: Plan & Enjoy Your Cruise* (available in bookstores everywhere).

CUSTOMS AND DUTIES

When shopping abroad, **keep receipts** for all purchases. Upon reentering the country, **be ready to show customs officials what you've bought.** If you feel a duty is incorrect, appeal the assessment. If you object to the way your clearance was handled, note the inspector's badge number. In either case, first ask to see a supervisor. If the problem isn't resolved, write to the appropriate authorities, beginning with the port director at your point of entry.

IN AUSTRALIA

Australian residents who are 18 or older may bring home A$400 worth of souvenirs and gifts (including jewelry), 250 cigarettes or 250 grams of tobacco, and 1,125 ml of alcohol (including wine, beer, and spirits). Residents under 18 may bring back A$200 worth of goods. Prohibited items include meat products. Seeds, plants, and fruits need to be declared upon arrival.

➤ INFORMATION: **Australian Customs Service** (Customs Head Office, ✉ Customs House, 5 Constitution Ave., Canberra, ACT 2601, Australia, ☎ 02/9213–2000 or 1300/363263, FAX 02/9213–4043, WEB www.customs.gov.au).

IN CANADA

Canadian residents who have been out of Canada for at least seven days may bring in C$750 worth of goods duty-free. If you've been away fewer than seven days but more than 48 hours, the duty-free allowance drops to C$200; if your trip lasts 24 to 48 hours, the allowance is C$50. You may not pool allowances with family members. Goods claimed under the C$750 exemption may follow you by mail; those claimed under the lesser exemptions must accompany you. Alcohol and tobacco products may be included in the seven-day and 48-hour exemptions but not in the 24-hour exemption. If you meet the age requirements of the province or territory through which you reenter Canada, you may bring in, duty-free, 1.5 liters of wine *or* 1.14 liters (40 imperial ounces) of liquor *or* 24 12-ounce cans or bottles of beer or ale. If you are 19 or older you may bring in, duty-free, 200 cigarettes and 50 cigars. Check ahead of time with the Canada Customs and Revenue Agency or the Department of Agriculture for policies regarding meat products, seeds, plants, and fruits.

You may send an unlimited number of gifts (only one gift per recipient, however) worth up to C$60 each duty-free to Canada. Label the package UNSOLICITED GIFT—VALUE UNDER $60. Alcohol and tobacco are excluded.

➤ INFORMATION: **Revenue Canada** (✉ 2265 St. Laurent Blvd. S, Ottawa, Ontario K1G 4K3, Canada, ☎ 613/

991–0501; 800/461–9999, FAX 613/991–1407, WEB www.ccra-adrc.gc.ca).

IN MEXICO

Upon entering Mexico, you'll be given a baggage declaration form and asked to itemize what you're bringing into the country. You are allowed to bring in 2 liters of spirits or wine for personal use; 400 cigarettes, 50 cigars, or 250 grams of tobacco; a reasonable amount of perfume for personal use; one movie camera and one regular camera and 12 rolls of film for each; and gift items not to exceed a total of $300. If driving across the U.S. border, gift items must not exceed $50. You are not allowed to bring firearms, meat, vegetables, plants, fruit, or flowers into the country.

IN NEW ZEALAND

All homeward-bound residents may bring back NZ$700 worth of souvenirs and gifts; passengers may not pool their allowances, and children can claim only the concession on goods intended for their own use. For those 17 or older, the duty-free allowance also includes 4.5 liters of wine or beer; one 1,125-ml bottle of spirits; and either 200 cigarettes, 250 grams of tobacco, 50 cigars, *or* a combination of the three up to 250 grams. Meat products, seeds, plants, and fruits must be declared upon arrival to the Agricultural Services Department.

➤ INFORMATION: **New Zealand Customs** (Head office: ✉ The Customhouse, 17–21 Whitmore St., Box 2218, Wellington, ☎ 09/300–5399 or 0800/428–786, WEB www.customs.govt.nz).

IN THE U.K.

From countries outside the European Union, including Mexico, you may bring home, duty-free, 200 cigarettes or 50 cigars; 1 liter of spirits or 2 liters of fortified or sparkling wine or liqueurs; 2 liters of still table wine; 60 ml of perfume; 250 ml of toilet water; plus £145 worth of other goods, including gifts and souvenirs. Prohibited items include meat products, seeds, plants, and fruits.

➤ INFORMATION: **HM Customs and Excise** (✉ Portcullis House, 21 Cowbridge Rd. E, Cardiff CF11 9SS, ☎ 029/2038–6423 or 0845/010–9000, WEB www.hmce.gov.uk).

IN THE U.S.

U.S. residents who have been out of the country for at least 48 hours may bring home, for personal use, $400 worth of foreign goods duty-free, as long as they haven't used the $400 allowance or any part of it in the past 30 days. This exemption may include 1 liter of alcohol (for travelers 21 and older), 200 cigarettes, and 100 non-Cuban cigars. Family members from the same household who are traveling together may pool their $400 personal exemptions. For fewer than 48 hours, the duty-free allowance drops to $200, which may include 50 cigarettes, 10 non-Cuban cigars, and 150 milliliters of alcohol (or perfume containing alcohol). The $200 allowance cannot be combined with other individuals' exemptions, and if you exceed it, the full value of all the goods will be taxed. Antiques, which the U.S. Customs Service defines as objects more than 100 years old, enter duty-free, as do original works of art done entirely by hand, including paintings, drawings, and sculptures.

➤ INFORMATION: **U.S. Customs Service** (for inquiries, ✉ 1300 Pennsylvania Ave. NW, Washington, DC 20229, WEB www.customs.gov, ☎ 202/354–1000; for complaints, ✉ Customer Satisfaction Unit, 1300 Pennsylvania Ave. NW, Room 5.5A, Washington, DC 20229; for registration of equipment, ✉ Office of Passenger Programs, 1300 Pennsylvania Ave. NW, Room 5.4D, Washington, DC 20229, ☎ 202/927–0530).

DINING

Mexican restaurants run the gamut from humble hole-in-the-wall shacks, street stands, *taquerías,* and American-style fast-food joints to internationally acclaimed gourmet restaurants. Prices, naturally, follow suit. To save money, **look for the fixed-menu lunch** known as *comida corrida* or *menú del día,* which is served 1–4 almost everywhere in Mexico.

The restaurants we list are the cream of the crop in each price category. Price categories are based on either a full three-course meal or the main course alone. For more information on local foods throughout Mexico, *see* "La Cocina Mexicana" in Mexico City (Chapter 1) and the Dining sections that appear under Pleasures and Pastimes at the beginning of each chapter.

Properties indicated by an ✕▣ are lodging establishments whose restaurant warrants a special trip.

MEALTIMES

In Mexico, lunch is the big meal; dinner is rarely served before 8 PM. Unlessotherwise noted, the restaurants listed in this guide are open daily for lunch and dinner.

PAYING

Credit cards—especially American Express, MasterCard, and Visa—are widely accepted at pricier restaurants. Bargains are usually cash only.

RESERVATIONS AND DRESS

Reservations are always a good idea; we mention them only when they're essential or not accepted. Book as far ahead as you can, and reconfirm as soon as you arrive. (Large parties should always call ahead to check the reservations policy.) We mention dress only when men are required to wear a jacket or a jacket and tie.

DISABILITIES AND ACCESSIBILITY

Mexico is poorly equipped for travelers with disabilities. There are no special discounts or passes for such travelers in Mexico, nor is public transportation, including the Mexico City Metro, wheelchair accessible. An exception is the city of Veracruz, where street corners have ramps in the downtown area. Roads and sidewalks are most often crowded and without ramps—in colonial cities cobblestone sidewalks and streets are unnavigable—and people on the street will not usually assist you unless expressly asked. You cannot rent vehicles outfitted for travelers with disabilities in Mexico, so your best bet for exploring comfortably is to **bring a car or van.**

Most hotels and restaurants have at least a few steps, and although rooms considered "wheelchair accessible" by hotel owners are usually on the ground floor, the doorways and bathroom may not be maneuverable. It's a good idea to call ahead to find out what a hotel or restaurant can offer. Despite these barriers, Mexicans with disabilities manage to negotiate places that most travelers outside Mexico would not consider accessible.

LODGING

The best choices of accessible lodging are found in major resort towns such as Acapulco, Cancún, and Mazatlán, and big cities such as Mexico City and Guadalajara.

RESERVATIONS

When discussing accessibility with an operator or reservations agent, **ask hard questions.** Are there any stairs, inside *or* out? Are there grab bars next to the toilet *and* in the shower/tub? How wide is the doorway to the room? To the bathroom? For the most extensive facilities meeting the latest legal specifications, **opt for newer accommodations.** If you reserve through a toll-free number, consider also calling the hotel's local number to confirm the information from the central reservations office. Get confirmation in writing when you can.

➤ COMPLAINTS: **Aviation Consumer Protection Division** for airline-related problems (✉ U.S. Department of Transportation, Aviation Consumer Protection Division, Room 4107, C-75, Washington, DC 20590, ☎ 800/255–1111, WEB www.dot.gov/airconsumer/problems.htm). **Civil Rights Office** (✉ U.S. Department of Transportation, Departmental Office of Civil Rights, S-30, 400 7th St. SW, Room 10215, Washington, DC 20590, ☎ 202/366–4648, FAX 202/366–3571, WEB www.dot.gov/ost/docr/index.htm) for problems with surface transportation. **Disability Rights Section** (✉ NYAV, U.S. Department of Justice, Civil Rights Division, 950 Pennsylvania Ave. NW, Washington, DC 20530; ☎ ADA information line 202/514–0301, 800/514–0301, 202/514–0383 TTY, 800/514–0383 TTY, WEB www.usdoj.gov/crt/ada/adahom1.htm).

TRAVEL AGENCIES

In the United States, the Americans with Disabilities Act requires that travel firms serve the needs of all travelers. Some agencies specialize in working with people with disabilities.

➤ TRAVELERS WITH MOBILITY PROBLEMS: **Access Adventures** (✉ 206 Chestnut Ridge Rd., Scottsville, NY 14624, ☎ 716/889–9096, dltravel@prodigy.net), run by a former physical-rehabilitation counselor. **CareVacations** (✉ No. 5, 5110–50 Ave., Leduc, Alberta T9E 6V4, Canada, ☎ 780/986–6404 or 877/478–7827, FAX 780/986–8332, WEB www.carevacations.com), for group tours and cruise vacations. **Flying Wheels Travel** (✉ 143 W. Bridge St., Box 382, Owatonna, MN 55060, ☎ 507/451–5005, FAX 507/451–1685, WEB www.flyingwheelstravel.com).

➤ TRAVELERS WITH DEVELOPMENTAL DISABILITIES: **New Directions** (✉ 5276 Hollister Ave., Suite 207, Santa Barbara, CA 93111, ☎ 805/967–2841 or 888/967–2841, FAX 805/964–7344, WEB www.newdirectionstravel.com).

DISCOUNTS AND DEALS

Be a smart shopper and **compare all your options** before making decisions. A plane ticket bought with a promotional coupon from travel clubs, coupon books, and direct-mail offers or purchased on the Internet may not be cheaper than the least expensive fare from a discount ticket agency. And always keep in mind that what you get is just as important as what you save.

DISCOUNT RESERVATIONS

To save money, **look into discount reservations services** with Web sites and toll-free numbers, which use their buying power to get a better price on hotels, airline tickets, even car rentals. When booking a room, always **call the hotel's local toll-free number** (if one is available) rather than the central reservations number—you'll often get a better price. Always ask about special packages or corporate rates.

When shopping for the best deal on hotels and car rentals, **look for guaranteed exchange rates,** which protect you against a falling dollar. With your rate locked in, you won't pay more, even if the price goes up in the local currency.

➤ AIRLINE TICKETS: ☎ **800/AIR–4LESS.**

➤ HOTEL ROOMS: **Hotel Reservations Network** (☎ 800/964–6835, WEB www.hoteldiscount.com). **Steigenberger Reservation Service** (☎ 800/223–5652, WEB www.srs-worldhotels.com). **Turbotrip.com** (☎ 800/473–7829, WEB www.turbotrip.com).

PACKAGE DEALS

Don't confuse packages and guided tours. When you buy a package, you travel on your own, just as though you had planned the trip yourself. Fly/drive packages, which combine airfare and car rental, are often a good deal.

ELECTRICITY

For U.S. and Canadian travelers, electrical converters are not necessary because Mexico operates on the 60-cycle, 120-volt system; however, many Mexican outlets have not been updated to accommodate three-prong and polarized plugs (those with one larger prong), so to be safe **bring an adapter.**

If your appliances are dual-voltage, you'll need only an adapter. Don't use 110-volt outlets marked FOR SHAVERS ONLY for high-wattage appliances such as blow-dryers. Most laptops operate equally well on 110 and 220 volts and so require only an adapter.

EMBASSIES

Australia, Canada, New Zealand, the United Kingdom, and the United States all have embassies in Mexico City. If you need assistance in an emergency, you can go to your country's embassy. Proof of identity and citizenship are generally required to enter.

➤ AUSTRALIA: **Australian Embassy** (✉ Rubén Darío 55, Col. Polanco, ☎ 55/5531–5225).

➤ CANADA: **Canadian Embassy** (✉ Schiller 529, Col. Polanco, ☎ 55/5724–7900, WEB www.canada.org.mx).

➤ NEW ZEALAND: **New Zealand Embassy** (✉ José Luis LaGrange 103, 10th floor, Col. Polanco, ☎ 55/5283–9460).

➤ UNITED KINGDOM: **British Embassy** (✉ Río Lerma 71, Col. Cuauhtémoc, ☎ 55/5207–2089).

➤ UNITED STATES: **U.S. Embassy** (✉ Paseo de la Reforma 305, Col. Cuauhtémoc, ☎ 55/5080–2000, WEB www.usembassy-mexico.gov/emenu.html).

EMERGENCIES

You're not protected by the laws of your native land once you're on Mexican soil. If you get into a scrape with the law, you can call the Citizens' Emergency Center in the United States. You can also call the 24-hour English-language hot line of the Procuraduría de Protección al Turista (Attorney General for the Protection of Tourists) in Mexico City; it can provide immediate assistance as well as general, nonemergency guidance. **In an emergency, dial 080 from any phone in Mexico City.**

➤ CONTACTS: **Citizens' Emergency Center** (☎ 202/647–5225 weekdays 8:15 AM–10 PM EST, Sat. 9 AM–3 PM; 202/634–3600 after hours and Sun.). **Procuraduría de Protección al Turista** (Attorney General for the Protection of Tourists; ☎ 55/5625–8153; 800/482–9832 from the U.S.).

ENGLISH-LANGUAGE MEDIA

English-language magazines and books can be found at some of the larger grocery stores in Mexico, but they're expensive—usually at least double what you'd pay back home. Several stores in Mexico City sell English-language publications and you can probably find at least one place in other major cities to buy them. However, in most smaller towns, you won't have much luck.

NEWSPAPERS AND MAGAZINES

Mexico has one major English-language newspaper: *The News,* available at hotels and newsstands in the tourist areas.

ETIQUETTE AND BEHAVIOR

In the United States, for example, being direct, efficient, and succinct is highly valued. But in Mexico, where communication tends to be more subtle, this style is often perceived as curt and aggressive. Mexicans are extremely polite, so losing your temper over delays or complaining loudly will get you branded as rude and make people less inclined to help you. **Remember that things move at a slow pace** here and that there's no stigma attached to being late; accept this gracefully. Learning basic phrases in Spanish such as "please" and "thank you" will make a big difference in how people respond to you.

BUSINESS ETIQUETTE

Personal relationships always come first here, so developing rapport and trust is essential. A handshake and personal greeting is appropriate along with a friendly inquiry about family, especially if you have met the family. In established business relationships, do not be surprised if you're greeted with a kiss on the cheek or a hug. Always be respectful toward colleagues in public and keep confrontations private. Meetings may or may not start on time, but you should be patient. When invited to dinner at the home of a client or associate, bring a gift and be sure to send a thank-you note afterward.

GAY AND LESBIAN TRAVEL

Mexican same-sex couples keep a low profile, and foreign same-sex couples may want to do the same. Two people of the same gender can often have a hard time getting a *cama matrimonial* (double bed), especially in smaller hotels. This could be attributed to the influence of the Catholic Church—Mexico is a devoutly Catholic country. The same rule that applies all over the world holds in Mexico as well: alternative lifestyles in general are more accepted in cosmopolitan areas, such as Mexico City, Acapulco, Ajijic, Cancún, Cuernavaca, Guadalajara, Puerto Vallarta, San Miguel de Allende, and Veracruz City.

➤ GAY- AND LESBIAN-FRIENDLY TRAVEL AGENCIES: **Different Roads Travel** (✉ 8383 Wilshire Blvd., Suite 902, Beverly Hills, CA 90211, ☎ 323/651–5557 or 800/429–8747, FAX 323/651–3678, lgernert@tzell.com). **Kennedy Travel** (✉ 314 Jericho Turnpike, Floral Park, NY 11001, ☎ 516/352–4888 or 800/237–7433, FAX 516/354–8849, WEB www.kennedytravel.com). **Now, Voyager** (✉ 4406 18th St., San Francisco, CA 94114, ☎ 415/626–1169 or 800/255–6951, FAX 415/626–8626, WEB www.nowvoyager.com). **Skylink Travel and Tour** (✉ 1006 Mendocino Ave., Santa Rosa, CA 95401, ☎ 707/546–9888 or 800/225–

5759, FAX 707/546–9891), serving lesbian travelers.

GUIDEBOOKS

Plan well and you won't be sorry. Guidebooks are excellent tools—and you can take them with you. You may want to check out color-photo-illustrated *Fodor's Exploring Mexico,* which is thorough on culture and history. It's available at on-line retailers and bookstores everywhere.

AIR POLLUTION

Air pollution in Mexico City can pose a health risk. The sheer number of cars and industries in the capital, thermal inversions, and the inability to process sewage have all contributed to the high levels of lead, carbon monoxide, and other pollutants in Mexico City's atmosphere. Though the long-term effects are not known, children, the elderly, and those with respiratory problems should avoid jogging, outdoor sports, and being outdoors more than necessary on days of high smog alerts. If you have heart problems, keep in mind that Mexico City is, at 7,556 ft, the highest metropolis on the North American continent. This compounded with the smog may pose a serious health risk, so check with your doctor before planning a trip.

The Australian, British, Canadian, New Zealand, and U.S. embassies in Mexico City can provide lists of English-speaking doctors.

DIVERS' ALERT

Do not fly within 24 hours of scuba diving.

FOOD AND DRINK

In Mexico the major health risk, known as *turista,* or traveler's diarrhea, is caused by eating contaminated fruit or vegetables or drinking contaminated water. So **watch what you eat.** Stay away from ice, uncooked food, and unpasteurized milk and milk products, and **drink only bottled water** or water that has been boiled for at least 10 minutes (ask: *quiero el agua hervida por diez minutos*), even when you're brushing your teeth. Mild cases may respond to Imodium (known generically as loperamide or Lomotil) or Pepto-Bismol (not as strong), both of which can be purchased over the counter; keep in mind, though, that these drugs can complicate more serious illnesses. Drink plenty of purified water or tea; chamomile tea (*te de manzanilla*) is a good folk remedy and it's readily available in restaurants throughout Mexico. In severe cases, rehydrate yourself with Gatorade or a salt-sugar solution (½ teaspoon salt and 4 tablespoons sugar per quart of water).

When ordering cold drinks at untouristed establishments, **skip the ice:** *sin hielo.* (You can usually identify ice made commercially from purified water by its uniform shape and the hole in the center.) Hotels with water-purification systems will post signs to that effect in the rooms. *Tacos al pastor*—thin pork slices grilled on a spit and garnished with the usual cilantro, onions, and chili peppers—are delicious but dangerous. It's also a good idea to pass up *ceviche,* raw fish cured in lemon juice—a favorite appetizer, especially at seaside resorts. The Mexican Department of Health warns that marinating in lemon juice does not constitute the "cooking" that would make the shellfish safe to eat. Also, be wary of hamburgers sold from street stands, because you can never be certain what meat they are made with (horse meat is common).

MEDICAL PLANS

No one plans to get sick while traveling, but it happens, so **consider signing up with a medical-assistance company.** Members get doctor referrals, emergency evacuation or repatriation, hot lines for medical consultation, cash for emergencies, and other assistance.

➤ MEDICAL-ASSISTANCE COMPANIES: **International SOS Assistance** (WEB www.internationalsos.com; ✉ 8 Neshaminy Interplex, Suite 207, Trevose, PA 19053, ☎ 215/244–1500 or 800/523–6586, FAX 215/244–2227; ✉ 12 Chemin Riantbosson, 1217 Meyrin 1, Geneva, Switzerland, ☎ 22/785–6464, FAX 22/785–6424; ✉ 331 N. Bridge Rd., 17-00, Odeon Towers, Singapore 188720, ☎ 338–7800, FAX 338–7611).

PESTS AND OTHER HAZARDS

Caution is advised when venturing out in the Mexican sun. Sunbathers lulled by a slightly overcast sky or the sea breezes can be burned badly in just 20 minutes. To avoid overexposure, **use strong sunscreens and avoid the peak sun hours** of noon to 2 PM. Sunscreen, including many American brands, can be found in pharmacies, supermarkets, and resort gift shops.

SHOTS AND MEDICATIONS

According to the U.S. National Centers for Disease Control and Prevention (CDC), there is a limited risk of malaria and dengue fever in certain rural areas of Mexico. In most urban or easily accessible areas you need not worry. However, if you plan to visit remote regions or stay for more than six weeks, **check with the CDC's International Travelers Hotline.** In areas where malaria and dengue, both of which are carried by mosquitoes, are prevalent, use mosquito nets, wear clothing that covers the body, apply repellent containing DEET, and use spray for flying insects in living and sleeping areas. Repellents (*repelentes contra moscos*) and sprays (*repelentes de sprie contra moscos*) can be purchased at pharmacies. In some places you see mosquito coils (*espirales contra moscos*) used; they can be purchased in hardware stores (*ferretería*) as well as in pharmacies. Also **consider taking antimalarial pills** if you are doing serious adventure activities in subtropical areas. There is no vaccine to combat dengue, which if you are reasonably healthy is usually not serious (only dengue hemorrhagic fever is potentially fatal).

➤ HEALTH WARNINGS: **National Centers for Disease Control and Prevention** (CDC; National Center for Infectious Diseases, Division of Quarantine, Traveler's Health Section, ✉ 1600 Clifton Rd. NE, Atlanta, GA 30333, ☎ 888/232–3228 general information, 877/394–8747 travelers' health line, 800/311–3435 public inquiries, FAX 888/232–3299, WEB www.cdc.gov).

HOLIDAYS

Banks and government offices close on January 1, February 5 (Day of the Constitution), March 21 (Benito Juárez's birthday), May 1 (Labor Day), September 16 (Independence Day), November 20 (Day of the Revolution), and December 25. They may also close on unofficial holidays, such as Day of the Dead (November 2), and during Holy Week (the days leading to Easter Sunday). Government offices usually have reduced hours and staff from Christmas through New Year's Day.

INSURANCE

The most useful travel-insurance plan is a comprehensive policy that includes coverage for trip cancellation and interruption, default, trip delay, and medical expenses (with a waiver for preexisting conditions).

Without insurance you will lose all or most of your money if you cancel your trip, regardless of the reason. Default insurance covers you if your tour operator, airline, or cruise line goes out of business. Trip-delay covers expenses that arise because of bad weather or mechanical delays. Study the fine print when comparing policies.

If you're traveling internationally, a key component of travel insurance is coverage for medical bills incurred if you get sick on the road. Such expenses are not generally covered by Medicare or private policies. U.K. residents can buy a travel-insurance policy valid for most vacations taken during the year in which it's purchased (but check preexisting-condition coverage). British and Australian citizens need extra medical coverage when traveling overseas.

Always **buy travel policies directly from the insurance company**; if you buy them from a cruise line, airline, or tour operator that goes out of business you probably will not be covered for the agency or operator's default, a major risk. Before making any purchase, **review your existing health and home-owner's policies** to find what they cover away from home.

➤ TRAVEL INSURERS: In the U.S.: **Access America** (✉ 6600 W. Broad St., Richmond, VA 23230, ☎ 804/285–3300 or 800/284–8300, FAX 804/673–1424, WEB www.accessamerica.com). **Travel Guard International** (✉ 1145 Clark St., Stevens Point, WI 54481, ☎ 715/345–0505 or 800/826–1300, FAX 800/955–8785, WEB www.noelgroup.com).

➤ INSURANCE INFORMATION: In the U.K.: **Association of British Insurers** (✉ 51 Gresham St., London EC2V 7HQ, ☎ 020/7600–3333, FAX 020/7696–8999, WEB www.abi.org.uk). In Canada: **RBC Travel Insurance** (✉ 6880 Financial Dr., Mississauga, Ontario L5N 7Y5, ☎ 905/791-8700 or 800/668–4342, FAX 905/813–4704, WEB www.rbcinsurance.com). In Australia: **Insurance Council of Australia** (✉ Level 3, 56 Pitt St., Sydney, NSW 2000, ☎ 02/9253–5100, FAX 02/9253–5111, WEB www.ica.com.au). In New Zealand: **Insurance Council of New Zealand** (✉ Level 7, 111–115 Customhouse Quay, Box 474, Wellington, ☎ 04/472–5230, FAX 04/473–3011, WEB www.icnz.org.nz).

LANGUAGE

Spanish is the official language of Mexico, although Indian languages are spoken by approximately 8% of the population and some of those people speak no Spanish at all. Basic English is widely understood by most people employed in tourism, less so in the less-developed areas. At the very least, shopkeepers will know the numbers for bargaining purposes.

As in most other foreign countries, knowing the mother tongue has a way of opening doors, so **learn some Spanish words and phrases.** Mexicans welcome even the most halting attempts to use the language.

Castilian Spanish—which is different from Latin American Spanish not only in pronunciation and grammar but also in vocabulary—is most widely taught outside Mexico. Words or phrases that are harmless or everyday in one country can offend in another. Unless you are lucky enough to be briefed on these nuances by a native coach, the only way to learn is by trial and error.

LANGUAGES FOR TRAVELERS

A phrase book and language-tape set can help get you started. *Spanish for Travelers* (available at bookstores everywhere) is excellent.

LANGUAGE-STUDY PROGRAMS

Language institutes are pretty widespread in Mexico, and attending one is an ideal way not only to learn Mexican Spanish but also to acquaint yourself with the customs and the people of the country. For total immersion, most language schools offer boarding with a Mexican family, but your choice of lodgings and of length of stay is generally flexible.

We recommend the places listed below for learning Spanish and living with a Mexican family. AmeriSpan Unlimited, based in the United States, can arrange for language study and homestays. Special programs include those at the Centro de Idiomas de la Universidad Autónoma Benito Juárez, which offers classes in Mixtec and Zapotec as well as in Spanish, and at Cemanáuac, which has an emphasis on Latin American studies as well as language acquisition.

➤ LANGUAGE INSTITUTES: **AmeriSpan Unlimited** (✉ Box 40007, Philadelphia, PA 19106, ☎ 800/879–6640 or 215/751–1100, FAX 215/751–1986, WEB www.amerispan.com). **Centro de Idiomas de la Universidad Autónoma Benito Juárez** (✉ Burgoa at Bustamante, Oaxaca 68000, ☎ FAX 951/516–5922). **Centro Internacional de Estudios para Estranjeros** (✉ Tomás V. Gómez 125, Guadalajara, Jalisco 44600, ☎ 33/3616–4399; ✉ Libertad 42, Local 1, Puerto Vallarta, Jalisco 48360, ☎ 322/223–2082, FAX 322/223–2982). **Cemanahuac** (✉ Apartado 5-21, Cuernavaca, Morelos CP 62051, ☎ 777/318–6407, FAX 777/312–5418, WEB www.cemanahuac.com). **Iberoamerican University Programs for Foreign Students** (✉ Prolongación Paseo de la Reforma 880, Lomas de Santa Fe, Mexico, D.F. 01210, ☎ FAX 55/5267–4243). **Instituto Allende** (✉ Ancha de San Antonio 20, San Miguel de Allende, Guanajuato 37700, ☎ 415/152–0190 or 415/152–0226, FAX 415/152–4538, WEB www.instituto-allende.edu.mx). **Instituto Falcon** (✉ Callejón de la Mora 158, Guanajuato, Guanajuato 36000, ☎ 473/731–0745, WEB www.institutofalcon.com). **Instituto de Lenguas Jovel, A.C.** (✉ A.P. 62, Ma. Adelina Flores 21, San Cristóbal de las Casas, Chiapas 29200, ☎ FAX 967/678–4069, WEB www.institutojovel.com). **National Autonomous University of Mexico School for Foreign Students** (✉ Ex-Hacienda El Chorillo,

A.P. 70, Taxco, Guerrero 40200, ☎ FAX 762/622–0124). **SLI–Spanish Language Institute** (✉ Bajada de la Pradera 208, Col. Pradera, Cuernavaca, Morelos 62170, ☎ 777/311–0063, FAX 777/317–5294; in the U.S. contact Language Link Inc. ✉ Box 3006, Peoria, IL 61612, ☎ 800/552–2051, FAX 309/692–2926, WEB www.sli-spanish.com.mx).

LODGING

The price and quality of accommodations in Mexico vary about as much as the country's restaurants: from superluxurious, international-class hotels and all-inclusive resorts to modest budget properties, seedy places with shared bathrooms, *casas de huéspedes* (guest houses), youth hostels, and *cabañas* (beach huts). You may find appealing bargains while you're on the road, but if your comfort threshold is high, **look for an English-speaking staff, guaranteed dollar rates, and toll-free reservation numbers.**

The lodgings we list are the cream of the crop in each price category. Properties are assigned price categories based on the range from their least-expensive standard double room at high season (excluding holidays) to the most expensive. We always list the facilities that are available—but we don't specify whether they cost extra; when pricing accommodations, **always ask what's included and what costs extra.** Lodgings are denoted in the text with a house icon, 🏨 ; establishments with restaurants that warrant a special trip have ✕🏨 .

Assume that hotels operate on the **European Plan** (EP, with no meals) unless we specify that they use either the **Continental Plan** (CP, with a Continental breakfast), **Breakfast Plan** (BP, with a full breakfast), or the **Modified American Plan** (MAP, with breakfast and dinner) or are **all-inclusive** (including all meals and most activities).

APARTMENT AND VILLA RENTALS

If you want a home base that's roomy enough for a family and comes with cooking facilities, **consider a furnished rental.** These can save you money, especially if you're traveling with a group. Home-exchange directories sometimes list rentals as well as exchanges.

➤ INTERNATIONAL AGENTS: **At Home Abroad** (✉ 405 E. 56th St., Suite 6H, New York, NY 10022, ☎ 212/421–9165, FAX 212/752–1591, WEB www.athomeabroadinc.com). **Hideaways International** (✉ 767 Islington St., Portsmouth, NH 03801, ☎ 603/430–4433 or 800/843–4433, FAX 603/430–4444, WEB www.hideaways.com; membership $129). **Vacation Home Rentals Worldwide** (✉ 235 Kensington Ave., Norwood, NJ 07648, ☎ 201/767–9393 or 800/633–3284, FAX 201/767–5510, WEB www.vhrww.com). **Villanet** (✉ 1251 N.W. 116th St., Seattle, WA 98177, ☎ 206/417–3444 or 800/964–1891, FAX 206/417–1832, WEB www.rentavilla.com). **Villas and Apartments Abroad** (✉ 1270 Ave. of the Americas, 15th floor, New York, NY 10020, ☎ 212/897–5045 or 800/433–3020, FAX 212/897–5039, WEB www.ideal-villas.com). **Villas International** (✉ 4340 Redwood Hwy., Suite D309, San Rafael, CA 94903, ☎ 415/499–9490 or 800/221–2260, FAX 415/499–9491, WEB www.villasintl.com).

BED-AND-BREAKFASTS

The bed-and-breakfast craze hasn't missed Mexico, and the same delights that you find elsewhere in the world apply here, too—personable service, interesting local furnishings and decorative talent, and tasty morning meals. San Miguel de Allende and other Heartland cities have their share of charming places, as do Mexico City and parts of the Yucatán. If you arrive in Mexico City without a reservation, the Mexico City Hotel and Motel Association operates a booth at the airport that will assist you.

➤ RESERVATION SERVICES: **Mexico City Hotel and Motel Association** (☎ 55/5571–3268 or 55/5571–3262).

CAMPING

A host of camping opportunities exist in Mexico, but don't expect the typical U.S.-style campground. Mexico's are usually trailer parks with running water, cooking areas, and room to pitch tents; sites can cost $1–$10. To enjoy more rustic surroundings, you can set up camp off the road or on the beach in relative safety, and save loads of money. Usually, you can camp at an *ejido* (farming community) or on someone's land for free as long as you ask permission first; **ask locals about the safest and best spots.** The beaches at night aren't as safe as they once were; **be alert and don't camp alone.** And don't camp at archaeological sites.

Camping supplies are scarce in Mexico. Before you begin packing loads of camping gear, however, consider how much camping you'll actually do versus how much trouble it will be to haul around your tent, sleeping bag, stove, and accoutrements. Finding a place to store your gear can be difficult—lockers tend to be small.

In many towns along the Pacific and Caribbean coasts, beachside *palapas* (thatch-roof huts) are an excellent alternative to tent camping. All you'll need for a night in a palapa is a hammock (they don't cost much in Mexico), some mosquito netting, and a padlock for stashing your belongings in a locker.

HOME EXCHANGES

If you would like to exchange your home for someone else's, **join a home-exchange organization,** which will send you its updated listings of available exchanges for a year and will include your own listing in at least one of them. It's up to you to make specific arrangements.

➤ EXCHANGE CLUBS: **HomeLink International** (✉ Box 47747, Tampa, FL 33647, ☎ 813/975–9825 or 800/638–3841, FAX 813/910–8144, WEB www.homelink.org; $106 per year).

HOSTELS

No matter what your age, you can **save on lodging costs by staying at hostels.** In Mexico, however, high-school and college students are more often the norm at hostels than older travelers. In some 4,500 locations in more than 70 countries around the world, Hostelling International (HI), the umbrella group for a number of national youth-hostel associations, offers single-sex, dorm-style beds and, at many hostels, rooms for couples and family accommodations. Membership in any HI national hostel association, open to travelers of all ages, allows you to stay in HI-affiliated hostels at member rates; one-year membership is about $25 for adults (C$35 for a two-year minimum membership in Canada, £13 in the U.K., A$52 in Australia, and NZ$40 in New Zealand); hostels run about $10–$30 per night. Members have priority if the hostel is full; they're also eligible for discounts around the world, even on rail and bus travel in some countries.

➤ ORGANIZATIONS: **Hostelling International—American Youth Hostels** (✉ 733 15th St. NW, Suite 840, Washington, DC 20005, ☎ 202/783–6161 Ext. 29 or 30, FAX 202/783–6171, WEB www.hiayh.org). **Hostelling International—Canada** (✉ 205 Catherine St., Suite 400, Ottawa, Ontario K2P 1C3, Canada, ☎ 613/237–7884 or 800/663–5777, FAX 613/237–7868, WEB www.hostellingintl.ca). **Youth Hostel Association of England and Wales** (✉ Trevelyan House, Dimple Road, Matlock, Derbyshire DE4 3YH, U.K., ☎ 0870/8708808, FAX 0169/592–702, WEB www.yha.org.uk). **Australian Youth Hostel Association** (✉ 10 Mallett St., Camperdown, NSW 2050, Australia, ☎ 02/9565–1699, FAX 02/9565–1325, WEB www.yha.com.au). **Youth Hostels Association of New Zealand** (✉ Box 436, Christchurch, New Zealand, ☎ 03/379–9970, FAX 03/365–4476, WEB www.yha.org.nz).

HOTELS

It's essential to **reserve in advance** if you're traveling during high season or holiday periods. Overbooking is a common practice in some parts of Mexico, such as Cancún and Acapulco. Travelers to remote areas will encounter little difficulty in obtaining rooms on a walk-in basis unless it's during a holiday season.

Hotel rates are subject to the 17% value-added tax (it's 10% in the states of Quintana Roo, Baja California, and Baja California Sur). In addition, many states charge a 2% hotel tax, and the revenue is being used for tourism promotion. Service charges and meals generally are not included in the hotel rates. The Mexican government categorizes hotels, based on qualitative evaluations, into *gran turismo* (superdeluxe, or five-star-plus, properties, of which there are only about 30 nationwide); five-star down to one-star; and economy class. Keep in mind that many hotels that might otherwise be rated higher have opted for a lower category to avoid higher interest rates on loans and financing.

High- versus low-season rates can vary significantly. Hotels in this guide have private bathrooms with showers, unless stated otherwise; bathtubs are not common in inexpensive hotels and properties in smaller towns.

If you're particularly sensitive to noise, you should **call ahead to learn if your hotel of choice is located on a busy street.** Many of the most engaging accommodations in Mexico are on downtown intersections that experience heavy automobile and pedestrian traffic. And large hotels are known to have lobby bars with live music in the middle of an open-air atrium leading directly to rooms. When you book, **request a room far from the bar.**

All hotels listed have private bath unless otherwise noted.

RESERVING A ROOM

➤ TOLL-FREE NUMBERS: **Best Western** (☏ 800/528–1234, WEB www.bestwestern.com). **Choice** (☏ 800/424–6423, WEB www.choicehotels.com). **Days Inn** (☏ 800/325–2525, WEB www.daysinn.com). **Doubletree and Red Lion Hotels** (☏ 800/222–8733, WEB www.hilton.com). **Four Seasons** (☏ 800/332–3442, WEB www.fourseasons.com). **Hilton** (☏ 800/445–8667, WEB www.hilton.com). **Holiday Inn** (☏ 800/465–4329, WEB www.sixcontinentshotels.com). **Howard Johnson** (☏ 800/654–4656, WEB www.hojo.com). **Hyatt Hotels and Resorts** (☏ 800/233–1234, WEB www.hyatt.com). **Inter-Continental** (☏ 800/327–0200, WEB www.intercontinental.com). **Marriott** (☏ 800/228–9290, WEB www.marriott.com). **Le Meridien** (☏ 800/543–4300, WEB www.lemeridien-hotels.com). **Nikko Hotels International** (☏ 800/645–5687, WEB www.nikkohotels.com). **Omni** (☏ 800/843–6664, WEB www.omnihotels.com). **Radisson** (☏ 800/333–3333, WEB www.radisson.com). **Ritz-Carlton** (☏ 800/241–3333, WEB www.ritzcarlton.com). **Sheraton** (☏ 800/325–3535, WEB www.starwood.com/sheraton). Westin Hotels and Resorts (☏ 888/625–5144, WEB www.starwood.com/westin). **Wyndham Hotels and Resorts** (☏ 800/822–4200, WEB www.wyndham.com).

MAIL AND SHIPPING

The Mexican postal system is notoriously slow and unreliable; **never send packages** or expect to receive them, as they may be stolen. (For emergencies, use a courier service or the express-mail service, with insurance). If you're an American Express cardholder, your best bet is to have packages sent to the nearest AmEx office.

Post offices (*oficinas de correos*) are found in even the smallest villages. International postal service is all airmail, but even so your letter will take anywhere from 10 days to six weeks to arrive. Service within Mexico can be equally slow.

OVERNIGHT SERVICES

Federal Express, DHL, and United Parcel Service are available in major cities and many resort areas, but Federal Express is the most widespread. They offer office or hotel pickup with 24-hour advance notice and are very reliable. From Mexico City to anywhere in the United States, the minimum charge is around $23 for a package weighing about one pound. Starting prices are higher for Australia, Canada, New Zealand, and the U.K., and deliveries take longer.

➤ MAJOR SERVICES: In Mexico City: **DHL** (☏ 55/5345–7000). **Federal Express** (☏ 55/5228–9904). **United Parcel Service** (☏ 55/5228–7900).

POSTAL ABBREVIATIONS

Mexican states have postal abbreviations of two or more letters. To send mail to Mexico, use the following Mexican state postal codes: **Baja California**: B.C.; **Baja California Sur**: B.C.S.; **Campeche**: Camp.; **Chiapas**: Chis.; **Chihuahua**: Chih.; **Distrito Federal (Mexico City)**: D.F.; **Guanajuato**: Gto.; **Guerrero**: Gro.; **Jalisco**: Jal.; **Estado de Mexico**: Edo. de Mex.; **Michoacán**: Mich.; **Morelos**: Mor.; **Nuevo Leon**: N.L.; **Oaxaca**: Oax.; **Querétaro**: Qro.; **Quintana Roo**: Q. Roo; **Sinaloa**: Sin.; **Sonora**: Son.; **Tabasco**: Tab.; **Veracruz**: Ver.; **Yucatán**: Yuc.; **Zacatecas**: Zac.

POSTAL RATES

It costs 4.80 pesos (about 50¢) to send a postcard or letter weighing under 20 grams to the United States or Canada; it's 5.90 pesos (about 60¢) to Europe or Australia.

RECEIVING MAIL

To receive mail in Mexico, you can have it sent to your hotel or use *poste restante* at the post office. In the latter case, the address must include the words "a/c Lista de Correos" (general delivery), followed by the city, state, postal code, and country. To use this service, you must first register with the post office at which you wish to receive your mail. The post office posts and updates daily a list of names for whom mail has been received. Holders of American Express cards or traveler's checks can have mail sent to them in care of the local American Express office. For a list of offices worldwide, write for the *Traveler's Companion* from **American Express** (✉ Box 678, Canal Street Station, New York, NY 10013, WEB www.americanexpress.com).

MONEY MATTERS

Prices in this book are quoted most often in U.S. dollars. We would prefer to list costs in pesos, but because the value of the currency fluctuates considerably, what costs 90 pesos today might cost 120 pesos in six months.

Mexico is less expensive than other North American vacation spots, such as the Caribbean. In general, costs will vary with the when, where, and how of your travel in Mexico. If you travel only by air or package tour, stay at international hotel-chain properties, and eat at tourist restaurants, you might not find Mexico such a bargain. If you want a closer look at the country and are not wedded to standard creature comforts, you can spend as little as $25 a day on room, board, and local transportation. Speaking Spanish is also helpful in bargaining situations and when asking for dining recommendations.

Cancún, Puerto Vallarta, Mexico City, Monterrey, Acapulco, Ixtapa, Los Cabos, Manzanillo, and, to a lesser extent, Mazatlán and Huatulco are the most expensive places to visit in Mexico. All the beach towns, however, offer budget accommodations, and the smaller, less accessible ones are often more moderately priced, examples being the Gulf coast and northern Yucatán, parts of Quintana Roo, some of the less developed spots north and south of Puerto Vallarta in the states of Jalisco and Nayarit, Puerto Escondido, and the smaller Oaxacan coastal towns as well as those of Chiapas and Tabasco.

Average costs in major cities vary, although less than in the past because of an increase in business travelers. A stay in one of Mexico City's top hotels can cost more than $200 (as much or more than at the coastal resorts), but you can get away with a tab of $45 for two at what was once an expensive restaurant.

Probably the best value for your travel dollar is in smaller, inland towns, such as San Cristóbal de las Casas, Mérida, Morelia, Guanajuato, and Oaxaca, where tourism is less developed. Although Oaxaca lodging can run more than $150 a night, simple colonial-style hotels with adequate accommodations for under $40 can be found, and tasty, filling meals are rarely more than $15.

Prices throughout this guide are given for adults. Substantially reduced fees are almost always available for children, students, and senior citizens. For information on taxes, *see* Taxes.

ATMS

ATMs (*cajeros automáticos*) are becoming commonplace in more and more Mexican towns and cities. Cirrus and Plus are the most commonly found networks in Mexico. Before you leave home, **ask what the transaction fee will be** for withdrawing money in Mexico. (It's usually $3 a pop.) Many Mexican ATMs cannot accept PINs (personal identification numbers) that have more than four digits; if yours is longer, **ask your bank about changing your PIN (*número de clave*) before you leave home,** and keep in mind that processing such a change often takes a few weeks.

If your transaction still cannot be completed—an annoyingly commonoccurrence—chances are that the computer lines are busy or that the machine has run out of money or is being serviced.

For cash advances, plan to use Visa or MasterCard, as many Mexican ATMs don't accept American Express. The ATMs at Banamex, one of the oldest nationwide banks, tend to be the most reliable. Bancomer is another bank with many ATM locations, but they usually provide only cash advances. The newer Serfín banks have reliable ATMs that accept credit cards as well as Plus and Cirrus cards.

See Safety, on avoiding ATM robberies.

CREDIT CARDS

Traveler's checks and all major U.S. credit cards are accepted in most tourist areas of Mexico. Smaller, less expensive restaurants and shops, however, tend to take only cash. In general, credit cards aren't accepted in small towns and villages, except for tourist-oriented hotels. Diners Club is usually accepted only in major hotel chains; the most widely accepted cards are MasterCard and Visa. When shopping, you can usually get better prices if you **pay with cash.**

At the same time, when traveling internationally you'll **receive wholesale exchange rates** when you make purchases with credit cards. These exchange rates are usually better than rates that banks give you for changing money. In Mexico the decision to pay cash or use a credit card might depend on whether the establishment in which you are making a purchase finds bargaining for prices acceptable. To avoid fraud, it's wise to **make sure that "pesos" is clearly marked on all credit-card receipts.**

Throughout this guide, the following abbreviations are used: **AE**, American Express; **DC**, Diners Club; **MC**, MasterCard; and **V**, Visa.

Before you leave for Mexico, be sure to **find out your credit-card companies' toll-free card-replacement numbers** that work at home as well as in Mexico; they could be impossible to find once you get to Mexico, and the calls you place to cancel your cards can be long ones. **Carry these numbers separately from your wallet** so you'll have them if you need to call to report lost or stolen cards.

➤ REPORTING LOST CARDS: **American Express** (☎ 801/965–2060). **Diners Club** (☎ 702/797–5532). **MasterCard** (☎ 800/307–7309). **Visa** (☎ 800/847–2911).

CURRENCY

In spring 2002, the peso was still "floating" after the devaluation enacted by the Zedillo administration in late 1994. Although exchange rates have been as favorable as 9.2 pesos to US$1, 5.7 pesos to C$1, 13 pesos to £1, 4.8 pesos to A$1, and 4 pesos to NZ$1, the market and prices continue to adjust. **Check with your bank or the financial pages of your local newspaper for current exchange rates.** For quick estimates of how much something costs in U.S. dollar terms, divide prices given in pesos by 10. For example, 50 pesos would be about $5.

Mexican currency comes in denominations of 10-, 20-, 50-, 100-, 200-, 500-, and 1,000-peso bills. Coins come in denominations of 20, 10, 5, and 1 pesos and 50, 20, 10, and 5 centavos. Many of the coins and bills are very similar, so check carefully.

U.S. dollar bills (but not coins) are widely accepted in many parts of the Yucatán, particularly in Cancún and Cozumel, where you'll often find prices in shops quoted in dollars. However, you'll get your change in pesos. Many tourist shops and market vendors as well as virtually all hotel service personnel also accept dollars.

CURRENCY EXCHANGE

ATM transaction fees may be higher abroad than at home, but ATM currency-exchange rates are the best of all because they're based on wholesale rates offered only by major banks. And if you take out a fair amount of cash per withdrawal, the transaction fee becomes less of a strike against the exchange rate (in percentage terms). However, most ATMs allow only up to $300 a transaction. Banks and *casas de cambio* (money-exchange houses) have the second-best exchange rates. The difference from one place to another is usually only a few centavos.

Most banks change money on weekdays only until 1 (though they stay open until 5), although casas de cambio generally stay open until 6 and often operate on weekends. Bank rates are regulated by the federal government and are therefore invariable, whereas casas de cambio have slightly more variable rates. Some hotels also exchange money, but for providing you with this convenience they help themselves to a bigger commission than banks.

You can do well at most airport exchange booths, except in Cancún, but not necessarily at rail and bus stations, in hotels, in restaurants, or in stores.

When changing money, count your bills before leaving the bank or casa de cambio, and don't accept any partially torn or taped-together notes; they won't be accepted anywhere. Also, many shop and restaurant owners are unable to make change for large bills. Enough of these encounters may compel you to request *billetes chicos* (small bills) when you exchange money.

For the most favorable rates, **change money through banks.** Although ATM transaction fees may be higher abroad than at home, ATM rates are excellent because they are based on wholesale rates offered only by major banks. You won't do as well at exchange booths in airports or rail and bus stations, in hotels, in restaurants, or in stores. To avoid lines at airport exchange booths, **get a bit of local currency before you leave home.**

➤ EXCHANGE SERVICES: International Currency Express (☎ 888/278–6628 orders). Thomas Cook Currency Services (☎ 800/287–7362 orders and retail locations, WEB www.us.thomascook.com).

TRAVELER'S CHECKS

Do you need traveler's checks? It depends on where you're headed. If you're going to rural areas and small towns, go with cash; traveler's checks are best used in cities. Lost or stolen checks can usually be replaced within 24 hours. To ensure a speedy refund, buy your own traveler's checks—don't let someone else pay for them: irregularities like this can cause delays. The person who bought the checks should make the call to request a refund.

OUTDOORS AND SPORTS

Mexico offers golf, waterskiing, diving, and hiking. Mexico City, Guadalajara, Monterrey, and smaller cities as well as beach resorts all have golf facilities. Courses abound in Los Cabos, an area that's been gearing up to become Mexico's premier golf resort.

Waterskiing is very popular at beach resorts, and the scuba diving in Cozumel, the Caribbean coast, and Cancún is excellent. Renting equipment isn't a problem in the larger resort areas.

Mexico's volcanoes and mountains provide many hiking opportunities. The Copper Canyon is a favorite destination for this.

PACKING

When traveling internationally, it's always a good idea to pack a change of clothes in your carry-on bag in case your other luggage is lost. Take at least a change of underwear, essential toiletries, and a shirt—add to that a bathing suit if you're heading to a beach resort. In your carry-on luggage, **pack an extra pair of eyeglasses or contact lenses and enough of any medication** you take to last a few days longer than the entire trip. You may also ask your doctor to write a spare prescription using the drug's generic name, since brand names may vary from country to country. In luggage to be checked, **never pack prescription drugs or valuables.** And don't forget to carry with you the addresses of offices that handle refunds of lost traveler's checks. Check *Fodor's How to Pack* (available in bookstores everywhere) for more tips.

To avoid customs and security delays, carry medications in their original packaging. Don't pack any sharp objects in your carry-on luggage, including knives of any size or material, scissors, manicure tools, and corkscrews, or anything else that might arouse suspicion.

For resorts, bring lightweight sportswear, bathing suits, and cover-ups for the beach. Bathing suits and immodest clothing are inappropriate for shopping and sightseeing, both in cities and beach resorts. Mexico City is a bit more formal than the resorts and, because of its high elevation, cooler. Men will want to bring lightweight suits or slacks and blazers for fancier restaurants; women should pack tailored dresses or pants suits. Many Mexico City restaurants require jacket and tie; jeans are acceptable for shopping and sightseeing, but shorts are frowned upon for men and women. You'll need a lightweight topcoat for winter and an all-weather coat and umbrella in case of sudden summer rainstorms. Lately the rains have been appearing at other times of the year, so always **pack a small umbrella** at least.

Cancún and Acapulco are both casual and elegant; you'll see high-style sportswear, cotton slacks and walking shorts, and plenty of colorful sundresses. The sun can be fierce; **bring a sun hat and sunscreen** for the beach and for sightseeing. You'll need a sweater or jacket to cope with hotel and restaurant air-conditioning, which can be glacial, and for occasional cool spells. Few restaurants require a jacket and tie.

Luggage carts are free at the Mexico City airport, practically the only airport where you'll find them; bus and train stations do not have carts.

CHECKING LUGGAGE

You are allowed one carry-on bag and one personal article, such as a purse or a laptop computer. Make sure that everything you carry aboard will fit under your seat or in the overhead bin. Get to the gate early, so you can board as soon as possible, before the overhead bins fill up.

If you are flying internationally, note that baggage allowances may be determined not by piece but by weight—generally 88 pounds (40 kilograms) in first class, 66 pounds (30 kilograms) in business class, and 44 pounds (20 kilograms) in economy.

Airline liability for baggage is limited to $2,500 per person on flights within the United States. On international flights it amounts to $9.07 per pound or $20 per kilogram for checked baggage (roughly $640 per 70-pound bag) and $400 per passenger for unchecked baggage. You can buy additional coverage at check-in for about $10 per $1,000 of coverage, but it excludes a rather extensive list of items, shown on your airline ticket.

Before departure, **itemize your bags' contents** and their worth, and label the bags with your name, address, and phone number. (If you use your home address, cover it so potential thieves can't see it readily.) Inside each bag, **pack a copy of your itinerary.** At check-in, **make sure that each bag is correctly tagged** with the destination airport's three-letter code. If your bags arrive damaged or fail to arrive at all, file a written report with the airline before leaving the airport.

PASSPORTS AND VISAS

When traveling internationally, **carry your passport** even if you don't need one (it's always the best form of I.D.) and **make two photocopies of the data page** (one for someone at home and another for you, carried separately from your passport). If you lose your passport, promptly call the nearest embassy or consulate and the local police.

U.S. passport applications for children under age 14 require consent from both parents or legal guardians; both parents must appear together to sign the application. If only one parent appears, he or she must submit a written statement from the other parent authorizing passport issuance for the child. A parent with sole authority must present evidence of it when applying; acceptable documentation includes the child's certified birth certificate listing only the applying parent, a court order specifically permitting this parent's travel with the child, or a death certificate for the nonapplying parent. Application forms and instructions are available on the Web site of the U.S. State Department's Bureau of Consular Affairs (www.travel.state.gov).

ENTERING MEXICO

For stays of up to 180 days, Americans must prove citizenship through either a valid passport, certified copy of a birth certificate, or voter-registration card (the last two must be accompanied by a government-issue photo ID). Minors traveling with one parent need notarized permission from the absent parent. For stays of more than 180 days, all U.S. citizens, even infants, need a valid passport to enter Mexico. Minors also need parental permission.

Canadians need only proof of citizenship to enter Mexico for stays of up to six months.

U.K. citizens need only a valid passport to enter Mexico for stays of up to three months.

Mexico has instituted a $17 visitor fee that applies to all visitors—except those entering by sea at Mexican ports who stay less than 72 hours, and those entering by land who do not stray past the 26–30-km (16–18-mi) checkpoint into the country's interior. For visitors arriving by air, the fee, which covers visits of more than 72 hours and up to 30 days, is usually tacked on to the airline-ticket price. You must pay the fee each time you extend your 30-day tourist visa.

PASSPORT OFFICES

The best time to apply for a passport or to renew is in fall and winter. Before any trip, check your passport's expiration date, and, if necessary, renew it as soon as possible.

➤ AUSTRALIAN CITIZENS: **Australian State Passport Office** (☎ 131–232, WEB www.passports.gov.au).

➤ CANADIAN CITIZENS: **Passport Office** (to mail in applications: ✉ Department of Foreign Affairs and International Trade, Ottawa, Ontario K1A 0G3; ☎ 800/567–6868 toll-free in Canada or 819/994–3500, WEB www.dfait-maeci.gc.ca/passport).

➤ NEW ZEALAND CITIZENS: **New Zealand Passport Office** (☎ 0800/22–5050 or 04/474–8100, WEB www.passports.govt.nz).

➤ U.K. CITIZENS: **London Passport Office** (☎ 0870/521–0410, WEB www.passport.gov.uk) for application procedures and emergency passports.

➤ U.S. CITIZENS: **National Passport Information Center** (☎ 900/225–5674, 35¢ per minute for automated service or $1.05 per minute for operator service, WEB www.travel.state.gov).

REST ROOMS

Expect to find clean flushing toilets, toilet tissue, soap, and running water in the major tourist destinations. Other places should have simple but clean toilets. The more primitive rest rooms, usually in public areas with little tourist traffic, will have no paper, no water at times, and no toilet seats. Some public places, like bus stations, charge one or two pesos to use the facility, but toilet paper is included in the fee. Keep tissues with you, just in case.

SAFETY

The U.S. State Department has warned of "critical levels" of crime against tourists in Mexico, noting an increase in the level of violence of the crimes committed and what appeared to be a significant incidence of sexual assaults against women. Reports indicated that uniformed police officers were on occasion perpetrating the nonviolent crimes, sometimes stopping cars and seeking money.

The largest increase in crime has taken place in Mexico City, where the age-old problem of pickpocketing has been overshadowed by robberies at gunpoint. Another development has been abductions and robberies in taxicabs hailed from the street (as opposed to hired from a hotel or taxi stand).

Many foreigners are aware of Mexico's reputation for corruption. The patronage system is a well-entrenched part of Mexican politics and industry, and workers in the public sector—notably policemen and customs officials—are notoriously underpaid. Everyone has heard some horror story about highway assaults, pickpocketing, bribes, or foreigners languishing in Mexican jails. These reports of crimes apply in large part to Mexico City and more-remote areas of Oaxaca and Chiapas. So far, crime is not such a problem in the Heartland (cities like San Miguel de Allende), Puerto Vallarta, Cancún, and much of the rest of the country. Pickpocketing is usually the biggest concern.

Use common sense everywhere, but **exercise particular caution in Mexico City.** In addition, **avoid remote, less-traveled areas of Oaxaca, Chiapas, and Guerrero,** as crime in these areas can be more life-threatening. Do not pick up hitchhikers or hitchhike yourself. Also, try to use luxury buses (rather than second- or third-class vehicles), which use the safer toll roads—and it's best to travel only during the day. For the time being, **women should not venture alone onto uncrowded beaches,** and everyone should **avoid urges to get away from it all** on your own (even as a couple) to go hiking in remote national parks.

In Mexico City, **don't wear any valuables, including watches,** and try not to act too much like a tourist. Wear a money belt, put valuables in hotel safes, avoid driving on untraveled streets and roads at night, and carry your own baggage whenever possible, unless in a luxury hotel. Also, you won't need your passport in the city, so leave it in the hotel safe—replacing it would be more trouble than you need.

Take only registered hotel taxis or have a hotel concierge call a *sitio* (stationed cab)—**do not hail taxis on the street under any circumstances.** Use ATMs during the day and in big, enclosed commercial areas. Avoid the glass-enclosed street variety of banks where you may be more vulnerable to thieves who force you to withdraw money for them; abduction is also possible. This cannot be stressed strongly enough.

Bear in mind that reporting a crime to the police is often a frustrating experience unless you speak excellent Spanish and have a great deal of patience. If you are the victim of an assault, contact your local consular agent or the consular section of your country's embassy in Mexico City, especially if you need medical attention. For more-detailed information on travel safety, consult the Mexican Ministry of Tourism's Web site at www.safemexico.com.

WOMEN IN MEXICO

Don't wear a money belt or a waist pack, both of which peg you as a tourist. If you carry a purse, choose one with a zipper and a thick strap that you can drape across your body; adjust the length so that the purse sits in front of you at or above hip level. Store only enough money in the purse to cover casual spending. Distribute the rest of your cash and any valuables (including credit cards and your passport) between a deep front pocket, an inside jacket or vest pocket, and a hidden money pouch. Do not reach for the money pouch once in public.

Women traveling alone are likely to be subjected to *piropos* (catcalls). To avoid this, don't wear tight or provocative clothes or enter street bars or cantinas alone; in some very conservative rural areas, even sleeveless shirts or Bermuda shorts may seem inappropriate to the locals. Your best strategy is always to ignore the offender, do not speak to him, and go on about your business. If the situation seems to be getting out of hand, don't hesitate to ask someone for help. Piropos are one thing, but more aggressive harassment of women is not considered acceptable behavior. If you express outrage, you should find no shortage of willing defenders.

SENIOR-CITIZEN TRAVEL

To qualify for age-related discounts, **mention your senior-citizen status up front** when booking hotel reservations (not when checking out) and before you're seated in restaurants (not when paying the bill). Be sure to have identification on hand. When renting a car, ask about promotional car-rental discounts, which can be cheaper than senior-citizen rates.

Mexican senior citizens must present a special government-issued credential to obtain discounts at any facility; foreign-issued credentials (such as from AARP) are not recognized in the country, and it's not enough to mention that you are a senior citizen.

➤ EDUCATIONAL PROGRAMS: **Elderhostel** (✉ 11 Ave. de Lafayette, Boston, MA 02111-1746, ☎ 877/426–8056, FAX 877/426–2166, WEB www.elderhostel.org). **Interhostel** (✉ University of New Hampshire, 6 Garrison Ave., Durham, NH 03824, ☎ 603/862–1147 or 800/733–9753, FAX 603/862–1113, WEB www.learn.unh.edu/interhostel).

SHOPPING

At least three varieties of outlets sell Mexican crafts: indoor and outdoor municipal markets, shops run by Fonart (a government agency to promote Mexican crafts), and tourist boutiques in towns, shopping malls, and hotels. If you buy in the municipal shops or markets, you can avoid the value-added tax (*impuesto de valor agregado,* or IVA), but you should pay in pesos because paying in dollars won't give you a good exchange rate most of the time. Be sure to **take your time and inspect merchandise closely**: you'll find bargains, but quality can be inconsistent. Fonart shops are a good reference for quality and prices (the latter are fixed), and they accept credit cards. Boutiques also accept credit cards if not dollars; although their prices may be higher, they are convenient and sometimes carry one-of-a-kind items. (You may be asked to pay up to 10% more on credit-card purchases; savvy shoppers with cash have greater bargaining clout.) The 15% IVA (10% in the states of Quintana Roo, Baja California, and Baja California Sur) is charged on most purchases but is often included in the price or disregarded by eager or desperate vendors.

It is not always true that the closer you are to the source of an article, the better the selection and price are likely to be. Mexico City, Guadalajara, Páztcuaro, San Miguel de Allende, Puerto Vallarta, Oaxaca, San Cristóbal de las Casas, and Mérida have some of the best selections of crafts—and bargains as well. Prices are usually higher and selections more touristy at beach resorts.

Bargaining is widely accepted in markets, but you should understand that not all vendors will start out with outrageous prices. If you feel the price quoted is too high, start off by offering half the asking price and then slowly go up, usually to about 70% of the original price. Always **shop around.** In major shopping areas such as San Miguel, shops will wrap and send purchases back to the United States via a package-delivery company. Items made from tortoiseshell and black coral are not allowed into the United States.

STUDENTS IN MEXICO

➤ I.D.S AND SERVICES: **Council Travel** (✉ 205 E. 42nd St., 15th floor, New York, NY 10017, ☎ 212/822–2700 or 888/226–8624, FAX 212/822–2719, WEB www.counciltravel.com). **Travel Cuts** (✉ 187 College St., Toronto, Ontario M5T 1P7, Canada, ☎ 416/979–2406 or 888/838–2887, FAX 416/979–8167, FAX 416/979–8167, WEB www.travelcuts.com).

TAXES

Mexico charges an airport departure tax of US$18 or the peso equivalent for international and domestic flights. This tax is usually included in the price of your ticket, but check to be certain. Traveler's checks and credit cards are not accepted at the airport as payment for this.

Many states are charging a 2% tax on accommodations, the funds from which are being used for tourism promotion.

VALUE-ADDED TAX

Mexico has a value-added tax of 15% (10% in the states of Quintana Roo, Baja California, and Baja California Sur), called IVA (*impuesto de valor agregado*), which is occasionally (and illegally) waived for cash purchases. Other taxes and charges apply for phone calls made from your hotel room.

TAXIS

Government-certified taxis have a license with a photo of the driver and a taxi number prominently displayed, a meter, and either an orange or green stripe at the bottom of the license plate. In many cities, taxis charge by zones. In this case, be sure to agree on a fare before setting off. For reasons of security, especially in Mexico City, it's always best to call a *sitio* (stationed) cab rather than to flag one on the street. Tipping is not necessary unless the driver helps you with your bags, in which case a few pesos are appropriate.

AT THE AIRPORT

From the airport, **take the authorized taxi service.** Purchase the taxi vouchers sold at stands inside or just outside the terminal, which ensure that your fare is established beforehand. However, before you purchase your ticket, it's wise to locate the taxi originating and destination zones on a map and make sure your ticket is properly zoned; if you need a ticket only to Zone 3, don't pay for a ticket to Zone 4 or 5. Don't leave your luggage unattended while making transportation arrangements.

IN CITIES AND BEACH RESORTS

In Mexican cities, **take a taxi rather than public transportation,** which, though inexpensive, is frequently slow and sometimes patrolled by pickpockets. (The exceptions are the air-conditioned buses in Acapulco, Cancún, and Mérida.) Always **establish the fare beforehand,** and **count your change.** In most of the beach resorts, there are inexpensive fixed-route fares, but if you don't ask, or your Spanish isn't great, you may get taken. In cities, especially the capital, be certain that the meter runs before getting in, and remember that there is usually an extra charge after 10 PM. For out-of-town and hourly services, negotiate a rate in advance; many drivers will start by asking how much you want to pay to get a sense of how street-smart you are. In all cases, if you are unsure of what a fare should be, ask your hotel's front-desk personnel or bell captain.

Hire taxis only from hotels and taxi stands *(sitios)*, or use those that you have summoned by phone. Street taxis might be the cheapest, but an alarming increase in abductions and violent crime involves street cabs—for safety's sake, under no circumstances should you take one. And never leave luggage unattended in a taxi.

In addition to private taxis, many cities have bargain-price collective taxi services using Volkswagen minibuses (called *combis*) and sedans. The service is called *colectivo* or *pesero*. Peseros run along fixed routes, and you hail them on the street and tell the driver where you are going. The fare—which you pay before you get out—is based on distance traveled. We recommend that you take only the *colectivos* (special airport taxis) that transport passengers from—and sometimes to—airports. In places like Cozumel you'll find that colectivos only—not taxis—are permitted to take passengers from airport terminals into town.

TELEPHONES

Many phones, especially in the better city hotels, have Touch-Tone (digital) circuitry. If you think you'll need to access an automated phone system or voice mail in the United States or elsewhere and you don't know what phone service will be available, it's a good idea to take along a Touch-Tone simulator (you can buy one for about $17 at most electronics stores).

AREA AND COUNTRY CODES

The country code for Mexico is 52. When calling a Mexico number from abroad, dial the country code and then all of the numbers listed for the entry.

The country code is 1 for the United States and Canada, 61 for Australia, 64 for New Zealand, and 44 for the United Kingdom.

DIRECTORY AND OPERATOR ASSISTANCE

Directory assistance is 040 nationwide. For international assistance, dial 00 first for an international operator and most likely you'll get one who speaks English; tell the operator in what city, state, and country you require directory assistance, and he or she will connect you with directory assistance there.

INTERNATIONAL CALLS

To make an international call, **dial 00 before the country code, area code, and number.** When calling home, the country code for the U.S. and Canada is 1, the U.K. 44, Australia 61, New Zealand 64, and South Africa 27.

LOCAL CALLS AND LONG-DISTANCE CALLS

In February 2002, Mexico implemented a national numbering program that entailed switching to a new 10-digit dialing plan. **Only 10-digit calls can be connected** throughout the country. Two-digit regional codes now precede the old eight-digit numbers for Mexico City (55), Guadalajara (33), and Monterrey (81). To call Mexico City from within Mexico, you must still dial 01, then the new regional code (55) followed by the old eight-digit number. From outside the country, you now dial the country code (52) followed by the 10-digit number. In other areas in Mexico, eight-digit numbers will drop their first number and be preceded by new three-digit regional codes. To convert any old number into a 10-digit number, use the converter on www.sprint.com/mexico/mexicodialplanchange.

For local or long-distance calls, one option is to find a *caseta de larga distancia,* a telephone service usually operated out of a store such as a *papelería* (stationery store), pharmacy, restaurant, or other small business; look for the phone symbol on the door. Casetas may cost more to use than pay phones, but you have a better chance of immediate success. To make a direct long-distance call, tell the person on duty the number you'd like to call, and she or he will give you a rate and dial for you. Rates seem to vary widely, so shop around. Sometimes you can make collect calls from casetas, and sometimes you cannot, depending on the individual operator and possibly your degree of visible desperation. Casetas will generally charge 50¢–$1.50 to place a collect call (some charge by the minute); it's usually better to call *por cobrar* (collect) from a pay phone.

LONG-DISTANCE SERVICES

AT&T, MCI, and Sprint access codes make calling long distance relatively convenient, but you may find the local access number blocked in many hotel rooms. First ask the hotel operator to connect you. If the hotel operator balks, ask for an international operator, or dial the international operator yourself. One way to improve your odds of getting connected to your long-distance carrier is to travel with more than one company's calling card (a hotel may block Sprint, for example, but not MCI). If all else fails, call from a pay phone.

➤ ACCESS CODES: **AT&T Direct** (☎ 01-800/288–2872 or 01-800/112–2020). **MCI WorldPhone** (☎ 01-800/021–8000 or 001-800/674–7000).

PHONE CARDS

In most parts of the country now, pay phones accept prepaid cards, called Ladatel cards, sold in 30-, 50- or 100-peso denominations at newsstands or pharmacies. Many pay phones in Mexico accept only these cards; coin-only pay phones are usually broken. Still other phones have two unmarked slots, one for a Ladatel (a Spanish acronym for "long-distance direct dialing") card and the other for a credit card. These are primarily for Mexican bank cards, but some accept Visa or MasterCard, though *not* U.S. telephone credit cards.

To use a Ladatel card, simply insert it in the appropriate slot, dial 001 (for calls to the States) or 01 (for calls in Mexico) and the area code and number you're trying to reach. Local calls may also be placed with the card. Credit is deleted from the card as you use it, and your balance is displayed on a small screen on the phone.

TOLL-FREE NUMBERS

Toll-free numbers in Mexico start with an 800 prefix. To reach them, you need to dial 01 before the number. In this guide, Mexico-only toll-free numbers appear as follows: 01-800/12–345 (numbers can also have six or seven digits). The 800 numbers listed simply 800/123–4567 work in the U.S. only.

TIME

Mexico has three time zones; most of the country falls in Central Standard Time, which includes Mexico City and is in line with Chicago. Baja California is on Pacific Standard Time—the same as California. Baja California Sur and parts of the northwest coast, including Sonora, are on Mountain Standard Time.

TIPPING

When tipping in Mexico, remember that the minimum wage is the equivalent of $3 a day and that the vast majority of workers in the tourist industry live barely above the poverty line. However, there are Mexicans who think in dollars and know, for example, that in the United States porters are tipped about $2 a bag. Many of them expect the peso equivalent from foreigners and may complain if they feel they deserve more—you and your conscience must decide. Following are some guidelines. Naturally, larger tips are always welcome.

Porters and bellhops at airports and at moderate and inexpensive hotels: $1 per bag.

Porters at expensive hotels: $2 per person.

Maids: $1 per night (all hotels).

Waiters: 10%–15% of the bill, depending on service (make sure a 10%–15% service charge hasn't already been added to the bill, although this practice is more common in resorts).

Taxi drivers: Tipping is necessary only if the driver helps with your bags—5 pesos to 10 pesos should be sufficient, depending on the extent of the help.

Tour guides and drivers: at least $1 per half day, minimum.

Gas-station attendants: 3 pesos to 5 pesos; if they check the oil, tires, etc., tip more.

Parking attendants and theater ushers: 5 pesos to 10 pesos. Some restaurants and theaters charge for valet-parking service; it's still customary to tip the attendant at least 10 pesos.

TOURS AND PACKAGES

Because everything is prearranged on a prepackaged tour or independent vacation, you spend less time planning—and often get it all at a good price.

BOOKING WITH AN AGENT

Travel agents are excellent resources. But it's a good idea to collect brochures from several agencies, as some agents' suggestions may be influenced by relationships with tour and package firms that reward them for volume sales. If you have a special interest, **find an agent with expertise in that area**; the American Society of Travel Agents (ASTA; ☞ Travel Agencies) has a database of specialists worldwide.

Make sure your travel agent knows the accommodations and other services of the place being recommended. Ask about the hotel's location, room size, beds, and whether it has a pool, room service, or programs for children, if you care about these. Has your agent been there in person or sent others whom you can contact?

Do some homework on your own, too: local tourism boards can provide information about lesser-known and small-niche operators, some of which may sell only direct.

BUYER BEWARE

Each year consumers are stranded or lose their money when tour operators—even large ones with excellent reputations—go out of business. So **check out the operator.** Ask several travel agents about its reputation, and try to **book with a company that has a consumer-protection program.** (Look for information in the company's brochure.) In the United States, members of the National Tour Association and the United States Tour Operators Association are required to set aside funds to cover your payments and travel arrangements in the event that the company defaults. It's also a good idea to choose a company that participates in the American Society of Travel Agents' Tour Operator Program (TOP); ASTA will act as mediator in any disputes between you and your tour operator.

Remember that the more your package or tour includes the better you can predict the ultimate cost of your vacation. Make sure you know exactly what is covered, and **beware of hidden costs.** Are taxes, tips, and transfers included? Entertainment and excursions? These can add up.

➤ TOUR-OPERATOR RECOMMENDATIONS: **American Society of Travel Agents** (☞ Travel Agencies). **National Tour Association** (NTA; ✉ 546 E. Main St., Lexington, KY 40508, ☎ 859/226–4444 or 800/682–8886, WEB www.ntaonline.com). **United States Tour Operators Association** (USTOA; ✉ 275 Madison Ave., Suite 2014, New York, NY 10016, ☎ 212/599–6599 or 800/468–7862, FAX 212/599–6744, WEB www.ustoa.com).

THEME TRIPS

➤ ART & ARCHAEOLOGY: **Archaeological Conservancy** (✉ 5301 Central Ave. NE, #1218, Albuquerque, NM 87108-1517, ☎ 505/266–1540, WEB www.americanarchaeology.com). **Crow Canyon Archaeological Center** (✉ 23390 Road K, Cortez, CO 81321, ☎ 970/565–8975 or 800/422–8975, FAX 970/565–4859, WEB www.crowcanyon.com). **Far Horizons Archaeological & Cultural Trips** (✉ Box 91900, Albuquerque, NM 87199-1900, ☎ 505/343–9400 or 800/552–4575, FAX 505/343–8076, WEB www.farhorizons.com).

➤ BICYCLING: **Backroads** (✉ 801 Cedar St., Berkeley, CA 94710-1800, ☎ 510/527–1555 or 800/462–2848, FAX 510/527–1444, WEB www.backroads.com). **Imagine Tours** (✉ Box 475, Davis, CA 95617, ☎ 530/758–8782 or 800/924–2453, FAX 530/758–8778, WEB www.imaginetours.com).

➤ BIRDING: **Field Guides** (✉ 9433 Bee Cave Rd., Bldg. 1, Suite 150, Austin, TX 78733, ☎ 512/263–7295 or 800/728–4953, FAX 512/263–0117, WEB www.fieldguides.com). **Victor Emanuel Nature Tours** (✉ Box 33008, Austin, TX 78746, ☎ 512/328–5221 or 800/328–8368, FAX 512/328–2919, WEB www.ventbird.com). **Wings** (✉ 1643 N. Alvernon Way, Suite 105, Tucson, AZ 85712, ☎ 888/293–0443 or 520/320–9868, FAX 520/320–9373).

➤ BUTTERFLY SANCTUARIES: **Natural Habitat Adventures** (✉ 2945 Center Green Ct., Boulder, CO 80301, ☎ 303/449–3711, FAX 303/449–3712, WEB www.gaiam.com/gaiam/NaturalHabitat). **Remarkable Journeys** (✉ Box 31855, Houston, TX 77231–1955, ☎ 713/721–2517 or 800/856–1993, FAX 713/728–8334, WEB www.remarkablejourneys.com).

➤ HORSEBACK RIDING: **Equitour FITS Equestrian** (✉ Box 807, Dubois, WY 82513, ☎ 307/455–3363 or 800/545–0019, FAX 307/455–2354).

➤ WALKING: **Backroads** (☞ Bicycling). **Butterfield & Robinson** (✉ 70 Bond St., Toronto, Ontario, Canada M5B 1X3, ☎ 416/864–1354; 800/678–1147 in the U.S. and Canada, FAX 416/864–0541, WEB www.butterfield.com).

➤ WHALE-WATCHING: **American Cetacean Society** (✉ Box 1391, San Pedro, CA 90733, ☎ 310/548–6279, FAX 310/548–6950, WEB www.acsonline.org). **Baja Discovery** (✉ 202 Cypress St., Chula Vista, CA 91910, ☎ 800/829–2252 or 619/262–8900, WEB www.bajadiscovery.com).

TRAIN TRAVEL

By late 1997 private companies operating the Mexican railroads decided that passenger service was not profitable enough, mainly because of the North American Free Trade Agreement, which rendered the freight service more valuable. The next few years saw passenger cars removed from almost all trains as Mexico's first-class bus service began to flourish.

The only passenger train route to survive the privatization process is, fortunately, also the most spectacular: the 16-hour ride through the gorgeous Copper Canyon in Northern Mexico. The route—between Chihuahua City and Los Mochis on the Pacific coast—crosses dozens of picturesque mountain bridges and burrows through the native lands of the Tarahumara Indians. Known as the *Chepe,* this route was privatized in 1998 and remodeled cars went into service in 1999. There are no sleeping cars on these trains, but the first-class routes do have dining cars, a bar, reclinable seats, and climate control. For more information, call Ferrocarriles Mexicanos (☎ 888/484–1623 in the U.S. or 1-800/122–4373 in Mexico.

TRAVEL AGENCIES

A good travel agent puts your needs first. Look for an agency that has been in business at least five years, emphasizes customer service, and has someone on staff who specializes in your destination. In addition, **make sure the agency belongs to a professional trade organization.** The American Society of Travel Agents (ASTA)—the largest and most influential in the field with more than 24,000 members in some 140 countries—maintains and enforces a strict code of ethics and will step in to help mediate any agent-client disputes involving ASTA members if necessary. ASTA (whose motto is "Without a travel agent, you're on your own") also maintains a Web site that includes a directory of agents. (If a travel agency is also acting as your tour operator, *see* Buyer Beware *in* Tours and Packages.)

➤ LOCAL AGENT REFERRALS: **American Society of Travel Agents** (ASTA; ✉ 1101 King St., Suite 200, Alexandria, VA 22314, ☎ 800/965–2782 24-hr hot line, FAX 703/739–3268, WEB www.astanet.com). **Association of British Travel Agents** (✉ 68–71 Newman St., London W1T 3AH, ☎ 020/7637–2444, FAX 020/7637–0713, WEB www.abtanet.com). **Association of Canadian Travel Agents** (✉ 130 Albert St., Suite 1705, Ottawa, Ontario K1P 5G4, ☎ 613/237–3657, FAX 613/237–7052, WEB www.acta.ca). **Australian Federation of Travel Agents** (✉ Level 3, 309 Pitt St., Sydney, NSW 2000, ☎ 02/9264–3299, FAX 02/9264–1085, WEB www.afta.com.au). **Travel Agents' Association of New Zealand** (✉ Level 5, Tourism and Travel House, 79 Boulcott St., Box 1888, Wellington 6001,

☎ 04/499–0104, FAX 04/499–0827, WEB www.taanz.org.nz).

VISITOR INFORMATION

➤ MEXICO TOURISM BOARD: **United States** (☎ 800/446–3942 nationwide; ✉ 21 East 63rd St., 3rd floor, New York, NY 10021, ☎ 212/821–0314, FAX 212/821–0367; ✉ 300 North Michigan Ave., 4th floor, Chicago, IL 60601, ☎ 312/606–9252, FAX 312/606–9012; ✉ 2401 West 6th St., 5th floor, Los Angeles, CA 90057, ☎ 213/351–2075, FAX 213/351–2074; ✉ 4507 San Jacinto, Suite 308, Houston, TX 77096, ☎ 713/772–2581, FAX 713/772–6058; ✉ 1200 NW 78th Ave., Suite 203, Coral Gables, FL 33126, ☎ 305/718–4095, FAX 305/718–4098).

Canada (✉ 1 Place Ville Marie, Suite 1931, Montréal, Québec H3B 2C3, ☎ 514/871–1052, FAX 514/871–3825; ✉ 2 Bloor St. W, Suite 1502, Toronto, Ontario M4W 3E2, ☎ 416/925–0704, FAX 416/925–6061; ✉ 999 W. Hastings St., Suite 110, Vancouver, British Columbia V6C 2W2, ☎ 604/669–2845, FAX 604/669–3498).

United Kingdom (✉ 42 Hertford St., London W1Y 7TF, ☎ 020/7488–9392, FAX 020/7265–0705).

Mexico (✉ Presidente Masaryk 172, Mexico, D.F. 11550, ☎ 55/5250–0123 or 1-800/903–9200).

➤ U.S. GOVERNMENT ADVISORIES: **U.S. Department of State** (✉ Overseas Citizens Services Office, Room 4811, 2201 C St. NW, Washington, DC 20520, ☎ 202/647–5225 interactive hot line or 888/407–4747, WEB www.travel.state.gov); enclose a business-size SASE.

WEB SITES

Do check out the World Wide Web when planning your trip. You'll find everything from weather forecasts to virtual tours of famous cities. Be sure to **visit Fodors.com** (www.fodors.com), a complete travel-planning site. You can research prices and book plane tickets, hotel rooms, rental cars, vacation packages, and more. In addition, you can post your pressing questions in the Travel Talk section. Other planning tools include a currency converter and weather reports, and there are loads of links to travel resources.

WHEN TO GO

Mexico is sufficiently large and geographically diverse enough that you can find a place to visit any time of year. October through May are generally the driest months; during the peak of the rainy season (June–September), it may rain for a few hours daily. But the sun often shines for the rest of the day, and the reduced off-season rates may well compensate for the reduced tanning time.

From December through the second week after Easter, the Mexican resorts—where the vast majority of tourists go—are the most crowded and therefore the most expensive. This also holds true for July and August, school-vacation months, when Mexican families crowd hotels. To avoid the masses, the highest prices, and the worst rains, **consider visiting Mexico during October, November, April, or May,** just not during the traditional holiday periods. Hotel rates at the beach resorts can fall as much as 30% in the shoulder season, 50% in the off-season.

Mexicans travel during traditional holiday periods—Christmas through January 6, Three Kings Day, *Semana Santa* (Holy Week, the week before Easter), the week after Easter—and summertime school vacations as well as over extended national holiday weekends, called *puentes* (bridges). Festivals play a big role in Mexican national life. If you plan to travel during a major national event, reserve both lodgings and transportation well in advance.

CLIMATE

Mexico's coasts and low-lying sections of the interior are often very hot if not actually tropical, with temperatures ranging from 17°C to 31°C (63°F to 88°F) in winter and well above 32°C (90°F) in summer. A more temperate area ranging from 16°C to 21°C (60°F to 70°F) is found at altitudes of 1,220–1,830 m (4,000–6,000 ft). In general, the high central plateau on which Mexico City, Guadalajara, and many of the country's colonial cities are located is springlike year-round.

➤ FORECASTS: **Weather Channel Connection** (☎ 900/932–8437), 95¢ per minute from a Touch-Tone phone.

ACAPULCO (PACIFIC COAST)

Jan.	88F	31C	May	90F	32C	Sept.	90F	32C
	72	22		75	24		75	24
Feb.	88F	31C	June	90F	32C	Oct.	90F	32C
	72	22		77	25		75	24
Mar.	88F	31C	July	90F	32C	Nov.	90F	32C
	72	22		77	25		73	23
Apr.	90F	32C	Aug.	91F	33C	Dec.	88F	31C
	73	23		77	25		71	22

COZUMEL (CARIBBEAN COAST)

Jan.	84F	29C	May	91F	33C	Sept.	89F	32C
	66	19		73	23		75	24
Feb.	84F	29C	June	89F	32C	Oct.	87F	31C
	66	19		75	24		73	23
Mar.	88F	31C	July	91F	33C	Nov.	86F	30C
	69	21		73	23		71	22
Apr.	89F	32C	Aug.	91F	33C	Dec.	84F	29C
	71	22		73	23		68	20

ENSENADA (BAJA CALIFORNIA)

Jan.	66F	19C	May	70F	21C	Sept.	79F	26C
	45	7		52	11		59	15
Feb.	68F	20C	June	73F	23C	Oct.	75F	24C
	45	7		54	12		54	12
Mar.	68F	20C	July	77F	25C	Nov.	72F	22C
	46	8		61	16		48	9
Apr.	69F	21C	Aug.	79F	26C	Dec.	68F	20C
	48	9		61	16		45	7

LA PAZ (BAJA CALIFORNIA SUR)

Jan.	73F	23C	May	91F	33C	Sept.	95F	35C
	54	12		59	15		73	23
Feb.	77F	25C	June	95F	35C	Oct.	91F	33C
	54	12		64	18		66	19
Mar.	80F	27C	July	97F	36C	Nov.	84F	29C
	54	12		71	22		61	16
Apr.	86F	30C	Aug.	97F	36C	Dec.	77F	25C
	55	13		73	23		54	12

MEXICO CITY (CENTRAL MEXICO)

Jan.	70F	21C	May	79F	26C	Sept.	72F	22C
	44	6		54	12		52	11
Feb.	73F	23C	June	77F	25C	Oct.	72F	22C
	45	7		54	12		50	10
Mar.	79F	26C	July	73F	23C	Nov.	72F	22C
	48	9		52	11		46	8
Apr.	81F	27C	Aug.	73F	23C	Dec.	70F	21C
	50	10		54	12		45	7

MONTERREY (NORTHEAST MEXICO)

Jan.	68F	20C	May	88F	31C	Sept.	88F	31C
	48	9		68	20		70	21
Feb.	73F	23C	June	91F	33C	Oct.	81F	27C
	52	11		72	22		63	17
Mar.	79F	26C	July	91F	34C	Nov.	73F	23C
	57	14		72	22		55	13
Apr.	86F	30C	Aug.	93F	34C	Dec.	70F	21C
	64	18		72	22		50	10

SAN MIGUEL DE ALLENDE (HEARTLAND)

Jan.	75F	24C	May	88F	31C	Sept.	79F	26C
	45	9		59	15		59	15
Feb.	79F	26C	June	88F	30C	Oct.	79F	26C
	48	9		59	15		54	12
Mar.	86F	30C	July	82F	28C	Nov.	75F	24C
	54	12		59	15		50	10
Apr.	88F	31C	Aug.	82F	28C	Dec.	75F	24C
	57	14		59	15		46	8

FESTIVALS AND SEASONAL EVENTS

Mexico is the land of festivals; if you reserve lodging well in advance, they're a golden opportunity to experience Mexico's culture. January is full of long, regional festivals. Notable are the **Fiesta de la Inmaculada Concepción** (Feast of the Immaculate Conception), which transforms the city of Morelia into a sea of lights and flowers for much of the month, and a series of folkloric dances in Chiapa de Corzo, Chiapas, that culminates in the **Feast of San Sebastian,** the third week in January.

➤ JAN. 1: **New Year's Day** is a major celebration throughout the country. Agricultural and livestock fairs are held in the provinces.

➤ JAN. 6: **Feast of Epiphany** is the day the Three Kings bring gifts to Mexican children.

➤ JAN. 17: **Feast of San Antonio Abad** honors animals all over Mexico. Pets and livestock are decked out with flowers and ribbons and taken to church for a blessing.

➤ FEB. 2: **Día de la Candelaria,** or Candlemas Day, means fiestas, parades, bullfights, and lantern-decorated streets. Festivities include a running of the bulls through the streets of Tlacotalpan, Veracruz.

➤ FEB.–MAR.: **Carnaval** is celebrated throughout Mexico—most notably in Mazatlán and Veracruz, with parades of floats and bands.

➤ MAR. 21: **Benito Juárez's Birthday,** a national holiday, is most popular in Guelatao, Oaxaca, where Juárez, the beloved 19th-century president of Mexico and champion of the people, was born. This is also the day that Cuernavaca's **Fiesta de la Primavera** marks the beginning of spring.

➤ MAR.–APR.: **Semana Santa** (Holy Week), the week leading to Easter Sunday, is observed with parades and passion plays.

➤ APR.–MAY: **San Marcos National Fair,** held in Aguascalientes, is one of the country's best fairs. It features Indian *matachnes* (dances performed by grotesque figures), mariachi bands, and bullfights. Also during this time, the 10-day **Festival de las Artes** (Arts Festival) brings music, theater, and dance troupes from all over Latin America to San Luis Potosí.

➤ MAY 1: **Labor Day** is a day for workers to parade through the streets.

➤ MAY 5: **Cinco de Mayo** marks, with great fanfare countrywide, the anniversary of the French defeat by Mexican troops in Puebla in 1862.

➤ MAY 15: **Feast of San Isidro Labrador** is noted nationwide by the blessing of new seeds and animals. In Cuernavaca, a parade of oxen wreathed in flowers is followed by street parties and feasting.

➤ JUNE 1: **Navy Day** is commemorated in all Mexican seaports and is especially colorful in Acapulco, Mazatlán, and Veracruz. The **Feast of Corpus Christi** is celebrated in different ways. In Mexico City, children are dressed in native costumes and taken to the cathedral on the zócalo for a blessing. In Papantla, Veracruz, the Dance of the Flying Birdmen—a pre-Hispanic ritual to the sun—is held throughout the day.

➤ JUNE 24: **Saint John the Baptist Day,** a popular national holiday, sees many Mexicans observing a tradition of tossing a "blessing" of water on most anyone within reach.

➤ EARLY JULY: The **Feria Nacional** (National Fair) in Durango runs from the Day of Our Lady of Refuge (July 4) to the anniversary of the founding of Durango in 1563 (July 22). The old-time agricultural fair has become known across the country for its carnival rides, livestock shows, and music. The **Guelaguetza Dance Festival,** a pre-Columbian Oaxacan affair, usually falls on the first and third Monday of July.

➤ JULY 16: **Our Lady of Mt. Carmel Day** is celebrated with fairs, bullfights, fireworks, even a major fishing tournament.

➤ LATE JULY: The **Feast of Santiago** features *charreadas,* Mexican-style rodeos.

➤ AUG.: The **Feast of St. Augustine** brings a month of music, dance, and fireworks to Puebla. On August 26 (feast day) it is customary to prepare the famous *chiles en nogada.*

➤ AUG. 15: **Feast of the Assumption of the Blessed Virgin Mary** is celebrated nationwide with religious processions. In Huamantla, Tlaxcala, the festivities include a running of the bulls and a carpet of flowers laid out in front of the church.

➤ AUG. 25: **San Luis Potosí Patron Saint Fiesta** is the day the town honors its patron, San Luis Rey, with traditional dance, music, and foods.

➤ SEPT. 15–16: **Independence Day** is marked throughout Mexico with fireworks and parties that outblast those on New Year's Eve. The biggest celebrations are in Mexico City.

➤ SEPT. 29: **San Miguel Day** honors St. Michael, the patron saint of all towns with San Miguel in their names—especially San Miguel de Allende—with bullfights, folk dances, concerts, and fireworks.

➤ OCT.: **October Festival** means a month of cultural and sporting events in Guadalajara.

➤ OCT. 4: **Feast of St. Francis of Assisi** is a day for processions dedicated to St. Francis in parts of the country.

➤ OCT. 12: **Día de la Raza** (Day of the Race) is comparable to Columbus Day in the United States.

➤ OCT.–NOV.: **International Cervantes Festival** in Guanajuato is a top cultural event that attracts dancers, singers, and actors from various countries.

➤ NOV. 1–NOV. 2: On **All Souls' and All Saints' Day,** or Day of the Dead, families welcome back the spirits of departed relatives to elaborate altars and refurbished gravesites. Especially intriguing are the celebrations in Pátzcuaro and Oaxaca.

➤ NOV. 20: **Anniversary of the Mexican Revolution** is a national holiday.

➤ NOV.–DEC.: **National Silver Fair,** an annual Taxco event, is an occasion for even more silver selling than usual, the crowning of a Silver Queen, and jewelry and silver exhibitions.

➤ DEC. 12: On **Feast Day of the Virgin of Guadalupe,** Mexico's patron saint is feted with processions and native folk dances, particularly at her shrine in Mexico City. In Puerto Vallarta, 12 days of processions and festivities lead up to the night of Dec. 12.

➤ DEC. 16–25: **The Posadas and Christmas** include candlelight processions that lead to holiday parties and the breaking open of piñatas. Mexico City is brightly decorated, but don't expect any snow.

➤ DEC. 23: **Night of the Radishes,** a pre-Christmas tradition in Oaxaca, is one of the most colorful in Mexico: participants carve giant radishes into amusing shapes and display them in the city's main plaza.

1 DESTINATION: MEXICO

The Many Faces of Mexico

What's Where

Pleasures and Pastimes

Fodor's Choice

Great Itineraries

THE MANY FACES OF MEXICO

MEXICO ITSELF is something like a *mole,* that complex and uniquely Mexican sauce whose myriad variations appeal to so many tastes at once.

It is a nation so diverse that most Americans have only a vague inkling of what it's about. Its landscapes range from ethereal cloud forests to terrain so barren it was the setting for *Dune,* the science fiction film about a desert planet. It reaches to chill mountain heights and plunges into tropical jungles shrill with monkeys and spilling over with mango, papaya, and avocado. Its dimensions can be mind-boggling: sections of the Copper Canyon are one-and-a-half times deeper than the Grand Canyon in Arizona.

Worlds collide in Mexico. Its muralists have chronicled the grinding struggles of its masses—in stark contrast to its enclaves of Spanish formality. Then fast-forward to today's imported California-style casualness, in which businesspeople dress in flip-flops and shorts, cellular telephones poking out of their shirt pockets.

It is a vacation mecca of computer-designed resorts—sites chosen for their perfect confluence of white beach and crystal sea, where hotels have sprouted shoulder to shoulder as high-glitz temples to sand, sun, and fun.

Yet much of it remains unchanged since the days of the conquistadors. In Chiapas, native Maya still work their fields with little more than machetes and hand-plows, smiling with benign amusement at the mountains of gear that adventure-travel outfitters use for rafting the rivers that have served as Maya highways for more than a millennium.

A past that is still very much a part of the present is central to Mexico's allure. In Mexico City's *Zócalo*—the name of the main square of any Mexican town or city—the drama of the pre-Hispanic Templo Mayor is created in part by its juxtaposition with the 16th-century Cathedral and the 17th-century National Palace. Nearby, the ruins of another Aztec temple have been incorporated into a subway stop.

Some contrasts verge on the comic. Even as Jack Nicklaus declares an oceanfront hole in one of his courses in Cabo San Lucas his favorite, drivers on the four-lane highway nearby must beware of the area's greatest traffic hazard in the cool desert night: cows drawn to the pavement, which retains the sun's warmth hours after sunset. Fences remain a relatively new concept in Cabo, but neon-hued collars are beginning to adorn the necks of cows.

Halfway up the Baja Peninsula from Los Cabos, where bulldozers and construction crews are busily erecting condos for golfers, 1,000-year-old polychrome paintings of men and women, sea turtles, and whales lie hidden in the Sierra San Francisco, mountainous terrain so rough that the only way you can get into it is on the backs of burros.

Pan east, across the Golfo de California and into the Copper Canyon, where passengers on private trains ride the rails in cruise ship–style luxury, disembarking to wander through tiny gems of colonial villages and watch the dances of the Tarahumara, indigenous people who live in caves or stone huts, just one step removed from their hunter-gatherer ancestors.

South along the Pacific coast, the resort of Mazatlán's old city is a mix of Spanish and French-style buildings carefully restored, while a string of modern, beachfront hotels lines the water's edge. Beyond the city limits lie the Sierra Madres and the mountain villages where the veins of gold that first attracted the fortune-seeking, empire-building conquistadors are still mined.

Mexico's heartland cities, such as Querétaro, San Miguel de Allende, and Morelia, were also of major importance in the days of colonial Mexico—at one point, a third of the world's silver came from the mines of Guanajuato. Their architecture—European Baroque facades and French doors opening onto wrought-iron balconies—has the feel of a Parisian neighborhood suddenly relocated to the American West.

In the south central highlands, the colorful colonial capital of Oaxaca is itself a babe compared with the Zapotec pyramids outside the city, which date back to 500 BC. Villagers living in the ring of settlements that surround Oaxaca like moons still practice crafts honed and perfected by their ancestors centuries before Europeans arrived.

And from the tip of the Yucatán Peninsula, you can take an air-conditioned bus from ultramodern Cancún to legendary Maya pyramids, built with such skill that on vernal and autumnal equinoxes, shadows look like a giant serpent descending its steps, joining with a carved serpent's head at its base. Some temples have sprouted tent cities of vendors hawking souvenirs. Others remain entwined in jungle vines, looking much as they did when the first tourists sought them out a century ago.

M**EXICO'S IDENTITY** is so potent that it transforms everyday experiences—like seemingly familiar foods. A simple cup of American hot chocolate tastes pale and insipid next to Mexican hot chocolate, a vital, lusty drink thickened with cornmeal, and spiced to perfection.

Much of Mexico is familiar to many travelers—more than 20 million people visit annually. With the advent of the wide-bodied jet and cheap charters, resorts such as Acapulco and Puerto Vallarta, once getaways for movie stars and the superrich, opened to the masses. More recently, isolated enclaves like Cabo San Lucas, whose private airstrips had kept it accessible only to fanatical and idiosyncratic fishermen and their celebrity cronies, opened international airports. The result: a desert-by-the-sea golf mecca.

Even though Mexico is America's next-door neighbor, it is no less remote, no less exotic. Only recently has Mexico's Ministry of Tourism sought to deal with the red tape that made it almost impossible for American motor coaches to drive across the border. Now you no longer need to switch to a Mexican bus when continuing into Mexico. Driving a car into Mexico, however, has veered toward bureaucratic madness, requiring precise documentation and an official car permit.

An airline system centered on Mexico City can make domestic travel roundabout—often the only way to get from one resort to another is via Mexico City. After the privatization of Mexican railroads, most companies eliminated passenger cars, but the bus network has become increasingly extensive and more comfortable, more than compensating for the loss.

Communication with home can be tough, too—even at major resorts. Anyone who has actually tried to use Mexican phones can do nothing but marvel at the popularity of Telmex, the Mexican phone company, on the stock market. Cellular phones abound because they are easier to get and often more reliable.

Violent crime targeted at tourists, it is sad to say, has escalated in parts of Mexico. The places that have been most affected are Mexico City and the Pacific coast and some less-visited parts of Oaxaca and Chiapas. *See* the Safety section of the Smart Travel Tips A to Z for further advice.

The election of President Vicente Fox in December 2000 ushered in more assertive approaches to social and economic change, including an emphasis on broadening tourism options. The government is pursuing everything from golf-centered megaresorts to ecological concerns to overlooked archaeological sites.

— Kate Rice

WHAT'S WHERE

The geographical organization of the following paragraphs mirrors the organization of the book. Beginning with Mexico City, coverage then shifts up to Baja California and works south to the Yucatán Peninsula.

Mexico City

Two volcanoes and a pyramid complex flank Mexico's capital, once the center of Aztec civilization and now the country's cosmopolitan business, art, and culinary hub. From the Alameda, a leafy center of activity since Aztec times, to the Zona Rosa, a chic shopping neighborhood, and the marvelous Chapultepec Park, with its many museums, gardens, and walking paths, Mexico City offers endless options for exploration.

Baja California

Lively border traffic colors the culture of the upper reaches of the Baja California peninsula, where seaside towns absorb floods of weekenders. But you can't say you've really experienced the 1,000-mi-long finger of land until you head south, off the beaten path. Boulder-strewn deserts, soaring mountain peaks, fishing villages, and pristine beaches can be found between the busy northern border and the highly developed Los Cabos resort at the southernmost tip.

Sonora

Imagine Arizona a hundred years ago, when cowboys drove cattle across wide-open ranch land. Then add a coastline—a fringe of beach washed by a turquoise sea—and you've conjured up Sonora, Mexico's northernmost state. The sea may lure you for swimming, kayaking, and snorkeling, but the foothills of the Sierra Madre hold their own treasures, such as colonial Alamos, once a silver-mining center, and a sprinkling of adobe missions.

The Copper Canyon: From Los Mochis to Chihuahua City

The so-called Copper Canyon is in fact a series of gorges, some of them deeper than the Grand Canyon in the United States. These gorges are home to the Tarahumara Indians, who are renowned for their running ability. And there is hiking—from pleasant walks to daylong descents to the canyon floor. A train trip through this magnificent, largely uncharted region usually begins or ends in Chihuahua, a lively midsize city with a museum devoted to Pancho Villa.

Guadalajara

Mexico's second-largest metropolis fully lives up to its reputation for being *señorial y moderna* (lordly and modern). The city retains a generous measure of colonial charm thanks to the landmarks of its historic center. Strolling through the quarter's squares, you'll likely encounter sombrero-topped bands of mariachis. Some of the country's best arts and crafts can be found at Tlaquepaque, on the city's outskirts, and Tonalá, about 10 minutes farther away. And at Tequila you can drink at the source of Mexico's famous firewater.

The Heartland

Rich with the history of Mexico's revolution, the heartland is a treasury of colonial towns—Guanajuato, Zacatecas, Querétaro, Morelia, and Pátzcuaro, among others—whose residents lead quiet, largely traditional lives. Even in San Miguel de Allende, an expatriate art colony and home to a well-known language institute, women wash their clothes and gossip at the local *lavandaría* as they have for hundreds of years.

Pacific Coast Resorts

People call it the Mexican Riviera and Gold Coast, but the most apt way to refer to this jungle-backed coastline might be Tropical Paradise. Sun worshippers, water-sports lovers, cruise ships, and anglers all converge on the cove-scalloped Pacific coast. Ixtapa/Zihuatanejo is a two-for-one attraction, a laid-back fishing village adjoining a glitzy resort.

Acapulco

The beaches and nightlife of Acapulco have proved their staying power; for decades vacationers have planned their days around lying on their beach towels or hammocks and their nights around the buzzing restaurants and dance clubs. The cobblestone streets of nearby Taxco, the silver city, are lined with master jewelers.

Oaxaca

The prime appeal of Oaxaca state and its eponymous colonial capital is the old and the older. Baroque buildings from the Spanish conquest pass almost for new when compared with the magnificent, millennia-old remnants of the native Zapotec and Mixtec civilizations. Though less exotic than Oaxaca City, the state's coastal developments of Puerto Escondido and Bahías de Huatulco are beloved by surfers and beach bums.

Chiapas and Tabasco

The state of Chiapas has always been off the beaten path, best known for the colonial town of San Cristóbal and the jungle-covered ruins of the exquisite Maya city of Palenque, arguably the most fascinating ancient site in Mexico. If you're thinking of just passing through on the way to Guatemala, you might find that the region has plenty to keep you lingering on.

Veracruz and the Northeast

Many Texans get their first taste of Mexico in the northeastern border towns of Nuevo Laredo, Reynosa, and Matamoros. Texan or otherwise, if you venture farther down to Monterrey, you'll find far more sophisticated dining, shopping, and cultural attractions of the country's third-largest city. The superb but little-explored pyramids of El Tajín and the raffish charm of Veracruz, the first European city established on the North American mainland, are among the many reasons to continue south.

The Yucatán Peninsula

Mexico's most-visited region will reward you with both spectacular beaches and evocative ruins—sometimes simultaneously, as at Tulum. After being mesmerized by the grace and power of sites such as Chichén Itzá and Uxmal, allow yourself to be taken in by the irresistible mix of sun, sand, and sea. Cancún was purpose-built for pleasure, while Isla Mujeres provides a more peaceful retreat. The world's second-largest barrier reef lies just off the island of Cozumel, and there are two huge coastal ecozones: Sian Ka'an Biosphere Reserve and Río Lagartos National Park, a migration stopover for thousands of flamingos and other birds.

PLEASURES AND PASTIMES

Arts and Crafts

Mexico is one of the best countries in the world to purchase *artesanías* (handicrafts), and many items are exempt from duty. The work is varied, original, colorful, and inexpensive, and it supports millions of families who are carrying on ancient or more recent traditions. Though cheap, shoddy merchandise masquerading as "native handicraft" is increasingly common, careful shoppers who take their time can come away with real works of folk art.

Mexican craftspeople excel in ceramics, woodwork, lacquerware, leather, weaving and textiles, silver, gold, and semiprecious stone jewelry. Each region has its specialty.

Ceramics Blue majolica (Talavera-style) tiles and other ceramic ware are at their best in Puebla. Oaxaca state is known for its burnished black, unglazed pottery. Inventive masks and figurines come from Michoacán, Jalisco, Taxco, Valle de Bravo, Tlaquepaque, and Chiapas.

Jewelry Silver is best bought in Taxco, San Miguel de Allende, and Oaxaca; be sure purchases are stamped "925," which means 92.5% pure silver. Gold filigree is sold in Oaxaca and Guanajuato. Oaxaca and Chiapas are also known for their amber, but beware, because much of what is sold as amber is in fact glass or plastic. (Good rules of thumb: don't buy amber off the street, and if it seems like a great bargain, it's probably fake.) For semiprecious stones, try the jewelers of Puebla and Querétaro. Coral jewelry is sold in the Yucatán and other coastal areas, but buying it is discouraged, because of the massive ecological damage caused by coral harvesting.

Leather The Yucatán, Chiapas, Oaxaca, and Jalisco are key destinations.

Metalwork Look for copper in Santa Clara del Cobre in Michoacán, and tin in San Miguel de Allende and Oaxaca.

Weavings and Textiles Options are many and varied: shawls (*rebozos*) and blankets around Oaxaca, Guadalajara, Jalapa, and Pátzcuaro; *huipiles* (heavily embroidered tunics worn by Indian women) and other embroidered clothing in Oaxaca state, Chiapas, the Yucatán, and Michoacán; masterfully woven rugs, some colored with natural dyes, in Oaxaca; hammocks and baskets in Oaxaca and the Yucatán; lace in the colonial cities of the heartland area; *guayaberas* (comfortable, embroidered and/or pleated men's dress shirts, now usually mass-produced) along the Gulf coast; and reed mats in Oaxaca and Valle de Bravo. The Mezquital region east of Querétaro can also be rewarding, as can shopping for Huichol Indian yarn paintings and embroidery near Puerta Vallarta.

Woodwork Best bets include masks (Guerrero, Mexico City), *alebrijes* (painted wooden animals, Oaxaca), furniture (Guadalajara, Michoacán, San Miguel de Allende, and Cuernavaca), lacquerware (Uruapan and Pátzcuaro, as well as Chiapa de Corzo in Chiapas and Olinalá in Guerrero), and guitars (Paracho, Michoacán).

Beaches

Beaches are the reason most tourists visit Mexico. Generally speaking, the Pacific is rougher and the waters less clear than the Caribbean, which is a better choice for snorkeling and scuba diving. Cancún, Cozumel, and Isla Mujeres, as well as what has come to be called the Cancún–Tulum Corridor, are among the best and most popular beach destinations on the Caribbean coast. Beaches on the Gulf of Mexico are often covered with tar. The Acapulco waters, though much improved by a cleanup effort, are still somewhat polluted, but there is no such problem at the other Pacific resorts. All beach resorts offer a variety of water sports, including waterskiing, windsurfing, parasailing, and if the water is clear enough, snorkeling and scuba diving. Surfers favor Puerto Escondido, near Huatulco.

Bullfighting

An import of the Spanish conquistadors, bullfighting was refined and popularized over the centuries, until every major city and most small towns had a bullring or some semblance of an arena. As in Spain, the last few decades have seen some decline of the popularity of the sport in Mexico, where it has been superseded by such modern games as soccer and has been the object of negative publicity by animal-rights activists. It remains a strong part of the Latin American culture, however, and can be thrilling to watch when performed by a skilled toreador. Ask at your hotel about arenas and schedules. Most fights are held on Sunday afternoon, and the most prestigious toreadors perform during the fall season.

Charreada

This Mexican rodeo is a colorful event involving elegant flourishes and maneuvers, handsome costumes, mariachi music, and much fanfare. There are *charreadas* (Mexican-style rodeos) most Sunday mornings at Mexico City's Rancho del Charro; inquire at your hotel or at a travel agency.

Dining

Mexico's food is as diverse and abundant as its geography. Distinct regional specialties typify each of the republic's 32 states and even the different provinces within the states. Fresh ingredients are bountiful, recipes are passed down through generations, and preparation requires much patience and loving care. (Mexican gastronomes are dismayed by foreigners' glaring misconceptions of Mexican food as essentially tacos, enchiladas, and burritos; they are bewildered by Tex-Mex and appalled by Taco Bell.)

The staples of rice, beans, chilies, and tortillas on which the poor subsist form the basis for creative variations of sophisticated national dishes but are by no means the only ingredients commonly used. As Mexican cooking continues to develop an international reputation, more people are recognizing its versatility.

Seafood is abundant, not just on the coasts but also in the lake regions around Guadalajara and in the state of Michoacán. Ceviche—raw fish and shellfish (*mariscos*) marinated in lime juice and topped with cilantro (coriander), onion, and chili—is almost a national dish, though it originated in Acapulco. It is worth trying, but make sure it's fresh. Shrimp, lobster, and oysters can be huge and succulent. Bear in mind the folk adage about eating oysters only in months with names that contain the letter *r,* and be sure to avoid raw shellfish in any area where cholera or water pollution may be a risk. Other popular seafood includes *huachinango* (sea bass), abalone, crab, and swordfish.

Mexicans consume lots of beef, pork, and barbecued lamb (*barbacoa*), with a variety of sauces. Chicken is often roasted, served in sauces such as mole, or tucked in enchiladas, tacos, or burritos. Mole, a complex, spicy sauce with more than 100 ingredients, including many kinds of chilies and even a bit of chocolate, is one of Mexico's proudest culinary inventions. It is usually served over chicken or lamb. Regional variations are described in the appropriate chapters.

Maize was sacred to the Indians, who invented innumerable ways of preparing cornmeal, from the faithful tortilla to the tamale (cornmeal wrapped in banana leaves or corn husks), tostada (lightly fried, open tortilla topped with meat, lettuce, and the like) and simple taco (a tortilla briefly heated, filled, and wrapped into a slim cylinder). *Atole* (a sweet, corn-based drink similar in consistency to hot chocolate) is a favorite breakfast or before-bed treat.

Fresh fruits and vegetables are another Mexican pleasure. Jicama, papaya, mamey, avocado, mango, guayaba, peanuts, squash, and tomatoes are just some of the produce native to Mexico. (All fresh produce should be washed in water with a commercial disinfectant, however, because bacteria exist in Mexico to which foreigners may not have been exposed.)

Other Mexican specialties less common abroad are any number of local *antojitos* or *botanas* (appetizers), *chilaquiles* (a rich breakfast dish made with tortilla strips scrambled with chili, tomatoes, onions, cream, and cheese), and *chiles en nogada* (a large poblano chili stuffed with beef or cheese, raisins, onion, olives, and almonds and topped with a creamy walnut sauce and pomegranate seeds). Soups are hearty—particularly the corn-and-pork-based *pozole, sopa azteca* (avocado and tortilla in a broth) and *sopa de flor de calabaza* (squash-flower soup).

But this barely touches on the plenitude and diversity of Mexican cuisine, which also encompasses an astonishing assortment of breads, sweets, beers, wines (which are fast improving), and cactus-based liquors. Freshly squeezed fruit juices and fruit shakes (*licuados*) are safe to drink—if ordered in a restaurant with hygienic practices—and taste heavenly. Coffee varies from standard American-style and Nescafé to espresso to the newer organic varieties to *café de olla,* which is laced with spices and served in a coarse clay mug. Imported liquor is very expensive; middle-class Mexicans stick with the local rum and tequila.

Horseback Riding

The dry ranch lands of northern Mexico have countless stables and dude ranches, as do San Miguel de Allende and Querétaro in the heartland. Horses can be rented by the hour at most beaches, and horseback expeditions can be arranged to the Copper Canyon in Chihuahua and the forest near San Cristóbal, Chiapas.

Hot Springs

Mexico is renowned for its *balnearios* (mineral bath springs), which today are surrounded by a cluster of spa resorts and hacienda-type hotels. Most spas are in the center of the country, in the states of Aguascalientes, Guanajuato, México, Morelos, Puebla, and Querétaro.

Music

From *norteño* to *mariachi* to *banda,* Mexico's varieties of music have at their core expressive power and verve that make their popularity instantly understandable.

Banda rose to fame in the 1990s—brass bands small and large arranging tunes from other styles, including ranchera and cumbia. Among its premier practitioners is Banda del Recodo.

Cumbia has its roots in Colombia, where it is also a favorite. Immensely danceable, cumbia was *the* craze before banda came along.

Danzón is a European-influenced style, accompanying dignified dancing, that came originally to Veracruz from Cuba. The style's popularity there has waned, but not so in Mexico.

Mariachi might seem to be Mexico's signature musical style, even though it is just one of many. It originated in the state of Jalisco, by some accounts at a garden party that dictator Porfirio Díaz threw for Americans in 1907. Mariachi bands play in plazas countrywide, their signature brass sounds backed up with guitars, most noticeably the huge, shoulder-strapped acoustic basses.

Norteño, characteristically sung without passion, is known for lyrics that pull no punches when it comes to the tragedies of life. It comes from northern Mexico—border country. Accordions are usually a part of norteño bands.

Ranchero is as passionate as Mexican music gets. Ranchero ("country") is often compared to American country music; its powerfully direct, relatively simple style was traditionally linked to the working class.

Ruins

Amateur archaeologists will find heaven in Mexico, where some of the greatest ancient civilizations—among them, the Aztecs, the Olmecs, and the Maya—left their mark. Pick your period and your preference, whether for well-excavated sites or overgrown, out-of-the-way ruins barely touched by a scholar's shovel. The Yucatán is, hands down, the greatest source of ancient treasure, with such heavy hitters as Chichén Itzá and Uxmal, but you're unlikely to find any region in the country that doesn't have some interesting vestige of Mexico's pre-Columbian past. A visit to Mexico City's archaeological museum, one of the best in the world, could ignite the imagination of even those who thought they had no interest in antiquity, and help others focus on the places they'd most like to explore further.

Soccer

As in Europe, this is Mexico's national sport (known as *futból*). It is played almost year-round at the Estadio Azteca in Mexico City, as well as in other large cities.

Tennis and Golf

Most major resorts have lighted tennis courts, and there is an abundance of 18-hole golf courses, many designed by such noteworthies as Percy Clifford, Joe Finger, and Robert Trent Jones. At private golf and tennis clubs, you must be accompanied by a member to gain admission. Hotels that do not have their own facilities will often secure you access to ones in the vicinity.

FODOR'S CHOICE

Archaeological Sites

Chichén Itzá. The best-known Maya ruin, Chichén Itzá was the most important city in the Yucatán from the 10th to 12th centuries. Its eclectic architecture is evidence of a complex intermingling of ancient cultures.

El Tajín. The centerpiece of this Veracruz site, the Pyramid of the Niches, is surely one of the finest pre-Columbian structures in Mexico.

Palenque. In a rain forest in Chiapas, these Maya ruins have a magical quality, perhaps because of their intimacy. The most magnificent royal tomb in the Maya empire was uncovered here.

Teotihuacan. Predating the Aztecs and believed by them to be the birthplace of the gods, this pyramid complex outside Mexico City was one of the largest cities in the ancient world.

Tulum. The spectacular backdrop of the Caribbean and proximity to Cancún explain why Tulum is the most visited archaeological site in the Yucatán.

Uxmal. Arguably the most beautiful of Mexico's ruins, Uxmal represents Maya style at its purest, including ornate stone friezes, intricate cornices, and soaring arches.

Beaches

Lo de Marcos, Sayulita, and San Francisco. These are just a few of the dozens of beautiful, unspoiled beaches north of Puerto Vallarta, across the state line in Nayarit. Sayulita is often described as Puerto Vallarta some 40 years ago.

Playa de Amor, Cabo San Lucas. From this secluded cove at the very tip of Baja California you can see the azure Sea of Cortez on one side, the churning Pacific Ocean on the other.

Playa Norte, Isla Mujeres. The beach on the northern tip of sleepy Isla Mujeres is ideal for both water sports and lounging under grass-roofed *palapa*.

Zicatela, Oaxaca Coast. A long stretch of cream-color sand, Zicatela is one of the top-10 surfing beaches in the world.

Dining

Coyuca 22, Acapulco. Some diners book a year in advance to ensure a table at this Continental restaurant for high season; it's one of the most expensive dining rooms in town, and one of the most beautiful. *$$$$*

Casa Cenote, Mexico's Caribbean coast. This unique restaurant near the ruins of Tulum allows you to plunge into a large natural pool before enjoying tasty American and Mexican fare. *$$*

La Bella Epoca, Mérida. Middle Eastern, French, and Yucatecan specialties star in this former ballroom of an elegant mansion. *$$*

La Valentina, Mexico City. Devoted to promoting historic native cuisine from across the country, La Valentina is known for its balanced, flavorful dishes. *$$*

Mariscos Villa Rica Mocambo, Veracruz. This apparently casual open-air *palapa* eatery turns out seriously terrific seafood. *$$*

L' Recif, Manzanillo. For a fantastic dinner with a view, feast on shrimp in this huge clifftop *palapa*; around March, you may spot migrating whales. *$–$$*

Lodging

Las Brisas, Acapulco. Jeeps transport guests around this secluded hillside haven, set on

110 acres that offer every imaginable activity and amenity. $$$$

La Casa Que Canta, Zihuatanejo. Perched on a cliff overlooking Zihuatanejo Bay, this thatched-roof complex features individualized suites with handcrafted furnishings. $$$$

Quinta Real, Guadalajara. Classical Mexican architecture and Spanish-style furnishings distinguish this luxury hotel in a quiet residential neighborhood. $$$$

Ritz-Carlton Cancún. The Cancún link of this international chain adds class to the beachfront hotel zone. Its facilities and restaurants are superb. $$$$

Las Ventanas al Paraíso, Cabo San Lucas. This waterside architectural wonder is the last word in earthy elegance—and reason enough to hop on the next plane to the southern tip of the Baja Peninsula. $$$$

Chan Kah, Palenque. A resident monkey is among the charms of this jungle retreat near the Maya ruins; accommodations are in comfortable bungalows. $$$

La Casa de Espiritus Alegres Bed and Breakfast, Guanajuato. This renovated hacienda is a folk-art paradise filled with whimsical treasures from every state in Mexico. $$$

El Fuerte Lodge, El Fuerte. A restored 380-year-old mansion welcomes canyon travelers with a flower-filled courtyard and wonderful *artesanía* (folk art). $$

Na Bolom, San Cristóbal de las Casas. Doubling as a center for the study and preservation of the Lacandon Maya and the rain forest, this hotel stands out for its beautiful gardens and its incorporation of native crafts. $$

Museums

Parque Museo La Venta, Villahermosa. Giant Olmec heads placed along a jungle pathway are among the most fascinating exhibits of the pre-Hispanic jaguar cult on which this park complex focuses.

Museo de Frida Kahlo, Mexico City. The decor and memorabilia in the former home of the formidable Kahlo amply demonstrate her originality and vitality.

Museo Nacional de Antropología, Mexico City. There are 100,000 square ft of displays at the greatest museum in the country, which hosts archaeological treasures from all of Mesoamerica.

Museo de Arte Contemporaneo, Monterrey. The best of postmodern Latin American art is gathered at this gallery, where a chic coffeehouse attracts the city's intellectuals.

Na-Bolom, San Cristobal de las Casas. Franz and Gertrude Blom lived in a lovely, rambling home surrounded by gardens. Their former residence contains displays reflecting their extensive archaeological, ethnological, and ecological interests.

Shopping

Tlaquepaque, outside Guadalajara. Crafts seekers throng to this village where some of the most talented glassblowers, potters, and jewelers in Mexico gather.

Saturday market, Oaxaca. At the largest Indian market in Mexico you'll find a wealth of colorful wares, including native huipiles, hand-carved wooden animals, and black regional pottery.

Zona Rosa, Mexico City. Antiques, crafts, and the latest fashions are abundant in this tony neighborhood, chock-full of galleries, boutiques, and cafés.

Casa de las Artesanías and San Jolobil, San Cristóbal de Las Casas. Stop here for some of Mexico's most striking Indian weavings, hand-embroidered blouses and tunics, multicolored *fajas* (sashes), and beribboned hats.

El Centro (downtown), Puerto Vallarta. Few Mexican cities have a collection of native crafts, among them clothing and household goods, as representative as that of Puerto Vallarta.

Special Moments

Whale-watching at Scammon's and San Ignacio lagoons, Baja. Go out on a boat for the best views of the great gray mammals, who pass here en route from Alaska each winter.

***Los voladores,* Papantla.** A precursor of bungee jumping, this ancient ceremony involves five "flyers" who hurl themselves from a tiny platform set atop a 100-ft pole.

Overlooking the Copper Canyon from Divisadero. Whether you just get off the train briefly or stop overnight, you'll be astounded by the vista of the grand abyss.

Don Porfirio's Bar, Querétaro, the Heartland. After a day of exploring, stop in at the bar of the Casa de la Marquesa hotel for a drink, and to drink in the old-world elegance of this 18th-century house.

Sunsets, Puerto Vallarta. The setting sun is bigger and more fiery here than any place else in the world and spreads like orange mercury over Banderas Bay before disappearing behind the horizon.

The divers at La Quebrada, Acapulco. It's heart-stopping to see these swimmers take the plunge off 130-ft-high cliffs—after praying at a small cliff-side chapel.

A *calesa* (horse-drawn carriage) ride through Mérida. Discover old-world graciousness by trotting slowly through the wide streets and French-style neighborhoods of Yucatán's capital.

GREAT ITINERARIES

Canyons and Coasts

8 to 12 days

Natural wonders never cease in northern and western Mexico. From the heart-stopping views and hikes into the Barranca del Cobre—the Copper Canyon—to Baja Sur's inland deserts, its annual migrations of whales, and the beaches of Los Cabos, opportunities for adventure and relaxation are everywhere.

The Copper Canyon *3 to 4 days.* Riding the Chihuahua al Pacífico rail line from west to east affords the most stunning views of the Copper Canyon. So start off in Los Mochis and make the mountain village of Cerocahui your first stop. From here, views of Urique Canyon—and the cave paintings at the Cueva de las Cruces—are superb. Head up the line to Divisadero, the place for sunset views and horseback trips to the Tarahumara village of Bacajipare. Farther on, the 806-ft Basaseachi Falls are one of North America's highest cascades. If a dose of urban life feels like the appropriate tonic after taking in the canyons, spend the night in Chihuahua before catching a plane for La Paz.

La Paz *1 to 2 days.* Begin with a kayaking, snorkeling, or diving trip to Isla Espíritu Santo or Isla Partida in the Sea of Cortez—you're almost guaranteed to spot sea lions and whales. Spend the rest of the day in town; as sunset nears, head for the seaside malecón where couples and families stroll beside playgrounds on the sand. If you're here in the winter, join a tour to Bahía Magdalena, where migrating gray whales give birth.

Loreto *1 to 2 days.* Visitors to Loreto are largely intent on fishing in the rich waters off nearby islands, and even nonanglers enjoy a boat ride at dawn. Loreto's laid-back hotels are also the perfect base for exploring the nearby mountains and coast. Drive about two hours past cattle ranches and boulder-strewn hills to the well-preserved Misión San Javier, or drive a couple of hours north to the incomparably picturesque Bahía Concepción and the town of Mulegé, in an oasis by the sea.

Los Cabos *3 to 4 days.* Spend your first day in Los Cabos fishing for marlin, golfing at a championship course on the Sea of Cortez, or swimming and sunbathing at Playa Médano. Sample Cabo San Lucas's theme restaurants and trendy cafés that night. Begin Day 2 with breakfast at one of the Corridor's lavish resorts and snorkeling at Bahía Chileno. Stroll through San José del Cabo's plazas and galleries in the evening, and end the day dining on fresh fish. Spend the rest of your days exploring Baja's incomparable desert and sea scenery: head for the artsy enclave of Todos Santos, or to the East Cape for long drives on sandy desert roads beside the sea.

By Public Transportation

Distances here demand a fair amount of air travel: first from Mexico City to Los Mochis, then from Chihuahua to La Paz—which flies you over the canyons. The entire rail trip from Los Mochis to Chihuahua is a 15-hour proposition, but it's best to stop at towns along the way and reboard later in the day or the next day, or even the next. From La Paz, tour companies will take you to Bahía Magdalena to see whales. To get to Loreto (three hours north of La Paz), the East Cape (one hour south), and Los Cabos (two hours south), rent a car so you can explore the quieter coastal stretches on your own. Buses also run throughout Baja Sur.

Colonial Mexico

7 to 10 days

Remarkably well preserved, these colonial cities are full of atmospheric haciendas and richly decorated cathedrals—along with intriguing juxtapositions of the colonial and the indigenous that are classic Mexico.

Querétaro *1 day.* This Heartland city has been called the cradle of independence. Its restored Plaza de la Independencia is filled with grand mansions once belonging to titled friends of the Crown. Amble around the square and nearby streets to see the Baroque Museo de Arte de Querétaro, housed in an 18th-century monastery, the Palacio del Gobierno del Estado, and the Jardín de la Corregidora.

San Miguel de Allende *1 to 2 days.* A cultural hub of the region, this friendly city is full of bookstores, art galleries, coffee shops, and American expats. Take time to visit churches—the Gothic Revival Parroquia, the churrigueresque Iglesia de San Francisco, and the unique Oratorio de San Felipe Neri. Consider a side trip to the historic village of Dolores Hidalgo, home of the insurgent priest whose cry for independence started the 1810 war.

Guanajuato *2 to 3 days.* Splendid buildings rising above labyrinthine streets give Guanajuato its medieval appearance. Make your way to the main square and the impressive Teatro Juárez. El Museo Casa Diego Rivera, birthplace of the famed muralist, and the hulking Alhóndiga de Granaditas fortress are nearby. On Day 2, visit the Basílica Colegiata de Nuestra Señora de Guanajuato and La Valenciana—the former for its 8th-century statue of the Virgin, the latter for its elaborately carved pink facade and gilded altars.

San Cristóbal de las Casas *1 to 2 days.* San Cristóbal is a walking city, and on foot you encounter the same mix of colonial and indigenous cultures—from the iconic ochre-colored cathedral to the mercado municipal bustling with Lacandon Maya merchants—that exists between the city and the surrounding Indian villages.

Mérida *2 days.* No city in Mexico has anything like Mérida's quirky self-confidence and cosmopolitan flair. At the same time the jaunty metropolis is just as Maya as San Cristóbal. Urbane streets like Paseo de Montejo are offset by the chilies-to-crafts mercado. And the cathedral, built with stone from a Maya temple, contains a dark-skinned Christ that aimed to reconcile people of Maya and Spanish descent. Mérida, the Yucatán's largest city, is at heart a typical Yucatecan town.

By Public Transportation

The easiest way to get to and between Querétaro, San Miguel de Allende, and Guanajuato is by luxury bus. From Mexico City the bus from the Observatorio or Northern bus terminals to Querétaro takes about two hours. From Querétaro it's another two hours to San Miguel. San Miguel to Guanajuato is a 2½-hour ride. Nearby León's airport has flights to Mexico City (one hour), from which you can fly to Tuxtla Gutiérrez (two hours), an hour west of San Cristóbal by bus. Then fly out of Tuxtla straight to Mérida (one hour).

The Lost Cities of Ancient Mexico

9 to 11 days

Inhabited by numerous cultures in pre-Columbian days, Mexico has one of the world's most impressive collections of archaeological sites. The monumental Maya cities, the standout, are at their finest on the Yucatán Peninsula and in jungly Tabasco and mountainous Chiapas.

Teotihuacán *1 day.* For the 14th- to 16th-century Aztecs, this was the birthplace of the gods. At its 8th-century peak Teotihuacán hummed with as many as 250,000 people, its massive, spellbinding pyramids symbolizing the ordered lives of people in the ancient Valley of Mexico. Just an hour outside of Mexico City by bus, these ruins are an essential first site.

Villahermosa *2 to 3 days.* Villahermosa is roughly at the midpoint between ancient culture and modern development. Head for the Parque Museo La Venta, with its enormous Olmec stone heads, for an in-depth look at a culture that preceded the Maya by several centuries. Later in the day, swing north out of town to Comalcalco, a Maya site with the only known brick temples in the Maya world. Save the best for last and make your way to Chiapas to see Palenque; its classicism is akin to that of Greek architecture.

Mérida *6 or 7 days.* A capital city of the Yucatán and the most Maya of all Yucatecan cities, Mérida is a perfect base for seeing the region's ruins. Take in the Museum of Anthropology to preview Maya art, and walk around the lively main square to view its colonial mansions, cathedral, small churches, and shady plazas. On your second day, head to Chichén Itzá, an extensive site built by two different Maya empires. Later in the afternoon visit the Cave of Balancanchén, with its ceremonial artifacts, and the Maya village of Izamal, on the way back to Mérida. Spend all of day three at beautiful Uxmal, the sterling example of the graceful Puuc architectural style. If time permits, you can spend a day at the smaller Puuc ruins of Kabah, Sayil, and Labná. Consider planning your trip around a local Maya festival to see the intriguing blend of pre-Hispanic beliefs and Catholic rituals.

By Public Transportation

In Villahermosa you can take a cab to the Parque Museo La Venta but need to book an excursion to Comalcalco. Buses are unreliable. To get to Palenque you can catch a luxury bus from the ADO terminal; the trip takes about 2½ hours. There are also full-day excursions to Palenque from Villahermosa. From Tuxtla Gutiérrez there is a one-hour flight to Mérida. You can take day trips to the major Yucatán sites from Mérida. Second-class buses do run to Chichén Itzá and Uxmal from Mérida's main bus terminal, but they have no air-conditioning and are a bit uncomfortable.

2 MEXICO CITY

Two volcanoes and a pyramid complex flank Mexico's capital, once the center of Aztec civilization and now the country's cosmopolitan business, cultural, and culinary hub. From the buzzing Alameda Park, where lovers cluster and jugglers entertain crowds, and the grand historic center to Polanco, a chic shopping and dining neighborhood by some of the major hotels, Mexico City offers endless options to urban adventurers. Longer-term visitors are enticed farther south by the churches, convents, and museums on the cobbled streets of San Ángel and leafy Coyoacán, or a canal trip by the floating gardens of Xochimilco.

Updated by Barbara Kastelein

MEXICO CITY IS A CITY OF SUPERLATIVES. It is both the oldest (founded in 1325) and the highest (2,200 m/7,350 ft) metropolis on the North American continent. And with nearly 24 million inhabitants, it's the most populous city in the world. At the southern edge of the Mesa Central region of the Plateau of Mexico, the city remains Mexico's industrial, financial, cultural, and political core. Fast, thrilling, and hard to get your head around, it seems permanently in the thrall of turbulent and exciting change—braving the 21st century while clinging to its deeply entrenched Aztec heritage.

As the gargantuan pyramids of Teotihuacán attest, the area around Mexico City was occupied from early times by a great civilization, probably Nahuatl in origin. The founding farther south of the Aztec capital, Tenochtitlán, did not occur until more than 600 years after Teotihuacán was abandoned, around AD 750. Between these periods, from 900 to 1200, the Toltec Empire controlled the Valley of Mexico. As the story goes, the nomadic Aztecs were searching for a promised land in which to settle. Their prophecies announced that they would recognize the spot when they encountered an eagle, perched on a prickly pear cactus and holding a snake in its beak. In 1325, the disputed date of Tenochtitlán's founding, they discovered this eagle in the valley of Mexico. They settled on what was then an island in shallow Lake Texcoco and connected it to lakeshore satellite towns by a network of *calzadas* (canals and causeways, now freeways). Even then it was the largest city in the Western Hemisphere and, according to historians, one of the three largest cities on Earth. When he first laid eyes on Tenochtitlán in the early 16th century, Spanish conquistador Hernán Cortés was dazzled by the glistening lacustrine metropolis, which reminded him of Venice.

A combination of factors made the Spanish conquest possible. The superstitious Aztec emperor Moctezuma II believed the white, bearded Cortés on horseback to be the mighty plumed serpent-god Quetzalcóatl, who, according to a tragically ironic prophecy, was supposed to arrive from the east in the year 1519 to rule the land. Moctezuma therefore welcomed the foreigner with gifts of gold and palatial accommodations.

In return, Cortés initiated a bloody massacre, assisted by a huge army of Indians from other settlements such as Cholula and Tlaxcala, who saw a chance to end their submission to the Aztec empire. Along with the European tactical advantages of horses, firearms, and, inadvertently, the introduction of smallpox and the common cold—Cortés succeeded in devastating Tenochtitlán only two centuries after it was founded.

Cortés began building the capital of what he patriotically dubbed New Spain, the Spanish empire's colony that would spread north to cover what is now the southwestern United States, and south to Panama. *Mexico* comes from the word *Mexica* (pronounced *meh*-shee-ka), which was the Aztecs' name for themselves. (Aztec is the Spaniards' name for the Mexica.) At the site of Tenochtitlán's demolished ceremonial center—now the 10-acre Zócalo—Cortés started building a church (the precursor of the impressive Metropolitan Cathedral), mansions, and government buildings. He utilized the slave labor—and the artistry—of the vanquished native Mexicans. On top of the ruins of their city, and using rubble from it, they were forced to build what became the most European-style city in North America. But instead of having the random layout of contemporary medieval cities, it followed the sophisticated grid pattern of the Aztecs. For much of the construction material the Spaniards quarried the local porous, volcanic reddish stone called *tezontle*. The Spaniards also drained the lakes, preferring wheels and horses (which they introduced to Mexico) over canals and canoes for transport. The land-filled lake bed turned out to be a soggy support for the immense buildings that have been slowly sinking into it since they were built.

The city grew during the colonial period, and the Franciscans and Dominicans converted the Aztecs to Christianity. In 1571 the Spaniards established the Inquisition in New Spain and burned heretics at its palace headquarters, which still stands in Plaza de Santo Domingo.

It took almost three centuries for Mexicans to rise up successfully against Spain. The historic downtown street 16 de Septiembre commemorates the "declaration" of the War of Independence. On that date in 1810, Miguel Hidalgo, Father of the Catholic Church—and of a couple of illegitimate daughters—rang a church bell and cried out his history-making *grito* (shout): "Death to the *gachupines!* (wealthy Spaniards living in Mexico)! Long live the Virgin of Guadalupe!" Excommunicated and executed the following year, Hidalgo is one of many independence heroes who fostered a truly popular movement, culminating in Mexico's independence in 1821. The liberty bell that now hangs above the main entrance to the National Palace is rung on every eve of September 16 by the president of the republic, who then shouts a revised version of the patriot's cry: "¡Viva México!"

Flying in or out of Mexico City, you get an aerial view of the remaining part of Lake Texcoco on the eastern outskirts of the city. In daylight you can notice the sprawling flatness of the 1,480-square-km (570-square-mi) Meseta de Anáhuac (Valley of Mexico), completely surrounded by mountains. On its southeastern side, two usually snow-capped volcanoes, Popocatépetl and Iztaccíhuatl, are both well over 5,100 m (17,000 ft) high. After a period of relative tranquility, Popocatépetl awoke and began spewing smoke, ash, and some lava in the mid-1990s; it has remained intermittently active since then.

Unfortunately, the single most widely known fact about Mexico City is that its air is polluted. You might picture the city wrapped daily in a cloak of black smog, its streets packed with vehicles. In reality, strict legislation in recent years has led to cleaner air and the capital has some of the clearest, bluest skies anywhere, especially in summer and fall. At 2,200 m (7,350 ft), the city often has mild daytime weather perfect for sightseeing and cool evenings. Mornings can be glorious—chilly and bright with the promise of the warming sun.

If notoriety for smog brings Los Angeles to mind, so might the fault line that runs through the valley. In 1957 a major earthquake took a tragic toll, which was exceeded by the devastating 1985 earthquake—8.1 on the Richter scale. The government reported 10,000 deaths, but locally it's said to be closer to 50,000.

Growing nonstop, Mexico City—which goes by just "México" in Mexico—is surrounded on three sides by the state of Mexico and bordered on the south by the state of Morelos. Glossy magazine ads usually tout Mexico's paradisiacal beach resorts and ancient ruins, but cosmopolitan, historic Mexico City is a vital destination in itself—more diverse and fascinating than many major capitals.

Pleasures and Pastimes

Dining

Mexico City has been a culinary capital ever since the time of Moctezuma. Chronicles tell of the extravagant banquets prepared for the Aztec emperor by his palace chefs. More than 300 different dishes were served for every meal—vast assortments of meat and fowl seasoned in dozens of ways, and limitless fruit, vegetables, herbs, and freshwater fish.

Until the 15th century, Europeans had never seen indigenous Mexican edibles such as corn, chilies of all varieties, tomatoes, potatoes, pumpkin, squash, avocado, turkey, cocoa, and vanilla. In turn, the colonization brought European gastronomic influence and ingredients—wheat, onions, garlic, olives, citrus fruit, cattle, sheep, goats, chickens, domesticated pigs (and lard for frying)—and ended up broadening the already complex pre-Hispanic cuisine into one of the most multifaceted and exquisite in the world: traditional Mexican.

Today's cosmopolitan Mexico City is a gastronomic melting pot with some 15,000 restaurants. You'll find everything from simple family-style eateries to five-star world-class restaurants. The number and range of international restaurants is growing and diversifying—although Spanish, Italian, and Argentine are dominant.

During the 1990s, a renaissance of Mexican cuisine brought about a fashion often referred to as *nueva cocina mexicana* (nouvelle Mexican cuisine), variants of which are served by many of the trendier Mexico City restaurants. Emphasis is on presentation and intriguing or far-fetched combinations of ingredients from the Old World with that of the new. In the more serious or purist restaurants that aim to rescue recipes from the pre-Hispanic past, you can enjoy the delicate tastes of traditional regional dishes gleaned from colonial reports, and ancient indigenous cooking techniques such as steaming and baking. In market eateries and in the provinces, you may come across seasonal delicacies such as crunchy fried grasshoppers and fried *maguey* (agave) larva.

Lodging

As might be expected of a megalopolis, Mexico City has more than 25,000 hotel rooms—enough to accommodate every taste and budget. You can lodge in the quaint or the colonial, the smoked-glass-and-steel high-rise, or the elegant replica of an Italianate palace.

Museums

Mexico City is the cultural as well as political capital of the country, as evidenced by its 80-plus museums—some of the finest in Latin America. In buildings of architectural merit, you can see the stirring murals of such native sons as Diego Rivera, José Clemente Orozco, David Alfaro Siqueiros, and Juan O'Gorman; the haunting paintings of Frida Kahlo; stunning pre-Hispanic ceremonial pieces; and outstanding collections of religious art.

Nightlife and the Arts

Mexico City is the cultural capital of Latin America and, with the exception of Río de Janiero (or maybe São Paolo), has the liveliest nightlife. There's something for every taste: opera and symphonies; modern theater and performance; a renowned folklore ballet; and a lively square where mariachi play. You'll also find trendy discos and steamy dance halls where salsa, merengue, and *danzón* (elegant Cuban dance music) are headliners.

Shopping

Native crafts and specialties from all over Mexico are available in the capital, as are designer clothing, ceramics, and furniture. You'll also find a trove of contemporary art by Mexico's best painters and sculptors. And of course Mexican goods are a far better deal here than they are in overseas outlets.

Sports and the Outdoors

Latin sports such as the *fiesta brava* (bullfighting)—brought to Mexico by the conquistadores—have enjoyed popularity for more than four centuries in the capital, which attracts the country's best athletes. And although the roots of soccer ("fútbol") are probably English, a weekend afternoon game at Mexico City's colossal Estadio Azteca leaves no question that this is the sport Mexicans are craziest about. Ecotourism and adventure-travel agencies have also opened in Mexico City to offer great weekend getaways such as white-water rafting in nearby Veracruz or paragliding in Valle del Bravo.

EXPLORING MEXICO CITY

Most of Mexico City is aligned on two major intersecting thoroughfares: Paseo de la Reforma and Avenida Insurgentes—at 34 km (21 mi), the longest avenue in the city. Administratively, Mexico City is divided into 16 *delegaciones* (districts) and about 400 *colonias* (neighborhoods), each with street names fitting a given theme, such as a river, philosopher, or revolutionary hero. The same street can change names as it goes through different colonias. Hence, most street addresses include their colonia (abbreviated as Col.). Unless you're going to a landmark, it's important to tell your taxi driver the name of the colonia.

The principal sights of Mexico City fall into three areas. Allow a full day to cover each thoroughly, although you could race through them in four or five hours apiece. You can cover the first area—the Zócalo and Alameda Central—on foot. Getting around the Zona Rosa Bosque de Chapultepec and Colonia Condesa will require a taxi ride or two, as will Coyoacán and San Ángel in southern Mexico City.

Numbers in the text correspond to numbers in the margin and on the Zócalo and Alameda Central; Zona Rosa, Bosque de Chapultepec, and Condesa; and San Ángel and Coyoacán maps.

Great Itineraries

You can spend a month in Mexico City and just begin to grasp the tip of its iceberg of sights, sounds, and tastes. For stays shorter than this, here are some highlights.

IF YOU HAVE 3 DAYS

Start with the **Casa de los Azulejos** ⑬ for a Mexican breakfast, which you can digest with a stroll around the **Alameda Central** ⑱; visit the **Palacio de Bellas Artes** ⑮ and then wind your way through the historic center on Calle Tacuba to have lunch in the historic Café de Tacuba; here, you are right on the corner of the **Zócalo** ①, with its exotic ruins, museums, and public buildings, and you could end your day overlooking it all from the bars in either the Hotel Majestic or the Holiday Inn Zócalo. Day 2, head for the **Museo Nacional de Antropología** ㉖ in the morning and enjoy lunch in one of the many swank eateries in the Polanco neighborhood; head to the **Zona Rosa** in the afternoon, when it starts to come alive. Visit the **Mercado Insurgentes** for some fun shopping, or any of the stores on our list. Consider an evening in the fashionable **Colonia Condesa** for cocktails and dinner. On Day 3, go to **Bosque de Chapultepec** ㉑ to stroll the green pathways past the rowing lake and visit the **Castillo de Chapultepec** ㉒, the **Museo Nacional de Arte Moderno** ㉔, **Museo Rufino Tamayo** ㉕, and, of course, the **Zoológico** ㉗ to see the pandas. Visit downtown's **Plaza Garibaldi** on your last night in town for a rousing mariachi send-off. If the Classic period site of **Teotihuacán** intrigues you, however, you could spend the third day there.

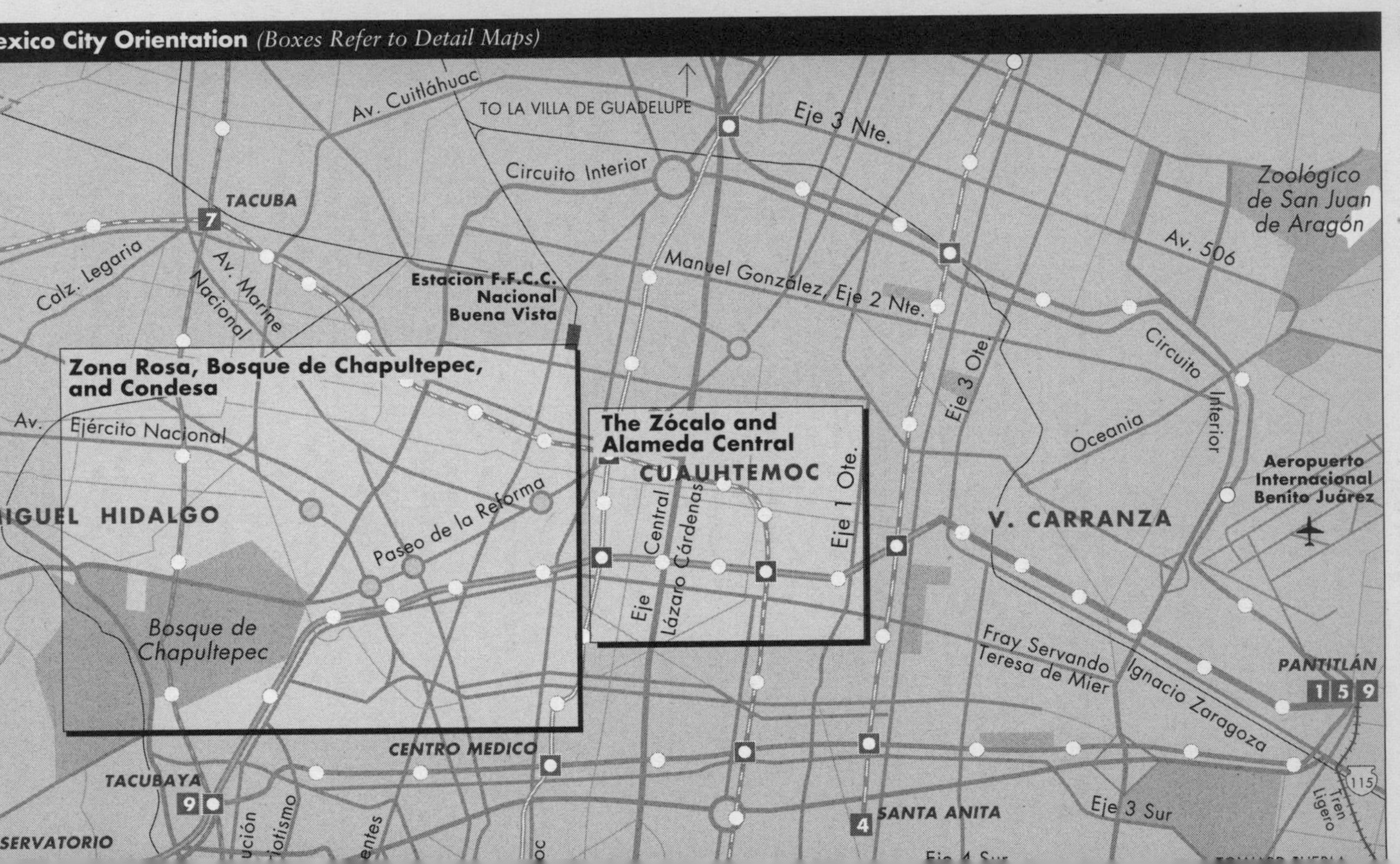
Mexico City Orientation (Boxes Refer to Detail Maps)
Av. Cuitláhuac
TO LA VILLA DE GUADELUPE
Eje 3 Nte.
Circuito Interior
TACUBA
7
Zoológico de San Juan de Aragón
Av. 506
Calz. Legaria
Av. Marina Nacional
Estacion F.F.C.C. Nacional Buena Vista
Manuel González, Eje 2 Nte.
Circuito Interior
Zona Rosa, Bosque de Chapultepec, and Condesa
Av. Ejército Nacional
Eje 3 Ote.
Oceania
The Zócalo and Alameda Central
CUAUHTEMOC
Eje 1 Ote.
Aeropuerto Internacional Benito Juárez
MIGUEL HIDALGO
Paseo de la Reforma
Eje Central Lázaro Cárdenas
V. CARRANZA
Bosque de Chapultepec
Fray Servando Teresa de Mier
Ignacio Zaragoza
PANTITLÁN
1 5 9
CENTRO MEDICO
TACUBAYA
9
SANTA ANITA
4
Eje 3 Sur
115
Tren Ligero
OBSERVATORIO

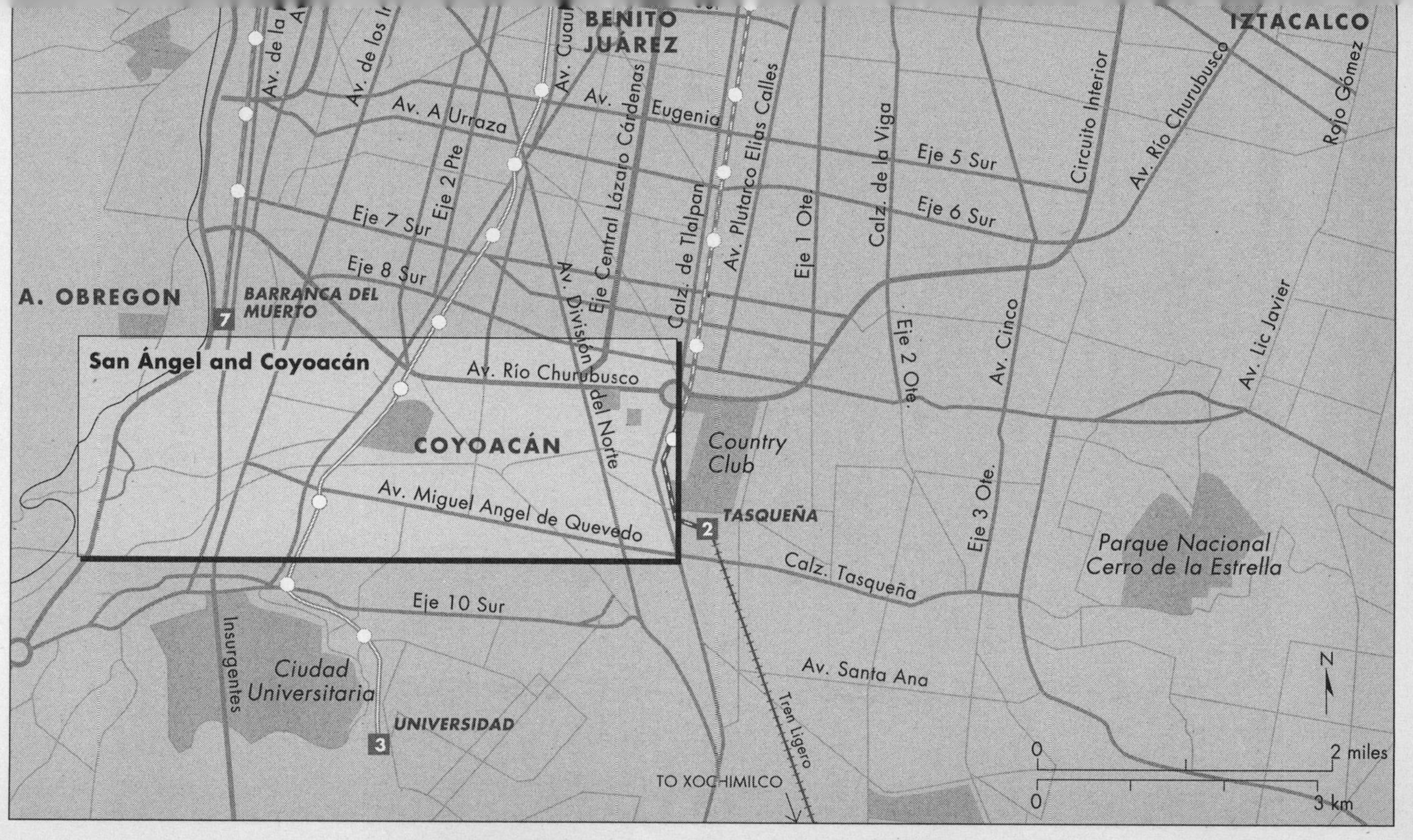
IZTACALCO
BENITO JUÁREZ
A. OBREGON
BARRANCA DEL MUERTO
7
San Ángel and Coyoacán
COYOACÁN
Country Club
TASQUEÑA
2
Parque Nacional Cerro de la Estrella
Ciudad Universitaria
UNIVERSIDAD
3
Insurgentes
Av. A Urraza
Av. Eugenia
Eje 2 Pte
Eje 7 Sur
Eje 8 Sur
Eje 10 Sur
Eje Central Lázaro Cárdenas
Av. División del Norte
Calz. de Tlalpan
Av. Plutarco Elías Calles
Eje 1 Ote.
Calz. de la Viga
Eje 5 Sur
Eje 6 Sur
Circuito Interior
Av. Río Churubusco
Rojo Gómez
Eje 2 Ote.
Av. Cinco
Eje 3 Ote.
Av. Lic Javier
Av. Río Churubusco
Av. Miguel Angel de Quevedo
Calz. Tasqueña
Av. Santa Ana
Tren Ligero
TO XOCHIMILCO
N
0
2 miles
0
3 km

Mexico City Metro

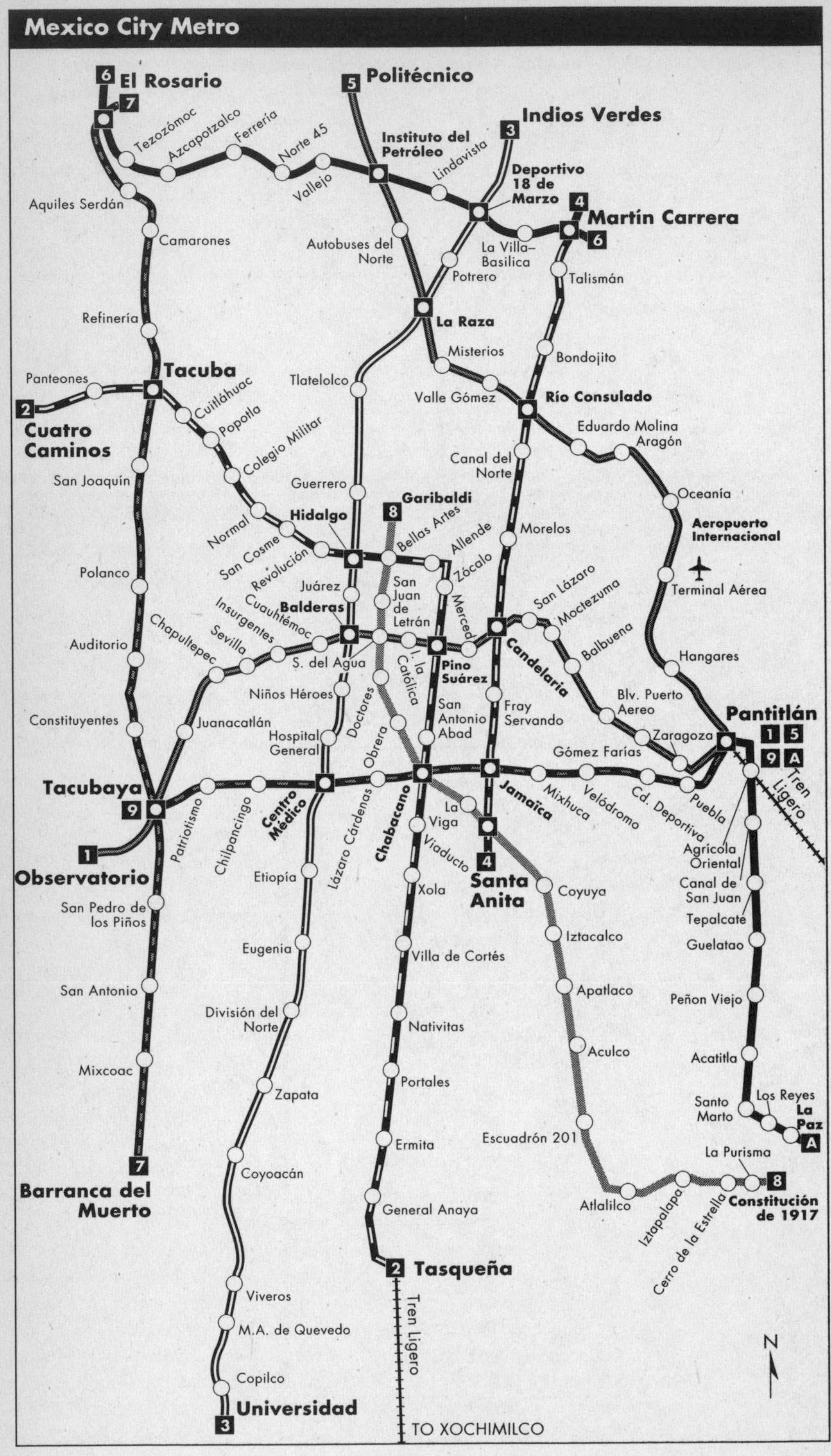

IF YOU HAVE 5 DAYS

Follow the three-day itinerary, going to **Bosque de Chapultepec** ㉑ on Day 3. On Day 4 spend time in **San Ángel**—start with the Bazar Sábado (if your plans bring you here on a Saturday) or the **Museo Estudio Diego Rivera** ㉞ and lunch in the San Ángel Inn—and in **Coyoacán,** with its lovely casa-museums, especially the **Museo de Frida Kahlo** ㊲ and **Museo de Leon Trotsky** ㊴. On Day 5 take an excursion to the **Basílica of the Virgin of Guadalupe,** Latin America's holiest shrine, and if you are back by midday you could just make it to the pyramids of **Teotihuacán,** where a powerful regime held sway over the region more than a millennium before the arrival of the Spanish. Climb at least one pyramid, visit the museum, and head back to Mexico City.

IF YOU HAVE 10 DAYS

Follow the five-day option and add a visit to the resort town of **Cuernavaca,** just over an hour's drive southeast of Mexico City. Spend the day in its museums and browsing its pretty main square, then overnight at one of the town's converted mansions. On Day 7 head back to Mexico City via Highway 95 and stop in **Xochimilco,** where you can ride through the floating gardens on a gondola-like boat and view an outstanding private collection of works by Diego Rivera and Frida Kahlo at the Dolores Olmedo Patino Museum. On Day 8 drive to the ancient Toltec ruins at **Tula** and continue to the village of **Tepotzotlán,** which has a beautiful Jesuit church. The next day, head to **Puebla** for a two-hour tour, including the main square and the fine Amparo Museum, then pop over to the nearby town of **Cholula,** once a sacred ceremonial site. Climb to the top of the church built over a pyramid, and return to Puebla for the night. En route back to Mexico City on the last day, drive to **Cacaxtla** to see some of the best-preserved Mesoamerican murals in Mexico.

The Zócalo and Alameda Central

This area is all about history: the Zócalo, its surrounding Centro Histórico, and Alameda Park were the heart of both the Aztec and Spanish cities. Several streets in the downtown area have been converted into pedestrian-only thoroughfares.

A Good Walk

An excellent point of departure for any tour of the city's center is the **Zócalo** ①, the heart and soul of old downtown. From here you can literally see the layers of history in the buildings around you. On the north side of this huge square you'll see the tilting **Catedral Metropolitana** ② and adjacent to it the 18th-century Sagrario Chapel. The **Templo Mayor** ③, ruins from the Aztec capital, with its superb museum, is northeast of the cathedral, across the pedestrian plaza. Modern art lovers should walk east on Calle Moneda to Academia to find the **Museo José Luis Cuevas** ④. Take Moneda back (west) to the Zócalo. The building on your left is the monumental **Palacio Nacional** ⑤, covering two city blocks. Its interior is lined with Diego Rivera's profound mural of Mexican history. Walk south past the palacio to the corner and turn right, crossing the street to get to the section of the Zócalo occupied by the 1722 **Ayuntamiento** ⑥. Recross the street and walk northwest through the open square to Calle Cinco de Mayo and the National Pawn Shop in the **Monte de Piedad** ⑦. Three-and-a-half blocks north is the historic **Plaza de Santo Domingo** ⑧. Walk one block east along Calle República de Cuba and one block south on Calle República de Argentina to get to Calle Justo Sierra and the **Antiguo Colegio de San Idelfonso** ⑨, now an art and history museum. Turn west and follow Calle Justo Sierra three blocks—it will change into Calle Donceles—to Calle

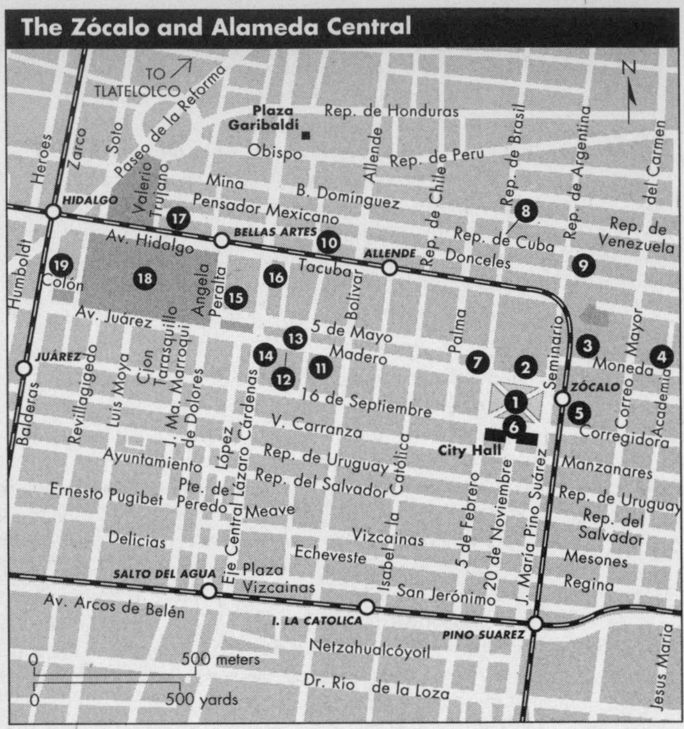

The Zócalo and Alameda Central

República de Chile, then turn left (south) a block to Calle Tacuba. Turn right and walk one block to have a scrumptious lunch at the Café de Tacuba on the right side of the street. Or, you can continue west on Tacuba 1½ blocks to the **Museo Nacional de Arte** ⑩ in the colonial Plaza Manuel Tolsa.

From Calle Tacuba, head two short blocks south to Calle Madero, one of the city's most architecturally varied streets. On the south side of Madero, between Bolivar and Gante, is the 1780 Baroque **Palacio de Iturbide** ⑪. Go west along on the south side of Madero; less than a block past the palacio you'll come to the **Iglesia de San Francisco** ⑫, with its beautifully painted walls. The stunning tilework of the **Casa de los Azulejos** ⑬ will draw your eye across Calle Madero.

The ultimate goals of the remainder of this walk are an antiques museum and a Diego Rivera mural museum. From Calle Madero, walk less than a half block west to Eje Central Lázaro Cárdenas, a wide four-lane avenue. At the corner and on your left, you can't miss the 1950s-style skyscraper, the **Torre Latinoamericana** ⑭, which has one of the best aerial views of the city as well as a sky-high aquarium. Cross the avenue and turn right (north) to explore the beautiful **Palacio de Bellas Artes** ⑮ opera house, the long side of which skirts Lázaro Cárdenas (its entrance is on Juárez). The 1908 post office building of **Dirección General de Correos** ⑯ is up Lázaro Cárdenas another 150 ft, across from Bellas Artes.

Pass the post office to Calle Tacuba and cross Lázaro Cárdenas one last time, where Calle Tacuba turns into Avenida Hidalgo. One block west, you'll come to the antiques-filled **Museo Franz Mayer** ⑰, which often hosts world-class art and photography exhibitions. Across Avenida Hidalgo is the north end of the leafy park **Alameda Central** ⑱. At its south end, on Avenida Juárez, **Fonart** is a government-owned arts and crafts store. To get to the **Museo Mural Diego Rivera** ⑲, take Juárez west to Calle Balderas, about 3½ blocks from Fonart. Turn right and walk a short block to Calle Colón.

TIMING

The Zócalo area will be quietest on Sunday, when bureaucrats have their day of rest. But Alameda Park will be jumping with children and their parents enjoying a Sunday outing. The park will be particularly festive during December, when dozens of "Santas" will appear with plastic reindeer to take wish lists. Although Mexicans celebrate on the night of December 24, the tradition of giving presents—especially to children—kicks in January 5, the eve of the Day of the Three Kings, and the Three Wise Men of biblical lore replace the Santas in the Alameda. Gorgeous Christmas-light sculptures deck the Zócalo from end to end and stream up Calle Madero past Alameda Park to Paseo de la Reforma beyond the museums in Bosque de Chapultepec.

During the daytime, the downtown area is vibrant with activity. As in any capital, watch out for pickpockets, especially on crowded buses and subways, and avoid deserted streets at night.

The streets in the walking tour are fairly close to one another and can be covered in a day if you're short on time; otherwise, a couple of days will make for a more leisurely tour. The National Palace, Templo Mayor and its museum, and Franz Mayer Museum are worth an hour each of your time; you can cover the Palace of Fine Arts in a half hour unless you stumble upon one of its marvelous and epic temporary exhibitions.

Sights to See

THE ZÓCALO

9 **Antiguo Colegio de San Ildefonso** (College of San Ildefonso). This colonial building with lovely patios started out as a Jesuit school for the sons of wealthy Mexicans in the 18th century. It is now a splendid museum that showcases outstanding regional exhibitions. The interior contains murals by Diego Rivera, José Clemente Orozco, and Fernando Leal. ✉ *Justo Sierra 16, Col. Centro, almost at the corner of República de Argentina, 2 blocks north of the Zócalo,* ☎ *55/5789–0485,* WEB *www.sanildefonso.org.mx.* 🎟 *$3.50, free Tues.* ⏲ *Tues.–Sun. 10–6.*

6 **Ayuntamiento** (City Hall). The two buildings of Mexico's city hall stand on the south side of the Zócalo; colonial tiles of the arms of Cortés and other conquistadores decorate the one on the west. Originally built in 1532, it was destroyed by fire in 1692 and rebuilt in 1722. In 1935 the Distrito Federal needed more office space, and to maintain the architectural integrity of the Zócalo, the "matching" structure across the street (20 de Noviembre) was built. Toward the end of the 20th century, for the first time in 70 years, Mexico City residents were allowed to elect their own mayor (the post had previously been appointed by the president). Thus did the city's first leftist administration begin, continuing under the feisty and contentious leadership of Manuel López Obrador. ✉ *Zócalo, Col. Centro.*

2 **Catedral Metropolitana** (Metropolitan Cathedral). Construction on this oldest and largest cathedral in Latin America began in 1573 on the north side of the Zócalo and continued intermittently throughout the next three centuries. The result is a medley of Baroque and neoclassical touches. Inside are four identical domes, their airiness grounded by rows of supportive columns. There are five altars and 14 chapels, mostly in the churrigueresque style, an ornate Baroque style named for

Spanish architect José Churriguera (d. 1725). Like most Mexican churches, the cathedral itself is all but overwhelmed by the innumerable paintings, altarpieces, and statues—in graphic color—of Christ and the saints. Over the centuries, this cathedral began to sink into the spongy subsoil, but a major engineering project to stabilize the structure was declared successful in 2000. ✉ *Zócalo, Col. Centro.*

7 **Monte de Piedad** (Mountain of Pity). This structure from the late 18th century houses the National Pawn Shop. It's on the northwest corner of the Zócalo, on what was once the site of an Aztec palace. ✉ *Monte de Piedad 7, Col. Centro,* ☎ *55/5278–1800,* WEB *www.nmp.org.mx.* ⏲ *Mon.–Sat. 8:30–6.*

4 **Museo José Luis Cuevas.** Installed in a refurbished former convent, this attractive museum displays international modern art as well as work by Mexico's enfant terrible, José Luis Cuevas, one of the country's best-known contemporary artists. The highlight is the sensational *La Giganta* (*The Giantess*), Cuevas's 8-ton bronze sculpture in the central patio. Up-and-coming Latin American artists appear in temporary exhibitions throughout the year. ✉ *Academia 13, Col. Centro,* ☎ *55/5522–0156.* 🎫 *90¢, free Sun.* ⏲ *Tues.–Sun. 10–5:30.*

★ 5 **Palacio Nacional** (National Palace). This grand government building was initiated by Cortés on the site of Moctezuma's home and remodeled by the viceroys. Its current form dates from 1693, although a third floor was added in 1926. Now the seat of government, it has always served as a public-function site. In fact, during colonial times, the first bullfight in New Spain took place in the inner courtyard.

Diego Rivera's sweeping, epic murals on the second floor of the main courtyard exert a mesmeric pull. For more than 16 years (1929–45), Rivera and his assistants mounted scaffolds day and night, perfecting techniques adapted from Renaissance Italian fresco painting. The result, nearly 1,200 square ft of vividly painted wall space, is grandiosely entitled *Epic of the Mexican People in Their Struggle for Freedom and Independence.* The paintings represent two millennia of Mexican history, filtered through Rivera's imagination. He painted pre-Hispanic times in innocent, almost sugary scenes of Tenochtitlán. Only a few vignettes—a man offering a human arm for sale, and the carnage of warriors—acknowledge the darker aspects of ancient life. As you walk around the floor, you'll pass images of the savagery of the conquest and the hypocrisy of the Spanish priests, the noble independence movement, and the bloody revolution. Marx appears amid scenes of class struggle, toiling workers, industrialization (which Rivera idealized), bourgeois decadence, and nuclear holocaust. These are among Rivera's finest work—as well as the most accessible and probably most visited. The palace also houses a minor museum that focuses on 19th-century president Benito Juárez and the Mexican Congress.

The liberty bell rung by Padre Hidalgo to proclaim independence in 1810 hangs high on the central facade. It chimes every eve of September 16, while from the balcony the president repeats the historic shout of independence to throngs of *chilangos* (Mexico City residents) below. Usually the people demand that the chief executive continue shouting until he loses his voice. ✉ *East side of the Zócalo, Col. Centro,* ☎ *55/5542–6466.* 🎫 *Free; you'll be asked to leave an I.D. at the front desk.* ⏲ *Mon.–Sat. 9–6, Sun. 9–2.*

8 **Plaza de Santo Domingo** (Santo Domingo Plaza). The Aztec emperor Cuauhtémoc built a palace here, where heretics were later burned at the stake in the Spanish Inquisition. The plaza was the intellectual hub of the city during the colonial era. Today, its most colorful feature is

the **Portal de los Evangelistas** (Portal of the Evangelists), filled with scribes at old-fashioned typewriters who are filling in official forms, printing invitations, or composing letters for love-stricken swains.

The gloomy-looking **Palacio de la Escuela de Medicina Mexicana** (✉ Palace of Medicine; ☎ *55/5529–7543*; free; daily 9–6), once the headquarters for the Inquisition, is catercorner to the lively portal. Founded by the Catholic Church in 1571 (50 years after the conquest) and closed by government decree in 1820, it was a medical school for many years. Now it serves as a fascinating museum portraying the history of medicine in this country.

The 18th-century Baroque **Santo Domingo church,** slightly north of the portal, is all that remains of the first Dominican convent in New Spain. The convent building was demolished in 1861 under the Reform laws that forced clerics to turn over all religious buildings not used for worship to the government. Today, you can still see white-robed Dominican nuns visiting the church. ✉ *Between República de Cuba, República de Brasil, República de Venezuela, and Palma, Col. Centro,* ☎ *no phone.*

★ 3 **Templo Mayor** (Great Temple). The ruins of the ancient hub of the Aztec empire were unearthed accidentally in 1978 by telephone repairmen and have since been turned into a vast archaeological site and museum. At this temple, dedicated to the Aztec cult of death, captives from rival tribes—as many as 10,000 at a time—were sacrificed to the bloodthirsty god of war, Huitzilopochtli. Seven rows of leering stone skulls adorn one side of the structure.

The adjacent **Museo del Templo Mayor** contains 3,000 pieces unearthed from the site and from other ruins in central Mexico; they include ceramic warriors, stone carvings and knives, skulls of sacrificial victims, a rare gold ingot, models and scale reproductions, and a room on the Spaniards' destruction of Tenochtitlán. The centerpiece is an 8-ton disk discovered at the Templo Mayor. It depicts the moon goddess Coyolxauhqui, who, according to myth, was decapitated and dismembered by her brother Huitzilopochtli. Call six weeks ahead to schedule free English-language tours by museum staff in the mornings. ✉ *Seminario 8, at República de Guatemala; entrance on the plaza, near Catedral Metropolitana, Col. Centro,* ☎ *55/5542–4784, 55/5542–4785, or 55/5542–4786,* WEB *templo-mayor.dieich.com or azteca.conaculta.gob.mx/templomayor.* *$3.50, free Sun.* *Tues.–Sun. 9–5.*

1 **Zócalo** (formal name: Plaza de la Constitución). Mexico City's historic plaza and the buildings around it were built by the Spaniards, using local slaves. This enormous paved square, the largest in the Western Hemisphere, occupies the site of the ceremonial center of Tenochtitlán, the capital of the Aztec empire, which once comprised 78 buildings. Throughout the 16th, 17th, and 18th centuries, elaborate churches and convents, elegant mansions, and stately public edifices were constructed around the square; many of these buildings have long since been converted to other uses. There's an air of Old Europe in this part of the city, which, in its entirety (the Centro Histórico), is a national monument that has undergone major refurbishing. Clusters of small shops, eateries, cantinas, street vendors, and a few women in native Indian dress contribute to an inimitably Mexican flavor and exuberance.

Zócalo literally means "pedestal" or "base": in the mid-19th century, an independence monument was planned for the square, but it was never built. The term stuck, however, and now the word "zócalo" is applied to the main plazas of most Mexican cities. Mexico City's Zócalo (because it's the original, it's always capitalized) is used for government rallies, protests, sit-ins, and festive events. It's the focal point for Independence Day celebrations on the eve of September 16 and is spectacularly festooned during the Christmas season. Flag-raising and -lowering ceremonies take place here in the early morning and late afternoon. ✉ *Bounded on the south by 16 de Septiembre, north by 5 de Mayo, east by Pino Suárez, and west by Monte de Piedad, Col. Centro.*

ALAMEDA CENTRAL

18 **Alameda Central** (Alameda Park). Since Aztec times, when the Indians held their *tianguis* (market) on the site, this park has been one of the capital's oases of greenery and centers of activity. In the early days of the Viceroyalty, the Inquisition burned its victims at the stake here. Later, national leaders, from 18th-century viceroys to Emperor Maximilian and President Porfirio Díaz, envisioned the park as a symbol of civic pride and prosperity: over the centuries, it has been endowed with fountains, railings, a Moorish kiosk imported from Paris, and ash, willow, and poplar trees. The semicircular, white-marble **Hemiciclo a Benito Juárez** (monument to Juárez) stands on the Avenida Juárez side of the park. It's a fine place for strolling, relaxing, and listening to live music on Sunday and holidays.

13 **Casa de los Azulejos** (House of Tiles). Built as the palace of the counts of the Valle de Orizaba, an aristocratic family from the early period of Spanish rule, this 17th-century masterpiece acquired its name from the tilework installed by a later descendant. The facade also has iron grillwork balconies and gray stonework. One of the prettiest Baroque structures in the country, it is currently occupied by Sanborns, a chain store–restaurant. The dazzling interior, which includes a Moorish patio, a monumental staircase, and a mural by Orozco, is worth seeing. If you have plenty of time—service is slow—this is a good place to stop for a meal. ✉ *Calle Madero 4, at Callejón de la Condesa, Alameda Central,* ☎ *55/5512–9820 Ext. 103.* ⏲ *Daily 7* AM*–1* AM.

16 **Dirección General de Correos** (General Post Office). Mexico City's main post office building is a fine example of Renaissance revival architecture. Constructed of cream-color sandstone in 1908, it epitomizes the grand imitations of European architecture common in Mexico during the Porfiriato—the long dictatorship of Porfirio Díaz (1876–1911). Upstairs, the **Museo del Palacio Postal** shows Mexico's postal history. ✉ *Calle Tacuba and Eje Central Lázaro Cárdenas, Alameda Central,* ☎ *55/5510–2999 museum; 55/5521–7394 post office.* 🎟 *Free.* ⏲ *Museum weekdays 9–4, weekends 10–2; post office weekdays 8–8, Sat. 9–1.*

12 **Iglesia de San Francisco.** On the site of Mexico's first convent (1524)—and supposedly the site of Moctezuma's zoo before that—this church's current 18th-century French Gothic incarnation is one of the newest buildings on the street. ✉ *Calles Madero and 16 de Septiembre, Alameda Central,* ☎ *no phone.* ⏲ *Daily 7* AM*–8:30* PM.

17 **Museo Franz Mayer.** Housed in the 16th-century Hospital de San Juan de Dios, this museum exhibits 16th- and 17th-century antiques, such as wooden chests inlaid with ivory, tortoiseshell, and ebony; tapestries, paintings, and lacquerware; rococo clocks, glassware, and architectural ornamentation; and an unusually large assortment of Talavera ceramics. The museum also has more than 700 editions of Cervantes's *Don Quixote.* The old hospital building is faithfully restored, with pieces of the original frescoes peeking through. ✉ *Av. Hidalgo 45, at Plaza Santa Veracruz, Alameda Central,* ☎ *55/5518–2267,* WEB *www.museosmexico.com.mx.* 🎟 *$2, free Tues.* ⏲ *Tues.–Sun. 10–5. Call 1 wk ahead for an English-speaking guide.*

19 **Museo Mural Diego Rivera.** Diego Rivera's controversial mural, *Sunday Afternoon Dream in the Alameda Park,* originally was painted on a lobby wall of the Hotel Del Prado in 1947–48. Its controversy grew out of Rivera's Marxist inscription, "God does not exist," which the artist later replaced with the bland "Conference of San Juan de Letrán" to placate Mexico's dominant Catholic population. The 1985 earthquake destroyed the hotel but not the poetic mural. This museum was built across the street from the hotel to house the work. ✉ *Calles Balderas and Colón, Alameda Central,* ☎ *55/5510–2329.* 🎟 *$1, free Sun.* ⏲ *Tues.–Sun. 10–6.*

10 **Museo Nacional de Arte** (National Art Museum). This neoclassical building contains examples of nearly every school of Mexican art, with a concentration on work made between 1810 and 1950. On display are Diego Rivera's portrait of Adolfo Best Maugard, José María Velasco's *Vista del Valle de México desde el Cerro de Santa Isabel (View of the Valley of Mexico from the Hill of Santa Isabel),* and Ramón Cano Manilla's *El Globo (The Balloon). El Caballito (The Little Horse),* a statue of Spain's Carlos V on horseback, stands out front. ✉ *Calle Tacuba 8, Col. Centro,* ☎ *55/5130–3400.* 🎟 *Free.* ⏲ *Tues.–Sun. 10:30–5:30.*

★ 15 **Palacio de Bellas Artes** (Fine Arts Palace). Construction on this colossal white-marble opera house was begun in 1904 by Porfirio Díaz, who wanted to add yet another ornamental building to his accomplishments. He was ousted seven years later and the building wasn't finished until 1934. Today the theater serves as a handsome venue for international and national artists, including the Ballet Folklórico de México. The palace is indeed renowned for its architecture, the work of Italian Adamo Boari, who also designed the post office; it includes an art deco facade trimmed in pre-Hispanic motifs. Inside are a Tiffany stained-glass curtain depicting the two volcanoes outside Mexico City and paintings by several celebrated Mexican artists, including Rufino Tamayo and Mexico's trio of muralists: Rivera, Orozco, and Siqueiros. Temporary art exhibitions are also held here. ✉ *Eje Central Lázaro Cárdenas and Av. Juárez, Alameda Central,* ☎ *55/5512–3633.* 🎟 *$2.50 for exhibitions, free Sun.; no charge to look at the building and gift shops inside.* ⏲ *Building Tues.–Sun. 10–9; exhibits Tues.–Sun. 10–6.*

OFF THE BEATEN PATH

TLATELOLCO – At Paseo de la Reforma's northern end, about 2 km (1 mi) north of the Palacio de Bellas Artes, the area known as Tlatelolco (pronounced tla-tel-*ohl*-coh) was the domain of Cuauhtémoc (pronounced kwa-oo-*teh*-mock)—the last Aztec emperor before the conquest—and the sister city of Tenochtitlán. In modern times its name continues to make residents shudder, as it was here that the Mexican army massacred several hundred protesting students in 1968. In addition, the 1985 earthquake destroyed several high-rise apartments in Tlatelolco, killing hundreds. The center of Tlatelolco is the **Plaza de las Tres Culturas,** so named because Mexico's three cultural eras—pre-Hispanic, colonial, and contemporary—are represented on the plaza in the form of the small ruins of a pre-Hispanic ceremonial center (visible from the roadway); the Iglesia de Santiago Tlatelolco (1609) and Colegio de la Santa Cruz de Tlatelolco (1535–36); and the modern Ministry of Foreign Affairs (1970). The *colegio* (college), founded by the Franciscans after the conquest, was once attended by the sons of the Aztec nobility. ✉ *Plaza bounded on the north by Manuel González, on the west by Av. San Juan de Letrán Nte., and on the east by Paseo de la Reforma, between Glorietas de Peralvillo and Cuitláhuac, Tlatelolco.*

11 **Palacio de Iturbide** (Emperor Iturbide's Palace). Built in 1780, this handsome Baroque structure—note the imposing door and its carved-stone

trimmings—became the residence of Iturbide in 1822. One of the heroes of the independence movement, the misguided Iturbide proclaimed himself emperor of a country that had thrown off the imperial yoke of the Hapsburgs only a year before. His own empire, needless to say, was short-lived. Now his home is owned by Banamex (Banco Nacional de México), which sponsors cultural exhibitions in the atrium. ✉ *Calle Madero 17, Col. Centro,* ☎ *55/5225–0281.* 🎟 *Free.* ⏲ *Inner atrium daily 10–7.*

⑭ **Torre Latinoamericana** (Latin American Tower). This 47-story skyscraper, the second-tallest building in the capital, was completed in 1956. On clear days the observation deck and café on the top floors afford fine views of the city. The **Fantastic World of the Sea,** a sky-high aquarium, miraculously transported small sharks and crocodiles to the 38th floor. ✉ *Calle Madero and Eje Central Lázaro Cárdenas, Alameda Central,* ☎ *55/5521–0844 observation deck; 55/5521–7455 aquarium.* 🎟 *Deck $3.50, aquarium $2.20.* ⏲ *Deck daily 9:30 AM–11 PM; aquarium daily 9:30 AM–10 PM.*

Zona Rosa, Bosque de Chapultepec, and Colonia Condesa

Bosque de Chapultepec, named for the *chapulines* (grasshoppers) that populated it long ago, is the largest park in the city, a great green refuge from concrete, traffic, and dust. Housing five world-class museums, a castle, a lake, an amusement park, and the Mexican president's official residence, Chapultepec is a saving grace for visitors and locals. If you have time to visit only one of these museums, make it the Museo Nacional de Antropología—you won't find the likes of its exhibits anywhere else.

Stores, hotels, travel agencies, and restaurants line the avenues of the Zona Rosa, once a cultural center of Mexico City, now a first stop for shopping. Nearby Colonia Condesa—a more recent tourist destination—is filled with fading art deco architecture, casual cafés, and inexpensive eateries that cater to the city's young and trendy.

A Good Walk

Emperor Maximilian built the Paseo de la Reforma in 1865, modeling it after the Champs-Élysées in Paris. Its purpose was to connect the Palacio Nacional with his residence, the Castillo de Chapultepec. At the northeastern end of Reforma are Tlatelolco, the Lagunilla Market, and Plaza Garibaldi, where the mariachis cluster and strut. To the west, Reforma winds its leisurely way west into the wealthy neighborhoods of Lomas de Chapultepec, where posh houses and estates sit behind stone walls.

Start your exploration of the Zona Rosa at the junction of Reforma, Avenida Juárez, and Bucareli, just west of the Alameda Central. Along the stretch of Reforma west of this intersection are a number of statues erected at the request of former Mexican president Porfirio Díaz to honor illustrious men, including Simón Bolívar, Columbus, Pasteur, and the Aztec emperor Cuauhtémoc. The best known, the **Monumento a la Independencia** ⑳, also known as The Angel, marks the western edge of the Zona Rosa. To get the best of the area's sights, walk along Hamburgo, Londres, and Copenhague streets—like others in the Zona, named for Continental cities. There's a crafts market, Mercado Zona Rosa, on Londres.

Four blocks southwest of the Zona Rosa, at Avenida Chapultepec, you'll come to the main entrance of **Bosque de Chapultepec** ㉑, or Chapultepec Park. Uphill from the entrance is the **Castillo de Chapultepec** ㉒

Bosque de Chapultepec . . 21
Castillo de Chapultepec . . 22
Monumento a la Independencia (El Ángel) . . . 20
Museo del Caracol 23
Museo Nacional de Antropología . 26
Museo Nacional de Arte Moderno . . . 24
Museo Rufino Tamayo 25
Zoológico . . . 27

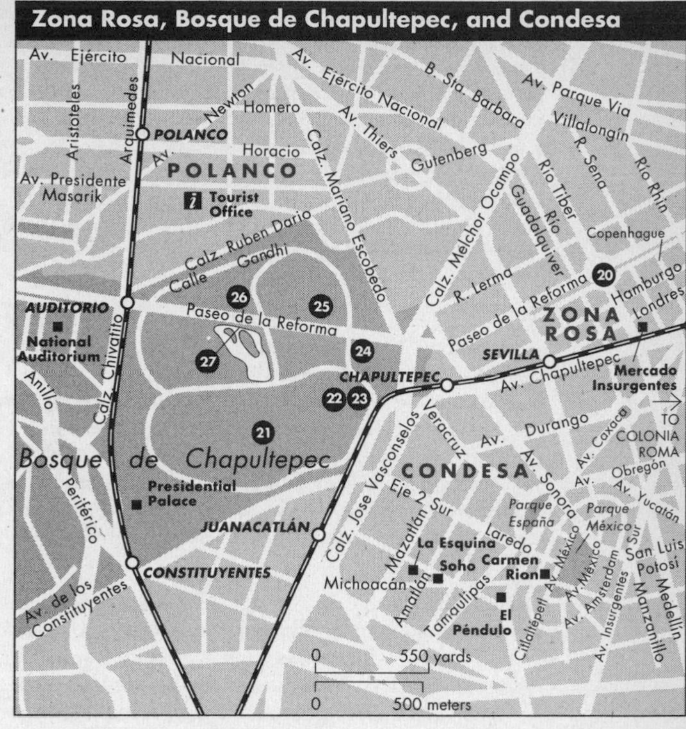

and its National History Museum. Heading downhill again after leaving the Castillo, you'll go past the much smaller, also historical, **Museo del Caracol** ㉓. North of the Castillo on the near side of Paseo de la Reforma is the **Museo Nacional de Arte Moderno** ㉔. Almost directly across Paseo de la Reforma on its north side and west of Calle Gandhi, you'll see the **Museo Rufino Tamayo** ㉕, in which you'll find Tamayo's paintings as well as those of other outstanding modern artists. West of the Museo Tamayo on the same side of Reforma is the **Museo Nacional de Antropología** ㉖, with its world-renowned collections of Mesoamerican art and artifacts. Cross Reforma again and you'll come to the entrance to the **Zoológico** ㉗.

Southeast of Bosque de Chapultepec, **Colonia Condesa** and **Colonia Roma** are attractive tree-lined neighborhoods where meandering streets make for pleasant strolling, especially in spring, when plentiful jacarandas are in bloom. From the Bosque de Chapultepec, take a *pesero* (minibus) from beside the Chapultepec metro or a five-minute taxi ride to the buzzing restaurant zone of Calle Michoacán. If you choose to walk, it'll take 25 minutes: walk along Calle Veracruz going away from the park, turn right on Avenida Mazatlán, then left onto Calle Michoacán.

TIMING

You can easily spend an hour at each Bosque de Chapultepec museum, with the exception of the National Museum of Anthropology, which is huge compared with its sister institutions. You can have a quick go-through in two hours, but to really appreciate the fine exhibits, anywhere from a half day to two full days is more appropriate. Tuesday to Friday are good days to visit the museums and stroll around the park. On Sunday and Mexican holidays, when museum entry is free, every inch is packed with families. Adding Colonia Condesa and Colonia Roma to the end of a day of museum visits will make for a delightful evening.

Sights to See

BOSQUE DE CHAPULTEPEC

21 **Bosque de Chapultepec** ("The Woods of Chapultepec," or Chapultepec Park). This 1,600-acre green space, divided into three sections, draws families on weekend outings, cyclists, and joggers. Its museums rank among the finest in Mexico. This is one of the oldest parts of Mexico City, having been inhabited by the Mexica (Aztec) tribe as early as the 13th century. The Mexica poet-king Nezahualcoyotl had his palace here and ordered construction of the aqueduct that brought water to Tenochtitlán. Ahuehuete trees (Moctezuma cypress) still stand from that era, when the woods were used as hunting preserves.

At the park's principal entrance, one block west of the Chapultepec metro station, the **Monumento a los Niños Héroes** (Monument to the Boy Heroes) consists of six marble columns adorned with eaglets. Supposedly buried in the monument are the young cadets who, it is said, wrapped themselves in the Mexican flag and jumped to their deaths rather than surrender to the Americans during the U.S. invasion of 1847. To Mexicans, that war is still a troubling symbol of their neighbor's aggressive dominance: the war cost Mexico almost half of its national territory—the present states of Texas, California, Arizona, New Mexico, and Nevada.

Other sights in the first section of Bosque de Chapultepec include three small boating lakes, a botanical garden, and the Casa del Lago cultural center, which hosts free plays, cultural events, and live music on weekends. **Los Pinos,** the residential palace of the president of Mexico, is on a small highway called Avenida Constituyentes, which cuts through the park; it's heavily guarded and cannot be visited.

The less crowded second and third sections of Bosque de Chapultepec contain a fancy restaurant; **La Feria de Chapultepec; El Papalote, Museo del Niño**; the national cemetery; and the Lienzo Charro (Mexican rodeos), held on Sunday afternoon.

22 **Castillo de Chapultepec** (Chapultepec Castle). On Cerro del Chapulín (Grasshopper Hill), the Castillo has borne witness to all the turbulence and grandeur of Mexican history. In its earliest permutations, it was a Mexica palace, where the Indians made one of their last stands against the Spaniards. Later it was a Spanish hermitage, gunpowder plant, and military college. Emperor Maximilian used the castle, parts of which date from 1783, as his residence, and his example was followed by various presidents from 1872 to 1940, when Lázaro Cárdenas decreed that it be turned into the **Museo Nacional de Historia** (National History Museum).

Displays on the museum's ground floor cover Mexican history from the conquest to the revolution. The bathroom, bedroom, tea salon, and gardens were used by Maximilian and his wife, Carlotta, during the 19th century. The ground floor also contains works by 20th-century muralists O'Gorman, Orozco, and Siqueiros, and the upper floor is devoted to temporary exhibitions, Porfirio Díaz's malachite vases, and religious art. A 40¢ shuttle bus runs between this museum and the Museo del Caracol. ✉ *Section 1, Bosque de Chapultepec,* ☎ *55/5553–6224 or 55/5286–9920.* 🎫 *$3, free Sun.* ⏲ *Tues.–Sun. 9–4.*

La Feria de Chapultepec. This children's amusement park has various games and more than 50 rides, including a truly hair-raising haunted house and a *montaña rusa*—"Russian mountain," or roller coaster. Admission price varies, depending on which rides are covered and whether meals are included. ✉ *Section 2, Bosque de Chapultepec,* ☎ *55/5230–2112.* 🎫 *$7–$15.* ⏲ *Tues.–Fri. 11–6, weekends 10–9.*

24 **Museo Nacional de Arte Moderno** (National Museum of Modern Art). One room here is devoted to Mexican plastic arts from the 1930s to the 1960s; four others feature revolving exhibitions of contemporary international painters, sculptors, lithographers, and photographers. ✉ *Paseo de la Reforma and Calle Gandhi, Section 1, Bosque de Chapultepec,* ☎ *55/5553–9394.* *$1.50, free Sun.* ⌚ *Tues.–Sun. 10–5:45.*

23 **Museo del Caracol.** Officially it's the Galería de la Lucha del Pueblo Mexicano por su Libertad, but most people refer to it by the more fanciful name Museum of the Snail because of its spiral shape. The gallery concentrates on the 400 years from the establishment of the Viceroyalty to the Constitution of 1917, using dioramas and light-and-sound displays that children can appreciate. ✉ *Section 1, Bosque de Chapultepec, on the ramp up to the Castillo,* ☎ *55/5553–6285.* *$2.50, free Sun.* ⌚ *Tues.–Sun. 9–5:30.*

★ 26 **Museo Nacional de Antropología** (National Museum of Anthropology). A distinguished architectural design by Pedro Ramírez Vázquez graces this archaeological museum, one of the finest in the world. Each salon on the museum's two floors displays artifacts from a particular geographic region or culture. The collection is so extensive—covering some 100,000 square ft—that you could easily spend a day here, and that might be barely adequate. Labels and explanations are in Spanish and English, and free tours are available at set times between 3 and 6. You can also reserve a special tour with an English-speaking guide by calling the museum one week in advance, or opt for an English audio guide ($3.50) or English-language guidebooks for sale in the bookshop.

A good place to start is in the Orientation Room, where a film is shown in Spanish nearly every hour on the hour weekdays and every two hours on weekends. The film traces the course of Mexican prehistory and the pre-Hispanic cultures of Mesoamerica. The 12 ground-floor rooms treat pre-Hispanic cultures by region—such as Sala Teotihuacána, Sala Tolteca, Sala Oaxaca (Zapotec and Mixtec peoples), Sala Maya (Maya groups from many areas, including Guatemala), and so on. You will find the famous Aztec calendar stone—the original *Piedra del Sol* (Stone of the Sun)—in Room 7, the Sala Mexica, which describes Aztec life. A copy of the Aztec ruler Moctezuma's feathered headdress is displayed nearby in the same salon—strangely, the original headdress is in Vienna. An original stela from Tula, near Mexico City, massive Olmec heads from Veracruz, and vivid reproductions of Maya murals in a reconstructed temple are some of the other highlights. The magnificent tomb of 8th-century Maya ruler Pacal, which was discovered in the ruins of Palenque, is another must to explore (Sala Maya). The perfectly preserved skeletal remains lie in state in an immense stone chamber, and the stairwell walls leading to it are beautifully decorated with bas-relief scenes of the underworld. Pacal's jade death mask is also on display nearby. The ground floor is filled with everything from the early remnants of nomadic societies to the statuary, jewelry, weapons, figurines, and pottery that evoke the intriguing, complex, and frequently bloodthirsty civilizations that peopled Mesoamerica for the 3,000 years that preceded the Spanish invasion.

The nine rooms on the upper floor contain faithful ethnographic displays of current indigenous peoples, using maps, photographs, household objects, folk art, clothing, and religious articles. When leaving the museum, take a rest and watch the famous Voladores de Papantla (flyers of Papantla) as they swing by their feet down an incredibly high maypolelike structure. ✉ *Paseo de la Reforma at Calle Gandhi, Section 1, Bosque de Chapultepec,* ☎ *55/5286–2923 or 55/5553–6381; 55/5553–6386 for a guide.* *$3, free Sun.* ⌚ *Tues.–Sun. 9–7.*

★ 25 **Museo Rufino Tamayo** (Rufino Tamayo Museum). Within its modernist shell, this sleek museum contains the paintings of the noted Mexican artist, works from his private collection, and temporary exhibitions that feature contemporary artists from around the world. The majority of paintings are by Tamayo; those from his collection, which demonstrate his unerring eye for great art, include a Picasso and a few works by Joan Miró, René Magritte, Francis Bacon, and Henry Moore. ⊠ *Paseo de la Reforma at Calle Gandhi, Section 1, Bosque de Chapultepec,* ☎ *55/5286–6519.* *$1.50, free Sun.* *Tues.–Sun. 10–6.*

El Papalote, Museo del Niño (The Butterfly–Kite, Children's Museum). Five theme sections compose this excellent interactive museum: *Our World; The Human Body; Con-Sciencia,* with exhibits relating to both consciousness and science; *Communication,* on topics ranging from language to computers; and *Expression,* which includes art, music, theater, and literature. There are also workshops, an IMAX theater, a store, and a restaurant. ⊠ *Av. Constituyentes 268, Section 2, Bosque de Chapultepec,* ☎ *55/5237–1781.* *$4.50.* *Weekdays 9–1 and 2–6, weekends 10–2 and 3–7.*

Ripley's Museo de lo Increíble (Ripley's Museum of the Incredible) and the **Museo de Cera de la Ciudad de Mexico** (Mexico City Wax Museum). Although these museums lack the polish of their equivalents in, say, Hollywood, they are nonetheless fun for children of all ages. The Ripley's museum has 14 exhibit rooms chockablock with believe-it-or-not items, and in the wax museum, Plácido Domingo and Mexican politicians come to life. ⊠ *Londres 4, Bosque de Chapultepec, east of Zona Rosa,* ☎ *55/5546–3784.* *$3 each museum or $5 for both.* *Weekdays 11–7, weekends 10–7.*

27 **Zoológico.** During the early 16th century, Mexico City's zoo housed a small private collection of animals belonging to Moctezuma II; it became quasi-public when he allowed favored subjects to visit it. The current zoo opened in the 1920s and has the usual suspects as well as some superstar pandas. A gift from China, the original pair—Pepe and Ying Ying—produced the world's first panda baby born in captivity (much to competitive China's chagrin). The zoo includes the Moctezuma Aviary and is surrounded by a miniature train depot, botanical gardens, and lakes where you can go rowing. You'll see the entrance on Paseo de la Reforma, across from the Museo Nacional de Antropología. ⊠ *Section 1, Bosque de Chapultepec,* ☎ *55/5553–6263 or 55/5256–4104.* *Free, English audio guide $3.50.* *Tues.–Sun. 9–4.*

COLONIA CONDESA AND COLONIA ROMA

Colonia Condesa. The neighborhood sprang up in the early 1900s around the city's elite, who quickly abandoned it in the 1940s for more fashionable areas, leaving decaying mansions and parks behind. Before the 21st century, the neighborhood had been spruced up by an influx of younger residents, artists, entrepreneurs, and foreigners. A multitude of midprice eateries soon followed, mimicking different kinds of cuisines, and transforming Condesa into a place to be seen.

Condesa is the perfect place to break from a hectic day of sightseeing—just sit back in one of the neighborhood's relaxed sidewalk cafés and watch the hip young world go by. The main drag is Avenida Michoacán, from which restaurants radiate out in every direction. Avenida México loops the main park in the area, Parque México, and Avenida Amsterdam makes another loop around the area. The park area used to be a racetrack, which explains the circular roads.

You'll encounter an abundance of fashionable clothing shops, the best-known of which are on Michoacán. **Soho** (⊠ Vicente Suarez 100, between Michoacán and Tamalipas, Col. Condesa, ☏ 55/5553–1730) is a clothing store whose name refers to the rather hopeful comparison of Condesa to New York's SoHo neighborhood in the 1950s. The trendy **La Esquina** clothing store (✉ Av. Michoacán 118, corner of Amatlán, Col. Condesa, ☏ 55/5211–2951) down the street is similar. You can also admire designer clothes in **Carmen Rion** (✉ Av. Michoacán 30–A, local 3, corner of Parque México, Col. Condesa, ☏ 55/5264–6179). A great shop to browse through is **El Péndulo** (✉ Nuevo León 115, Col. Condesa, ☏ 55/5286–9493, WEB www.pendulo.com), a sort of cultural center. It has a large selection of Spanish books and an international collection of CDs, and the restaurant has a great breakfast menu, with classical guitarists playing on Saturday and Sunday from 11 to 1. El Péndulo often hosts other performers—jazz, classical, folk, or rock bands—on weekends.

Farther east on Michoacán, you can head to the Parque México, complete with duck pond and kids' funfair, or the smaller Parque España for a picnic or a stroll. An amusing movie theater right on the Parque España—the **Plaza Condesa** (☏ 55/5286–4973)—shows American and Mexican films; waiters will serve you popcorn and drinks during the flick. From Michoacán, take Tamaulipas north about four blocks to arrive at the park and theater.

Condesa doesn't have much in the way of museums or monuments, but neighboring **Colonia Roma** is home to some good private art galleries and independent, lively, artist-run spaces. This former aristocratic area—one defined by late-20th-century French-style mansions—also has fewer, but better, restaurants than Colonia Condesa.

The first serious art galleries in Mexico City opened in Colonia Roma in the 1980s. More recent galleries, bookstores, and cafés have also helped transform the old neighborhood into the capital's art district. The **Galería OMR** (✉ Plaza Rio de Janeiro 54, Col. Roma, ☏ 55/5525–3095 or 55/5511–1179) is housed in a typical Colonia Roma house, with a late-20th-century stone facade and quirkily lopsided exhibition rooms. This active gallery has a strong presence in international art fairs and art magazines. A short walk from OMR, **Galería Nina Menocal** (✉ Zacatecas 93, Col. Roma, ☏ 55/5564–7443, WEB www.artnet.com/nmenocal.html; ⏲ Mon.–Fri. 10–7, Sat. 10–2, closed Sun.) is directed by the enthusiastic, Cuban-born Nina Menocal. The gallerist radically influenced the art scene in Mexico by organizing exciting exhibitions with major Cuban artists.The **Casa Lamm Cultural Center** (✉ Av. Álvaro Obregón 99, Col. Roma, ☏ 55/5525–0019, WEB www.nueve.com.mx/casalamm), a small mansion and national monument, is a haven for artists and browsers with three exhibition spaces, a bookstore, a wide range of courses, and a superb restaurant.

ZONA ROSA

Thanks to a plethora of restaurants, cafés, art and antiques galleries, hotels, discos, and shops, the touristy Zona Rosa has been a favorite part of the city for years. With the mushrooming of fast-food spots and some tacky bars and stores, however, the area has lost some of its former appeal. Most of the buildings were built in the 1920s, as two- to three-story private homes for the well-to-do. All the streets are wistfully named after European cities; some, such as Génova, are garden-lined pedestrian malls accented with contemporary bronze statuary.

To enjoy the Zona Rosa, walk the lengths of Hamburgo and Londres and some of the side streets, especially Copenhague—a veritable restaurant row. The large crafts market on Londres is officially called Mercado Insurgentes, although most people refer to it as either Mercado

Zona Rosa or Mercado Londres. Opposite the market's Londres entrance is Plaza del Ángel, a small upscale shopping mall, the halls of which are crowded by antiques vendors on weekends.

20 **Monumento a la Independencia** (Independence Monument). Known as El Ángel, this Corinthian column topped by a gold-covered angel is the city's most uplifting monument, built to celebrate the 100th anniversary of Mexico's War of Independence. Beneath the pedestal lie the remains of the principal heroes of the independence movement; an eternal flame burns in their honor. ✉ *Traffic circle between Calle Río Tiber, Paseo de la Reforma, and Calle Florencia, Zona Rosa.*

San Ángel and Coyoacán

Originally separate colonial towns and then suburbs of Mexico City, San Ángel and Coyoacán were both absorbed by the ever-growing capital. But in the process they've managed to retain their original pueblo charm and tranquility.

San Ángel is a little colonial enclave of cobblestone streets, stone walls, pastel houses, rich foliage, and gardens drenched in bougainvillea. It became a haven for wealthy Spaniards during the Viceroyalty period, around the time of the construction of the Ex-Convento del Carmen. The elite were drawn to the area because of its rivers, pleasant climate, and rural ambience, and proceeded to build haciendas and mansions that, for many, were country homes.

Coyoacán means "Place of the Coyotes." According to local legend, a coyote used to bring chickens to a friar who had saved the coyote from being strangled by a snake. Coyoacán was founded by Toltecs in the 10th century and later settled by the Aztecs, or Mexica. Bernal Díaz Castillo, a Spanish chronicler, wrote that there were 6,000 houses at the time of the conquest. Cortés set up headquarters in Coyoacán during his siege of Tenochtitlán and kept his famous Indian mistress La Malinche here. At one point he considered making Coyoacán his capital; many of the Spanish buildings left from the two-year period during which Mexico City was built still stand.

Coyoacán has had many illustrious residents from Mexico's rich and intellectual elite, including Miguel de la Madrid, president of Mexico from 1982 to 1988; artists Diego Rivera, Frida Kahlo, and José Clemente Orozco; Gabriel Figueroa, cinematographer for Luis Buñuel and John Huston; film star Dolores del Río; film director El Indio Fernández; and writers Carlos Monsiváis, Jorge Ibargüengoitia, and Nobel laureate Octavio Paz. It's also the neighborhood where the exiled Leon Trotsky met his violent death. Although superficially it resembles San Ángel, Coyoacán has a more animated street life and focuses around a *zócalo* (central square), second in importance and popularity only to the Zócalo downtown. Most of the houses and other buildings honor the traditions of colonial Mexican architecture, and the neighborhood is well kept by residents, many of whose families have lived here for generations.

A Good Tour

Weekends are best for exploring the southern part of the city. Take a taxi or pesero down Avenida Insurgentes and get off at Avenida de la Paz, where you'll find many fine restaurants. On the east side of Insurgentes is the **Monumento al General Álvaro Obregón** ㉘. Cross Insurgentes on Avenida de la Paz, and take the southern fork off Avenida de la Paz (Calle Madero) until you come to San Ángel's center, **Plaza San Jacinto** ㉙. Stroll to the **Casa del Risco** ㉚ on the north side of the plaza and, if it's a Saturday, head to the north end for arts and crafts at the **Bazar Sábado.**

Retrace your steps on Avenida La Paz, to Avenida Revolución and Plaza del Carmen, which lies at the corner of Calle Monasterio. Inside is the colonial **Ex-Convento del Carmen** ㉛, interesting as an example of sacred architecture and for its religious artifacts. Now take Avenida Revolución one long block north to see the modern Mexican and European works at the **Museo de Arte Carrillo Gil** ㉜ (known as the Carrillo Gil). Unless you have plenty of energy, get a taxi to take you up Altavista to the **Museo Estudio Diego Rivera** ㉝ (and to an elegant lunch in the San Ángel Inn or Il Fornaio).

The next part of the tour goes to Coyoacán, which extends east of Avenida Insurgentes about 1 km (½ mi) from San Ángel. You're best off taking a taxi to the **Plaza de Santa Catarina** on Avenida Francisco Sosa, about halfway into the center of Coyoacán, because the tour involves a lot of walking.

The pretty 16th-century Iglesia de Santa Catarina dominates this tiny plaza. It also contains a bust of Mexican historian Francisco Sosa. Across the street is the **Casa de Jesús Reyes Heroles** (☒ Avenida Francisco Sosa 202); the former home of the ex-minister of education is a fine example of 20th-century architecture on the colonial model. It's now used as a cultural center. Continue east on Francisco Sosa and you'll pass **Casa de Diego de Ordaz** at the corner of Tres Cruces. This *mudéjar* (Spanish-Arabic) structure, adorned with inlaid tiles, was the home of a former captain in Cortés's army.

Now you're standing at the entrance of the **Jardín Centenario** ㉞. The Templo de San Juan Bautista and the picturesque **Casa de Cortés** ㉟ sit in the small Plaza Hidalgo adjacent to and north of the garden. Walk two blocks southeast of Plaza Hidalgo on Calle Higuera to the corner of Calle Vallarta, where you'll find the **Casa de la Malinche** ㊱. The house, darkened with age, faces an attractive cobbled park called Plaza de la Conchita and houses a tiny, ornate church that Mexican girls long to wed in.

Return to Plaza Hidalgo and walk five blocks north on Calle Allende to the corner of Calle Londres and the **Museo de Frida Kahlo** ㊲. It's linked both historically and romantically with the fortresslike **Museo de Leon Trotsky** ㊳, east of it on Londres, then two long blocks north on Morelos. If you have time, hop in a taxi and head south to the **Museo del Anahuacalli** ㊴, a virtual shrine to Diego Rivera.

TIMING

You're likely to want to linger in these elegant and beautiful sections of town, especially in Coyoacán. The Frida Kahlo and Leon Trotsky museums give intense, intimate looks at the lives of two famous people who were friends and lovers, and who breathed their personalities into the places where they lived. Allow at least an hour at each. The other museums are much smaller and merit less time. Weekends are liveliest at the Plaza Hidalgo and its neighboring Jardín Centenario (usually referred to as *la plaza* or *el zócalo*), where street life explodes into a fiesta with balloons, clowns, cotton candy, live music, and hypnotic dancing to the sound of drums.

Sights to See

SAN ÁNGEL

㉚ **Casa del Risco** (Risco House). This 1681 mansion is one of the prettiest houses facing the Plaza San Jacinto. A huge free-form fountain sculpture—exploding with colorful porcelain, tiles, shells, and mosaics—covers the entire eastern wall of its patio. Although it's not ranked among the city's top museums, the **Museo de la Casa del Risco** houses a splendid collection of 17th- and 18th-century European and colonial Mexican

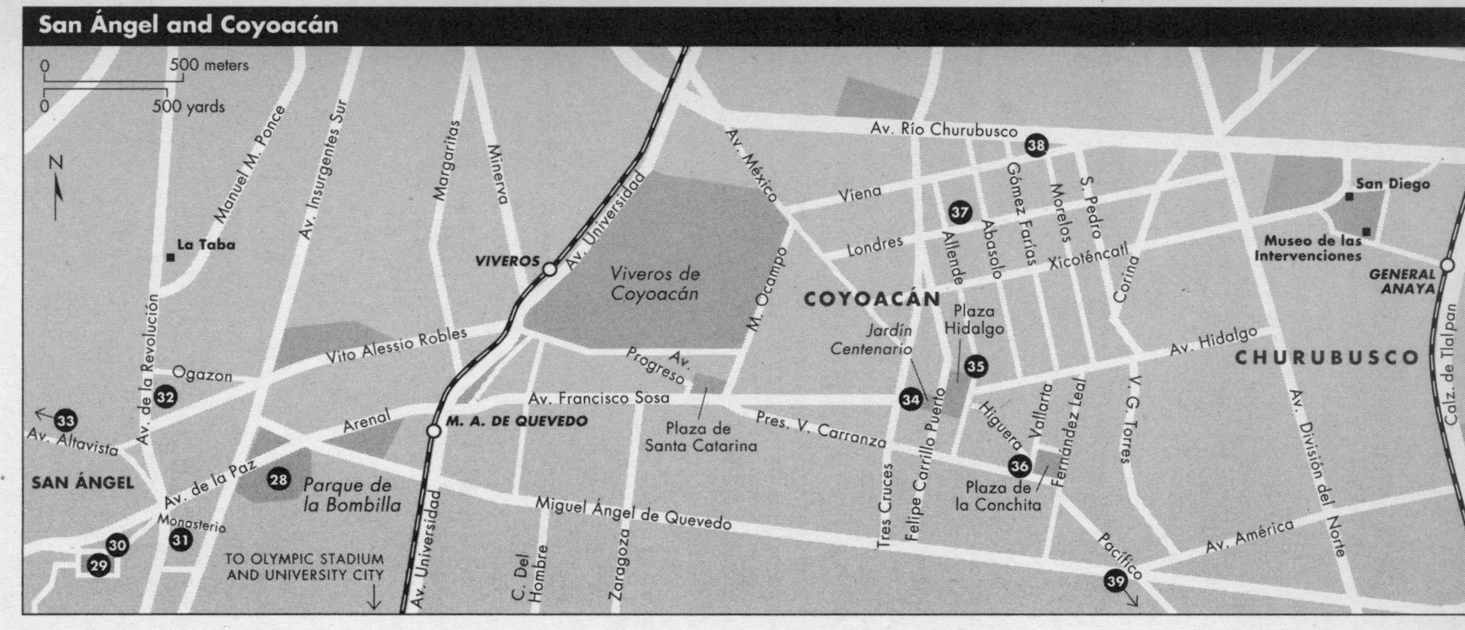

Casa de Cortés 35
Casa de la Malinche. 36
Casa del Risco. 30
Ex-Convento del Carmen 31
Jardín Centenario. . . 34
Monumento al General Álvaro Obregón. 28
Museo de Arte Carrillo Gil 32
Museo Estudio Diego Rivera 33
Museo de Frida Kahlo 37
Museo de Leon Trotsky. 38
Museo del Anahuacalli. 39
Plaza San Jacinto . . . 29

paintings, as well as period furnishings. ✉ *Plaza San Jacinto 15, San Ángel,* ☎ *55/5616–2711.* 🎟 *Free.* ⏲ *Tues.–Sun. 10–5.*

31 **Ex-Convento del Carmen** (Carmelite Convent and Church). Erected by Carmelite friars with the help of an Indian chieftain between 1615 and 1628, this cloister, with its tile-covered domes, fountains, and gardens, is one of the most interesting examples of colonial religious architecture in this part of the city. The church still operates, but the convent is now the **Museo Regional del Carmen,** with a fine collection of 16th- to 18th-century religious paintings and icons. It's worth visiting the 12 mummified corpses tucked away in the crypt. ✉ *Av. Revolución 4, at Monasterio, San Ángel,* ☎ *55/5616–2816 or 55/5616–1177.* 🎟 *$2.50, free Sun.* ⏲ *Tues.–Sun. 10–4:45.*

28 **Monumento al General Álvaro Obregón.** This somber gray granite monument marks the spot where reformer and national hero Obregón was gunned down by a religious zealot in a restaurant in 1928, soon before he was to begin his second term as president. It used to house a gruesome display of the general's hand, which he lost in battle, but it was removed in the interest of good taste. ✉ *Parque de la Bombilla, San Ángel, east of Av. La Paz at Av. Insurgentes.*

32 **Museo de Arte Carrillo Gil.** Considerably superior in terms of design and natural lighting to the city's Museo Nacional de Arte Moderno, this private collection contains early murals by Orozco, Rivera, and Siqueiros; works by modern European artists such as Klee and Picasso; and temporary exhibitions of young Mexican artists. ✉ *Av. Revolución 1608, at Altavista, San Ángel,* ☎ *55/5550–1254.* 🎟 *$1.* ⏲ *Tues.–Sun. 10–6.*

33 **Museo Estudio Diego Rivera.** Some of Rivera's last paintings are still resting here on ready easels, and his denim jacket and shoes sit on a wicker chair, waiting. The museum that once was home to Diego Rivera and his artist wife, Frida Kahlo, appears as if the two could return at any moment to continue work. Juan O'Gorman, a famous architect and close friend of Rivera, designed the house in the functionalist spirit, with an intent to economize space. ✉ *Diego Rivera 2, at Altavista, San Ángel,* ☎ *55/5616–0996.* 🎟 *$1.50.* ⏲ *Tues.–Sun. 10–6.*

★ 29 **Plaza San Jacinto.** This cozy plaza with a grisly history is the center of San Ángel. In 1847 about 50 Irish soldiers of St. Patrick's Battalion, who had sided with the Mexicans in the Mexican-American War, had their foreheads branded here with the letter *D*—for deserter—and were then hanged by the Americans. These men had been enticed to swim the Rio Grande, deserting the ranks of U.S. General Zachary Taylor, by pleas to the historic and religious ties between Spain and Ireland. As settlers in Mexican Texas, they felt their allegiance lay with Catholic Mexico, and they were among the bravest fighters in the war. They met their end when the American flag flew over Castillo de Chapultepec after the death of the *niños héroes.* A memorial plaque (on a building on the plaza's west side) lists their names and expresses Mexico's gratitude for their help in the "unjust North American invasion." Off to one side of the plaza, the excellent arts and crafts market, Bazar Sábado, is held on Saturday. ✉ *Between Miramon, Cda. Santisima, Dr. Galvez, and Madero, San Ángel.*

COYOACÁN

35 **Casa de Cortés** (Cortés's House). The place where the Aztec emperor Cuauhtémoc was held prisoner by Cortés is reputed to have been rebuilt in the 18th century from the stones of his original house by one of Cortés's descendants; the municipal government now has offices here. Dominating the little square on which it sits, this was almost the city's first city hall, but Cortés decided to rebuild Tenochtitlán instead. The

Close-Up

FRIDA KAHLO: A RIBBON AROUND A BOMB

OF COURSE, HE DOES PRETTY WELL for a little boy, but it is I who am the big artist."

Frida Kahlo's tongue-in-cheek comment about her husband to the *Detroit News* in 1933 seems less and less a joke as the years go by. This petite painter, who has gained international recognition since the 1980s for her colorful but pained self-portraits, has begun to overshadow the massive muralist Diego Rivera. Considered one of the last century's major artistic figures, Rivera created images—especially those rounded peasant women with braided hair, arms brim-full of creamy lilies—that have typified this country for more than a half century. The bizarre Beauty-and-the-Beast dynamics and sordid drama of the couple's relationship ensure the popularity of many of Mexico's museums and murals. But, if Diego dwarfed Frida in stature, he no longer does in fame.

Now, Kahlo's hauntingly beautiful face, broken body, and bright Tehuana costumes, along with a few exotic accessories such as monkeys, parrots, and hairless dogs, have become the trademark of Mexican femininity. Life-size cardboard cutouts with her bat-wing brows, moustache, and clunky ethnic earrings are as familiar here as Marilyn's pout and puffed-up white dress are in the United States.

In fact, Frida didn't even need to paint to make it into the history books. The controversy and scandal that surrounded her two marriages to Diego include his affair with her younger sister—the same year Frida suffered a third miscarriage and had toes removed from her right foot—and her affair with Communist exile Leon Trotsky. It's hard not to become mired in the tragic twists and turns of her life—from childhood polio to a tram accident that smashed her pelvis, a gangrenous foot that resulted in the amputation of a leg, as well as bouts of anorexia and alcoholism.

But she was also a groundbreaking artist who pioneered a new expressivism, and her unique iconography of suffering transcended self-pity to create an existential art. Kahlo was the first Latin American woman to have a painting in the Louvre; her work caused a storm in Paris in 1939 (at an exhibition entitled *Méxique*), and the surrealists claimed it as supremely illustrative of their ideas. It was André Breton who described her art as "a ribbon around a bomb."

Frida, who was always frank about her start in painting—she did it to kill time in one of her many convalescences—had doubts that her paintings were surrealist, saying, "they are the most frank expression of myself." Later she expressed unease with her art for not being suitable to serve the aims of the Communist Party, of which she and Diego were avid supporters. Her gargantuan husband was more generous, emphasizing how the influence of the religious retablo (ex-voto) that Frida collected was transformed in her art to an exploration of the permanent miracle of life. "Frida . . . tore open her chest and heart to reveal the biological truth of her feelings," he wrote.

And Frida tried hard to be as much the comrade and revolutionary as the icon of long-suffering Mexican femininity. Her last public appearance was 11 days before her death, in a wheelchair at Diego's side, protesting the intervention of the United States in Guatemala.

— Barbara Kastelein

two-story, deep-red house, with its wide arches and tile patio, is gorgeous. The house is not open to the public, but there's an information booth in the front room that's staffed by friendly employees. ✉ *Plaza Hidalgo between Calles Carillo Puerto and Caballo Calco, Coyoacán.*

36 **Casa de la Malinche.** One of the most powerful symbols of the Spanish conquest is located in Coyoacán but, significantly perhaps, is not even marked. It's the somber-looking residence of La Malinche, Cortés's Indian mistress and interpreter, whom the Spaniards called Doña María and the Indians called Malintzín. La Malinche aided the conquest by enabling Cortés to communicate with the Nahuatl-speaking tribes he met en route to Tenochtitlán. Today she is a reviled Mexican symbol of a traitorous xenophile—hence the term *malinchista,* used to describe a Mexican who prefers things foreign. Legend says that Cortés's wife died in this house, poisoned by the conquistador. The house is not open to the public. ✉ *2 blocks east of Plaza Hidalgo on Calle Higuera at Vallarta, Coyoacán.*

34 **Jardín Centenario** (Centenary Gardens). Small fairs, amateur musical performances, and poetry and palm readings are frequent occurrences in this large park surrounded by outdoor cafés. At the far end of the Jardín you'll see **Templo de San Juan Bautista,** one of the first churches to be built in New Spain. It was completed in 1582, and its door has a Baroque arch. ✉ *Between Calle Centenario, Av. Hidalgo, and Caballo Calco, Coyoacán.*

★ 37 **Museo de Frida Kahlo.** Kahlo has become a sort of cult figure, not only because of her paintings—55 of 143 are self-portraits—but also because of her bohemian lifestyle and flamboyant individualism. The "Blue House" where Kahlo was born in 1907 (not 1910, as she wanted people to believe) and died 47 years later, is both museum and shrine. Kahlo's astounding vitality and originality are reflected in the house, from the giant papier-mâché skeletons outside and the *retablos* (small religious paintings on tin) on the staircase to the gloriously decorated kitchen and the bric-a-brac in her bedroom. You can admire her early sketches, diary entries, tiny outfits, wheelchair at the easel, plus her four-poster bed conveniently fitted with mirror above. Even if you know nothing about Kahlo, a visit to the museum will leave you with a strong, visceral impression of this pivotal feminist artist. ✉ *Londres 247, at Allende, Coyoacán,* ☎ *55/5554–5999.* 🎟 *$2.* ⏲ *Tues.–Sun. 10–5:45.*

38 **Museo de Leon Trotsky.** Resembling an anonymous and forbidding fortress, with turrets for armed guards, this house is where Leon Trotsky lived and was murdered. It's difficult to believe that it's the final resting place for the ashes of one of the most important figures of the Russian Revolution, but that only adds to the allure of this austere dwelling, which is owned by Trotsky's grandson.

Anyone taller than 5 ft must stoop to pass through doorways to Trotsky's bedroom—with bullet holes still in the walls from the first assassination attempt, in which the muralist Siqueiros was implicated—his wife's study, the dining room, and the study where assassin Ramón Mercader—a man of many aliases—allegedly drove a pickax into Trotsky's head. On his desk, cluttered with writing paraphernalia and an article he was revising in Russian, the calendar is open to that fateful day, August 20, 1940. The volunteers will tell you how Trotsky's teeth left a permanent scar on Mercader's hand, how he clung to life for 26 hours, what his last words were, and how his death was sponsored by the United States (others would say Stalin). Not all the volunteers, however, speak English. ✉ *Río Churubusco 410, Coyoacán,* ☎ *55/5658–8732.* 🎟 *$1.* ⏲ *Tues.–Sun. 10–5.*

39 **Museo del Anahuacalli.** Diego Rivera built his own museum for the thousands of pre-Columbian artifacts he collected over the years. The third-floor studio that Rivera did not live long enough to use displays sketches for some of his most controversial murals. The huge dark-gray building, constructed in the 1950s from volcanic rock, resembles an aboveground tomb. If you visit between October and the end of December you'll see one of the city's finest altars to the dead in honor of Rivera himself. ✉ *Calle del Museo 150, Coyoacán,* ☎ *55/5617–4310 or 55/5617–3797.* 🎫 *$1.* ⏲ *Tues.–Sun. 10–6.*

OFF THE BEATEN PATH

SIX FLAGS OF MÉXICO – This 100-acre theme park on the southern edge of the city comprises seven "villages": Mexican, French, Swiss, Polynesian, Moroccan, the Wild West, and Children's World. Shows include performances by trained dolphins. ✉ *Southwest of Coyoacán on Carretera Picacho a Ajusco at Km 1.5,* ☎ *55/5645–5434 or 55/5728–7200.* 🎫 *$20 includes entrance and all rides.* ⏲ *Tues.–Thurs. 10–6, Fri.–Sun. 10–7.*

DINING

Mexico City restaurants open 7–11 AM for breakfast (*desayuno*) and 1:30–5 for lunch (*comida*)—although it's rare for Mexicans to eat lunch before 3 and you are likely to feel lonely if you arrive at a popular restaurant before 2. Lunch is an institution in this country, often lasting two hours, and until nightfall on Sundays. Consequently, evening meals may often be very light, consisting of sweet bread and coffee, a few tacos, or traditional *tamales* and *atole,* which can double up as breakfast.

When dining, most locals start out at 9 PM for dinner (*cena*); restaurants stay open until 11:30 during the week and a little later on weekends. At deluxe restaurants, dress is generally formal (jacket at least), and reservations are almost always advised; see reviews for details. If you're short on time, you can always head to American-style coffee shops (VIPS, Denny's, and Sanborns) or recognizable fast-food chains that offer the tired but reliable fare of burgers, fried chicken, and pizzas all over the city; many are open 24 hours.

The popular *Cafe Chino* (Chinese cafés) all over town are a cheap and hearty option for a quick bite. Asian cuisine is still limited here, but you will find some good Japanese and a few real Chinese restaurants. Similarly, there are very few vegetarian restaurants, but you will have no trouble finding nonmeat dishes wherever you grab a bite. Vegans, however, may have a more difficult time finding desired ingredients.

Hygiene practices in food preparation are improving greatly as establishments learn about catering to foreign tourists with more vulnerable stomachs. If you want to avoid trouble, avoid sauces that have fresh cilantro or dishes garnished with lettuce shreds. The Distintivo H, a rigorous standard for disinfection and cleanliness, is an important step in the right direction. It is backed by the Tourism Ministry, and numerous upper-end restaurants are striving to meet its specifications.

Colonia Polanco is an attractive, upscale neighborhood on the edge of Chapultepec Park that has some of the best and most expensive dining (and lodging) in the city. Zona Rosa restaurants get filled pretty quickly on Saturday night, especially on Saturdays coinciding with most people's paydays: the 1st and 15th of each month. The same is true of San Ángel, whereas the Condesa neighborhood buzzes with a younger crowd Thursday to Saturday.

Close-Up

LA COCINA MEXICANA

TO ENTERTAIN THE NOTION that Mexican food is little more than tacos, enchiladas, and burritos—or Tex-Mex or Taco Bell—would be culinary blasphemy to native gastronomes. Regional cooking is the heart and soul of Mexico, multiplied by the republic's 32 states and the provinces within them. Fresh ingredients abound, recipes are passed down through generations (think *Like Water for Chocolate*), and preparation requires much patience and loving care. With the staples—rice, beans, chilies, and corn—chefs are turning out ever more sophisticated variations on national dishes. But, of the Mexican chef's arsenal of ingredients, they're only the beginning.

Maize was sacred to the Indians, who have innumerable ways of preparing it—from faithful tortillas and tamales (cornmeal wrapped in banana leaves or corn husks) to tostadas (lightly fried, open tortillas topped with meat, lettuce, and the like) and tacos (tortillas briefly heated, filled, and wrapped into slim cylinders). *Pozole* (made with hominy) is a delicious pork-based soup. The sweet, corn-based drink *atole,* similar in consistency to hot chocolate, is a favorite breakfast or before-bed treat.

You'll find fish not just on the coasts but also in the lake regions around Guadalajara and in the state of Michoacán. *Huachinango* (red snapper), abalone, crab, and swordfish are all popular. And ceviche—raw *mariscos* (shellfish) marinated in lime juice then topped with chopped chilies, onions, and cilantro—is almost a national dish; just make sure it's fresh. Shrimp, lobster, and oysters can be huge and succulent; bear in mind the folk adage and eat oysters only in months with names that contain the letter *r.* Likewise avoid raw shellfish wherever cholera or water pollution might be a risk.

Mexicans love beef, pork, and *barbacoa* (barbecued lamb) with a variety of sauces. The complex, spicy mole—its ingredients can number more than 100, among them many kinds of chilies, and in one mole, chocolate—is one of Mexico's proudest culinary inventions. It is usually served over chicken or turkey. Chicken is often roasted, served in sauces like mole, or tucked in enchiladas, tacos, or burritos.

Fresh fruits and vegetables are another Mexican pleasure. Jicama, papaya, mamey, avocado, mango, guayaba, squash, and tomatoes are just some of the produce native to Mexico. (All fresh produce should be washed in water with a commercial disinfectant—bacteria exist in Mexico that your stomach might not be happy with. For this reason, avoid eating at street stalls and beware of uncooked herbs such as cilantro).

Other Mexican specialties are less common abroad: *antojitos* or *botanas* (appetizers), *chilaquiles* (breakfast dishes made with tortilla strips scrambled with chilies, tomatoes, onions, cream, and cheese), and *chiles en nogada* (a large poblano chili stuffed with beef or cheese, raisins, onion, olives, and almonds and topped with a creamy walnut sauce and pomegranate seeds). Soups are hearty—particularly pozole, *sopa azteca* (avocado, chicken chunks, and tortilla in a broth), and don't forget to try the lighter *sopa de flor de calabaza* (zucchini-flower soup) or, if you get a chance, *sopa de colorin,* made from a bright red flower.

The astonishing assortment of breads, sweets, beers, wines (which are fast improving), and agave-based (cactus-related) liquors goes on and on. Sadly, shortage of the blue agave has caused tequila prices to soar, so watch out for cheap varieties that add sugar cane liquor or less digestible substances. Freshly squeezed fruit juices and fruit shakes (*licuados*) are safe to drink—if ordered in a restaurant with hygienic practices—and taste heavenly. And coffee ranges from americano (black) to organic varieties to sweet *café de olla,* which is laced with spices.

CATEGORY	COST*
$$$$	over $15
$$$	$10–$15
$$	$5–$10
$	under $5

**per person for a main course at dinner*

Argentine

$$ ✕ **Cambalache.** If you come with a few people to this ever-busy beef-lover's dream, try the Super Lomo Cambalache, a steak big enough for three—four people. Or try the Don Ignacio, a boneless chicken breast served in a mushroom sauce with pineapple and fresh sweet peppers. And why not sink your fork into the potato soufflé–a house specialty? ✉ *Arquímedes 85, Col. Polanco,* ☎ *55/5280–2080 or 55/5282–2922,* FAX *55/5280–2957. AE, MC, V.*

$$ ✕ **Rincón Argentino.** This established Argentine restaurant is known as much for its decor as for its exquisite cuts of beef. The ceiling is painted to resemble the sky, the bar is covered by a thatch roof, and the dining areas call to mind a stone-and-wood lodge. Most Argentines prefer their beef *bien cocida* (well-done), but you can have it any way you like. ✉ *Presidente Masarik 177, Col. Polanco,* ☎ *55/5531–8617 or 55/5254–8775,* FAX *55/5231–8877. AE, MC, V.*

$$ ✕ **La Taba.** This smart, yet unpretentious, restaurant in the south of the city is characterized by its generous portions of top-quality beef, done perfectly to your choice of five options—from blue to well-done. The flavorful *provoleta* (smoked provolone cheese) and *chistorra* (a semicured chorizo-type sausage) stand out from the wide range of starters; vegetarians will be content with the variety of soups, pastas, and salads. The *bife de chorizo* (rump steak) is unforgettable, and big eaters might find room for one of the traditional Argentine desserts. ✉ *Revolución 1398, Col. Guadalupe Inn,* ☎ *55/5662–3165 or 55/5662–2670,* FAX *55/5662–2670,* WEB *www.lataba.com.mx. AE, MC, V.*

$$ ✕ **Entrevero.** A Uruguayan may own this friendly eatery on the square of Coyoacán, but rest assured that all Argentine attractions appear on the menu—chistorra and provoleta among them. Entrevero is also one of the few restaurants in the capital where you will find good pizza, calzones, and gnocchi, and the *crema quemada* (a version of crème brulée) is sinful. Fair prices and the excellent location guarantee it is always busy, so arrive a little early on weekends to get a table. ✉ *Jardín Centenario 14-C, Col. Villa Coyoacán,* ☎ *55/5659–0066,* FAX *55/5658–5644. AE, MC, V. No dinner Sun.*

Chinese

$$–$$$ ✕ **Chez Wok.** Above an elegant ladies' boutique on the corner of posh Polanco's Avenida Mazaryk and Tennyson, two Chinese chefs trained in Hong Kong prepare top quality food from an extensive menu. Start with exotic frogs' legs Mandarin-style, served with lychees and shiitake mushrooms and steamed in lotus leaves. Three can share a hot pot of leg of venison with bamboo shoots in oyster sauce. A business crowd generates a lively lunchtime bustle. ✉ *Tennyson 117, Col. Polanco,* ☎ *55/5281–3410 or 55/5281–2921. AE, MC, V.*

$$–$$$ ✕ **Mandarin House.** Standing proudly at the head of the eateries that line San Ángel's cobbled Avenida de la Paz, this spacious restaurant offers predominantly Mandarin cuisine. The chef's specialties include *Pato Pekin* (duck with plum sauce and cucumber in crêpes) and *Pollo Mo Su* (chicken with bamboo, cabbage, mushroom, and hoisin sauce). You may feel more comfortable in formal dress. ✉ *Av. de la Paz 57,*

San Ángel, ☎ *55/5616–4410 or 55/5616–4434;* ✉ *Cofre de Perote 205-B, Col. Lomas de Chapultepec,* ☎ *55/5520–9870 or 55/5540–1683,* WEB *www.mandarin-house.com. AE, MC, V. No dinner Sun.*

French

$$–$$$ ★ ✕ **Au Pied de Cochon.** Open round the clock on the ground floor inside the Hotel Presidente, this fashionable bistro continues to seduce Mexico's celebrities with everything from oysters to oxtail. The roasted leg of pork with béarnaise sauce is the signature dish; the green-apple sorbet with calvados is a delicate finish. The daily three-course set menu—which may include seafood, a perfect crème brûlée, as well as a glass of house wine—is only $16. ✉ *Campos Elíseos 218, Col. Polanco,* ☎ *55/5327–7700 or 55/5327–7756,* FAX *55/5327–7767. Reservations essential. AE, MC, V.*

$$–$$$ ★ ✕ **Le Bistro Littéraire.** At the far end of a French bookshop in the south of the city, this gem is open only for lunch. Clearly run out of love rather than for profit, the bistro lets you delight in redolent escargots, couscous, duck, or moules marinières—but expect slow service. The wine list keeps in tune with the accessible prices of the cuisine. ✉ *Inside "La Bouquinerie" French bookshop, Camino al Desierto de los Leones 40, San Ángel, Prolongación Altavista, between Insurgentes and Revolución,* ☎ *55/5616–0632,* FAX *55/5550–0632. AE, MC, V. Closed Sun.*

$$–$$$ ★ ✕ **Champs Élysées.** Commanding a superb view of the Independence Monument is one of the bastions of haute cuisine in Mexico City. The variety of sauces served with both meat and fish dishes is impressive—tarragon sauce over salmon, and sea urchin over bass take top honors. ✉ *Paseo de la Reforma 316, at Estocolmo, Zona Rosa,* ☎ *55/5525–7259,* FAX *55/5208–2302. AE, DC, MC, V. Closed Sun.*

Greek

$–$$ ✕ **Agapi Mu.** Rambunctious Greek song and dance enliven this friendly Greek bistro Thursday through Saturday nights. Tucked away in a snug room of the converted Colonia Condesa home, you'll hum along as you partake of the atmosphere and the *paputsáka* (stuffed eggplant), *kalamárea* (fried squid Greek-style), and *dolmádes* (stuffed grape leaves). ✉ *Alfonso Reyes 96, Col. Condesa,* ☎ *55/5286–1384,* FAX *55/5286–1942. AE, MC, V.*

International

$$$–$$$$ ✕ **Bellini.** While its great turntable slowly revolves on the 45th floor of the World Trade Center, Bellini draws executives from surrounding offices at lunchtime. The view of the city by night is romantic, but the view by day—when it's clear and you can see the volcanoes—is truly breathtaking. The majority of the dishes here aren't Italian but Mexican and international, with lobster as the house special. Finish in style with a flambéed dessert, such as strawberries jubilee or crêpes suzette. ✉ *Av. de las Naciones 1, World Trade Center, Col. Napoles, 20 mins by car south of Zona Rosa,* ☎ *55/5628–8305,* FAX *55/5628–8325. AE, DC, MC, V.*

$$$–$$$$ ★ ✕ **Estoril.** French cuisine with a Mexican flair is served in this fine 1930s town house in fashionable Colonia Polanco. *Perejil frito* (fried parsley) is a popular starter, and main dishes offer some unusual combinations: giant prawns in Chablis or curry sauce, and sea bass in fresh coriander sauce. If you have a sweet tooth, try either the delicious tarte Tatin—an upside-down apple tart with caramel—or the homemade mint sorbet. ✉ *Alejandro Dumas 24, Col. Polanco,* ☎ *55/5280–9828,* FAX *55/5280–9311. AE, MC, V. Closed Sun.*

Mexico City Dining

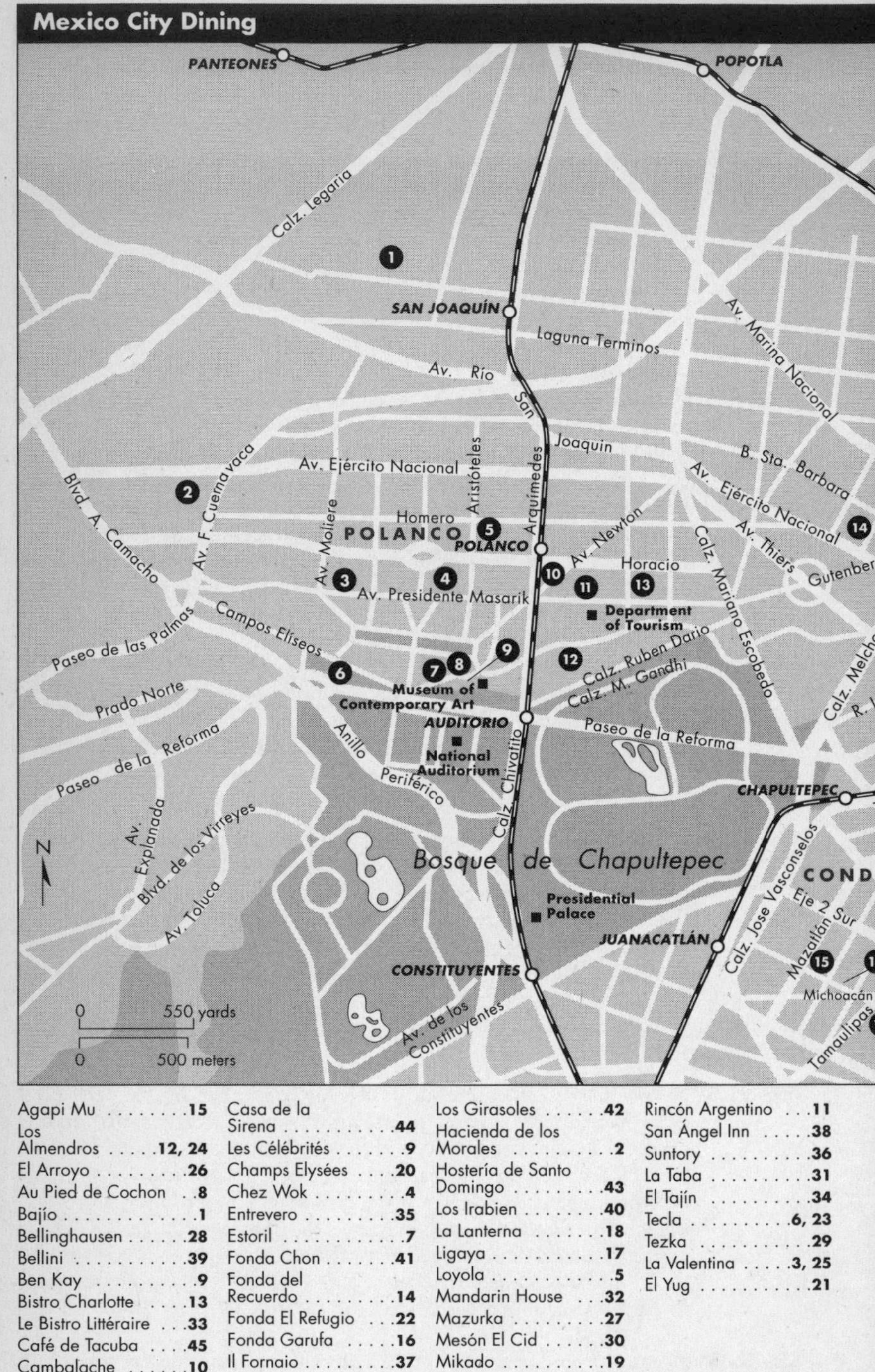

Agapi Mu 15
Los Almendros 12, 24
El Arroyo 26
Au Pied de Cochon . . 8
Bajío 1
Bellinghausen 28
Bellini 39
Ben Kay 9
Bistro Charlotte 13
Le Bistro Littéraire . . . 33
Café de Tacuba 45
Cambalache 10
Casa de la Sirena 44
Les Célébrités 9
Champs Elysées 20
Chez Wok 4
Entrevero 35
Estoril 7
Fonda Chon 41
Fonda del Recuerdo 14
Fonda El Refugio . . . 22
Fonda Garufa 16
Il Fornaio 37
Los Girasoles 42
Hacienda de los Morales 2
Hostería de Santo Domingo 43
Los Irabien 40
La Lanterna 18
Ligaya 17
Loyola 5
Mandarin House . . . 32
Mazurka 27
Mesón El Cid 30
Mikado 19
Rincón Argentino . . . 11
San Ángel Inn 38
Suntory 36
La Taba 31
El Tajín 34
Tecla 6, 23
Tezka 29
La Valentina 3, 25
El Yug 21

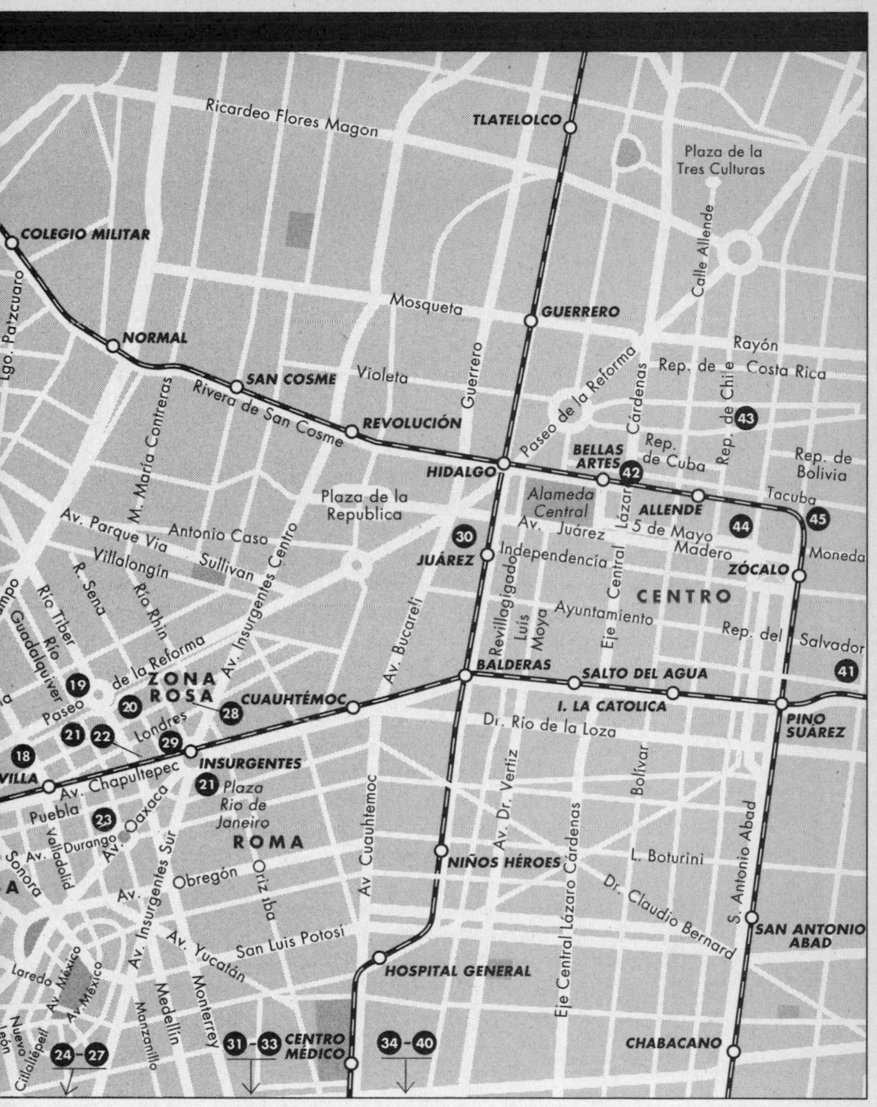

Ricardeo Flores Magon
TLATELOLCO
Plaza de la Tres Culturas
COLEGIO MILITAR
Calle Allende
Mosqueta
GUERRERO
NORMAL
Lgo. Patzcuaro
Rayón
SAN COSME
Violeta
Paseo de la Reforma
Rep. de Costa Rica
Cárdenas
Rep. de Chile
Guerrero
Rivera de San Cosme
REVOLUCIÓN
M. María Contreras
BELLAS ARTES
Rep. de Cuba
Rep. de Bolivia
HIDALGO
Alameda Central
ALLENDE
Tacuba
Plaza de la Republica
Av. Juárez
Lázaro
5 de Mayo
Av. Parque Via
Antonio Caso
JUÁREZ
Independencia
Madero
Moneda
Villalongín
Sullivan
Av. Insurgentes Centro
ZÓCALO
R. Sena
Río Rhin
Eje Central
CENTRO
Río Tiber
Ayuntamiento
Revillagigado
Luís Moya
Río Guadalquivir
Rep. del Salvador
Paseo de la Reforma
Av. Bucareli
BALDERAS
SALTO DEL AGUA
ZONA ROSA
CUAUHTÉMOC
I. LA CATOLICA
PINO SUÁREZ
Londres
Dr. Río de la Loza
INSURGENTES
VILLA
Av. Chapultepec
Plaza Rio de Janeiro
Puebla
Av. Oaxaca
Bolívar
Av. Durango
Valladolid
ROMA
Av. Cuauhtemoc
Av. Dr. Vertiz
Eje Central Lázaro Cárdenas
S. Antonio Abad
NIÑOS HÉROES
L. Boturini
Sonora
Av. Obregón
Oriz iba
Av. Insurgentes Sur
Dr. Claudio Bernard
SAN ANTONIO ABAD
San Luis Potosí
Av. Yucatán
Laredo
Av. México
HOSPITAL GENERAL
Medellín
Monterrey
Manzanillo
Nuevo León
Citlaltépetl
CENTRO MÉDICO
CHABACANO

$$$–$$$$ ✕ **Hacienda de los Morales.** This Mexican institution, set in a former hacienda that dates back to the 16th century, is grandly colonial in style, with dark-wood beams, huge terra-cotta expanses, and dramatic torches. You could start with the delicate walnut soup and follow with one of the chef's highlights, duck in raspberry sauce. Live trio music (three voices and guitars that play melodic traditional Mexican ballads) completes the atmosphere. ✉ *Vázquez de Mella 525, Col. Bosque Polanco,* ☎ *55/5281–4554,* FAX *55/5096–3056,* WEB *www.haciendadelosmorales.com.mx. AE, DC, MC, V.*

$$–$$$ ✕ **Bellinghausen.** This cherished Zona Rosa lunch spot is one of the capital's classics. The partially covered hacienda-style courtyard at the back, set off by an ivy-laden wall, is a midday magnet for executives and tourists. A veritable army of waiters scurries back and forth serving such tried-and-true favorites as *sopa de hongos mexicana* (mushroom soup) and *filete chemita* (broiled steak with mashed potatoes). ✉ *Londres 95, Zona Rosa,* ☎ *55/5207–6149,* FAX *55/5208–9843,* WEB *www.grupo-bellinghausen.com. AE, DC, MC, V. No dinner.*

$$–$$$ ✕ **Fonda Garufa.** Its tables spilling out onto a Condesa sidewalk, this cheerful place for people-watching will often subject you to rather noisy street performers. Go for the tasty filet mignon, served with mushrooms and watercress, or choose from the diverse and very affordable menu offerings, many of which have an Argentine bent. A quirky favorite is fettuccine Hindú: half a chicken breast bathed in a yogurt sauce laced with cilantro, ginger, onion, and chili. ✉ *Michoacán 93, Col. Condesa,* ☎ *55/5286–8295. MC, V.*

$$ ★ ✕ **Bistro Charlotte.** You may get addicted to dining at Charlotte's intimate neighborhood bistro. At lunchtime regulars flock like clockwork to the quirky, chatty English chef for inspired culinary surprises. Most dishes are prepared with French and Mediterranean accents, yet Thai flourishes appear with increasing regularity. A small lament: there's only one Charlotte's. ✉ *Lope de Vega 341, Col. Polanco,* ☎ *55/5250–4180,* FAX *55/5511–0032. MC, V. No dinner. Closed weekends.*

$$ ✕ **Ligaya.** The trendiest eatery in Colonia Condesa is replete with white padding, frosted glass, and aluminum flower vases. Here posing is more important than eating, and it's worth lingering over your cocktail. But if your eyes are not bigger than your stomach, try the gruyère and beer soup or fresh tuna steak in a subtle creamy sauce. Portions are not large, but desserts will make up for it. ✉ *Nuevo León 68, Col. Condesa,* ☎ *55/5286–6268 or 55/5286–6380. MC, V.*

Italian

$$ ✕ **Il Fornaio.** A steady stream of well-heeled diners come here to taste *carpaccio di salmone* dressed with Belgian endive, grapefruit, cress, and a lightly citric vinegar, or enjoy an excellent *linguine ai sapori di mare* (linguine with seafood). The chef refuses to use anything but Italian ingredients; notice the authentic cheeses (as in the succulent veal in Gorgonzola sauce). The desserts, such as the sweet crêpes (*crespelle al caffè*), are unforgettable. ✉ *Altavista 192, San Ángel,* ☎ *55/5616–5985. AE, DC, MC, V. No dinner Sun.*

$–$$ ✕ **La Lanterna.** The Petterino family has run this two-story restaurant since 1966. The downstairs has the rustic feel of a northern Italian trattoria, with the cramped seating adding to the intimacy. All pastas are made on the premises; the Bolognese sauce is a favorite. Raw artichoke salad, *conejo al Salmi* (rabbit in a wine sauce), and *filete al burro nero* (steak in black butter) are all worthy dishes. ✉ *Paseo de la Reforma 458, Col. Juárez,* ☎ *55/5207–9969,* FAX *55/5525–4357. AE, DC, MC, V. Closed Sun. and Dec. 25–Jan. 1.*

Japanese

$$$–$$$$ ✕ **Ben Kay.** The silk-clad staff includes a sake sommelier in this prestigious restaurant in the Hotel Nikko. *Keiseki* is the specialty, a series of small, exquisite dishes. The menu is organized in helpful groupings that limit the anxiety of choice. Prices are high, but you're getting the best. ✉ *Campos Elíseos 204, Col. Polanco 11560,* ☎ *55/5280–1111 Ext. 8600,* FAX *55/5280–9191. AE, DC, MC, V.*

$$ ✕ **Mikado.** Strategically positioned between the Zona Rosa and the U.S. embassy, this treasure offers all you could hope for from Japanese cuisine at very fair prices. Immaculate hygiene, a fine sushi chef, an extensive menu, and a cheerful, bustling atmosphere downstairs make Mikado both welcoming and a real treat for the palate. ✉ *Paseo de la Reforma 369, Col. Cuauhtémoc,* ☎ *55/5525–3096,* FAX *55/5207–1296. MC, V. No dinner Sun.*

$$ ✕ **Suntory.** This main branch of the Suntory restaurants in Mexico welcomes you with a Japanese garden at the entryway. You can choose between the teppanyaki room, the sushi bar, and the shabu-shabu room, with its wafer-thin sashimi and a copper pot of steaming vegetable broth for cooking wafer-thin slices of beef. ✉ *Torres Adalid 14, Col. del Valle,* ☎ *55/5536–9432,* FAX *55/5543–0031,* WEB *www.restaurantesuntory.com.mx. AE, DC, MC, V. No dinner Sun.*

Mexican

$$$–$$$$ ★ ✕ **San Ángel Inn.** In the south of the city, this magnificent old hacienda and ex-convent is a joy to behold. Dark mahogany furniture, crisp white table linens, and beautiful blue-and-white Talavera place settings strike a note of restrained opulence. For a classic treat, have the *sopa de tortilla* (tortilla soup); note that the *puntas de filete* (sirloin tips) are liberally laced with chilies. Desserts—from light and crunchy meringues to pastries bulging with cream—can be rich to the point of surfeit. ✉ *Diego Rivera 50, at Altavista, San Ángel,* ☎ *55/5616–0537 or 55/5616–2222,* FAX *55/5616–0977. AE, DC, MC, V.*

$$–$$$ ✕ **Fonda Chon.** This unpretentious family-style restaurant, deep in a downtown working-class neighborhood, is famed for its pre-Hispanic Mexican dishes. A knowledge of zoology, Spanish, and Nahuatl helps in making sense of a menu that takes in a gamut of ingredients from throughout the republic. *Escamoles de hormiga* (red-ant roe) is known as the "caviar of Mexico" for its costliness, but you may have to acquire a taste for it. Among the exotic dishes are armadillo in mango sauce and fillet of wild boar. ✉ *Regina 160, Col. Centro, near La Merced market,* ☎ *55/5542–0873. MC, V. Closed Sun. No dinner.*

$$–$$$ ✕ **Hostería de Santo Domingo.** This genteel institution near downtown's Plaza Santo Domingo has been serving colonial dishes since the late 19th century in an atmospheric town house. Feast on tried-and-true favorites such as stuffed cactus paddles, thousand-flower soup, pot roast, and a stunning array of quesadillas. Among what may be the best homemade Mexican desserts in town are the comforting flan and *arroz con leche* (rice pudding). The place is open for breakfast and is always full at lunch. Get there early to avoid standing in line. ✉ *Belisario Dominguez 72, Col. Centro,* ☎ *55/5510–1434 or 55/5526–5276. AE, DC, MC, V. Closes 9:30 PM Sun.*

$$ ✕ **Casa de la Sirena.** Dining is picturesque at the foot of the Templo Major ruins, which supplied some of the building blocks for this 16th-century mansion. The atmospheric second-floor terrace is within sight and sound of numerous Indian dances honoring the spirits of the crumbling Aztec temples below. At night, it's utterly romantic dining under the stars. The nouvelle cuisine pairs Cornish hen with a mango mole sauce and adds a spark to a plethora of meat and fish dishes. ✉

Guatemala 32, Zócalo, ☎ *55/5704–3225,* FAX *55/5704–3465. AE, MC, V. No dinner Sun.*

$$ ✕ **Fonda El Refugio.** Since it opened in 1954, this restaurant has served dishes from each major region of the country. Along with a varied regular menu, there's a daily selection of appetizers and entrées; you might find a mole made with pumpkin seeds or *huachinango a la veracruzana* (red snapper cooked in onions, tomatoes, and olives). Try the refreshing *aguas* (fresh-fruit and seed juices) with your meal and the *café de olla* (clove-flavored coffee sweetened with brown sugar) afterward. ✉ *Liverpool 166, Zona Rosa,* ☎ *55/5207–2732 or 55/5525–8128,* FAX *55/5207–8802. AE, DC, MC, V.*

$$ ✕ **Los Almendros.** If you can't make it to the Yucatán, try the peninsula's unusual and lively food at one of this restaurant's two locations. The habañero chilies, red onions, and other native Yucatecan ingredients are a delightful surprise for those not yet in the know. Traditional dishes, such as a refreshing lime soup, share the menu with impossible-to-pronounce Maya cuisine. Especially worth trying is the *pescado tikinxic*—white fish in a mild red marinade of achiote seed and bitter orange juice. ✉ *Campos Elíseos 164, Col. Polanco,* ☎ *55/5531–6646;* ✉ *Insurgentes Sur 1759, Col. Guadalupe Inn,* ☎ *55/5663–5151.*

$$ ✕ **Los Girasoles.** Two prominent Mexico City society columnists own this downtown spot. Los Girasoles (which means sunflowers) is on a lovely old square in a restored three-story colonial home and serves light, tasty, and innovative nueva cocina Mexicana. There are also pre-Hispanic delicacies such as *escamoles* (ant roe), *gusanos de maguey* (chilied worms), and *mini chapulines* (tiny crispy fried grasshoppers). ✉ *Plaza Manuel Tolsa on Xicoténcatl 1, Col. Centro,* ☎ *55/5510–0630,* FAX *55/5510–0630. AE, MC, V. No dinner Sun. or Mon.*

$$ ✕ **Los Irabien.** This beautiful dining area filled with plants and the owner's impressive art collection is a worthwhile stop for foodies and culture vultures. Featuring Mexican traditional and international cuisine, the *filete de res en salsa de fresas* triumphs as a blend of beef with peppered strawberry sauce. Los Irabien is one of the city's breakfast spots par excellence—tempting you with *huevos de codorniz huitzilopochtli*—quail eggs with tortilla in a zucchini-blossom sauce. ✉ *Av. de la Paz 45, San Ángel,* ☎ *55/5616–0014. Jacket and tie. AE, DC, MC, V. No dinner Sun.*

$$ ✕ **El Tajín.** Named after El Tajín Pyramid in Veracruz, this elegant lunchtime eatery serves innovative Mexican cooking that sizzles with authentic pre-Hispanic influences. The dazzling main dishes include soft-shell crab accented by sesame seeds and a whisper of chipotle. The restaurant is hidden in the Veracruz Cultural Center. Ancient Huastecan faces grinning from a splashing fountain add a bit of levity to the dining experience. ✉ *Miguel Angel de Quevedo 687, Col. Coyoacán,* ☎ *55/5659–4447 or 55/5659–5759. AE, MC, V. No dinner.*

$$ ★ ✕ **La Valentina.** The epitome of elegance and good taste in all things Mexican, La Valentina is devoted to rescuing and promoting historic native cuisine. It avoids gimmicks with balanced dishes that are soft on the palette, yet fragrant with blends of chilies, herbs, nuts, and flowers. Starters reflect regional specialties from across the country: from the far northern Chilorio tacos from Sinaloa to the famous *Panuchos Yucatecos*. The appetizing tamarind mole intensifies any poultry dish; the seductively titled "Symphony in Mexican Rose" bathes chicken in a walnut and chipotle sauce. ✉ *Insurgentes Sur 1854B, Col. Florida, San Ángel,* ☎ *55/5662–0872 or 55/5662–0177,* FAX *55/5662–5049;* ✉ *Av. Presidente Mazaryk 393, Col. Polanco,* ☎ *55/5282–2297. AE, DC, MC, V. No dinner Sun.*

$–$$ ★ ✕ **Fonda del Recuerdo.** The popular *fonda* (modest restaurant) has made a name for itself with fish and seafood platters from the gulf state of Veracruz. Sharing their fame is the *torito,* a potent drink made from sugarcane liquor, and exotic tropical fruit juices. Portions are huge, but if you have room for dessert, try *crepas de cajeta al tequila* (milk-caramel crêpes lightly sauced with tequila). Every day from 1 to 10, five lively jarocho and mariachi groups provide festive music. ✉ *Bahía de las Palmas 37, Col. Veronica Anzures,* ☎ *55/5260–7339 or 55/5260–1292. Reservations essential. AE, DC, MC, V.*

$ ✕ **El Arroyo.** Complete with its own bullring, this huge dining complex is an attraction in itself from May to September, when you can see *novilleros* (novice toreros) trying out their skills. Traditional Mexican specialties are prepared in open kitchens. There's jarocho music from Veracruz and the full gamut of Mexican drinks, including *pulque,* a classic alcoholic Aztec beverage made from the maguey cactus. The restaurant is near the beginning of the highway to Cuernavaca; breakfast starts at 8 AM, and lunch is served until 8 PM. ✉ *Av. Insurgentes Sur 4003, Col. Tlalpán, a 40-min drive south of Zona Rosa,* ☎ *55/5573–4344,* WEB *www.arroyo.com.mx. AE, DC, MC, V. No dinner.*

$ ✕ **Bajío.** Decorated in bright colors, Bajío attracts Mexican families and is run by vivacious Carmen "Titita" Ramírez—a culinary expert who has been featured in various food magazines. The 30-ingredient mole, a Bajío signature dish, is to die for; also excellent are *empanadas de platano rellenos de frijol* (tortilla turnovers filled with bananas and beans) and *carnitas* (roast pork). You may have to go a little off the beaten track to get here, but it's worth it. ✉ *Cuitláhuac 2709, Col. Azcapotzalco, about a 20-min ride north of Zona Rosa,* ☎ *55/5341–9889. AE, MC, V. No dinner.*

$ ✕ **Café de Tacuba.** An essential breakfast, lunch, dinner, or snack stop downtown, this Mexican classic has been charming the hungry since it opened in 1912 in a section of an old convent. At the entrance to the atmospheric main dining room are huge 18th-century oil paintings depicting the invention of *mole poblano,* a complex sauce with a variety of chilies and chocolate that was created by the nuns in the Santa Rosa Convent of Puebla. A student group dressed in medieval capes and hats serenades Thursday–Sunday 3:30–11:30; mariachis play during dinner on other days. ✉ *Tacuba 28, Col. Centro,* ☎ *55/5518–4950. AE, MC, V.*

$ ★ ✕ **Tecla.** This see-and-be-seen eatery is an established veteran of Mexico City's nueva cocina Mexicana scene and the restaurants' locations and newsprint collage set a hip tone. The appetizers are especially intriguing, including squash flowers stuffed with goat cheese in a chipotle sauce and a spicy crab-stuffed chili. ✉ *Moliere 56, Col. Polanco,* ☎ *55/5282–0010;* ✉ *Durango 186A, Col. Roma,* ☎ *55/5525–4920. AE, MC, V. No dinner Sun.*

Polish

$$–$$$ ★ ✕ **Mazurka.** The capital's first and only establishment to offer Polish food enjoys a glowing reputation among older Mexican families. Settle in with complimentary starters of blini with herring paste and cucumber, dill, and cream salad, as Chopin's polonaises trill and leap in the background. The "star of the house" is a crispy, oven-baked duck, stuffed with bitter apple and blueberries. Or try the juicy, sweet duck and pear with cassis. The generous "Pope's Menu" includes two sets of entrees and is only $21 a head. ✉ *Nueva York 150, Col. Napoles,* ☎ *55/5543–4509 or 55/5523–8811. AE, MC, V. No dinner Sun.*

Spanish

$$$ ★ ✕ **Les Célébrités.** Known for superb Basque fare, this elegant hotel restaurant has refreshed the menu with Mediterranean selections. The sunny yellow decor and a profusion of flowers enhance the pleasing, light-filled ambience. The restaurant is known for its one-of-a-kind combinations, such as an appetizer of king crab with asparagus cream, sauce of caviar, and passion-fruit vinaigrette. For dessert, there's a sinfully rich chocolate mousse cake and a light, flaky hazelnut pastry with profiteroles in a chocolate-coriander sauce. The restaurant is open for breakfast as well. ✉ *Nikko México hotel, Campos Elíseos 204, Col. Polanco,* ☎ *55/5280–1111. Reservations essential. Jacket and tie. AE, DC, MC, V. Closed weekends.*

$$–$$$ ✕ **Tezka.** This Zona Rosa restaurant specializing in nueva cocina Basque was created by famous chef Arzac, who transposed many of his best dishes to Mexico from his restaurant in San Sebastían, Spain. Feast on yellow tuna in a fluffy sweet and spicy sauce, or liver prepared with beer, green pepper, and malt. The starters are exquisite, both to look at and taste; the *caldo de xipiron* (broth of baby squid) is the best in the city. There are tempting and original desserts, and the servings are small enough that you'll have room. A decent list of Spanish wines includes Cune, Vina Ardanza, and Reserva 904. ✉ *Royal Hotel, Amberes 78, at Liverpool, Col. Juárez,* ☎ *55/5228–9918,* FAX *55/5514–3330. AE, DC, MC, V. Closed Sun. No dinner Sat.*

$$ ✕ **Loyola.** A Basque tour de force, the ample menu with unpronounceable but delicious items includes *kokotxas* (fish cheeks), tapas, black rice simmered in squid ink, oxtail, and many other such regional delicacies. Great salads and wines are another welcome feature. Courteous service, stained glass, Basque coats of arms, and the cozy hum of conversation from contented connoisseurs make this an excellent and authentic dining experience. ✉ *Aristóteles 239, Col. Polanco,* ☎ *55/5250–6756 or 55/5250–9097. AE, MC, V. No dinner.*

$$ ✕ **Mesón El Cid.** This charming *mesón* (tavern) exudes an atmosphere of Old Spain. During the week, classic dishes such as paella, spring lamb, suckling baby pig, and Cornish hens with truffles keep customers happy, but on Saturday night this place comes into its own with a medieval banquet, including a procession of costumed waiters carrying huge trays of steaming hot viands. Further entertainment is provided by a student singing group dressed in medieval Spanish capes and hats. ✉ *Humboldt 61, Col. Centro,* ☎ *55/5521–1940, 55/5512–8881, or 55/5512–7629. AE, MC, V. No dinner Sun.*

Vegetarian

$ ✕ **El Yug.** Within the confines of an esoteric bookshop, this vegetarian spot offers delicious fare to the accompaniment of New Age music. Heaping salads, homemade soups, and main courses such as *chiles rellenos* (poblano chili stuffed with cheese) come with whole-grain bread. You can choose the daily *comida corrida* (fixed-price menu) for just over $4 or order à la carte. The sister restaurant in Colonia Juárez is open daily for breakfast, lunch, and dinner. ✉ *Puebla 326-6, Col. Roma,* ☎ *55/5553–3872;* ✉ *Varsovia 3, Col. Juárez,* ☎ *55/5525–5330. AE, MC, V. No dinner. Closed Sun.*

LODGING

Although the city is huge and spread out, most hotels are clustered in a few neighborhoods. Stylish Colonia Polanco and Bosque de Chapultepec are on the west side of the city. Paseo de la Reforma runs from Chapultepec, northeast through "midtown," and intersects with Avenida

Juárez at the beginning of the downtown area. Juárez becomes Calle Madero, which continues east to the downtown historic district and its very core, the Zócalo. The Zona Rosa is literally across Reforma (south), in the western midtown area. The only pleasant tourist area still poorly served for accommodation is the south.

Business travelers tend to fill up deluxe hotels during the week; some major hotels discount their weekend rates. If you reserve through the toll-free reservations numbers, you may find rates as much as 50% off during special promotions. You can expect hotels in the $$$ and $$$$ categories to have purified water, air-conditioning, cable TV, radio, minibars, and extended (often 24-hour) room service.

CATEGORY	COST*
$$$$	over $250
$$$	$175–$250
$$	$110–$175
$	under $110

**All prices are for a standard double room, excluding service charge and tax.*

Colonia Polanco and Bosque de Chapultepec

$$$$ **Casa Vieja.** This sumptuously decorated Colonia Polanco mansion is a dream come true. Tastefully selected folk art, handsomely hand-carved furniture, and gilded wall trimmings complement patios and splashing fountains. Each suite has a full kitchen, fax machine, CD and videocassette players, hot tub, and picture window overlooking an inside garden. The hotel's Mexican restaurant is named after its huge floor-to-ceiling *Árbol de la Vida (Tree of Life)* sculpture. Rates include breakfast. ✉ *Eugenio Sue 45, Col. Polanco 11560,* ☎ *55/5282–0067,* FAX *55/5281–3780,* WEB *www.casavieja.com. 9 suites. Restaurant, bar, concierge, free parking. AE, MC, V.*

$$$$ **J. W. Marriott.** In posh Colonia Polanco, this hotel was designed as a boutique property with personalized service and small, clubby public areas; nothing overwhelms here. Rooms are done with plenty of wood and warm colors but are otherwise unremarkable in decor. Each has a work desk with an outlet for a personal computer and modem. The hotel has a well-equipped 24-hour business center. Attractive weekend rates range between $130 and $185. ✉ *Andrés Bello 29, at Campos Elíseos, Col. Polanco 11560,* ☎ *55/5282–8888 or 800/228–9290,* FAX *55/5282–8811,* WEB *www.marriotthotels.com. 311 rooms. 2 restaurants, coffee shop, pool, gym, bar, business services, meeting rooms, car rental, travel services. AE, DC, MC, V.*

$$$$ **Nikko México.** Part of the Nikko chain, this 42-floor high-rise occupies a prime Polanco position: adjacent to Bosque de Chapultepec, just a five-minute walk from the Anthropology Museum. With signage and menus in Japanese, English, and Spanish, it caters especially to business travelers and conferences. It's the second-largest hotel in the city and has marvelous views from the top floor. Each room has at least three telephones with two lines and business services are excellent. Four top restaurants excel in their gastronomic specialties. ✉ *Campos Elíseos 204, Col. Polanco 11560,* ☎ *55/5280–1111, 800/908–8800, or 800/645–5687,* FAX *55/5280–9191,* WEB *www.nikkohotels.com. 744 rooms, 24 suites. 4 restaurants, driving range, 4 tennis courts, indoor pool, gym, sauna, steam room, 2 bars, dance club, business services, meeting rooms, car rental, travel services. AE, DC, MC, V.*

$$$ ★ **Camino Real.** About the size of Teotihuacán's Pyramid of the Sun, this sleek, minimalist, bright pink and yellow, 8-acre city-within-a-city was designed by Mexico's modern master, Legorreta. Impressive artworks embellishing the public spaces include Rufino Tamayo's mural

Mexico City Lodging

Aristos **15**	Four Seasons Mexico City. **9**	Holiday Inn Zócalo. **26**	María Cristina **14**	Misión Park Plaza México **19**
Calinda Geneve. . . . **18**	Galería Plaza **8**	Hotel de Cortés **23**	María Isabel Sheraton **12**	Nikko México **4**
Camino Real **6**	Gran Hotel de la Ciudad de México **24**	Imperial **22**	Marquis Reforma . . . **10**	Plaza Florencia **16**
Casa Vieja **1**	Habita. **5**	J.W. Marriott **2**	Marriott Aeropuerto **28**	Presidente Inter-Continental México **3**
La Casona. **11**	Hilton Aeropuerto . . . **29**	Krystal Rosa **17**	Melía México Reforma **21**	Sevilla Palace **20**
Catedral **27**		Majestic **25**		
Fiesta Americana Gran Chapultepec. . . . **7**		Marco Polo **13**		

Man Facing Infinity and a Calder sculpture. The fifth-floor executive level has 100 extra-large guest rooms with special amenities. El Centro Castellano restaurant offers free child care for long weekend lunchtimes, and Le Cirque, an upscale French restaurant, was due to open by fall 2002. ✉ *Mariano Escobedo 700, Col. Polanco 11590,* ☎ *55/5263–8888 or 800/722–6466,* FAX *55/5263–8898,* WEB *www.caminoreal.com-mexicocity. 620 rooms, 89 suites. 3 restaurants, 4 tennis courts, 2 pools (1 indoor), gym, 3 bars, business services. AE, DC, MC, V.*

$$$ **Habita.** Characterized by pale colors and a spa-like atmosphere, Mexico's first design hotel strikes a harmonious balance between style statements and minimalism. New-Age voices are piped into the rooms (you can turn them off, of course), and tasteful bowls of limes sit by state-of-the-art TV sets. Offering beautiful open-air views one floor above the pool and gym, the swanky tapas bar Área also draws Mexico City's chic nonguests Thursday to Saturday. ✉ *Av. Presidente Masarik 201, Col. Polanco 11560,* ☎ *55/5282–3100,* FAX *55/5282–3101,* WEB *www.hotalhabita.com. 32 rooms, 4 suites. Restaurant, gym, spa, bar, business services, meeting rooms, free parking. AE, MC, V.*

$$–$$$ **Presidente Inter-Continental México.** This Inter-Continental has a dramatic five-story atrium lobby—a hollow pyramid of balconies—with music performed daily at the lively lobby bar. Rooms are spacious, and all have work areas. On clear days, the top two floors have views of the nearby snowcapped volcanoes. The executive floors have a lounge, concierge, and extra amenities. A number of smart stores and six eateries are on the premises, including Au Pied de Cochon. ✉ *Campos Elíseos 218, Col. Polanco 11560,* ☎ *55/5327–7700 or 800/447–6147,* FAX *55/5327–7730,* WEB *www.interconti.com. 629 rooms, 30 suites. 6 restaurants, coffee shop, gym, lobby lounge, baby-sitting, business services, meeting rooms, car rental, travel services, parking (fee). AE, DC, MC, V.*

$$ **Fiesta Americana Gran Chapultepec.** Sleek and contemporary, this stylish new hotel is located opposite Chapultepec Castle and Park, close to the city's main shopping area and five minutes from the National Auditorium. The spa, beauty salon, and barbershop guarantee you will be presentable for the ultramodern Asian bar, where you can hang out for sushi and cocktails. ✉ *Mariano Escobedo 756, Col. Anzures 11590,* ☎ *55/2581–1500,* FAX *55/2581–1501,* WEB *www.fiestaamericana.com.mx. 204 rooms, 14 suites. Restaurant, gym, spa, 2 bars, business services, meeting rooms, free parking. AE, DC, MC, V.*

Zona Rosa

$$ **Calinda Geneve.** A Quality Inn, referred to locally as El Génova, this five-story 1906 hotel is fitted with traditional colonial-style carved-wood chairs and tables in the pleasant lobby; guest rooms are small but comfortable. The attractive Salón Jardín is part of the popular Sanborns restaurant chain. ✉ *Londres 130, Zona Rosa 06600,* ☎ *55/5211–0071,* FAX *55/5207–4160,* WEB *www.hotelescalinda.com.mx. 300 rooms. Restaurant, café, room service, gym, bar, laundry facilities, business services. AE, DC, MC, V.*

$$ **La Casona.** This charming hotel is an elegant, understated former mansion, registered as an artistic monument by Mexico's Institute of Fine Arts. Filled with sunny patios and sitting rooms, the hotel is decorated in the spirit of the days of the Porfiriato. No two rooms are alike, but all have hair dryers, fluffy bathrobes and slippers, and good-size bathtubs. The two-story hotel building, with its salmon-color facade, looks out on a tree-lined street in Colonia Roma, about a 10-minute walk south of the Zona Rosa. A Continental breakfast is included in the price of a room. ✉ *Durango 280, at Cozumel, Zona Rosa, 06700,* ☎ *55/*

5286–3001, FAX *55/5211–0871,* WEB *www.hotellacasona.com.mx. 29 rooms. Restaurant, room service, gym, bar. AE, DC, MC, V.*

$$ ★ **Galería Plaza.** This ultramodern property is on a quiet street in elegant Zona Rosa—ideal for shopping, enjoying nightlife, and dining out. Service and facilities are faultless; advantages include voice mail in all rooms, a heated rooftop pool with sundeck, a secure underground parking lot, and a 24-hour restaurant. ✉ *Hamburgo 195, at Varsovia, Zona Rosa 06600,* ☎ *55/5230–1717 or 888/559–4329,* FAX *55/5207–5867,* WEB *www.brisas.com. 420 rooms, 19 suites. 3 restaurants, room service, pool, gym, lobby lounge, concierge, travel services, parking (fee). AE, DC, MC, V.*

$$ **Krystal Rosa.** Part of the Mexican Krystal Hotel chain, this superbly run high-rise hotel is in the heart of the Zona Rosa and has an excellent view of the city from the rooftop pool terrace. There's a stylish lobby cocktail lounge, a bar with local entertainers, and a restaurant, Hacienda del Mortero, which serves excellent classic Mexican cuisine. Two club floors have VIP check-in and service, complimentary Continental buffet breakfast, and rooms with extra amenities. ✉ *Liverpool 155, Zona Rosa 06600,* ☎ *55/5228–9928,* FAX *55/5228–9929,* WEB *www.krystal.com.mx. 267 rooms, 35 suites. Restaurant, pool, bar, concierge, business services, parking (fee). AE, DC, MC, V.*

$$ ★ **Marco Polo.** Ultramodern and intimate, the central Zona Rosa all-suites Marco Polo has the amenities and outstanding personalized service often associated with a small European hotel. North-facing top-floor rooms have excellent views of Paseo de la Reforma and the Ángel monument; the four penthouse suites have terraces—and the U.S. Embassy is close by. Breakfast is included. ✉ *Amberes 27, Zona Rosa 06600,* ☎ *55/5207–1893,* FAX *55/5533–3727,* WEB *www.marcopolo.com.mx. 60 suites, 4 penthouse suites, 9 long-stay apartments. Restaurant, bar, business services. AE, DC, MC, V.*

$ **Aristos.** On bustling Paseo de la Reforma, a few blocks east of the U.S. Embassy and near the Mexican Stock Exchange, this 15-story Zona Rosa–fringe hotel wears its age well (it was one of the first luxury hotels in the area). Rooms are well supplied and decorated in shades of peach and mauve, with brass and wood accents. The business center has a bilingual staff and a message service. ✉ *Paseo de la Reforma 276, Zona Rosa 06600,* ☎ *55/5211–0112,* FAX *55/5514–3543,* WEB *www.aristoshotels.com.mx. 320 rooms, 25 suites. 3 restaurants, gym, hair salon, sauna, bar, travel services, parking (fee). AE, DC, MC, V.*

$ **Misión Park Plaza México.** A part of the Misión chain, this very comfortable hotel a few blocks from the Zona Rosa's eastern end is well placed for shopping and sightseeing. Mirrors, good light, and like-new bathrooms make the rooms pleasant; all have air-conditioning and color TV with U.S. channels. Sixteen rooms have work areas, and you can use an Internet connection in an office off the lobby. The staff is friendly and accommodating. ✉ *Napoles 62, Zona Rosa 06600,* ☎ *55/5533–0535,* FAX *55/5533–1589,* WEB *www.hotelesmision.com.mx. 50 rooms. Coffee shop, gym, lobby lounge, meeting rooms. AE, MC, V.*

$ **Plaza Florencia.** On a busy avenue that borders the Zona Rosa, this modern hotel invites you to relax in a lodgelike lobby with heavy furniture and dark colors. Rooms are bright and soundproofed against the location's heavy traffic noise; higher floors have views of the Ángel monument. Some large family suites are available. A business center offers fax, copy, computer, and Internet-access services. ✉ *Florencia 61, Zona Rosa 06600,* ☎ *55/5242–4700,* FAX *55/5242–4785,* WEB *www.florencia.web.com.mx. 130 rooms, 12 suites. Restaurant, coffee shop, bar, business services. AE, DC, MC, V.*

Midtown and along the Reforma

$$$$ ★ **Four Seasons Mexico City.** Ranking among the most luxurious hotels in the capital, the Four Seasons repeatedly has won the AAA Five Diamond Award. The eight-story building was modeled after the 18th-century Iturbide Palace downtown and surrounds a traditional courtyard with a fountain. Half the rooms overlook the lush inner courtyard garden. Geared to business travelers, rooms have data ports and the full-service business center houses a reference library. A well-stocked tequila bar off the lobby is a perfect predinner option. Excellent cultural tours of the city are offered free to guests on weekends. ✉ *Paseo de la Reforma 500, Col. Juárez 06600,* ☎ *55/5230–1818 or 800/332–3442,* FAX *55/5230–1808,* WEB *www.fourseasons.com. 200 rooms, 40 suites. 2 restaurants, in-room data ports, pool, gym, bar, business services, meeting rooms. AE, DC, MC, V.*

$$$$ **María Isabel Sheraton.** Don Antenor Patiño, the Bolivian "Tin King," inaugurated this Mexico City classic in 1969 and named it after his granddaughter, socialite Isabel Goldsmith. All guest and public rooms are impeccably maintained; penthouse suites in the 22-story tower are extra-spacious and exceptionally luxurious. The location—across from the Ángel monument and the Zona Rosa, with Sanborns next door and the U.S. Embassy a half block away—is prime. The conference room holds 1,500. ✉ *Paseo de la Reforma 325, Col. Cuauhtémoc 06500,* ☎ *55/5242–5555 or 800/903–2500,* FAX *55/5207–0684,* WEB *www.sheraton.com. 681 rooms, 74 suites. 3 restaurants, room service, pool, gym, massage, sauna, 2 bars, concierge floor, business services, meeting rooms, parking (fee). AE, DC, MC, V.*

$$$ ★ **Marquis Reforma.** This plush, privately owned member of the Leading Hotels of the World is within walking distance of the Zona Rosa. Its striking art nouveau facade combines pink stone and curved glass, and the seventh-floor suites afford picture-perfect views of the Castillo de Chapultepec. An art deco theme defines the rooms. You can enjoy Mexican cuisine at the La Jolla restaurant and take advantage of hard-to-find holistic, stress-busting massages at the health club. ✉ *Paseo de la Reforma 465, Col. Cuauhtémoc 06500,* ☎ *55/5229–1200 or 800/235–2387,* FAX *55/5229–1212,* WEB *www.hotelmarquisrsma.com.mx. 133 rooms, 84 suites. 2 restaurants, in-room data ports, gym, bar, business services, meeting rooms. AE, DC, MC, V.*

$$$ **Melía México Reforma.** This flashy 22-story smoked-glass behemoth is convenient to downtown, the Zona Rosa, and the Stock Exchange. It touts the ultimate in high-tech amenities for business travelers: a stock-market indicator, computers, cellular phones, and secretarial, translation, messenger, and shipping services. Public areas include a coffee bar with 20 java concoctions. ✉ *Paseo de la Reforma 1, Col. Tabacalera 06030,* ☎ *55/5128–5000,* FAX *55/5128–5050,* WEB *www.solmelia.com. 424 rooms, 30 suites. 2 restaurants, room service, in-room data ports, hair salon, 2 bars, shops, business services, car rental, travel services. AE, DC, MC, V.*

$$ **Imperial.** The Imperial occupies a stately late-19th-century European-style building right on the Reforma alongside the Columbus Monument. Quiet elegance and personal service are keynotes of this privately owned property. The hotel's Restaurant Gaudí has an understated, tony atmosphere and serves Continental cuisine with some classic Spanish selections. ✉ *Paseo de la Reforma 64, Col. Juárez 06600,* ☎ *55/5705–4911,* FAX *55/5703–3122,* WEB *www.hotelimperial.com.mx. 50 rooms, 10 junior suites, 5 master suites. Restaurant, café, in-room safes, bar, business services, meeting rooms, travel services. AE, DC, MC, V.*

$$ **Sevilla Palace.** This glistening modern showplace has five panoramic elevators for its 23 floors, a covered rooftop pool with hot tub, a health

club, a top-floor supper club with entertainment, a terraced rooftop lounge with a city view, and convention halls with capacities of up to 1,000. It's near the Columbus traffic circle and attracts lots of tourists from Spain. ✉ *Paseo de la Reforma 105, Col. Revolución 06030,* ☎ *55/5705–2800 or 800/732–9488,* FAX *55/5703–1521,* WEB *www.sevillapalace.com.mx. 413 rooms. 2 restaurants, pool, gym, 3 bars, nightclub, meeting rooms. AE, MC, V.*

$ ★ **María Cristina.** Brimming with old-world charm, this Spanish colonial-style gem is a Mexico City classic. Impeccably maintained since it was built in 1937, the building surrounds a delightful garden courtyard—the setting for its El Retiro bar. Three apartment-style master suites come complete with hot tubs. In a quiet residential setting near Parque Sullivan, the hotel is close to the Zona Rosa. ✉ *Río Lerma 31, Col. Cuauhtémoc 06500,* ☎ *55/5603–1212 or 55/5566–9688,* FAX *55/5566–9194. 140 rooms, 8 suites. Room service, in-room safes, hair salon, bar, travel services. AE, MC, V.*

Downtown

$$ **Majestic.** If you're interested in exploring the historic downtown, you will find the atmospheric, colonial-style Majestic is perfectly located. It's also ideal for viewing the Independence Day (September 16) celebrations, for which many people reserve a room a year in advance. Although the front units have balconies and a delightful view, they can be noisy with car traffic until about 11 PM. Live Mexican music accompanies the Sunday buffet (1–5) on the terrace of the seventh-floor La Terraza restaurant—which serves international and Mexican specialties. ✉ *Madero 73, Downtown 06000,* ☎ *55/5521–8600 or 800/528–1234,* FAX *55/5512–6262,* WEB *www.majestic.com.mx. 85 rooms. Restaurant, coffee shop, bar, travel services. AE, DC, MC, V.*

$ ★ **Catedral.** In the heart of historic downtown, this refurbished older hotel is a bargain, with many of the amenities of the more upscale hotels at less than half the price. Public areas sparkle with marble and glass. Guest rooms are done in a generic but cheerful contemporary fashion, and all have color TVs (local channels only) and phones. You can get a room with a view of the namesake Catedral, but keep in mind that its bells chime every 15 minutes, late into the night. El Retiro bar attracts a largely Mexican clientele to hear live Latin music. ✉ *Donceles 95, Col. Centro 06000,* ☎ *55/5512–8581,* FAX *55/5512–4344,* WEB *www.hotelcatedral.com.mx. 116 rooms, 8 suites. Restaurant, coffee shop, room service, bar, nightclub, dry cleaning, laundry service, business services, travel services, free parking. AE, MC, V.*

$ **Gran Hotel de la Ciudad de México.** Ensconced in a former 19th-century department store, this hotel has rooms furnished in a modern style. Its distinctive Belle Epoque lobby—with a striking stained-glass Tiffany dome, chandeliers, gilded birdcages, and 19th-century wrought-iron elevators—is worth a visit in its own right. The Mirador breakfast restaurant overlooks the Zócalo. Run by Delmónicos, the Del Centro restaurant-bar is one of Mexico City's best. ✉ *16 de Septiembre 82, Col. Centro 06000,* ☎ *55/5510–4041 or 55/5510–4046,* ☎ FAX *55/5510–4040. 124 rooms. 2 restaurants, bar, concierge, travel services, parking (fee). AE, DC, MC, V.*

$ **Holiday Inn Zócalo.** This hotel couldn't have a better location—on the Zócalo and close to a gaggle of museums, restaurants, and historic buildings. The building may be historic, but the interior has the feel of a Holiday Inn. Although the glass-front lobby lacks personality, there's more flavor to the terrace restaurant, which is set with old-fashioned wrought-iron tables and has an amazing view of the Metropolitan Cathedral and National Palace. Rooms are small but well-equipped and all suites have data ports; five have Jacuzzi bathtubs. ✉ *5 de Mayo at Zócalo, Centro Histórico, Col. Centro 06000,* ☎ *55/5521–2121 or 800/465–4329,* FAX *55/5521–2122,* WEB *www.holidayinnzocalo.com.mx. 100 rooms, 10 suites. 2 restaurants, room service, in-room safes, gym, bar, meeting rooms, travel services, parking (fee). AE, MC, V.*

$ **Hotel de Cortés.** This darling small hotel, managed by Best Western, is housed in a 1780 colonial building that's also a national monument. Rooms, in colonial style, are small and simply furnished; they open onto an enclosed central courtyard. Two comfortable soundproof suites overlook Alameda Park across the busy street. The Franz Mayer Museum is a block away, and it's an easy walk to Palacio de Bellas Artes. Loyal guests reserve many months in advance. ✉ *Av. Hidalgo 85, Col. Guerrero 06000,* ☎ *55/5518–2184 or 800/509–2340,* FAX *55/5512–1863,* WEB *www.hoteldecortes.com.mx. 19 rooms, 10 suites. Restaurant, bar. AE, DC, MC, V.*

Airport

$$ **Hilton Aeropuerto.** Cool and compact—with a distinctive gray marble lobby and a bar with a wide-angle view of landing planes—the hotel feels like a private club, enhanced by an attentive but unobtrusive staff. Rooms come with full working gear for a traveling executive: two phone lines, modem connection, ergonomic chairs, and coffeemaker. Rooms have four different views—airstrip, street, atrium, or garden (bamboo plants set along a concrete ledge). ✉ *Benito Juárez International Airport, at international terminal, 15620,* ☎ *55/5133–0505 or 800/445–8667,* FAX *55/5133–0500,* WEB *www.nhhoteles.com.mx. 129 rooms. Restaurant, in-room data ports, gym, bar, business services, meeting rooms, parking (fee). AE, DC, MC, V.*

$$ **Marriott Aeropuerto.** Over a short covered footbridge from the airport terminal, this deluxe hotel is sleek and modern. There's a pool on the eighth floor. Even if you're only between flights and don't overnight, you can sit in one of the overstuffed chairs in the soothing lobby to get away from the frantic energy of the airport, or catch a meal in the restaurant. ✉ *Benito Juárez International Airport, 15520,* ☎ *55/5133–0033 or 800/228–9290,* FAX *55/5133–0030,* WEB *www.marriott.com. 600 rooms, 8 suites. Restaurant, coffee shop, pool, gym, sauna, bar, meeting rooms, car rental, free parking. AE, DC, MC, V.*

NIGHTLIFE AND THE ARTS

Good places to check for current events include the Friday edition of *The News,* a daily English-language newspaper (WEB www.thenewsmexico.com), and *Tiempo Libre,* a weekly magazine listing activities and events in Spanish (WEB www.tiempolibre.com.mx). Both are available at newsstands.

Citywide festivals with free music, dance, and theater performances by local groups take place all year long but especially in July and August. A three-week spring cultural and gastronomic festival with international headliners takes place in the Historic Center between March and April. Check with the Mexico City Tourist Office for dates and details (WEB www.mexicocity.com.mx).

The Arts

Dance

The world-renowned **Ballet Folklórico de México,** of Amalia Hernández, is a visual feast of Mexican regional folk dances in whirling colors. Lavish and professional, as you can see from the Web site (WEB www.

balletamalia.com), it's one of the most popular shows in Mexico. Performances Wednesday at 8:30 PM and Sunday at 9:30 AM and 8:30 PM are at the beautiful Palacio de Bellas Artes (Palace of Fine Arts; ✉ Av. Juárez at Eje Central Lázaro Cárdenas)—it's a treat to see its Tiffany-glass curtain lowered. Call the Palacio de Bellas Artes box office (☎ 55/5512–3633) or Ticketmaster (☎ 55/5325–9000) for information on prices and for reservations. Hotels and travel agencies can also secure tickets.

The **National Dance Theater** (☎ 55/5280–8771) is a good forum for contemporary dance behind the National Auditorium on Paseo de la Reforma, and the **Miguel Covarrubias Hall** (✉ National Autonomous University of Mexico [UNAM], Av. Insurgentes Sur 3000, Ciudad Universitaria, ☎ 55/5665–6825), home of the university's dance department, frequently sponsors modern-dance performances. Check the National Arts Council Web page (in Spanish) for a wide range of cultural activities, including dance: www.cnca.gob.mx.

Music

The primary venue for classical music is the **Palacio de Bellas Artes** (✉ Eje Central Lázaro Cárdenas and Av. Juárez, Col. Centro, ☎ 55/5512–3633), which has a main auditorium and the smaller Manuel Ponce concert hall. The National Opera performs from February through November at the palace. The National Symphony Orchestra stages classical and modern pieces at the palace in spring and fall.

The top concert hall, often touted as the best in Latin America, is **Ollin Yolitzli** (✉ Periférico Sur 5141, Col. Isidro Favela, ☎ 55/5606–0016 or 55/5606–8558); it hosts the Mexico City Philharmonic several times a year. The National Autonomous University of Mexico's Philharmonic orchestra performs at **Nezahualcoyotl Hall** (✉ National Autonomous University of Mexico, Av. Insurgentes Sur 3000, Ciudad Universitaria, ☎ 55/5622–7112 or 55/5606–8933).

For pop, rock, and Latin music stars such as Luis Miguel, Lou Reed, and Mercedes Sosa, check newspapers for attractions. The **Auditorio Nacional** (✉ Paseo de la Reforma 50, Col. San Miguel Chapultepec, across from Nikko México hotel, ☎ 55/5280–9250 or 55/5280–9979, WEB www.auditorio.com.mx) is smart and modern, with great acoustics. A choice venue, the **Hard Rock Cafe** (✉ Campos Elíseos 278, Col. Chapultepec Polanco, ☎ 55/5327–7171) is intimate with state-of-the-art sound. **Palacio de los Deportes** (✉ Av. Río Churubusco and Calle Añil, Col. Granjas México, ☎ 55/5237–9999 Ext. 4264) has an open air venue called the *Foro Sol* where you'll catch the glitzy shows of Madonna or the Rolling Stones. Though it's in need of an overhaul, the ambience is good at the **Teatro Metropolitano** (✉ Independencia 90, Downtown, ☎ 55/5510–1035 or 55/5510–1045).

Theater

You might find some English-language plays by checking listings in *The News*. If you understand Spanish (or are content to watch), you'll be able to enjoy a wider range of theatrical entertainment in Mexico City, including recent Broadway hits. Prices are reasonable compared with those for stage productions of a similar caliber in the United States. Although Mexico City has no central theater district, most theaters are within a 15- to 30-minute taxi ride from the major hotels. Top venues include **Hidalgo** (✉ Av. Hidalgo 23, at Eje Central Lázaro Cárdenas, Col. Centro, ☎ 55/5521–5859), **Manolo Fabregas** (✉ Joaquín Velázquez de León 31, Col. San Rafael, ☎ 55/5566–4321), **Silvia Pinal** (✉ Yucatán 160, at Coahuila, Col. Roma, ☎ 55/5264–1172), and **Teatros**

Alameda (✉ Av. Cuauhtémoc at Av. Chapultepec, Col. Roma, ☎ 55/ 5207–1498). Theater tickets are available through **Ticketmaster** (☎ 55/ 5325–9000).

Nightlife

Night is the key word to understanding the timing of going out in Mexico City. People generally have cocktails at 7 or 8, take in dinner and a show at 10 or 11, head to discos at midnight, then find a spot for a nightcap or tacos somewhere around 3 AM. The easiest way to do this if you don't speak Spanish is on a nightlife tour. If you set off on your own you should have no trouble getting around, but for personal safety absolutely avoid taking taxis off the street—take official hotel taxis or call a *sitio* (stationed) taxi.

Niza and Florencia streets in the Zona Rosa are practically lined with nightclubs, bars, and discos that are especially lively Friday and Saturday nights. Big hotels have bars and places to dance or be entertained, and they are frequented by locals. Outside the Zona Rosa, Paseo de la Reforma and Avenida Insurgentes Sur have the greatest concentration of nightspots. Mexico City has something for everyone in the way of night entertainment, but remember that the capital's high altitude makes liquor extremely potent, even jolting. Imported booze is expensive, so you may want to stick with what the Mexicans order: tequila, *cerveza* (beer), and rum, usually as a *cuba libre* (with Coke).

Dancing

Dance emporiums in the capital run the gamut from cheek-to-cheek romantic to throbbing strobe lights and ear-splitting music. Most places have a cover charge, but it's rarely more than $10. Some of the clubs require that reservations be made one to two days beforehand for Thursday through Saturday nights, if you want a table.

To really experience the nightlife Mexico has to offer, it's imperative to visit a dance club. **Bar León** (✉ República de Brasil 5, Col. Centro, behind the Catedral Metropolitana in the Zócalo, ☎ 55/5510–2979) is a traditional salsa bar with great live music and a kitschy feel. So popular you can barely move is the friendly **Mama Rumba** (✉ Querétaro 230, at Medillín, Col. Roma, ☎ 55/5564–6920; ✉ Plaza San Jacinto 23, San Ángel, ☎ 55/5550–8099), a 10-minute cab ride from the Zona Rosa. A nondescript Cuban restaurant during the day, it turns on the heat Wednesday through Saturday nights. **Meneo** (✉ Nueva York 315, Col. Napoles, just off Av. Insurgentes Sur, ☎ 55/5523–9448) is a modern dance hall for live salsa and merengue with two dance floors. **Salón Los Ángeles** (✉ Lerdo 206, Col. Guerrero, ☎ 55/5597–5181) takes you back in time to the 1930s, with decor straight out of a movie. The grand, open dance floor swings to the rhythms of danzón and salsa. When renowned Latin musicians such as Celia Cruz come to town, this is often where they perform.

If Latin music isn't your thing, two of the hippest discos in the city stand close to each other in the center. **Colmillo** (✉ Versailles 52, Col. Juárez, ☎ 55/5553–0262) spins techno music downstairs and has an exclusive jazz bar upstairs. The **Pervert Lounge** (✉ Uruguay 70½, Col. Centro, ☎ 55/5518–0976) is for the young and trendy.

Bars

Nice bars to sit and have a few drinks in are hard to come by in Mexico City. Often they are either too noisy (the rougher cantina variety) or too seedy. Bars are usually open Tuesday–Saturday 8–3 and generally don't charge a cover.

Baracuda (✉ Nuevo León 4A, Col. Condesa, ☎ 55/5211–9346) is a trendy cocktail bar that also offers good food, tempting martinis, and live jazz (on Wednesday nights). **Bar Mata** (✉ Filomeno Mata 11, at 5 de Mayo, Col. Centro, ☎ 55/5518–0237) is on the fourth and fifth floors of a colonial building near Palacio de Bellas Artes in the Centro. The atmosphere is conducive to dancing and mingling, especially in the rooftop bar, which has great views of the city and is a place to escape the cigarette smoke. **Bar Milán** (✉ Milán 18, at General Prim, Col. Juárez, ☎ 55/5592–0031) is a local favorite with the young and hip; the music is good but very loud. Upon entering you need to change pesos into *milagros* (miracles), which are notes necessary to buy drinks throughout the night. The catch is to remember to change them back for pesos before last call. **La Bodeguita del Medio** (✉ Cozumel 37, Col. Roma Norte, ☎ 55/5553–0246; ✉ Av. Insurgentes Sur 1798, Col. Florida, ☎ 55/5661–4400) is a sit-down joint full of life, with every surface splashed with graffiti. Inspired by the original Havana establishment where Hemingway lapped up rum-and-mint mojitos, you can also try cheap Cuban food, but most people just drink.

A sophisticated crowd and mellow music set the scene at the **Camino Real** bar (✉ Mariano Escobedo 700, Col. Nueva Anzures, ☎ 55/5263–8888). **La Guadalupana** (✉ Higuera 14, Coyoacán, ☎ 55/5554–6253), a famous Coyoacán cantina dating from 1932, is always packed and heavy on local color. The crowd is overwhelmingly male, so unaccompanied women will be showered with attention. Students and hip intellectuals of all ages pack **El Hijo del Cuervo** (✉ Jardín Centenario 17, Coyoacán, ☎ 55/5658–5306) for an interesting mix of rock and nueva canción, and the occasional theater show. Covers vary (up to $7), depending on the show. **El Nivel** (✉ Calle de Moneda, near the Templo Mayor, Col. Centro, ☎ 55/5522–9755), Mexico City's first cantina, opened in 1855, is right off the Zócalo. It's a small traditional cantina where you can get a cheap beer or tequila and be served free appetizers like peanuts and *chicharrón* (crisp fried meat) as long as you keep ordering drinks. The bar is named after a water marker outside (called "el nivel") that warned the city about imminent floods during the 20th century. **La Nueva Ópera** (✉ 5 de Mayo 10, at Filomeno Mata, Col. Centro, ☎ 55/5512–8959) is one of the city's most elegant watering holes, and it's brought in top personalities since it opened in 1870. The bar provides a relaxing atmosphere, Mexican appetizers and entrées, and an expansive drink list. Don't forget to have your waiter point out the bullet hole allegedly left in the ceiling by Mexican revolutionary hero Pancho Villa. With glass walls and three split-levels, **Rexo** (✉ Saltillo 1, corner of Vicente Suarez, Col. Condesa, ☎ 55/5553–1300 or 55/5553–5337) is a popular meeting place for the well-heeled young things of the Condesa district. The food is good.

Dinner Shows

The liveliest shows are in clubs downtown and in the Zona Rosa. The mazelike **La Bodega** (✉ Popocatepetl 25, corner of Amsterdam, Col. Hipodromo, ☎ 55/5525–2473; 🎫 $4, more for theater) is a lively place for drinks and decent Mexican food. A quirky band of old chaps plays relaxed Latin and Caribbean dance music in the small front room, and the upstairs theater hosts visiting musicians. Try to catch Astrid Haddad, a wild feminist cabaret artiste. You won't get the jokes without excellent Spanish, but you'll be laughing anyway. At **Focolare** (✉ Hamburgo 87, at Río Niza, Zona Rosa, ☎ 55/5207–8257), you can watch a cockfight, mariachi singers, and traditional folk dancers Thursday through Saturday nights. The show costs $8.50; Mexican dinner and drinks are separate.

Mariachi Music

The traditional last stop for nocturnal Mexicans is **Plaza Garibaldi** (✉ Col. Cuauhtémoc, east of Eje Central Lázaro Cárdenas, between República de Honduras and República de Perú), where exuberant and often inebriated mariachis gather to unwind after evening performances—by performing even more. There are roving mariachis, as well as *norteño* (country-style) music and white-clad *jarocho* bands (Veracruz-style), peddling songs in the outdoor plaza, where you can also buy beer and shots of tequila. Well-to-do Mexicans park themselves inside one of the cantinas or clubs surrounding the plaza and belt out their favorite songs with the hired musicians.

Tenampa is one of the better cantinas, with some great paintings on the walls. Order a tequila and the musicians will be around shortly, offering to serenade you (a song costs about $5, though Mexicans typically haggle for a dozen), so the bar is rarely without the wailing mariachis for more than 10 minutes. These places stay open Sunday through Thursday until at least 2 AM, and even later Friday and Saturday.

Note: the square was spruced up in the early 1990s to improve its seedy image, but things still get rough late at night. Furthermore, leaving Plaza Garibaldi can be dangerous—be sure to arrange for transportation ahead of time. You may call a travel agency, drive your car and park in the well-lit ramp below the plaza, or call a safe sitio taxi.

OUTDOOR ACTIVITIES AND SPORTS

Adventure Sports

A number of adventure-travel agencies have sprouted up to entice both tourists and locals out of the smog and chaos of Mexico City for a weekend of white-water rafting, rappelling, or biking. One of the best is **México Verde Expeditions** (✉ Homero 526, Int. 801, Col. Polanco, ☎ 55/5255–4400 or 55/5255–4465), whose guides speak English and lead tours to the pristine areas of such nearby states as Veracruz and Morelos. Call a week in advance to make reservations and bring a sleeping bag and sunblock. Or check the adventure and ecotours directory at www.mexonline.com/tours.htm.

Bullfighting

The main season for bullfighting is the dry season, around November through March, when celebrated *matadores* appear at **Plaza México** (✉ Calle Agusto Rodín 241, at Holbein, Col. Ciudad de los Deportes, ☎ 55/5563–3959), the world's largest bullring (it seats 40,000). Tickets, about $2–$25, can be purchased at hotel travel desks or at the bullring's ticket booths weekends 9:30–2 and 3:30–7. The show goes on at 4 Sunday.

Golf

All golf courses are private in Mexico City, but you can play if you're the guest of a member. If you stay at the Camino Real hotel, you can have the hotel arrange admittance to the **Bella Vista Golf Club** (☎ 55/5360–3501), off the Querétaro Highway. Greens fees Tuesday through Friday are $100; weekends, $200. You can try the 18-hole **Club de Golf Chaputepec** (☎ 55/5589–1408) in Col. Lomas Hipódromo. Toward the south of the city, you'll find the **Club de Golf México** (✉ Av. Glorieta Sur No. 64, Col. San Buenaventura Tlalpan, ☎ 55/5573–2000).

Soccer

Fútbol is the sport that Mexicans are most passionate about, which is evident in the size of their soccer stadium, **Estadio Azteca** (✉ Calzada de Tlalpan 3465, Tlalpan), the second largest in Latin America. The

World Cup Finals were held here in 1970 and 1986. You can buy tickets outside the stadium in the south of the city on the same day of any minor game. For more-important games, buy tickets a week in advance. The Pumas, a popular university-sponsored team, play at **Estadio Olímpica** (✉ Av. Insurgentes Sur at Universidad Nacional Autónoma de México, Ciudad Universitaria).

Tennis

Tennis clubs are private in Mexico, so if you want to play, consider staying at a hotel that has courts on-site.

Water Sports

The best place for swimming is your hotel pool. If you're desperate to row a boat, however, you can rent one in the lakes of Bosque de Chapultepec, near the Zoológico. The nearest sailing you'll get is in Valle de Bravo in Mexico State, and Lake Tequesquitengo in Morelos State caters well to water-skiers.

SHOPPING

The finest, most-concentrated shopping area is the **Zona Rosa,** a 29-square-block area bounded by Paseo de la Reforma on the north, Niza on the east, Avenida Chapultepec on the south, and Varsovia on the west. It's chock-full of boutiques, jewelry stores, leather-goods shops, antiques stores, and art galleries, as well as dozens of restaurants and coffee shops. Day or night, the Zona Rosa is always lively.

Polanco, a choice residential neighborhood along the northeast perimeter of Bosque de Chapultepec, has blossomed into a more upscale shopping area. Select shops line the huge, ultramodern **Plaza Polanco** mall (✉ Jaime Balmes 11, Polanco). You can also head to the **Plaza Masarik** (✉ Presidente Masarik and Anatole France, Polanco). **Plaza Moliere** (✉ Moliere between Calles Horacio and Homero, Polanco) is another upscale shopping area.

Hundreds of shops with more modest trappings and better prices are spread along the length of Avenida Insurgentes, as well as along Avenida Juárez and in the old downtown area.

Department Stores, Malls, and Shopping Arcades

Department stores are generally open Monday, Tuesday, Thursday, and Friday 10–7, and Wednesday and Saturday 10–8.

Bazar del Centro (✉ Isabel la Católica 30, just below Calle Madero, Col. Centro) is a restored, late-17th-century noble mansion built around a garden courtyard that houses several chic boutiques and prestigious jewelers such as **Aplijsa** (☎ 55/5521–1923), known for its fine gold, silver, pearls, and gemstones, and **Ginza** (☎ 55/5518–6453), which has Japanese pearls, including the prized cultured variety. Other shops sell Taxco silver, Tonalá stoneware, and Mexican tequilas and liqueurs. This complex is elegant and also has a congenial bar.

Liverpool (✉ Av. Insurgentes Sur 1310, Col. Guadalupe Inn; ✉ Mariano Escobedo 425, Col. Polanco; and in the Plaza Satélite and Perisur shopping centers) often has bargains on clothes.

El Palacio de Hierro (✉ Calles Durango and Salamanca, Col. Condesa; in the Plaza Moliere in Col. Polanco, and in the Plaza Coyoacán in Col. Xoco) is noted for items by well-known designers and seductive advertising campaigns.

Perisur shopping mall (✉ Periférico Sur, Perisur), on the southern edge of the city, near where the Periférico Expressway meets Avenida Insurgentes, is posh and pricey.

Plaza La Rosa, a modern shopping arcade (✉ between Amberes and Génova, Zona Rosa), has 72 prestigious shops and boutiques, including Aldo Conti and Diesel. It spans the depth of the block between Londres and Hamburgo, with entrances on both streets.

Portales de los Mercaderes (Merchants Arcade; ✉ extending the length of the west side of the Zócalo between Calles Madero and 16 de Septiembre, Col. Centro) has attracted merchants since 1524. It's lined with jewelry shops selling gold (often by the gram) and authentic Taxco silver at prices lower than those in Taxco itself, where the overhead is higher. In the middle of the Portales de los Mercaderes is **Tardán** (✉ Plaza de la Constitución 7, Col. Centro, ☎ 55/5512–2459), an unusual shop specializing in fashionable men's hats of every shape and style.

Sanborns is a chain of mini–department stores with some 65 branches in Mexico City. The most convenient are at Madero 4 (its original store in the House of Tiles, downtown); several along Paseo de la Reforma (including one at the Angel monument and another four blocks west of the Diana Fountain); and in the Zona Rosa (one at the corner of Niza and Hamburgo and another at Londres 130 in the Hotel Calinda Geneve). They carry quality ceramics and crafts (and can ship anywhere), and most have restaurants or coffee shops, a pharmacy, ATMs, and periodical and book departments with English-language publications.

Santa Fe (✉ Salida a Toluca, Santa Fe) is the largest mall in Latin America, with 285 stores, a movie theater, an international exhibition center, hotels, and several restaurants. It's in the wealthy Santa Fe district, which in recent years has become the favored office real-estate property in the city. To get here, take the Periférico Expressway south to the exit marked CENTRO SANTA FE.

Markets

A "must"—even for browsers—is a visit to the **Bazar Sábado** (Saturday Bazaar; ✉ Plaza San Jacinto, San Ángel). Hundreds of vendors sell tons of crafts, silver, wood carvings, embroidered clothing, leather goods, wooden masks, beads, *amates* (bark paintings), and trinkets at stalls on the network of cobbled streets outside. Inside the bazaar building, a renovated two-story colonial mansion, are the better-quality—and higher-priced—goods, including *alebrijes* (painted wooden animals from Oaxaca), glassware, pottery, jewelry, and papier-mâché flowers. A patio buffet and an indoor restaurant will help you conquer hunger and thirst. The market is open 10–7.

Open every day from about 10–5, the bustling **Mercado Artesanal La Ciudadela** (✉ Balderas, one block south of Parque José María Morelos, Col. Juárez) offers crafts, from talavera pottery, leather belts, guitars, tile-framed mirrors, hammocks, silverware, and papier-mâché skeletons to rugs, trays from Olinalá, and the ubiquitous sombrero. Prices are good but you can still haggle. A number of casual restaurants serve up hearty set-menu lunches for $2–$4. Covered stalls take up a whole square a 10–15 minute walk from the Alameda.

Sunday 10–4, more than 100 artists exhibit and sell their painting and sculpture at the **Jardín del Arte** (Garden of Art; ✉ Río Nevada, between Sullivan and Manuel Villalongín, Parque Sullivan, Col. Cuauhtémoc, northeast of the Reforma-Insurgentes intersection). Along the west side of the park, a colorful weekend mercado with scores of food stands is also worth a visit.

The **Mercado Insurgentes** (also called Mercado Zona Rosa; ✉ between Florencia and Amberes, Zona Rosa) is an entire block deep, with entrances on both Londres and Liverpool. This typical neighborhood public market distinguishes itself from others in one noticeable way: most of the stalls (222 of them) sell crafts. You can find all kinds of handmade items—including serapes and ponchos, baskets, pottery, silver, pewter, fossils, and onyx, as well as regional Mexican clothing.

The Zona Rosa's pink neocolonial Plaza del Ángel has a **Centro de Antigüedades** (antiques center; ✉ Londres 161, Zona Rosa) with several fine shops. On Saturday, together with other vendors, the dealers set up a flea market in the arcades and patios. On Sunday, bibliophiles join the antiques vendors to sell, peruse, and buy collectors books and periodicals.

The enormous **La Lagunilla** market (✉ Libertad, between República de Chile and Calle Allende, Col. Centro and Col. Cuauhtémoc) has been a site for local trade and bartering for more than five centuries. The best day is Sunday, when flea-market and antiques stands are set up outside. Dress down and watch out for pickpockets; it's known affectionately as the Thieves Market—local lore says you can buy back on Sunday what was stolen from your home Saturday.

Specialty Shops

Antiques

Antigüedades Coloniart (✉ Estocolmo 37, Zona Rosa, ☎ 55/5514–4799) has good-quality antique paintings, furniture, and sculpture. The store is open weekdays noon–3 and 4–7, Saturday 10–2. **Antigüedades Imperio** (✉ Hamburgo 149, Zona Rosa, ☎ 55/5525–5798) specializes in 19th-century European furniture, paintings, glass, and vases. It's open weekdays 11–2 and 4–7, Saturday 11:30–3.

Art

The **Juan Martín Gallery** (✉ Dickens 33-B, Col. Polanco, ☎ 55/5280–0277, WEB www.arte-mexico.com/juanmartin) is an avant-garde studio. **Misrachi** (✉ Presidente Masarik 523, Col. Polanco, ☎ 55/5250–4105), a long-standing gallery, promotes well-known Mexican and international artists. The **Nina Menocal de Rocha Gallery** (✉ Zacatecas 93, Col. Roma, ☎ 55/5564–7209) specializes in up-and-coming Cuban painters. The **Oscar Roman Gallery** (✉ Julio Verne 14, Col. Polanco, ☎ 55/5280–0436, WEB www.arte-mexico.com/romanosc) is packed with work by good Mexican painters with a contemporary edge. The store and gallery of the renowned **Sergio Bustamante** (✉ Nikko México hotel, Campos Elíseos 204, Col. Polanco, ☎ 55/5282–2638; ✉ Amberes 13, Zona Rosa, ☎ 55/5525–9059; ✉ Camino Real hotel, Mariano Escobedo 700, Col. Polanco, ☎ 55/5254–7372) displays and sells the artist's wild sculpture, jewelry, and interior-design pieces.

Candy

Celaya (✉ 5 de Mayo 39, Col. Centro, ☎ 55/5521–1787), in the downtown historic section, is a decades-old haven for those with a sweet tooth. It specializes in candied pineapple, sweet potato, guava, and other exotic fruit; almond paste; candied walnut rolls; and *cajeta,* a typical Mexican dessert of thick caramelized milk.

Clothing

The Spanish designer store **Zara** (✉ Londres 102, Zona Rosa, ☎ 55/5525–1516; ✉ Presidente Masarik 332, at Tennyson, Col. Polanco, ☎ 55/5280–1529; ✉ Plaza Coyoacán, Col. Xoco, ☎ 55/5605–7944; and other locations) has sleek women's fashions. **Guess** (✉ Presidente Masarik 326, Col. Polanco, ☎ 55/5282–0133) sells chic denim sportswear.

Designer Items

Cartier (✉ Amberes 9, Zona Rosa, ☎ 55/5207–6109; ✉ Presidente Masarik 438, Col. Polanco, ☎ 55/5281–5528) sells genuine designer jewelry and clothes, under the auspices of the French Cartier. **Via Spiga** (✉ Hamburgo 136, Zona Rosa, ☎ 55/5207–9997) has a fine selection of shoes, gloves, and handbags.

Jewelry

Taxco silver of exceptional style is sold at **Arte en Plata** (✉ Londres 162-A, Zona Rosa, ☎ 55/5511–1422), with many designs inspired by pre-Columbian art. The owner of **Los Castillo** (✉ Amberes 41, Zona Rosa, ☎ 55/5511–8396) developed a unique method of melding silver, copper, and brass, and is considered by many to be Taxco's top silversmith. His daughter Emilia Castillo displays fine ceramic dishes with tiny inlaid silver figures, such as fish and birds. **Pelletier** (✉ Torcuato Caso 237, Col. Polanco, ☎ 55/5250–8600) sells fine jewelry and watches. **Tane** (✉ Amberes 70, Zona Rosa, ☎ 55/5511–9429; ✉ Presidente Masarik 430, Col. Polanco, ☎ 55/5281–4775; ✉ Santa Catarina 207, San Ángel Inn, ☎ 55/5616–0165; and other locations) is a treasure trove of perhaps the best silver work in Mexico—jewelry, flatware, candelabra, museum-quality reproductions of archaeological finds, and bold new designs by young Mexican silversmiths.

Leather

For leather goods you have a few choices in Mexico City. **Aries** (✉ Florencia 14, Zona Rosa, ☎ 55/5533–2509) is Mexico's finest purveyor of leather goods, with a superb selection of bags and accessories for men and women; prices are high. **Las Bolsas de Coyoacán** (✉ Carrillo Puerto 9, Col. Coyoacán, ☎ 55/5554–2010) specializes in high-quality leather goods. **Gaitán** (✉ Calle Sarasete 95-B, at Tetracini, Col. Peralvillo downtown, ☎ 55/5759–3393) carries an extensive array of leather coats, luggage, golf bags, and saddles.

Mexican Crafts

Browse for folk art, sculpture, and furniture in the gallery **Artesanos de México** (✉ Londres 117, Zona Rosa, ☎ 55/5514–7455). **Arte Popular en Miniatura** (✉ Hamburgo 85, Col. Juárez, ☎ 55/5525–8145) is a tiny shop filled with tiny things, from dollhouse furniture and lead soldiers to miniature Nativity scenes. **Flamma** (✉ Hamburgo 167, Zona Rosa, ☎ 55/5511–8499 or 55/5511–0266) is a town house that sells beautiful handmade candles. You can find handwoven wool rugs, tapestries, and fabrics with original and unusual designs at **Tamacani** (✉ Av. Insurgentes Sur 1748B, Col. Florida, ☎ 55/5662–7133).

Under the auspices of the National Council for Culture and Arts, **Fonart** (National Fund for Promoting Arts and Crafts) operates two stores in Mexico City, and others around the country. Prices are fixed (and high), but the diverse, top-quality folk art and hand-crafted furnishings from all over Mexico represent the best artisans. The best location is downtown (✉ Juárez 89, Col. Juárez, ☎ 55/5521–0171), west of Alameda Park. Major sales at near wholesale prices are held from time to time at the main store–warehouse (✉ Av. Patriotismo 691, Col. Mixcoac, ☎ 55/5563–4060).

Outskirts of Mexico City

As the capital continues to expand, many attractions that used to be side trips are becoming more accessible. To the north of Mexico City stands the Basílica de Guadalupe, a church dedicated to Mexico's patron saint. It can be enjoyed in a half-day tour; if you get an early start, you could combine your visit with a jaunt to the pyramids of Teotihuacán in the afternoon. Xochimilco (pronounced kso-chee-*meel*-co), famous for its floating gardens, lies on the southern outskirts of the city. You can ride in gondolalike boats and get a fleeting sense of a pre-Hispanic Mexico City. The western extremes of the capital offer the popular Parque Nacional Desierto de los Leones—a forested national park whose centerpiece is an intriguing Carmelite monastery.

La Villa de Guadalupe

North of the Zócalo.

"La Villa"—the local moniker of the site of the two basilicas of the Virgin of Guadalupe—is Mexico's holiest shrine. Its importance derives from the miracle that the devout believe transpired here on December 12, 1531: an Aztec named Juan Diego received from the Virgin a cloak permanently imprinted with her image so he could prove to the priests that he had had a holy vision. On that date each year millions of pilgrims arrive, many crawling on their knees for the last few hundred yards, praying for cures and other divine favors. Pope John Paul II blessed the statue of Juan Diego outside the **Antigua Basílica** (Old Basilica; ⊠ Paseo Zumarraga, Atrio de América, Col. Villa de Guadalupe). Juan Diego was canonized in summer 2002. The Antigua Basílica dates from 1536; various additions have been made since then. The altar was executed by sculptor Manuel Tolsá. The basilica now houses a museum of ex-votos (hand-painted depictions of miracles, dedicated to Mary or a saint in thanks) and popular religious art, paintings, sculpture, and decorative and applied arts from the 15th through 18th centuries.

Because the structure of the Antigua Basílica had weakened over the years and the building was no longer large enough or safe enough to accommodate all the worshipers, Pedro Ramírez Vázquez, the architect responsible for Mexico City's splendid National Museum of Anthropology, was commissioned to design a new shrine, consecrated in 1976. In this case, alas, the architect's inspiration failed him: the **Nueva Basílica** (⊠ Paseo Zumarraga, Atrio de América 1, Col. Villa de Guadalupe, ☎ 55/5577–3654) is a gigantic, circular mass of wood, steel, and polyethylene that feels like a stadium rather than a church. The famous image of the Virgin is encased high up in its altar at the back and can be viewed from a moving sidewalk that passes below. The church is open daily from 6 AM to 9 PM.

Xochimilco

21 km (13 mi) south of Mexico City center.

When the first nomadic settlers arrived in the Valley of Mexico, they found an enormous lake. As the years went by and their population grew, the land could no longer satisfy their agricultural needs. They solved the problem by devising a system of *chinampas* (floating gardens), rectangular structures akin to barges, which they filled with reeds, branches, and mud. They planted the barges with willows, whose roots anchored the floating gardens to the lake bed, making a labyrinth of small islands and canals on which vendors carried flowers and produce grown on the chinampas to market.

Today Xochimilco is the only place in Mexico where the gardens still exist. Go on a Saturday, when the *tianguis* (market) is most active, or on a Sunday. (Note that Xochimilco can become crowded on Sunday.) On weekdays the place is practically deserted, so it loses some of its charm. Hire a *trajinera* (flower-painted boat); an arch over each spells out its name in flowers. As you sail through the canals, you'll pass mariachis and women selling tacos from other trajineras.

★ People also flock to Xochimilco for the **Museo Dolores Olmedo Patino,** which holds a superb collection of paintings by Frida Kahlo and the largest private collection of works by Kahlo's husband, the flamboyant muralist Diego Rivera. The museum was established by Olmedo, his lifelong model, patron, and onetime mistress. The lavish display of nearly 140 pieces from his cubist, post-cubist, and mural periods hangs in a magnificent 17th-century hacienda with beautiful gardens. Concerts and entertainment for children are held on weekends, while gaggles of geese and strutting peacocks add to the clamor. This is also the place to see the strange Mexican hairless dog: Ms. Olmedo shares Rivera's passion for these funny-looking creatures and keeps a few as pets on the grounds. The museum also has works by Rivera's common-law wife, Angelina Beloff. ✉ *Av. México 5843,* ☎ *55/5555–1016.* 🎫 *$2.50.* ⏲ *Tues.–Sun. 10–6.*

Parque Nacional Desierto de los Leones

25 km (16 mi) west of Mexico City center.

Several walking trails crisscross this 5,000-acre national park's pine forest. Pack a lunch and enjoy it at one of the picnic tables. The park's focal point is the ruined 17th-century **ex-monastery of the Carmelites,** isolated amid an abundance of greenery; it's open weekends 10–4. The park played a significant role in the War of Independence: in late October 1810, at a spot called **Las Cruces,** Father Hidalgo's troops trounced the Spaniards but resolved not to go on to attack Mexico City, an error that cost the insurgents 10 more years of fighting.

Outskirts of Mexico City A to Z

BUS TRAVEL

Some tour companies offer combination visits to La Villa de Guadalupe and Teotihuacán. Ask at your hotel.

CAR TRAVEL

To get to **La Villa de Guadalupe,** take Paseo de la Reforma Norte until it forks into Calzada de Guadalupe, which leads directly to the shrine.

To get to Xochimilco, take Periférico Sur to the extension of División del Norte. Xochimilco is 21 km (13 mi) from the Zócalo in Mexico City; the trip should take between 45 minutes and one hour, depending on traffic. (You may be better off taking a taxi, which may cost anywhere from $5 to $25, depending on the taxi company.)

For Parque Nacional Desierto de los Leones, follow Paseo de la Reforma all the way west. It eventually merges with the Carretera Libre at Toluca, and after 20 km (12 mi), you'll see signs for the turnoff; it's another 10 km (6 mi) to the park.

SUBWAY TRAVEL

You can reach **La Villa de Guadalupe** by taking the No. 3 metro line from downtown to Deportivo 18 de Marzo. Here, change to line No. 6 in the direction Martin Carrera, getting off at La Villa–Basílica stop.

For Xochimilco take metro line No. 2 to Taxqueña; here hop on the *tren ligero* ("light" train) that continues south to Xochimilco, or catch any bus marked Xochimilco.

MEXICO CITY A TO Z

To research prices, get advice from other travelers, and book travel arrangements, visit www.fodors.com.

AIR TRAVEL

Mexico City's airport, Aeropuerto Internacional Benito Juárez, is the main gateway to the country. Many American carriers fly direct to Mexico City, and most Mexican carriers have flights here from elsewhere in the country.

Construction was expected to begin on a six-runway international airport in Texcoco in 2003.

CARRIERS

Major North American carriers, including Air Canada, Alaska Airlines, American, America West, Canadian, Continental, Delta, Northwest, Trans World Airlines, United, and USAirways–Air France fly nonstop between Houston and Mexico City.

Mexicana has scheduled service from Chicago, Denver, Las Vegas, Los Angeles, Miami, New York, Orlando, San Antonio, San Francisco, and San Jose, as well as direct or connecting service at 30 locations throughout Mexico. Aeroméxico serves Mexico City daily from Dallas, Houston, Los Angeles, Miami, Orlando, New Orleans, Atlanta, New York, Phoenix, San Antonio, San Diego, and Tucson (as well as Tijuana). Aeroméxico serves some 35 cities within Mexico. Aerolitoral, a subsidiary of Aeroméxico based in Monterrey, serves north-central cities as well as San Antonio, Texas, via Monterrey from Mexico City.
➤ AIRLINES AND CONTACTS: **Aerocaribe** (☎ 55/5536–9046 or 55/5448–3284, WEB www.aerocaribe.com). **Aerolitoral** (☎ 55/5133–4000, WEB www.aerolitoral.com.mx). **Aeroméxico** (☎ 55/5133–4000, WEB www.aeromexico.com.mx). **Mexicana** (☎ 55/5448–0990, WEB www.mexicana.com.mx).

AIRPORTS AND TRANSFERS

The newest wing of Mexico City's Aeropuerto Internacional Benito Juárez is a high-tech elongation of the airport's east end. It has four banks and seven currency exchanges (*casas de cambio*); Cirrus and Plus ATMs that disburse pesos; places to rent cellular phones; an Internet room; and a food court, pharmacy, bookstore, and pricey shops. A multilevel parking garage charges $2 an hour for short-term parking.

Porters and free carts are available in the baggage-retrieval areas. Banks and currency exchanges rotate their schedules to provide 24-hour service. You can also use your ATM card to take pesos directly out of your U.S. account at ATMs (called *cajero automático* locally) here and throughout the city—and you'll get an even better exchange rate. Just remember that your home bank may charge $3 or more per transaction. The Mexico City Tourist Office, Mexican Ministry of Tourism (Sectur), and the Hotel Association have stands in the arrival areas that can provide information and find visitors a room for the night.
➤ AIRPORT INFORMATION: **Aeropuerto Internacional Benito Juárez** (☎ 55/5571–3600, WEB www.asa.gob.mx).

AIRPORT TRANSFERS

If you're taking a taxi, be sure to purchase your ticket at an official airport taxi counter marked Transportación Terrestre (ground transportation), located in the baggage-carousel areas as well as in the concourse area and curbside. Under no circumstance take a *pirata* taxi (unofficial drivers offering their services). Government-controlled fares are based on which colonia you are going to and are usually $10–$12 (per car, not per person) to most hotels. A 10% tip is customary for airport drivers if they help with baggage. All major car-rental agencies have booths at both arrival areas.

To get a taxi into the city, head to the official ticket windows just before customs, or those to your left immediately afterward. Taxis are priced by zones; figure out your zone from the big map on the wall (if you're in the central part of the city, you'll probably need Zone 4 or 5, which will cost $12–$15). To get to the taxi rank, head left from the arrivals area and out of the building. Touts stand at the exit; if you don't have a ticket in your hand, they will attempt to charge you more for the same taxi ride. The yellow-and-white airport taxis are safe. Avoid the others.

Reaching the city center takes 15 minutes to an hour depending on the traffic. If you're leaving from the city center in the morning, going against traffic, you will reach the airport quickly. In the evening allow at least an hour, count on more time in the rainy season.

Your taxi driver will ask which terminal you want: "Nacional o Internacional?" This question refers to your airline, not your destination. Be careful: some flights have code-sharing between a Mexican and a foreign airline, and check-in could be in either terminal. (Note that you will not lose more than 10 minutes if you arrive at the wrong terminal, since both share the same building.)

BUS TRAVEL TO AND FROM MEXICO CITY

Greyhound buses make connections to major U.S. border cities, from which Mexican bus lines depart throughout the day. Reserved seating is available on first-class coaches, which are comfortable but not nearly as plush as the intercity buses. If you plan stopovers en route, make sure in advance that your ticket is written up accordingly. In Mexico, platform announcements are in Spanish only.

Within Mexico, buses are the most popular way to travel: you can board ultramodern, superdeluxe motor coaches that show U.S. movies and serve soft drinks and coffee. ETN (Enlaces Terrestres Nacionales) serves cities to the west and northwest, such as Guadalajara, Morelia, Querétaro, Guanajuato, San Miguel de Allende, and Toluca. ADO buses depart southeast to such places as Puebla, Oaxaca, Veracruz, Mérida, and Cancún. Reserved-seat tickets can be purchased at Mexico City travel agencies.

Various other classes of intercity bus tickets can be purchased at most travel agencies in the city (there are many agencies in the Zona Rosa). Buses depart from four outlying stations (*terminales de autobuses*), where tickets can also be purchased: Central de Autobuses del Norte, going north; Central de Autobuses del Sur, going south; Central de Autobuses del Oriente, going east; and Terminal de Autobuses del Poniente, going west.

➤ BUS INFORMATION: **ADO** (☎ 55/5133–2424, 55/5133–2444, or 800/702–8000). **Central de Autobuses del Norte** (✉ Av. Cién Metros 4907, Col. Magdalena de la Salina, ☎ 55/5587–1552). **Central de Autobuses del Sur** (✉ Tasqueña 1320, Tasqueña, ☎ 55/5689–9745 or 55/5689–4987). **ETN** (☎ 55/5577–6529, 55/5271–1262, or 55/5277–6529). **Greyhound** (☎ 55/5669–1287, 55/5669–0986, or 800/010–0600, WEB www.greyhound.com.mx). **Terminal de Autobuses del Oriente** (✉ Ignacio Zaragoza 200, Col. 7 de Julio, ☎ 55/5762–5977). **Terminal de Autobuses del Poniente** (also known as "Observatorio," (✉ Río Tacubaya and Sur 122, Col. Real del Monte, ☎ 55/5271–4519).

BUS TRAVEL WITHIN MEXICO CITY

The Mexico City bus system is used by millions of commuters because it's cheap and goes everywhere. Buses are packed during rush hours so, as in all big cities, you should be wary of pickpockets. One of the principal bus routes runs along Paseo de la Reforma, Avenida Juárez, and Calle Madero. This west–east route connects Bosque de Chapultepec with the Zócalo. A southbound bus may be taken along Avenida Insurgentes Sur to San Ángel and University City, or northbound along Avenida Insurgentes Norte to the Guadalupe Basílica. Mexico City tourism offices provide free bus-route maps. The price is between 1 and 4 pesos (about 40¢), depending on your destination.

CAR TRAVEL

Major arteries into Mexico City include Highway 57 to the north, which starts at Laredo, Texas, and goes through Monterrey and Querétaro. Highway 95 comes in from Cuernavaca to the south, and Highway 190D from Puebla to the east. Highway 15 via Toluca is the main western route.

Millions of intrepid drivers brave Mexico City's streets every day and survive, but for out-of-towners the experience can be frazzling. One-way streets are confusing, rush-hour traffic is nightmarish, and parking places can be hard to find. Police tow trucks haul away illegally parked vehicles, and the owner is heavily fined. Getting your car back here is a tedious process. Locatel is an efficient 24-hour service for tracing vehicles that are towed, stolen, or lost (in case you forgot where you parked). There's a chance an operator on duty may speak English, but the service is primarily in Spanish. You can hire a chauffeur for your car through a hotel concierge or travel service such as American Express.

Also, the strictly enforced law *Hoy No Circula* (Today This Car Can't Circulate) applies to all private vehicles, including your own. One of several successful efforts to reduce smog and traffic congestion, this law prohibits every privately owned vehicle (including out-of-state, foreign, and rental cars) from being used on one designated weekday. All cars in the city without a Verification "0" rating (usually those built before 1994) are prohibited from driving one day a week (two days a week during alert periods, which are usually in December and January). Cars in violation are inevitably impounded by the police. Expect a hefty fine as well.

The weekday you can't drive is specified by the last number or letter of the license plate: on a nonemergency week, 5–6 are prohibited on Monday; 7–8 on Tuesday; 3–4 on Wednesday; 1–2 on Thursday; and 9–0 on Friday. For further information, contact the Mexican Government Tourism Office nearest you, or log on to www.mexicocity.com.mx/nocircula.html, or the English-language www.t1msn.imeca.com.mx/t1msn_valle_de_mexico/vehicula.asp, and plan your schedule accordingly.
➤ CONTACT: **Locatel** (☎ 55/5658–1111).

E-MAIL

Many hotels have complimentary e-mail service for guests. There's also a proliferation of Internet cafés in areas such as the Colonia Condesa, Coyoacán, and Zona Rosa. Charges can be as little as $3.50 an hour for access. At Bits Café, you can have a cappuccino and cheesecake, or a beer and a sandwich, while you catch up on your e-mail. It's open Monday–Saturday 10–10. Open 10–10 daily, JavaChat offers free bottomless coffee while you're on the computer.
➤ INTERNET SERVICES: **Bits Café** (✉ Hamburgo 165-C, at Florencia, 1 block south of the Angel monument, Col. Juárez, ☎ 55/5525–0144). **JavaChat** (✉ Génova 44-K, next to McDonald's, Zona Rosa, ☎ 55/5514–6856 or 55/5525–6853).

EMBASSIES

The U.S. Embassy is open weekdays 9–5, but is closed for American and Mexican holidays; however, there's always a duty officer to take emergency calls on holidays and after closing hours. The embassy keeps a list of English-speaking local doctors on hand if you need to consult one. The Canadian Embassy is open weekdays 9–1 and 2–5 and is closed for Canadian and Mexican holidays. The British Embassy is open weekdays 8:30–3:30.

➤ CONTACTS: **British Embassy** (✉ Río Lerma 71, Col. Cuauhtémoc, ☏ 55/5207–2449, WEB www.embajadabritanica.com.mx). **Canadian Embassy** (✉ Schiller 529, Col. Polanco, ☏ 55/5724–7900, WEB www.canada.org.mx). **U.S. Embassy** (✉ Paseo de la Reforma 305, Col. Juárez, ☏ 55/5209–9100, WEB www.usembassy-mexico.gov).

EMERGENCIES

Dial **060, 065,** or **080** for police, Red Cross, ambulance, fire, or other emergency situations. If you are not able to reach an English-speaking operator, call the Sectur hot line (☏ 55/5212–0260). For missing persons or cars call Locatel (☏ 55/5658–1111). You'll find English-speaking staff at both the American British Cowdray Hospital and Hospital Español.

➤ HOSPITALS: **American British Cowdray Hospital** (✉ Calle Sur 136–116, corner of Observatorio, Col. las Américas ☏ 55/5230–8161 for emergencies; 55/5230–8000 switchboard). **Hospital Español** (✉ Ejército Nacional 613, Col. Granada, ☏ 55/5203–3735).

ENGLISH-LANGUAGE MEDIA

The best place for English- and foreign-language newspapers and magazines is Casa de la Prensa, which has two locations in the Zona Rosa. Sanborns carries a few U.S. newspapers but an ample supply of magazines, paperbacks, and guidebooks. The American Book Store has an extensive selection of publications. A daily English-language newspaper, *The News,* is widely available at hotels and at newsstands; it provides a summary of what's happening in Mexico and the rest of the world with cultural and entertainment listings and daily stock-market reports. Remember that most U.S. or foreign-published publications are about double the price you'd pay for them at home.

The Benjamin Franklin Library, actually a part of the U.S. Embassy, was instituted to create greater understanding and cultural exchange between the United States and Mexico. The library, open weekdays noon–7, has a substantial collection of English novels, a good reference section, and many U.S. periodicals. You must be at least 20 years old, fill out an application, and have a Mexican resident sign it in order to check out books, but anyone can browse through the stacks.

➤ ENGLISH-LANGUAGE MEDIA OUTLETS: **American Book Store** (✉ Bolivar 23, Col. del Valle, ☏ 55/5575–2372; ✉ Insurgentes Sur 1188, Col. del Valle, ☏ 55/5575–2372). **Benjamin Franklin Library** (✉ Londres 16, Zona Rosa, ☏ 55/5209–9100 Ext. 3482). **Casa de la Prensa** (✉ Florencia 57, Col. Juárez; ✉ Hamburgo 141, Zona Rosa, ☏ 55/5208–1419).

PESERO TRAVEL

Originally six-passenger sedans, now minibuses, peseros operate on a number of fixed routes and charge a flat rate (a peso once upon a time, hence the name). They're a good alternative to buses and taxis; however, be prepared for a jolting ride because many drivers like to turn their buses into bucking broncos. Likely routes for tourists are along the city's major west–east axis (Bosque de Chapultepec–Paseo de la Reforma–Avenida Juárez–Zócalo) and north–south along Avenida Insurgentes, between the Guadalupe Basílica and San Ángel–University City. Peseros pick up passengers at bus stops and outside almost all metro stations. Just stand on the curb, check the route sign on the oncoming pesero's windshield, and hold out your hand. Tell the driver where to stop, or press the button by the back door. If it's really crowded and you can't reach the back door in time, just bang on the ceiling and yell, "Baja," which means "getting down." Base fares are 2 pesos (about 20¢) with the price going up to 3.50 pesos (about 35¢) according to how far you travel. Exact change is appreciated by drivers and will save you a lot of fuss. Peseros are also known as "combis," "micros," and "rutas."

SIGHTSEEING TOURS

Various travel agencies run tourist-friendly, English-guided tours of Mexico City and surrounding areas. The basic city tour ($39) lasts eight hours and takes in the Zócalo, Palacio Nacional, Catedral Metropolitana, and Bosque de Chapultepec. A four-hour pyramid tour costs around $23 and covers the Basílica de Nuestra Señora de Guadalupe and the major ruins at Teotihuacán. Except for the Tren Turístico, the tours described below can be booked through the agents listed in Travel Agencies; most agencies offer some version of each tour.

BULLRING TOUR

There are trips to the bullring on Sunday with a guide who will explain the finer points of this spectacle. This three-hour afternoon tour can usually be combined with the Ballet Folklórico–Xochimilco trip.

CULTURAL TOUR

A seven-hour cultural tour is run Sunday morning only and usually includes a performance of the folkloric dances at the Palacio de Bellas Artes, a gondola ride in the canals of Xochimilco's floating gardens, and a visit to the modern campus of the National University.

NIGHTLIFE TOUR

Nightlife tours are among the most popular tours of Mexico City. The best are scheduled to last five hours and include transfers by private car rather than bus; dinner at an elegant restaurant (frequently Bellini or at the Del Lago); a drink and a show at the Plaza Garibaldi, where mariachis play; and a nightcap at one of the cantinas around the square, which features Mexican folk dancers.

TROLLEY TOUR

A good way to see the historic downtown—if you know some Spanish—is on Tren Turístico's charming replicas of 20-passenger trolleys from the 1920s. The 50-minute narrated tour ($3.50) includes the Zócalo, Colegio de San Idelfonso, Plaza de Santo Domingo, Plaza Manuel Tolsá (location of the Palacio de Minería and Museo Nacional de Arte), Plaza de la Santa Veracruz (Museo Franz Mayer), and the Palacio de Iturbide. Trolleys depart hourly 10–5 daily from the train's offices in front of Alameda Park.

➤ CONTACTS: **Tren Turístico's** (✉ Av. Juárez 66, at Revillagigedo, Col. Centro, ☏ 55/5512–1013).

SUBWAY TRAVEL

Transporting 5 million passengers daily, Mexico City's metro is one of the world's best, busiest, and cheapest transportation systems—a ride costs 1.50 pesos (about 15¢). The clean marble-and-onyx stations are brightly lighted, and modern French-designed trains run quietly on rubber tires. Some stations, such as Insurgentes, are shopping centers. Even if you don't take a ride, visit the Zócalo station, which has large models of central Mexico City during three historic periods. Many stations have temporary cultural displays, from archaeological treasures to contemporary art; the Pino Suárez station has a small Aztec pyramid inside, a surprise discovery during construction.

There are 10 intersecting metro lines covering more than 160 km (100 mi). It's a bit confusing: the No. 8 previously had been assigned to a line whose construction was canceled because it would have destroyed unearthed Aztec ruins. Line 9 was subsequently built. Now No. 8 designates the newest (10th) line. The ninth line was A. Segments of Lines 1 and 2 cover most points of interest to foreigners, including Zona Rosa, Bellas Artes, and Centro Histórico. At the southern edge of the city, the Tasqueña station (Line 2) connects with the electric train (*tren eléctrico*) that continues south to Xochimilco. To the southeast, the *tren ligero* ("light" train) from the Pantitlán station (Lines 1, 5, and 9) heads east to Chalco in the state of Mexico. The various lines also serve all four bus stations, the Buenavista train station, and the airport; however, only light baggage is allowed on board during rush hours. User-friendly, color-coded maps are sometimes available free at metro-station information desks (if there's an attendant) and at Mexico City tourism offices; color-keyed signs and maps are posted all around.

Trains run frequently (about two minutes apart) and are least crowded 10–4 and at night. To reduce incidences of harassment during crowded rush hours, regulations may require men to ride separate cars from women and children. Hours vary somewhat according to the line, but service is essentially 5 AM–midnight weekdays; 6 AM–2 AM Saturday; 6 AM–1 AM Sunday and holidays.

TAXIS

The Mexico City variety comes in several colors and sizes. Unmarked, or *turismo,* sedans with hooded meters are usually stationed outside major hotels and in tourist areas; however, they are uneconomical for short trips. Their drivers are almost always English-speaking guides and can be hired for sightseeing on a daily or hourly basis (always negotiate the price in advance). Sitio taxis operate out of stands, take radio calls, and are authorized to charge a small premium over the meter rate or will offer a set rate. Among these, Servi-Taxis, Radio-Taxi, and Taxi-Mex, which accepts American Express, offer 24-hour service.

Unauthorized cab drivers (often criminals who have stolen the cabs they drive) pose probably the single greatest danger to tourists in the capital, but this danger is easily avoided. Although the situation has improved slightly, outsiders are especially vulnerable to their assaults, and many have been robbed or forced to withdraw money from ATMs. Take only registered hotel taxis or have a hotel concierge call a more economical, but equally reliable sitio cab—**do not hail taxis on the street** under any circumstances. Be sure to establish the fare in advance if the sitio does not work with meter and premium.

Taxi drivers are authorized to charge 10% more at night, usually after 10. Taking even a sitio taxi in Mexico City is inexpensive and tips are not expected unless you have luggage—then 10% is sufficient.
➤ TAXI SERVICES: **Servi-Taxis** (☎ 55/5271–2560). **Radio-Taxi** (☎ 55/5566–0077). **Taxi-Mex** (☎ 55/5538–0912 or 55/5538–0573).

TELEPHONE CODES

In February 2002 Mexico switched to a 10-digit dial plan; all phone numbers were revised and extended. A regional code for Mexico City—55—now precedes all original eight-digit numbers. To reach Mexico City from elsewhere in Mexico, dial 01 plus the 10-digit number; from abroad, dial 52 plus the 10-digit number.

TRAIN TRAVEL

The train system in Mexico is in the process of being privatized and is depressingly moribund given its romantic history. Currently, trains are used almost exclusively for cargo, and the very few existing passenger services take at least twice as long as road transportation. If you are a train lover determined to go by rail, try to get information from English-speaking operators about schedules and prices from Ferrocarriles Nacionales de Mexico in Mexico City.

➤ TRAIN INFORMATION: **Ferrocarriles Nacionales de Mexico** (National Mexican Railways; ☎ *55/5547–9458* or *55/5659–7512*).

TRANSPORTATION AROUND MEXICO CITY

You can get around Mexico City in the popular public buses, the subway, taxis, or the idiosyncratic peseros—minibuses that follow designated routes through the city. The subway is cheap, fast, and efficient, and routes are easy to understand. Along with taxis (which are more expensive), the subway is the best option for those who don't speak much Spanish. Buses and peseros are something of a nightmare if you don't speak the language (and confusing and hectic even for people who do). Note that peseros can also be unsafe.

TRAVEL AGENCIES

➤ LOCAL AGENT REFERRALS: **American Express** (✉ Paseo de la Reforma 234, Col. Ciudad de los Deportes, ☎ *55/5326–3521*, WEB www.vacaciones.amex.com). **Grey Line Tours** (✉ Londres 166, Zona Rosa, ☎ *55/5208–1163*, WEB www.greyline.com.mx). **Mexico Travel Advisors** (MTA; ✉ Génova 30, Col. Juárez, ☎ *55/5525–7520* or *55/5525–7534*).

VISITOR INFORMATION

The Mexico City Tourist Office (Departamento de Turismo del Distrito Federal, or DDF) maintains information booths at both the international and domestic arrival areas at the airport. In town, visit the city's tourism module in the Zona Rosa. This office also gives information by phone with its Infotur service 9–7 daily. Multilingual operators are available and have access to an extensive data bank.

The Secretariat of Tourism (Sectur) operates a 24-hour multilingual hot line that provides information on both Mexico City and the entire country. If lines are busy, keep trying. Outside Mexico City, call the Sectur Tourist Information Center in Colonia Polanco toll-free weekdays 8–8.

➤ TOURIST INFORMATION: **Mexico City Tourist Office** (✉ Amberes 54, at the corner of Londres, Zona Rosa, ☎ *55/5525–9380*, WEB www.mexicocity.gob.mx). **Secretariat of Tourism** (✉ Presidente Masarik 172, Col. Polanco, ☎ *55/5250–0123, 55/5250–0493, 55/5250–0027, 55/5250–0589, 55/5250–0151, 55/5250–0292, 55/5250–0741*, or *55/5212–0260*; 01–800/903–9200 outside Mexico City; 800/482–9832 outside Mexico City, WEB www.mexico-travel.com).

3 SIDE TRIPS FROM MEXICO CITY

If the pace—or smog—of the megalopolis begins to run you down, simply abscond from Mexico City to find fulfillment in a plethora of archaeological sites and vivid rural towns, old-fashioned and frozen in simpler times. After two nights or more, you are guaranteed to feel that you've turned back the clock on the concrete jungle. You can take a deep breath of fresh air while you hike up the Tepozteco mountain or sail at Valle de Bravo, relax amid the bougainvillea in the perennial spring of Cuernavaca, feast your eyes on the intricate churches and ex-convents of Puebla, or marvel at the spectacular pyramids at Teotihuacán.

Updated by Barbara Kastelein

ALTHOUGH THE URBAN lifestyle in Mexico City has all the frenzy and rush of any major capital in the world, you'll be pleasantly surprised to find that just a short drive or bus ride can place you in a small-town church, in the middle of a densely forested national park, or on top of intoxicating ancient ruins. Cholula is famous for its friendly townsfolk and colonial churches. Tepoztlán has a curious cultural mix of its indigenous community and the New Age proselytes drawn by the town's mystic reputation. An hour north of the city you can climb the famous pyramids of the sun and the moon in the mammoth and mysterious ruins of Teotihuacán. Other historically significant pyramids can be seen in the former Toltec capital of Tula and the splendid ruins at Cacaxtla and Xochicalco to the southeast.

Two nearby state capitals, the cities of Cuernavaca and Puebla, are windows on the diversity of Mexican life. Cuernavaca's deliciously warm climate and abundance of flowers have made it a favorite weekend getaway for *chilangos* (Mexico City residents), as well as a center for Spanish-language schools that draw people from around the world. Puebla, on the other hand, is a beautifully preserved and conservative colonial city, surrounded by important agricultural valleys and abounding in churches, chapels, ex-convents, and monasteries.

NORTH OF MEXICO CITY

Hugging the roads to the north of Mexico City are several of the country's most celebrated pre-Columbian and colonial monuments. The pyramids of Teotihuacán can be best enjoyed in a day tour; if you get an early start, your trip can entail a visit to the Basílica of Guadalupe (☞ *see* Chapter 2), as well as the ex-convent at Tepotzotlán (now a magnificent museum of the viceregal period), and the ruins at Tula.

There are no tourist offices in the area, but a good English-language guidebook to Teotihuacán is sold at the site. Useful maps and information can also be found on archaeology.la.asu.edu/teo and www.mexicocity.com.mx/teoti_i.html.

Teotihuacán

50 km (31 mi) northeast of Mexico City center.

This Mesoamerican Giza is one of the most powerful sites in Mexico; from its size and scale, there's no doubting Teotihuacán's (*teh*-oh-tee-wa-*can*) monumental place in history. It was likely a small town by 100 BC; four centuries later it had reached its zenith. At the time of its decline during the 8th century, it was one of the largest cities in the world. The sacred metropolis lay in the midst of rich obsidian mines, which provided the means for its rise as a major regional trading power and center for the arts—its influence on Maya pottery stretched as far away as Tikal in present-day Guatemala. Just who lived here isn't exactly clear—even the original name of the city is lost. It is believed that water shortages and crises caused by local deforestation contributed to Teotihuacán's downfall. It was set on fire and destroyed by raiders around AD 650. Centuries later, the Aztecs arrived in the Valley of Mexico. Because the memory of the grandeur of this city survived the passage of time, these new settlers named the site Teotihuacán, meaning "place of the gods." It was here, the Aztecs believed, that the gods created the universe.

The awe-inspiring **Pirámide del Sol** (Pyramid of the Sun), with a base as broad as that of the pyramid of Cheops in Egypt, is off the center

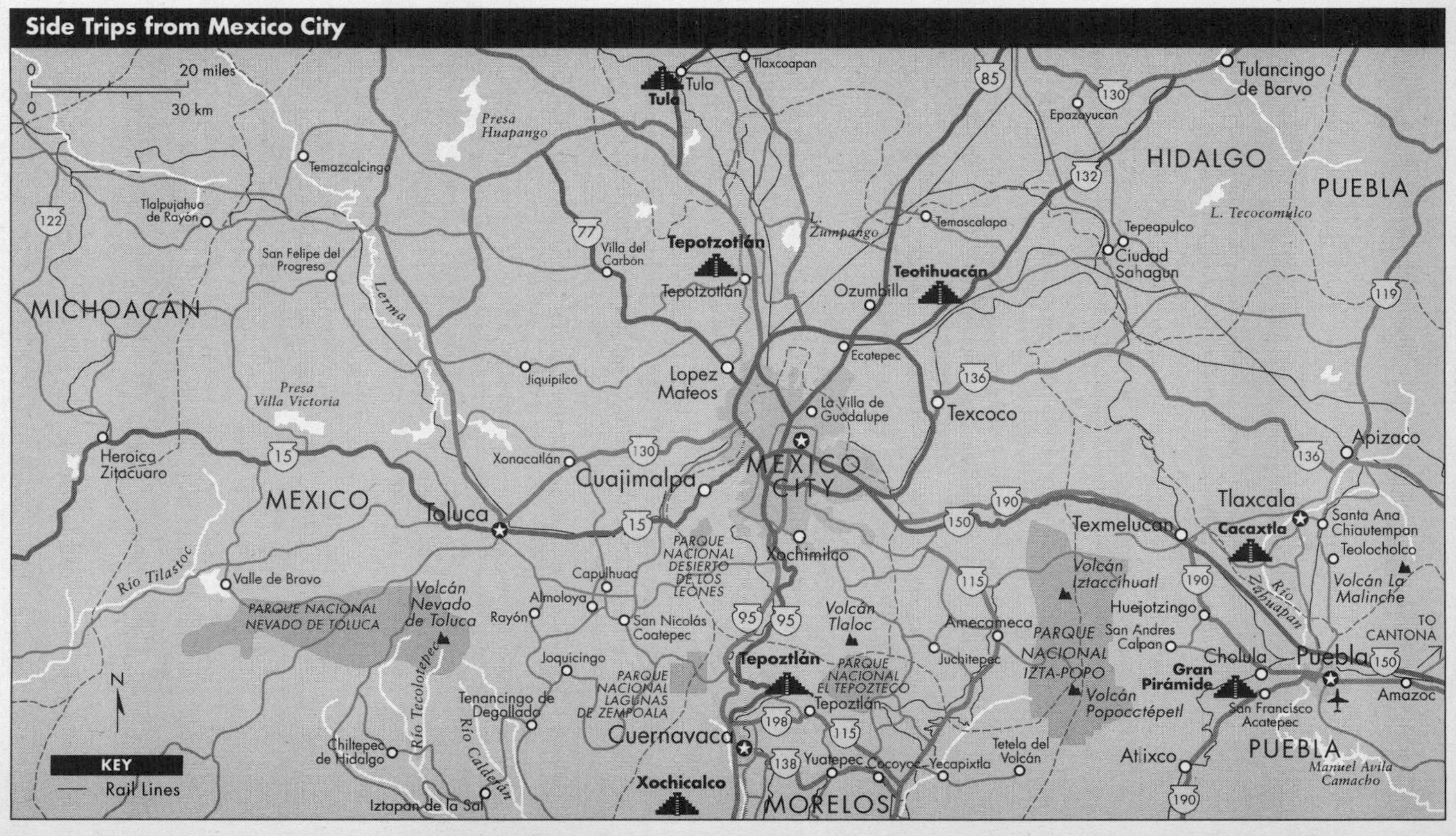
Side Trips from Mexico City
0 20 miles
0 30 km
Tula
Tlaxcoapan
Tulancingo de Barvo
Epazoyucan
HIDALGO
PUEBLA
L. Tecocomulco
Presa Huapango
Temazcalcingo
Tlalpujahua de Rayón
Villa del Carbón
Tepotzotlán
L. Zumpango
Temascalapa
Tepeapulco
Ciudad Sahagun
San Felipe del Progreso
Lerma
Teotihuacán
Ozumbilla
MICHOACÁN
Ecatepec
Jiquipilco
Lopez Mateos
Presa Villa Victoria
La Villa de Guadalupe
Texcoco
Apizaco
Heroica Zitácuaro
Xonacatlán
MEXICO CITY
Cuajimalpa
MEXICO
Toluca
Tlaxcala
Santa Ana Chiautempan
Texmelucan
Cacaxtla
Teolocholco
PARQUE NACIONAL DESIERTO DE LOS LEONES
Xochimilco
Río Tilastoc
Valle de Bravo
Capulhuac
Volcán Iztaccíhuatl
Volcán La Malinche
Río Zahuapan
PARQUE NACIONAL NEVADO DE TOLUCA
Volcán Nevado de Toluca
Almoloya
Rayón
San Nicolás Coatepec
Volcán Tlaloc
Amecameca
Huejotzingo
San Andres Calpan
TO CANTONA
PARQUE NACIONAL IZTA-POPO
Joquicingo
Tepoztlán
PARQUE NACIONAL EL TEPOZTECO
Juchitepec
Cholula
Puebla
Gran Pirámide
Amazoc
PARQUE NACIONAL LAGUNAS DE ZEMPOALA
Volcán Popocatépetl
Río Tecolotepec
Tenancingo de Degollado
Río Calderón
San Francisco Acatepec
Cuernavaca
Chiltepec de Hidalgo
Tetela del Volcán
PUEBLA
KEY
Rail Lines
Yuatepec
Cocoyoc
Yecapixtla
Atlixco
Manuel Avila Camacho
Xochicalco
Iztapan de la Sal
MORELOS
N
85
130
132
119
122
77
136
15
190
150
115
95
198
138

of Teotihuacán's main axis. Estimated to have been built between AD 100 and AD 250, it is the site's oldest structure. Its planes and angles were precisely built in relation to the movement of the sun—marking the equinoxes, for example—and the Pleiades constellation. The 242 steps of the 215-ft pyramid face west, the cardinal point where it was believed that the sun was transformed into a jaguar in order to pass nightly through the darkness of death.

The most impressive sight in Teotihuacán is the 4-km-long (2½-mi-long) **Calzada de los Muertos** (Avenue of the Dead), the main axis of the ancient city along which six major structures lie. The Aztecs gave the avenue this name because of the stepped platforms lining it, which they mistook for tombs. The graceful 126-ft-high **Pirámide de la Luna** (Pyramid of the Moon) dominates the northern end of the avenue, and the compact, square **Ciudadela** (Citadel) flanks the opposite end. More than 4,000 one-story dwellings constructed of adobe and stone and occupied by artisans, warriors, and tradesmen once surrounded the avenue. On the west side of the spacious plaza facing the Pyramid of the Moon are the **Palacio del Quetzalpápalotl** (Palace of the Plumed Butterfly), **Templo de las Conchas Emplumados** (Temple of Plumed Conch Shells), and **Palacio de los Jaguares** (Palace of the Jaguars), which is where the priests resided. The palaces are best known for the spectacular bird and jaguar murals in their winding underground chambers.

The Ciudadela, with the decorative **Templo de Quetzalcóatl y Tlaloc** (Temple of the Plumed Serpent and the Rain God), shows off the plastic arts of the time with its brawny toothed serpent heads jutting out of the temple facade. Quetzalcóatl and Tlaloc together represent the fusion of Earth and sky.

Climbing one pyramid is probably enough for most people. The Pyramid of the Sun is the taller by 89 ft, and affords a spectacular view of the entire area. Wear comfortable clothes (especially shoes) and bring sunscreen or a visored hat when you visit.

Many of the artifacts uncovered at Teotihuacán are on display at the Museum of Anthropology in Mexico City. The **on-site museum** near the Pyramid of the Sun contains fabulous pieces from the archaeological zone—such as the stone sculpture of Tlaloc, the goggle-eyed god of rain; black and green obsidian arrowheads; and simulated burial sites of exalted personages of the empire, their skeletons arranged as they were when discovered.

Seeing the ruins will take two–four hours, depending on how smitten you are by the place—or when your tour bus leaves. ☎ *594/956–0052 or 594/956–0276.* 🎫 *$3.50, free Sun.* 🕓 *Daily 7–6.*

Many tour buses to the ruins stop briefly in **San Agustín Acolmán,** about 20 km (12 mi) south of Teotihuacán, to see the outstanding plateresque (an ornate 16th-century Spanish style) church and ex-convent, now a museum. The original Augustinian church (1539) is noteworthy for its vaulted roof and pointed towers. The ornate cloister and plateresque facade, set off with candelabralike columns, were added a century later by the monks. ☎ *No phone.* 🎫 *$3.*

Dining and Lodging

CATEGORY	COST*
$$$$	over $15
$$$	$10–$15
$$	$5–$10
$	under $5

**per person for a main course at dinner*

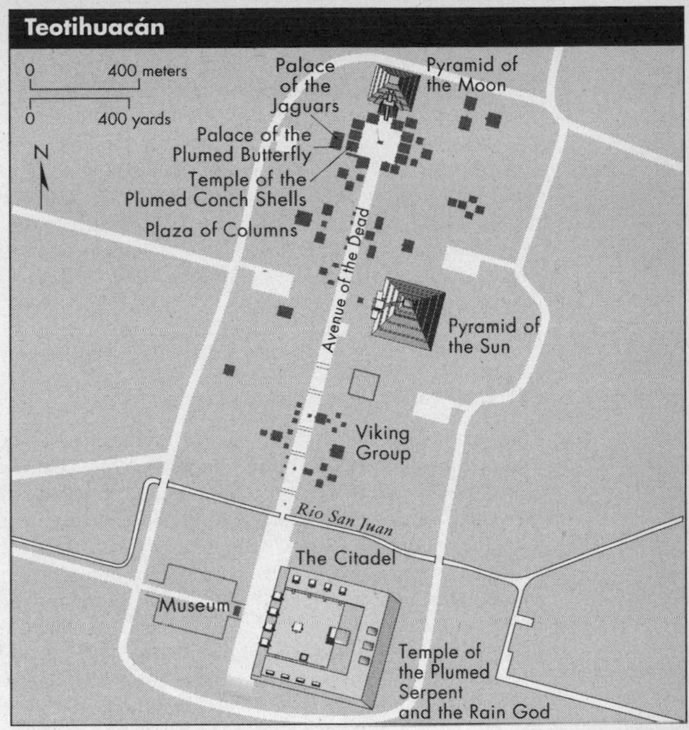

$ Villa Arqueológica. Overnight at the pyramids in this Club Med across the road from the fenced-off site. It has snug rooms and a huge garden and patio restaurant-bar surrounding a pool and tennis court. ✉ *Villa Arqueológica Teotihuacán, San Juan de Teotihuacán 55800,* ☎ *594/956–0909; 55/5254–7077 in Mexico City; 800/514–8244,* WEB *www.teotihuacaninfo.com. 39 rooms. Restaurant, tennis court, pool. AE, MC, V.*

Tepotzotlán

35 km (22 mi) north of Mexico City center.

The **Museo del Virreinato,** which entails a Jesuit church and the School of San Francisco Javier at Tepotzotlán (pronounced teh-po-tzot-*lan*), ranks among the masterpieces of Mexican churrigueresque architecture. The unmitigated Baroque facade of the church (1682) will catch your eye immediately, but you'll also see that inside and out, every square inch has been worked over, like an overdressed Christmas tree. Note the gilded, mirrored Chapel of the Virgin of Loreto. ✉ *Plaza Hidalgo 99,* ☎ *55/5876–0332 or 55/5876–2771,* *$3.*

In pre-Hispanic times, the settlement was an important stop along the salt route—salt was used as money—between Toluca and Texcoco (near Teotihuacán) and had a prestigious school of dance and art. In 1580 four Jesuit priests arrived, learned the local language, and turned the village into a center of evangelization by setting up a school for the young nobles of the conquered nation. The church, of course, was built with Indian slave labor, but as a concession to the slaves, many of the angels decorating the chambers have been painted with dark-skinned indigenous faces. This church is probably the only one in Mexico where you'll find such paintings. In the complex you'll find a museum of religious art, which has a coffee shop. Directly across the square from the church is restaurant **Casa Mago,** (☎ 55/5876–0229) whose owners will proudly recount how Elizabeth Taylor dropped by in 1963 to have a beer.

This village is also famous for its traditional Christmas *pastorela,* a charming and humorous morality play that has been performed for more than 30 years. The play tells the story of the birth of Jesus Christ. A few professional cast members are joined by loads of extras from the town who portray shepherds, angels, and, of course, the Devil. The play is staged every year December 16–23 in the patio of the church at night. Tickets are a little pricey ($35), but include a meal and a tequila; they're available through Ticketmaster (☎ 55/5325–9000 in Mexico City).

Tula

75 km (47 mi) north of Mexico City center.

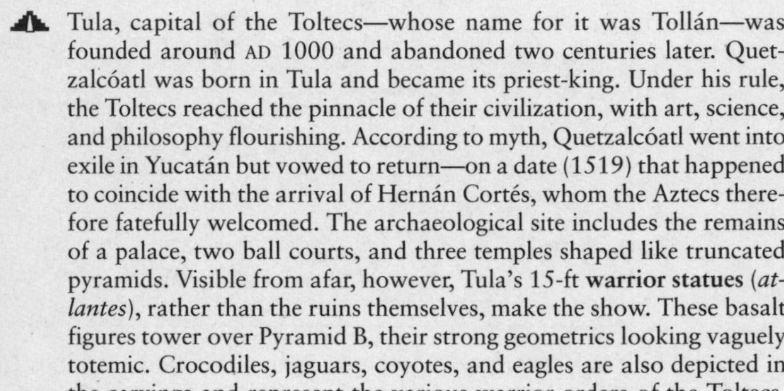

Tula, capital of the Toltecs—whose name for it was Tollán—was founded around AD 1000 and abandoned two centuries later. Quetzalcóatl was born in Tula and became its priest-king. Under his rule, the Toltecs reached the pinnacle of their civilization, with art, science, and philosophy flourishing. According to myth, Quetzalcóatl went into exile in Yucatán but vowed to return—on a date (1519) that happened to coincide with the arrival of Hernán Cortés, whom the Aztecs therefore fatefully welcomed. The archaeological site includes the remains of a palace, two ball courts, and three temples shaped like truncated pyramids. Visible from afar, however, Tula's 15-ft **warrior statues** (*atlantes*), rather than the ruins themselves, make the show. These basalt figures tower over Pyramid B, their strong geometrics looking vaguely totemic. Crocodiles, jaguars, coyotes, and eagles are also depicted in the carvings and represent the various warrior orders of the Toltecs. ☎ *No phone,* WEB *www.tourbymexico.com/hidalgo/tula/tula.htm.* *$2.50, free Sun.* *Tues.–Sun. 9:30–4:30.*

North of Mexico City A to Z

To research prices, get advice from other travelers, and book travel arrangements, visit www.fodors.com.

BUS TRAVEL

Buses run every 20 minutes between 7 AM and 3 PM from the Central de Autobuses del Norte (☎ 55/5587–1552) to **Teotihuacán**; the trip takes about one hour. Tour companies also offer combination visits to Teotihuacán and La Villa de Guadalupe. Línea Teotihuacán (☎ 55/5587–0501) buses leave every 15 minutes from 7 AM; a trip costs about $2.

Buses to **Tula and Tepotzotlán** leave Mexico City every 15 to 30 minutes, also from the Central de Autobuses del Norte. You can make reservations on-line at www.ticketbus.com.mx.

CAR TRAVEL

From the city, follow Periférico Norte to **Tepotzotlán.** After 41 km (25 mi), you'll come to the exit for Tepotzotlán. **Tula** is about 8 km (5 mi) north of Tepotzotlán.

To ensure your safety on the roads, avoid stopping in the middle of nowhere. Watch out for drunk drivers if you are traveling around Easter or Christmas, or during fiesta time. Avoid heavy traffic on weekends when returning from Cuernavaca and Tepoztlán after 4 PM on Sunday.

SOUTH OF MEXICO CITY

In the neighboring state of Morelos, **Cuernavaca** is a sunny weekend retreat for wealthy chilangos and foreigners. Now a thriving city, it has a few good museums, decent nightlife and dining as well as signature excellent hotels and spas. **Tepoztlán** can be visited either as a detour from Cuernavaca, or as a pleasant day- or weekend trip in itself. Surrounded by glorious mountains, this quaint town has a 16th-century Dominican convent, a lively weekend market, its own little pyramid, and plenty of New Age devotees.

Cuernavaca

85 km (53 mi) south of Mexico City center.

The climate in Cuernavaca, a trifling 85 km (53 mi) from Mexico City, changes dramatically to lush and semitropical as the altitude descends almost 2,500 ft. In fact, it was the balmy springlike temperature that first attracted the rich and famous to what has become a resort: Cortés built the first summer place—read palace—here in the 16th century and even the Aztec emperors kept botanical gardens in the area. Spectacular restaurants and hotels await you in addition to the beautiful Borda Gardens and Diego Rivera murals in the Palacio de Cortés. An overnight stay is highly recommended.

Cuernavaca is built on a series of small hills whose streets intertwine in a byzantine maze. If you're not used to driving in San Francisco, say, it's better to get around by cab, especially on weekends, when the number of cars swells to disproportionate numbers.

Most sights are concentrated around the central **Plaza de Armas,** which is surrounded by crafts shops, sidewalk cafés, and government buildings. The square itself is filled with vendors from neighboring villages. Throughout the week they hawk local arts and crafts; on weekends, one side of the square is taken over by stalls in which you'll find silver and gold jewelry and leather goods from elsewhere in the country.

Jardín Juárez (Juárez Gardens), a smaller square across the street from Plaza de Armas, puts on free band concerts Thursday evenings at 6 under its colonial arcade. Either of these two squares is the perfect place for whiling away a pleasant afternoon after a visit to the tourist sights.

The **Plazuela del Zacate** (✉ Galeana and Fray Bartolomé de Las Casas, 2 blocks from the Plaza de Armas) is lively with sidewalk cafés and bars. Beware that the mood can turn aggressive after dark.

The Palacio de Cortés (Cortés's palace-cum-fortress) houses the **Museo de Cuauhnáhuac**—Cuauhnáhuac being the pre-Hispanic name for Cuernavaca—which focuses on Mexican history before and after the Spanish conquest. Diego Rivera painted some of his finest murals on the palace's top floor in 1930–32. Like those of Mexico City's National Palace, the murals dramatize the history and the horrors of the conquest, colonialism, and the revolution. Former U.S. Ambassador to Mexico Dwight Morrow commissioned Rivera to paint the murals for $30,000. ✉ *Juárez and Hidalgo,* ☎ *77/7312–8171.* 🎫 *$3, free Sun.* ⏲ *Tues.–Sun. 9–6.*

The beautiful, spacious **Jardín Borda** (Borda Gardens) is the most visited sight in Cuernavaca. The jardín was designed in the late 18th century by a member of the Borda family—rich miners of French extraction—for one of his relatives; Maximilian and Carlotta visited the gardens frequently. Here Maximilian had a dalliance with the gardener's wife, La India Bonita, who was immortalized in a portrait by a noted painter of the time. Novelist Malcolm Lowry turned the gardens into a sinister symbol in his 1947 *Under the Volcano.* A pleasant café and bookshop round out the gardens. ✉ *Av. Morelos 103, at Hidalgo, 3 blocks west of Palacio de Cortés,* ☎ *77/7312–9237,* WEB *www.arte-cultura-morelos.com.* 🎫 *$1, free Sun.* ⏲ *Tues.–Sun. 10–5:30.*

The **Catedral de la Asunción,** an eclectic structure begun in 1529 by Cortés, is noteworthy for the skull and crossbones over its main entrance and its 17th-century Japanese wall paintings. Paintings inside the **Palacio Municipal,** diagonally opposite the cathedral, depict pre-Hispanic city life. ✉ *Hidalgo and Av. Morelos, opposite Borda Gardens.* ⏲ *Daily 8 AM–6 PM.*

Near Plaza de Armas, the **Robert Brady Museum** is a delightful restored colonial mansion housing a diverse collection of art and artifacts assembled by the late Brady—an artist, antiquarian, and decorator from Fort Dodge, Iowa. You can see ceramics, antique furniture, sculptures, paintings, and tapestries, all beautifully arranged in rooms painted with bright Mexican colors and more than a hint of kitsch. ✉ *Calle Netzahuacóyotl 4, between Hidalgo and Abasolo,* ☎ *77/7318–8554,* WEB *www.geocities.com/bradymuseum.* 🎫 *$2.* ⏲ *Tues.–Sun. 10–6.*

★ The beautifully restored ruins of **Xochicalco** ("place of flowers") are the most fascinating in Morelos state. They sit atop terraced hills overlooking a valley and include a pyramid, ball court, and underground observatory. Showing Maya, Toltec, and Zapotec influences, the ancient fortified city reached its peak between AD 700 and 900. It was of great astronomical significance for the whole region and seems to have been a ceremonial center where scholars met to calibrate their calendars. A solar-powered museum has six rooms of artifacts, including beautiful sculptures of Xochicalco deities found on-site. English-speaking guides have an extensive knowledge of the site and its history, so feel free to ask questions. The museum has a café, bookstore, and gift shop. ✉ *23 mi southwest of Cuernavaca; take Hwy. 95D south; look for the sign for the turnoff,* ☎ *no phone; information in Cuernavaca 77/7312–5955,* WEB *www.tourbymexico.com/morelos/xochical.htm.* 🎫 *$3, free Sun.* ⏲ *Tues.–Sun. 10–5.*

Dining and Lodging

If you've missed getting invited to one of the wealthy weekenders' mansions set in the hills on the edge of town, not to worry: there are a number of remarkable hotels and restaurants with equally remarkable gardens—several of them in restored colonial mansions and even haciendas—where you can get a taste of the high life behind the high stone walls. Many people come here to do just that, and many Cuernavaca hostelries began as restaurants: they added on rooms to satisfy clients who felt too relaxed to drive back to Mexico City after their elaborate meals.

$$ ✕ **Casa Hidalgo.** Offering a marvelous view of the Palacio de Cortés on two floors, Casa Hidalgo's blend of Mexican and international cuisine has become a great hit among the foreigners in town. Begin your evening with *hojaldre de queso de cabra al tamarindo* (goat cheese pastry with tamarind sauce), followed by the *filetón hidalgo* (breaded veal stuffed with serrano ham and manchego cheese). Keep your eye out for the lively saxophonist in the jazz band that plays Thursday through Saturday night. ✉ *Hidalgo 6, Col. Centro,* ☎ *77/7312–9605 or 77/7312–2749,* WEB *www.casahidalgo.com. AE, DC, MC, V.*

$$ ✕ **El Gallinero** (The Chicken Coop). Let yourself be seduced by savorsome starters such as banana-steamed lamb or the generous Hesch salad composed of asparagus, pumpkin seed, goat cheese, and fresh greens. As intimated by the restaurant's name, chicken courses are done to perfection. Portions are not large, so you may still have room for the flambéed wonders and exotic ice creams on the dessert menu. ✉ *Fco. Leyva 94, Col. Centro,* ☎ *77/7312–7425 or 77/7312–7444,* WEB *www.tourbymexico.com/gallinero. AE, MC, V.* ⊙ *No dinner Sun. Closed Mon.*

$$ ✕ **La Pancha.** Perched on the edge of a gulley, dining is picturesque as well as tasty. The fare is beautifully presented and has Italian leanings, but portions are on the small side. Salads are fresh and creative, and the lamb broth is exquisite. You can dine by the pool or in the garden, and the bar space is popular with a younger crowd. ✉ *Rufino Tamayo 26, Col. Acapantzingo,* ☎ *77/7312–8186,* FAX *77/7318–9477,* WEB *www.tourbymexico.com/ctamayo. AE, MC, V.*

$$ ✕ **La Strada.** For a change from Mexican food, come to this old-timer to enjoy a good Italian meal on a colonial candlelit patio. You can't go wrong with the fish dishes, pizzas (ask for the pizza menu), or the house beef specialty—*filete de Estrada,* served with homemade pasta. A guitarist plays Wednesday and Friday night, and the chef whips up weekend specials each Friday. ✉ *Salazar 38, around the corner from Palacio de Cortés,* ☎ *77/7318–6085. AE, MC, V.*

$$$–$$$$ ✕🏨 **Las Mañanitas.** An American expat opened this praised hotel in the 1950s, granting rooms and suites traditional fireplaces, hand-carved bedsteads, hand-painted tiles in the bathrooms, and gilded crafts. The president and European princes stay here, and chilangos drive an hour on weekends just to dine at the restaurant, with its spectacular open-air terraces and garden inhabited by flamingos, peacocks, and African cranes. The *sopa de tortilla* is a classic, and don't miss the black-bottom (chocolate) pie. ✉ *Ricardo Linares 107, 62000,* ☎ *77/7314–1466; 01-800/221–5299 in Mexico; 888/413–9199 from the U.S.,* FAX *77/7318–3672,* WEB *www.lasmananitas.com.mx. 1 room, 21 suites. Restaurant, pool, bar. AE.*

$$$ 🏨 **Camino Real Sumiya.** Woolworth heiress Barbara Hutton built this romantic hideaway amid formal Japanese gardens (including a contemplative rock garden) that contain an original Kabuki theater brought over from Kyoto. A concierge takes care of every need. The rooms, which are equipped with modern furniture, two queen-size beds, and color satellite TVs, are set in the far part of the garden for privacy. Nonguests can eat in the restaurant. ✉ *Col. José Parres, Juitepec, Morelos 62550, take Civac exit on Acapulco Hwy., about 15 mins south of town at Interior del Fracc. Sumiya,* ☎ *77/7320–9199,* FAX *77/7320–9142,* WEB *www.caminoreal.com/sumiya. 163 rooms. 2 restaurants, 7 tennis courts, 2 pools, bar. AE, DC, MC, V.*

$$ 🏨 **Clarion Cuernavaca Racquet Club.** This posh tennis club–turned–hotel is less expensive than most lodgings, and its appeal is in its beautiful gardens and spacious two-room suites equipped with romantic fireplaces. Families converge here on weekends. The restaurant admits nonguests. ✉ *Francisco Villa 100, Fracc. Rancho Cortés, 62120,* ☎ *77/7311–2400,* FAX *77/7317–5483. 39 rooms, 13 suites. Restaurant, 9 tennis courts, pool, bar. AE, DC, MC, V.*

$$ 🏨 **Hacienda de Cortés.** This old hacienda dates from the 16th century and *did* belong to the conquistador. Wandering at dusk around the secret gardens and discovering cascades, fountains, and sculptures is an enchanting experience. Rooms are decorated in traditional Mexican furnishings; they have lovely patios and gardens that will beckon you outdoors. Nonguests can eat in the restaurant, and concerts of classical music are often held on weekends. ✉ *Plaza Kennedy 90, Col. At-*

lacomulco, 62250, ☎ *77/7315–8844,* FAX *77/7315–0035,* WEB *www.haciendadecortes.com. 22 rooms. Restaurant, pool, bar. MC, V.*

$$ **Hacienda San Gabriel de las Palmas.** A colorful history pervades the walls of this grand hacienda built under the orders of Cortés in 1529. A palm-lined promenade leads you into the pristine garden and stables, and the pool is a haven surrounded by lush vegetation. Suites are laden with art objects and decorated with period furnishings. The restaurant makes an ideal lunch stop for those visiting the Xochicalco ruins. Its location in Morelos state but outside Cuernavaca facilitates visits to Taxco, the caves of Cacahuamilpa, and the lake of Tequesquitengo. ✉ *Km 41.8 Carretera Federal Cuernavaca–Chilpancingo, Amacuzac, Morelos 62642,* ☎ *55/5616–6032 in Mexico City; 800/347–2642,* FAX *55/5550–0657 in Mexico City,* WEB *www.hacienda-sangabriel.com.mx. 13 suites. Restaurant, tennis court, pool, croquet, horseback riding, squash, bar. AE, MC, V.*

Tepoztlán

75 km (47 mi) south of Mexico City center.

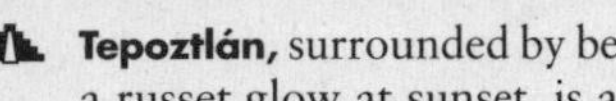

Tepoztlán, surrounded by beautiful sandstone monoliths that throw off a russet glow at sunset, is a magical place. It attracts practitioners of yoga, meditation, crystal healing, herbal medicine, astrology, and native sorcery and is a favorite for UFO congresses. The New Age attractions have struck a comfortable balance with traditional Mexican life, however, and Tepoztlán accommodates both a gentle affluence marked by Internet cafés and barefoot Indian women selling local produce and chatting in indigenous tongues. This town of 13,000, with a village atmosphere and cobblestone streets, is primarily known for its tiny **Tepozteco pyramid,** probably of Aztec origin and perched on top of a hill; hundreds of people climb it every weekend. Although steep, the hour-long trek is not arduous as long as you wear comfortable shoes. Near the summit, however, you have to scale a ladder, so it may not be appropriate for small children. The view over the valley is delightful. Just remember that it closes at 4:30, so set out no later than 3.

Other points of interest include the lively **weekend market,** with its fruits, vegetables, and crafts (a slightly smaller version is held on Wednesday), the **dances** held during Mardi Gras, and the pre-Lenten Carnival, when celebrants don bright masks depicting birds, animals, and Christian figures. Tepoztlán's landmark is the multibuttressed 1559 **Templo y Ex-Convento de la Natividad de la Virgen María** (Temple and Ex-Convent of the Birth of the Virgin Mary), its fine paneled doors adorned with Indian motifs. Yearly on September 8 the faithful assemble here to celebrate the birth of the Virgin Mary, the town's patron saint. The date also commemorates the baptism of the legendary ruler Tepoztecatl, for whom the pyramid is named; there's a colorful indigenous festival held at the ruins the day before. Both pyramid and convent are closed Monday. For more information, call the Morelos State Tourist Office (☎ 77/7314–3872).

Tepoztlán drew national attention in the 1990s, when townspeople stormed the city hall and took government officials hostage to protest the proposed building of a mega–golf resort on their revered Tepozteco terrain. They eventually ousted the mayor and town police and continued protesting until the developers abandoned the project. They finally elected a member of the Party of the Democratic Revolution, but governed themselves for more than a year.

Close-Up

THE TEMAZCAL: TRADITIONAL MEDICINE MAKES A COMEBACK

HERBAL MEDICINE REMAINS an integral part of Mexican life, and still predominates in remote areas where modern medicines are hard to come by or too expensive for rural laborers. Even in the capital, most markets will have distinctive stalls piled with curative herbs and plants. Vendors will happily tell you how to prepare teas, poultices, and steam baths for inhalation.

The Aztecs were excellent botanists, and their extensive knowledge impressed the Spanish, who borrowed from Mexico's indigenous herbolarium and catalogued the intriguing new plants. Consequently, medicine remains one of the few examples of cultural practices and indigenous wisdom that has not been lost to history. Visitors to the capital can find a very informative display of medicinal plants used by the Aztecs in the Museum of Medicine, in the former Palace of the Inquisition, at the northwest corner of Plaza Santo Domingo.

A rich variety of herbs is harvested in the 300 rural communities of the fertile state of Morelos, where *curanderos* (natural healers) flock to the markets on weekends to offer advice and sell their concoctions. Armed with their wares and a good patter, they line the busier roads, and sometimes get a chance to hawk on buses. Stores in the state capital, Cuernavaca, sell natural antidotes for every ailment imaginable and potions for sexual prowess, lightening the skin, colic in babies, and IQ enhancement.

Chamanes (shamans) and healers abound at the weekend market in the main square of the picturesque mountain village of Tepoztlán. Long known for its *brujos* (witches), Tepoztlán continues to experience a boom in spiritual retreats and New Age shops. Visitors can benefit from the healing overload without getting hoodwinked by booking a session in one of the many good *temazcales* (Aztec sweat lodges) in town, such as the one in the elegant Posada del Tepozteco hotel on Calle del Paraíso, or at an excellent retreat, Hostal de la Luz on the road to Amatlán.

The temazcal is a "bath of cleansing" for body, mind, and spirit; a session consists of a ritual that lasts at least an hour, ideally (for first-timers) with a guide. Temazcales are igloo-shaped clay buildings, round so as not to impede the flow of energy. They usually seat 6 to 12 people, who can participate either naked or in a bathing suit. Each guide develops his own style, under the tutelage of a shaman, so practices vary. In general, your aura (or energy field) is cleaned with a bunch of plants before you enter the temazcal, so that you start off as pure as possible. You will have a fistful of the same plants—usually rosemary, sweet basil, or eucalyptus—to slap or rub against your skin. You walk in a clockwise direction and take your place, and water is poured over red-hot stones in the middle to create the steam. Usually silence is maintained, although the guide may chant or pray, often in Nahuatl. The procedure ends with a warm shower followed by a cold one to close the pores.

The experience helps eliminate toxins, cure inflammations, ease pains in the joints, and relieve stress. Consequently, temazcales are growing in popularity, even drawing city executives from the capital on the weekends. You can find some of the most outstanding temazcales in Morelos's top spas, such as the Misión del Sol in Jiutepec and Hostería las Quintas in Cuernavaca. Less pricey are El Centro Mayahuel in Ahuacatitlán, or the temazcales of Teresa Contreras or Dr. Horacio Rojas in Cuernavaca. You could also try La Casa de los Árboles in Zacualpan de Amilpas.

— Barbara Kastelein

Dining and Lodging

$ ✕ **Axitla.** This smart establishment is surrounded by ponds and bridges right in the skirts of the mountain (where it can get chilly as the sun sets). Amicable gringo William Grady lets his international culinary leanings inspire his creations; try one of the generous salads and the superb baked bass *a la talla* (charcoal grilled, with a creamy sauce). ✉ *Av. del Tepozteco, at the road to the Pyramid,* ☎ *739/395–0519 or 739/395–2555. MC, V. No dinner.*

$ ✕ **Los Colorines.** Folksy and full of colored *papel picado* (frilly paper cutouts), this popular fonda serves great bean soup, stuffed chilies, and grilled meat from an attractive open kitchen. Special dishes include *huauzontles* (a fine, broccoli-like vegetable you scrape from the stalk with your teeth) and *sopa de colorín,* a soup made from the red blossom of the flower that gives the cheerful family restaurant its name. ✉ *Av. del Tepozteco 13,* ☎ *739/395–0198. No credit cards. No dinner Sun.*

$ ✕ **La Luna Mextli.** Across the road from the church, La Luna is one of the oldest restaurants in the village. Its sunny patio is especially inviting for laid-back breakfasts and slow leafing through the newspaper. Wooden masks and flying mermaids provide the principal adornment, and local women patting fresh tortillas add to the ambience. ✉ *Av. Revolución 16,* ☎ *739/395–1114 or 739/395–0800. AE, MC, V. No breakfast weekdays.*

$$ 🏨 **Posada del Tepozteco.** Enjoy splendid views of both the village and the pyramid as you stroll from the resort's two pools or tennis court to terraced gardens bursting with bougainvillea. A favorite for weddings and with honeymooners, the Posada is also a good place for children, with a trampoline, swings, a pair of rabbits discreetly tucked away in the lower garden, and a video room with giant-screen TV. Most rooms have balconies and Jacuzzis, and a temazcal steam room is available. Reservations for weekend stays should be made two weeks in advance. ✉ *Calle del Paraíso 3, 62520,* ☎ *739/395–0010,* FAX *739/395–0323. 19 rooms. Restaurant, tennis court, 2 pools, massage, steam room, bar, playground. AE, MC, V.*

South of Mexico City A to Z

To research prices, get advice from other travelers, and book travel arrangements, visit www.fodors.com.

BUS TRAVEL

Buses run every 10 minutes to Cuernavaca and every 15 minutes to Tepoztlán from Mexico City's Metro Taxqueña bus station. **Pullman de Morelos** (☎ 55/5549–3505 in Mexico City; 77/7318–4638 in Cuernavaca) is the most reliable bus line, with the most frequent service.

CAR TRAVEL

To head south by car, find the Periférico Sur, turn left (south) on Viaducto Tlalpán, and watch for signs to **Cuernavaca** in about a half hour. The *cuota* (toll road, Route 95D) costs about $10 but is much faster than the *carretera libre* (free road, Route 95). On Route 95D, it will take you about 1½ hours to cover 85 km (53 mi).

Tepoztlán is 26 km (16 mi) east of Cuernavaca via Route 95D.

VISITOR INFORMATION

The Morelos State Tourist Office in Cuernavaca is open weekdays 8–8 and 9–2 on Saturdays; weekends there's a stand in the square opposite the Universal cafeteria from 10 to 4.

➤ TOURIST INFORMATION: **Morelos State Tourist Office** (✉ Av. Morelos Sur 187, Colonia Las Palmas, ☎ 77/7314–3872, WEB www.turismomorelos.com.mx).

SOUTHEAST OF MEXICO CITY

Well-preserved colonial Puebla was once the center of the Spanish tile industry. Nearby Cholula is a sacred spot in ancient Mexico and home to an important pyramid and scores of churches. On the way you can size up the volcanoes, Popocatépetl (pronounced poh-poh-kah-*teh*-pettle) and Iztaccíhuatl (pronounced ees-tah-*see*-wattle), which tower over the valley. On your way back to the capital, leave time—an entire day would be best—to visit the city of Tlaxcala, with its rare church and former convent, and a marvelous archaeological site nearby.

The Volcanoes

Leaving Mexico City on Route 150D (known as the Carretera to Puebla or the Puebla Highway), you'll see **Popocatépetl** and **Iztaccíhuatl** to your right—if the clouds and smog allow. "Popo," 17,887 ft high, is the pointed volcano farther away, usually topped with a plume of smoke; "Izta" is the larger, rugged one covered with snow. Popo last erupted in 1802, but has seen a renewed period of activity since the mid-1990s; a moderate eruption in 2000 resulted in the temporary evacuation of nearby villagers. Popo remains off-limits for climbing and Izta can be explored only up to the Paso de Cortés. Check with the U.S. State Department for the latest developments, as even the Parque Nacional, a verdant pine forest, may no longer be recommended for picnics. A useful English-language Web site is www.txinfinet.com/mader/ecotravel/mexico/mexparks.html.

The legend states that Popocatépetl, an Aztec warrior, had been sent by the emperor—father of his beloved Iztaccíhuatl—to bring back the head of a feared enemy in order to win Iztaccíhuatl's hand. He returned triumphantly only to find that Iztaccíhuatl had killed herself, believing him dead. The grief-stricken Popo laid out her body on a small knoll and lit an eternal torch that he watches over, kneeling. Each of Iztaccíhuatl's four peaks is named for a different part of her body, and its silhouette conjures up its nickname, "Sleeping Woman."

Lodging

$ **Los Volcanes.** This venerable hotel is about an hour from Popocatépetl and Iztaccíhuatl, but it's the closest one and has fine views of both volcanoes. All 38 rustic rooms have potbellied stoves. The restaurant is open only for Easter and at the end of the year. ✉ *Blvd. Los Volcanes, Popo Park 56970, at Km 66.5 on Carretera Mexico–Cuautla,* ☎ *597/976–0294. 40 rooms. Restaurant, in-room safes, dance club, free parking; no room phones. MC, V.*

Cholula and the Colonial Treasures of Puebla State

Before the Spanish Conquest, Cholula, 8 km (5 mi) west of Puebla, reportedly had hundreds of temples and rivaled Teotihuacán as a cultural and ceremonial center. The *mercado santuario* (market sanctuary) system was developed here in AD 1200, whereby satellite cities of Cholula exchanged cultural ideas and began trading with the Gulf region and Oaxaca. On his arrival, Cortés ordered every temple destroyed, and a church built in its place. The town fathers claim that Cholula has 365 church cupolas, one for every day in the year.

Thanks in part to the student presence at the respected Universidad de las Americas in Cholula, some pleasant eateries (with menus in English) have popped up downtown. The liveliest time to visit Cholula is Sunday and Wednesday, which are market days. For a unique experience, stop and knock on the door of the gaudy and eccentric house on your left as you approach the center of town on the main route (known as the Carretera a Cholula). A famous local witch and his various companions live here; depending on his mood, visitors may enter to hear their fortune told.

Although many of the 39 churches in Cholula—and the 128 in the surrounding area—are in poor condition, work is gradually taking place to restore and preserve this region's heritage. Two astonishing churches lie about 6½ km (4 mi) south of town, in **San Francisco Acatepec** and **Santa María Tonantzintla.**

If you would like to spend some time in Cholula, consider the attractive Club Med villas (WEB www.come2clubmed.com/mexican_villas.htm) or ask Gregorio Porras at the the local tourist office (☎ 22/2247–3116) for other accommodations.

The **Gran Pirámide** (Great Pyramid) was the centerpiece of Olmec, Toltec, and Aztec religious centers and is, by volume, the largest pyramid in the world. It consists of seven superimposed structures (one for every tribe) connected by tunnels and stairways. The Spaniards built a chapel to **Nuestra Señora de los Remedios** (Our Lady of the Remedies) on top of it. Almost toppled by a quake in 1999, it was being restored at this writing. Behind the pyramid is a vast 43-acre temple complex, once dedicated to Quetzalcóatl. From the top of the pyramid, or from the smaller, earth-covered pyramid in front of it, you have a clear view of the surrounding area. Note the many churches, color-coded by period: oxidized red was used in the 16th century, yellow in the 17th and 18th, and pastel colors in the 19th. You can obtain an English-language guide for $6. ✉ *Calzada San Andrés at Calle 2 Nte.,* ☎ *22/2247–9081,* *$3 includes museum, free Sun.* ⏲ *Daily 9–6.*

The huge **Ex-Convento de San Gabriel** is an impressive structure that includes three churches. The most unusual is the Moorish-style **Capilla Real,** with 49 domes. It was built in 1540 and originally was open on one side, to facilitate conversion of huge masses of people. About 20 Franciscan monks still live in one part of the premises, so be respectful of their privacy. ✉ *2 Norte s/n, east of Cholula Zócalo,* ☎ *no phone.* ⏲ *10–12:30 and 4:30–6.*

★ **San Francisco Acatepec** has one of the most stunning, well-preserved churches in the country. Covered with Puebla tiles, it is said to have the most ornate rococo Poblano facade in Mexico. ✉ *6½ km (4 mi) south of Cholula,* ☎ *no phone.*

★ The church of **Santa María Tonantzintla**'s polychrome wood-and-stucco carvings—inset columns, altarpieces, and the main archway—are the essence of churrigueresque. Set off by ornate gold-leaf figures of plant forms, angels, and saints, the carvings were made by local craftspeople. The church slipped into a new coat of paint in 2002. Puebla municipal tourism officers run excellent day tours from $18 to $50. ✉ *Av. Reforma, 5 km (3 mi) south of Cholula.* ⏲ *9–6.*

Huejotzingo is a must for lovers of religious art and history. The sleepy town, which offers pristine views of Iztaccíhuatl, is known for its cider but is truly swamped with visitors only at carnival time (on the Saturday before Ash Wednesday and on Shrove Tuesday). The battle against the French is reenacted on May 5; the concomitant masked dance comes closer to recalling the festivities of the agricultural year of Tlaloc (the Aztec rain god). The town also produces a Festival of Cider from September 22 to October 2.

Famous for the well chapels at its four angles, the **Ex-Convento de Huejotzingo** is a 16th-century Franciscan monastery on the Plaza de Huejotzingo. Note the marvelous carved stonework and the complete altar paintings. Original onyx windows allow a mysterious light to filter through, onto the frescos. The museum on the side documents Spanish missions in the area, but information is poor and not available in English. ⊠ *Plazuela de San Francisco de Asís s/n, 15 km (9 mi) northwest of Cholula on Hwy. 150.* 🎫 *$2.* ⏲ *Monastery, daily 8–7; museum, Tues.–Sun. 10–4:30, closed Mon.*

Africam Safari. A 25-minute drive from the city brings you to vampire bats, Bengal tigers, zebras, and chimps, as well as a well-kept botanical garden. Check dates for the occasional night safaris that give visitors a chance to see the big cats and other nocturnal creatures at their most perky. ⊠ *Km 16.5 on the road to Valsequillo, Puebla,* ☎ *22/2236–1212 or 11/2235–8713; 55/5575–2731 in Mexico City,* WEB *www.africamsafari.com.* 🎫 *$7.50.* ⏲ *10–5.*

Puebla

120 km (75 mi) east of Mexico City center.

Maize was first cultivated in the Tehuacán Valley around 5000 BC. Later, the region was a crossroads for many Mesoamerican cultures, including the Olmecs and Totonacs. The young Spanish colony Puebla had the first glass factory, the first textile mill, and the second hospital. The battle of May 5, 1862—resulting in a short-lived victory against French invaders—took place north of town. A procession is the highlight of celebrations held to commemorate that date every Cinco de Mayo, the national holiday. Throughout the month of May bullfights are held in the city's quaint and intimate bullring.

Puebla (the fourth-largest city in Mexico) today retains a strong conservative religious element. Overflowing with religious structures, this city probably has more ex-convents and monasteries, chapels, and churches per square mile than anywhere else in the country. In fact, the valley of Puebla, which includes Cholula, was said to have 224 churches and 10 convents and monasteries in its heyday.

The city is full of idiosyncratic Baroque structures built with red bricks, gray stone, white stucco, and the beautiful Talavera tiles produced from local clay. Puebla is one of the few cities in Mexico declared a Patrimony of Humanities site by the United Nations because of the splendor of its colonial architecture. With a population approaching 2 million, it remains a prosperous and civilized town, with textiles, ceramics, and a Volkswagen plant bolstering the local economy. An international convention center (El Centro de Convenciones Puebla; ☎ 22/2223–6400, WEB www.convenciones-puebla.com.mx) has provided a further boost, and good restaurants and hotels are proliferating. Streets are safe and women will feel comfortable walking alone. For information on ecotourism in the region, go to Puebla ecotourism: www.amtave.com/amtave/estados/puebla.ph.

7 **Barrio del Artista.** You can watch painters and sculptors working in the galleries here 10–6 daily. You may also purchase pieces, or continue walking down Calle 8 Norte and buy Talavera pottery, cheaper copies of Talavera, and other local crafts and souvenirs from the dozens of small stores and street vendors along the way. ⊠ *Calle 8 Nte. and Av. 6 Ote.* ⏲ *10–4:30.*

6 **La Calle de las Dulces** (or Calle de Santa Clara). Puebla is famous for *camote,* a popular candy made from sweet potatoes and fruit. Sweets Street is lined with shops competing to sell a wide variety of freshly made camote and many other sugary treats in the shape of sombreros,

Barrio del Artista 7
La Calle de las Dulces . . .6
Callejón de los Sapos . . .12
Catedral 8
Centro Cultural Santa Rosa . .3
Ex-Convento Secreto de Santa Mónica 4
Iglesia de Santo Domingo 5
Mercado de Artesaníans El Parián 9
Museo Amparo 10
Museo Nacional de los Ferrocarriles . .1
Museo-Taller Erasto Cortès 11
Uriarte Talavera 2

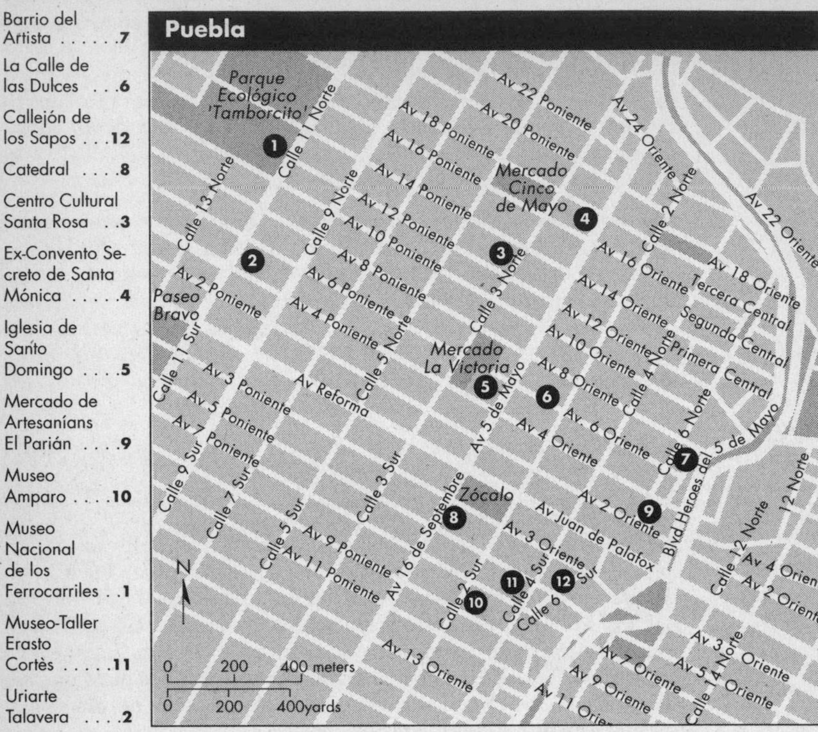

guitars, sacred hearts, and pistols. Packed in pretty baskets, these make good presents. Don't fail to try the cookies you see in Puebla—they're even more delicious than they look. ✉ *Av. 6 Ote. between Av. 5 de Mayo and Calle 4 Nte.* ⏲ *9–8.*

⓬ **Callejón de los Sapos.** Toad Alley cuts diagonally behind the cathedral, and the attached square, Plazuela de los Sapos, is the up-and-coming antiques market and café area for the trendy. It brims with bright young things on Sunday and is a good place to hang out for a beer and live music on Friday and Saturday nights. ✉ *Av. 5 Ote. and 6 Sur.* ⏲ *10–7.*

❽ **Catedral.** The cathedral was partially financed by Puebla's most famous son, Bishop Juan de Palafox y Mendoza—who donated his personal fortune to build its famous tower, the second-largest church tower in the country. Palafox was the illegitimate son of a Spanish nobleman who grew up poor but inherited his father's wealth. Onyx, marble, and gold adorn the cathedral's high altar, designed by Mexico's most illustrious colonial architect, Manuel Tolsá. ✉ *Calle 2 Sur, south of the Zócalo.* ⏲ *10–6.*

❸ **Centro Cultural Santa Rosa.** The colonial former convent houses a museum of crafts from the state's seven regions; wandering through the well-designed rooms will give you a good introduction to traditional Mexican arts. The museum also contains the intricately tiled kitchen where Puebla's renowned chocolate mole sauce is believed to have been invented—by the nuns as a surprise for their demanding gourmet bishop. ✉ *Av. 14 Pte. between Calles 3 and 5 Nte.,* ☎ *22/2232–9242 or 22/2232–7792.* 🎟 *$1.* ⏲ *Tues.–Sun. 10–5.*

❹ **Ex-Convento Secreto de Santa Mónica.** Quirky and large, the ex-convent originally opened in 1688 as a spiritual refuge for women whose husbands were away on business. Despite the Reform Laws of the 1850s, it functioned as a convent until 1934, requiring that the nuns withdraw completely from the outside world. You can see the peepholes through which the nuns watched mass in the church next door and tour the crypt where they are buried. Curiosities include the gruesome display of the preserved heart of the convent's founder, and the velvet paintings in the *Sala de los Terciopelos* in which the feet and faces seem to change position as you view them from different angles. ✉ *Av. 18 Pte. 103, near 5 de Mayo,* ☎ *22/2232–0178.* 🎟 *$2.* ⏲ *Tues.–Sun. 9–6.*

5 **Iglesia de Santo Domingo** (Santo Domingo Church). The beautiful church is especially famous for its overwhelming **Rosary Chapel,** where almost every inch of the walls, ceilings, and altar is covered with gilded carvings and sculpture. Dominican friars arrived in Puebla as early as 1534, only 13 years after the conquest, and the chapel of La Tercera Orden (The Third Order) was originally called "the chapel of the dark-skinned," so designated for the mixed-race population that shortly ensued. ✉ *Av. Cinco de Mayo at Av. 4 Pte.* ⏲ *10–6.*

9 **Mercado de Artesanías El Parián.** This attractive collection of stalls and shops sells regional craftwork, such as onyx, Talavera, silverware, basketwork, clothing, papier-mâché figurines, candles, and sweets. Also good for getting a bite to eat. ✉ *Av. 4 Ote. and 6 Nte.* ⏲ *Daily 10–7:30.*

★ 10 **Museo Amparo.** Home to the private collection of pre-Columbian and colonial art of Mexican banker and philanthropist Manuel Espinoza Yglesias, the museum was a pioneer in interactive information systems. Accessible (in four different languages) and modern, it exhibits unforgettable pieces from diverse regions of the country. Displays are organized clearly and artfully, with evocative videos and ancient poems. Temporary exhibitions often showcase current international work, as well as the museum's own collection of contemporary and modern pieces. The museum also functions as a cultural center and library, hosting events and conferences. One of the most beautiful museums in Mexico, it does full justice to its philosophy that art is "an aesthetic through which humanity has endeavored to represent and understand the world." ✉ *Calle 2 Sur at Av. 9 Ote.,* ☎ *22/2246–4646,* FAX *22/2246–6333,* WEB *www.museoamparo.com.* 🎟 *$2.50, free Mon.* ⏲ *Wed.–Mon. 10–6.*

1 **Museo Nacional de los Ferrocarriles** (National Railway Museum). Housed in the shell of a 19th-century railway station, this quaint museum offers a nostalgic treat. Period engines sit on the disused platforms. ✉ *Calle 11 Nte. and 12 Pte.,* ☎ *22/2232–4988,* FAX *22/2232–7848.* 🎟 *Free.* ⏲ *Tues.–Sun. 10–5.*

11 **Museo-Taller Erasto Cortés.** Erasto Cotés Juárez was Puebla's most important 20th-century artist. This museum of modern art opened its doors in 2000 as a real contribution to the Mexican scene: temporary exhibitions showcase up-and-coming international artists, and the permanent display of Cortés' vibrant work is a pleasure. You will find a shop and a library, as well as children's art programs. ✉ *7 Ote. 4 Sur, Centro,* ☎ *22/2232–1277 or 22/2232–1966.* 🎟 *Free, temporary exhibitions $1.20.* ⏲ *Tues.–Sun. 10–5.*

2 **Uriarte Talavera.** This pottery factory was founded in 1824 and is one of the few authentic Talavera workshops left today. To be authentic, the pieces must be hand-painted in intricate designs with natural dyes derived from minerals, which is why only five colors are used: blue, black, yellow, green, and a reddish pink. There's a shop on site, and free tours of the factory are given Monday through Saturday 10–2. ✉ *Av. 4 Pte. 911, between Avs. 9 and 11 Nte.,* ☎ *22/2232–1598,* FAX *22/2242–2943,* WEB *www.uriartetalavera.com.* ⏲ *Weekdays 9–6:30, Sat. 10–6:30, Sun. 11–6.*

Dining and Lodging

Puebla is noted for its regional cuisine. Two of Mexico's most popular dishes were supposedly created here to celebrate special occasions. One is mole, a sauce made with as many as 100 ingredients, the best-known mole being one with bitter chocolate. The other local specialty, believed to have been initiated by the town's nuns, is *chiles en nogada,* a green poblano chili filled with ground meats, fruits, and nuts, then covered with a sauce of chopped walnuts and cream, and topped with red pomegranate seeds; the colors represent the red, green, and white of the Mexican flag.

For after-dinner drinks, head to Avenida Juárez. Mariachis keep the songs coming at **La Cantina de Los Remedios** (✉ Av. Juárez 2504, Col. la Paz, ☎ 22/2249–0843).

$$ ✕ **Fonda de Santa Clara.** Founded in 1965, this popular spot is a classic, with two branches in Puebla (other branches are in Acapulco and Mexico City). Typical regional fare is offered in a super setting in the Puebla locales. The original has a cozy and home-style atmosphere and is only a few blocks from the zócalo; the larger newcomer (Paseo Bravo) has a shop and banquet hall attached, but still maintains a very attractive colonial flavor. It's open for breakfast, lunch, and dinner. ✉ *Calle 3 Pte. 307,* ☎ *22/2242–2659,* FAX *22/2232–7674;* ✉ *Paseo Bravo, Calle 3 Pte. 920,* ☎ *22/2246–1919,* FAX *22/2232–0503, MC, V.*

$$ ✕ **La Piccola Italia.** The business lunch crowd jostles with local notable families in this prestigious restaurant, whose specialty is pasta. A display of homemade varieties greets you in the entranceway and owner Gino has no doubts you will be more than happy with the wide range of choices. ✉ *Teziutlán Nte. 1, Col. La Paz,* ☎ *22/2231–3220,* FAX *22/2230–4833.*

$ ✕ **Las Bodegas del Molino.** In a 16th-century hacienda at the edge of town, this elegant restaurant is notable for both its setting and its fine cuisine. If you're not sure about mole, give it a try here: the same woman has been making it since 1982, and her seductive, fruity blend will probably win you over. Make time to request a tour (Matthijs de Kool speaks excellent English) of the fabulous premises, which are being renovated with admirable care. Romantics should book a private dinner in the "French Room." ✉ *Molino de San José del Puente,* ☎ *22/2249–0483 or 22/2249–0399. AE, MC, V.*

$ ✕ **La Tecla.** Modish, spacious design, and decently priced nouvelle Mexican cuisine has made this branch of the Mexico City restaurant a hit in Puebla. Try the duck tacos in green sauce, or fillet of veal bathed in corn fungus and Roquefort. ✉ *Ave. Juárez 1909, between 19 and 21 Sur,* ☎ *22/2246–2616,* FAX *22/2246–6066. AE, MC, V.*

$ ★ ✕ **Villa Rica.** This buzzing eatery evokes its sister restaurant in Veracruz, one of the best seafood restaurants in the country. Elegant wooden decor and a grand thatched roof create the seaside palapa ambience, and live music makes Villa Rica a firm lunchtime favorite. Noticeably fresh products are fused to produce specialties such as *chilpachole* (crabmeat soup flavored with epazote) and conch fillet. You can also enjoy mussels, grouper, crab claws, and octopus prepared as you wish. In addition to kids' menus and, a game area, there is free weekend nanny service from 2 to 6. ✉ *Calle 14 Sur 3509, Col. Anzures,* ☎ *22/2211–2060 or 22/2211–2061,* FAX *22/2211–2062. AE, DC, MC, V.*

$$ ✕🏨 **Mesón Sacristía de la Compañía.** Each individually decorated room in this converted colonial mansion is outfitted with antiques that are also for sale. The rich colors of folk art pervade the cozy but stylish bar, and the patio is a feast for the eyes. The attractive restaurant serves tasty regional dishes. Breakfast is included in the room rate. ✉ *Calle 6 Sur 304, at Callejón de los Sapos, 72000,* ☎ *22/2242–3554,* FAX *22/*

2232–4513, WEB *www.mesones-sacristia.com. 9 rooms. Restaurant, bar. AE, MC, V.*

$$$ **Mesón Sacristía de Capuchinas.** In the center of Puebla, but very quiet, this 17th-century building is a luxurious sanctuary if you want to rest without distractions or disturbances. The suites have thick walls and are decorated in a contemporary style. The staff is friendly and guests are surrounded by antiques and artwork. ✉ *Av. 9 Ote. 16, 72000,* ☎ *22/2232–8088 or 22/2246–6084,* WEB *www.g-networks.net/sacristia. 7 suites. Restaurant, bar. AE, MC, V.*

$$ ★ **Camino Real.** The accommodations are deluxe in this former 16th-century convent, with luminous restored fresco murals and heaps of historical character. Each room is appointed differently, based on the original look, which varied depending on each nun's donation to the order. The junior suite was once the convent's chapel, and the presidential suite has original 16th-century gilded furnishings and carpeting. The entire property has been sensitively restored, and the staff is warm and professional. ✉ *Av. 7 Pte. 105, 72000,* ☎ *22/2229–0909, 22/2229–0910, or 800/901–2300,* FAX *22/2232–9251,* WEB *www.caminoreal.com/puebla. 70 rooms, 9 suites. 2 restaurants, in-room data ports, bar, business services. AE, DC, MC, V.*

$$ **El Mesón del Ángel.** At the city's entrance—a bit far from the attractions—is this quiet and cheery hotel with spacious and colorful gardens. The executive area is designed for business travelers; it consists of a separate building with 70 rooms and its own pool, restaurant, and business area. Breakfast is included in room rates. ✉ *Av. Hermanos Serdan 807, 72100,* ☎ *22/2223–8300 or 800/223–3300,* FAX *22/2223–8301,* WEB *www.mesondelangel.com.mx. 192 rooms. Restaurant, room service, in-room safes, 2 pools, bar, business services, meeting rooms. AE, DC, MC, V.*

$ **Royalty.** Small and well maintained, this hotel on the main square is one of the less expensive choices in Puebla. ✉ *Portal Hidalgo 8, 72000,* ☎ *22/2242–4740,* FAX *22/2242–4743,* WEB *www.hotelr.com. 45 rooms. Restaurant, bar. AE, MC, V.*

Cantona

170 km (106 mi) east of Mexico City; 107 km (67 mi) northeast of Puebla.

Puebla state is home to the fascinating **Cantona,** which has 24 ball courts where a precursor to soccer was played. It's built into a hillock and is larger than Teotihuacán. It supposedly reached its pinnacle in AD 950, and we can judge its importance from the fact that about 500 cobblestone streets and lanes crisscross its 13-square-km (5-square-mi) area. Note that in the rainy season (August–October), you can navigate the site only with a four-wheel-drive. ✉ *Take Hwy. 150 to Hwy. 129; turn off Hwy. 129 at Oriental.* *$2.50.* ⏲ *Tues.–Sun. 10–5.*

Tlaxcala

30 km (19 mi) north and 120 km (75 mi) east of Puebla.

The warriors of the state of Tlaxcala (pronounced tlas-*ca*-la) played a pivotal role in the Spanish conquest by aligning themselves with Cortés against their enemy Aztecs, thus swelling the conqueror's military ranks by 5,000 men. The state capital, seat of the ancient nation of the same name, will interest both archaeology buffs and church-lovers.

A former Franciscan church, now called the **Catedral de Nuestra Señora de la Asunción** (Our Lady of the Assumption Cathedral), with its adjoining **monastery** (1537–40), stands atop a hill one block from the handsome main square. This was the first permanent Catholic edifice in the New World. The most unusual feature of the church is its wood ceiling beams, carved and gilded with gold studs after the Moorish fashion. There are only three churches of this kind in Mexico. (Moorish, or mudéjar, architecture appeared in Mexico only during the very early years after the Spanish conquest, when the Moorish occupation was still recent enough to influence Spain with Arabic architectural styles.) The austere monastery, now a museum of history, displays 16th- to 18th-century religious paintings and a small collection of pre-Columbian pieces. A beautiful outdoor **chapel** near the monastery has notable Moorish and Gothic traces. ✉ *Convento Franciscano Catedral de Tlaxcala s/n.* ⏲ *Daily 9–6.*

The **Palacio de Gobierno** (Government Palace), which occupies the north side of the zócalo, was built about 1550. Inside are vivid epic murals of Tlaxcala before the conquest, painted in the 1960s by local artist Desiderio Hernández Xochitiotzin. ☎ *No phone.* ⏲ *9–6.*

About 1 km (½ mi) west of Tlaxcala is the large, ornate **Santuario de la Virgen de Ocotlán** (Basilica of Our Lady of Ocotlán). The legend of the Virgin dates from 1541, when, during a severe epidemic, she appeared to a poor Indian and told him to cure his people with water from a stream that had miraculously appeared. The villagers recovered. The Virgin then asked for the Franciscan monks from a nearby monastery. When they arrived in her forest, they were temporarily blinded by the raging flames of a fire that didn't harm the trees. They returned the next day with an axe to cut open one particular pine (*ocotlán*) tree that had caught their attention. When they split it open, they discovered the wooden image of the Virgin, which they installed in the present basilica. Many miracles have been attributed to the Virgin since then. Noteworthy sights of the church are the churrigueresque white-plaster facade, which conjures up images of a wedding cake; the two white Poblano towers adorned with the apostles; and, inside, the brilliantly painted and gilded **Camarín de la Virgen** (Virgin's Dressing Room) with figures on each of its eight sides portraying the history of the Lady of Ocotlán. ☎ *246/465–0960.* ⏲ *9–6.*

Cacaxtla

100 km (63 mi) east of Mexico City center.

The archaeological site at **Cacaxtla,** accidentally discovered in 1975 by a *campesino* (peasant) working the land, contains a breathtaking series of murals (AD 650–700) depicting scenes of a fierce battle between Maya and Central Mexican warriors. It's considered a major breakthrough in tracing the immigration and trade patterns of pre-Hispanic Mexico. The site is thought to have been settled around 2000 BC by the Olmeca-Xicalancas, a transition culture between the Olmecs and the peoples of central Mexico. It reached its height between AD 600 and 900 and was abandoned by 1000. The vividly portrayed battle scenes with life-size figures show warriors in lofty bird headdresses and plumage being vanquished by victors wearing jaguar skins and wielding spears, obsidian knives, and lances. The murals—painted on the walls of a series of palaces built one on top of another—are protected under a huge roof. Give yourself at least three hours to see both Cacaxtla and Xochitécatl. Make a right before you reach Puebla on Carretera Federal 119; after Nativitas, go to San Miguel del Milagro, the village where Cacaxtla lies. ✉ *About 19 km (12 mi) southwest of Tlaxcala on Carretera Federal 119,* ☎ *246/416–0477,* WEB *www.cnca.gob.mx/cnca/inah/zonarq/cacaxtla.html or www.tourbymexico.com/tlaxcala/cacaxtla/cacaxtla.htm.* 🎫 *$3.50, free Sun.* ⏲ *Tues.–Sun. 10–4:30.*

Xochitécatl

1½ km (1 mi) north of Cacaxtla; 100 km (63 mi) east of Mexico City center.

Dedicated to a bevy of important goddesses, little Xochitécatl is decidedly soft and feminine. Four Classic period **pyramids** are built on a hill that affords a spectacular view of the Tlaxcala and Puebla valleys. A small on-site **museum** has a good collection of sculpted stone heads and pregnant women. ✉ *Less than 1½ km (1 mi) north of Cacaxtla on the route to Xochitecatitla.* 🎫 *$2.50.* ⏲ *Tues.–Sun. 10–4:30.*

Southeast of Mexico City A to Z

To research prices, get advice from other travelers, and book travel arrangements, visit www.fodors.com.

BUS TRAVEL

Buses from different lines run every 20 minutes to Puebla from the Mexico City's Terminal del Oriente (TAPO). **ADO** (☎ 55/5133–2424 in Mexico City) is the cleanest and most reliable bus line; you can call the Freephone Central Reservations Center toll free (☎ 1-800/702-8000).

A few services leave from Taxqueña bus station in the south of the capital. Buses to Tlaxcala also leave from the TAPO in Mexico City. To get to Cacaxtla you can take a bus either from Puebla bus station (take the Zacatelo–San Martín bus) or in Tlaxcala.

CAR TRAVEL

From Mexico City, head east on the Viaducto Miguel Aleman toward the airport and exit right onto Calzada Zaragoza, the last wide boulevard before arriving at the airport; this becomes the Puebla Highway at the tollbooth. Route 150D is the toll road straight to Puebla; Route 190 is the scenic—and bumpy—free road (the trip takes about 1½ hours on 150D, three hours on 190). To go directly to Cholula, take the exit at San Martín Texmelucan and follow the signs. From Puebla, Cholula is 8 km (5 mi) west. You'll need to go to Puebla to get to Tlaxcala; from there, take Highway 119 north.

INTERNET

The Cyberbyte Café on Calle 2 between Avs. 5 and 7 Ote. is open daily 10–9 and charges $2 an hour.

➤ CYBERCAFÉ: **Cyberbyte Café** (✉ Calle 2 Sur 505B, Puebla, ☎ 22/2217–5523).

VISITOR INFORMATION

The Puebla Municipal Tourist Office is open Monday–Friday 9–5, Sunday 9–3. Be sure to get the new state and city map "Puebla Destinos a tu alcance." Ask for Rene Paredes or Manuel Salazar; both speak English and can set you up on a tour to churches in the countryside, Cholula, and Huejotzingo. The Tlaxcala Tourist Office is open weekdays 9–6; weekends a stand is open downstairs 9–6.

➤ TOURIST INFORMATION: **Cholula Tourist Office** (✉ Calle 4 Pte. 103, San Pedro Cholula, ☎ 22/2247–3116. **Puebla Municipal Tourist Office** (✉ Portal Hidalgo 14, Centro Histórico, ☎ 22/2246–1890 or 22/2246–1580, FAX 22/2242–4980, WEB www.ayuntamiento.pue.gob.mx). **Tlaxcala Tourist Office** (✉ Av. Juárez 18, corner with Lardizabal, ☎ 246/465–0960, WEB www.tlaxcala.gob/turismo.com).

WEST OF MEXICO CITY

Toluca, renowned for its Friday market, makes a good day trip from Mexico City. For a longer stay, stop over in Valle de Bravo, a lovely lakeside village popular with vacationing chilangos; it's often called Mexico's Switzerland because of its green, hilly setting. A quick trip is into Parque Nacional Desierto de los Leones—a forested national park whose centerpiece is an intriguing Carmelite monastery; make a detour from Toluca for a picnic at Parque Nacional Nevado de Toluca.

Parque Nacional Desierto de los Leones

30 km (19 mi) west of Mexico City center.

Several walking trails crisscross this 5,000-acre national park's pine forest. Its focal point is the ruined 17th-century **ex-monastery of the Carmelites,** isolated amid an abundance of greenery and open daily 9–5; the entrance fee is about 20¢. The park played a significant role in the War of Independence in late October 1810. At a spot called **Las Cruces,** Father Hidalgo's troops trounced the Spaniards but resolved not to go on to attack Mexico City, an error that cost the insurgents 10 more years of fighting.

Parque Nacional Nevado de Toluca

65 km (40 mi) west of Mexico City center.

At 4,527 m (15,090 ft), the Nevado de Toluca, an extinct volcano, is Mexico's fourth-tallest mountain; on clear days its crater affords wonderful views of the valley. You can hire a guide at the entrance to go with your car to the top of the crater and lead you down to its sandy floor, which surrounds two lakes. Self-guided hiking trails are plentiful.

Valle de Bravo

75 km (47 mi) west of Mexico City center.

A few hours here explains why "Valle" is often billed as Mexico's best-kept secret. You are not likely to expect such a picturesque, yet manageable, town south of the Río Bravo. Reminiscent of Switzerland, or England's Lake District, this colonial lake-side treasure is peppered with white stucco houses trimmed with wrought-iron balconies, red-tile roofs, and red-potted succulents cluttering doorways. Valle and its suburb of Avandaro are enclaves for established artists and the extremely wealthy, and the pines, clear air, and sparkling lake make it very different from most people's idea—and experience—of Mexico.

A hilly town that rises from the shores of Lake Avandaro and is surrounded by pines and mountains, Valle was founded in 1530 but has no historical monuments to speak of other than the town church. The area's geography lends itself to many costly and healthful diversions: boating, waterskiing, and swimming in the lake and its waterfalls—and motorcross and hang gliding for the adventurous (hang gliders can check www.flymexico.com/Valle.html). It has a verdant European feel and a lot of class, and is truly fresh and beautiful. But it is an enclave, and therefore more an escape from Mexico City (two to three hours by road) than a settlement with its own heart and character. Valle also has a pleasant Sunday market, where outstanding pottery is the draw, along with vegetarian restaurants and short-lived jazz clubs.

But the area's main attraction is the migration of monarch butterflies November through March, when you hike through the butterfly sanctuaries. Other sights in the area include the Hacienda Santa María Pi-

pioltepec, whose name means "hill of the bees"; Amanalco de Becerra Parish, where there's a fine nursery; the Franciscan temple in Amanalco; the San Lucas Waterfall; and the Carmel Maranatha prayer house and retreat. Valle is a big weekend-vacation town for well-to-do Mexicans (and foreigners) from Mexico City; locals like to keep a low profile, and the population shrinks when the weekend is over.

Lodging

$$$ **Avandaro Golf & Spa Resort.** For a weekend stay, head for this posh former country club, where all the rooms have romantic fireplaces and great views of the pine forest. In addition to its golf course, the resort has a high-tech spa equipped with hot tubs and offering massage, facials, body toning, and aerobics and yoga classes. ✉ *Vega del Río, Fracc. Avandaro, 52100,* ☎ *726/266–0366 or 726/266–0303; 55/5280–1532 in Mexico City; 800/223–6510,* FAX *726/266–0905. 66 rooms. Restaurant, 18-hole golf course, 2 pools, health club, spa, bar. AE, MC, V.*

West of Mexico City A to Z

To research prices, get advice from other travelers, and book travel arrangements, visit www.fodors.com.

BUS TRAVEL

Buses headed to Toluca depart Terminal Poniente every 20 minutes.

CAR TRAVEL

By car from Mexico City, follow Paseo de la Reforma all the way west. It eventually merges with the Carretera Libre at Toluca, and after 20 km (12 mi), you'll see signs for the turnoff to the Parque Nacional Desierto de los Leones; it's another 10 km (6 mi) to the park. To go straight to Toluca, take the toll highway (expensive, but worth it). To reach Parque Nacional Nevado de Toluca, make a 44-km (27-mi) detour south of Toluca on Route 130.

To reach Valle de Bravo, take the Carretera Federal 15 to Toluca and then continue on the Federal 134 to Valle de Bravo.

VISITOR INFORMATION

The Mexico State Tourist Office in Toluca is open weekdays 9–6.

➤ TOURIST INFORMATION: **Mexico State Tourist Office** (✉ Urawa 100, Gate 110, Toluca, ☎ 722/219–5190 or 722/219–6158, WEB www.gem.uaemex.mx/turismo).

4 BAJA CALIFORNIA

Separated from mainland Mexico by the Sea of Cortez, the Baja California peninsula stretches 1,625 km (1,000 mi) from Tijuana to Los Cabos. The desert landscape harbors isolated fishing retreats, Prohibition-era gambling palaces, world-class golf courses, and one of the busiest international borders in the world. Adventurers delight in kayaking alongside migrating gray whales, diving with hammerhead sharks, and hiking to hidden cave paintings.

BAJA (MEANING LOWER) CALIFORNIA is an arid stretch of land dipping southward from the international boundary that divides California and Mexico. The 240-km-wide (150-mi-wide) Sea of Cortez—also called the Gulf of California—separates Baja from the Mexican mainland. Both Baja and the gulf are part of Mexico.

By Maribeth Mellin

Although only 21 km (13 mi) across at one point and 193 km (120 mi) at its widest, Baja has one of the most varied and beautiful terrains on the planet. The peninsula's two coasts are separated by great mountain ranges, with one peak soaring more than 3,000 m (10,000 ft) high. Countless bays and coves with pristine beaches indent both shores, and islands big and small—many inhabited only by sea lions—dot the 3,364 km (2,086 mi) of coastline. You'll find stretches of desert as dry as the Sahara, as well as cultivated farmlands, vineyards, and resorts lush with swaying palm trees.

Varied, too, is the demographic makeup of Baja. The border strip of northern Baja is densely populated. Tijuana is home to more than 2 million people, making it more populous than the entire remainder of the peninsula. La Paz, with about 175,000 residents, is the only city of any size south of Ensenada. The two towns at Los Cabos (The Capes) have yet to reach city status.

Baja is divided politically into two states—Baja California (also called Baja Norte, meaning North Baja) and Baja California Sur (South)—at the 28th parallel, about 710 km (440 mi) south of the border. Near the tip of the peninsula, a monument marks the spot where the Tropic of Cancer crosses the Transpeninsular Highway (Mexico Highway 1).

Baja travelers have traditionally been adventurous, and the peninsula has become a cult destination. Back in the days of Prohibition, the Hollywood crowd learned the joy of having an international border so near. John Steinbeck brought attention to La Paz when he made it a setting for his novella *The Pearl*. Bing Crosby is said to have put up some of the money for the first resort hotel in San José del Cabo when the only way to get there was aboard a yacht or private plane.

Today you'll fly in on commercial jets and check into thoroughly modern hotels. The rich and famous still find Baja, particularly the southern tip, an ideal escape, and you can see them in secluded hotels along the Los Cabos Corridor. But Baja is no longer the exclusive turf of adventurers. Caravans of motor homes and pickups occasionally clog the Transpeninsular Highway, and flights into Loreto, La Paz, and Los Cabos are often packed with regular folks. Baja's resort towns have become mainstream, but you can still find adventure and sublime solitude at the peninsula's hidden beaches and bays.

Pleasures and Pastimes

Dining

Baja's cuisine highlights food from the sea. Fresh fish, lobster, shrimp, and abalone are particularly good. In both states, scores of restaurants and kitchens serve great authentic Mexican seafood dishes. Beef, pork, and local quail are also excellent, both grilled and marinated. Many restaurants serve regional Mexican cuisine, and plenty of spots throughout the peninsula combine U.S. and Mexican flavors in tacos, burritos, burgers, and pizza.

Two dishes that originated in Baja have become standard fare in southern California. Lobster Puerto Nuevo–style (shellfish grilled or boiled in oil and served with beans, rice, and tortillas) comes from the fishing settlement of the same name near Tijuana. Fish tacos (chunks of deep-fried fish wrapped with condiments in a corn tortilla) are said to have begun in the northern Baja town of San Felipe. Mexico's best domestic wines are nurtured in the vineyards in the Santo Tomás and Guadalupe valleys outside Ensenada, and one of the country's most popular beers, Tecate, comes from the Baja Norte town of the same name.

Restaurants as a rule are low-key, except in Tijuana, Ensenada, and Los Cabos, where dining options range from *taquerías* (taco stands) to upscale Continental dining rooms. Dress is accordingly casual at nearly all Baja restaurants, and reservations are not required unless otherwise noted. Moderate prices prevail even in city restaurants—except in Los Cabos, which can be surprisingly expensive. Some places add a 15% service charge to the bill.

CATEGORY	COST*
$$$	over $15
$$	$10–$15
$	under $10

**per person for a main course at dinner*

Fishing
Baja is considered one of the world's great sportfishing destinations. The fishing is best in the south, with large fishing fleets in Loreto, La Paz, and Los Cabos. Although summer brings the most fish, anglers are sure to catch something year-round. Fishing from Ensenada and San Quintín is best in summer and early fall.

Golf
With well-established courses in Tijuana, Rosarito, and Ensenada, Baja is growing in popularity among golfers. Los Cabos has experienced a particular boom, with several excellent, championship-level courses open and others in development stages.

Kayaking
Both the Pacific Ocean and the Sea of Cortez have isolated bays and coves ideal for kayaking. Some hotels and outfitters in Ensenada, Loreto, La Paz, and Los Cabos offer kayak rentals and excursions, and some U.S. companies offer kayaking trips to the Sea of Cortez.

Lodging
Baja lodging is mostly low-key—except world-class Los Cabos. Until the 1980s, Los Cabos's hotels were mostly fishing lodges where die-hard sportsmen took refuge. Now the area draws golfers to deluxe hotels that front championship courses. In the rest of Baja, you can find great deals at small, one-of-a-kind hostelries.

Reservations are a must on holiday weekends for most of Baja's coastal towns; some hotels require a minimum two-night stay for a confirmed reservation. Several hotels in Baja have toll-free numbers that connect directly to the hotel; although the operator may answer in Spanish, there is usually someone who speaks English in the reservations office. Some hotels have fax numbers, although you may have to ask them to turn on the fax machine when you call. Many have Web sites or e-mail addresses you can use to confirm reservations. Ask for a confirmation, and print it out before you leave. A few of the out-of-the-way and budget-price hotels do not accept credit cards; some of the more lavish places add a 10%–20% service charge to your bill. Most properties also raise their rates for the December–April high season (and raise them even higher for the days around Christmas). Some resorts also have a three-night minimum stay requirement on weekends. Rates here are based on high-season standards. Expect to pay 25% less during the off-season. Many hotels offer midweek discounts of 30%–50% off the weekend rates; always ask about special promotions.

Several agencies in the United States book reservations at Baja hotels, condos, and time-share resorts, which may actually cost less than hotel rooms if you are traveling with a group of four or more.

CATEGORY	COST*
$$$$	over $160
$$$	$90–$160
$$	$50–$90
$	under $50

**All prices are for a standard double room, excluding service charge and 12%–17% hotel occupancy tax.*

Whale-Watching

Gray whales migrate to the Pacific coast of Baja from January through March. Whale-watching expeditions are available in Ensenada, Guerrero Negro, San Ignacio, Loreto, La Paz, and Los Cabos.

Exploring Baja California

The Baja Peninsula is made up of two Mexican states: Baja California, which begins at the U.S. border, and Baja California Sur. The northern half of the Baja peninsula, Baja California, contains the largest cities and highest population. Tijuana, Tecate, and Mexicali—the peninsula's border cities—have close ties to the Southwestern United States. San Felipe, the northernmost town on the Sea of Cortez, is a popular weekend escape for Arizonans and southern Californians. Similarly, Rosarito and Ensenada, on Baja's northern Pacific coast, are practically extensions of the southern California coast. South of Ensenada the natural side of Baja appears in desolate mountain ranges and fields of cacti and boulders.

Baja California Sur is more remote, in spite of its strong American influences. The most populated areas lie on the Sea of Cortez coast. The Pacific side is more popular with migrating gray whales, who travel by the thousands every winter from the Bering Strait to isolated coves and lagoons along this coast. For those few months, people come from around the world to Guerrero Negro and a few bays and lagoons farther south. Loreto, on the Sea of Cortez, is beloved by sportfishers who find seclusion in this small, largely undiscovered town. La Paz is the capital of Baja California Sur, the region's major port, and a busy center of commerce and government. Los Cabos, made up of the two towns of Cabo San Lucas and San José del Cabo, has become one of the fastest-growing and most expensive resort areas in Mexico. Despite all the development and steep prices, it remains a mysteriously natural hideaway.

Numbers in the text correspond to numbers in the margin and on the Tijuana, Ensenada, La Paz, Los Cabos Coast, San José del Cabo, and Cabo San Lucas maps.

Great Itineraries

Baja aficionados will tell you that you haven't really explored the peninsula unless you've driven its entire length, stopping at small towns and secluded beaches along the way. That's a major journey, requiring at least 10 days of travel time—one way—if you plan to stop at many of the sights along the way. Keep in mind that regulars who boast of making the drive in two or three days are actually pelting along the roads, stopping only to eat and sleep.

If you plan to drive the peninsula, you must have Mexican auto insurance (about $18 per day) for the length of your drive. Always carry water, and make sure your vehicle is in good condition. Keep your gas tank at least half full at all times—remote gas stations may be out of gas just when you need it. For the most part, the Transpeninsular Highway is well maintained, although some areas are marred by potholes or gravel and rocks. In addition, it often has only two lanes, and sharing them with semis and speeding buses can be somewhat unnerving.

Even if you don't have 10 days you can still see plenty of the peninsula's attractions by focusing on the area around where you enter Baja. A full week allows a quick jaunt through the peninsula (one way) or a more leisurely exploration of northern Baja or Baja Sur. If you have five days, you can see the most interesting towns in one state and still linger a bit. With three days you're best off staying within the immediate vicinity of your entry point.

IF YOU HAVE 3 DAYS

In northern Baja, you can explore Tijuana, Rosarito, and Ensenada. Start in **Tijuana** ①–⑪ at the **Centro Cultural** ⑧, then stroll down **Avenida Revolución** ②. Head south before nightfall to a hotel in **Rosarito** or **Puerto Nuevo.** Tour **Ensenada** ⑫–⑲ the next day, taking in the **Fish Market** ⑭, the **Riviera del Pacífico** ⑱, and the shops on **Paseo Calle Primera** ⑰. Take the third day in Rosarito before heading back to the border.

In Baja Sur, you're best off staying in **Los Cabos,** allowing time for golf, sportfishing, and snorkeling at **Bahía Santa María** or **Bahía Chileno.**

IF YOU HAVE 5 DAYS

You can do a thorough tour of northern Baja, starting with a full day and overnight in **Tijuana** ①–⑪. From there head to the small town of **Tecate,** then on to **Mexicali** and **San Felipe.** Overnight in San Felipe, and spend Day 3 checking out the beaches before driving the backcountry to **Ensenada** ⑫–⑲. Devote Day 4 to exploring **La Bufadora** and downtown Ensenada; then head up the coast for a lobster feast at **Puerto Nuevo.** On Day 5, head back to Tijuana and the border.

If you'd rather tour Baja Sur, begin in **Los Cabos,** spending the night there and starting out early the next day for **La Paz** ⑳–㉘. Spend Day 2 exploring downtown La Paz, making sure to see the **malecón** ㉑, or seaside walkway, and the **Plaza Constitución** ㉕. On Day 3, head up the coast to the small mission town of **Loreto.** Spend Days 4 and 5 making your way back to Los Cabos at a leisurely pace, stopping to explore the desert and coast along the way.

IF YOU HAVE 7 DAYS

If you want to cover great distances—and spend much time in the car—you could drive the length of the peninsula in a week, especially if you arrange to begin in the north and drop off your car in the south. Most rental-car agencies will charge you a whopping drop-off fee, however, and the terrain covered isn't always awe-inspiring. (A leisurely roundtrip takes about 14 days, especially as many of Baja's treasures take some extra time and effort to reach.) Start in **Tijuana** ①–⑪ on Day 1. Head south before nightfall to a hotel in **Rosarito** or **Puerto Nuevo.** On Day 2, move on to **Ensenada** ⑫–⑲ for a brief tour of the city; then head south to **San Quintín** and **Guerrero Negro.** If you're traveling between January and March, arrange for a whale-watching tour for the next day. If not, overnight in Guerrero Negro and then move on for a full day's trip to **Mulegé** on the Sea of Cortez. The drive between the two coasts, through stark desert scenery, is one of the most beautiful and desolate in Baja. Spend Night 3 or 4 in Mulegé. Move on to **Loreto,** stopping for a swim at **Bahía Concepción** along the way, and spend the next night there. If you didn't stay in Guerrero Negro for whale-watching, spend an extra night in Loreto and arrange a boat tour of the Sea of Cortez. Devote Day 6 of the drive to **La Paz** ⑳–㉘, spending the evening strolling the waterfront **malecón** ㉑. On Day 7, continue on to **Los Cabos.**

When to Tour Baja

Baja's climate is extreme, thanks to its desert locale. Temperatures in Tijuana, Ensenada, and Rosarito are similar to those in southern California. Mexicali gets extremely hot in the summer. Northern Baja's resort cities are crowded on holiday weekends, and advance reservations are a must.

Baja Sur's winters are mild, but not warm; Loreto, La Paz, and Los Cabos can get downright chilly in the evening. Sportfishing aficionados prefer the summer months: although the temperatures are high, the fish are abundant. Loreto and La Paz tend to be crowded only on holiday weekends, but Los Cabos is crowded through much of the year, except at the height of the summer heat.

BAJA CALIFORNIA NORTE

The most densely populated area of the Baja California Peninsula, the state of Baja California begins at the U.S. border and extends 699 km (433 mi) to the border with Baja California Sur. Tijuana, just 29 km (18 mi) south of San Diego, is Baja's largest city. Its promoters like to call it "the most visited city in the world," and the border crossing to Tijuana is the busiest in the United States.

By comparison, the state's capital, Mexicali, has a population of only 850,000 residents and attracts few tourists. Tecate, located between Tijuana and Mexicali, is a typical village famous for its beer of the same name. Travelers who do pass through Tecate and Mexicali are usually en route to San Felipe, the northernmost town on the Sea of Cortez.

On Baja's Pacific coast, travelers stream down the Transpeninsular Highway (Highway 1) to the beach communities of Rosarito and Ensenada. English is spoken as freely as Spanish here, and the dollar is as readily accepted as the peso. Between Baja's towns, the landscape is unlike any other, with cacti growing beside the sea, and stark mountains and plateaus rising against clear blue skies.

Highway 3 runs east from Ensenada to San Felipe through the foothills of the Sierra San Pedro Martir. The same highway runs north from Ensenada to Tecate through the Guadalupe Valley, where you'll find many of the area's vineyards and wineries. If you're traveling south, Ensenada is the last major city on the northern section of Mexico Highway 1. San Quintín, 184 km (114 mi) south of Ensenada, is an agricultural community said to be the windiest spot in Baja. Sportfishing is particularly good here. Farther south are turnoffs for a dirt road to San Felipe and a paved road to Bahía de los Angeles, a remote bay beloved by fishermen and naturalists.

At the end of the northern section of Baja, 595 km (369 mi) from Ensenada, stands a steel monument in the form of an eagle, 138 ft high. It marks the border between the states of Baja California and Baja California Sur, and the time changes from Pacific to Mountain as you cross that 28th parallel. Guerrero Negro, Baja Sur's northernmost town, with hotels and gas stations, is 2 km (1 mi) south.

Baja California Norte

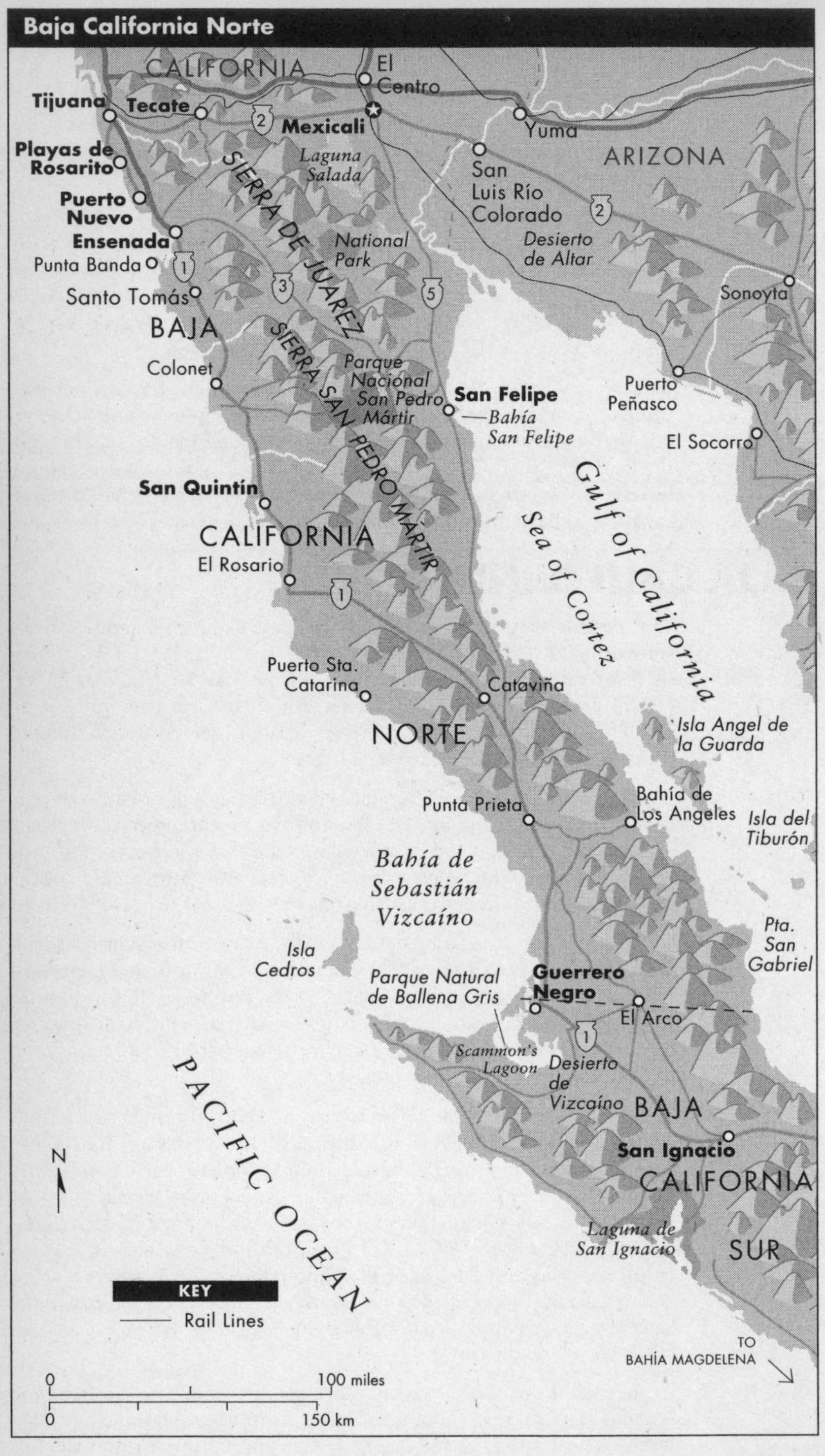

CALIFORNIA
El Centro
Tijuana
Tecate
Mexicali
Yuma
Playas de Rosarito
Laguna Salada
San Luis Río Colorado
ARIZONA
Puerto Nuevo
SIERRA DE JUAREZ
Ensenada
National Park
Desierto de Altar
Punta Banda
Santo Tomás
Sonoyta
BAJA
SIERRA SAN PEDRO MÁRTIR
Colonet
Parque Nacional San Pedro Mártir
San Felipe
Bahía San Felipe
Puerto Peñasco
El Socorro
San Quintín
Gulf of California
Sea of Cortez
CALIFORNIA
El Rosario
Puerto Sta. Catarina
Cataviña
NORTE
Isla Angel de la Guarda
Punta Prieta
Bahía de Los Angeles
Isla del Tiburón
Bahía de Sebastián Vizcaíno
Pta. San Gabriel
Isla Cedros
Parque Natural de Ballena Gris
Guerrero Negro
El Arco
Scammon's Lagoon
Desierto de Vizcaíno
BAJA
San Ignacio
CALIFORNIA
PACIFIC OCEAN
Laguna de San Ignacio
SUR
N
KEY
Rail Lines
TO BAHÍA MAGDELENA
0
100 miles
0
150 km

Tijuana

29 km (18 mi) south of San Diego.

Tijuana is the only part of Mexico many people see—a distorted view of the country's many cultures. Before the city became a gigantic recreation center for southern Californians, it was a ranch populated by a few hundred Mexicans. In 1911 a group of Americans invaded the area and attempted to set up an independent republic; they were quickly driven out by Mexican soldiers. When Prohibition hit the United States in the 1920s and the Agua Caliente Racetrack and Casino opened (1929), Tijuana boomed. Americans seeking alcohol and gambling flocked across the border, spending freely and fueling the region's growth. Tijuana became the entry port for what some termed a "sinful, steamy playground" frequented by Hollywood stars and the idle rich.

Then Prohibition was repealed, Mexico outlawed gambling, and Tijuana's fortunes declined. Although the flow of travelers from the north slowed to a trickle for a while, Tijuana still captivated those in search of the sort of fun that was not allowed back home. Drivers heading into Baja's wilderness passed through downtown Tijuana, stopping along Avenida Revolución and its side streets for supplies and souvenirs.

When the toll highway to Ensenada was finished in 1967, travelers bypassed the city and tourism dropped again. But Tijuana began attracting residents from throughout Latin America. The city's population mushroomed from a mere 300,000 in 1970 to more than 2 million today. As the government struggles to keep up with the growth and demand for services, thousands live without electricity, running water, or adequate housing in squatters' villages along the border. Crime is now a significant problem in Tijuana. Poverty is vast, and petty crime is on the rise. Moreover, the area has become headquarters for serious drug cartels, and violent crime—reaching the highest levels of law enforcement and business—is booming. You're unlikely to witness a shooting or some other frightening situation, but be mindful of your surroundings and guard your belongings.

City leaders, realizing that tourism creates jobs and bolsters Tijuana's fragile economy, are working hard to attract visitors. Avenida Revolución, the main street, is lined with tourist-oriented shopping arcades, restaurants, and bars. The city has an international airport; a fine cultural center that presents international music, dance, and theater groups; and deluxe high-rise hotels. The demand for high-end accommodations has increased with the growth of *maquiladoras* (foreign manufacturing plants). Although it's no longer considered just a bawdy border town, the city remains best known as a place for an intense, somewhat exotic daylong adventure.

Tijuana's tourist attractions have remained much the same throughout the century. The impressive El Palacio Frontón (Jai Alai Palace) no longer hosts jai alai games but is occasionally used as a concert venue. Some of Mexico's greatest bullfighters appear at the oceanfront and downtown bullrings, and an extraordinary number of places in town serve up good food and drinks.

And then, of course, there's shopping. From the moment you cross the border, people will approach you or call out and insist that you look at their wares. If you drive, workers will run out from auto-body shops to place bids on new paint or upholstery for your car. All along Avenida Revolución and its side streets, shops sell everything from tequila to Tiffany-style lamps. If you intend to buy food in Mexico, get the

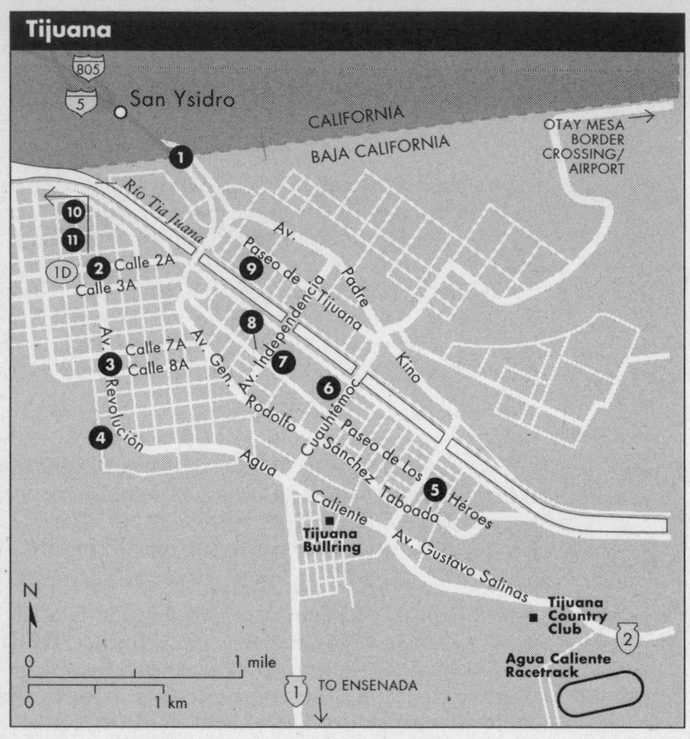

U.S. customs list of articles that are illegal to bring back so that your purchases won't be confiscated.

❷ **Avenida Revolución.** This infamous strip, lined with an array of shops and restaurants that cater to uninhibited travelers, has long been Tijuana's main tourism zone. Shopkeepers call out from their doorways, offering low prices for an assortment of garish souvenirs and genuine folk art treasures. Many shopping arcades open onto Avenida Revolución; inside the front doors are mazes of stands with low-priced pottery and other crafts.

❽ **Centro Cultural.** The Cultural Center was designed by architects Manuel Rosen and Pedro Ramírez Vásquez, who also created Mexico City's famous Museum of Anthropology. The center's Museum of the Californias provides an excellent overview of the history, geography, and flora and fauna of Baja. Exhibits include replicas of several Baja missions and prehistoric cave paintings, along with a nearly full-size sailing ship filled with interactive exhibits for children. The Omnimax Theater, with its curved 180-degree screen, shows films on a rotating schedule; some are in English. Exhibitions on art and culture change frequently, and the center's stage hosts musical and dance performances by international groups. The bookstore has an excellent selection of Mexican history, culture, and arts, mostly in Spanish. ✉ *Paseo de los Héroes and Av. Independencia, Zona Río,* ☎ *664/687–9600 or 664/684–1125.* 🎫 *Museum $2, museum and Omnimax Theater $4.* ⏲ *Tues.–Fri. 10–6, weekends 10–8, closed Mon.*

❹ **L.A. Cetto Winery.** Most of Baja's legendary wineries are in the Ensenada region, but Tijuana does have this branch of one of Mexico's finest wineries. You can tour the bottling plant, sample the excellent wines while watching a video on the winery's operations in the Guadalupe Valley. The wine shop's prices are far lower than those in regular liquor stores. ✉ *Cañon Johnson 8151, at Av. Constitución Sur, Centro,* ☎ *664/685–3031 or 664/685–1644.* 💵 *$2 for tour and tasting 4 wines; $6 for tour and tasting 11 wines.* ⏲ *Mon.–Sat. 10–5.*

5 **Mundo Divertido.** This popular amusement park in the Río zone includes a miniature golf course, batting cages, bumper boats, go-carts, a roller coaster, and a video-game parlor. Admission is free, and the rides cost just a few pesos. ✉ *Paseo de los Héroes at Calle Velasco, Zona Río,* ☎ *664/634–3213 or 664/634–3214.* ⏲ *Weekdays noon–8:30, weekends 11–9:30.*

3 **El Palacio Frontón** (Jai Alai Palace). For many years, the magnificent Moorish-style Jai Alai Palace hosted fast-paced jai alai games. The sport has declined in popularity, however, and the Palacio is now occasionally used for boxing contests and concerts. ✉ *Av. Revolución at Calle 7, Downtown,* ☎ *664/685–7833.*

10 **Playas Tijuana.** Along the oceanfront is this mix of modest and expensive residential neighborhoods, with a few restaurants and hotels. The isolated beaches are visited mostly by residents.

11 **Plaza de Toros Monumental.** The "Bullring by the Sea" sits at the northwest corner of the beach area near the U.S. border. The bullring is occasionally used for summer concerts.

7 **Plaza Río Tijuana.** The area's largest shopping complex has good restaurants, department stores, hundreds of shops, and the Cineopolis, a multiplex theater where several English-language films are usually shown. Shade trees and flowers line the sidewalks that lead from the shopping complex to the Cultural Center. ✉ *Paseo de los Héroes, across from the Centro Cultural, Zona Río,* ☎ *664/684–0402.*

9 **Pueblo Amigo.** This entertainment center was built to resemble a colonial Mexican village, replete with stucco facades and tree-lined pathways leading to a domed gazebo. The complex includes a hotel, several restaurants and clubs, a huge grocery store, and a large branch of the Caliente Race Book, where gambling on televised races and sporting events is legal. It's more interesting at night. ✉ *Paseo de Tijuana between Puente Mexico and Av. Independencia, Zona Río.*

1 **San Ysidro Border Crossing.** Locals and tourists jostle each other along the pedestrian walkway through the Viva Tijuana dining and shopping center and into the center of town. Artisans' stands line the walkway and adjoining streets, offering a quick overview of the wares to be found all over town.

6 **Zona Río.** The section that runs along Avenida Paseo de los Héroes, parallel to the dry Tia Juana River, is one of the city's main thoroughfares, with large statues of historic figures, including Abraham Lincoln. With its impressive **Centro Cultural,** several shopping complexes, fine restaurants, and fashionable discos, this part of town rivals Avenida Revolución for tourists' as well as locals' attention. A massive 10-story-high cathedral dedicated to the Virgin of Guadalupe is under construction in this neighborhood; when completed (construction is expected to take several years) it will surely be a city landmark. ✉ *Paseo de los Héroes between Blvd. Sanchez Taboada and the border, Zona Río.*

Dining and Lodging

$$–$$$ ✕ **Señor Frog's.** Kitschy license plates, posters, and Mexican crafts cover the walls of this wildly popular restaurant where waiters encourage patrons to eat, drink, and sing along with the blaring music. Known for its barbecued ribs and chicken, the kitchen also prepares good Mexican standards such as tacos and carne asada. ✉ *Pueblo Amigo, Paseo*

Tijuana between Puente México and Av. Independencia, ☏ *664/682–4964. MC, V.*

$$–$$$ ✕ **Villa Saverios.** Well-dressed Tijuanans savor exceptional pastas, gourmet pizzas, and unusual entrées in this elegant dining room reminiscent of a Mediterranean café. Starters include foie gras, carpaccio, sashimi, lobster taquitos, and tiny mesquite-grilled quail with a tamarind glaze. Canneloni is stuffed with eggplant, spinach, and mushrooms; duck is marinated with raspberry liqueur; and Calvados scents the sweetbreads. The menu is ambitious, the service attentive. ✉ *Escuadrón 201 at Blvd. Sánchez Taboada, Zona Río,* ☏ *664/686–6502. AE, MC, V.*

$$ ✕ **Cien Años.** In this gracious Spanish colonial–style restaurant, dishes include crêpes filled with *huitlacoche* (fungus that grows on corn), shrimp with nopal cactus, and tender beef with avocado and cheese. Each has an unusual blend of flavors—tamarind, Mexican oregano, mango, poblano chilies—that distinguishes the taste of even the *queso fundido* (melted cheese wrapped in tortillas). ✉ *Av. José María Velasco 1407, Zona Río,* ☏ *664/634–3039. MC, V.*

$–$$ ✕ **Carnitas Uruapan.** You'll need to take a cab to this festive restaurant, where patrons mingle at picnic tables and toast one another to live mariachi music. The main attraction here is *carnitas* (marinated pork roasted over an open pit), sold by weight and served with homemade tortillas, salsa, cilantro, guacamole, and onions. ✉ *Paseo de los Héroes at Av. Rodríguez, Zona Río,* ☏ *no phone. No credit cards.*

$–$$ ✕ **El Faro de Mazatlán.** Fresh fish prepared simply is the hallmark of one of Tijuana's best seafood restaurants. This is the place to try ceviche, abalone, squid, and lobster without spending a fortune. Frequented by professionals, the dining room is a peaceful spot for a long, leisurely lunch. Appetizers and soup are included in the price of the meal. ✉ *Blvd. Sanchez Taboada 9542, Zona Río,* ☏ *664/684–8883. MC, V.*

$–$$ ✕ **La Fonda de Roberto.** Roberto's is the best restaurant in Tijuana for traditional cuisine from the diverse culinary regions of Mexico. Try the *chiles en nogada* (chilies stuffed with raisins and meat and topped with cream and pomegranate seeds), meats with spicy *achiote* (a blend of seasonings) sauce, and many varieties of mole. Portions are small, so order liberally and share samples of many dishes. ✉ *La Siesta Motel, Blvd. Cuauhtémoc Suroeste 2800, also called Old Ensenada Hwy., near Blvd. Agua Caliente, Agua Caliente,* ☏ *664/686–1601. MC, V.*

$ ★ ✕ **La Especial.** At the foot of the stairs leading to an underground shopping arcade, this place serves up home-style Mexican cooking. The gruff, efficient waiters shuttle platters of *carne asada* (grilled strips of marinated meat), enchiladas, and burritos, all with a distinctive flavor found only at this busy, cavernous basement dining room. ✉ *Av. Revolucion 78, Centro,* ☏ *664/685–6654. No credit cards.*

$$$$ 🏨 **Camino Real.** This fashionable, modern purple-and-yellow hotel near the Centro Cultural is the most prestigious hotel in town. Business guests abound, but tourists also appreciate the plush rooms decorated in browns and gold, an excellent restaurant, and the perfect location, though the lack of a swimming pool is a detraction. ✉ *Paseo de los Héroes 10305, Zona Río 22320,* ☏ *664/633–4000 or 800/722–6466,* FAX *664/633–4001,* WEB *www.tjcamino.com. 235 rooms, 15 suites. Restaurant, room service, gym, 2 bars, laundry service. AE, MC, V.*

$$$–$$$$ 🏨 **Grand Hotel.** The twin, mirrored towers of the hotel and a high-rise office building are Tijuana's most ostentatious landmarks. The rooms could use modernization, but are large; ask for one with good views of the city. It's a good spot for business travelers and anyone looking for a touch of luxury. The hotel mall has an Internet café. ✉ *Blvd. Agua Caliente 4500, Zona Río 22420,* ☏ *664/681–7000,* FAX *664/681–7016. 422 rooms. Restaurant, 2 tennis courts, pool, gym, shops, nightclub, travel services. AE, MC, V.*

$$$ **Fiesta Inn.** It's hard to resist this quirky hotel set between two boulevards on a landscaped island. The building stands beside the thermal spring for the1920s-era Agua Caliente Spa. Today's rooms are modern and comfortable. The Vita Spa includes individual and couples' hot tubs fed from the healing spring and a cozy relaxation room. ✉ *Paseo de los Héroes 18818, Zona Río 22320,* ☎ *664/634–6901 or 800/343–7821,* FAX *664/634–6912,* WEB *www.fiestainn.com. 122 rooms, 5 suites. Restaurant, pool, spa. AE, MC, V.*

$$$ **Lucerna.** Once one of the most charming hotels in Tijuana, the Lucerna is now showing its age. Still, the lovely gardens, large pool surrounded by palms, touches of tile work, and folk art lend the hotel a distinct Mexican character. ✉ *Paseo de los Héroes 10902, at Av. Rodríguez, Zona Río 22320,* ☎ *664/633–3900 or 800/582–3762,* FAX *664/634–2400,* WEB *www.hotel-lucerna.com.mx. 167 rooms, 11 suites. Restaurant, coffee shop, pool, nightclub, travel services. MC, V.*

$$ **Bugambilias.** Proximity to the Tijuana airport makes this modest hotel a great find. The pink three-story building has motel-like rooms; suites have kitchenettes. The hotel offers free transportation to and from the Tijuana airport. ✉ *Av. Tijuana 1600, Otay Mesa 22450,* ☎ *664/623–7600 or 800/472–1153. 132 rooms, 9 suites. Restaurant, pool, gym, bar. MC, V.*

$$ **La Villa de Zaragoza.** Some rooms in this brown stucco motel have kitchenettes, and all offer air-conditioning and cable TV. The location, near the Jai Alai Palace and around the corner from Avenida Revolución, is ideal. The neighborhood can be noisy, so it's best to choose a room at the back. The guarded parking lot is a major plus. The motel is used by tour groups, so book ahead for holidays and weekends. ✉ *Av. Madero 1120, Downtown 22000,* ☎ *664/685–1832,* FAX *664/685–1837. 66 rooms. Restaurant, free parking. MC, V.*

$ **Hotel Nelson.** Were it better cared for, the Nelson's pale pink, five-story corner building might be considered a historic landmark. It feels like an older downtown inn, with a barbershop, somewhat noisy bar, and coffee shop on the ground floor. The rooms are serviceable and clean; the best have air-conditioning, heat, and cable TV. ✉ *Av. Revolución 721, Downtown 22000,* ☎ *664/685–4302,* FAX *664/685–4304. 92 rooms. Restaurant, bar, parking (fee). MC, V.*

Nightlife and the Arts

Tijuana has toned down its Sin City image, but there are still plenty of raucous bars on Avenida Revolución. Locals, however, prefer the classier nightclubs in the Zona Río. Tijuana's discos usually have strict dress codes—no T-shirts, jeans, or sandals allowed.

Baby Rock (✉ Calle Diego Rivera 1482, Zona Río, ☎ 664/634–2404), an offshoot of a popular Acapulco disco, attracts a young, hip crowd.

The **Hard Rock Cafe** (✉ Av. Revolución 520, between Calles 1 and 2, Downtown, ☎ 664/685–0206) has the same menu and decor as other branches of the ubiquitous club.

Businessmen (there's a definite shortage of women here) favor **María Bonita** (✉ Camino Real hotel, Paseo de los Héroes 10305, Zona Río, ☎ 664/633–4000). Designed after the famed L'Opera bar in Mexico City, this small clublike tavern serves several brands of fine tequila along with beer and mixed drinks, and patrons are encouraged to play dominoes, chess, and card games at the tables.

Tijuana has its own brand name beer, thanks to the Czech brewmaster at **Tijuana Brewery Company/La Cervecería** (✉ Blvd. Fundadores 2951, Downtown, ☎ 664/638–8662). The European-style pub serves only two drinks—Tijuana Claro and Tijuana Oscura, the light and dark beers brewed in the glassed-in brewery beside the bar. *Botanes,* or appetizers, include *chiles rellenos,* queso fundido, and smoked tuna; live music is offered some nights. The bar is a popular after-work spot, and is usually crowded by 7 PM.

One of the hottest nightspots with the fashionable set is **Zka** (✉ Blvd. Paseo de los Heroes, at Av. Diego Rivera, Zona Río, ☎ 664/634–7140). Dancers take a break from the action on the large disco floor by settling in on comfy couches in the quieter cocktail lounge.

Outdoor Activities and Sports

BULLFIGHTING

Bullfights feature skilled matadors from throughout Mexico and Spain. Admission to bullfights varies, depending on the fame of the matador and the location of your seat—try for one in the shade. Fights are held at **El Toreo de Tijuana** (✉ Blvd. Agua Caliente, Zona Río, ☎ 664/686–1510) Sunday at 4:30, June through October. In July and August you can see bullfights at the **Plaza de Toros Monumental** (✉ Playas Tijuana area, Ensenada Hwy., Playas Tijuana, ☎ 664/685–2210) Sunday at 4:30.

GOLF

The **Tijuana Country Club** (✉ Blvd. Agua Caliente, east of downtown, Zona Río, ☎ 664/681–7855) is open to the public. You can rent clubs, electric and hand carts, and caddies for the 18-hole course.

Shopping

The Avenida Revolución shopping area spreads across Calle 2 to the pedestrian walkway leading from the border. Begin by checking out the stands along the border-crossing walkway, comparing prices as you travel toward Avenida Revolución. You may find that the best bargains are closer to the border; you can pick up your piñatas and serapes on your way out of town. The traditional shopping strip is Avenida Revolución between Calles 1 and 8; it's lined with shops and arcades that display a wide range of crafts and curios. Bargaining is expected on the streets and in the arcades, but not in the finer shops.

Importaciones Sara (✉ Av. Revolución at Calle 4, Downtown, ☎ 664/688–0482), one of the best department stores in Tijuana, features a wide selection of imported perfumes and fine clothing at attractive prices. High-quality furnishings and art are tastefully displayed at **Mallorca** (✉ Calle 4 at Av. Revolución, Downtown, ☎ 664/688–8224). The **Mexicoach Terminal** (✉ Av. Revolución between Calles 6 and 7, Downtown, ☎ 664/685–1470) is a one-stop center. **La Piel** (✉ Av. Revolución between Calles 4 and 5, Downtown, ☎ 664/687–2398) has dependable quality in its leather jackets, backpacks, and luggage.

The shops in **Plaza Revolución** (✉ Calle 1 and Av. Revolución, Downtown) sell quality crafts. **Sanborns** (✉ Av. Revolución at Calle 8, Downtown, ☎ 664/688–1462) has beautiful crafts from throughout Mexico, an excellent bakery, and chocolates from Mexico City. The nicest folk-art store, **Tolán** (✉ Av. Revolución between Calles 7 and 8, Downtown, ☎ 664/688–3637), carries everything from antique, carved wooden doors to tiny, ceramic miniature village scenes.

MARKET

The **Mercado Hidalgo** (✉ Av. Independencia at Av. Sanchez Taboada, Downtown, two blocks south of Paseo de los Héroes) is Tijuana's municipal market, with rows of fresh produce, grains, herbs, some souvenirs, and the best selection of piñatas in Baja.

SHOPPING CENTERS

You can find great buys on fashionable clothing and shoes at **Plaza Río Tijuana** (✉ Paseo de los Héroes, Zona Río).

Playas de Rosarito

29 km (18 mi) south of Tijuana.

For better or worse, Rosarito has seen a transformation during the past few decades. The onetime small seaside community, once part of the municipality of Tijuana, had been an overlooked suburb on the way to the port city of Ensenada. But as the roads improved—and particularly after the 1973 completion of Baja's Transpeninsular Highway—Rosarito began to flower. Rosarito is now a municipality separate from Tijuana and is self-governed. Rosarito attracted considerable attention when 20th Century Fox built a permanent movie-production studio on the coastline south of town to film the mega-success *Titanic.* Today, the studio is home to an exciting theme park. Rosarito's leaders had hoped their town would become a cruise-ship port, and funded construction of a long pier at the Rosarito Beach Hotel. The sea, however, is too rough and shallow for the ships, so the pier has become a bustling outdoor café.

Meanwhile, Rosarito's population, now about 110,000, has been growing steadily. The city's main drag, alternately known as the Old Ensenada Highway and Boulevard Benito Juárez, reflects the unrestrained growth and speculation that have both helped and harmed Rosarito. The street is packed with restaurants, bars, and shops in a jarring juxtaposition of building styles. Fortunately, the building boom has slowed and the town's boosters are attempting to beautify the boulevard.

Southern Californians have made Rosarito their weekend getaway, and the crowd is far from subdued. Surfers, swimmers, and sunbathers come here to enjoy the beach, which stretches from the power plant at the north end of town to about 8 km (5 mi) south. Horseback riding, jogging, and strolling are popular along this uninterrupted strand, where whales swim within viewing distance on their winter migration.

Rosarito has always attracted a varied group. These days it's made up of prosperous young Californians building villas and vacation developments, retired Americans and Canadians homesteading in gated communities, and an abundance of young adults seeking cheap food, drink, and an escape from supervision. It often seems that spring break is a year-round event here, with much of the action centered on the Festival Plaza hotel. The police do their best to control the revelers, but spring and summer weekend nights can be outrageously noisy.

Hedonism and health get equal billing in Rosarito. People cast off their inhibitions, at least to the degree permitted by local constables. A typical Rosarito day might begin with a breakfast of eggs, refried beans, and tortillas, followed by a few hours of horseback riding on the beach. Lying in the sun or browsing in shops takes care of midday. Siestas are imperative and are usually followed by more shopping, strolling, or sunbathing before a night of dinner and dancing.

Rosarito has few historic or cultural attractions, beaches and bars being the main draws. Sightseeing consists of strolling along the beach or down **Boulevard Benito Juárez,** which runs parallel to it. An immense Pemex gasoline installation and electric plant anchor the northern end of Boulevard Juárez, which then runs along a collection of shopping arcades, restaurants, and motels.

Nearly everyone stops at the Rosarito Beach Hotel, the town's landmark historic hotel. Built during Prohibition, it has huge ballrooms, tiled fountains and stairways, murals, and a glassed-in pool deck overlooking the sea. A wooden pier stretches over the ocean; on calm days, there's no better place to watch the sunset than from the café tables along its glassed-in edges. Azteca, the main restaurant, is a good place to stop for Sunday brunch.

Museo Wa-Kuatay. Rosarito's history is illustrated in exhibits on the Kumiai Indians, the early missions, and ranching in the region at this small museum. The hours are inconsistent. ✉ *Blvd. Juárez next to the Rosarito Beach Hotel,* ☎ *no phone.* *Free.* ⏲ *Closed Tues.*

Foxploration. Fox Studios has expanded its operation to include a film-oriented theme park. Guests learn how films are made by visiting a set resembling a New York street scene, and another filled with props from *Titanic.* Exhibits on filming, sound and light effects, and animation are both educational and entertaining, and Fox's most famous films are shown in the large state-of-the-art theater. The park includes a children's playroom where kids can shoot thousands of foam balls out of air cannons, a food court with U.S. franchises, and a large retail area. ✉ *Old Ensenada Hwy. Km 32.8, Popotla,* ☎ *661/614–9499,* WEB *www.foxploration.com.* *$9–$12.* ⏲ *Mon., Thurs., Fri. 9–5:30, weekends 10–6:30.*

Galería Giorgio Santini. Baja's finest painters and sculptors now have a worthwhile venue for their works, which are handsomely displayed in this architecturally stunning gallery. Stop by for a glass of wine or an espresso in the coffee shop, and learn something about Baja's vibrant art scene. ✉ *Old Ensenada Hwy. Km 40,* ☎ *661/614–1459,* WEB *www.giorgiosantini.com.* *Free.* ⏲ *Closed Wed.*

Dining and Lodging

$–$$$ ✕ **El Nido.** A dark, wood-paneled restaurant with leather booths and a large central fireplace, this is one of the oldest eateries in Rosarito. Diners unimpressed with newer, fancier places come here for mesquite-grilled steaks and for grilled quail from the owner's farm in the Baja wine country. ✉ *Blvd. Juárez 67,* ☎ *661/612–1430. MC, V.*

$–$$$ ✕ **El Patio.** Calm amid the bustle of the Festival Plaza complex, this tasteful, colonial-style restaurant is the best spot for a relaxed, authentic Mexican meal. Umbrella-covered tables are framed by soft-blue and azure walls, and the aromas of chilies, mole, and grilled meats spark the appetite. The menu favors dishes like savory grilled quail, shrimp crêpes, and chicken with poblano sauce. The bar is peaceful as well—a good place to enjoy a cocktail away from the streetside crowds. ✉ *Festival Plaza, Blvd. Juárez,* ☎ *661/612–2950. AE, MC, V.*

$–$$ ★ ✕ **La Leña.** The cornerstone restaurant of the Quinta Plaza shopping center, La Leña is spacious and impeccably clean, with tables spread far enough apart for privacy. Try any of the beef dishes, especially the tender carne asada with tortillas and guacamole or the steak and lobster combo. ✉ *Quinta Plaza, Blvd. Juárez,* ☎ *661/612–0826. MC, V.*

$ ✕ **La Flor de Michoacán.** Michoacán-style carnitas, served with homemade tortillas, guacamole, and salsa, are featured at this rustic Rosarito landmark, established in 1950. The tacos, *tortas* (sandwiches), and tostadas are great. Takeout is available. ✉ *Blvd. Juárez 291,* ☎ *661/612–1858. No credit cards. Closed Wed.*

$ ✕ **Tacos El Yaqui.** For true down-home Mexican cooking, nothing beats this taco stand. Carne asada tacos wrapped in fresh corn tortillas are superb and the perfect fix for late-night munchies. The stand is clean and the cooks use purified water. ✉ *Calle de la Palma off Blvd. Juárez across from the Rosarito Beach Hotel,* ☎ *no phone. No credit cards.*

$$$–$$$$ 🏨 **Rosarito Beach Hotel and Spa.** Charm rather than comfort is the main reason for staying here. The rooms in the oldest section have hand-painted wooden beams and heavy dark furnishings. Those in the tower have air-conditioning and a more modern pastel look. Reduced midweek rates and special packages are often available. ✉ *Blvd. Juárez, south end of*

town, (Box 430145, San Diego, CA 22710), ☎ 661/612–1106 or 800/343–8582, FAX 661/612–1125, WEB www.rosaritobeachhotel.com. 180 rooms, 100 suites. 3 restaurants, tennis court, 2 pools, gym, spa, beach, bar, playground. MC, V.

$$–$$$$ ✕🏨 **Marriott Real Del Mar Residence Inn.** Golfers and escapists relish this all-suites hotel with faraway views of the sea. Accommodations have living rooms with vaulted brick ceilings, fireplaces, kitchens, and two double beds; some have one or two bedrooms. Greens fees at the on-site golf course are included in packages. Both restaurants attract diners from Tijuana and Rosarito for their fresh seafood and nouvelle Mexican preparations. ✉ *Ensenada toll road Km 19.5, 22710,* ☎ *661/631–3670 or 800/331–3131,* FAX *661/631–3677,* WEB *www.realdelmar.com.mx. 75 suites. 2 restaurants, snack bar, 18-hole golf course, pool, gym, spa, bar. AE, MC, V.*

$–$$$ ✕🏨 **Calafia.** This complex, a 10-minute car ride south of Rosarito, houses an eclectic array of attractions—all perched above the intractable sea. The walls are a nascent museum dedicated to the missionary conquests in Baja. The restaurant, with tables posed on cliffs over the crashing waves, features fresh seafood and creative Mexican cuisine. Hotel rooms are available in a variety of buildings; the best are right above the water. ✉ *Old Ensenada Hwy. Km 35.5,* ☎ *661/612–1581,* FAX *661/612–0296,* WEB *www.calafia.com.mx. 52 rooms. Restaurant, pool, beach, bar. MC, V.*

$$$–$$$$ ★ 🏨 **Las Rocas.** This white hotel with blue-tile domes is the most romantic in the area. All rooms have ocean views. The least expensive ones are small; others are larger and have fireplaces and microwaves. The pool and whirlpool seem to spill into the ocean. An excellent full spa offers state-of-the-art treatments at reasonable prices. Ask about spa packages and midweek specials. ✉ *Old Ensenada Hwy. Km 38.5, 22710,* ☎ *888/527–7622,* ☎ FAX *661/612–2140,* WEB *www.lasrocas.com. 40 rooms, 34 suites. Restaurant, 2 pools, hot tub, spa, beach, 2 bars. AE, MC, V.*

$$–$$$ 🏨 **Festival Plaza.** Designed with unrestrained fun in mind, the motel-like rooms are in an eight-story building beside the road and bars. The casitas close to the beach are the quietest accommodations and have small hot tubs, living rooms with foldout couches, but no kitchen facilities. The 13 villas just south of Rosarito have full kitchens. The central courtyard serves as a concert stage, playground, and party headquarters. Discounted room rates are often available, especially in winter. ✉ *Blvd. Juárez 11, 22710,* ☎ *624/612–0842, 661/612–2950, or 800/453–8606,* FAX *661/612–0124,* WEB *www.festivalbaja.com. 217 rooms, 5 suites, 7 casitas, 13 villas. 4 restaurants, pool, 6 bars, dance club. AE, MC, V.*

$$ 🏨 **Brisas del Mar.** This roadside motel is especially good for families—the large pastel rooms comfortably accommodate four people. A few of the suites on the second story have hot tubs and ocean views; all have air-conditioning and TV. The motel is on the inland side of Boulevard Juárez, and traffic noise can be a problem. ✉ *Blvd. Juárez 22, 22710,* ☎ FAX *661/612–2547 or 888/871–3605,* WEB *www.hotelbrisas.com. 69 rooms, 2 suites. Coffee shop, pool, bar. AE, MC, V.*

$–$$ 🏨 **Los Pelicanos Hotel.** Guests return annually to their favorite rooms in this small hotel by the beach. Those without ocean views are inexpensive; rates are higher for rooms on the top floors. The restaurant is a local favorite for sunset cocktails. ✉ *Calle Ebano 113, 22710,* ☎ FAX *661/612–0445. 39 rooms. Restaurant, bar. No credit cards.*

Nightlife and the Arts

Rosarito's many restaurants keep customers entertained with live music, piano bars, or *folklórico* (folk music and dance) shows, and the bar scene is hopping as well. Drinking-and-driving laws are stiff; the police will fine you no matter how little you've had. If you drink, take a cab or assign a designated driver. The police are also enforcing laws that prohibit drinking in the streets: confine your revelry to the bars.

The **Festival Plaza** (✉ Blvd. Juárez 11, ☎ 661/612–0842) has become party central for Rosarito's younger crowd and presents live concerts on the hotel's courtyard stage most weekends. In the hotel complex are **El Museo Cantina Tequila** (☎ 661/612–2950), dedicated to the art of imbibing tequila and stocked with more than 130 brands of the fiery drink—including the house rattlesnake tequila, said to be an aphrodisiac. Also at Festival Plaza, **Rock & Roll Taco** is a taco stand and boisterous bar with several sections, including an outdoor area backed by hotel rooms. It's the largest (and probably the most rambunctious) dancing and drinking hangout in town.

Papas and Beer (✉ On the beach off Blvd. Juárez near Rosarito Beach Hotel, ☎ 661/612–0444) draws a young, energetic crowd for drinking and dancing on the beach and small stages.

Rene's Sports Bar (✉ Carretera Transpeninsular Km 28, ☎ 661/612–1061) draws a somewhat quieter, older crowd; the restaurant isn't great, but a few pool tables, TVs broadcasting sporting events, and a convivial gaggle of gringos make the bar a great hangout.

There's a lot going on at night at the **Rosarito Beach Hotel** (✉ Blvd. Juárez, ☎ 661/612–1106): live music at the ocean-view **Beachcomber Bar**; a Mexican Fiesta on Friday and Saturday nights; and occasional live bands and dances in the cavernous ballroom.

Sports

GOLF

The **Real del Mar Golf Club** (✉ 18 km [11 mi] south of the border on Ensenada toll road, ☎ 661/631–3401) has 18 holes overlooking the ocean. Golf packages are available at some Rosarito Beach hotels.

HORSEBACK RIDING

You can hire horses at the north and south ends of Boulevard Juárez and on the beach south of the Rosarito Beach Hotel for $10 per hour. If you're a dedicated equestrian, ask about tours into the countryside, which can be arranged with the individual owners.

SURFING

The waves are particularly good at **Popotla** (Km 33), **Calafia** (Km 35.5), and **Costa Baja** (Km 36) on the Old Ensenada Highway.

Shopping

Shopping is far better in Rosarito than in most Baja cities, especially for pottery, wood furniture, and high-end household items favored by condo-owners in nearby expat clusters. Curio stands and open-air artisans' markets line Boulevard Juárez both north and south of town. Major hotels have shopping arcades with decent crafts stores.

Apisa (✉ Blvd. Juárez 2400, ☎ 661/612–0125) is said to be the finest home-decor shop in town, and sells contemporary furnishings and iron sculptures from Guadalajara. **Casa la Carreta** (✉ Old Ensenada Hwy. Km 29, ☎ 661/612–0502), one of Rosarito's best furniture shops, is worth a visit just to see the wood-carvers shaping elaborate desks, dining tables, and armoires. **Casa Torres** (✉ Rosarito Beach Hotel Shopping Center, Blvd. Juárez, ☎ 661/612–1008) carries a wide array of imported perfumes. There are several shops in this center by the hotel's parking lot, along with an Internet café. **Don Quijote Furniture** (✉ Blvd. Juárez s/n, across from Quinta Plaza, ☎ no phone) is a great outlet for custom furnishings and wrought iron. Resembling a colonial church with its facade of hand-painted tiles, **La Misión** (✉ Blvd. Juárez s/n, across from Ortega's, ☎ 661/612–1576) displays hand-carved chairs, tin lamps shaped like stars, and glazed pottery.

Puerto Nuevo (Newport)

Old Ensenada Hwy. Km 44, 12 km (7½ mi) south of Rosarito.

Southern Californians regularly cross the border to indulge in the classic Puerto Nuevo meal: grilled lobster, refried beans, rice, homemade tortillas, salsa, and lime. At least 30 restaurants are packed into this village; nearly all offer the identical menu. An artisans' market sits at the entrance to the restaurant row, and stands selling pottery, serapes, and T-shirts line the highway. Several longtime favorite inns and restaurants hug the road south to Ensenada. A marina is under construction at Puerto Salina south of Puerto Nuevo; when completed, it will allow private boaters to anchor and refuel before reaching Ensenada.

Dining and Lodging

Don't expect much variety in the food at any of the Puerto Nuevo restaurants: people come here for the classic lobster meal. Some places have full bars; others serve only wine and beer. **Ortega's,** with several branches in Puerto Nuevo and Rosarito, is the most crowded; **Ponderosa** is smaller and quieter and is run by a gracious family; **Puerto Nuevo II** offers unusual preparations of scallops and abalone (when it's available); and **La Casa de la Langosta** serves grilled fish along with lobster and shrimp. Lobsters in most places are priced as small, medium, and large—medium is about $15. Some of the lobster comes from the waters off Baja's shores (where pollution is not a concern), and is frozen when not in season (October through March). Many places import frozen lobster from the mainland; most are open for lunch and dinner on a first-come, first-served basis. Some take credit cards.

$$$–$$$$ 🏨 **Hacienda Bajamar.** On the grounds of the Bajamar golf resort, south of Puerto Nuevo and about halfway between Rosarito and Ensenada, this hacienda-style hotel surrounds a central courtyard. Rooms have hand-carved furnishings and French doors leading to landscaped patios. Private condos (some for rent) edge the golf course and the cliffs overlooking the ocean. ✉ *Old Ensenada Hwy. Km 77.5, Ensenada 22800,* ☎ *661/155–0151 or 800/225–2418,* FAX *661/155–0150,* WEB *www.bajamar.com. 81 rooms. Restaurant, golf course, 2 tennis courts, pool, bar. AE, MC, V.*

$$–$$$$ 🏨 **New Port Beach Hotel.** The closest accommodations to the lobster restaurants are in this sand-color complex with ocean views. Rooms have heaters for chilly winter nights, along with cable TV, small balconies, and simple blue-gray and white furnishings. The hotel has dance bands in the upstairs lounge, marimba music on the weekend in the lobby bar, and classical music on Sunday. ✉ *Old Ensenada Hwy. Km 45, 22712,* ☎ *661/614–1166 or 800/582–1018,* FAX *661/614–1174,* WEB *www.newportbeachhotel.com. 147 rooms. Restaurant, 2 tennis courts, pool, gym, bar. MC, V.*

$$ ★ 🏨 **La Fonda.** Landmark La Fonda has well-worn rooms decorated with carved-wood furniture, old bullfighting posters, and local folk art; most have ocean views. There are no phones or televisions, just the beach to keep you entertained. The bar is packed on weekend nights. Ask for a room as close to the sounds of the surf as possible. ✉ *Old Ensenada Hwy. Km 59, 22710 (Box 430268, San Ysidro, CA 92143),* ☎ *661/155–0307,* FAX *661/155–0390. 26 rooms. Beach, bar. No credit cards.*

Outdoor Activities and Sports

GOLF

Bajamar (✉ Old Ensenada Hwy. Km 77.5, ☎ 661/155–0151; 661/155–0161 for tee times) has 18 holes of championship-level golf on the cliffs above the ocean and another nine holes near the beach.

En Route Open views of pounding surf and jagged cliffs are interspersed with one-of-a-kind hotels and restaurants along the coastline between Rosarito and Ensenada. The paved highway (Mexico Highway 1) between the two cities often cuts a path between low mountains and high oceanside cliffs. Exits lead to rural roads, oceanfront campgrounds, and an ever-increasing number of resort communities. The small fishing villages of **San Miguel** and **El Sauzal** sit off the highway to the north of Ensenada, and you can see the **Coronado Islands** clearly off the coast.

Ensenada

104 km (65 mi) south of Tijuana, 75 km (47 mi) south of Rosarito.

In 1542 Juan Rodríguez Cabrillo first discovered the seaport that Sebastián Vizcaino named Ensenada-Bahía de Todos Santos (All Saints' Bay) in 1602. Since then the town has drawn a steady stream of explorers and developers. First ranchers made their homes on large plots along the coast and into the mountains. Gold miners followed, turning the area into a boomtown in the late 1800s. After mine stocks were depleted, the area settled back into a pastoral state, but the harbor gradually grew into a major port for shipping agricultural goods from the nearby ranches and farms. Today, with a population of some 369,000, it's one of Mexico's largest seaports and has a thriving fishing fleet and fish-processing industry. The smell of fish from the canneries lining the north and south sides of the city can be overpowering at times.

There are no beaches in Ensenada proper, but beaches north and south of town are satisfactory for swimming, sunning, surfing, and camping. On summer and holiday weekends the population swells, but the town rarely feels overcrowded. Ensenada tends to draw those who want to explore a more traditional Mexican city.

Ensenada, the third-largest city in Baja, hugs the harbor of Bahía de Todos Santos. The city is undergoing a boom, thanks in part to the cruise-ship industry. Many cruise ships stop for at least a few hours in Ensenada to clear Mexican customs; thus, Ensenada is called Baja's largest cruise-ship port. A hotel and shopping center in a complex to be called Cruise Port Village are in the planning stages. Both the waterfront and downtown's main street are pleasant places to stroll, especially since the city leaders have incurred considerable expenses to beautify the tourist areas. If you are driving, be sure to take the Centro exit from the highway, since it bypasses the commercial port area.

⓭ **Las Bodegas de Santo Tomás.** One of Baja's oldest wineries gives tours and tastings at its downtown winery and bottling plant. The local restaurant, La Embotelladora Vieja, is one of Baja's finest. The winery also operates La Esquina de Bodegas, a café, shop, and gallery in a bright-blue building across Avenida Miramar. ✉ *Av. Miramar 666, Downtown,* ☎ *646/178–3333 or 800/336–5454.* *$2.* ⏲ *Tours, tastings daily at 11, 1, and 3.*

⓮ **Fish Market.** At the northernmost point of Boulevard Costero, the main street along the waterfront, is an indoor-outdoor market where row after row of counters display piles of shrimp, tuna, dorado, marlin, snapper, and dozens of other species of fish caught off Baja's coasts. Outside, stands sell grilled or smoked fish, seafood cocktails,

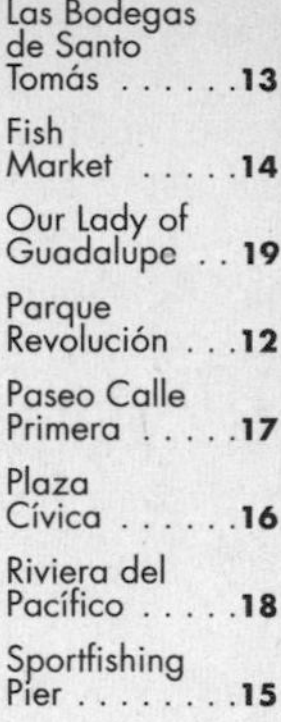

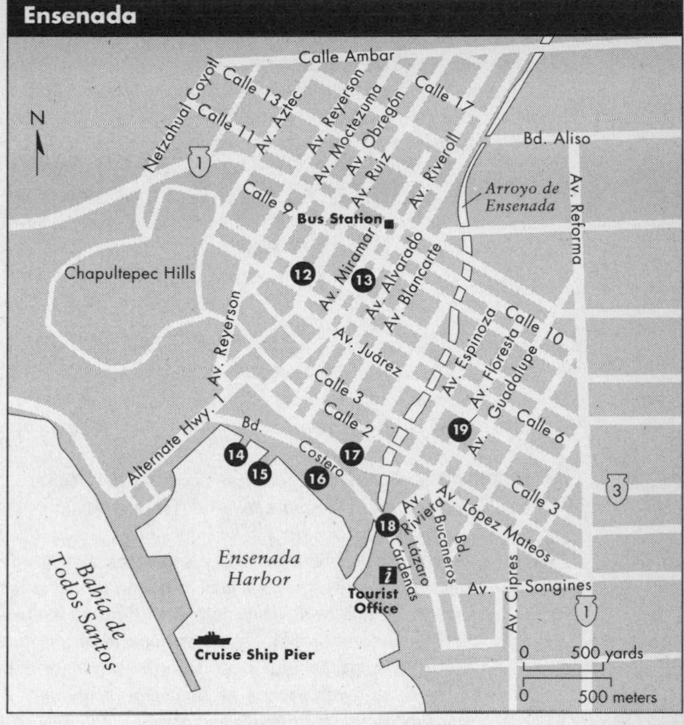

and fish tacos. Browsers can pick up some standard souvenirs, eat well for very little money, and take some great photographs. The original fish taco stands line the dirt path to the fish market. If your stomach is on the delicate side, try the fish tacos at the cleaner, quieter **Plaza de Mariscos** in the shadow of the giant beige **Plaza de Marina** that blocks the view of the traditional fish market from the street.

19 **Our Lady of Guadalupe.** The city's largest cathedral is the heart of Ensenada for many residents. ✉ *Av. Floresta at Av. Juárez, Downtown.*

12 **Parque Revolución.** Revolution Park is the most traditional plaza in Ensenada, with a bandstand, playground, and plenty of benches in the shade. The plaza takes on a festive feeling weekend evenings, when neighbors congregate on the benches and children chase seagulls. ✉ *Av. Juárez at Av. Obregón, Downtown.*

17 **Paseo Calle Primera.** The renamed Avenida López Mateos is the center of Ensenada's traditional tourist zone. High-rise hotels, souvenir shops, restaurants, and bars line the avenue for eight blocks, from its beginning at the foot of the Chapultepec Hills to the dry channel of the Arroyo de Ensenada. Tourist promoters have sponsored a beautification project along the avenue, which now has sidewalks, outdoor cafés, and restored storefronts. Businesses use one or both street names for their addresses, though most stick with López Mateos. Locals shop for furniture, clothing, and other necessities a few blocks inland on **Avenida Juárez,** in Ensenada's downtown area.

16 **Plaza Cívica.** The block-long concrete park has sculptures of Mexican heroes Benito Juárez, Miguel Hidalgo, and Venustiano Carranza. ✉ *Blvd. Costero at Av. Riveroll, Downtown.*

18 **Riviera del Pacífico.** Officially called the Centro Social, Cívico y Cultural de Ensenada (Social, Civic and Cultural Center of Ensenada), the Riviera is a rambling white, hacienda-style mansion built in the 1920s.

An enormous gambling palace, hotel, restaurant, and bar, the glamorous Riviera was frequented by wealthy U.S. citizens and Mexicans, particularly during Prohibition. When gambling was outlawed in Mexico and Prohibition ended in the United States, the palace lost its raison d'être. You can tour some of the elegant ballrooms and halls, which occasionally host art shows and civic events. Many of the rooms are locked; check at the main office to see if someone is available to show you around. The gardens alone are worth visiting, and the building now houses the **Museo de Historia de Ensenada,** a museum on Baja's history. ✉ *Blvd. Costero and Av. Riviera, Downtown,* ☎ *646/176–4310; 646/177–0594 for museum.* *Building and gardens free, museum donations requested.* ⏲ *Daily 9:30–2 and 3–5.*

15 **Sportfishing Pier.** Fishing and whale-watching boats depart from the pier. The area around the pier has been remodeled, and a broad *malecón* (seaside walkway) with park benches and palms runs along the waterfront. ✉ *Blvd. Costero at Av. Alvarado, Downtown.*

OFF THE BEATEN PATH

LA BUFADORA – Seawater splashes up to 75 ft in the air, spraying sightseers standing near this impressive tidal blowhole (*la bufadora* means the buffalo snort) in the coastal cliffs at Punta Banda. Legend has it that the blowhole was created by a whale or sea serpent trapped in an undersea cave; both these stories, and the less romantic scientific facts, are posted on a roadside plaque here. The road to La Bufadora along Punta Banda, an isolated, mountainous point that juts into the sea, is lined with stands selling olives, tamales, strands of chilies and garlic, and terra-cotta planters. The drive gives short-term visitors a sampling of Baja's wilderness and is well worth a half-day excursion. Public rest rooms are available. There's a small fee to park near the blowhole. There's a public bus that runs from the downtown Ensenada bus station to Maneadero, the nearest town on the highway to La Bufadora. There, you can catch a minibus labeled Punta Banda that goes to La Bufadora. ✉ *Hwy. 23, 31 km (19 mi) south of Ensenada, Punta Banda.*

Beaches

The waterfront in Ensenada proper is taken up by fishing boats, repair yards, and commercial shipping. The best swimming beaches are south of town. **Estero Beach** is long and clean, with mild waves; the Estero Beach Hotel takes up much of the oceanfront, but the beach is public. Surfers populate the beaches off Highway 1 north and south of Ensenada, particularly **San Miguel, California, Tres Marías,** and **La Joya;** scuba divers prefer **Punta Banda,** by La Bufadora. Lifeguards are rare, so swimmers should be cautious. The tourist office in Ensenada has a map that shows safe diving and surfing beaches.

Dining and Lodging

$–$$$ ✕ **Bronco's Steak House.** A great find near the Riviera del Pacífico, Bronco's serves exceptional steaks and Mexican specialties. Try the Boca del Río, a New York steak stuffed with grilled onions and fiery serrano chilies. Tripe appears frequently on the menu, satisfying the cravings of the local diners gathered at many of the wood tables. Brick walls, wood-plank floors, and hanging spurs and chaps give the place a Wild West feel, but the mood is subdued and relaxed. Locals rave about the weekend breakfast buffet. ✉ *Av. López Mateos 1525, Downtown,* ☎ *646/176–4900. MC, V.*

$–$$$ ★ ✕ **La Embotelladora Vieja.** The most elegant restaurant in Ensenada is this converted wine-aging room at the Santo Tomás winery. The Baja French menu could include smoked tuna, grilled lobster in cabernet sauvignon sauce, or quail with sauvignon blanc sauce. Some dishes are available without alcohol-enhanced sauces. ✉ *Av. Miramar 666, Downtown,* ☎ *646/174–0807. MC, V. Closed Tues.*

$–$$$ ★ ✕ **El Rey Sol.** From its chateaubriand *bouquetière* (garnished with a bouquet of vegetables) to the savory chicken chipotle, this family-owned French restaurant sets the standard for fine dining in Baja. Open since 1947, the restaurant is comfortable and elegant, with Louis XIV–style furnishings, and the service is attentive. The sidewalk tables are a perfect place to dine and enjoy people-watching. The small café in the front sells pastries, all made on the premises, to go. ✉ *Av. López Mateos 1000, Downtown,* ☎ *646/178–1733. AE, MC, V.*

$–$$ ★ ✕ **Mariscos de Bahía de Ensenada.** Red lights flicker around the front door, making this popular seafood house just off the main drag easy to spot. The place is packed on weekends. Clams, shrimp, lobster, red snapper, squid, and other fresh seafood are fried, baked, broiled, or grilled, and served with a basic iceberg-lettuce salad, white rice, and tortillas made fresh at the window-front tortillería. A few canopied sidewalk tables allow for outdoor dining. ✉ *Av. Riveroll 109, Downtown,* ☎ *646/178–1015. MC, V.*

$–$$ ✕ **Oxidos Café.** Baja meets L.A. at this new-wave café where the metal sculptures and other original art are as interesting as the food. The menu aims to satisfy hungry diners with hearty burgers, ribs, and pasta. The bar is a gathering spot for local artistes. You're sure to get into some interesting conversations if you hang out here. ✉ *Av. Ruíz 108, Downtown,* ☎ *646/178–8827. No credit cards.*

$ ★ ✕ **El Charro.** Hungry patrons hover over platters of *chiles rellenos* (cheese-stuffed chilies deep-fried in batter), enchiladas, and fresh chips and guacamole at heavy wooden picnic tables. Plump chickens slowly turn over a wood fire by the front window, and the aroma of simmering beans fills the air. ✉ *Av. López Mateos 475, Downtown,* ☎ *646/178–3881. No credit cards.*

$$$–$$$$ ★ **Hotel Coral & Marina.** The largest resort on the Baja Norte coast features a marina with slips for 600 boats and customs-clearing facilities. All rooms here are suites. Those in the two eight-story towers are decorated in burgundy and dark green; most have waterfront balconies, seating areas, cable TV, and international phone service. The full-service spa, tennis courts, and water-sports center are added attractions that keep the hotel full during boat races and holidays. The rates are often lower on winter weekdays. ✉ *Mexico Hwy. 1 Km 103, Zona Playitas* ☎ *646/175–0000 or 877/233–5839,* FAX *646/175–0005,* WEB *www.hotelcoral.com. 147 suites. Restaurant, 2 tennis courts, 3 pools (1 indoor), gym, hot tub, spa, boating, fishing. MC, V.*

$$$–$$$$ ★ **Punta Morro.** Just five minutes from Ensenada, this secluded all-suites hotel is a great place to relax. The restaurant, perched above the crashing waves, has an excellent combination of Continental cuisine and fresh seafood. All rooms have seaside terraces and fireplaces. Studios with kitchens are the least expensive units; two- and three-bedroom suites are available for groups and families. ✉ *Mexico Hwy. 1, 3 km (2 mi) north of town, Zona Playitas,* ☎ *646/178–3507 or 800/526–6676,* FAX *646/174–4490,* WEB *www.punta-morro.com. 30 suites. Restaurant, pool, hot tub, beach, bar. MC, V.*

$$$ ★ **Las Rosas.** This elegant all-suites hotel north of Ensenada is both intimate and upscale. The atrium lobby has marble floors, mint-green-and-pink couches that look out at the sea, and a glass ceiling that glows at night. All rooms face the ocean and pool; some have fireplaces and hot tubs, and even the least expensive are lovely. Make reservations far in advance. *Mexico Hwy. 1, north of Ensenada, Zona Playitas,* ☎ *646/174–4320,* FAX *646/174–4595,* WEB *www.lasrosas.com. 32 suites. Restaurant, pool, hot tub, bar. AE, MC, V.*

$$–$$$ **Estero Beach Resort.** Families love this long-standing resort on Ensenada's best beach. The best rooms (some with kitchenettes) are by the sand; the worst are by the parking lot. Nonguests should check out the outstanding collection of folk art and artifacts in the resort's small museum. Midweek winter rates are a real bargain. ✉ *Mexico Hwy. 1, 10 km (6 mi) south of Ensenada, Estero Beach,* ☎ *646/176–6230,* FAX *646/176–6925,* WEB *www.hotelesterobeach.com. 106 rooms, 2 suites, RV park. Restaurant, kitchenettes, 4 tennis courts, pool, horseback riding, volleyball, bar, shops, playground. MC, V.*

$ **Hotel del Valle.** Fishermen and budget travelers frequent the clean, basic rooms in this small hotel on a relatively quiet side street. Although the rooms lack air-conditioning, they're well maintained and have fans, phones, and TVs (with local stations only). Guests have use of a coffeemaker in the lobby and parking spaces in front of the rooms. Ask about rate discounts—those posted behind the front desk are about 40% higher than guests in the know normally pay. ✉ *Av. Riveroll 367, Downtown 22800,* ☎ *646/178–2224,* FAX *646/174–0466. 42 rooms. MC, V.*

$ **Joker Hotel.** A bizarre, colorful mishmash of styles makes it hard to miss the Joker, which is conveniently located for those traveling south of Ensenada. Spacious rooms have private balconies, satellite TV, and phones. Traffic noise from the highway and from guests leaving at the crack of dawn can be a problem; try to stay away from the road and the busiest parts of the parking lot. ✉ *Mexico Hwy. 1 Km 12.5, Ejido Chapultepec 22800,* ☎ *646/176–7201,* FAX *646/176–4460. 40 rooms. Pool, hot tub. MC, V.*

Nightlife and the Arts

Ensenada is a party town for college students, surfers, and other young tourists, though it's also possible to enjoy a mellow evening out. **La Capilla** (✉ Hotel El Cid, Blvd. López Mateos 993, Downtown, ☎ 646/174–2401) is better suited to an older crowd who enjoy live Cuban music and romantic ballads in a relaxed setting. **Hussong's Cantina** (✉ Av. Ruíz 113, Downtown, ☎ 646/178–3210) has been an Ensenada landmark since 1892 and has changed little since then. A security guard stands by the front door to handle the often rowdy crowd—a mix of locals and tourists of all ages over 18. The noise is usually deafening, pierced by mariachi and ranchera musicians and the whoops and hollers of the inebriated. **Papas and Beer** (✉ Av. Ruíz at López Mateos, Downtown, ☎ 646/178–0145) attracts a collegiate crowd.

Outdoor Activities and Sports

FISHING

Boats leave the Ensenada **Sportfishing Pier** regularly. The best angling is from April through November, with bottom fishing good in winter. Charter vessels and party boats are available from several outfitters along Avenida López Mateos and Boulevard Costero and off the sportfishing pier. Trips on group boats cost about $45 for a half day or $100 for a full day. Mexican fishing licenses for the day or year are at the tourist office or from charter companies.

You can book sportfishing packages including transportation, accommodations, and fishing through **Baja California Tours** (☎ 858/454–7166; 800/336–5454 in the U.S., FAX 858/454–2703, WEB www.bajatours.signonsandiego.com). **Ensenada Clipper Fleet** (✉ Sportfishing Pier, Blvd. Costero at Av. Alvarado, Downtown, ☎ 646/178–2185) has charter and group boats. **Sergio's Sportfishing** (✉ Sportfishing Pier, Blvd. Costero at Av. Alvarado, Downtown, ☎ 646/178–2185, FAX 646/178–2377), one of the best sportfishing companies in Ensenada, has charter and group boats, and slips for guests' boats.

GOLF

The **Baja Country Club** (✉ Mexico Hwy. 1 south of Ensenada, Maneadero, ☎ 646/177–5523) has a secluded 18-hole course in a resort development.

KAYAKING

Estero Beach and Punta Banda (en route to La Bufadora south of Ensenada) are both good kayaking areas, although facilities are limited. **Dale's La Bufadora Shop** (✉ Rancho La Bufadora, Punta Banda, ☎ 646/154–2092) offers kayak rentals. The shop is open on weekends or by advance reservation. **Expediciones de Turismo Ecológico y Aventura** (✉ Blvd. Costero 1094-14, Downtown, ☎ 646/178–3704) runs kayaking trips and other adventure tours in the region.

WHALE-WATCHING

Boats leave the Ensenada **Sportfishing Pier** for whale-watching trips from December through February. The gray whales migrating from the north to bays and lagoons in southern Baja pass through Todos Santos Bay, often close to shore. There are restrictions on how close the boats can get to the whales, but you should be able to get good photos. Binoculars and telephoto camera lenses come in handy. The trips last about three hours. Vessels and tour boats are available from several outfitters, including Sergio's, along Avenida López Mateos and Boulevard Costero and off the sportfishing pier. You can book whale-watching packages, which include transportation, accommodations, and the boat trips, through the American company **Baja California Tours** (☎ 800/336–5454; 858/454–7166 in the U.S., FAX 858/454–2703, WEB www.bajatours.signonsandiego.com).

Shopping

Most of the tourist shops are located along Avenida López Mateos beside the hotels and restaurants. There are several two-story shopping arcades, many with empty shops. Dozens of curio shops line the street, all selling similar selections of pottery, serapes, and more.

Artes Don Quijote (✉ Av. López Mateos 503, Downtown, ☎ 646/176–9476) has an impressive array of carved wood doors, huge terra-cotta pots, and crafts from Oaxaca. **Bazar Casa Ramirez** (✉ Av. López Mateos 510, Downtown, ☎ 646/178–8209) sells high-quality Talavera pottery and other ceramics, wrought-iron items, and papier-mâché figurines. Be sure to check out the displays upstairs. At **Los Castillo** (✉ Av. López Mateos 815, Downtown, ☎ 646/176–1187), the display of silver jewelry from Taxco is limited but of excellent quality. **Mario's Silver** (✉ Calle Primera 1090-6, Downtown, ☎ 646/178–2451) has several branches along the main street tempting shoppers with displays of silver and gold jewelry. **La Mina de Salomón** (✉ Av. López Mateos 1000, Downtown, ☎ 646/178–2836) carries elaborate jewelry in a tiny gallery next to El Rey Sol restaurant.

The **Centro Artesenal de Ensenada** has a smattering of galleries and shops.By far, the best shop at the Centro Artesenal is **Galería de Pérez Meillón** (✉ Blvd. Costera 1094–39, Downtown, ☎ 646/174–0394), with its museum-quality Casas Grandes pottery and varied folk art by indigenous northern Mexican peoples. **La Esquina de Bodegas** (✉ Av. Miramar at Calle 6, Downtown, ☎ 646/178–3557) is an innovative gallery, shop, and café in a century-old winery building. Baja's finest wines are sold here at reasonable prices, and an upstairs gallery sells glassware, pottery, and books. Bargain hunters are delighted with **Los Globos** (✉ Calle 9, three blocks east of Reforma, Downtown, ☎ no phone), a daily open-air swap meet. Vendors and shoppers are most abundant on weekends.

Side Trip to the Guadalupe Valley

Most of Baja's wineries are in the Guadalupe Valley northeast of Ensenada on Highway 3 to Tecate. The valley, originally settled by Russian immigrants, is one of the loveliest parts of the state, with vast vineyards and rambling hacienda-style estates. A few of the wineries are open to the public. **Baja California Tours** (☏ 800/336–5454; 858/454–7166 in the U.S., FAX 858/454–2703, WEB www.bajatours.signonsandiego.com) frequently offers winery tours, which include visits to several wineries, a historical overview of the valley, transportation from the border, and lunch.

Domecq (✉ Hwy. 3 Km 73, ☏ 646/155–2249) offers wine tastings and tours. Call ahead for hours. **L.A. Cetto** (✉ Hwy. 3 Km 73.5, ☏ 646/155–2264) has wine tastings and tours daily 10–4.

The **Museo Comunitario del Valle de Guadalupe** (✉ Hwy. 3 Km 70, ☏ 646/155–2030), open Tuesday–Sunday 9–5, contains a display of Russian household items from the local indigenous settlements in a 1905 Russian home. If it's not open, ask around for the caretaker.

Tecate

32 km (20 mi) east of Tijuana, 112 km (69 mi) northeast of Ensenada.

Tecate is a quiet border community with a population of about 100,000 and the pleasant ambience of a small Mexican town. Visitors stop by on day trips from Tijuana, Ensenada, or San Diego to shop and to have lunch at modest cafés facing the pleasant Parque Hidalgo. Tecate's most famous attraction is Rancho la Puerta.

One of the area's largest pottery yards is **Baja-Mex-Tile** (✉ Blvd. Juárez 9150, Carretera Tecate a Tijuana, ☏ 665/654–0204). Downtown Tecate is centered on the **Parque Hidalgo.** A few cabdrivers, shoe-shine boys, schoolchildren, and snuggling couples hang out around the small gazebo. On summer evenings, dance and band concerts are held in **Parque López Mateos,** on Highway 3 south of town.

Dining and Lodging

$–$$ ✕ **El Tucan.** Fancy by local standards, this motel restaurant is the current favorite for everything from hamburgers to spicy beefsteaks. The full bar and banquet facilities draw *maquiladora* executives and local bigwigs, and everyone enjoys the lively ambience in the dining room. ✉ *Av. Juárez 1100,* ☏ *665/654–1102. MC, V.*

$ ✕ **Panadería de Tecate.** Open 24 hours every day except Christmas and New Year's, this simple bakery is famed throughout the region. The kitchen whips up more than 100 types of cookies, doughnuts, *pan dulce* (sweet bread), crunchy *bolillos* (rolls), and cakes. ✉ *Av. Juárez 331,* ☏ *665/654–0040. No credit cards.*

$ ✕ **Plaza Jardín.** The setting is plain and the food simple Mexican fare, but the café tables outside have a pleasant view of the plaza. ✉ *Callejón Libertad 274,* ☏ *665/654–3453. No credit cards.*

$$$$ **Rancho la Puerta.** Spanish-style buildings and modern glass-and-wood structures are spread throughout the sprawling ranch at this isolated spa. Guests stay in luxurious private cottages and check in for at least a week to indulge in the perfect blend of exercise, diet, and pampering. Advance reservations are essential. Transportation is available to and from the San Diego airport. ✉ *Hwy. 2, 5 km (3 mi) west of Tecate, 21275,* ☏ *665/654–1155 or 800/443–7565; 760/744–4222 in the U.S.,* FAX *760/744–5007 in the U.S.,* WEB *www.rancholapuerta.com. 80 rooms. Restaurant, 4 tennis courts, pool, 2 health clubs, hair salon, spa. AE, MC, V.*

$$ **Hacienda Santa Veronica.** The Hacienda is a pretty countryside resort whose rooms are furnished with Mexican colonial beds, bureaus, and fireplaces. Off-road trails etch the 5,000-acre property, making it a popular stop-off for motorcyclists and mountain bikers. Horseback riding is available in the summer, and bullfights are occasionally held at the ranch's bullring. ✉ *30 km (19 mi) east of Tecate off Hwy. 2,* ☎ *665/648–5234; 619/423–3830 in the U.S. 55 rooms. Restaurant, 8 tennis courts, pool, horseback riding, bar. No credit cards.*

Mexicali

136 km (84 mi) east of Tijuana.

Mexicali, with a population of about 850,000, shares the Imperial Valley farmland and the border crossing with Calexico, a small California city. The capital of Baja California, Mexicali sees a great deal of government activity and a steady growth of maquiladoras. Most visitors come to town on business, and the city's sights are few and far between. A tourist-oriented strip of curio shops, restaurants, and bars is along Avenida Francisco Madero, a block south of the border.

Dining and Lodging

$$–$$$ ✕ **La Misión Dragon.** Chinese laborers came to Mexicali in the early 20th century to work on irrigation and railroad projects. As a result, the city has one of the largest Chinese populations (and some of the best Chinese restaurants) in Mexico. The most famous restaurant is renowned for its crispy special duck and suckling pig in plum sauce. ✉ *Lázaro Cárdenas 555,* ☎ *686/566–4400. MC, V.*

$$$ ✕ **La Lucerna.** The prettiest hotel in Mexicali, the colonial-style Lucerna has plenty of palms and fountains around the pools and carved-wood furnishings in the dark, somber rooms. A newer section has suites with separate seating areas and modern furnishings. The two restaurants have local decor and good Mexican meals. Conventions and business meetings sometimes fill the hotel; advance reservations are advised. ✉ *Av. Benito Juárez 2151, 21270,* ☎ *686/564–7000 or 800/582–3762,* FAX *686/566–4706,* WEB *www.hotel-lucerna.com.mx. 175 rooms, 28 cabins, 4 suites. 2 restaurants, 2 pools, bar. MC, V.*

En Route **Parque Nacional San Pedro Mártir.** Baja's interior mountain ranges are filled with hidden caves and mountain hideaways. This park is more accessible than most, and even a short drive or hike up its rough trails offers a different perspective on Baja. As long as it hasn't been raining, a regular car can handle the dirt road into the park. ✉ *140 km (87 mi) south of Ensenada, turn off Hwy. 1 south of Colonet and drive 98 km (61 mi) east to the park.*

San Quintín

191 km (118 mi) south of Ensenada.

Agricultural fields line the highway as you enter San Quintín, the largest producer of tomatoes in Baja. The Oaxacan migrant workers who plant and pick the fertile valley's produce live in squalid camps out of the view of travelers. **Bahía de San Quintín,** which fronts a few small hotels, is among northern Baja's best fishing grounds, along with **Bahía Falsa** and **Bahía Santa Maria,** and the area's few hostelries tend to cater to anglers. Roadside stands sell the local delicacy, Pismo clams, fresh and cooked. Travelers often stop here for essentials en route farther south; this is the last major outpost until Guerrero Negro (a drive of about six hours).

Lodging

$ **Old Mill.** Anglers ease their boats into the sheltered bay at this longtime favorite hideaway and set up housekeeping in a variety of rooms, some with kitchens and fireplaces. The lodge-style bar with its huge fireplace is filled with locals and travelers on weekend nights. ✉ *South of San Quintín on a dirt road leading to the bay,* ☎ FAX *616/165–3376, 800/479–7962, or 877/800–4081,* WEB *www.oldmillbaja.com. 30 rooms, 2 suites. Restaurant, fishing, bar. No credit cards.*

San Felipe

198 km (123 mi) south of Mexicali, 244 km (151 mi) southeast of Ensenada.

San Felipe (pop. 25,000) is the quintessential fishing village with one main street (two if you count the highway into town). It sits at the edge of the northern Sea of Cortez, which is protected as an ecological reserve in this region. The ***malecón*** (seaside walkway) runs along a broad beach with a swimming area. Taco stands, bars, and restaurants are clustered at the south end of the beach.

In 1948 the first paved road from Mexicali was extended into town, at which point San Felipe became significant. Prior to that time only a few fishermen and their families lived along the coast; now there are impressive fishing and shrimping fleets.

A getaway spot for years, San Felipe has several campgrounds and modest hotels, which fill up quickly during winter and spring holidays. Snowbirds arrive in recreational vehicles in winter, setting up huge vacation communities in local trailer parks. On holiday weekends San Felipe can be boisterous—dune buggies, motorcycles, and off-road vehicles abound—but most of the time it's a quiet, relaxing place. The town also appeals to sportfishers, especially in spring. Launches, bait, and supplies are readily available. Locals, including a large population of retired Americans, are working to improve San Felipe's image and have opened small galleries and shops.

The main landmark in San Felipe is the **shrine of the Cerro de la Virgen** (Virgin of Guadalupe), at the north end of the malecón on a hill overlooking the sea.

The **Bahía San Felipe** has dramatic changes in its tides. They crest at 20 ft, and because the beach is so broad, the waterline can move in and out up to 1 km (about ½ mi). Local fishermen are well aware of the peculiarities of this section of the Sea of Cortez; many of them visit the shrine of the Cerro de la Virgen before setting sail.

Dining and Lodging

$$–$$$ ✕ **El Nido.** One in a chain of reliable steak houses, this comfy restaurant is known for its good burgers, steaks, and seafood platters. The Mexican specialties are toned down for tourists' palates. You can order imported whiskey or scotch to go with your beef, but beware of high prices. ✉ *Av. Mar de Cortés 348,* ☎ *686/577–1660. MC, V.*

$–$$ ✕ **Red Lobster.** A Mexican combo plate featuring grilled chicken rather than the ubiquitous carne asada is a good choice, as are all the shrimp dishes at this slightly fancy (by local standards) restaurant in a small hotel. Ask what the fishermen have brought in that day—it could be anything from clams to *huachinango* (red snapper). ✉ *Av. Mar de Cortés at Chetumal,* ☎ *686/577–1571. No credit cards.*

$ ✕ **Rice and Beans.** The name nearly says it all—the word "fish" should precede it. This is the place to try *mantaraya* (stingray) tacos and fish soup, along with San Felipe's famous shrimp. It's a casual hangout for the expat-retiree gang. ✉ *Malecón at Av. Chetumal,* ☎ *no phone. No credit cards.*

$$$ **San Felipe Marina Resort.** Most rooms at this low-slung terra-cotta building facing the sea have kitchens, woven rugs on white-tile floors, folk-art decorations, and balconies or patios with sea views. The least expensive rooms lack kitchens and ocean views. The pool sits above the beach next to a *palapa* (thatch-roof) bar; a second, indoor pool is a delight on cold winter days. The resort is a five-minute drive south of town and has an RV campground next door. ✉ *Carretera San Felipe Aeropuerto Km 4.5, 21850,* ☎ *686/577–1455,* FAX *686/577–1568. 60 rooms, 123 RV spaces. Restaurant, 2 tennis courts, 2 pools (1 indoor), gym, bar, shops. AE, MC, V.*

$$–$$$ **El Cortez.** Easily the most popular hotel in San Felipe, El Cortez has several types of accommodations, including moderate-price bungalows and modern hotel rooms. The hotel's beachfront and second-story bars are both enduringly beloved, and the restaurant is the nicest water-view dining spot in town. The hotel is a five-minute walk from the malecón. ✉ *Av. Mar de Cortés s/n, 21850 (Box 1227, Calexico, CA 92232),* ☎ *686/577–1055,* FAX *686/577–1056. 77 rooms, 4 suites, 24 bungalows. Restaurant, pool, 2 bars. MC, V.*

$$ **Las Misiones.** A pretty oasis of blue pools and green palms by the beach, this resort is big with group tours. It's also a good choice if you want to get away from it all—but you'll need a car or cab to get to town. A building down the street from the hotel has suites with kitchens. ✉ *Av. Misión de Loreto 148, 21850,* ☎ *686/577–1280 or 858/454–7166; 800/336–5454 in the U.S.,* FAX *686/577–1283,* WEB *www.hotellasmisiones.com. 186 rooms, 31 suites. Restaurant, 2 tennis courts, 2 pools, bar. MC, V.*

Outdoor Activities and Sports

FISHING

The northern part of the Sea of Cortez offers plentiful sea bass, snapper, corbina, halibut, and other game fish. Clamming is good here as well. It's important to use a well-established company when fishing off San Felipe, as there have been several serious incidents involving anglers lost at sea. **Alex Sportfishing** (☎ 686/577–1052), runs day trips on small skiffs. Casey's Baja Tours (☎ 686/577–2739) runs tours to Puertocitos, a small community with natural hot springs south of San Felipe, along with other desert and sea activities. **Tony Reyes Sportfishing** (☎ 686/577–1120; 714/538–9300 in the U.S., FAX 714/538–1368 in the U.S.) is one of the most reputable companies offering multiday trips, and uses a U.S.-based company to organize trips.

BAJA NORTE A TO Z

To research prices, get advice from other travelers, and book travel arrangements, visit www.fodors.com.

AIR TRAVEL

There are few international flights into Baja Norte; most travelers access the area from the border at San Diego. Several airlines offer flights between mainland Mexico and Tijuana or Mexicali, which currently have the only commercial flights in the region. Tijuana's Aeropuerto Alberado Rodriguez is on the eastern edge of the city, near the Otay Mesa border crossing. The Tijuana airport is served from cities in Baja and mainland Mexico. Mexicali's international airport, Aeropuerto Internacional General Rodolfo Sánchez Taboada, is about 11 km (7 mi) east of the city.

CARRIERS

Mexicana flies from Tijuana to Los Cabos Hermosillo, Monterrey, Mexico City, and Guadalajara, connecting with other national and international flights. Aeroméxico flies to Los Cabos, La Paz, and Mexicali on the Baja Peninsula and to several cities in mainland Mexico. AeroCalifornia flies to La Paz.

➤ AIRLINES AND CONTACTS: **AeroCalifornia** (☎ 664/684–2100; 664/684–2876 in Tijuana). **Aeroméxico** (☎ 664/686–5588 in Tijuana; 686/557–2551 in Mexicali). **Mexicana** (☎ 664/634–6596 in Tijuana; 686/552–9391 in Mexicali).

BUS TRAVEL

Greyhound serves the border from San Diego several times daily. Buses to San Diego and Los Angeles depart from the Greyhound terminal in Tijuana at Avenida Mexico at Madero. Mexicoach runs buses from the trolley depot and the large parking lot on the U.S. side of the border to its depot on Avenida Revolución. Buses also run from Tijuana to Rosarito several times daily.

Buses connect all the towns in Baja Norte and are easy to use; stations are in Ensenada, Mexicali, San Felipe, Tecate, and Tijuana. Buses traveling to Rosarito stop at the Rosarito exit on the toll road where taxis wait to transport passengers to town. There is no official bus station here; check at the hotels for bus-schedule information.

Autotransportes de Baja California covers the entire Baja route and connects in Mexicali with buses to Guadalajara and Mexico City. Elite has first-class service to mainland Mexico. Transportes del Pacífico goes to Mexico City and other points on the mainland from Mexicali; Transportes Norte de Sonora frequents border towns in Baja and on mainland Mexico.

➤ BUS INFORMATION: **Greyhound** (☎ 664/621–2951 or 664/686–0695 in Tijuana; 619/239–3266 in the U.S.; 800/231–2222). **Mexicoach** (☎ 664/685–1470; 619/428–9517 in the U.S., WEB www.mexicoach.com).

➤ BUS STATIONS: **Ensenada bus station** (✉ Av. Riveroll 1075 between Calles 10 and 11, Ensenada, ☎ 646/178–6680). **Mexicali bus station** (✉ Centro Cívico, Av. Independencia, Mexicali, ☎ 686/557–2410). **San Felipe bus station** (✉ Av. Mar Caribe at Av. Manzanillo, San Felipe, ☎ 686/577–1516). **Tecate bus station** (✉ Av. Benito Juárez and Calle Abelardo Rodríguez, Tecate, ☎ 665/654–1221). **Tijuana bus station** (✉ Calzada Lázaro Cárdenas and Blvd. Arroyo Alamar, Tijuana, ☎ 664/621–2982).

TIJUANA BUS TRAVEL

The downtown station for buses within the city is at Calle 1a and Avenida Madero (☎ 664/686–9515). Most city buses at the border will take you downtown; look for the ones marked CENTRO CAMIONERA. To catch the bus back to the border from downtown, go to Calle Benito Juárez (also called Calle 2a) between Avenidas Revolución and Constitución. *Colectivos* (small, often striped vans) cover neighborhood routes in most Baja cities and towns. The destination is usually painted on the windshield; look for them on main streets.

CAR RENTAL

Many U.S. car-rental companies do not allow you to drive their cars into Mexico. Avis permits its cars to go from San Diego into Baja as far as 724 km (450 mi) south of the border. Cars must be returned by the renter to San Diego, and you must declare your intention to take the car into Mexico and purchase Mexican auto insurance. Southwest

Car Rentals allows its cars as far as Ensenada. You must purchase Mexican insurance when you rent the car. California Baja Rent-A-Car rents four-wheel-drive vehicles, convertibles, and sedans for use throughout Mexico (the only company to do this). If you plan to rent your car in Tijuana or San Diego and drop it in Los Cabos, be prepared to pay a hefty sum (up to $900) on top of the rental price.

Fiesta Rent-a-Car and Hertz have offices in Ensenada. The larger U.S. rental agencies have offices at the Tijuana International Airport (Aeropuerto Alberado Rodriguez), and Avis and Budget have offices in downtown Tijuana.

California Baja Rent-A-Car has a fabulous fleet of vehicles you can drive all over Mexico. Vans, recreational vehicles, off-road four-by-fours, and regular sedans are all available. You can drop the car off in Cabo San Lucas; the fee is $600–$800.

➤ MAJOR AGENCIES: **Avis** (✉ Av. Agua Caliente 3310, Tijuana, ☎ 664/686–4004, 664/686–3718, or 800/331–1212). **Budget** (✉ Paseo de los Héroes 77, Tijuana, ☎ 664/634–3303). **California Baja Rent-A-Car** (✉ 9245 Jamacha Blvd., Spring Valley, CA 91977, ☎ 619/470–7368 or 888/470–7368). **Fiesta Rent-a-Car** (✉ Hotel Corona at Blvd. Costero, Ensenada, ☎ 646/176–3344). **Hertz** (✉ Av. Blancarte between Calles 1 and 2, Ensenada, ☎ 646/178–2982).

CAR TRAVEL

The best way to tour Baja Norte is by car, although the driving can be difficult and confusing. If you're just visiting Tijuana, Tecate, or Mexicali, it's easiest to park on the U.S. side of the border and walk across.

From San Diego, U.S. 5 and I–805 end at the San Ysidro border crossing; Highway 905 leads from I–5 and I–805 to the Tijuana border crossing at Otay Mesa. U.S. 94 from San Diego connects with U.S. 188 to the border at Tecate, 57 km (35 mi) east of San Diego. I–8 from San Diego connects with U.S. 111 at Calexico—203 km (126 mi) east—and the border crossing to Mexicali. San Felipe lies on the coast, 200 km (124 mi) south of Mexicali via Highway 5.

To head south into Baja from Tijuana, follow the signs for Ensenada Cuota, the toll road (also called Highway 1 and, on newer signs, the Scenic Highway) that runs south along the coast. There are two clearly marked exits for Rosarito, and one each for Puerto Nuevo, Bajamar, and Ensenada. The road is excellent, although it has some hair-raising curves atop the cliffs and is best driven in daylight (the stretch from Rosarito to Ensenada is one of the most scenic drives in Baja). Tollbooths accept U.S. and Mexican currency; tolls are usually just over $3. Rest rooms are available near toll stations. The alternative free road—Highway 1D or Ensenada Libre—has been vastly improved, but it's difficult for the first-timer to navigate. Highway 1 continues south of Ensenada through San Quintín to Guerrero Negro, at the border between Baja California and Baja Sur, and on to the southernmost tip of Baja; there are no tolls past Ensenada.

Mexico Highway 2 runs east from Tijuana to Tecate and Mexicali. There are toll roads between Tijuana and Tecate and between Tecate and Mexicali. The 134-km (83-mi) journey from Tecate east to Mexicali on La Rumorosa, as the road is known, is as exciting as a roller-coaster ride, with the highway twisting and turning down steep mountain grades and over flat, barren desert.

If you're traveling only as far as Ensenada or San Felipe, you do not need a tourist card, unless you stay longer than 72 hours. If you know you'll be traveling south of Ensenada, you can get the form at the Mexican Customs Office. You must have Mexican auto insurance, available at agencies near the border.

The combination of overpopulation, lack of infrastructure, and heavy winter rains makes many of Tijuana's streets difficult to navigate by automobile. It's always best to stick to the main thoroughfares. There are parking lots along Avenida Revolución and at most major attractions. Most of Rosarito proper can be explored on foot, which is a good idea on weekends, when Boulevard Juárez has bumper-to-bumper traffic. To reach Puerto Nuevo and other points south, continue on Boulevard Juárez (also called Old Ensenada Highway and Ensenada Libre) through town. Most of Ensenada's attractions are within five blocks of the waterfront; it's easy to take a long walking tour of the city. A car is necessary to reach La Bufadora and most of the beaches.

When driving farther south to San Quintín, Guerrero Negro, and Baja Sur, be sure to fill up your gas tank when it's half full. Few towns appear on the highway, and you quickly have the feeling you are headed into the unknown (unless you're following a caravan of RVs). Don't drive at night, and watch your speed. You never know when a pothole or arroyo will challenge your driving skills.
➤ CONTACT: **Mexican Customs Office** (✉ inside San Ysidro border crossing, ☎ 664/682–3439 or 664/684–7790).

EMBASSIES

➤ UNITED STATES: **U.S. Consulate** (✉ Tapachula 96, Tijuana, ☎ 664/681–7400).

EMERGENCIES

In an emergency anywhere in Baja Norte, dial **060** for the police, **066** for Red Cross, and **068** for the fire department.

Tijuana operates a bilingual Tourist Assistance Hot Line, and the city's Tourist Assistance Office takes calls on weekdays to help with tourist complaints and problems.
➤ CONTACTS: **Tourist Assistance Hot Line** (☎ 078). **Tourist Assistance Office** (☎ 664/688–0555).

LANGUAGE

A great way to get to know Ensenada and improve your Spanish is to attend weekend or weeklong classes at the International Spanish Institute of Ensenada.
➤ SPANISH CLASSES: **International Spanish Institute of Ensenada** (☎ 646/176–0109; 858/755–7044 in the U.S.).

LODGING

RESERVING A ROOM

Several companies specialize in arranging hotel reservations in northern Baja. Baja Information is one of the oldest and best agencies working with Baja hotels and tourism departments. Baja California Tours books hotel rooms in the cities and outlying areas. Mexico Condo Reservations books hotel and condo accommodations and represents La Pinta Hotels, a chain with several hotels on the peninsula.
➤ CONTACTS: **Baja California Tours** (✉ 7734 Herschel Ave., Suite O, La Jolla, CA 92037, ☎ 858/454–7166; 800/336–5454 in the U.S., FAX 858/454–2703, WEB www.bajatours.signonsandiego.com). **Baja Information** (✉ 6855 Friars Rd., Suite 26, San Diego, CA 92108, ☎ 619/298–4105; 800/522–1516 in CA, NV, AZ; 800/225–2786 elsewhere, FAX 619/294–7366). **Mexico Condo Reservations** (✉ 4420 Hotel Circle Ct., Suite 230, San Diego, CA 92108, ☎ 619/275–4500 or 800/262–9632, FAX 619/456–1350, WEB www.gobaja.com).

TOURS AND PACKAGES

Baja California Tours (*See under* Lodging) has comfortable, informative bus trips throughout northern Baja. Seasonal day and overnight trips focus on whale-watching, fishing, shopping, wineries, sports, dude ranches, and art and cultural events in Tijuana, Rosarito, Ensenada, and San Felipe.

TROLLEY TRAVEL

The San Diego Trolley travels from the Santa Fe Depot in San Diego, at Kettner Boulevard and Broadway, to within 100 ft of the border every 15 minutes from 5 AM to midnight. The 45-minute trip costs $3.
➤ CONTACT: **San Diego Trolley** (☎ 619/233–2004).

VISITOR INFORMATION

Baja tours, Mexican auto insurance, a monthly newsletter, and workshops are available through Discover Baja, which is a membership club for Baja travelers.

Baja's largest cities have several tourism offices operated by different agencies. These regional tourist offices are usually open weekdays 9–7 (although some may close in early afternoon for lunch) and weekends 9–1. Some of the smaller areas do not have offices. The excellent Baja California State Secretary of Tourism distributes information on the entire state.

Ensenada's most comprehensive office is at Boulevard Costera 1477. A second office is on Boulevard Costera at the entrance to town. Mexicali has both a Convention and Tourism Bureau, and a State Secretary of Tourism office, as does Tijuana. Tijuana Convention and Tourism Bureau has two offices, one within the San Ysidro border crossing, and one on Avenida Revolución. The Tijuana Tourist Board operates an office in the Zona Río. Rosarito, San Felipe, and Tecate also each have a tourist office. The best Web sites for different cities are often private ones that are casually linked to the tourism bureau.
➤ TOURIST INFORMATION: **Baja California State Secretary of Tourism** (✉ Paseo de los Héroes 10289, Tijuana, ☎ 664/634–6330, FAX 664/634–7157, WEB www.turismobc.gob.mx). **Discover Baja** (✉ 3089 Clairemont Dr., San Diego, CA 92117, ☎ 619/275–4225 or 800/727–2252, FAX 619/275–1836, WEB www.discoverbaja.com). **Ensenada Tourism** (✉ Blvd. Costera 1477, ☎ 646/172–3022, www.ensenada-tourism.com). Ensenada Tourist Board (✉ Blvd. Cárdenas 609, ☎ FAX 646/178–2411, WEB www.enjoyensenada.com. **Mexicali Convention and Tourism Bureau** (✉ Calz. López Mateos at Calle Compresora, ☎ 686/552–2376, ☎ FAX 686/557–2561). **Mexicali State Secretary of Tourism Office** (✉ Calle Calafia at Calzada Independencia, ☎ 686/566–1277). **Rosarito Tourist Board** (✉ Blvd. Juárez 907, Oceana Plaza Shopping Center, ☎ 624/612–0396 or 800/962–2252, WEB www.rosaritobch.com). **San Felipe Tourist Information Office** (✉ Av. Mar de Cortés, ☎ 686/577–1155 or 686/577–1865, WEB www.sanfelipe.com.mx). **Tecate Tourist Information** (✉ Callejón Libertad, ☎ 665/654–1095). **Tijuana Convention and Tourism Bureau** (✉ inside the San Ysidro border crossing, ☎ 664/683–1405; ✉ Av. Revolución between Calles 3 and 4, ☎ 664/684–0481 or 664/684–7790). **Tijuana Tourist Board** (✉ Paseo de los Héroes 9365-201, in the Zona Río, ☎ 664/684–0537 or 888/775–2417, WEB www.seetijuana.com).

BAJA CALIFORNIA SUR

With the completion in 1973 of the Transpeninsular Highway, also called Mexico Highway 1, travelers gradually started finding their way down

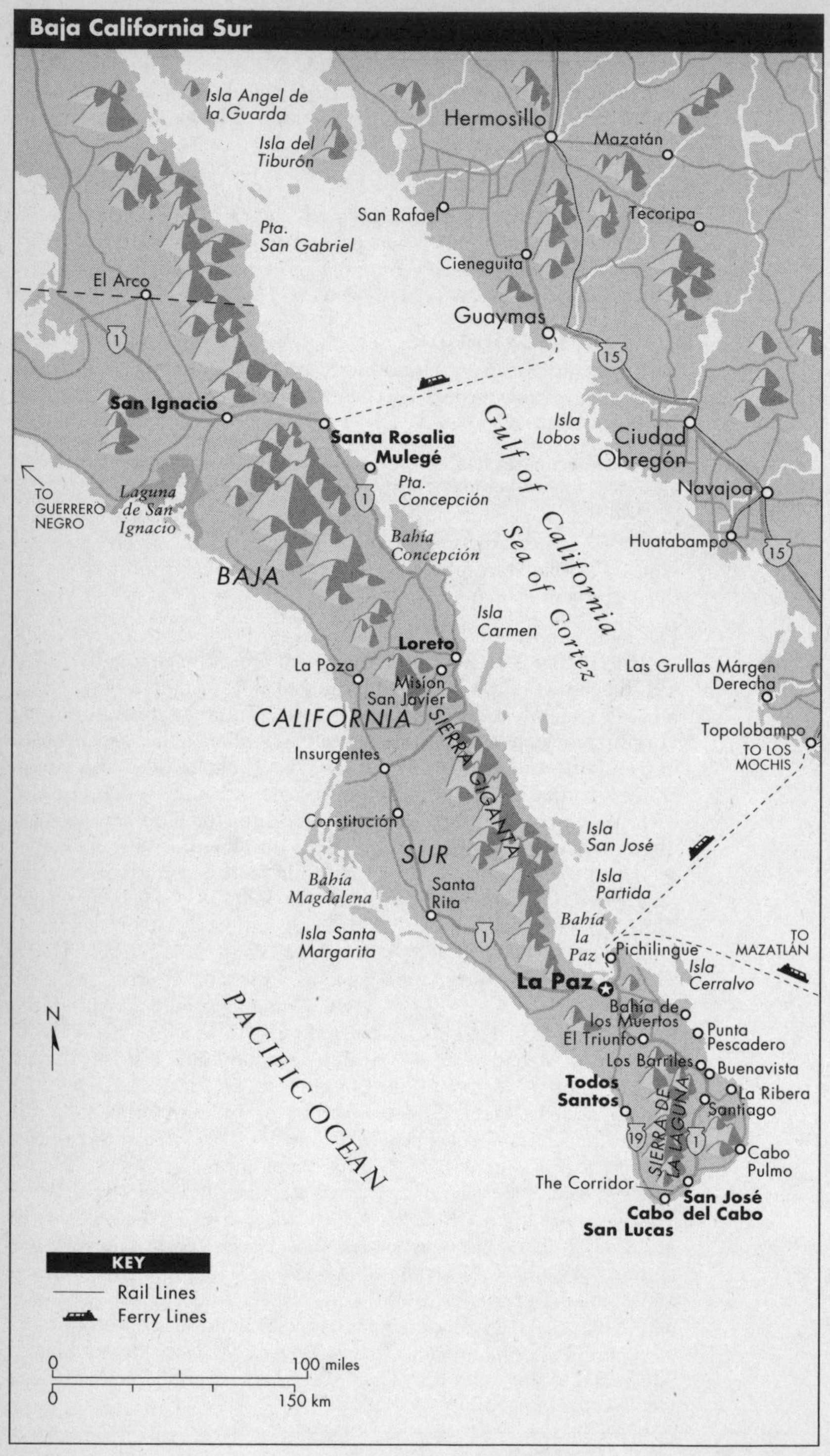
Baja California Sur
Isla Angel de la Guarda
Isla del Tiburón
Hermosillo
Mazatán
San Rafael
Tecoripa
Pta. San Gabriel
Cieneguita
El Arco
Guaymas
1
15
San Ignacio
Santa Rosalia
Mulegé
Isla Lobos
Ciudad Obregón
Gulf of California
Sea of Cortez
TO GUERRERO NEGRO
Laguna de San Ignacio
Pta. Concepción
Navajoa
Bahía Concepción
Huatabampo
BAJA
Isla Carmen
Loreto
La Poza
Misión San Javier
Las Grullas Márgen Derecha
CALIFORNIA
SIERRA GIGANTA
Topolobampo
TO LOS MOCHIS
Insurgentes
Constitución
Isla San José
SUR
Bahía Magdalena
Santa Rita
Isla Partida
Isla Santa Margarita
Bahía la Paz
Pichilingue
TO MAZATLÁN
Isla Cerralvo
La Paz
PACIFIC OCEAN
N
Bahía de los Muertos
El Triunfo
Punta Pescadero
Los Barriles
Buenavista
Todos Santos
La Ribera
Santiago
SIERRA DE LA LAGUNA
19
Cabo Pulmo
The Corridor
San José del Cabo
Cabo San Lucas
KEY
Rail Lines
Ferry Lines
0
100 miles
0
150 km

the 1,708-km (1,059-mi) road, drawn by the wild terrain and the pristine beaches of both coastlines. Baja California Sur became Mexico's 30th state in 1974, and the population and tourism have been growing. Still, Baja Sur remains a rugged and largely undeveloped land. Many people opt to fly to the region rather than brave Highway 1. The road is in fairly good repair, but there are potholes in some stretches, and services (gas, rest rooms) may not be available. Those venturing on the Transpeninsular Highway should be well prepared with water and other provisions for a long drive in desolate but beautiful country.

Whale-watching in Guerrero Negro, Scammon's Lagoon, San Ignacio Lagoon, Magdalena Bay, and throughout the Sea of Cortez is a main attraction in winter. History buffs enjoy Loreto, where the first mission in the Californias was established. La Paz, today a busy governmental center and sportfishing city, was the first Spanish settlement in Baja. At the southernmost tip of the peninsula, fishing aficionados, golfers, and sun worshippers gather in Los Cabos, one of Mexico's most popular and most expensive coastal resorts.

Guerrero Negro and Scammon's Lagoon

720 km (446 mi) south of Tijuana, 771 km (478 mi) north of La Paz.

Every December through March, thousands of gray whales swim 8,000 km (5,000 mi) south from Alaska's Bering Strait to the tip of the Baja Peninsula. Up to 6,000 whales swim past and stop close to the shore at several spots along the Baja coast—including Scammon's Lagoon near **Guerrero Negro**—to give birth to their calves. These newborns each weigh about half a ton and consume nearly 50 gallons of milk a day. In the past, Guerrero Negro was the headquarters for whale-watching trips, but many of the whale-watching operators have moved farther south, to Laguna de San Ignacio and Bahía Magdalena. Still, it's easiest to spot whales from shore or to arrange for a boat in Guerrero Negro.

If it weren't for the whales and the Transpeninsular Highway, which passes near town, few would venture to Guerrero Negro, a town of 10,000. Those traveling south can easily bypass the town. The name Guerrero Negro, which means Black Warrior, was derived from a whaling ship that ran aground in Scammon's Lagoon in 1858. Near the Desierto de Vizcaíno (Vizcaíno Desert), on the Pacific Ocean, the area is best known for its salt pans, which provide work for much of the town's population and produce one-third of the world's salt supply. Salt water collects in some 780 square km (300 square mi) of sea-level ponds and evaporates quickly in the desert heat, leaving great blocks of salt. The town is dusty, windy, and generally unpleasant, but it happens to be a favored roosting spot for osprey, which build huge nests on power poles around town.

Scammon's Lagoon is about 27 km (17 mi) south of Guerrero Negro, down a rough but passable sand road that crosses the salt flats. The lagoon got its name from U.S. explorer Charles Melville Scammon of Maine, who came here in the mid-1800s. On his first expedition to the lagoon, Scammon and his crew collected more than 700 barrels of valuable whale oil, and the whale rush was on. Within 10 years, nearly all the whales in the lagoon had been killed, and it took almost a century for the whale population to increase to what it had been before Scammon arrived. It wasn't until the 1940s that the U.S. and Mexican governments took measures to protect the whales.

These days, whale-watching boats—most of them *pangas* (small skiffs)—must get permission from the Mexican government to enter

Scammon's Lagoon, now a national park called **Parque Natural de Ballenas Gris** (Gray Whale Natural Park). The other major whale-watching spots (also protected by the government) are farther south, at Laguna de San Ignacio and Bahía Magdalena, both on the Pacific coast. If traveling on your own, you can reach Laguna de San Ignacio from the town of San Ignacio. Bahía Magdalena—regulars call it "Mag Bay"—is about a four-hour drive across the peninsula from La Paz. Fishermen will take you out in their boats to get closer to the whales at both places. But for a better view, and an easier stay in this rugged country, travel with an outfitter who will arrange your transportation, accommodations, and time on the water. Whales will come close to your boat, rising majestically from the water, and sometimes swim close enough to be patted on the back.

Dining and Lodging

There are several hotels in Guerrero Negro, none of which is worth visiting for its own sake. Double-occupancy rooms cost from about $25 to $70 a day; rates tend to increase during the peak whale-watching season from January through March. None of the hotels has heat, and winter nights can be downright frigid. Credit cards aren't normally accepted, but the hotels do take traveler's checks. The food in the hotel restaurants recommended below is far from haute cuisine, but it's about as good as you're going to get in the area.

$$ **La Pinta.** A few kilometers outside of town, looking like an oasis of palms in the desert, La Pinta is the largest hotel in the area. The clean, functional rooms are dependable, the setting more attractive than that of other local lodgings, and the American-Mexican restaurant decent, but the rates are high for the area. Whale-watching excursions can be arranged here. ✉ *La Pinta Hwy. 1 at 28th parallel, Domicilio Conocido, 23940,* ☏ *615/157–1301 or 800/800–9632; 619/275–4500 in the U.S.,* FAX *615/157–1306,* WEB *www.lapintahotels.com. 26 rooms. Restaurant. MC, V.*

$ **El Morro.** This simple motel with serviceable rooms, hot water showers, and rough towels is a popular layover for drivers heading south. ✉ *Blvd. Zapata 23940,* ☏ *615/157–0414. 34 rooms. No credit cards.*

$ **Malarrimo.** This trailer park cum Mexican and seafood restaurant has a 10-room motel—Cabañas San Miguelito—with private baths and TV. It fills up quickly and is one of the best deals in town. The restaurant's grilled or steamed fresh fish, lobster, and clams are legendary, and the dining-room walls are covered with maps and photos of Baja. Whale-watching excursions from the hotel are also immensely popular and are run by knowledgeable local guides. ✉ *Blvd. Zapata, 23940,* ☏ *615/157–0250,* FAX *615/157–0100. 10 rooms. Restaurant. No credit cards.*

Outdoor Activities and Sports

WHALE-WATCHING

The gray whales that migrate from the Bering Strait are Guerrero Negro's biggest attraction. With a sturdy vehicle, you can drive the 24-km (15-mi) washboard dirt and sand road to Scammon's Lagoon and arrange a trip with the boat captains who await passengers there. Trips usually cost $25 per person and boats stay on the water for about an hour. Start early to take advantage of the calmest water and best viewing conditions. Whale-watching from the shores of the lagoon can be disappointing without binoculars. But it is still an impressive sight to see the huge mammals spouting water high into the air.

Eco-Tours Malarrimo (✉ Blvd. Zapata, 23940, ☏ 615/157–0250) is the best tour operator in the area. It offers four-hour trips with bus transportation to and from the lagoon (about 75% of the trip is spent in small skiffs among the whales with English-speaking guides) and lunch for $40 per person. Reserve several months in advance, especially for February, when whales appear in abundance.

San Ignacio

227 km (141 mi) southeast of Guerrero Negro.

San Ignacio is an oasis amid the Desierto de Vizcaíno. Date palms, planted by Jesuit missionaries in the late 1700s, sway gently, in sync with the town's laid-back air. San Ignacio is primarily a place to organize whale-watching and cave-painting tours or to stop and cool off in the shady *zócalo* (town square).

Lodging

$$ 🏨 **La Pinta.** This simple, functional hotel is a pleasant place to stay on your transpeninsular journey—although you may wish for a bit more for the money. White arches frame the courtyard and pool, and the rooms are decorated with folk art and wood furnishings. Both the river and town are within walking distance. The hotel staff can set up whale-watching trips with local guides. ✉ *2 km (1 mi) west of Hwy. 1 on an unnamed road into town, Apdo. 37, 23943,* ☎ *624/154–0300 or 800/800–9632; 619/275–4500 in the U.S.,* WEB *www.lapintahotels.com. 28 rooms. Restaurant, pool, bar. No credit cards.*

Outdoor Activities and Sports

WHALE-WATCHING

San Ignacio is the base for trips to Laguna de San Ignacio, 59 km (35 miles) from San Ignacio on the Pacific coast. The lagoon is one of the best places to watch the gray-whale migration, and local boat captains will usually take you close enough to pet the new baby whales. Tours arranged through **Baja Discovery** (✉ Box 152527, San Diego, CA 92195, ☎ 619/262–0700 or 800/829–2252, WEB www.bajadiscovery.com) include round-trip transport from San Diego to San Ignacio Lagoon, by van to Ensenada and private plane to the lagoon. The company operates a comfortable camp at the lagoon with solar-heated showers and private tents facing the water. **Baja Expeditions** (✉ 2625 Garnet Ave., San Diego, CA 92109, ☎ 858/581–3311 or 800/843–6967, FAX 858/581–6542) operates a camp at the lagoon and offers tours including air transportation from San Diego. **Ecoturísticos Kuyima** (☎ 615/154–0070) in San Ignacio offers transport between the town and the lagoon, operates a campground at an isolated area of the lagoon, and has tours including overnights in San Ignacio and at the lagoon. You may also be able to use your own camping gear at their site for a fee.

Santa Rosalia

77 km (48 mi) southeast of San Ignacio.

You'll find a fascinating mix of French, Mexican, and American Old West–style architecture in this dusty mining town. Santa Rosalia is known for its **Iglesia Santa Barbara,** a prefabricated iron church designed by Alexandre-Gustave Eiffel, creator of the Eiffel Tower. Be sure to stop by **El Boleo** (✉ Av. Obregón at Calle 4), where fresh breads tempt customers weekday mornings at 10. A fire demolished many of the old wooden houses in the center of town in 2001; fortunately, it was extinguished before reaching the church and businesses by the sea.

Lodging

$ 🏨 **Hotel Frances.** The former glory of this 1886 French mansion shines through despite its modest furnishings. The Frances sits on a steep hill, and many of its refurbished rooms open onto a second-story porch with views of town and the sea. There's a small pool in the courtyard. ✉ *Av. 11 de Julio at Calle Jean M. Cousteau, 23920,* ☎ FAX *615/152–2052. 17 rooms. Restaurant, pool. MC, V.*

$ **El Morro.** Santa Rosalia's version of a resort hotel is on the waterfront a bit south of town. Rooms, in a series of one-story buildings connected by rock arches and tile mosaics, are large and comfortable; some have terraces and tile bathrooms. The rooms are a bit worn, but the reasonable price and the proximity of the sea even the score. The bar is a popular gathering spot for travelers. ✉ *1½ km (1 mi) south of Santa Rosalia on Hwy. 1, 23900,* ☎ FAX *615/152–0414. 39 rooms. Restaurant, pool, bar. MC, V.*

Mulegé

64 km (40 mi) south of Santa Rosalia.

Mulegé has become a popular base for exploring the nearby **Sierra de Guadalupe** mountains, the site of several prehistoric rock paintings. Access to the paintings is good, though you must have a permit and go with a licensed guide. The paintings are a UNESCO World Heritage Site. Tours typically involve a bumpy ride followed by an even bumpier climb on *burros* (donkeys). Kayaking in **Bahía Concepción,** the largest protected bay in Baja, is spectacular. Once a mission settlement, this charming tropical town of some 3,500 residents swells in winter, when Americans and Canadians fleeing the cold arrive in motor homes. There are several campgrounds outside town.

Lodging

$$$$ **Posada de los Flores.** A sister property to Loreto's most charming hotel, Punta Chivato is far removed from civilization. Yet the lovely rooms have air-conditioning, fireplaces, and terraces facing the sea. The restaurant serves everything from lobster salad to chocolate mousse, along with bountiful breakfast and lunch. Smoking is not allowed in the rooms, and the hotel does not accept children under 12. ✉ *20 km north of Mulege, Hwy. 1, 23880,* ☎ *615/153–0188; 877/245–2860 in the U.S.,* FAX *615/155–5600,* WEB *www.posadadelasflores.com. 10 rooms, 10 junior suites. 2 restaurants, snack bar, pool, 2 bars, car rental. MC, V.*

$$–$$$ **Hotel Serenidad.** A Mulegé mainstay for Baja aficionados since the late 1960s, the Serenidad is owned by the Johnson family, longtime Baja residents. The hotel is a delightful escape, with simple rooms in brick and stucco buildings scattered under bougainvillea vines and fruit trees. Some rooms have fireplaces and/or air-conditioning. The Saturday night pig roast is a Baja tradition. ✉ *2½ km (1½ mi) north of Mulegé, Hwy. 1, 23900,* ☎ *615/153–0530 or 800/346–3942,* FAX *615/153–0311. 29 rooms. Restaurant, pool, bar, airstrip. AE, MC, V.*

$ **Hacienda.** Guests read and lounge in rocking chairs by the pool or along the bar at this small, comfortable hotel steps from the town plaza. Kayak trips and tours to cave paintings in the mountains can be arranged, and special fiestas are planned for groups. Rooms are spartan but work fine for a night or two. ✉ *Calle Madero 3, 23900,* ☎ FAX *615/153–0021 or 800/346–3942. 24 rooms. Restaurant, pool, bar, travel services. MC, V.*

Outdoor Activities and Sports

DIVING

Cortez Explorers (✉ Calle Moctezuma 75A, 23900, ☎ 615/153–0500, FAX 615/153–0500, WEB www.cortez-explorer.com) conducts dive trips to the rocky reefs off the Santa Inez Islands in the Sea of Cortez. They rent dive equipment, mountain bikes, and ATVs, and offer resort courses and snorkeling trips.

KAYAKING

Baja Tropicales (✉ Apdo. 60, 23900, ☎ 615/153–0409, FAX 615/153–0190) rents kayaks, wet suits, and other gear and has several types of kayaking tours, including day and overnight trips in the area of Mulegé. Whale-watching trips on the Pacific coast are also available. Their Eco-Mundo center on Bahía Concepción includes a learning center, cafeteria, and a center for participants in the tours.

Seafaris (✉ 5095 Comanche Dr., La Mesa, CA 91941, ☎ FAX 619/462–3761) operates eight-day kayaking trips between Mulegé and Loreto from October through April. The trips include gear, meals, and accommodations in camps along the way.

Loreto

134 km (83 mi) south of Mulegé.

Loreto's setting on the Sea of Cortez is truly spectacular: the gold and green hills of the Sierra Gigante seem to tumble into the cobalt water. According to local promoters, the skies are clear 360 days of the year, and the desert climate harbors few bothersome insects.

The Kikiwa, Cochimi, Cucapa, and Kumyaii Indian tribes first inhabited the barren lands of Baja. Jesuit priest Juan María Salvatierra founded the first California mission at Loreto in 1697, and not long after, the indigenous populations were nearly obliterated by disease and war. Seventy-two years later, a Franciscan monk from Mallorca, Spain—Father Junípero Serra—set out from here to establish a chain of missions from San Diego to San Francisco, in the land then known as Alta California.

In 1821 Mexico achieved independence from Spain, which ordered all missionaries home. Loreto's mission was abandoned and fell into disrepair. Then in 1829, a hurricane swept through the remains, virtually destroying the settlement, capital of the Californias at the time. The capital was moved to La Paz, and Loreto languished for a century. In 1976, when oil revenue filled government coffers, the area was tapped for development. Streets were paved, and phone service, electricity, potable water, and sewage systems were installed in both the town and the surrounding area. Even an international airport was built. A luxury hotel and tennis center were opened in nearby Nopoló. Eventually, the pace of development slowed as the money dried up.

With a population of 10,000, Loreto is a good place to escape the crowds, relax, and go fishing. The fears of sports enthusiasts that the town would be spoiled have thus far been largely unfounded, although the residential trailer parks are filling up and private homes are clustered in secluded enclaves. The Loreto National Marine Park protects much of the Sea of Cortez in this area.

The **malecón** is a pleasant place for a stroll along downtown's waterfront. A marina shelters yachts and the panga fleet; the adjoining beach is a popular gathering spot for locals, especially on Sunday afternoon, when kids hit the playground.

Loreto's main historic sight is **La Misión de Nuestra Señora de Loreto.** The stone walls, gilded altar, and primitive-style portraits of its priests are worth seeing.

El Museo de los Misiones, also called the Museum of Anthropology and History, contains religious relics, tooled leather saddles used in the 19th century, and displays of Baja's history. ✉ *Next door to La Misión de Nuestra Señora de Loreto,* ☎ *613/135–0441.* *$2.* *Tues.–Sun. 9–1 and 2–6.*

Nopoló, an area that was slated for luxury resorts, is about 8 km (5 mi) south of Loreto. There's a nine-court tennis complex and an 18-hole golf course, and a few private homes, but Nopoló has yet to become a major resort area.

Puerto Escondido, 16 km (10 mi) down the road from Nopoló, has an RV park, **Tripui** (☏ 613/133–0818), with a good restaurant, a few motel rooms, a snack shop, bar, stores, showers, laundry, a pool, and tennis courts. There's a boat ramp at the marina close to Tripui; to pay the fee required to launch here, go to the port captain's offices (☏ 613/135–0656, FAX 613/135–0465) just south of the ramp; the offices are open weekdays 8–3.

Isla Danzante, 5 km (3 mi) southeast of Puerto Escondido, has good reefs and diving opportunities. Picnic trips to **Coronado Island,** inhabited only by sea lions, may be arranged in Loreto, Nopoló, or Puerto Escondido. The snorkeling and scuba diving on the island are excellent. Danzante and other islands off Loreto are now part of the Parque Marítimo Nacional Bahía de Loreto. Commercial fishing boats are not allowed within the 60-square-km (23-square-mi) park.

A trip to **Misión San Javier,** 32 km (20 mi) southwest of Loreto, is one of the best ways to see Baja at its most picturesque. A high-clearance vehicle is essential for the three-hour drive to the mission—and don't even try getting here if the dirt and gravel road is muddy. The road climbs past small ranches, palm groves, and the steep cliffs of the Cerro de la Giganta. Unmarked trails lead off the road to caves and remnants of **Indian cave paintings.** The mission village is a remote community of some 300 residents, many of whom come outdoors when visitors arrive. The church, built in 1699, is impressive and well preserved, set amid fruit orchards. It's often locked; ask anyone hanging about to find the person with the keys, and you'll be allowed to go inside to look at the stained-glass windows and ornate altar. Slip a few pesos into the contribution box as a courtesy to the village's inhabitants, who need all the help they can get to keep the church well maintained. Although you can drive to San Javier on your own, it helps to have a guide along to lead you to the caves and Indian paintings. Most hotels, or the tour companies listed below, can arrange tours.

Dining and Lodging

$–$$$ ✕ **El Nido.** If you're hungry for steak, chicken, and hearty Mexican combo plates, then this is your place. As close as you'll get to a steak house in these parts, El Nido caters to a meat-and-potatoes crowd. The brass and woodwork and courteous waiters make up for prices that seem outrageously high for the neighborhood. ✉ *Calle Salvatierra 154,* ☏ *613/135–0027. No credit cards.*

$–$$$ ✕ **La Palapa.** A favorite with kayakers and travelers, this thatch-roof restaurant one block from the waterfront serves up a good combination of Mexican plates. This is the only place in town to get fried red snapper, the house specialty. ✉ *Paseo Hidalgo between Calle Francisco Madero and the malecón,* ☏ *613/135–0284. No credit cards.*

$ ✕ **Café Olé.** This local and gringo hangout is the best taquería in town, but it also serves good burgers, ice cream, and french fries. ✉ *Calle Francisco Madero,* ☏ *613/135–0496. No credit cards.*

$$$–$$$$ **Hotel Posada de los Flores.** Charm and attention to detail set this gorgeous hotel apart from the rest. Exposed beams and locally crafted tile adorn the remodeled colonial mansion. Above the atrium lobby sits a crystal-bottom pool. Two restaurants serve up Loreto's finest Mexican and Italian fare; breakfast is included in the room rate. Smoking is not allowed in the rooms, and the hotel does not accept children. ✉

Calle Salvatierra at Madero, 23880, ☎ *613/135–1162; 877/245–2860 in the U.S.,* WEB *www.posadadelasflores.com. 10 rooms, 5 junior suites. 2 restaurants, snack bar, pool, 2 bars, car rental. MC, V.*

$$$–$$$$ **Oasis.** One of the original fishing camps, Oasis remains a favorite with those who want to spend as much time as possible on the water. Many of the rooms, set amid an oasis of palms, have a view of the water and hammocks on the front terraces. The hotel has its own fleet of skiffs. You can opt for a meal plan; cabins are also available at San Javier. ✉ *Calle de la Playa at Zaragoza, Apdo. 17, 23880,* ☎ *613/135–0112 or 800/497–3923,* FAX *613/135–0795,* WEB *www.hoteloasis.com. 39 rooms. Restaurant, pool, boating, fishing, bar. MC, V.*

$$$ **Danzante Resort.** This all-inclusive hilltop resort is architecturally stunning and ecologically sensitive. Owners Michael and Lauren Farley are Baja experts, writers, and underwater photographers specializing in the Sea of Cortez. There's a dive shop on the premises; you must show your open-water certification card. Rates include meals and many activities. There's cellular phone service at the hotel. Smoking is not allowed in the rooms. Advance reservations are essential; guests must be at least eight years old. ✉ *32 km (20 mi) south of Loreto off Hwy. 1, 23800,* ☎ *no phone at hotel; 408/354–0042 in the U.S.,* FAX *408/354–3268 in the U.S.,* WEB *www.danzante.com. 9 suites. Restaurant, pool, beach, horseback riding. No credit cards.*

$$–$$$ **Villas de Loreto.** This hideaway's smoke-free rooms have refrigerators and porches by a large pool and the beach. Bikes are available and horseback riding, kayaking (for experienced paddlers), and fishing tours can be arranged. There's a dive shop on the premises. Rates include Continental breakfast. To get here, turn right off Calle Salvatierra onto Calle Francisco Madero and follow signs for the hotel. ✉ *Antonio Mijares at beach, 23880,* ☎ FAX *613/135–0586,* WEB *www.villasdeloreto.com. 10 rooms. Pool, laundry service. MC, V.*

$$ **La Pinta.** Part of a Baja California hotel chain, La Pinta is a collection of pastel brick buildings right on the beach. The rooms are spacious but unremarkable, with air-conditioning and satellite TVs. ✉ *Blvd. Misión de Loreto, 23880,* ☎ *624/135–0025 or 800/800–9632; 619/275–4500 in the U.S.,* FAX *624/135–0026,* WEB *www.lapintahotels.com. 48 rooms. Restaurant, tennis court, pool, fishing, bar. MC, V.*

$$ **Plaza Loreto.** Plaza Loreto has a loyal following of regulars who appreciate the prime downtown location near the old mission. The two-story hotel has an upstairs bar overlooking the street. Rooms aren't consistently maintained—the best of the lot have TVs and huge showers. Check a few before choosing one. ✉ *Paseo Hidalgo, 23880,* ☎ *613/135–0280,* FAX *613/135–0855. 25 rooms. Restaurant, bar. MC, V.*

Outdoor Activities and Sports

FISHING

Fishing put Loreto on the map, especially for American enthusiasts. Cabrillo and snapper are caught year-round; yellowtail in spring; and dorado, marlin, and sailfish in summer. If you plan to fish, bring tackle, as top-notch gear can be difficult to find, although some sportfishing fleets do update their equipment regularly. All Loreto-area hotels can arrange fishing, and many own skiffs. Local anglers congregate with their small boats on the beach at the north and south ends of town. **Alfredo's Sportfishing** (✉ Blvd. Mateos at Juárez, across from the marina, ☎ 613/135–0132, FAX 613/135–0590) has good fishing guides. **Arturo's Fishing Fleet** (✉ Calle Hidalgo between the plaza and marina, ☎ 613/135–0409, FAX 613/135–0022, WEB www.arturosport.com) has several types of boats and fishing packages. **The Baja Big Fish Company** (✉ Paseo Hidalgo 19, by the plaza, ☎ 613/135–1603 or 888/533–2252, FAX 613/135–0078) has full fishing packages from the United States, which include air and hotel, as well as fishing trips from Loreto. Baja Big Fish specializes in tag-and-release and in light tackle and fly-fishing.

GOLF

The 18-hole **Loreto Campo de Golf** (☎ 613/135–0788 or 613/133–0554) is along Nopoló Bay at the south side of the Fonatur resort. Several hotels in Loreto have golf packages and reduced or free greens fees.

KAYAKING

Ideal sites for kayakers are just off Loreto's shores. Tours and rentals can be arranged through the **Baja Outpost** (✉ Blvd. Mateos near the Oasis Hotel, ☎ 613/135–1134 or 888/649–5951). Loreto outdoor specialists **Las Parras Tours** (✉ Calle Salvatierra at Madero, ☎ 613/135–1010, FAX 613/135–0900) provides experienced local guides for kayaking, as well as for whale-watching, scuba diving, visiting San Javier, and hiking to cave paintings in the mountains. The U.S.-based company **Sea Quest** (✉ 360/578–5767, WEB sea-quest-kayak.com) offers several trips that begin in Loreto. Options include kayaking with gray whales in Magdalena Bay or San Ignacio Lagoon. Or you can stick close to Loreto and spend several days camping on nearby islands.

SCUBA DIVING

Arturo's Fishing Fleet (✉ Calle Hidalgo between the plaza and marina, ☎ 613/135–0409, FAX 613/135–0022, WEB www.arturosport.com) offers dive services. The **Baja Outpost** (✉ Blvd. Mateos near the Oasis Hotel, ☎ 613/135–1134 or 888/649–5951) has scuba certification courses, dive trips to the islands, gear rental, and guest rooms for clients. They also offer kayaking, whale-watching, and hiking tours. Extremely knowledgeable guides from the **Danzante Resort** (☎ 408/354–0042 in the U.S., FAX 408/354–3268 in the U.S., WEB www.danzante.com) take dedicated divers to explore the Loreto Marine Sanctuary. **Las Parras Tours** (☎ 613/135–1010, FAX 613/135–0900) offers certification courses, guided tours, and gear rental.

TENNIS

The **Loreto Tennis Center** (☎ 613/135–0408), 8 km (5 mi) south of town, has nine courts open, for a fee, to the public.

Shopping

Loreto has limited shopping opportunities. **El Alacrán,** in the small complex behind the church on Calle Salvatierra, has remarkable folk art, jewelry, and sportswear. You can also find some nice silver shops in this complex. Groceries and ice are available on Calle Salvatierra at **El Pescador,** the town's only supermarket.

La Paz

354 km (220 mi) south of Loreto.

La Paz is one of those cities that makes you wish you'd been here 30 years ago. In the slowest of times, in late summer when the heat is oppressive, you can easily see how it must have been when it was a quiet place, living up to its name: "Peace." Today the city has a population of 180,000, with a large contingent of retirees from the United States and Canada. Travelers use La Paz as both a destination in itself and a stopping-off point en route to Los Cabos. Some call it the most traditional city on the peninsula, with the feel of a mainland community that has adapted to tourism while retaining its character. There's always excellent scuba diving and sportfishing in the gulf—La Paz is the stop-off for divers and fishermen headed for **Cerralvo, La Partida,** and the **Espíritu Santo** islands, where parrot fish, manta rays, neons, and angels blur the clear waters by the shore, and marlin, dorado, and yellowtail leap out of the sea.

Hernán Cortés and his soldiers were drawn to La Paz in 1535 by stories of magnificent pearls and women. In 1720 the Jesuits arrived to deliver their message of salvation to the indigenous Pericú people. Instead, they inadvertently introduced smallpox, which decimated the local populace within 30 years. La Paz became the capital of the Californias in 1829 after a hurricane nearly leveled Loreto. In 1853 a group of U.S. Southerners, led by William Walker, tried to make La Paz a slave state, but Mexicans quickly banished them. Peace reigned for the next century. In 1940 disease wiped out the oyster beds, and with the pearls gone, La Paz no longer attracted prospectors.

La Paz officially became the capital of Baja California Sur in 1974 and is now the state's largest settlement. It is the site of the governor's house and the state's bureaucracy, jail, and power plant, as well as the ferry port to Mazatlán.

Sights to See

23 **Biblioteca de las Californias.** Specializing in the history of Baja California, the library houses the best collection of historical documents on the peninsula. Unfortunately, it has been relegated to a small section of this building, which has been turned into a children's cultural center. You can look at the books in small cartels; they cannot be removed from the building. Films and lectures are sometimes presented in the evening. Check the bulletin board outside the library or ask the clerk for information. ✉ *Madero at 5 de Mayo, Downtown,* ☎ *612/122–0162.* ⌚ *Weekdays 9–6.*

24 **La Catedral de Nuestra Señora de La Paz** (Our Lady of La Paz Cathedral). Downtown's big attraction was built in 1860 near the site of La Paz's first mission, which was established that same year by Jesuit Jaime Bravo. You'll see it just across from the town's main square.

27 **Ferry Terminal.** The busy warehouselike spot has a large parking lot. Roadside stands serving oysters and grilled fish line the highway across the street.

20 **Fidepaz Marina.** At La Paz's west end is the construction zone for the 500-acre marina, a long-term development that has yet to reach completion. There is a resort hotel by the waterfront.

21 **Malecón.** La Paz's seawall, tourist zone, and main drag are all rolled into one. As you enter town from the southwest (near Fidepaz Marina), Paseo Al´varo Obregón turns into the malecón at a cluster of high-rise condos.

22 **Malecón Plaza.** A two-story white gazebo is the focus at this small concrete square where musicians sometimes appear on weekend nights. The tourist-information center sits beside the gazebo. Across the street, Calle 16 de Septiembre leads inland to the city center. Around the plaza and all along the malecón, a steady stream of teens cruises through town, red and yellow car lights twinkling and radios blaring.

Marina La Paz. At the southwest end of the malecón, this ever-growing development is home to condominiums, vacation homes, and a pleasant walkway lined with casual cafés.

26 **Museum of Anthropology.** La Paz's culture and heritage is well represented here, with re-creations of Comondu and Las Palmas Indian villages, photos of cave paintings found in Baja, and copies of Cortés's writings on first sighting La Paz. Many exhibit descriptions are written only in Spanish, but the museum's staff will help you translate. ✉

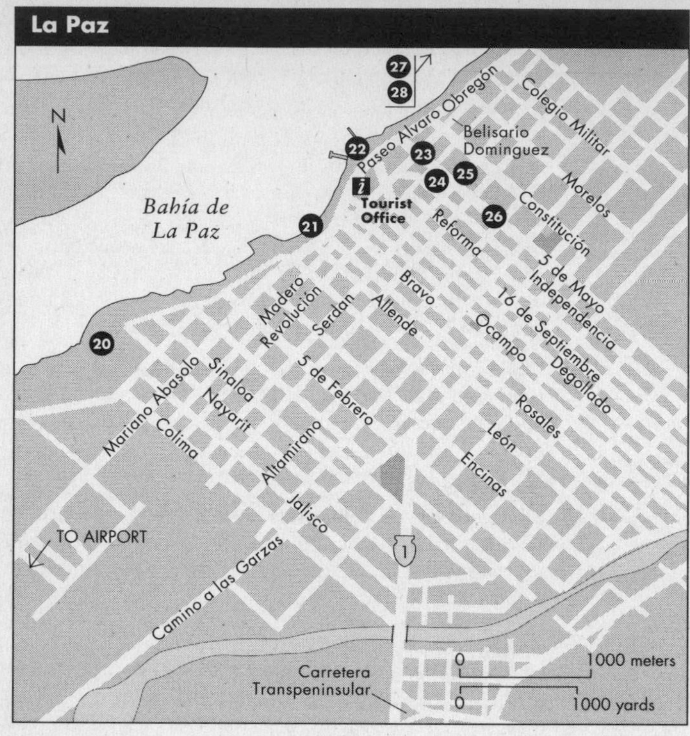

Altamirano and 5 de Mayo, Downtown, ☎ *612/122–0162.* *Donation.* ⏲ *Weekdays 8–6, Sat. 9–2.*

28 **Pichilingue.** Since the time of pirate ships and Spanish invaders, Pichilingue was known for its preponderance of oysters bearing black pearls. In 1940 an unknown disease killed them off, leaving the beach deserted. Today it's a pleasant place for sunbathing and watching sportfishing boats bring in their hauls. Palapa restaurants on the beach serve cold beer and oysters *diablo* (raw oysters steeped in a fiery-hot sauce), as well as fresh and inexpensive grilled fish.

Pichilingue Road. Northeast of town, Paseo Álvaro Obregón, or the malecón, becomes what is commonly known as the Pichilingue Road. It curves northeast along the bay about 16 km (10 mi) to the terminals where the ferries from Mazatlán and Topolobampo arrive and many of the sportfishing boats depart.

25 **Plaza Constitución.** This zócalo also goes by the name Jardín Velazco.

Beaches

Off a dirt road just past Pichilingue, **Playa Tecolote** and **Playa Coyote** are adjacent crystal-blue coves with clean beaches. Both have restaurants, water-sports equipment rentals, and palapas for shade. This is a good place to test your kayaking skills, and rentals are available on site. Camping is allowed in the parking lots. **Playa Balandra,** on a side road between Pichilingue and Tecolote, is a peaceful cove favored by kayak and snorkeling operations from town. There are no facilities or rentals at this beach. Make arrangements in advance in town.

Dining and Lodging

$$–$$$ ★ ✕ **El Bismark.** You've got to go a bit out of your way for a local home-style Mexican restaurant. Specialties include carne asada served with beans, guacamole, and homemade tortillas; and enormous grilled lob-

sters. You'll see families settle down for hours at long wood tables, while waitresses divide their attention between patrons and soap operas on the TV above the bar. The desultory service is a drawback. ✉ *Santos Degollado and Av. Altamirano, Downtown,* ☎ *612/122–4854. MC, V.*

$$–$$$ ✕ **Carlos 'n' Charlie's.** The noise level here is deafening, but it's a fun place, with a wide-screen TV in the bar and waiters so jolly you expect them to break into song. The food—basic beef, chicken, fish, and Mexican selections—is good and plentiful. Live bands appear weekend evenings on the back patio and attached dance club, one of the hottest nightlife spots in town. ✉ *Obregón at Calle 16 de Septiembre, Malecón,* ☎ *612/122–9290. MC, V.*

$–$$ ✕ **El Cangrejo Loco.** A few sidewalk tables sit outside this tiny family-run cafe; seats are hard to come by at lunchtime. A long list of seafood cocktails offers shrimp, crab, and clams with lime, chilies, or soy sauce. Entrees include a great quesadilla with cheese and crab, manta ray tacos, and stuffed crab. The setting is simple, and the food and camaraderie will make you want to return ASAP. ✉ *Obregón between Bravo and Ocampo, Malecón,* ☎ *no phone. No credit cards.*

$–$$ ✕ **La Pazta.** Locals who crave international fare rave about this trattoria with sleek black-and-white decor and excellent homemade pasta and pizzas. Imported cheeses and wines, and bracing espresso and cappuccino are all welcome changes from the local seafood and taco fare. ✉ *Allende 36, Downtown,* ☎ *612/125–1195. MC, V.*

$ ✕ **El Quinto Sol Restaurante Vegetariano.** El Quinto's brightly painted exterior walls are covered with snake symbols and smiling suns. The all-vegetarian menu can be a nice change of pace, and there's a wide selection of fresh juices and herbal elixirs. The four-course prix-fixe comida corrida (noon–4 PM) is a bargain. The back half of the space is a bare-bones natural-foods store offering grains, fresh breads, soaps, oils, bulk herbs, and homeopathic remedies. ✉ *Belisario Domínguez and Independencia, Downtown,* ☎ *612/122–1692. No credit cards.*

$ ✕ **Taco Hermanos Gonzalez.** La Paz has plenty of great taco stands, but the Gonzalez brothers still corner the market with their hunks of fresh fish wrapped in corn tortillas. Bowls of condiments line the small stand, and the top quality draws crowds of sidewalk munchers. ✉ *Mutualismo and Esquerro, Downtown,* ☎ *no phone. No credit cards.*

$$$ ✕🏨 **Crowne Plaza Resort.** By far the most modern resort in La Paz, this hacienda-style inn sits beside the Fidepaz Marina. Its suites range in size and style; the largest have two bedrooms and a kitchenette. The pool flows through several levels in the courtyard, and there's a children's playground. The restaurant, with its cordial service, serene ambience, and excellent cuisine, has become a favorite among local executives. ✉ *Lote A, Marina Fidepaz, Apdo. 482, Fidepaz 23000,* ☎ *612/124–0830 or 800/227–6963,* FAX *612/124–0837,* WEB *www.crowneplaza.com. 54 suites. Restaurant, pool, gym, bar, nightclub, business services, travel services. AE, MC, V.*

$$$–$$$$ 🏨 **Hotel Marina.** Lush gardens surround the pool and Jacuzzi and a seaside promenade lines the property. The full-service marina offers fishing, scuba diving, and kayaking. Private charters are available. Most rooms have terraces with water views and are airy, clean, and functional. ✉ *Carretera a Pichilingue Km 2.5, Marina 23000,* ☎ *612/121–6254 or 800/826–1138,* FAX *612/121–6177,* WEB *www.hotelmarina.com.mx. 70 rooms, 16 junior suites, 5 master suites. Restaurant, tennis court, pool, hot tub, marina, bar. MC, V.*

$$$ 🏨 **Los Arcos.** This colonial-style 1950s hotel is a La Paz landmark. The lobby leads to the central courtyard, where the rush of water in the fountain drowns out the noise from the street. Most rooms have balconies, some facing the bay. The Cabañas de Los Arcos next door consists of several small brick cottages surrounded by gardens and a small hotel

with a pool. ✉ *Obregón 498, between Rosales and Allende, 23000, Malecón* ☎ *612/122–2744 or 800/347–2252; 520/529–4529 in the U.S.,* FAX *612/125–4313; 520/529–4549 in the U.S.,* WEB *www.losarcos.com. 93 rooms and 18 suites at hotel, 20 bungalows and 23 rooms at Cabañas. Restaurant, coffee shop, 2 pools, sauna, fishing, bar. MC, V.*

$$$ ★ **La Concha Beach Resort.** The beach, modern rooms, complete water-sports center, and very good restaurant are this hotel's assets. All rooms have tile floors, TVs, and small refrigerators. A separate building houses condos with kitchenettes, living rooms, and bedrooms, and has its own pool. Another section, in town, has six suites for long-term rental. There's a shuttle to town and back. ✉ *Carretera a Pichilingue Km 5, between Downtown and Pichilingue, 23010,* ☎ *612/121–6344, 612/121–6161, or 800/999–2252,* FAX *612/121–6218; 619/294–7366 in the U.S.,* WEB *www.laconcha.com. 107 rooms. Restaurant, pool, dive shop, 3 bars, shops, car rental, travel services. AE, MC, V.*

$$–$$$ ★ **El Ángel Azul.** La Paz's historic center has finally attracted entrepreneurs. The city's historic courthouse has been converted into a charming bed-and-breakfast whose nonsmoking rooms frame a central courtyard and are decorated with original artwork (which also fills the walls in the restaurant). The rooftop suite overlooks the city. Breakfast is included in the rate; children over 12 are welcome. ✉ *Independencia 518, at Guillermo Prieto, Downtown,* ☎ *612/125–5130,* WEB *www.elangelazul.com. 11 rooms. Bar, no-smoking rooms. MC, V. Restaurant closed Mon.*

$$ **Club Hotel Cantamar.** Fernando Aguilar, a longtime scuba diving master in La Paz, owns this small sports lodge beside a private marina, 14 km (9 mi) north of town. Rooms have balconies that look out on the pool and the sea. The restaurant is in the clubhouse beside the dive boats. This is the ideal hangout for divers, who have easy access to the Sea of Cortez. ✉ *Carretera a Pichilingue (Calle Obregon 1665, Apdo. 782) Pichilingue 23000.* ☎ *612/122–1826 or 612/122–7010,* FAX *612/122–8644,* WEB *www.clubcantamar.com. 18 rooms. Restaurant, pool, dive shop, snorkeling, boating, fishing, bar. MC, V.*

$$ **Hotel Suites Club El Moro.** A vacation-ownership resort with suite rentals on a nightly and weekly basis, El Moro has a garden of lush palms and a densely landscaped pool area. You can recognize the building by its stark-white turrets and domes. Rooms are Mediterranean-style, with arched windows, Mexican tiles, and private balconies. Some rooms have kitchens and can sleep up to five people. A small café serves light fare. ✉ *Carretera a Pichilingue Km 2, between Downtown and Pichilingue 23010,* ☎ FAX *612/122–4084 or 612/125–2828,* WEB *www.clubelmoro.com. 21 suites. Café, pool, bar. AE, MC, V.*

$$ **La Perla.** This brown low-rise hotel has a long-standing reputation as one of the best places to stay in La Paz. Rooms have white walls and light-wood furnishings; some have king-size beds. The pool is on a second-story sundeck away from main street traffic. Noise is a factor in the oceanfront rooms; the trade-off is wonderful sunset views over the malecón. ✉ *Paseo Obregón 1570, Malecón 23010,* ☎ *612/122–0777,* FAX *888/242–1577 or 612/125–5363. 101 rooms. Restaurant, pool, bar, shops. AE, MC, V.*

$ **Pensión California.** This run-down hacienda does have clean blue-and-white rooms with baths and draws backpackers and low-budget travelers. The courtyard has picnic tables and a TV. A laid-back camaraderie prevails. ✉ *Av. Degollado 209, Downtown 23000,* ☎ *612/122–2896. 25 rooms. No credit cards.*

Nightlife and the Arts

El Teatro de la Ciudad (✉ Av. Navarro 700, Downtown, ☎ 612/125–0004) is La Paz's cultural center. The theater seats 1,500 and stages shows by visiting performers as well as by local ensembles. **La Terraza** (✉ La Perla hotel, Paseo Obregón 1570, Malecón, ☎ 612/122–0777) is the best spot for both sunset- and people-watching along the malecón. The hotel also has a disco open on weekend nights.

Outdoor Activities and Sports

BOATING AND FISHING

The considerable fleet of private boats in La Paz now has room for docking at three marinas: **Fidepaz Marina** at the north end of town, and the **Marina Palmira** and **Marina La Paz** south of town. Most hotels can arrange sportfishing trips. Tournaments are held in August and November. The **Jack Velez Fleet** (✉ Apdo. 402, Downtown 23000, ☎ 612/122–2744 Ext. 608, FAX 612/125–5313), operated in Los Arcos hotel, has cabin cruisers; charters start around $240 per day.

KAYAKING

The calm waters off La Paz are perfect for kayaking, and novice and experienced kayakers enjoy multiday trips along the coast to Loreto or out to the nearby islands. **Baja Expeditions** (✉ 2625 Garnet Ave., San Diego, CA 92109, ☎ 800/843–6967; 858/581–3311 in the U.S., FAX 858/581–6542, WEB www.bajaex.com), one of the oldest outfitters working in Baja, offers several options for kayaking tours, including multinight trips between Loreto and La Paz. A support boat carries all gear, including ingredients for great meals. **Baja Quest** (✉ Sonora 174, Downtown, ☎ 612/123–5320, FAX 612/123–5321) has day and overnight trips. **Mary Aventuras** (✉ Calle Topete 564, Downtown, ☎ FAX 612/123–0559, ☎ 800/355–7140 in the U.S., FAX 612/123–5321, WEB www.kayakbaja.com) offers group tours and customized trips and kayak rentals. **Nichols Expeditions** (✉ 497 North Main, Moab, UT 84532, ☎ 800/648–8488; 435/259–3999 in the U.S., FAX 435/259–2312, WEB www.nicholsexpeditions.com) offers kayaking tours to Isla Espiritu Santo and between Loreto and La Paz, with camping along the way.

SCUBA DIVING

Popular diving spots include the white coral banks off Isla Espíritu Santo, the sea lion colony off Isla Partida, and the seamount 14 km (9 mi) farther north. Almost every hotel has arrangements with a dive outfitter. **Baja Diving & Service** (✉ Paseo Obregón 1665-2, Malecón, ☎ 612/122–1826, FAX 612/122–8644) rents equipment and operates diving, snorkeling, and tours to Espíritu Santo, the wreck of the ferryboat *Salvatierra,* and a seamount where you can observe schools of hammerhead sharks. The outfitter is affiliated with the Club Hotel Cantamar. **Baja Expeditions** (✉ 2625 Garnet Ave., San Diego, CA 92109, ☎ 800/843–6967; 858/581–3311 in the U.S., FAX 858/581–6542 in the U.S.) runs multiday live-aboard dive trips as well as day trips. Tours must be booked in advance through the U.S. office. **Baja Quest** (✉ Sonora 174, Downtown, ☎ 612/123–5320, FAX 612/123–5321) has day trips and live-aboard dive cruises during the summer months. The **Cortez Club** at La Concha Beach Resort (✉ Carretera a Pichilingue Km 5, between Downtown and Pichilingue, ☎ 612/121–6344 or 612/121–6161) is a full-scale water-sports center with a bar, equipment rental, and scuba, snorkeling, kayaking, and sportfishing tours. Whale-watching trips are extremely popular in winter. The scuba operation is one of the best in La Paz, and you can arrange tours and rentals through the club even if you're not staying here. **Scuba Baja Joe** (✉ Malecón, ☎ 612/122–4006, FAX 612/122–4000) offers full equipment rentals and guided tours.

WHALE-WATCHING

La Paz has become a center for whale-watching expeditions to Magdalena Bay on the Pacific coast. Most hotels can make all the arrangements, but keep in mind that any whaling trip will entail about six hours' transportation from La Paz and back for two–three hours on the water. Serious whale fans with extra time can stay overnight in San Carlos, the small town by the bay. You can do the trip on your own by taking a public bus from La Paz to San Carlos and then hiring a boat captain to take you into the bay. Check with the tourist office before starting your trip for hotel arrangements. **Baja Expeditions** (✉ 2625 Garnet Ave., San Diego, CA 92109, ☎ 800/843–6967 or 858/581–3311, FAX 858/581–6542) also runs whale-watching trips to the bay. Advance reservations are required. In La Paz, you can arrange a trip through **Baja Quest** (✉ Sonora 174, Downtown, ☎ 612/123–5320, FAX 612/123–5321). **Discover Baja** (☎ 800/727–2252) has guided camping tours and whale-watching trips to Bahía Magdalena.

Shopping

Artesanías la Antigua California (✉ Obregón 220, Malecón, ☎ 612/125–5230) has the nicest selection of Mexican folk art in La Paz, including wooden masks and lacquered boxes from Guerrero, along with a good supply of English-language books on Baja. **Artesanía Cuauhtémoc** (✉ Av. Abasolo between Calles Nayarit and Oaxaca, south of downtown, ☎ no phone) is the workshop of weaver Fortunado Silva, who creates and sells cotton place mats, rugs, and tapestries. Julio Ibarra oversees the potters and painters at **Ibarra's Pottery** (✉ Calle Prieto 625, ☎ 612/122–0404). His geometric designs and glazing technique result in gorgeous mirrors, bowls, platters, and cups. Unusual pottery can be found at **Mexican Designs** (✉ Calle Arreola 41 Av. Zaragoza, Downtown, ☎ 612/123–2231.) The pottery boxes with cactus designs are good souvenirs. **La Tiendita** (✉ Malecón, ☎ 612/125–2744) has embroidered guayabera shirts and dresses, tin ornaments and picture frames, and some black pottery from Oaxaca.

Los Barriles and the East Cape

105 km (65 mi) south of La Paz.

The Sea of Cortez coast north of Los Cabos has long been a favored hideaway for anglers and adventurers. The area known as the East Cape consists of a string of settlements and fishing villages between La Paz and San José del Cabo—including Los Barriles, Buena Vista, and La Ribera, all accessible from Highway 1. From Punta Pescadero in the north to Cabo Pulmo in the south, the cape is renowned for its rich fishing grounds, top-notch diving, and, when the wind kicks up, excellent windsurfing. Moderately developed but growing, the cape makes a great day trip or, if you want more time away from the glitz (and prices) of Los Cabos, a nice place to overnight. Food and lodging tend to be modest affairs; most hotels have meal plans—a good idea since fine dining is scarce.

There's an outback feel to the East Cape, with a robust group of American "settlers" making their presence known and creating a real-estate market out of thin air. Many of the communities are accessible via paved road from Los Cabos. For the intrepid traveler, a three-hour drive on a dirt washboard takes you along the coast to La Ribera, Punta Colorado, and Cabo Pulmo—the latter a superb dive site within a national marine reserve. (This route is *not* recommended for those bothered by dust or long stretches of precipitous driving conditions.)

The village of Cabo Pulmo is home to 100 or so residents, depending on the season. Power comes from solar panels, and drinking water is trucked in over dirt roads. Near the beach, solar-powered cottages are for rent at the **Cabo Pulmo Beach Resort** (✉ Cabo Pulmo, ☎ 624/141–

0244, FAX 624/143–0371, WEB www.cabopulmo.com), which also has a full-service PADI dive facility. Cabo Pulmo is a magnet for serious divers, kayakers, and windsurfers, and remains one of southern Baja's natural treasures.

Windsurfers take over the East Cape in January, when stiff breezes provide ideal conditions. Water-sports equipment and boat trips are available through area hotels, although regulars tend to bring their own gear and rent cars for getting to isolated spots. The nearest airport is at San José del Cabo, about a two-hour drive from the farthest East Cape hotels; several car rental agencies have desks at the airport. Expensive shuttle service can be arranged through most hotels, and there are plenty of cabs in the area.

Dining and Lodging

$–$$ ✕ **Otra Vez.** Whether you're in the mood for some simple grilled seafood, an omelet, or lobster New Orleans, this great little California-style café is sure to please. This may be the only time you see sprouts in Baja, so stock up. The clientele largely consists of expat retirees and tourists who gossip freely while listening to the Beach Boys. ✉ *Calle 20 de Noviembre, Los Barriles,* ☎ *624/142–0249. MC, V.*

$$$–$$$$ **Hotel Buena Vista Beach Resort.** Sixty tile-roof bungalows sit along flower-lined paths next to pools and lawns. Some rooms have private terraces. The fishing fleet is excellent, as are other diversions, such as diving, snorkeling, kayaking, horseback riding, and trips to natural springs. ✉ *Hwy. 1 Km 105, Buena Vista 23500,* ☎ *624/141–0033 or 800/752–3555; 619/429–8079 in the U.S.,* FAX *624/141–0133,* WEB *www.hotelbuenavista.com. 60 rooms. Restaurant, tennis court, 2 pools, hot tub, massage, beach, fishing, horseback riding. AE, MC, V.*

$$$–$$$$ **Rancho Leonero.** Diehard anglers love this seaside hotel for its fishing; divers and kayakers are also regulars. The rooms have tile floors, hard mattresses, and powerful showers. Meals (included in the rate) are served family-style in the large dining room. Credit cards are not accepted for payment at the resort. ✉ *Carretera Transpeninsular Km 103, Buena Vista,* ☎ *624/141–0216; 800/646–2252 in the U.S.,* FAX *624/141–0216,* WEB *www.rancholeonero.com. 35 rooms. Restaurant, pool, beach, fishing. AE, MC, V for advance payment through the U.S. reservation line only.*

$$$ **Hotel Palmas de Cortés.** This casual lodge, often featured on sportfishing shows, is near the famed Cortez banks. The rooms and suites are sparsely furnished with basic comforts, and have powerful air-conditioners and hot showers. Caged parrots and macaws hang about the gardens among hammocks. A pool, playground, Internet café, and large-screen TVs in the bar bring the hotel up to par with its neighbors. Food is hearty, abundant, and included in room rates. ✉ *On the beach; take the road north through Los Barriles and continue to the beach, Los Barriles,* ☎ *624/141–0050; 800/368–4334 in the U.S.,* FAX *624/141–0046. 30 rooms, 15 suites, 10 condos. Restaurant, tennis court, pool, gym, fishing. MC, V.*

$$$ **Hotel Punta Pescadero.** This secluded resort is one of the most peaceful spots in Baja. Rooms have private waterfront terraces and are reserved far in advance by regulars who enjoy the sense of complete escape—miles of windswept beach and calm coves with superb snorkeling. The hotel can arrange for tours to local sights. ✉ *Camino de los Barriles a El Cardonal, Punta Pescadero 23000, 12 km (7 mi) north of Los Barriles,* ☎ *624/121–0101 or 888/765–0653,* FAX *624/126–1771,* WEB *www.puntapescadero.com. 22 rooms. Restaurant, pool, beach, dive shop, fishing, airstrip. MC, V.*

Shopping

The **Plaza Del Pueblo** (✉ Hwy. 1, Los Barriles) is just about the area's only shopping opportunity. At the **East Cape Smoke House** (☎ 624/141–0294) you can sample and purchase freshly smoked seafood, and get a report on the local fishing conditions. The Smoke House also specializes in custom smoking and vacuum-packing your fresh catch. The small shopping center also includes an Internet café, a tackle store, an ice cream parlor, and a bakery.

Los Cabos

195 km (121 mi) south of La Paz.

At the southern tip of the 1,625-km (1,000-mi) Baja California peninsula, the land ends in a rocky point called El Arco (The Arch), a place of stark beauty. The warm waters of the Sea of Cortez swirl into the Pacific Ocean's rugged surf as marlin and sailfish leap out of the waves. The desert ends in sandy coves, with cactus standing at their entrances like sentries under the soaring palm trees.

The conquistadors focused their attention on La Paz during expeditions from mainland Mexico in the mid-1500s. Well aware of the loot to be had, pirates found the tip of the Baja peninsula ideal for spotting Spanish galleons traveling from the Philippines to Spain's empire in central Mexico. In their turn, missionaries came to convert the few thousand local Indians who lived in mountain villages. The Jesuits established the mission of **San José del Cabo** in the mid-18th century, but their settlements didn't last long. The missionaries (and other Europeans) had brought syphilis and smallpox along with their preachings, and, like elsewhere on the peninsula, the susceptible indigenous population was nearly wiped out after a few decades.

Anglers rediscovered this remote region in the 20th century. When pilots flew over Baja during World War II, they spotted the swirling waters and fertile fishing grounds from the air, and word soon spread. Wealthy adventurers with private planes and boats created a demand for fishing lodges, airstrips, and other services, and the region became a cult destination. By the 1960s a half-dozen exclusive resorts were thriving on the cliffs and shores amid the barren landscape.

Connected by a 32-km (20-mi) stretch of highway called the **Corridor,** the two towns of Cabo San Lucas and San José del Cabo were distinct until the late 1970s, when the Mexican government's office of tourism development (Fonatur) targeted the southern tip of Baja as a major resort and dubbed the area Los Cabos. The destination now consists of three major areas: San José del Cabo, Cabo San Lucas, and the Corridor.

Los Cabos has become one of Mexico's most popular and most expensive coastal getaways, with deluxe hotels, championship golf courses, and some of the best sportfishing in the world. Hotels in this area have some of the highest room rates in the country. A few elegant spots command $500 or more a night for enormous suites; more mainstream accommodations run $200 or more per night. Budget rooms are extremely difficult to find. Expect to pay $60 for the most basic lodgings.

The population growth rate here is among the fastest in Mexico, and the inadequate infrastructure is becoming a problem. But despite all the development that has taken place, and the steep prices that have come along with it, the area remains a natural hideaway.

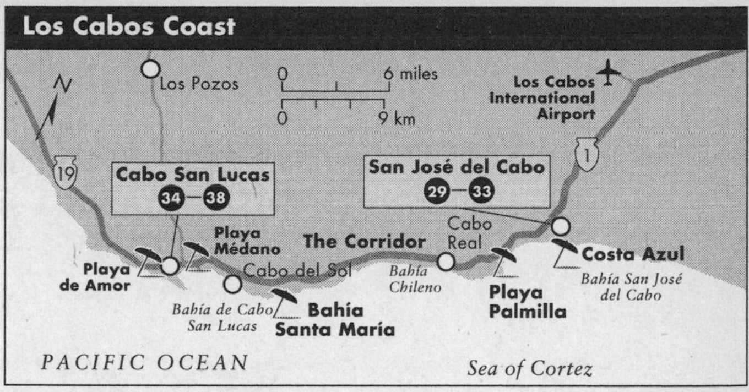

San José del Cabo

San José del Cabo is the municipal headquarters for the two Los Cabos towns. The hotel zone faces a long stretch of waterfront on the Sea of Cortez, where several large hotels and time-share projects are under construction. A 9-hole golf course and private residential community are well established south of the town center. The downtown area with its adobe houses and jacaranda trees is the loveliest part of Los Cabos. Entrepreneurs have converted old homes into stylish restaurants and shops, and the government has enlarged and beautified the main plaza. Unfortunately, bumper-to-bumper traffic often clogs the streets during weekday business hours. Despite the development, San José remains the more peaceful of the two towns—the one to come to for a quiet escape. If you are in search of an exciting nightlife and a rowdy beach scene, you may be better off staying in Cabo San Lucas; it costs at least $20 to take a taxi between the two towns.

30 **Boulevard Mijares.** The south end of the main street in San José del Cabo has been designated a tourist zone, with the Los Cabos Club de Golf as its centerpiece. A few reasonably priced hotels are situated perpendicular to the boulevard (about a 10-minute walk from shops and restaurants) on a beautiful long beach where the surf, unfortunately, is too dangerous for swimming. These small properties once laid claim to the long beach. Now, enormous all-inclusive and time-share hotels are rising on the sand.

31 **City Hall.** The modest yellow municipal building is near Avenida Zaragoza, where Boulevard Mijares ends—a spot marked by a long fountain. There is a small, shaded plaza here.

29 **Estero de San José.** The spot where the freshwater Río San José flows into the sea is at the end of the tourist strip, on Paseo San José by the Presidente Inter-Continental. The estuary is a natural preserve closed to boats, but supervision of the reserve is slack. More than 200 species of birds can be spotted here, and anglers enjoy fishing from shore where the river meets the sea. Hurricane Juliette ravaged the estuary in 2001, and it will take time for the wildlife to return.

33 **Iglesia San José.** The town's church looms above the plaza. Be sure to walk up to the front and see the tile mural of a captured priest being dragged toward a fire by Indians.

32 **Plaza Mijares.** Locals and travelers mingle at the large central plaza, which has a white wrought-iron gazebo and green benches set in the shade. The plaza was vastly enlarged and remodeled in 2001 and now hosts small concerts and art shows.

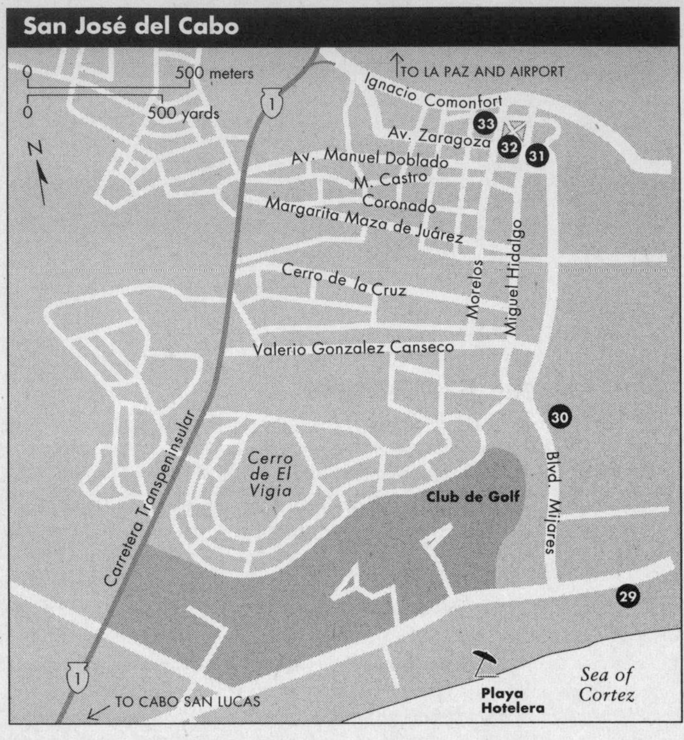

BEACHES

Playa Hotelera is the stretch of beach that most of the finer hotels use. It's beautiful, but the current is dangerously rough, and swimming is not advised. At the east end of the beach, near the Presidente Inter-Continental, there's a freshwater lagoon filled with tropical birds and plants. If you plan to spend time here, be sure to douse yourself with insect repellent. The best swimming beach near San José is **Playa Palmilla,** which is protected by a rocky point south of town. The northern part of the beach is cluttered with boats and shacks, but if you walk south you'll reach the Hotel Palmilla beach, a long stretch of white sand and calm sea.

DINING AND LODGING

$$$ ★ ✕ **Da Antonio.** Overlooking the estuary, this subdued Italian trattoria serves an antipasto that alone is worth the price of a meal. The restaurant is part of the all-inclusive Presidente, but is open to the public for a set price meal. The red snapper with asparagus is drizzled with a tomato and black olive sauce, and all the pastas are homemade. Wines from Italy, Chile, and the Napa Valley fill out the wine list. ✉ *Paseo San José, at the end of the hotel zone,* ☏ *624/142–0211. Reservations essential. AE, MC, V. Closed Mon.*

$–$$$ ★ ✕ **Damiana.** For a special night out, come to this small hacienda tucked beside the plaza, past the center of town. Bougainvilleas wrap around the tall pines shading the wrought-iron tables, and the pink adobe walls glow in the candlelight. Start with fiery oysters diablo, then move on to the tender chateaubriand, charbroiled lobster, or the restaurant's signature shrimp steak, made with ground shrimp. You'll find the setting so relaxing and charming that you might want to linger well into the night. ✉ *Blvd. Mijares 8,* ☏ *624/142–0499. AE, MC, V.*

$–$$$ ✕ **Tequila Restaurante.** An old adobe home serves as the setting for the classiest restaurant in town. The lengthy tequila list gives you a chance to savor the finer brands of Mexico's national drink, and the menu challenges you to decide between excellent regional dishes and innovative Pacific Rim spring rolls, salads, and seafood with mango, ginger, and citrus sauces. Take your time and sample all you can. ✉ *Manuel Doblado s/n,* ☎ *624/142–1155. No credit cards.*

$–$$$ ✕ **Tropicana Bar and Grill.** Start the day with coffee and French toast at this enduringly popular restaurant. The back patio quickly fills for every meal with a loyal clientele who enjoy the garden setting. The menu includes U.S. cuts of beef and imported seafood along with fajitas, chilies rellenos, and lobster, always in demand. ✉ *Blvd. Mijares 30,* ☎ *624/142–1580. AE, MC, V.*

$$ ✕ **Fandango.** This quirky restaurant has an excellent reputation among longtime residents, and its eclectic menu should please almost everyone. Try the sweet potato fritters, Greek salad, or baby green beans with chilies and toasted almonds. A festive mural, Chinese umbrellas, and a candlelit patio bespeak Fandango's carefree style. ✉ *Obregón 19 at Morelos,* ☎ *624/142–2226. MC, V. Closed Sun.*

$ ★ ✕ **Baan Thai.** An Asian furniture importer and a Thai chef teamed up to create an authentic Thai restaurant full of visual and culinary delights. The formal dining room is filled with antiques, and the patio has a murmuring fountain. Delicious, reasonably priced dishes are made with ingredients imported from Thailand. *Tom Kha Gai* (spicy chicken in coconut milk with lemongrass and mushrooms) and *Kao Pad Sap Pa Ros* (fried rice with shrimp and cashew nuts served in a half pineapple) are two highlights. ✉ *Morelos and Obregón, across from El Encanto Inn,* ☎ *624/142–3344. AE, MC, V. Closed Sun.*

$ ✕ **Baja Natural.** Tucked down a flight of steps away from the busy streets, this low-key kid-pleaser is a good place to cool off with fresh-fruit smoothies, juices, shakes, or power drinks. Hamburgers, hot dogs, and veggie burgers round out the options. ✉ *Manuel Doblado between Morelos and Hidalgo,* ☎ *624/142–3105. No credit cards. Closed Sun. No dinner.*

$ ✕ **Restaurant La Playita.** Local anglers bring their latest catch to this small, out-of-the-way restaurant. Dedicated locals and tourists stop here for lunch before strolling on the largely deserted beach. ✉ *Pueblo la Playa, 2 km (1 mi) south of San José,* ☎ *624/142–3774. MC, V.*

$$$$ 🏨 **Casa Natalia.** Standing gracefully at the north end of San José's most charming street is this beautiful boutique hotel. The rooms are decorated in regional Mexican motifs and have king-size beds, European linens, remote-control air-conditioning, and private patios. The restaurant features a delicious blend of traditional Mexican and European cuisine. ✉ *Blvd. Mijares 4, 23400,* ☎ *624/142–5100 or 888/277–3814,* FAX *624/142–5110,* WEB *www.casanatalia.com. 14 rooms, 2 suites. Restaurant, pool, massage, bar. AE, MC, V.*

$$$$ 🏨 **Presidente Inter-Continental Los Cabos.** The all-inclusive hotel sits amid cactus gardens next to the estuary and has three sections centered by pools and lounging areas. You can choose between gourmet restaurants and themed buffets at dinner, order 24-hour room service, or opt for fast-food nachos, hot dogs, and fries at several food carts. ✉ *Paseo San José, at the end of the hotel zone, 23400,* ☎ *624/142–0211 or 800/327–0200,* FAX *624/142–0232,* WEB *hotels.loscabos.interconti.com. 395 rooms, 4 suites, 3 restaurants, 3 tennis courts, 3 pools, beach, fishing, horseback riding, children's programs (ages 5–12). AE, MC, V.*

$$ 🏨 **Posada Terranova.** San José's best inexpensive hotel is a friendly place where guests return so frequently they're almost part of the family. The large, air-conditioned rooms have two double beds and tile bathrooms. You can congregate at the front patio tables or in the restaurant and it still feels like a private home. ✉ *Calle Degollado at Zaragoza,*

23400, ☎ *624/142–0534,* FAX *624/142–0902,* WEB *www.hterranova.com.mx. 20 rooms. Restaurant, bar. AE, MC, V.*

$$ **Tropicana Inn.** This small hotel is a great option if you aren't desperate to be on the beach. The stucco buildings decorated with tile murals of Diego Rivera paintings frame a pool and palapa bar in a quiet enclave behind San José's main boulevard. Rooms are air-conditioned, have satellite TV, and are maintained to look brand new. Book in advance in high season. ✉ *Blvd. Mijares 30, 23400,* ☎ *624/142–0907,* FAX *624/142–1590,* WEB *www.tropicanacabo.com. 39 rooms, 2 suites. Restaurant, room service, pool, bar. AE, MC, V.*

$–$$ **Posada Señor Mañana.** Budget travelers are relieved to find this quirky place where accommodations run the gamut from dark, humble cells to large rooms with air-conditioning, fans, and refrigerators. Hammocks hang on an upstairs deck (there's a great selection of books on the shelves), and you can store food and prepare meals in the communal kitchen. Bugs tend to migrate over from the nearby estuary, but all rooms have good screens on the windows. ✉ *Obregón by the Casa de la Cultura, 23400,* ☎ FAX *624/142–0462. 11 rooms. No credit cards.*

NIGHTLIFE AND THE ARTS

San José's nightlife is struggling; there are no bars like the rowdy joints in San Lucas. At **Havanas** (✉ Hwy. 1 Km 29, ☎ no phone), the excellent jazz band of owner-singer Sheila Mihevic plays in the hip club Wednesday through Friday. Local guides who work with kayaking and adventure-tourism companies hang out at **Rawhide** (✉ Obregón at Guerrero, ☎ 624/142–3626). Tropicana Inn guests, other tourists, and locals mingle at the **Tropicana Bar and Grill** (✉ Blvd. Mijares 30, ☎ 624/142–1580), an old standby.

OUTDOOR ACTIVITIES AND SPORTS

Ecotours. Baja Salvaje (✉ Obregón at Guerrero, San José, ☎ 624/142–5300, WEB www.bajasalvaje.com) offers a good selection of tours, including customized trips to La Sierra la Laguna, a series of mountain peaks that was submerged in water millions of years ago. At 7,000 ft above sea level, the highest peak is ringed by pure pine forests. Trips can include hikes to canyons, hot springs, a fossil-rich area, and caves with rock paintings. It also runs rock-climbing and rappelling trips.

Fishing. Most hotels in San José can arrange fishing trips. There's no marina in town, so you'll board your boat at the marina in Cabo San Lucas—hotels will also set up transportation to the marina and prepare lunches. The boats at **Gordo Banks Pangas** (✉ La Playa, near San José del Cabo, ☎ 624/142–1147; 800/408–1199 in the U.S.) have the advantage of pushing off from shore near some of the hottest fishing spots in the Sea of Cortez, the famed outer and Inner Gordo Banks.

Kayaking. Kayak tours and rentals are available through **Los Lobos del Mar** (✉ Brisas del Mar RV park, on the south side of San José, ☎ 624/142–2983). The tours paddle along the Corridor's peaceful bays and are especially fun in winter when gray whales pass by offshore. **Baja Salvaje** (✉ Obregón at Guerrero, San José, ☎ 624/142–5300) has two-hour sunrise and sunset kayak tours through the estuary. There's hotel pickup and drop-off, beverages, and a guide.

Surfing. For good surfing tips, rentals, and lessons, head to **Costa Azul Surf Shop** (✉ Hwy. 1 Km 27.5, along the Corridor, ☎ 624/142–2771).

SHOPPING

San José's shops and galleries carry a gorgeous array of high-quality folk art, jewelry, and housewares. In fact, serious shoppers staying elsewhere should plan on splurging here. **ADD** (✉ Av. Zaragoza at Hidalgo,

☎ 624/143–2055), an interior-design shop, sells gorgeous hand-painted dishes from Guanajuato and carved wood furniture from Michoacán. Across from City Hall is **Almacenes Goncanseco** (✉ Blvd. Mijares 18, ☎ no phone), where you can get film, postcards, groceries, and liquor. **Amigos Smokeshop and Cigar Bar** (✉ Calle Doblado and Morelos, ☎ 624/142–1138) is a classy shop and cigar bar selling fine Cuban and Mexican cigars and Casa Noble tequila. Look for visiting celebs here. **Los Castillo** (✉ Av. Zaragoza at Hidalgo, ☎ 624/142–4717) carries original jewelry pieces from the famed Taxco designers.

Copal (✉ Plaza Mijares, ☎ 624/142–3070) has an array of carved animals from Oaxaca, masks from Guerrero, and heavy wooden furnishings. **Daniel Espinosa Studio** (✉ Blvd. Mijares 2, ☎ 624/142–4696) displays handcrafted silver jewelry from some of the country's finest artists. For fresh produce, flowers, meat, fish, and a sampling of local life in San José, visit the **Mercado Municipal,** off Calle Doblado. **Veryka** (✉ Blvd. Mijares 6B, ☎ 624/142–0575) is associated with galleries in San Miguel de Allende and Oaxaca, two of the finest art centers in Mexico. This shop's selection of huipiles, masks, tapestries, and pottery is coveted by collectors.

The Corridor

Many of the legendary fishing lodges and exclusive resorts built before the government stepped in were located along the wild cliffs between San José del Cabo and Cabo San Lucas. Since the mid-1980s the area has developed as a destination unto itself. It has several private communities and large-scale resorts, and an ever increasing number of championship golf courses. Much of the development is centered on two major areas—Cabo Real and Cabo del Sol—both containing hotels, private homes, restaurants, and golf courses. The highway along the Corridor has been widened to four lanes. The road is in good shape most of the time, but tends to flood during heavy rains, especially between August and November.

BEACHES

Costa Azul is the most popular surfing beach in Los Cabos. A few small campgrounds and casual restaurants line the beach. **Playa Palmilla** is one of the Corridor's best swimming beaches.

Two bays, **Bahía Chileno** and **Bahía Santa María,** are terrific for diving and snorkeling.

DINING AND LODGING

$$–$$$ ✕ **Da Giorgio II.** The best sunset-watching in all of Los Cabos is at the cliffside tables outside this restaurant. Staggered along the cliffs and poised beside a small pond with a waterfall, the tables have great views of the arch at land's end. The menu focuses on pastas and pizza, and the salad bar has an abundance of fresh veggies. ✉ *Hwy. 1 Km 5 at Las Misiones,* ☎ *624/145–8160. MC, V.*

$$–$$$ ✕ **Pitahayas.** This elegant restaurant occupies a lovely niche above the beach at Cabo del Sol. The menu features Pacific Rim cuisine, blending touches of Thai, Polynesian, and Chinese cooking in unusual recipes. Lobster appears in the form of gourmet hash, duckling is served with a plum-tangerine sauce, and fresh organic vegetables are lightly stir-fried and served while still crisp. Soft jazz contributes to a romantic setting. ✉ *Hwy. 1 Km 10,* ☎ *624/145–8010. AE, MC, V.*

$ ✕ **Zippers.** Home to the surfing crowd and those who like a bit of sand in their burgers, this casual palapa-roof restaurant sits on Costa Azul beach just south of San José. It's the crowd that makes the place fun. ✉ *Hwy. 1 Km 18.5,* ☎ *no phone. No credit cards.*

$$$$ **Casa Del Mar.** This hacienda-style hotel is all about luxurious privacy. A hand-carved door leads into the courtyard-lobby, and stairways curve up to the rooms, spa, and library. Rooms have bathrooms with whirlpool bathtubs set a few steps above the main bedroom. A series of flowing streams, fountains, and gardens leads around the pool to a wide stretch of beach. The restaurant is excellent. ✉ *Hwy. 1 Km 19.5, Cabo San Lucas 23410,* ☎ *624/144–0030 or 888/227–9621,* FAX *624/144–0034,* WEB *www.mexonline.com/casamar.htm. 25 rooms, 31 suites. Restaurant, pool, spa, beach. AE, MC, V.*

$$$$ **Esperanza.** Created by the prestigious Auberge Resorts, this luxurious inn has only 50 suites and six villas. All have handcrafted furnishings, Frette linens, dual-head showers, and DVD players. French and Mexican recipes receive a Baja twist in the restaurant. ✉ *Hwy. 1 Km 3.5, 23410,* ☎ *624/145–8641; 866/311–2226 in the U.S.,* FAX *624/145–8651,* WEB *www.esperanzaresort.com. 50 suites, 6 villas. Restaurant, pool, spa, beach, shops. AE, MC, V.*

$$$$ **Hotel Cabo San Lucas.** Looking like a mountain lodge nearly buried in palms, this long-standing Corridor hotel is a favorite of Baja devotees. Rooms are furnished with cheery yellow and blue fabrics and lightwood pieces; suites and villas are more luxurious. The hacienda-style buildings are right above Chileno Beach, one of the best diving spots in Los Cabos. ✉ *Hwy. 1 Km 14.5, Cabo San Lucas 23410,* ☎ *624/144–0014 or 866/733–2226,* FAX *624/144–0015; 323/655–3243 in the U.S.,* WEB *www.hotelcabo.com. 89 rooms, 7 villas. Restaurant, pool, beach, dive shop, fishing. AE, MC, V.*

$$$$ **Meliá Cabo Real.** The Meliá sprawls over a hilltop with a crystal-blue pool, fountains, waterfalls, white canopies shading rest areas, and a private beach. Rooms are well suited to business travelers and those who prefer simplicity over fussy decor. For a fee, you can take advantage of wireless Internet access in the rooms. The Cabo Real resort development around the hotel includes two golf courses. A shuttle runs to its sister property in Cabo San Lucas. ✉ *Hwy. 1 Km 19.5, Cabo San Lucas 23400,* ☎ *624/144–0000 or 800/336–3542,* FAX *624/144–0101,* WEB *www.solmelia.com. 287 rooms, 15 suites. 4 restaurants, café, 2 tennis courts, pool, gym, beach, dive shop, fishing. AE, MC, V.*

$$$$ ★ **Palmilla.** At this gracious hacienda-style resort tile stairways lead from flower-lined paths to large suites with hand-carved furniture, private patios, and tile baths. The buildings are spread along a hillside overlooking the beach, the service is delightfully personalized, and the hotel's La Paloma restaurant is excellent. A 27-hole Jack Nicklaus–designed golf course surrounds the hotel, which manages to feel secluded and serene. Continental breakfast is included. ✉ *Hwy. 1 Km 7.5 San José del Cabo, 23400,* ☎ *624/144–5000 or 800/637–2226,* FAX *624/144–5100,* WEB *www.palmillaresort.com. 24 rooms, 91 suites, 1 villa. Restaurant, golf privileges, 2 tennis courts, pool, beach, bar. AE, MC, V.*

$$$$ ★ **Las Ventanas al Paraíso.** The service is sublime in this den of luxury. All suites have hot tubs, fireplaces, and telescopes for viewing whales at sea and stars at night. The hotel is filled with handcrafted lamps and doors, sculpture, and paintings. The restaurants are outstanding and the spa offers the latest luxurious treatments; nonguests must make advance reservations. There's even a luxury program for pets. ✉ *Hwy. 1 Km 19.5, Cabo San Lucas 23400,* ☎ *624/144–0300 or 888/767–3966,* FAX *624/144–0301,* WEB *www.lasventanas.com. 61 suites. 2 restaurants, 2 pools, hot tub, spa, beach, fishing, 2 bars. AE, MC, V.*

$$$–$$$$ **Calinda Cabo San Lucas.** One of the Corridor's oldest hotels, this modest inn sits right above the sea. It's not as fancy as its neighbors, but the rooms have minibars, satellite TV, and coffeemakers; some have balconies over the cliffs. You can watch the sun set in one of the large Jacuzzis on the edge of the cliff. The hotel often has air and lodging

packages. ✉ *Hwy. 1 Km 4.5, 23410,* ☎ *624/145–8044 or 877/657–5799,* FAX *624/145–8057,* WEB *www.hotelescalinda.com. 100 rooms. Restaurant, pool, beach, bar. MC, V.*

$$–$$$ **Casa Terra Cotta.** In the hills above Playa Costa Azul, this tiny bed-and-breakfast offers four secluded minivillas amid lush gardens. All have boveda-style arched brick roofs, terra-cotta tile floors, and verandas ideal for whale-watching. The enormous breakfasts, made entirely with homegrown or organic ingredients, are legendary. Reserve at least six weeks in advance. ✉ *Hwy. 1 Km 28.5, ¼ mi up hill, 23410,* ☎ *624/142–4250,* WEB *www.terracotta-mex.com. 3 rooms, 1 suite. Massage, bar. No credit cards.*

OUTDOOR ACTIVITIES AND SPORTS

ATV Tours. Desert Park (✉ Cabo Real, across from Meliá Cabo Real, Corridor, ☎ 624/144–0127) leads ATV (all-terrain vehicle) tours through the desert arroyos and canyons on the inland side of the Cabo Real development. The tours are more ecologically oriented than most, and guides point out geological formations and desert plants. There are three departures daily; fees start at $50 per person.

Diving and Snorkeling. Bahía Chileno, an underwater preserve, teems with marine life and is a wonderful place for snorkeling and diving. Concessionaires usually have gear for rent, but you're best off bringing your own. **Bahía Santa María,** a white-sand cove protected by towering brown cliffs, has superb snorkeling, with hundreds of colorful fish swarming through chunks of white coral. There's a concession stand on the beach with snorkeling-gear rental; its hours are erratic.

Fishing. Most Corridor hotels have excellent fishing fleets, with the boats anchored at the marina in Cabo San Lucas. Hotels can set up the trips and provide transportation to the marina and box lunches. **Victor's Sport Fishing** (☎ 624/142–1092, FAX 624/142–1093) has a fleet of pangas on the Palmilla resort's beach. **Jig Stop Tours** (☎ 800/521–2281) books fishing trips for several Los Cabos fleets.

Golf. Los Cabos is a hot spot for golf, hosting tournaments, including the PGA Senior Grand Slam. The courses that have brought so much attention this way are all in the Corridor and serve as the centerpieces for mega-resort developments. If you aren't staying at a hotel associated with one of the courses, reserve a tee time a week in advance. Expect to pay exorbitant greens fees—nearly $200 in winter, and $140 in summer. Among the most spectacular golf courses is the 27-hole Jack Nicklaus–designed course at the **Palmilla Golf Club** (✉ Palmilla resort, Hwy. 1 Km 1, ☎ 624/144–5250 or 800/637–2226). **Cabo del Sol** (☎ 624/145–8200 or 800/386–2405, a resort development in the Corridor, has an 18-hole Jack Nicklaus course and an 18-hole Tom Weiskopf course. The Robert Trent Jones II–designed **Cabo Real Golf Club** (✉ Meliá Cabo Real Hotel, ☎ 624/144–0040 or 800/393–0400 has 18 holes. The **El Dorado** (☎ 624/144–5451 or 800/393–0400) is the latest 18-hole course from Jack Nicklaus and covers rough seaside terrain in Cabo Real.

Horseback Riding. The **Cuadra San Francisco Equestrian Center** (✉ on Corridor highway across from Cabo Real development, ☎ 624/144–0260) is a professional center with training and trail rides. The ride through back canyons is more interesting than that of the beach, and the horses and guides are both excellent. Make advance reservations.

Cabo San Lucas

Cabo San Lucas, once an unsightly fishing town with dusty streets and smelly canneries, has become Los Cabos's center of tourism activity. The sportfishing fleet is headquartered here, and cruise ships anchor

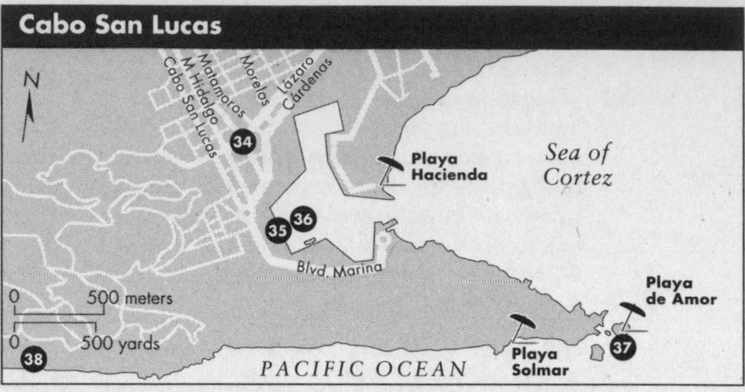

off the marina. Trendy restaurants and bars line the streets, and massive hotels have risen on every available plot of waterfront turf—alas, a five-story condo-hotel complex along the bay blocks the view from the town's side streets. Cabo San Lucas is decidedly *in*—for its rowdy nightlife, its slew of restaurants, and its shopping.

37 **El Arco.** The most spectacular sight in Cabo San Lucas, this natural rock arch is visible from the marina and from some of the hotels but is more impressive from the water. You should take at least a short boat ride out to the arch and Playa de Amor, the beach underneath, to fully appreciate Cabo.

36 **Bahía de Cabo San Lucas.** The sportfishing fleet is docked in this bay, and glass-bottom boats are available at the water's edge.

38 **El Faro de Cabo Falso.** The Lighthouse of the False Cape, built in 1890 and set amid sand dunes, is on the cliffs above the Pacific coast. You need a four-wheel-drive vehicle to reach the lighthouse by land; most hotels can arrange off-road-vehicle tours.

35 **Handicrafts Market.** Paved walkways run from the busy Boulevard Marina—formerly a dusty main drag—to the hotels and beaches on the east end of town and west to this market at the marina.

34 **Plaza Amelia Wilkes.** The main downtown street, Avenida Lázaro Cárdenas, passes this pretty square with its white wrought-iron gazebo. Buildings around the plaza house galleries and restaurants. Most of the shops, services, and restaurants are located between Avenida Cárdenas and the waterfront. The area around the Cárdenas stoplight leading into town is also an active center, especially with the addition of Puerto Paraíso, a shopping and entertainment mall.

BEACHES

Playa de Amor consists of a secluded cove at the very end of the peninsula, with the Sea of Cortez on one side and the Pacific Ocean on the other. The contrast between the peaceful azure cove on the Sea of Cortez and the pounding white surf of the Pacific is dramatic. **Playa Hacienda,** in the inner harbor by the Hacienda Hotel, has the calmest waters of any beach in town and there's good snorkeling around the rocky point. **Playa Médano,** just north of Cabo San Lucas, is the most popular stretch in Los Cabos (and possibly in all Baja) for sunbathing and people-watching. The 3-km (2-mi) span of white sand is always crowded, especially on weekends. **Playa Solmar,** on the fringe of the Solmar Hotel, is a beautiful wide beach but it has dangerous surf with a swift undertow. Stick to sunbathing here.

DINING AND LODGING

$$$ ★ ✕ **Edith's Café.** The Caesar salad and flambéed crêpes are served tableside at this small café, where dinners are accompanied by Mexican

trios or soft jazz. Even the simplest quesadilla is enhanced by Oaxacan cheese and homemade tortillas, and the meat and fish dishes are creative, with unusual chili or tropical fruit sauces. The excellent wine list and good coffees and desserts make for a long, romantic dinner. ✉ *Paseo del Pescador near Playa Médano,* ☎ *624/143–0801. MC, V.*

$$–$$$ ✕ **Capo San Giovannis.** Owner Gianfranco Zappata and his master pastry chef–wife, Antonella, perform a culinary concert that keeps you coming back for encores. Try their green salad with lobster chunks, cioppino Calabrese, salmon with champagne and leek sauce and *mela,* an apple and nut pastry topped with caramel. For a romantic touch, dine on the starlighted back patio. There's a 10% discount for cash. ✉ *Av. Guerrero at Cárdenas,* ☎ *624/143–0593. MC, V. Closed Mon.*

$$–$$$ ✕ **El Galeón.** Considered by some to be the most distinguished dining room in town, El Galeón is across from the marina. The choice seats are on the outside terraces facing the water; the inside is decorated with heavy wooden furniture. Traditional Italian, Mexican, and American dishes are prepared expertly, with an emphasis on thick, tender cuts of beef. ✉ *Across from marina by the road to the Finisterra Hotel,* ☎ *624/143–0443. AE, MC, V.*

$–$$$ ✕ **Mi Casa.** One of Cabo's best restaurants is in a cobalt-blue building painted with a mural of a burro, near the main plaza. Mexican cuisine reaches gourmet status here with fresh tuna and dorado served with tomatillo salsa or Yucatecan achiote, or with sophisticated dishes such as *chili en nogada* (chilies stuffed with raisins and meat). The large back courtyard is especially nice at night, when it's illuminated by candlelight. ✉ *Av. Cabo San Lucas,* ☎ *624/143–1933. No lunch Sun. MC, V.*

$–$$$ ★ ✕ **Mocambo.** Veracruz (known for its regional seafood preparations) meets Los Cabos in an enormous dining room packed with locals. The menu features hard-to-find regional dishes such as octopus ceviche, shrimp empanadas, and a heaping mixed seafood platter that includes sea snails, clams, and octopus, with lobster and shrimp. Musicians stroll among the tables and the chatter is somewhat cacophonous, but you're sure to have a great dining experience here. ✉ *Leona Vicario at 20 de Noviembre,* ☎ *624/143–2122. AE, MC, V.*

$–$$$ ✕ **Pancho's.** This festive restaurant, a favorite among locals, has an enormous collection of tequilas (almost 500 labels); take advantage of owner John Bragg's encyclopedic knowledge of tequila and sample a few. Oaxacan tablecloths, murals, painted chairs, and streamers add to the fun atmosphere. The menu offers a variety of delicious seafood and regional Mexican specialties; try the tortilla soup, chiles rellenos, or stuffed bacon-wrapped shrimp. ✉ *Hidalgo between Zapata and Serdan,* ☎ *624/143–0973,* FAX *624/143–5095. AE, MC, V.*

$–$$$ ✕ **Peacocks.** Romantics seeking a special night out are drawn to this classy dining spot. Seafood is mixed into tender dumplings, blackened and served with a papaya glaze, or tossed with pasta. If you're only in the mood for dessert, stop by for a cappuccino and a tequila mousse. The candlelit two-level dining room is topped by an enormous palapa; you can also dine on an outdoor patio. ✉ *Paseo Pescador near Playa Médano,* ☎ *624/143–1858. AE, MC, V.*

$–$$$ ★ ✕ **Sancho Panza.** The sophisticated menu, decor, and wine list make this small bistro an excellent spot for dining, drinking, and enjoying live jazz. Try the steamed mussels, flank steak stuffed with goat cheese, and sublime wahoo in a savory broth. The menu changes constantly, as does the art in the Dalíesque bar and the extraordinary selection of imported wines in the wine warehouse. ✉ *Blvd. Marina, behind KFC and Plaza Las Glorias,* ☎ *624/143–3212. AE, MC, V. Closed Sun.*

$–$$ ★ ✕ **Marisquería Mazatlán.** The crowds of locals lunching at this simple restaurant are a good sign—as are the huge glasses packed with shrimp, ceviche, and other seafood cocktails. You can dine inexpensively on wonderful seafood soup, or spend a bit more for tender *pulpo ajillo* (marinated octopus with garlic, chilies, onion, and celery). The menu is a seafood lover's delight, and it's hard to choose among oysters, blue crab, 12 shrimp preparations, or whole grilled snapper. ✉ *Mendoza at 16 Septiembre,* ☎ *624/143–8565. MC, V.*

$–$$ ✕ **The Office.** Playa Médano is lined with cafés on the sand, some with lounge chairs, others with more formal settings. All serve the same basics—cold beer, snacks, fish tacos, french fries—and most accompany the meal with loud American rock. The Office, which has provided perfect vacation photo opportunities for more than a decade, is the best. ✉ *Playa Médano,* ☎ *624/143–3464. MC, V.*

$–$$ ✕ **El Shrimp Bucket.** This is the calmest of the three Carlos Anderson restaurants in Cabo San Lucas. A few tables are set out on the walkway that runs along the marina in front of the Marina Fiesta Hotel, a good spot to relax and watch the boats rock on the water. The indoor dining room has the chain's typical mishmash decor and quirky adornments. The food—barbecued ribs and chicken, burgers, piles of fried shrimp—is dependable and abundant. ✉ *Blvd. Marina in Marina Fiesta complex,* ☎ *624/143–2598. AE, MC, V.*

$ ✕ **Señor Greenberg's Mexicatessen.** Pastrami, chopped liver, knishes, bagels, lox, cheesecake—such wonders you can find behind the glass counters at this decent Mexican incarnation of a New York deli. It's open 24 hours; the tables, air-conditioning, stacks of newspapers, and soft music encourage frequent visits. ✉ *Plaza Nautica on Blvd. Marina,* ☎ *624/143–5630. AE, MC, V.*

$ ✕ **Swiss Pastry Shop.** This is your chance to indulge. But be prepared to choose your vice: pastries, danish, cheesecake, black forest cake, chocolate bonbons, bagels, croissants—the list goes on. Swiss chef Peter Straub starts baking at dawn each morning. Sit inside amid local artists' paintings, or on the front patio, which faces the town square. Daily lunch specials are a bargain. ✉ *Hidalgo between Cárdenas and Madero,* ☎ *624/143–3494. No credit cards.*

$$$$ 🏨 **Finisterra.** An eight-story-high palapa covers this beachfront hotel's restaurant and bar next to two free-form swimming pools. Rooms with oceanfront balconies are by far the nicest, though longtime guests favor the less expensive older section of the hotel. The Whale Watcher bar atop a high cliff has the best view in town. ✉ *Blvd. Marina, 23410,* ☎ *624/143–3333 or 800/347–2252; 949/450–9000 in the U.S.,* FAX *624/143–0590; 949/450–9010 in the U.S.,* WEB *www.finisterrahotel.com. 286 rooms. 2 restaurants, 3 pools, 2 bars, travel services. AE, MC, V.*

$$$$ 🏨 **Hotel Hacienda.** Sitting at the edge of the bay, the Hacienda resembles a Spanish colonial inn with white arches and bell towers, stone fountains, and statues of Indian gods set amid hibiscus and bougainvillea. The white rooms have red-tile floors, tile baths, and folk art. The water-sports center has any gear you might need. The hotel has a three-night minimum stay on weekdays, and a four-night minimum on weekends in the high season. ✉ *Playa Médano, 23410,* ☎ *624/143–0665, 624/143–0666, or 800/733–2226,* FAX *624/143–0666,* WEB *www.haciendacabo.com. 60 rooms, 12 suites, 30 beachfront cabañas. Restaurant, pool, beach, bar. MC, V.*

$$$$ 🏨 **Meliá San Lucas.** The most popular beach in Los Cabos is where you'll find the Meliá and its huge, ever-packed pool areas, a hot tub under the palms, and all the equipment you could need for playing on and in the water. Early reservations are essential. ✉ *Playa Médano, 23410,* ☎ *624/143–4444 or 800/336–3542,* FAX *624/143–0418,* WEB *www.solmelia.com. 144 rooms, 6 suites. 3 restaurants, 2 pools, hot tub, beach. AE, MC, V.*

$$$$ 🏨 **Pueblo Bonito Rosé.** Mediterranean-style buildings curve around the elegant grounds at this Playa Médano resort. Flemish tapestries deco-

rate the spacious lobby; statues reminiscent of Roman busts guard reflecting pools. The spacious suites have private balconies overlooking the grounds; some have kitchenettes. The spa is one of the best in Los Cabos. Many of the suites are used as time-share units, with guests booking in for a week. ✉ *Playa Médano, 23410,* ☎ *624/143–5500 or 800/990–8250,* FAX *624/143–5979,* WEB *www.pueblobonito.com. 260 suites. 2 restaurants, pool, beach, snorkeling, jet skiing. MC, V.*

$$$$ ★ **Solmar Suites.** The Solmar sits against cliffs at the tip of Land's End, facing the Pacific. The rooms, decorated in Mexico–Santa Fe style, have separate sitting areas and tile baths. The adjacent time-share and condo units have kitchenettes and a private pool area. The surf here is far too dangerous for swimming, but don't miss a stroll along the wide strip of beach. The Solmar's sportfishing fleet is first-rate. The good restaurant hosts a Saturday night Mexican fiesta and buffet dinner. ✉ *Av. Solmar at Blvd. Marina, Apdo. 8, 23410,* ☎ *624/143–3535 or 800/344–3349; 310/459–9861 in the U.S.,* FAX *624/143–0410; 310/454–1686 in the U.S.,* WEB *www.solmar.com. 82 junior suites, 14 studios, 27 deluxe suites. Restaurant, 3 pools, beach, fishing, bar. AE, MC, V.*

$$–$$$ **The Bungalows Breakfast Inn.** If solitude and a reasonable room rate are more important than being in the center of the action, this is your place, 10 blocks from the beach. Several two-story buildings frame a small, heated pool. Rooms are beautifully decorated with Mexican textiles and art. Breakfast is included; smoking is not permitted. ✉ *Calle Constitución, 5 blocks from main plaza, 23410,* ☎ FAX *624/143–5035,* WEB *www.cabobungalows.com. 16 suites. Pool. No credit cards.*

$$ **Cabo Inn.** What this small palapa-roof hotel lacks in luxury, it makes up for in character. The small, comfortable rooms feature tangerine and cobalt sponge-painted walls and stained-glass windows above the headboards. The eight rooms on the lower level have refrigerators; a kitchen, barbecue and picnic area, and a television round out the communal amenities. ✉ *20 de Noviembre and Vicario, 23410,* ☎ FAX *624/143–0819,* WEB *www.mexonline.com/caboinn.htm. 23 rooms. Picnic area, refrigerators. No credit cards.*

$$ **Chile Pepper Inn.** Upon entering the pretty garden patio, you'll be greeted with a warm *hola,* either by the friendly staff or the resident parrot. A few blocks off the town center, this tiny inn offers delightful rooms at unbeatable prices. Each is named for a type of chili and features handmade wooden furniture and chili tiles around the doorway and in the bathroom. Internet access and local calls are toll free; rooms are smoke free. Reserve a few months in advance; the inn fills quickly. ✉ *Calle 16 de Septiembre and Calle Abosolo, 23410,* ☎ *624/143–8611 or 877/708–1918,* FAX *624/143–0510,* WEB *www.chilepepperinn.com. 9 rooms, 1 suite. Pool. MC, V.*

$ **Siesta Suites.** This oasis of calm off the main drag scene offers you a lot for the money. There's no pool, but the suites have full-size refrigerators, and between the two double beds and wide padded couches that make excellent beds even for grown-ups, you'll have room to sleep quite a crew. The three-story hotel sits two blocks from the marina, and the proprietors keep a close eye on the place and offer great budget tips. ✉ *Calle Zapata, Apdo. 310, 23410,* ☎ FAX *624/143–6494; 602/331–1354 in the U.S.,* WEB *www.cabosiestasuites.com. 5 rooms, 15 suites. Kitchenettes. No credit cards.*

NIGHTLIFE AND THE ARTS

Some travelers choose Cabo San Lucas for its nightlife, which consists mainly of noisy bars with blaring music and plenty of dancing, flirting, and imbibing. The latest U.S. rock plays over an excellent sound system at **Cabo Wabo** (✉ Calle Guerrero, ☎ 624/143–1198), but the impromptu jam sessions with appearances by Sammy Hagar—an owner—and his many music-business friends are the real highlight. **Edith's** (✉ Paseo del Pescador at Playa Médano, ☎ 624/143–0801) presents live jazz in a tasteful garden setting. **El Galeón** (✉ Blvd. Marina, ☎ 624/143–0443) is a welcome refuge for the quieter crowd, who sip brandy by the piano bar. **Giggling Marlin** (✉ Blvd. Marina, ☎ 624/143–1182) seems to have been around forever as the favorite watering hole for anglers. **Sancho Panza Wine Bistro** (✉ Blvd. Marina in the Plaza Las Glorias Hotel, ☎ 624/143–3212) is the place to sip imported wines served by the glass while listening to live soft jazz. **Squid Roe** (✉ Av. Cárdenas, ☎ 624/143–0655) is the rowdiest spot in town, packed with young foreigners who work in the local tourist industry and know how to party. **Wild Coyote** (✉ Puerto Paraíso, Av. Cárdenas, ☎ 624/143–6969, WEB www.coyoteugly.com.mx) features sexily clad Coyote Girls tending bar and dancing for patrons. There are several dance floors where music ranges from rock to salsa. The clientele is better dressed than that at Cabo's rowdy nightspots.

OUTDOOR ACTIVITIES AND SPORTS

Diving. El Arco is a prime diving and snorkeling area, as are several rocky points off the coast. Divers consider the sandfalls, an underwater cascade of sand that flows from 27 to 360 m (90 to 1,200 ft) below sea level, an essential experience; many also undertake the two-hour boat trip to the coral reefs off Cabo Pulmo, off the East Cape. Most hotels can arrange diving trips and equipment rental. **The Activity Center** (✉ Playa Médano, ☎ 624/143–03093) has every type of water and land sports equipment, including diving gear, wave runners, windsurfers, and parasails. The oldest and most complete dive shop in the area is **Amigos del Mar** (✉ Blvd. Marina across from sportfishing docks at the marina, ☎ 624/143–0505 or 800/344–3349, FAX 624/143–0887). **Cabo Acuadeportes** (✉ Hotel Hacienda, Playa Médano, ☎ 624/143–0117) offers diving trips along with all other imaginable water sports. The ***Solmar V*** (✉ Solmar Suites Hotel, Blvd. Marina, ☎ 624/143–0022 or 800/344–3349), a live-aboard dive boat, takes weeklong trips to the islands of Socorro, San Benedicto, and Clarion, and the coral reefs at Cabo Pulmo. It has 12 cabins with private baths (maximum 24 passengers).

Ecotours. Capeland Tours & Expeditions (✉ Playa Médano beside Billygans bar, ☎ 624/143–0775) offers ecotours to Caduaño, a small community near the Sierra la Laguna. The tour includes a bumpy, exciting ride in a four-wheel-drive vehicle to a region rich in fossils. During the ride you also pass by small ranches and vast fields of cardon cacti; bird-watching is excellent if you arrive early in the morning. Other tours include visits to the woodworkers and leather factories in Miraflores and the waterfalls and lakes in the mountains. Trips include a great barbecue lunch at a small ranch, and hotel pickup and drop-off.

Fishing. More than 800 species of fish teem in the waters off Los Cabos. Most hotels will arrange fishing charters, which include a captain and mate, tackle, bait, licenses, and drinks. Prices start at $295 per day for a 25-ft cruiser. Some charters provide lunch, and most can arrange to have your catch mounted, frozen, or smoked. Most of the boats leave from the sportfishing docks in the Cabo San Lucas marina. Usually there are a fair number of pangas for rent at about $30 per hour with a five-hour minimum. **The Gaviota Fleet** (✉ Bahía Condo Hotel, Playa Médano, ☎ 624/143–0430 or 800/932–5599, WEB www.grupobahia.com) currently holds the record for the largest marlin caught in Cabo's waters. The company has charter cruisers and pangas. Minerva and John Smith oversee **Minerva's** (✉ Av. Madero, between Blvd. Marina and Guerrero, ☎ 624/143–1282, WEB www.

minervas.com), the renowned tackle store in San Lucas. The Minerva fleet has four charter fishing boats. Some of the Corridor's priciest hotels choose the **Pisces Sportfishing Fleet** (✉ Cabo Maritime Center on Blvd. Marina, ☎ 624/143–1288, WEB www.piscessportfishing.com) for their guests. The fleet includes the usual 31-ft Bertrams and extraordinary 50- to 70-ft Hatteras cruisers with tuna towers and staterooms. The **Solmar Fleet** (✉ Blvd. Marina, across from the sportfishing dock, ☎ 624/143–0646, 624/143–4542, or 800/344–3349, FAX 624/143–0410; 310/454–1686 in the U.S., WEB www.solmar.com) is one of the oldest and most reputable companies in the area. The boats and tackle are always in good shape, and regulars wouldn't fish with anyone else.

Horseback Riding. Cantering down an isolated beach or up a desert trail is one of the great pleasures of Baja (as long as the sun isn't beating down on your head). Horses are available for rent in front of the Playa Médano hotels; contact **Rancho Collins Horses** (☎ 624/143–3652). **Red Rose Riding Stables** (✉ Hwy. 1 Km 4, ☎ 624/143–4826) has healthy horses for all levels of riders and an impressive array of tack.

Whale-Watching. The gray whale migration doesn't end at Baja's Pacific lagoons. Plenty of whales of all sizes make it down to the warmer waters off Los Cabos and into the Sea of Cortez. Several companies run whale-watching trips from Cabo San Lucas. Check with **Cabo Acuadeportes** (✉ Hotel Hacienda, Playa Médano, ☎ 624/143–0117) for excursions. **Cabo Expeditions** (✉ Plaza las Glorias hotel, Blvd. Marina, ☎ 624/143–2700) offers snorkeling and whale-watching tours in rubber boats. The tour boats that run snorkeling and sunset cruises also offer whale-watching tours in winter. To watch whales from shore, go to the beach at the Solmar Suites or any Corridor hotel, or the lookout points along the Corridor highway.

SHOPPING

Boulevard Marina and the side streets between the waterfront and the main plaza are filled with an ever changing parade of small shops. **El Callejón** (✉ Guerrero between Cárdenas and Madero, ☎ 624/143–1139) has multiple showrooms with gorgeous furniture, lamps, dishes, and pottery. **Galería Gatemelatta** (✉ on dirt road to Hotel Hacienda, ☎ 624/143–1166) specializes in colonial furniture and antiques. Need a new bathing suit? Check out the selection at **H2O de los Cabos** (✉ Madero at Guerrero, ☎ 624/143–1219), where you can choose between skimpy thongs and modest one-piece suits. **J&J Habanos** (✉ Madero between Blvd. Marina and Guerrero, ☎ 624/143–6160) is a cigar aficionado's heaven, with a walk-in humidor stocked with pricey cigars. The shop also sells expensive tequilas. **Libros** (✉ Blvd. Marina 20, ☎ 624/143–3172) carries a good selection of books on Baja and some English-language novels and magazines. **Magic of the Moon** (✉ Hidalgo near Blvd. Marina, ☎ 624/143–3161) is the place to shop for handmade women's sundresses, skirts, and lingerie in fashionable fabrics and styles. **Mama Eli's** (✉ Av. San Lucas, ☎ 624/143–1616) is a three-story gallery with fine furnishings, ceramics, appliquéd clothing, and children's toys. **Necri** (✉ Blvd. Marina between Madero and Ocampo, ☎ 624/143–0283) has an excellent selection of folk art and furnishings. One of the oldest folk-art shops in the area, **Zen Mar** (✉ Cárdenas beside the Mar de Cortés hotel, ☎ 624/143–0661) displays an excellent selection of masks from Oaxaca and Guerrero.

Puerto Paraíso (✉ Av. Cárdenas at the entrance to town, Cabo San Lucas) has completely changed the shopping scene for the region. The palatial entrance on Cárdenas leads into a three-story marble and glass enclosed mall. In 2002, a few businesses had moved in, mostly U.S. chains including two Häagen-Dazs shops, a Johnny Rockets diner, and a Ruth's Chris steak house. Clothing shops including Hugo Boss, Benetton, Guess, Polo, and Ralph Lauren are slated to open in the plaza, as are several jewelry shops.

Cartes (✉ Plaza Bonita, Blvd. Marina, ☎ 624/143–1770) is the best of Los Cabos's many home-furnishing stores, with an irresistible array of hand-painted pottery and tableware, pewter frames, handblown glass, and carved furniture. **Dos Lunas** (✉ Plaza Bonita, Blvd. Marina, ☎ 624/143–1969) has a trendy selection of colorful sportswear and straw hats.

At the **crafts market** in the marina, you can pose for a photo with an iguana, plan a ride in a glass-bottom boat, or browse to your heart's content through stalls packed with blankets, sombreros, and pottery.

Todos Santos

72 km (45 mi) north of Cabo San Lucas.

The Pacific side of the tip of Baja has remained largely undeveloped. The exception is the small agricultural town of Todos Santos, which has become a haven for artists, architects, and speculators who have contributed to a rapid rise in real estate prices. The town sits a bit inland from the rugged coast and is classically charming with its 19th-century brick-and-stucco buildings and small central plaza. It's an ideal haven if you deplore the overdevelopment of Baja's tip, since both Los Cabos and La Paz are within easy driving distance (for shopping, dining, and taking care of business). New homes continue to rise in the outskirts of town, usually before electricity, telephone lines, and water pipes are installed. Entrepreneurs have turned some of the plaza-front buildings into galleries and cafés, and there's always a new spot to check out. Business hours are erratic, especially in summer.

Los Cabos regulars typically drive up the coast to Todos Santos on day trips, stopping to watch surfers at Playa Migriño, Playa los Cerritos, and Punta Gaspareo. El Pescadero is the largest settlement before Todos Santos, populated by ranchers and farmers who grow herbs and vegetables for the restaurants in Los Cabos. Seasonal produce is sold at small stands by the side of the road. Dirt roads intersect the highway at several points along the way to Todos Santos, but you should attempt these roads only with four-wheel-drive vehicles—sands on the beach or in the desert will stop conventional vehicles in their tracks.

During high season, you may find tour buses clogging the streets around the plaza in Todos Santos; it's a pit stop on tours between Cabo San Lucas and La Paz. When the buses leave, the town is a pleasant and peaceful place to wander through shops and galleries. If you drive to Todos Santos on your own, head back to Cabo before dark; Highway 19 between the two towns is unlighted and is prone to high winds and flooding. When you get to town, be sure to pick up *El Calendario de Todos Santos,* a free guide (published eight times a year) with the most current events and developments.

Dining and Lodging

$$–$$$ ✕ **Cafe Santa Fe.** The setting, with tables amid herb gardens in an overgrown courtyard, is part of the appeal, but the main highlight is the food—salads and soups made from homegrown organic vegetables and herbs, homemade pastas, and fresh fish with light herbal sauces. Many Cabo residents lunch here weekly. ✉ *Calle Centenario,* ☎ *612/145–0340. No credit cards. Closed Tues. and parts of Sept. and Oct.*

$$–$$$ ✕ **Posada La Poza.** This gourmet restaurant on a lagoon by the beach serves an unusual selection of delicacies, from fondue and tortilla soup as starters to rack of lamb and fettuccine with white truffle sauce for entrées. Tables are set on the patio overlooking the lagoon or in the tasteful dining room decorated with lighting fixtures and tableware imported from Switzerland. Don't let the bumpy, unmarked road deter you—just keep heading toward the ocean. Eventually, this gorgeous complex will include high-end hotel rooms. ✉ *Follow the signs on Hwy. 19 and on Av. Juárez to the beach,* ☎ *612/145–0400,* WEB *www.lapoza.com. No credit cards.*

$–$$ ✕ **Mi Costa.** Locals crave the shrimp with garlic and oil served at this concrete-floor, palapa-covered café. On Sunday, families fill the dining area, feasting on peeled shrimp, fish tacos, and grilled fish fillets. The ambience is Mexican casual—feel free to fetch your own napkins and condiments. ✉ *Militar at Ocampo,* ☎ *no phone. No credit cards.*

$ ✕ **Caffé Todos Santos.** Omelets, bagels, granola, and delicious whole-grain breads delight the breakfast crowd at this small café; deli sandwiches, fresh salads, and an array of tamales, *flautas* (tortillas rolled around savory fillings), and combo plates are lunch and dinner highlights. Check for fresh seafood on the daily specials board, and pick up a loaf of bread for the road. You'll enjoy the high ceilings and quirky charm of the main dining room or the shady calm of the outdoor patio. ✉ *Calle Centenario 33,* ☎ *612/145–0300. No credit cards. Closed Mon.*

$$–$$$ ★ **Todos Santos Inn.** The four guest rooms in this converted 19th-century house are unparalleled in design and comfort. Gorgeous antiques are set against stone walls under brick ceilings. Ceiling fans and the shade from garden trees keep the rooms cool and breezy. The absence of telephones and TVs makes a perfect foil for the conceits of Los Cabos. And good restaurants are within easy walking distance. ✉ *Calle Legaspi, 23300,* ☎ FAX *612/145–0040,* WEB *www.mexonline.com/todassantosinn.htm. 4 rooms. No credit cards.*

$$ **Hostería Las Casitas.** If Los Cabos has got you feeling like turning down the volume (and the cash flow), this B&B in a lush garden setting might give you the quiet you're looking for—and great breakfasts. The buildings' traditional Mexican architecture makes for cool accommodations. Owner Wendy Faith's art-glass studio is also on-site. ✉ *Calle Rangel at Obregón and Hidalgo, Apdo. 73, 23300,* ☎ FAX *612/145–0255. 2 rooms, private bath and shared showers, 2 suites with bath. No credit cards.*

$ **Hotel Misión del Pilar.** Offering comfortable but spartan accommodations, this hotel is fine if you don't mind close quarters with no frills. The hotel is three blocks from Pilar's Taco Stand, the town bus stop. ✉ *Colegio Militar and Hidalgo, 23300,* ☎ *612/145–0114. 12 rooms. No credit cards.*

BAJA SUR A TO Z

To research prices, get advice from other travelers, and travel arrangements, visit www.fodors.com.

AIR TRAVEL

Baja Sur has airports in La Paz, Los Cabos, and Loreto, all serviced by many domestic and international airlines.

CARRIERS

AeroCalifornia serves the La Paz airport from Tijuana and Los Angeles, has daily flights from Los Angeles to Loreto's airport, and flies to Los Cabos from Los Angeles and Tijuana. Aeroméxico flies to La Paz from Los Angeles, Tucson, Tijuana, Mexico City, and other cities within Mexico; it flies to Los Cabos from San Diego and Mexico City. Mexicana has flights to the Los Cabos airport from Guadalajara, Mexico City, and Los Angeles. Alaska Airlines operates its own terminal at the Los Cabos airport and has flights from Anchorage, Fairbanks, Portland, Phoenix, San Francisco, San Diego, Los Angeles, and Seattle. America West flies into Los Cabos from Phoenix, Continental from Houston. American flies nonstop from Dallas–Fort Worth, Chicago, and Los Angeles; Delta flies from Atlanta. Other international airlines may have service in winter. Many of the U.S. carriers do not have offices or customer phone numbers in Los Cabos. Ask the hotel's concierge or tour desk to reconfirm your flight.

➤ AIRLINES AND CONTACTS: **AeroCalifornia** (☏ 612/125–1023 in La Paz; 624/143–3700 in Los Cabos; 613/135–0500 in Loreto; 800/237–6225). **Aeroméxico** (☏ 612/122–0091 in La Paz; 624/146–5097 in Los Cabos; 800/237–6639). **Alaska Airlines** (☏ 624/146–5097 in Los Cabos; 800/426–0333). **American** (☏ 800/904–6000; 800/433–7300 in the U.S.). **America West** (☏ 800/363–2597). **Continental** (☏ 624/142–3880 in Los Cabos; 800/525–0280). **Delta** (☏ 800/902–2100; 800/241–4141 in the U.S.). **Mexicana** (☏ 624/142–0230 in Los Cabos).

AIRPORTS

The La Paz airport is about 16 km (10 mi) north of town. Loreto's airport is 7 km (4½ mi) southwest of town. The Los Cabos International Airport is about 11 km (7 mi) north of San José del Cabo and about 48 km (30 mi) from Cabo San Lucas.

➤ AIRPORT INFORMATION: **Los Cabos International Airport** (☏ 624/146–5013). **Loreto Airport** (☏ 613/135–0565). **La Paz Airport** (☏ 612/112–0082).

BOAT AND FERRY TRAVEL

The ferry system connecting Baja to mainland Mexico is constantly undergoing rate and schedule changes. Sematur ferries connect La Paz and Mazatlán (an 18-hour trip) every day except Saturday. Ferries also head from La Paz to Topolobampo, the port at Los Mochis, every day except Sunday. Tickets are available at the La Paz Terminal at the dock on the road to Pichilingue. Tickets are also available at the Sematur Office. The Sematur Web site *should* have the most up-to-date information, but isn't always accurate. Purchase your ticket in advance—it's probably best to use a Mexican travel agent—and expect confusion. Continuous changes in Sematur procedure and pricing make it difficult for even ferry personnel to keep up with the latest policy.

If you plan to take a car or a motor home on the ferry to the mainland, you must obtain a vehicle permit before boarding the ferry and must have Mexican auto-insurance papers; everyone crossing to the mainland also needs a tourist card. Tourism officials in La Paz strongly suggest that you obtain the vehicle permit when crossing the U.S. border into Baja; although permits are not needed in Baja, offices at the border are better equipped to handle the paperwork than those in La Paz. Tourist cards also are available at the border. It's wise to take copies of the following, in triplicate, plus the original: passport, tourist card, birth certificate, and vehicle registration.

Ferries travel from Santa Rosalia to Guaymas on the mainland Pacific coast. They depart for the six-hour trip to the mainland at 9 AM on Thursday and arrive in Santa Rosalia at 3 PM Tuesday. Buy tickets in advance at the Santa Rosalia ferry terminal, just south of town on Highway 1. Schedules are often erratic.

➤ BOAT AND FERRY INFORMATION: **La Paz Terminal** (☏ 612/125–4440, FAX 624/125–6588). **Santa Rosalia ferry terminal** (☏ 615/152–0014, FAX 615/152–0013). **Sematur Office** (✉ Calle 5 de Mayo 502, ☏ 612/125–3833, FAX 612/125–6588, WEB www.ferrysematur.com.mx).

BUS TRAVEL TO AND FROM BAJA SUR

The Autotransportes de Baja California bus line runs from Tijuana to La Paz, stopping at towns en route; the peninsula-long trip takes 22 hours. It also has a route from La Paz to Guerrero Negro (the bus stops at the highway entrance to town). Loreto is serviced by both Autotransportes de Baja California and Aguila. The Loreto bus terminal sits at the entrance to town. The Aguila bus line runs from Santa Rosalia and La Paz to Los Cabos.

➤ BUS INFORMATION: **Aguila** (☎ 612/122–4270 or 612/122–3063). **Autotransportes de Baja California** (☎ 612/122–6476 or 612/122–7094). **Loreto bus terminal** (✉ Calles Salvatierra and Tamaral, ☎ 613/135–0767).

BUS TRAVEL WITHIN BAJA SUR

In La Paz it's fairly easy to get around by bus: city buses run along the malecón and into downtown. Buses run between Cabo San Lucas and San José del Cabo, and will stop along the Corridor if you ask the driver.

CAR RENTAL

California Baja Rent-A-Car rents four-wheel-drive vehicles, convertibles, and sedans for use throughout Mexico; you can pick up a car in San Diego and drop it off in Los Cabos, but expect to pay a hefty additional charge.

Thrifty has an office south of Loreto in Nopoló. They'll deliver your car to town. Budget in Loreto has a few four-wheel-drive vehicles available.

Avis and Hertz have desks at the La Paz airport. Hertz has an additional office on Avenida Obregon in town.

Several car-rental agencies have desks at the airport and in San José or Cabo San Lucas. Reserve a car in advance during high season, especially if you want a van, four-wheel-drive, or air-conditioning. Most agencies rent VW bugs and topless VW bugs, which seem like fun until you're under the blazing sun for several hours.

➤ MAJOR AGENCIES: **Avis** (☎ 612/124–6312; 612/122–2651 in La Paz; 624/146–0388 at Los Cabos airport). **Budget** (✉ Paseo Hidalgo at the malecón, Loreto, ☎ 613/135–1090; ✉ Paseo Obregón at Hidalgo La Paz, ☎ 612/122–1919 or 612/122–7655; 624/146–5333 Los Cabos). **California Baja Rent-A-Car** (✉ 9245 Jamacha Blvd., Spring Valley, CA 91977, ☎ 888/470–7368; 619/470–8368 in the U.S.). **Dollar** (☎ 624/142–0100; 624/143–1250 in Los Cabos). **Hertz** (☎ 612/124–6330 at La Paz airport; 624/142–0375 at Los Cabos airport; ✉ Av. Obregon 2130, La Paz, ☎ 612/122–5300; 612/122–0919 at La Paz airport). **Thrifty** (✉ Loreto airport, ☎ 613/133–0612).

CAR TRAVEL

Mexico Highway 1, also known as the Transpeninsular Highway, runs the entire 1,700 km (1,060 mi) from Tijuana to Cabo San Lucas. The highway's condition varies depending on the weather and intervals between road repairs. Don't drive it at high speeds or at night—it's not lighted. There are exits for all the principal towns in Baja Sur.

The road between San José del Cabo and Cabo San Lucas was widened to four lanes and is in good condition, although dips and bridges become flooded in heavy rains.

CRUISE TRAVEL

Several cruise lines use Cabo San Lucas as a port of call. Carnival makes a short stop during its cruise between Los Angeles and Mexico's mainland Pacific coast. Princess has cruises to Los Cabos and the Mexican Riviera from Los Angeles and San Francisco. Royal Caribbean stops off during its Panama Canal and Mexican Riviera cruises. **Cruise West, Lindblad Expeditions,** and **Clipper Cruise Line** run cruises in the Sea of Cortez, focusing on nature, and combine the Sea of Cortez with the Copper Canyon on the mainland. Baja Expeditions has live-aboard ships for diving and whale-watching trips.

➤ CRUISE LINES: **Carnival** (☏ 800/327–9501). **Princess** (☏ 800/421–0522). **Royal Caribbean** (☏ 800/327–6700). **Cruise West** (☏ 800/888–9378). **Clipper Cruise Line** (☏ 800/325–0010). **Lindblad Expeditions** (☏ 800/397–3348; 212/765–7740 in the U.S., WEB www.expeditions.com). **Baja Expeditions** (✉ 2625 Garnet Ave., San Diego, CA 92109, ☏ 800/843–6967; 858/581–3311, FAX 858/581–6542, WEB www.bajaex.com).

EMERGENCIES

The state of Baja California Sur has instituted an **emergency number** for police, fire, and medical problems: **060.** The number can be used throughout the state.

➤ CONTACTS: **Fire** (☏ 612/122–7474 in La Paz). **Hospital** (☏ 612/122–7377 in La Paz; 624/143–1594 in Cabo San Lucas; 624/142–0013 in San José del Cabo). **Police** (☏ 612/122–122-0054 in La Paz; 624/143–3977 in Cabo San Lucas; 624/142–2835 in San José del Cabo). **Red Cross** (☏ 612/122–1111 in La Paz; 624/143–3300 in Cabo San Lucas; 624/142–0316 in San José del Cabo).

INTERNET

Galería Don Tomás in La Paz has Internet access in artful surroundings. Baja Net in La Paz has ports for laptops along with many computer terminals. Dr. Z's Internet Café and Bar in Cabo San Lucas has a full bar and casual menu, and charges $9 an hour for Internet access. Cabocafe in San José del Cabo offers access for $9 an hour.

➤ INTERNET CAFÉS: **Baja Net** (✉ Av. Madero 430, La Paz, ☏ 612/125–9380). **Cabocafe** (✉ Plaza José Green, Suite 3, Blvd. Mijares, San José del Cabo, ☏ 624/142–5250). **Dr. Z's Internet Café and Bar** (✉ Blvd. Cárdenas across from Pemex, Cabo San Lucas, ☏ 624/143–5390). **Galería Don Tomás** (✉ Av. Obregón 229, La Paz, ☏ 612/128–5508).

TAXIS

In Loreto, taxis are in good supply and fares are inexpensive; it costs $5 or less to get anywhere in town. Taxi fares in Los Cabos, however, are steep. A car isn't necessary if you plan to stay in La Paz; taxis are readily available and inexpensive. A ride within town costs under $5; a trip to Pichilingue costs between $7–$10. If you'd like to explore the remote beaches, however, *see* Car Rental. Illegitimate taxis are not a problem in this region. The cars are often Volkswagen bugs.

TOURS AND PACKAGES

Eco-Tours Malarrimo is the best tour operator in Guerrero Negro. The company runs four-hour tours ($40 per person) by bus to and from Scammon's Lagoon, three hours in small skiffs among whales with English-speaking guides, and lunch. Reserve several months in advance, especially for February, when whales appear in abundance.

There are several options for tours from Loreto, including trips inland to Misión San Javier and prehistoric rock paintings, as well as kayaking, sportfishing, diving, and day trips north to Mulegé. Las Parras Tours has the most options for local-guided adventure tours focusing on natural history and conservation.

The Cortez Club at La Concha Beach Resort has diving, fishing, whale-watching, and cruising tours and is the most complete tour facility in La Paz.

With the water as the main attraction in Los Cabos, most tours involve getting into a boat and diving or fishing. It's a must to take a ride to El Arco, the natural rock arches at Land's End, and Playa de Amor, where the Sea of Cortez merges with the Pacific. Nearly all hotels have frequent boat trips to these destinations; the fare depends on how far your hotel is from the point. Tour boats dock by the arts-and-crafts market in the Cabo San Lucas marina, and the sidewalk along the water is lined with salespeople offering boat rides. Check out the boat before you pay, and make sure there are life jackets on board.

Contactours has land and sea tours of Los Cabos for groups, and booking agents at several hotels. TourCabos runs boat trips, offers horseback riding, and can provide information on water sports. Nomadas de Baja offers hiking, snorkeling, and kayaking tours of Los Cabos with an ecological bent. Pez Gato, on the marina near Plaza Las Glorias hotel in Los Cabos, has sailing and sunset cruises on a 46-ft catamaran, with live music as well as snorkeling and sailing tours. All trips depart from the marina in Cabo San Lucas; call or stop by the booth at the marina for further information.

➤ TOUR OPERATOR RECOMMENDATIONS: **Baja California Tours** (✉ 7734 Herschel Ave., Suite O, La Jolla, CA 92037, ☎ 858/454–7166, FAX 800/336–5454 or 858/454–2703, WEB www.bajatours.signonsandiego.com). **Baja Expeditions** (✉ 2625 Garnet Ave., San Diego, CA 92109, ☎ 800/843–6967; 858/581–3311 in the U.S., FAX 858/581–6542, WEB www.bajaex.com). **Contactours** (✉ Blvd. Marina, Los Cabos, ☎ 624/143–3333 or 624/143–2439). **Discover Baja** (✉ 3089 Clairemont Dr., San Diego, CA 92117, ☎ 800/727–2252; 619/275–4225 in the U.S., FAX 619/275–1836, WEB www.discoverbaja.com). **Eco-Tours Malarrimo** (✉ Blvd. Zapata, Guerrero Negro 23940, ☎ 615/157–0250). **Las Parras Tours** (✉ Salvatierra at Madero, Loreto, ☎ 624/135–1010, FAX 624/135–0900). **Nomadas de Baja** (☎ 624/148–1468 in Los Cabos, ☎ FAX 624/142–4388). **Lindblad Expeditions** (✉ 720 5th Ave., New York, NY 10019, ☎ 800/397–3348; 212/765–7740 in the U.S., WEB www.expeditions.com). **Pez Gato** (☎ 624/143–3797 in Los Cabos). **TourCabos** (✉ Plaza los Cabos, Paseo San José, ☎ 624/142–4040 in Los Cabos, FAX 624/142–0782).

TRANSPORTATION AROUND LOS CABOS

The best way to see the sights of Los Cabos is on foot. Downtown San José and Cabo San Lucas are compact, with the plaza, church, shops, and restaurants within a few blocks of one another. Bus service runs between the towns, with stops along the Corridor. If you plan to dine at the Corridor hotels or travel frequently between the two towns, it's a good idea to rent a car for a few days.

VISITOR INFORMATION

The Baja California Sur State Tourist Office is in La Paz on Mariano Abasolo s/n, and a more convenient location on the malecón near Calle 16 de Septiembre.

The Loreto Tourist Information Office is in the Municipal Building on the main plaza.

There are no official tourist-information offices in Los Cabos; hotel tour desks are the best sources of information. Avoid tour stands on the streets; they are usually associated with time-share operations. Baja tours, Mexican auto insurance, a monthly newsletter, and workshops are available through Discover Baja, which is a membership club for Baja travelers.

➤ Tourist Information: **Baja California Sur State Tourist Office** (✉ Mariano Abasolo s/n, ☎ 612/124–0100, 612/122–5939, or 612/124–0100; 612/122–5939 at the malecón, FAX 612/124–0722). **Discover Baja** (✉ 3089 Clairemont Dr., San Diego, CA 92117, ☎ 619/275–4225 or 800/727–2252, FAX 619/275–1836, WEB www.discoverbaja.com). **Loreto Tourist Information Office** (✉ Municipal Building on Plaza Principal, ☎ 613/135–0411; 866/465–6738 in the U.S., WEB www.gotoloreto.com). **La Paz Hotel Association** (✉ Obregón at 16 de Septiembre, ☎ 612/125–6844; 866/733–5272 in the U.S., WEB www.vivalapaz.com).

5 SONORA

Cowboys still ride the range in Mexican ranch country, but beaches have upstaged beef as this northwestern state's economic indicator. Along with relatively unspoiled and inexpensive coastal towns such as Puerto Peñasco, Bahía Kino, and San Carlos, Sonora's lures include a sprinkling of Spanish missions and colonial Alamos, an immaculate former silver-mining center with cobblestone streets and restored haciendas that evoke the spirit of Old Mexico.

Revised by Jane Onstott

SONORA, Mexico's second-largest state, is also its second richest. Ranch lands feed Mexico's finest beef cattle, and rivers flowing west from the Sierra Madre are diverted by giant dams to irrigate a low-rainfall area. Among Sonora's many crops are wheat and other grains, cotton, vegetables, nuts, and fruit—especially citrus, peaches, and apples. Hermosillo, Sonora's capital, bustles with agricultural commerce in the midst of the fertile lands that turn dry again toward the coast.

In the more rural areas, this stretch of the Mexican northwest is reminiscent of the American Wild West: *rancheras,* ballads of love and deception, blare from saloons and truck radios, and tiny *ranchitos* (small ranches) dot the sage-strewn countryside.

The Sonoran desert dominates the landscape through northern Sonora and into southern Arizona. Long stretches of flat scrub are punctuated by brown hills and mountains, towering saguaros, and organ-pipe cacti. This arid landscape, especially at the sea, is a vacation and retirement paradise for neighbors in Arizona, for whom the beaches of Sonora are closer, cheaper, and more interesting than those of southern California. In fact, good highways south of Nogales, Mexico, make the beaches of Puerto Peñasco (Rocky Point) and San Carlos–Guaymas as accessible to Tucson natives as those of Los Angeles or San Diego, California.

Highway 15 begins at the border town of Nogales, Sonora, adjacent to the U.S. town of Nogales, Arizona. It continues south through Hermosillo and reaches the Sea of Cortez (officially called the Gulf of California) at Guaymas, 418 km (259 mi) from the Arizona border. South of Guaymas, the harsh Sonoran desert is left behind, and the landscape begins to take on a more tropical character as it enters the state of Sinaloa just north of the city of Los Mochis. Except in the mountains, the entire region is hot between May and late September, with afternoon temperatures in midsummer sometimes exceeding 120°F.

In 1540 Francisco Vázquez de Coronado, governor of the provinces to the south, became the first Spanish leader to visit the plains of Sonora. More than a century later, Father Francisco Kino led a missionary expedition to Sonora and what is now southern Arizona—an area referred to as the Pimería Alta for the band of Pima Indians still living there. The Italian-born padre and his fellow friars founded half a dozen missions there. Although Alamos, in the south of Sonora, boomed with silver-mining wealth in the late 17th century, no one paid much attention to the northern part of the region. When the United States annexed a giant chunk of Mexico's territory after the Mexican-American War (1846–1848), northern Sonora suddenly became a border area—and a haven for Arizona outlaws. International squabbles bloomed and faded over the next decades as officials argued over issues such as the right to pursue criminals across the border. Porfirio Díaz, dictator of Mexico for most of the years between 1876 and 1911, finally moved to secure the state by settling it.

Settlers from Sonora, however, proved a hardy and independent bunch ill-suited to accepting the dictums of politicos in faraway Mexico City. Sonorans and their neighbors, the Chihuahenses, were major players in the Mexican Revolution, and the republic was ruled by three Sonorans: Plutarco Elías Calles, Adolfo de la Huerta, and Abelardo Rodríguez. Despite the enormous cost and destruction to railroads and other infrastructure, the Mexican Revolution brought prosperity to Sonora. With irrigation from the state's dams, inhabitants have been able to grow enough wheat not only for Mexico but also for export.

Pleasures and Pastimes

Beaches

Lively hotels and restaurants line the coastal areas around San Carlos, Guaymas, and Puerto Peñasco, but if you are willing to take more time for travel and forgo facilities, you'll find miles and miles of more-secluded beaches along the Sea of Cortez. Most of Sonora's main beaches have paved access roads, but some of the best—like pristine Playa San Nicolás just south of Bahía Kino (Kino Bay)—await the adventurous at the end of rutted, washed-out dirt tracks.

Dining

Sonoran cuisine is distinguished by its abundance of steaks and, on the coast especially, its fresh fish and seafood. Sonora is also the home of the giant flour tortilla, *machaca* (air-dried beef), and some of the best *carne asada* (thin, grilled, marinated meat) in Mexico. Seafood lovers will find shrimp, scallops, octopus, clams, and fish, both freshwater and ocean species. Traditional-Mexican foodies will be contented as well, with an abundance of dishes such as enchiladas, tacos, and tamales. Indeed, the style of Mexican cooking with which most Americans are familiar derives from this region. Casual dress (but not beachwear) is always acceptable, and reservations are rarely needed.

CATEGORY	COST*
$$$$	over $20
$$$	$15–$20
$$	$10–$15
$	under $10

**per person for a main course at dinner*

Lodging

In Sonora you might find yourself sleeping in a converted mansion or convent in fashionable Alamos, growing a Hemingway beard in a beach bungalow at Bahía Kino, or luxuriating in a posh resort in San Carlos. Lodging in Sonora is no longer the bargain it once was, and winter prices are similar to those of comparable accommodations in other parts of Mexico.

CATEGORY	COST*
$$$$	over $150
$$$	$100–$150
$$	$60–$100
$	under $60

**All prices are for a standard double room, excluding 17% tax.*

Missions

Among Sonora's hills and river valleys are a handful of almost forgotten missions that were founded by Jesuit fathers in the 17th and early 18th centuries and completed by the Franciscans in the late 18th and 19th centuries. Some of the churches, such as San Ignacio, still serve the small agricultural communities around them, whereas others, like Cocóspera, are simply shadows of their remarkable past.

Exploring Sonora

Sonoran landscapes are as varied as the state is vast. From the seemingly endless tracts of desert that tumble into the Gulf of California to the mountains of the Sierra Madre and the fields and valleys that nurture its produce and livestock, Sonora is a place of dramatic contrasts.

Mexico Highway 2 enters Sonora's far northwest from Baja California, paralleling the U.S. border. There are several crossing points, but

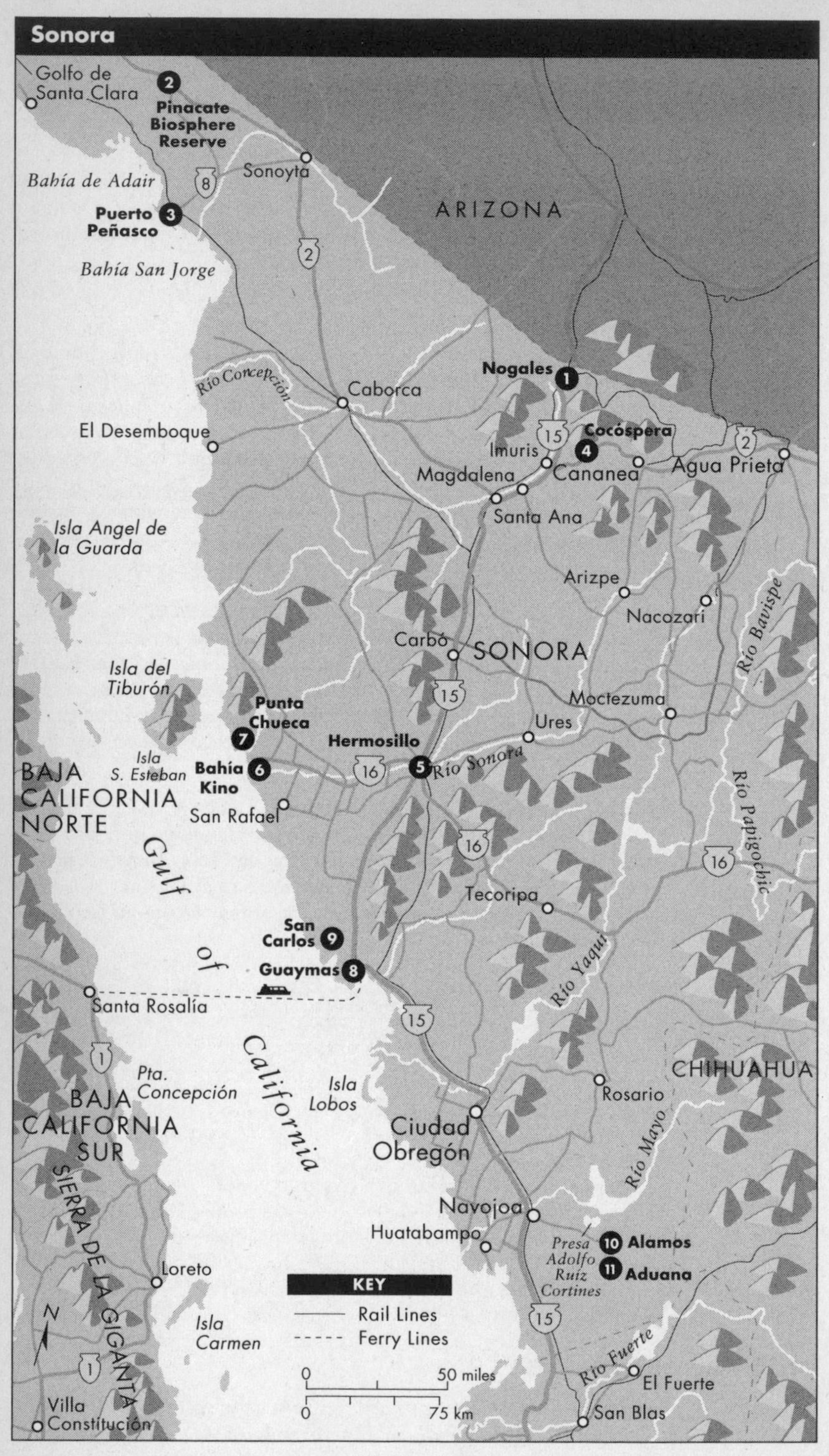
Sonora
Golfo de Santa Clara
2 Pinacate Biosphere Reserve
Sonoyta
Bahía de Adair
Puerto Peñasco 3
Bahía San Jorge
ARIZONA
Río Concepción
Caborca
Nogales 1
El Desemboque
Cocóspera
4
Imuris
Magdalena
Cananea
Agua Prieta
Santa Ana
Isla Angel de la Guarda
Arizpe
Nacozari
Río Bavispe
Carbó
SONORA
Isla del Tiburón
Punta Chueca
7
Moctezuma
Ures
Hermosillo
5 Río Sonora
Isla S. Esteban
Bahía Kino 6
BAJA CALIFORNIA NORTE
San Rafael
Río Papigochic
Gulf of California
Tecoripa
San Carlos 9
Guaymas 8
Río Yaqui
Santa Rosalía
CHIHUAHUA
Pta. Concepción
Isla Lobos
Rosario
BAJA CALIFORNIA SUR
Ciudad Obregón
Río Mayo
SIERRA DE LA GIGANTA
Navojoa
Huatabampo
Presa Adolfo Ruiz Cortines
10 Alamos
11 Aduana
Loreto
KEY
Rail Lines
Ferry Lines
Isla Carmen
N
0
50 miles
0
75 km
Río Fuerte
El Fuerte
Villa Constitución
San Blas

most people entering Sonora from the United States do so at Nogales, south of Tucson, Arizona. It's also a point of entry for winter fruit and vegetables exported to the United States.

Numbers in the text correspond to numbers in the margin and on the Sonora map.

Great Itineraries

Because it is so large and spread out, the state of Sonora demands eight days or more to really do it justice. With less time, you'll do best to choose one area and concentrate on exploring it. Most visitors to Sonora choose the sea, where desert landscapes collide with the shimmering blue Gulf of California.

IF YOU HAVE 3 DAYS

Take Highway 15 south from Nogales to the state capital, **Hermosillo** ⑤, where you will find a variety of good hotels and restaurants. Overnight here and spend the next morning touring the city or browsing through the Centro Ecológico, which is of special interest to children. After lunch, drive west on Highway 16 to **Bahía Kino** ⑥, a perfect beach for a one- or two-night retreat. The drive back to the Arizona border from Kino Bay is about six hours.

An alternative three-day itinerary is to cross the U.S. border at Lukeville-Sonoyta and head straight for the beaches of **Puerto Peñasco** ③ for the rest of the first day. The next day you can continue to lounge, lunch overlooking the beach, and tap your feet to live jazz in the evening, or spend the day exploring the lunarlike regions of the **Pinacate Biosphere Reserve** ②. On your last day, admire the formidable desert scenery as you loop east to **Nogales** ①. Spend an afternoon shopping there before you cross the U.S. border.

IF YOU HAVE 5 DAYS

Take Highway 15 from **Nogales** ① to **Guaymas** ⑧; the drive will take six or seven hours. Exploring the town of Guaymas and the adjacent resort area of **San Carlos** ⑨ will give you plenty to do for two days and nights. Continue south and then east for 3½ hours to charming colonial **Alamos** ⑩, in the foothills of the Sierra Madre. After one or two nights in Alamos, head back north. You might consider spending the night along the tranquil shores of **Bahía Kino** ⑥ on your way home.

IF YOU HAVE 8 DAYS

Combine the second of the three-day itineraries with the five-day itinerary, but stop off at **Hermosillo** ⑤ on the way down to **Guaymas** ⑧. If you have extra time, you might want to take a short side trip from Alamos to **Aduana** ⑪, former site of a thriving silver mine and current location of a thriving gourmet restaurant.

When to Tour

Summer temperatures in Sonora are as high as they are in southern Arizona, so unless you're prepared to broil, plan your trip for sometime between October and May.

Nogales

1 *100 km (62 mi) south of Tucson via Hwy. 19, on the Arizona-Mexico border.*

Bustling Nogales can become fairly rowdy on weekend evenings, when underage Tucsonans head south of the border to drink. It has some good restaurants, however, and visitors can find fine-quality crafts in addition to the usual souvenirs. If you're just coming for the day, it's

Close-Up

THE MAQUILA'S MARCH TO MODERNITY

WHEN MEXICO BEGAN ITS Border Industrialization Program in 1965, few could have imagined the social and environmental ills that open markets and prosperous free-trade deals would spawn three decades later. Mexico's *maquiladoras* (also known as *maquilas*) are foreign-owned assembly plants that produce cars, electronics, and garments for export to the First World; the passage of the North American Free Trade Agreement (NAFTA), which relaxed tariffs on goods moving across North American borders, made the maquila a profitable tool in getting cheap products to the United States. Even prior to NAFTA, repeated recessions and peso devaluations in the 1980s, combined with drought and chronic poverty in many of the northern and central agricultural states, brought both multinational companies and desperate migrant workers to Tijuana and Ensenada in Baja California, Nogales in Sonora, Matamoros in Tamaulipas, and above all, Ciudad Juárez in the state of Chihuahua.

Shantytowns sprang up, most of which are still lacking in clean water, sanitation, schools, electricity, and other basic infrastructure; companies and city governments have had no legal obligation, no financial incentive, and in the case of the local governments, no tax revenue, to provide for inhabitants. With time, the living conditions have improved marginally in some areas, but even with the meager allowances for housing or health care, workers here are still exploited by American labor standards. And because NAFTA has only an impotent Commission on Environmental Cooperation (CEC) to evaluate, but not enforce, the safe environmental procedures outlined in the agreement, hundreds of maquilas regularly dump hazardous waste along the border. It's estimated that less than half of American maquilas follow Mexican law and return their toxic waste to the United States. Many maquila workers live with contaminated water as a result.

But the maquila industry also created hundreds of thousands of jobs, gave impetus to Mexico's economy, and effectively threw a grenade in the midst of rural Mexico's family mores and values—for better and worse. Academic studies chart devastating social disintegration and the heartbreaking effect on young children; but Mexican women—who for the first time earn a wage and decide what to do with it—are viewed by many to have finally found liberation from rural, macho servitude.

Ciudad Juárez sits above anonymous swathes of the huge state of Chihuahua, just over the Río Bravo (or Rio Grande) from El Paso, Texas. Over the last three decades more than a million souls have come to toil in the maquilas, assembling televisions, clothes, car parts, calculators, telephones, and other appliances for the wealthiest market in the world. Juárez became a magnet for young women, lured from the interior of the country by plentiful jobs. As it turned out, though, not only was their labor cheap, but so were their lives: by the year 2001, more than 200 female corpses had been found in the desert or side streets around town. Murders of women in Juárez (most of whom worked in the maquilas) has become a scandal of international proportions, and although most cases remain unsolved, local, state, and even international protest is beginning to mount.

The maquila zone poses profound questions with no easy answers, but it still looks a long way from resolution, as a quick drive into the hills reveals the squalor in which people live. Hopeful young men and women are carted in from their rank little huts every day to make gadgets for others, before they can make a life for themselves.

— Barbara Kastelein

best to park on the Arizona side of the border—you'll see many guarded lots that cost about $8 for the day—and walk across. Most of the good shopping is within easy strolling distance of the border.

The shopping area centers mainly on Avenida Obregón, which begins a few blocks west of the border entrance and runs north–south; just follow the crowds. Most of the good restaurants are also on Obregón. Take Obregón as far south as you like; you'll know you have entered workaday Mexico when the shops are no longer fronted by English-speaking hustlers trying to lure you in the door.

Dining

$$ ✕ **El Cid.** This clean, festive restaurant has something for everyone. The menu features a variety of burgers, fresh seafood, and traditional Mexican specialties such as *camarones ajo* (grilled garlic shrimp) and carne asada. Be sure to wash it all down with a house-special margarita. ✉ *Av. Obregón 124, Centro,* ☎ *631/312–1113. MC, V.*

$$ ✕ **Elvira.** The free shot of tequila that comes with each meal complements Elvira's fine fish Mexican classics. There are 10 different types of mole served, from the rich, exotic, and dark *mole poblano,* made with nuts, seeds, tortillas, chocolate, and chiles, to the *manchamanteles,* a sweet stew built around pineapple, banana, and apple. This large, friendly restaurant next to the border is divided into intimate dining areas, including a pleasant outdoor patio. ✉ *Av. Obregón 1, Centro,* ☎ *631/312–4773. MC, V.*

$–$$ ★ ✕ **La Roca.** An elegant restaurant within walking distance of the border, this old stone house has a variety of dining rooms—some with fireplaces—and a balcony overlooking the magnolia trees and gurgling fountain on the patio below. There's excellent seafood, and an assortment of grilled meats served with stuffed chilies and a cheese enchilada. The *queso la Roca* (seasoned potato slices covered with melted cheese) makes a fine starter. Reservations are suggested weekend nights. ✉ *Calle Elias 91, Centro,* ☎ *631/312–0891. MC, V.*

Shopping

Nogales's wide selection of crafts, furnishings, and jewelry makes for some of Sonora's best shopping. At more informal shops, bargaining is not only acceptable but expected. The following shops tend to have fixed prices. East of the railroad tracks, **El Changarro** (✉ Calle Elias 93, Centro, below Restaurant La Roca, ☎ 631/312–0545) carries high-quality furniture, including both antiques and rustic-style modern pieces, blown glass, and pewter. **Mickey** (✉ Av. Obregón 128–130, Centro, ☎ 631/312–2299) has two floors of handcrafted Mexican treasures, *equipale* (pigskin) furniture, Talavera ceramic dishes, pottery, and glassware. **El Sarape** (✉ Av. Obregón 161, Centro, ☎ 631/312–0309) specializes in sterling-silver jewelry from Taxco and pewter housewares and crafts from all over Mexico.

Pinacate Biosphere Reserve

❷ *50 km (31 mi) west of Lukeville-Sonoyta.*

Midway between the Arizona border and the beach town of Puerto Peñasco, Pinacate Biosphere Reserve is best known for its volcanic rock formations and craters so moonlike that they were used for training the Apollo astronauts. The diversity of the lava flows makes Pinacate unique, as does the striking combination of Sonoran desert and volcanic field. Highlights of the area include **Santa Clara peak,** a little more than 4,000 ft high and 2.5 million years old, and **El Elegante crater,** 1½ km (1 mi) across and 750 ft deep, created by a giant steam eruption 150,000 years ago.

There are no facilities of any kind at Pinacate. You'll need to bring your own water—take plenty of it—food, and extra gasoline, as well as a good map, which you can get at Si Como No bookstore in Ajo, Arizona, Tucson's Map and Flag Center, or at the Intercultural Center for the Study of Desert and Oceans (CEDO) in Puerto Peñasco, Mexico. A high-clearance vehicle is strongly advised, and four-wheel-drive is recommended. Primitive camping is allowed with a permit obtainable from the Oficina Cerro del Pinacate in Sonoyta, a block south of the border crossing. You must register at the park entrance. For current park information, contact the International Sonoran Desert Alliance in Ajo, Arizona, at ☎ 520/387–6823.

Summer temperatures can be blistering. The best time to visit is between November and March, when daytime temperatures range between 60°F and 90°F. Tours can be arranged through the tourism office in Puerto Peñasco. An excellent naturalist-led day tour in English from Ajo is available from **Ajo Stage Lines** (✉ 321 Taladro, Ajo, AZ 85321, ☎ 520/387–6559 or 800/942–1981, WEB www.ajostageline.com) for about $85.

Puerto Peñasco

❸ *104 km (65 mi) south of the Arizona border at Lukeville on Mexico Hwy. 8.*

Puerto Peñasco was dubbed Rocky Point by British explorers in the 18th century, and that's the name most Americans know it by today. The town itself was established about 1927, after Mexican fishermen found abundant shrimp beds in the area and American John Stone built the first hotel. Al Capone was a frequent visitor during the Prohibition era, when he was hiding from U.S. law.

The real appeal of Puerto Peñasco, at the north end of the Sea of Cortez, is the miles of sandy beaches punctuated by stretches of black, volcanic rock. A remarkably high tide change—as much as 23 ft—makes for great exploring among countless tide pools.

To the beaches add low prices for accommodations, food, and drink, and you've got a popular wintering spot for American RVers and retirees and a favorite weekend getaway for Arizonans. Although Rocky Point is rather faceless, the "old town" has a number of interesting shopping stalls, fish markets, and restaurants.

This coastline is rapidly changing, however. A number of major projects have been developed—including a complex with a shopping center, a luxury hotel, condos and villas, a yacht club, a golf course, and a marina—all designed to attract an upscale clientele. Even more dramatic changes to the landscape may result from the $2.5 million "Escalera Náutica" (Nautical Ladder), a series of high-end marinas up and down the Baja Peninsula and Sonora and Sinaloa coasts, being pushed by the Fox administration. Only time will tell whether these plans will reach fruition, and if they do, what their impact on ecology and the local economy will be.

Thanks to the Only Sonora program, you needn't post a bond when driving into the state of Sonora, and you are also exempt from a tourist tax (technically, if spending 72 hours or less). Simply tell the border guards that you are heading for Puerto Peñasco as you drive through—but don't neglect to get Mexican auto insurance.

The northern Gulf area forms an impressive desert-coast ecosystem, and scientists from both the United States and Mexico conduct research programs at the **Intercultural Center for the Study of Desert and Oceans** (known as CEDO, its acronym in Spanish), about 3 km (2 mi) east of town on Fremont Boulevard, Fracc. Las Conchas. You can take a free English-language tour of the facility (Tuesday at 2, Saturday at 4; donation encouraged) to learn about the ecology of the area and its history, or just pick up a tide calendar (useful if you're planning beach activities) or field guide from the gift shop. Talks and nature outings—including tide-pool walks, Pinacate excursions, and kayaking expeditions of area estuaries—are offered sporadically. ✉ *Turn east at municipal building and follow signs for Caborca Rd., where there will be signs for Las Conchas Beach and CEDO,* ☎ *638/382–0113,* WEB *www.cedointercultural.org.* *Free.* ⏲ *Mon.–Sat. 9–5, Sun. 10–2.*

Dining and Lodging

$$–$$$ ✕ **Costa Brava.** In town, this small, split-level restaurant has excellent service and a great view of the Gulf. The house specialties are succulent prawns Costa Brava, breaded shrimp stuffed with cheese, wrapped in bacon, and fried, and the prawns Carlos Quinto, with a sweet sauce made of apples. Great for fishermen and early risers, this restaurant opens at 6 AM. ✉ *Blvd. Kino 41, at Paseo Estrella, Col. Puerto,* ☎ *638/383–3130. MC, V.*

$$ ✕ **La Casa del Capitán.** Perched atop Rocky Point's tallest point, this restaurant has the best views over the bay and the town below. There's inside dining, but the long outdoor porch overlooking the sea is the place to be. A wide-ranging menu includes everything from nachos and quesadillas to flaming brandied jumbo shrimp. ✉ *Av. del Agua 1 Cerro de la Ballena,* ☎ *638/383–5698. MC, V.*

$$ ✕ **Friendly Dolphin.** This bright blue-and-pink palace feels like a wealthy Mexican family home, with nicely stuccoed ceilings, wood-paneled windows, hand-painted tiles, and an upstairs porch overlooking the harbor. Unique family recipes include foil-wrapped shrimp or fish prepared *estilo delfín*—steamed in orange juice, herbs, and spices. Gaston, the operatic owner, often bursts into song in the dining room, singing in a baritone as rich and robust as the food he serves. ✉ *Av. Alcantar 44, Col Puerto,* ☎ *638/383–2608. MC, V.*

$$ ★ ✕ **Puesta del Sol.** As the name ("setting of the sun") implies, this is a perfect place to see the sun set, with plenty of outdoor seating on a patio overlooking the beach. The menu features such seafood dishes as fish Mornay (with a creamy cheese sauce) and grilled lobster, with appetizers to appeal to American tastes. Don't miss the margaritas—they're to die for. ✉ *Hotel Playa Bonita, Paseo Balboa, Playa Bonita,* ☎ *638/383–2586. MC, V.*

$–$$ ✕ **La Curva.** This friendly family restaurant with great Mexican food is easy to spot if you look for the mermaid on the sign. The menu lists more than 100 items, including shrimp cooked 20 ways. Hawaiian-style shrimp is wrapped in bacon and served in a sweet sauce; the filet mignon, doused in mushroom sauce. ✉ *Blvd. Kino and Comonfort, Centro,* ☎ *638/383–3470. MC, V.*

$$ 🏨 **Playa Bonita.** One of the first three hotels in Rocky Point, Playa Bonita offers clean, comfortable rooms; ask for one facing the hotel's broad, sandy beach. This place is very popular with Americans, who also enjoy the Puesta del Sol restaurant. An RV park offers 300 hookups at $17–$20 a day. ✉ *Paseo Balboa 100, Paseo Balboa, 85550,* ☎ *638/383–2586; 638/383–2596 for RV Park. 120 rooms, 6 suites. Restaurant, pool, hot tub, beach, bar. MC, V.*

$$ 🏨 **Plaza Las Glorias.** Sitting like a sand-color fortress overlooking the beach, Plaza Las Glorias was the first large chain hotel to hit town. Its open lobby with towering quadrangular ceiling and bamboo-covered skylights draws gasps of admiration from the busloads of tourists who flock here. Rooms are standard; for just a bit more money, junior suites offer refrigerator, microwave, and ocean view. ✉ *Paseo Las Glorias, Las Explanadas, Playa Bonita 83550,* ☎ *638/833–6010, 800/342–2644, or 800/515–4321,* FAX *638/383–6015. 210 rooms. 2 restaurants, pool, hot tub, beach, snorkeling, 2 bars. MC, V.*

$ **Costa Brava.** All the rooms in this small, clean downtown hotel overlook the Gulf. Down the street are the fish markets, popular with those who bring the catch of the day back across the border. ✉ *Malecón Kino and Paseo Estrella, Col. Puerto, 83550,* ☎ *638/383–4100 or 638/383–4101,* FAX *638/383–3621. 25 rooms. Restaurant, bar, free parking. MC, V.*

Nightlife

Nightlife in Puerto Peñasco centers around bars and drinking. **Latitude 31** (✉ Av. Benito Juárez, en route to Col. Puerto, ☎ 638/388–4311) is a sports bar with a great view of the harbor. **The Lighthouse** (✉ Lote 2, Fracc. el Cerro, ☎ 638/383–2389), a pretty restaurant-bar overlooking the harbor, appeals to a more sophisticated crowd. The owners are jazz musicians, and you can dance to live music between 6 and 10 every night except Monday. Popular among the young and those who don't want to put too much distance between the water's edge and their next margarita is **Manny's Beach Club** (✉ Avs. Coahuila and Primera, El Mirador, ☎ 638/383–3605), where recorded music is always blaring.

Outdoor Activities and Sports

WATER SPORTS

At **Sun and Fun Dive Shop** (✉ Blvd. Benito Juárez s/n at Calle 1, entrance to old port, ☎ 638/383–5450) you can rent diving or snorkeling equipment or receive PADI and NAUI scuba instruction. Sunset cruises, fishing charters, and snorkeling trips can all be booked here.

Cocóspera

4 *104 km (65 mi) southeast of Nogales, between Imuris and Cananea.*

The ruined mission church of Our Lady of Pilar and Santiago de Cocóspera was one of more than a dozen churches established in the state of Sonora and Arizona by Father Eusebio Francisco Kino between 1687 and 1711. The crumbling adobe mission sits on a bluff above an oak forest and farmlands in a mountain pass in the Sierra Madre Occidental. This is the only mission church in Sonora that retains parts of the original foundation and adobe. To get here from Nogales, take Highway 15 Libre to Highway 2.

Hermosillo

5 *185 km (115 mi) south of Magdalena on Hwy. 15.*

Hermosillo (pop. 850,000) is the capital of Sonora, a status it has held on and off since 1831. It's the seat of the state university and benefits from that institution's cultural activities. If you know a bit of Spanish, you might think the city's name means "little beauty." In fact, it honors José María González Hermosillo, one of the leaders in Mexico's War of Independence.

Settled in 1742 by Captain Augustín de Vildosola and a contingent of 50 soldiers, Hermosillo was originally called Pitic, the Pima Indian name for "the place where two rivers meet." The city's most prestigious neighborhood—home to the governor and U.S. consul, among other prominent citizens—still bears the name Pitic. Located immediately north of the highway into town and behind the Hotel Bugambilia, the area is worth an hour's stroll to view the creative handling of concrete, tile, and other materials in the homes of Hermosillo's affluent residents.

A business center for the state of Sonora, Hermosillo is largely modern, but some lovely plazas and parks hark back to a more graceful past. Although Hermosillo is usually just considered a jumping-off point for Bahía Kino or Guaymas, it has a number of attractions in its own right, as well as the best accommodations and restaurants until you reach Guaymas or San Carlos.

At the center of town, look for charming **Plaza Zaragoza,** a town square shaded by orange trees and towering figs. The centerpiece of this pretty park, set about with comfortable wooden benches, is a lovely Victorian gazebo, restored between 1997 and 2000. Facing the park on the south side, **Catedral de San Agustín** (1878) has been regilded.

Overlooking the city on the Cerro la Campana (Hill of Bells), the **Museo de Sonora** has displays of regional history, geology, geography, and culture. The building in which it's housed served as a penitentiary for 70 years beginning in 1907; displays are found in the many cells. The bulk of the exhibits are graphic displays, including charts and maps of trade routes and native populations. Each display has a short summary in English. ✉ *Jesús García Final at Calle California, Col. La Matanza,* ☎ *662/217–2714.* 🎫 *$3.* ⏲ *Tues.–Sat. 10–5, Sun. 9–4.*

On the highway south of town, stop at the **Centro Ecológico,** an environmental and ecological park with more than 500 species of plants and animals—both native to Sonora as well as exotic. It's modeled after the Arizona–Sonora Desert Museum in Tucson and is best visited November through March because of the heat and lack of shade the rest of the year. ✉ *Carretera a Guaymas Km 35; 5 km (3 mi) south of Hermosillo,* ☎ *622/250–1225.* 🎫 *$2.20.* ⏲ *Daily 8–5.*

Dining and Lodging

$$ ✕ **Sonora Steak.** Here in a sophisticated, understated, and elegant old house you can enjoy the finest cuts of the famous Sonoran beef at reasonable prices. The specialty, rib-eye steak, is aged 10–18 days at 12–18 degrees centigrade. Vegetarians can graze on watercress salad, or opt for cream of green chili soup or penne with fresh tomato and basil. The restaurant is a good spot for a late-night meal—it's open until 2 AM. ✉ *Blvd. Kino 914, Zona Hotelera,* ☎ *662/210–0313. MC, V.*

$$ ✕ **Xochimilco.** If you want to try regional specialties and are willing to go with the set meal, come to this large, institutional-looking place on a narrow side street near town center. Popular with locals and regulars from across the border, Xochimilco's meals are designed for two or more, and include carne asada, ribs, tripe, vegetable salad, beans, and fresh flour tortillas. ✉ *Av. Obregón 51, at Gutiérrez, Col. Villa de Seris,* ☎ *622/250–4089. MC, V.*

$$$$ 🏨 **Fiesta Americana.** Hermosillo's premier hotel, this full-service property is the largest in town and popular among business travelers. Guest rooms feature tasteful decor, with a beige-and-forest-green color scheme. The adjacent disco is one of the most popular in town. ✉ *Blvd. Kino 369, Col. Lomas Pitic 83010,* ☎ *622/259–6000 or 800/343–7821,* FAX *622/259–6062,* WEB *www.fiestaamericana.com. 221 rooms. Restaurant, cafeteria, tennis court, pool, gym, bar, shop, dance club, business services, meeting rooms, car rental, travel services. AE, MC, V.*

$$$ 🏨 **Holiday Inn Hermosillo.** Two-thirds of the attractive rooms in this contemporary, two-story hotel surround a large green lawn and a good-size pool. Rooms have comfortable molded plastic bathtubs as well as coffeemakers and radio alarm clocks. Free airport transfer is included in room price. ✉ *Blvd. Kino and Ramón Corral 1110, Zona Hotelera 83010,* ☎ *662/214–4570 or 800/623–3330,* FAX *662/214–6473. 132 rooms, 10 suites. Restaurant, pool, gym, bar, meeting rooms, travel services, free parking. AE, MC, V.*

$$ **Hotel Bugambilia.** This pleasant small property has reasonable prices, comfortable rooms, a convenient location in the hotel zone, and a good restaurant. The bougainvillea-drenched bungalows facing the parking spaces are most popular; other rooms surround the pool. Rates include breakfast, and guests can use the facilities at the Holiday Inn, across the street. ✉ *Blvd. Kino 712, Zona Hotelera 83010,* ☎ *662/214–5050,* FAX *662/214–5252. 104 rooms. Restaurant, room service, pool, free parking. AE, MC, V.*

$ **San Andrés.** The owner of this friendly, family-owned hotel, 75-year-old don Andrés, inherited the three-story downtown hotel from his dad. Three floors of rooms surround courtyards with wrought-iron tables and chairs. Rooms have flowered bedspreads, coffeemakers, air-conditioning, and heat. Beds are a bit hard, carpeting is industrial-strength, and bathrooms are super simple, but the pluses by far outweigh the minuses. ✉ *Oaxaca 14, at Juárez, Centro 83000,* ☎ *662/217–3099,* FAX *662/217–3139,* WEB *www.naftaconnect.com/sanandres. 80 rooms, 1 suite. Restaurant, cable TV, bar, meeting room, free parking. AE.*

Nightlife and the Arts

Hermosillo is home to several lively nightspots. **Bar Freedom** (✉ Blvd. Kino 1012, Zona Hotelera, ☎ 662/215–1340) is a popular upscale joint for the youngish set. **Joy's** (✉ Fiesta Americana, Blvd. Kino 369, Zona Hotelera, ☎ 622/259–6000) attracts an affluent clientele; it's open Thursday–Saturday only. **Marco n' Charlie's** (✉ Blvd. Rodríguez at Calle San Luis Potosí, Zona Hotelera, ☎ 662/215–3061) is a watering hole for the town's upper crust. **La Trova** (✉ Calle Guerrero and Tamaulipas, Zona Hotelera, ☎ 662/214–2861) has musicians playing romantic music for dancing Wednesday through Saturday.

Shopping

In the downtown markets of Hermosillo, particularly along Avenidas Serdán and Monterrey, you can buy anything from blankets and candles to wedding attire, as well as a selection of cowboy boots. The variety of goods concentrated in this area equals what you'll find in Nogales, and the prices are better. Typical local sweets, called *coyotas* (pie crust surrounding brown sugar or a treaclelike sweet), can be purchased in the Villa de Seris neighborhood, near restaurant Xochimilco. At **Ehui!** (✉ Av. Serdáb at Pino Suárez, Centro, ☎ 662/212–4010) the friendly Mexican and American owners will tell you the history behind *torote* grass baskets, beautifully carved rain sticks, reproductions of Yaqui testaments, and more typical souvenirs.

Bahía Kino

❻ *107 km (64 mi) west of Hermosillo on Hwy. 16.*

On the eastern shore of the Sea of Cortez lies Bahía Kino, home to some of the prettiest beaches in northwest Mexico. For many years, Bahía Kino was undiscovered except by RV owners and other aficionados of the unspoiled. In the past decade or so, great change has come at the hands of North Americans who have been building condos and beach houses here. The moniker "Bahía Kino" actually refers to twin towns: Kino Viejo (Old Kino, the Mexican village) and Kino Nuevo (New Kino), where facing a long strand of creamy beach you'll find private homes, condos, RV sites, and other tourist facilities.

There's little to do in Bahía Kino, so after hanging around a few days, you might consider taking a run across the narrow channel to **Isla del Tiburón** (Shark Island), designated an ecological preserve in 1963. Permission to visit Tiburón may be obtained from the Seri Indian government; they can also provide a reliable boatman—guide. Only the

Seri Indians, for whom Isla del Tiburón is a traditional fishing ground, are permitted to ferry travelers across and guide them around the island. The trip, which is of most interest to anglers and bird-watchers, costs about $100 per boatload of one to four passengers. ✉ *Seri Indian government: main street, across from the Pemex station, Kino Viejo,* ☎ *662/242–0557 or 662/242–0590.*

For a crash ethnography lesson, poke around the interesting if hodgepodge collection of photographs, musical instruments, and dioramas in the **Museo de los Seris.** ✉ *Blvd. Mar de Cortés at Calle Progreso,* ☎ *no phone.* 💵 *60¢.* ⏲ *Wed.–Sun. 8–6.*

If you'll be in town a week or more, it's worthwhile to obtain a temporary membership to the **Club Deportivo.** For $15 a month, you'll be introduced to most of the town's temporary residents and some locals as well. The club offers everything from quilting and Spanish classes to dances and other social activities. By spring of 2002 the club plans to be operating its new golf course, where for a $5 greens fee even duffers can attempt the 9-hole sand-and-cottonseed-grass course. ✉ *Calle Cadiz s/n, at Plaza del Mar RV Park,* ☎ *662/242–0321.*

Dining and Lodging

$$ ✕ **La Palapa.** This thatch-roof restaurant, with a plain interior and a small balcony overlooking the beach, has great seafood, as well as the best cheeseburger in town. The shrimp brochette with green chilies is memorable, and the owner, Julian (who practically grew up in his dad's seafood restaurant in Old Kino), recommends the breaded oysters. ✉ *Blvd. Mar de Cortés and Wellington, on the way into Kino Nuevo,* ☎ *662/242–0210. AE, MC, V.*

$$ ✕ **El Pargo Rojo.** The best known restaurant in town is decorated with fishnets and realistic reproductions of the fish you'll be eating; its name means "red snapper." The catch of the day varies, but you can depend on consistent quality, including such classics as a brimming shrimp cocktail followed by fish stuffed with shrimp, clams, squid, and octopus. Fine cuts of meat are available and, depending on your luck, you'll be serenaded either by Mexican musicians or by the ceaseless wailing of recorded, polkalike *norteña* music on Mexican MTV. ✉ *Blvd. Mar de Cortés 1426, Kino Nuevo,* ☎ *662/242–0205. MC, V.*

$$ ★ ✕ **Restaurant Marlin.** This restaurant in Kino Viejo is hard to find only the first time; after that, you will return frequently, drawn by the clean, unpretentious atmosphere and congenial service—not to mention margaritas as big as fishbowls. Superb seafood dishes include *sopa de siete mares* (soup of the seven seas) and *jaiba a la diabla* (a spicy hot crab dish). ✉ *Calles Tastiota and Guaymas, Kino Viejo,* ☎ *662/242–0111. MC, V. Closed Mon.*

$ ✕ **Jorge's Restaurant.** This clean, comfortable family restaurant overlooks the bay: a perfect spot for morning coffee, pancakes, and pelican viewing. At other meals portions tend to be small, but the food is quite good, and the owner and his daughters play the guitar and sing in the evening. ✉ *Near the end of Blvd. Mar de Cortés at Alecantres, Kino Nuevo,* ☎ *662/242–0049. No credit cards.*

$ 🏨 **Posada Las Aves.** There's a lot to love about these comfortable, clean, and new one- and two-bedroom apartments. It's a great deal: the two largest units—which sleep five or six comfortably in two bedrooms—have a fireplace in the living room, full kitchen and dining room, and cost just $115 a night. All of the units are spacious, with sturdy wood cabinets, clunky wood and vinyl couches, and sparkling tile bathrooms. ✉ *Calle Veracruz between Calle Nautla and Calle Tecolutla, Kino Nuevo 83340,* ☎ *662/242–0242. 15 apartments. Picnic area, pool, playground, free parking. No credit cards.*

$ **Posada del Mar.** Across the street from the beach, this hotel is landscaped in shrubs and cacti surrounding a central fountain and walkways of hewn stone. One of the first hotels built in Kino Nuevo, it has dark rooms that could use some sprucing up. You can see the sea from comfortable chairs on the wide second-story balcony, and barbecue on outdoor grills in a picnic area. ✉ *Blvd. Mar de Cortés and Calle Creta, Kino Nuevo 83340,* ☎ FAX *662/242–0155. 42 rooms, 2 suites, 2 bungalows. Pool, free parking. MC, V.*

Shopping

Kino has little in the way of crafts or even souvenirs, but **Alcatraz** (✉ Tastiota 12, Kino Nuevo, ☎ 662/242–0570), which is Spanish for calla lily, offers Talavera-style plates, mounted deer heads, shell ornaments, and plenty of gift items and housewares from all over Mexico.

Punta Chueca

❼ *27 km (17 mi) north of Bahía Kino.*

This rustic Seri fishing village perches at the end of a bumpy, winding dirt road. You'll pass exquisite vistas of the bay, distant empty beaches, and rolling mountains. The inhabitants of this community live a subsistence lifestyle, relying on the sea and desert much as they have for hundreds of years.

With fewer than 700 remaining members, the Seri tribe represents an ancient culture on the verge of dying out. The Seris' love for their natural surroundings is evident in the necklaces that they have traditionally worn and now create to sell. Pretty little shells are wound into the shape of flowers and strung with wild desert seeds and tiny bleached snake vertebrae to result in delicate necklaces. Seri women weave elaborate *canastas* (baskets) of torote grass, which have become highly prized and expensive.

As you get out of your car anywhere in town, be prepared to encounter an entourage of Seri women dressed in colorful ankle-length skirts, their heads covered with scarves and their arms laden with necklaces for sale. The Seri are best known, however, for the carved ironwood figurines that represent the animal world around them, including dolphins, turtles, and pelicans. Many Mexican merchants have taken to machine-making large figures out of ironwood for the tourist trade, thereby seriously depleting the supply of the lilac-blossomed tree that grows only in the Sonoran desert. (If the bottom of the statuette is clean cut, it was cut with an electric saw and not made by the Seri.) For this reason, the Seri now carve figures out of several types of stone, including soapstone.

Guaymas

❽ *128 km (79 mi) south of Hermosillo.*

The buzz and bustle of Guaymas—Mexico's seventh-largest port—has a pleasant backdrop of rusty red, saguaro-speckled mountains that nudge the deep-blue waters of a sprawling bay on the Sea of Cortez. The Spanish arrived in this "port of ports" by the mid-16th century. In 1701, two Jesuit priests, Father Kino and his colleague Juan María Salvatierra, erected a mission base here intended to convert the native Guaimas, Seri, and Yaqui Indians.

Guaymas was declared a commercial port in 1814 and became an important center of trade with Europe as well as within Mexico. In 1847, during the Mexican-American War, U.S. naval forces attacked and occupied the town for a year. Bumbling filibuster William Walker also managed to take Guaymas for a short time in 1853, and in 1866, during Maximilian's brief reign, the French took control. Today's foreign invaders are mostly travelers passing through on their way somewhere else. Given its proximity to the beaches of San Carlos and Mazatlán, as well as the twice-weekly ferry that travels between Guaymas and Santa Rosalía on the Baja peninsula, modern Guaymas is more a steppingstone than a destination. That said, it's a congenial seaside town that some folks prefer to more tourist-oriented, spread-out San Carlos.

No visit to a Mexican town is complete without a trip to the *mercado*, or municipal market, bursting with colors and smells and a glimpse at daily life. After the throngs, you'll find quiet at the 19th-century church **Parroquia de San Fernando.** Or you might relax across the street at **Plaza 13 de Julio,** a typical Mexican park with a Moorish-style bandstand and matching benches.

Dining and Lodging

$–$$ ✕ **Los Barcos.** Across the street from the harbor, Los Barcos offers a predictable seafood-and-steak menu. The main room is large and somewhat sterile, with an enormous bar along the back wall. More beachy is the fan-cooled, thatch-roofed adjoining room, with a juke box and walls painted with smiling dolphins and octopi. The crab tostadas are especially recommended. ✉ *Calle 22 and Malecón, Centro,* ☎ *622/222–7650. MC, V.*

$$ ✕🏨 **Hotel Armida.** On the edge of town but still close to downtown, this sand-color hotel has a large, well-kept pool, and a good coffee shop where locals gather for power breakfasts. At the excellent steak house, El Oeste ("The West"), the stuffed and mounted heads of mountain goats, cougars, and bison gaze down at diners. Large, bright accommodations are plain but serviceable, with comfortable beds; many have balconies overlooking the pool. The economy rooms at the back are a great bargain. ✉ *Carretera Internacional, Salida Norte 85400,* ☎ *622/222–5220,* FAX *622/224–0448. 125 rooms. Restaurant, coffee shop, room service, pool, bar, meeting rooms, free parking. AE, MC, V.*

$$ 🏨 **Playa de Cortés.** This fine, sprawling old hotel overlooking Bacochibampo Bay has a traditional, hospitable main lobby with towering wooden beam ceilings and a lavish fireplace. Combining semitropical landscaping and a sweeping view of the bay, this hotel evokes memories of a more genteel past. Some rooms are furnished with hand-carved antiques; many have fireplaces and balconies. Private casitas are less attractively furnished, but are closest to the beach. ✉ *Bahía Bacochibampo, Col. Miramar,* ☎ *622/221–0135, 01–800/623–4400, or 800/782–7608,* FAX *622/221–0135. 89 rooms, 22 suites, 9 bungalows. Restaurant, tennis court, pool, beach, bar. AE, MC, V.*

Nightlife and the Arts

The younger set heads to **Charles Baby** (✉ Av. Serdán and Malecón, Centro, ☎ no phone), open Friday–Sunday. Also open on the weekends is **Xanadu** (✉ Malecón at Malpica, Centro, ☎ no phone).

San Carlos

❾ *32 km (20 mi) northwest of Guaymas.*

Long considered an extension of Guaymas, this resort town—on the other side of the rocky peninsula that separates Bacochibampo Bay from San Carlos Bay—has a personality of its own. Whitewashed houses with red-tile roofs snuggle together along the water where countless yachts and motorboats are docked. The town is a laid-back favorite among professional anglers, North American tourists, and the time-share crowd, as well as wealthy Mexican families from Guaymas. There's a growing assortment of hotels and condominiums, as well as a country club with an 18-hole golf course.

The overlapping of desert and semitropical flora and fauna has created a fascinating diversity of species along this coast. Among marine life, more than 650 species of fish exist here; red snapper, marlin, corbina, yellowtail, sea bass, and flounder are commonly caught. Whales have occasionally been spotted in San Carlos Bay, but more common are dolphins and pelicans. The water is calm and warm enough through October to enjoy excellent swimming. Scuba, snorkeling, fishing, and boat excursions are popular, too.

The quiet 5-km (3-mi) stretch of sandy beach at **Los Algodones,** where the San Carlos Plaza Hotel and Club Med are now, was in the 1960s a location site for the film *Catch 22*. Mexico's first man-made marina lies in the shadow of the jagged twin-peak **Tetakawi mountain,** a sacred site where Indian warriors once gathered to gain spiritual strength. **La Martinica** beach, near the San Carlos Marina, is a great place for snorkeling in shallow waters. An interesting day trip can be made by boat out to the pristine **San Pedro Island,** where sea lions frolic on the rocks.

To reach San Carlos from Guaymas, take Mexico 15 north for about 8 km (5 mi) to a well-marked turnoff. San Carlos itself has no real city center; instead, it stretches for miles along the four-lane **Corredor Escénico** (Scenic Corridor), which was completed in 1995 to replace an infamously bumpy road.

Dining and Lodging

$$$ ✕ **El Pueblito.** Although some find the Mexican decor here a bit excessive, to others it's a truly gracious and romantic place—especially when trios begin to seranade diners at candlelit tables. You'll be treated to creative international cuisine, as well as regional favorites. The Tetakawi prawns, stuffed with other shellfish and served in a rich and creamy béchamel sauce, are a heavenly indulgence. ✉ *San Carlos Plaza Hotel, Paseo Mar Barmejo Nte., Apdo. 441, Los Algodones,* ☎ *622/226–0777 Ext. 510. AE, MC, V. Closed Mon.*

$$ ✕ **Rosa's Cantina.** Bearing little resemblance to the saloon in Marty Robbins's song "El Paso," this cozy, pink, laid-back restaurant has two large dining rooms filled with picnic tables. Ask anyone in town and they'll tell you Rosa's ample breakfasts are the best way to start the day. Try the *machaca* (dried beef) with eggs and yummy salsa; the tortilla soup is great for lunch or dinner. Gringos who miss being pampered will appreciate the nonsmoking section, decaf coffee, and salad bar. ✉ *Calle Aurora 297, Creston,* ☎ *622/226–1000. MC, V.*

$$$$ **San Carlos Plaza Hotel and Resort.** Rising from San Carlos Bay, this huge, striking pink edifice is the most luxurious hotel in Sonora. The arresting atrium lobby opens onto a large pool and beach. Attractive rooms—all with an ocean view—have contemporary furnishings, and rooms on the first two floors have balconies overlooking the sea. Children love the swimming-pool slide and horseback riding on beautiful Algodones Beach. ✉ *Paseo Mar Barmejo Nte. 4, Los Algodones 85506,* ☎ *622/227–0077 or 800/854–2320,* FAX *622/227–0098,* WEB *www.guaymassancarlos.net. 132 rooms, 41 suites. 3 restaurants, snack bar, in-room safes, minibars, 2 tennis courts, 2 pools, gym, hot tub, beach, 2 bars, meeting rooms. AE, MC, V.*

$$$ **Plaza Las Glorias.** This condo-hotel complex overlooks the San Carlos marina. It's smaller than the San Carlos Plaza Hotel but nearly as impressive. Subtle pastels prevail in the comfortable rooms, and most accommodations have a tiny kitchenette. Corner rooms—about $15 more than standard rooms—have hot tubs on the outdoor patios. A shuttle takes guests to the hotel beach club, with restaurant, pool, and beach toys. ✉ *Calle Gabriel Estrada s/n, Sector La Herradura 85506,* ☎ *622/226–1021 or 622/226–1034,* FAX *622/226–1035,* WEB *www.sidek.com.mx. 105 rooms. Restaurant, snack bar, 2 pools, baby-sitting, car rental, travel services. AE, MC, V.*

$ **Fiesta San Carlos.** This small hotel on the bay has a lot of charm and is clean and comfortable. Some rooms with kitchens are available. The cost is the same for one or two guests and includes an American breakfast. ✉ *Carretera Escénico San Carlos Km 8.5, Carretera Escénico 85506,* ☎ *622/226–0229 or 662/226–1318. 31 rooms. Restaurant, pool, bar, free parking; no room phones, no room TVs. AE, MC, V.*

$ **Hacienda Tetakawi.** This hotel and trailer park across from the beach on the main street of town is a Best Western. Rooms are generic but clean, and each has a balcony, a few with a view of the sea. ✉ *Carretera Escénico San Carlos Km 10, Carretera Escénico 85000,* ☎ *622/226–0248. 22 rooms. Restaurant, pool, bar. AE, MC, V.*

Nightlife and the Arts

For two floors of paintings and sculpture by a variety of Mexican and foreign artists, stop by the **Galería Bellas Artes** (✉ Villa Hermosa 111, Sector Villahermosa, ☎ 622/226–0073), where their work is for sale. It's open Monday–Saturday 9:30–5. Every Tuesday the San Carlos Plaza hotel hosts an evening of folkloric dancing and singing along with dinner buffet and open bar ($18; ☎ 622/226–0545). Reservations are encouraged, and the hotel will provide transportation from some hotels. For conversation and exotic drinks, try **Mai-Tai Bar** (✉ Plaza las Glorias, ☎ 622/226–1021). **Ranas Ranas** (✉ Carretera San Carlos Km 9.5, Carretera Escénico, ☎ 622/226–0610) is a party-down bar with a beach view. During the filming of *Mask of Zorro,* Antonio Banderas hung out at **Tequilas Bar** (✉ Camino a la Marina San Carlos, La Marina, ☎ 622/226–0545), still a popular nightspot.

Outdoor Activities and Sports

GOLF

Anyone can get a tee time at the 18-hole golf course at the **Club de Golf San Carlos** (✉ Av. de los Yaquis between Loma Bonita and Solimar, ☎ FAX 622/226–1102), although those staying in area hotels usually get lower greens fees.

WATER SPORTS

Gary's Dive Shop (✉ Blvd. Beltrones Km 10, ☎ 622/226–0049; 622/226–0024 after hours, WEB www.garysdivemexico.com) runs fishing, snorkeling, and PADI-certified diving excursions. You can also book sunset cruises, and whale-watching and customized expeditions.

Shopping

Kiamy's Gift Shop (✉ Carretera San Carlos Km 10, ☎ 622/226–0400) is like a bazaar, with something for everyone: silver jewelry, earrings, leather bags, ceramics, Yaqui Indian masks, T-shirts, and caps, as well as a variety of souvenirs. **Sagitario's Gift Shop** (✉ Carretera San Carlos 132, ☎ 622/226–0090), across from the entrance to the San Carlos Country Club, features clothing and a variety of crafts, including wood carvings, baskets, high-quality rugs, and Talavera tile.

Alamos

10 *257 km (160 mi) southeast of Guaymas.*

With its cobblestone streets, charming central plaza, 250-year-old Baroque church, and thoughtfully restored haciendas, Alamos is the most authentically restored colonial town in Sonora. In the ecologically rich zone where the Sonoran desert meets a dry tropical forest (also called the semitropical thorn forest) in the foothills of the Sierra Madre, the entire town is designated a national historic monument.

Coronado camped here in 1540, and a Jesuit mission (later destroyed in an Indian rebellion) was established in 1630, but the town really boomed when silver was discovered in the area during the 1680s. Wealth from the mines financed Spanish expeditions to the north—as far as Los Angeles and San Francisco during the 1770s and '80s—and the town became the capital of the state of Occidente, which combined the provinces of Sinaloa and Sonora, from 1827 to 1832. A government mint was established here in 1864. The mines closed by the end of the 19th century, and the town went into decline.

These days, Alamos is reinventing itself as a tourist spot. Leading the movement are a relatively large number of expats who have bought and restored sprawling haciendas near the center of town, turning some into luxurious private homes, others into hotels. So far, the foreigners' efforts to keep the town producing magical, postcard moments seem to be successful.

Points of interest include the impressive **Parroquia de Nuestra Señora de la Concepción,** constructed on the site of a 17th-century adobe church destroyed in an Indian uprising. Fronting the parrish church is the beautiful central square, the **Plaza las Armas,** where the ornate Moorish-style wrought-iron gazebo was brought from Mazatlán in 1904. To the west of the square, on Guadalupe Hill, the old Alamos **jail** is still in use. You can purchase belts and other accessories made by the prisoners.

If possible, time your trip to Alamos to include a Saturday **house and garden tour** of some of the superbly restored mansions and their interior patios and gardens. The tourist office and all the local hotels have listings of the times and rates.

Not to be missed, the **Museo Costumbrista de Sonora** gives an excellent overview of the cultural history of the state of Sonora. The numerous well-marked displays include artifacts from the nearby silver mines and coins from the mints of Alamos and Hermosillo, as well as typical examples of the clothing and furnishings of prominent local families. ✉ *Calle Guadalupe Victoria 1, on Plaza las Armas,* ☎ *647/428–0053.* *$1.* ⏲ *Wed.–Sun. 9–6.*

Fishing is a popular pastime in this area. Not far from Alamos, Presa (Reservoir) Adolfo Ruíz Cortines—as well as the smaller Presa Tatjiosa and Presa El Veranito—are full of black bass, catfish, and other freshwater species. For information on fishing trips, call the tourism office.

Dining and Lodging

$ ★ ✕ **Las Palmeras.** This Mexican family restaurant is crammed onto the sidewalk across the street from the Museo Costumbrista de Sonora and right on the main square. Here you might get homemade *rosca* bread (a sweet, round loaf) with your coffee and an assortment of daily specials. The corn tamales are hard to beat; other specialties include the chilies relleno and the *carne milanesa*: similar to chicken-fried steak. ✉ *Lázaro Cárdenas 9,* ☎ *647/428–0065. Reservations not accepted. No credit cards.*

$ ✕ **Polo's.** One of the few hangouts for locals, this place is not unfriendly to the many gringos who flock to this beautiful colonial town—but it's not the most welcoming either. That said, Polo's does have many loyal gringo customers. The food is simple but very good: sandwiches and shish kebab. Sonoran steaks are the specialty. ✉ *Calle Zaragoza 4,* ☎ *647/428–0001. Reservations not accepted. No credit cards.*

$ ✕ **Los Sabinos.** This small, unpretentious family home–turned–mini café has seating indoors and out, and an extensive menu. House specials include beef tips and ranch-style shrimp, along with fried fillet of sole in garlic butter and lots of things kids will like, including tacos, quesadillas, hamburgers, and club sandwiches. No alcoholic beverages are sold here. ✉ *Calle 2 de Abril No. 15,* ☎ *647/428–0598. Reservations not accepted. No credit cards.*

$$$$ ★ **Hacienda de los Santos.** Alamos's most opulent hotel rambles across the lushly landscaped grounds of four restored and linked colonial mansions. In gracious courtyards and lining long porticos are centuries-old pieces of religious art, hand-carved antique furniture, and inviting leather sofas. Spacious bedrooms are appointed with antiques, comfortable beds, and fireplaces. A spa offers massage and beauty treatments; park your plane for free in the on-site hangar. Price includes full breakfast. ✉ *Calle Molina 8, 85763,* ☎ *647/428–0222,* FAX *647/428–0367,* WEB *www.haciendadelossantos.com. 8 rooms, 5 suites. Restaurant, 3 pools, spa, bar. AE, MC, V.*

$$ **Casa Encantada.** Just off the main square, this lovely converted 250-year-old mansion was once owned by one of Alamos's wealthy Spanish mine owners. Rooms retain a colonial character, with high-beamed ceilings, fireplaces, and carved-wood furnishings; all have air-conditioning, tile baths, and good lighting. The price includes breakfast. ✉ *Calle Juárez 20, 85760,* ☎ *647/428–0482,* FAX *647/428–0400. 10 rooms. Pool; no room phones, no room TVs. V.*

$$ **Casa de los Tesoros.** This hotel, the House of Treasures, is a picturesque and romantic converted 18th-century convent. The rooms are former nuns' cells and have fireplaces, tile baths, antique furnishings, and high-quality arts and crafts on the walls. Room rates include breakfast, and the restaurant is excellent. ✉ *Av. Obregón 10, 85763,* ☎ *647/428–0010,* FAX *647/428–0400,* WEB *www.tesoros-hotel.com. 13 rooms, 2 suites. Restaurant, pool, bar. MC, V.*

Shopping

It's worth a peek into the three crowded rooms of **El Nicho Curios** (✉ Calle Juárez 15, ☎ 647/428–0213), filled with treasures ranging from Mexican religious paintings to old jewelry and regional pottery. In addition, small stores lining **Plaza Alameda** (northwest of the central plaza) sell Mexican sweets, fabrics, belts, and hats, among other items.

Aduana

11 *10 km (6 mi) west of Alamos.*

Aduana was formerly the site of one of the richest mines in the district. Today it's the unlikely location of one of Sonora's best restaurants, **Casa la Aduana** (✉ Domicilio Conocido, ☎ 642/482–2525). Mexican tourists and expats living in Alamos spill from the nondescript dining room onto the patio of this gourmet eatery run by California exile Samuel Beardsley. A four-course, prix-fixe menu ($17 to $25) is served at both lunch and dinner, and entrée selections might include chicken in apple-chipotle cream or grilled Norwegian salmon. The desserts are sublime.

Across the plaza from Casa la Aduana is the **Iglesia de Nuestra Señora de Balvanera.** A cactus that grows out of one of the church's walls is said to mark the spot where the Virgin appeared to the Yaqui Indians in the late 17th century, an event that is celebrated by a procession every November 21 and festivities in the preceding week.

SONORA A TO Z

To research prices, get advice from other travelers, and book travel arrangements, visit www.fodors.com.

AIR TRAVEL

AeroCalifornia offers daily nonstop jet service from Los Angeles and Tucson to Hermosillo. Aeroméxico and its subsidiary Aero Litoral have daily flights to Hermosillo from Tucson, and flights from Los Angeles to Hermosillo. Aeroméxico has direct flights to Hermosillo from many cities in Mexico—including Mexico City, Tijuana, Chihuahua, and Guadalajara, with connections to Guaymas. Mexicana de Aviación offers domestic service as well. America West Express has daily flights to Hermosillo and Guaymas from Phoenix.

CARRIERS

➤ AIRLINES AND CONTACTS: **AeroCalifornia** (☎ 662/260–2555 or 800/237–6225). **Aeroméxico** (☎ 01–800/021–4000 or 800/237–6639). **America West Express** (☎ 01–800/235–9292 or 800/235–9292). **Mexicana de Aviación** (☎ 662/261–0112 or 01–800/849–1529).

BOAT AND FERRY TRAVEL

Ferries from Guaymas to Santa Rosalía on the Baja coast leave two or three times a week, usually departing at 11 AM and arriving at 6:30 PM. You can buy tickets in advance or the morning of the day you plan to travel unless you have a car, for which you should make reservations three weeks in advance. Fares are about $50 for an assigned seat in the upper salon; $115 for cabin without toilet; $140 for cabin with toilet; and $163 for a "suite," with bathroom, TV, VCR, and sitting area. Car transportation is priced by car size, with the smallest cars costing around $240. Purchase tickets at the Sematur ferry terminal, just east of the center of Guaymas. Check with the Guaymas or San Carlos tourist offices for the latest information and schedules.

➤ BOAT AND FERRY INFORMATION: **Sematur ferry terminal** (✉ Av. Serdán s/n, ☎ 622/222–2324 or 01-800/696–9600).

BUS TRAVEL

Frequent buses travel to Hermosillo and Guaymas from Nogales, Tijuana, and Mexicali via Grupo Estrella Blanca. Golden State Buses travel between Tucson, Arizona, and Hermosillo 10 times daily. TUFESA has frequent service between Hermosillo and Guaymas, Nogales, and other destinations within Sonora and northern Mexico. TAP connects Hermosillo to other Sonoran cities as well as to Mazatlán, Guadalajara, Tepic, and Tijuana.

➤ BUS INFORMATION: **Golden State Buses** (☎ 520/623–1675 in the U.S.). **Grupo Estrella Blanca** (☎ 662/213–4050). **TAP** (☎ 662/212–6870). **TUFESA** (☎ 662/213–0442).

CAR RENTAL

In Guaymas, the agencies to contact are Budget and Hertz, both on the main highway. Budget and Hertz are also in Hermosillo.

➤ MAJOR AGENCIES: **Budget** (✉ Garmendia 46, at Tamaulipas, Col. San Benito, Hermosillo, ☎ 622/222–1430; ✉ Blvd. Augustín García López s/n, Col. Delicias, Guaymas, ☎ 662/222–1450 or 622/222–5500). **Hertz** (✉ Airport, Hermosillo, ☎ 662/261–0110; ✉ Calzada Agustin Garcia Lopez 625 Norte, Col. las Villas, Guaymas, ☎ 622/222–1000).

CAR TRAVEL

Many visitors to Sonora travel by car from Tucson via I–19 to the border in Nogales, Arizona. Mexico's Highway 15, a divided four-lane road, begins in Nogales, Sonora. This highway makes travel to Hermosillo and Guaymas–San Carlos faster. However, expect to pay approximately $35 in tolls. The alternative "Libre" (free) routes are generally slower and not as well maintained, though by no means problematic.

There are two points of entry into Nogales. Most drivers take U.S. I–19 to the end and then follow the signs to the border crossing. This route, however, will take you through the busiest streets of Nogales. It's better to take the Mariposa exit west from I–19, which leads to the international truck crossing and joins a small periphery highway that connects with Highway 15 after skirting the worst traffic.

The official checkpoint for entering Mexico is 21 km (13 mi) south of Nogales. It's here that you have to buy insurance and complete paperwork to bring in your car if you haven't already done so in Tucson at either Sanborn's Mexico Insurance or the Arizona Automobile Association.

As a result of the Only Sonora program, tourists driving into Mexico through Nogales and not intending to leave the state need not make a deposit for the vehicle (though insurance is still required). Fill out necessary paperwork at the Sonora Only booth at the Km 21 checkpoint. Bring a valid driver's license and vehicle registration. A six-month tourist visa ($20) is required of anyone planning to stay longer than three days. Keep the receipt if you'll be making more than one foray into Sonora over a period of six months.
➤ CONTACTS: **Arizona Automobile Association** (✉ 8204 E. Broadway, Tucson, AZ, ☎ 520/296–7461; ✉ 6950 N. Oracle Rd., Phoenix, AZ, ☎ 520/885–0694 or 800/352–5382). **Sanborn's Mexico Insurance** (✉ 105 W. Grant, Tucson, AZ, ☎ 520/882–5000).

CONSULATES

There is a U.S. Consulate in Hermosillo, in back of Hotel Calinda near downtown.
➤ UNITED STATES: **U.S. Consulate** (✉ Calle Monterrey 140, ☎ 662/217–2375 or 662/212–5885).

EMERGENCIES

For emergency fire, police, or medical attention call **060.**

The Green Angels in Hermosillo is a very helpful state-run roadside assistance service for travelers in distress.
➤ EMERGENCY CONTACTS: **Green Angels** (☎ 662/269–2714 in Hermosillo; 01–800/903–9200 around the state). **Hospitals** (☎ 662/259–0900 in Hermosillo; 622/222–0122 in Guaymas). **Red Cross** (☎ 662/214–0010 in Hermosillo; 622/222–0101 in San Carlos).

TOURS

Arizona Coach Tours runs mostly senior-citizen package tours to Alamos, San Carlos, Puerto Peñasco, and the Copper Canyon. Mexico Tours offers escorted and unescorted bus tours, hotel and condo reservations, and general advice about Pacific coast destinations.
➤ TOUR OPERATOR RECOMMENDATIONS: **Arizona Coach Tours** (✉ 200 E. 35th St., Tucson, AZ, ☎ 520/791–0210). **Mexico Tours** (✉ 1604 E. Seneca, Tucson, AZ, ☎ 520/325–3284 or 800/347–4731).

TRANSPORTATION AROUND SONORA

By far the easiest way to get around is by automobile—San Carlos and Bahía Kino are particularly spread out, and Bahía Kino has no taxi service of any kind. Most hotels have car-rental agencies. Buses between towns are frequent and inexpensive.

VISITOR INFORMATION

In addition to the tourism offices listed below, the Sonora Department of Tourism, in Hermosillo, will send you mounds of information and a helpful, full-color magazine. The tourism folks at Hermosillo, Bahía Kino, and San Carlos speak great English and take their jobs seriously; the office in Guaymas is often closed for no reason.

➤ TOURIST INFORMATION: **Alamos** (✉ Main Plaza, Calle Juárez 6, ☎ 647/428–0450). **Bahía Kino** (✉ Calle Mar de Cortez at Catalina, Kino Nuevo, ☎ 662/242–0447). **Guaymas** (✉ Calle 19 and Av. 6, ☎ 622/226–0313). **Hermosillo** (✉ Paseo del Canal and Comonfort, Edificio Sonora, 3rd floor, ☎ 662/217–0076 or 800/476–6672, WEB www.sonoraturismo.gob.mx). **Puerto Peñasco** (✉ Blvd. Juárez 320-B at V. Estrella, ☎ 888/850–8122, 638/383–6122, or 638/383–5010). **San Carlos** (✉ Corredor Escénico San Carlos, Edificio Hacienda Plaza, ☎ 622/226–0202).

6 THE COPPER CANYON: FROM LOS MOCHIS TO CHIHUAHUA CITY

Ancestral home to the private, self-sufficient Tarahumara Indians, the rugged Copper Canyon, or Sierra Tarahumara, is increasingly accessible to adventurous travelers. A series of interconnected gorges—several of them deeper than the U.S. Grand Canyon—provides a gorgeous backdrop for hikes ranging from pleasant walks to steep and scary descents to the canyon floor. Those who prefer to experience their adventure from afar can ride the 410-mi (661-km) Chihuahua al Pacífico railroad, beginning or ending their journey in the lively city of Chihuahua.

Revised by Jane Onstott

THE MAGNIFICENT series of gorges known collectively as Las Barrancas del Cobre, the Copper Canyon is the real treasure of the Sierra Madre. Inaccessible to the casual visitor until the early 1960s and still largely uncharted, the canyons may now be explored by taking one of the most breathtaking rides in North America. The Chihuahua al Pacífico railroad passes through 87 tunnels and crosses 39 bridges on its journey through country as rich in history and culture as it is in physical beauty.

The *barrancas* (canyons) of the Sierra Tarahumara, as this portion of the Sierra Madre Occidental is known, form part of the Pacific "Ring of Fire," a belt of seismic and volcanic activity ringing the globe. As a result of its massive geologic movement, a large quantity of the earth's buried mineral wealth was shoved toward the surface. The canyons were then carved over eons by the Urique, Septentrión, Batopilas, and Chínipas rivers and further defined by wind erosion. Totaling more than 1,452 km (900 mi) in length and roughly four times the area of the Arizona Grand Canyon, the gorges are nearly a mile deep and wide in places. The average height of the peaks is 8,000 ft, and some rise to more than 12,000 ft. Four of the major barrancas—Copper, Urique, Sinforosa, and Batopilas—descend deeper than the Grand Canyon, Urique by nearly 1,500 ft.

The idea of building a rail line to cross this region was first conceived in 1872 by Albert Kinsey Owen, an idealistic American socialist. Owen met with some success initially. More than 1,500 people came from the states to join him in Topolobampo, his utopian colony on the Mexican west coast, and in 1881 he obtained a concession from Mexican president General Manuel Gonzales to build the railroad. Construction on the flat stretches near Los Mochis and Chihuahua presented no difficulties, but eventually the huge mountains of the Sierra Madre got in the way of Owen's dream, along with the twin scourges of typhoid and disillusionment within the community.

Owen abandoned the project in 1893, but it was taken up in 1900 by American railroad magnate and spiritualist Edward Arthur Stilwell. One of Stilwell's contractors in western Chihuahua was Pancho Villa, who ended up tearing up his own work during the Mexican Revolution in order to impede the movement of government troops. By 1910, when the revolution began, the Mexican government had taken charge of building the railroad line. Progress was painfully slow until 1940, when surveying the difficult Sierra Madre stretch finally began in earnest. Some 90 years and more than $100 million after it was started, the Ferrocarril Chihuahua al Pacífico was dedicated on November 23, 1961.

The railroad no longer starts at Topolobampo but at nearby Los Mochis, and Chihuahua City—capital of the eponymous state—is at the other end of the line. Chihuahua was established in 1709, after the Spanish discovered silver in the area around 1649. Chihuahua still derives some of its wealth from mining, as well as from ranching, agriculture, and lumber.

Closely related to the Pima Indians of southern Arizona, the Tarahumara once occupied the entire state of Chihuahua—Mexico's largest state. They are renowned for their running ability—Tarahumara is a Spanish corruption of their word Rarámuri, which means "running people." Still renowned for their endurance (and today winners of international marathon races), the Tarahumara in earlier times hunted deer by chasing them to the point of collapse. Like other native groups, the Tarahumara's way of life was totally disrupted by the arrival of the Europeans. The Spanish forced them to labor in the mines, and later both Mexicans and Americans put them to work on the railroads. The threat of slavery and the series of wars that began in the 1600s and continued until the 20th century forced them to retreat deeper into the canyons, where they are still subject to having their lands taken over by loggers and drug lords. Some are still seminomadic, moving to the high plateaus of the Sierra Madre in summer and down to the warmer canyon floor in winter. Their population, diminished over the years by disease, drought, and poverty, is estimated today at 50,000 to 60,000.

Pleasures and Pastimes

Dining

Outside small Copper Canyon villages such as Creel and Batopilas, there are few eateries except those connected with lodges: at Cerocahui, Divisadero, and Posada Barrancas, hearty meals are generally included in room rates. There are a few more dining options in Creel, where, in addition to hotel dining rooms, you'll find small cafés along the town's main street, Avenida López Mateos.

You'll have the greatest choice of restaurants in Chihuahua City. The state is a large producer of beef, so steak houses and informal eateries serving *carne asada* (charbroiled strips of marinated beef) abound, but Mexican specialties and seafood flown in from the coast are also available. Some of Chihuahua's best known restaurants are in the Zona Dorada, on Calle Juárez starting at its intersection with Calle Colón. In Los Mochis your best bet is seafood.

Dress is casual everywhere except at some of Chihuahua's pricier restaurants. Unless otherwise indicated, reservations aren't necessary.

CATEGORY	COST*
$$$$	over $20
$$$	$15–$20
$$	$8–$15
$	under $8

**per person for a main course at dinner*

Hiking

Hiking in the Copper Canyon is fantastic if you take the proper precautions. *Mexico's Copper Canyon Country,* by M. John Fayhee, is a good source of information. But even the most experienced trekkers should enlist the help of local guides, who can be contacted through area hotels or through travel agents in Los Mochis, El Fuerte, and Chihuahua. Few adequate maps are available, and many of the better-worn routes into the canyon are made by the Tarahumara, whose prime concern is getting from one habitable area to the next rather than getting to the canyon floor. Also, the presence of well-guarded marijuana plantations throughout the canyon makes it safer to travel with a local guide who knows which areas are best avoided.

Urique Canyon is most easily reached—by horse, bus, sturdy vehicle, or on foot—from Cerocahui. Hotels in Divisadero and Posada Barrancas offer tours ranging from easy rim walks to a 27-km (17-mi) descent to the bottom. If you're in Cusárare, a gentle and rewarding hike is the 6-km (4-mi) walk from the Copper Canyon Lodge to 100-ft-high Cusárare Falls. More challenging but also more impressive is a full-day trek to the base of Basaseachi Falls. The descent into Batopilas Canyon from Creel—not for the faint of heart—requires an overnight stay.

Horseback Riding

Hotels throughout the canyons can arrange for local guides and reasonably gentle horses; however, these trips aren't for couch potatoes. The trails into the canyon are narrow and rocky as well as slippery if the weather is icy or wet. At rough spots you might be asked to dismount and walk part of the way. A fairly easy and inexpensive ride is to Wicochic Falls at Cerocahui, about two hours round-trip, including a half-hour hike at the end, where the trail is too narrow for the horses. From Divisadero, horses can be hired to the tiny settlement of Wacajipare, deep within the canyon. The vistas are stunning, but again, it's not for the fainthearted.

Lodging

The hotels in Chihuahua City, including several international chains, cater to both tourists and business travelers. In Cerocahui, Divisadero, Posada Barrancas (*posada* means "inn"), and Creel, most hotels are pine-log types heated by gas furnaces or wood-burning stoves. The lodges send buses or cars to meet the train, and for this reason, reservations are recommended. In summer, October, and around Christmas and Easter, it's important to book in advance. Where indicated, rates for hotels include meals.

CATEGORY	COST*
$$$$	over $170
$$$	$120–$170
$$	$60–$120
$	under $60

**All prices are for a standard double room, excluding 15% tax.*

Nightlife

Conversing with fellow guests in your lodge or stargazing from a balcony are about the extent of nighttime activities in the heart of the Sierra, although occasionally one of the larger hotels will have performances in the evening by Tarahumara dancers or Mexican musicians. There are more options in commercially oriented Los Mochis and Chihuahua, although the latter is more subdued than you'd think for a capital city.

Shopping

A main source of cash income for the Tarahumara is their crafts, including simple handwoven baskets made from sotol (an agavelike plant) or pine needles, carved wooden dolls, rustic pottery, brightly colored woven belts and sashes made on back-strap looms, and wooden fiddles from which the men produce haunting music. The Tarahumara women, who are generally shy about talking with tourists, sell their wares throughout the Copper Canyon area. Their prices are fair, so bargaining is unnecessary. Tarahumara wares are sold at the Divisadero train station and at shops in Creel; in fact, wherever a tourist sets foot, women or children will soon appear with a few items for sale. Chihuahua is known for affordable cowboy boots, and *bota* (boot) shops proliferate downtown.

Exploring the Copper Canyon

Imagine visiting the Grand Canyon in the days before it was tamed by tourist facilities and you'll have some sense of what a trip through the Copper Canyon will be like—for better and for worse. That is, with the opportunity to encounter a relatively untouched natural site come some of the discomforts of the rustic experience. But if you are careful in your choice of time to visit and are properly prepared, the trip's myriad rewards should far outstrip any inconveniences.

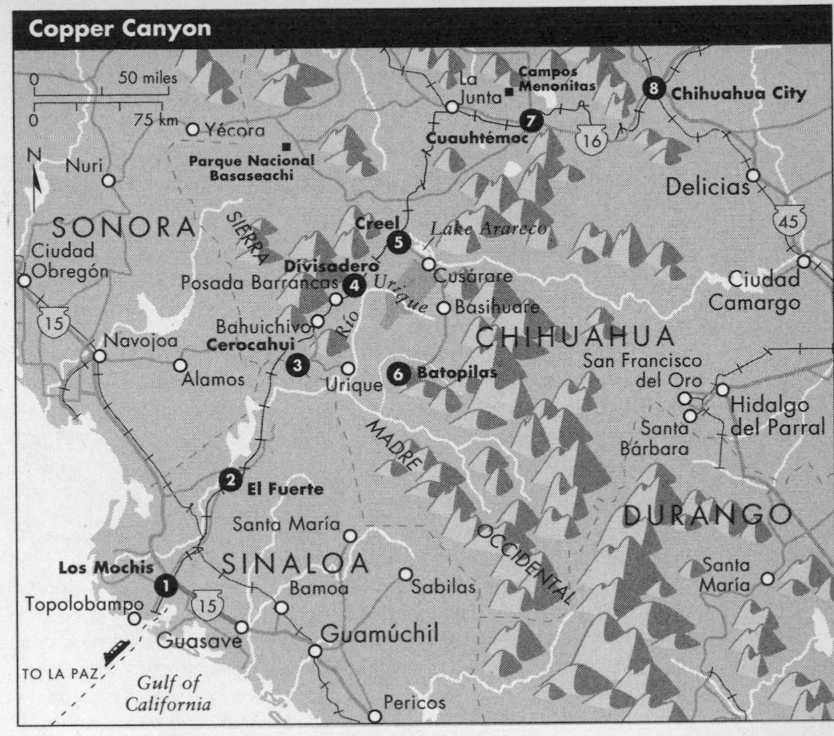

Numbers in the text correspond to numbers in the margin and on the Copper Canyon map.

Great Itineraries

You'll see some beautiful scenery even if you only ride the railroad—including a look into the canyons during a 15-minute stop at Divisadero—but you'll take in only a fraction of what the canyons have to offer if you don't get off the train. If possible, plan one or more nights in Cerocahui (Bahuichivo stop), one at Posada Barrancas or Divisadero (the train stations are five minutes apart), and one or two at Creel.

Most people make their way into the Copper Canyon via Los Mochis, which is the easiest route if you're coming from California or Arizona. More important, the most dramatic canyon scenery is at the western end of the ride, and you're likely to miss it if you approach Los Mochis in the evening. Train delays of three hours or more are not unusual, so even during the extended daylight hours of summer, you can't count on reaching the scenic end of the route before dark.

Even if you drive down to either Los Mochis or Chihuahua, your itinerary will be largely dependent on the schedule of the Chihuahua al Pacífico train: it runs in each direction only once a day, so you must plan the time spent in each stop accordingly. (Alternatively, you can drive or take a bus as far as Creel from Chihuahua, and arrange hikes or ride the train from there through some of the canyon's best scenery.) The following itineraries assume you will add on a day's train ride to return to your starting point—unless you catch one of the Aerolitoral flights between Los Mochis and Chihuahua. The small turboprops fly low over the mountains and canyons, providing magnificent views.

Note: The Sinaloa-Chihuahua state border divides two time zones: Mountain Time to the west and Central Time to the east.

IF YOU HAVE 3 DAYS

Departing from **Los Mochis** ①, take the 6 AM Chihuahua al Pacífico train and get off at Bahuichivo, where you can explore the 18th-century church at **Cerocahui** ③ and the overlook into Urique Canyon. The next day, continue to **Divisadero** ④, where it's practically impossible not to get a room with a view. Spend your last day exploring **Creel** ⑤ and taking a short hike to the falls near Cusárare. If you begin the trip in **Chihuahua City** ⑧, make Cerocahui your final stop.

IF YOU HAVE 5 DAYS

Starting in the west, consider bypassing Los Mochis and spending a day in the old colonial town of **El Fuerte** ②, catching the train through the canyons the next morning. Follow the three-day itinerary above, and use the last day and night to extend your time in **Creel** ⑤, with a visit to the mission church of San Ignacio or a drive and hike to Basaseachi Falls. If you start in the east, you might take the extra day to explore **Chihuahua City** ⑧. Don't miss the home of Pancho Villa's wife, now a great museum.

IF YOU HAVE 8 OR MORE DAYS

Spend a day each in **El Fuerte** ②, **Cerocahui** ③, and **Divisadero** ④, then extend your stay in **Creel** ⑤ to include a trip down to the former silver mining town of **Batopilas** ⑥. It's six to eight hours each way by car (preferably four-wheel-drive) or bus, so you'll want to spend two nights to make the trip worthwhile. (Alternately, extend your stay in Cerocahui to allow an overnight visit to the small town of Urique, in the canyon of the same name.) You'll be ready for modern conveniences after that, so plan to enjoy the restaurants and museums of **Chihuahua City** ⑧ for an additional day. Another option would be to visit the new Mennonite museum near **Cuauhtémoc** ⑦ and tour one of the surrounding farms before going on to Chihuahua.

When to Tour

Unless you're planning to head deep into the barrancas, winter—December through February—is not the best time to come. Some of the hotels in the region are inadequately prepared for the cold. The warmest months are May, June, and July. The rainy season, late June through September, brings precipitation for a short period every day, but this shouldn't interfere with your enjoyment in any way. It's temperate in the highlands in summer. If you're planning to hike down into the canyons, however, remember that the deeper you go, the hotter it will get. The best months to visit are September and October, when the weather is still warm, and rains have brought out all the colors in the Sierra Tarahumara.

Many people come during Easter and Christmas, specifically to see the Tarahumaras' colorful take on church holidays. On these and other religious feast days, many Tarahumara communities dance throughout the night, and villages challenge one another in races that can go for days. The men run in small groups, upward of 161 km (100 mi) or more, all the while kicking a wooden ball. It's not *just* fun and games—each village places a huge communal wager for this winner-take-all event.

Los Mochis

❶ *763 km (473 mi) south of Nogales on the Arizona-Mexico border.*

At the western end of the rail line, Los Mochis (population 331,000) is an agricultural boomtown. The rail terminus and the city's location about 19 km (12 mi) from the harbor at Topolobampo make it the export center of the state of Sinaloa. You can tour Benjamin Johnston's sugar refinery, the **Ingenio Azucarero,** around which the town grew.

Near Johnston's estate you can still see the American colony—the group of brick bungalows that housed his associates.

The **Museo Regional del Valle del Fuerte** rotates work by local, regional, national, and international artists, and has a didactic exhibit on the area's history. A replica of a railroad steam engine is on permanent display. Labels are in Spanish only. ✉ *Obregón and Mina,* ☎ *668/812–4692.* *$1.* *Tues.–Sun. 9–1 and 4–7.*

Cottonwood trees and bougainvillea line the highway from Los Mochis to **Topolobampo.** Fields en route are planted with crops ranging from sugarcane to marigolds and mangoes. Once the site of Albert Owen's utopian colony and the center of the railroad-building activity in the area, it is now a suburb of Los Mochis. **Isla El Farallón,** off the coast, is a breeding ground for the sea lions that gave the town its name: in the language of the Mayo Indians who once dominated the area, *Topolobampo* means "watering place of the sea lions."

Dining and Lodging

$$ ✕ **El Farallón.** Nautical decor and murals set the tone for the excellent fish served at this simple restaurant. Sushi and sashimi are especially good, as are the taquitos of marlin or shrimp. For dessert sample some *pitalla* (cactus fruit) ice cream. ✉ *Obregón 593, at Ángel Flores,* ☎ *668/812–1428 or 668/812–1273. AE, MC, V.*

$$ ✕ **Las Fuentes.** This unpretentious, colonial-style restaurant specializes in Sinaloan and U.S. beef cuts. Try the local favorite, *cabreria*—a thinly cut, tender fillet. Yummy *queso fundido* (cheese fondue) is made with fresh flour tortillas; the corn tortillas are also made on the premises throughout the day. ✉ *Blvd. López Mateos 1070 Nte., at Jiquilpan,* ☎ *668/812–4770. AE, MC, V.*

$$ ✕ **Restaurante España.** This slightly upscale restaurant in downtown Los Mochis is popular with the local business crowd. Good seafood, U.S. cuts of beef, and Spanish dishes are served around an indoor fountain. The house specialty is paella. As in Spain (and Mexico), lunch is late: the restaurant is open from 3 to 11 PM. ✉ *Obregón 525,* ☎ *668/812–2221 or 668/812–2335. AE, MC, V.*

$$ ✕ **Hotel Plaza Inn.** Los Mochis's only five-star hotel caters to businesspeople and tourists, offering bathtubs, room safes, hair-dryers, and coffeemakers. Despite these and other numerous amenities, rooms suffer from a disconcerting color palette combining various hues of pink, coral, and sea-foam green. Duck hunters and fishermen are lured here with sporting packages. ✉ *Av. Leyva and Cárdenas, 81200,* ☎ *668/818–1042 or 800/862–9026,* FAX *668/812–1590. 100 rooms, 27 suites. 2 restaurants, in-room safes, pool, bar, nightclub, meeting rooms, travel services. AE, MC, V.*

$$ **Hotel Santa Anita.** The central reservations link of the Balderrama chain, this downtown hotel will book tours in its sister hotels in El Fuerte, Cerocahui, and Divisadero. Built in 1959, the four-story property has midsize, dim rooms fitted with comfortable modern furniture; most have air-conditioning. ✉ *Av. Leyva and Hidalgo, 81200,* ☎ *668/818–7046 or 800/896–8196,* FAX *668/812–0046,* WEB *www.mexicoscoppercanyon.com. 110 rooms, 6 suites. Restaurant, cable TV, bar, business services, meeting rooms, travel services, free parking. AE, MC, V.*

$ **Corintios Hotel.** Rooms here are plain and looking a bit long in the tooth, but this modern-style hotel with a dark-glass facade is centrally located and offers services often not available in this price range, including data ports, remote-control cable TV, and room service. The three-story hotel has no elevator. ✉ *Obregón 580 Pte., 82000,* ☎ *668/818–2300,* FAX *668/818–2224. 34 rooms, 1 suite, 6 junior suites. Restaurant, in-room data ports, cable TV, gym, hot tub, bar, travel services. AE, MC, V.*

$ **Taj Majal.** Rooms are standard and uninspired, despite the Indian affect and graceful pointed arches of the building's facade and interior hallways, but this inexpensive new hotel (a younger sister to the aging Corintios Hotel) offers free Internet access on a common computer, plus comfortable beds, room service, and coffeemakers. ✉ *Av. Obregón 400 Ote., 81200,* ☎ *668/818–6095 or 688/818–6095,* FAX *668/818–6095. 23 rooms, 3 suites. Restaurant. AE, MC, V.*

Nightlife

Friends (✉ Hotel Plaza Inn, Av. Leyva and Cárdenas, ☎ 668/818–7046), the most popular bar and disco in town, is open Friday and Saturday nights only. Music, often live, varies from techno to rock en español. **Yesterday** (✉ Obregón 579 and Guerrero, ☎ 668/815–3810) has live bands playing different types of music, but predominantly oldies. It's open Wednesday to Sunday 9 PM–midnight.

Shopping

If you're headed to Divisadero, Creel, or beyond, snacks and reading material can help pass the long train journey. **La Cava Deli** (✉ Av. Leyva 425, ☎ 614/410–9940) sells American and Mexican beers, a good selection of wines and liquors, Cuban cigars, and snack foods. **Librería Los Mochis** (✉ Calle Madero Pte. 402, at Av. Leyva) has a limited selection of English-language magazines and plenty of Spanish-language daily newspapers.

El Fuerte

❷ *80 km (50 mi) northeast of Los Mochis.*

If you prefer a peaceful, laid-back small town to the bustle and traffic of commercial Los Mochis, take a bus to El Fuerte (instead of the train that leaves at the crack of dawn), stay the night, and sleep in an hour longer before grabbing the 7:30 train to points east. A bus with comfortable seats leaves from **Mercado Independencia** (✉ Avs. Independencia and Degollado) every half hour 7:30 AM–8:30 PM for the two-hour trip. Fresh foods are available at the mercado.

Originally named for Saint John the Baptist, this small colonial town is known today as El Fuerte for its 17th-century fort, built by the Spaniards to protect against attacks by the local Mayo, Sinaloa, Zuaque, and Tehueco Indians. Conquistador Don Francisco de Ibarra and a small group of soldiers founded it as San Juan Bautista de Carapoa in 1564. Located along El Camino Real (literally, the "Royal Road"), El Fuerte was one of the frontier outposts from which the Spanish set out to explore and settle New Mexico and California. For three centuries, it was a major trading post for gold and silver miners from the nearby Sierras and the most important commercial and farming center of the area. It was chosen as Sinaloa's capital in 1824 and remained so for several years.

Now a rather sleepy town of some 45,000 residents, El Fuerte has intact colonial mansions, two of the most accessible being the Posada del Hidalgo and El Fuerte Lodge. Most of the historic houses are set off the cobblestone streets leading from the central plaza. A 4-km (2.5-mi) float along the river outside town is offered through area hotels. You'll see heron and egrets as well as magpies, kingfishers, and many other birds as you float downstream past willow trees, cacti, and lilac bushes that grow along shore.

Dining and Lodging

$$ ✕ **El Mesón del General.** Just a block off the main plaza, this is the best bet in town for black bass (*lobina*) caught in one of the nearby

reservoirs, as well as for crayfish and shrimp. A varied menu includes Mexican fare and and tasty steaks; you can also order Chinese dishes from the restaurant at the back, run by the same owners. ✉ *Benito Juárez 202,* ☎ *698/893–0260. MC, V.*

$$ ★ 🏨 **El Fuerte Lodge.** Years ago, longtime hunting guide Robert Brand married a local woman and restored this 380-year-old mansion to offer comfortable and lovely accommodation to canyon travelers. A flower-filled courtyard has been fitted with a waterfall and hidden Jacuzzi, and examples of some of Mexico's best *artesanía* (folk art) adorns the rooms and common areas. ✉ *Montesclaro 37, 81820,* ☎ *698/893–0226. 36 rooms. Dining room, hot tub, bar. MC, V.*

$$ ★ 🏨 **Posada del Hidalgo.** You'll be transported back to a more gracious era at this restored hacienda, with its gardens and cobblestone paths, built in 1895. It's difficult to choose between the larger rooms with balconies, set off a lobby filled with period artifacts, and those that open onto the gardens. All are decorated with rough-hewn handcrafted furniture. ✉ *Hidalgo 101,* ☎ *698/893–0242 or 668/812–1929. Reservations: Hotel Santa Anita, Av. Leyva and Hidalgo, Apdo. 159, Los Mochis 81200,* ☎ *668/818–7046 Ext. 432 or 800/896–8196,* FAX *668/812–0046. 50 rooms, 1 suite. Dining room, pool, bar, dance club; no room phones, no room TVs. AE, MC, V.*

$ ★ 🏨 **Río Vista Lodge.** On the Cerro de las Pilas, the highest spot in El Fuerte, is this small, adobe-and-wood posada owned by local guide Eleazar Gamez. Rooms are rustic but creatively decorated with family heirlooms and antiques from friends in town, each piece with its own story that the owner gladly shares. Continental breakfast is included in the room price (first night only). ✉ *Cerro de las Pilas,* ☎ *698/893–0413. 12 rooms. Restaurant. No credit cards.*

En Route As the train ascends almost 5,906 ft from El Fuerte to Bahuichivo, it passes through or over the majority of the rail line's tunnels and bridges, including the longest and highest of both. The scenery shifts from Sinaloan thorn forest, with cactus and scrublike vegetation, to the pools, cascades, and tropical trees of the Río Septentrión canyon. Past Temoris, where a plaque marks the 1961 dedication of the railroad by President López Mateos, the setting shifts to the oak and pine forest that characterizes the higher elevations.

Cerocahui

❸ *160 km (100 mi) northeast of El Fuerte.*

The quiet mountain village of Cerocahui, just inside the Sinaloa state border, is a good place to get a sense of how people live in the canyon area. Across the dirt street from the Hotel Misión is **Misión San Francisco Javier,** a pretty church established by the Jesuits. Although the order arrived in the area in 1680, Tarahumara Indian uprisings and other difficulties delayed construction of the church until 1741. It is said that this was the favorite church of the founder, Father Juan María de Salvatierra, because the Tarahumara were the most difficult Indians to convert. Near the church is a boarding school for Tarahumara children, which tour groups sometimes visit. Both of the town's hotels provide transportation to and from the train station at Bahuichivo, about a 40-minute drive along a bumpy, mostly unpaved road.

The prime reason to come to Cerocahui is its accessibility to **Urique Canyon.** It's a lovely ride to the **Cerro del Gallego lookout,** one of the best spots for viewing the magnificent Urique Canyon. From there you can make out the slim thread of the Urique River and the old mining town of Urique, a dot on the distant canyon bottom. From Cerro del Gallego the road continues down into the canyon, which has a few basic hotels and restaurants. A public bus makes the trip from Cerocahui daily after the late arrival of the second-class train, but many people opt for the local hotels' full-day or overnight tours.

OFF THE BEATEN PATH

URIQUE – A journey to the small town of Urique offers a fascinating glimpse into canyon life. At the bottom of the system's deepest canyon—1,640 ft above sea level—Urique enjoys an excellent climate. At the semitropical canyon bottom, residents plant orchards of citrus and guava trees, and sycamore and fig trees dot the landscape. The Urique River, which carved the great canyon, slides lazily along in the dry season but races briskly after the summer rains. In town, browse in the old general store, El Central, and the town church, and then munch on a lunch of chicken wings, fresh avocado, fried potatoes, and refried beans at the town's best restaurant, **La Plaza**, on the main square.

In the surrounding countryside, the Tarahumara eschew town life, preferring to live in separate family enclaves throughout the valley, while the mestizos form communities such as Guadalupe, 7 km (4½ mi) from Urique. The most direct path to this town is across a 400-ft-long suspension bridge that rocks and sways above the river. It's not for the faint-of-heart, although the tiny town can also be accessed by car.

You can visit Urique as a day trip from Cerocahui, two to three hours by car, or ride horses or hike down into the canyon. Tours are also offered through Cerocahui hotels Paraíso del Oso and Misión. The best lodgings in Urique are **Hotel Estrella del Río**, which has large rooms, hot water, and impossibly hefty pillows ($35 double).

Dining and Lodging

$$$$ ✕🏨 **Hotel Misión.** Part of the Balderrama chain, this is the only accommodation in Cerocahui itself. The main house, which looks like a cross between a ski lodge and a hacienda, contains the hotel's office, small shop, and a combined dining room, bar, and lounge surrounding two large fireplaces. The plain rooms have beam ceilings, Spanish colonial–style furnishings, and wood-burning stoves. Rates include meals. ✉ *Cerocahui. Reservations: Hotel Santa Anita, Av. Leyva and Hidalgo, Apdo. 159, Los Mochis 81200,* ☎ *668/818–7046 Ext. 432 or 800/896–8196,* FAX *668/812–0046. 38 rooms. Restaurant, bar, lounge, shop. AE, MC, V.*

$$$ ★ ✕🏨 **Paraíso del Oso Lodge.** Doug "Diego" Rhodes runs this lodge where many guests overnight in relative luxury before and after adventurous horseback rides down into the canyons to the towns of Urique or Batopilas. Ranch-style rooms facing a grassy courtyard feature handmade wooden furniture, cozy beds, and wood-burning stoves. A generator provides electricity for guest rooms, although the fireplace in the bar and kerosene lamps in the restaurant-lounge keep the common areas romantic and quaint. Rates include meals. ✉ *5 km (3 mi) outside of Cerocahui. Reservations:* ✉ *Box 31089, El Paso, TX 79931,* ☎ FAX *614/421–3372 in Chihuahua City,* WEB *www.mexicohorse.com. 21 rooms. Dining room, horseback riding, free parking. MC, V.*

Divisadero and Posada Barrancas

❹ *80 km (50 mi) northeast of Cerocahui, in the state of Chihuahua.*

There's little to do in Divisadero and Posada Barrancas, two whistle stops five minutes apart on the Continental Divide. Nonetheless, the canyon scenery and refreshing lack of man-made distractions provide a breath of fresh air, and it's impossible to be unmoved by their Copper Canyon vistas—especially marvelous at sunset. A popular excursion that takes about seven to eight hours round-trip on foot is to

Wacajipare, a Tarahumara village in the canyon. The Hotel Cabañas Divisadero-Barrancas offers a $38 guided trip October–March only, for a minimum of two clients. To do this daylong tour you must spend two nights at Divisadero.

Dining and Lodging

$$$$ ✕🏨 **Hotel Divisadero-Barrancas.** The dining room and Rooms 1–10 in the old section and 35–52 in the newer section of this canyon-rim hotel have panoramic views. There's a reading room and a café with many types of coffee and tea; the view from the second-story dining room and lounge is magnificent, and the food is good. Rooms are also top-notch, with beautiful comforters on the beds. Rates include meals. ✉ *Divisadero train station. Reservations:* ✉ *Av. Mirador 4516, Apdo. 661, Col. Residencial Campestre, Chihuahua, Chihuahua 31000,* ☎ *614/415–1199,* FAX *614/415–6575,* WEB *www.hoteldivisadero.com.mx. 52 rooms. Restaurant, bar, meeting room. AE, MC, V.*

$$$$ ★ ✕🏨 **Hotel Posada Barrancas Mirador.** This beautiful pink hotel—another link in the Balderrama chain—perches on the edge of the Copper Canyon. The dining room and all the guest rooms have spectacular views; balconies seem to hang right over the abyss. Accommodations are bright and comfortable, although when overbooked, the hotel sends guests down the hill to its sister property, Posada Barrancas Rancho, with no price break. Meals are included in the rates. ✉ *Posada Barrancas train station. Reservations:* ✉ *Hotel Santa Anita, Av. Leyva and Hidalgo Los Mochis 81200,* ☎ *668/818–7046 or 800/862–9026,* FAX *668/812–0046. 51 rooms. Restaurant, bar, meeting room. AE, MC, V.*

$$$ ★ ✕🏨 **Hotel Mansión Tarahumara.** It's a bit disconcerting to come across a red-turreted castle out in barranca country, but somehow this whimsical fancy works. All rooms (15 in separate cabins) have Spanish contemporary-style light-pine furniture and individual heaters, with walls of stone and pine paneling and exposed beam ceilings. The staff is typically helpful and courteous. Three meals are included. ✉ *Posada Barrancas train station. Reservations: Av. Juárez 1602-A, Col. Centro, Chihuahua, Chihuahua 31000,* ☎ *614/415–4721,* FAX *614/416–5444. 57 rooms, 1 suite. Restaurant, indoor pool, lake, sauna, steam room, bar, dance club, meeting room, travel services. MC, V.*

$$ ✕🏨 **Rancho Posada Mirador.** This is a good base from which to explore the Barranca del Cobre. Rooms have ochre stucco walls, ceramic-tile floors, and colonial-style, hand-painted furniture; some have cozy fireplaces. The lobby–dining room has a massive stone fireplace, beamed ceiling, and wood furniture. Rate includes breakfast only; American Plan also available. ✉ *Posada Barrancas train station. Reservations:* ✉ *Hotel Santa Anita, Apdo. 159, Los Mochis 81200,* ☎ *668/818–7046 Ext. 432 or 800/896–8196,* FAX *668/812–0046. 38 rooms. Restaurant, bar. AE, MC, V.*

Creel

❺ *60 km (37 mi) northeast of Divisadero.*

Surrounded by pine-covered mountains, Creel is a mining, ranching, and logging town that grew up around the railroad station. The largest settlement in the area, it's also a gathering place for Tarahumara Indians seeking supplies and markets for their crafts. It's easy to imagine American frontier towns at the turn of the 20th century looking like Creel—without, of course, the international backpacking contingent that makes this town its base. For the number of lodgings and restaurants, the availability of nearby excursions, and the existence of simple yet sound infrastructure for overnight guided trips into the canyon, Creel is the most convenient base for visitors to the Sierra Tarahumara.

Right in the middle of the town plaza, a cooperative group of tour guides specializes in day trips to areas of interest around Creel. One of the most common day tours is a visit to **Lake Arakeko,** a nearby mission church, a Tarahumara cave dwelling, and rock formations in a variety of weird shapes. The lake visit is a simple "stop and look," with a chance to buy Tarahumara crafts. The two- to three-hour tour also includes visits to **Valle de los Hongos** (Valley of the Mushrooms), where rocks perch atop each other precariously. Nearby, at **Valle de los Monjes** (Valley of the Monks), the monolithic rocks resemble towering figures. The Tarahumara call this the Valley of the Erect Penises, but tourism pundits have changed the name. Before you reach this spot you'll stop at **Valle de las Ranas** (Valley of the Frogs), where a few of the formations do look quite froglike.

Many half-day tours also include a visit to **Cusárare,** whose Tarahumara name means "eagle's nest." Located 26 km (16 mi) from Creel, it's the site of a Jesuit mission, built in 1741, that still serves as a center for religious and community affairs for the Tarahumara who live in the area. Inside the simple whitewashed structure, men and women stand for the Sunday service, women on one side, men on the other. The main reason to visit, however, is to take the easy 6-km (4-mi) hike through a lovely piñon forest to see the **Cusárare waterfall,** most impressive during or just after the rainy months.

A popular way to spend the day is to hike to **Recohuata Hot Springs,** which involves climbing down from the canyon rim into the Tararecua Canyon. Some tour guides leave their clients at the rim to be guided down to a series of pools by youngsters stationed at the trailhead for this purpose. This tour can be combined with a trip to the magnificent canyon lookout point at **Divisadero,** some 43 km (27 mi) away on a windy road.

Several other worthwhile day trips along the way to the colonial town of Batopilas are **Basihuare,** where wide horizontal bands of color cross huge vertical outcroppings of rock; the **Urique Canyon overlook,** a perspective that differs from the one at Divisadero; and **La Bufa,** site of a former Spanish silver mine. Seventy-three km (45 mi) northwest of Creel, along an unpaved, winding road, the 806-ft **Basaseachi Falls** are among the highest cascades in North America.

Dining and Lodging

$ ★ ✕ **Tungar.** "The Hangover Hospital," as it is nicknamed, is a home-style, counter-only café with probably the best, most authentic Mexican food in town. The menu includes such traditional morning pick-me-ups—and hangover cures—as *pozole* (hominy soup with chunks of pork, which when doctored with lime and chili, produces a powerful sweat). For lunch consider a few delicious stingray tostadas. ✉ *Calle Francisco Villa s/n, next to train depot,* ☎ *no phone. No credit cards. No dinner. No lunch or dinner Sun.*

$ ✕ **Veronica's.** This clean, simple eatery on the main street is popular with locals and tourists for its economical meals, although service is spotty and some cuts of meat can be tough. *Comidas corridas*—set meals with soup and main course—are available; or order enchiladas, tacos, and other simple dishes off the back of the menu. Try the *sopa de verduras* (vegetable soup) or the vegetarian tacos. The salsa is sublime. ✉ *Av. López Mateos 34,* ☎ *635/456–0631. No credit cards.*

$$ 🏨 **Best Western: The Lodge at Creel.** This simple lodge has several wings of log cabin-like rooms with pine floors and walls. Gas-log heaters controlled by wall thermostats are disguised as wood-burning stoves, giving cheer to otherwise plain accommodations. The main lodge has a cozy bar and a dining room that can be chilly in winter. ✉ *Av. López*

Mateos 61, 33200, ☎ 635/456–0071 or 800/879–4071, FAX 635/456–0082, WEB www.thelodgeatcreel.com. 28 rooms, 1 suite. Restaurant, bar, free parking. AE, MC, V.

$$ **Cabañas Pueblo Viejo.** This funky complex has cabins individually designed and decorated to resemble an old Mexican village. Owner-manager don Francisco swears newlyweds love the squeaky, steel-bed-framed bed in the "jail," room; soon to be completed are the "church" and "town hall." Despite the whimsy and the numerous antiques, rooms are comfortable and have TVs and heaters; the well-designed kitchenettes have toasters, coffeemakers, and small refrigerators; some are family-size, with separate sleeping quarters and multiple beds. Breakfast in the large dining room surrounding a huge fireplace is included in the room rate. ✉ *Atras del Hotel KOA, ☎ 635/456–0295; 614/411–3706 reservations in Chihuahua City, FAX 614/418–2516. 20 rooms. Restaurant, bar, travel services, free parking. MC, V.*

$ ★ **Copper Canyon Sierra Lodge.** In a peaceful piñon forest near Cusárare Falls and an old mission church, this natural beauty has no electricity: no TV, phones, fax, or cell phones here. The pine-panel rooms with antique furnishings and tile, hot-water baths are romantically equipped with kerosene lamps and woodstoves. The unbeatable price includes three excellent meals served in the beautiful yet simple dining room; the large kitchen is immaculate. This rustic chic hotel is best for those with wheels or who want a night or two of quiet revelry; it's 26 km (16 mi) from Creel. ✉ *Cusárare, FAX 635/456–0036. (✉ Copper Canyon Lodges, 2741 Paldan, Auburn Hills, MI 48326, ☎ 248/340–7220 Ext. 233 in Michigan; 800/776–3942, WEB www.sierratrail.com). 22 rooms. Restaurant, bar, free parking. No credit cards.*

$ ★ **Margarita's.** Tiny touts at the train station will guide you to one of the best deals in town. Catercorner from the town plaza, this backpackers' haven has a single dorm room (about $8 gets you a bunk, breakfast, and dinner) as well as private rooms with bath, also with breakfast and dinner. The rooms—with wrought-iron lamps and light-wood furnishings—are as pleasant as anything at three times the price. A second-story addition, to be completed by summer 2002, will house a restaurant and Internet café, and free up space for several new rooms below. ✉ *Av. López Mateos 11, 33200, ☎ 635/456–0045 or 635/456–0245. 17 rooms, 1 dorm. Restaurant. No credit cards.*

$ **Margarita's Plaza Mexicana.** This pretty, two-story hotel is one of the town bargains, serving up honest hospitality (as well as breakfast and dinner, included in the room price) at low prices. Each room has a wall heater and a different wall mural. One disadvantage is that the nightly tequila parties in the central courtyard can get quite noisy. ✉ *Calle Elfido Bautista s/n, off Av. López Mateos, 33200, ☎ 635/456–0245 or 635/456–0045. 26 rooms. Restaurant, bar; no TV in some rooms. No credit cards.*

$ **Parador de la Montaña.** This plain hotel has large, clean, no-frill rooms with local TV only and a secure parking area. Nicer than the guest rooms is the wood-paneled lounge surrounding a huge stone fireplace, and the adjacent dining room, where long, family-size tables invite mingling with other guests. ✉ *Av. López Mateos 44, 32300, ☎ 635/456–0075, FAX 635/456–0085, WEB www.members.tripod.com/copperinn. 50 rooms. Restaurant, bar, free parking. AE, MC, V.*

Nightlife

Most visitors recreate in the hotels where they are staying, as there are only a few other options. When the sun goes down on weekend evenings, **Laylo's Lounge** (✉ Av. López Mateos 25, next to El Caballo Bayo restaurant, ☎ 635/456–0136) has music and sometimes other types of performers; it can get rowdy at times. The hotel **Sierra Bonita**

(✉ Carr. Gran Visión s/n, ☎ 635/456–0615), on a hill west of town, has a disco Friday through Sunday that sometimes hosts live bands playing norteño tunes or Caribbean *cumbia.* When the music is canned, you might get some pop or rock thrown in.

Shopping

At the west end of Avenida López Mateos, **Artesanías Victoria** (☎ 635/456–0030) sells huge Tarahumara pots and other artifacts, some from elsewhere. On the plaza, **Casa de las Artesanías** (☎ 635/456–0080) is an excellent museum focusing on traditional Tarahumara life, including a beautiful exhibit of black-and-white photographs. The gift shop has Tarahumara crafts and dolls. Be sure to pay a visit to **Misión Tarahumara** (☎ 635/456–0097), on the east side of the plaza. The shop sells only Tarahumara handiwork, including violins, woven belts, and simple pots of pine needles or unglazed clay. Here you'll also find English-language books on the culture. Proceeds benefit the mission hospital.

Batopilas

❻ *80 km (50 mi) southeast of Creel.*

Veins of silver—mined on and off from the time of the conquistadors—made this remote village of about 800 people one of the wealthiest towns in colonial Mexico. At one time it was the only place in the country besides Mexico City that had electricity. The hair-raising, 80-km (50-mi) ride down a narrow, unpaved road to the languid town at the bottom of Batopilas Canyon takes about six hours by car from Creel (closer to seven hours on the local bus, which runs back and forth every day except Sunday). Sights in this relatively lush oasis, in the middle of the semitropical thorn forest, include the ruined **hacienda of Alexander Shepherd,** built in the late 1800s by one of the town's wealthiest mine owners; the original **aqueduct,** which still serves the town; and the triple-dome 17th-century **Satevó mission church,** mysteriously isolated in the Satevó Valley on a scenic 16-km (10-mi) round-trip hike from town. Because it takes most of the day to get down to Batopilas, you'll need to spend at least one night at one of the town's modest posadas; allow more time to explore the canyon's depths.

Lodging

$ **Real de Minas.** Owner Martín Alcaraz earned his stripes during his years as manager of the nearby Copper Canyon Riverside Lodge, now closed, before opening his own small hotel. It's a charming spot, but some have complained of reservations not honored, and advance communication is difficult, as there are only a few phones in all of town. ✉ *Donato Guerra at Pablo Ochoa,* ☎ *649/456–9045. 6 rooms. No credit cards.*

Cuauhtémoc

❼ *128 km (79 mi) northeast of Creel, 105 km (65 mi) southwest of Chihuahua.*

A rather anomalous experience in Mexico is a visit to the **Campos Menonitas,** individual family farms of a large Mennonite community surrounding Cuauhtémoc. Some 20,000 Mennonites came to the San Antonio Valley in 1922 at the invitation of President Alvaro Obregón, who gave them the right to live freely and autonomously in return for farming the land. Set up a tour in Cuauhtémoc at Mennonite David Friesen's travel agency, Cumbres Friesen (✉ Calle 3A No. 466, ☎ 625/582–4292, FAX 625/582–4060), or in Chihuahua (☎ 614/414–6046).

Also worth a visit is the **Mennonite Museum and Cultural Center** (✉ Carr. Cuauhtémoc–Alvaro Obregón Km 10.5, ☎ 625/842–2340). Inaugurated in October 2001, the first phase of this museum shows a typical Mennonite house from the first pioneers, combining living quarters, kitchen, and stable under one roof.

Dining and Lodging

$–$$ ✕ **Rancho Viejo.** People from Chihuahua City make regular pilgrimages to Cuauhtémoc just to dine at this simple but charming country restaurant in the town center. Steaks are the specialty—rib eye, T-bone, or New York cuts— but seafood and Mexican *antojitos* (enchiladas, tacos, and the like) are also served. ✉ *Av. V. Guerrero at Calle Tercera 303,* ☎ *625/582–4360. MC, V.*

$ **Motel Tarahumara Inn.** You'll find most of the creature comforts you need at this two-story motel just a few blocks from the main plaza. Rooms have heat; suites have sofa beds and kitchenettes with refrigerator and stove but no dishes. ✉ *Av. Allende 373,* ☎ FAX *625/581–1919. 55 rooms, 15 suites. Restaurant, kitchenettes, cable TV, gym, bar, shop, meeting rooms, free parking. AE, MC, V.*

Chihuahua City

8 *375 km (233 mi) south of the El Paso–Ciudad Juárez border, 1,440 km (893 mi) northwest of Mexico City.*

If you're arriving from the peaceful Copper Canyon, the sprawling city of Chihuahua—with more than 670,000 inhabitants—might come as a bit of a jolt. But then, the city is known for its jolting nature: two of Mexico's most famous revolutionaries are closely tied to Chihuahua. The father of Mexican independence, Father Miguel Hidalgo, and his coconspirators were executed here by the Spanish in 1811. And Chihuahua was home to General Pancho Villa. His revolutionary army, the División del Norte (Northern Army Division), was decisive in overthrowing dictator Porfirio Díaz in 1910 and securing victory in the ensuing civil war. A half-century earlier, Benito Juárez, known as the Abraham Lincoln of Mexico, made Chihuahua his base when the French invaded the country in 1865.

Whatever you do, don't miss the **Museo de la Revolución Mexicana,** better known as La Casa de Pancho Villa. Villa lived in this 1909 mansion, also called the "Quinta Luz" (*quinta* means "manor," or "country house"), with his wife, Luz Corral. Although Villa married dozens of women, Corral was considered his only legitimate wife, as the couple was married in both civil and church ceremonies. She lived in this house until her death on June 6, 1981, willing the residence to the government. The 50 small rooms that used to board Villa's bodyguards now house a vast array of artifacts of Chihuahua's cultural and revolutionary history. Parked in the museum's courtyard is the bullet-ridden 1919 Dodge in which Villa was assassinated in 1923 at the age of 45. ✉ *Calle Décima 3010, near Calle Terrazas, Iglesia Corazón de Jesús,* ☎ *614/416–2958.* *$1.* ⊙ *Tues.–Sat. 9–1 and 3–7, Sun. 9–5.*

Known as the **Parroquia del Sagrado,** the cathedral is also worth a visit. Construction on this stately Baroque structure on the Plaza de Armas was begun by the Jesuits in 1726 and—because of local Chichimeca Indian uprisings and the expulsion of the Jesuits—not completed until 1825. The opulent church has Carrara marble altarpieces and a ceiling studded with 24-karat gold ornaments; the huge German-made pipe organ from the late 18th century is still used on special occasions. In the basement, the **Museum of Sacred Art** displays 18th-century paintings primarily in the Mexican Baroque tradition. ✉ *Plaza de Armas, Centro,* ☎ *614/410–3238.* *$1.70.* ⊙ *Weekdays 10–2 and 4–6.*

The **Palacio de Gobierno** (State Capitol) was built by the Jesuits as a monastery in 1882. Converted into government offices in 1891, it was destroyed by a fire in the early 1940s and rebuilt in 1947. Murals around the patio depict famous episodes from the history of the state of Chihuahua. A plaque commemorates the spot where Father Hidalgo was executed on the morning of July 30, 1811. ✉ *Calle Aldama, at Plaza Hidalgo, Centro,* ☎ *614/410–1077.* 🎫 *Free.* 🕐 *Daily 8–8.*

The **Palacio Federal** (Federal Building) houses the city's main post office and telegraph office, as well as the cell where Hidalgo was imprisoned before he was executed by the Spanish. His pistols, traveler's trunk, crucifix, and reproductions of his letters are on display. ✉ *Av. Juárez between Calles Neri Santos and Carranza, Centro,* ☎ *no phone.* 🎫 *50¢.* 🕐 *Tues.–Sun. 9–7.*

The 1721 **Iglesia de San Francisco** (San Francisco Church) is the oldest church in Chihuahua. Father Hidalgo's decapitated body was interred in the chapel of this simple church from 1811 to 1827, when it was sent to Mexico City. His head was publicly displayed for 10 years by Spanish Royalists in Guanajuato on the Alhóndiga de Granaditas. ✉ *Av. Libertad at Calle 15, Centro,* ☎ *no phone.* 🎫 *Free.* 🕐 *Daily 7–2 and 5–7.*

Slightly outside the center of town but worth a visit is the Cultural Center of the University of Chihuahua, known as **Quinta Gameros.** This hybrid French Second Empire–art nouveau mansion, with stained-glass windows, ornate wooden staircases, rococo plaster wall panels, and lavish ironwork, was begun in 1907 by architect Julio Corredor Latorre, a Colombian architect, for Manuel Gameros, a wealthy mining engineer. On the ground floor are changing archaeological or fine arts exhibits; on the second floor, the mismatched and rather amateurish contemporary paintings belonging to the state university. ✉ *Calle Bolívar 401, at Calle de la Llave, Centro,* ☎ *614/416–6684.* 🎫 *$2.50.* 🕐 *Tues.–Sun. 11–2 and 4–7.*

Not to be confused with the University Cultural Center, the **Chihuahua Cultural Center** displays Paquimé ceramics from the pre-Columbian settlement of Casas Grandes northwest of Chihuahua. Music, dance, and other cultural performances and events are held here throughout the year. ✉ *Aldama 430, at Ocampo, Centro,* ☎ *614/416–1336.* 🎫 *Free.* 🕐 *Tues.–Sun. 10–2 and 4–7.*

A restoration project has made the site of the town's original settlement, **Santa Eulalia,** particularly appealing. The 30-minute drive southeast of town, about $14 one-way by taxi (significantly less by bus), is repaid by the colonial architecture and cobblestone streets of this village, which was founded in 1652. The religious artwork in the 18th-century cathedral is noteworthy.

Opened in 2001, the **Nombre de Dios caverns** are just outside the northeast side of the city, about 30 minutes from the city center. An illuminated, 1.6-km (1-mi) path takes you past rock formations and stalactites and stalagmites, which have been given names such as Christ, the Waterfall, and the Altar. ✉ *H. Colegio Militar s/n, Sector Nombre de Dios,* ☎ *614/400–7059.* 🎫 *Weekdays $2.20, weekends $3.* 🕐 *Tues.–Fri. 9–4, weekends 10–5.*

OFF THE BEATEN PATH

CASAS GRANDES – Some 350 km (161 mi) northwest of Chihuahua, the twin towns of Nuevo Casas Grandes and Casas Grandes are the gateways to the ancient area known as Paquimé, declared a UNESCO World Heritage site in 1998. Nuevo Casas Grandes, a two-horse town with wide, dusty streets and cowboys en regalia, has the hotels and most of the local restaurants. Sleepy Casas Grandes, 8 km (5 mi) away, is officially a one-horse town.

Near the aspen-lined Casas Grandes River, sheltered by the burnt-sienna peaks of the Sierra Madre Occidental, Paquimé was inhabited by peoples of the Oasis America culture between AD 700 and 1500. The trading and ceremonial city was poised between the Pueblo cultures of today's Southwestern United States (to whom they were related) to the north and their Mesoamerican neighbors to the south. Architecture and possibly cultural traditions were borrowed from each; Paquimé was a cosmopolitan commercial center whose residents raised fowl and manufactured jewelry. Evidence of their engineering and architectural savvy still stands, in the form of heat-shielding walls, T-shaped doorways for defense, and intricate indoor plumbing systems. The high-tech museum on-site houses Paquimé artifacts and ceramics and has bilingual descriptions of local cultural, religious, and economic practices. ☏ *636/692–4140.* 🎫 *Museum $1.* ⏲ *Tues.–Sun. 10–5.*

In Nuevo Casas Grandes, **Restaurante Constantino** (✉ Minerva 112, across from Hotel Paquimé, ☏ 636/694–1005) makes great enchiladas and has a full breakfast menu. In Casas Grandes, **El Pueblo** (✉ off Juárez, ☏ no phone) draws residents from all around with great food (no breakfast) and a full bar. **Hotel Piñon** (✉ Juárez 605, Nuevo Casas Grandes, ☏ 636/694–0655) has a swimming pool and a private collection of ancient *ollas* (clay pots) from Paquimé. **Hotel Hacienda** (✉ Av. Juárez 2603 Nte., Nuevo Casas Grandes, ☏ 636/694–1046), with 117 rooms, 7 suites, and a swimming pool, is one of the best places to stay in town.

Omnibus de México makes the 5½-hour trip from Chihuahua to Nuevo Casas Grandes (about $15). To get to the ruins, hop a blue-and-gold CASAS GRANDES bus (30¢) at Constitución and 16 de Septiembre. After 15 minutes, get off at Casas Grandes *zócalo* (main square). Paquimé is a 10-minute walk from town—follow the PAQUIMÉ sign on Constitución. The last bus returns to Nuevo Casas Grandes at 9 PM.

Dining and Lodging

$$$ ✕ **La Calesa.** A large, dimly lighted, and rather elegant room with wood paneling and red tablecloths and curtains, this looks like the classic steak house it is. The filet mignon and rib-eye steaks are particularly recommended; try the former cooked with mushrooms. ✉ *Av. Juárez 3300,* ☏ *614/410–1038 or 614/416–0222. AE, MC, V.*

$$ ✕ **Café del Paseo.** Two doors down from Quinta Gameros, this casual, friendly evening hot spot is known for good service and a cozy ambience that is attractive to people of all ages. Original art decorates walls painted Santa Fe pinks, peaches, and ochre yellows, and a *trova* group sings popular ballads Wednesday to Sunday after 8:30 PM. The specialty is *arrachera,* tenderized beef, served with quesadilla and baked potato. The veggie tacos with melted cheese are another good bet. ✉ *Bolivar 411,* ☏ *614/410–3200. AE, MC, V. No lunch.*

$$ ✕ **Rincón Mexicano.** Chihuahua natives return again and again to this traditional eatery for dependable Mexican food in a festive atmosphere. Mariachis serenade patrons in both the restaurant and the adjacent bar. ✉ *Av. Cuauhtémoc 2224, Col. Cuauhtémoc,* ☏ *614/411–1427 or 614/411–8410. AE, MC, V.*

$–$$ ✕ **Café Mandala.** If you need your palm or tarot cards read, or just want to sit back and smell the incense, head for this New Age eatery at a lookout above Chihuahua. Tables crowding the outdoor terrace are popular on summer evenings, and the food—tacos, tostadas, and other Mexican fare with a healthful and sometimes vegetarian slant—

is tasty and very reasonably priced. ✉ *Mirador de la Calle 11,* ☎ *614/416–0266. Reservations not accepted. No credit cards. No lunch.*

$ ✕ **Ah Chiles.** If you like it hot, this is the spot. A block from Plaza Hidalgo, this informal Chihuahua chain restaurant serves *norteño* (northern Mexican) food along with an array of different salsas. ✉ *Aldama 712, at Guerrero, Centro,* ☎ *614/437–0977. No credit cards.*

$ ✕ **La Casa de Los Milagros.** According to legend, the owner of this house fell in love with one of Pancho Villa's "girls." The owner's wife prayed to Saint Anthony, and when her husband returned, the house was dubbed "House of Miracles." Today it's *the* place for light snacks, coffee, drinks, and, Thursday through Saturday after 9 PM, live romantic music. High-ceilinged rooms painted salmon or deep blue are often adorned with the paintings or photos by local talent. ✉ *Victoria 812, near Ocampo, Centro,* ☎ *614/437–0693. No lunch. AE, MC, V.*

$$$ ★ **Holiday Inn Hotel & Suites.** This appealing property combines comfort, style, and convenience; it's 10 minutes from the downtown sights. Each guest room has a kitchen with stove, refrigerator, dishwasher, and coffeemaker, and a long counter where you can eat or work. The TV swivels between the comfortable living area and the bedroom, and comes with a VCR. The English-speaking staff is friendly and helpful and there's a complimentary Continental breakfast buffet. ✉ *Escudero 702, Col. San Felipe 31000,* ☎ *614/439–0000 or 800/465–4329,* FAX *614/414–3313. 74 suites. Restaurant, kitchens, cable TV, in-room VCRs, pool, gym, spa, basketball, free parking. AE, DC, MC, V.*

$$$ **Westin Soberano Chihuahua.** Atop a rise that has magnificent views of the city and surrounding mountains, Chihuahua's most elegant hotel sparkles with fountains and marble. Designed around an atrium with a cascading waterfall, the hotel is a contemporary palace in contrast to the rustic accommodations of the Copper Canyon. Rooms are plush, with richly patterned textiles, comfortable furniture, TV in a tall chest, and bath with both tub and shower. ✉ *Barranca del Cobre 3211, Fracc. Barrancas 31125,* ☎ *614/429–2929 or 888/625–5144,* FAX *614/429–2900,* WEB *www.westinsoberano.com. 194 rooms, 10 suites. 2 restaurants, cable TV, tennis court, pool, gym, 2 bars, business services, meeting rooms, free parking. AE, DC, MC, V.*

$$ ★ **Hotel San Francisco.** A favorite of Mexican business travelers, this modern five-story hotel has a prime location behind the Plaza de Armas. Clean and comfortable rooms are equipped with air-conditioning and heat, firm mattresses, large TVs, bathtubs, and desks. The lobby, adjacent to an open lounge–bar, is decorated with classic-style statues and urns, and massive floral arrangements. Local calls are free, as are fax, Internet, and some secretarial services. The coffee shop overlooking the street is always full of locals. ✉ *Victoria 409, Centro 31000,* ☎ *614/416–7550 or 800/847–2546,* FAX *614/415–3538,* WEB *www.hotelsanfrancisco.com.mx. 111 rooms, 20 suites. Restaurant, cable TV, bar, business services, meeting rooms, free parking. AE, MC, V.*

$$ **Palacio del Sol.** The high-rise downtown hotel looks faded from the outside, but inside, rooms and public spaces are redecorated on a regular basis. Comfortable if plain rooms have computer ports and radio, although they lack the Mexican charm of some less prestigious hotels. From the revolving front door to the stained-glass "sun" mural in the lobby bar, the public spaces seem permanently stuck in an earlier, less sophisticated era. ✉ *Independencia 116, Centro,* ☎ *614/416–6000 or 800/852–4049,* FAX *614/416–9947,* WEB *www.hotelpalaciodelsol.com. 174 rooms, 26 suites. 2 restaurants, in-room data ports, cable TV, gym, bar, shop, laundry service, meeting rooms, car rental, travel services, free parking. AE, DC, MC, V.*

$ **Posada Tierra Blanca.** Across the street from the Palacio del Sol but considerably less expensive, this modern motel-style property is convenient to downtown sights. Redecorated in 2001 with new mattresses, pseudo-antique furnishings, and larger cable TVs, the rooms are well heated in winter. ✉ *Niños Héroes 102, Centro,* ☎ *614/415–0000,* FAX *614/416–0063. 98 rooms, 5 suites. Restaurant, pool, piano bar, free parking. AE, MC, V.*

Nightlife and the Arts

This large city is more sedate than one might expect; and its hardworking residents generally wait for the weekends to kick up their heels. **La Casa de Los Milagros** starts to groove after 8:30 PM. **Hotel Sicomoro** (✉ Blvd. Ortiz Mena 411, Col. Unidad Presidentes, ☎ 614/413–5445) offers live romantic and folk music nightly in the lobby bar.

Cervecería La Taberna (✉ Av. Juárez 3331, Centro, ☎ 614/415–8380) is a glass-encased, neon-laced restaurant and bar within a former brewery where you can play pool or dance to a DJ. **El Grotto** (✉ Calle Ernesto Talavera between el Canal and Cuauhtémoc, Auditorio Municipal, ☎ no phone) plays salsa (live or canned) for an energetic crowd 25 years and older; it's open Thursday to Saturday after 9 PM.

Shopping

In addition to selling gems and geodes from the area, the **Artesanías y Gemas de Chihuahua** (✉ Calle Décima 3015, across from the Museum of the Mexican Revolution Iglesia Corazón de Jesús, ☎ 614/415–2882, closed Mon.) carries exceptional silver jewelry and a variety of other crafts. Across the street from the *calabozo* (jail) where Father Hidalgo was held, the **Casa de las Artesanías del Estado de Chihuahua** (✉ Av. Juárez 705, Centro, ☎ 614/437–1292) carries the best selection of Tarahumara and regional crafts in the city. **Mercado de Artesanías** (✉ Calle Victoria 506 [another entrance on Aldama 511] between Calles Quinta and Guerrero, Centro, ☎ 614/416–2716), a block wide with two entrances, sells everything from inexpensive jewelry, candy, and T-shirts to mass-produced crafts from all over the region.

COPPER CANYON/CHIHUAHUA A TO Z

To research prices, get advice from other travelers, and book travel arrangements, visit www.fodors.com.

AIR TRAVEL

You can fly into either Chihuahua or Los Mochis from Los Angeles, Tucson, Mexico City, or other major U.S. and Mexican cities.

CARRIERS

Aeroméxico and its feeder airline, Aerolitoral, have daily flights to Chihuahua from Los Angeles, Phoenix, Tucson, San Antonio, and El Paso. Within Mexico, the airlines have daily flights from Mexico City, Monterrey, Guadalajara, and Tijuana. AeroCalifornia has daily flights to Los Mochis from Los Angeles, Tucson, Tijuana, Mexico City, and Guadalajara.

➤ AIRLINES AND CONTACTS: **AeroCalifornia** (✉ Leyva 99 Nte., Centro, Los Mochis, ☎ 668/818–1616); (✉ Lateral Periférico Ortíz Mena 1809, Col. Campestre Virreyes, Chihuahua, ☎ 614/437–1022). **Aeroméxico** (✉ Paseo Bolívar 405, next to Quinta Gameros, Centro, Chihuahua, ☎ 614/415–6303 in Chihuahua; 668/815–2570 in Los Mochis).

BOAT AND FERRY TRAVEL

The Sematur ferry (for cars and passengers) runs two to four times per week between La Paz and Topolobampo, weather permitting. Hours and days of the week for sailings change constantly, so it's important to check in advance of your departure and again a few days before. At press time one-way car rate was about $240; salon, $40; cabin, $88; "suite," $115. In Los Mochis, contact Agencia de Viajes Ahome for information and reservations. In Topolobampo, contact Sematur.

➤ BOAT AND FERRY INFORMATION: **Agencia de Viajes Ahome** (✉ Morelos 392A Pte., Los Mochis, ☎ 668/815–6120; 01-800/201–9383 in Mexico). **Sematur** (☎ 668/862–0035 or 668/862–0141 in Topolobampo; 01-800/696–9600 in Mexico, WEB www.ferrysematur.com.mx).

BUS TRAVEL

The Omnibus de México lines run clean, air-conditioned buses from Ciudad Juárez to Chihuahua. These leave approximately every hour from 7 AM to 8 PM. The cost of the 4½-hour trip is approximately $20 for first class. Buses shuttle between El Paso and Ciudad Juárez every two hours; the price is $5. This line also has buses between these and other northern Mexico cities and Guadalajara and Mexico City.

Grupo Estrella Blanca (which includes Chihuahuenses, Elite, and other lines) buses connect the border cities to Puerto Peñasco, other northern cities, and as far south as Huatulco, in Oaxaca state. TUFESA is another reliable company serving cities and towns throughout northern Mexico.

➤ BUS INFORMATION: **Grupo Estrella Blanca** (☎ 614/429–0242 or 614/429–0240 in Chihuahua; 631/313–1603 in Nogales; 668/815–0062 in Los Mochis). **Omnibus de México** (☎ 614/420–1580 in Chihuahua). **TUFESA** (☎ 631/313–3862 in Nogales).

CAR RENTAL

Avis, Budget, and Hertz all have offices at the airport in Chihuahua. Car companies at the airport in Los Mochis and in town include Budget and Hertz.

➤ MAJOR AGENCIES: **Avis** (✉ Av. Universidad 1703, Universidad, Chihuahua, ☎ 614/414–1003). **Budget** (✉ Ortiz Mena 3322, Col. Magesterial, Chihuahua, ☎ 614/414–2171; ✉ Guillermo Prieto 850 Nte., Los Mochis, ☎ 668/812–5360). **Hertz** (✉ Av. Revolución 514, Centro, Chihuahua, ☎ 614/416–6473; ✉ Av. Leyva 171 Nte., Los Mochis, ☎ 668/812–1122).

CAR TRAVEL

Most U.S. and Canadian visitors drive to Chihuahua via Mexico Highway 45 from the El Paso–Ciudad Juárez border, a distance of 375 km (233 mi), or up from Mexico City, 1,440 km (893 mi). The drive down to Los Mochis from Nogales on the Arizona border via Mexico Highway 15, four lanes much of the way, is 763 km (473 mi).

Paved roads connect Chihuahua City to Creel and Divisadero: take Mexico Highway 16 west to San Pedro, then State Highway 127 south to Creel. The 300-km (186-mi) trip takes 3½–4 hours in good weather. This drive, through the pine forests of the Sierra Madre foothills, is more scenic than the railroad route via the plains area. Driving is a good option if you have a four-wheel-drive vehicle, because there are many worthwhile, if difficult, excursions into the canyons from Creel. From Divisadero to Bahuichivo, the dirt road is full of potholes and is especially dangerous in rain or snow.

EMERGENCIES

To contact the police, fire department, or an ambulance in Chihuahua or Los Mochis dial **060**. In case of a medical problem that does not require an ambulance, contact the Red Cross or the local hospital or clinic in Chihuahua or Los Mochis.

Chihuahua has an abundance of pharmacies with late-night service in the city center. Farmacia Cosmos will deliver at no cost.

➤ CONTACTS: **Red Cross** (☎ 668/815–0808 or 668/812–0292 in Los Mochis; 614/411–1619 in Chihuahua).

➤ HOSPITALS: **Clínica del Parque** (✉ Calle Dr. Pedro Leal 1802, Centro, Chihuahua, ☎ 614/415–7411 or 614/415–7339). **Hospital del Centro del Estado** (✉ Calle 33 and Rosales, Colonia Obrera, Chihuahua, ☎ 614/415–9000). **Hospital Santa Rita** (✉ Calle Angel Flores 266 Sur, Los Mochis, ☎ 668/815–4800).

➤ PHARMACIES: **Farmacia del Ahorro** (✉ Calle Aldama at Calle 13A, Centro, Chihuahua, ☎ 614/410–9017). **Farmacia Cosmos** (✉ Blvd. Rosendo G. Castros at Guillermo Prieto, Centro, Chihuahua, ☎ 614/812–9660. **Farmacia Internacional** (✉ Avs. Leyva at Rendón, Los Mochis, ☎ 668/812–5556).

MONEY MATTERS

Be sure to change money before you get into the Copper Canyon: there are no banks in Cerocahui, Divisadero, or Posada Barrancas, and no guarantee that the hotels in those places will have enough cash to accommodate you. In Creel, there's a Serfín just across from the train station. It's open weekdays 9–3 and, more important, it has a 24-hour ATM that accepts Cirrus and Plus system cards. In Los Mochis, most banking hours are weekdays between 8:30 and 4:30; some banks open Saturday morning. The Banamex there has a 24-hour ATM. In Chihuahua, most banks open weekdays from 9 to 1:30 and from 3:30 to 7:30, and Saturday from 9 to 1:30. Banco Bital in downtown Chihuahua is open Monday through Saturday 8–7. In El Fuerte, Bancomer is open Monday through Saturday 8:30–3. Hotels have slightly lower exchange rates but charge no commission, and you normally won't have to wait in line.

➤ BANKS: **Banamex** (✉ Guillermo Prieto and Hidalgo, Los Mochis, ☎ 668/812–0116). **Banco Bital** (✉ Av. Libertad 1922, Centro, Chihuahua, ☎ 614/416–0880). **Bancomer** (✉ Constitución and Juárez, El Fuerte). **Banco Serfín** (✉ Creel, ☎ 635/456–0060).

TAXIS

In Chihuahua and Los Mochis, taxis are easy to find and can be engaged at hotels or hailed on the street. The trip from the airport into town costs $8–$10 ($16 for a private taxi) in Chihuahua and $14 in Los Mochis. Always agree on a price before getting into the cab.

TOURS

Most large hotels in Los Mochis and Chihuahua have in-house travel agencies that arrange tours of the Copper Canyon area, as well as hiking, hunting, and fishing expeditions. In Los Mochis, tours arranged by Hotel Santa Anita will book you almost exclusively into their own line of hotels throughout the Copper Canyon. In El Fuerte, contact Copper Canyon Adventures, which offers individualized and group tours from sedate to adventurous. In Chihuahua, both Rojo y Casavantes and Turismo Al Mar offer plane and train tickets as well as city tours, Mennonite Camps, and Copper Canyon sojourns. In Cuauhtémoc, Cumbres Friesen, owned by Mennonite David Friesen, can arrange Mennonite tours.

From the United States, the oldest operator in the area is Pan American Tours. Prices for tours between Los Mochis and Chihuahua range from about $410 to $875 per person (three to seven nights); custom tours are arranged. Synergy Tours runs individual and group trips about 10 times a year, including off-the-beaten-path treks. California Native runs independent and small-group escorted trips through the

Copper Canyon. Four- to 11-day trips for individuals start around $650; group trips last one to two weeks and begin at $1,690. Doug Rhodes, of Paraíso del Oso Hotel in Cerocahui, leads horseback tours into the Urique Canyon on his stable of some 30 horses and offers day rentals of mountain bikes and rafting trips (mid-July to mid-September only for rafting). Communications to Cerocahui are spotty, so e-mail, phone, or fax with plenty of lead time.

➤ TOUR OPERATOR RECOMMENDATIONS: **California Native** (✉ 6701 W. 87th Pl., Los Angeles, CA 90045, ☎ 800/926–1140, WEB www.calnative.com). **Copper Canyon Adventures** (☎ FAX 698/893–0915, FAX 603/696–7713 in the U.S., WEB www.coppercanyonadventures.com). **Cumbres Friesen** (✉ Calle 3A No. 466, Cuauhtémoc, ☎ 625/582–5457, FAX 625/582–4060). **Pan American Tours** (✉ 5959 Gateway W. 160-B, El Paso, TX 79925, ☎ 800/876–3942, WEB www.panamericantours.com). **Paraíso del Oso** (✉ Box 31089, El Paso, TX 79931, ☎ 800/884–3107, FAX 915/585–7027, WEB www.mexicohorse.com). **Rojo y Casavantes** (✉ Av. Vincent Guerrero 1207, Centro, Chihuahua, ☎ 614/439–5858 or 614/415–5787, FAX 614/415–5384). **Synergy Tours** (✉ 7335 E. Indian Plaza, Suite 120, Scottsdale, AZ 85251, ☎ 800/569–1797, FAX 480/994–4439, WEB www.synergytours.com). **Turismo Al Mar** (✉ Calle Verna 2202, Colonia Mirador, Chihuahua, ☎ FAX 614/416–6589, ☎ 614/416–5950).

TRAIN TOURS

Sierra Madre Express of Tucson runs its own deluxe trains (with dome-dining and Pullman cars) to the Copper Canyon from Tucson via Nogales on eight-day, seven-night trips about six times a year. Its trips combine the charm of sleeping on the train with first-class accommodations, starting at $2,795 per person. The company's slogan is "soft adventure of a lifetime"; the trips are geared toward older folks and those who want to view the canyon scenery and experience Tarahumara culture without roughing it.

➤ FEES AND SCHEDULES: **Sierra Madre Express of Tucson** (✉ Box 26381, Tucson, AZ 85726, ☎ 520/747–0346 or 800/666–0346, WEB www.sierramadreexpress.com).

TRAIN TRAVEL

Other than the private train cars of the Sierra Madre Express, there is no passenger service from any U.S. border city to either Los Mochis or Chihuahua.

The Ferrocarril Chihuahua al Pacífico line (CHEPE) runs a first-class and a second-class train daily in each direction from Chihuahua and Los Mochis through the Copper Canyon. For long-term reservations and price information, your best bet may be using one of the private train companies or tour operators.

The first-class train departs from Los Mochis at 6 AM (sit on the right side of the train for the best views) and arrives in Chihuahua about 15 hours later. Delays of several hours are not unusual. Westbound, it departs from Chihuahua at 6 AM and arrives in Los Mochis around 9 PM. The price of a first-class ticket is about $110 each way; you should arrange stopovers when you buy tickets.

State police with automatic weapons travel aboard to discourage would-be thieves. Food and drink in the dining car and bar are predictably expensive, and although it is technically forbidden to bring your own food and drink, conductors generally ignore this bending of rules.

Make reservations a week or more in advance during the busy months of July, August, and October, and around Christmas and Easter. Some find it most convenient to book through a hotel, tour company, or travel agency, although you can also buy tickets at the train station or major hotels in Los Mochis or Chihuahua.

The second-class train, *El Pollero*, leaves an hour later from each terminus but makes many stops and is scheduled to arrive 3½ hours later in both directions than the first-class train. It is less comfortable, more crowded, and harder to see the scenery, and there are no dining or bar coaches. No reservations are needed; prices are approximately $56 each way.

If you're driving down to Los Mochis, you're better off leaving your car there and taking the train round-trip. Or, take the train to Chihuahua and fly back to Los Mochis via Aerolitoral. If you're coming via Chihuahua, however, consider driving to Creel or Divisadero and doing a round-trip from there. In either case, El Fuerte is a more charming starting and ending point than Los Mochis, and if you start there, you'll get another hour's sleep on departure day.

➤ TRAIN INFORMATION: **Ferrocarril Chihuahua al Pacífico** (☎ 614/439–7210 in Chihuahua; 668/824–1167 in Los Mochis; 800/367–3900 information within Mexico; 888/416–5420 for information outside Mexico, WEB www.ferromex.com.mx).

VISITOR INFORMATION

The Government Tourist Office in Chihuahua is open weekdays 9–4. A smaller office at the State Government Building, on Plaza Hidalgo, is open weekdays 9–7. At the former, Sonia Estrada, who speaks fluent English, will answer questions and help visitors (in person or over the phone) make travel arrangements all over the state.

The Oficina de Turismo in Los Mochis, on the first floor of the Unidad Administrativa del Gobierno del Estado building, is generally lacking in information.

➤ TOURIST INFORMATION: **Government Tourist Office** (✉ Av. Libertad and Calle 13, 2nd floor, Centro, Chihuahua, ☎ 614/429–3421; 614/429–3300 Ext. 4511 or 4512; Palacio de Gobierno, Calle Aldama between Avs. Guerrero and Carranza, Centro, Chihuahua, ☎ 614/429–3300 Ext. 1061). **Oficina de Turismo** (✉ Allende and Ordoñez, Los Mochis, ☎ 668/815–1090).

7 GUADALAJARA

INCLUDING TLAQUEPAQUE, TONALÁ, AND LAKE CHAPALA

Colonial architecture that dates from the city's heyday as the center of regional commerce is among the lures of Guadalajara, which introduced the world to mariachis, tequila, and the Mexican hat dance. On the city's outskirts, Tlaquepaque and Tonalá produce some of Mexico's finest crafts. A near-perfect semitropical climate and proximity to the Pacific Ocean—240 km (149 mi) away—ensure warm, sunny days and cool, clear nights.

Updated by Paul Davidson

TRADITIONS ARE PRESERVED and customs perpetuated in Guadalajara; it's a place where the siesta is an institution and the fiesta an art form. Mexico's second-largest city, and the capital of the state of Jalisco, Guadalajara is engaged in a struggle to retain its provincial ambience and colonial charm as its population surpasses 7 million. Émigrés who left Mexico City after the devastating 1985 earthquake and staggering numbers of the rural poor seeking employment created a population explosion that continues to strain public services and increase pollution. Despite these problems, visitors still can enjoy the tree-lined boulevards, parks, plazas, and stately churrigueresque architecture.

Guadalajara has always been one of the most socially traditional and politically conservative cities in Mexico. It has also been a seat of Christian fundamentalism and was one of the strategic areas of the *cristeros,* a movement of Catholic zealots in western Mexico in the 1920s. Tapatíos, as the city's residents are called (the name may come from *tlapatiotl,* three units or purses of cacao or other commodities used as currency by the Indians of the area), even seem to take a certain amount of pride in their rather straight and narrow outlook.

Still, Tapatíos are historically accustomed to challenge and change. Within 10 years of its founding in 1531, the location of the city changed three times. In 1542 the city council followed the advice of Doña Beatriz Hernández to build the city in the center of the Atemajac Valley, where it could expand. Guadalajara was thus placed on a mile-high plain of the Sierra Madre, bounded on three sides by rugged cliffs and on the fourth by the spectacular Barranca de Oblatos (Oblatos Canyon).

Geographically removed from the rest of the republic during the nearly 300 years of Spanish rule, the city cultivated and maintained a political and cultural autonomy. By the end of the 16th century, money was flowing into Guadalajara from the rich farms and silver mines in the region, creating the first millionaires of what was then known as New Galicia. Under orders from Spain, much of the wealth was lavished on magnificent churches, residences, and monuments. Many of these reminders of the golden era still stand in downtown Guadalajara.

The suburbs of Tlaquepaque (pronounced tla-kay-*pah*-kay) and Tonalá (pronounced toe-na-*la*) produce some of Mexico's finest and most popular traditional crafts and folk art. Lake Chapala—Mexico's largest body of fresh water—and the nearby towns Chapala and Ajijic have lured retirees from the United States and Canada, who enjoy most of the amenities they were accustomed to north of the border.

Pleasures and Pastimes

Arts and Architecture

You can find all kinds of Mexican and international arts in Guadalajara—from the traditional Ballet Folklórico at the Teatro Degollado to rock groups at the Instituto Cultural Cabañas. Galleries and museums around town also offer the best of modern and traditional work. Numerous 16th-century colonial buildings fill the downtown area, connected by a series of large, Spanish-style plazas.

Churches

Guadalajara seems to have a church every block or two—there are 15 in the downtown area alone, all dating from the colonial era. Some have elaborately carved facades, and others conceal ornate Baroque altars and priceless colonial oil paintings behind sober stone exteriors.

Dining

The variety of Guadalajara's restaurants includes classic Mexican dishes, Continental delicacies, Argentine-style steaks, and fresh seafood. Savory regional specialties—often served in simpler places—include *birria,* a spicy stew prepared with goat, lamb, or beef in a light tomato broth; *pozole,* a thick pork and hominy soup; and *carne en su jugo,* consisting of steak bits in a clear spicy broth with bacon, beans, and cilantro, usually served with a side of tiny, grilled whole onions.

CATEGORY	COST*
$$$	$15–$25
$$	$10–$15
$	under $10

**per person for a main course at dinner*

Lodging

Hotels run the gamut from older establishments in the downtown historic district to representatives of the large chains, most of which are on or near Avenida López Mateos Sur, a 16-km (10-mi) strip extending from the Minerva Fountain to the Plaza del Sol shopping center. In the mid-1990s several hotels were built close to the ExpoGuadalajara convention center, which opened in 1987.

CATEGORY	COST*
$$$$	over $160
$$$	$90–$160
$$	$40–$90
$	under $40

**All prices are for a standard double room, excluding 15% VAT and 2% hotel tax.*

Shopping

Blown glass, hand-carved wood furniture, fine leatherwork, and hand-glazed pottery are local traditions. Two of the most common ceramic techniques are *barro bruñido,* in which the pieces are hand-burnished to a soft sheen, and *petatillo,* in which glaze is applied to earthenware in a fine crosshatch pattern. Guadalajara is also home to a thriving shoe industry. At sprawling markets you can bargain for anything from embroidered shirts to *huaraches* (woven leather sandals), and sleek shopping malls have full-service department stores and trendy boutiques.

Sports

Highly stylized *charreadas,* traditional equestrian events with teams of elegantly clad women and men, are presented weekly, and bullfights are held in October and November. Late August through May, soccer fans crowd Estadio Jalisco (Jalisco Stadium).

EXPLORING GUADALAJARA

Metropolitan Guadalajara consists of a historic city center and nearby urban districts, including Tlaquepaque, Tonalá, and Zapopan. Just outside are the tranquil villages on Lake Chapala's receding shores.

Numbers in the text correspond to numbers in the margin and on the Downtown Guadalajara, Tlaquepaque, Tonalá, and Lake Chapala Area maps.

Great Itineraries

It's not surprising that Guadalajara has been described as *señorial y moderna* (lordly and modern). In fact, although the graciousness of colonial Mexico is still readily apparent, it now takes a backseat to contemporary culture, for both better and worse. The once-separate satellite pueblos of Tlaquepaque and Tonalá are now the best places to feel the pulse of traditional pueblo life. Seven days would allow you to fully explore the city and villages surrounding Lago de Chapala, as well as to take an excursion or two to points farther afield. With five days to spend, you'll have time to see most of the city's highlights and to get to know Tlaquepaque, Tonalá, and the Lake Chapala area. In three days, you can take in the historic center and make day trips to Tlaquepaque and Tonalá.

IF YOU HAVE 3 DAYS

Spend your first day in the historic **centro** ①–⑩ (town center). The next day, spend the morning and have lunch in **Tlaquepaque** ⑳–㉗, and visit **Tonalá** ㉘–㉝ in the afternoon. These two towns are the best places in Guadalajara to shop. On your third day, see more of the city sights, including an evening performance of theater or dance, or head to one of the thermal spas southwest of town.

IF YOU HAVE 5 DAYS

See **el centro** ①–⑩ on your first day, and then consider your interests. If traditional crafts or outstanding furniture and housewares lure you, devote a day to **Tlaquepaque** ⑳–㉗ and Day 3 to **Tonalá** ㉘–㉝. Alternatively, explore the two towns in one day, and leave a day to spend around **Lake Chapala.** Spend your final day back in Guadalajara in museums and the **Basílica de la Virgen de Zapopan** ⑮, for which you'll need several hours, or even the **Zoológico Guadalajara** ⑭. Plan an afternoon of strolling past the mansions that were built by Guadalajara's upper classes in the glorious twilight before the 1910 revolution; the best area is in a six-block radius around Avenida Vallarta west of Avenida Chapultepec. If you'd like to get your feet on the ground in more natural surroundings, hike in the nearby **Barranca de Oblatos.**

IF YOU HAVE 7 DAYS

You will be able to cover all of **el centro** ①–⑩ plus the other city sights, and **Tlaquepaque** ⑳–㉗, **Tonalá** ㉘–㉝, and the area of **Lake Chapala.** Fill in the gaps with a visit to Tequila and a soak in the soothing thermal waters of **San Juan Cosalá,** on the shores of Lake Chapala, or one of the thermal pools around **Villa Corona,** southwest of Guadalajara.

Guadalajara

Beginning around 1960, 20th-century architecture started to threaten the aesthetic of this provincial state capital. During the 1980s the city declared 30 blocks in the heart of downtown a cultural sanctuary. With the additional help of private-sector groups, **el Centro Histórico** has now been restored to the polished charm of its elegant past. The 16th-century buildings here are connected by a series of large Spanish-style plazas where children chase balloons, young lovers coo on tree-shaded park benches, and grandparents stroll past vendors and marble fountains. At the nearby **Plaza de los Mariachis,** sombreroed troubadours stroll about, strumming their guitars and singing traditional songs.

Outside the historic center, most tourist sights and large hotels are located in three areas: near Avenida Chapultepec, near the Minerva Fountain and Los Arcos monument, and near the Plaza del Sol shopping mall and ExpoGuadalajara convention center.

A Good Walk

Guadalajara's 17th-century **Catedral** ①, on the north side of Plaza de Armas, is the place to start exploring downtown. After you've marveled at the interior, exit through the main doors and cross Avenida Alcalde to Plaza de la Ciudad de Guadalajara, with its large fountain, outdoor café, and benches scattered beneath square-cut laurel trees.

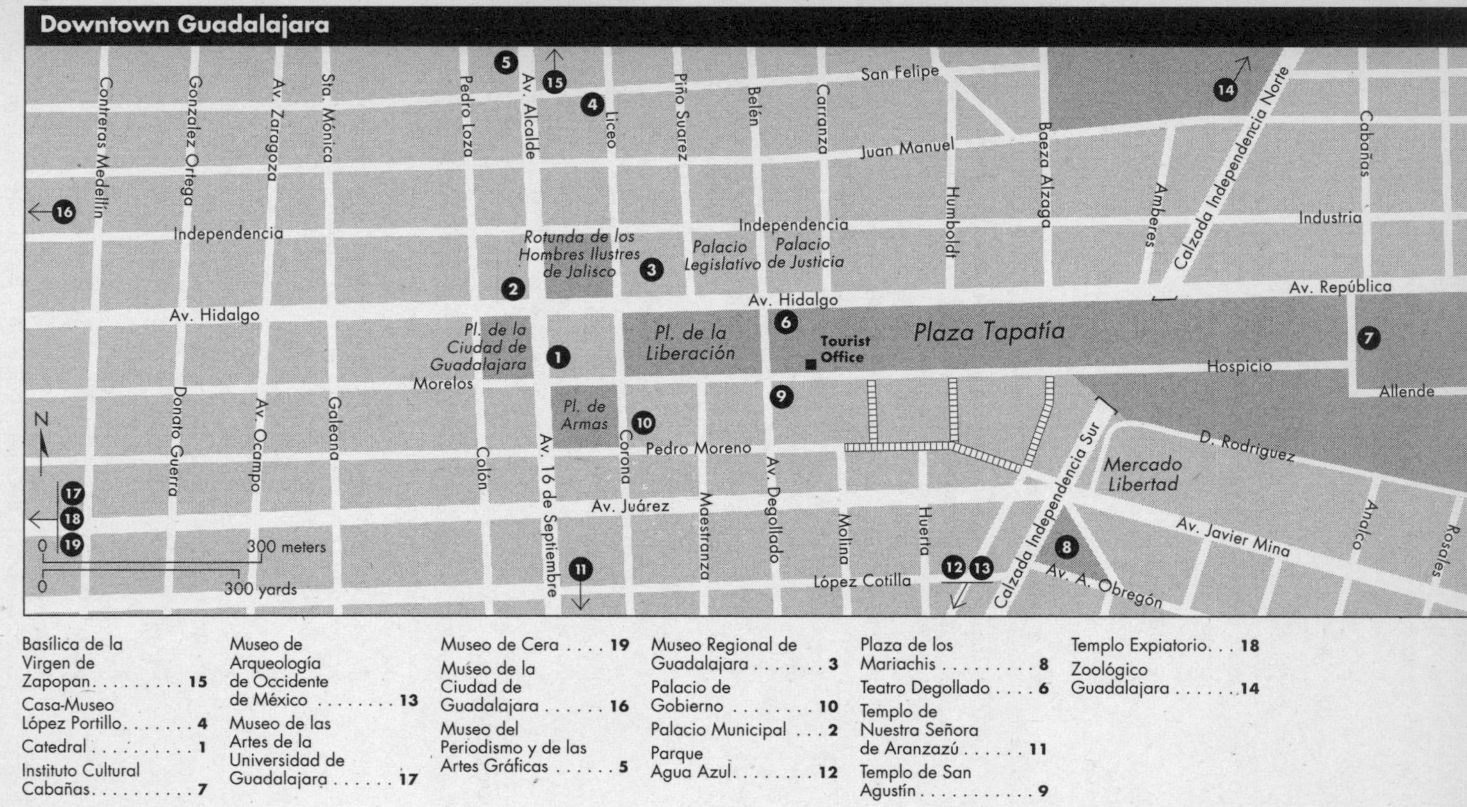

Basílica de la Virgen de Zapopan. **15**
Casa-Museo López Portillo. **4**
Catedral **1**
Instituto Cultural Cabañas. **7**
Museo de Arqueología de Occidente de México **13**
Museo de las Artes de la Universidad de Guadalajara **17**
Museo de Cera **19**
Museo de la Ciudad de Guadalajara **16**
Museo del Periodismo y de las Artes Gráficas **5**
Museo Regional de Guadalajara **3**
Palacio de Gobierno **10**
Palacio Municipal . . . **2**
Parque Agua Azul. **12**
Plaza de los Mariachis **8**
Teatro Degollado **6**
Templo de Nuestra Señora de Aranzazú **11**
Templo de San Agustín **9**
Templo Expiatorio. . . **18**
Zoológico Guadalajara **14**

To your right (with your back toward the cathedral) across Avenida Hidalgo is the **Palacio Municipal** ②, built in the mid-20th century to match surrounding buildings. The second-floor Salón Guadalajara often features cultural exhibits.

From the corner of Avenidas Alcalde and Hidalgo, head one block east to Calle Liceo, where you'll see the **Museo Regional de Guadalajara** ③. You'll pass the Rotunda de los Hombres Ilustres de Jalisco, a tree-shaded square whose central colonnaded rotunda covers a mausoleum containing the remains of 17 of the state of Jalisco's most eminent people.

After you leave the museum, turn right and walk three blocks on Calle Liceo to **Casa-Museo López Portillo** ④. North and west of here, on Avenida Alcalde, is the fascinating **Museo del Periodismo y de las Artes Gráficas** ⑤.

Return to the Museo Regional, make a left, and head east along Avenida Hidalgo, past the Palacio Legislativo—a former customhouse, tobacco warehouse, and inn that today houses Jalisco's state legislature—and the Palacio de Justicia, which was built in 1588 as part of Guadalajara's first convent and now is the state courthouse. Across Avenida Hidalgo on your right sprawls the Plaza de la Liberación, at the east end of which rises the spectacular **Teatro Degollado** ⑥. Behind it begins the Plaza Tapatía, a five-block-long pedestrian mall lined with shops, trees, and whimsical sculpture. At the end, visit the **Instituto Cultural Cabañas** ⑦. Then proceed back west to the modernistic Quetzalcóatl Fountain in the center of the plaza outside the institute. (Too heavy for its base, the statue's 5-ton serpent head lies in one of the patios of the Instituto Cabañas.) Turn left and walk down the stairs to the sprawling **Mercado Libertad.** Turn left again when you leave the market and cross the pedestrian bridge over Avenida Javier Mina to the **Plaza de los Mariachis** ⑧.

Return to Plaza Tapatía by heading right to the intersection of Calzada Independencia Sur and Avenida Javier Mina, in front of the Iglesia de San Juan de Dios. Continue two blocks past the church and go back up the stairs. Turn left and walk west four blocks (so you can see the stores on the south side of the plaza) to the **Templo de San Agustín** ⑨.

As you leave the church, turn left on Calle Morelos and then turn left onto Avenida Corona. A half block south is the main entrance of the **Palacio de Gobierno** ⑩ to see two of José Clemente Orozco's murals. Exit the palacio back onto Avenida Corona (the way you came in) and cross the street to the Plaza de Armas, where you can rest on a wrought-iron bench, imagining yourself in the Porfiriato—Mexico's Victorian period—when wealthy *dons* and *doñas* strolled amid the trees and flower beds around the ornately sculpted kiosk, a gift from France in 1910. With the cathedral to your right, you've come full circle back to the north side of the plaza.

TIMING

You can take in most of downtown Guadalajara in a day or two. The sights outside of the center can easily take a half or full day each. Most museums, the zoo, and the planetarium are closed Monday. In early September Guadalajara hosts the international mariachi and tequila festival, bringing traditional troubadours from as far away as Japan and running daily train trips to Tequila. In October the city puts on the Fiestas de Octubre, a monthlong cultural festival that exudes a county fair–like atmosphere and is sprinkled with top-flight international entertainment.

Sights to See

15 **Basílica de la Virgen de Zapopan.** This vast church, with an ornate plateresque facade and *mudéjar* (Moorish) tile dome, was consecrated in 1730. It is known throughout Mexico as the home of La Zapopanita, Our Lady of Zapopan. The 10-inch-high statue is venerated as the source of many miracles in and around Guadalajara. Every October 12, more than a million people crowd the streets leading to the basilica, to which the Virgin is returned after a five-month tour of parish churches throughout the state. In the right side of the basilica is the **Museo Huichol Wixarica de Zapopan** (✉ 152 Av. Hidalgo, Zona Zapopan Norte, ☎ 33/3636–4430; 🎫 50¢; ⏲ 9:30–1:30 and 3–6), a small gallery and shop with exquisite beadwork and other crafts by the Huichol Indians of northern Jalisco and neighboring states Zacatecas and Nayarit; it's open Monday–Saturday 10–2 and 4–6, and Sunday 10–2. The basilica is 7 km (4½ mi) northwest of downtown. ✉ *Av. Hidalgo at Morelos, Zona Zapopan Norte,* ☎ *33/3633–0141 or 33/3633–6614.*

4 **Casa-Museo López Portillo.** Guadalajara's López Portillo family included prominent writers and politicians, such as an early 20th-century Jalisco governor and his Mexico City–born grandson, José López Portillo, president of Mexico from 1976 to 1982. As is typical of homes built by Mexico's 19th-century upper class, the plain stucco exterior belies the rich interior, where French Baroque–style rooms ring a spacious interior patio. ✉ *Liceo 177, Centro Histórico, at San Felipe,* ☎ *33/3613–2411 or 33/3613–2435.* 🎫 *Free.* ⏲ *Mon.–Sat. 10–6.*

★ 1 **Catedral.** Begun in 1561 and consecrated in 1618, this focal point of downtown is an intriguing mélange of Baroque, Gothic, and other styles, the result of design and structural modifications made during its 57 years of construction. Its emblematic twin towers replaced the originals, which fell in the earthquake of 1818. Ten of the silver-and-gold altars were gifts from King Fernando VII, donated in appreciation of Guadalajara's financial support of Spain during the Napoleonic Wars. Some of the world's most beautiful *retablos* (altarpieces) hang on the cathedral walls; above the sacristy (often closed to the public) is the priceless 17th-century painting by Bartolomé Esteban Murillo, *The Assumption of the Virgin.* In a loft high above the main entrance is a magnificent late-19th-century French organ, which is played during the afternoon mass on the third Sunday of the month, and in May's organ festival. ✉ *Av. Alcalde between Av. Hidalgo and Calle Morelos, Centro Histórico.* ⏲ *Daily 8–7.*

★ 7 **Instituto Cultural Cabañas.** This landmark neoclassical-style cultural center was designed by the famous Spanish architect-sculptor Manuel Tolsá. Originally a shelter for widows, the elderly, and orphans, the building was later home to 400 indigent children, until the 1970s, when the orphanage moved. The rooms, which surround 23 flower-filled patios, contain permanent and revolving art exhibitions. The central dome and walls of the main chapel display a series of murals painted by José Clemente Orozco in 1938–39, including *The Man of Fire,* widely considered his finest work. Room 33 has a permanent exhibition of Orozco's paintings, cartoons, and drawings. Ask the attendant at the front desk for an English-speaking guide. ✉ *Calle Cabañas 8, Centro Histórico, at Plaza Tapatía,* ☎ *33/3668–1640.* 🎫 *$1.20, free Sun.* ⏲ *Tues.–Sat. 10–6, Sun. 10–3.*

13 **Museo de Arqueología de Occidente de México.** The Archaeological Museum of Western Mexico houses pottery and other artifacts used by ancient peoples of what are now the states of Colima, Jalisco, and Nayarit. It's across from the entrance to Parque Agua Azul. ✉ *Av. 16*

de Septiembre 889, Zona Olimpica, ☎ *33/3619–0104.* *50¢.* *Daily 10–2 and 4–7.*

17 **Museo de las Artes de la Universidad de Guadalajara.** The University of Guadalajara's impressive contemporary art museum is housed in an exquisite early 20th-century building. In addition to its permanent collection of 20th-century drawings and paintings, the museum shows revolving exhibitions of contemporary Latin American, U.S., and European work. Look for the murals Orozco painted upon returning to Guadalajara at age 53. ✉ *Lopez Cotilla 930, Centro Histórico, at Diaz de Leon,* ☎ *33/3826–9183.* *Free.* *Tues.–Sun. 10:30–6.*

19 **Museo de Cera.** At Guadalajara's 120-figure wax museum in the historic downtown area across from Plaza de la Liberación, go eye-to-eye with Madonna, Mahatma Gandhi, beloved Mexican comic Cantinflas, and a host of other Mexican and international political and artistic luminaries. Visit the underground Aztec sacrificial chamber and a chamber of horrors. A wax mariachi, playing "Guadalajara, Guadalajara," greets you at the door. Next door, with the same phone and address, is the Ripley's Believe-It-Or-Not Museum. ✉ *Calle Morelos 217, Centro Histórico,* ☎ *33/3614–8487.* *$3.* *Daily 11–8.*

16 **Museo de la Ciudad de Guadalajara.** In a series of rooms surrounding the tranquil interior patio of this spacious remodeled colonial home, you'll find informative artwork, artifacts, and reproductions of documents about the city's development from pre-Hispanic times through the 20th century. ✉ *Calle Independencia 684, Centro Histórico, between Contreras Medellín and Mariano Bárcenas,* ☎ *33/3658–2531 or 33/3658–3706.* *50¢, free Sun.* *Tues.–Sun. 10–5.*

5 **Museo del Periodismo y de las Artes Gráficas.** In 1792 Guadalajara's first printing press was set up on this site. Today you can see displays of historic newspapers, printing presses, recording equipment, and a complete television studio in this fine old mansion, long known as the Casa de los Perros because of the two wrought-iron dogs (*perros*) guarding the roof. ✉ *Av. Alcalde 225, Centro Histórico, between Reforma and San Felipe,* ☎ *33/3613–9285 and 33/3613–9286.* *$1.* *Tues.–Sat. 10–6, Sun. 10:30–3.*

★ 3 **Museo Regional de Guadalajara.** Constructed as a seminary and public library in 1701, this distinguished building has been home to the Regional Museum (also known as the State Museum) since 1918. The first-floor galleries, which surround a garden courtyard, contain artifacts and memorabilia that trace the history of western Mexico from prehistoric times through the Spanish conquest; revolving exhibitions of art and crafts are also on display. On the second-floor balcony are five 19th-century carriages; the galleries here offer an impressive collection of paintings by European and Mexican artists, including Bartolomé Esteban Murillo. ✉ *Liceo 60, Centro Histórico,* ☎ *33/3614–9957.* *About $3.20, free Tues.* *Tues.–Sun. 9–5:45.*

10 **Palacio de Gobierno.** The initial adobe structure of 1643 was replaced with this churrigueresque and neoclassical stone structure in the 18th century. Within are Jalisco's state government offices and two of José Clemente Orozco's most passionate murals. The mural just past the entrance, in the stairwell to the right, depicts a gigantic Father Miguel Hidalgo looming amid shadowy figures—including the Pope, Hitler, and Mussolini—representing oppression and slavery. The other mural, in the former state-legislature quarters on the upper level, portrays Juárez and other figures of the 1850s Reform era. ✉ *Av. Corona between Calle Morelos and Pedro Moreno, Centro Histórico,* ☎ *no phone.* *Daily 9–8:45.*

❷ **Palacio Municipal.** Guadalajara's city hall was designed and built in 1952 with an arched facade and interior patios to fit in with neighboring buildings. Inside are colorful murals of the city's founding, painted by Guadalajara native Gabriel Flores. ✉ *Av. Hidalgo at Av. Alcalde, Centro Histórico,* ☎ *no phone.* ⏲ *Daily 9–9.*

⓬ **Parque Agua Azul.** Amid acres of trees and flowers, this popular park has carnival rides, tropical birds in cages, an orchid house, and a geodesic dome covering a semitropical garden. Next to the park entrance, the small **Teatro Experimental** (☎ 33/3619–1176) is a venue for Spanish-language plays, as well as for chamber music and other cultural events. The **Museo de la Paleontología** (✉ Dr. R. Michel 520, at González Gallo, Zona Olimpica, ☎ 33/3619–7043), on the southeast side of the park, displays regional animal and plant fossils and mammoth bones as well as exhibits—some hands-on for kids—on the origin of the planet. Free guided tours are offered at 11, 12:30, and 4:30; with advance notice English-language guides are available. ✉ *Calzada Independencia Sur, Zona Olimpica, between González Gallo and Las Palmas,* ☎ *33/3619–0332.* *50¢.* ⏲ *Tues.–Sun. 10–6.*

★ ❽ **Plaza de los Mariachis.** Experience the most Mexican of music in this picturesque little plaza surrounded by honky-tonks, where strolling mariachi groups perform for paying customers. Mariachi serenades are about $4 a song. Although the action lasts all night, it's safer to visit during the day or early evening. Use the pedestrian overpass from the Mercado Libertad to avoid the heavy traffic. ✉ *Calzada Independencia Sur, Zona Centro, between Av. Javier Mina and Álvaro Obregón.*

★ ❻ **Teatro Degollado.** Inaugurated in 1866, this magnificent theater was modeled after Milan's La Scala. Above the Corinthian columns gracing the entrance is a relief depicting Apollo and the nine Muses. Inside, the refurbished theater has kept its traditional red-and-gold color scheme, and the balconies ascend to a multitier dome adorned with Gerardo Suárez's depiction of Dante's *Divine Comedy.* The theater is the permanent home for the Jalisco Philharmonic and the Ballet Folclórico of the University of Guadalajara and hosts visiting orchestras, plays, and numerous other performances. According to legend, Guadalajara was founded on the site of what is now the **Plaza de los Fundadores,** which flanks the east side of the theater. A sculpted frieze on the rear wall of the Teatro Degollado depicts the historic event. ✉ *Av. Degollado, Centro Histórico, between Av. Hidalgo and Calle Morelos,* ☎ *33/3614–4773 or 33/3613–1115.* ⏲ *Weekdays 10–2.*

⓫ **Templo de Nuestra Señora de Aranzazú.** Don't be fooled by Our Lady of Aranzazú's drab brown stone exterior: inside is a spectacular Baroque gilt altar whose 14 niches contain life-size statues of saints. The intricate floral details on the walls and ceilings are painted in various hues and shades of blues, reds, and greens. The church is on the west side of Parque San Francisco, a small green oasis that draws food vendors, families, and senior citizens. ✉ *Av. 16 de Septiembre and Prisciliano Sánchez, Centro Histórico,* ☎ *33/3614–4083.* ⏲ *Weekdays 10–2 and 4–7, Sat. 10–2, Sun. 11:30–8:30.*

❾ **Templo de San Agustín.** One of the city's oldest churches, the venerable templo has been remodeled many times since its consecration in 1574, but the sacristy is original. The building to the left of the church, originally an Augustinian cloister, is now the **Escuela de Música** (School of Music) of the University of Guadalajara. Free recitals and concerts are held on its patio. ✉ *188 Calle Morelos at Av. Degollado, Centro Histórico,* ☎ *33/3614–5365.* ⏲ *Daily 8–1 and 5–8.*

18 **Templo Expiatorio.** The Church of Atonement is a striking Gothic structure. Modeled after the Orvieto Cathedral in Italy, it has a beautiful rose window above the choir and pipe organ, and lovely stained glass throughout. ✉ *930 Calle Díaz de León at Escorza, Centro Histórico,* ☎ *33/3825–3410.*

14 **Zoológico Guadalajara.** On the edge of the jagged Barranca Huentitán (Huentitán Canyon), the impressive zoo has more than 1,500 animals representing some 360 species. There's a kids' zoo, two aviaries, and a herpetarium with 130 species of reptiles, amphibians, and fish. For 50¢ you can take a guided train tour around part of the 40-hectare grounds. The adjacent **Selva Mágica,** or Magic Jungle amusement park, has carnival rides and attractions for about $1.30. Spanish speakers will enjoy the comical trained-animal shows, usually at 2 PM. The complex is 6 km (nearly 4 mi) northeast of downtown, near the planetarium. ✉ *Paseo del Zoológico 600, Zona Huentitlán,* ☎ *33/3674–4488 or 33/3674–3976.* *$3.15.* *Wed.–Sun. 10–6.*

OFF THE BEATEN PATH

BARRANCA DE OBLATOS – A spectacular 2,000-ft-deep gorge, Oblatos Canyon has hiking trails and the narrow Cola de Caballo waterfall, named for its horse-tail shape. You can see the falls from the zoo, or better yet, catch an Ixcantantus-bound bus from Glorieta La Normal, 10 blocks north of the cathedral. Ask to be let off at the view point, *mirador de la cascada.* You'll have about 20 minutes to view the falls before catching the bus upon its return to Guadalajara. ✉ *10 km (6 mi) northeast of downtown Guadalajara via Calzada Independencia Nte.*

DINING

Guadalajara eateries continue to be very affordable. Most are open throughout the evening, although seafood restaurants often close earlier. A number of places listed below have branches elsewhere in the city; our choices are either the most colorful, original locations, or those most convenient to the hotel areas. Because Guadalajara is a big, business-oriented city, it is advisable to dress well for more expensive restaurants.

$$–$$$ ✕ **El Farallón de Tepic.** Set underneath a bright-blue awning, this open-air establishment is reminiscent of beach restaurants in the nearby state of Nayarit. Order fresh *pescado*—usually red snapper or an equally mild fish—grilled with garlic or butter, in classic tomato sauce, breaded, or stuffed with seafood and cheese. Pescado *sarandeado* (Jalisco-style whole barbecued fish stuffed with vegetables) is worth every second of the 30-minute wait. Try the homemade flan for dessert. ✉ *Av. Niño Obrero 560, Zona Zapopan Sur,* ☎ *33/3121–2616 or 33/3121–9616. AE, MC, V. No dinner.*

$$ ✕ **Casa Bariachi.** This grand mariachi restaurant and bar is a favorite among locals, a place to celebrate with friends and enjoy some of Guadalajara's finest mariachi bands. Expect waiters as well as diners to sing along. The menu highlights steaks and alcoholic drinks, and the fiesta continues until 3 AM. ✉ *Av. Vallarta 2221, Zona Minerva,* ☎ *33/3615–0029. AE, MC, V. Closed Sun.*

$$ ✕ **La Destilería.** If you can't make it to the village of Tequila, here's the next best thing: a restaurant-cum-tequila-museum that serves novel Mexican specialties and 240 varieties of the fiery liquor. Antique photos of tequila distilleries and bilingual plaques explaining the history of tequila line the brick walls. ✉ *Av. México 2916, Zona Minerva,* ☎ *33/3640–3110. AE, MC, V. No dinner Sun.*

Guadalajara Dining and Lodging

Dining
Casa Bariachi 9
La Chata 25
La Destilería 13
La Estancia Gaucha . .11
El Farallón de Tepic . . .7
La Feria 27
Formosa Gardens . . .17
Karne Garibaldi 19
Mondo Cafe 20
La Pianola 8
Pierrot 18
La Rinconada 23
Santo Coyote 16
La Trattoria 10

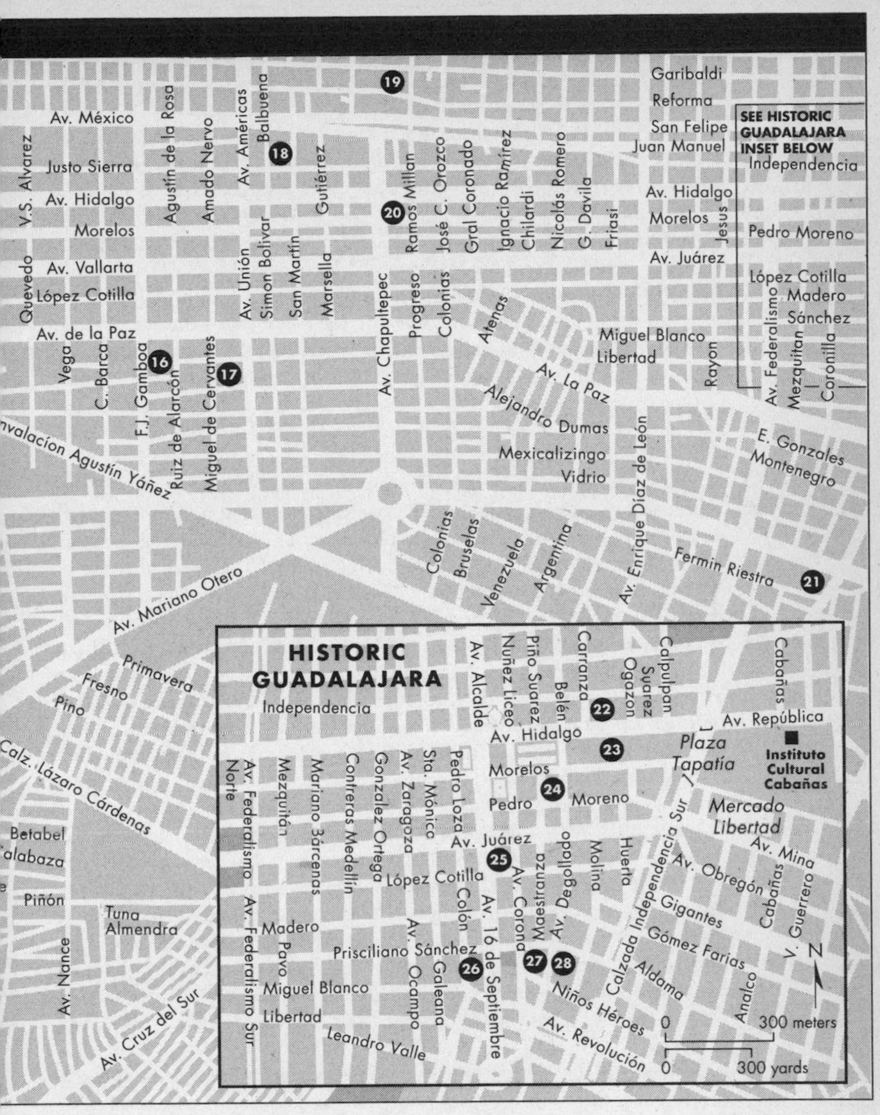

Lodging

Camino Real 6
Crowne Plaza Guadalajara 1
De Mendoza 22
Diana 15
Fiesta Americana . . .12
Francés 24
Hilton 5
Misión Carlton 21
Posada Guadalajara 4
Presidente Inter-Continental 2
Quinta Real 14
San Francisco Plaza 28
Santiago de Compostela 26
Vista Plaza del Sol . . .3

$$ ✕ **La Estancia Gaucha.** In a town that loves Argentine cuisine, this no-nonsense steak establishment is widely considered the cream of the crop. Among the best cuts here are the *churrasco estancia* (rib eye) and the *bife de chorizo* (essentially New York strip). The empanadas and the *parillada* (a mixed grill that often includes beef, sausages, and selected organ meats) are also delicious. Piano music accompanies dinner Wednesday through Saturday. ✉ *Av. Niños Héroes 2860, Zona Minerva,* ☎ *33/3122–6565 and 33/3122–9985. AE, MC, V. No dinner Sun.*

$$ ★ ✕ **La Feria.** Mariachis, *charros* (talented, elegantly clad equestrians performing rope tricks), and traditional Mexican folkloric dances make for a festive atmosphere at La Feria. Come for a late lunch or appetizers to catch the afternoon show, or for a late-night dinner to catch the evening show. The shrimp tacos are scrumptious, and meat lovers will want to share the parillada for two. After the show, play *lotería* (a type of bingo) for a bottle of tequila or have a parakeet choose your fortune. ✉ *Av. Corona 291, Zona Centro,* ☎ *33/3613–1812 or 33/3613–7150. AE, MC, V.*

$$ ★ ✕ **Pierrot.** This quiet French dining room offers mouthwatering pâtés followed by seafood, chicken, and beef entrées—among them trout almondine, osso buco, and pâté-stuffed chicken breast in tarragon sauce. Wall-mounted lamps with fringed velvet shades and fresh flowers on each table lend a gracious touch. ✉ *Justo Sierra 2355, Zona Minerva,* ☎ *33/3630–2087 or 33/3615–4758. AE, MC, V. Closed Sun.*

$$ ★ ✕ **La Rinconada.** Popular for its old Guadalajara charm, La Rinconada has appeared in numerous Mexican movies and TV comedies. The heart of an 1897 farm, its dining area has arched pillars and high vaulted ceilings. Local businesspeople in search of excellent steak and other international and Mexican dishes fill the colonial dining room, which feels equally welcoming to casually dressed tourists. Breakfast is served daily beginning at 8. ✉ *Calle Morelos 86, Centro Histórico, at Plaza Tapatía,* ☎ *33/3613–9914 or 33/3613–9925. AE, MC, V.*

$$ ★ ✕ **Santo Coyote.** At this haven of Mexican *nouvelle cuisine* in the former U.S. Consul General's residence, murals of goddesses adorn one dining area, waterfalls flow, and candles burn at a huge shrine to Mexico's patron saint—the Virgin of Guadalupe. Try the wood-fired roast or grilled *cabrito* (goat)—a house specialty—or consider the baby back ribs topped with a tamarind and pepper sauce, or marrow soup. Service and presentation are excellent. ✉ *Lerdo de Tejada 2379, Zona Minerva,* ☎ *33/3616–6978. AE, MC, V.*

$$ ✕ **La Trattoria.** Guadalajara's top Italian restaurant has retained its reputation as a family place committed to good value. Pictures of Italian piazzas decorate the dining room, which has closely spaced tables. The menu's best options include *spaghetti frutti di mare* (seafood spaghetti) and *scaloppine alla Marsala* (beef medallions with Marsala and mushrooms). The homemade bread is delicious, and all meals include the salad bar. ✉ *Av. Niños Héroes 3051, Zona Minerva,* ☎ *33/3122–1817 and 33/3122–4425. AE, MC, V.*

$ ✕ **La Chata.** Black-and-white photos of old Guadalajara and exquisitely glazed plates adorn the white walls of this popular, casual downtown eatery. Start off with guacamole and then savor the zesty *chiles rellenos* (stuffed peppers). Or try one of the spicy roasted meat dishes, such as *carne tampiqueña,* served with rice, beans, taco, guacamole, and enchilada. Complement your meal with a tangy *jugo de lima,* the distinctive lime juice popular throughout Jalisco. Breakfast is served as well. ✉ *Av. Corona 126, Zona Centro, between Avs. López Cotilla and Juárez,* ☎ *33/3613–0588. AE, MC, V.*

$ ✕ **Formosa Gardens.** For a taste of home, it's no wonder Guadalajara's Asian residents visit Formosa Gardens, which has sister restaurants in Beijing and Taiwan. Peking duck is crisp and tasty here, but go for the deep-fried orange beef—sweet and tangy. This beautiful mansion opens onto a garden dining area, where each table is set with crisp linens. ✉ *Av. Union 322, Zona Centro,* ☎ *33/3615–7415. MC, V. No dinner Sun.*

$ ✕ **Karne Garibaldi.** According to the *Guinness Book of World Records,* this Tapatío institution has the fastest service in the world—at 13.5 seconds. This lightning service is possible because there's only one thing on the menu: *carne en su jugo,* a tasty combination of finely diced beef and bacon simmered in a rich beef broth. Served with grilled onions, tortillas, and refried beans mixed with corn, it's a great down-home meal. ✉ *Garibaldi 1306, Zona Centro,* ☎ *33/3826–1286. AE, MC, V.*

$ ✕ **Mondo Cafe.** The alluring fragrance from Mondo's coffee roaster wafts into wide, tree-lined Avenida Chapultepec. Foreign and local students frequent this favorite coffee house for its large picture-window views onto the busy avenue and for various blends of fresh-roasted coffee. Hearty breakfasts are served daily beginning at 7, along with mixed fruit and vegetable juices and flavored coffees. The American owner offers beer and wine as well. ✉ *Av. Chapultepec 48, Zona Centro, at Pedro Moreno,* ☎ *33/3616–2709. V.*

$ ★ ✕ **La Pianola.** The entrance—through what looks like an open-air kitchen where costumed women are making tortillas—may be misleading to first-timers: in back is a large restaurant and garden with an excellent, varied Mexican menu. Specialties include pozole and chilies *en nogada,* spicy stuffed chili peppers in a walnut cream sauce. The signature player-piano music accompanies the meal. ✉ *Av. México 3220, Zona Minerva,* ☎ *33/3813–1385 or 33/3813–2412. AE, MC, V.*

LODGING

Guadalajara has a variety of hotels in all price ranges. Call ahead if you're apprehensive about noise levels outside your hotel room; many hotels are on busy intersections, in which case rooms higher up or in the back tend to be less noisy. If fresh air is important to you, ask if there are windows or balconies, as some of the most exclusive hotels have windows that won't open.

The rates given are based on the year-round or peak-season price; promotional rates may be lower, and business-oriented hotels may offer lower rates on weekends. You can expect hotels in the $$$ and $$$$ categories to have purified-water systems, English-language TV channels, a concierge, and laundry and dry cleaning service. Many hotels now offer in-room data ports and room safes.

$$$$ 🏨 **Hilton.** Adjacent to the Guadalajara World Trade Center and Expo, the Hilton is a premier business destination. Although the hotel lacks character, it has modern furnishings and considerable business services, including a multilingual staff, a private executive floor, and a well-equipped business center. The hotel caters to convention goers. ✉ *Av. de las Rosas 2933, Zona Cruz del Sur 44540,* ☎ *33/3678–0505, 800/003–1400, or 800/445–8667,* FAX *33/3678–0511,* WEB *www.guadalajara.hilton.com. 402 rooms, 20 suites. 2 restaurants, in-room data ports, pool, gym, hair salon, massage, bar, concierge floor, business services, meeting rooms, no-smoking rooms. AE, DC, MC, V.*

$$$$ ★ 🏨 **Quinta Real.** Stone and brick walls, colonial arches, and objets d'art highlight public areas of this luxury hotel on the city's west side. Suites are plush and intimate, with select neocolonial furnishings, including glass-top writing tables with carved-stone pedestals and fireplaces with marble mantelpieces. Tile bathrooms have marble sinks and bronze fixtures; some suites have sunken hot tubs. Deluxe tower accommodations are the most lavish, although removed from the gar-

dens below. The hotel provides 24-hour medical service. ✉ *Av. México 2727, Zona Minerva 44680, at Av. López Mateos Norte,* ☎ *33/3615–0000, 800/713–1966, or 800/457–4000,* FAX *33/3630–1797,* WEB *www.quintareal.com. 152 suites. Restaurant, in-room data ports, pool, bar, baby-sitting, concierge, business services, meeting rooms, car rental, no-smoking rooms. AE, MC, V.*

$$$ **Camino Real.** A 15-minute cab ride from downtown will bring you to the first of Guadalajara's luxury hotels. Although its five stars are likely posted more for reputation and atmosphere than for actual creature comforts, guest rooms are large and well decorated, with many surrounding the hotel pool and gardens, where trios serenade during the excellent Sunday morning buffet brunch. Rooms in the rear face noisy Avenida Vallarta. ✉ *Av. Vallarta 5005, Zona Minerva 45040,* ☎ *33/3134–2424, 800/901–2300, or 800/722–6466,* FAX *33/3134–2404,* WEB *www.caminoreal.com/guadalajara. 195 rooms, 10 suites. 3 restaurants, coffee shop, in-room data ports, putting green, tennis court, 4 pools, bar, baby-sitting, playground, concierge, no-smoking rooms. AE, DC, MC, V.*

$$$ **Crowne Plaza Guadalajara.** Well-tended gardens and towering shade trees full of birds surround a large pool, bringing a bit of nature to this hotel near the convention center. The hotel's public areas are tastefully decorated with antiques and reproductions. Rooms have marble baths and lots of natural light. Tower rooms have city views; those in the two-story building surround the pool and gardens. Rooms in the back are loud: they're near the children's play area and caged, shrieking macaws. ✉ *Av. López Mateos Sur 2500, Zona Minerva 45050,* ☎ *33/3634–1034, 800/365–5500, or 800/227–6963,* FAX *33/3631–9393,* WEB *www.basshotels.com/crowneplaza. 380 rooms, 4 suites. 3 restaurants, in-room data ports, miniature golf, 2 tennis courts, pool, gym, hair salon, bar, shops, baby-sitting, playground, concierge floor, business services, airport shuttle, car rental, no-smoking floor. AE, DC, MC.*

$$$ ★ **Fiesta Americana.** The dramatic glass facade of this luxury high-rise faces the Minerva Fountain, on the city's west side. Four glass-enclosed elevators ascend above the 14-story atrium lobby to the city's largest guest rooms, which have modern furnishings, marble bathrooms, and panoramic views. The business center is one of the best-equipped in the city. ✉ *Aurelio Aceves 225, Zona Minerva 44100,* ☎ *33/3825–3434, 800/504–5000, or 800/343–7821,* FAX *33/3630–3725,* WEB *www.fiestamericana.com. 352 rooms, 39 suites. Restaurant, coffee shop, in-room data ports, 2 tennis courts, pool, gym, hair salon, bar, shops, baby-sitting, concierge, business services, meeting rooms, car rental, no-smoking floor. AE, DC, MC, V.*

$$$ **Presidente Inter-Continental.** A modern hotel with a multiplane mirrored facade and a 12-story atrium lobby, the Inter-Continental attracts sophisticated business clientele. For the best city view, request a room on an upper floor facing the Plaza del Sol shopping center. There's a Tane silver shop on the premises, and you can use nearby golf and tennis facilities. The hotel's health club is the best in the city. ✉ *Av. López Mateos Sur and Moctezuma, Zona Minerva 45050,* ☎ *33/3678–1234, 800/904–4400, or 800/327–0200,* FAX *33/3678–1222,* WEB *www.interconti.com. 381 rooms, 30 suites. Restaurant, coffee shop, in-room data ports, pool, health club, massage, sauna, spa, steam room, bar, shops, baby-sitting, concierge floor, business services, meeting rooms, airport shuttle, car rental. AE, DC, MC, V.*

$$ ★ **De Mendoza.** This downtown hotel is convenient—on a quiet side street a block from the Teatro Degollado—and elegant, with its impressive postcolonial architecture and refined atmosphere. Low, beamed ceilings, hand-carved furniture and doors, and wrought-iron railings decorate

public areas and the clean, comfortable rooms. Twenty rooms have balconies with tables and chairs overlooking the small but inviting courtyard pool, outside the hotel's acclaimed international restaurant. ✉ *Calle Venustiano Carranza 16, Centro Histórico 44100,* ☎ *33/3613–4646 or 800/361–2600,* FAX *33/3613–7310,* WEB *www.demendoza.com.mx. 87 rooms, 17 suites. Restaurant, in-room data ports, pool, meeting rooms, no-smoking room. AE, DC, MC, V.*

$$ **Diana.** Mexican and European travelers favor this hotel two blocks from the Minerva Fountain. The white stucco lobby adjoins a small lounge and busy restaurant. Standard-size rooms have white-on-white walls and ceilings and brightly patterned curtains and bedspreads; the quietest rooms are on the upper floors in the rear. Some suites have private saunas. The small Internet center has three computers. ✉ *Circunvalación Agustín Yáñez 2760, Zona Minerva 44100,* ☎ *33/3615–5510, 33/3615–6428, or 800/024–8181,* FAX *33/3630–3685. 134 rooms, 15 suites. Restaurant, coffee shop, pool, bar, airport shuttle. AE, DC, MC, V.*

$$ ★ **Francés.** Guadalajara's oldest hotel, dating from 1610, is also a national monument. Stone columns and colonial arches surround a three-story enclosed atrium lobby with a polished marble fountain and cut-crystal chandeliers. Rooms vary in size, and the authentic colonial ambience—with white stucco walls, polished wood floors, and high-beam ceilings—seems a touch spare by modern standards. Rooms facing Calle Maestranza have tiny 17th-century balconies, but also street noise. The location in the historic center is a plus. ✉ *Calle Maestranza 35, Centro Histórico 44100,* ☎ *33/3613–1190, 3613–0936, or 800/718–5309,* FAX *33/3658–2831,* WEB *www.hotelfrances.com. 50 rooms, 10 suites. Restaurant, fans, bar, dance club, car rental. AE, MC, V.*

$$ **Misión Carlton.** This modern 20-story hotel on the edge of downtown has large rooms; those on the upper floors have spectacular city views and provide a retreat from the horrendous street noise. Ivy-draped walls surround the rear gardens and fountain. Although the hotel is convenient for tourists, it caters to the business traveler. ✉ *Av. Niños Héroes 125, Zona Centro 44100, at Av. 16 de Septiembre,* ☎ *33/3614–7272 or 800/967–6400,* FAX *33/3613–5539. 193 rooms, 1 suite. Restaurant, pool, hair salon, 2 bars, shop, baby-sitting, concierge, meeting rooms, no-smoking floor. AE, MC, V.*

$$ **Posada Guadalajara.** Rooms in this colonial-style hotel open onto airy hallways with wrought-iron rails that overlook the small patio and its enormous stone fountain. Accommodations are clean and comfortable, with carved-wood furniture. In addition to its loyal international patrons, the Posada welcomes visiting sports teams, so evenings here can be festive or raucous. The hotel is south of Calzada Lázaro Cárdenas, about 1½ km (1 mi) northeast of Plaza del Sol. ✉ *Av. López Mateos Sur 1280, Centro Histórico 45040,* ☎ *33/3121–2022 or 33/3121–2424,* FAX *33/3122–1834,* WEB *www.posadaguadalajara.com.mx. 152 rooms, 18 suites. Restaurant, pool, bar, baby-sitting. AE, DC, MC, V.*

$$ **Santiago de Compostela.** This cozy downtown hotel in a converted 19th-century building is across from the Parque San Francisco and offers simple, modern accommodations. More expensive rooms overlooking the park and Templo de Nuestra Señora de Aranzazú have tall, narrow windows with iron balconies. Inside rooms open onto an atrium. All the bathrooms here have tubs, and the suites have Jacuzzis. The open-air pool and sunning area on the fifth floor overlook the park. A drawback is that only one small elevator services the six floors. ✉ *Colón 272, Centro Histórico 44100,* ☎ *33/3613–8880 or 800/365–5300,* FAX *33/3658–1925. 91 rooms, 4 suites. Restaurant, pool, bar, shop. AE, DC, MC, V.*

$$ **Vista Plaza del Sol.** Location and price bring families, visiting soccer teams, and tour groups to this two-building hotel at the south end of the Plaza del Sol shopping center. Rooms and public areas are painted glossy white; accommodations in the cylindrical tower are a bit larger and have views of the shopping center. The popular restaurant has piping hot coffee and buffet or à la carte dining for all three meals. ✉ *Avs. López Mateos Sur 2375 at Mariano Otero, Zona Minerva 45050,* ☎ *33/3647–8790 or 888/300–6394,* FAX *33/3122–9685,* WEB *www.vistahotel.com. 341 rooms, 16 suites. Restaurant, coffee shop, pool, hair salon, bar, shop, baby-sitting, concierge floor, meeting rooms, car rental, travel services. AE, DC, MC, V.*

$ **San Francisco Plaza.** On a quiet downtown side street in the historic district, this attractive two-story colonial-style building is easy to spot thanks to its pale orange facade. Potted palms and geraniums surround a gurgling stone fountain in the pleasant courtyard sitting area, and copper wall lamps lend an old-fashioned air to the sparsely furnished rooms, with somewhat threadbare furnishings. ✉ *Calle Degollado 267, Centro Histórico 44100,* ☎ *33/3613–8954,* FAX *33/3613–3257. 74 rooms, 2 suites. Restaurant, laundry service. AE, MC, V.*

NIGHTLIFE AND THE ARTS

Guadalajara is an active cultural and performing-arts center, with excellent local talent and well-known artists and entertainers from abroad. The U.S. and Canadian communities around Lake Chapala have developed a schedule of English-language cultural events. During the afternoon and evening, many cafés along Avenida Chapultepec also have live music.

The Arts

DANCE

Ballet Folclórico of the University of Guadalajara. The university's internationally acclaimed troupe offers traditional Mexican folkloric dances and music in the Teatro Degollado every Sunday at 10 AM. ☎ *33/3614–4773.* *$2.50–$11.*

PERFORMANCE VENUES

Cine Cinematógrafo I, II, and III. Founded by two Guadalajara-area movie buffs, these theaters present mostly art-house variety films—often in English with Spanish subtitles. ✉ *Av. Vallarta 1102, Zona Minerva,* ☎ *33/3825–0514;* ✉ *Av. México 2222, Zona Centro, at Plaza Amistad,* ☎ *33/3630–1208;* ✉ *Av. Patria 600, Zona Centro,* ☎ *33/3629–4780.*

Ex-Convento del Carmen. Classical music performances are held in the former convent during "Martes Musical," Tuesdays at 8:30 PM; literature-oriented Wednesdays are dedicated to book presentations or poetry readings. Fridays and Saturdays at 8:30 PM and Sundays at 6 PM different theatrical presentations are the norm. There's also a spacious art gallery and bookshop. It's 6½ blocks west of Avenida 16 de Septiembre. ✉ *Av. Juárez 638, Centro Histórico,* ☎ *33/3614–7184.*

Instituto Cultural Cabañas. Large-scale theater, dance, and musical performances take place on a patio here. The Tolsá Chapel hosts more intimate events, and subtitled English-language films are often shown in the theater. Exhibitions of both Mexican and foreign art are on display, and free art classes are given. ✉ *Calle Cabañas 8, Centro Histórico, at Plaza Tapatía,* ☎ *33/3617–4322 or 33/3617–4440.*

Plaza de Armas. The State Band of Jalisco, the Municipal Band, and sometimes even the Philharmonic play at the bandstand on Tuesday, Thursday, and Sunday evenings around 6:30. ✉ *Av. Corona, Centro*

Histórico, between Calle Morelos and Pedro Moreno, across from Palacio de Gobierno.

Teatro Degollado. Nationally and internationally famous artists perform here year-round. The refurbished velvet seats are comfortable, the acoustics are excellent, and the central air-conditioning can be a treat. ✉ *Calle Degollado, Centro Histórico, between Av. Hidalgo and Calle Morelos,* ☎ *33/3614–4773 or 33/3613–1115.*

SYMPHONY

Orquesta Filarmónica de Jalisco. Conducted by Maestro Guillermo Salvador, performances take place Sunday at 12:30 PM and Friday night at 8:30 at the Teatro Degollado. ☎ *33/3658–3812 or 33/3658–3819.* *$2–$12.*

Nightlife

A string of Guadalajara nightspots generally geared to the under-30 crowd lines Avenida Vallarta and the Centro area. Live tropical tunes Wednesday through Saturday after 10 draw crowds to **Cubilete** (✉ General Río Seco 9, Centro Histórico, in the Nine Corners area of downtown, ☎ 33/3613–2096). The Fiesta Americana hotel's sleek **Lobby Bar** has live but low-key entertainment, with jazz most nights after 8. For a bit of local color, stop downtown at **La Maestranza** (✉ Calle Maestranza 179, Centro, ☎ 33/3613–5878), a renovated 1940s cantina chock-full of bullfighting memorabilia. The Crowne Plaza's jungle-theme **Manglar** (✉ Av. López Mateos Sur 2500, Zona Minerva, ☎ 33/3634–1034) has a game room and large-screen TV in addition to live Latin music.

A visit to central Guadalajara wouldn't be complete without a stop at **La Fuente** (✉ Calle Suarez, Centro Histórico, ☎ no phone, ⏲ noon–after midnight), perhaps the most charming and unpretentious cantina in town. You'll find it around the corner from the Palacio Legislativo, directly behind the famed statue of a raving Miguel Hidalgo, attracting an eclectic crowd of business types, bohemian intellectuals, and working-class people who come for the cheap drinks, lively conversation, and live traditional music. For a few pesos, the regular trio—made up of a pianist, bassist, and violinist—will play requests, even allowing would-be singers to take the stage and make fools of themselves. Nightly after 9 (except Monday), patrons cluster around the small stage at **La Peña Cuicacalli** (✉ Av. Niños Héroes 1988, Zona Centro, at Suarez traffic circle, ☎ 33/3825–4690). There's *rock en español* on Tuesday, and folk music from Mexico, Latin America, and Spain most other nights.

DANCE CLUBS AND DISCOS

A hot spot in town is the 94th **Hard Rock Cafe** (✉ Av. Vallarta 2125, Zona Minerva, ☎ 33/3616–4560), in the Centro Magno mall. Live bands play rock, naturally, Wednesday through Saturday from 10 PM on. Well-dressed professional types 25 and older like the classic rock at **El Mito** (✉ Vallarta 2425, Zona Minerva, at Centro Magno shopping center, ☎ 33/3615–7246). You can dance most of the night to popular Latin and European music at the multilevel **Tropigala** (✉ Av. López Mateos Sur 2188, Zona Minerva, across from Plaza del Sol shopping center, ☎ 33/3122–5553 or 33/3122–7903).

Maxim's (✉ Calle Maestranza 35, Zona Centro, ☎ 33/3613–1190, 33/3613–0936, or 800/718–5309) in the Hotel Francés, is one of the better downtown discos. **Salón Veracruz** (✉ Manzano 486, Zona Centro, behind the Hotel Carlton, ☎ 33/3613–4422) is a spartan, old-style dance hall where a 15-piece band keeps hundreds of hoofers moving to Colombian cumbia, Dominican merengue, and *danzón,* a waltzlike dance invented in Cuba and favored in Veracruz. It's open Wednesday through Sunday 10 PM–3:30 AM.

OUTDOOR ACTIVITIES AND SPORTS

Participant Sports

Fitness Clubs

Celebrities visit **Gold's Gym** (✉ Av. Xóchitl 4203, Zona Minerva, ☎ 33/3647–0420) for its unique amenities, such as a climbing wall, a full basketball court, and Tae Kwon Do lessons. Guest passes are available for about $7 a day. The health club at the **Presidente Inter-Continental** (☎ 33/3678–1227) is open 5:30 AM–11 PM to nonguests for about $12 a day. It includes a fitness center, heated pool, massage, and spa.

Golf

Several golf clubs admit nonmembers upon payment of a greens fee of $40–$100. Across from Montenegro Park is the **Atlas Chapalita Golf Club** (✉ Carretera Guadalajara-Chapala Km 6.5, El Salto, ☎ 33/3689–2620 or 33/3689–0240; 🎫 $47; ⏲ closed Mon.). Tuesday and Thursday are the least-crowded nights at **Las Cañadas Country Club** (✉ Av. Bosques San Isidro 777, ☎ 33/3685–0285 or 33/3685–0412; 🎫 $50–$55; ⏲ closed Mon.). As is the case at most courses, rates rise on weekends at the **Club de Golf Santa Anita** (✉ Carretera a Morelia Km 6.5, ☎ 33/3686–0321). **El Palomar** (✉ Paseo del Palomar 220, ☎ 33/3684–4434 or 33/3684–4436) is the most exclusive country club in Guadalajara.

Tennis

Nonguests are allowed to use the **Camino Real** court (✉ Av. Vallarta 5005, Zona Minerva, ☎ 33/3134–2424) for a fee. It's open 7 AM–10 PM. English is spoken at the **Club de Tenis Royal** (✉ San Ignacio 316, Zona Minerva, ☎ 33/3647–5348), where you can take lessons. It's open weekdays 7 AM–10 PM, Saturday 7–7, and Sunday 7–3. The **Crowne Plaza Guadalajara** (✉ Av. López Mateos Sur 2500, Zona Minerva, ☎ 33/3634–1034) allows nonguests to use its two courts, open 7 AM–dark, for a fee.

Water Parks

Approximately 50 km (31 mi) from Guadalajara are two water parks with thermal pools and lots of entertainment for adults and children. The parks can be reached most easily by taxi, or by bus from the old or new bus terminals to Villa Corona. **Agua Caliente** (✉ Carretera a Barra de Navidad Km 56, Villa Corona, ☎ 33/3778–0022 or 33/3778–0784; 🎫 $2) has a large artificial wave pool and large water slides as well as thermal pools, gardens, and restaurants. All of the pools and facilities are open on weekends; some are closed midweek. **Chimulco** (✉ Camino Real Km ½, ☎ 33/3778–0014, in the village of Villa Corona; 🎫 $4), in a more intimate setting, serves hot food and has a thermal pool, water slides, boat rides, and a large children's play area.

Spectator Sports

Bullfighting

Corridas (bullfights) are held Sunday at 4:30 PM at **Plaza Nuevo Progreso.** Tickets are sold for the *sol* (sunny) or *sombra* (shady) side of the bullring. You can buy tickets at the bullring (about 5 km [3 mi] northeast of downtown) or at the bullring's booth in Plaza México. *Novilleros* (apprentice matadors) work the cape many mornings between 7 AM and 1 PM, and it doesn't cost anything to watch them practice. ✉ *M. Pirineos 1930 and Calzada Independencia Nte., Zona Huentitlán, across from Estadio Jalisco,* ☎ *33/3637–9982 or 33/3651–8378.* 🎫 *$9–$60.*

Charreadas

Charreadas take place year-round at the **Lienzo Charros de Jalisco** Sunday at noon. The competitors participate in 10 equestrian and roping events, mariachis or *bandas* (brass bands) perform during breaks, and food and drinks are available. ✉ *Av. Dr. R. Michel 577, Zona Olimpica, next to Parque Agua Azul,* ☎ *33/3619–3232.* 🎫 *About $2.*

Soccer

Two professional teams (and a university team) play at **Estadio Jalisco,** including one of Mexico's favorite teams, Las Chivas ("the she-goats") de Guadalajara, who generally play on Sunday. The two regular seasons run January through April or May and July through December. ✉ *Siete Colinas 1772 and Calzada Independencia Nte., Zona Huentitlán, across from the bullring,* ☎ *33/3637–0301 or 33/3637–0299.* 🎫 *$1.50–$26.*

SHOPPING

Guadalajara has a great variety of high-quality merchandise at low prices, although you also can find high-priced low-quality items. Store hours tend to be Monday through Saturday 9 or 10 until 8, and Sunday 10–2; some shops close during lunch, usually 2–4 or 2–5, and others close all day on Sunday. In Guadalajara, shopping malls are springing up everywhere: the metropolitan area now has more than 50. Shopping-mall stores generally stay open during lunch and on weekends. *Tianguis* (street markets) run every day throughout the Guadalajara area. If you're interested in traditional arts and crafts, browse about in Tlaquepaque and Tonalá.

Malls and Shops

Centro Magno. A number of upscale boutiques and bistros, along with a large cineplex and a Hard Rock Cafe, make this center a trendy shopping and dining spot. It's a few blocks from the Minerva. ✉ *Av. Vallarta 2425, Zona Minerva,* ☎ *33/3630–1113 or 33/3630–1776.* ⏲ *Daily 10–10.*

El Charro, an excellent leather-goods store, has branches in Plaza del Sol (☎ 33/3122–5148 or 33/3647–5731) as well as downtown (✉ Av. Juárez 148, Zona Centro, ☎ 33/3614–7599 or 33/3614–9743).

Galería del Calzado. The 60 stores in this westside complex all sell shoes. Guadalajara is one of Mexico's leading shoe centers, and high-quality footwear and accessories are available here, many at lower prices than you find in the States. ✉ *Avs. México 3225, Zona Minerva,* ☎ *33/3647–6422.* ⏲ *Mon.–Sat. 11–9, Sun. 11–8:30.*

La Gran Plaza. A sleek glass-and-steel exterior houses 334 commercial spaces and a 14-plex cinema, surrounded by a large food court and some quality restaurants. It's east of the Guadalajara Chamber of Commerce and the Camino Real hotel. ✉ *Av. Vallarta 3959, Zona Minerva,* ☎ *33/3122–3004.* ⏲ *Daily 10–9:30.*

Plaza del Sol. The city's largest mall sprawls like a park, with 270 commercial spaces, outdoor patios, trees and garden areas, and parking for 2,100 cars. It's across from the Presidente Inter-Continental hotel. ✉ *Avs. López Mateos Sur 2375, Zona Minerva, at Mariano Otero,* ☎ *33/3121–5950.* ⏲ *Weekdays 10–8, Sat. 10–9, Sun. 10–7.*

Markets and Arts and Crafts

Although the shops listed below are great for shopping for crafts from the area and from throughout Mexico, the best shops—for crafts, fine furniture, and home furnishings—are found in the satellite towns of Tlaquepaque and Tonalá.

El Baratillo. This flea market—one of the world's largest—encompasses 30 city blocks lined with stalls, tents, and blankets, all piled high with new, used, and antique merchandise. ✉ *On and around Calle Esteban Loera, Zona Centro, some 15 blocks east of Mercado Libertad.* ⊙ *Sun. 7–5.*

Bazar Capitán. Serious art-, crafts-, and antiques-lovers may want to consult with Roberto Alvarado, who has devoted decades to the art and antiques business. Alvarado runs personalized buying tours, scheduling appointments in private homes depending on clients' interests. One month's advance notice is requested, although visits can sometimes be accommodated at shorter notice. ✉ *Argentina 73, Zona Minerva, ½ block off Av. Vallarta,* ☎ *33/3827–1990,* FAX *33/3640–1292.*

Calle Esteban Alatorre. Several blocks of stores selling shoes and leather goods—all reasonably priced—line this street. ✉ *East of Calzada Independencia Nte. and 4 blocks north of Av. Hidalgo, Centro.*

Instituto de Artesanías Jaliscienses. Run by the state government, this store has a wide selection of the exquisite blown glass and hand-glazed pottery typical of Jalisco artisans. Merchandise—including belts, wood furniture, silver, and Huichol art—is sold at fixed prices. ✉ *Calzadas González Gallo 20 and Independencia Sur, Zona Olimpica, next to Parque Agua Azul,* ☎ *33/3619–4664.* ⊙ *Weekdays 10–6, Sat. 10–5, Sun. 10–3.*

Mercado Libertad. Also known as the Mercado San Juan de Dios, the Liberty Market is one of Latin America's largest enclosed markets. Within a three-square-block area, you can browse through more than 1,000 stalls selling everything from clothing and crafts to live animals and gold watches. It's a good place to shop for typical silver jewelry. ✉ *Calzada Independencia Sur between Dionísio Rodríguez and Av. Javier Mina, Zona Centro.* ⊙ *Daily 10–8.*

SIDE TRIPS FROM GUADALAJARA

No trip to Guadalajara is complete without an excursion out of the city, whether you're into shopping for crafts in Tlaquepaque and Tonalá, taking in the towns surrounding Lake Chapala, or unlocking the secrets of Mexican firewater in Tequila.

Tlaquepaque and Tonalá

For inveterate shoppers, a combined visit to the crafts meccas of Tlaquepaque and Tonalá makes a perfect day trip from Guadalajara. You'll find at least one good bed-and-breakfast in Tlaquepaque if you really want to shop until you drop, or if you'd just like to relax in a charming town that's reminiscent of Guadalajara, but less congested and more picturesque. Those preferring a more tranquil base of operations might even consider staying in Tlaquepaque and taking one or more day trips into Guadalajara, only 15–20 minutes away by cab.

Tlaquepaque

7 km (4½ mi) southeast of downtown Guadalajara.

Tlaquepaque is known throughout Mexico as an arts-and-crafts center. Among its offerings are intricate blown-glass miniatures; exquisite pottery; jewelry, silver, and copperware; leather and hand-carved wood furniture; and handwoven clothing. More than 300 shops—many of which are run by families with centuries-old traditions of workmanship—line pedestrian malls and plazas in this charming town.

Tlaquepaque's craft heritage began with the distinctive decorated pottery fashioned by the Tonaltecan Indians, who lived in the area in the

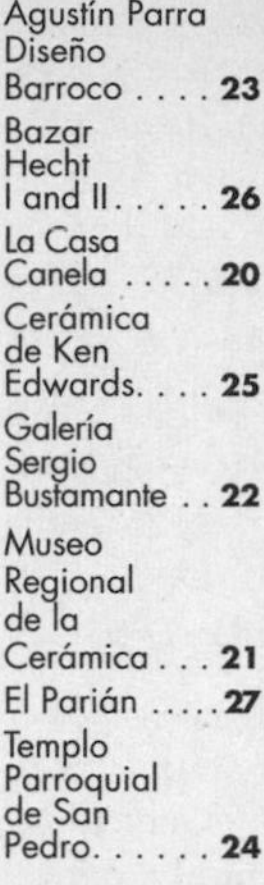

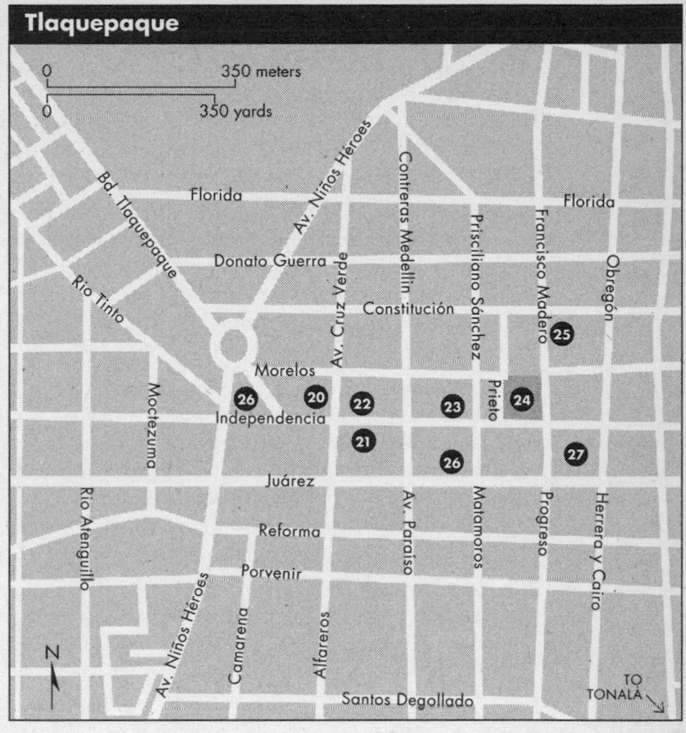

mid-16th century. After local authorities met here to sign a regional proclamation of independence from Spain in 1821, the village emerged from obscurity as wealthy Guadalajara residents began to build palatial summer houses—many of which have been restored and now house shops and restaurants. As more people came to purchase the pottery and intricate glass creations (glass-blowing was introduced from Europe in 1870), weavers, jewelers, and wood-carvers also arrived and built workshops. In 1973 downtown Tlaquepaque underwent a major renovation, the highlight of which was the creation of a wide pedestrian mall, Calle Independencia. More shops line Calle Juárez, a block south, as well as the many side streets.

A GOOD WALK

Begin your tour near the west end of pedestrian-only Calle Independencia, at **La Casa Canela** ⑳, a pretty venue with plenty of crafts for sale. A half block southeast, the modest but worthwhile **Museo Regional de la Cerámica** ㉑ shows the different styles of regional pottery through the ages, while across the street, **Galería Sergio Bustamante** ㉒ sells contemporary ceramics and folk art. Continue east on Calle Independencia, cross Avenida Paraíso, and you will come upon exquisite Baroque-style statues, wood-and-gilt altarpieces, and other treasures for sale at **Agustín Parra Diseño Barroco** ㉓. One block east, on the lively main plaza, is tiny **Templo Parroquial de San Pedro** ㉔. After visiting the parish church, walk north on Madero from the northeast corner of the square to **Cerámica de Ken Edwards** ㉕, the town's first stoneware workshop. Shopping opportunities continue at **Bazar Hecht** ㉖, on Juárez just west of Sánchez and at the newer Independencia location. You can now celebrate your fine purchases (or your admirable restraint) with a drink and appetizer at the festive **El Parián** ㉗, catercorner from the Plaza Hidalgo, at Independencia near Calle Progreso.

23 **Agustín Parra Diseño Barroco.** Behind the doors of this shop is a mystical gallery of carved wooden pieces and ceramic figurines. Influenced by the unique Baroque style of 17th-century New Spain, artist Agustín Parra creates everything from ornate tables and doors to religious icons. ✉ *Calle Independencia 158,* ☎ *33/3657–8530 or 33/3657–0316.* ⏲ *Weekdays 10–2 and 3–7, Sat. 10–7, Sun. 10–4.*

26 **Bazar Hecht (I and II).** The Hecht brothers opened their second store after outgrowing the showroom in their first one on Juárez. Visit both and see why the Hecht family is known throughout Mexico for its high-quality, ornately sculpted tables, armoires, and chairs. ✉ *Juárez 162,* ☎ *33/3659–0205;* ✉ *Independencia 280-A,* ☎ *33/3635–1961.* ⏲ *Weekdays 10–2:30 and 3:30–7, Sat. 10:30–2:30 and 3:30–7.*

20 **La Casa Canela.** Color seems to explode in the extensive shop's more than 24 rooms, each exquisitely decorated with vivid papier-mâché flowers, finely glazed pottery, and elegant furniture. All surround a courtyard blooming with tropical plants. Free tequila and snacks are served on Saturday. ✉ *Calle Independencia 258,* ☎ *33/3635–3717 or 33/3657–1343.* ⏲ *Weekdays 10–2 and 3–7, Sat. 10–6, Sun. 11–3.*

25 **Cerámica de Ken Edwards.** In 1959 Ken Edwards introduced more durable stoneware (which is by nature lead-free) into the Tonalá pottery vernacular—the original local earthenware is more fragile. His store is filled with brightly colored, hand-decorated plates, cups, and vases. Edwards also has a store in Tonalá. ✉ *Francisco Madero 70,* ☎ *33/3635–5456.* ⏲ *Mon.–Sat. 10:30–6:30.*

22 **Galería Sergio Bustamante.** Sergio Bustamante's work is found in galleries throughout the world, but you can purchase his whimsical sculpture or silver- and gold-plated jewelry for less here. At the back of the store is an art gallery featuring work by Mexican artists. The flamingos under the waterfall in the rear are real. ✉ *Calle Independencia 238,* ☎ *33/3639–5519, 33/3659–7110, 33/3657–8354, or 800/024–2727.* ⏲ *Mon.–Sat. 10–7, Sun. 11–4.*

★ 21 **Museo Regional de la Cerámica.** Housed in a colonial mansion, the museum covers the evolution of ceramic wares in the Atemajac Valley during the 20th century. Free guided tours in Spanish or English will enrich your visit and make for more enlightened shopping. ✉ *Calle Independencia 237,* ☎ *33/3635–5404.* 🎟 *Free.* ⏲ *Tues.–Sat. 10–6, Sun. 10–3.*

27 **El Parián.** When you're ready for lunch or a drink, head for this enormous, partly covered cantina south of Calle Independencia. This former marketplace dates from 1883; for a few dollars the local mariachis will treat you to a song or two as you slide down a margarita or *cazuela,* a traditional drink made of fruit and tequila and served in a ceramic pot. ✉ *Jardín Hidalgo,* ☎ *33/3659–2362.*

24 **Templo Parroquial de San Pedro.** The Franciscan friars who founded this tiny parish church during the Spanish conquest named it after San Pedro de Analco. In keeping with the Mexican custom of adding to the town's name the name of its patron saint, Tlaquepaque was officially changed to San Pedro Tlaquepaque in 1915. The altars of Our Lady of Guadalupe and the Sacred Heart of Jesus are intricately carved in silver and gold. ✉ *In square at Calles Guillermo Prieto and Morelos,* ☎ *33/3635–1001.* ⏲ *Daily 7 AM–9 PM.*

DINING

$ ✕ **El Abajeño.** Quality Mexican specialties are served on the outdoor patio of this converted hacienda, including *carnitas* (shredded pork) or *filete tapado* (cheese-topped fillet of beef) for two. Mexican dance performances and mariachi music take place weekends at 4:30. ✉ *Juárez 231,* ☎ *33/3635–9015 or 33/3635–9097. MC, V.*

$ ✕ **Casa Fuerte.** Dine on such gourmet Mexican dishes as chicken stuffed with *huitlacoche* (a corn fungus known as Mexico's answer to the truffle) and shrimp in tamarind sauce. There are tables on the front sidewalk or in the verdant patio garden, decorated with palms and a fountain. ✉ *Calle Independencia 224,* ☎ *33/3639–6481. AE, MC, V.*

$ ✕ **Restaurant sin Nombre.** The "Restaurant with No Name" serves Mexican cuisine, a combination of pre-Hispanic and modern recipes. High adobe walls surround the 18th-century colonial building and interior gardens. Afternoon entertainment includes jazz and traditional Mexican music. ✉ *Francisco Madero 80,* ☎ *33/3635–4520. AE, MC, V. Closed Mon.*

LODGING

$$ 🏨 **La Villa del Ensueño.** If you prefer a hotel out of the fray and near the region's fabulous shopping, choose this intimate B&B in the heart of Tlaquepaque, about 20 minutes outside downtown Guadalajara. The restored 19th-century hacienda maintains a rustic air, with thick white adobe walls, exposed beam ceilings, and plants in huge unglazed pots. Smokers should request a room with private balcony, as no smoking is allowed inside the hotel. ✉ *Florida 305, Tlaquepaque 45500,* ☎ *33/3635–8792,* FAX *33/3659–6152,* WEB *www.bestinns.net/mexico/ensueno. 14 rooms, 4 suites. 2 pools, bar, no-smoking rooms.*

Tonalá

8 km (5 mi) east of Tlaquepaque.

Tonalá is 10 minutes away but centuries removed from its more tourist-oriented, spruced-up neighbor, Tlaquepaque. One of the region's oldest pueblos, Tonalá is a quiet but prosperous village with dusty, cobblestone streets and adobe houses covered in stucco. The village was both the pre-Hispanic capital of the Atemajac Valley Indians and the capital of New Spain when Captain Juan de Oñate moved Guadalajara here in 1532. Within three years, however, Indians and a lack of water forced the Spaniards out.

Although it's been swallowed by the ever-expanding city of Guadalajara, Tonalá preserves the character of a small town. It's homey, independent, and industrious. Municipal officials estimate that more than 6,000 artisans live and work here. Indeed, much of the ceramics and pottery sold in Tlaquepaque (and in many other parts of the world) are made in Tonalá. In small home studios, families create the lovely pieces, cobalt-blue glassware, and playful animals with the same materials and techniques their ancestors used. More than 20 techniques of producing barro are used in the village. You can visit many home studios on free tours offered by the Tonalá municipal tourist office, beginning from the Casa de Artesanos, with a minimum of one-day advance notice.

On Thursday, much Tonalá merchandise is sold at bargain prices at one of the best tianguis in all of Mexico. Most stores are open Monday through Saturday 10–2 and 4–7; some are open Sunday 10–2. As opposed to Tlaquepaque, where shops line up shoulder to shoulder along pedestrian-only Calle Independencia and surrounding streets, Tonalá's shops and factories are spread throughout the area, with a special concentration on Avenida Tonalteca, the main street into town.

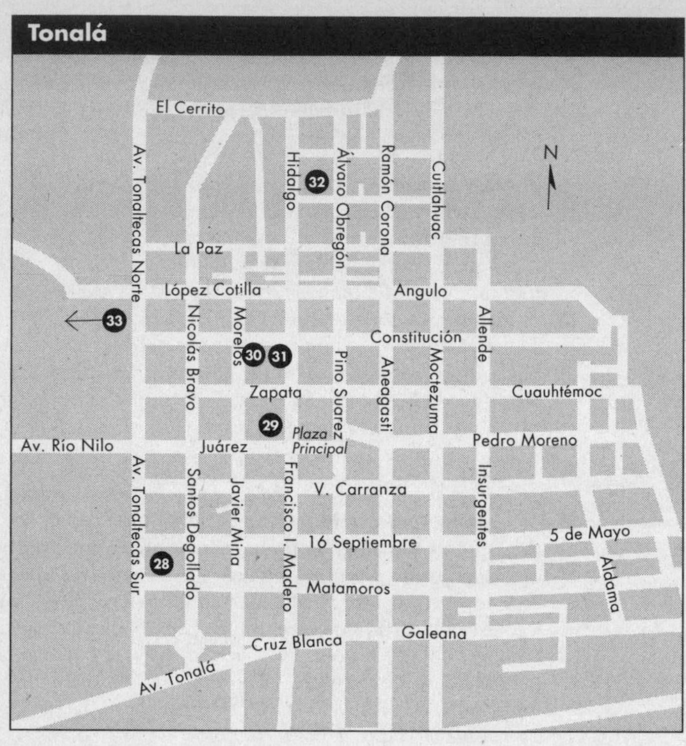

A GOOD WALK

Begin your tour at the many different workshops that make up la **Casa de los Artesanos** ㉘, on Avenida Tonaltecas between 16 de Septiembre and Matamoros. From there you'll pass scores of stores and workshops as you cruise north along the broad, busy avenue. Turn right onto Juárez and enter the downtown area where the town church, the **Santuario** ㉙, the municipal palace, and the tourism office surround the open plaza. Walk north on Morelos to **Erandi** ㉚ and **Galería José Bernabe** ㉛, both specializing in typical local ceramics. Continue north on Morelos several long blocks, turning east (right) on La Paz and left onto Álvaro Obregón to see handmade wooden masks at **El 7** ㉜. Return the way you came, this time turning west (right) onto López Cotilla. Not far past Avenida Tonaltecas is **La Casa de Salvador Vásquez Carmona** ㉝, where the owner sells his fanciful ceramic pottery.

SIGHTS TO SEE

㉘ **Casa de los Artesanos.** This virtual department store of Mexican folk art and crafts displays an excellent selection of works by the best of Tonalá's artisans. The work of generations is here, including items made of wood, glass, wrought iron, brass, and of course clay. Prices are reasonable, and the staff can direct you to local artisans' studios. ✉ *Av. de los Tonaltecas Sur 140,* ☎ *33/3683–0590.* ⏲ *Weekdays 9–7, weekends 9–3.*

㉝ **Casa de Salvador Vásquez Carmona.** On a small patio behind his home, Carmona molds enormous ceramic pots and glazes them with intricate designs. Numerous award certificates hang in his living room. Call before visiting. ✉ *Av. de los Maestros 328, west of Av. de los Tonaltecas,* ☎ *33/3683–2896.*

30 **Erandi.** One of Tonalá's largest exporters of hand-painted ceramics abroad has its exhibition center in founder Jorge Wilmot's former workshop. To see artisans in action, stop by their factory three blocks away. ✉ *Calle Morelos 86,* ☎ *33/3683–0101.* ⏲ *Mon.–Sat. 9–6 (Thurs. 9–2 only), Sat. 9–2. Factory:* ✉ *López Cotilla 118,* ☎ *33/3683–0253.* ⏲ *Weekdays 9:30–6, Sat. 9:30–2.*

31 **Galería José Bernabe.** The Bernabe family has made exquisite petatillo ceramics for generations, as well as simpler stoneware. The sprawling workshop in back of the gallery is open to visitors. ✉ *Hidalgo 83, between Zapata and Constitución,* ☎ *33/3683–0040 or 33/3683–0877.* ⏲ *Weekdays 10–3 and 4–7, weekends 10–3. Workshop closed weekends.*

29 **Santuario.** In the parish church, paintings of the 14 stations of the cross fill the walls. Next door is the simple **Palacio Municipal,** or City Hall. The **Plaza Principal** is across the street. ✉ *Juárez at Hidalgo.*

32 **El 7.** Tonalá native J. Cruz Coldívar Lucano, who signs his work and named his shop El 7 (*el siete*), makes striking hand-painted masks, as well as decorative plates and other wall hangings. He has exhibited throughout Mexico, and also in North and South America and Europe. The Spanish Crown owns a number of his works. ✉ *Álvaro Obregón 28,* ☎ *33/3683–1122.* ⏲ *Weekdays 9–6, Sat. 9–2.*

DINING

$ ✕ **Restaurant Jalapeños.** Steaks are the house specialty in this small but clean restaurant decorated with bright *papel picado* (cut paper streamers). Come for a late breakfast or dinner, or enjoy the daily lunch special, with soup, main dish, drink, and dessert for under $5. ✉ *Madero 23, ½ block from town hall,* ☎ *33/3683–0344. MC, V.*

$ ✕ **El Rincón del Sol.** A peaceful covered patio invites you to sip margaritas while listening to live guitar music that begins around 3:30. Try the chilies en nogada or one of the steak or chicken dishes. Hours are about 8:30 AM to 8 PM. ✉ *Av. 16 de Septiembre 61,* ☎ *33/3683–1989 or 33/3683–1940. AE, MC, V.*

Tlaquepaque and Tonalá A to Z

BUS TRAVEL

Frequent public bus service connects downtown Guadalajara to Tlaquepaque and Tonalá. The trips take around 30 and 45 minutes, respectively. You can also catch the number 707 bus to Tonalá from the Plaza del Sol mall.

CAR TRAVEL

From Guadalajara, take Avenida Revolución southeast. At the Plaza de la Bandera, jog right onto Boulevard General Marcelino García Barragán, which becomes Boulevard Tlaquepaque as it leads into town. When you reach the *glorieta* (traffic circle), follow the circle around to Avenida Niños Héroes. The first intersection is Calle Independencia, the pedestrian mall. From the Plaza del Sol area, take Calzada Lázaro Cárdenas southeast to the Alamo traffic circle. Fork off to the north onto Avenida Niños Héroes. Both routes take around 20 minutes.

To get from Tlaquepaque to Tonalá, take Avenida Río Nilo southeast directly into town, to the intersection of Avenida de los Tonaltecas.

TAXIS

The fare from downtown Guadalajara to Tlaquepaque comes to about $6, a bit more to Tonalá. A cab from Tlaquepaque to Tonalá runs about $4.

VISITOR INFORMATION

Both the Tlaquepaque and Tonalá tourist offices will cheerfully dispense maps and whatever brochures are available. At least one of the attendants usually speaks some English.

➤ CONTACT INFORMATION: **Tlaquepaque municipal tourist office** (✉ Morelos 288, Tlaquepaque, ☎ 33/3635–5756 or 33/3657–3846; ⏲ weekdays 9–7). **Tonalá municipal tourist office** (✉ Av. Hidalgo 21, Tonalá, ☎ 33/3683–0047 or 33/3683–0048; ⏲ weekdays 9–3).

Around Lake Chapala

The jagged mountains that ring Lake Chapala, Mexico's largest inland lake, make it seem a world away from Guadalajara; and the tranquility of lakeshore towns offers a welcome contrast to the bustling city. Sunsets are spectacular, and there's just enough humidity to keep the abundant bougainvillea blooming.

In the 1960s, Mexico's favorable rate of exchange and the springlike climate around Lake Chapala began to woo U.S. and Canadian retirees to the area. More than 40,000 expats now call this area their home at least part of the year, lending it the feel of a southern Californian retirement community. Many were surely dismayed when the lake began shrinking in the early 1990s and their waterfront property suddenly overlooked muddy marshlands. Every governor of Jalisco and every president of the republic has promised to save this national heritage site, yet Lake Chapala continues to shrink, withdrawing from the once prestigious towns that adjoin its former shoreline.

Spanish settlement in the area dates from 1538, when Franciscan friar Miguel de Bolonio arrived to convert the Taltica Indians to Christianity. Their chief was named Chapalac, from which the name Chapala may have originated. Today, Chapala is the area's largest settlement; although 8 km (5 mi) to the west, Ajijic is now the more vital and attractive. The latter has been home to expat artists and writers since the 1920s. The towns and villages along the lake are linked by one highway with multiple names, such as Carretera Chapala–Ajijic or Carretera Ajijic–Jocotepec.

Chapala

45 km (28 mi) south of Guadalajara.

With Chapala's proximity to rapidly growing Guadalajara, as well as its comfortable climate, it is surprising that tourists didn't frequent the area until the late 19th century. Then-president Porfirio Díaz heard that aristocrats had discovered this ideal place for weekend getaways, and he began spending holidays here in 1904. Soon summer homes were built, and in 1910 the Chapala Yacht Club opened. Word of the town, with its lavish lawn parties and magnificent estates, spread quickly to the United States and Europe. Along the main street, Avenida Madero, you can see the still-functioning (but now rather decrepit) Hotel Nido, built in the early 1900s to accommodate Díaz and his entourage. In the 1940s, Mexican film star María Félix spent the first of her numerous honeymoons there.

Nowadays the town of Chapala attracts a less influential assortment of visitors. On weekends the town still fills with Mexican families, although the once-bustling promenade is a shadow of its former self. Vendors sell refreshments and souvenirs, while dilapidated buses carry visitors across mudflats to the lake's edge—now nearly a half mile away.

Avenida Madero, the town's main drag, is lined with restaurants, shops, and cafés. On Madero, three blocks north of the promenade, the **plaza,** at the corner of López Cotilla, is a relaxing spot to sit and read the paper, or to succumb to ice cream or doughnuts from the surrounding shops. Two blocks south of the plaza, the **Iglesia de San Francisco** is easy to spot by the blue neon crosses on its twin steeples. The church was built in 1528 and reconstructed in 1580. On weekends, the rather forlorn **Parque la Cristianía,** on the south side of the *malecón* (boardwalk), fills with Tapatíos taking a respite from the city and browsing the remaining souvenir booths. Boys compete in energetic games of volleyball, while kids play on jungle gyms and swings. Indoor/outdoor cafés at the end of the promenade serve up seafood (but—because of the shrinking lake—no longer the native whitefish, *pescado blanco*).

DINING AND LODGING

$$ ✕ **Mariscos Guicho's.** The best of the waterfront seafood joints, Guicho's serves savory caviar tostadas, frogs' legs, garlic shrimp, and spicy seafood soup. The bright gold-and-green walls and tomato-red tablecloths lend the place an authentic Mexican charm. ✉ *Paseo Ramón Corona 20,* ☎ *33/3765–3232. No credit cards. Closed Tues.*

$ ✕ **El Árbol del Café** (The Coffee Tree). Local expatriates cherish this modest café for its roasted-on-the-premises specialty coffee, imported teas, and homemade cakes. Sip a decaffeinated cappuccino (hard to find in Mexico) and peruse the day's English-language papers. ✉ *Av. Hidalgo 236,* ☎ *no phone. No credit cards. Closed Sun.*

$ ✕ **Cozumel.** Ajijic residents regularly drive over to Chapala for the Wednesday chicken Cordon Bleu special, which includes wine or a margarita in addition to an opening cocktail and nachos. Other days choose from seafood and international dishes (you still get the free wine), and listen to a mini-mariachi band on Wednesday and Friday. Reservations are essential for Wednesday night. ✉ *Paseo Corona 22-A,* ☎ *33/3765–4606. MC, V. Closed Mon.*

$ ✕ **Restaurant Cazadores.** This grandly turreted brick building was once the summer home of the Braniff family, owners of the now-defunct airline. On the menu are seafood and beef dishes, which are a bit overpriced. But the lovely patio overlooking the boardwalk is pleasant, especially in the evening. ✉ *Av. Madero and Paseo Ramón Corona, northeast corner,* ☎ *33/3765–2162. AE, MC, V. Closed Mon.*

$$ 🏨 **Lake Chapala Inn.** It's a pity this charming inn was built just about the time the lake began to recede. Three of the four rooms in this renovated mansion face the dusty lake bed; all have whitewashed oak furniture, TVs, and phones. A dining room, library, large garden terrace, and kitchen are on-site, and an English-style breakfast is included in the rate (with a Continental breakfast on Sunday). ✉ *Paseo Ramón Corona 23, 45900,* ☎ FAX *33/3765–4786. 6 rooms. Pool, laundry service, Internet. No credit cards.*

$$ 🏨 **Villa Montecarlo.** The simple rooms here are housed in three-story contiguous units and are popular with Mexican families. One of the two swimming pools (the biggest in the area) is filled with natural thermal water. ✉ *Av. Hidalgo 296, 45900, about 1 km (½ mi) west of Av. Madero,* ☎ FAX *33/3765–2216, 33/3765–2120, or 33/3765–3366. 46 rooms, 2 suites. Restaurant, 2 tennis courts, 2 pools, bar, laundry service, free parking. V.*

OUTDOOR ACTIVITIES AND SPORTS

The **Chapala Country Club** (✉ Vista del Lago 1, San Nicholás Ibarra, ☎ 33/3763–5136) is open daily to nonmembers from dawn to dusk, except Tuesday and Wednesday, when it's open to nonmembers after noon. Fees are $22–$38.

Ajijic

8 km (5 mi) west of Chapala.

Despite blocks of galleries and crafts shops, Ajijic's small-town ambience is still defined by its narrow cobblestone streets, pastel-color buildings, and gentle pace. Still, the foreign influence is unmistakable: English is spoken almost as widely here as Spanish, and license plates run the gamut from British Columbia to Texas. Although Lago de Chapala has receded here also, the change is less dramatic and desultory than in nearby Chapala, and the arts scene gives Ajijic a raison d'être independent of the lake's existence.

The **Plaza Principal** (also called the Plaza de Armas or El Jardín) is a tree- and flower-filled central square at the corner of Avenidas Colón and Hidalgo. The **Iglesia de San Andrés** (Church of St. Andrew) sits on the Jardín's north side, shaded by laurel and tulip trees and brightened with roses, lilies, and hibiscus bushes in the courtyard. In late November the plaza fills for the saint's nine-day fiesta.

Walk down Calle Morelos (the continuation of Avenida Colón) toward the lake and you'll find stores and boutiques that sell everything from designer fashions to traditional arts and crafts. Turn left onto Independencia to find about a dozen art galleries and studios.

Just northeast of the plaza, activity centers surround the soccer field, which doubles as a venue for bullfights and concerts. Locals and visitors frequent the movie theater, cybercafé, athletic club, and Salvador's restaurant, a local institution.

DINING AND LODGING

In addition to the establishments listed below, there are other good-quality lodgings in the area. Consult the tourist office in Chapala, the *Ojo del Lago* newspaper, or the *Guadalajara Colony Reporter.* Note that restaurants in Ajijic seem to come and go frequently.

$$ ★ ✕ **Ajijic Grill.** The *yakitori* and *tempura* in this Japanese restaurant are better than average, though the sushi leaves much to be desired. The large patio in the center is prettiest at night, when it's softly lighted by tiny white lights. ✉ *Calle Morelos 5,* ☎ *33/3766–2458. MC, V. Closed Tues.*

$$ ✕ **Johanna's.** If you tire of Mexican or Continental cuisine, come to this intimate bit of Bavaria on the lake. The authentic German cuisine includes a variety of excellent sausages and homemade goose or duck pâté. Main dishes come with soup or salad as well as applesauce and cooked red cabbage. For dessert indulge in plum strudel or blackberry-topped torte. ✉ *Blvd. Ajijic 118A, in front of the La Floresta Auditorium,* ☎ *33/3766–0437. No credit cards. Closed Mon.*

$ ✕ **La Casa del Waffle.** Stop in this bright, cheery spot on the outskirts of town for breakfast and choose from 12 varieties of Belgian waffles and numerous other favorites. ✉ *Carretera Chapala–Jocotepec Pte. 75, on the highway west of Ajijic,* ☎ *33/3766–2301. No credit cards. Closed Tues. No dinner.*

$ ✕ **Salvador's.** An afternoon hangout for local expats looking for a great value, this restaurant has a well-kept salad bar and specialties from both south and north of the border. A musician tickles the ivories during the fabulous Sunday brunch, as well as during Wednesday lunch. On Friday locals come in droves for the well-loved fish and chips lunch special. ✉ *Carretera Chapala–Jocotepec Oriente 56, in Plaza Bugambilias,* ☎ *33/3766–2301.* ⏲ *Closed Sat. No credit cards.*

$$ ★ ✕🏨 **La Nueva Posada.** Luxuriant gardens framed in bougainvillea define this charming inn. There's fine entertainment most evenings (typically a jazz trio or tropical music) in the cozy bar, with its brick domed

ceilings, hanging reed lamps, and leather chairs surrounding custom-made tables. Out in the garden restaurant, strands of tiny white lights set the mood for an evening meal, where anything from chef Lorraine Rousseau's eclectic menu is recommended. ✉ *Donato Guerra 9, Apdo. 30, 45920,* ☎ *33/3766–1344,* FAX *33/3766–1444,* WEB *www.mexconnect.com/amex/np. 17 rooms. Restaurant, fans, pool, bar, laundry service. MC, V.*

$$ **Los Artistas.** Surrounded by an acre of splendidly landscaped gardens, this cozy inn has rooms with white textured walls and red tile floors. Each is uniquely decorated with colorful handwoven Mexican bedspreads, wrought iron or carved wood bedframes, and fresh-cut bouquets; most have patios made intimate by bowers of blooming things; four have fireplaces. Rates include a generous breakfast of egg dishes, local fruits, and fresh homemade yogurt, granola, and breads. ✉ *Constitución 105, 45920,* ☎ *33/3766–1027,* FAX *33/3766–1762. 6 rooms. Pool. No credit cards.*

$$ **Inn at San Andres.** Hand-painted tiles and rustic furniture define each one-of-a-kind suite in this small B&B. A full breakfast is included with a night's stay. ✉ *Galeana 22-A, 45920, one block off plaza,* ☎ *33/3766–1250; 703/830–8398 in the U.S.,* FAX *33/3766–1250. 6 suites. Pool. No credit cards.*

NIGHTLIFE AND THE ARTS

Art classes, exhibitions, and informal gallery space characterize **CABA** (✉ Colón 43, ☎ FAX 33/3766–1920). The rambling, hacienda-style **Posada Ajijic** (✉ Calle Morelos, facing the lake, ☎ 33/3766–0744 or 33/3766–0430) is a restaurant, bar, and popular weekend dance place with an unobstructed view of the lake bed. A cozy, candlelit nightclub, **Viva María** (✉ Donato Guerra 20-A, ☎ 33/3766–0984) presents an eclectic range of live musical offerings Wednesday through Saturday.

SHOPPING

Along the shores of Lake Chapala are workshops creating export-quality crafts. **La Casa de las Artesanías Ajijik** (✉ Carretera Chapala-Jocotepec Km 6.5, ☎ 33/3766–0548) is a branch of the state-run Instituto de Artesanías Jaliscienses crafts shop. It's open weekdays 10–6, Saturday 10–4, and Sunday 10–2. **La Colección Bárbara** (✉ Av. Independencia 7A–9A, ☎ 33/3766–1824), open Friday 9–5:30, Saturday 9–4, sells traditional crafts, antiques, jewelry, and fine furniture. You can find exhibitions of sculpture, paintings, prints, photography, pottery, and other artworks by local and Guadalajara artists at **Galería Américas** (✉ Ramón Corona 11, across from the Lake Chapala Society, ☎ 33/3766–1292, ⏲ Mon.–Sat. 10–4). The **Mi México** (✉ Morelos 8, ☎ 33/3766–0133, ⏲ Mon.–Sat. 10–2 and 3–6, Sun. 11–3) boutique sells women's clothing and jewelry as well as pottery, blown glass, and other crafts and gifts.

HORSEBACK RIDING

You can mount lively horses for about $2.50 an hour at **Caballos** (✉ Paseo Delgado and Camino Real, ☎ 33/3766–1319), at a narrow grassy plaza shaded by oak trees in Ajijic.

San Juan Cosalá

10 km (6 mi) west of Chapala.

San Juan Cosalá is known for its natural thermal-water spas on the shores of Lake Chapala, with the mountains rising to the north. The **Hotel Balneario San Juan Cosalá** (✉ La Paz 420, ☎ 33/3761–0222, 🎟 $6) welcomes day-trippers and overnight guests to its four large swimming pools and two wading pools. A restaurant with international fare is on the premises. Although **Villas Buenaventura Cosalá** (✉ Km 13.5

Carretera Chapala–Jocotepec, ☎ 33/3761–0202) doesn't accept day-trippers, guests can enjoy thermal waters in their hotel suite's bathtubs as well as in the property's hot tubs and swimming pools. Facilities include six one-bedroom suites and 11 with two bedrooms; most have kitchenettes. There's a two-night minimum on weekends; the nightly rate is $69.

Lake Chapala A to Z

BUS TRAVEL

Autotransportes Guadalajara Chapala and other bus lines have frequent service to Chapala, Ajijic, and other lakeside towns from Guadalajara's Antigua Central Camionera (Old Bus Station). It's about 45 minutes to Chapala and another 10–15 minutes to Ajijic. Make sure you ask for the *directo* (direct) as opposed to *clase segunda* (second class), which stops at every little pueblo en route.

➤ BUS INFORMATION: **Autotransportes Guadalajara Chapala** (☎ 33/3619–5365).

CAR TRAVEL

From downtown Guadalajara take Calzada Independencia Sur to Dr. R. Michel, turn left, and follow the signs to Chapala and the other lakeside towns. The trip takes 40 minutes.

ENGLISH-LANGUAGE MEDIA

The *Ojo del Lago* monthly newspaper is available free throughout Chapala and Ajijic. The monthly *Lake Chapala Review* sells for less than a dollar. The *Guadalajara Reporter* weekly newspaper devotes a section to lakeside news and events. Libros de Chapala, open daily 9–2 and 3–6, has an extensive range of English-language magazines, U.S. and Canadian newspapers, and a large selection of books on Mexico in English.

➤ BOOKSTORES: **Libros de Chapala** (✉ Av. Madero, Chapala, across from the plaza, ☎ no phone).

VISITOR INFORMATION

The Jalisco state tourism office in Chapala is open weekdays 9–7, and weekends 9–5. In Ajijic, the nonprofit Lake Chapala Society, open Monday–Saturday 10–1, provides information about the area.

➤ TOURIST INFORMATION: **Jalisco state tourism office** (✉ Madero 407-A, 2nd floor, ☎ FAX 33/3765–3141). **Lake Chapala Society** (✉ Av. 16 de Septiembre 16, ☎ no phone).

Tequila

56 km (35 mi) northwest of Guadalajara.

For a close look at how Mexico's most famous liquor is made from the spiny blue agave plant that grows in the fields alongside the highway, spend part or all of a day in this tidy village, about 59 km (37 mi) from outside the city of Guadalajara. It's said that centuries ago, the Tiquilas, a small Nahuatl-speaking tribe, discovered that the heart of the agave produced a juice that could be fermented to make intoxicating drinks. When distilled (an innovation introduced after the arrival of the Spanish in the 16th century), the fermented liquid turns into the heady liquor, which in this and only a few other regions can be rightfully labeled tequila.

You can tour the famous Sauza Distillery or one of the other modern tequila distilleries here—it's best to make reservations ahead of time or to take a tour. Most distilleries prefer to receive visitors weekdays between 10 AM and 1 PM. Bus service is available from Guadalajara's

Old Bus Station, and various Guadalajara tour companies offer guided excursions. Each Saturday the Tequila Express leaves Guadalajara on a 10-hour trip that includes a tour of the Hacienda San José del Refugio distillery, in Amatitlán, a satisfying lunch, a folkloric ballet performance serenaded by mariachis, and an unlimited supply of Mexico's most famous liquor. Tickets are available through Guadalajara's **Chamber of Commerce** (☎ 33/3880–9099).

GUADALAJARA A TO Z

To research prices, get advice from other travelers, and book travel arrangements, visit www.fodors.com.

AIR TRAVEL

The main gateway to Guadalajara is Los Angeles, but you can also fly direct from other cities such as Atlanta, Dallas, Houston, and Phoenix on some airlines.

CARRIERS

Aero California serves Tucson and Los Angeles as well as many Mexican cities. Aeroméxico has nonstop service to Guadalajara from Los Angeles and extensive internal flights. Mexicana has direct flights from Chicago, Los Angeles, San Francisco, and San José. Through Dallas, American Airlines provides service to Guadalajara from all cities in its system. Flights on Continental are routed through the Houston hub. Delta Air Lines flies direct from Los Angeles and Atlanta.

➤ AIRLINES AND CONTACTS: **Aero California** (☎ 33/3616–2525). **Aeroméxico** (☎ 33/3669–0202). **Mexicana** (☎ 33/3678–7676). **American Airlines** (☎ 33/3616–4090 or 33/3688–5518). **Continental** (☎ 33/3688–5141 or 33/3647–4251). **Delta Air Lines** (☎ 33/3630–3530).

AIRPORTS AND TRANSFERS

Libertador Miguel Hidalgo International Airport is 16½ km (10 mi) south of Guadalajara, en route to Chapala. A new international terminal is under construction to help meet the demands of increased air service to the area.

➤ AIRPORT INFORMATION: **Libertador Miguel Hidalgo International Airport** (✉ Av. Solidaridad Iberoamericana Km 17.5, Tlaquepaque, ☎ 33/3688–5248 or 33/3688–5127).

AIRPORT TRANSFERS

The Chapala Highway stretches north from the airport to the city. The 30-minute trip can be delayed by slow-moving caravans of trucks and weekend recreational traffic.

Autotransportaciones Aeropuerto is 24-hour airport taxi service that goes anywhere in the Guadalajara area in VW buses (*combis*). Fares, based on distance, range from $8 to $12 for up to three people going in the same part of the city. At the airport, buy a ticket from the booth outside the terminal exit. To the airport, hotel taxis have set rates, as do regular city taxis.

➤ TAXI AND SHUTTLES: **Autotransportaciones Aeropuerto** (☎ 33/3812–4278 or 33/3812–4308).

BUS TRAVEL TO AND FROM GUADALAJARA

First-class, air-conditioned buses with rest rooms run daily to Guadalajara from most major cities on the border. Greyhound has schedule and fare information for service into Mexico, although you'll have to change to a Mexican carrier at the border. Guadalajara's Nueva Central Camionera (New Bus Station) is 10 km (6 mi) southeast of downtown Guadalajara on the highway to Zapotlanejo. Elite has first-class service to Mexico City and many other destinations. One of the most reliable lines is ETN. Primera Plus has first- and second-class buses serving mainly central and western Mexico. Omnibus de México serves the U.S. border and intermediate destinations.

Buses to and from such nearby destinations as Chapala, Ajijic, and Tequila depart from the Antigua Central Camionera, northeast of the Parque Agua Azul on Avenida Dr. R. Michel, between Calles Los Angeles and 5 de Febrero.

➤ BUS INFORMATION: **Greyhound** (☎ 800/712–8819 or 800/231–2222). **Elite** (☎ 33/3679–0404). **ETN** (☎ 33/3600–0477 or 800/360–4200). **Omnibus de México** (☎ 33/3600–0469). **Primera Plus** (☎ 33/3600–0398).

BUS TRAVEL WITHIN GUADALAJARA

FARES AND SCHEDULES

Buses run every few minutes between 6 AM and 11 PM to all local attractions, including Tlaquepaque, Tonalá, and Zapopan. Fares are roughly 40¢, making buses the preferred mode of transportation for Guadalajara natives, so expect to stand during daytime. Various "luxury" buses—which run on some of the main routes through the city, including out to Tlaquepaque and Tonalá—cost $1–$2 and are much less crowded and vastly more comfortable.

CAR RENTAL

All the major international players, including Avis, Budget, Dollar, and Hertz have offices in Guadalajara's airport. Downtown, you can walk into Budget or the local agency, Express.

➤ MAJOR AGENCIES: **Avis** (☎ 33/3688–5528 or 33/3688–5656). **Budget** (✉ Av. Niños Héroes 934, Centro, Sector Reforma, at Av. 16 de Septiembre, ☎ 33/3613–0027). **Dollar** (✉ Av. Federalismo Sur 540A, Centro, at Av. de la Paz, ☎ 33/3826–7959). **Express Rent a Car** (✉ Manzano 444, Zona Centro, ☎ 33/3614–1465 or 33/3614–1865). **Hertz** (☎ 33/3688–5403 [airport]; ✉ Av. 16 de Septiembre 738-B, Zona Centro, Sector Reforma, ☎ 33/3614–6162).

CAR TRAVEL

Major routes include Highway 54, which leads south to Colima (220 km [136 mi]) and north to Zacatecas (320 km [198 mi]). Highway 15 hugs the southern shore of Lake Chapala before continuing southeast to Morelia (255 km [58 mi]) and Mexico City (209 km [130 mi]). Highway 15D is the toll road to Mexico City. Heading northwest from Guadalajara, both Highways 15 and 15D pass through some of the most beautiful country in Jalisco and neighboring Nayarit state. If you have a choice between a free or toll road, remember that the latter tend to be quite expensive but in better condition than their free counterparts.

In Guadalajara, beware of heavy traffic and *topes* (speed bumps). Traffic circles are common at many busy intersections. Parking in the city center can be scarce, so take a taxi or bus if you're not staying nearby; otherwise, try the underground lots across from the Palacio Municipal (✉ Av. Hidalgo and Calle Pedro Loza) and below the Plaza de la Liberación (✉ Av. Hidalgo and Calle Belén, in front of the Teatro Degollado). If you park illegally, the police may tow your vehicle: you'll have to go to the municipal transit office to pay a fine and then to one of the *correlones* (holding areas) to pay the tow charge (around $15) and retrieve your car.

EMBASSIES

For information about consulates other than those listed below, call Guadalajara's consular association, open weekdays 9–3 and 5–8.

The U.S. Consulate is open weekday mornings 8:30–11:30. The Canadian Consulate is open weekdays 8:30–2 and 3–5. The British Consulate is open only by appointment.

➤ CONSULAR INFORMATION: **Asociación Consular de Guadalajara** (☎ 33/3616–0629).

➤ CONSULATES: **British Consulate** (✉ Eulogio Parra 2539, Zona Centro, ☎ 33/3616–0629). **Canadian Consulate** (✉ Fiesta Americana, Aurelio Aceves 225, Zona Centro, ☎ 33/3616–5642; 800/706–2900 after-hours emergency). **United States Consulate** (✉ Progreso 175, Zona Centro, between Av. López Cotilla and Libertad, ☎ 33/3825–2700 or 33/3825–1717; 33/3826–5553 after-hours emergency).

EMERGENCIES

Dialing **080** will connect you with a central emergency system (for all of the organizations listed below and other metro-area police stations). Ask for an English-speaking operator.

➤ EMERGENCY SERVICES: **Cruz Roja** (Red Cross; ☎ 33/3614–5600 or 33/3614–2707). **Cruz Verde** (Green Cross municipal emergency medical service; ☎ 33/3812–5143 or 33/3614–5252). **Guadalajara City police** (☎ 33/3668–0800). **Highway patrol** (☎ 33/3629–5082 or 33/3629–5085). **State police** (☎ 33/3617–0770 or 33/3614–7374). **Theft Line** (☎ 33/3618–2539).

➤ HOSPITALS: **Hospital del Carmen** (✉ Tarascos 3435, Zona Minerva, ☎ 33/3813–1224 or 33/3813–0025). **Hospital México-Americano** (✉ Colomos 2110, Zona Centro, ☎ 33/3641–3141). **Hospital San Javier** (✉ Av. Pablo Casals 640, Col. Providencia, Zona Minerva, ☎ 33/3669–0222).

ENGLISH-LANGUAGE MEDIA

Sandi Bookstore, open weekdays 9:30–2:30 and 3:30–7 and Saturday 9:30–2, sells many newspapers, magazines, and books. Sanborn's has a good selection of books, periodicals, and music.

The *Guadalajara Reporter,* a weekly newspaper sold for 90¢ at newsstands and hotels, includes excellent community and cultural listings. You can also get the paper off the Web at www.guadalajarareporter.com. The monthly newspaper *Ojo del Lago* covers the Lake Chapala area. An excellent source of general information on the Lake Chapala area as well as 40 different day excursions from Guadalajara is *Outdoors in Western Mexico* by John and Susana Pint (Editoriales Agata, 1998).

➤ BOOKSTORES: **Sanborn's** (✉ Av. 16 de Septiembre 127, Centro Histórico, ☎ 33/3613–6693; ✉ Av. López Mateos 2718, Plaza del Sol mall, Zona Cruz del Sur, ☎ 33/3647–2510). **Sandi Bookstore** (✉ Av. Tepeyac 718, Chapala, ☎ 33/3121–0863).

HEALTH

DOCTORS AND DENTISTS

The U.S. Consulate maintains a list of English-speaking doctors and dentists. All major hotels have the names of doctors who are on 24-hour call.

PHARMACIES

Several branches of Farmacias Guadalajara are open 24 hours. Benavides is another ubiquitous drugstore chain. Convenient branches are located downtown, and in Zapopan.

➤ PHARMACY INFORMATION: **Benavides** (✉ Morelos 468, Centro Histórico, near el Palacio Municipal, ☎ 33/3614–7676; ✉ Hidalgo 307-A, Centro Histórico, ☎ 33/3633–2510). **Farmacias Guadalajara** (✉ Av. Javier Mina 221, Zona Centro, between Calle Cabañas and Vicente Guerrero, ☎ 33/3618–3767).

MAIL AND SHIPPING

The main post office is open weekdays 8–7.

Sending e-mail from an Internet café is an increasingly popular alternative to Mexico's slow postal service. Both CCCP and Cybercentro are inexpensive, and Cybercentro also serves coffee.

➤ INTERNET CAFÉS: **CCCP** (✉ Av. Alcade 159, Centro Histórico, ☎ 33/3614–5311). **Cybercentro** (✉ Santa Mónica 208, Zona Centro, near San Felipe, ☎ 33/3613–4259).

➤ POST OFFICE: **Post Office** (✉ Administración de Correos 1, Zona Centro, ☎ 33/3614–8125).

MONEY MATTERS

The most convenient places to change currency are *casas de cambio,* generally open weekdays 9–7 and Saturday until 1 PM. Many of them are on Calle López Cotilla downtown and in the Plaza del Sol area. Banks tend to have more limited hours, longer waits, and a similar rate of exchange.

SIGHTSEEING TOURS

Most tour operators in Guadalajara have guided city tours and excursions to Tequila, Lake Chapala, Tlaquepaque, and Tonalá. Free three-hour guided bus and walking tours are offered periodically by the tourist office. They usually leave from the Municipal Palace Saturday at 10 AM. Call 33/3616–3333 to confirm. Free guided trolley tours of Zapopan are offered for groups by the Zapopan Tourist Board; call 33/3110–0754 for information and reservations.

You can hire a horse-drawn carriage (*calandrias*) in front of the Museo Regional, the Mercado Libertad, or Parque San Francisco. The charge is about $15 for an hour-long tour for up to five passengers. Few drivers speak English.

Panoramex offers lake tours and arranges bus tickets and excursions to Tequila. The bilingual guides of Ajijic's Charter Club Tours lead tours to Guadalajara, shopping and factory tours to Tlaquepaque and Tonalá, and to lesser known yet scenic towns throughout the state of Jalisco. Sonrisa Tours is another established, reliable tour operator.

➤ TOUR INFORMATION: **Charter Club Tours** (✉ Carretera Oriente 1, Ajijic, Plaza Moñana mall, ☎ 33/3766–1777). **Panoramex** (✉ Av. Federalismo Sur 944, Zona Centro, ☎ 33/3810–5057 or 33/3810–5005). **Sonrisa Tours** (✉ Paseo del Hospicio 63, Plaza Tapatía, Centro Histórico, ☎ 33/3618–9601, 33/3617–2511, or 33/3617–2590).

SUBWAY TRAVEL

Guadalajara's underground *tren ligero* (light train) system is clean, safe, and efficient. Line 1 runs north–south along Avenida Federalismo from the Periférico (city beltway) Sur to Periférico Norte, near the Benito Juárez Auditorium. The central terminal is at Parque Revolución. Line 2 runs east–west along Avenida Javier Mina (which becomes Avenida Juárez at Calzada Independencia) from Tetlán in eastern Guadalajara to Avenida Federalismo. Trains run about every 15 minutes from 6 AM to 11 PM; a token for one trip costs about 30¢. Juárez Station, where Lines 1 and 2 meet, serves as a public art gallery, with changing exhibits of works by Mexican artists.

TAXIS

Taxis are readily available and reasonably economical. All cabs are supposed to use meters. Schedules listing fares to downtown and all major attractions are posted in most hotel lobbies, and cab drivers should produce a copy upon request. *Sitios* (cab stands) are near all hotels and attractions. Fares go up about 25% after 10 PM.

TELEPHONES

As part of the national phone number conversion to a 10-digit dial plan, **all eight-digit Guadalajara numbers must be preceded by the regional code 33** as of February 17, 2002.

TRAIN TRAVEL

Train tickets for a full-day, round-trip Saturday excursion to Tequila are available from the Cámera de Comercio (Chamber of Commerce) for $40. The trip runs from 10:30 AM to 8:30 PM.

➤ TRAIN INFORMATION: **Cámera de Comercio** (☎ 33/3122–9020).

TRANSPORTATION AROUND GUADALAJARA

Guadalajara's major attractions are best seen on foot. For points outside the city center, Guadalajara has an inexpensive, well-organized public-transportation system.

Buses are without a doubt the cheapest and most efficient—but sometimes least comfortable—means of traversing the city.

TRAVEL AGENCIES

Many of the city's 100-plus travel agencies are in the two hotel zones, el Centro and Avenida López Mateos Sur, on the city's southwest side. Near the Minerva Fountain you'll find American Express. Copenhagen Tours sells bus and plane tickets.

➤ LOCAL AGENT REFERRALS: **American Express** (✉ Av. Vallarta 2440, Zona Minerva, ☎ 33/3818–2323 or 33/3818–2325). **Copenhagen Tours** (✉ Av. J. Manuel Clouthier 156, Col. Prados Vallarta, Zona Minerva, ☎ 33/3629–7957 or 33/3629–4758).

VISITOR INFORMATION

The Jalisco state tourist offices have information about Guadalajara and other parts of Mexico.

Guadalajara's Municipal Tourist Office, in front of the Municipal Palace, also has kiosks downtown in the Plaza Guadalajara, in Los Arcos monument on Avenida Vallarta east of the Minerva Fountain, in Parque San Francisco, in front of the Instituto Cultural Cabañas, in front of Mercado Libertad, at Vicente Guerrero 233 (open weekdays only), and at the airport.

The Tourist Board of Zapopan provides information and maps about metropolitan Guadalajara, including Zapopan, Tonalá, and Tlaquepaque.

➤ TOURIST INFORMATION: **Jalisco state tourist offices** (✉ Calle Morelos 102, Centro Histórico, in Plaza Tapatía, ☎ 33/3668–1600, 33/3613–0306, or 800/363–2200; ⏲ weekdays 9–8, weekends 9–1; ✉ Palacio de Gobierno, Centro Histórico ☎ no phone; ⏲ weekdays 8:30–7:30, Sat. 10–1). **Municipal Tourist Office** (☎ 33/3616–3333 or 33/3616–3300; ⏲ Mon.–Sat. 9–7). **Tourist Board of Zapopan** (✉ Av. Vallarta 6501, Ciudad Granja, Zapopan, ☎ 33/3110–0754; ⏲ weekdays 9–7:30).

8 THE HEARTLAND

Rich with the history of Mexico's revolution, the heartland is a treasury of colonial towns—Guanajuato, Zacatecas, Querétaro, Morelia, and Pátzcuaro, among others—whose residents lead quiet, largely traditional lives. Even in San Miguel de Allende, an American art colony and home to a well-known language institute, women wash their clothes and gossip at the local lavandería as they have for hundreds of years.

Updated by Amy Mansell

MEXICO'S HEARTLAND, so named for its central position in the country, is known for its well-preserved colonial architecture, its fertile farmland and surrounding mountains, and its leading role in Mexican history, particularly during the War of Independence (1810–21). The Bajío (ba-*hee*-o), as it is also called, corresponds roughly to the states of Guanajuato and parts of Querétaro and Michoacán. In the hills surrounding the cities of Guanajuato, Zacatecas, Querétaro, and San Miguel de Allende, the Spanish found silver in the 1500s, leading them to colonize the area heavily.

Three centuries later, wealthy Creoles (Mexicans of Spanish descent) in Querétaro and San Miguel took the first audacious steps toward independence from Spain. When their clandestine efforts were discovered, two of the early insurgents, Ignacio Allende and Father Miguel Hidalgo, began in earnest the War of Independence.

When Allende and Hidalgo were executed in 1811, another native son, José María Morelos, picked up the independence banner. This mestizo (mixed race) mule skinner–turned–priest–turned–soldier, with his army of 9,000, came close to gaining control of the land before he was killed in 1815. Thirteen years later, the city of Valladolid was renamed Morelia in his honor.

Long after the War of Independence ended in 1821, the cities of the Bajío continued to play a prominent role in Mexico's history. Three major events took place in Querétaro alone: in 1848 the Mexican-American War ended with the signing of the Treaty of Guadalupe Hidalgo; in 1867 Austrian Maximilian of Hapsburg, crowned Emperor of Mexico by Napoleon III of France, was executed in the hills north of town; and in 1917 the Mexican Constitution was signed here.

The heartland honors the events and people that helped shape modern Mexico. In ornate cathedrals or bucolic plazas, down narrow alleyways or atop high hillsides, you'll find monuments—and remnants—of a heroic past. During numerous fiestas, you can savor the region's historic spirit. On a night filled with fireworks, off-key music, and tireless celebrants, it's hard not to be caught up in the vital expression of national pride.

Tourism is welcomed in the heartland, especially in these hard economic times, and, for the most part, it doesn't disrupt the normal routines of residents. Families visit parks for Sunday picnics, youngsters tussle in school courtyards, old men chat in shaded plazas, and Purépecha women in traditional garb sell their wares in crowded *mercados* (markets). Unlike areas where attractions have been specifically designed for tourism, the Bajío relies on its historic ties and the architectural integrity of its cities to appeal to travelers. Although this is an interesting area to tour by car, there is frequent inexpensive bus service from one city to the next throughout the Bajío.

Pleasures and Pastimes

Architecture

Financed largely by the region's fabulously wealthy silver mines, the cities of the heartland are architectural masterpieces full of buildings richly worked with curvaceous lines, human, animal, plant, and geometric motifs, and sculptural depth that accents the play of light and shadow. From the stately, almost European grandeur of Morelia to the steep, labyrinthine allure of Guanajuato and the sandstone pink splendor of Zacatecas, no two towns are alike. San Miguel de Allende's

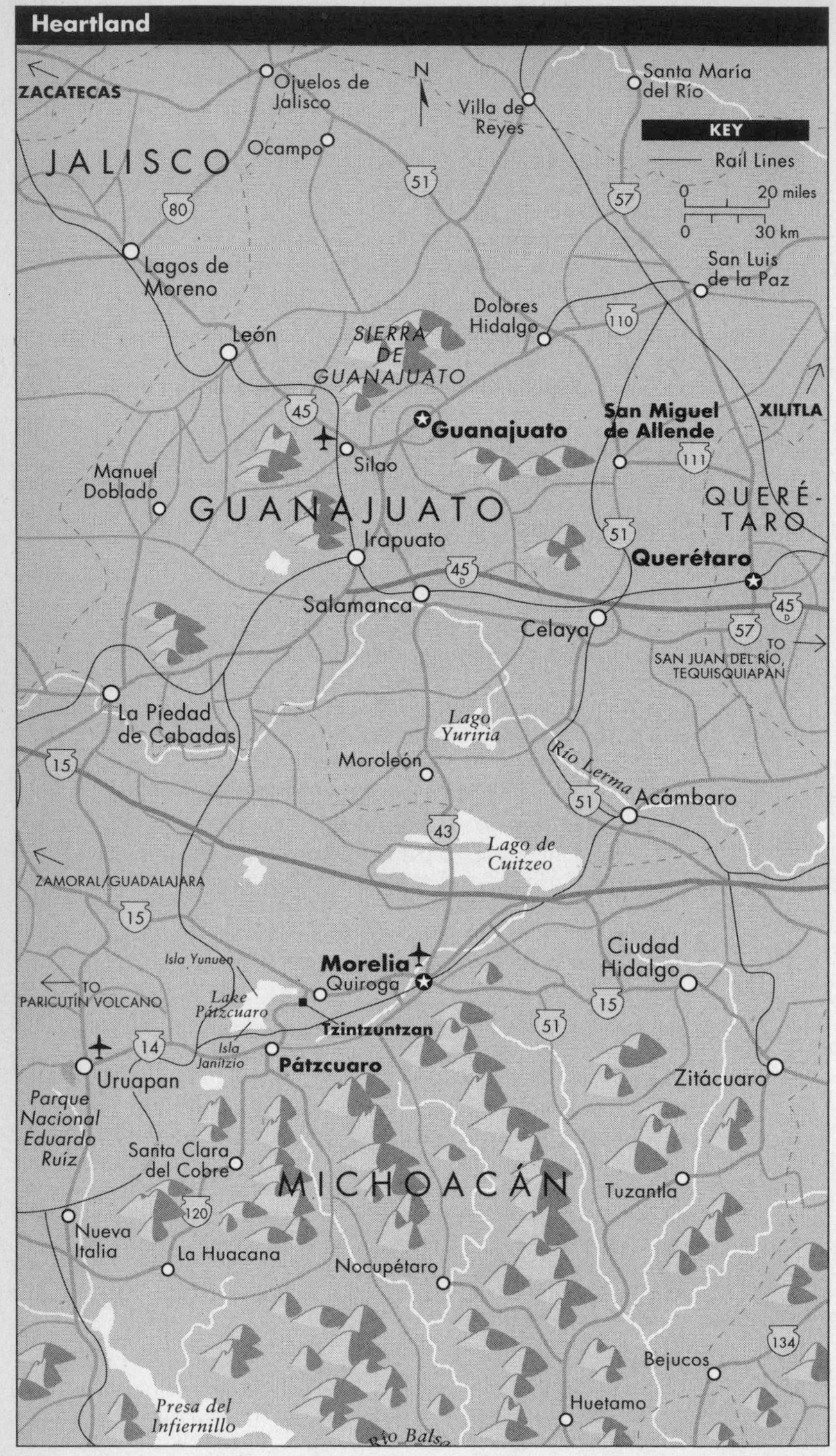
Heartland
ZACATECAS
Ojuelos de Jalisco
N
Villa de Reyes
Santa María del Río
KEY
Rail Lines
0 20 miles
0 30 km
JALISCO
Ocampo
51
80
57
Lagos de Moreno
San Luis de la Paz
Dolores Hidalgo
110
León
SIERRA DE GUANAJUATO
45
Guanajuato
San Miguel de Allende
XILITLA
Silao
111
Manuel Doblado
GUANAJUATO
QUERÉTARO
Irapuato
51
Querétaro
45 D
Salamanca
Celaya
45 D
57
TO SAN JUAN DEL RÍO, TEQUISQUIAPAN
La Piedad de Cabadas
Lago Yuriria
15
Moroleón
Río Lerma
51
Acámbaro
43
Lago de Cuitzeo
ZAMORAL/GUADALAJARA
15
Ciudad Hidalgo
Isla Yunuen
Morelia
Quiroga
TO PARICUTÍN VOLCANO
Lake Pátzcuaro
15
Tzintzuntzan
51
14
Isla Janitzio
Pátzcuaro
Uruapan
Zitácuaro
Parque Nacional Eduardo Ruíz
Santa Clara del Cobre
MICHOACÁN
Tuzantla
120
Nueva Italia
La Huacana
Nocupétaro
134
Bejucos
Presa del Infiernillo
Huetamo
Río Balsa

Gothic-style parish church puts a Gallic touch on an otherwise very Mexican skyline. And in Pátzcuaro and Querétaro, the ornate 16th-century colonial mansions surrounding the city squares have been converted into hotels and government offices, making their interior patios accessible to the public.

Dining

It's no surprise that culinary tastes vary widely in the heartland, which spans a large area across central Mexico. In the state of Michoacán, Purépecha Indian influences predominate. The tomato-based *sopa tarasca* (a soup with cheese, cream, and tortillas) is one of the best-known regional specialties. Because of the numerous lakes and rivers in the state, several types of freshwater fish are often served in Michoacán restaurants.

At the northern end of the heartland, in Zacatecas, the hearty, meat-eating tastes of the *norteños* (northerners) rule the dinner table. Although beef is the favored dish, other specialties include *asado de boda* (wedding barbecue), pork in a spicy but semisweet sauce. The region is also known for its cheese and wine. And because of San Miguel's expatriate community, the city has a wealth of worthy eateries.

CATEGORY	COST*
$$$$	over $15
$$$	$10–$15
$$	$5–$10
$	under $5

**per person for a main course at dinner*

Hiking and Walking

With its rolling farmland, lofty volcanoes, lakes, and Indian villages, Michoacán is a perfect area for day hikes. Trails near Pátzcuaro wind up to nearby hilltops for great views across town and the surrounding countryside, and in Uruapan—64 km (40 mi) away and 2,000 ft lower in elevation—you can walk along a lush river valley. And no tour of the heartland would be complete without a few days of leisurely strolling on the avenues and back streets of colonial cities and towns.

Lodging

In many of the heartland's colonial cities, restored haciendas of the fabulously rich residents of centuries past make the best lodgings. Often near the center of town, sometimes facing directly onto plazas, some of these mansions date from the 16th century. There are also deluxe modern high-rises and functional, low-cost hotels. Except for five-star hotels, most properties in the region aren't heated; you may want to bring warm, comfortable clothes for indoor wear, or to inquire in advance if heating is important to you. In restored colonial properties, rooms often vary dramatically as to size and furnishings, so if you aren't satisfied with the one you are shown, ask to see another. High season, for the most part, is limited to specific dates surrounding Christmas, Easter, and regional festivals. Most moderate and inexpensive hotels quote prices with 15% value-added tax already included.

CATEGORY	COST*
$$$$	over $200
$$$	$100–$200
$$	$50–$100
$	under $50

**All prices are for a standard double room, excluding 15% tax.*

Exploring the Heartland

Many travelers barrel past the heartland to points north or west of Mexico City, but there are plenty of reasons to stop here: browsing in the shops of San Miguel or Guanajuato for bargains in silver and other local crafts, or heading to the state of Michoacán, renowned for its folklore and folk crafts, especially ceramics and lacquerware. Stay longer to linger over the wealth of architectural styles that each of the colonial cities has to offer.

Numbers in the text correspond to numbers in the margin and on the San Miguel de Allende, Guanajuato, Zacatecas, Querétaro, Morelia, and Pátzcuaro maps.

Great Itineraries

If you have only a couple of days to spare, stop in any of several colonial cities for a taste of life in the heartland—each one has its own particular flavor. If you happen to fall under the heartland's peaceful, friendly spell, you'll want a week to 10 days to give yourself time to drink in the atmosphere of two or three of the region's cities.

IF YOU HAVE 3 DAYS

Head to **Guanajuato** 12–22 (365 km [226 mi] from Mexico City), the most architecturally dramatic of the heartland cities. Make a day trip from here to the picturesque town of **San Miguel de Allende** 1–11, 90 minutes away by car or bus, to shop for crafts.

Another option is to go from Mexico City to the Michoacán capital of **Morelia** 40–49 (about four hours by car) and spend a day taking in its stately architecture and café-lined plaza. The next day, drive on to **Pátzcuaro** 50–56, set among volcanoes in the center of Purépecha Indian country. Spend the morning in the bustling market or strolling in the surrounding countryside before making a late-afternoon return to Mexico City.

IF YOU HAVE 5 DAYS

Make **Guanajuato** 12–22 your base and allow an extra day to see its churches and museums—perhaps even the gruesome Mummy Museum. Stop off at the town of Dolores Hidalgo, home of Mexican independence, on your way to a day of shopping in San Miguel. Overnight in San Miguel and the next morning head for **Querétaro** 32–39, 63 km (39 mi) away. This quiet colonial city is considered the capital of the Bajío. After a night in a downtown hotel, return to Mexico City (three hours) or to the airport outside Guanajuato (2½ hours).

If you decide to spend several days in Michoacán, you can easily fill your time exploring the state's colonial towns and enjoying the lush, mountainous countryside. After three days in **Morelia** 40–49 and **Pátzcuaro** 50–56, take a day trip to explore the crater on an extinct volcano in **San Juan Parangaricútiro** or the ruins of an ancient Purépecha Indian capital, **Tzintzuntzan** (both are easy day trips from Pátzcuaro), before returning on the final day to Morelia and Mexico City.

IF YOU HAVE 7 DAYS

From your base in **Guanajuato** 12–22, consider adding to the first of the five-day itineraries a round-trip flight from León's Guanajuato International Airport to **Zacatecas** 23–31. This would give you a day and a half to explore the northern colonial mining city. Because it lies off the main tourist track, Zacatecas has a refreshingly unself-conscious attitude. Another possibility for a week in the heartland would be to make a loop from Mexico City that includes both Morelia and Guanajuato. You'd have time for leisurely side trips to **Pátzcuaro** 50–56 and **San Miguel de Allende** 1–11 and a stop in **Querétaro** 32–39. When in

Pátzcuaro, be sure to take a boat out to the island town of **Janítzio** on nearby Lake Pátzcuaro, home of Mexico's most famous Day of the Dead festival (lasting up to two days), or to the island of **Yunuen**, which isn't as yet besieged by tourists.

When to Tour the Heartland

One of the most pleasing aspects of the heartland is its superb climate—it rarely gets overly hot, even in the middle of summer, and although winter days can get nippy, especially in northern Zacatecas, they are generally temperate. Average temperatures in the southern city of Morelia range from 20°C (68°F) in May to just under 10°C (49°F) in January. Zacatecas is more extreme, with winter temperatures as low as 0°C (32°F) and snow flurries every several years, and summer highs of 28°C–30°C (81°F–85°F). Nights are cool all year in most of the region's cities. The rainy season across the heartland hits between June and October and is generally strongest in July and August.

Consider going to the heartland for cultural festivals or religious events: in October Guanajuato's three-week-long International Cervantes Festival, which brings actors, musicians, painters, and hundreds of thousands of visitors to town; in late November San Miguel's Jazz Festival International; and November 1–2 on the island of Janítzio, where local Purépecha (also called Tarascan) Indians hold a Day of the Dead in honor of their ancestors. Millions of monarch butterflies arrive near Morelia between early November and early March.

SAN MIGUEL DE ALLENDE

San Miguel de Allende first began luring foreigners in the late 1930s when American Stirling Dickinson and prominent local residents founded an art school in this mountainous settlement. The school, now called the Instituto Allende, has grown in stature over the years—as has the city's reputation as a writers' and artists' colony. Walk down any cobblestone street and you're likely to see residents of a variety of national origins. Some come to study at the Instituto Allende or the Academia Hispano-Americana, some to escape the harsh northern winters, and still others to retire.

Cultural offerings in this town of about 110,000 reflect its large American and Canadian community. There are literary readings, art shows, a yearly jazz festival, psychic fairs, aerobics and past-life regression classes, and a lending library. International influence notwithstanding, San Miguel, declared a national monument in 1926, retains its Mexican characteristics. Wandering down streets lined with 18th-century mansions, you'll also discover fountains, monuments, and churches—all reminders of the city's illustrious, and sometimes notorious, past. The onetime headquarters of the Spanish Inquisition in New Spain, for example, is at the corner of Calles Hernández Macías and Pila Seca. The former Inquisition jail stands across the way. Independence Day is celebrated with exceptional fervor in San Miguel, with fireworks, dances, and parades September 15 and 16, and bullfights and cultural events for the remainder of the month, including the running of the bulls.

Exploring San Miguel de Allende

You'll find most of San Miguel's sights in a cluster downtown, which you can visit in a couple of hours.

A Good Walk

Begin at the main plaza, otherwise known as **El Jardín** ①. After you get a feel for the square, stop into **La Parroquia** ②, the sandstone

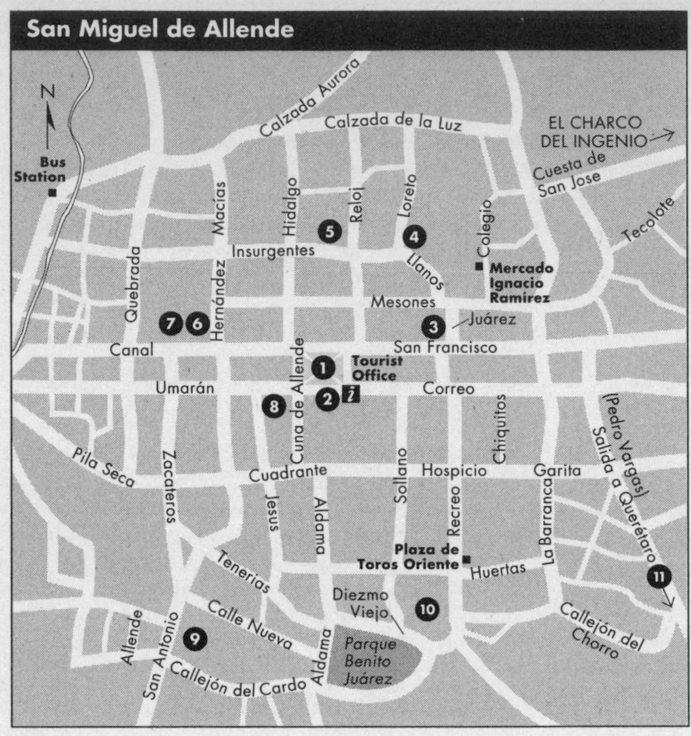

church on its south side. Three blocks northeast of La Parroquia (take Calle San Francisco, on the north side of El Jardín, to Calle Juárez) is the **Iglesia de San Francisco** ③, with a fine churrigueresque (heavily ornamented) facade. Take a few steps north on Calle Juárez to Calle Mesones, then east to Calle Colegio, where the colorful **Mercado Ignacio Ramírez** occupies a cavernous structure off the west side of the street. The dome of the **Oratorio de San Felipe Neri** ④ is visible just before the market.

A block west of the church on Calle Insurgentes, **La Biblioteca Pública** ⑤ is a great place to catch up on town events. Continue west from the library two blocks to Calle Hernández Macías, then head south to the **Bellas Artes** ⑥ cultural center at No. 75 and the ornate **Iglesia de la Concepción** ⑦ behind it. Take Hernández Macías south for a block and turn left on Calle Umarán to reach the **Casa de Ignacio Allende** ⑧, birthplace of the Mexican national hero. You've circled back to the southwest corner of El Jardín.

After making your way around the center of town, consider a leisurely stroll to sights a bit farther afield. From the south side of the plaza (by La Parroquia), head west four blocks on Calle Umarán until you reach Calle Zacateros. Turn south on this narrow cobblestone street for some of the town's most interesting crafts shops—stocked with everything from silver jewelry to Mexican ceremonial masks.

Past the shops, Calle Zacateros becomes Ancha de San Antonio. On your left at No. 20 is the renowned **Instituto Allende** ⑨, where many of San Miguel's foreign visitors come to study. From the institute, continue south on Ancha de San Antonio until you reach Callejón del Cardo on your left. Continue past St. Paul's Episcopal Church, an expat house of worship, until you arrive at the cobblestone Calle Aldama on your left. Head downhill and walk briefly through a neighborhood of whitewashed houses before reaching the north entrance to the 5-acre Parque Benito Juárez, an oasis of evergreens, palm trees, and gardens.

From the north edge of the park, follow Calle Diezmo Viejo to the terra-cotta–color mansion known as La Huerta Santa Elena. From here turn left and walk one block uphill to the **Lavaderos Publicos** ⑩, San Miguel's outdoor laundry and a favorite gathering spot for local women. Calle Recreo, above the Lavandería, heads north back toward the plaza: follow Recreo until reaching Calle Correo, turn left, and walk three blocks to return to El Jardín.

Sights to See

6 **Bellas Artes.** This impressive cloister across the street from the U.S. Consulate was once the Royal Convent of the Conception. Since 1938 it has been an institute for the study of music, dance, and the visual arts. There are rotating exhibits and a cafeteria on the patio. A bulletin board at the entrance lists cultural events. ✉ *Calle Hernández Macías 75, El Centro,* ☎ *415/152–0289.* 🎟 *Free.* ⏲ *Mon.–Sat. 9–8, Sun. 10–2.*

5 **La Biblioteca Pública.** Notices—about such things as literary readings and yoga and aerobics classes—are posted on the bulletin board in the entranceway to the library. There's a lovely courtyard café inside, as well as the offices of the English-language newspaper *Atención San Miguel* and reading rooms with back issues of popular publications and books in English. On Sundays at noon a two-hour house-and-garden tour (about $15) of San Miguel leaves from the library. ✉ *Calle Insurgentes 25, El Centro,* ☎ *415/152–0293,* FAX *415/152–7048.* ⏲ *Weekdays 10–2 and 4–7, Sat. 10–2.*

8 **Casa de Ignacio Allende.** Now housing a museum and gallery, this is the birthplace of Ignacio Allende, one of Mexico's great independence heroes. Allende was a Creole aristocrat who, along with Father Miguel Hidalgo, plotted in the early 1800s to overthrow the Spanish regime. At clandestine meetings held in San Miguel and nearby Querétaro, the two discussed strategies, organized an army, gathered weapons, and enlisted the support of clerics for the struggle ahead.

Spanish Royalists learned of their plot and began arresting conspirators in Querétaro on September 13, 1810. Allende and Hidalgo received word of these actions and hastened their plans. At dawn on September 16, they rang out the cry for independence, and the fighting began. Allende was captured and executed by the Royalists the following year. As a tribute to his brave efforts, San Miguel El Grande was renamed San Miguel de Allende in the 20th century. ✉ *Calle Cuna de Allende 1, El Centro,* ☎ *415/152–2499.* 🎟 *$3.* ⏲ *Tues.–Sun. 10–4.*

El Charco del Ingenio. Northeast of the city center, San Miguel's botanical garden is an enjoyable place to walk or cycle, particularly in the early morning or late afternoon. Its five-odd miles of pathways wind past more than 1,500 species of cacti and succulents. ✉ *1½ km (1 mi) northeast of El Jardín; signs point the way off Cuesta de San Jose.* 🎟 *$1.* ⏲ *Sunrise–sunset.*

7 **Iglesia de la Concepción.** Just behind the Bellas Artes cultural center, this church has one of the largest domes in Mexico. The two-story dome (completed in 1891) and the elegant Corinthian columns and pilasters gracing its drum are said to have been inspired by the dome of the Hôtel des Invalides in Paris. Ceferino Gutiérrez (of La Parroquia fame) is credited with its design. ✉ *Calle Canal between Calles Hernández Macías and Zacateros, El Centro.*

3 **Iglesia de San Francisco.** The San Francisco Church has one of the finest churrigueresque facades in the state of Guanajuato. This term for the

style refers to José Churriguera, a 17th-century (Baroque) Spanish architect, noted for his extravagant surface decoration. Built in the late 18th century, it was financed by donations from wealthy patrons and by revenue from bullfights. Topping the elaborately carved exterior is the image of Saint Francis of Assisi. Below, along with a crucifix, are sculptures of Saint John and Our Lady of Sorrows. ✉ *Calle Juárez between Calles San Francisco and Mesones, El Centro.*

9 **Instituto Allende.** The school is in the former country estate of the Count of Canal. Since its founding in 1951, thousands of students from around the world have come to learn Spanish and to take classes in the arts here. Courses last from a couple of weeks to a month or longer. Lush with bougainvillea, rosebushes, and ivy vines, the grounds provide a quiet refuge for students and visitors alike. ✉ *Ancha de San Antonio 20, El Centro,* ☎ *415/152–0190,* FAX *415/152–4538,* WEB *www.instituto-allende.edu.mx.* ⏲ *Weekdays 8–6, Sat. 9–1.*

1 **El Jardín** (The Garden). The heart of San Miguel is the plaza commonly known as El Jardín. Seated on one of its wrought-iron benches, you'll quickly get a feel for the town: old men with canes exchange tales, young lovers smooch, and bells from nearby La Parroquia pierce the thin mountain air at each quarter hour. At dusk thousands of grackles make a fantastic ruckus as they return to roost in the laurel trees. ✉ *Bounded by Calle Correo on the south, Calle San Francisco on the north, Portal Allende on the west, and Portal Guadalupe on the east, El Centro.*

NEED A BREAK?

On the southwest corner of the main plaza is **Café del Jardín** (✉ Portal Allende 2, El Centro, ☎ 415/152–5006). This unassuming little café has excellent coffee, cappuccino, hot chocolate, and, in the evening, pizza. Breakfasts are tasty and inexpensive, and the service is friendly.

10 **Lavaderos Publicos.** At this outdoor public laundry—a collection of red concrete tubs set above Parque Benito Juárez—local women gather daily to wash clothes and chat as their predecessors have done for centuries. Although some women claim to have more-efficient washing facilities at home, the lure of the spring-fed troughs—not to mention the chance to catch up on the news—brings them to this shaded courtyard. ✉ *Calle Diezmo Viejo at Calle Recreo, El Centro.*

11 **El Mirador.** Climb El Mirador (The Lookout) for a panorama of the city, mountains, and reservoir below. The vista is great at sunset, and chances are you won't be alone. Locals and tourists like to join Pedro Vargas, whose bronze image commands this spot. ✉ *1 block before town turn right off Calle Recreo onto Calle Hospicio, follow Hospicio 3 blocks to Calle Pedro Vargas, turn right, and head uphill to the overlook, El Centro.*

4 **Oratorio de San Felipe Neri.** Built by local Indians in 1712, the original chapel can still be glimpsed in the eastern facade, made of pink stone and adorned with a figure of Our Lady of Solitude. The newer, southern front was built in an ornate Baroque style. In 1734 the wealthy Count of Canal paid for an addition to the Oratorio. His **Templo de Santa Casa de Loreto,** dedicated to the Virgin of Loreto, is just behind the Oratorio. Its main entrance, now blocked by a grille, is on the Oratorio's left rear side. Peer through the grille to see the heavily gilded altars and effigies of the count and his wife, under which they are buried. ✉ *Calles Insurgentes and Loreto, El Centro.*

2 **La Parroquia.** This towering Gothic Revival parish church, made of local *cantera* sandstone, was designed in the late 19th century by self-trained mason Ceferino Gutiérrez, who sketched his designs in the sand

with a stick. Gutiérrez was purportedly inspired by postcards of European Gothic cathedrals. Since the postcards gave no hint of what the back of those cathedrals looked like, the posterior of La Parroquia was done in quintessential Mexican style.

La Parroquia still functions as a house of worship, although its interior has been changed over the years. Gilded wood altars, for example, were replaced with neoclassical stone altars. The original bell, cast in 1732, still calls parishioners to mass several times daily. ✉ *South side of El Jardín on Calle Correo, El Centro.*

Dining

For its size, San Miguel has a surprisingly large number of international restaurants. The steady influx of American and Canadian visitors supports a variety of Tex-Mex and health-food places. A European influence has contributed to variations on French, Italian, and Spanish themes.

$$$$ ★ ✕ **El Market Bistro.** Fine French cuisine is served in a lush, stone-paved garden with a piano or in a private dining room enhanced by a roaring fire. For a special evening try the *tournedos rossini,* a marinated sirloin smothered in foie gras, red wine sauce, and mushrooms. The leek and potato soup and goat cheese salad are delectable. ✉ *Hernandez Macias 95, El Centro,* ☎ *415/152–3229. AE, MC, V.*

$$$$ ✕ **Tio Lucas.** This is possibly the most popular restaurant in San Miguel as much for the nightly jazz music and covered-patio ambience as for the grilled fare. Share an *ensalada César,* created at your table by one of the talented and friendly waiters. The sumptuous house specialty, *filete Chemita,* is a thick-cut fillet crowned in a secret recipe garlic sauce. ✉ *Mesones 103, El Centro,* ☎ *415/152–4996. AE, MC, V.*

$$$ ✕ **Bugambilia.** Founded in 1945, Mercedes Arteaga Tovar's restaurant has a well-earned reputation for serving fine traditional Mexican cuisine. Try such classic specialties as *pollo en mole poblano* (chicken coated in a traditional mole sauce) and *sopa azteca* (classic tortilla soup served with a variety of toppings). The candlelit, tree-filled colonial courtyard and live classical guitarist make for a romantic setting. ✉ *Calle Hidalgo 42, El Centro,* ☎ *415/152–0127. AE, MC, V.*

$$$ ★ ✕ **L'Invito.** Indulge in Sylvia's authentic Italian cuisine beneath the soft lights of a romantic courtyard. Enjoy a glass of wine and the prosciutto and mozzarella cheese panini, then select from a menu of traditional pastas, Italian meat dishes, and side vegetables like the carrots flambéed in cognac. The daily special includes soup, meat, vegetables, and homemade dessert; the peanut ice cream is delicious. Portions are designed to leave you satisfied, not stuffed. ✉ *Umarán 19, El Centro,* ☎ *415/152–7333. AE, MC, V.*

$$ ✕ **Cafe Olé Olé.** Dine in this lively steak house and survey the collection of posters, paintings, and other bullfight memorabilia from around the country. For starters, savor the favorite *champiñones ajillio,* mushrooms floating in a bath of garlic and butter. The *Fajitas Olé Olé,* with chicken, beef, or shrimp are served with fresh tortillas and guacamole. If you're feeling adventurous, order the ostrich kabobs. ✉ *Loreto 66-A, El Centro,* ☎ *415/152–0896. No credit cards. Closed Sun.*

$ ✕ **The Bagel Café.** A popular hangout for breakfast and lunch, this cozy café offers patio or indoor dining near El Jardín. Revive with a fresh-baked bagel topped with Alaskan lox, or linger over iced tea and a chicken breast sandwich. ✉ *Correo 19, El Centro,* ☎ *415/152–2497. No credit cards.*

$ ★ ✕ **La Buena Vida.** Don't miss this fabulous bakery and tiny coffee shop and its mouthwatering orange scones, chocolate-chip cookies, lemon bread, and breakfast specials. If the few patio tables are full, take your treats to the plaza. ✉ *Hernández Macías 72–5, El Centro,* ☎ *415/152–2211. No credit cards.*

Lodging

San Miguel has a wide selection of lodging, from cozy bed-and-breakfasts to elegant all-suites properties. Rooms fill up quickly in summer and winter, when northern tourists migrate here in droves. Make reservations several months in advance if you plan to visit at these times or during the September Independence Day festivities.

$$$$ **Casa de Sierra Nevada.** Built in 1580 as the residence of the archbishop of Guanajuato, this elegant country-style inn still attracts ambassadors, diplomats, film stars, and other luminaries; children under 16 aren't admitted, however, and the formerly attentive service has declined. Lace curtains, handwoven rugs, and chandeliers adorn some rooms; fireplaces, cozy terraces, and skylights enhance others. The hotel runs the separate **Casa de Sierra Nevada en el Parque** (✉ Santa Elena 2, El Centro), an exquisitely restored 18th-century ex-hacienda with just five guest rooms. Its restaurant serves refined versions of traditional Mexican dishes and has a wonderful view of Parque Benito Juárez. ✉ *Calle Hospicio 46, El Centro 37700,* ☎ *415/152–7040,* FAX *415/152–1436. 17 rooms, 16 suites. 2 restaurants, pool, massage, spa, horseback riding, bar. AE, MC, V.*

$$$$ ★ **La Puertecita Boutique Hotel.** In a secluded, wooded canyon in the tony Atascadero neighborhood, this luxury no-smoking hotel has uniquely decorated rooms with rustic Mexican furnishings, domed vaulted ceilings, and in many cases private patios, fireplaces, and bathrooms with small indoor gardens. Customized vacation packages including room, meals, mountain biking, horseback riding, hot-springs excursions, and yoga, cooking, art, or Spanish classes are available. You can use the golf and tennis facilities at Club Malanquin. ✉ *Santo Domingo 75, Colonia Atascadero 37740,* ☎ *415/152–5011 or 415/152–2250,* FAX *415/152–5505,* WEB *www.lapuertecita.com. 18 rooms, 6 suites. Restaurant, 2 pools, massage, billiards. AE, MC, V.*

$$$ ★ **Casa Luna.** In a restored 300-year-old Spanish colonial house, this lovely B&B has 2-ft-thick walls, 20-ft-high ceilings, and tranquil fountain- and flower-filled patios. Rooms have antiques, fireplaces, featherbeds, and bathtubs. The rooftop honor bar is spectacular at night, lighted by some two dozen miniature tin star lights. Cooking classes are frequently available on-site. A three-night minimum stay is required; children are allowed only when the entire house is rented to one party. ✉ *Pila Seca 11, El Centro 37700,* ☎ FAX *415/152–1117,* WEB *www.casaluna.com. 8 rooms, 1 suite. Dining room, massage, shop. MC, V.*

$$$ **Villa Jacaranda.** Near the Parque Benito Juárez, the Villa Jacaranda has a full range of amenities. Rooms, though decorated without imagination, have space heaters, tile bathtubs, and cable TV. The hotel's Cine-Bar shows American movies daily at 7:30 PM; the price of admission—roughly $5—includes a drink. The restaurant serves international and Mexican cuisine in the homey dining room or in a stained-glass gazebo, and there's a delicious Sunday champagne brunch for about $8. ✉ *Calle Aldama 53, El Centro 37700,* ☎ *415/152–1015, 415/152–0811, or 800/310–9688,* FAX *415/152–0883,* WEB *www.villajacaranda.com. 5 rooms, 11 suites. Restaurant, hot tub, bar, cinema, free parking. AE, MC, V.*

$$$ **Villas Mirasol.** Each of this lodge's rooms is tastefully decorated with original prints, oil paintings, pastels, or small sculptures. Most rooms are flooded with sunlight during the day, and all have a private or shared terrace. A second branch (✉ Callejón del Pueblito 4–A, El Centro) is

located in a cozy house near the Mercado Ignacio Ramírez. Both locations are on quiet streets, each about a 10-minute walk from the main plaza. A rich breakfast is included in the rate. Children under 12 are discouraged from staying in either hotel. ✉ *Pila Seca 35, Apdo. 409, El Centro 37700,* ☎ *415/152–6685 or 415/154–5113,* FAX *415/152–1564,* WEB *www.infosma.com/villamirasol. 13 rooms, 6 suites. Dining room. AE, MC, V.*

$$ **Casa Carmen.** Run by a friendly San Miguel family, this pension is an oasis of peace in the center of town. The 200-year-old house two blocks from El Jardín has large, clean rooms, each with desk or writing table and portable gas heater, and two small patios. The large suite on the top floor has a great view of the city for the same price, but is often booked far in advance. Rates include breakfast and lunch. ✉ *Calle Correo 31, El Centro 37700,* ☎ *415/152–0844. 12 rooms. Dining room. No credit cards.*

$$ **Villa Scorpio al Puente.** Located next to the Heroes Bridge (where couples meet to enjoy enchanting sunsets), this cozy B&B boasts a stunning rooftop-patio view of San Miguel and the surrounding countryside. A well-stocked library, three gardens, and an elegant salon provide comfortable places to visit with friends or enjoy a quiet afternoon. You'll find a fresh bouquet of flowers, down bedding, and a gas fireplace in every room. The 250-year-old house was connected to an underground tunnel system used during the revolution. ✉ *Quebrada 93, El Centro 37700,* ☎ FAX *415/152–7575,* WEB *www.villascorpio.com. 5 rooms. Dining room, spa, bar. No credit cards.*

$ **Posada de las Monjas.** This 19th-century inn has been operating as a hotel for more than 50 years. Rooms are simply furnished in a colonial style. Some in the old wing are uncomfortably dark and cramped. The rooftop public terrace has tables and lounge chairs and offers commanding views of mountains and city. Some rooms have fireplaces, and there's a communal TV in the lobby, which looks like a formal Mexican living room. ✉ *Calle Canal 37, El Centro 37700,* ☎ *415/152–0171,* FAX *415/152–6227. 65 rooms. Restaurant, bar, laundry service, free parking. MC, V.*

$ **Quinta Loreto.** Clean, plain, comfortable rooms, shady and pleasantly kept grounds, and excellent *comida casera* (home cooking) make this inexpensive hotel a favorite with snowbirds and other San Miguel aficionados. There's a dilapidated tennis court and an unheated pool, which is dirty and uninviting. The hotel is about a 10-minute walk north of the main plaza, near the market. Many nonguests take their *comida corrida* (fixed-menu lunch) in the unpretentious dining room. ✉ *Calle Loreto 15, El Centro 37700,* ☎ *415/152–0042,* FAX *415/152–3616. 40 rooms. Restaurant, tennis court, pool. AE, MC, V.*

Nightlife and the Arts

The Arts

San Miguel, long known as an artists' colony, continues to nurture that image today. Galleries, museums, and arty shops line the streets near El Jardín, and two government-run salons—at **Bellas Artes** and **Instituto Allende**—feature the work of Mexican artists. The **Galería de Arte Contemporáneo** (✉ Plaza Principal 14, El Centro, ☎ 415/152–0454) sells works by contemporary Mexican artists. For a sampling of both regional and international talent, visit **Galería Atenea** (✉ Jesús 2, El Centro, ☎ 415/152–0785). The rambling rooms of **Galería Duo Duo** (✉ Pila Seca 3, El Centro, ☎ 415/152–6211) features local and international artists. **Galería del Pueblo** (✉ Calle Correo 12A, El Centro, ☎ 415/152–1448) shows an extensive collection of Huitchol beadwork and yarn paintings. For a taste of contemporary Mexican art stop by **Galería San Miguel** (✉ Plaza Principal 14, El Centro, ☎ 415/152–0454). **Kligerman Gallery** (✉ Calle San Francisco 11, El Centro, ☎ 415/152–0951) has contemporary Mexican and American art. Most close weekdays between 2 and 4 and are open Sunday 10 or 11 to 2 or 3.

For more than 20 years, San Miguel has played host to the world-class **Festival de Musica de Camara** in August, a feast of classical chamber music that in past years has included the illustrious Tokyo String Quartet. The **Jazz Festival International** takes place around the last week in November. Tickets for the concerts, workshops, and after-hour jam sessions may be purchased individually or for the series. Call the tourist office for dates and details.

Nightlife

On most evenings in San Miguel you can readily satisfy a whim for a literary reading, an American movie, a theatrical production, or a turn on a disco dance floor. The most up-to-date listings of events can be found in the English-language paper *Atención San Miguel,* published every Sunday. The bulletin board at the public library (✉ Calle Insurgentes 25) is also a good source of current events.

Agave Azul (✉ Calle Mesones 99, El Centro, ☎ 415/152–1958) draws a crowd for live music and, of course, tequila. **Mama Mia** (✉ Calle Umarán 8, El Centro, ☎ 415/152–2063) presents everything from Peruvian folk music, classical guitar, and flamenco to salsa and rock. The rotating art exhibitions and comfortable leather chairs at **El Petit Bar** (✉ Hernandez Macias 95, El Centro, ☎ 415/152–3229) attract an eclectic mix of locals and tourists. **Plum** (✉ Zacateros 21, El Centro, ☎ 415/154–8323) offers a variety of international cocktails and music in a distinctly purple setting.

Outdoor Activities and Sports

The **Club de Golf Malanquin** (✉ Celaya Hwy., Km 3, ☎ 415/152–0516) has a heated pool, steam baths, tennis courts, and 9 holes of golf, all of which are open to the public for a guest fee of $45 on weekdays or $70 on weekends; it's closed Monday. The exclusive **Hotel Hacienda Taboada** (✉ Dolores Hidalgo Hwy., Km 8, ☎ 415/152–0888, FAX 415/152–1798) has several geothermal pools, manicured grounds, and tennis courts. It's open to the public for about $15, which includes lunch; closed Wednesday. **Taboada** (✉ Dolores Hidalgo Hwy., Km 8) has three outdoor geothermally heated pools, one of which is Olympic-size and good for doing laps. They are open to the public for $3.50; closed Tuesday.

Ballooning

Gone with the Wind Balloon Adventures (✉ Calle Recreo 68, El Centro, ☎ 415/152–6735) offers hot-air balloon rides over town and the surrounding countryside with licensed-certified pilots from Napa Valley, California. The one-hour flights depart at 6 or 7 AM, depending on the season. The $150 cost includes breakfast upon landing.

Biking

Aventuras San Miguel (✉ Calle Recreo 10, El Centro, ☎ 415/152–6406, FAX 415/152–6153) rents bicycles at reasonable prices. **Bici-Burro** (✉ Calle Hospicio 1, esq. Barranca, El Centro, ☎ 415/152–1526) rents and services bikes for exploring San Miguel and environs.

Bullfights

To witness the pageantry of a traditional Mexican bullfight, go to the **Plaza de Toros Oriente** (✉ off Calle Recreo, El Centro), which has events several times a year. The most important contest takes place in the last week of September during *la fiesta de San Miguel.* Call the tourist office for more information.

Horseback Riding

Aventuras San Miguel (✉ Calle Recreo 10, El Centro, ☎ 415/152–6406) rents horses at reasonable rates. The equestrian center of the hotel **Casa de Sierra Nevada** offers riding lessons, carriage rides, and horse rental at its 500-acre ranch for about $50 per hour.

Shopping

For centuries San Miguel's artisans have been creating crafts ranging from straw products to metalwork. Although some boutiques in town may be a bit pricey, you can find good buys on silver, brass, tin, woven-cotton goods, and folk art. Store hours tend to be erratic, but most stores open daily at around 9, shut their doors for the traditional afternoon siesta (2 to 4 or 5), then reopen in the afternoon until 7 or 8, and open for just a half day on Sunday. Most San Miguel shops accept MasterCard and Visa.

Markets

Spilling out for several blocks behind the Mercado Ignacio Ramírez, the **Mercado de Artesanías** (artisans' market) is where you'll find vendors of local work—glass, tin, and papier-mâché—as well as some of the best prices on silver jewelry in town. **Mercado Ignacio Ramírez,** a traditional Mexican covered market off Calle Colegio, one block north of Calle Mesones, is a colorful jumble of fresh fruits and vegetables, flowers, bloody butchers' counters, inexpensive plastic toys, taco stands, and Mexican-made cassettes.

Specialty Shops

FOLK ART

Artes de México (✉ Calz. Aurora 47, at Dolores Hidalgo exit, Colonia Guadalupe, ☎ 415/152–0764) has been producing and selling traditional crafts, including furniture, metalwork, and ceramics, for more than 40 years. **La Calaca** (✉ Calle Mesones 93, El Centro, ☎ 415/152–3954) focuses on quality antique and contemporary Latin American folk and ceremonial art. Although the inventory at the **Casa Maxwell** (✉ Calle Canal 14, El Centro, ☎ 415/152–0247) has slipped in quality, there's still a reasonable selection of folk art. **La Guadalupana** (✉ Jesus 25-A, inside Jasmine Day Spa, El Centro, ☎ 415/152–7973) sells all manner of items adorned with images of Mexico's beloved Virgin of Guadalupe—from temporary tattoos to coffee mugs. **Talisman Boutique 2** (✉ San Francisco 7, El Centro, ☎ 415/152–0438) sells beautiful embroidered *huipiles* (tunics or blouses) from southern Mexico and Guatemala.

HOUSEWARES

Casa Canal (✉ Calle Canal 3, El Centro, ☎ 415/152–0479), in a beautiful old hacienda, sells new furniture, much of it in traditional styles. **Casa María Luisa** (✉ Calle Canal 40, El Centro, ☎ 415/152–0130) focuses on a wild combination of contemporary Mexican furniture, household items, and art. **Casa Vieja** (✉ Calle Mesones 83, El Centro, ☎ 415/152–1284) has tons of glassware and ceramics, housewares, picture frames, furniture, and more. **CLAN destino** (✉ Zacateros 19, El Centro, ☎ FAX 415/152–1623) features an eclectic international mix of antiques, contemporary art, and jewelry. **México Lindo** (✉ Calle Mesones 85, El Centro, ☎ 415/152–0730) sells a good selection of hand-painted tiles and ceramics from Dolores Hidalgo. **La Zandunga** (✉ Calle Hernández Macías 129, El Centro, ☎ 415/152–4608) sells high-quality, 100% wool rugs from Oaxaca.

Close-Up

MÉXICO: HECHO A MANO

HANDMADE IN MEXICO: some of the world's finest *artesanías* (crafts) come from this country. Artisanal work is varied, original, colorful, and inexpensive, and it supports millions of families who are carrying on ancient and more recent traditions. Although cheap, shoddy items masquerading as "native crafts" are certainly common, careful shoppers who take their time can come away with real works of folk art. Also keep in mind that many items are exempt from duty.

The crafts to look for are ceramics, woodwork, lacquerware, leather, weaving and textiles, and silver, gold, and semiprecious-stone jewelry. Each region has its specialty. Cities that are noted for the quality of their crafts are Puebla (Chapter 3); Nogales in Sonora (Chapter 5); Guadalajara, Tlaquepaque, and Tonalá in Jalisco (Chapter 7); San Miguel de Allende, Guanajuato, and Pátzcuaro in the heartland (Chapter 8); Taxco in Morelos (Chapter 9); Oaxaca City in Oaxaca (Chapter 11); San Cristóbal de las Casas in Chiapas (Chapter 12); and Mérida in Yucatán (Chapter 14).

Ceramics. Talavera-style tiles (blue majolica) and other ceramic ware are at their best in Puebla. Oaxaca state is known for its unglazed, burnished black pottery. Inventive masks and figurines come from Valle de Bravo, Pátzcuaro in the state of Michoacán, Tonalá outside of Guadalajara, Taxco, and Chiapas.

Jewelry. Silver is best in Taxco, San Miguel de Allende, and Oaxaca; be sure purchases are stamped "925," which means 92.5% pure silver. You can find gold filigree in Guanajuato and Oaxaca. Oaxaca and Chiapas are also known for their amber, but be aware that much of what is sold as amber is in fact glass or plastic. Good rules of thumb: don't buy amber off the street; and if it seems like a great bargain, it's probably fake. For semiprecious stones, go to jewelers' shops in Puebla and Querétaro. Coral jewelry is sold in the Yucatán and other coastal areas, but because of the massive ecological damage caused by coral harvesting, the practice around it is environmentally unsound.

Leather. The key places to find quality leatherwork are Guadalajara, Oaxaca (for sandals), Chiapas (for belts and purses), and the Yucatán (for bags).

Metalwork. Look for copper in Santa Clara del Cobre in Michoacán, and tin in San Miguel de Allende and Oaxaca.

Weavings and Textiles. Fabric work is quite varied: you'll find *rebozos* (shawls) and blankets around Oaxaca, Guadalajara, Jalapa, and Pátzcuaro; *huipiles* (heavily embroidered tunics worn by Indian women) and other embroidered clothing in Michoacán, Oaxaca state, Chiapas, and the Yucatán; masterfully woven rugs, some colored with natural dyes, in Oaxaca; hammocks and baskets in Oaxaca and the Yucatán; lace in the colonial cities of the heartland area; *guayaberas* (comfortable, embroidered or pleated men's dress shirts, now usually mass-produced) along the Gulf coast; and reed mats in Oaxaca and Valle de Bravo. The Mezquital region east of Querétaro can also be rewarding, as can shopping for Huichol Indian yarn paintings and embroidery near Puerto Vallarta.

Woodwork. Look for masks in Mexico City; *alebrijes* (painted wooden animals) in Oaxaca; furniture in Cuernavaca, Guadalajara, San Miguel de Allende, Querétaro, Tequisquiapan, and Pátzcuaro; lacquerware in Uruapan and Pátzcuaro in Michoacán, Chiapa de Corzo in Chiapas, and Puerto Vallarta for pieces from Olinalá in Guerrero state; and guitars in Paracho, Michoacán.

JEWELRY

Established in 1963, **Joyería David** (✉ Calle Zacateros 53, El Centro, ☎ 415/152–0056) has an extensive selection of gold, silver, copper, and brass jewelry, all made on the premises. A number of pieces contain Mexican opals, amethysts, topaz, malachite, and turquoise. **Platería Cerroblanco** (✉ Calle Canal 17, El Centro, ☎ 415/152–0502) creates and crafts its own silver and gold jewelry and will arrange a visit to its *taller* (workshop) on request. The reputable **7th Heaven** (✉ Sollano 31, El Centro, ☎ 415/154–4677) designs and creates its own silver, gold, and carved amber pieces.

Side Trip to Dolores Hidalgo

50 km (31 mi) north of San Miguel via Rte. 51.

Dolores Hidalgo played an important role in the fight for independence. It was here, before dawn on September 16, 1810, that local priest Father Miguel Hidalgo gave an impassioned sermon to his clergy that ended with the *grito* (cry), "Death to bad government!" At 11 PM on September 15, politicians throughout the land repeat a revised version of the grito—"Viva Mexico! Viva Mexico! Viva Mexico!"—signaling the start of Independence Day celebrations. On September 16 (and only on this day), the bell in Hidalgo's parish church is rung.

Casa Hidalgo, the house where Father Hidalgo lived, is now a museum. It contains copies of important letters Hidalgo sent or received, and other independence memorabilia. ✉ *Calle Morelos 1,* ☎ *418/182–0171.* *About $3, free Sun.* ⏲ *Tues.–Sat. 10–5:45, Sun. 10–4:45.*

Dolores Hidalgo is famous for its lovely hand-glazed Talavera-style ceramics, most notably tiles and tableware. There are good prices at the town's many stores and factories. After shopping, head for the plaza for some of the most exotic ice creams you'll taste—flavors such as mole, avocado, beer, and corn. The town is an easy one-hour bus ride from San Miguel de Allende's Central de Autobuses.

San Miguel de Allende A to Z

To research prices, get advice from other travelers, and book travel arrangements, visit www.fodors.com.

AIR TRAVEL

Many international airlines fly into León's Guanajuato International Airport, which is about 1½ hours from San Miguel. Aeroméxico flies from Los Angeles. American travels from Dallas–Fort Worth. Continental has service from Houston. Mexicana comes from Chicago. Taxis from León's Guanajuato International Airport to downtown San Miguel cost about $60.

➤ AIRLINES AND CONTACTS: **Aeroméxico** (☎ 477/714–7156 or 477/716–6226). **American** (☎ 477/714–0483 or 477/716–5551). **Continental** (☎ 477/718–5254 or 477/718–5199). **Mexicana** (☎ 477/716–3697 or 477/714–9500).

BUS TRAVEL

Daily buses run direct from Mexico City's Central del Norte (North Bus Station) to the Central de Autobuses in San Miguel. Several major lines have frequent service. They include ETN, Flecha Amarilla, Primera Plus, Herradura de Plata, and Pegasso Plus. Travel time is about four hours.

➤ BUS INFORMATION: **ETN** (☎ 415/154–5135 or 415/152–6407). **Flecha Amarilla** (☎ 415/152–7323). **Herradura de Plata** (☎ 415/152–0725). **Pegasso Plus** (☎ 415/152–0725). **Primera Plus** (☎ 415/152–0084).

CAR RENTAL

Hola Rent a Car has a limited selection of manual-transmission compacts available.

➤ LOCAL AGENCIES: **Hola Rent a Car** (✉ Plaza Principal 2, Int. 5, El Centro, ☎ 415/152–0198).

CAR TRAVEL

Driving time from Mexico City to San Miguel is roughly four hours via Route 57 (to Querétaro) then Route 111. Traveling on Route 45 from Mexico City, a road connecting to Routes 57 and 111 bypasses Querétaro, saving a half hour. Guanajuato is 100 km (62 mi), about 1½ hours, west of San Miguel.

EMBASSIES

The U.S. Consulate is open weekdays 9–1.

➤ UNITED STATES: **U.S. Consulate** (✉ Calle Hernández Macías 72, El Centro, ☎ 415/152–2357 during office hours; 415/152–0068 or 415/152–0653 for emergencies).

EMERGENCIES

The staff at Hospital de la Fé can refer you to an English-speaking doctor.

San Miguel has many pharmacies. American residents recommend Botica Agundis, where English speakers are often on hand. It's open daily 10:30 AM–11 PM.

➤ EMERGENCY CONTACTS: **Ambulance–Red Cross** (☎ 415/152–4121 or 415/152–4225). **Fire Department** (☎ 415/152–2888). **Police** (☎ 415/152–0022). **Traffic Police** (☎ 415/152–0538).

➤ HOSPITAL: **Hospital de la Fé** (✉ Libramiento a Dolores Hidalgo 43, Mesa el Malanquin, ☎ 415/152–2233 or 415/152–2320).

➤ PHARMACY: **Botica Agundis** (✉ Calle Canal 26, El Centro, ☎ 415/152–1198).

ENGLISH-LANGUAGE MEDIA

Warren Hardy Spanish offers two-and-a-half-week classes in beginning, intermediate, and advanced Spanish.

El Colibrí has a good selection of paperback novels, magazines, and a few art supplies. Libros el Tecolote has a great selection of new and used books on Mexican art, history, literature, and cooking.

➤ BOOKSTORES AND LANGUAGE SCHOOL: **El Colibrí** (✉ Sollano 30, El Centro, ☎ 415/152–0751). **Libros el Tecolote** (✉ Calle Jesús 11, El Centro, ☎ FAX 415/152–7395). **Warren Hardy Spanish** (✉ San Rafael 6, El Centro, ☎ 415/154–4017 or 415/152–4728).

MAIL, INTERNET, AND SHIPPING

Border Crossings offers 24-hour answering and fax service, a Mexico address for receiving mail, packing and shipping, e-mail, a gift shop and art gallery, and other services. Internet San Miguel charges $5 an hour for the fastest Internet access in town. Coffee, beer, and fresh juices are available.

➤ CONTACTS: **Border Crossings** (✉ Correo 19, Int. 2, El Centro, ☎ 415/152–2497, FAX 415/152–3672). **Internet San Miguel** (✉ Mesones 57, side entrance at Reloj, El Centro, ☎ 415/154–4634, WEB www.internetsanmiguel.com).

MONEY MATTERS

A better bet for money exchange than the slow-moving bank lines is Intercam, open weekdays 9–6, Saturday 9–2.

➤ EXCHANGE SERVICES: **Intercam** (✉ Calles San Francisco 4, Correo 15, or Juárez 27, El Centro, ☎ 415/154–6660).

TAXIS

You can easily hail a taxi on the street or find one at taxi stands—Sitio Allende in the main plaza, Sitio San Francisco on Calle Mesones, or Sitio San Felipe on Calle Juárez. Flat rates to the bus terminal, train station, and other parts of the city apply.

➤ TAXI COMPANIES: **Sitio Allende** (☎ 415/152–0192).

TOURS

Aventuras San Miguel has off-the-beaten-track mountain-bike treks, "ghost town" trips, even nighttime full-moon excursions. Colonial México Tours runs historical tours to Guanajuato, Querétaro, and Dolores Hidalgo. Recommended for local tours is PMC (Promotion of Mexican Culture).

➤ TOUR OPERATOR RECOMMENDATIONS: **Aventuras San Miguel** (✉ Calle Recreo 10, El Centro, ☎ 415/152–6406, FAX 415/152–6153). **Colonial México Tours** (✉ Plaza Portal Allende 4, 2nd floor, El Centro, ☎ FAX 415/152–5794). **PMC** (✉ Calle Cuna de Allende 11, El Centro, ☎ 415/152–1630, FAX 415/152–0121).

TRANSPORTATION AROUND SAN MIGUEL DE ALLENDE

San Miguel de Allende is best covered on foot, keeping in mind two pieces of advice. The city is more than a mile above sea level, so you might tire quickly during your first few days here if you aren't accustomed to high altitudes. Streets are paved with rugged cobblestones, and some have no sidewalks. Sturdy footwear, such as athletic or other rubber-sole walking shoes, is recommended.

TRAVEL AGENCIES

Viajes Vértiz is the American Express representative in San Miguel.

➤ LOCAL AGENT REFERRALS: **Viajes Vértiz** (✉ Calle Hidalgo 1A, El Centro, ☎ 415/152–1856 or 415/152–1695, FAX 415/152–0499).

VISITOR INFORMATION

Delegación de Turismo, on the southeast corner of El Jardín, in a glassed-in office next to la Terraza restaurant, is open weekdays 10–5, Saturday 10–2.

➤ TOURIST INFORMATION: **Delegación de Turismo** (☎ 415/152–6565).

GUANAJUATO

100 km (62 mi) west of San Miguel de Allende, 365 km (226 mi) northwest of Mexico City.

Once Mexico's most prominent silver-mining city, Guanajuato is a colonial gem, tucked into the mountains at 6,700 ft. This provincial state capital is distinguished by twisting cobblestone alleyways, colorful houses, 15 shaded plazas, and a vast subterranean roadway where a rushing river once coursed. In the center of town is **Alhóndiga de Granaditas,** an 18th-century grain-storage facility that was the site of Mexico's first major victory in its War of Independence from Spain.

The city fills to overflowing in mid-October with the International Cervantes Festival, a three-week celebration of the arts. During the rest of the year, things regain a semblance of normalcy. Students rush to class with books tucked under their arms, women eye fresh produce at the Mercado Hidalgo, and old men utter greetings from behind whitewashed doorways. On weekend nights, *estudiantinas* (student minstrels dressed as medieval troubadours) serenade the public in the city squares.

Exploring Guanajuato

Although Guanajuato's many plazas and labyrinthine streets may seem confusing at first, this is not a bad city in which to get lost. The center is small, and there are wonderful surprises around every corner. Remember that the top of the Alhóndiga (which you can see from many spots in town) points north, and the spires of the Basílica Colegiata Nuestra Señora de Guanajuato, at Plaza de la Paz, point south.

A Good Walk

The tourist office, at Plaza de la Paz 14, is a good place to begin a walking tour. Turn right and walk up Obregón to reach **Jardín Unión** ⑫, Guanajuato's central square. The ornate **Teatro Juárez** ⑬ is just past the Jardín to your right on Calle Sopeña. The hardy might want to make a detour and take a half-hour climb to **El Pípila** ⑭, a monument to a hero of the War of Independence of 1810 that looms over the center of the city. If you're interested, bear right on Calle Sopeña just past Teatro Juárez. A sign marked EL PÍPILA will direct you onto Callejón de Calvario, which eventually leads to the hillside memorial.

Head back into town on Calle Cantarranas, a main street that winds down the hill and around the Jardín Unión. Just before Calle Cantarranas changes its name to Calle Pozitos, you'll see the **University of Guanajuato** ⑮. A short way down from where Calle Cantarranas becomes Calle Pozitos is **El Museo Casa Diego Rivera** ⑯, birthplace of Mexico's famous muralist. Calle Pozitos weaves past more residences and eventually becomes Calle 28 de Septiembre. On the left, just past the junction with Mendizabal, is the **Alhóndiga de Granaditas** ⑰, a former fortress converted into a state museum. Head one block south to return to Avenida Juárez and the glassed-in **Mercado Hidalgo** ⑱.

Turn right on Juárez as you leave the market and continue until the road splits near the Jardín Reforma. Bear left and cut down Calle Reforma, a short alley lined with shops. Keep right at the end of the street and you'll come to two pleasant courtyards: Plaza de San Roque, which hosts outdoor performances during the Cervantes Festival, and Plaza de San Fernando, a shady square where many book fairs are held. After the Plaza de San Roque continue southeast and this short detour will return you to Avenida Juárez, where it's a slight climb up to Plaza de la Paz, a 19th-century square surrounded by some of the city's finest colonial buildings, including the 18th-century **Mansión del Conde de Rul** ⑲. The bright-yellow 17th-century Baroque **Basílica Colegiata de Nuestra Señora de Guanajuato** ⑳ dominates the plaza. If you continue up Avenida Juárez about a half block past the plaza, you'll pass the tourist office again and arrive back at the Jardín Unión.

Sights to See

⓱ **Alhóndiga de Granaditas.** A massive stone structure with horizontal slit windows, this 18th-century grain-storage facility served as a jail under Emperor Maximilian and as a fortress during the War of Independence, where El Pípila committed his courageous act. It's now a state museum with exhibits on local history, archaeology, and crafts. The hooks on which the Spanish Royalists hung the severed heads of Father Hidalgo, Ignacio Allende, and two other independence leaders still dangle on the exterior. ✉ *Calle 28 de Septiembre 6, El Centro,* ☎ *473/732–1112.* 🎫 *About $3, free Sun.* ⏲ *Tues.–Sat. 10–1:30 and 4–5:30, Sun. 10–2:30.*

⓴ **Basílica Colegiata de Nuestra Señora de Guanajuato.** A 17th-century Baroque church painted a striking shade of yellow, the Basílica dominates Plaza de la Paz. Inside is the oldest Christian statue in Mexico,

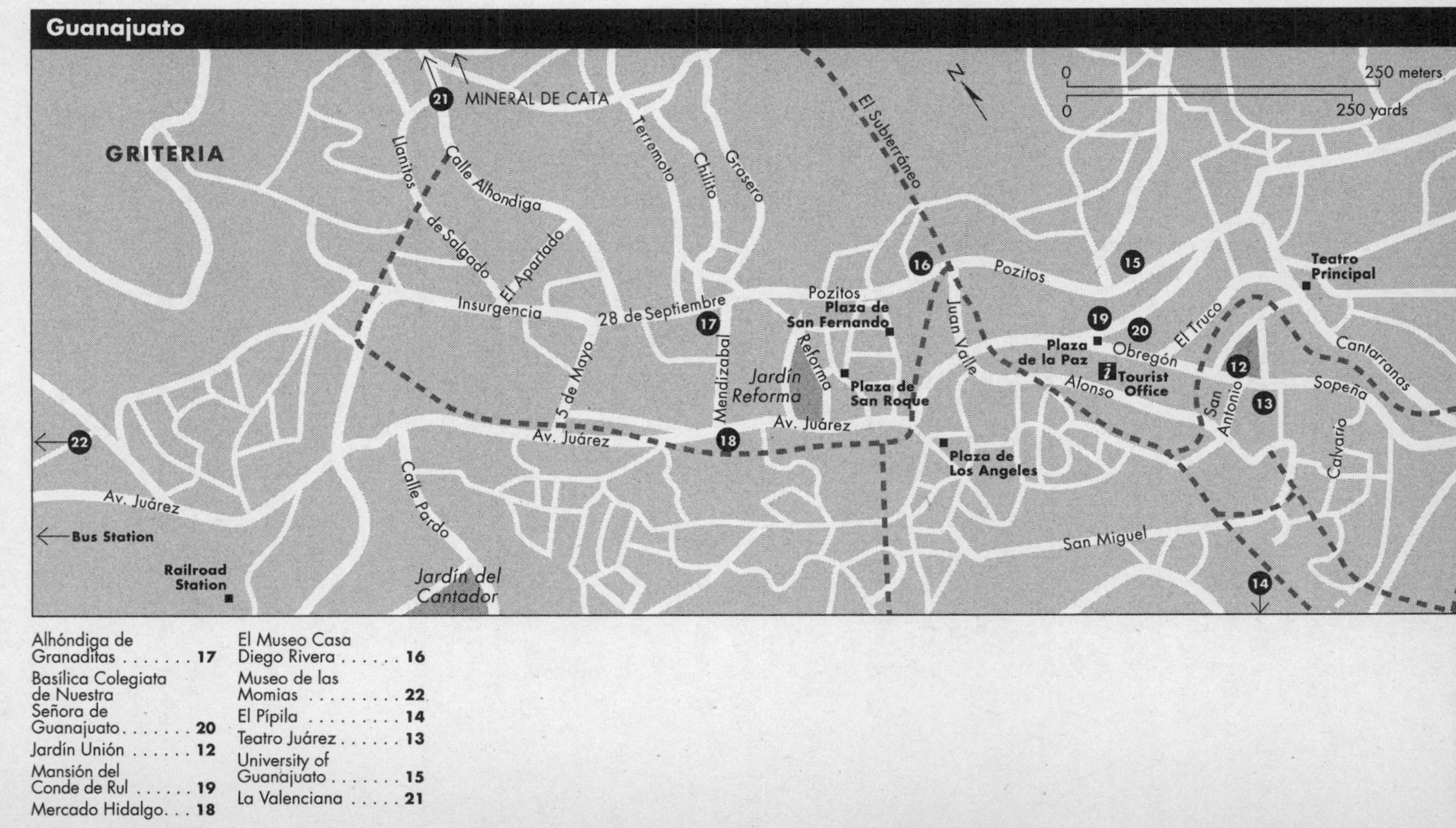

Alhóndiga de Granaditas 17
Basílica Colegiata de Nuestra Señora de Guanajuato 20
Jardín Unión 12
Mansión del Conde de Rul 19
Mercado Hidalgo. . . 18
El Museo Casa Diego Rivera 16
Museo de las Momias 22
El Pípila 14
Teatro Juárez 13
University of Guanajuato 15
La Valenciana 21

a bejeweled 8th-century statue of the Virgin. The highly venerated figure was a gift from King Philip II of Spain in 1557. On the Friday preceding Good Friday, miners, accompanied by floats and mariachi bands, parade to the Basílica to pay homage to the Lady of Guanajuato. ✉ *Plaza de la Paz, El Centro.* ⏲ *Daily 9–8.*

12 **Jardín Unión.** This tree-lined, wedge-shape plaza is Guanajuato's central square. All three sides of the wedge are pedestrian walkways. Tuesday, Thursday, and Sunday evenings, musical performances take place in the band shell here; at other times, groups of musicians break into impromptu song along the plaza's shaded tile walkways.

NEED A BREAK?

For alfresco dining at the Jardín, try the terrace at the **Hotel Museo Posada Santa Fé** (✉ Jardín Unión 12, El Centro, ☎ 473/732–0084). You can order a cappuccino and a slice of cake, or a full meal. Try the *pozole estilo Guanajuato* (hominy soup into which you spoon, or squeeze, onions, radishes, lettuce, lime, and chili peppers).

El Cafe (✉ Calle Sopeña 10, El Centro, ☎ 473/732–2566) has indoor and outdoor tables next to Teatro Juárez and serves good soups and sandwiches, as well as an interesting assortment of spiked specialty coffees—among them *cafe diable* (coffee, rum, and lemon juice).

19 **Mansión del Conde de Rul.** This 18th-century residence, now a government office, housed the count of Rul and Valenciana, who owned La Valenciana, which was then the country's richest silver mine. The two-story structure was designed by famed Mexican architect Eduardo Tresguerras. ✉ *Plaza de la Paz at Av. Juárez and Callejón del Estudiante, El Centro,* ☎ *no phone.* 🎫 *Free.* ⏲ *Weekdays 8–6.*

18 **Mercado Hidalgo.** You can't miss this 1910 cast-iron-and-glass structure, designed by the one-and-only Gustave Eiffel. Though the balcony stalls are filled with T-shirts and cheap plastic toys, the lower level is full of authentic local wares and colorful basketry, as well as fresh produce, peanuts, and honey-drenched nut candies shaped like mummies. ✉ *Calle Juárez near Mendizabal, El Centro.* ⏲ *Daily 8–8.*

16 **El Museo Casa Diego Rivera.** This museum, birthplace of Mexico's best known muralist, Diego Rivera, contains family portraits and furniture as well as works by the master, among them his studies for the controversial mural commissioned for New York City's Rockefeller Center. Completed in 1933, the mural contained a portrait of Lenin and had a decidedly Communist bent, which caused it to be destroyed immediately after it was displayed. The museum's upper galleries show revolving contemporary art exhibitions. ✉ *Calle Pozitos 47, El Centro,* ☎ *473/732–1197.* 🎫 *$2.* ⏲ *Tues.–Sat. 10–6:30, Sun. 10–2:30.*

22 **Museo de las Momias.** For a macabre thrill, check out this unique museum at the municipal cemetery off Calzada del Panteón, at the west end of town. In the museum, mummified human corpses—once buried in the cemetery—are on display. Until the law was amended in 1858, if a grave site hadn't been paid for after five years, the corpse was removed to make room for new arrivals. Because of the mineral properties of the local soil, these cadavers (the oldest is more than 130 years old) were in astonishingly good condition upon exhumation. Some of them are exhibited in glass cases. ✉ *Panteón Municipal,* ☎ *473/732–0639.* 🎫 *$3.* ⏲ *Daily 9–6.*

14 **El Pípila.** A half-hour's climb from downtown is the monument to Juan José de los Reyes Martínez, a young miner and hero of the War of Independence of 1810. Nicknamed El Pípila, De los Reyes crept into the Alhóndiga de Granaditas, where Spanish Royalists were hiding. With

a stone shield strapped to his back, he set the front door ablaze. The Spanish troops were captured by Father Hidalgo's army in this early battle, giving the independence forces their first major military victory. There's a splendid view of the city from the monument. It's easiest to take a taxi or a bus (marked PÍPILA) from the Jardín. ✉ *Carretera Panorámica, on bluff above south side of Jardín Unión, El Centro.*

⓭ **Teatro Juárez.** Adorned with bronze lion sculptures and a line of large Greek muses overlooking the Jardín Unión from the roof, the theater was inaugurated by Mexican dictator Porfirio Díaz in 1903 with a performance of *Aïda*. It now serves as the principal venue of the annual International Cervantes Festival. A brief tour of the art deco interior is available. ✉ *Calle Sopeña s/n, El Centro,* ☎ *473/732–0183.* 🎫 *$1.20.* ⏲ *Tues.–Sun. 9–1:45 and 5–7:45.*

⓯ **University of Guanajuato.** Founded in 1732, the university was formerly a Jesuit seminary. The original churrigueresque church, **La Compañía,** still stands next door. The facade of the university building, built in 1955, was designed to blend in with the town's architecture. If you do wander inside, check out the bulletin boards for notices of cultural events in town. ✉ *Calle Lascurain de Retana 5, ½ block north of Plaza de la Paz, El Centro,* ☎ *473/732–0006.* ⏲ *Weekdays 8–3:30.*

㉑ **La Valenciana.** Officially called La Iglesia de San Cayetano, this is one of the best known colonial churches in all of Mexico. The mid- to late-18th-century pink stone facade is brilliantly ornate. Inside are three altars, each hand-carved in wood and gilded, in different styles: plateresque, churrigueresque, and Baroque. There are also fine examples of religious painting from the viceregal period.

The silver mine near the church, Mina y Bocamina Valenciana, was discovered in 1529 and continued to produce until the early 1800s. An excellent guided tour of the mine (in Spanish only) includes the history of the mine, miners, and the creation of the 1,650-ft-deep mine shaft. The mine and the church are also included in any guided tour of Guanajuato, and buses (marked LA VALENCIANA) frequently make the trip from the city center. ✉ *Carretera Guanajuato–Dolores Hidalgo, Km 2, La Valenciana.* ⏲ *Daily 9–6.* 🎫 *Mine tour: $3.*

OFF THE BEATEN PATH

MINERAL DE CATA – The modest church at Mineral de Cata, officially called Señor de Villaseca, is a moving testament to religious faith. Since its founding in 1725, silver miners and their families have come here to offer heartfelt *ex-votos* (also called *retablos*)—folk paintings with text about prayer and gratitude. The church is now covered floor to ceiling with these remarkable offerings. Those near the ceiling are a couple hundred years old, painted on tin. The recent, lower paintings deal with contemporary issues, such as immigration. It's best to take a taxi here and have the driver wait (which will run you about $8 an hour) while you look inside. ✉ *Callejón del Quijote.*

Dining

Guanajuato's better restaurants are in hotels near the Jardín Unión and on the highway to Dolores Hidalgo. For simpler fare, private eateries around town offer a good variety of Mexican and international dishes. Dress tends to be casual.

$$$ ★ ✕ **Casa del Conde de la Valenciana.** Come to this refurbished 18th-century home across the street from La Iglesia de San Cayetano (La Valenciana) for superbly prepared traditional Mexican and international fare. Fresh gazpacho comes in a bowl made of ice, and the tender *lomo*

en salsa de ciruela pasa (pork shoulder in prune sauce) and *pollo a la flor de calabaza* (chicken with poblano chili slices and squash-blossom sauce) are delicious. Sample the luscious mango ice cream served in the shell, or round out the meal with a honeyed house cappuccino. ✉ *Carretera Guanajuato–Dolores Hidalgo, Km 5, La Valenciana,* ☏ *473/732–2550. MC, V. Closed Sun. No dinner.*

$$$ ★ ✕ **El Comedor Real.** Continental cuisine served in a medieval environment defines this bright whitewashed restaurant in the Hotel Castillo Santa Cecilia. Indulge in the chef's special—the award-winning *Filete Domenech* (named after the chef), a tender fillet of beef served over a potato pancake and wrapped in a woven pasta basket. Troubadours perform every Friday and Saturday at 10:30 PM at La Cava, the bar next door. ✉ *Camino a la Valenciana s/n, Km 1, La Valenciana,* ☏ *473/732–0485. AE, MC, V.*

$$ ✕ **El Gallo Pitagórico.** Prevail over the 100-plus steps that lead to the threshold of El Gallo Pitagórico and bask in the exceptional view of downtown Guanajuato. Your efforts are further rewarded by a plate of the house specialty, *Filetto Claudio,* (Italian-style fillet marinated in olive oil, capers, parsley, and garlic). The salmon fettuccine is savory, but make room for dessert—a velvety tiramisu. If the weather is fair, ask to have your aperitif in the top-story bar, which offers a view surpassing that of the restaurant. ✉ *Constancia 10, behind the Teatro Juárez, El Centro,* ☏ *473/732–9489. MC, V.*

$$ ✕ **Tasca de los Santos.** This cozy restaurant, across the street from the Basílica, specializes in Spanish and international fare. Recommended dishes include the *sopa de mariscos* (a rich broth with shrimp, mussels, clams, and crabs, all in their shells) and *filete parrilla* (grilled beef with baked potatoes and spinach). Dine inside or out under umbrellas on the plaza, with a view of the sculpture *Monumento a La Paz,* created in 1895 by Jesús Contreras in honor of peace. ✉ *Plaza de la Paz 28, El Centro,* ☏ *473/732–2320. AE, MC, V.*

$$ ★ ✕ **Truco 7.** Red-tile floors, *equipale* (pigskin) chairs, and original art enliven this cozy coffeehouse and restaurant. In the morning, serious students hunch over coffee and textbooks. Later in the day locals and savvy tourists pile in for the inexpensive comida corrida, sandwiches, or grilled chicken. The atmosphere is also lively at night, when Mexican wines are served by the glass. ✉ *Calle Truco 7, El Centro,* ☏ *473/732–8374. No credit cards.*

$ ✕ **El Pingüis Cafeteria.** Cheap and plentiful food attracts the university crowd to this spartan eatery decorated with Mexican art posters. For about $2.50, a midday meal consists of soup, Mexican rice, a chicken or beef dish, dessert, and coffee. *Consumé de verduras* (vegetable soup) is good, as is the *café americano.* Service can be slow, but vibrant music and a lively crowd will keep you entertained. ✉ *Jardín Unión at Allende 3, El Centro,* ☏ *473/732–1414. Reservations not accepted. No credit cards. No dinner.*

$ ✕ **El Unicorno Azul.** If you're growing weary of heavy meat dishes, stop by this food counter just behind Jardín Unión: it serves fruit, yogurt, and vegetarian burgers and sandwiches. The owner will cheerfully recommend other health-food places and yoga classes. ✉ *Plaza del Baratillo 2, El Centro,* ☏ *473/732–0700. No credit cards. Closed Sun.*

Lodging

Guanajuato's less expensive hotels are along Avenida Juárez and Calle de la Alhóndiga. Moderately priced and upscale properties are near the Jardín Unión and on the outskirts of town. It's best to secure reservations at least six months in advance if you plan to attend the Cervantes Festival, which usually runs from mid- to late October.

$$$ ★ **La Casa de Espiritus Alegres Bed and Breakfast.** A paradise for folk-art lovers, this "house of good spirits" is filled with extraordinary crafts from every state in Mexico. Owned by a California artist, the lovingly restored hacienda (circa 1700) has thick stone walls and serene grounds lush with bougainvillea, banana trees, and calla lilies. All rooms have hand-glazed tile baths, fireplaces, and private terraces. Rates include a sumptuous breakfast served in a glassed-in atrium overlooking the garden. Children under 13 are not admitted. Marfil is about a 15-minute drive from the center of town—frequent bus service is available. ✉ *La Ex-Hacienda La Trinidad 1, Marfil 36250,* ☎ FAX *473/733–1013. 5 rooms, 3 suites. Bar, library, shop, free parking. No credit cards.*

$$$ **Parador San Javier.** This immaculately restored hacienda was converted into a hotel in 1971. A safe from the Hacienda San Javier and old wood trunks still decorate the large, plant-filled lobby. Rooms are clean and spacious with inviting blue-and-white-tile baths. A few of the 16 colonial-style rooms reached via a stone archway have fireplaces. Newer rooms in the adjoining high-rise have satellite TVs. A word of caution: large convention groups sometimes crowd the facility. ✉ *Plaza Aldama 92, El Centro 36000,* ☎ *473/732–0626,* FAX *473/732–3114. 100 rooms, 12 suites. 2 restaurants, café, pool, bar, dance club, free parking. AE, MC, V.*

$$ **Hostería del Frayle.** A half block off Jardín Unión, this quiet four-story lodging was once the Casa de Moneda, where ore was taken to be refined after it was brought out of the mines. Built in 1673 and turned into a hotel in the mid-1960s, it has whitewashed plaster and wood-beam rooms (which nonetheless are somewhat dark), arranged around a small maze of stairways, landings, and courtyards. All have phones and cable TV, and some have excellent views of the Pípila, Teatro Juárez, and Jardín Unión. The staff is extremely friendly and helpful. ✉ *Calle Sopeña 3, El Centro 36000,* ☎ FAX *473/732–1179. 32 rooms, 5 suites. Restaurant, cable TV, bar, laundry service. MC, V.*

$$ **Hotel Museo Posada Santa Fé.** This colonial-style inn, at the Jardín Unión, has been in operation since 1862. Large historic paintings by local artist Don Manuel Leal hang in the wood-paneled lobby. A sweeping, if tattered, carpeted stairway leads to second-floor quarters. Each room has cable TV and a phone. Rooms facing the plaza can be noisy; quieter rooms face narrow alleyways. ✉ *Plaza Principal at Jardín Unión 12, El Centro 36000,* ☎ *473/732–0084,* FAX *473/732–4653. 47 rooms, 9 suites. Restaurant, bar, laundry service, free parking. AE, MC, V.*

$ **Hotel Socavón.** One of Guanajuato's newer hotels, this modest five-story property was built in 1981. Don't be put off by the gloomy, tunnel-like entrance: open-air walkways, with views of surrounding mountains, lead to guest quarters. Each small room—simply furnished with a bed, desk, and tiny TV—has a wood-beam ceiling and a modern bath. Fourth-floor corner rooms have some good views. ✉ *Calle de la Alhóndiga 41A, El Centro 36000,* ☎ *473/732–6666,* ☎ FAX *473/732–7344. 40 rooms. Restaurant, bar. AE, MC, V.*

Nightlife and the Arts

Guanajuato, on most nights a somnolent provincial capital, awakens each fall for the **International Cervantes Festival.** For three weeks in October world-renowned actors, musicians, and dance troupes perform nightly at the Teatro Juárez and other venues in town. Plaza San Roque, a small square near the Jardín Reforma, hosts a series of *Entremeses Cervantinos*—swashbuckling one-act farces by classical Spanish writers. Grandstand seats require advance tickets, but crowds often gather by the edge of the plaza and watch for free. Hundreds of thousands of people attend the festivities each year. If you plan to be in Guanajuato for the festival, contact the Festival Internacional Cervantino office (✉ Plaza de San Francisquito 1, El Centro, ☎ 473/731–1150, 473/731–1161, or 532/325–9000, FAX 473/732–6775) or Ticketmaster (☎ 473/731–1150, 473/731–1161, or 532/325–9000) at least six months in advance for top-billed events.

At other times of the year, nightlife in Guanajuato consists of dramatic, dance, and musical performances at **Teatro Juárez** (✉ Calle de Sopeña s/n, El Centro, ☎ 473/732–0183). Friday and Saturday at 8 PM, *callejoneadas* (mobile musical parties) begin in front of Teatro Juárez and meander through town (don't forget to tip the musicians). You'll find several nightclubs in or near the downtown area, including **El Bar** (✉ Sopeña 10, El Centro, ☎ 473/732–2566), where students gather for drinks and salsa dancing. The **Castillo Santa Cecilia** (✉ Camino a la Valenciana s/n, Km 1, La Valenciana, ☎ 473/732–0485) offers live music on Friday and Saturday nights. For an evening of hopping music and lively dancing visit **La Dama de las Camelias** (✉ Calle de Sopeña 32, El Centro). **Teatro Principal** (✉ Calle Hidalgo, El Centro, ☎ 473/732–1523) shows American movies several times a week.

Shopping

Artesanías Vázques (✉ Cantarranas 8, ☎ FAX 473/732–5231) carries Talavera ceramics from Dolores Hidalgo. You'll find painterly, old-style majolica ceramics at **Capelo** (✉ Cerro de la Cruz s/n, a dirt road off the Guanajuato–Dolores Hidalgo Hwy, past La Valenciana, ☎ 473/732–8964). **Casa del Conde de la Valenciana** (✉ Carretera Guanajuato–Dolores Hidalgo, Km 5, La Valenciana, ☎ 473/732–2550) specializes in brass, tin, ceramic, and wrought-iron home decorations from Mexico and Africa. The **Gorky González Workshop** (✉ Pastita Ex-huerta de Montenegro s/n, past the baseball stadium, ☎ 473/731–0389) offers high-quality ceramics (at a higher price). Both venerable studios now use lead-safe glazes. Some jewelry and regional knickknacks are sold at the **Mercado Hidalgo.** Other shops around Plaza de la Paz and Jardín Unión sell ceramics and woolen shawls and sweaters. Silver is available from street vendors and shops clustered near La Valenciana and El Pípila.

Side Trip to León

56 km (35 mi) northwest of Guanajuato.

Best known as the shoemaking capital of Mexico, León is also an important center for industry and commerce. With more than 1 million people, it is the state's most populous urban area.

If you know footwear and have the time (and patience) to browse through the downtown shops, you might find some good buys in León. First try the **Plaza del Zapato,** a mall with 70 stores on Boulevard Adolfo López Mateos, roughly one block from the bus station. From here take a taxi west (about a 10-minute ride) to the **Zona Peatonal,** a pedestrian zone with several shoe stores. On **Calle Praxedis Guerrero,** various artisans' stands sell leather goods.

Flecha Amarilla **buses** leave Guanajuato's Central Camionera every 15 minutes for León; the ride takes about 45 minutes and costs less than $1. **Taxis** cost about $17 one way. Pick up a map of León at the tourist office in Guanajuato.

Guanajuato A to Z

To research prices, get advice from other travelers, and book travel arrangements, visit www.fodors.com.

AIR TRAVEL

León's Guanajuato International Airport is 40 km (25 mi) west of the city of Guanajuato. The taxi ride from the airport to Guanajuato costs about $17 and takes around 45 minutes.

BUS TRAVEL

Direct bus service is available between the Central del Norte (North Bus Station) in Mexico City and Guanajuato's Central Camionera. Flecha Amarilla offers hourly service. For frequent first-class service use Estrella Blanca. Travel time is about five hours. Deluxe buses, including those of Primera Plus (Flecha Amarilla's first-class service) and ETN, connect Guanajuato to Mexico City, San Miguel, and Guadalajara. There are several departures daily. Taxis to downtown Guanajuato from the Camionera cost $2–$3.

➤ BUS INFORMATION: **Estrella Blanca** (☎ 473/733–1344). **ETN** (☎ 473/733–1579). **Flecha Amarilla** (☎ 473/733–1332 or 473/733–1333). **Primera Plus** (☎ 473/733–1332 or 473/733–1333).

CAR RENTAL

Avis will drop a car at your hotel in Guanajuato.

➤ MAJOR AGENCIES: **Avis** (✉ Hotel Fiesta Americana, Los Gabilanes, León, ☎ FAX 471/713–6040).

CAR TRAVEL

Guanajuato is 365 km (226 mi), about five hours, northwest of Mexico City via Route 57 (to Querétaro), then via Route 45.

Don't bother with a car in Guanajuato. Many of the attractions are within strolling distance of one another and located between Avenida Juárez and Calle Pozitos, the city's two major north–south arteries. The twisting subterranean roadway—El Subterráneo—also has a primarily north–south orientation.

EMERGENCIES

Few people in Guanajuato have a good command of English, so in an emergency it's best to contact your hotel manager or the tourist office.

El Fénix (pharmacy) is open Monday–Saturday 8 AM–9:45 PM, Sunday 9–9.

➤ CONTACTS: **Ambulance–Red Cross** (☎ 473/732–0487). **El Fénix** (✉ Av. Juárez 104, El Centro, ☎ 473/732–6140). **Hospital General** (☎ 473/733–1577). **Police** (☎ 473/732–0266).

INTERNET

Redes Internet, open weekdays 9:30–8 and Saturday 10–3, charges $3 an hour for Internet access.

➤ INTERNET CAFÉS: **Redes Internet** (✉ Alonso 70, El Centro, ☎ 473/732–0611).

TAXIS

You can find taxis at *sitios* (taxi stands) near the Jardín Unión, Plaza de la Paz, and Mercado Hidalgo.

TOURS

The following tour operators give half- and full-day tours with English-speaking guides. These tours typically include the Museum of Mummies, the church and mines of Valenciana, the monument to Pípila, the

Panoramic Highway, subterranean streets, and residential neighborhoods. Night tours often begin at the Pípila Monument for a nighttime city view and end at a dance club. Estudiantinas usually perform during the weekend tours.

Transporte Exclusivo de Turismo has several tours of Guanajuato and its environs. Transporte Turísticos de Guanajuato also has a kiosk at the main bus terminal.

➤ TOUR OPERATOR RECOMMENDATIONS: **Transporte Exclusivo de Turismo** (✉ Av. Juárez and Calle 5 de Mayo, El Centro, ☎ 473/732–5968). **Transporte Turísticos de Guanajuato** (✉ Plaza de la Paz 2, by Basílica de Guanajuato, El Centro, ☎ 473/732–2134 or 473/732–2838).

TRAVEL AGENCIES

Viajes Georama is the local American Express representative. Viajes Frausto is reliable for hotel and airline reservations.

➤ LOCAL AGENT REFERRALS: **Viajes Frausto** (✉ Calle González Obregón 10, El Centro, ☎ 473/732–3580, FAX 473/732–6620). **Viajes Georama** (✉ Plaza de la Paz 34, El Centro, ☎ 473/732–5909, FAX 473/732–1954).

VISITOR INFORMATION

The Guanajuato tourist office is open daily 9–7.

➤ TOURIST INFORMATION: **Guanajuato tourist office** (✉ Plaza de la Paz 14, El Centro, ☎ 473/732–1574 or 473/732–1982 Ext. 107, FAX 473/732–4251).

ZACATECAS

In colonial days Zacatecas was the largest silver-producing city in the world, sending great treasures of the precious metal to the king of Spain. Still a large silver-mining center, with factories producing silver jewelry and trade schools training apprentices in the fine art of handmade silver craft, Zacatecas is relatively undiscovered by foreigners. Although it is a state capital with a population of some 300,000, it has the feel of a much smaller place. Zacatecas is kept spotlessly clean, thanks to civic pride and a mandate by the governor of the state of Zacatecas. This city is rightly famous for its historic role as the scene of one of Pancho Villa's most spectacular battles and for its 18th-century colonial architecture.

One of the town's unique charms is the *tambora,* a musical walk up and down the streets and alleyways led by a *tamborazo,* a typical local band that shatters the evening quiet with merriment. Also known as a callejoneada (*callejón* means "alley"), the tambora is a popular free-for-all, in which everyone along the way either joins in the procession or leans from balconies and doorways to cheer the group. During the December *feria* (festival), the tamborazos play night and day as they serenade the Virgin of Zacatecas.

Exploring Zacatecas

Most of Zacatecas's colonial sights are near the city center, making it an easy place to explore on foot—and there's rarely much traffic in town. For an overview of Zacatecas, you can walk or taxi up to the mine, catch an elevator to a nearby hilltop, take the cable car across the city, then return to your starting point below by taxi or bus.

A Good Walk

Start your tour at the Plaza de Armas, in the center of the city. Here you'll find the stunning **Catedral de Zacatecas** ㉓ and the **Palacio del Gobierno** ㉔. Across the street from the plaza are two beautiful colo-

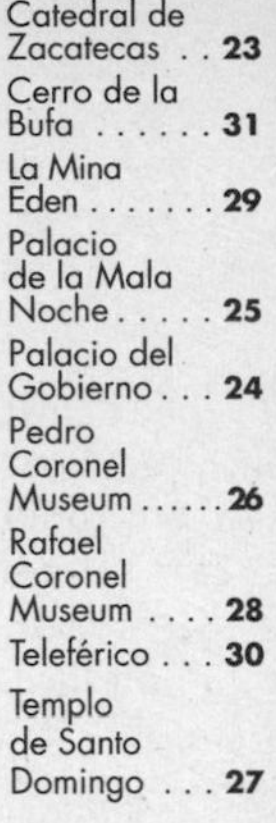

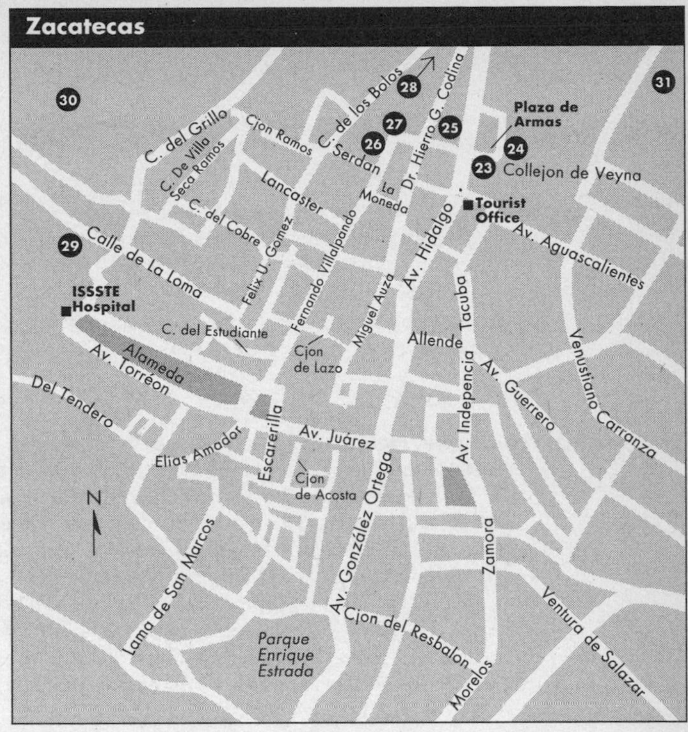

nial buildings worth exploring; one is known as the **Palacio de la Mala Noche** ㉕ because of a local legend. Go to the Plaza Santo Domingo, two blocks west of the cathedral, to see the art in the **Pedro Coronel Museum** ㉖ and the Baroque **Templo de Santo Domingo** ㉗ right next door. To visit the museum of the other Coronel brother—both were equally fanatical art collectors—return to the cathedral, turn left on Avenida Hidalgo, and walk about 1 km (½ mi) north of the plaza to the **Rafael Coronel Museum** ㉘.

For a longer walk, head south on Avenida Hidalgo until you come to Juárez, then go right (roughly west) up the hill, passing the several-block-long Alameda park and the Social Security Hospital to get to **La Mina Eden** ㉙. After touring the mine, you can take an elevator up to Cerro del Grillo (Cricket Hill) and catch the **Teleférico** ㉚ cable car across the city to **Cerro de la Bufa** ㉛, the site of Pancho Villa's famous battle.

Sights to See

23 **Catedral de Zacatecas.** This is one of Mexico's finest interpretations of Baroque style. Each of the facades tells a different legend. According to one of them, an anticlerical governor of the state used the cathedral's silver cross and baptismal font to mint Zacatecas's first silver coins. ✉ *South side of Plaza de Armas on Av. Hidalgo.* ⏲ *Daily 8–2 and 4–6.*

31 **Cerro de la Bufa.** The city trademark, this rugged hill is the site of Pancho Villa's definitive battle against dictator Victoriano Huerta in June 1914. The spacious **Plaza de la Revolución,** paved with the three shades of pink Zacatecan stone, is crowned with three huge equestrian statues of Villa and two other heroes, Felipe Angeles and Panfilo Natera. Also on site are the **Sanctuary of the Virgin of Patrocinio,** a chapel dedicated to the patron of the city, and the **Museo de la Toma de Zacatecas** (☎ 492/922–8066; 🎫 $1), which has nine rooms filled with

historic objects such as guns, newspapers, furniture, and clothing from the days of Pancho Villa. It's open Tuesday–Sunday 10–4:30. ✉ *If driving, follow Av. Hidalgo north from town to Av. Juan de Tolosa; turn right and continue until you come to a fountain; take 1st immediate right off retorno (crossover) onto Calle Mexicapan, which leads to Carretera Panorámica. Turn right to signposted Carretera La Bufa, which leads to the top of the hill.*

29 **La Mina Eden.** Now a tourist attraction, the Eden Mine supplied most of Zacatecas's silver from 1586 until 1960. An open mine train runs down into the underground tunnels. The tour is in Spanish, but you'll have no trouble imagining what the life of the miners was like. Be sure to wear sturdy shoes. Farther down the train track is another stop at, of all places, a discotheque. There's a small gift shop at the entrance. ✉ *Entrance on Antonio Dovali off Av. Torreon beyond Alameda García de la Cadena,* ☎ *492/922–3002.* 🎟 *$2.* ⏲ *Daily 10–6.*

25 **Palacio de la Mala Noche.** The Palace of the Bad Night is one of two beautiful 18th-century colonial buildings across from the downtown plaza. Both declared national monuments, they are built from native pink stone and have lacy ironwork balconies. One of them now houses the Continental Plaza hotel, and the other is a municipal building known as El Palacio de la Mala Noche. Legend has it that this was the home of a silver-mine owner who was called upon so often to help the needy that he built a hidden door from which he could enter and leave the palace undisturbed. Up the hill along the side of the palace, you can find the so-called hidden door. ✉ *Av. Hidalgo 639.* 🎟 *Free.* ⏲ *Weekdays 8:30–3 and 5–8, weekends 10–2.*

24 **Palacio del Gobierno.** The Governor's Palace is an 18th-century mansion with flower-filled courtyards and, on the main staircase, a powerful mural painted in 1970 by António Pintor Rodríguez that depicts the history of Zacatecas. ✉ *East side of Plaza de Armas.* 🎟 *Free.* ⏲ *Daily 9–2 and 5–8.*

NEED A BREAK?

El Teatro Caffé (✉ Av. Hidalgo 501, inside Teatro Caldreon, ☎ 492/922–8620), in a restored 100-year-old theater adorned in celestial murals, is a hopping coffee shop where students swap ideas over a cappuccino or a *Neive Opera* (vanilla ice cream topped with chocolate syrup, espresso, and cream).

★ 26 **Pedro Coronel Museum.** Originally a Jesuit monastery, this building was used as a jail in the 18th century. The museum houses the work of Zacatecan artist and sculptor Pedro Coronel and his extensive collection of works by Picasso, Dalí, Miró, Braque, and Chagall, among others, as well as art from Africa, China, Japan, India, Tibet, Greece, and Egypt. ✉ *Av. Fernando Villalpando at Plaza Santo Domingo,* ☎ *492/922–8021.* 🎟 *About $2.* ⏲ *Fri.–Wed. 10–5.*

★ 28 **Rafael Coronel Museum.** The museum is in the Ex-Convento de San Francisco, northeast of the town center toward Lomas del Calvario. Its mellowed pink 18th-century facade conceals a rambling structure of open, arched corridors, all leading through garden patios to rooms that contain an amazing collection of some 4,500 *máscaras* (masks)—saints and devils, wise men and fools, animals and humans—used in regional festivals all over Mexico. There's also an outstanding display of puppets. ✉ *Off Vergel Nuevo between Chaveño and Garcia Salinas,* ☎ *492/922–8116.* 🎟 *About $2.* ⏲ *Thurs.–Tues. 10–5.*

30 **Teleférico.** The only cable car in the world that crosses an entire city, the Teleférico runs from **Cerro del Grillo** (Cricket Hill) above the Eden

Mine to Cerro de la Bufa. True, it crosses at the narrowest point, but it presents a magnificent panoramic view of the city and its many Baroque church domes and spires. It's also well worth the cost to get the ride up to Cerro de la Bufa, which is quite a climb otherwise. ✉ *Cerro del Grillo station is off Paseo Díaz Ordaz, a steep walk from Plaza de Armas,* ☎ *492/922–5694.* 🎫 *About $2.* ⏲ *Daily 10–6, except when there are high winds.*

27 **Templo de Santo Domingo.** This 18th-century Jesuit church has an ornamented facade and a rich interior that includes gold-leaf religious paintings. The sacristy also contains an impressive collection of religious art. ✉ *Av. Fernando Villalpando at Plaza Santo Domingo.* ⏲ *Daily 7:30–3 and 5:30–8:30.*

Dining and Lodging

Several of Zacatecas's better restaurants are in hotels, and many of the best lodgings are in beautiful, well-preserved 18th- and 19th-century buildings. Other popular restaurants are on Avenida Juárez, which intersects Avenida Hidalgo.

$$$ ★ ✕ **La Cuija.** Regional food is the strength of this large restaurant, whose name means "the gecko." Start off with an appetizer of three quesadillas: one each of squash blossoms, cheese, and *huitlacoche* (a corn fungus delicacy). Also recommended are the *crema de labor* (a cream soup with corn and squash blossoms) and *asado de boda* (pork in a semisweet and spicy sauce). The decor approximates a wine cellar, and in addition to fine food, the restaurant serves wine from the owner's Cachola Vineyards in Valle de las Arsinas. A traditional Mexican trio plays Thursday–Sunday afternoons. ✉ *Centro Commercial El Mercado, bottom level,* ☎ *492/922–8275. AE, V.*

$$ ✕ **Café y Nevería Acrópolis.** This quaint diner is trimmed with paintings and sketches given to the owner by some of the famous people who have eaten here, including a small acrylic by Rafael Coronel. Enjoy a strong Turkish coffee and watch the locals flood in for breakfast. The *chiliquiles verdes* (strips of fried tortilla smothered in a tangy green sauce and white cheese) is served with an alluring basket of pastries and bread. Traditional café fare like hamburgers, sandwiches, and fruity shakes are available for lunch. ✉ *Av. Hidalgo at Plazuela Candelario Huizar, alongside the cathedral,* ☎ *492/922–1284. MC, V.*

$$ ✕ **El Paraiso.** The fashionable cantina for the Zacatecano elite more than 100 years ago, El Paraiso is still a town favorite today. Rich burgundy walls, green velvet curtains, and brass accents impart a wealthy Old West–saloon look. The extensive menu of Zacatecas appetizers offers an ideal opportunity to sample various traditional dishes. *Enchiladas de ayer* (yesterday's enchiladas) may sound like leftovers, but the friendly waiters promise that the flavor is enhanced by the second day. ✉ *Av. Hidalgo y Plaza Goitia,* ☎ *492/922–6164. AE, MC, V.*

$ ✕ **El Recoveco.** Choose from 25 different steaming plates of traditional Mexican dishes at this rustic, full-buffet diner. The breakfast buffet includes coffee, juices, and a variety of egg, chicken, and beef delights. You'll likely find Spanish rice, beans, *pollo en mole* (chicken in a mole sauce), an array of fresh salads, and fruit water—just to name a few choices—at the daily lunch buffet. The staff is friendly and the price is right at just $4 for an all-you-can-eat lunch, $3.50 for breakfast. ✉ *Av. Torreón 513, in front of the Alameda,* ☎ *492/924–2013. No credit cards.*

$$$$ ★ ✕🏨 **Quinta Real.** This hotel must be one of the most unusual in the world: it's built around Mexico's oldest bullring, the second one constructed in the Western Hemisphere. Large and bright, the plush rooms are decorated in pastel fabrics that complement the dark traditional furniture. The bar occupies some of the former bull pens, and an outdoor café with bright-white umbrella tables takes up two levels of the spectator area. Fine Continental cuisine is served in the elaborate, formal restaurant, with an awesome view of the *plaza de toro* (bullring) and the aqueduct beyond. ✉ *Av. Gonzales Ortega s/n, to the side of the aqueduct, 98000,* ☎ *492/922–9104,* FAX *492/922–8440,* WEB *www.quintareal.com. 49 suites. Restaurant, minibars, bar, shops, laundry service, free parking. AE, MC, V.*

$$$ **Continental Plaza.** This beautiful old colonial building faces the Plaza de Armas and the cathedral in the heart of the city. The pinkstone facade dates from the 18th century; unfortunately the modern interior is rather stark and charmless. Rooms are fitted with new but unexceptional furniture. Those facing the plaza are within earshot of late-night and early morning tamborazo music during festivals. That said, you'll get a great view of the goings-on from your small balcony. The hotel's restaurant, Candiles, offers both Continental and regional dishes, and there's a daily breakfast buffet. ✉ *Av. Hidalgo 703, 98000,* ☎ *492/922–6183,* FAX *492/922–6245. 86 rooms, 13 suites. Restaurant, bar, laundry service, convention center, free parking. AE, MC, V.*

$$$ ★ **Mesón de Jobito.** This early 19th-century apartment building stood for well over a hundred years before its conversion to a four-star hotel. The two levels of guest rooms are done in tasteful modern decor, with wall-to-wall carpet and striped drapes. The restful atmosphere is enhanced by the Mesón's perfect location on a blissfully quiet little plaza a few blocks from the cathedral. ✉ *Jardín Juárez 143, 98000,* ☎ FAX *492/924–1722. 53 rooms, 6 suites. 2 restaurants, cable TV, bar, laundry service, parking (fee). AE, MC, V.*

$$ **Hostal del Vasco.** For a truly Zacatecano hotel, consider the clean, cozy, and quiet Hostal del Vasco. Spacious brown-carpeted suites are decorated in dark antiques and include telephones, cable TV, and marble bathrooms; some are equipped with a small kitchen (but no cookware). Sprawling plants and singing birds—Pepe the parrot leads the choir—enliven the two-story interior courtyard. ✉ *Alameda y Velasco 1, 98000,* ☎ FAX *492/922–0428. 18 suites. Some kitchenettes, cable TV, hair salon, laundry service, free parking. AE, MC, V.*

$ **Posada de la Moneda.** This very Mexican hotel in the middle of downtown is adequate if you're on a budget. Everything is highly polished, especially the lobby's tile floor. If the room furnishings are a bit threadbare, they are clean, and the carpet is relatively new. ✉ *Av. Hidalgo 413, 98000,* ☎ FAX *492/922–0881. 34 rooms, 2 suites. Restaurant, cable TV, bar. AE, MC, V.*

Nightlife and the Arts

There's live music in the lobby bar of the **Continental Plaza.** A must-see if only for its uniqueness, **El Malacate** (✉ La Mina Eden, ☎ 492/922–3002), the discotheque in the Eden Mine, is more than 1,000 ft underground. It's best to make reservations at this popular place, which is both crowded and noisy. It's open Thursday–Saturday night; the cover charge is about $7. **Quinta Real** features a nightly band in a romantic bar located to one side of the old bullring.

Shopping

Don't expect to find quality crafts in Zacatecas; souvenirs are more along the line of tacky knickknacks than handmade crafts. There's some decent silver jewelry, although not as much as you would expect.

Crafts

Opposite the east end of Plaza de Armas is **La Cazzorra** (✉ Av. Hidalgo 713, ☎ 492/924–0484), a collectibles shop with authentic antiques, books about Zacatecas, Huichol art, *rebosos* (a traditional woven wrap still widely used for warmth), and a fine selection of jewelry from the local silver factory. The owners are a good source of information about the city. **Güichito** (✉ Av. Hidalgo 126, ☎ 492/922–1907) specializes in handmade traditional candies from the region.

Silver

The **Centro Comercial El Mercado** (✉ Calle Hidalgo, next to cathedral) has a few shops with silver goods. **Centro Platero Zacatecas** (☎ 492/923–1007) sells silver jewelry with regional designs, made in its factory in nearby Guadalupe. **Sa Pe Ca** (☎ 492/922–0273) sells a large selection of silver jewelry and accessories for women and men.

Side Trips from Zacatecas

Guadalupe

7 km (4½ mi) southeast of Zacatecas.

If you're interested in colonial art and architecture, don't miss this small town. Its centerpiece is the **Ex-Convento de Guadalupe,** founded by Franciscan monks in 1707. It currently houses the **Museo de Arte Virreinal** (*virreinal* means "viceregal," or "colonial"), run by the Instituto Nacional de Antropología e Historia. The convent is itself a work of art, with its Baroque **Templo de Guadalupe** and the **Capilla de Nápoles,** but even more impressive is the stunning collection of religious art under its roof. Works by Miguel Cabrera, Nicolás Rodríguez Juárez, Cristóbal de Villalpando, and Andrés López are included. ✉ *Jardín Juárez s/n,* ☎ *492/923–2386.* *$3, free Sun.* *Daily 10–4:30.*

In the 18th-century mansion of don Ignacio de Bernárdez, the **Centro Platero Zacatecas** is a school and factory for handmade silver jewelry and other items. Stop in to watch student silversmiths master this fine tradition. ✉ *Casco de la Ex-Hacienda Bernárdez,* ☎ *492/923–1007.* *Weekdays 10–6, Sat. 10–2.*

Zona Arqueológica La Quemada

50 km (31 mi) southwest of Zacatecas on Hwy. 54, 3 km (2 mi) off highway.

This ancient city was already a ruin before the Spaniards arrived in the 16th century. The site's original name, "Chicomostoc," means "place of the seven tribes." Although it was once believed that seven different Native American cultures built here, one community atop the other, this theory is currently under scrutiny. The remaining edifices appear to be constructed of thin slabs of stone wedged into place. The principal draw is a group of rose-color ruins containing 11 large, round columns built entirely of the same small slabs of rock seen in the rest of the ruins. An impressive site museum has a scale model of the ruins and some interesting artifacts. To get here, take a bus toward Villanueva, get off at the entrance to La Quemada, and walk 3 km (2 mi). The bus ride takes about an hour. Alternatively, take a taxi or guided tour. ☎ *No phone.* *$3, free Sun.* *Site and museum daily 10–4:30.*

Zacatecas A to Z

To research prices, get advice from other travelers, and book travel arrangements, visit www.fodors.com.

AIR TRAVEL

Mexicana has direct service to Zacatecas from Chicago, Denver, and Los Angeles. In Zacatecas, the Mexicana office is at Avenida Hidalgo 406. The airport is 29 km (18 mi) north of town. Aerotransportes makes the trip for about $5; private taxis cost about $15.

➤ AIRLINES AND CONTACTS: **Aerotransportes** (☎ 492/922–5946). **Mexicana** (☎ 492/922–7470 or 492/922–3248).

BUS TRAVEL

Major bus lines run several first- and second-class buses daily from Mexico City to Zacatecas. Estrella Blanca is the first-class service offered by Futura. The trip takes eight to nine hours.

➤ BUS INFORMATION: **Estrella Blanca** (☎ 492/922–0042). **Futura** (☎ 492/922–0042). **Omnibus de México** (☎ 492/922–5495).

CAR TRAVEL

Zacatecas is 603 km (375 mi), about 7½–8 hours, northwest of Mexico City via Route 57 (to Querétaro and San Luis Potosí) and Route 49.

EMERGENCIES

English is not generally spoken in Zacatecas, so it's best to contact your hotel manager or the tourist office in case of an emergency. The emergency line for fire, police, or medical attention is **066.**

Pharmacies are abundant; try Farmacia Isstezac, open daily 8 AM–10 PM.

➤ CONTACTS: **Farmacia Isstezac** (✉ Tacuba 153, ☎ 492/924–0690). **Hospital General** (☎ 492/923–3004). **Police** (☎ 492/922–0180). **Red Cross** (☎ 492/922–3005).

INTERNET

Cronos, open Monday–Saturday 9–8, Sunday 10:30–8, charges $2 an hour for Internet access.

➤ INTERNET CAFÉ: **Cronos** (✉ Av. Rayon 212, ☎ 492/922–1548).

TOURS

Viajes Mazzoco, a well-established travel agency and the local American Express representative, gives a four-hour tour of the city center, the Eden Mine, the Teleférico, and La Bufa for about $12 a person. There are also tours to La Quemada ruins and environs ($16).

Operadora Zacatecas is recommended by the tourism office, and offers tours of the city center and elsewhere in the area. Juan Dela O of DelaOTours offers a lively introduction to the sights of Zacatecas.

➤ TOUR OPERATOR RECOMMENDATIONS: **DelaOTours** (✉ 2 da. de Matamoros 153-C, ☎ FAX 492/922–3464). **Operadora Zacatecas** (✉ Av. Hidalgo 630, ☎ 492/922–2552). **Viajes Mazzoco** (✉ Calle Fatima 115, ☎ FAX 492/922–0859).

TRANSPORTATION AROUND ZACATECAS

You can get to most of the town-center attractions on foot, although you might want to hire a taxi if you want to tour a mine or take a ride on the Teleférico (cable car) to the top of Cerro de la Bufa. The city has an excellent and inexpensive bus system.

VISITOR INFORMATION

The tourist information office is open weekdays 9–8, weekends 9–7.

➤ TOURIST INFORMATION: **Tourist information office** (✉ Av. Hidalgo 403, 2nd floor, ☎ 492/924–4047 or 492/924–0552).

QUERÉTARO

In 1810 the first plans for independence were hatched at the Querétaro home of Josefa Ortiz de Domínguez—known as La Corregidora, wife of El Corregidor, Querétaro's mayor of the time. She was a heroine of the independence movement. In 1848 the Mexican–American War was concluded in this city with the signing of the Treaty of Guadalupe Hidalgo. Emperor Maximilian made his last stand here in 1867 and was executed by firing squad on the Cerro de las Campanas (Hill of the Church Bells), north of town. A small memorial chapel, built by the Austrian government, marks the spot. A gigantic statue of Benito Juárez crowns a park on the crest of the hill just above it. Also, in 1917, the Mexican Constitution, which is still in force, was signed here. Now Querétaro is a state capital and an industrial center of more than 1 million people.

Throughout Querétaro are markers, museums, churches, and monuments that commemorate the city's heroes and historic moments. A prevailing sense of civic pride is evident in the impeccably renovated mansions, the flower-draped cobblestone pedestrian walkways, and the plazas, which are softly lighted at night. On Sunday evening couples dance to live *danzón* music in the main plaza, or simply chat with their friends. The people are among the most congenial in central Mexico and are quick to share their favorite sites and tales with travelers.

Querétaro is also renowned for opals—red, green, honey, and fire stones. Caveat emptor: some street vendors sell opals so full of water that they crumble shortly after purchase. Buy from reputable dealers.

Exploring Querétaro

Although Querétaro extends for some distance, the historic district is in the heart of town. You can easily spend a day or two here visiting museums, admiring architecture, and taking in local history.

A Good Walk

Most sights are near the **Plaza de la Independencia** ㉜. The **Palacio del Gobierno del Estado** ㉝ is on the plaza's northwest corner. If you walk around the square counterclockwise, you'll come to the Palacio de Justicia, originally built as a mansion for the wealthy Domingo Iglesia and, beside it, the **Casa de Ecala** ㉞. Just past the Casa de Ecala is Avenida Libertad Oriente, one of the city's bougainvillea-draped pedestrian walkways. Turn west here and walk two blocks to reach Calle Corregidora. Bear right again, and in the middle of a long block you'll find the entrance to the **Museo Regional de Querétaro** ㉟. Cross the street to Avenida Madero, another "pedway," this one lined with shops. The city's main square, Jardín Obregón, will be on your right.

One block past Avenida Juárez on the corner of Calle Allende Sur and Madero you'll see the former **Casa de la Marquesa** ㊱, an 18th-century mansion converted into a hotel. Across Allende, next to the Church of Santa Clara, is the neoclassical **Fountain of Neptune** ㊲. From the fountain, head south on Calle Allende and walk almost a block to a fine example of Baroque architecture, the **Museo de Arte de Querétaro** ㊳. Retrace your steps to Calle Corregidora. Make a left and walk one block to Calle 16 de Septiembre. Across the street is the **Jardín de la Corregidora** ㊴.

Sights to See

34 **Casa de Ecala.** Currently housing the offices of DIF, a family-services organization, this Mexican Baroque palace has its original facade. As the story goes, its 18th-century owner adorned his home elaborately

Casa de Ecala 34
Casa de la Marquesa . . 36
Fountain of Neptune. . . . 37
Jardín de la Corregidora 39
Museo de Arte de Querétaro . . 38
Museo Regional de Querétaro . . 35
Palacio del Gobierno del Estado . . 33
Plaza de la Independencia 32

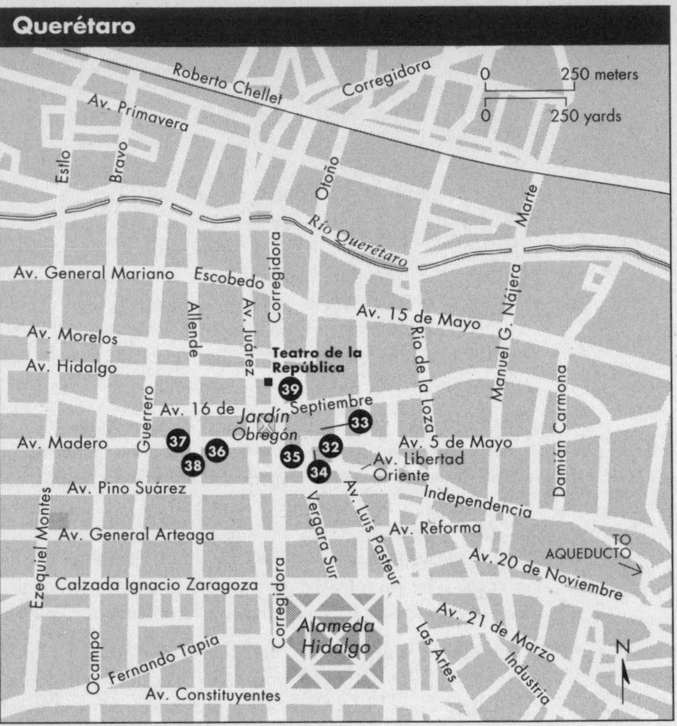

to outdo his neighbor, starting a remodeling war in which the Casa de Ecala eventually triumphed. Visitors are welcome to walk around the courtyard when the offices are open. ✉ *Pasteur Sur 6, Plaza de la Independencia.* ⏲ *Daily 9–2 and 4–6.*

36 **Casa de la Marquesa.** Today a five-star hotel, this beautifully restored 18th-century house was built by the second Marqués de la Villa del Villar del Aguila. Most of the legends about the house's construction suggest that it was built to impress a nun with whom the marquis was terribly smitten. But he didn't live to see the casa completed in 1756, and its first resident was his widow, who had a penchant for things Arabic. The interior is *mudéjar* (Moorish) style, with lovely tile work. Stop in for a drink and the elegant atmosphere of **Don Porfirio's Bar.** ✉ *Madero 41.*

NEED A BREAK?

Cafeteria El Naranjo (✉ Av. Madero 48, ☎ 421/224–0136 Ext. 109) has a wide selection of specialty coffee, including the Sexy Coffee (coffee, rum, Kahlúa, and whole cream).

37 **Fountain of Neptune.** Built in 1797 by Eduardo Tresguerras, the renowned Mexican architect and a native of the Bajío, the fountain originally stood in the orchard of the Monastery of San Antonio. According to one story, when the monks faced serious economic problems, they sold part of their land and the fountain along with it. It now stands next to the Church of Santa Clara. ✉ *Calle Allende at Madero.*

39 **Jardín de la Corregidora.** This plaza is prominently marked by a statue of the War of Independence heroine—Josefa Ortiz de Domínguez—whose moniker it bears. Behind the monument stands the **Arbol de la Amistad** (Tree of Friendship). Planted in 1977 in a mixture of soils from around the world, the tree symbolizes Querétaro's hospitality to all trav-

elers. This is the calmest square in town, with plenty of choices for patio dining. ✉ *Calle Corregidora and Av. 16 de Septiembre.*

38 **Museo de Arte de Querétaro.** A fine example of Baroque architecture, the museum is housed in an 18th-century Augustinian monastery. Its collection focuses on European and Mexican paintings from the 17th through 19th centuries, and there are rotating exhibits of 20th-century art. Note the elegant and fascinating Baroque patio, and ask for an explanation of the symbolism of its columns and the figures in the conch shells at the top of each arch. ✉ *Calle Allende 14 Sur,* ☎ *421/212–2357.* 🎫 *About $1.50, free Tues.* ⏲ *Tues.–Sun. 10–6.*

35 **Museo Regional de Querétaro.** This bright-yellow, 17th-century Franciscan monastery displays the works of colonial and European artists in addition to historic memorabilia, including early copies of the Mexican Constitution and the table on which the Treaty of Guadalupe Hidalgo was signed. ✉ *Calle Corregidora 3, at Av. Libertad Oriente,* ☎ *421/212–2031.* 🎫 *About $3, free Sun.* ⏲ *Tues.–Sun. 10–7.*

33 **Palacio del Gobierno del Estado.** Also known as La Casa de la Corregidora, in 1810 this was the home of Querétaro's mayor-magistrate (El Corregidor) and his wife, Josefa Ortiz de Domínguez (La Corregidora). On many evenings, conspirators—including Ignacio Allende and Father Miguel Hidalgo—came here under the guise of participating in La Corregidora's literary salon. When El Corregidor learned that they were actually plotting the course for independence, he imprisoned his wife in her room. La Corregidora managed to whisper a warning to a coconspirator, who notified Allende and Hidalgo. A few days later, on September 16, Father Hidalgo tolled the bell of his church to signal the beginning of the fight for freedom. A replica of the bell can be seen atop the building. Now the Palacio houses municipal government offices. ✉ *Northwest corner of Plaza de la Independencia.* 🎫 *Free.* ⏲ *Weekdays 8 AM–9 PM, Sat. 8–3.*

32 **Plaza de la Independencia.** Bordered by carefully restored colonial mansions, this immaculate square, also known as Plaza de Armas, is especially lovely at night, when the central fountain is lighted. Built in 1842, the fountain is dedicated to the Marqués de la Villa del Villar, who constructed Querétaro's elegant aqueduct and provided the city with drinking water. The old stone aqueduct with its 74 towering arches still stands at the east end of town. ✉ *Bounded by Av. 5 de Mayo on the north, Av. Libertad Oriente on the south, Luis Pasteur on the east, and Vergara Sur on the west.*

Dining

Many of Querétaro's dining spots are near the main plaza (Jardín Obregón), along Calle Corregidora, near the Teatro de la República, and particularly in the Jardín de la Corregidora. There are more-upscale restaurants in hotels on the Plaza de la Independencia and off Route 57, north of the city.

$$$$ ★ ✕ **Restaurante Josecho.** Bullfight aficionados and other sports fans frequent this highway road stop next to the bullring at the southwest end of town as much for the lively atmosphere as for the food. Wood-paneled walls are hung with hunting trophies, including peacocks, elk, bears, and lions; waiters celebrate patrons' birthdays by singing and blasting a red siren. In the evenings a classical guitarist or pianist performs. House specialties include *filete Josecho* (steak with cheese and mushrooms) and *filete Chemita* (steak sautéed in butter with onions). Save room for the creamy coconut ice cream. ✉ *Dalia 1, next to Plaza de Toros Santa María,* ☎ *421/216–0229 or 421/216–0201. AE, MC, V.*

$$$ ✕ **El Mesón de Chucho el Roto.** Named after Querétaro's version of Robin Hood, this restaurant is on the quiet Plaza de Armas. The interesting menu highlights regional cooking, including exotic tacos of either steamed goat, shrimp with nopal cactus, or squash blossoms. You can enjoy a variety of breakfast foods here as well, either overlooking the plaza from the café tables outside, indoors, or on the back patio. ✉ *Plaza de Armas,* ☎ *421/212–4295. AE, MC, V.*

$$$ ★ ✕ **La Nueva Fonda del Refugio.** Situated in the Jardín de la Corregidora, this restaurant offers intimate indoor and outdoor dining. Inside, fresh flowers adorn brightly clothed tables; outside, comfortable *equipale* chairs face the surrounding gardens. For a delicious regional twist order the *filete de huitlacoche,* a steak filet smothered in a corn fungus sauce. Cocktails are served on the terrace at night, when diners are often serenaded by guitar-playing trios. ✉ *Jardín de la Corregidora 26,* ☎ *421/212–0755. AE, MC, V.*

$$ ✕ **Bisquets Bisquets.** Mexican families flock to this friendly spot after church for good and hearty inexpensive food. The specialty of the house is—you guessed it—biscuits, made fresh on the premises, with such traditional toppings as butter and jelly or with more unusual ones such as mole or tuna. There are good enchiladas *Queretanas,* with cheese, potatoes, carrots, and cream, and *huevos al albañil* (eggs with red sauce and beans). ✉ *Av. Pino Suarez 7,* ☎ *421/214–1481. No credit cards.*

$ ✕ **La Mariposa.** Celebrating more than 50 years in business, La Mariposa is easily recognized by the wrought-iron butterfly (*mariposa*) over the entrance. This is the place for coffee and cake or a light Mexican lunch: tacos, tamales, and *tortas* (sandwiches). It's a favorite among locals despite its very plain, cafeterialike appearance. ✉ *Angela Peralta 7,* ☎ *421/212–1166 or 421/212–4849. No credit cards.*

Lodging

Querétaro offers a variety of elegant and unique restored properties, including the Casa de la Marquesa. Lower-price hotels are near the main plaza and thus tend to be noisy; restored colonial mansions are on or near the city's many plazas in the heart of town; and deluxe properties are on the outskirts of town.

$$$$ ★ **Casa de la Marquesa.** This handsomely restored property, originally an 18th-century private home, is in the heart of Querétaro. Each large guest room is furnished in antiques, tasteful art, parquet floors, and area rugs. Rooms in the main building are more elegant and expensive than those in La Casa Azul (children under 12 are not admitted in the main building). The property's award-winning restaurant, Comedor de la Marquesa, is elegant and a bit austere. It specializes in such regional rarities as boar, venison, and *escamole* (ant eggs) in season, as well as more-traditional international cookery. ✉ *Madero 41, 76000,* ☎ *421/212–0092,* FAX *421/212–0098. 25 suites. 2 restaurants, room service, bar, shop. AE, MC, V.*

$$$ ★ **Hacienda Jurica.** A favorite getaway for Mexico City families, this sprawling 16th-century ex-hacienda has nearly 30 acres of grassy sports fields, topiary gardens, a horse stable, and you can play golf at a nearby course. The grounds and courtyards are dotted with antique horse-drawn carriages, and the spacious earth-tone rooms have substantial dark-wood furniture. The hacienda is in Jurica, an upscale residential neighborhood 13 km (8 mi) northwest of the city off Highway 57 and is easiest to reach by car. ✉ *Carretera Mexico–San Luis Potosí, Km 229, Apdo. 338, 76100,* ☎ *421/218–0022,* FAX *421/218–0136. 176 rooms, 6 suites. Restaurant, minibars, 2 tennis courts, pool, billiards, horseback riding, bar, free parking. AE, MC, V.*

$$$ **Holiday Inn Querétaro.** This gracious, well-run establishment has a lot more charm than others in the chain. Located 3 km (about 2 mi) west of the historic district off Highway 57, the contemporary building incorporates many colonial touches such as stone archways and domed *boveda* (vaulted) ceilings. Sunny, ample rooms are comfortably appointed with rustic Mexican furnishings and cheery pastel bedspreads. ✉ *Av. 5 de Febrero 110, 76000,* ☎ *421/216–0202,* FAX *421/216–8902,* WEB *www.holidayinn.com.mx. 171 rooms, 4 suites. 2 restaurants, minibars, cable TV, pool, gym, piano bar, baby-sitting, travel services, free parking, no-smoking rooms. AE, MC, V.*

$$$ ★ **Mesón de Santa Rosa.** On the quiet Plaza de la Independencia, this elegant property was used almost 300 years ago as a stopover for travelers to the north. Rooms are clustered around a quiet courtyard; lace-hung glass doors and wood-beam ceilings maintain the colonial charm. ✉ *Pasteur Sur 17, 76000,* ☎ *421/224–2623,* FAX *421/212–5522. 5 rooms, 16 suites. Restaurant, minibars, cable TV, pool, bar. AE, MC, V.*

$$ **Hotel Mirabel.** A favorite among business travelers and conventioneers, this modern high-rise at the bottom of its price range hums with activity. Its carpeted rooms are insulated and quiet and have wooden desks. Some double rooms have views of the Alameda Hidalgo park; some singles overlook a soccer stadium. ✉ *Av. Constituyentes Ote. 2, 76000,* ☎ *421/214–3099 or 421/214–3444,* FAX *421/214–3585. 170 rooms, 10 suites. Restaurant, cable TV, bar, free parking. AE, MC, V.*

Nightlife and the Arts

Band concerts are held in the **Jardín Obregón,** Querétaro's main square, every Sunday evening at 6. A monthly publication called *Tesoro Turístico,* available at the tourist office, provides information about current festivals, concerts, and other cultural events.

Shopping

A number of stores around town sell opals (not milky white, like Australian opals, but beautiful nonetheless) and other locally mined gems. If you're in the market for loose stones or opal jewelry, do some comparison shopping, as you're apt to find better prices here than in the United States. **Lapidaria Querétaro** (✉ Corregiedora 149 Nte., ☎ 421/212–0030) is a reputable dealer of loose stones and opals. **Villalone y Artesanos** (✉ Av. Libertad 24-A, ☎ 421/212–8414) offers friendly service and authentic stones.

El Globo (✉ Corregidora 41, at Independencia, ☎ 421/212–1019 or 421/212–8883), boasting more than 100 hundred years of service in Querétaro, offers a variety of extravagant cookies, chocolates, freshly baked breads, cakes, and pies.

Side Trips from Querétaro

San Juan del Río and Tequisquiapan are both within an hour's drive of Querétaro. The highway between Querétaro and San Juan del Río is paved with factories, and San Juan is a bustling manufacturing center whose only real appeal is the semiprecious gems—especially opals, topaz, and amethyst—sold here, both loose and in settings. Tequisquiapan, on the other hand, is a tranquil and pretty *pueblo* (town) drenched in sun and bougainvillea and flowering trees, and known as a producer of wicker and other crafts. Once frequented by harried Mexican urbanites who came to soak in the area's thermal waters, Tequis (as the locals call it) now suffers a dearth of hot water.

A car is the best means to get around. Buses serve both towns from Querétaro, but the trip is longer. If you go to both towns, shop first in San Juan del Río, then head to Tequisquiapan to look around, shop a bit, and perhaps have a meal or a snack. A taxi between the two towns costs about $4.50.

San Juan del Río

51 km (32 mi) southeast of Querétaro via Rte. 57.

Most of San Juan's gem shops are near the main plaza downtown, and along Avenida Juárez and Calle 16 de Septiembre. **Lapidaria Guerrero** (✉ Av. Juárez Pte. 4, ☎ 427/272–1481) has an exceptionally large collection of opal, amethyst, turquoise, and topaz jewelry. The store is open daily 10–2 and 3–7:30.

Tequisquiapan

19 km (12 mi) east of San Juan del Río, off Rte. 120.

This town, famous for centuries for its restorative thermal waters, has in recent years lost much of its thermal flow, reportedly due to the extraordinary water consumption of a paper mill in the area. Many spas struggle on as simple swimming pools–recreation areas, but as the main tourist draw has receded with the once-warm waters, most are deserted midweek. Things do liven up on hot weekends, however. The **tourist office** (✉ Andador Independencia 1, Plaza Miguel Hidalgo, ☎ 427/273–0295), open daily 9–7, will cheerfully direct you to one or more of the spas, most of which are outside of town.

After lunch or a snack, head to the shops or to the **Mercado de Artesanías** (✉ Calzado de los Misterios s/n, ☎ no phone), where woven goods, jewelry, and locally made furniture are sold. The **Templo de Santa María de la Asunción,** on the main plaza, was begun in 1874 in the neoclassical style, but not completed until the beginning of the 20th century. In late May or early June, the city hosts a weeklong wine and cheese festival.

Xilitla

Approximately 320 km (198 mi) northeast of Querétaro.

Feel the ordinary world fade away with a trip to the decidedly off-the-beaten-path **Las Pozas** (The Pools), the extraordinary sculpture garden of the late, eccentric English millionaire Edward James (1907–84). Friend of artists Dalí and Picasso and rumored to be the illegitimate son of King Edward VII, James spent 20 years building 36 surrealist concrete structures deep in the waterfall-filled Xilitla jungle. These amazing structures are half-finished fantasy castles, gradually falling to ruin as the rain forest slithers in to claim them. It's like the ultimate child's fort. The castles don't have walls—just vine-entwined pillars, secret passageways, and operatic staircases leading nowhere.

It's a six- to seven-hour thrilling but exhausting mountainous drive to Xilitla, with hairpin turns and spectacular desert, forest, and jungle vistas. Plan on staying at least two nights, as you'll want time to soak up the jungle magic. If you choose not to drive, you can take a bus to Ciudad Valles (1½-hour drive from Xilitla) or fly to Tampico (3½-hour drive from Xilitla), and arrange ahead for the staff of Posada El Castillo to pick you up. ✉ *From Querétaro, head north on Hwy. 57 (Carretera Mexico–San Luis Potosí). Take the* PEÑA DE BERNAL *turnoff, marked on a bridge overpass and also on a smaller sign at the Cadareyta exit. Continue north through Bernal, after which the road will join Rte. 120. Take 120 through Jalpan and then on to Xilitla, just across the border in the state of San Luis Potosí. The turnoff to Las Pozas is just beyond Xilitla on the left after passing a small bridge.* 🎫 *$1.50.* ⏲ *Daily dawn–dusk.*

LODGING

$$ **Posada El Castillo.** When he wasn't living in his jungle hut, Edward James stayed in town (a 10-minute drive away) in a whimsical house that feels like an extension of the garden structures at Las Pozas—except that it has walls. That house, El Castillo (the castle), is now a quirky inn run by Lenore and Avery Danziger, who have made an award-winning documentary film about James that they happily screen for guests. Rooms are adorned with simple wooden furnishings; the best rooms have huge Gothic windows and panoramic mountain views. You can arrange to have meals here; otherwise there are few dining options in the area. ✉ *Ocampo 105, Xilitla, San Luis Potosí 79900,* ☎ *136/365–00–38,* FAX *136/365–00–55,* WEB *www.junglegossip.com. 8 rooms. Pool. No credit cards.*

Querétaro A to Z

To research prices, get advice from other travelers, and book travel arrangements, visit www.fodors.com.

BUS TRAVEL

Daily buses run direct between Mexico City's Central del Norte (North Bus Station) and Querétaro's Central de Autobuses. Major lines have frequent service; travel time is about three hours. Buses also leave several times a day for Guanajuato, San Miguel de Allende, and Morelia.

➤ BUS INFORMATION: **ETN** (☎ 421/229–0078 or 421/229–0019). **Flecha Amarilla** (☎ 421/211–4001). **Futura** (☎ 421/229–0022). **Omnibus de México** (☎ 421/229–0029).

CAR RENTAL

Two major car rental agencies are available in Querétaro. Both are located downtown.

➤ MAJOR AGENCIES: **Avis** (✉ Prol. Corregidora Nte. 318, Col. Alamos, 3a sección, ☎ 421/224–1785 or 421/224–1786, FAX 421/224–1786). **Budget** (✉ Av. Constituyentes Ote. 73, ☎ FAX 421/213–4498).

CAR TRAVEL

Querétaro is 220 km (136 mi) northwest of Mexico City, a three-hour drive on Route 57.

EMERGENCIES

Dial **066** for medical, fire, and theft emergencies. Oficinas Para la Seguridad de la Turista offers a countrywide 24-hour toll-free hot line to provide legal and medical help for tourists.

➤ CONTACTS: **Ambulance–Red Cross** (☎ 421/229–0545 or 421/229–0665). **Emergency** (☎ 066). **Fire Department** (☎ 421/212–3939 or 421/212–0627). **Oficinas Para la Seguridad de la Turista** (☎ 800/903–9200). **Police** (☎ 421/220–8303 or 421/220–9191). **Sanatorio Alcocer Pozo (Hospital)** (✉ Calle Reforma 23, ☎ 421/212–0149 or 421/212–1787). **Traffic Police** (☎ 421/213–8424).

MONEY MATTERS

Casa de Cambio Acueducto is open weekdays 9–2 and 4–6, Saturday 9–1.

➤ EXCHANGE SERVICES: **Casa de Cambio Acueducto** (✉ Av. Juárez Sur 58, ☎ 421/212–9304).

INTERNET

Web Café, open Monday–Saturday 10–10, Sunday 4–10, charges $3 an hour for Internet access.

➤ INTERNET CAFÉS: **Web Café** (✉ Ezequiel Montes Sur 67, ☎ 421/216–0250 or 421/216–7272).

TOURS

The tourist office conducts hour-long trolley tours of the city's historic landmarks at 9, 10, and 11 AM and at 4, 5, and 6 PM Tuesday–Sunday. To arrange a city tour in English, call the office—one day in advance if possible. The cost is about $1.50.

TRANSPORTATION AROUND QUERÉTARO

Most of Querétaro's historic sites are within walking distance of one another in the downtown district and can be reached by a series of walkways that are closed to car traffic most of the day. If you want to venture farther afield, you will find that buses and taxis run frequently along the main streets and are inexpensive.

TRAVEL AGENCIES

Turismo Beverly offers full travel services.
➤ LOCAL AGENT REFERRALS: **Turismo Beverly** (✉ Av. Tecnologia 118, ☎ 421/216–1500 or 421/216–1260, FAX 421/216–8524).

VISITOR INFORMATION

Dirección de Turismo del Estado is open weekdays 8–8, weekends 9–8.
➤ TOURIST INFORMATION: **Dirección de Turismo del Estado** (✉ Plaza de Armas, ☎ 421/212–1412 or 421/212–0907, FAX 421/212–1094).

MORELIA

With its long, wide boulevards and earth-tone colonial mansions, Morelia is the gracious capital of the state of Michoacán. Founded in 1541 as Valladolid (after the Spanish city), it changed its name in 1828 to honor José María Morelos, the town's most famous son. The legendary mule skinner–turned–priest took up the battle for independence after its early leaders were executed in 1811.

Morelos began with an ill-equipped army of 25 but soon organized a contingent of 9,000 that nearly gained control of the country. Although he was defeated and executed in 1815, he left behind a longstanding reformist legacy that called for universal suffrage, racial equality, and the demise of the hacienda system. The city today still pays tribute to Morelos—his former home has been turned into a museum, and his birthplace is now a library.

Morelianos love music, and several annual festivals are designed to indulge them. Each May the city celebrates the International Organ Festival in the cathedral, giving voice to its outstanding 4,600-pipe organ. The last two weeks in July are given to the Festival International de Música, featuring Baroque and chamber music, with orchestras participating from throughout Mexico.

Morelia has the delicious distinction of being the candy capital of Mexico. So strong is the sweet-eating tradition that the city has a **Mercado de Dulces**—a sweets market.

Exploring Morelia

To explore Morelia and its surrounding hillside neighborhoods thoroughly would take some time. However, if you stroll through the historic plazas and frequent the cafés (as many locals do), you will begin to feel the city's vitality. Although the vehicle and sidewalk traffic can get a little heavy at times, Morelia is a pedestrian-friendly city.

A Good Walk

Begin your walk in Morelia's tree-lined downtown **Plaza de Armas** ㊵, on the east side of which is the city's famed **Catedral** ㊶. As you leave

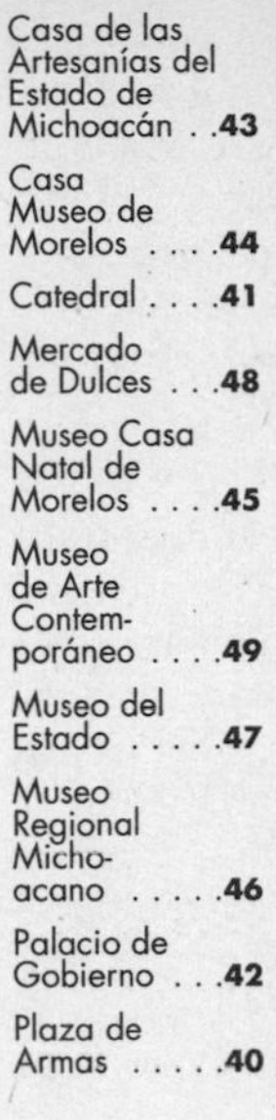

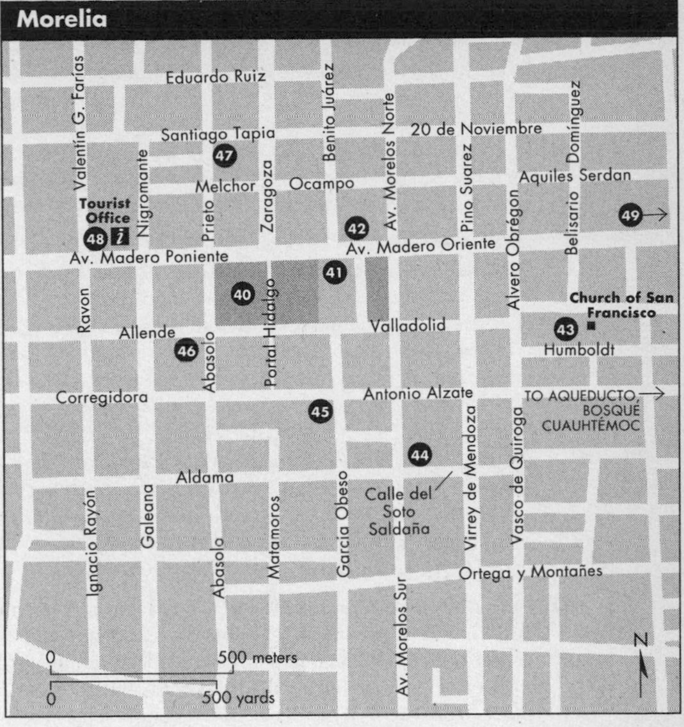

the cathedral, cross Avenida Madero Oriente to the **Palacio de Gobierno** ㊷, a former seminary. From the palace it's four blocks east along Avenida Madero Oriente to Calle de Belisario Domínguez. Make a right and walk one block south to the Church of San Francisco. To the rear of the church, in the former convent of San Francisco, is the entrance to the **Casa de las Artesanías del Estado de Michoacán** ㊸, a virtual cornucopia of crafts from around the state.

Walk two blocks south on Calle Vasco de Quiroga, a street lined with vendors, until you come to Calle del Soto Saldaña. Head west another two blocks to Avenida Morelos Sur. The corner building on the right is the **Casa Museo de Morelos** ㊹, which displays memorabilia of the independence leader. It's one block north from the museum to Calle Antonio Alzate and then one block west (where the street name changes to Calle Corregidora) to Calle García Obeso. On this corner stands the **Museo Casa Natal de Morelos** ㊺, Morelos's birthplace. Continue west on Calle Corregidora until you reach Calle Abasolo. On Calle Allende, one block to the north, you'll find the **Museo Regional Michoacano** ㊻.

After leaving the museum take Calle Abasolo back to the plaza; 2½ blocks to the north, you'll see the **Museo del Estado** ㊼ on the right side of the street (which changes to Calle Guillermo Prieto at Avenida Madero Oriente). Return to Avenida Madero Oriente and then go two blocks to the right to the corner of the Valentín Gómez Farías, to the **Mercado de Dulces** ㊽.

For a longer stroll, take Avenida Madero Oriente east a dozen blocks or so to where it forks. Stay to the right; you'll see the **Fountain of the Tarascans** on a traffic island to your left. Just past the fountain, Morelia's mile-long **aqueduct** begins. This 1875 structure, which consists of 253 arches, once carried the city's main source of drinking water.

It's particularly beautiful at night when its arches—some rising to 30 ft—are illuminated. Two blocks farther along (Madero is now called Avenida Acueducto) is the entrance to **Bosque Cuauhtémoc,** Morelia's largest park. If you happen by during the week, you may encounter university students studying (or lounging) beneath the palms and evergreens. On weekends, especially Sunday, families on outings take over. Two blocks past the park entrance, you'll see the **Museo de Arte Contemporáneo** ㊾, also on the right side of the street.

Sights to See

43 **Casa de las Artesanías del Estado de Michoacán.** In the 16th century, Vasco de Quiroga, the bishop of Michoacán, helped the Purépecha Indians develop artistic specialties so they could be self-supporting. At this two-story museum and store, you can see the work that the Purépechas still produce: copper goods from Santa Clara del Cobre, lacquerware from Uruapan, straw items and pottery from Pátzcuaro, guitars from Paracho, fanciful ceramic devil figures from Ocumicho. At the **Museo Michoacana de las Artesanías** in the two main floors around the courtyard, some of these items are showcased behind glass while artists demonstrate how they are made. ✉ *Calle Fray Juan de San Miguel 129,* ☎ *443/312–2486 museum; 443/312–1248 store.* 🎫 *Free.* ⏲ *Mon.–Sat. 10–3 and 5–8, Sun. 10–4:30.*

44 **Casa Museo de Morelos.** What is now a two-story museum was acquired in 1801 by José María Morelos and served as home to generations of the Mexican independence leader's family until 1934. Owned by the Mexican government, it contains family portraits, various artifacts from the independence movement (such as a camp bed used by Ignacio Allende), and the blindfold Morelos wore for his execution. The excellent free tour is in Spanish only. ✉ *Av. Morelos Sur 323,* ☎ *443/313–2651.* 🎫 *About $2, free Sun.* ⏲ *Daily 9–7.*

41 **Catedral.** Morelia's cathedral is a majestic structure built between 1640 and 1744. It is known throughout Mexico for its 200-ft Baroque towers, among the tallest in the land, and for its 4,600-pipe organ, one of the finest in the world. The organ is the vehicle for the international organ festival held here each May. ✉ *Av. Madero between Plaza de Armas and Av. Morelos.*

48 **Mercado de Dulces.** If you have a sweet tooth, don't miss Morelia's famous candy market, behind the tourist office. All sorts of local sweets are for sale, such as *ate* (a candied fruit) and *cajeta* (heavenly caramel sauce made from goat's milk). ✉ *Av. Madero Pte. and Valentín Gómez Farías.* ⏲ *Daily 10–9.*

45 **Museo Casa Natal de Morelos.** José María Morelos's birthplace is now a library and national monument housing mostly literature and history books (as well as two murals by Moreliano Alfredo Zalce). Be sure to visit the courtyard in back: it's a tranquil square, adjacent to the Church of San Agustín; a marker and an eternal flame honor the fallen hero. ✉ *Calle Corregidora 113,* ☎ *443/312–2793.* 🎫 *Free.* ⏲ *Daily 9–7.*

49 **Museo de Arte Contemporáneo.** The works of contemporary Mexican and international artists are on view at this well-lighted museum near the Bosque Cuauhtémoc. ✉ *Av. Acueducto 18,* ☎ *443/312–5404.* 🎫 *Free.* ⏲ *Tues.–Sun. 10–2 and 4–8.*

47 **Museo del Estado.** Across from a small plaza with statues of Bishop Vasco de Quiroga and Spanish writer Miguel de Cervantes, this history museum is in a stately mansion that was once the home of the wife of Agustín de Iturbide, Mexico's only native-born emperor. A high-

light of the collection is a complete Morelia pharmacy dating from 1868. ✉ *Guillermo Prieto 176,* ☎ *443/313–0629.* 🎫 *Free.* ⏲ *Tues.–Sun. 10–2 and 4–8.*

46 **Museo Regional Michoacano.** An 18th-century former palace, the museum traces the history of Mexico from its pre-Hispanic days through the Cardenista period, which ended in 1940. President Lázaro Cárdenas, a native of Michoacán, was one of Mexico's most popular leaders because of his nationalization of the oil industry and his support of other populist reforms. The ground floor contains an art gallery, plus archaeological exhibits from Michoacán. Upstairs is an assortment of colonial objects, including furniture, weapons, and religious paintings. ✉ *Calle Allende 305,* ☎ *443/312–0407.* 🎫 *About $3, free Sun.* ⏲ *Tues.–Sat. 9–7, Sun. 9–4.*

NEED A BREAK? When you've finished your tour of the Museo Regional Michoacano, walk across the street to the colonial stone *portales* (arcades). The portales on one side of the square contain popular sidewalk cafés. For a sandwich, an order of guacamole with chips, or a good selection of juices, coffees, and teas, try **Hotel Casino** (✉ Portal Hidalgo 229, ☎ 443/313–1328). No one will mind if you linger over a book or newspaper for the better part of an hour sipping an excellent *café con leche.*

42 **Palacio de Gobierno.** This former Tridentine seminary, built in 1770, has had such notable graduates as independence hero José María Morelos, social reformer Melchor Ocampo, and the first emperor of Mexico, Agustín de Iturbide. Striking murals decorate the stairway and second floor. Painted by local artist Alfredo Zalce in the early 1960s, they depict dramatic, often bloody scenes from Mexico's history. ✉ *Av. Madero 63,* ☎ *443/312–8598.* 🎫 *Free.* ⏲ *Weekdays 8 AM–10 PM.*

40 **Plaza de Armas.** During the War of Independence, several rebel priests were brutally murdered on this site, and the plaza, known as Plaza de los Mártires, is named after them. Today, however, the square belies its violent past: sweethearts stroll along the tree-lined walks and friends chat under the colossal silver-domed gazebo. A welcoming peace has settled over the plaza: for the first time in almost 20 years the square is devoid of the overwhelming crush of street vendors. ✉ *Bounded on the north by Av. Madero, on the south by Calle Allende, on the west by Calle Abasolo, and on the east by the cathedral.*

Dining

Some of Michoacán's tastiest dishes—tomato-based Tarascan soup, corn products such as *huchepos* (sweet tamales) and *corundas* (savory triangular tamales), and game (rabbit and quail)—are served at Morelia restaurants. Traditional chicken and beef fare are also available, as are international dishes. As a rule, more-upscale restaurants are in hotels near the plaza and on the outskirts of town.

$$$ ✕ **Boca del Río.** Large picture windows opening onto a busy intersection provide ample light for this cheerful yet cafeterialike restaurant, which has fresh fish and seafood trucked in daily from Sinaloa and Veracruz. There are light snacks like the popular *coctel de camarones* (shrimp cocktail), along with heartier fare, such as the *jaiba rellena* (mushroom-and-cheese-stuffed crabs liberally seasoned with garlic). Beef and chicken dishes are also offered. After lunch, head to the sprawling Mercado de Dulces, across the street, for dessert. ✉ *Valentín Gómez Farías 185,* ☎ *443/312–9974. MC, V.*

$$$ ★ ✕ **Casa de la Calzada.** In a restored weekend home a block and a half from the aqueducts, this elegant restaurant offers contemporary Mexican food with an eye on Morelia's rich past. Dine under umbrellas on the courtyard beside a peaceful fountain or in one of the richly painted dining rooms hung with contemporary art. Enjoy pasta citrus, a tantalizing dish topped with a citrus, olive oil, and macadamia nut sauce and sprinkled with fried parsley, or the taste-bud fiesta of *pollo del jardín de los naranjos,* chicken stuffed with Mexican sausage and shrimp and coated in a citrus sauce. ✉ *Calz. Fray Antonio de San Miguel 344,* ☏ *443/313–5319. AE, MC, V.*

$$$ ★ ✕ **Fonda Las Mercedes.** This delightful restaurant's arty, modern furnishings somehow fit perfectly in the plant-filled stone patio of this restored colonial mansion. The inside dining room, which is equally pleasant, may be cozier on chilly days or evenings. Offerings from the eclectic menu include lots of soups and six kinds of crêpes. If you dare, try the sinfully rich pasta with pistachios and pine nuts in cream sauce. ✉ *León Guzmán 47,* ☏ *443/312–6113. AE, MC, V. No dinner Sun.*

$$ ✕ **La Casa del Portal.** Overlooking the Plaza de Armas and quartered in four distinctly decorated dining rooms, this venerable restaurant features a variety of local dishes. Served in a succulent red sauce, the *corundas* (small triangle tamales) are topped with chopped pork, sour cream, and chili poblano strips. Don't miss the *arrachera Valladolid,* a succulent slice of skirt steak served with *nopales* (sliced and steamed cactus), guacamole, and beans. ✉ *Guillermo Prieto 30,* ☏ *443/317–4217 or 443/313–4899. AE, MC, V.*

$ ★ ✕ **Taquería Pioneros.** There's a reason the tables are full at lunch at this positively plain taco shop: it has delicious grilled meats, served Michoacán style with salsas and mountains of fresh, hot tortillas made on site. The *pionero* (beef, ham, bacon, onions, and cheese, all grilled) is the only style served in a half portion, which is plenty for most appetites. Quesadillas, *sincronizadas* (quesadillas with ham), and beans are also served, as is beer and soda. ✉ *A. Serdán 7, at Ocampo,* ☏ *443/313–4938. Reservations not accepted. No credit cards.*

Lodging

Morelia offers a number of pleasant colonial-style hotels both in the downtown and outlying areas. Generally, the cheapest properties are near the bus station, moderately priced selections are clustered around the plaza (or on nearby side streets), and deluxe resort hotels are in or near the Santa María hills.

$$$ ★ **Hotel Virrey de Mendoza.** Built in 1565 to house a Spanish nobleman, this downtown hotel still radiates plenty of old-world atmosphere. The elegant lobby lounge is fitted with an enormous stone fireplace and cushy black leather couches. Guest rooms have dark colonial-style furnishings, lace curtains, soaring ceilings, and creaking hardwood floors, and the bathrooms have porcelain tubs. ✉ *Av. Madero Pte. 310, 58000,* ☏ *443/312–0633 or 443/312–4940,* FAX *443/312–6719,* WEB *www.hotelvirrey.com. 40 rooms, 15 suites. Restaurant, coffee shop, cable TV, bar, laundry service, free parking. AE, MC, V.*

$$$ ★ **Villa Montaña.** French count Philippe de Reiset has fitted this villa with all the trappings of a wealthy Mexican estate. High above Morelia in the Santa María hills, its five impeccably groomed acres are dotted with stone sculptures. Each individually decorated unit has at least one piece of antique furniture, and most have a fireplace and private patio. The hotel's renowned restaurant serves North American, French, and Mexican cuisine, and huge windows afford a marvelous view of Morelia, especially at night. Children under age eight are discouraged from dining in the restaurant. ✉ *Calle Patzimba 201, 58000,* ☏ *443/*

314–0231 or 443/314–0179, FAX *443/315–1423,* WEB *www.villamontana.com.mx. 15 rooms, 25 suites. Restaurant, in-room safes, tennis court, pool, piano bar, baby-sitting, laundry service, business services, meeting rooms, free parking. AE, MC, V.*

$$ **Hotel Mansión Acueducto.** An elaborate wood and wrought-iron staircase leads from the elegant lobby to more-modest quarters upstairs. Rooms have dark, colonial-style furniture; older units overlook the aqueduct and nearby park. Rooms in the motel-like wing have views of the garden, pool, and surrounding city. At times, student groups book the entire property. ✉ *Av. Acueducto 25, 58000,* ☎ *443/312–3301,* FAX *443/312–2020. 36 rooms, 1 suite. Restaurant, cable TV, pool, bar, free parking. MC, V.*

$$ ★ **Hotel Posada de la Soledad.** In a restored private mansion built in the late 17th century, this charming hotel is one block from the Plaza de Armas. Rooms vary in size, decoration, amenities, and price. The rooms in the original section surround an elegant patio with a large fountain and massive bougainvilleas. Rooms in a newer section are smaller and plain but quiet; rooms on Calle Ocampo get loud traffic noise from the street. If you're not impressed with the room you are shown, ask to see another. ✉ *Ignacio Zaragoza 90, 58000,* ☎ *443/312–1888 or 443/312–8990,* FAX *443/312–2111,* WEB *www.hsoledad.com. 48 rooms, 9 suites. Restaurant, cable TV, bar. AE, MC, V.*

$ **Hotel Valladolid.** Right on the Plaza de Armas, this property has plain but clean rooms with brick floors and striped bedspreads. The price includes coffee and juice. Although the accommodations are far from deluxe, this location offers easy access to downtown, and the staff is friendly. ✉ *Portal Hidalgo 245, 58000,* ☎ *443/312–0027,* FAX *443/312–4663. 25 rooms. Restaurant, no room phones. AE, MC, V.*

Nightlife and the Arts

Morelia has two lively folk-music clubs, both in beautiful locations downtown. **Colibri** (✉ Galeana 36, ☎ 443/312–2261) has folk music from throughout Latin America every night from 9:30 PM to 1 AM. **La Porfiriana** (✉ Calle Corregidora 694, ☎ 443/312–2663) presents spirited salsa music Tuesday–Saturday from 7 PM to 3 AM.

Side Trip to Santuario de Mariposas el Rosario

Approximately 115 km (71 mi) east of Morelia.

Every year 100 million monarch butterflies migrate from the United States and Canada to winter in the easternmost part of Michoacán, near the border of México state. A visit to the **Santuario de Mariposas el Rosario** (El Rosario Monarch Butterfly Sanctuary) between early November and early March is an awesome sensory experience. Caked with orange and black butterflies, the pine forest looks like it's on fire. Listen closely and you'll hear the rustle of millions of wings beating. The hike to the groves is a steep climb, and the high altitude (10,400 ft) will require that you take it slowly.

This day trip takes about 10 hours, but it's well worth the effort. If you choose not to drive the rough roads, catch a guided tour in Morelia. ✉ *Hwy. 15 east to Zitácuaro, then take marked but unnumbered road north to Angangueo, and on to sanctuary entrance.* 🎫 *$2 (plus tip for guide).* ⏲ *Daily 10–5.*

Morelia A to Z

To research prices, get advice from other travelers, and book travel arrangements, visit www.fodors.com.

AIR TRAVEL

There are daily flights between Francisco Mujica International Airport and Mexico City's International Airport on Aeroméxico.

➤ AIRPORT INFORMATION: **Francisco Mujica International Airport** (✉ 24 km [15 mi] north of Morelia).

CARRIERS

Mexicana has direct flights to and from Los Angeles, San Francisco, and Chicago. Flights are subject to cancellation; flight times change often and must be confirmed one day in advance. The 45-minute taxi ride from the airport to Morelia costs about $20.

➤ AIRLINES AND CONTACTS: **Aeroméxico** (☎ 800/021–4000). **Mexicana** (☎ 443/324–3808 or 443/324–3818).

BUS TRAVEL

Direct bus service is available daily between the Terminal Poniente (West Terminal, commonly referred to as the Observatorio) in Mexico City and Morelia's Central de Autobuses. Several bus lines have frequent service; the most direct trip ($18) takes four hours on ETN. Herradura de Plata is another bus line. Buses leave every hour or two around the clock.

➤ BUS INFORMATION: **Central de Autobuses** (✉ Eduardo Ruiz, between Valentín Gómez Farías and Guzmán, ☎ 443/312–5664). **ETN** (☎ 443/313–7440 or 443/313–4137). **Herradura de Plata** (☎ 443/312–2988).

CAR RENTAL

Budget has an office at the Francisco Mujica International Airport. National's office is beside the airport on Acueducto.

➤ MAJOR AGENCIES: **Budget** (✉ Francisco Mujica International Airport, ☎ 443/313–3399). **National** (✉ Av. Acueducto 3891, ☎ 443/324–6747).

CAR TRAVEL

The drive from Mexico City to Morelia (302 km [187 mi]) on the toll road through Toluca, Atlacamulco, Contepec, and Maravatio takes about four hours.

EMERGENCIES

Dial **070** for medical, fire, and theft emergencies. The Green Angels provide emergency roadside assistance.

➤ CONTACTS: **Ambulance–Red Cross** (☎ 443/314–5151). **Consumer Protection Office** (☎ 443/315–6202). **Fire Department** (☎ 443/320–1780). **Green Angels** (☎ 443/312–7777). **Hospital de la Cruz Roja** (☎ 443/314–5073). **Hospital Memorial** (☎ 443/315–1047 or 443/315–1099). **Police** (☎ 443/326–8522).

INTERNET

Chat Room Cyber Café, open Monday–Saturday 9 AM–10 PM and Sunday noon–9, charges $2 an hour for Internet access.

➤ INTERNET CAFÉS: **Chat Room Cyber Café** (✉ Nigromante 132-A, ☎ 443/312–9222).

MONEY MATTERS

Consultoría Internacional Casa de Cambio is open Monday–Saturday 9:30–5:30.

➤ CONTACT: **Consultoría Internacional Casa de Cambio** (✉ Prieto 48, ☎ 443/313–8308).

TOURS

Several worthy operators conduct tours of Morelia and the butterfly sanctuary. Contact Ayangupani through David Saucedo Ortega at the Villa Montaña front desk.

➤ Tour Operator Recommendations: **Ayangupani** (✉ Calle Patzimba 201, ☎ FAX 443/315–4045). **Explora Viajes** (✉ Av. Madero Ote. 493B, ☎ 443/312–7766, FAX 443/312–7660). **Morelia Operadores de Viajes** (✉ Isidro Huarte 481, ☎ 443/312–8723 or 443/312–8747, FAX 443/312–9591).

TRANSPORTATION AROUND MORELIA

As in many heartland cities, Morelia's major sights are near the center of town and easy to get to on foot. Street names in Morelia change frequently, especially on either side of Avenida Madero, the city's main east–west artery. Taxis can be hailed on the street or found near the main plaza. Buses run the length of Avenida Madero.

TRAVEL AGENCIES

Gran Turismo is the American Express representative.

➤ Local Agency: **Gran Turismo** (✉ Edificio Ejecutivo Camelinas, Av. Camelinas 3233, Int. 102–103, ☎ 443/324–0484, FAX 443/324–0495).

VISITOR INFORMATION

Secretaría Estatal de Turismo is open weekdays 9–8, Saturday 9–7, and Sunday 9–3.

➤ Tourist Information: **Secretaría Estatal de Turismo** (✉ Palacio Clavijero, Calle Nigromante 79, ☎ 443/317–2371, FAX 443/312–9816).

PÁTZCUARO

Pátzcuaro, the 16th-century capital of Michoacán, cxists in a time warp. A bit more than an hour by car from Morelia, this beautiful lakeside community at 7,250 ft in the Sierra Madre is home to the Purépecha Indians, who fish, farm, and ply their crafts as they have for centuries. Women wrapped tightly in their striped wool *rebozos* (shawls) hurry to market in the chilly morning air. Men in traditional straw hats wheel overburdened carts down crooked, dusty backstreets.

The architecture, too, has remained largely unchanged over the years. In the 16th century, under kindly Bishop Vasco de Quiroga, Pátzcuaro underwent a building boom. After he died in 1565, the state capital was moved to Morelia, and the town became a cultural (and architectural) backwater for hundreds of years. These days 16th-century mansions surround the downtown plazas; one-story whitewashed houses with sloping red tile roofs line the side streets and hills.

Despite the altitude, the weather in Pátzcuaro is temperate year-round. (Autumn and winter nights, however, are cold; sweaters and jackets are a must.) On November 1 the town is inundated with tourists en route to Janítzio, an island in Lake Pátzcuaro, where one of the most elaborate Day of the Dead graveyard ceremonies in all of Mexico takes place. Go to the island of Yunuen for an authentic glimpse of daily island life, and you can stay overnight. At numerous small towns around the lake you can buy craft items from their makers, in the process absorbing a bit of small-town rural Mexico. The Delegación de Turismo can share suggestions for adventures outside Pátzcuaro, as can expert local tour guides Francisco Castilleja and Marilyn Mayo.

Exploring Pátzcuaro

Most of Pátzcuaro's sights can be seen in a few hours, but the town and outlying areas deserve to be explored at a leisurely pace. There can be some traffic in the Plaza Bocanegra and on the main road coming into town, but elsewhere it is blissfully quiet.

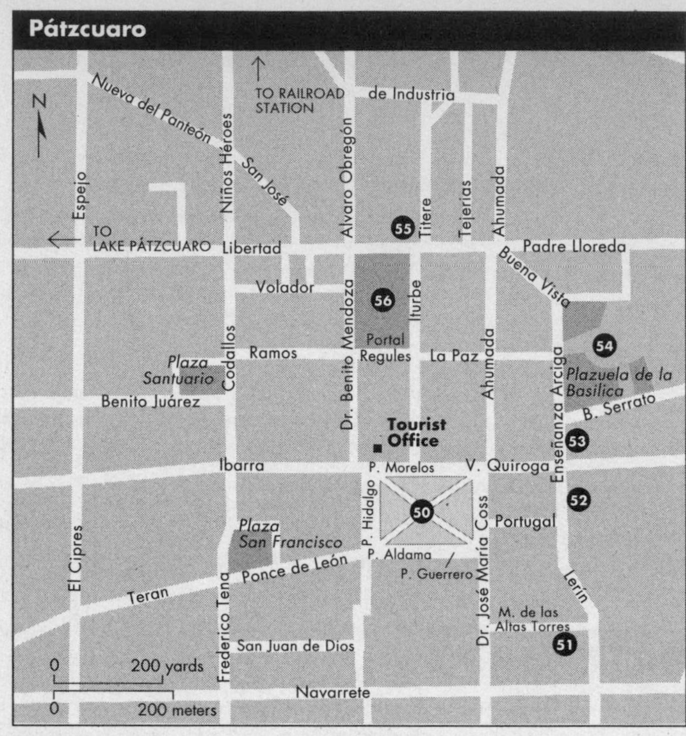

A Good Walk

Start your stroll at the **tourist office** (Plaza Vasco de Quiroga 50A), where you can pick up maps and brochures. Walk across the large **Plaza Vasco de Quiroga** ⑩ to the east side of the square and turn right on Calle Dr. José María Coss; in less than a block you'll see a long cobblestone walkway leading to **La Casa de los 11 Patios** ⑪, a former convent now housing a number of crafts shops. As you leave the complex, continue up a stone walkway to Calle Lerín. To the north (past Calle Portugal) is the **Templo de la Compañía** ⑫, the state's first cathedral. After visiting the church, continue another half block along Calle Lerín to the **Museo de Artes Populares** ⑬ on your right.

Directly down Enseñanza Arciga and across a cobblestone courtyard is **La Basílica de Nuestra Señora de la Salud** ⑭. Walk downhill from the basilica (take Buena Vista to Libertad and turn left) to reach the **Biblioteca Pública Gertrudis Bocanegra** ⑮. For a nice detour from the library, continue for a half block to the large outdoor **mercado** sprawled along Calle Libertad and its side streets. At times the road is so crowded with people and their wares—fruit, vegetables, beans, rice, herbs, and other necessities of daily life—that it's difficult to walk. If you press on for about a block, you'll see an indoor market to your left, filled with more produce, large hanging slabs of meat, hot food, and a variety of cheap trinkets. When you're finished with your market tour, retrace your steps down Calle Libertad. Across the street from the library, you can rest at **Plaza Bocanegra** ⑯, one block north of your starting point, Plaza Vasco de Quiroga.

Sights to See

54 **La Basílica de Nuestra Señora de la Salud** (Basilica of Our Lady of Health). The church was begun in 1554 by Vasco de Quiroga, and throughout the centuries others—undaunted by earthquakes and fires—

took up the cause and constructed the church in honor of the Virgin of Health. Near the main altar is a statue of the Virgin made of derivatives of cornstalks and orchids. Several masses are still held here daily; the earliest begins shortly after dawn. Out front, Purépecha women sell hot tortillas, herbal mixtures for teas, and religious objects. You can glimpse Lake Pátzcuaro in the distance. ⊠ *Enseñanza Arciga, near Calle Benigno Serrato.*

55 **Biblioteca Pública Gertrudis Bocanegra.** In the back of this library, a vast mural painted by Juan O'Gorman in 1942 depicts in great detail the history of the region and of the Purépecha people. In the bottom right of the mural, you can see Gertrudis Bocanegra, a local heroine who was shot in 1814 for refusing to divulge the revolutionaries' secrets to the Spaniards. ⊠ *North side of Plaza Bocanegra.* ⏲ *Weekdays 9–7, Sat. 10–2.*

51 **La Casa de los 11 Patios.** An 18th-century convent, 11 Patios houses a number of high-quality shops featuring Purépecha handiwork. As you meander through the shops and courtyards, you'll encounter weavers producing large bolts of cloth, artists trimming black lacquerware with gold, and seamstresses embroidering blouses. If you plan to shop in Pátzcuaro, this is a good place to start. ⊠ *Calle Madrigal de las Altas Torres s/n.* ⏲ *Daily 10–2 and 4–8.*

53 **Museo de Artes Populares.** Home to the Colegio de San Nicolás Obispo in the 16th century, the building today houses displays of colonial and contemporary crafts, such as ceramics, masks, lacquerware, paintings, and ex-votos in its many rooms. Behind this building is a *troje* (traditional Purépecha wooden house) braced atop a stone platform. ⊠ *Enseñanza Arciga,* ☎ *434/342–1029.* 🎫 *About $3, free Sun.* ⏲ *Tues.–Sat. 9–7, Sun. 9–2:30.*

56 **Plaza Bocanegra.** The smaller of the city's two squares (it's also called Plaza Chica), this is the center of Pátzcuaro's commercial life. Bootblacks, pushcart vendors, and bus and taxi stands are all in the plaza, which is embellished by a statue of the local heroine, Gertrudis Bocanegra. ⊠ *Bounded by Av. Libertad on the north, Portal Regules on the south, Dr. Benito Mendoza on the west, and Iturbe on the east.*

50 **Plaza Vasco de Quiroga.** A tranquil courtyard surrounded by ash and pine trees and 16th-century mansions (since converted into hotels and shops), the larger of the two downtown plazas commemorates the bishop who restored dignity to the Purépecha people. During the Spanish conquest, Nuño de Guzmán, a lieutenant in Hernán Cortés's army, committed atrocities against the local population in his efforts to conquer western Mexico. He was eventually arrested by the Spanish authorities, and in 1537 Vasco de Quiroga was appointed bishop of Michoacán. Attempting to regain the trust of the indigenous people, he established a number of model villages in the area and promoted the development of *artesanía* (crafts) commerce among the Purépechas. Quiroga died in 1565, and his remains were consecrated in the **Basílica de Nuestra Señora de la Salud.** ⊠ *Bounded by Calle Quiroga on the north, Av. Ponce de León on the south, Portal Hidalgo on the west, and Dr. José María Coss on the east.*

NEED A BREAK?

Before heading to Lake Pátzcuaro, sit in **Plaza Vasco de Quiroga** for a moment and enjoy a rich Michoacán ice cream you can buy under the portals on the west side of the plaza. Or sip a warming Doña Paca cappuccino spiked with *rompope* (egg liqueur) at the sidewalk café in front of **Mansión Iturbe.**

52 **Templo de la Compañía.** Michoacán's first cathedral was begun in 1540 by order of Vasco de Quiroga and completed in 1546. When the state capital was moved to Morelia some 20 years later, the church was taken over by the Jesuits. Today it remains much as it was in the 16th century. Moss has grown over the crumbling stone steps outside; the dank interior is planked with thick wood floors and lined with bare wood benches. ✉ *Calle Lerín s/n, near Calle Alcantaría.*

OFF THE BEATEN PATH

LAKE PÁTZCUARO – A 10-minute taxi ride from downtown are the tranquil shores of Lake Pátzcuaro. A few lakeside restaurants here serve fresh whitefish and other local catches. Amble along the dock or peek into the waterfront crafts shops. A boat trip to Janítzio (the largest of Lake Pátzcuaro's five islands) or to tiny Yunuen, which offers a cleareyed view of island life, is recommended. Wooden launches, with room for 25 people, depart for Janítzio and the other islands daily 9–6. Purchase round-trip tickets for $3 at a dockside office (prices are controlled by the tourist department). The ride to Janítzio takes about 30 minutes and is particularly beautiful in late afternoon, when the sun is low in the sky. Once you're out on the lake, fishermen with butterfly nets may approach your boat. The nets are no longer used for fishing, but for a small donation these locals will let you take their picture.

On most days (November 1 being the exception), Janítzio is a quiet albeit touristy island inhabited by Purépecha Indians. It's crowned by a huge statue of independence hero José María Morelos, which is accessible by a cobblestone stairway. Although the road twists past many souvenir stands as it ascends, don't be discouraged. The view from the summit—of the lake, the town, and the surrounding hills—is well worth the climb. Inside the statue are some remarkable murals that spiral up from the base to the tip of the monument.

Although Janítzio has succumbed to tourism, the small island of Yunuen is just beginning to attract visitors. This tranquil town has just 21 families, and provides a more accurate picture of island life than does Janítzio. You can get a boat to here from the ferry landing, or arrange to stay overnight in simple yet clean cabins available for visitors. The office of tourism can provide information.

Dining

Many restaurants in Pátzcuaro specialize in seafood. In addition to whitefish, look for *trucha* (trout) and *charales* and *boquerones* (two small, locally caught fish served as appetizers). Finding a satisfying meal in Pátzcuaro can be a challenge; focusing on local Purépecha dishes, such as *sopa tarasca*, may prove most rewarding. As a rule, restaurants are around the two plazas and in hotels. Since the large meal is served at midday, many dining establishments are shuttered by 9.

$$ ✕ **El Patio.** Although this low-key restaurant features mouthwatering whitefish platters (including salsa, vegetables, and french fries), it's possible to duck in at midday for just a strong cappuccino or glass of Mexican wine. For a late-afternoon snack, a plate of quesadillas with a side order of guacamole is highly recommended, and the sopa tarasca is superb. ✉ *Plaza Vasco de Quiroga 19,* ☎ *434/342–0484. MC, V.*

$$ ★ ✕ **El Primer Piso.** This second-floor restaurant overlooks Plaza Vasco de Quiroga, and on warm nights you can watch the comings and goings from a balcony table. There's plenty to look at inside as well; the restaurant doubles as an art gallery. The eclectic menu provides a break from the rather monotonous Pátzcuaro fare: try the pear salad with goat cheese, walnuts, and watercress, or the white-chocolate

mousse with blackberries and melon cream. ✉ *Plaza Vasco de Quiroga 29,* ☎ *434/342–0122. AE, MC. Closed Tues.*

$$ ✕ **El Viejo Gaucho.** Join the crowd for a festive night of live music from North, Central, and South America performed in front of a mural, repainted each season. Try the *Churrasco Argentino* (seasoned steak) and don't forget to top it with *chimichurri* (an Argentine sauce made with fresh herbs and olive oil). Most entrées are pseudo-Argentinian, but pizza, hamburgers, and American-style french fries are also available. ✉ *Iturbe 10,* ☎ *434/342–3627. AE, MC, V. No lunch.*

Lodging

Although Pátzcuaro has no deluxe hotels, there is an ample number of clean, moderately priced properties. Most are on or within a few blocks of the Plaza Vasco de Quiroga. Several more-expensive hotels are on Avenida Lázaro Cárdenas, the road to Lake Pátzcuaro. If you're planning to be in town on or near November 1–2, the Day of the Dead, make hotel reservations at least six months in advance.

$$ ★ **Hotel Posada La Basílica.** This colonial-style inn, housed in a 17th-century building, faces the Basílica de Nuestra Señora de la Salud, and on some mornings strains from a postdawn mass filter softly into the hotel. The property has comfortable, individually decorated rooms, some with fireplaces. Thick wood shutters cover floor-to-ceiling windows, and walls are trimmed in hand-painted colonial designs. The restaurant has views of the mountains, the lake, and tile-roof homes. Open for breakfast and lunch only, it offers such regional specialties as broiled trout with garlic and tamales with sweet cream. Service can be slow. ✉ *Enseñanza Arciga 6, 61600,* ☎ *434/342–1108,* FAX *434/342–0659. 12 rooms. Restaurant, free parking. AE, MC, V.*

$$ **Hotel Posada de Don Vasco.** Located several minutes out of town on the road to Lake Pátzcuaro, this sprawling resort hotel offers a wide range of amenities but often mediocre service. Its 30 newer rooms are thickly carpeted and have balconies or patios; the older quarters, which are oddly decorated with bright checkered bedspreads, are smaller and open onto a courtyard. Request a room on the main property for better service and less traffic noise. The restaurant is decorated like a prosperous country estate; unfortunately, the food is uninspired. At the Saturday buffet dinner, the regional Dance of the Old Men is performed at 8:30 PM. ✉ *Av. Las Americas 450, 61600,* ☎ *434/342–3971 or 434/342–2490,* FAX *434/342–0262. 99 rooms, 4 suites. Restaurant, tennis court, pool, badminton, billiards, bowling. AE, MC, V.*

$$ ★ **Mansión Iturbe.** Housed in a 17th-century mansion, this hotel still retains much of its colonial charm. Plant-filled courtyards are ringed by stone archways. Rooms, with large wood-and-glass doors, are partially carpeted. Bicycles are lent to guests for a few hours per stay, and every fourth night is free. Breakfast at Café Dona Paca is included in the room rate. The owners are an excellent source of information regarding Pátzcuaro and the surrounding areas. ✉ *Portal Morelos 59, 61600,* ☎ *434/342–0368 or 434/342–3628,* FAX *443/313–4593 in Morelia,* WEB *www.mexonline.com/iturbe.htm. 10 rooms, 4 suites. 3 restaurants, bicycles, travel services. AE, MC, V.*

$ **Cabañas Yunuen.** This complex was built on the island of Yunuen in collaboration with the Department of Tourism to promote visits to some of the area's more authentic communities. There are six cabins in all: two each for 2, 4, and 16 people; each has a kitchenette with small refrigerator. Breakfast or dinner and round-trip transportation by boat is included in the price, about $38 for two people. Be sure to call ahead for reservations. ✉ *Domicilio Conocido, Isla de Yunuen,*

☎ 434/342–4473. 6 cabins. Dining room, kitchenettes, billiards, Ping-Pong. No credit cards.

$ **Los Escudos.** Today a cozy hotel, this property was originally a 16th-century home. Its courtyards bloom with potted plants, and guest rooms contain small murals. Ten rooms situated in back and shielded from street noise open onto an outdoor patio; five rooms have fireplaces. The adjoining restaurant has a varied menu, including a tempting *pollo especial Los Escudos* (chicken sautéed in tomato sauce and vegetables). *✉ Portal Hidalgo 73, 61600, ☎ 434/342–0138 or 434/342–1290, FAX 434/342–0649. 31 rooms, 2 suites. Restaurant, free parking. MC, V.*

Nightlife and the Arts

The **Danza de los Viejitos** (Dance of the Old Men), a widely known regional dance, is performed during Saturday dinner at Hotel Posada de Don Vasco for approximately $12 (includes dinner). The dance is also performed Saturday night at 9 PM at Los Escudos, on Plaza de Quiroga.

Shopping

Pátzcuaro has some of Mexico's finest folk-art shopping. **Artesanias El Naranjo** (✉ Plaza Vasco de Quiroga 29-2), an intimate group of stores, offers a variety of ceramics, clothing, and folk art. **Bordados Santa Cruz** (✉ Calle Dr. Coss 3, ☎ 433/338–1425) is a women's embroidery collective. For fresh-ground local coffee appealingly packaged in burlap bags, visit **El Café Urapan** (✉ Benito Mendoza 3, ☎ 434/342–5061). Since 1898, the family-run **Chocolate Casero Joaquinita** (✉ Enseñanza 38, ☎ 434/342–4514) has been concocting delectable homemade cinnamon-spiced hot-chocolate tablets. Don't miss the stands in front of the basilica and at the daily mercado west of Plaza Chica for an array of inexpensive local crafts. **Mantas Tipicas** (✉ Calle Dr. Coss 5, ☎ 434/342–1324) sells hand-loomed tablecloths and more. Visit the doorway of Jesús García Zavala at **Plateria García** (✉ Enseñanza Arciga 28, ☎ 434/342–2036) for hand-worked silver Purépecha jewelry in the pre-Columbian tradition. **Santa Teresa Velas y Cirios** (✉ Portugal 1, ☎ 434/342–0918) sells handsome handmade candles.

Side Trips from Pátzcuaro

Tzintzuntzan

17 km (10½ mi) northeast of Pátzcuaro.

When the Spanish came to colonize the region in the 16th century, some 40,000 Purépechas lived and worshiped in this lakeshore village, which they called "place of the hummingbirds." The ruins of the pyramid-shape temples, or *yacatas,* found in the ancient capital of the Purépecha kingdom, still stand today and are open to the public for $2. There are also vestiges of a 16th-century Franciscan monastery where Spanish friars attempted to convert the Indians to Christianity. Although Tzintzuntzan lost some prominence when Bishop Vasco de Quiroga moved the seat of his diocese to Pátzcuaro in 1540, the village is still well known for the straw and ceramic crafts made by the Purépecha Indians and sold in numerous shops along the main street of town. The bus marked QUIROGA takes a half hour to get from Pátzcuaro's Central Camionera to Tzintzuntzan.

Santa Clara del Cobre

20 km (12½ mi) south of Pátzcuaro.

Since before the conquest, Santa Clara del Cobre has been a center for copper arts. Now the local copper mines are empty, but the artisans still make gorgeous vessels, plates, napkin rings, and jewelry using the traditional method of pounding out each piece of metal by hand. For an introduction to quality and range of styles available, visit the **Museo del Cobre** (✉ Calles Morelos and Pino Suárez, near the plaza), open Tuesday–Sunday 10–3 and 5–7. Admission is 50¢. Then explore the 50-some little shops and factories in town. The friendly owners speak English at **Arte y Cobre** (✉ Pino Suárez 53, ☎ no phone). Although the selection isn't as extensive as other shops along the square, the prices are often less expensive. The bus to Santa Clara del Cobre from Pátzcuaro's Central Camionera takes 40 minutes.

Uruapan

64 km (40 mi) west of Pátzcuaro.

The subtropical town of Uruapan is distinctly different from its lakeside neighbor: some 2,000 ft lower than Pátzcuaro, although still at an elevation of 5,300 ft, it's a populous commercial center with a warm climate and lush vegetation. The town's name is derived from the Purépecha word *urupan,* meaning "where the flowers bloom." Uruapan celebrates Palm Sunday with a lively procession through the streets, brass bands, and a spectacular, bargain-filled crafts market in the central plaza—one of the best in all of Mexico.

You can get to Uruapan from Pátzcuaro by car or bus. Route 14 and the toll road are the most direct routes between the two cities. There's also frequent bus service on the Flecha Amarilla and other major lines; travel time is about 70 minutes.

You can see several points of interest within a few hours. The **Mercado de Antojitos,** an immense, sprawling market, begins in back of the Museo Regional de Arte Popular and extends quite a distance north along Calle Constitución. Along the road, Purépecha Indians sell large mounds of produce, fresh fish, beans, homemade cheese, and a variety of cheap manufactured goods. If you travel south along Calle Constitución, you'll come to a courtyard where vendors sell hot food.

The **Museo Regional de Arte Popular,** opposite the north side of Uruapan's Plaza Principal, was a 16th-century hospital before its conversion. It houses a collection of crafts from the state of Michoacán, including an excellent display of lacquerware made in Uruapan. ☎ *452/524–3434.* 🎫 *Free.* ⏲ *Tues.–Sun. 9:30–1:30 and 3:30–6.*

★ **Parque Nacional Eduardo Ruiz** (about six long blocks from the Plaza Principal off Calle Independencia) is a gem of an urban park. Its paved paths meander through verdant tropical acreage past abundant waterfalls, fountains, and springs to the source of the Río Cupatitzio. A trout farm and a popular playground also are here.

Eleven km (7 mi) south along the Río Cupatitzio is the magnificent waterfall at **Tzaráracua.** At this point the river plunges 150 ft off a sheer rock cliff into a riverbed below; a rainbow seems to hang perpetually over the site. Buses marked TZARÁRACUA leave sporadically from the Plaza Principal in Uruapan. You can also take a taxi for about $3, or drive there via Avenida Lázaro Cárdenas.

Farther afield, about 32 km (20 mi) north of Uruapan, lies the dormant **Paricutín volcano.** Its initial burst of lava and ashes wiped out the nearby village of San Juan Parangaricútiro in 1943. Today travelers can visit this buried site by hiring gentle mountain ponies and a Purépecha guide in the town of Angahuan. To reach Angahuan, take the Los Reyes bus from Uruapan's Central Camionera or go by car via the Uruapan-Carapan highway.

DINING

For good home cooking, try **El Rincón del Burrito** (✉ Portal Matamorros 7, ☎ no phone). In the national park at the mouth of the Río Cupatitziothe is the restaurant at **Mansión de Cupatitzio** (✉ Parque Nacional s/n, ☎ 452/523–2070 or 452/523–2100).

Pátzcuaro A to Z

To research prices, get advice from other travelers, and book travel arrangements, visit www.fodors.com.

BUS TRAVEL

Buses run daily between the Terminal Poniente (West Terminal, commonly referred to as the Observatorio) in Mexico City and Pátzcuaro's Central Camionera on El Libramiento, on the southwestern outskirts of town. Several lines offer frequent service; the most direct trip, which takes five hours, is on either Herradura de Plata, Pegasso Plus, or ETN. Transportation coming from most heartland cities goes to Morelia; buses leave about every 15 minutes from there on the 45-minute trip to Pátzcuaro.

➤ BUS INFORMATION: **ETN** (☎ 434/342–1060, 443/313–7440 in Morelia). **Herradura de Plata and Pegasso Plus** (☎ 434/342–1045).

CAR TRAVEL

The Mexico City–Guadalajara tollway cuts driving time to Pátzcuaro to 4½ or 5 hours, and the trip on to Guadalajara to four hours by car. From Morelia, the excellent free road to Pátzcuaro takes just over an hour. You'll have to rent a car in Mexico City or Morelia, as there are no rental outlets in Pátzcuaro.

EMERGENCIES

Pharmacies are plentiful; Farmacia Gems is popular with residents. Pátzcuaro offers medical services through Hospital Civil.

➤ CONTACTS: **Farmacia Gems** (✉ Benito Mendoza 21, ☎ 434/342–0332). **Hospital Civil** (✉ Romero 10, ☎ 434/342–0285). **Police** (☎ 434/342–0004). **Traffic Police** (☎ 434/342–0565).

MONEY MATTERS

Bancomer–BBVA has a 24-hour ATM. Banamex has an ATM for use during business hours.

➤ EXCHANGE SERVICES: **Banamex** (✉ Portal Juárez 32, ☎ 434/342–1550 or 434/342–1031). **Bancomer–BBVA** (✉ Benito Mendoza 23, ☎ 434/342–0901).

INTERNET

Informatica Integral de Pátzcuaro, open daily 9–9, charges $1.50 an hour for Internet access.

➤ INTERNET CAFÉS: **Informatica Integral de Pátzcuaro** (✉ Plaza Vasco de Quiroga 64, ☎ no phone).

TOURS

Marilyn Mayo designs custom tours based on your interests. She can take you to exuberant fiestas in tiny villages, to the home studios of master artisans, to the butterfly sanctuary, or any other place you want to go.

Guide Francisco Castilleja is highly knowledgeable about pre-Hispanic philosophy, history, archaeology, and medicinal herbs. He speaks fluent English, German, French, and Spanish.

➤ TOUR OPERATOR RECOMMENDATIONS: **Francisco Castilleja** (✉ Centro Eronga, Profr. Urueta 105, ☎ 434/344–0167). **Marilyn Mayo** (✉ Apdo. 416, 61600, ☎ 434/342–2301, FAX 434/342–2756).

TRANSPORTATION AROUND PÁTZCUARO

Many of Pátzcuaro's principal sights are near the Plaza Vasco de Quiroga and Plaza Bocanegra in the center of town. Taxis and buses to the lake can also be found at the latter square. If you want to visit surrounding villages, taxi drivers will drive you for a reasonable rate. Be sure to agree on a fee before setting out.

VISITOR INFORMATION

Delegación de Turismo is the official tourism office, and although you may not find anyone here who speaks English, they will do their best to provide information regarding excursions outside Pátzcuaro. It's open Monday–Saturday 9–2 and 4–7, Sunday 9–2.

Dirección de Orientación y Fomento al Turismo offers maps and can answer basic questions about tourist facilities in Pátzcuaro. It's open daily 9–3 and 5–7.

➤ TOURIST INFORMATION: **Delegación de Turismo** (✉ Plaza Vasco de Quiroga 50A, ☎ FAX 434/342–1214). **Dirección de Orientación y Fomento al Turismo** (✉ Portal Hidalgo 1, on Plaza de Quiroga, ☎ 434/342–0215 or 434/342–0216, FAX 434/342–0967).

9 PACIFIC COAST RESORTS

Hollywood introduced us to two of the Mexican Riviera's most popular towns: Ava Gardner and Richard Burton's sleepy, steamy Puerto Vallarta in *The Night of the Iguana* and the sparkling Manzanillo coast that served as the backdrop to Bo Derek—and Dudley Moore's antics—in *10*. These days both places are prime stops, as is Mazatlán, a bustling port that attracts sportfishing enthusiasts, surfers, and snowbirds. Ixtapa/Zihuatanejo has two-for-one appeal as one of Mexico's most charming fishing villages adjoining a pristine resort.

Updated by Rob Aikins

ACROSS THE GULF OF CALIFORNIA from the Baja California Peninsula lies Mazatlán, Mexico's largest Pacific port and the major Mexican resort closest to the United States, some 1,200 km (745 mi) south of the Arizona border. This is the beginning of "the Gold Coast," what cruise-ship operators now call the Mexican Riviera: with ports-of-call at Mazatlán, Puerto Vallarta, Manzanillo, and Ixtapa/Zihuatanejo. The coastline for the next 1,400 km (870 mi) is Mexico's tropical paradise. The Gulf of California, or the Sea of Cortez, as it is also called, ends just below the Tropic of Cancer, leaving the Pacific coastline open to fresh sea breezes. The farther south you travel, the warmer both air and water temperatures become.

Although Mexico's Pacific Coast cultures were in some ways as fascinating as that of the better known Aztecs, they left behind no major monuments, and so have been largely ignored by archaeological research teams. Not the place to see ruins, museums, and cathedrals, it's a gathering spot for sun worshipers, sportfishing enthusiasts, surfers, and swimmers. Not far from the resort regions are jungle streams and ocean coves, but the majority of visitors prefer only to immerse themselves in the simultaneously bustling and restful resort lifestyle, where great dining, shopping, and sunbathing are the major draws.

Thanks to its excellent port and the fertility of the surrounding countryside, **Mazatlán** is a busy commercial center. More than 600,000 acres of farmland near Mazatlán produce tomatoes, melons, cantaloupes, wheat, and cotton. Many of these products—along with tens of thousands of tons of shrimp, tuna, and sardines hauled in annually—are processed and frozen for the American and Japanese markets.

Proximity to the United States and excellent sportfishing account for Mazatlán's popularity as a resort. The port sits at the juncture of the Pacific and the Sea of Cortez, forming what has been called the world's greatest natural fish trap. Hunters are drawn to the quail, duck, and dove that thrive in the hillsides, and surfers find great waves on nearby beaches. Another draw is that accommodations are about half the cost of those in Cancún or Los Cabos. Additionally, downtown Mazatlán has several charming plazas and some beautifully restored buildings.

Some 323 km (200 mi) south of Mazatlán, **Puerto Vallarta** is the best-known resort on the upper Pacific Coast. Late film director and sometime resident John Huston put the town on the map when he filmed Tennessee Williams's *The Night of the Iguana* on the outskirts of the village in 1963. Elizabeth Taylor accompanied Richard Burton during the filming, and the gossip about their romance (both were married at the time, but not to each other) brought this quaint Mexican fishing village to the public's attention. Before long, travel agents were deluged with queries about Puerto Vallarta.

Today the fabled cobblestone streets can become clogged with bumper-to-bumper traffic, but Puerto Vallarta is still picturesque. For a sense of the Eden that once was, travel south of town to where the Río Tomatlán tumbles over boulders into the sea, or north to Punta de Mita on the northern tip of Bahía de Banderas (Bay of Flags).

Conquistador Hernán Cortés envisioned **Manzanillo** as a gateway to the Orient: from these shores, Spanish galleons would bring in the riches of Cathay to be trekked across the continent to Veracruz, where they would fill vessels headed for Spain. But Acapulco, not Manzanillo, became the port of call for the Manila galleons that arrived each year with riches from beyond the seas. Pirates are said to have staked out

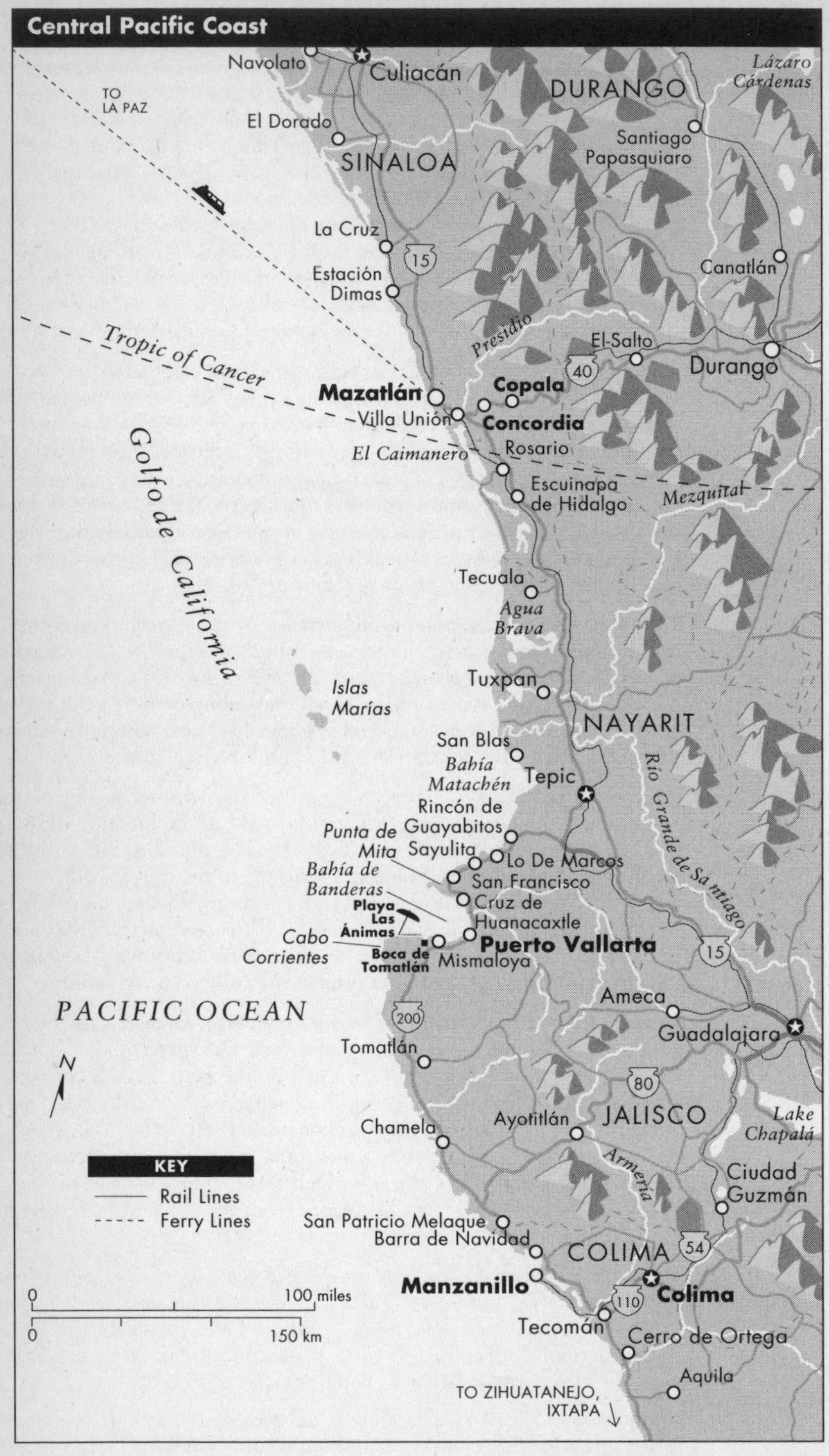
Central Pacific Coast
Navolato
Culiacán
Lázaro Cárdenas
DURANGO
TO LA PAZ
El Dorado
Santiago Papasquiaro
SINALOA
La Cruz
15
Estación Dimas
Canatlán
Presidio
Tropic of Cancer
El-Salto
40
Durango
Mazatlán
Copala
Villa Unión
Concordia
El Caimanero
Rosario
Escuinapa de Hidalgo
Mezquital
Golfo de California
Tecuala
Agua Brava
Islas Marías
Tuxpan
NAYARIT
San Blas
Bahía Matachén
Tepic
Río Grande de Santiago
Rincón de Guayabitos
Punta de Mita
Sayulita
Lo De Marcos
Bahía de Banderas
San Francisco
Playa Las Ánimas
Cruz de Huanacaxtle
Cabo Corrientes
Boca de Tomatlán
Puerto Vallarta
Mismaloya
15
PACIFIC OCEAN
Ameca
200
Guadalajara
Tomatlán
80
N
Ayotitlán
JALISCO
Lake Chapalá
Chamela
Armería
KEY
Rail Lines
Ferry Lines
Ciudad Guzmán
San Patricio Melaque
Barra de Navidad
COLIMA
54
Manzanillo
Colima
0
100 miles
110
Tecomán
0
150 km
Cerro de Ortega
Aquila
TO ZIHUATANEJO, IXTAPA

Manzanillo during the colonial era, and chests of loot are rumored to be buried beneath the sands.

With the coming of the railroads, Manzanillo became a major port of entry. It is now Mexico's second-busiest port, and the lights of freighters at anchor can be seen along the southern beaches. Fifty years ago, a few seaside hotels opened up on the outskirts of town, which vacationers reached by train. The jet age, however, seemed to doom the port as a sunny vacation spot. Then Bolivian tin magnate Antenor Patiño built **Las Hadas** (The Fairies), a lavish Moorish-style resort inaugurated in 1974. It attracted the beautiful people, and for a while Las Hadas was better known than Manzanillo itself.

The Mexican government has steadily worked to develop for tourism the pristine coast between Manzanillo and Puerto Vallarta. A four-lane toll road now cuts the driving time between Manzanillo and Guadalajara, Mexico's second-largest city, to three hours. Older hotels have been spruced up, and all-inclusive resorts constructed. About an hour north of Manzanillo, at the Jalisco state line across from Barra de Navidad, the **Grand Bay hotel** is but one example of the newer luxury resorts. The complex spreads over some 1,200 acres on a peninsula between the Pacific Ocean and the Navidad Lagoon, 20 minutes west of the Manzanillo airport.

Of the Gold Coast resorts, **Ixtapa/Zihuatanejo,** some 500 km (300 mi) south of Manzanillo, is the destination whose popularity is growing the fastest. Like Cancún, Ixtapa was the brainchild of the Mexican government in the early 1970s. With an offshore island and many beautiful beaches, this resort comprises two distinct destinations only 7 km (4½ mi) from each other. Ixtapa is the glitzier of the two, with international chain hotels lining its hotel zone, but it's far smaller and more low-key than resorts such as Puerto Vallarta and Cancún. Its development put neighbor Zihuatanejo, a sleepy fishing village virtually unknown even among Mexicans, on the tourist map. In Zihuatanejo, La Casa Que Canta is one of the finest small hotels in the world.

Pleasures and Pastimes

Beaches

Mexico's Pacific Coast doubtless has some of North America's most inviting beaches, with deliciously warm waters and spectacular sunsets. There are beaches for every taste: long stretches of creamy sand, crescents of soft gold-and-black volcanic grains, secluded coves, and pristine shores accessible only by boat.

Dining

Up and down the coast, the emphasis is on delicious seafood. Visitors savor traditional *pescado sarandeado* (whole fish marinated and grilled over hot coals) as well as elaborate dishes devised by imported European chefs. Shrimp, octopus, oysters, and fresh fish are the highlights; be sure to have a seafood cocktail along the beach. Mazatlán has a number of casual, lively restaurants serving surf-and-turf and traditional Mexican favorites, and prices are reasonable. Puerto Vallarta has the widest array of restaurants, some with spectacular views, others hidden in the small, romantic patios of former homes, and still others as popular for people-watching as they are for their great seafood. Several Manzanillo dining spots have scenic views of the jungle and water that compensate for their lack of culinary excitement. In Ixtapa/Zihuatanejo, restaurants range from open-air *palapas* on the beach to deluxe establishments with international chefs.

Some hotel restaurants add 15% IVA (value-added tax) as well as a service charge to your tab. Many more humble establishments charge neither, so check your bill and tip accordingly.

CATEGORY	COST*
$$$$	over $30
$$$	$20–$30
$$	$15–$20
$	under $15

**per person for a main course at dinner*

Fishing

Mazatlán is tops in the Mexican Pacific for billfishing. Sailfish run from March through December, blue and black marlin from May through December, and swordfish and striped marlin from December through April. Other sportfish include rooster fish, wahoo, yellowfin tuna, bonito, mahimahi, and shark. Light-tackle fishing in the lagoons and just off the beach in *pangas* (small boats) for *huachinango* (red snapper) is also popular. Bass anglers will be pleased with the freshwater lakes in the foothills of the Sierra Madre.

Sportfishing is good off Puerto Vallarta most of the year, particularly for billfish, rooster fish, mahimahi, yellowtail, and bonito. Manzanillo claims to be the sailfish capital of the world; the season runs from mid-October through March. Blue marlin and dorado are also abundant. Ixtapa/Zihuatanejo is one of Mexico's most popular sportfishing destinations. Anglers revel in the profusion of sailfish (November through March), black and blue marlin (May through January), yellowfin tuna (November through June), and mahimahi (November through January). In November, Mazatlán, Puerto Vallarta, and Manzanillo host international fishing tournaments. Competitors often employ the increasingly popular catch-and-release methods.

Horseback Riding

In most Pacific Coast resorts, horseback riding along the shore is popular, and horses can be rented by the hour at major beaches. Most resorts have at least one stable offering half-day or even overnight rides to colonial villages in the Sierra Madre.

Lodging

Although not known for its upscale resorts, Mazatlán has its share of comfortable beachfront hotels, and one of the highest concentrations of trailer parks in the country. In Puerto Vallarta, accommodations range from tiny inns to luxury waterfront hotels and spectacular resorts on secluded coves. Big beachfront properties are the norm in Ixtapa; Zihuatanejo has budget hotels and several of the most exclusive small hotels in Mexico.

Most hotels raise their rates for the high season (December 15 through Easter week); rates are lowest in May, June, September, and October. Though less common than in the Caribbean, hurricanes may crop up between late September and early November. Despite the rain and humidity, rates rise somewhat during July and August when Mexican families take advantage of the warm waters and swarm the beaches for their summer vacations. Price categories are based on high-season rates; expect to pay at least 25% less during the off-season.

CATEGORY	COST*
$$$$	over $250
$$$	$100–$250
$$	$60–$100
$	under $60

**All prices are for a standard double room, excluding 17% tax.*

Shopping

You can spend as much time shopping in Puerto Vallarta as you can lazing in the sun. Shops selling excellent crafts from around the country vie with upscale art galleries and clothing and jewelry boutiques for buyers' attention, especially in the downtown area. Mazatlán and Ixtapa/Zihuatanejo also have some colorful markets and folk art shops. Look for masks from Jalisco and Guerrero states, and beaded masks, bowls, and statuettes made by the Huichol Indians.

Water Sports

Parasailing, swimming, windsurfing, sailing, kayaking, and waterskiing are popular at Pacific Coast resorts. Manzanillo, Mazatlán, and San Blas have some of the finest surfing in Mexico, and the best diving spots in this area are found around the islands off Puerto Vallarta, Ixtapa, and Mazatlán. Puerto Vallarta hosts Mexico's annual boat show each November, as well as various sailing regattas in winter.

Exploring the Pacific Coast Resorts

Resorts on this coastal stretch are at their best in winter, with temperatures in the 70s and 80s (a bit higher in Ixtapa/Zihuatanejo). The off-season brings humidity, mosquitoes, and higher temperatures (northernmost Mazatlán remains coolest), but also emptier beaches, warmer water (well into the 70s), and less-crowded streets—plus 25%–35% lower room rates and cheaper rental-car costs. Toward the end of the rainy season, which involves mostly brief daily showers, the countryside and the mountainous backdrop of the Sierra Madre Occidental and Sierra Madre del Sur turn a brilliant green.

MAZATLÁN

Mazatlán is the Aztec word for "place of the deer," and long ago its islands and shores sheltered far more deer than humans. Today it is a city of almost 700,000 residents and draws about 1 million tourists a year. Sunning, surfing, fishing, and sailing are the primary attractions, and in the winter months visitors from inland Mexico, the United States, and Canada flock to Mazatlán for a break in the sun. Hotel and restaurant prices are substantially lower than elsewhere on the coast. Although the ambience downtown is that of a dignified port city, the Zona Dorada—lined with hotels, shops, and tourist-oriented restaurants—certainly has the feel of a tourist town.

Hunting and fishing were the original draw for visitors. At one time, duck, quail, pheasant, and other wildfowl fed in the lagoons, and mountain lions, rabbits, and coyotes roamed the surrounding hills. Today the more popular sport—at least among visitors—is deep-sea fishing. Mazatlán has one of Mexico's largest sportfishing fleets, and anglers haul in some of the coast's biggest catches, both in size and number. Approximately 12,000 billfish are caught and released each year, including some of gargantuan proportions.

The Spanish settled in the Mazatlán region in 1531 and used the indigenous people as a labor force to create the port and village. In the ensuing centuries, the center of Mazatlán gradually moved north. The original site is now the village of Villa Unión, 24 km (15 mi) southeast of the harbor.

In the early 1600s, the colonial government built a small fort and watchtowers atop the hills in the city to discourage attacks on the rich Spanish galleons by English and French pirates. The buccaneers were gone by 1800, but legends of buried treasure along the coast still circulate.

Acuario Mazatlán . . . 2
Cerro del Vigía 7
Mazatlán Catedral 4
Museo Arquelógico de Mazatlan. 6
Museo de Arte de Mazatlán. 5
Plaza República 3
Zona Dorada 1

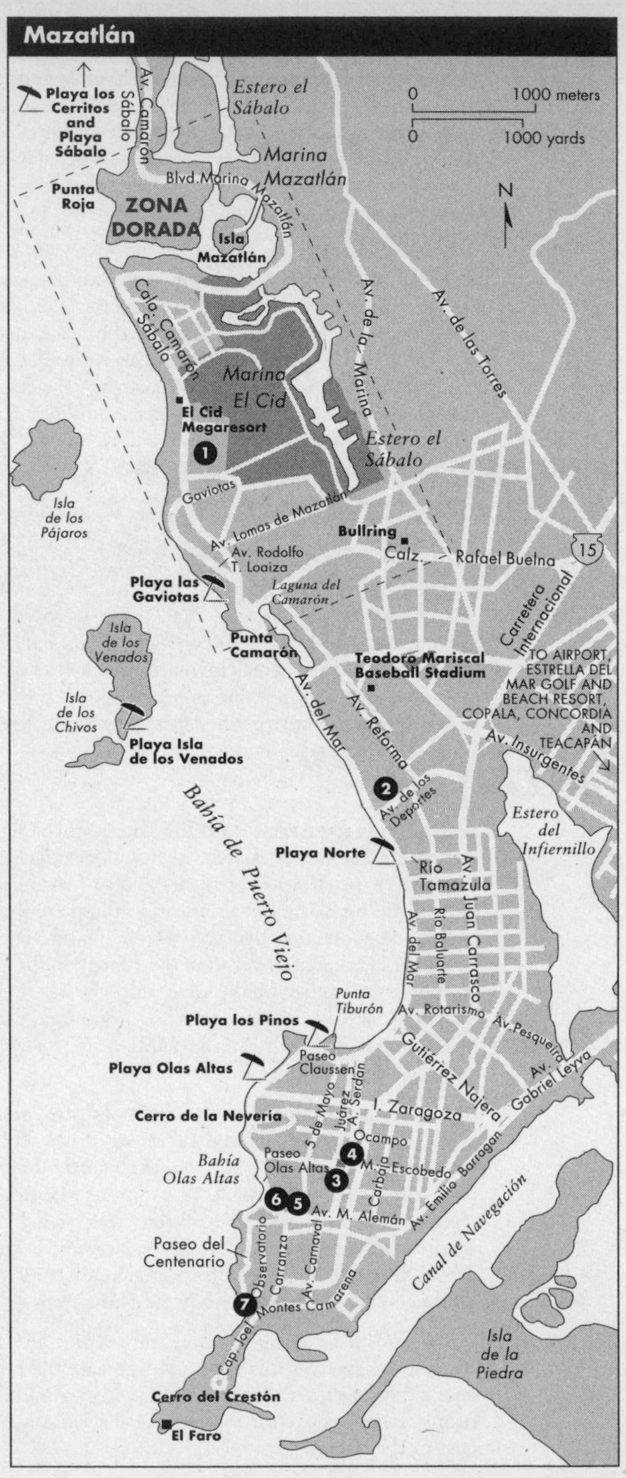

The port has a history of blockades. In 1847, during the Mexican-American War, U.S. forces marched down from the border through northeast Mexico and closed it. In 1864, the French bombarded the city and then controlled it for several years. The British occupied the port for a short period in 1871. Mexico's own internal warring factions took over from time to time. And after the Civil War in the United States, a group of Southerners tried to turn Mazatlán into a slave city.

Exploring Mazatlán

Downtown Mazatlán is a fun place to walk and explore, though many visitors never leave the Zona Dorada (Golden Zone), a broad avenue lined with hotels, shops, and party-down restaurants.

Numbers in the text correspond to numbers in the margin and on the Mazatlán map.

A Good Tour

Start from the **Zona Dorada** ①, Mazatlán's tourist area, at Punta Camarón (Shrimp Point). Stretching north along Avenida Camarón Sábalo is the stuff resorts are made of: bars and restaurants, shell and souvenir shops, and beachfront hotels. This route affords a good view of Mazatlán's three Pacific islands—Isla de los Pájaros, Isla de los Venados, and Isla de los Chivos. Just past the Playa Real resort, Avenida Camarón Sábalo becomes Avenida Sábalo Cerritos and crosses over the Estero del Sábalo lagoon. The area north of here is being developed as "Nuevo Mazatlán," an exclusive resort area.

South of the Zona Dorada, the main road changes names frequently. Mazatlán's main highway begins at Punta Camarón and is here called Avenida del Mar. About halfway between Punta Camerón and downtown and a few blocks inland is the city's highly recommended aquarium, **Acuario Mazatlán** ②, on Avenida de los Deportes. Avenida del Mar continues past beaches popular with residents and travelers staying at the budget hotels across the street. You're sure to notice the avenue's main landmark, the Monumento al Pescador: an enormous statue of a voluptuous, nude woman reclining on an anchor, her hand extended toward a nude fisherman dragging his nets.

After the monument, Avenida del Mar becomes Paseo Claussen. Calles Juárez and Cinco de Mayo lead from the coast-hugging road to Mazatlán's busy downtown. The heart of the city is **Plaza República** ③, also called *el zócalo* (main square) or Plaza Revolución. On the north side of the square you'll see the twin-spired **Mazatlán Catedral** ④; on facing streets are the City Hall, banks, and post office. About three blocks south of the zócalo, the Teatro Angela Peralta, built in 1860 and since beautifully restored, is now an official historic monument. Stop for a drink or a bite at any one of the establishments around the nearby Plazuela Machado, known for its lively neighborhood fiestas. Head three blocks west to the Casa de la Cultura, which houses the **Museo de Arte de Mazatlán** ⑤. Just a few doors away is another restored building housing the **Museo Arqueológico de Mazatlán** ⑥.

Back along the waterfront, Paseo Claussen and the malecón continue past El Fuerte Carranza, an old Spanish fort built to defend the city against the French. Next you'll come to Playa Olas Altas, where at High-Divers Park, young men plunge into the sea, Acapulco-style, from a small white platform. It's spectacular at night, when the divers leap carrying flaming torches. Continuing south you'll see La Mazatleca, a bronze nymph, and across the street, a small bronze deer, the symbol of Mazatlán. Just down the road is the Monument to the Continuity of Life, a large fountain with a handsome couple on top of a large conch shell and a school of porpoises leaping from the water. Looming above the Olas Altas area is **Cerro del Vigía** ⑦ (Lookout Hill).

Sights to See

❷ **Acuario Mazatlán.** A perfect child-pleaser, Mazatlán's aquarium features tanks of sharks, sea horses, and multicolor salt- and freshwater fish. Kids will also enjoy the skating macaw and penny-pinching parrot at bird shows held four times daily, as well as the sea-lion show and diving exhibition. There are botanical gardens, a large playground, an aviary, gift shop, and snack bars. ✉ *Av. de los Deportes 111, Telleria,* ☎ *669/981–7815.* *$4.50.* ⏲ *Daily 9:30–6:30.*

❼ **Cerro del Vigía** (Lookout Hill). The view from this windy hill above Olas Altas is fantastic: you can see both sides of Mazatlán, the harbor, and the Pacific. The steep road up is better suited for a private car or taxi than for walking. At the top of the hill you'll see a rusty cannon and the **Centenario Pérgola,** built in 1848 to celebrate the end of the U.S. invasion.

❹ **Mazatlán Catedral.** The bright yellow spires of the downtown cathedral are a city landmark. Begun in 1855, the church was not completed until the end of the century, and embraces a variety of architectural styles. Made a basilica in 1935, it has a gilded and ornate triple altar, with murals of angels overhead and many small altars along the sides. ✉ *Calles Juárez and 21 de Marzo, Centro.*

❻ **Museo Arqueológico de Mazatlán.** The town's archaeological museum houses a small but interesting collection of artifacts from the region. Among these are exquisite black and red pottery left behind by the Totorames, an indigenous tribe that inhabited the area up until 200 years before the Spanish arrived. ✉ *Sixto Osuna 76, off Paseo Olas Altas, Centro,* ☎ *669/981–1455.* *Free.* ⏲ *Daily 10–2.*

NEED A BREAK? The sidewalk tables at **Copa de Leche** and **Fonda Santa Clara** (✉ Paseo Olas Altas, near Sixto Osuna, Centro) are perfect for watching sunsets.

❺ **Museo de Arte de Mazatlán.** This small museum shows the work of local, regional, and national artists, including Gerardo Santamarino, José Luis Cuevas, and Armando Nava. Daily painting classes are offered. ✉ *Sixto Osuna and Venustiano Carranza, Centro,* ☎ *669/985–3502.* *90¢.* ⏲ *Tues.–Sun. 10–2 and 4–7.*

❸ **Plaza República.** At the center of downtown, this city square hosts one of the most fascinating gazebos in Mexico—what looks like a '50s diner inside the lower level and a wrought-iron bandstand on top. The multicolor tiles on floors and walls, ancient jukebox, and soda fountain couldn't make a more surprising sight. Tourists and locals surround the bandstand Sunday afternoon to hear local musicians play. ✉ *Bounded by 21 de Marzo to the north, Flores to the south, Benito Juárez to the east, and Nelson to the west, Centro.*

❶ **Zona Dorada.** Marking the beginning of Mazatlán's tourist zone is **Punta Camarón,** the rocky outcropping on which the disco Valentino sits, resembling a Moorish palace perched above the sea. To the north, Avenida Rodolfo T. Loaiza splits off from Avenida Camarón Sábalo, running closer to the beach before rejoining Camarón Sábalo. In this four-block pocket are many hotels, shops, and restaurants. This is the place to souvenir-shop, hit the discos, and check out the hotel bars.

NEED A BREAK? **No Name Café** (✉ Av. Rodolfo T. Loaiza 417, Zona Dorada, ☎ 669/913–2031), in the Mazatlán Arts and Crafts Center, is a good spot for barbecued ribs and beer. At the **Panadería Panamá** (✉ Av. Camarón

Sábalo across from Las Palmas hotel, Zona Dorada, ☏ 669/913–6977), you can sit at a table and enjoy fragrant cinnamon-flavored coffee with fresh-baked pastries.

Around Mazatlán

CONCORDIA

48 km (30 mi) east of Mazatlán.

A pleasant yet relatively unexceptional small town, Concordia is known for its furniture makers, its 18th-century church, and its unglazed clay pottery. Lined with organ cactus and mango trees, the drive is especially pretty after the summer rains cover nearby hills and distant mountains in green.

COPALA

25 km (15 mi) east of Concordia.

Huddled at the foot of the Sierra Madre Occidental, Copala's single cobblestone street winds through town to the tiny town square and 18th-century church, which perches above a gorge. As you amble about this small but picturesque former mining town, you'll pass old homes with colorful facades enlivened with flowering vines and trees and embellished with ironwork balconies and window coverings. Refresh yourself at one of the town's simple yet charming restaurants before heading back down the hill.

TEACAPÁN

25 km (15 mi) south of Mazatlán.

A serene drive into cattle and coconut country is a great way to see the countryside outside Mazatlán. Tour companies such as Marlin Tours visit en route the 17th-century mining town of El Rosario, including the Spanish cemetery and lovely old church and a visit to nearby thermal springs, before visiting the Haas hacienda in Teacapán, with many exotic plants.

Beaches

Playa los Cerritos. A long stretch of sand running for several miles from the Marina Mazatlán to Punta Cerritos, Playa los Cerritos is still relatively unpopulated, although the construction of condos along its length may change that. A steep drop-off and undertow make it less than ideal for swimming. Around Punta Cerritos are thatch-roof eateries frequented by locals and surfers.

Playa Isla de la Piedra. Sixteen kilometers (10 miles) of unspoiled beaches allow enough room for all visitors to spread out and claim their own space. This is the place to rent a horse for a good long ride on the beach. On Sunday, the beach looks like a small village, with lots of music and fun. Many of the small palapas set up along the north end of the beach serve a tasty smoked marlin and other seafood treats.

Playa Isla de los Venados. Boats make frequent departures from the Zona Dorada hotels for this beach on Deer Island. It's only a 10-minute ride, but the difference in ambience is striking. The beach is pretty, uncluttered, and clean, and you can hike around the southern point of the island to small, secluded coves covered with shells. El Cid hotel employs a 1964 army surplus amphibious vehicle, affectionately known as *el tiburón* (the shark), to take you to the island and back.

Playa Norte. This strand begins at Punta Camarón (the Fiestaland complex is a landmark) along Avenida del Mar and runs to the Fisherman's Monument. The dark brown sand is dirty and rocky at some points, but clean at others, and is popular with those staying at hotels across the avenue. Palapas selling cold drinks (including whole chilled coconuts), tacos, and fresh fish line the beach. Fishermen land their skiffs on the south end of this beach, sometimes referred to as Los Pinos (the pines).

Playa Olas Altas. This beach, whose name means "high waves," was the first tourist beach in Mazatlán, running south along the malecón from the Fisherman's Monument. Surfers congregate here during the summer months, when the waves are at their highest.

Playa Sábalo and Playa las Gaviotas. Mazatlán's two most popular beaches parallel la Zona Dorada. Both are crowded with vendors selling pottery, lace tablecloths, and silver jewelry and renting boats, windsurfers, and other toys. The beach is protected from heavy surf by the three islands—Venados, Pájaros, and Chivos. When you tire of sand and sun, repair to one of the many beachfront hotel restaurants willing to accommodate skimpily clad and somewhat sandy customers.

Dining

$$$ ★ ✕ **Angelo's.** With its fresh flowers, cream-and-beige decor, gentle piano music, and soft candlelight, this is by far the most elegant restaurant in Mazatlán. The Italian and Continental cuisine is outstanding—try the veal scallopini with mushrooms or shrimp marinara on pasta—and the service is impeccable. ✉ *Pueblo Bonito, Av. Camarón Sábalo 2121, Zona Dorada,* ☎ *669/914–3700. AE, MC, V. No lunch.*

$$ ✕ **Sr. Peppers.** Elegant yet unpretentious, with ceiling fans, lush foliage, and candlelit tables, Sr. Peppers serves choice, mesquite-grilled steaks and lobsters. This is the place locals go for a fancy night out, and to enjoy the dance floor and live music. ✉ *Av. Camarón Sábalo across from Playa Real, Zona Dorada,* ☎ *669/914–0101. AE, MC, V. No lunch.*

$ ✕ **La Casa Country.** This festive restaurant across from the Holiday Inn serves a variety of steaks and Mexican dishes to a country-loving crowd. Steaks are grilled over charcoal or firewood—the *arrachera* (skirt steak) served with kettle beans and guacamole is a good bet, as is the rib eye with baked potato. Margaritas and piña coladas are served by the pitcher; at night, country-music fans are brought to their feet for dancin' and carousin' until 2 AM. ✉ *Av. Camarón Sábalo s/n, Zona Dorada,* ☎ *669/916–5300. AE, MC, V.*

$ ★ ✕ **La Concha.** One of the prettiest waterside dining spots, La Concha is a large enclosed palapa with three levels of seating, including a spacious dance floor adorned with twinkling lights and tables by the sand. Adventurous types might attempt the stingray with black butter or calamari in its ink, and the more conservative can try a thick filet mignon. During the winter season there's live music in the evenings. La Concha is also open for breakfast as well as lunch and dinner. ✉ *El Cid Megaresort, Av. Camarón Sábalo s/n, Zona Dorada,* ☎ *669/913–3333. AE, MC, V.*

$ ✕ **Karnes en Su Jugo.** A small family-run café on the malecón, with a few outdoor tables and a large indoor restaurant, this establishment specializes in *karnes en su jugo* (literally, "beef in its juice"), a Mexican stew with chopped beef, onions, beans, and bacon. It's a satisfying meal, especially when eaten with a basket of homemade tortillas. ✉ *Av. del Mar 550, Zona Costera,* ☎ *669/982–1322. No credit cards.*

$ ✕ **El Paraíso Tres Islas.** With a good view of the three islands, this wonderful palapa on the beach is a favorite with families. Entire Sunday afternoons can be spent feasting on fresh fish; try the smoked marlin, oysters diablo, octopus, or the seafood platter. ✉ *Av. Rodolfo T. Loaiza 404, Zona Dorada,* ☎ *669/914–2812. MC, V.*

$ ★ ✕ **Pedro & Lola.** Authentic Mexican seafood is served in this 19th-century building in the heart of the historic center, decorated with contemporary art. Try the *papillot,* the day's fresh catch cooked in foil with white wine, shrimp, and mushrooms. Named after Mexican *ranchera* singers Pedro Infante and Lola Beltrán, the restaurant hosts excellent live music in the evening. Reservations recommended Thursday through Saturday. ✉ *Carnaval 1303, next to Plazuela Machado, Centro,* ☎ *669/982–2589. AE, MC, V. No lunch.*

$ ✕ **Restaurante Pancho's.** Upstairs or down, inside or out, seafood is the specialty at this bustling, casual, and friendly seaside restaurant. Choose from enormous seafood platters to share, seafood soup, ceviche, or many other dishes. You can also order fresh salads, hearty tortilla soup, and filet mignon smothered in mushrooms and served with rice, steamed veggies, baked potato, and thick Texas-style toast. Portions are generous, and the food is so good that you'll most likely clean your plate. ✉ *Rodolfo T. Loaiza 408, Centro Comercial Las Cabanas, Local 11-B, Zona Dorada,* ☎ *669/914–0911. MC, V.*

$ ✕ **El Shrimp Bucket.** In Old Mazatlán, facing the water, this was the original Carlos 'n' Charlie's. The garden patio restaurant (part of the inexpensive Hotel Siesta) is much quieter than its predecessors—some would call it respectable. This is the in spot for Mazatlán businessmen and social mavens at breakfast (from 6 AM). For lunch or dinner, best bets are fried shrimp served in clay buckets and barbecued ribs. Portions are large, and there's live music at night. ✉ *Paseo Olas Altas 11–126 Sur, Zona Costera,* ☎ *669/981–6350. AE, MC, V.*

Lodging

Most of Mazatlán's hotels are in the Zona Dorada, along the beaches. Less expensive places are in Old Mazatlán, the original tourist zone along the malecón on the south side of downtown.

$$$$ ★ **El Cid Megaresort.** Mazatlán's largest resort, El Cid has four different properties, three of which are grouped together in the Zona Dorada. The fourth, the upscale Marina El Cid Hotel and Yacht Club, is at the north end of town and has 210 suites and a 100-slip marina; a free shuttle connects the properties. Suites in the El Moro tower overlooking the ocean are nicer (but more expensive) than rooms in the older Castilla tower. All guests can enjoy such perks as a full-service spa and fitness center, golf school and 27-hole course, deep-sea fishing fleet, and aquatic sports center. Its size is a drawback for those looking to get away from it all. ✉ *Av. Camarón Sábalo s/n, Zona Dorada 82110,* ☎ *669/913–3333 or 800/525–1925,* FAX *669/914–1311* WEB *www.elcid.com. 1,320 rooms, suites, and studios. 8 restaurants, room service, cable TV, 27-hole golf course, 11 tennis courts, 8 pools, gym, spa, beach, marina, mountain bikes, 5 bars, dance club, shops, children's programs (ages 4–12), laundry service, Internet, business services, meeting rooms, car rental, travel services, free parking, no-smoking rooms. AE, DC, MC, V.*

$$$–$$$$ ★ **Pueblo Bonito.** One of the comeliest properties in Mazatlán, this all-suites hotel and time-share resort has an enormous lobby with chandeliers and beveled-glass doors; terra-cotta-color rooms have domed ceilings. Pink flamingos stroll manicured lawns, golden koi swim in small ponds, and bronzed sunbathers repose on padded white lounge chairs by the crystal-blue pool. Angelo's is a dining must—as elegant as Mazatlán gets. ✉ *Av. Camarón Sábalo 2121, Zona Dorada 82110,* ☎ *669/914–3700 or 800/990–8250,* FAX *669/914–1723,* WEB *www.pueblobonito.com. 250 suites. 3 restaurants, room service, in-room safes, kitchenettes, cable TV, 2 pools, gym, massage, sauna, beach, bar, chil-*

dren's programs (ages 6–12), laundry service, concierge, Internet, car rental, travel services, free parking. AE, MC, V.

$$$ **Fiesta Inn.** One of Mazatlán's newer hotels, the Fiesta Inn is operated by the Mexican hotel chain Posadas, and attracts primarily business travelers. The nine-story tower is on a nice stretch of beach in the Zona Dorada. Guest rooms are rather plain, with tile floors, light-wood furniture, and tiny balconies. Public areas are pleasant, however, and the gym is roomy and well equipped. ✉ *Av. Camarón Sábalo 1927, Zona Dorada 82110,* ☎ *669/989–0100, 800/504–5000, or 800/343–7821,* FAX *669/989–0130. 117 rooms. 2 restaurants, in-room safes, minibars, cable TV, pool, gym, beach, bar, business services, meeting rooms, car rental, travel services, no-smoking rooms. AE, MC, V.*

$$$ **Holiday Inn Sunspree Resort.** A consistently good hotel, the Holiday Inn attracts tour and convention groups that fill the rooms and create a party mood by the pool and on the beach. The Kid's Spree program provides activities for children while adults can attend tennis clinics and borrow snorkel equipment or boogie boards. Rooms are done in whites and pastels, with large sliding doors that open to views of the islands. ✉ *Av. Camarón Sábalo 696, Zona Dorada 82110,* ☎ *669/913–2222 or 800/465–4329,* FAX *669/914–1287. 160 rooms, 23 suites. 3 restaurants, refrigerators, cable TV, pool, gym, beach, volleyball, 2 bars, children's programs (ages 6–15), business services, meeting rooms, no-smoking rooms. AE, MC, V.*

$$$ ★ **Pueblo Bonito Emerald Bay.** The first major resort property in Nuevo Mazatlán, it offers a seclusion and exclusivity lacking in the bustling, crowded Zona Dorada. This all-suites property is designed with freestanding villas nestled among a stand of old-growth mangrove trees, with neoclassical design features reminiscent of a luxurious European palace. The grounds feature lakes, fishponds, and tropical gardens maintained by biologists and inhabited by tropical birds. Additionally, the private beach is a natural sea turtle nesting site, which, in season, proves an added attraction. ✉ *Av. Ernesto Coppel Campaña 201, Nuevo Mazatlán 82110,* ☎ *669/989–0525 or 800/937–9567,* FAX *669/914–1723,* WEB *www.pueblobonito.com. 258 suites. Restaurant, room service, in-room safes, kitchenettes, cable TV, pool, gym, hair salon, massage, sauna, beach, 2 bars, children's programs (ages 6–12), laundry service, concierge, Internet, airport shuttle, car rental, travel services, free parking. AE, MC, V.*

$$$ ★ **Royal Villas Resort.** Panoramic elevators transport you from the cool marble atrium lobby of this pyramid-shape, 12-story structure to the upper floors. More ample and functional than elegant, one- and two-bedroom suites have ocean views, remote-control TVs, direct-dial phones, balconies, and kitchenettes. Access to the inviting pool is by a bridge that crosses over a fish-filled pond. ✉ *Av. Camarón Sábalo 500, Zona Dorada 82110,* ☎ *669/916–6161 or 800/898–3564,* FAX *669/914–0777,* WEB *www.royalvillas.com.mx. 125 suites. 2 restaurants, room service, kitchenettes, cable TV, pool, gym, hot tub, beach, bar, laundry service, business services, meeting rooms, travel services, free parking, no-smoking rooms. AE, MC, V.*

$$–$$$ **Los Sábalos.** Smack in the center of the Zona Dorada, this white high-rise perches on a long clean beach. Rooms are boldly decorated in bright blue and stark white, and have such perks as satellite TV, coffeemakers, and hair dryers. You'll be in the thick of the action here, and it's the home of Joe's Oyster Bar, one of the most popular dance venues in town. ✉ *Av. Rodolfo T. Loaiza 100, Zona Dorada 82110,* ☎ *669/983–5333 or 800/528–8760; 877/756–7532 in the U.S.,* FAX *669/983–8156,* WEB *www.lossabalos.com. 85 rooms, 100 suites. 3 restaurants, room service, in-room safes, cable TV, 2 tennis courts, pool, gym,*

spa, beach, volleyball, 2 bars, dance club, shops, baby-sitting, concierge, convention center. AE, MC, V.

$$ 🏨 **Azteca Inn.** At the low end of this price category, this property across the street from the Playa Mazatlán hotel is a great find for budget travelers who like to be in the center of things. The brown-and-white exterior color scheme gives way for the rooms' bright reds and yellows. Rooms in the three-story low-rise—all with satellite TV and direct-dial phones—surround the courtyard pool and hot tub. The staff couldn't be friendlier. ✉ *Av. Rodolfo T. Loaiza 307, Zona Dorada 82110,* ☎ *669/913–4477,* FAX *669/913–7476,* WEB *www.aztecainn.com.mx. 74 rooms. Cafeteria, pool, hot tub, bar. AE, MC, V.*

$$ ★ 🏨 **Casa Contenta.** A small surprise on the beach near the north end of Av. Rodolfo T. Loaiza, this property has seven one-bedroom apartments in a colonial-style building. The large beachfront house boasts three bedrooms, three baths, living and dining room, and even servants' quarters; it accommodates eight people. All units have equipped kitchens and TVs, but no phones. The bargain prices bring many repeat clients, so book this one well in advance. ✉ *Av. Rodolfo T. Loaiza 224, Zona Dorada 82110,* ☎ *669/913–4976,* FAX *669/913–9986. 8 units. Kitchenettes, cable TV, pool, parking; no room phones. MC, V.*

$$ 🏨 **Hotel Plaza Marina.** Near the Fisherman's Monument downtown, all suites at this hotel have ocean views as well as kitchenettes, bedrooms with king-size beds, and bathtubs. Rooms face the pool and are done in pastels. Don't be frightened by the lifelike, 4-ft-tall wooden cobra in the lobby. ✉ *Av. del Mar 73, Zona Costera 82110,* ☎ *669/982–3622 or 800/711–9465,* FAX *669/982–3499. 56 rooms, 43 suites. Restaurant, kitchenettes, pool, gym, bar, travel services. AE, MC, V.*

$$ ★ 🏨 **Playa Mazatlán.** Palapas are set up on the patios by the rooms in this casual low-rise hotel on Gaviotas Beach, popular with Mexican families and laid-back singles more concerned with comfort than style. The bright, sunny rooms have comfy beds with tile headboards, tile tables by the windows, and terraces or balconies. At night candles flicker in the breeze at the open-air restaurant right on the beach. Mazatlán's first resort is known for its thrice-weekly Mexican Fiesta. ✉ *Av. Rodolfo T. Loaiza 202, Zona Dorada 82110,* ☎ *669/913–7989 or 800/762–5816,* FAX *669/914–0366,* WEB *www.playamazatlan.com.mx. 413 rooms. Restaurant, snack bar, room service, cable TV, 3 pools, gym, hair salon, hot tub, beach, bar, shops, dry cleaning, laundry service, concierge, convention center, meeting rooms, car rental, travel services. AE, MC, V.*

$$ 🏨 **El Quijote Inn.** A great bargain on the beach in the midst of the hotel zone, this five-story inn is a tranquil alternative to some of the more frenzied facilities. A range of accommodations includes mainly one- and two-bedroom suites with full kitchens. All units have tile floors, rattan furnishings, cable TV, and patios or balconies. The outdoor bar and restaurant overlook both the beach and the nicely landscaped pool area with large hot tub. ✉ *Avs. Camarón Sábalo and Tiburón, Zona Dorada 82110,* ☎ *669/914–1134,* FAX *669/914–3344. 18 rooms, 52 suites. Restaurant, some kitchens, pool, hot tub, beach, bar, shop, meeting room, car rental. AE, MC, V.*

$ 🏨 **Hotel Siesta.** At well below $50 per double, you can't beat the price of this comfortable budget hotel. The beach across the street is rocky, but the hotel's location in the Olas Altas is great for those who want to explore the "real" Mazatlán, downtown. Rooms are plainly furnished, but do have cable TV and air-conditioning. Interior-facing rooms overlook the courtyard and the Shrimp Bucket restaurant, where live music is played nightly in high season until 11. ✉ *Paseo Olas Altas 11 Sur, Zona Costera 82110,* ☎ *669/981–2640,* FAX *669/982–2633,* WEB *www.lasiesta.com.mx. 57 rooms. Restaurant, car rental, travel services. AE, MC, V.*

$ **Plaza Gaviotas.** You don't get a whole lot of perks here, but the location across from Gaviotas Beach, for which it is named, is good, and the salmon-color rooms in this clean, colonial-style budget hotel have small balconies, although without chairs or table. ✉ *Av. Rodolfo T. Loaiza 100 and Bugambilias, Zona Dorada 82110,* ☎ *669/913–4322,* FAX *669/913–6685. 67 rooms. Restaurant, pool, bar. MC, V.*

Nightlife

Marking the southern edge of the Golden Zone, Valentino, Bora Bora, Pepe's & Joe, and Sheik are all part of the complex known as **Fiesta Land** (✉ Av. Camarón Sábalo at Calzada Rafael Buelna, Zona Dorada, ☎ 669/984–1006 or 669/984–1666). Valentino, with its stark white towers rising above Punta Camarón, has two dance clubs—one geared toward a younger crowd, the other with more tranquil, romantic music—as well as a karaoke salon. Bora Bora is a palapa restaurant and bar renowned for its raucous disco music and table-dancing; like Valentino, it opens after 9 PM. Pepe's & Joe is a microbrewery with American-style burgers and dogs. Extravagant Sheik restaurant delights diners with waterfalls, ocean views, Moorish-inspired stained-glass windows, marble floors, and a central domed skylight—a nice place for viewing the beaches south of Zona Dorada.

In the historic center near the Angela Peralta theater, **Café Pacífico** (✉ Constitución 501, Centro, ☎ 669/981–3972) sometimes hosts jazz, bohemian guitarists, or other musicians Thursday through Saturday. **El Caracol Disco Club** (✉ Av. Camarón Sábalo s/n, Zona Dorada, ☎ 669/913–3333), at El Cid Megaresort, has a high-tech disco, billiards, board and arcade games, and different theme nights throughout the week. A hefty $20 cover includes all drinks and games. **Joe's Oyster Bar** (✉ Los Sábalos hotel, Av. Rodolfo T. Loaiza 100, Zona Dorada, ☎ 669/983–5333) is a popular beachfront spot where the dancing starts at noon and lasts until 2 AM.

The **Mexican Fiesta** held Tuesday, Thursday, and Saturday 7–10:30 at the Playa Mazatlán is a good entertainment bet. The $25 fee includes a Mexican buffet dinner, open bar, entertainment, and live music for dancing. A favorite with young revelers bent on belting down tequila shooters and generally whooping it up is **Señor Frog's** (✉ Av. del Mar s/n, Zona Costera, ☎ 669/982–1925). This member of the Carlos Anderson chain is a restaurant as well, serving good barbecued ribs and chicken with corn on the cob. Bandidos carry tequila bottles and shot glasses in their *bandoliers,* Revolution-era ammunition belts.

Outdoor Activities and Sports

Participant Sports

ECOTOURS

Mazatleco Sport Center (✉ Av. Rodolfo T. Loaiza s/n, next to Hotel Flores, Zona Dorada, ☎ 669/916–5933) leads Hobie Cat sailing tours and kayaking tours to Isla de los Venados, where paddlers can then hike or snorkel (4 hours, $37). They also lead kayaking trips (best in winter) to bird-watch among the mangroves south of town ($45, includes lunch). If you prefer to go solo, Mazatleco rents kayaks, snorkel gear, and ice chests. **Pronatura** (✉ Av. Camarón Sábalo s/n, Centro Comercial de El Cid, Local 2627, Zona Dorada, ☎ 669/916–7720), in the El Cid complex, offers a variety of tours, including daily adventure tours via trimaran to Isla de los Venados ($37, includes lunch and open bar) for snorkeling and kayaking, and five-hour tours to El Verde ($32) to learn about marine tortoise protection programs. **Robert Hudson** (☎ 669/913–1764, WEB www.hudsontours.com), an American who has lived in Mazatlán for many years, offers spearfishing, snorkeling, kayaking, and other tours tailored to fit your needs.

FISHING

There are nine sportfishing fleets that operate from the docks south of the lighthouse and one in Marina Vallarta. Hotels can arrange charters, or you can contact the companies directly. Charters include a full day of fishing, bait, and tackle. Prices range from $80 to $100 per person on a party boat, or from $200 to $380 to charter a boat for 1 to 5 passengers. The very reputable **Aries Fleet** (☎ 669/916–3468) is connected with the El Cid Megaresort and operates from Marina Vallarta. **Bill Heimpel's Star Fleet** (☎ 669/982–2665), which boasts fast twin engine boats that meet U.S. Coast Guard standards, is also well regarded.

GOLF

The spectacular 27-hole course at **El Cid Megaresort** (☎ 669/913–3333), with 9 holes designed by Lee Trevino, is reserved for members of the resort, hotel guests, and their guests. At the **Estrella del Mar Golf and Beach Resort** (☎ 669/982–3300), south of Mazatlán proper on Isla de la Piedra (Stone Island), you'll find a championship 18-hole Robert Trent Jones golf course open to the public.

HORSEBACK RIDING

You can rent horses on **Isla de la Piedra** for about $5 per hour, guide included, unless you ask to go it alone.

TENNIS

Many of the hotels have courts, some of which are open to the public, and there are a few public courts not connected to the hotels. Call in advance for reservations at **El Cid Megaresort** (☎ 669/913–3333), which has nine courts. Three courts are available at **Costa de Oro** (✉ Av. Camarón Sábalo s/n, ☎ 669/913–5344). The **Racquet Club Las Gaviotas** (✉ Av. Ibis s/n, at corner of Av. Rio Bravo, ☎ 669/913–5939) has seven courts.

WATER SPORTS

Jet Skis, Hobie Cats (a two-person catamaran), and windsurfers are available for rent at most beachfront hotels, and parasailing is popular along the Zona Dorada. Scuba diving and snorkeling are catching on, but there are no really great diving spots; the best are around Isla de los Venados. For rentals and trips, contact one of the many operators. **Centro Acuático El Cid** (✉ Av. Camarón Sábalo s/n, Zona Dorada, ☎ 669/913–3333 Ext. 3341) has parasailing and rents Wave Runners, kayaks, boogie boards, sailboats, and banana boats. They also arrange four-hour boat trips to Isla de los Venados aboard *el Colonage,* docked at Hotel Marina el Cid.

Parque Acuático Mazagua (✉ Av. Sábalo Cerritos and Entronque Habal Cerritos, Nuevo Mazatlán, ☎ 669/988–0041 or 669/988–0152) has water slides, wading pools, and a pool with man-made waves—a total of 20 water activities on 4 acres. Entrance is about $9 per person.

Spectator Sports

BASEBALL

The people of Mazatlán loyally support their team, **Los Venados** (☎ 669/981–1710), a Pacific League Triple A team. Regular season games are played at the Teodoro Mariscal Baseball Stadium (✉ Blvd. Justo Sierra, Zona Estadio) October through December.

BULLFIGHTS AND CHARREADAS

Bullfights are held most Sunday afternoons at 3:30 from January through April at the bullring on Calzada Rafael Buelna. *Charreadas* (rodeos) take place year-round. Tickets (about $10–$20) are available at the **Monumental Plaza de Toros** (☎ 669/984–1666), through most hotels and travel agencies, and from Valentino nightclub.

Shopping

Zona Dorada

Mazatlán may not be a shopper's mecca, but like most Mexican resort towns, it has a range of souvenirs and folk art from around the country. Some of the best shops are located in the Zona Dorada, particularly along Avenidas Camarón Sábalo and Rodolfo T. Loaiza, where you can buy everything from piñatas to silver jewelry.

CRAFTS

A good place for browsing is the **Mazatlán Arts and Crafts Center** (✉ Av. Rodolfo T. Loaiza 417, Zona Dorada, ☎ 669/913–2120), originally designed as a place to view artisans at work. The center, open 9–6, has a good sampling of the city's souvenir selection—onyx chess sets, straw sombreros, leather jackets, sandals, coconut masks, and Mickey Mouse piñatas.

One of the most unique shops in town is **Casa Maya** (✉ Av. Rodolfo T. Loaiza 411, Zona Dorada, ☎ 669/916–7220), which is housed in a building designed to look like a Mayan pyramid. They sell onyx, talavera pottery, leather goods, and jewelry from all over Mexico.

Possibly Mazatlán's most beautiful shop is **Gallery Michael** (✉ Camarón Sábalo 19, Zona Dorada, ☎ 669/916–7816), with several rooms of tastefully chosen folk art, religious icons, and jewelry.

If floor-to-ceiling shells that have been glued, strung, and molded into every imaginable form—from necklaces to kitschy statuettes—interest you, you'll love **Sea Shell City** (✉ Av. Rodolfo T. Loaiza 407, Zona Dorada, ☎ 669/913–1301), a rather tacky seashell emporium.

JEWELRY

Madonna (✉ Av. Las Garzas 1, at Calle Laguna, Zona Dorada, ☎ 669/914–2389) displays an extensive collection of silver and gold jewelry as well as masks and handicrafts.

Rubio Jewelers (✉ Costa de Oro hotel, Av. Camarón Sábalo s/n, Zona Dorada, ☎ 669/914–3167) carries fine gold, silver, and platinum jewelry as well as ceramics. It's also Mazatlán's exclusive distributor of Sergio Bustamante's whimsical sculptures of ceramics and bronze.

Downtown

The gigantic **Mercado Central,** between Calles Juárez, Ocampo, Serdán, and Leandro Valle, is open daily and filled with produce, pungent meat and fish, and a sprinkling of handicrafts. Although the latter are more along the lines of souvenirs than fine folk art, it's fun to search the market for great buys.

Nidart gallery and workshop (✉ Libertad 45 and Carnaval, Centro, ☎ 669/981–0002) shows and sells handcrafted leather masks, ceramic figurines and sculptures, contemporary black-and-white photos, and other Mexican arts and crafts in a beautiful setting. Artisans can be seen producing these wares in open workshops. The gallery and workshop are open Monday–Saturday 10–2.

Mazatlán A to Z

AIR TRAVEL

You can fly to Mazatlán from major U.S. cities, including Houston, Los Angeles, and Denver, or from Mexico City or other cities in Mexico.

CARRIERS

Aeroméxico has daily flights from multiple U.S. and Mexican cities. Alaska Airlines flies direct daily from Los Angeles. Continental flies daily, direct from Houston. AeroCalifornia has direct flights twice weekly from Los Angeles, and daily from La Paz, Guadalajara, and Mexico City. Mexicana flies in daily from Mexico City, twice weekly direct from Denver, and daily from Los Angeles with a stop in Los Cabos. America West links Mazatlán with Phoenix.

➤ AIRLINES AND CONTACTS: **AeroCalifornia** (☏ 669/913–2042). **Aeroméxico** (☏ 669/913–0772). **Alaska Airlines** (☏ 669/985–2730). **America West** (☏ 669/981–1184). **Continental** (☏ 800/525–1700). **Mexicana** (☏ 669/982–7722).

AIRPORTS AND TRANSFERS

Mazatlán's Rafael Buelna International Airport is served by several airlines. The airport is a good 40-minute drive from town.

➤ AIRPORT INFORMATION: **Rafael Buelna International Airport** (☏ 669/985–2272).

AIRPORT TRANSFERS

Autotransportes Aeropuerto charges about $19 for a private car and $5 per person on its Volkswagen van shuttles into town. Private taxis charge approximately $19.

➤ TAXIS AND SHUTTLES: **Autotransportes Aeropuerto** (☏ 669/981–5554).

BOAT AND FERRY TRAVEL

Ferry service between La Paz and Mazatlán is fairly reliable. The car-and-passenger ferry takes about 17 hours to reach La Paz. One-way fares start at $51 for regular passage and $300 per car. Check the schedule and purchase tickets in advance, as the schedule is subject to change.

Royal Caribbean, Holland America, and Princess, among other cruise lines, include Mazatlán on their seven-day Mexican Riviera cruises.

➤ BOAT AND FERRY INFORMATION: **Ferry service** (✉ Prong. Carnaval s/n, Fracc. Playa Sur, ☏ 669/981–7020 or 800/696–9600).

BUS TRAVEL

The Mazatlán bus terminal is at Carretera Internacional 1203, three blocks behind the Sands Hotel. Elite, one of the area's best bus lines, has service to the U.S. border and south to Guadalajara, Mexico City, and the southern coast. Estrellas del Pacífico serves western Mexico.

Buses and minibuses run frequently along all main avenues. Fares start at about 50¢ and increase slightly, depending on the destination.

➤ BUS INFORMATION: **Elite** (☏ 669/981–3811). **Estrellas del Pacífico** (☏ 669/984–2817).

CAR RENTAL

The following rental firms have desks at Rafael Buelna International Airport as well as the addresses given here. Hertz rents cars and trucks. Budget has the usual assortment of vehicles. National has cars at the cruise ship terminal (no phone) as well as two Zona Dorada locations. They rent everything from VW Beetles and compacts without air-conditioning to Suburbans and 4x4s.

➤ MAJOR AGENCIES: **Hertz** (✉ Av. Camarón Sábalo 314, Zona Dorada, ☏ 669/913–4955). **Budget** (✉ Av. Camarón Sábalo 402, Zona Dorada, ☏ 669/913–2000). **National** (✉ Av. Camarón Sábalo 7000, Zona Dorada, ☏ 669/913–6000; ✉ El Campanario shopping center, Av. Camarón Sábalo s/n, Zona Dorada, ☏ 669/984–4077).

CAR TRAVEL

Mazatlán is 1,212 km (751 mi) from the border city of Nogales, Arizona, via Mexico Route 15, either on the good but quite expensive toll road or on the federal highway. At least one overnight stop is recommended.

EMBASSIES

Agents of the U.S. Consul can be reached weekdays 8–1 and 1:30–4. The Canadian Consulate is open weekdays 9–1.

➤ CANADA: **Canadian Consulate** (✉ Av. Rodolfo T. Loaiza 202, Zona Dorada, ☎ 669/914–6655).

➤ UNITED STATES: **U.S. Consul** (✉ Av. Rodolfo T. Loaiza 201, Zona Dorada, ☎ 669/916–5889).

EMERGENCIES

Dial **060** for all emergencies. Sharp Hospital, at Calzada Rafael Buelna at Avenida Dr. Jesus Kumate, has English-speaking doctors.

➤ CONTACTS: **Toll-free medical or travel advice** (☎ 800/903–9200). **Sharp Hospital** (☎ 669/986–5676; 669/986–7911 for emergencies).

ENGLISH-LANGUAGE MEDIA

The best place for English-language paperbacks, dictionaries, and maps is Mazatlán Book and Coffee Company, across from the Costa de Oro Hotel behind Banco Santander Mexicano. The store is open daily 9–7 and has copies of Mazatlán's English newspaper, *Pacific Pearl*.

➤ BOOKSTORE: **Mazatlán Book and Coffee Company** (☎ 669/916–7899).

MAIL, INTERNET, AND SHIPPING

The main post office is downtown, across from the main plaza. However, if you are in the Zona Dorada, it's easier to go to Mail Boxes Etc., which offers fax and e-mail services in addition to regular postal services.

➤ MAIL SERVICES: **Mail Boxes Etc.** (✉ Av. Camarón Sábalo 310, Zona Dorada, ☎ 669/916–4009). **Post office** (✉ Juárez at 21 de Marzo, Centro, ☎ 669/981–2121).

TAXIS

Most tourist hotels are located in the Zona Dorada, about 3 km (2 mi) north of downtown, but taxis cruise the strip regularly. Fares start at $3. A fun way to get around is on the *pulmonías* (VW Beetles without tops), so you can sunbathe and take pictures as you cruise along, although there are no windows to raise against rain or automobile fumes. The fare, for up to three passengers, starts at about $3 and increases according to the distance of the trip.

TOURS

Two- or three-hour city tours, which generally cost $15–$25, are a good way to get the lay of the land; the historical section downtown is small but interesting.

Bay cruises are available daily (except Monday) aboard *Costalegre* at 11 AM. Tickets are $14 and include round-trip transportation from Zona Dorada hotels and two drinks aboard. Centro Aquatico El Cid offers tours to Isla de los Venados, including lunch and, for those who wish, snorkeling and kayaking (4 hours, $35). Viajes el Sábalo runs a five-hour bay tour ending at Isla de la Piedra, with time for lunch and a swim. Included in the $28 price is a choice of two activities; choose from snorkeling, horseback riding, or banana boats.

Also available are country tours to Concordia and Copala (about $28–$35, including lunch). Marlin Tours runs an eight-hour excursion

($42) ending in Teacápan, near the Nayarit border. The bus tour makes stops in towns, ranches, and sometimes a thermal spring, and includes Continental breakfast and drinks. Lunch at a seaside restaurant and an optional boat ride of the estuary are not included in the price.

➤ TOUR OPERATOR RECOMMENDATIONS: **Centro Acuático El Cid** (☎ 669/913–3333 Ext. 3341). **Costalegre** (☎ 669/916–5747). **Marlin Tours** (✉ Calle Laguna 300, Zona Dorada, ☎ 669/913–5301). **Viajes el Sábalo** (✉ Los Sábalos shopping center, Zona Dorada, ☎ 669/983–1933 or 669/913–1111; ✉ Hotel Los Sábalos, Zona Dorada, ☎ 669/981–3009).

TRAVEL AGENCIES

American Express offers local tours and sells airline tickets. Agencies are generally open weekdays 10–2 and 4–7, Saturday 10–2.

➤ LOCAL AGENT REFERRALS: **American Express** (✉ Av. Camarón Ŝbalo 500, Plaza Balboa, Zona Dorada, ☎ 669/913–0600).

VISITOR INFORMATION

The State Tourism Office is open weekdays 9–5.

➤ TOURIST INFORMATION: **State Tourism Office** (✉ Av. Camarón Sábalo, Banrural Bldg., 4th floor, Zona Dorada, ☎ 669/916–5160 through 669/916–5165).

PUERTO VALLARTA

On the edge of the Sierra Madre range sits one of the most popular vacation spots in Mexico. When Puerto Vallarta first entered the public's consciousness, with John Huston's 1964 movie *The Night of the Iguana,* it seemed an almost mythical paradise. At the time it was a quiet fishing and farming community in an exquisite tropical setting.

Puerto Vallarta's Bahía de Banderas attracted pirates and explorers as early as the 1500s; it was used as a stopover on long trips as a place for the crew to relax (or maybe plunder and pillage). Sir Francis Drake apparently stopped here. In the mid-1850s, Don Guadalupe Sánchez Carrillo developed the bay as a port for the silver mines by the Río Cuale. Then it was known as Puerto de Peñas and had about 1,500 inhabitants. In 1918 it was made a municipality and renamed for Ignacio L. Vallarta, a governor of Jalisco. "Puerto" is Spanish for port.

In the 1950s Puerto Vallarta was essentially a pretty hideaway for those in the know—the wealthy and some hardy escapists. After the publicity brought on by *The Night of the Iguana,* tourism began to boom. PV—as the former fishing village is called these days—is now a city with some 250,000 residents. Airports, hotels, and highways have supplanted palm groves and fishing shacks. About 3 million people visit each year, and from November through April cobblestone streets are clogged with pedestrians and cars. There are now more than 16,000 hotel rooms in Puerto Vallarta, with another 4,000 in Nuevo Vallarta, on the northern edge of the enormous bay, in Nayarit state.

Despite the transformation, every attempt has been made to keep the town's character and image intact. City ordinances require houses in town to be painted white, with restrictions on number of floors and architectural details. Houses with red-tile roofs perch on hills above the glistening blue bay and line the streets downtown, where pack mules still occasionally clop down the cobblestone streets. Within 16 km (10 mi) of town are rocky coves, rushing rivers, and steep mountain roads that curve and twist through jungles of pines and palms.

Exploring Puerto Vallarta

Central Puerto Vallarta has several major components. North of town, hotels and resorts surround Marina Vallarta, a public marina sharing space with restaurants, condos, and stores. Downtown, aka Viejo Vallarta, is the heart of the old city, where many two- and three-story houses have been converted to shops, galleries, and restaurants. Dividing downtown in two is el Río Cuale. This river—which ranges from ebullient to anemic, depending on the rains—embraces a sliver of an island with cultural center, museum, restaurants, and shops. Beginning just south of the river, Playas Olas Altas and Los Muertos are two beaches backed by lively outdoor restaurants and modest hotels.

A cab or rental car is helpful to fully explore the hotel zone—a long stretch of shopping centers, restaurants, and hotels—although buses cruise continually up and down as well. A car is a serious hindrance, however, downtown and in the Río Cuale area. Most of the interesting sights can be covered on foot—just be sure you wear comfortable shoes for the cobblestone streets.

Numbers in the text correspond to numbers in the margin and on the Puerto Vallarta map.

A Good Walk

When you start seeing cobblestone streets, you're in the downtown area, also known as **Old Town,** or Viejo Vallarta. This is the heart of PV, a vestige of old Puerto Vallarta. Start your walk at the northern end of the delightful **malecón** ⑧, which runs parallel to Díaz Ordáz beginning at 31 de Octubre. Nine blocks south, Díaz Ordáz merges with Calle Morelos at the old lighthouse tower. Two blocks farther south is the town's main square, Plaza de Armas. On the northern side of the busy, tree-shaded plaza you'll see the **Palacio Municipal** ⑨ (City Hall), and one block east, **La Iglesia de Nuestra Señora de Guadalupe** ⑩, which is topped by a distinctive crown. Los Arcos Amphitheater, across the street from the plaza on the malecón, is host to a number of concerts. Local artists show their wares here in the evenings.

Head south a few blocks and turn left on A. Rodríguez. After a few blocks you'll come to the bustling **Mercado Municipal** at the foot of the upper bridge over the Río Cuale. The steep hillside above, dotted with vine-drenched villas, is called **Gringo Gulch** ⑪. Reach it by climbing the steps on Calle Zaragoza. In the middle of the Río Cuale lies the **Isla Río Cuale** ⑫ (accessible by bridges for both pedestrians and autos), an inviting place for dining, strolling, and shopping.

Sights to See

11 **Gringo Gulch.** The most famous attraction in this neighborhood, named after the hundreds of U.S. expats who settled here in the 1950s and '60s, is Elizabeth Taylor's former home, **Casa Kimberly.** It's connected to Richard Burton's former home across the street by the pink-and-white "love bridge" he had constructed. Part of the house has been converted into an unattractive bed-and-breakfast, but its other areas can be toured daily 9–6. Burton bought the 24,000-square-ft home for Taylor's 32nd birthday after their much-publicized romance during his filming of *The Night of the Iguana* with Ava Gardner, Deborah Kerr, and Sue Lyon. Taylor owned the house for 26 years, and left the majority of her possessions behind (all on display) when she sold it. ✉ *Calle Zaragoza 445, Centro,* ☎ FAX *322/222–1336.* 🎫 *$6.*

10 **La Iglesia de Nuestra Señora de Guadalupe** (Church of Our Lady of Guadalupe). The town's main church is topped by an ornate crown that replicates the one worn by Carlota, the empress of Mexico in the

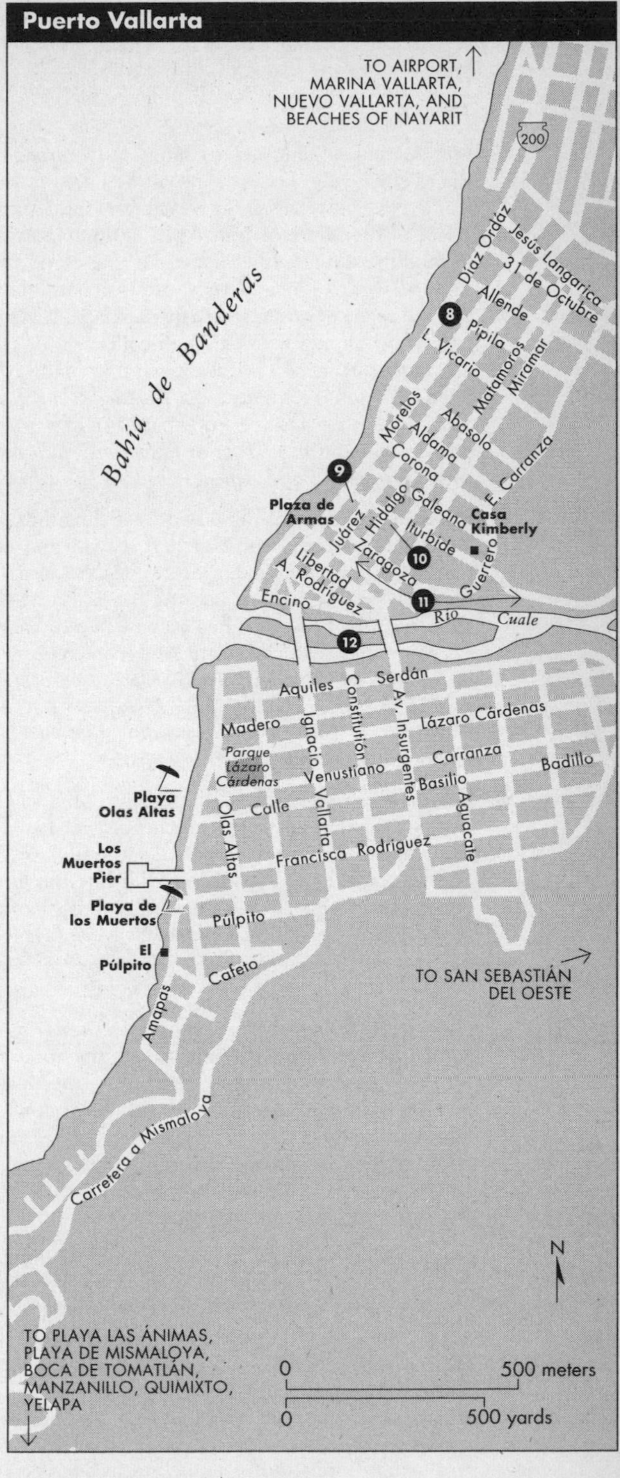
Puerto Vallarta
TO AIRPORT, MARINA VALLARTA, NUEVO VALLARTA, AND BEACHES OF NAYARIT
200
Bahía de Banderas
Díaz Ordáz
Jesús Langarica
31 de Octubre
Allende
Pípila
L. Vicario
Matamoros
Miramar
Morelos
Abasolo
Aldama
Corona
E. Carranza
Plaza de Armas
Juárez
Hidalgo
Galeana
Casa Kimberly
Iturbide
Guerrero
Libertad
Zaragoza
A. Rodríguez
Encino
Río Cuale
Aquiles
Serdán
Constitución
Av. Insurgentes
Madero
Ignacio Vallarta
Lázaro Cárdenas
Parque Lázaro Cárdenas
Venustiano Carranza
Badillo
Basilio
Aguacate
Playa Olas Altas
Calle
Olas Altas
Los Muertos Pier
Francisca Rodriguez
Playa de los Muertos
Púlpito
El Púlpito
Cafeto
Amapas
TO SAN SEBASTIÁN DEL OESTE
Carretera a Mismaloya
N
TO PLAYA LAS ÁNIMAS, PLAYA DE MISMALOYA, BOCA DE TOMATLÁN, MANZANILLO, QUIMIXTO, YELAPA
0
500 meters
0
500 yards

late 1860s. The crown toppled during an earthquake that shook this area of the Pacific Coast, but was quickly replaced with a fiberglass version in time for the celebration of the Feast of the Virgin of Guadalupe (December 12). ✉ *Calle Hidalgo, 1 block east of zócalo, Centro.* ⏲ *7:30 AM–8 PM.*

12 **Isla Río Cuale** (Cuale River Island). Surrounded by the Río Cuale, this island effectively slices the downtown area in two. It has an outdoor marketplace as well as trendy restaurants and inexpensive cafés. A bronze statue of film director John Huston dominates the central plaza. Just beyond the statue at the east end of the island, the **Casa de la Cultura** sells the work of local artists, offers art and dance classes, and hosts cultural events. The **Museo Arqueológico** (✉ western tip of island, Centro, ☎ no phone) hosts a small collection of pre-Columbian figures and Indian artifacts. The museum is open daily 10–6. Admission is free, but a donation is requested. ✉ *To reach Isla Río Cuale from north side of town, cross bridge at Encino and Juárez or at Libertad and Miramar. From the south, cross at Ignacio L. Vallarta and Aquiles Serdán, or at Insurgentes and Aquiles Serdán, Isla Río Cuale.*

8 **Malecón.** The malecón is downtown's main drag, a nice place to rest on a white wrought-iron bench. A seawall and sidewalk run along the bay, and restaurants, cafés, and shops are across the street. You'll see some interesting sculpture along the walkway—among other pieces, the bronze sea horse that has become Puerto Vallarta's trademark, and *La Nostalgia,* a bronze statue of a seated couple, inspired by the love life of author Ramiz Barquet. The latest sculptural addition is **Rotunda del Mar,** a collection of whimsical statues by artist Alejandro Colunga. ✉ *Parallel to Díaz Ordáz, extending about 16 blocks from Río Cuale northeast to 31 de Octubre, Centro.*

9 **Palacio Municipal** (City Hall). The late Manuel Lepe's 1981 mural depicting Puerto Vallarta as a fanciful seaside fishing and farming village hangs above the stairs on city hall's second floor. Puerto Vallarta's most famous artist, Lepe is known for his blissful, primitive-style scenes of the city, filled with smiling angels. The tourism office is on the first floor. ✉ *Av. Juárez by zócalo, Centro.* ⏲ *Weekdays 9–5.*

Beaches

Puerto Vallarta's stellar attraction is its amazing beaches: crescents of golden sand fringed with palms along the hotel zone; endless stretches of gloriously unpopulated beaches to the north; and soft, creamy beaches on craggy coves to the south. Near downtown, Olas Altas and Los Muertos—popular with visitors, families, and vendors—are closest to all that downtown has to offer, including shops, budget hotels, and sidewalk cafés. Beaches below are described in order from the southern part of the bay to the north.

Playa Las Ánimas and beyond. Yelapa, Quimixto, and Playa de Las Ánimas are three secluded fishing villages accessible by boat. Yelapa is approximately an hour southeast of downtown; Quimixto and Las Ánimas are a bit to the north. From the beach at Yelapa, take a 20-minute hike into the jungle to see the waterfalls. Quimixto's beautiful beach boasts calm, clear waters. Horses can be rented for a 15-minute ride to a spectacular large clear pool under a waterfall for swimming. Day excursions visit these beaches daily from the Marina Vallarta cruise-ship terminal; or hire a motor launch from Boca de Tomatlán ($43 round-trip for 1–6 people to Playa Las Ánimas; about $86 to Yelapa). Water taxis ($6.50 round-trip) depart the pier at Los Muertos at 10:30 and 11 AM for Yelapa and return to pick you up at 3 or 4 PM.

Boca de Tomatlán. This small village at the mouth of the Río Tomatlán (Tomatlán River) is about 17 km (10½ mi) south of Puerto Vallarta and 4 km (2½ mi) south of Mismaloya. Just off the coast road down a short but bumpy dirt driveway is a beautiful, generally uncrowded cove. Both locals and visitors enjoy the scene while relaxing at one of several palapa restaurants on the sand. Water taxis leave from Boca to Los Arcos, an offshore rock formation popular with skin and scuba divers, and the more secluded beaches of Playa Las Ánimas and Yelapa. About halfway between Boca and Playa de Mismaloya, Chee Chee's, a massive, terraced restaurant and swimming-pool complex, spreads down a steep hillside like a small village. Next door, similarly terraced Le Kliff restaurant is a great spot for a sunset cocktail. Just south of Boca is Chico's Paradise, and a bit farther on, Las Orquidias. Both are riverfront restaurants where you can swim in clear river pools.

Playa de Mismaloya. This once pristine cove is where "the movie" was made. The 13-km (8-mi) drive south from the center of town on Highway 200 passes spectacular houses, some of PV's oldest and quietest resorts, and a slew of condo and time-share developments. You can take a taxi or one of the bright green Mismaloya buses from Calles Vallarta and Badillo, in downtown PV. Although the jungle-fringed cove was spoiled by the construction of La Jolla de Mismaloya (a huge hotel complex), it still affords a good view of Los Arcos. From Mismaloya you can catch a cab inland 2 km (1 mi) on the dirt road to the jungle restaurant Chico's Paradise.

Playa de los Muertos and Playa Olas Altas. These two contiguous beaches south of the Río Cuale have long been a budget traveler's domain, although they have some of the more expensive restaurants and shops. Proximity to lively sidewalk bars and cafés here has made them the most popular and crowded beaches in Puerto Vallarta. Long ago, Playa de los Muertos was the site of a battle between pirates and Indians, hence the name, which means "Beach of the Dead." The area around the beach is now promoted as the Zona Romántica, but locals still call it Los Muertos. Strolling vendors selling lace tablecloths, kites, and jewelry are almost as abundant as sunbathers. Beach toys for rent include everything from rubber inner tubes to windsurfers. To the south, Playa de los Muertos ends at a rocky point called El Púlpito. Walking up the steps (more than 100) at the east end of Púlpito street leads to a lookout with a great view of the beach and the bay.

La Zona Hotelera. Stretching north from downtown to the marina and cruise-ship terminal area is a string of beaches often collectively called "la zona hotelera," or hotel zone. The beach changes a bit with the character of each hotel it fronts, but it is particularly nice by the Fiesta Americana and the Krystal hotels.

Nuevo Vallarta and Nayarit. When PV swells with tourists, local families head out of town to relax and play on the unpopulated beaches at the north end of Bahía de Banderas, in the state of Nayarit. Twelve kilometers (7 miles) north of Nuevo Vallarta (Puerto Vallarta's newest hotel and marina development, which is actually in Nayarit), on yet another beautiful beach, is the simple town of **Bucerías,** where a loyal flock of snowbirds has encouraged the growth of small hotels and restaurants. Beyond Bucerías there are long stretches of deserted beach around **Cruz de Huanacaxtle** and La Manzanilla, where kids play in the shallow waters while their parents sip beer or soft drinks at beachfront restaurants. **Destiladeras** is a long, semirocky beach with good surf. The coast road continues to the popular beach at **El Anclote,** with simple restaurants. Just beyond El Anclote is **Punta de Mita,** on the northern tip of Bahía de Banderas. Home of the posh Four Seasons Resort,

Punta de Mita has blue bay water that's nice for swimming; around the bend are waves for surfing. This is a prime spot for viewing a sunset and, during the winter months, the whales that come here to mate in the warm waters of the Mexican Pacific. Scuba divers like the fairly clear waters and abundance of tropical fish and coral on the bay side of the Isla Marietas, about a half hour offshore.

From Punta de Mita, a dirt road can be slowly traversed in dry weather to **Sayulita** (which can also be reached in about 45 minutes from Puerto Vallarta by staying on Highway 200 past Bucerías). In addition to hotels and restaurants, Sayulita has excellent surfing and a great beach hidden behind a hill only 10 minutes on foot north of the town center. Some say Sayulita is like Puerto Vallarta 40 years ago. Fifteen minutes north of Sayulita is **San Francisco,** unofficially known as San Pancho, with modest rental bungalows and eateries and a 1½-km-long (1-mi-long), barely developed stretch of beach. A half hour beyond San Francisco, the pretty beach at **Lo de Marco** is popular with surfers.

Dining

Wonderful restaurants are concentrated downtown, especially along the part of Calle Basilio Badillo known as "restaurant row," one block south of Parque Lázaro Cárdenas in the Los Muertos area.

$$$–$$$$ ✕ **Café des Artistes.** A beautiful garden with a breathtaking view of the Pacific, this is Puerto Vallarta's most sophisticated—and expensive—dining spot. Owner/chef Thierry Blouet blends Mexican ingredients with European techniques to produce such interesting combinations as cream of prawn and pumpkin soup, mussels in a scallop mousse, and roast duck with soy and honey. A piano and flute duo provides musical accompaniment. ✉ *Guadalupe Sánchez 740, Centro,* ☎ *322/222–3228. Reservations essential. AE, MC, V. No lunch.*

$$–$$$ ✕ **Felipe's.** Sitting high on a hill, Felipe Palacio's gracious family home has the charm of old Vallarta mixed with spectacular views of the bay and town from its multilevel terraces. Try the grilled seafood, or the superbly prepared steaks served with baked potato and veggies. The strains of live jazz drift down nightly from the restaurant's upper terrace. ✉ *Av. Insurgentes 466, Col. Alta Vista,* ☎ *322/222–3820. AE, MC, V. Closed Sun. No lunch.*

$$–$$$ ✕ **River Cafe.** Candles flicker at romantic tables lining the riverbank, and tiny white lights wrap the palm trees surrounding the restaurant's multilevel terrace. Attentive waiters serve such international dishes as steak, lobster, and pasta to a well-dressed crowd. If you're not into a romantic dinner, stop in for breakfast, or belly up to the intimate bar for a drink. ✉ *Isla Río Cuale, Local 4, Isla Río Cuale,* ☎ *322/223–0788. AE, MC, V.*

$$ ✕ **Archie's Wok.** Although the lumpia can be limp and the salads overdressed, the Asian-fusion cuisine here is a great break from Continental and Mexican food. International music at a discreet level permits conversation, and ceiling fans rustle the lacy limbs of potted ferns and palms. There are plenty of choices for noncarnivores, including stir-fry pastas with green veggies and mushrooms, Chinese sesame cucumber salad, and Vietnamese fish in banana leaves. ✉ *Francisca Rodriguez 130, Los Muertos,* ☎ *322/222–0411. AE, MC, V. Closed Sun.*

$$ ★ ✕ **Chef Roger.** The cozy patio of a typical Puerto Vallarta house is the unpretentious setting for one of the best restaurants in town. Roger Dreier, the Swiss owner and chef, combines his European training with Mexican ingredients, and the results are superb. Don't leave town without trying the pork tips "Zurich style," served in a light mushroom sauce with *rösti* potatoes (a grated-potato pancake), and for dessert, the fried apples with vanilla sauce. ✉ *Calle Basilio Badillo 180–B, Col. E. Zapata,* ☎ *322/222–5900. AE, MC, V. Closed Sun. No lunch.*

$$ ✕ **Daiquiri Dick's.** The beachside patio dining room of this longtime *vallartense* favorite frames one of the best views of the bay at Playa de los Muertos. The Caesar salad explodes with flavor, and the medallions of beef tenderloin demi-glacé and the lobster tacos are superb. Finish off with a hazelnut daiquiri. ✉ *Olas Altas 314, Olas Altas,* ☎ *322/222–0566. MC, V.*

$$ ★ ✕ **Trio.** Two young German chefs, Bernhard Guth and Peter Lodes, have become the favorites of local diners with their avant-garde Mediterranean creations—such as orange-crusted sea bass with a sweet purée of garbanzo, dates, olives, and cider, or the rack of lamb and ravioli with lamb ragout. The artsy crowd and professional staff make for a wonderful dining experience. The kitchen often stays open until midnight, and there's a rooftop terrace on which to dine or have drinks. ✉ *Guerrero 264, Centro,* ☎ *322/222–2196. AE, DC, MC, V.*

$–$$ ✕ **Adobe Café.** Minimalist decor in shades of white and earth tones, stark trees, and fresh flowers make for a delightful dining experience. Specialties include black bean soup, pork tenderloin in rum, and one of the best desserts in town: a sinfully rich chocolate mousse between two layers of chocolate cake and chocolate icing. ✉ *Calle Basilio Badillo 252, Col. E. Zapata,* ☎ *322/222–6720. MC, V. Closed Tues. Closed June–Sept. No lunch.*

$–$$ ✕ **The Blue Shrimp.** This downtown eatery certainly lives up to its name. The ambience, heavy on blue light, makes you feel like you're underwater. The menu consists of shrimp (any style you like). Choose your shrimp by size and weight, and the kitchen then prepares it to order. And if the menu doesn't have your favorite shrimp recipe, you can even bring your own. Lobster and a variety of fish plates are also available. ✉ *Calle Morelos 779, Centro,* ☎ *322/222–4246. MC, V.*

$–$$ ✕ **Café Maximilian.** Efficient and fluid service accompanied by genuine smiles from both diners and staff make this a top spot to eat around Olas Altas. Viennese and other European entrées dominate the menu, including braised baby lamb strips with rosemary and an excellent pork loin escallop with homemade noodles. These items can also be ordered from the delightful, European-style coffeehouse next door, open all day and specializing in desserts and sandwiches. ✉ *Olas Altas 380, Olas Altas,* ☎ *322/223–0760. AE, MC, V. Closed Sun.*

$ ✕ **Andale.** An Olas Altas hangout and a good spot for an afternoon beer with the locals, this restaurant serves giant shrimp, great herb-garlic bread, and delicious black-bean soup as well as nightly drink specials at the chummy bar. Despite the open storefront, the inside is cool, dark, and informal; two rows of tables line the narrow outdoor patio. ✉ *Olas Altas 425, Olas Altas,* ☎ *322/222–1054. MC, V.*

$ ✕ **La Bodeguita del Medio.** Near the north end of the malecón, this attractive restaurant/bar has a view of the sea from the second-floor dining room. Like its Havana namesake (established in 1942), La Bodeguita del Medio sells Cuban rum and cigars, and the music, and the cuisine, naturally, are pure Caribbean. ✉ *Paseo Díaz Ordaz 858, Centro,* ☎ *322/223–1584 or 322/223–1585. No credit cards.*

$ ★ ✕ **Cafe de Olla.** This is the place for cheap, down-to-earth Mexican food—enchiladas, *carne asada* (grilled strips of marinated meat), and *chiles rellenos* (stuffed chili peppers). Service is excellent and the atmosphere inviting: trees extend from the dining-room floor through the roof, local artwork adorns the walls, and salsa music often plays in the background. The restaurant is hugely popular and you may need to wait a short while for a table. ✉ *Calle Basilio Badillo 168-A, Los Muertos,* ☎ *322/223–1626. No credit cards. Closed Tues.*

$ ★ ✕ **Chico's Paradise.** It's easy to while away hours—or even the day—under the huge, multilevel palapa, taking a dip in the river or watching tortillas being made by hand. Seafood, including fresh jumbo shrimp and stuffed crab, is a specialty, but chiles rellenos and chicken burritos are also popular. Or just come for some of the huge tropical drinks. In the off-season, Chico's closes just after sunset. ✉ *Carretera a Manzanillo Km 20, just south of Boca de Tomatlán,* ☎ *322/222–0747. No credit cards.*

$ ★ ✕ **Don Pedro's.** Everything is a treat at this giant beachfront palapa in Sayulita, a half hour north of the airport, where European-trained chef and co-owner Nicholas Parrillo serves an array of fish, seafood, and poultry sprinkled with herbs and grilled over mesquite. From the crusty herbed breads and pizzas to the rich mango ice cream, everything is as fresh as can be. ✉ *Calle Marlin 2, midway along Sayulita town beach, 35 km (22 mi) north of Puerto Vallarta airport, Sayulita,* ☎ *322/275–0229. AE, MC, V. Closed Aug.–Oct.*

Lodging

Most of PV's deluxe resorts are to the north of downtown. Many are concentrated in the Marina Vallarta complex, practically a town unto itself with a 355-slip marina, hundreds of condominiums, shopping centers, an 18-hole golf course, the Royal Pacific Yacht Club, and the cruise-ship pier. Farther north is Nuevo Vallarta, just over the state line in Nayarit, at the mouth of the Río Ameca. This beautiful community with beachfront houses and condos on canals with direct access to the bay is home to several all-inclusive resorts. South of downtown and the Río Cuale, around Olas Altas and Playa de los Muertos, the rates are lower. If you head farther south still, the prices go up again: some spectacular properties are tucked away on hidden coves on the road to Manzanillo.

Rates at most hotels usually go down 25%–30% just after Easter week through December 15, although they may rebound during July and August when nationals take a two-week vacation. Reservations are a must at Christmas, New Year's, Easter, and in July and August.

$$$$ ★ **Four Seasons Resort.** Ensconced at the northern end of Bahía de Banderas, at Punta de Mita (a 40-minute drive northwest of the PV Airport), this hotel has been designed for exclusivity. Rooms, which start at $620, are housed in red-tile-roof Mexican-style casitas of one, two, and three stories. Furnished like luxurious Mexican homes and fitted with traditional Four Seasons amenities, spacious rooms feature private terraces or balconies with sweeping sea views. The Jack Nicklaus–designed 18-hole championship golf course has a challenging, optional 19th island hole. Other sports facilities include tennis courts, a health club, and beach activities. ✉ *Punta de Mita, Bahía de Banderas, Nayarit 63732,* ☎ *322/291–6000 or 800/819–5053,* FAX *322/291–6060,* WEB *www.fourseasons.com. 140 rooms, 27 suites. 3 restaurants, room service, in-room data ports, in-room safes, minibars, cable TV, 18-hole golf course, 4 tennis courts, pool, wading pool, gym, spa, beach, snorkeling, windsurfing, bicycles, horseback riding, 2 bars, baby-sitting, children's programs (ages 5–12), dry cleaning, laundry service, concierge, meeting rooms, car rental. AE, DC, MC, V.*

$$$$ **Hotel Sierra Nuevo Vallarta.** Situated on a long, wide expanse of creamy sand beach in Nuevo Vallarta, the Sierra is a deluxe all-inclusive property. The rooms are light and airy, with tile floors, light-wood and wicker furniture, and the ubiquitous pastel bedspreads. Activities are nonstop: cookouts, beach parties, Mexican fiestas, disco blasts, theme nights, musicals, and karaoke. Daytime activities include aerobics,

volleyball, tennis, minigolf, windsurfing, and kayaking, as well as jungle and city tours. A golf course is minutes away. ✉ *Paseo de los Coteros 19, Nuevo Vallarta 63732,* ☎ *322/297–1300 or 800/448–5028,* FAX *322/297–1162,* WEB *www.sidek.com.mx. 350 rooms and suites. 3 restaurants, in-room safes, minibar, cable TV, 2 tennis courts, 4 pools, aerobics, beach, windsurfing, bicycles, billiards, horseback riding, volleyball, 3 bars, concierge, meeting rooms. AE, MC, V.*

$$$–$$$$ ★ **Camino Real.** One of PV's first hotels, this property sits on a lovely small bay south of town. Rooms have marble floors with white furniture and bright pink, yellow, and purple highlights against stark white walls. The hotel has five-star touches—from plush robes in the rooms to the fragrant white jasmine blooming along the natural waterfall. La Brisa restaurant serves superb seafood lunches; elegant, upscale La Perla has excellent international food and inspired desserts. An 11-story tower houses the Camino Real Club, where guests receive upgraded amenities and breakfast on a terrace overlooking the sea. ✉ *Playa Las Estacas Km 3.5, 48300,* ☎ *322/221–5000 or 800/722–6466,* FAX *322/221–6000,* WEB *www.caminoreal.com. 326 rooms, 11 suites. 4 restaurants, room service, in-room safes, minibars, cable TV, 2 tennis courts, 2 pools, wading pool, health club, beach, 2 bars, baby-sitting, children's programs (ages 5–10), laundry service, concierge, meeting rooms, travel services. AE, DC, MC, V.*

$$$–$$$$ **Meliá Puerto Vallarta.** On the beach in Marina Vallarta, this sprawling, top-of-the-line all-inclusive resort is close to the marina's 18-hole golf course. The lobby is an odd blend of cool marble and tile floors, industrial-strength rust-and-marine-blue paint with lilac accents, and wicker furniture. The large rooms are more pleasingly decorated in soft natural tones of blue, cream, and sand; all have balconies with chairs. Amenities include a large pool, the Mini Club (for kids), an outdoor theater, and nightly shows. Two children under age seven can stay free (including meals and activities) if they share a room with their parents. ✉ *Paseo de la Marina Sur 7, Marina Vallarta 48354,* ☎ *322/221–0200 or 800/336–3542,* FAX *322/221–0118,* WEB *www.solmelia.es. 380 rooms, 3 suites. 3 restaurants, in-room safes, cable TV, 2 tennis courts, pool, gym, beach, archery, 3 bars, shops, children's programs (ages 4–12), laundry service, concierge, meeting room. AE, DC, MC, V.*

$$$ ★ **Buenaventura.** An excellent value, this hotel has an ideal location on the northern edge of downtown, about 10 blocks from the *malecón* and, in the opposite direction, the shops, hotels, and restaurants on the airport highway. The bright, cheerful rooms have beam ceilings and pale-wood furnishings. Many rooms have views of both arms of the bay, and some have equipped kitchenettes. The seven-story luxury tower has six different styles of suites, many with Jacuzzis. An all-inclusive plan, adding $100 more per person per night, includes food, drinks, room tax, and tip. ✉ *Av. México 1301, Centro 48350,* ☎ *322/222–3737 or 888/859–9439,* FAX *322/222–6242,* WEB *www.buenaventurahoteles.com. 199 rooms, 37 suites. 3 restaurants, room service, cable TV, 2 pools, hot tub, massage, beach, snorkeling, jet skiing, volleyball, 2 bars, baby-sitting, laundry service, car rental, travel services. AE, DC, MC, V.*

$$$ **Continental Plaza Beach and Tennis Club.** An all-inclusive that's ideal for tennis lovers, this hotel offers a tennis club with eight courts and daily tennis clinics. In addition, there's a shopping plaza, several restaurants and bars, and a large swimming pool with little shade. Furnishings are simple and motel-like, and few rooms in this four-story low-rise have an ocean view. ✉ *Blvd. Francisco Medina Ascencio s/n, Zona Hotelera Las Glorias, Zona Hotelera 48300,* ☎ *322/224–0123,* FAX *322/224–3932. 430 rooms. 3 restaurants, 8 tennis courts, pool, gym, beach, 2 bars. AE, DC, MC, V.*

$$$ **Fiesta Americana.** The dramatically designed terra-cotta building rises above a deep-blue pool that flows under bridges, palm oases, and palapa restaurants; a seven-story palapa covers the lobby and a large round bar. The ocean-view rooms have a modern pink and terra-cotta color scheme, and each has beige marble floors, tile bath with powerful shower, and balcony. The beach bustles with activity and equipment rentals. Located in the hotel zone, it's about halfway between the Marina Vallarta complex and downtown. ✉ *Blvd. Francisco Medina Ascencio Km 2.5, Zona Hotelera 48300,* ☎ *322/224–2010 or 800/343–7821,* FAX *322/224–2108,* WEB *www.fiestaamericana.com.mx. 255 rooms, 36 suites. 2 restaurants, pool, beach, 3 bars, concierge, meeting rooms, car rental, travel services. AE, DC, MC, V.*

$$$ **La Jolla de Mismaloya.** Although the overpowering design of this resort has virtually ruined Mismaloya Bay for visitors, hotel guests have half the bay to themselves, as well as a fabulous view of Puerto Vallarta's famous Los Arcos rock formations. In its favor, the hotel's huge, brightly decorated one- and two-bedroom suites have terraces and well-equipped kitchens, and there are many activities for children. Booked on the European Plan or as an all-inclusive, this hotel consistently gets high marks from guests. ✉ *Zona Hotelera Sur Km 11.5, Mismaloya 48300,* ☎ *322/228–0660 or 800/322–2343,* FAX *322/228–0853,* WEB *www.lajollademismaloya.com. 303 suites. 6 restaurants, room service, in-room data ports, minibars, cable TV, tennis court, 4 pools, gym, hot tub, spa, beach, dive shop, snorkeling, 5 bars, shops, baby-sitting, children's programs (ages 5–11), laundry service, concierge, business services, convention center, car rental, travel services. AE, MC, V.*

$$$ **Krystal Vallarta.** A full-service resort that sprawls like a small town, the Krystal has pretty, bright hotel rooms and villas, many with private pools. The accommodations exude Mexican character, with tile floors and Spanish colonial-style furnishings. Not all rooms are by the ocean, but the secluded beach can accommodate all sunseekers. ✉ *Carretera Aeropuerto, Zona Hotelera 48300,* ☎ *322/224–0202 or 800/231–9860,* FAX *322/224–0111,* WEB *www.krystal.com.mx. 291 rooms, 114 villas. 5 restaurants, in-room safes, minibars, cable TV, 2 tennis courts, 3 pools, 3 wading pools, gym, massage, beach, racquetball, 3 bars, dance club, baby-sitting, dry cleaning, laundry service, concierge, car rental, travel services. AE, DC, MC, V.*

$$$ **Marriott Casa Magna.** Located on the beach in Marina Vallarta, this is one of Vallarta's largest and most glamorous hotels. The vast, plant-filled marble lobby is hung with wrought-iron chandeliers, the adjacent bar is wide open to the sea air and view, and the huge infinity pool is right on the beach. Rooms have polished and unpolished marble, blond woods, and floral-print spreads. And if the water sports, kid's club, and other hotel amenities aren't enough, you also have access to the facilities of the Marina Vallarta complex, including a huge shopping center, a yacht club, and more restaurants. ✉ *Paseo de la Marina 5, Marina Vallarta 48354,* ☎ *322/221–0004 or 800/228–9290,* FAX *322/221–0760,* WEB *www.marriott.com. 433 rooms, 29 suites. 4 restaurants, in-room data ports, in-room safes, minibars, cable TV with movies, 3 tennis courts, pool, gym, spa, beach, 3 bars, baby-sitting, children's programs (ages 5–12), laundry service, concierge, business services, convention center, car rental, no-smoking rooms. AE, DC, MC, V.*

$$$ **Paradise Village.** Built like an Aztec pyramid, this Nuevo Vallarta hotel and time-share property has its own marina and hosts an international sailing regatta each March. All suites have tile floors and balconies with either marina or ocean views. Furnishings are functional: there are sofa beds and a full kitchen—including stove, microwave, refrigerator, and plenty of cookware. Locals come by to visit the spa, which is noted for its massages and facials. ✉ *Paseo de los Cocoteros 18, Nuevo Vallarta*

63732, ☎ 322/297–0770, FAX 322/297–0980, WEB www.paradisevillage.com. 510 suites. 2 restaurants, snack bar, room service, kitchens, cable TV, 4 tennis courts, 3 pools, aerobics, gym, spa, beach, windsurfing, jet skiing, basketball, volleyball, 4 bars, dance club, convention center, car rental, travel services. AE, DC, MC, V.

$$$ ★ **Westin Regina.** Architecturally dramatic, this elegant yet spare and modern 14-story hotel sits on a choice 21-acre site in Marina Vallarta. In addition to four pools, a long stretch of beach, and a full range of facilities and activities, the Westin has spacious balconied rooms with marble bathrooms and brightly colored, handwoven spreads and drapes. Rooms above the sixth floor have ocean views; those below face the 600 palm trees surrounding the beautiful pools. Concrete-and-stone floors massage bare feet, and top-of-the-line mattresses with whisper-soft duvets make for heavenly siestas. Most suites have Jacuzzis. ✉ *Paseo de la Marina Sur 205, Marina Vallarta 48321, ☎ 322/221–1100 or 800/228–3000, FAX 322/221–1121, WEB www.westin.com. 266 rooms, 14 suites. 2 restaurants, room service, in-room safes, kitchenettes, cable TV, 3 tennis courts, 4 pools, gym, spa, beach, 3 bars, baby-sitting, children's programs (ages 3–7), laundry service, concierge, car rental, no-smoking rooms. AE, DC, MC, V.*

$$ ★ **Casa Dulce Vida.** Popular with family groups as well as solo travelers, this hidden villa four blocks off the bustling malecón has seven suites of various sizes decorated with Mexican art and comfortable furniture. All have well-equipped kitchens and most have ocean-view terraces; the largest has two bedrooms, two baths, and a separate dining room. There's a red-tile pool, tropical gardens, and Continental breakfast daily. ✉ *Calle Aldama 295, Centro 48300, ☎ 322/222–1008 or 800/600–6026, FAX 322/222–5815, WEB www.dulcevida.com. 7 suites. Kitchens, pool. MC, V.*

$$ **Hotel Rosita.** Rosita, the city's first official hotel, opened its doors in 1948. Since then, this family-run business has served many repeat guests. On the northern edge of the malecón, it's a great spot for budget travelers who want to be close to the action. ✉ *Paseo Díaz Ordaz 901, Centro 48380, ☎ FAX 322/223–2000 or 322/222–1033, WEB www.hotelrosita.com. 112 rooms. Restaurant, pool, bar; no air-conditioning in some rooms. AE, MC, V.*

$–$$ **Playa Los Arcos.** By far the most popular hotel on the beach near the Río Cuale, the Los Arcos has a friendly, casual air and an open central courtyard with pool. A glass elevator rises to the simple yet comfortable rooms, which are fitted with rustic light-wood and pastel furnishings and have small balconies. There's live music nightly until 11:30, and a Mexican fiesta on Saturday evenings. ✉ *Olas Altas 380, Olas Altas 48380, ☎ 322/222–0583, FAX 322/222–2418. 170 rooms, 5 suites. Restaurant, cable TV, pool, beach, bar. AE, MC, V.*

$–$$ **Villa Amor.** What began as a home on top of a hill was transformed into luxury palapa suites among the trees, with more outdoor than indoor living and beautiful views of Sayulita's coast. Accommodations range from a basic room for two (with hot plate and small fridge) to two-bedroom suites for four with terrace and plunge pool. The restaurant is good and has live music on weekends. The hotel staff is quite friendly, and a beautiful beach is just a short walk away. ✉ *Playa Sayulita, Sayulita, Nayarit 63842, ☎ 322/275–0196 or 888/295–1667, FAX 322/275–0263, WEB www.villaamor.com. 18 villas. Restaurant, kitchenettes, massage, beach, snorkeling, fishing, bicycles, laundry service, concierge. No credit cards.*

$ **Posada de Roger.** You'll enjoy the company of savvy budget travelers from Europe and Canada hanging around the pool—an international meeting spot. The spare, simple rooms have telephones, TVs, and air-conditioning; the showers are hot, the beds comfortable—if you like a very firm mattress. The location a few blocks from Los Muertos beach and in the heart of "restaurant row" is a plus. ✉ *Basilio Badillo 237, Col. E. Zapata 48380,* ☎ *322/222–0836 or 322/222–0639,* FAX *322/223–0482,* WEB *www.puerto-vallarta.com/posada. 48 rooms. Restaurant, pool, bar. AE, MC, V.*

En Route to Manzanillo

The coastline south of Puerto Vallarta is sprinkled with some of the Mexican Riviera's most exclusive and secluded one-of-a-kind resorts. But you'll never see them from Highway 200 as you head south—it's a rugged, twisting road a short distance from the coast that runs through a tropical forest of pines and palms. Most resorts are on unpaved roads. To get there, fly to Puerto Vallarta or Manzanillo and take a taxi or hotel van to your resort (which can run well over $100). Having arrived, you're likely to stay put for a week or more, leaving only for the requisite shopping spree in PV—or, for the well-heeled, a chartered-plane shopping spree to Tlaquepaque and Tonalá, outside Guadalajara.

Lodging

$$$$ ★ **Las Alamandas.** Personalized service and exclusivity lure movie stars and Danish princes to this lovely but low-key environment. Surrounded by a nature preserve with abundant wildlife, the property's villas and suites are decorated with folk art and traditional Mexican furnishings. Among the outdoor activities are golf, horseback riding, fishing, and boat rides along the Río San Nicolás. Guests can fly in via the small airstrip or take the hotel's limo from either the airport at Puerto Vallarta or Manzanillo—each about 1½ hours away. There's a two-night minimum; meal packages are available. ✉ *A.P. 201, San Patricio Melaque, Jalisco 48980 (3525 Sage Rd., Houston, TX 77056);* ☎ *322/285–5500 or 888/882–9616,* FAX *322/285–5027,* WEB *www.alamandas.com. 8 suites, 4 villas. 2 restaurants, room service, tennis court, pool, gym, beach, snorkeling, mountain bikes, croquet, Ping-Pong, volleyball, 2 bars, shops, laundry service, concierge, meeting room. AE, MC, V.*

$$$$ **Careyes.** Resembling a boldly painted village nestled on a gorgeous bay, this pioneering resort is situated on Mexico's "Turtle Coast," 98 km (60 mi) north of Manzanillo airport and 172 km (107 mi) south of Puerto Vallarta. There are 51 rooms and suites, all decorated in warm tones—yellow ochre, coral, and sapphire blue. The full-service spa features European beauty and body treatments and has a deli/snack bar selling fine wines, prosciutto, and other necessities of the good life. At the beach await a full range of water-sports equipment. Excursions can be made to lagoons, tropical forests, and local beaches. ✉ *Barra de Navidad Hwy. Km 53.5, Costa Careyes, Jalisco 48970,* ☎ *315/351–0000,* FAX *315/351–0100,* WEB *www.careyes.com.mx. 48 rooms, 4 suites, 100 condominiums. Restaurant, 2 tennis courts, pool, gym, spa, beach, snorkeling, boating, fishing, bar. AE, DC, MC, V.*

$$$$ **Hotelito Desconocido.** This isolated hotel on a long stretch of beach is an idyllic escape for those willing to pay a high price for simple pleasures. Individual *casitas* incorporate local building materials and styles, including plank floors, reed mats, bamboo walls, and palm frond roofs; rustic-style bathrooms have tile floors. Solar power runs essential equipment, but rooms are cooled only by battery-powered fans and lit by lanterns and candles, with no TV or telephone. In the morning, signal for coffee and croissants by running the flag up the flagpole. ✉ *Cruz de Loreto Tomatlán,* ☎ *315/222–2526 or 877/486–3372,* FAX *315/223–0293,* WEB *www.hotelito.com. 19 rooms, 10 suites. 2 pools, massage, spa, beach, billiards. AE, MC, V.*

$$$$ ★ **El Tamarindo.** This magical resort, nestled in palms and surrounded by more than 2,000 acres of ecological reserve and jungle, lies on 16 km (10 mi) of private coast. The secluded villas all have private plunge pools and outdoor living rooms. Decorated in nubby fabrics, oiled wood, and other classy elements, this casually elegant hotel embodies the "Careyes style" of architecture that first appeared in the 1960s, rendering simple design elements in local building materials. At night, the gracious staff lights more than 1,500 candles around the villas to create a truly enchanting setting. ✉ *Melaque–Puerto Vallarta Hwy. Km 7.5, Cihuatlán, Jalisco 48970,* ☎ *315/351–5032,* FAX *315/351–5070. 28 villas. Restaurant, 18-hole golf course, 2 tennis courts, pool, beach, dive shop, snorkeling, bar. AE, DC, MC, V.*

Nightlife and the Arts

Puerto Vallarta is a party town, where the discos open at 10 PM and stay open until at least 3 or 4 AM. A $20 cover charge is not uncommon (at least for men) in the popular discos, many of which are at hotels. **Cactus Club** (✉ Ignacio L. Vallarta 399, Los Muertos, ☎ 322/222–6037) attracts a youngish crowd. The Krystal Vallarta hotel has **Christine's** (☎ 322/224–0202), which features a spectacular light show set to music from disco to techno. **Club Roxy** (✉ Ignacio L. Vallarta 217, Col. E. Zapata, ☎ 322/223–2424) has live rock and R&B, with an occasional reggae set, nightly beginning at 10 PM. **J.&B.** (✉ Blvd. Fco. Medina Ascencio 2043, Zona Hotelera, ☎ 322/224–4616), pronounced "Jota Bay," is popular for dancing to live salsa. **The Zoo** (✉ Paseo Díaz Ordaz 630, Centro, ☎ 322/222–4945), facing the boardwalk near Olas Altas, attracts a youngish crowd.

As its name implies, **Collage** (☎ 322/221–0505), on the highway at the Marina Vallarta complex, has several restaurants, a bowling alley, billiards, two bars, shuffleboard, a video arcade, and a disco. **El Faro** (✉ Royal Pacific Yacht Club, Marina Vallarta, ☎ 322/221–0541) is a romantic spot from which to watch a lightning storm roll into the bay in hurricane season, or just to admire the bay and marina from the top of the 110-ft lighthouse.

Mexican fiestas are popular at the hotels and can be lavish affairs with buffet dinners, folk dances, and even fireworks. Reservations may be made with the hotels or travel agencies. The **Camino Real** (☎ 322/221–5000) hosts cultural events, such as music concerts and folkloric dances, on the first Thursday of every month at 9 PM.

Outdoor Activities and Sports

Swimming, sailing, windsurfing, and parasailing are popular sports at the beachfront hotels, which have stands on the beach offering boat trips and equipment. You needn't be a guest to rent these services.

Biking

B-B-Bobby's Bikes (✉ Miramar 399, at Iturbide, Centro, ☎ 322/223–0008) rents mountain bikes, beach cruisers, and "shopper's bikes" (with carrier racks) by the day or week and leads guided tours.

Bike Mex (✉ Guerrero 361, Centro, ☎ 322/223–1680) provides the gear (21-speed mountain bikes and helmets) and snacks for several different bike tours, which can be tailored to riders' experience and fitness level. The most popular is a three- to four-hour trip inland to bathe in an impressive waterfall. Guided hikes are also offered.

Fishing

The sailfishing tournament in November draws dedicated fishermen from all over the world. Canadian Candice Shaw runs a bilingual-crewed boat, ***Fishing with Carolina*** (☎ 322/224–7250), with three chairs; an all-day trip costs $300. Throughout the year, the **Progreso Fishermen's Cooperative** offers a variety of fishing trips from its shack on the north end of the malecón; most hotels can arrange your reservations. Large group boats cost about $60 per person for a day's fishing. Cruisers may be chartered for $150–$350 a day, and include a skipper, fishing license, bait, and tackle; some also include lunch.

Golf

The 18-hole course at **Los Flamingos Country Club** (✉ 12 km [8 mi] north of airport, Nuevo Vallarta, ☎ 322/298–0606), designed by Percy Clifford, has a putting green, driving range, and tennis courts. There is a Joe Finger–designed 18-hole course at the **Marina Vallarta** complex (☎ 322/221–0545 or 322/221–0073) with caddies, carts, pro shop, lessons, and driving range. Make reservations for both through your hotel a day in advance.

Horseback Riding

Horseback riding along the shore is popular, and horses can be rented by the hour at area beaches. **Rancho Charro** (✉ Poblano de Playa Grande, Playa Grande, ☎ 322/224–0114) provides transportation to and from your hotel for three- to five-hour rides to area rivers and waterfalls. **Rancho El Ojo de Agua** (✉ Cerrada de Cardenal 227, Fracc. Aralias, ☎ 322/224–8240 or 322/224–0607) also runs horseback sunset and half-day rides, some including lunch and time for a swim in a mountain stream. Excursions of up to five nights can be arranged to some of the colonial villages in the Sierra Madre.

Tennis

Most of the larger hotels have tennis courts for their guests' use. Courts are also available at the **Los Flamingos Country Club.**

Water Park

Children love **Splash** (✉ Carretera a Tepic Km 155, Nuevo Vallarta, Nayarit, ☎ 322/297–0723 or 322/297–0724, 🎫 $13), where they can swim with dolphins, slide down enormous water slides, swim, and play on playground equipment and carnival rides. There are restaurants and bars as well as sea lion shows. The park is open daily 9–7.

Water Sports

Snorkeling and diving are most common at Los Arcos, a natural underwater preserve located near the Los Arcos rock formation off Mismaloya beach. Quimixto Bay, about 32 km (20 mi) south of PV and accessible only by boat, has some good diving spots, as does Punta de Mita, about 80 km (50 mi) north. Experienced divers head for Las Marietas and El Morro islands, off Punta de Mita.

Many of the larger resort hotels rent snorkeling and diving equipment and offer short diving courses at their pools. For intensive certification courses, dive trips, and equipment rentals, contact **Chico's Dive Shop** (✉ Paseo Díaz Ordaz 772, Centro, ☎ 322/222–1895). **Pacific Scuba** (✉ Juárez 722, Centro, ☎ 322/222–4741) also rents equipment and arranges trips.

Shopping

Puerto Vallarta has been described as a shopper's paradise punctuated with hotels and beaches. There are plenty of shopping malls and small shops selling folk art, as well as more than 20 fine-art galleries. Prices in the shops are fixed, and U.S. dollars and credit cards are accepted. Bargaining is expected in the markets and by the vendors on the beach, who also freely accept American money. Most stores are open 10–8. A few close for siesta at 1 or 2, then reopen at 4.

Art

Galería Arte Latinoamericano (✉ Josefa Ortiz Domínguez 155, Centro, ☎ 322/222–4406) features contemporary art, sculptures, and lithographs. **Galería Dante** (✉ Basilio Badillo 269, Col. E. Zapata, ☎ 322/222–2477) has a 6,000-square-ft gallery and sculpture garden with classical, contemporary, and abstract works from more than 50 Latin American artists. One of PV's best-known artists is the late Manuel Lepe, whose primitive-style prints can be seen in the galleries around town, including the one run by his family, **Galería Lepe** (✉ Juárez 533, Centro, ☎ 322/222–5515). Contemporary paintings and sculpture are displayed in **Galería Pacífico** (✉ Calle Aldama 174, Centro, ☎ 322/222–1982), a pioneer gallery nearly 20 years old. **Galería Rosas Blancas** (✉ Juárez 523, Centro, ☎ 322/222–1168) combines fine art with folk art. Wonderful, varied art in many media is found at **Galería Uno** (✉ Calle Morelos 561, Centro, ☎ 322/222–0908). Owners Jan Lavender and Martina Goldberg love to showcase local talent. Internationally known Sergio Bustamante—the creator of life-size brass, copper, and ceramic animals—has several galleries: **Sergio Bustamante** (✉ Av. Juárez 275, Centro, ☎ 322/222–1129; ✉ Paseo Díaz Ordaz 716, Centro, ☎ 322/223–1407; ✉ Paseo Díaz Ordaz 542, Centro, ☎ 322/222–5480).

Clothing

Most of the brand-name sportswear shops are located along the malecón and down its side streets. **La Bohemia** (✉ Constitución at Basilio Badillo, Col. E. Zapata, ☎ 322/222–3164; ✉ Plaza Neptuno Interior, Marina Vallarta, ☎ 322/221–2160) displays contemporary resort wear, designer art wear, unique jewelry, and accessories. **Express–Guess** (✉ Paseo Díaz Ordaz 660, Centro, ☎ 322/222–6470) carries its own line of quality sportswear. **Güeros** (✉ Calle Zaragoza 160, Centro, ☎ 322/222–0633) carries contemporary clothing for men, women, and children, as well as shoes, handbags, straw, leather, and home furnishings.

María de Guadalajara (✉ Puesta del Sol condominiums, Marina Vallarta, ☎ 322/221–2566; ✉ Plaza Malecón and Paseo Díaz Ordaz, Centro, ☎ 322/222–4735; ✉ Calle Morelos 550, Centro, ☎ 322/222–2387) carries easy-to-wear clothing for women in gauzy fabrics dyed in luscious colors. **Nina & June** (✉ Hidalgo 226, 227–8, upstairs, Centro, ☎ 322/222–3099) sells handwoven, originally designed fashions, fanciful accessories, and silver jewelry as well as outfits from Indonesia, Guatemala, New York, Mexico City, and Guadalajara. Tropical-print dresses and boxy cotton blouses and pants can be found at **Sucesos Boutique** (✉ Libertad and Hidalgo, Centro, ☎ 322/222–1002).

Folk Art

Puerto Vallarta is known for the variety of handicrafts sold, both from the region and throughout Mexico. Masks, pottery, lacquerware, clothing, mirrors, glass dishes, lamps, carved-wood animals, antiques and modern art, hand-dyed woven rugs, and embroidered clothing are all available in shops and markets, but look before you buy, as quality varies. **Galería de Ollas** (✉ Calle Morelos 101, Centro, ☎ 322/223–1045) has the wondrous pottery of the village of Juan Mata Ortiz exclusively. Highly prized beaded masks and statuettes, yarn art, and other folk crafts are found downtown at the **Huichol Collection Gallery** (✉ Morelos 490, Centro, ☎ 322/222–0182) or its sister store at Marina Vallarta. **Mundo de Azulejos** (✉ Venustiano Carranza 374, Col. E. Zapata, ☎ 322/222–2675) sells a line of decorative tiles and will re-create your favorite scene or work of art in a series of tiles in 24 to 48 hours. Glassblowers at the **Mundo de Cristal** (✉ Av. Insurgentes 333, at Basilio Badillo, Col. E. Zapata, ☎ 322/222–4157) factory create both avant-garde and classic designs to be sold in their store.

Olinalá (✉ Lázaro Cárdenas 274, Centro, ☎ 322/222–4995) specializes in painted ceremonial masks from throughout Mexico and sells contemporary paintings. **Puerco Azul** (✉ Marina Las Palmas II promenade, Marina Vallarta, ☎ 322/221–1985) carries one-of-a-kind items for the home, including furniture, ceramics, antiques, glassware, and whimsical pig figurines. **Querubines** (✉ Juárez 501–A, Centro, ☎ 322/222–2988) sells a wealth of utilitarian and decorative folk art, especially woven goods: linens, place mats, and Guatemalan fabrics as well as painted gourds from Michoacán, tin, and ceramics. **Talavera Etc.** (✉ Ignacio L. Vallarta 266, Col. E. Zapata, ☎ 322/222–4100) has a small but fine selection of majolica ceramics and handcrafted jewelry. Original hand-loomed rugs, fabrics, and hand-painted furniture are on display at **Tamacani** (✉ Plaza Marina D-2, Marina Vallarta, ☎ 322/221–0982).

Jewelry

There's a good selection of Mexican silver in Puerto Vallarta, but watch out for *chapa,* a combination of alloys. Real silver carries the.925 stamp required by the government. **Joyas Finas Suneson** (✉ Calle Morelos 593, Centro, ☎ 322/222–5715) specializes in silver jewelry and objets d'art by some of Mexico's finest designers. At **Ric Taxco** (✉ Pueblo Viejo shopping center, Versalles, ☎ 322/224–4598; ✉ Villa Vallarta shopping center, Versalles, ☎ 322/223–0143), much of the sterling silver and gold jewelry is inspired by pre-Hispanic designs. **Viva** (✉ Basilio Badillo 274, Col. E. Zapata, ☎ 322/222–4078) represents jewelers from around world, and has a large inventory of jewelry in silver, gold, and gemstones, as well as shoes and purses.

Markets

The **Mercado Municipal,** at Avenida Miramar and Libertad, is a typical market plopped down in the busiest part of town. Flowers, piñatas, produce, and plastics are all shoved together in indoor and outdoor stands that cover a full city block. The strip of **shops along Isla Río Cuale** is an outdoor market of sorts, with souvenir stands and exclusive boutiques interspersed with restaurants and cafés.

Shopping Centers

The highway on the north side of town is lined with small arcades and large shopping centers that are occupied by handicrafts and sportswear shops. The best selections are at the **Gigante Plaza,** by the Fiesta Americana hotel; **Plaza Malecón,** at the beginning of Paseo Díaz Ordaz; **Plaza Marina,** on the highway at Marina Vallarta; and **Villa Vallarta,** by the Plaza las Glorias hotel.

Puerto Vallarta A to Z

AIR TRAVEL

Puerto Vallarta's Gustavo Díaz Ordaz International Airport is 7½ km (4.5 mi) north of town, not far from the resorts at Marina Vallarta. Volkswagen vans provide economical transportation from the airport to PV hotels.

CARRIERS

Mexicana has direct service from Chicago, Denver, and Mexico City. Aeroméxico has flights from multiple U.S. and Mexican cities. Alaska Airlines serves the western United States, with direct flights from Los

Angeles, Phoenix, San Francisco, and Seattle. American has daily nonstop flights from Dallas/Fort Worth. Continental flies direct from Houston. America West has direct flights from Phoenix.

➤ AIRLINES AND CONTACTS: **Aeroméxico** (☎ 322/221–1030 or 322/224–1799). **Alaska Airlines** (☎ 322/221–1353 or 322/221–1350). **America West** (☎ 322/235–9292 or 322/221–1025). **American** (☎ 322/221–1799). **Continental** (☎ 322/221–2213 or 322/221–1025). **Mexicana** (☎ 322/221–1266 or 322/224–8900).

➤ AIRPORT INFORMATION: **Gustavo Díaz Ordaz International Airport** (✉ Hwy to Tepic Km 7.5, Zona Aeropuerto, ☎ 322/221–1298 or 322/221–1325).

BOAT AND FERRY TRAVEL

Several cruise lines, including Carnival, Holland America Line, Princess Cruises, and Royal Caribbean Cruises, sail to Puerto Vallarta, most frequently during the winter months.

BUS TRAVEL

One km (½ mi) north of the airport is PV's Central Camionero, or central bus station. ETN has the most luxurious service to Guadalajara and Mexico City, with roomy, reclining seats. Transportes del Pacífico serves the region. Elite, which incorporates three lines (Estrella Blanca, Tres Estrellas de Oro, and Norte de Sonora), has first-class service to Guadalajara, Aguascalientes, and Mexico City. Primera Plus serves destinations throughout Mexico.

City buses serve downtown, the northern hotel zone, and the southern beaches. Bus stops—marked by blue-and-white signs—are located every two or three blocks along the highway (Carretera Aeropuerto) and in town. Buses to Playa Mismaloya and Boca de Tomatlán run about every 15 minutes from the corner of Avenida Insurgentes and Basilio Badillo, downtown.

➤ BUS INFORMATION: **Central Camionero** (✉ Puerto Vallarta–Tepic Hwy. Km 9, Las Mojoneras, ☎ 322/221–0739). **Elite** (☎ 322/223–1117 or 322/221–0848). **ETN** (☎ 322/221–0550). **Primera Plus** (☎ 322/221–0095). **Transportes del Pacífico** (☎ 322/222–1015 or 322/221–0021).

CAR RENTAL

During the high season, rentals start at $50 per day, including mileage; always ask about special promotions. All the car-rental agencies below have desks at the airport; some have offices along the highway.

Alamo offers free pickup. Prices at Budget range from $50 to $78 a day. Dollar has branches at the Krystal and Buenaventura hotels. National is another well-known international chain.

➤ MAJOR AGENCIES: **Alamo** (✉ Blvd. Francisco Medina Ascencio 1851, Centro, ☎ 322/221–3030). **Budget** (✉ Av. Paseo de las Palmas 1680, Col. Olimpica, ☎ 322/222–2980). **Dollar** (✉ Av. Paseo de las Palmas 1728, Marina Vallarta, ☎ 322/223–1354). **National** (✉ Carretera Aeropuerto Km 1.5, Marina Vallarta, ☎ 322/222–0515).

CAR TRAVEL

Puerto Vallarta is about 1,900 km (1,200 mi) south of Nogales, Arizona, at the U.S.–Mexico border, 354 km (220 mi) from Guadalajara, and 167 km (104 mi) from Tepic.

Driving in the city can be very unpleasant. From December through April—peak tourist season—traffic clogs the small cobblestone streets. During the rainy season, from July through October, the streets become flooded and the city's steep hills are muddy and slippery. Parking is nearly nonexistent.

EMBASSIES

The U.S. and Canadian consulates are in the same building on the main plaza.

➤ CANADA: **Canadian Consulate** (✉ Calle Zaragoza 160, Centro, ☎ 322/222–5398).

➤ UNITED STATES: **U.S. Consulate** (✉ Calle Zaragoza 160, 2nd floor, Centro, ☎ 322/222–0069).

EMERGENCIES

Dial **060** in emergency situations.

➤ CONTACTS: **Ambulance** (☎ 322/222–1533). **Farmacia California** (✉ Francisco Villa 880, Marina Vallarta, ☎ 322/225–0635). **Hospital** (✉ Plaza Neptuno, Marina Vallarta, ☎ 322/221–0023). **Police** (✉ City Hall, Calles Morelos and Iturbide, Centro, ☎ 322/222–0123 or 322/223–2500). **Red Cross** (☎ 322/222–1533).

ENGLISH-LANGUAGE MEDIA

There's no shortage of printed English-language information in PV. In addition to lots of slick (and truly helpful) map guides, check out the ad-driven but informative *PV Tribune*. The *Vallarta Voice* is a monthly English-language paper.

MAIL, INTERNET, AND SHIPPING

For sending and receiving mail and packages, go to Mail Boxes Etc., which also offers fax and e-mail services. The Net House is open from dawn to the wee hours, and has computers with English-language keyboards.

➤ INTERNET CAFÉS: **The Net House** (✉ Ignacio L. Vallarta 232, Col. E. Zapata, ☎ 322/222–6953) has an air-conditioned computer room and serves coffee drinks as well.

➤ MAIL SERVICES: **Mail Boxes Etc.** (✉ Blvd. Francisco Medina Ascencio, Edificio Andrea Mar Local 7, Marina Vallarta, ☎ 322/224–9434).

TAXIS

The ride from the north-side hotels to downtown costs about $10; within downtown, a ride is $2; from Marina Vallarta to downtown, about $4. Be sure to agree on a fare before embarking.

TOURS

The five-hour city tour is a good way to get the lay of the land, from Marina Vallarta and Gringo Gulch to the Río Cuale and Playa Mismaloya. Almost everyone goes on at least one daytime or sunset cruise of the bay. Daytime cruises go to Los Arcos, Yelapa, Quimixto, and Playa Las Ánimas, and to Isla Marietas for whale-watching (during winter months), snorkeling, swimming, and lunch, departing from the Terminal Marítima at around 9 AM.

Local fishermen at Punta de Mita have formed the Sociedad Cooperativa Corral de Risco, offering fishing, whale-watching, and snorkel trips around the Marieta islands at reasonable rates. Intermar Vallarta offers a dinner cruise to movie director John Huston's former home, on a private bay south of the city, with dancing on the return trip. Vallarta Adventure arranges transportation and tours to destinations such as San Sebastian del Oeste, an interesting old mining town high in the Sierra Madre, 62 km (38 mi) from Puerto Vallarta; or to shopping or tequila-tasting expeditions outside Guadalajara. Harris Tours offers city tours for about $16; tours to Yelapa run about $30; and tours to Las Ánimas and Quimixto cost approximately $40. It's worth the few extra dollars to go on a private tour (small groups) in a van rather than with a large group on a tour bus. Natura Tours offers numerous types of nature-oriented excursions, including bass and deep-sea fishing, hiking, scuba diving, and biking. Their subsidiary, Viva Tours, books cruises and air travel.

Tropical tours visit mango and banana plantations in Nayarit. These often include stops in Nayarit's capital, Tepic, and a boat ride on the scenic Río Tovara, through jungle thick with tropical birds, with a stop for a refreshing swim in a natural spring.

➤ TOUR OPERATOR RECOMMENDATIONS: **Harris Tours** (☎ 322/223–2972). **Intermar Vallarta** (✉ Paseo de la Marina s/n, Condominio Via Golf, Marina Vallarta, ☎ 322/221–0734). **Natura Tours** (✉ Carr. Aeropuerto Km 5.5, Las Flores, ☎ FAX 322/224–0410). **Sociedad Cooperativa Corral de Risco** (✉ Av. el Anclote, Manzana 17, No. 1, Nuevo Vallarta, ☎ 322/291–6298). **Vallarta Adventure** (✉ Av. de las Palmas at Nayarit, Nuevo Vallarta, ☎ 322/221–0657).

TRAVEL AGENCIES

➤ LOCAL AGENT REFERRALS: **American Express** (✉ Morelos 660, Centro, ☎ 322/223–2955).

VISITOR INFORMATION

The municipal tourist office, open weekdays 9–5, is on the Plaza Principal. The state tourism office is open weekdays 9–7, Saturday 9–1.

➤ TOURIST INFORMATION: **Municipal Tourist Office** (✉ Independencia 123, Centro, ☎ 322/223–2500 Ext. 230 to 232). **State Tourism Office** (✉ Plaza Marina shopping center, Local 144 & 146, Marina Vallarta, ☎ 322/222–0242 or 322/221–2676).

MANZANILLO

Manzanillo is not your typical resort destination. Crystal blue waters lap the black-and-gold volcanic sand on its twin bahías, Manzanillo and Santiago, which host not only resort hotels but a major industrial port. Twin towns of the same name, with little polish, have a dearth of shops, museums, or other tourist attractions. Still, it's the very lack of sophistication combined with inviting beaches and some great resorts that attract a certain type of tourist. In the July–September rainy season, rivers and lagoons swell, forming waterfalls and ponds.

La Península de Santiago, which separates Bahía de Santiago and Bahía de Manzanillo, is a spit of land on which perches Las Hadas resort. From the water or points above the beach, the resort seems a mirage, a mass of white domes and peaks that radiate pink in the midday heat. When Bolivian tin magnate Antenor Patiño conceived of this dazzling palace in the early 1960s, Manzanillo was easier to reach by sea than by land, a rugged, primitive port that attracted hardy sailors and beachcombers bent on creating their own tropical paradise. When Patiño's retreat was completed in 1974, the international social set began to visit Manzanillo. Even then, Manzanillo remained essentially a port city with only a few tourist attractions.

Manzanillo is still relatively undeveloped, a sleeper compared with other Pacific Coast resorts. Many shops and hotel desks close for afternoon siesta, and on Sunday most businesses (including restaurants) shut down and everyone heads for the beach.

Along with the rest of the Gold Coast, this area is being developed. The latest prize to be carved out of the wilderness by big-time investors is Isla Navidad, a 1,230-acre resort complex on a peninsula about 20 minutes north of the Manzanillo international airport and an hour north of Manzanillo proper. Robert Von Hagge designed the 27-hole golf course, and other amenities include a full-service marina.

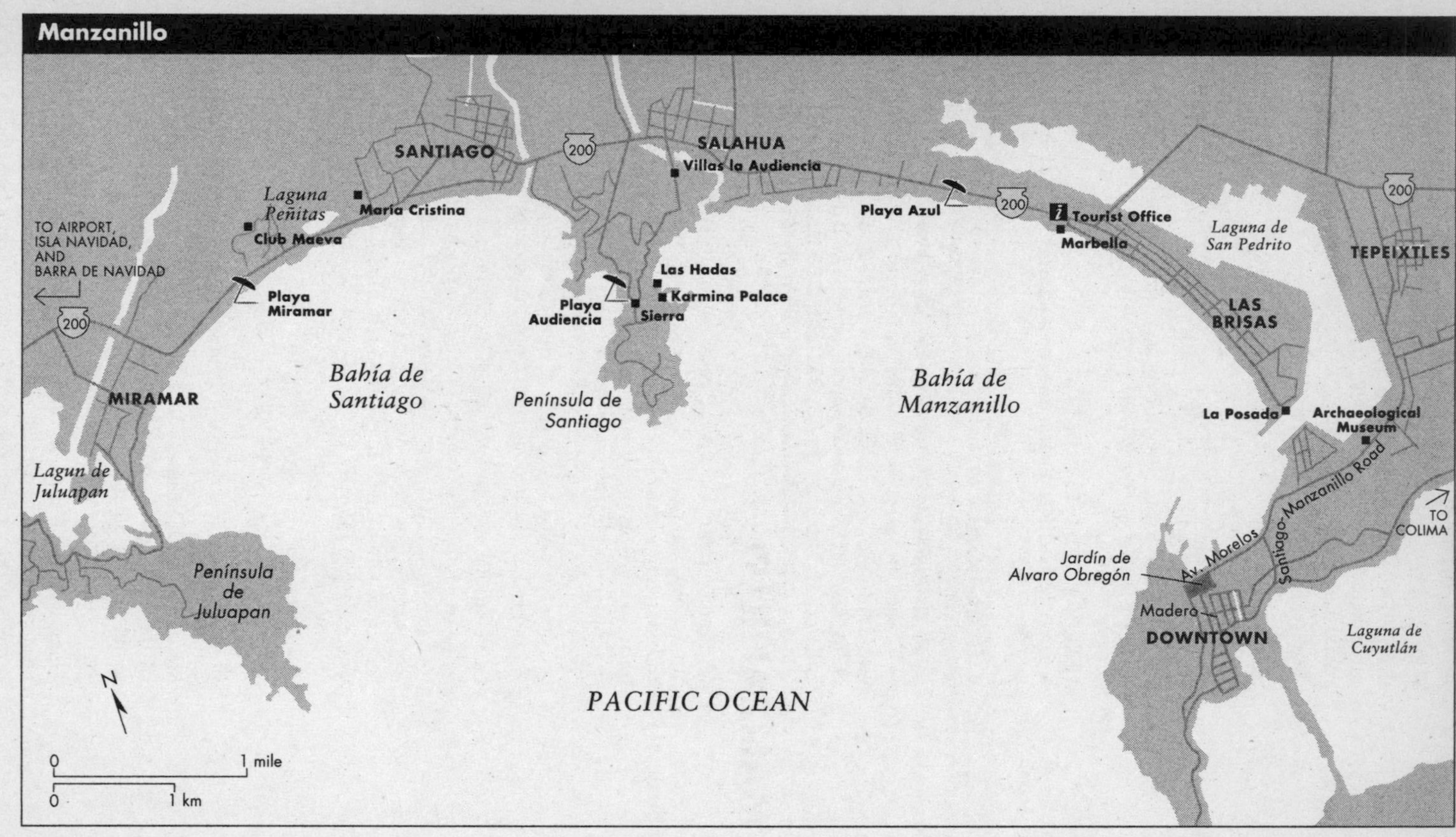
Manzanillo
SANTIAGO
SALAHUA
Villas la Audiencia
Laguna Peñitas
María Cristina
TO AIRPORT, ISLA NAVIDAD, AND BARRA DE NAVIDAD
Club Maeva
Playa Miramar
200
Playa Audiencia
Las Hadas
Karmina Palace
Sierra
Playa Azul
Tourist Office
Marbella
Laguna de San Pedrito
TEPEIXTLES
LAS BRISAS
MIRAMAR
Bahía de Santiago
Península de Santiago
Bahía de Manzanillo
La Posada
Archaeological Museum
Santiago-Manzanillo Road
Lagun de Juluapan
TO COLIMA
Av. Morelos
Jardín de Alvaro Obregón
Madero
DOWNTOWN
Laguna de Cuyutlán
Península de Juluapan
N
PACIFIC OCEAN
0
1 mile
0
1 km

Exploring Manzanillo

A vacation in Manzanillo is not spent shopping and sightseeing. There's little in the way of folk art to buy, and visitors generally stay put and relax on the beach, venturing out to survey the local scene only when boredom or sunstroke strike.

A Good Tour

The **Santiago** area, on Santiago Bay between the Santiago and Juluapan peninsulas, offers little indication that it's a tourist destination save a string of hotels and restaurants along the beach. The next area to the east, **Salahua,** is residential, with a baseball field and restaurants. Farther southeast on Manzanillo Bay, past the traffic circle and Avenida Morelos, you'll see **Las Brisas** beach, where some of the cheaper hotels are located.

Downtown is busy and jam-packed, but of little tourist interest, except for the bustling seaport and, just north of downtown, the **Museo Universitario Arqueolóico.** The museum displays 5,000 of its more than 18,000 artifacts, which come from the immediate region, the state of Colima, and throughout Mesoamerica. Chamber music, folkloric dance, and other cultural events are sometimes presented Friday evenings. ✉ *San Pedrito traffic circle, Centro,* ☎ *314/332–2256.* 🎫 *$1.* ⏲ *Tues.–Sat. 10–2 and 5–8, Sun. 10–1.*

At the beginning of the harbor, Highway 200 jogs around downtown and intersects with Highway 110 to Colima. Avenida Morelos leads past the shipyards and into town. Just before you reach the port, stop at **Laguna de San Pedrito,** where graceful white herons and vivid pink flamingos assemble at sunset. The zócalo, or **Jardín de Alvaro Obregón,** is right on the main road by the waterfront. It's small but quite lively in the evening.

Beaches

Manzanillo's biggest attraction is its beaches. Every day is a beach day, and Sundays are downright festive, with half the town gathered to play onshore. The volcanic sand is a mix of black, white, and brown, with the southernmost beaches the blackest.

Playa Miramar, at the north end of Santiago Bay, is populated by windsurfers and boogie-boarders. The beach in front of Club Santiago, once the favored hangout for locals, is now accessible only by walking north along the beach from the highway or by passing the guards at the club gates. The main stretch of beach is across the highway from Club Maeva. Manzanillo's best beach is probably **Playa Audiencia,** in a cove along the north side of Santiago Peninsula. The local Indians supposedly granted Cortés an audience here—thus the name. Located between two rock outcroppings, it's a good spot for snorkeling. The rocky beach at **Las Hadas,** directly behind Hotel La Sierra on Bahía de Manzanillo, is a good snorkeling spot. **Playa Azul,** also called Playa Santiago, is a long strand that runs from Santiago Peninsula along Manzanillo Bay to Playa Las Brisas. The surf gets rough along the north end; swimming is better toward Las Brisas.

To the north, **Barra de Navidad** has pretty beaches lined with open-air restaurants; it's popular with surfers when the autumn swells hit. Pangas access a small island just offshore, where unbroken seashells are abundant. When the tide is low, it is possible to walk along the beach from Barra to San Patricio Melaque, a distance of about 6 km (almost 4 mi). Having caught the eye of both government tourism officials and entrepreneurs, this area is destined to grow. For now, Barra is a smallish town with plenty of low-key, low-budget hotels and restaurants.

Dining

$$$–$$$$ ✕ **Legazpi.** Named for the navigator who put the Philippines on the map, this international restaurant at Las Hadas is beautiful. The service is white-glove perfection, but friendly rather than pretentious, and the food is decidedly elegant. The emphasis is on Continental cuisine with a Mexican touch, including Tulum salad (lettuce with crabmeat, avocado, and quail eggs) and grilled salmon with hibiscus-flower sauce. The only drawback is the difficulty of finding the restaurant open. ✉ *Las Hadas, Av. de los Riscos, Zona Hotelera,* ☎ *314/334–0101. AE, DC, MC, V. Closed Wed., Fri., Sun. Closed Mar.–Nov. No lunch.*

$$$ ✕ **Colima Bay Café.** A comely and lively seaside venue, the Colima Bay has a large second-story bar looking down onto another bar below, which has low tables of decorative tiles, leather *equipale* chairs, and giant plaster hippos and frogs for decoration. The cheerful restaurant overlooking the beach has cardboard menus in English and Spanish offering nachos, spaghetti, barbecued pork accompanied by a stuffed baked potato, and other familiar dishes. ✉ *Blvd. Costero 921, Las Brisas,* ☎ *314/333–1150. MC, V.*

$$$ ✕ **Toscana.** When the popular restaurant Willy's closed due to storm damage, the owners transferred customers' favorite dishes to their other restaurant, Toscana. Most tables at this French-Italian restaurant sit on the charming outdoor terrace adjacent to the beach. Specialties include smoked-salmon quiche, the San Remo salad (with tomatoes, onions, black olives, and Italian dressing), and a seafood assortment with scallop ceviche, shrimp, clams, and calamari. Live guitar music is offered nightly after 7 PM. ✉ *Blvd. Costero Miguel de la Madrid 3177, Zona Hotelera,* ☎ *314/333–2515. MC, V. No lunch.*

$$ ✕ **El Vaquero Campestre.** Its name means "the country cowboy," so it's no surprise to find a setting reminiscent of a ranch-land saloon. The menu at this restaurant en route to Las Hadas resort emphasizes fine cuts of beef—grilled without embellishment or marinated and seasoned carne asada. There are also burgers and shrimp; or try the *carne tampiqueña,* thin strips of grilled beef served with guacamole, beans, and quesadillas. ✉ *Av. la Audiencia Lote 2, Playa La Audencia,* ☎ *314/334–1548. MC, V.*

$–$$ ✕ **El Bigotes.** Good seafood is served at a leisurely pace in this restaurant, which is under open-air palapas on the beach. With no decoration save the oceanscape in front, the ambience comes from the lively patrons and canned music. The house specialty is the spicy Jalisco favorite *pescado sarandeado* (whole fish marinated and grilled over hot coals). Also recommended is Camerón Mustache: butterfly shrimp breaded in shredded coconut and sautéed. ✉ *Blvd. Costero Miguel de la Madrid 3157, Zona Hotelera,* ☎ *314/334–0831. MC, V.*

$–$$ ✕ **Club de Playa.** Situated on a rocky outcropping at Santiago Bay's midway point, this restaurant is effectively the starting point of Playa Miramar. Diners can take in a perfect view of the waves crashing all around them while enjoying a selection of seafood or more traditional Mexican dishes such as fajitas or steak tampiqueña. A good bet is the *filete de pescado relleno con mariscos,* a fish filet stuffed with shrimp, octopus, and vegetables. And even if you're not hungry, the bar is a prime spot to sip a cocktail and watch the sun set over the bay. ✉ *Carretera Manzanillo–Cihuatlan Km 15.5, Playa Miramar,* ☎ *314/333–1870. AE, MC, V.*

$–$$ ★ ✕ **L' Recif.** A huge palapa set on a cliff with a pool/bar to one side and waves crashing on the rocks below, this is undoubtedly the best dinner-with-a-view in the area, and around March, a great place to see migrating whales. Beef is the specialty, but also popular is the *camaron L'Recif,* shrimp sautéed with corn, zucchini, and carrots, served with mango sauce on a bed of mashed potatoes. ✉ *Cerro del Cenicero s/n, El Naranjo, Condominio Vida del Mar, Peninsula de Juluapan,* ☎ *314/ 335–0900. MC, V. Closed May–Oct. No lunch.*

$ ✕ **Juanito's.** Owned by an American who settled in Manzanillo in 1976, Juanito's is the spot to watch U.S. football in good company. It's the most popular place in town for breakfast, and also specializes in great burgers, malts, fries, barbecued ribs, and fried chicken. Decoration is minimal, but the service is quick and the coffee strong and hot. It's also one of Manzanillo's only Internet cafés. ✉ *Blvd. Costero Km 14, Olas Altas,* ☎ *314/333–1388. Reservations not accepted. AE, MC, V.*

Lodging

Although the $10 room is a thing of the past, there are still several decent places where you can lay your head for less than $60. Travelers on a tighter budget usually head to Barra de Navidad and Melaque, about an hour north. As with the rest of the Pacific Coast, Manzanillo is in the midst of a building boom, mainly condominiums, to accommodate the growing number of Canadian snowbirds and Guadalajara residents buying vacation homes here. The resorts are spread out along the Santiago-Manzanillo Road.

$$$$ ★ **Grand Bay.** Set on a 1,200-acre peninsula between the Pacific and the Navidad lagoon, 30 minutes north of Manzanillo airport, this no-holds-barred resort cascades down a hill to a delightful stretch of private beach. Rooms in this luxurious hotel, with Spanish arches, shady patios, fountains, and lush gardens, have mountain or sea views, imported-marble baths, original art, deluxe amenities, and balconies. Three striking tiered pools dot the gardens. Guests may play the adjacent 27-hole Robert Von Hagge–designed golf course; boat service is available to Barra de Navidad, across the bay. ✉ *Isla Navidad (A.P. 20), Jalisco 48987,* ☎ *315/355–5050 or 888/472–6229,* FAX *315/355–6071,* WEB *www.grandbay.com. 158 rooms, 41 suites. 3 restaurants, in-room safes, minibars, cable TV, golf privileges, 3 tennis courts, 3 pools, gym, beach, dive shop, snorkeling, jet skiing, marina, waterskiing, fishing, volleyball, 3 bars, shops, baby-sitting, children's programs (ages 4–12), concierge. AE, MC, V.*

$$$$ **Karmina Palace.** Manzanillo's newest all-inclusive, all-suites hotel is just a short walk from neighboring Las Hadas. Punctuating Karmina's spacious lawns are cascades, fountains, eight multitier lagoon-pools, and a beautiful palapa restaurant at the ocean's edge. Junior suites have two TVs, marble floors, refrigerator, balcony or terrace, and large tubs with separate shower facilities and double vanities in the bathrooms. The seven-story resort hotel has 24-hour concierge service and a well-equipped business center, but service is only average. ✉ *Av. Vista Hermosa 13, Fracc. Península de Santiago, Santiago, Colima 28200,* ☎ *314/334–1313 or 877/527–6462,* FAX *314/334–1915. 325 suites. 3 restaurants, in-room safes, minibars, cable TV, 8 pools, gym, spa, beach, shops, children's programs (ages 4–12), concierge. AE, V.*

$$$–$$$$ **Las Hadas.** For many years Manzanillo's premier resort, Las Hadas still delights with its exotic, "nouveau-Moorish" buildings set among six hectares of beautiful, flower-and-vine-covered grounds. Room rates are high considering the lackadaisical maintenance, however, and the resort no longer attracts the jet-set crowd of its glory days. The hotel has its own golf course and looks over a gorgeous bay and marina, and Legazpi restaurant is the city's most elegant. ✉ *Av. De los Riscos y Vista Hermosa s/n, Península de Santiago, Zona Hotelera 28867,* ☎ *314/331–0101 or 888/559–4329,* FAX *314/331–0125,* WEB *www.brisas.com.mx. 184 rooms, 36 suites. 4 restaurants, room service, in-room safes, cable TV, 18-hole golf course, 10 tennis courts, 2 pools, hair salon,*

massage, beach, 3 bars, shops, baby-sitting, laundry service, concierge, travel services. AE, DC, MC, V.

$$$ 🏨 **Sierra.** This 19-story white stucco giant is popular with families (up to two children under age six stay free in their parents' room) and conventioneers. All of the 339 inviting rooms and suites have private balconies; many have a bay view. A large free-form pool, four tennis courts, and several bars and restaurants round out the property. Light-wood and pastel colors dominate the pleasant decor. The all-inclusive resort includes buffet meals, snacks, dinners at a gourmet restaurant, domestic drinks, tennis, and water sports such as kayaking and windsurfing. ✉ *Av. de la Audiencia 1, Playa La Audiencia 28200,* ☎ *314/333–2000 or 800/448–5028,* FAX *314/333–2272. 328 rooms, 11 suites. 3 restaurants, cable TV, 4 tennis courts, pool, beach, 4 bars, children's programs (ages 4–12), meeting rooms. AE, MC, V.*

$$ ★ 🏨 **Marina Puerto Dorado.** There are excellent views of the bay and harbor from this family hotel, which looks a lot like condos. With 40 suites, 10 of them penthouse suites with Jacuzzis and wet bars, this is a good bet for large families. Continental breakfast included in the reasonable room price makes this a great bargain. ✉ *Av. Lázaro Cárdenas 101, Fracc. Las Brisas Playa Azul 28200,* ☎ FAX *314/334–1480. 40 suites. Restaurant, pool, beach, 2 bars. AE, MC, V.*

$$ ★ 🏨 **La Posada.** This "passionate pink" hotel has been a favorite with North Americans since 1957. With only 23 rooms, most guests get to know each other well, mingling in the *sala,* a large, open-air living-dining area with a communal coffeepot. Rooms are comfortable but not at all fancy; there's one on the beach. Old iron keys work the antique locks. The room rate includes a complete breakfast; beer and soft-drink service is on the honor system. ✉ *Lazaro Cardenas 201, at the end of the Old Hwy to Santiago, Las Brisas 28200,* ☎ FAX *314/333–1899. 23 rooms. Snack bar, pool, beach, bar. MC, V.*

$–$$ 🏨 **Villas la Audiencia.** A block from the Las Hadas turnoff and about 1 km (½ mi) from the beach, this small white-and-red hotel and villa complex overlooks the Mantarraya golf course. Clean, air-conditioned rooms are motel-like, yet comfortable; special deals often make the one-, two-, and three-bedroom "villas" just a bit more expensive than the small, plain rooms. Free transportation is provided to the beach. The lack of an elevator means lots of trudging up and down stairs. ✉ *Av. de la Audiencia and Las Palmas, off Santiago-Manzanillo Rd., La Audencia 28860,* ☎ *314/333–0861,* FAX *314/333–2653. 20 rooms, 26 villas. Restaurant, pool. AE, MC, V.*

$ 🏨 **María Cristina.** A clean but drab two-story motel in the Santiago area, it's just four blocks from the beach. All rooms have limited cable TV, but only three—they call them "bungalows"—are air-conditioned; they're well worth the difference in price. ✉ *Calle 28 de Agosto 36, Santiago 28860,* ☎ *314/333–0966,* FAX *314/334–1430. 21 rooms. Cable TV, pool; no air-conditioning in some rooms. MC, V.*

$ 🏨 **Marbella.** This hotel is one of the few reasonably priced places on the beach, which faces the open ocean, not the bay. The best rooms are on the beach; each has a tiny balcony under the palms. The accommodations have tile floors, air-conditioning, and TV. There's a good Spanish/seafood restaurant, El Marinero. ✉ *Santiago-Manzanillo Rd. Km 9.5, Zona Hotelera 28869,* ☎ *314/333–1103,* FAX *314/333–1222. 92 rooms. Restaurant, pool, bar. AE, MC, V.*

Nightlife and the Arts

For a rowdy drinking and dancing scene, head for **Colima Bay Café** (✉ Av. Audencia Plaza Pacífico, Blvd. Costero 921, Zona Hotelera, ☎ 314/333–0168), which has become *the* in spot. To dance to live, authentic salsa and other tropical tunes, your best bet is **Tropigala** (✉ Blvd. Miguel de la Madrid Km 14, Zona Hotelera, ☎ 314/333–2474 or 314/333–2475). Some nights there are specials such as free dinner buffets or dance performances. Friday is ladies' night: no cover until 11 PM. **VOG** (✉ Blvd. Miguel de la Madrid Km 9.5, Zona Hotelera, ☎ 314/333–1875) plays disco music Thursday through Saturday.

Outdoor Activities and Sports

Fishing

Billed the "Sailfish Capital of the World," Manzanillo has fleets that regularly hook marlin, dorado, roosters, and tuna. Sportfishing charters are available at major hotels and through tour agencies. Contact **Ocean Pacific Tours** (☎ FAX 314/335–0605) to charter a 28-ft boat (1–5 people) for $195, or a 40-ft cruiser (1–10 people) for $245. Both tours last five hours and include a case of beer as well as the usual ice, bait, and tackle.

Golf

The nine-hole course at **Club Santiago** (☎ 314/335–0410), designed by Larry Hughes, has the usual amenities, including carts, caddies, pro shop, and restaurant. Robert Von Hagge mapped out the 27-hole course on **Isla Navidad** (☎ 314/335–6439). **La Mantarraya** (☎ 314/331–0101), the 18-hole golf course designed by Roy Dye at Las Hadas, has been rated among the world's 100 best courses by *Golf Digest*.

Water Sports

The rocky points off Manzanillo's peninsulas and coves make for good snorkeling and scuba diving. Kayaks, paddleboats, windsurfers, and snorkel and scuba gear can be rented at the Las Hadas and other major hotels and at La Audiencia beach.

Shopping

Most of the hotels offer a small selection of folk art and beachwear, but in general, shopping in Manzanillo is poor. There are some shops around the main square, hardly worth the trip downtown, and others at Plaza Manzanillo, a shopping center at Km 7.5 on the Santiago–Manzanillo Road. Most of the shops are closed 2–4; many are open Sunday 10–2. **Centro Artesenal Las Primaveras** (✉ Juárez 40, Santiago, ☎ 314/333–1699) has a huge assortment of handicrafts of so-so quality.

Side Trip

Colima

98 km (61 mi) northeast of Manzanillo.

Colima, the capital of the eponymous state, is about an hour from Manzanillo via an excellent toll road that continues on to Guadalajara. An easygoing provincial city, Colima is most famous for the pre-Hispanic "Colima dog" figurines, which originated in this region and are on display—along with other archaeological pieces—at the **Museo de las Culturas del Occidente** (Museum of Western Cultures; ✉ Casa de la Cultura, Calzada Galván and Av. Manuel Gallardo, ☎ 312/313–0608; closed Mon.). The **Museo Universitario de Culturas Populares** (University Museum of Popular Culture; ✉ Calle Gabino Barreda and Manuel Gallardo, ☎ 312/312–6869) has a large collection of pre-Hispanic and contemporary Indian costumes, masks, instruments, and other artifacts. Entry to the museum, which is open Tuesday–Sunday 10–2 and 5–8, is free. The town of **Comala,** a 15-minute ride north of Colima, is noted for hand-carved furniture and ironwork.

Manzanillo A to Z

AIR TRAVEL

You can fly to Manzanillo from several United States cities as well as Mexico City.

CARRIERS

Aeroméxico has daily flights from Houston, Los Angeles, and Atlanta, with a plane change in Mexico City. Mexicana serves via Mexico City. Alaska Airlines flies out of Los Angeles. America West has twice-weekly flights from Phoenix. AeroCalifornia flies in from Mexico City and Los Angeles daily.

➤ AIRLINES AND CONTACTS: **AeroCalifornia** (☎ 314/334–1414). **Aeroméxico** (☎ 314/333–0151). **Alaska Airlines** (☎ 800/426–0333). **America West** (☎ 800/363–2597). **Mexicana** (☎ 314/333–2323).

AIRPORTS AND TRANSFERS

Manzanillo's Aeropuerto Internacional Playa de Oro is 32 km (20 mi) north of town, on the way to Barra de Navidad. Volkswagen vans transport passengers from the airport to major resorts; these shuttles are less expensive than taxis.

➤ AIRPORT INFORMATION: **Aeropuerto Internacional Playa de Oro** (☎ 314/333–2525).

BUS TRAVEL

The resorts in the Manzanillo area are several miles from the main bus stop (✉ Blvd. Costero Miguel de la Madrid Km 13.5), but city buses regularly make the trip, which costs 50¢. For longer trips, Elite and Estrella Blanca serve Manzanillo; the former has a longer list of destination cities. Primera Plus serves Puerto Vallarta, Guadalajara, Tijuana, Mexico City, Acapulco, and smaller coastal towns. ETN has comfortable buses with wide, almost totally reclining seats, to Guadalajara, Colima, Morelia, and Mexico City.

➤ BUS INFORMATION: **Elite** (☎ 314/332–0432). **Estrella Blanca** (☎ 314/332–0432). **ETN** (☎ 314/334–1050). **Primera Plus** (☎ 314/332–0515).

CAR RENTAL

Hertz has compact and midsize cars with and without air-conditioning. Dollar has no airport booth but will pick customers up there; they offer sedans, VW bugs, and minivans. National also has a desk at the airport.

➤ MAJOR AGENCIES: **Dollar** (✉ Hotel Karmina Palace, Zona Hotelera, ☎ 314/334–1313). **Hertz** (✉ Blvd. Costero Miguel de la Madrid 1246-B, Zona Hotelera, ☎ 314/333–3141). **National** (✉ Blvd. Costero Miguel de la Madrid 1070, Zona Hotelera, ☎ 314/333–1140).

CAR TRAVEL

The trip south from the Arizona border to Manzanillo is about 2,419 km (1,500 mi); from Guadalajara, it is 332 km (206 mi) over mostly well-kept highways; from Puerto Vallarta, 242 km (150 mi) on Highway 200, which winds through the mountains beginning in Tepic, in the state of Nayarit.

A car is almost essential for exploring the area on your own. Considering the high cost of rental cars, some folks opt to hire a taxi—about $13 per hour, or $50–$80 per day, depending on your destination. Agree on a price beforehand.

EMERGENCIES

There is no general emergency number in Manzanillo, so call the police, hospital, or fire department directly.

➤ CONTACTS: **Fire Department** (☎ 314/312–5858). **Hospital de Manzanillo** (☎ 314/336–7272). **Police** (☎ 314/334–0557 or 314/336–7300). **Public Security** (☎ 314/332–1004). **Red Cross** (☎ 314/336–5770).

TOURS

Manzanillo is spread out; you might consider a guided tour to get the lay of the land. More appealing, though, than the city tours are the sportfishing trips, sunset cruises, horseback outings, and excursions to Colima, Comala, and the volcanoes that can be arranged through area travel agencies.

Bahías Gemelas Agencia de Viajes offers city, walking, fishing, and horseback-riding tours. Viajes Héctur offers the same tours as Bahía Gemelas, plus shopping, bay cruises, tours on four-wheelers, and day excursions to the beach or area banana plantations.

➤ TOUR OPERATOR RECOMMENDATIONS: **Bahías Gemelas Agencia de Viajes** (✉ Blvd. Costero Miguel de la Madrid 1556, Zona Hotelera, ☎ 314/333–1000). **Hectour** (✉ Blvd. Costero Miguel de la Madrid 3147, Zona Hotelera, ☎ 314/333–1707).

VISITOR INFORMATION

The State Tourism Office is open weekdays 9–3 and 5–7, Saturday 10–2. The Municipal Tourism office is open weekdays 8–2.

➤ TOURIST INFORMATION: **Municipal Tourism Office** (✉ Juárez 100, Centro, ☎ 314/332–6238). **State Tourism Office** (✉ Blvd. Costero Miguel de la Madrid 1033, Zona Hotelera, ☎ 314/333–2277).

IXTAPA/ZIHUATANEJO

One of the most appealing of the Pacific Coast destinations, Ixtapa/Zihuatanejo is a taste of Mexico present and past. Ixtapa (pronounced eesh-*tah*-pa), where most Americans stay—probably because they can't pronounce Zihuatanejo (see-wa-ta-*nay*-ho)—is young and glitzy. Exclusively a vacation resort, it was created in the 1970s by Mexico's National Fund for Tourism Development, which also dreamed up Cancún and Huatulco, and developed Los Cabos. High-rise chains in the hotel zone rent water-sports equipment, and rocky islets offshore help to protect the ocean-facing beach from rough surf. Across the road from the hotel zone are clusters of commercial plazas housing cafés, restaurants, and shops.

Zihuatanejo, only 7 km (4 mi) down the coast (southeast) from Ixtapa, is an old fishing village on a picturesque sheltered bay. Until the advent of Ixtapa, it was hardly known. But long before Columbus sailed to America, Zihuatanejo was a retreat for indigenous nobility. Figurines, ceramics, stone carvings, and stelae verify the presence of civilizations dating as far back as the Olmecs (3000 BC). Weaving was likely the dominant industry, as evidenced by pre-Hispanic figurines, bobbins, and other related artifacts found in the area. The original Nahuatl name, Cihuatlán, means "place of women."

In 1527, Spanish conquistadors launched a trade route from Zihuatanejo Bay to the Orient. Galleons returned with silks, spices, and, according to some historians, the Americas' first coconut palms, brought from the Philippines. But the Spaniards did little colonizing here. A scout sent by Cortés reported back to the conquistador that the place was nothing great, tagging the name Cihuatlán with the less-than-flattering suffix "ejo"—hence "Zihuatanejo."

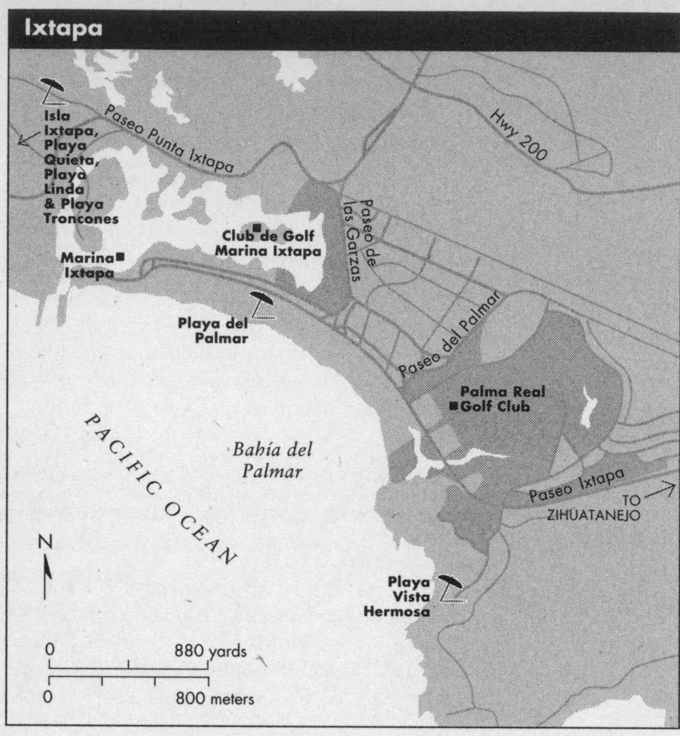

With the arrival of Highway 200 in the 1960s and the construction of Ixtapa the following decade, Zihuatanejo began to grow, and now its streets have been paved in brick. The place has managed to retain its charm, even if its malecón and narrow streets are lined with hotels, restaurants, and shops. Zihuatanejo is also home to some of Mexico's most exclusive boutique hotels, attracting discerning clients who prefer the intimacy of these secluded settings to the comfortable but more mainstream high-rises in neighboring Ixtapa.

Exploring Ixtapa/Zihuatanejo

Ixtapa and Zihuatanejo have few sights per se, but they're both pleasant places to stroll—the former especially if you enjoy a modern beach ambience and shops, the latter if you prefer local color.

A Good Tour

The **hotel zone** in **Ixtapa** extends along a 3-km (2-mi) strip of wide, sandy beach called Playa del Palmar, on the open Pacific. It's fun to walk along the beach to check out the various hotel scenes and water-sports activities. Alternatively, you can stroll the length of the zone on Paseo Ixtapa, a nicely landscaped and immaculate thoroughfare lined with a series of Mexican village–style shopping malls. At one end of the hotel zone (when you enter from Zihuatanejo) is the 18-hole Ixtapa Golf Club, and on the other (generally described as being "up the coast," but actually lying to the northwest) you'll come to the Marina Ixtapa development, with a 600-slip yacht marina, a promenade with restaurants and shops, and the 18-hole Marina Golf Course. If you want to venture out of this compact resort area, take a taxi 15 minutes up the coast to **Playa Linda.** It's a 10-minute boat ride from here to **Ixtapa Island,** where you can spend the day eating, sunning, and swimming.

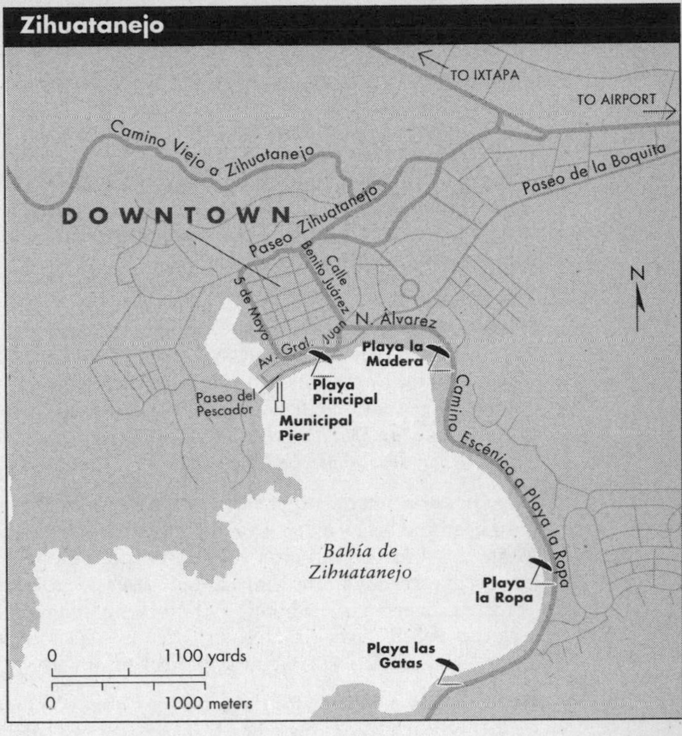

The town of **Zihuatanejo** (population about 37,000) lies near the back of a deep, enclosed bay with calm beaches. A simple way to tour the town is to take a taxi to the municipal pier (*muelle*), from which skiffs continually depart for the 10-minute ride to **Playa las Gatas,** most easily accessible by water. The sportfishing boats depart from this pier, too, and it's the beginning of the **Paseo del Pescador** (Fisherman's Walk), or malecón, which runs along the main beach, the most picturesque part of the town itself. The brick-paved seaside path, only ½ km (⅓ mi) long, is lined with small restaurants and overflowing shops; you'll pass a basketball court that doubles as the town square. The malecón ends at the **Museo Arqueológico de la Costa Grande** (✉ east end of Paseo del Pescador, ☎ 755/554–7552), where pre-Hispanic murals, maps, and archaeological pieces describing the Olmec, Tarascan, and Aztec cultures are on permanent display. It's open Tuesday–Sunday 9–6; admission is 50¢. If you continue beyond the museum, you can take a footpath cut into the rocks to **Playa la Madera.**

Beaches

Ixtapa

Ixtapa Island. The most popular beach on Ixtapa Island (and closest to the boat dock) is Playa Cuachalalate, named for a local tree whose bark has been used as a remedy for kidney ailments since ancient times. This beach is lined with seafood eateries and water equipment concessions and is excellent for swimming. A short walk across to the other side of the island takes you to the gorgeous Varadero Beach, also with informal eateries and water-sports equipment rentals. Just behind the restaurants is Playa Coral, with crystal-clear water that's ideal for snorkeling. Playa Carey, toward the south end of the island, is small and isolated. Pangas run between the boat landings at both Cuachalalate and Varadero beaches and Playa Linda on the mainland.

Playa del Palmar. Ixtapa's main beach, this 3-km-long (2-mi-long) broad sandy stretch runs along the hotel zone. Water-sports equipment is rented at many hotel concessions to guests and others. Since this is essentially open sea, the surf can be quite strong.

Playa Linda and Playa Quieta. About 10 minutes north of the Ixtapa hotel zone, thatch-roof restaurants dispense beer, sodas, and the catch of the day. The beach is protected by Ixtapa Island offshore, as is pretty Playa Linda, just beyond. Playa Linda is bordered at one end by an estuary with birds and gators, horses can be rented, and boats ($4 round-trip) run continually to Ixtapa Island.

Zihuatanejo

Playa la Madera. Across Zihuatanejo Bay from la Playa Principal, tiny Playa la Madera can be reached via a seaside footpath cut into the rocks. Also accessible by car, this pancake-flat beach has a sprinkling of small hotels and restaurants. It was named *madera,* or "wood," beach because it was a Spanish port for shipping oak, pine, cedar, and mahogany cut from the nearby Sierra Madre del Sur.

Playa la Ropa. On the other side of a rocky point, Playa la Ropa is the most beautiful beach in the area; it's a five-minute taxi ride from town. Along this 1-km (½-mi) stretch of soft sand are open-air restaurants (complete with hammocks for post-meal siestas), a few hotels, and rental of wave runners, banana boats, and snorkel equipment. It got its name ("clothes beach") when a cargo of Oriental silks and clothing washed ashore from a Spanish galleon shipwrecked offshore.

Playa las Gatas. Named for the *gatas* (nurse sharks) that used to linger here, this beach has a long row of hewn rocks just offshore that serves as a breakwater. Legend has it that a Tarascan king built it to shelter his royal daughter's private beach, now lined with simple seafood eateries that provide lounge chairs for sunning. The clear waters are ideal for swimming, snorkeling, and diving. You can walk to Las Gatas in about 20 minutes from La Ropa beach; most folks come in pangas that run continuously to and from the municipal pier from 8 to 5. Purchase your round-trip ticket (about $3.50) at the Cooperativa office at the pier; keep the ticket stub for your return trip.

Playa Principal. At the edge of town, the town's picturesque main beach (aka Playa Municipal) is rimmed by the Paseo del Pescador. Here local fishermen keep their skiffs and gear, used for nightly fishing journeys out to sea. They return here in the early morning to sell their catch to the local townspeople and to restaurateurs.

Dining

Ixtapa

$$$–$$$$ ✕ **Bogart's.** Anyone who's been to any of the links in the Krystal hotel chain is familiar with the strikingly Moroccan flavor of this exotic (and expensive) eatery. Tables are separated by palm trees, and a Moorish fountain and piano music add to the movie-theme atmosphere. The international menu includes Suprema Casablanca, breaded chicken breasts stuffed with lobster. ✉ *Krystal Ixtapa, Blvd. Ixtapa,* ☏ *755/553–0303. Reservations essential. MC, V. No lunch.*

$$–$$$ ★ ✕ **Beccofino.** This marina-side restaurant is always crowded, even when its neighbors are empty. That's partly due to the elegant yet accessible atmosphere. Dark, polished wood contrasts nicely with bright white linens; outside, there's alfresco seating on a canopied deck adjacent to the water. Among the best dishes on the Northern Italian menu are minestrone soup, *caprese* salad (with tomatoes, basil, and mozzarella), fish fillet (usually red snapper or mahimahi) with a champagne sauce,

salmon ravioli in cream, and chicken cacciatore. ✉ *Plaza Marina Ixtapa,* ☎ *755/553–1770. Reservations essential. AE, MC, V.*

$$–$$$ ✕ **El Galeón.** Seafood lovers and people-watchers like to settle in at Marina Ixtapa's nautical-decor bar, strewn with lots of rope and rigging, a ship's wheel, and other maritime knickknacks. Sit at the outdoor terrace or on a simulated galleon right on the water. The fresh tuna steak is outstanding, as are the pastas; upscale Mexican fare is also available. ✉ *Plaza Marina Ixtapa,* ☎ *755/553–2150. AE, MC, V.*

$–$$ ✕ **Casa Morelos.** Positioned next to party-hearty Señor Frog's, Casa Morelos offers excellent Mexican seafood on the patio or inside, where hand-loomed spreads, ochre walls, and wood furnishings give a homey feel. The *chile relleno de mariscos* (roasted chili stuffed with seafood), fish and octopus fajitas, and tuna steak topped with seven kinds of dry chilies are all filling and delicious. Save room for a margarita and a dance next door at Señor Frog's. Or, come for breakfast: la Casa opens at 7:30 AM. ✉ *La Puerta shopping center,* ☎ *755/553–0578. MC, V.*

$–$$ ✕ **El Infierno y la Gloria.** "Hell and Paradise" is both cantina and restaurant serving an array of dishes from throughout Mexico. The food is good, and you'll admire the walls, hand-painted with extravagant scenes and allegories. It opens early (8 AM) and closes around midnight. ✉ *La Puerta shopping center,* ☎ *755/553–0304. AE, MC, V.*

$–$$ ✕ **Mamma Norma & Deborah.** You can dine indoors or alfresco at this lively, casual restaurant/bar, which has the best pizza in town as well as tasty seafood, hummus with pita bread, vegetarian dishes, and wholesome salads. ✉ *La Puerta shopping center,* ☎ *755/553–0274. Reservations not accepted. MC, V.*

$ ✕ **Nueva Zelanda.** Although open all day, this sparkling little coffee shop is best known for its tasty breakfasts. This location opened after the success of the original eatery in downtown Zihuatanejo. Both kitchens produce fresh tropical fruit juices, fruit salads, and a variety of *tortas,* sandwiches on large, crusty rolls. ✉ *Los Patios shopping center, behind bandstand,* ☎ *755/554–2340;* ✉ *Calle Cuauhtémoc 30, Zihuatanejo,* ☎ *755/553–0838. Reservations not accepted. No credit cards.*

Zihuatanejo

$$ ✕ **Coconuts.** Its name reminiscent of Ixtapa's previous status as a coconut plantation, this downtown venue has become one of the top restaurants in Zihuatanejo. Under the direction of chef Patricia Cummings, Coconuts serves a variety of dishes, including roast pork loin, seafood tacos, sweet and zesty coconut shrimp, and a number of vegetarian items. Five different dessert coffees are prepared flaming at your table. Lunch is served noon–4, dinner 6–11. ✉ *Agustín Ramírez 1,* ☎ *755/554–2518. AE, DC, MC, V. Closed mid-July–mid-Oct.*

$$ ✕ **Rossy.** A local favorite for dining on the roof terrace or right on the beach, Rossy specializes in Mexican-style seafood, including a tempting shrimp-and-pineapple brochette. Musicians usually serenade diners on weekends. ✉ *South end of Playa la Ropa,* ☎ *755/554–4004. MC, V.*

$–$$ ✕ **Casa Elvira.** Named for the owner and onetime chef, this local institution near the town pier has a pleasant dining room and serves a variety of consistently good seafood and Mexican dishes. Lobster is the house specialty. ✉ *Paseo del Pescador 8,* ☎ *755/554–2061. MC, V.*

$–$$ ✕ **Kau-Kan.** Opened in the mid-1990s, this restaurant quickly became a local favorite. Owner-chef Ricardo Rodriguez, previously of Casa Que Canta, serves imaginative, exquisitely prepared seafood, including fillet of sea bass, melt-in-your-mouth abalone, and grilled mahimahi under a sweet, spicy pineapple sauce. Kau-Kan enjoys a gorgeous location overlooking Zihuatanejo Bay and is probably the most elegant restaurant in town. ✉ *Carretera Escénica, Playa la Ropa Lote 7,* ☎ *755/554–8446. AE, MC, V. No lunch.*

$–$$ ✕ **Paul's.** Like many of Mexico's other high-end eateries, Paul's doesn't open until 2 PM, but it's got some of the best food in town. The zany Swiss-German owner seems to have created an eclectic lifestyle here, and he may well greet you dressed in shorts and an unbuttoned Hawaiian shirt. Notwithstanding his fashion choices, Paul has crafted a small international menu of wonderful dishes. Start with a fresh artichoke or escargot appetizer or the lentil soup, followed by quail, pork chops, or poached mahimahi served with a dill sauce. ✉ *Benito Juárez 23,* ☎ *755/554–6528. MC, V. Closed May.*

$ ✕ **Casa Puntarenas.** Talk about homey: Casa Puntarenas is not only family-owned and -operated, but run out of the family residence. Select from a paper menu of seafood and Mexican specialties, which later becomes your check. To get here, cross the footbridge over the lagoon at the west end of town near the pier (or take a taxi). Come for breakfast until 11:30, or for the evening meal from 6:30 to 9. ✉ *Noria 12,* ☎ *755/554–2109. Reservations not accepted. No credit cards. Closed mid-Mar.–mid-Dec. No lunch.*

$ ✕ **La Mordida.** Join the throngs after 4 PM at this simple, popular eatery for pizza and tasty charcoal-broiled burgers. Although in Mexico "una mordida" usually refers to a bribe or a payoff, here it refers to its more literal meaning: "a bite." ✉ *Paseo de la Boquita 20,* ☎ *755/554–8216. Reservations not accepted. No credit cards. No lunch.*

$ ✕ **La Perla.** Eat indoors if you want sports-bar action, or begin your day at the beach with an omelet or invigorating ceviche in the alfresco patio overlooking Playa la Ropa. Among the seafood specialties, *filete La Perla* (fish fillet baked with cheese) is a favorite. ✉ *Playa la Ropa,* ☎ *755/554–2700. Reservations not accepted. AE, MC, V.*

$ ✕ **La Sirena Gorda.** Oil paintings and a bronze statue depict the namesake "fat mermaid" at this friendly restaurant near the pier. Specialties include seafood tacos and octopus kebab. The setting is casual, with an outdoor patio and a lively bar. ✉ *Paseo del Pescador 90,* ☎ *755/554–2687. Reservations not accepted. MC, V.*

Lodging

Pricier Ixtapa specializes in deluxe, beachfront properties located along Playa del Palmar. Most of the budget accommodations are in Zihuatanejo, where the most glamorous hotels are on or overlooking La Madera or La Ropa beach, and the least expensive are downtown. For out-of-the-way seclusion, venture to the tiny beach of Troncones, about 30 minutes northwest of Zihuatanejo by car.

Ixtapa

$$$$ ★ 🏨 **Las Brisas Ixtapa.** This immense, pyramid-shape architectural wonder slopes down a hillside to its own secluded cove and beach, Playa Vista Hermosa. The grounds are lush with jungle vegetation; fresh flowers decorate your room. Every unit has a private balcony with a hammock, ocean view, and a table for room-service dining; junior suites have larger balconies with hot tubs. Guests and nonguests enjoy the hotel's excellent Portofino and El Mexicano restaurants. ✉ *Playa Vista Hermosa, Apdo. 97, 40880,* ☎ *755/553–2121 or 888/559–4329,* FAX *755/553–0751,* WEB *www.brisas.com.mx. 423 rooms, 19 suites. 3 restaurants, room service, in-room safes, cable TV, 4 tennis courts, 4 pools, gym, hair salon, 2 bars, children's programs (ages 3–7), laundry service, concierge floor, business services, meeting rooms, travel services, car rental, no-smoking rooms. AE, DC, MC, V.*

$$$$ 🏨 **Presidente Inter-Continental Ixtapa.** One of Ixtapa's best all-inclusive properties, the Presidente has 24-hour beverage service, and various recreational activities—most of them centered on the pool. Rooms

are attractively decorated in creams and whites, and rates include all meals. If you want tranquility, request a room near the east pool, away from the action. ✉ *Blvd. Ixtapa s/n, 40880,* ☎ *755/553–0018 or 800/327–0200,* FAX *755/553–2312,* WEB *www.ixtapa.interconti.com. 420 rooms and suites. 4 restaurants, minibars, cable TV, 2 tennis courts, 2 pools, gym, sauna, steam room, beach, snorkeling, basketball, volleyball, bar, children's programs (ages 3–10), laundry service, concierge, meeting rooms, car rental, no-smoking rooms. AE, DC, MC, V.*

$$$ **Dorado Pacífico.** This privately owned beachfront hotel is known for its fine food and good service. The huge pool, with two water slides, makes it a favorite with youngsters. Modern rooms are decorated in soft colors, and all have ocean views. Glass elevators look out on the dramatic atrium lobby. Try the beachside Cebolla Roja restaurant for dinner. ✉ *Blvd. Ixtapa, 40880,* ☎ *755/553–2025 or 888/738–4205,* FAX *755/553–0126. 285 rooms and suites. 4 restaurants, minibars, cable TV, 2 tennis courts, pool, massage, 2 bars, shop, children's programs (ages 10+), meeting rooms, travel services, car rental. AE, MC, V.*

$$$ **Krystal Ixtapa.** Shaped like a boat with its bow pointing to the sea, this beachfront hotel is comfortable if lacking in charm. Rooms are standard contemporary style with ocean views. The Club Krystalito provides recreational activities for children, and because of its meeting facilities, the hotel is often filled with conventioneers. The Krystal is home to Christine, Ixtapa's most popular disco, and Bogart's. ✉ *Blvd. Ixtapa, 40880,* ☎ *755/553–0333 or 800/231–9860,* FAX *755/553–0336,* WEB *www.krystal.com.mx. 254 rooms, 20 suites. 4 restaurants, coffee shop, in-room safes, cable TV, 2 tennis courts, pool, gym, hair salon, dance club, children's programs (ages 3–10), concierge, meeting rooms, car rental, travel services, no-smoking floor. AE, DC, MC, V.*

$$ **Best Western Posada Real.** Despite its location in the midst of the hotel zone, there is a certain casual charm that makes this pleasant hotel more intimate than most of the others in Ixtapa. A good value, the beachfront low-rise has amenities such as a swim-up bar and putting green; rooms have remote-control satellite TV. ✉ *Blvd. Ixtapa s/n, 40880,* ☎ *755/553–1745 or 800/528–1234,* FAX *755/553–1805,* WEB *www.bestwestern.com. 110 rooms. Restaurant, cable TV, putting green, 2 pools, hot tub, volleyball, bar, shop, laundry service, car rental, travel services. AE, MC, V.*

Troncones

$$ **Casa Ki.** Bungalows at this homey haven in the wilds of Troncones have tiny refrigerators, but guests may also use the fully equipped kitchen and barbecue, and breakfast is included in the rates. The house, which can accommodate four adults and two children, has a full kitchen as well as two bedrooms, living room, and larger bath. ✉ *Troncones Beach, Apdo. 405, Zihuatanejo 40880,* ☎ *755/553–2815,* FAX *755/553–2417. 3 bungalows, 1 house. Beach. No credit cards.*

$ **El Burro Borracho.** Six comfortable stone cottages sit right on the 5-km-long (3-mi-long) beach. Relax in a hammock on your private patio, or go beachcombing, boogie-boarding, hiking, or cave exploring. Afterward, retreat to the congenial bar-restaurant, with menu options ranging from cheeseburgers to fresh lobster. For even cheaper digs, trailer spaces are available. Owners Dewey and Carolyn also own Casa de la Tortuga B&B, just up the beach. ✉ *Troncones Beach, Apdo. 277, Zihuatanejo 40880,* ☎ *755/553–2800,* FAX *755/553–2807. 6 bungalows. Restaurant, beach, hiking. No credit cards. Closed Sept.–Oct.*

Zihuatanejo

$$$$ ✕ **Casa Cuitlateca.** The smallest of Zihuatanejo's boutique hotels opened high above the bay, with spectacular views from three of the four individually decorated rooms. Rooms have handmade furnishings and

arts and crafts from four Mexican states. A beautiful infinity pool is surrounded by a small fishpond, and there's a cool-water whirlpool on the villa's rooftop. The patio restaurant, open to the public for dinner only, serves a nightly, prix fixe multicourse meal. The hotel's staff offers personalized attention and will arrange nearly any excursion you can think of. Unless one group books the entire hotel, children under 16 are not permitted. ✉ *Calle Playa la Ropa, Apdo. 124, 40880,* ☎ *755/554–2448 or 877/541–1234,* FAX *755/554–7394,* WEB *www.casacuitlateca.com. 3 rooms, 1 suite. Restaurant, pool, hot tub. AE, MC, V.*

$$$$ ★ **La Casa Que Canta.** One of the loveliest small hotels in the world, "The House That Sings" clings to a cliffside above Playa la Ropa. The lobby and rooms are adorned with folk-art furnishings, and each suite boasts gorgeous bay views from both the bedroom balcony and living-room terrace. Huge bathrooms and fresh flower petals on your bed are two of the hotel's hallmarks. Because of the stepped architecture, the main swimming pool seems to be airborne; below, a saltwater pool features a sea Jacuzzi (the beach is a short walk away). The outdoor restaurant serves Mexican and seafood dishes and opens to the public after 7 PM (reservations required). Children under 16 are not accepted at the hotel. ✉ *Camino Escénico a Playa la Ropa, 40880,* ☎ *755/554–6529 or 888/523–5050,* FAX *755/554–7900,* WEB *www.casaquecanta.com. 25 suites. Restaurant, in-room safes, minibars, pool, saltwater pool, gym, hot tub. AE, DC, MC, V.*

$$$–$$$$ **Villa del Sol.** This luxury hotel is set amid coconut palms, lush tropical gardens, fountains, and meandering paths leading to lovely Playa la Ropa. German-owned and -run, it is popular with European travelers. Rooms are artistically designed, with king-size beds draped in canopies, folk-art furnishings, and terraces or balconies. Beachfront and lagoon suites are much nicer than lower-price rooms. Elegant meals are served at the Villa del Sol restaurant, whereas the Cantina Bar and Grill is more casual. The Modified American Plan (including breakfast and dinner) is required in high season, when kids under 14 are not allowed. ✉ *Playa la Ropa, Apdo. 84, 40880,* ☎ *755/554–2239 or 888/389–2645,* FAX *755/554–2758,* WEB *www.hotelvilladelsol.com. 54 suites. 2 restaurants, in-room safes, cable TV, 2 tennis courts, 4 pools, beach, travel services, no-smoking rooms. AE, MC, V.*

$$ **Ávila.** Although somewhat institutional in character, this hotel is well situated in the center of town facing the beach at Paseo del Pescador. The large, clean rooms have TVs, air-conditioning, and ceiling fans. Visiting fisherfolk like to stay here during the March tournaments. ✉ *Calle Juan N. Álvarez 8, 40880,* ☎ *755/554–2010,* FAX *755/554–3299. 26 rooms. AE, MC, V.*

$$ **Bungalows Pacíficos.** Perched on three terraces above Playa la Madera, spacious but plain bungalows have no air-conditioning or TV, but do offer a sweeping view of the bay from the veranda, equipped with hammock, table, and chairs. Walk to Zihuatanejo's restaurants, just 10 minutes away, or cook in the room's fully equipped kitchen. The owner, who speaks Spanish, English, and German, enjoys sharing her knowledge of prime birding sites with her guests. ✉ *Cerro de la Madera, Apdo. 12, 40880,* ☎ FAX *755/554–2112,* WEB *www.zihuatanejo-ixtapa.com.mx/bungalowspacificos. 6 units. No credit cards.*

$$ **Irma.** One of Zihuatanejo's originals, this simple but comely colonial-style hotel sits on a bluff overlooking Madera Beach (accessible by a stairway). Rooms have both air-conditioning and fans, gleaming red-tile floors, and whitewashed walls with hand-painted headboards; those on the sixth floor have been remodeled. Ask for a room with a balcony and ocean view. ✉ *Playa la Madera s/n, Apdo. 4, 40880,* ☎ *755/554–2105,* FAX *755/554–3738,* WEB *www.ixtapazihuatanejo.com.mx/irma. 72 rooms. Restaurant, 2 pools, bar. AE, MC, V.*

$$ **Solimar Inn Suites.** Located on a quiet plaza four blocks from the main beach, this family-owned hotel has 12 suites with separate bedroom and both air-conditioning and fan. Thick white walls, tile floors, and bright accent colors give the rooms a distinctly Mediterranean flavor. Living/dining rooms have equipped kitchenettes, cable TV, and built-in couches that double as beds. Long-term guests receive discounts; some rent a blender, microwave, or coffeepot and stay for weeks. ✉ *Plazas los Faroles, 40880,* ☎ FAX *755/554–3692,* WEB *www.ixtapa-zihuatanejo.com/solimarinn. 12 rooms. Pool, bar. AE, MC, V.*

$$ **Villas Miramar.** Most of the rooms have views of the exuberant gardens; a few overlook Madera Beach. All have a small balcony and are decorated in Mexican folk art and cooled by ceiling fans as well as air-conditioning. An extra $50 gets you a two-bedroom suite with equipped kitchenette, living/dining room, and a larger terrace overlooking the sea. ✉ *Playa la Madera, Apdo. 211, 40880,* ☎ *755/554–2106,* FAX *755/554–2149. 16 rooms, 2 suites. Restaurant, 2 pools, bar. AE, MC, V.*

$–$$ **Catalina-Sotavento.** Really two hotels in one, this multilevel oldie-but-goodie sits on a cliff overlooking the bay. Below, accessible by extensive stairs, are Playa la Ropa and the hotel's beach bar and lounge chairs. Rooms are large and well maintained, with ceiling fans (but no air-conditioning) and ample terraces sporting hammocks and a chaise longue. ✉ *Playa la Ropa, Apdo. 2, 40880,* ☎ *755/554–2032,* FAX *755/554–2975. 126 rooms. 2 restaurants, pool, 4 bars, travel services. AE, DC, MC, V.*

Nightlife

A good way to start an evening is a happy hour at one of Ixtapa or Zihuatanejo's hotel bars. In Zihuatanejo, that will exhaust your nightlife options; all of the following are in Ixtapa. Sunset is an important daily ritual, and plans should be made accordingly. Tops for sunset viewing (with live music) is the beachfront **Lobby Bar** (☎ 755/553–2121) at the Las Brisas resort. **Christine** (☎ 755/553–0333), at the Krystal, is the town's most expensive disco, featuring varied music and high-tech light shows. You'll get a gorgeous nighttime view from atop the 85-ft-high faux-lighthouse tower of **El Faro** (☎ 755/553–2090), attached to El Galeón restaurant, in Marina Ixtapa. There's live piano music nightly, and if you sing well, Raymundo will invite you to croon a tune as he tickles the ivories.

Carlos 'n' Charlie's (✉ Playa el Palmar s/n, next to the Best Western Posada Real, ☎ 755/553–0085) has a party atmosphere, with late-night dancing on a raised platform by the beach. There's a desert-inspired disco, complete with blue sky and cactus, at **La Valentina** restaurant-video-bar-disco complex (✉ Blvd. Ixtapa next to the Radisson hotel, ☎ 755/553–1190). Or head over to often-rowdy **Señor Frog's** (✉ Centro Comercial La Puerta, opposite the Hotel Riviera Beach, ☎ 755/553–0692) for tequila shots and dancing. Except for the casual spots like Señor Frog's and Carlos 'n' Charlie's, most discos have dress codes, and may turn you away if you're wearing shorts or tennis shoes (also for men, tank tops or sandals).

A number of hotels feature **Mexican Fiesta** nights with buffets and folkloric dance performances. In high season you'll find Mexican Fiesta night Monday at the Hotel Krystal, Tuesday at the Dorado Pacífico, and Wednesday at the Barceló.

Outdoor Activities and Sports

Fishing

The area is best known for its feisty sailfish, hooked year-round. Seasonally one finds yellowfin tuna and yellowtail jacks, dorado, blue and black marlin, as well as mackerel, barracuda, bonito, and others. **Cooperativo Benito Juárez** (✉ Paseo del Pescador 20, Zihuatanejo municipal pier, ☎ 755/554–3758) offers day trips in boats from 26 to 36 ft. Prices range from $150 for up to four for close-to-shore fishing in a motor launch to $270 for deep-sea fishing. Another Zihuatanejo cooperative venture with similar prices is **Cooperativo de Pescadores** (✉ Paseo del Pescador 81, ☎ 755/554–2056). Bookings and information about sportfishing can be obtained through **Ixtapa Sportfishing Charters** (✉ 19 Depue La., Stroudsburg, PA 18360, ☎ 570/688–9466, FAX 570/688–9554). Cost ranges from $190 for 1–2 people to a luxury yacht accommodating 6 people for $900.

Golf

There are two 18-hole championship courses in Ixtapa. Each par-72 course has its own clubhouse with a restaurant, tennis courts, and pool. Part of the Marina Ixtapa complex, the challenging **Club de Golf Marina Ixtapa** (☎ 755/553–1410) was designed by Robert Von Hagge. Greens fees are $61 (including caddie or cart). The **Palma Real Golf Club** (☎ 755/553–1062), designed by Robert Trent Jones Jr., is on a wildlife preserve that runs from a coconut plantation to the beach. A round costs $48, plus cart ($25) and/or caddie ($6).

Horseback Riding

You can rent horses with guides at **Rancho Playa Linda** (☎ 755/554–3085) just up the coast from Ixtapa. **VIPSA** (☎ 755/553–2214 or 755/553–1858) tour operators also can arrange riding tours.

Scuba Diving

More than 30 dive sites in the area range from deep canyons to shallow reefs. The waters here are teeming with sea life, and visibility is generally excellent. On Ixtapa Island, **Centro de Buceo Oliverio** (✉ Playa de Cuachalalate, ☎ 755/554–3992) provides rental equipment, instruction, and guided dives ($50 per tank). Owned and operated by NAUI (National Association of Underwater Instructors) master diver and marine biologist Juan Barnard, the **Zihuatanejo Scuba Center** (✉ Centro Comercial Ixtapa, behind Restaurant Rafaello's, ☎ 755/553–0288) in Ixtapa runs one- and two-tank dives as well as five-day certification courses.

Tennis

All major Ixtapa hotels have lighted tennis courts. At the **Club de Golf Marina Ixtapa** (☎ 755/553–1410), fees are $10–$12 and equipment rentals are available. Fees are $10–$12 at the **Palma Real Golf Club** (☎ 755/553–1062 or 755/553–1163), where you can also rent equipment. In Zihuatanejo, **Villa del Sol** (☎ 755/554–2239) has courts available to nonguests.

Water Park

A treat for children is a trip to **Magic World** (✉ Paseo de las Garzas s/n, next to Ixtapa Palace Hotel, ☎ 755/553–1359), with wave pools, water slides, an artificial lake for boating, a pirate ship, and several restaurants. It's open Tuesday–Sunday 10:30–5:30 and costs about $6.50 per person.

Water Sports

You'll find a variety of water sports along Playa del Palmar in Ixtapa. Parasailing costs about $22 for an eight-minute ride or $32 for 15 minutes; waterskiing runs about $38 per half hour; banana-boat rides are about $5.50 per person for a 20-minute trip. On Playa la Ropa, next to La Perla restaurant in Zihuatanejo, Hobie Cats rent for about $27 an hour depending on the size of the boat, and classes cost $25 per half hour. Windsurfers—when you can find them—rent for $20 per hour; classes, which include six hours over four days, cost $40.

Shopping

Ixtapa

As you enter Ixtapa from the airport or from Zihuatanejo, you'll see a large handicrafts market, **Mercado de Artesanía Turístico,** on the right side of Boulevard Ixtapa. The result of an ordinance banning vendors from the beach, this market is open weekdays 10–10 and hosts some 150 stands, selling handicrafts, T-shirts, and kitschy souvenirs.

Across the street from the hotel zone, the shopping area is loosely divided into *centros comerciales,* or malls. These clusters of pleasant colonial-style buildings feature patios containing boutiques, restaurants, cafés, and grocery minimarkets.

Zihuatanejo

Downtown Zihuatanejo has a colorful **municipal market** with a labyrinth of small stands on the east side of the town center, on Calle Benito Juárez between Nava and González. On the western edge of town along three blocks of Calle Cinco de Mayo is the **Mercado de Artesanía Turístico,** similar to the craft and souvenir market in Ixtapa, but larger, with 255 stands. Good purchases include hand-painted wooden masks and ceramics made in small towns throughout the state, huaraches, and silver jewelry. Near the mercado, across from the Aeroméxico office and facing the waterfront, **Casa Marina** (☒ Paseo del Pescador 9, ☎ 755/554–2373) is a two-story building with individual boutiques selling folk art, hammocks, and hand-loomed rugs.

In addition to these shops, the tiny three-block nucleus of central Zihuatanejo has several worthwhile shops. Shop for silver and gold jewelry at **Alberto's** (☒ Calle Cuauhtémoc 12 and 15, ☎ 755/554–2161). **Coco Cabaña** (☒ Agustín Ramírez 1, ☎ 755/554–2518) is a fascinating folk-art shop at Coconuts restaurant. Over at Playa la Ropa, **Gala Art** (☒ Villa del Sol, ☎ 755/554–7774) exhibits and sells paintings, jewelry, and bronze, wood, and marble sculptures crafted by artists from throughout Mexico. **Galería Maya** (☒ Calle Nicolás Bravo 31, ☎ 755/554–4606) is very browseable for its folk art and women's clothing. **Lupita's** (☒ Juan N. Álvarez 5, ☎ 755/554–2238) has a good selection of colorful women's apparel, including handmade items from Oaxaca, Yucatán, Chiapas, and Guatemala. **Arte Mexicano Nopal** (☒ Av. Cinco de Mayo 56, ☎ 755/554–7530) sells Mexican handicrafts and natural pine furniture that can be finished according to the client's tastes.

Ixtapa/Zihuatanejo A to Z

To research prices, get advice from other travelers, and book travel arrangements, visit www.fodors.com.

AIR TRAVEL

You can fly to Ixtapa from Houston, Los Angeles, and other major cities. From the airport, the taxi fare to the Ixtapa hotel zone is about $15; the trip takes about 20 minutes. To Zihuatanejo, the 15-minute trip costs about $8.

CARRIERS

Mexicana has daily flights from the U.S. and Mexican cities. Aeroméxico flies from multiple U.S. and Mexican cities. Alaska Airlines has direct flights three times a week from Los Angeles. America West has direct service three times a week from Phoenix. Houston is the hub for Continental, which offers daily direct flights.

➤ AIRLINES AND CONTACTS: **Aeroméxico** (☎ 800/021–4010). **Alaska Airlines** (☎ 800/426–0333). **America West** (☎ 800/235–9292 or 800/356–6611). **Continental** (☎ 800/900–5000). **Mexicana** (☎ 755/554–2208 in Zihuatanejo; 755/553–2208 in Ixtapa).

BOAT AND FERRY TRAVEL

Several cruise lines, including Holland America Lines and Royal Cruise Lines, sail to Ixtapa/Zihuatanejo as part of their seven-day Riviera Mexicana trips.

BUS TRAVEL

Various bus companies run from the Central de Autobuses. Estrella de Oro has deluxe service to Acapulco, Cuernavaca, Taxco, and Mexico City. Estrella Blanca offers first-class service to the same destinations as well as Querétaro, Aguascalientes, and León.

➤ BUS INFORMATION: **Central de Autobuses** (✉ Paseo Zihuatanejo at Paseo de la Boquita). **Estrella Blanca** (☎ 755/554–3476 or 755/554–8477). **Estrella de Oro** (☎ 755/554–2175 or 755/554–3802).

CAR RENTAL

Hertz has desks in the airport and in Zihuatanejo. Quick Rent-A-Car, in the Riviera Beach hotel, rents cars and jeeps, and Suburbans with or without air-conditioning.

➤ MAJOR AGENCIES: **Budget** (☎ 755/553–0397 in Zihuatanejo; 755/554–4837 at the International Airport) is the only agency with an airport location. **Hertz** (☎ 755/554–2590; 755/554–2255 in Zihuatanejo). **Quick Rent-A-Car** (✉ Blvd. Ixtapa s/n, ☎ 755/553–1830).

CAR TRAVEL

The Autopista del Sol connects Ixtapa/Zihuatanejo to Mexico City passing Acapulco en route; tolls on the six-hour trip total around $55. Otherwise, the trip from Mexico City takes about eight hours. Acapulco is a 3½-hour drive on Highway 200, which passes through small towns and coconut groves and has some spectacular ocean views. The drive from Manzanillo takes about seven hours.

EMBASSIES

The U.S. Consulate has an office in Ixtapa.

➤ UNITED STATES: **U.S. Consulate** (✉ Paseo Ixtapa, Plaza Ambiente, local 9, ☎ 755/553–2100, FAX 755/554–6276).

EMERGENCIES

There is no general emergency number, so call the police or the hospital directly. Hospital de la Armada is next to the Mercado de Artesanía Turístico, across from Los Patios Shopping Center.

➤ CONTACTS: **Hospital de la Armada** (✉ Paseo del Palmar s/n, ☎ 755/554–3099). **Police** (☎ 755/554–2040). **Red Cross** (☎ 755/554–2009). **Tourist Protection** (☎ 755/554–2207).

INTERNET

CDNET Internet Provider in Zihuatanejo offers inexpensive Internet access.

➤ INTERNET CAFÉS: **CDNET Internet Provider** (✉ Av. La Boquita 205, ☎ 755/554–7384).

TAXIS AND MINIBUSES

Unless you plan to travel great distances or visit remote beaches, taxis and buses are by far the best way to get around. Taxis are plentiful, and fares are reasonable and fixed. The fare from the Ixtapa hotel zone to Zihuatanejo begins at a little more than $3. To order a cab, call APAAZ. A second radio cab company is UTAAZ. Minibuses run every

10–15 minutes between the Ixtapa hotels and downtown Zihuatanejo; fare is about 30¢.

➤ TAXI COMPANIES: **APAAZ** (☎ 755/554–3680). **UTAAZ** (☎ 755/554–4583).

TOURS

Moderate and high-end hotels will arrange tours for their guests. Two-and-a-half-hour sunset cruises ($49) and four-hour swim and snorkel cruises aboard the 65-ft trimaran *Tri-Star* set sail from Zihuatanejo Bay. Both include open bar (domestic drinks); the snorkel cruise includes lunch. Other half-day cruises access Ixtapa Island or Playa las Gatas (both $20). Details on all these cruises are available from Yates del Sol in Zihuatanejo.

You can hire a fisherman's boat from Zihuatanejo's municipal pier to go to scenic, remote Playa Manzanillo—great for snorkeling—or to Los Moros de Potosí, a group of large white rocks in the ocean where rare web-footed brown boobies congregate with cormorants, egrets, frigates, pelicans, and long-tailed white terns. To see pink flamingos and other wading birds, take a bus or taxi to Barra de Potosí (15 minutes past the airport), where a beautiful *laguna* (lake) is an unofficial bird sanctuary. You can arrange a cruise with the small fishing launches in front of the palapa restaurants there, but the fishermen probably don't speak English. Organized tours to Barra de Potosí are also available.

➤ TOUR OPERATOR RECOMMENDATIONS: **Yates del Sol** (☎ 755/554–2694).

TRAVEL AGENCIES

American Express in Ixtapa is open Monday–Saturday 9–6. In Zihuatanejo, TIP arranges snorkel and dive tours to beaches in and around Ixtapa/Zihuatanejo.

➤ LOCAL AGENT REFERRALS: **American Express** (✉ Krystal Ixtapa arcade, Blvd. Ixtapa, ☎ 755/553–0853, FAX 755/553–1206). **TIP** (✉ Juan N. Álvarez at Calle Benito Juárez, ☎ 755/554–7510).

VISITOR INFORMATION

The Guerrero State Tourism Office is open weekdays 8–9, Saturday 8–3.

➤ TOURIST INFORMATION: **Guerrerc State Tourism Office** (✉ La Puerta shopping center, across from Presidente Inter-Continental, Ixtapa, ☎ 755/553–1967).

10 ACAPULCO

After a half century, Acapulco endures at the top of the glitterati top-10 list as a sentimental favorite and a party-hearty resort town, with miles of beaches and some of the glitziest discos this side of the Pacific. A delightful three-hour drive from Acapulco is Taxco, a colonial treasure, where the Baroque towers of Santa Prisca church overlook cobblestone streets lined with silversmiths.

Updated by
Patricia Alisau

ACAPULCO IS A VIBRANT PORT CITY with one of the most beautiful bays in the world. Famed Mexican muralist Diego Rivera is said to have been so awestruck by the sunsets here that he re-created them on canvas. This beauty, no doubt, is what attracted the Hollywood celebrities of the 1950s who built homes and hotels as hideaways and places for entertaining their friends. The celebrity status continued. This is where John and Jackie Kennedy spent their honeymoon. Likewise, Bill and Hillary Clinton and Henry and Nancy Kissinger. And it's where Liz Taylor and Michael Todd ventured after tying the knot. In fact, Acapulco still ranks as one of the top honeymoon spots worldwide. It's also a much solicited movie location. Three Rambo flicks starring Sylvester Stallone were filmed here, as was *Blow* with Johnny Depp and Penélope Cruz. Singers such as Julio Iglesias and a host of others maintain residences here, carrying on the Hollywood tradition that started long ago.

Acapulco has managed to age gracefully over the years even as it's grown into a town of a million inhabitants. Care is especially lavished on its upkeep. The city fathers initiated a multimillion-dollar beautification program some time ago, which is renewed annually to keep the bay, beaches, and streets landscaped and clean.

Of course, anyone who ventures to this stretch of the Pacific, 433 km (268 mi) south of Mexico City, does so to relax. Swimming, shopping, enjoying the nightlife—everything takes place against a staggeringly beautiful backdrop. The natural harbor of Acapulco Bay is the city's centerpiece. By day the water looks temptingly deep blue; at night it flashes and sparkles with the city lights.

The weather is Acapulco's major draw—warm waters, almost constant sunshine, and year-round temperatures in the 80s. It comes as no surprise, then, that most people plan their day around laying their towel on some part of Acapulco's beaches. Both tame and wild water sports are available—everything from waterskiing to snorkeling, parasailing, and fishing. Championship golf courses, tennis courts, and the food and crafts markets also lure some visitors away from the beach.

Most people rise from their hammocks, deck chairs, or towels only when impelled by hunger, and eating is one of Acapulco's great pleasures. In addition to the showy places, there are plenty of good no-frills, down-home Mexican restaurants. Eating at one of these joints takes you to the real Mexico.

At night Acapulco rouses itself from the day's torpor and prepares for the long hours ahead. Though Acapulco's heyday is past, its nightlife is legendary, and the opening of new and ever more spectacular dance clubs is proof positive that this remains the disco capital of the world. Perpetually crowded, the discos are grouped in twos and threes, and most people go to several places in one night.

Since the late 1940s, Acapulco has expanded eastward so that today it is one of Mexico's larger cities, with a population of approximately one million. Former President Miguel Alemán Valdés bought up miles of the coast just before the road and airport were built—as his namesake Avenida Costera Miguel Alemán testifies. Under development is a 3,000-acre expanse known as Acapulco Diamante, which encompasses the areas known as Punta Diamante and Playa Diamante and some of the city's most sparkling hotels and residential developments.

Pleasures and Pastimes

Beaches

The lure of sun and sand in Acapulco is legendary. Every sport is available, and you can eat in a beach restaurant, dance, and sleep in a *hamaca* (hammock)—all without leaving the water's edge. There are also plenty of quiet and even isolated beaches within reach.

Dining

Dining in Acapulco is more than just eating out—it is the most popular leisure activity in town. Every night the restaurants fill up, and every night the adventurous diner can sample a different cuisine. The variety of styles matches the range of cuisines: from greasy spoons that serve regional favorites to gourmet restaurants with gorgeous views of Acapulco Bay. Most restaurants fall somewhere in the middle. On the Costera Miguel Alemán are dozens of beachside restaurants with *palapa* (palm frond) roofs, as well as wildly decorated rib and hamburger joints popular with visitors under 30—not necessarily in age, but definitely in spirit. Most establishments that cater to tourists purify their drinking water and use it to cook vegetables.

Lodging

Accommodations in Acapulco run the gamut from sprawling, big-name complexes with nonstop amenities to small, family-run inns where hot water is a luxury. Wherever you stay, however, prices will be reasonable compared with those in the United States, and service is generally good, as Acapulqueños have been catering to tourists for more than half a century.

Nightlife

Acapulco has always been famous for its nightlife, and justifiably so. For many visitors the discos and restaurants are just as important as the sun and the sand. The minute the sun slips over the horizon, the Costera comes alive with people milling around window-shopping, deciding where to dine, and generally biding their time till the disco hour. The legendary Acapulco discos are open 365 days a year from about 10:30 PM until they empty out. Cultural offerings are improving here; theater efforts are few and far between, but Placido Domingo gives the occasional benefit concert and the Acapulco Symphonic Orchestra rates as one of the best in the country. International pop-music fests and several film events such as black- and French-cinema festivals are gaining popularity.

Shopping

The abundance of air-conditioned shopping malls and boutiques makes picking up gifts and souvenirs a snap. Malls in Acapulco range from designer shopping arcades at several of the more lavish hotels to the huge, completely enclosed Plaza Bahía and Gran Plaza.

The state of Guerrero is especially known for hand-painted ceramics, items made from *palo de rosa* wood, primitive bark paintings depicting scenes of village life and local flora and fauna, and embroidered textiles. There are several good shops specializing in Mexican crafts, and the mercado municipal also is a good source of local handicrafts. Taxco is one of the silver capitals of the world.

Sports and the Outdoors

Acapulco has lots for sports-lovers to enjoy. Most hotels have pools, and many have private tennis clubs and gyms. Acapulco's waters are teeming with sailfish, marlin, shark, and mahimahi, and although the waters aren't as clear as in the Caribbean, waterskiing is popular as are windsurfing, kayaking, and bronco riding (one-person Jet Skis). Scuba diving is best in December, January, and February, when the water is the most transparent. A Canadian warship was purposely sunk to make diving more appealing. Golfers can tee off at the 9-hole municipal course, in town, or at one of the five 18-hole championship courses in Acapulco Diamante.

EXPLORING

It's possible to get a feel for Acapulco during a short stay if you take in some downtown sights along with your beach activities. Those who have a longer time to spend can really soak up the ambience of the place and can enjoy excursions to some isolated beaches as well as to Taxco.

Numbers in the text correspond to numbers in the margin and on the Acapulco and Taxco maps.

Great Itineraries

IF YOU HAVE 3 DAYS

Spend the first day enjoying your favorite beach activity, be it parasailing, waterskiing, or simply sunning. That evening, to get the lay of the land, take a sunset cruise that includes a ringside view of Acapulco's daredevil *clavadistas* (divers) at **La Quebrada** ⑨. The following day, experience Acapulco at its most authentic, paying an early visit to the **Mercado Municipal** ④, the **waterfront** ⑦, and the ***zócalo*** (town square) ⑧. Head for the beach for some rays after all that activity and later take in some late-afternoon shopping in the boutiques and handicrafts markets along the Costera Miguel Alemán. Come nightfall, "shake off the dust" (as they say in Mexico) at one of the city's glitzy discos. The next day you'll want to try to land a sailfish, take in the Mexican Fiesta at the **Acapulco International Center,** and bid farewell to Acapulco with a late candlelit dinner at one of the city's romantic dining spots.

IF YOU HAVE 5 DAYS

Add on to the three-day itinerary a visit to the newly renovated **El Fuerte de San Diego** ⑥, built in the 18th century to protect Acapulco from pirates, and today home of the Anthropology Museum. Then swing down the street to the **Casa de Mascaras** ⑤, with its collection of Guerrero masks. For a taste of the 1950s Acapulco of John Wayne and Johnny Weissmuller, hire a taxi to take you into the hills above Caleta and Caletilla; make it a point to drop into Los Flamingos Hotel, which Weissmuller once owned with others from the Hollywood gang. Head out to Pie de la Cuesta for a late lunch and boat ride or waterskiing on Coyuca Lagoon, and then cross the road and park your body under a palm-frond umbrella for a spectacular sunset on the beach. Save one morning for the thrilling **Shotover Jet** boat ride on the Papagayo River. Especially if you're traveling with children, devote a few hours to **Mágico Mundo Marino** ⑩.

IF YOU HAVE 7 DAYS

Follow the five-day itinerary above and then, for a complete change of pace, rent a car or arrange for a tour to **Taxco,** a colonial treasure of twisting cobblestone streets and some 2,000 silver shops, about a three-hour drive from Acapulco; plan to spend the night. For a change from shopping for silver, visit the **Iglesia de San Sebastián y Santa Prisca** ⑪, Taxco's most important landmark, on Plaza Borda, and the **Casa Humboldt** ⑬, which now houses a museum of viceregal art. Try to get a front-row seat at one of the bars or restaurants on the square and spend an hour watching the constant activity: weddings, funerals, baptisms, and vendors selling baskets and animal figurines. The following day, tour the **Grutas de Cacahuamilpa** ⑮, an amazing expanse of subterranean chambers.

Acapulco

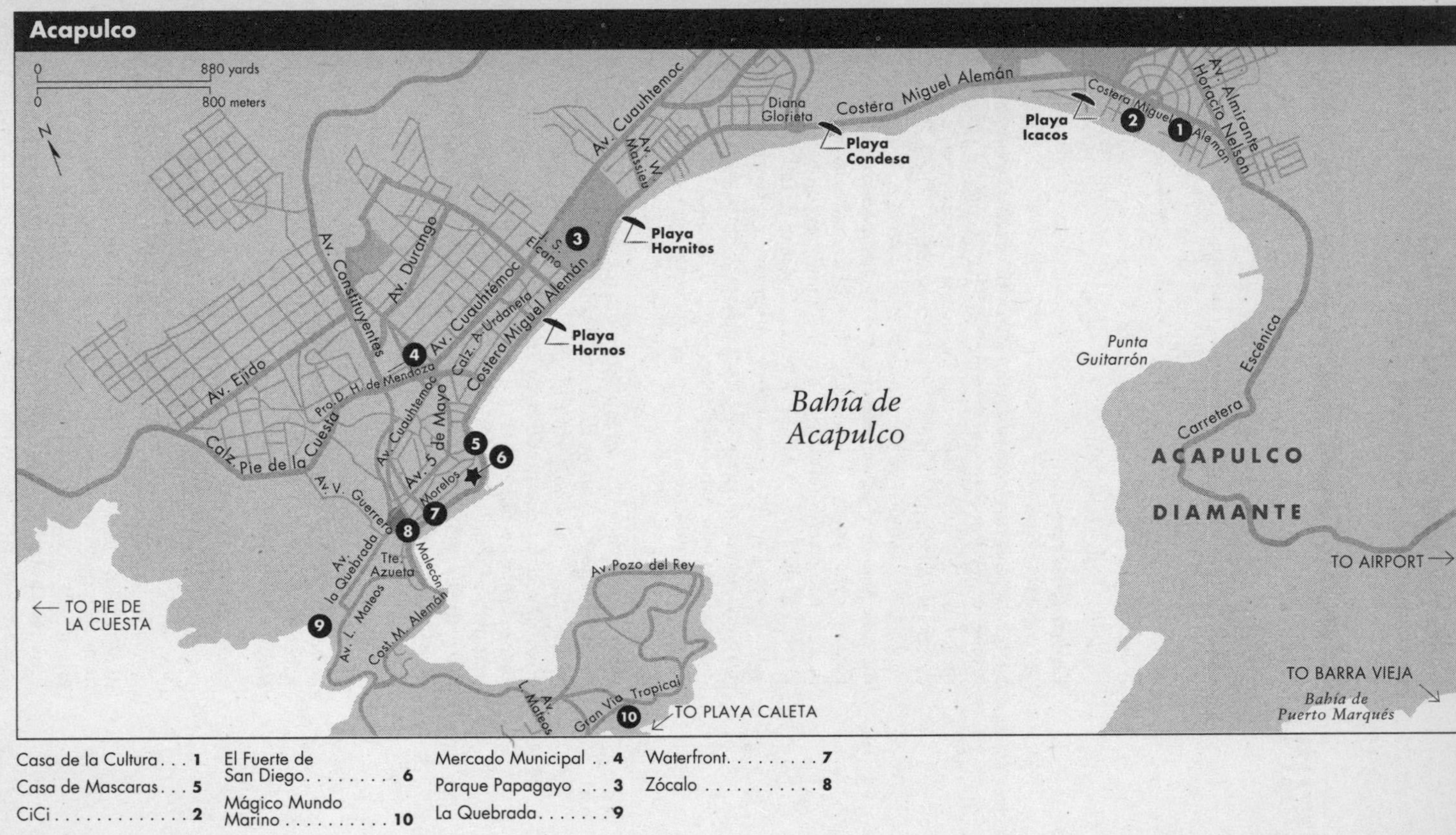

Casa de la Cultura . . . **1**	El Fuerte de San Diego. **6**	Mercado Municipal . . **4**	Waterfront. **7**
Casa de Mascaras. . . **5**	Mágico Mundo Marino **10**	Parque Papagayo . . . **3**	Zócalo **8**
CiCi **2**		La Quebrada. **9**	

Acapulco

Acapulco is easily explored. During the day the focus for most visitors is the beach and the myriad activities that happen on and off it. At night the attention shifts to the restaurants and discos. The Avenida Costera Miguel Alemán, the wide boulevard that hugs Acapulco Bay from the Scenic Highway to Playa Caleta (about 8 km, or 5 mi), is central to both day and night diversions. All the major beaches, shopping malls, and big hotels—minus the more exclusive Acapulco Diamante properties—are off the Costera, and "Costera" is the name given to the more exclusive area by the locals. Hence most of the shopping, dining, and clubbing takes place within a few blocks of this main drag, and many an address is listed only as "Costera Miguel Alemán." Because street addresses are not often used and streets have no logical pattern, directions are usually given from a major landmark.

Old Acapulco, one of the areas of Acapulco that can easily be visited on foot, is where the Mexicans go to dine at traditional restaurants, enjoy a town festival, run errands, and worship. Also known as El Centro, it's where you'll find the zócalo, the church, and El Fuerte de San Diego. Just up the hill from Old Acapulco is La Quebrada.

The southern peninsula of Old Acapulco contains remnants of the first version of Acapulco. This primarily residential area was prey to dilapidation and abandonment for many years, but efforts were made to revitalize it—such as reopening the Caleta Hotel and opening the aquarium and the zoo on Isla la Roqueta. Although its prime is definitely past, it is now a popular area for budget travelers, especially those seeking a retro experience of Acapulco. The **Plaza de Toros,** where bullfights are held on Sunday from the first week of January to Easter, is in the center of the peninsula.

If you arrived by plane, you've already had a royal introduction to Acapulco Bay. **Acapulco Diamante** is the area stretching east of Acapulco proper from Las Brisas to Barra Vieja beach. You'll need a car or a taxi to explore this area, where you'll find most of Acapulco's poshest hotels and residential developments, as well as several exclusive private clubs, pounding surf, and beautiful beaches.

A Good Tour

If you want to get the lay of the land, you might take a drive or taxi ride along the Costera Miguel Alemán, starting on its eastern edge at **La Base,** the Mexican naval base south of Playa Icacos. When you come to Playa Icacos, you'll see the **Casa de la Cultura** ① cultural complex on the beach side (just past the Hyatt Regency hotel); a little farther down is **CiCi** ②, a children's amusement park. About 1 km (½ mi) past CiCi, on the right side of the Costera, lies the **Acapulco International Center** (often called the Convention Center); you might return here in the evening to attend a Mexican Fiesta. Continue along through the commercial heart of the Costera until you reach **Parque Papagayo** ③, one of the top municipal parks in the country. When you arrive at the intersection of the Costera with Diego Hurtado de Mendoza, detour a few blocks inland to find Old Acapulco and the sprawling **Mercado Municipal** ④. You'll want to take the bus marked MERCADO or have your taxi drop you off; it's best to navigate this area by foot. A few blocks west and closer to the water, **El Fuerte de San Diego** ⑥ sits on the hill overlooking the harbor next to the army barracks. You'll next see the **waterfront** ⑦ (locally known as the *malecón*) with its series of docks and, adjoining it, the **zócalo** ⑧, the center of Old Acapulco. A 15-minute walk up the hill from the zócalo brings you to **La Quebrada** ⑨, where the famous cliff divers perform their daredevil stunts daily.

Sights to See

1 **Casa de la Cultura.** This cultural complex includes a small archaeological museum, first-class regional and Mexican handicrafts for sale, and the Ixcateopan art gallery. ✉ *Costera Miguel Alemán 4834, Costera,* ☎ *744/484–4004.* 🎫 *Free.* ⏲ *Weekdays 9–2 and 5–8, Sat. 9–2.*

5 **Casa de Mascaras.** A private home has been turned into a gallery for a stunning collection of 550 handmade ceremonial masks, most from the state of Guerrero. Some represent traditional ritualistic dances, such as "Moors and the Christians" and "Battle of the Tigers." ✉ *Calle Morelos S/N, ex-zona militar B, a half block from the Fuerte de San Diego, Old Acapulco,* ☎ *744/486–5577.* 🎫 *Free (donation suggested).* ⏲ *Mon.–Sat. 10–6.*

2 **CiCi** (Centro Internacional para Convivencia Infantil). A water-oriented theme park for children, CiCi has dolphin and seal shows, a freshwater pool with wave-making apparatus, a water slide, miniaquarium, and other attractions. Swim with the dolphins for $90 for an hour, $51 for a half hour, including transportation to or from your hotel. ✉ *Costera Miguel Alemán, across from Hard Rock Cafe, Costera,* ☎ *744/484–8210.* 🎫 *$3 (free admission when signing up to swim with dolphins).* ⏲ *Daily 10–6.*

6 **El Fuerte de San Diego.** Under the Spaniards, Acapulco became a very lucrative port for trade with the Philippines. Trade made the city so rich that the conquerers erected this impressive fortress to protect it from pirates. The original fort was built in 1616 but later destroyed in an earthquake; the current one went up in the 18th century. The pentagon-shape fort, restructured into 15 salons, houses the **Museo Historico de Acapulco.** The museum was stylishly renovated in 2000 with new acquisitions and retooled exhibit salons; it's the top cultural attraction in the state. Bilingual videos and text expound on the exhibits, which trace the city's history from the first pre-Hispanic settlements 3,000 years ago, to the exploits of famous pirates like Sir Francis Drake, through the era of the missionaries, and up to Mexico's independence from Spain in 1821. New air-conditioning makes the tour pleasant. ✉ *Calle Hornitos and Morelos, Old Acapulco,* ☎ *744/482–3828.* 🎫 *$3.25, free Sun.* ⏲ *Tues.–Sun. 10–5.*

10 **Mágico Mundo Marino.** In addition to an aquarium, Magic Marine World has a sea lion show, swimming pools, a toboggan, scuba diving, and (for rent) Jet Skis, inner tubes, and kayaks—not to mention clean rest rooms. From **Playa Caleta,** you can take the glass-bottom boat to **Isla la Roqueta** (about 10 minutes each way) for a visit to the small zoo and aquarium. ✉ *Playa Caleta, Old Acapulco,* ☎ *744/483–1215.* 🎫 *Aquarium $2; round-trip ferry service to Isla la Roqueta, including zoo, $5.* ⏲ *Mágico Mundo Marino daily 9–6, zoo daily 9–5.*

4 **Mercado Municipal.** Locals come to this sprawling municipal market to purchase their everyday needs, from fresh vegetables and candles to plastic buckets and love potions. The stalls within the mercado are densely packed together, but things stay relatively cool despite the lack of air-conditioning. There are baskets, pottery, hammocks, even a stand offering charms, amulets, and talismans. Come as early as possible to avoid the crowds. ✉ *Diego Hurtado de Mendoza and Av. Constituyentes, a few blocks west of Costera, Old Acapulco.* ⏲ *Daily 5 AM–7 PM.*

3 **Parque Papagayo.** Named for the hotel that formerly occupied the grounds, the park sits on 52 acres of prime real estate on the Costera, just after the underpass that begins at Playa Hornos. Youngsters enjoy the life-size model of a Spanish galleon, made to look like the ones that sailed into Acapulco when it was Mexico's capital of trade with the

Orient. There is an aviary, a roller-skating rink, a racetrack with mite-size race cars, a replica of the space shuttle *Columbia,* bumper boats in a lagoon, and other rides. ✉ *Costera Miguel Alemán, Old Acapulco,* ☎ *744/485–9623.* *No entrance fee, rides 45¢ each, $5 and $8 ride packages available.* ⏲ *Daily 10–8, rides section 4–11 nightly.*

9 **La Quebrada.** High on a hill above downtown Acapulco, La Quebrada (literally "gorge"; in this case cliffs) is home to the Mirador Hotel, *the* place for tourists in the 1940s. These days most visitors come here to see the famous cliff divers jump from a height of 130 ft daily at 1 PM and evenings at 7:30, 8:30, 9:30, and 10:30. The dives are thrilling, so be sure to arrive early. Before they take the plunge, the divers say a prayer at a small shrine near the jumping-off point. Sometimes they dive in pairs; often they carry torches. The hotel's La Perla supper club is the traditional and most comfortable viewing spot, but you will be obligated to buy a drinks-show-tips ($18) or buffet-show-tips package ($34). Be forewarned: the tequila, rum, and brandy drinks are watered down. By all means, don't let this dissuade you from seeing the show. The divers can also be seen from a general observation deck next to the hotel (about $2). When you exit, some of the divers may also be waiting to greet you—and to ask for tips; they get paid very little for risking their lives.

7 **Waterfront.** A stroll by the docks will remind you that Acapulco is still a lively commercial port and fishing center. The cruise ships anchor here, and at night Mexicans bring their children to play on the small tree-lined promenade. Farther west, by the zócalo, are the docks for the sightseeing yachts and smaller fishing boats, a good spot for people-watching. ✉ *Costera Miguel Alemán, between Calle Escudero on the west and El Fuerte de San Diego on the east, Old Acapulco.*

8 **Zócalo.** You'll find the hub of downtown and Old Acapulco at this shaded plaza, overgrown with dense trees. All day it's filled with vendors, shoeshine men, and people lining up to use the pay phones. After siesta, they drift here to meet and greet. On Sunday evening there's often music in the bandstand. The zócalo fronts **Nuestra Señora de la Soledad,** the town's modern but unusual church, with its stark-white exterior and bulb-shape blue-and-yellow spires. The church hosts the festive Virgin of Guadalupe celebration on December 12. ✉ *Bounded by Calle Felipe Valle on the north, Costera Miguel Alemán on the south, Calle J. Azueta on the west, and Calle J. Carranza on the east, Old Acapulco.*

NEED A BREAK?

Just off the zócalo, **Sanborns** attracts locals and tourists alike; many linger for hours over a newspaper and a cup of coffee. **Cafetería Astoria** is a little outdoor café on the zócalo where businesspeople stop in for breakfast before work or meet midmorning for a cappuccino and a sweet roll.

Beaches

The bay has been considerably cleaned up over the past few years due to the efforts of city officials, and maintaining it continues to be a top priority. However, some beaches, such as Revolcadero and Pie de la Cuesta, have very strong undertows and surf, so swimming isn't advised. In addition, although vending on the beach has been officially outlawed, you'll still be approached by souvenir hawkers. You can always follow the lead of the Mexican cognoscenti and enjoy the waters at your hotel pool.

Beaches in Mexico are public, even those that seem to belong to a big hotel.

Barra Vieja

About 27 km (17 mi) east of Acapulco, between Laguna de Tres Palos and the Pacific, this long stretch of uncrowded beach is somewhat more inviting than Pie de la Cuesta because the drive out is much more pleasant. Most people make the trip out here for the solitude and to feast on *pescado à la talla* (red snapper marinated in spices and grilled over hot coals).

Caleta and Caletilla

On the peninsula in Old Acapulco, these two beaches rivaled La Quebrada as the main tourist area in Acapulco's heyday. Now they attract families. Motorboats to Isla la Roqueta leave from here.

Condesa

Referred to as "the strip," this stretch of sand facing the middle of Acapulco Bay has more than its share of tourists, especially singles, and the beachside restaurants are lively joints.

Hornos and Hornitos

Running from the Plaza las Glorias Paraíso to Las Hamacas hotel, these beaches are packed shoulder to shoulder on the weekends with locals and Mexican tourists who know a good thing: graceful palms shade the sand, and there are scads of casual eateries within walking distance.

Icacos

Stretching from the naval base to El Presidente hotel, away from the famous strip, this beach is less populated than others on the Costera. The morning waves are especially calm.

Pie de la Cuesta

You'll need a car or cab to reach this relatively unpopulated spot, about a 25-minute drive west of Acapulco's downtown, through one of the least picturesque parts of town (where the roads are being repaired for the first time in many years). A string of simple, thatched-roof restaurants and new, rustic inns border the wide beach, and straw palapas provide shade. What attracts people to Pie de la Cuesta, besides the long expanse of beach and spectacular sunsets, is beautiful Coyuca Lagoon, a favorite spot for waterskiing, freshwater fishing, and boat rides. The boats will ferry you to La Laguna restaurant, where, some people claim, the pescado à la talla is even better than at Barra Vieja.

Puerto Marqués

Tucked below the airport highway, this strand is popular with Mexican tourists, so it tends to get crowded on weekends.

Revolcadero

A wide, sprawling beach fronting the Fairmont Pierre Marqués and Fairmont Acapulco Princess hotels, its water is shallow and its waves are fairly rough. People come here to surf and ride horses.

DINING

The top restaurants in Acapulco can be fun for a splurge and provide very good value. At the best places in town, a main dish of meat or fish can run up to $40, and the atmosphere and views are fantastic. Ties and jackets are out of place, but so are shorts or jeans. Unless stated otherwise, all restaurants are open daily for lunch and dinner; dinner-only places open around 6:30 or 7.

Note: Loud music blares from many restaurants along the Costera, especially those facing Condesa Beach, and proprietors will aggressively try to hustle you inside with offers of drink specials. If you're looking for a hassle-free evening, it's best either to avoid this area or decide in advance precisely where you want to dine.

CATEGORY	COST*
$$$$	over $40
$$$	$30–$40
$$	$20–$30
$	under $20

**per person for a main course at dinner*

American

$ ✕ **Carlos 'n' Charlie's.** An Acapulco landmark, this is still one of the most popular restaurants in town. Part of the Anderson group (with restaurants in the United States and Spain, too), Carlos 'n' Charlie's cultivates an atmosphere of controlled craziness. Prankster waiters, a jokester menu, and eclectic decor add to the chaos. The crowd is mostly young and relaxed, and the menu straddles the border, with ribs, stuffed shrimp, and oysters among the best offerings. ✉ *Costera Miguel Alemán 112, Costera,* ☎ *744/484–1285 or 744/484–0039. AE, DC, MC, V.*

$ ✕ **Hard Rock Cafe.** This link in the international Hard Rock chain is one of the most popular spots in Acapulco, and with good reason. The famous New York–cut steaks, hamburgers, and brownies plus Southern-style food—fried chicken, ribs—are well prepared, and the portions are more than ample. The taped rock music begins at noon, and a live group starts playing at 11 PM (except Tuesday). ✉ *Costera Miguel Alemán 37, Costera,* ☎ *744/484–6680. AE, MC, V.*

Belgian

$$ ★ ✕ **La Petite Belgique.** Mexican-born Yolanda Brassart, who spent years in Europe studying the culinary arts, reigns in the kitchen of this small bistro. Diners are greeted by the enticing aromas of goose-liver pâté, home-baked breads, and apple strudel. The menu changes every three months but usually includes boned duck stuffed with almonds and mushrooms and served with a white wine and mushroom sauce. ✉ *Plaza Marbella, Costera,* ☎ *744/484–7725. AE, MC, V.*

French

$$ ✕ **Le Jardín des Artistes.** This chic garden hideaway, once a scruffy parking lot, is thoroughly French: the tables bear fresh flowers and Tiffany lamps, and discreet waiters deliver deliciously rich dishes with classic cream and butter sauces. Swiss chef Richard has a local following for his escargots in garlic butter, red-snapper fillet with savory mustard sauce, and smoked trout soufflé. After dinner, stroll through the snazzy art gallery adjoining the garden. ✉ *Vicente Yañez Pinzón 11, Costera,* ☎ *744/484–8344. Reservations essential. AE, DC, MC, V.* ⊙ *Closed Sun.–Wed. in Sept. and Oct. No lunch.*

Health Food

$ ✕ **100% Natural.** Along the Costera Miguel Alemán are several of these 24-hour restaurants that specialize in light, healthful food—yogurt shakes, fruit salads, and sandwiches made with whole-wheat bread. You can order soy burgers or dishes with chicken, about the only meat you'll find on the menu. The service is quick, and the food is a refreshing alternative to heavy meals. You can recognize these eateries by the green signs with white lettering. The original—and best—is across from the Acapulco Plaza hotel. ✉ *Costera Miguel Alemán 200, near Acapulco*

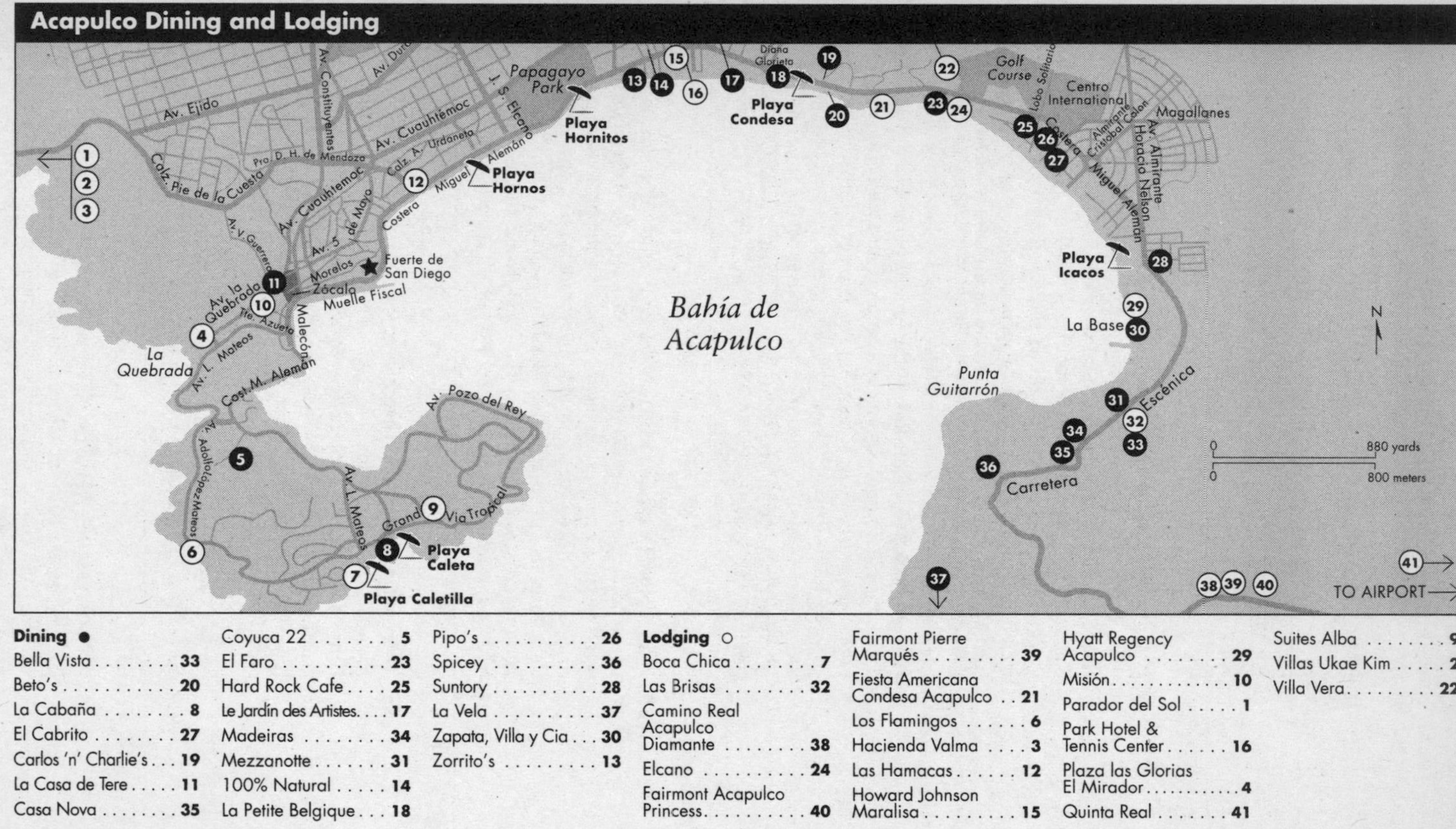

Dining ●

- Bella Vista 33
- Beto's 20
- La Cabaña 8
- El Cabrito 27
- Carlos 'n' Charlie's 19
- La Casa de Tere 11
- Casa Nova 35
- Coyuca 22 5
- El Faro 23
- Hard Rock Cafe 25
- Le Jardín des Artistes 17
- Madeiras 34
- Mezzanotte 31
- 100% Natural 14
- La Petite Belgique 18
- Pipo's 26
- Spicey 36
- Suntory 28
- La Vela 37
- Zapata, Villa y Cia 30
- Zorrito's 13

Lodging ○

- Boca Chica 7
- Las Brisas 32
- Camino Real Acapulco Diamante 38
- Elcano 24
- Fairmont Acapulco Princess 40
- Fairmont Pierre Marqués 39
- Fiesta Americana Condesa Acapulco 21
- Los Flamingos 6
- Hacienda Valma 3
- Las Hamacas 12
- Howard Johnson Maralisa 15
- Hyatt Regency Acapulco 29
- Misión 10
- Parador del Sol 1
- Park Hotel & Tennis Center 16
- Plaza las Glorias El Mirador 4
- Quinta Real 41
- Suites Alba 9
- Villas Ukae Kim 2
- Villa Vera 22

Plaza, Costera, ☎ *744/485–3982 or 744/484–8440;* ✉ *Next to Oceanic 2000 at Costera Miguel Alemán 3111, Costera,* ☎ *744/485–3982 or 744/484–8440. MC, V.*

International

$$$$ ★ ✕ **Coyuca 22.** This is Acapulco's most beautiful restaurant, and more celebrities have eaten here than you can shake a stick at. On hilltop terraces that overlook the bay, the understated decor includes Doric pillars and statuary; diners gaze down on an enormous illuminated obelisk and a small pool. It's like eating in a partially restored Greek ruin. Diners can choose from two fixed menus or order à la carte; either way, the food presentation is a work of art. Seafood and prime rib are house specialties. ✉ *Av. Coyuca 22 (10-min taxi ride from the zócalo), Old Acapulco,* ☎ *744/482–3468 or 744/483–5030. Reservations essential. AE, DC, MC, V. Closed Apr. 30–Nov. 1.*

$$$ ✕ **Bella Vista.** This alfresco restaurant in the exclusive Las Brisas area has fantastic sunset views of Acapulco. Its large menu includes items that range from Asian appetizers to Italian and seafood entrées. Try the delicious (and spicy) Thai shrimp, sautéed in sesame oil, ginger, Thai chili, and hoisin sauce; or the red snapper étouffée, cooked in a chardonnay, tomato, herbs, basil, and oyster sauce. For dessert the white/dark chocolate mousse is a treat. Part of the restaurant has been enclosed and air-conditioned for those who like it cool. ✉ *Carretera Escénica 5255, Las Brisas,* ☎ *744/469–6900 Ext. 500. Reservations essential. AE, DC, MC, V.*

$$ ★ ✕ **Madeiras.** At this local favorite, the bar-reception area is decorated with dramatic coffee tables whose glass tops rest on carved wooden animals; the dishes and flatware were created by silversmiths in nearby Taxco; and all tables have star-studded views of lovely Acapulco Bay. Dinner is a four-course, prix-fixe meal costing about $38 without wine. Specialties include a delicious red snapper baked in sea salt (a Spanish specialty), tasty chilled soups, and a choice of steaks and other seafood. Seatings are every 30 minutes from 7 PM to 10:30 PM. Reserve well in advance on weekends and for Christmas and Easter week. ✉ *Carretera Escénica 33-B, just past La Vista shopping center, Costera,* ☎ *744/446–5636. Reservations essential. AE, DC, MC, V. No lunch.*

$ ★ ✕ **Spicey.** In addition to another spectacular view of Acapulco's diamond-studded bay from the air-conditioned dining room or the terrace, this restaurant has an innovative menu of dishes that blend international techniques and spices. The results are delicious, as well as a delight to the eye: spring rolls filled with smoked salmon, cream cheese, and vegetables, served with a Chinese plum sauce, and whole red snapper flavored with star anise and rosemary, glacéed with honey. ✉ *Carretera Escénica, Fracc. Marina Las Brisas, Costera,* ☎ *744/446–6003. Reservations essential. AE, MC, V. No lunch.*

Italian

$$$$ ★ ✕ **Casa Nova.** Another ultraromantic spot, Casa Nova is carved out of a cliff that rises up from Acapulco Bay. The views, both from the terrace and the air-conditioned dining room, are spectacular, the service impeccable, and the Italian cuisine divine. Diners can choose the fixed-price menu (called *menu turístico*) or order à la carte. Favorites include antipasto, fresh pastas, a delightful *costoletta di vitello* (veal chops with mushrooms), lobster tail, and linguini *alle vongole* (with clams, tomato, and garlic). ✉ *Carretera Escénica 5256, Las Brisas,* ☎ *744/446–6237. Reservations essential. AE, DC, MC, V. No lunch.*

$$ ✕ **Mezzanotte.** If you fancy dancing with your waiter, even on the tabletops, this is the place. Attracting the who's who of Acapulco, Mezzanotte sits atop a rise off the Acapulco highway. The elegant and stylish interior features a large sunken dining area, original sculptures, and humongous bay windows looking out to sea. Clients rave about the fettuccine with smoked salmon in avocado sauce and the meatier charcoaled sea bass with shrimp and artichokes in a citrus sauce. Try the Italian gelato for a light finish to the meal. The waiters are personable and efficient and, Friday and Saturday nights after midnight, dance with diners. ✉ *Carr. Escenico 28–1, in the La Vista shopping center, Costera,* ☎ *744/446–5727. AE, DC, MC, V.*

Japanese

$$$ ✕ **Suntory.** At this traditional Japanese restaurant, you can dine either in a blessedly air-conditioned interior room or in the delightful Asian-style garden. It's one of the few Japanese restaurants in Acapulco and one of the only deluxe restaurants open for lunch. Most diners opt for the *teppanyaki*—thin slices of beef and vegetables prepared on a hot grill—prepared at your table by skilled chefs. ✉ *Costera Miguel Alemán 36, across from La Palapa hotel, Costera,* ☎ *744/484–8088. AE, DC, MC, V.*

Mexican

$ ✕ **El Cabrito.** This is a local favorite for true Mexican cuisine and ambience. The name—"The Goat"—is also its specialty, charcoal-grilled, that is. In addition, you can choose among chicken in *mole* (spicy chocolate-chili sauce); shrimp in tequila; jerky with egg, fish, and seafood; and other Mexican dishes. ✉ *Costera Miguel Alemán between CiCi and Centro Internacional, Costera,* ☎ *744/484–7711. AE, MC, V.*

$ ✕ **La Casa de Tere.** Hidden in a commercial district downtown (signs point the way), La Casa de Tere is in a league of its own—expect beer-hall tables and chairs, colorful Mexican decorations, and photos of Acapulco of yore. But that's part of the mix at this spotlessly clean, open-air establishment. And so is its small but varied menu, which includes an outstanding *sopa de tortilla* (tortilla soup), chicken mole, and flan, plus the daily fixed-price lunch for $6.50. ✉ *Alonso Martín 1721, 2 blocks from Costera Miguel Alemán, Old Acapulco,* ☎ *744/485–7735. No credit cards. Closed Mon.*

$ ✕ **Zapata, Villa y Cia.** The music and the excellent food at this Mexican version of the Hard Rock Cafe are strictly local, and the memorabilia recalls the Mexican Revolution—with guns, hats, and photographs of Pancho Villa. The highlight of an evening here is a visit from a sombrero-wearing baby burro, so be sure to bring your camera. (If per chance the burro is missing, it's likely that the search is on for a younger version.) The menu features the ever popular fajitas, tacos, and grilled chicken and meats. ✉ *Hyatt Regency Acapulco, Costera Miguel Alemán 1, Costera,* ☎ *744/469–1234. AE, DC, MC, V. No lunch.*

$ ✕ **Zorrito's.** When Julio Iglesias is in town, this is where he heads in the wee hours of the morning, after the discos close. The menu of this simple, open-air streetside eatery, which is open almost all the time, includes a host of steak and beef dishes, Acapulco's famous green-and-white *pozole* (pork and hominy soup), and the special, *filete tampiqueña* (a strip of tender grilled beef), which comes with tacos, enchiladas, guacamole, and beans. ✉ *Costera Miguel Alemán and Anton de Alaminos, next to Banamex, Costera,* ☎ *744/485–3735. AE, MC, V. Closed 7 AM–9 AM and Tues. 7 AM–2 PM.*

Seafood

$$$ ★ ✕ **La Vela.** Set on a wharf that juts out into Pichilingue Bay, this open-air dining spot is protected by a dramatic roof that simulates a huge white sail. It's very atmospheric after dark, when the lights of Puerto Marqués flicker in the distance. A variety of fish and shellfish dishes are on the menu, but the specialty of the house is the red snapper *à la talla* (basted with chili and other spices and broiled over hot coals). ✉ *Camino Real Acapulco Diamante, Carretera Escénica, Km 14, Costera,* ☎ *744/466–1010. AE, DC, MC, V.*

$$ ✕ **Beto's.** By day you can eat right on the beach and enjoy live music; by night this palapa-roof restaurant is transformed into a dim and romantic dining area lighted by candles and paper lanterns. Whole red snapper, lobster, and ceviche are recommended. At the Barra Vieja Beach branch, the specialty is pescado à la talla. ✉ *Beto's, Costera Miguel Alemán at Playa Condesa, Costera,* ☎ *744/484–0473;* ✉ *Beto's Barra Vieja, Barra Vieja,* ☎ *744/444–6071. AE, MC, V.*

$$ ✕ **El Faro.** A pleasant adjunct to the Elcano Hotel, the sleek, classy El Faro resembles a lighthouse down to its nautical interior, with portholes and gleaming sculptures that evoke anchors and giant waves. Spanish chef Jorge Pereira adds touches of Basque and Mediterranean cooking to his original creations for a knockout menu. For starters, there's a lettuce salad mixed with goat cheese, dried wild fruits, and herb-infused olive oil. Favorite main dishes are haddock with clams and seared tuna medallions with baby onions. A pianist tickles the ivories Tuesday through Sunday from 9 PM to midnight. ✉ *Costera Miguel Alemán 75, Costera,* ☎ *744/484–3100. AE, MC, V.*

$$ ★ ✕ **Pipo's.** Situated on a rather quiet part of the Costera, this old, family-run seafood restaurant doesn't have an especially interesting view, but diners come here for the fresh fish, good service, and reasonable prices for most dishes. *Huachinango veracruzano* (red snapper baked with tomatoes, peppers, onion, and olives) and fillet of fish in *mojo de ajo* (garlic butter) are about as sophisticated as the food preparation gets. The original location downtown is extremely popular, also with locals. ✉ *Costera Miguel Alemán and Nao Victoria, across from Acapulco International Center, Costera,* ☎ *744/484–0165;* ✉ *Almirante Bretón 3, Old Acapulco,* ☎ *744/482–2237. AE, MC, V.*

$ ✕ **La Cabaña.** This humble seaside restaurant run by the Alvarez family was a bohemian hangout that attracted famous bullfighters and Mexican songwriter Agustín Lara and his lady love María Félix in the 1950s. You can see their photo over the bar and sample the same dishes that made the place famous then, such as baby-shark tamales. For heartier appetites, there's steaming seafood casserole or shrimp prepared with sea salt, curry, or garlic. The restaurant is smack in the middle of Playa Caleta, where vendors stroll the beach with peeled mangoes and shells. There are free lockers for diners. ✉ *Playa Caleta Lado Ote. s/n, Fracc. Las Playas (a 5-min taxi ride east of town square), Old Acapulco,* ☎ *744/482–5007. AE, MC, V.*

LODGING

In Acapulco, geography is price, so where you stay determines what you pay. The most exclusive area is the Acapulco Diamante, home to some of the most luxurious hotels in Mexico—so lush and well equipped that most guests don't budge from the minute they arrive. The minuses: Playa Revolcadero is too rough for swimming (although great for surfing), and this area is a 25-minute (expensive: $8–$14) taxi ride from the heart of Acapulco.

There is much more activity on Avenida Costera Miguel Alemán, where the majority of large hotels, discos, American-style restaurants, and airline offices can be found, along with Acapulco's most popular beaches. All the Costera hotels have freshwater pools and sundecks, and most have restaurants and/or bars overlooking or on the beach. Hotels across the street are almost always less expensive than those directly on the beach; because there are no private beaches in Acapulco, all you have to do is cross the road to enjoy the sand.

Moving west along the Costera leads you to downtown Acapulco. The beaches and restaurants here are popular with Mexican vacationers; the hotels attract Canadian and European bargain-hunters.

You can assume that accommodations that cost more than $50 (double) will include a telephone, TV, and a view of the bay. All hotels have air-conditioning unless otherwise stated. Even the cheapest hotels have cooling ceiling fans.

Note: Most hotels are booked solid Christmas, Easter week, and during school vacations in July and August, so if you plan to visit then, it's wise to make reservations months in advance. Prices during Christmas week are 10% to 20% higher than the rest of the year.

CATEGORY	COST*
$$$$	over $250
$$$	$150–$250
$$	$75–$150
$	under $75

**All prices are for a standard double room, excluding 15% sales (called IVA) tax and 2% room tax.*

Acapulco Diamante

$$$$ ★ **Las Brisas.** Set high on a hillside, Las Brisas remains distinct in Acapulco for the secluded haven it provides its guests. This self-contained luxury complex has one-bedroom units to deluxe private casitas, complete with small private pools. All have beautiful bay views and a few have TVs. As the facilities are very spread out, transportation is by white-and-pink Jeep, which you can rent for $70 a day; otherwise, it's a wait for the staff to pick you up. Rates include a Continental breakfast stylishly delivered to your room. On Saturdays from December through April, the hotel puts on a rousing Fiesta Mexicana. ✉ *Carretera Escénica 5255, Las Brisas, 39868,* ☎ *744/469–6900 or 888/559–4329,* FAX *744/484–2269,* WEB *www.brisas.com.mx. 300 rooms. 2 restaurants, in-room data ports, 5 tennis courts, 3 pools, hair salon, hot tub, sauna, snorkeling, sailing, access to water skiing, fishing, 2 bars, dry cleaning, laundry service, concierge, meeting room, car rental, travel services. AE, DC, MC, V.*

$$$$ ★ **Camino Real Acapulco Diamante.** This stunning hotel is set at the foot of a lush tropical hillside on exclusive Pichilingue Beach, far from the madding crowd. All rooms are done in luscious pastels, with tile floors, balcony or terrace (most with ceiling fans), and luxurious baths. Each has a view of peaceful Puerto Marqués bay. Eleven extra-spacious club rooms have their own concierge and extra amenities. Some rates include a buffet breakfast. ✉ *Carretera Escénica, Km 14, Calle Baja Catita, Acapulco Diamante, 39867,* ☎ *744/466–1010 or 800/722–6466,* FAX *744/466–1111,* WEB *www.caminoreal.com/acapulco. 145 rooms, 11 suites. 3 restaurants, room service, in-room safes, minibars, cable TV, golf privileges, tennis court, 3 pools, gym, spa, beach, snorkeling, sailing, waterskiing, fishing, 2 bars, baby-sitting, children's programs* *(ages 5–15), laundry service, concierge, meeting room, car rental, travel services, no smoking rooms. AE, DC, MC, V.*

$$$$ **Quinta Real.** In the late 1990s, one of Mexico's most prestigious hotel chains inaugurated this exclusive low-slung resort in the posh Punta Diamante section, about a 10-minute drive from downtown Acapulco. The 74 suites built on a hillside overlooking the sea have Mexican-made hardwood furniture and earth-tone drapes, rugs, and bedcovers. All have balconies, marble floors, and closet door handles shaped like iguanas—the hotel's signature motif. Guests take advantage of the large freshwater pools and the endless stretch of lovely beach. ✉ *Paseo de la Quinta Lote 6, Desarrollo Turmstico Real Diamante, Acapulco Diamante 39907,* ☎ *744/469–1500 or 800/457–4000,* FAX *744/469–1515,* WEB *www.quintareal.com. 74 suites. Restaurant, room service, cable TV, 4 pools, gym, spa, beach, snorkeling, sailing, access to waterskiing, fishing, bar, baby-sitting, laundry service, concierge, Internet, car rental. AE, DC, MC, V.*

$$$ ★ **Fairmont Acapulco Princess.** The Princess is one of those luxury digs that lures the rich and famous. In fact, eccentric multimillionaire Howard Hughes rented a suite here in the 1970s before he died. The pool near the reception desk is sensational—fantastic tropical ponds with little waterfalls and a slatted bridge. Large, delightfully light and airy rooms have cane furniture, marble floors, plus Jacuzzi tubs in the bathrooms. A new full-service spa and a business center opened in 2002, and a new tennis stadium hosts international tournaments. The optional Modified American Plan (breakfast and dinner) costs $38 per person. ✉ *Playa Revolcadero (A.P. 1351), Revolcadero 39300,* ☎ *744/469–1000 or 800/441–1414,* FAX *744/469–1016,* WEB *www.fairmont.com. 927 rooms, 92 suites. 3 restaurants, café, room service, in-room safes, minibars, cable TV, 18-hole golf course, 11 tennis courts, 5 pools, gym, spa, beach, diving, snorkeling, sailing, waterskiing, fishing, basketball, 3 bars, dance club, shops, baby-sitting, children's programs (ages 3–12), laundry service, concierge, business services, meeting room, car rental, travel services. AE, DC, MC, V.*

$$$ ★ **Fairmont Pierre Marqués.** This hotel, built as a beach hideaway for J. Paul Getty in 1958, is especially blessed because guests have access to all the Princess's facilities without the crowds. A $30 million makeover added red-tile roofs and touches of the old Mexico hacienda; rooms are getting new floors, overhead fans, and natural wood furniture. In addition to standard rooms the Pierre Marqués offers guests villas and duplex bungalows with private patios. Executive premier rooms have a small fridge. ✉ *Apdo. 1351, Playa Revolcadero, Revolcadero 39907,* ☎ *744/466–1000 or 800/441–1414,* FAX *7/466–1046,* WEB *www.fairmont.com. 256 rooms, 80 suites. 2 restaurants, deli, room service, in-room safes, minibars, cable TV, 18-hole golf course, 5 tennis courts, 3 pools, beach, bar, shops, baby-sitting, children's programs (3–12), playground, laundry service, concierge, meeting room, car rental, travel services. AE, DC, MC, V.*

The Costera

$$$$ **Hyatt Regency Acapulco.** A luxurious oasis that you never have to leave, this property is popular with business travelers and conventioneers. The decor is striking, with strong Caribbean colors; in fact, the hotel's glamorous setting has appeared in many Mexican soap operas. Four outstanding eateries (including a kosher restaurant), a new spa, and a lavish shopping area are among the reasons for staying put. The Hyatt is also the only hotel in Latin America with an on-site synagogue, supervised by the orthodox rabbinate of Mexico City. The west side of the hotel insulates you from the noise of the maneuvers of the nearby

naval base. ✉ *Costera Miguel Alemán 1, Costera 39869,* ☎ *744/469–1234 or 800/233–1234,* FAX *744/484–3087,* WEB *www.hyatt.com. 607 rooms, 17 suites. 4 restaurants, snack bar, room service, in-room safes, minibars, cable TV, 5 tennis courts, 2 pools, gym, spa, beach, 3 bars, shops, baby-sitting, children's programs (ages 8–12) in high season only, laundry service, meeting room, car rental, travel services, free parking. AE, DC, MC, V.*

$$$ **Villa Vera.** A five-minute drive north of the Costera leads to what was once one of Acapulco's most exclusive hotels. This is where Elizabeth Taylor married Mike Todd and where Lana Turner put down roots for three years. Although it has many rivals, the name sells. Some of the villas, which were once private homes, have their own pools, and some standard rooms have been converted into suites. Units have coffeemakers, videocassette players, and other amenities, but are otherwise unremarkable. Although there's no beach, the main pool with its swim-up bar is the hotel's hub; the full-service spa soothes and relaxes. Children under 16 are now allowed. ✉ *Apdo. 560, Lomas del Mar 35, Costera 39690,* ☎ *744/484–0333 or 888/554–2361,* FAX *744/484–7479,* WEB *www.clubregina.com. 24 rooms, 25 suites, 6 villas. Restaurant, minibars, cable TV, 4 tennis courts, 15 pools, aerobics, gym, spa, bar, shop, laundry service, meeting room, concierge, car rental, travel services. AE, MC, V.*

$$ ★ **Elcano.** One of Acapulco's traditional favorites, this boutique hotel has been completely remodeled while still (thankfully) maintaining its '50s flavor. The rooms are snappily done in nautical white and navy blue, with white-tiled floors and beautiful modern bathrooms. There's a beachside restaurant with an outstanding breakfast buffet, a more elegant indoor restaurant, and a gorgeous pool that seems to float above the bay, with whirlpools built into its corners. ✉ *Costera Miguel Alemán 75, Costera 39690,* ☎ *744/484–1950 or 800/972–2162,* FAX *744/484–2230,* WEB *www.hotel-elcano.com. 163 rooms, 17 suites. 2 restaurants, room service, minibars, cable TV, golf privileges, pool, gym, beach, snorkeling, boating, waterskiing, fishing, bar, baby-sitting, laundry service, concierge, travel services. AE, DC, MC, V.*

$$ **Fiesta Americana Condesa Acapulco.** The Condesa is right in the thick of the main shopping and restaurant district, and it is ever popular with tour operators. And no wonder—it has one of the liveliest lobby bars and is located on one of the best beaches in town. Guest rooms are decorated in pastel tones. ✉ *Costera Miguel Alemán 97, Costera 39690,* ☎ *744/484–2828 or 800/343–7821,* FAX *744/484–1828,* WEB *www.fiestaamericana.com. 492 rooms, 8 suites. 2 restaurants, room service, minibars, cable TV, 2 pools, beach, parasailing, waterskiing, bar, shop, baby-sitting, children's programs (ages 4–12), dry cleaning, laundry service, concierge, business services, meeting room, car rental, travel services. AE, DC, MC, V.*

$$ **Las Hamacas.** Las Hamacas is a friendly, old-fashioned Acapulco hotel built in the 1950s with rooms surrounding a large inner courtyard. Across the street from the beach, it has a lovely garden of coconut palms from its former days as a plantation, as well as a beach club. A double costs $80. Rooms are spacious and light-filled with modern wood furnishings; those facing the leafy courtyard are the quietest. Junior suites sleep two adults and two children. The hotel is about a three-minute ride from downtown. Guests can play tennis at the nearby Municipal Golf Club. ✉ *Costera Miguel Alemán, Costera (near downtown) 39670,* ☎ *744/483–7006,* FAX *744/483–0575,* WEB *www.hamacas.com.mx. 100 rooms, 20 suites. Restaurant, room service, cable TV, golf privileges, 2 pools, hair salon, paddle tennis, Ping-Pong, bar, shop, meeting room, travel services, free parking. MC, V.*

$$ ★ **Howard Johnson Maralisa.** Formerly the sister hotel of the Villa Vera, this property, on the beach side of the Costera, is now part of the Howard Johnson chain. The rooms are light and decorated in pastels. This is a small, friendly place; some rooms have balconies, and the price is right. The penthouse suite with a refrigerator goes for $252. ✉ *Apdo. 721, Calle Alemania, Costera 39670,* ☎ *744/485–6677 or 800/446–4656,* FAX *744/485–9228,* WEB *www.acapulco-travel.com/hotels/maralis.html. 85 rooms, 5 suites. Restaurant, cable TV, 2 pools, beach, bar, dry cleaning, laundry service. AE, MC, V.*

$$ **Park Hotel & Tennis Center.** A helpful staff and prime location make this hotel an appealing, intimate, and cordial place. Rooms with colonial-style furnishings are well situated around a garden with a good-size pool. Other assets include refrigerators, TVs (Spanish channels only), and some rooms with kitchenettes (for a small fee) and balconies; all are spotlessly clean and well priced. The Park has an excellent tennis center and it's only a block to the beach. Rooms overlooking the tennis courts are the quietest. ✉ *Apdo. 269, Costera Miguel Alemán 127, Costera 39670,* ☎ *744/485–5992,* FAX *744/485–5489. 88 rooms. 3 tennis courts, pool, bar. MC, V.*

Old Acapulco

$ **Boca Chica.** This Old Acapulco mainstay may have peeling paint on the facade and an antique switchboard, but its old-time Mexican ambience is the best at a price that's hard to beat. It's a few short steps from a swimming cove, and the open-air lobby has lovely views of Caletilla Bay. Rooms are small—with old-fashioned slats on the door, little balconies, and nondescript furnishings—but they're very clean and have been freshly painted. The property also has a pretty palapa restaurant with sushi bar, landscaped jungle garden, and pool. An abundant Mexican breakfast is included in the price. ✉ *Playa Caletilla, across the bay from Isla la Roqueta and Mágico Mundo Marino, Old Acapulco 39390,* ☎ *744/483–6601 or 800/346–3942,* WEB *acapulco-travel.web.com.mx/hotels/bocachica. 42 rooms, 3 suites. Restaurant, pool, beach, bar, shops, laundry service, free parking. MC, V.*

$ **Los Flamingos.** Almost a historical monument, this hot-pink hotel was the favored hangout of John Wayne, Johnny ("Tarzan") Weissmuller, Errol Flynn, and the rest of the "Hollywood gang" back in the '50s. The hotel is strung along a cliff that has some of the finest views in Acapulco. Europeans love the place, especially the *coco locos,* which barman Esteban Castañeda will tell you were invented here in the 1960s. Rooms have bright pink walls and baths are spartan (shower only). A circular two-bedroom master suite was once Weissmuller's digs. The hotel provides free transportation to the beach and downtown. ✉ *Av. López Mateos, Old Acapulco,* ☎ *744/482–0690,* FAX *744/483–9806,* WEB *www.acapulco-cvb.org/losflamingos. 234 rooms, 2 suites. Restaurant, pool, bar, laundry service, free parking. MC, V.*

$ **Misión.** Two minutes from the zócalo, this charming, colonial-style hotel surrounds a greenery-rich courtyard with an outdoor dining area that functions only on Thursday. (Ask for the green-and-white pozole.) The rooms are small and by no means fancy, with wrought-iron beds, tile floors, painted brick walls, and ceiling fans (no air-conditioning, no TVs). Every room has a shower, and there's plenty of hot water. The best rooms are on the second and third floors; the top-floor room is large but hot in the daytime. ✉ *Calle Felipe Valle 12, Downtown 39300,* ☎ *744/482–3643,* FAX *744/482–2076. 20 rooms. No credit cards.*

$ **Plaza las Glorias El Mirador.** The old El Mirador has been taken over by the Plaza las Glorias chain, which is part of the Sidek conglomerate responsible for marina and golf developments all over Mexico. Very Mexican in style—white with red tiles and hand-carved Mexican furniture—Plaza las Glorias exudes nostalgia. The hotel is set high on a hill with a knockout view of Acapulco Bay and La Quebrada, where the cliff divers perform. Many of the suites have refrigerators, hot tubs, and stunning ocean vistas. Rates are highest ($170) December 20–January 6, then drop to $69 for the rest of the year. ✉ *Quebrada 74, Old Acapulco 39300,* ☎ *744/483–1155 or 800/342–2644,* FAX *744/482–4564,* WEB *www.sidek.com.mx. 72 rooms, 58 suites. 2 restaurants, minibars, cable TV, 3 pools (one saltwater), hair salon, sauna, bar, shops, children's programs (ages 3–12), laundry service, meeting room, travel services, free parking. AE, DC, MC, V.*

$ **Suites Alba.** On a quiet hillside, the Alba is a resort-style hotel with bargain prices, especially for groups. All suites sleep four and have a kitchenette, private bath, and terrace. There's no extra charge for up to two children under 12 sharing a room with relatives, which makes it especially popular with families. A cable car takes guests to the hotel's beach club on the bay, next door to the Club de Yates, with a 330-ft-long toboggan. During the high season (mid-December–mid-April) transportation from the hotel to Playa Caleta and downtown is free with more than one night's stay. ✉ *Grand Via Tropical 35, Old Acapulco 39390,* ☎ *744/483–0073,* FAX *744/483–8378,* WEB *www.acapulco-cvb.org/suites-alba. 244 suites. 3 restaurants, kitchenettes (some), tennis court, 3 pools, hot tub, beach, bar, shops, laundry service (Dec.–Apr. only), free parking. MC, V.*

Pie de la Cuesta

$$$ ★ **Parador del Sol.** If you want to get away from it all, this is the perfect place. Traversing both the lagoon and the Pacific Ocean sides of the Pie de la Cuesta road, this all-inclusive property gives the impression that it was designed as a luxury resort. The 150 rooms are distributed among pink villas scattered over gardens. Spacious, with tile floors and baths, each room has a fan-cooled terrace complete with hammocks. The rate includes all meals and refreshments, domestic drinks, tennis, dance class, shows, aerobics, and nonmotorized water sports. ✉ *Carretera Pie de la Cuesta–Barra de Coyuca, Km 5, Apdo. 1070, Pie de la Cuesta 39300,* ☎ *744/444–4050 or 800/515–4321,* FAX *744/444–4051. 150 rooms. Restaurant, fans, cable TV, miniature golf, 4 tennis courts, 2 pools, aerobics, gym, fishing, soccer, 2 bars, dance club, shops, children's programs (ages 4–12), laundry service, meeting rooms, free parking. AE, DC, MC, V.*

$$ ★ **Villas Ukae Kim.** You can't miss the bright colors of this rustic seaside lodge. The spacious rooms are tastefully painted in bright Mexican hues, and all have overhead fans (four have air-conditioning), mosquito nets slung over large double beds, and terraces. A perfect hideaway for a short or long stay, the hotel has 22 rooms, including a honeymoon suite with a private hot tub for $130. The price of a room includes $21 credit a day in the restaurant, which is expensive but good and overlooks the beach. Don't expect phones or TVs—come here to get away from them. ✉ *Av. Fuerza Aereo Mexicana 356, Pie de la Cuesta 39300,* ☎ FAX *744/460–2187. 21 rooms, 1 suite. Restaurant, pool, waterskiing, fishing, bar, laundry service, free parking. No credit cards.*

$ **Hacienda Valma.** Congenial hosts Philippe and Parwin run the place with European flair. Twenty white stucco bungalows (six with air-conditioning), named after famous musicians and painters, line the beachfront property. The plain and small rooms, which accommodate two, three, or five people, have huge beds protected by mosquito nets and tiny bathrooms but no hot water. The rates go up on weekends when the hotel fills with embassy personnel from nearby Mexico City.

A luxury wing has a spa with hot tub, massages, and the largest pool in Pie de la Cuesta. ✉ *Av. Fuerza Aereo Mexicana 356, Pie de la Cuesta 39300,* ☎ *744/460–2882,* FAX *744/460–0697,* WEB *www.vayma.com.mx. 20 rooms. Restaurant, fans, pool, waterskiing, boccie, horseback riding, volleyball, bar, laundry service, free parking. No credit cards.*

NIGHTLIFE AND THE ARTS

The companies listed in the Acapulco A to Z can organize evening jaunts to most of the dance and music places listed below. And don't forget the nightly entertainment at most hotels. The big resorts have live music to accompany the early evening happy hour, and some feature big-name bands from Mexico. Many hotels sponsor theme parties—Italian Night, Beach Party Night, and similar festivities.

Cultural Shows

Acapulco International Center (✉ Costera Miguel Alemán, Costera, ☎ 744/484–3218), also known as the Convention Center, has a Mexican Fiesta Wednesday and Friday (and Monday December–April), where you can take in mariachi bands, singers, and the *voladores* (flyers) from Papantla. The show with open bar and buffet costs about $52; entrance to the show alone is $30. The performance starts at 8. On Saturday December–April at **El Mexicano** restaurant (✉ Carretera Escénica 5255, Las Brisas, ☎ 744/469–6900) in Las Brisas hotel, the Mexican Fiesta starts off with a *tianguis* (marketplace) of handicrafts and ends with a spectacular display of fireworks.

Dance

Salon Q (✉ Costera Miguel Alemán 23, Costera, ☎ 744/484–3252), referred to as the "Cathedral of Salsa," is a combination dance hall and disco where the bands play salsas, merengues, and other Latin rhythms for young and old. There's a live show weekends—mostly impersonations of Mexican entertainers—as well as dance contests.

Discos

Reservations are advisable for a big group; late afternoon or after 9 PM are the best times to call. New Year's Eve requires planning.

Except for Palladium, Zucca, and Enigma, the discos are clustered on the Costera.

Alebrije is enormous, with seating for 2,000 people in love seats and booths. The most popular night is Friday, when everyone is bathed in foam, with a kind of wet-T-shirt effect. From 10:30 (opening time) to 11:30, the music is slow and romantic; then the disco music and the light show begin, and they go on until dawn. ✉ *Costera Miguel Alemán 3308, across from Hyatt Regency, Costera,* ☎ *744/484–5902.*

Andromeda is quite spectacular, even for a city known for its splendiferous discos; this one will impress even the most jaded discoers. Entrance to the Queen of the Sea's "castle" is over a torchlit moat; once inside, the impression is of being in a submarine, where live "mermaids" swim about. There are supposedly two dance floors, but the 18–25 crowd dances everywhere to the latest techno and techno-pop sounds. Open weekends only, May–November. ✉ *Costera Miguel Alemán 15, at Fragata Yucatán, Costera,* ☎ *744/484–8815.*

Baby O is a private club that is known to open its doors to a few select nonmembers. Eschewing the glitz and mirrors of Acapulco's older discos, Baby O resembles a cave in a tropical jungle. The crowd is 25 to 35, mostly well-dressed, wealthy Mexicans. ✉ *Costera Miguel Alemán 22, Costera,* ☎ *744/484–7474.*

Discobeach, right on the beach, is Acapulco's only alfresco disco and its most informal one. The under-30 crowd sometimes even turns up in shorts. The waiters are young and friendly—some people find them overly so. (In fact, this is one of Acapulco's legendary pickup spots.) One night they're all in togas carrying bunches of grapes; the next they're in pajamas. Every Wednesday, ladies' night, all the women receive flowers. During the day, you can try the bungee jump on the beach. ✉ *Playa Condesa, Costera,* ☎ *744/484–8230.*

★ **Enigma** (formerly called Extravaganzza) claims to have the ultimate in light and sound and is Acapulco's answer to the Luxor hotel in Las Vegas with its lavish, New Egyptian theme. It accommodates 700 at a central bar and in comfortable booths, and a glass wall provides an unbelievable view of Acapulco Bay, which includes fireworks on weekends. The music (which is for all ages) starts at 10:30. ✉ *On Carretera Escénica to Las Brisas, near Las Brisas,* ☎ *744/484–7164.*

Palladium is another spectacular production of Tony Rullán, creator of Enigma. A waterfall that cascades down the hill from the dance-floor level makes this place hard to miss. As at Enigma, the dance floor is nearly surrounded by 50-ft-high windows, giving dancers a wraparound view of Acapulco. ✉ *On Carretera Escénica to Las Brisas, near Las Brisas,* ☎ *744/481–0330.*

★ **Zucca** attracts a 25-and-up crowd—mainly couples—and is one of the few discos where people really dress up, with the men in well-cut pants and shirts and the women in racy outfits and cocktail dresses. Singles gravitate toward the two bars in the back. Zucca is quite snug, to put it nicely, and people tend to come here earlier to dance to music from the '70s, '80s, and '90s. At 2 AM there is a fireworks display. A glass elevator provides an interesting overview of the scene and leads upstairs to a little shop that stocks T-shirts and lingerie. ✉ *On Carretera Escénica to Las Brisas, near Las Brisas,* ☎ *744/484–6727.*

OUTDOOR ACTIVITIES AND SPORTS

Participant Sports

Fishing

Fishing trips can be arranged through your hotel, downtown at the Pesca Deportiva near the *muelle* (dock) across from the zócalo, or through travel agents. At the docks, you can hire a boat for $40 a day (two lines). Stick with one of the reliable companies whose boats and equipment are in good condition. Boats accommodating 4–10 people cost $200–$500 a day, $45–$60 by chair. Excursions leave about 7 AM and return at 1 PM or 2 PM. You are required to get a fishing license ($8–$10, depending on the season) from the Secretaría de Pesca; you'll find their representative at the dock. It's closed during siesta, between 2 and 4 in the afternoon.

Small boats for freshwater fishing can be rented at **Cadena's** and **Tres Marías** at Coyuca Lagoon.

Fitness and Swimming

Most of the time, Acapulco weather is like August in the warmest parts of the United States. This means that you should cut back on your workouts outdoors and maintain proper hydration by drinking plenty of water.

Villa Vera Spa and Fitness Center (☎ 744/484–0333) in the Villa Vera hotel is equipped with exercise machines (including step machines), free weights, and benches. Masseuses and cosmetologists give facials, milk baths, herbal wraps, algae marina treatments, and shiatsu, reflexology, couples, and Swedish massages. Both the beauty center and the gym are open to nonguests.

Spa Willow Stream (☎ 744/469–1000), in the Fairmont Princess hotel, opened at the beginning of 2002 as the largest full-service spa in Acapulco. The Atlantes Fitness Center, with trainer and Keizer equipment, is part of the complex. The spa offers traditional and New Age massages, facials, a hair salon, Jacuzzi, sauna, and Swiss showers. Nonguests are welcome at the spa and gym.

Golf

There is a public golf course at the **Club de Golf** (☎ 744/484–0781) on the Costera across from the Acapulco Malibú hotel. Greens fees are $35 for nine holes, $52 for 18. Two 18-hole championship golf courses are shared by the **Fairmont Acapulco Princess and Fairmont Pierre Marqués** hotels. Reservations should be made in advance (☎ 744/469–1000). Greens fees are $70 for guests and $90 for nonguests. At **Tres Vidas** (✉ Carretera al Aeropuerto, domicilio conocido, Tres Vidas, ☎ 744/444–5135), which is open to the public at large, greens fees are $75 for 18 holes. A round at the 18-hole **Mayan Palace** (✉ Playa Revolcadero, domicilio conocido, Revolcadero, ☎ 744/469–0201) course is $92 for guests, $103 for nonguests.

Jogging

If you don't like beach jogging, the only real venue for running in the downtown area is along the sidewalk next to the Costera Miguel Alemán at the seafront, but you'll have to go very early, before traffic fumes set in. Away from the city center, the best area for running is out at the Acapulco Princess hotel, on the airport road. A 2-km (1-mi) loop is laid out along a lightly traveled road, and in the early morning you can also run along the asphalt trails on the golf course.

Rollerblading

For a change of pace from sand and sea activities, come to **Roller Gran Prix** (✉ east of Costera Miguel Alemán, just before Los Rancheros restaurant, Brisamar, ☎ 744/484–9313) for rollerblading to disco music and racing Formula One–style go-carts. The $4 fee includes blades, and instruction is available. Go-carts cost $3.50 for five minutes.

Scuba Diving

Arnold Brothers (✉ Costera Miguel Alemán 205, near El Fuerte de San Diego, Old Acapulco, ☎ 744/482–1877), one of the best in town, has been running scuba-diving excursions and snorkeling trips for almost 50 years. Scuba trips cost $35; snorkeling costs $20. Lessons are included.

Tennis

Court fees range from about $9 to $26 an hour during the day and double in the evening. At the hotel courts, nonguests pay about $6 more per hour. Lessons with English-speaking instructors start at about $15 an hour; ball boys get a $2 tip.

There are several places in town to play tennis. **Costa Club** (☎ 744/485–9050) has three hard-surface courts, two lighted. In addition to five outdoor courts, the **Fairmont Acapulco Princess** (☎ 744/469–1000) has two air-conditioned indoor courts and a new multimillion-dollar tennis stadium for hosting international tournaments. The **Fairmont Pierre Marqués** (☎ 744/466–1000) has five courts. The **Hyatt Regency** (☎ 744/484–1225) has three lighted courts at the Municipal Golf Club. There are three lighted courts at the **Park Hotel & Tennis Center** (☎ 744/485–5992). You'll find five courts at **Tiffany's Racquet**

Club (✉ Av. Villa Vera 120, Costera, ☎ 744/484–7949). At **Mayan Palace** (☎ 744/469–1879), there are 12 lighted courts. **Villa Vera** (☎ 744/484–0333) has two outdoor lighted clay courts and two hard-surface courts.

Water Sports

Waterskiing, broncos (one-person Jet Skis), and parasailing can all be arranged on the beach. Parasailing is an Acapulco highlight; a five-minute trip costs $125. Waterskiing is about $40 an hour; broncos cost $40–$95 for a half hour, depending on the size. Windsurfing can be arranged at Caleta and most beaches along the Costera but is especially good at Puerto Marqués. The main surfing beach is Revolcadero.

Acapulco's latest attraction, the **Shotover Jet,** is an import from the rivers around Queenstown, New Zealand. For $60, you're driven via air-conditioned coach from the outfit's Acapulco offices to a site near the town of Tierra Colorado (35 minutes each way). There you climb aboard the 12-passenger craft for an exciting 30-minute boat ride on the Papagayo River, complete with several thrilling 360-degree turns—one of the Shotover Jet's trademarks—and vistas of local flora and fauna (cacti, bats, and iguanas). For more thrills, you can shoot the rapids for $60 an hour with a guide. For both rides, you pay $90. Rock climbing can be included in either for the same price. After the ride, you can return directly to Acapulco or take a later shuttle bus and linger at the riverside property, which has a swimming pool plus restaurant, souvenir shop, and an iguana nursery. ✉ *Continental Plaza, Costera Miguel Alemán, Locale 3, Costera,* ☎ *744/484–1154.*

Spectator Sports

Bullfights

The season runs from about the first week of January to Easter, and *corridas* (bullfights) are held on Sunday at 5:30. Tickets are available through your hotel or at the **Plaza de Toros** ticket window (✉ Av. Circunvalación, across from Playa Caleta, Playa Caleta, ☎ 744/482–1181) Monday–Saturday 10–2 and Sunday 10:30–5. Tickets in the shade (*sombra*)—the only way to go—cost about $16. Preceding the fight are performances of Spanish dances and music by the Chili Frito band.

Jai Alai

The **Jai Alai Acapulco Race & Sports Book** (✉ Costera Miguel Alemán 498, Costera, ☎ 744/484–31–95) has two restaurants and a bar, and capacity for 1,500 spectators. The fast-paced games take place Thursday through Sunday at 9 PM, mid-December through January 6, Easter week, and throughout July and August. Entrance is $7. The slower-paced game of bingo is played year-round, and Sports Book, or betting on major U.S. sporting events, is also a 365-day activity.

SHOPPING

The main shopping strip is on the Costera Miguel Alemán from the Costa Club to the El Presidente Hotel. Here you can find Guess, Peer, Aca Joe, Amarras, Polo Ralph Lauren, and other fashionable sportswear boutiques. Downtown (Old) Acapulco doesn't have many name shops, but this is where you'll find the inexpensive tailors patronized by the Mexicans, lots of little souvenir shops, and a vast flea market with crafts. Also downtown is Sanborns. Most shops are open from 10 to 7 Monday through Saturday and are closed on Sunday.

Department Stores and Supermarkets

Except for the waitresses' uniforms, the food, and a good handicrafts selection, **Sanborns** is very un-Mexican. Still, it is an institution throughout Mexico. It sells English-language newspapers, magazines, and books, as well as a line of high-priced souvenirs. The Calinda branch (✉ Costera Miguel Alemán 1226, Costera, ☎ 744/484–4413), the Oceanic 2000 branch (✉ Costera Miguel Alemán 3111, Costera, ☎ 744/484–2025), and the downtown branch (✉ Costera Miguel Alemán 209, Costera, ☎ 744/482–6167) are open 7 AM to midnight during the high season and 7:30 AM–11 PM the rest of the year.

Branches of **Aurrerá, Gigante, Price Club, Sam's, Wal-Mart** (in case you don't get enough of them back home), **Comercial Mexicana,** and the upscale **Liverpool** department store (called Fabricas de Francia) are all on the Costera and sell everything from liquor and fresh and frozen food to lightbulbs, clothing, medicines, garden furniture, and sports equipment.

Malls

Malls in Acapulco range from the delightful air-conditioned shopping arcade at the Princess hotel to rather gloomy collections of shops that sell cheap jewelry and embroidered dresses. Malls are listed below from east to west.

Aca Mall, which is next door to Marbella Mall, is all white and marble; here you'll find Tommy Hilfiger, Peer, and Aca Joe. The multilevel **Marbella Mall,** at the Diana Glorieta, is home to Martí, a well-stocked sporting-goods store; a health center (drugstore, clinic, and lab); the Canadian Embassy; and Bing's Ice Cream, as well as several restaurants. **Plaza Bahía,** next to the Costa Club hotel, is an air-conditioned mall with boutiques such as Dockers, Nautica, and Aspasia.

Markets

Not to be missed is the **Mercado Municipal,** where restaurants load up on the day's veggies, fruits, and meats in the early morning. It's also where the locals go to buy piñatas, serapes, leather goods, baskets, hammocks, and velvet paintings of the Virgin of Guadalupe. Many stands offer charms to attract a lover and amulets against your enemies. **El Mercado de Artesanías El Parazal,** a conglomeration of every souvenir in town, is a 15-minute walk from Sanborns downtown. You'll find fake ceremonial masks, the ever-present onyx chessboards, $20 hand-embroidered dresses, imitation silver, hammocks, and even skin cream made from turtles (don't buy it, because turtles are endangered and you won't get it through U.S. Customs). ✉ *From Sanborns downtown, head away from the Costera to Vásquez de León and turn right 1 block, Downtown.* ⏲ *Daily 9–9.*

In an effort to get the itinerant vendors off the beaches and streets, the local government set up a series of **flea markets** along the Costera, mostly uninviting dark tunnels of stalls that carry a large supply of inexpensive collectibles and souvenirs. The selections of archaeological-artifact replicas, bamboo wind chimes, painted wooden birds, shell earrings, and embroidered clothes begin to look identical. Prices at the flea markets are often quite low, but it's a good idea to compare prices of items you're interested in with prices in the shops, and bargaining is essential. It's best to buy articles described as being made from semiprecious stones or silver in reputable establishments, lest you end up with cleverly painted paste or a silver facsimile called *alpaca*. Always check to make sure that .925 is stamped on the silver piece; this verifies its authenticity. One large market with a convenient location is La Diana Mercado de Artesanías, a block from the Continental Plaza hotel, close to the Diana monument.

Specialty Shops

Art

Edith Matison's Art Gallery (✉ Av. Costera Miguel Alemán 2010, across from Club de Golf, Costera, ☎ 744/484–3084) shows the works of renowned international and Mexican artists, including Calder, Dalí, Siqueiros, and Tamayo, and a large line of Mexican crafts.

Galería Rudic (✉ Vicente Yañez Pinzón 9, across from Continental Plaza and adjoining the Jardín des Artistes restaurant, Costera, ☎ 744/484–1004) is one of the best galleries in town, with a good collection of top contemporary Mexican artists, including Armando Amaya, Leonardo Nierman, Gastón Cabrera, Trinidad Osorio, and Casiano García.

Pal Kepenyes (✉ Guitarrón 140, Lomas Guitarrón, ☎ 744/484–3738) gets good press for his sculpture and jewelry (some of it rather racy), on display in his workshop. The whimsical, painted papier-mâché and giant ceramic sculpture of **Sergio Bustamente** (✉ Costera Miguel Alemán 120–9, across from Fiesta American Condesa hotel, Costera, ☎ 744/484–4992) can also be seen at his gallery and at the Hyatt Regency Hotel.

Boutiques

Armando's (✉ Costera Miguel Alemán at the Hyatt Regency, Costera, ☎ 744/484–5111; ✉ Costera Miguel Alemán 1252–7, in La Torre de Acapulco, Costera, ☎ 744/469–1234) carries its own line of women's dresses, jackets, and vests with a Mexican flavor, as well as some interesting Luisa Conti accessories. **Nautica** (✉ Plaza Bahía, Costera, ☎ 744/484–1650; smaller shop at ✉ Las Brisas hotel, Carretera Escénica 5255, Las Brisas, ☎ 744/485–7511) is stocked with stylish casual clothing for men. **Men's and Ladies** (✉ Fairmont Princess hotel arcade, Playa Revolcadero, Revolcadero, ☎ 744/469–1000) has a smashing line of beach cover-ups and hand-painted straw hats, as well as Israeli bathing suits, Colombian sweaters, Walford bodywear, and light dresses. **St. Germaine** (✉ Costera Miguel Alemán, outside the entrance to Fiesta Americana Condesa hotel, Costera, ☎ 744/485–2515; ✉ Costa Club, Costera Miguel Alemán 123, Costera, ☎ 744/487–3712) carries a sensational line of swimsuits for equally sensational bodies.

Custom-Designed Clothes

Esteban's (✉ Costera Miguel Alemán 2010, across from Club de Golf, Costera, ☎ 744/484–3084) is the most glamorous shop in Acapulco, boasting a clientele of international celebrities and many of the important local families. Esteban's opulent evening dresses range from $200 to $3,000, although daytime dresses average $120. There's a men's clothing section on the second floor. If you scour the sale racks, you can find some items marked down as much as 80%.

Handicrafts

Alebrijes & Caracoles (✉ Plaza Bahía, Costera, ☎ 744/485–0490) comprises two shops designed to look like flea-market stalls. Top-quality merchandise is on display, including papier-mâché fruits and vegetables, Christmas ornaments, wind chimes, and brightly painted wooden animals from Oaxaca. **Arte Para Siempre** (✉ Costera Miguel Alemán 4834, near Hyatt Regency, Costera, ☎ 744/484–3624), in the Acapulco Cultural Center, sparkles with handicrafts from the seven regions of Guerrero, including hand loomed shawls, painted gourds, hammocks, baskets, Olinala boxes, and silver jewelry.

Silver and Jewelry

Minette (✉ Princess arcade, Playa Revolcadero, Revolcadero, ☎ 744/469–1000) has diamond jewelry of impeccable design by Charles Garnier and Nouvelle Bague that you wouldn't be surprised to find on Fifth Avenue. Also on display is jewelry set with Caledonia stones from Africa plus Emilia Castillo's exquisite line of brightly colored porcelain ware, inlaid with silver fish, stars, and birds. **Suzett's** (✉ Hyatt Regency, Costera Miguel Alemán 1, Costera, ☎ 744/469–1234), a tony shop that's been around for years, has a laudable selection of gold and silver jewelry. **Tane** (✉ Hyatt Regency, Costera Miguel Alemán 1, Costera, ☎ 744/469–1234; ✉ Las Brisas hotel, Carretera Escénica 5255, Las Brisas, ☎ 744/469–6900) carries small selections of the exquisite flatware, jewelry, and objets d'art created by one of Mexico's most prestigious (and expensive) silversmiths.

SIDE TRIP TO TAXCO, THE SILVER CITY

275 km (170 mi) north of Acapulco.

This is Mexico's most medieval-looking city—marvelously preserved colonial buildings nuzzle cobblestone streets that wind up and down the foothills of the Sierra Madre in the state of Guerrero. You could say that its white stucco buildings, red-tile roofs, and quaint inns and cafés make it a centuries-old Mexican town at its best—which is why the government declared the city a national monument in 1928. The city Taxco (pronounced *tahss*-ko) is a living work of art. For centuries its silver mines drew foreign mining companies here. Now its charm, mild temperatures, abundant sunshine, flowers, and silversmiths make Taxco a popular getaway.

Hernán Cortés discovered Taxco's mines in 1522 while looking for lead for his armory. The silver rush lasted until the next century, when excitement tapered off. Then, in the 1700s, a Frenchman who Mexicanized his name to José de la Borda discovered a rich lode that revitalized the town's silver industry and made him exceedingly wealthy. After Borda, however, Taxco's importance faded, until the 1930s and the arrival of William G. Spratling, a writer-architect from New Orleans. Enchanted by Taxco and convinced of its potential as a center for silver jewelry, Spratling set up an apprentice shop. His artistic talent and fascination with pre-Columbian design combined to produce silver jewelry and other artifacts that soon earned Taxco its worldwide reputation once more as the Silver City, this time known for its silver artisans. Spratling's inspiration lives on in his students and their descendants, many of whom are the city's current silversmiths.

Getting around Taxco is easy, especially if you're a sturdy walker. But be advised that Taxco's altitude is 5,800 ft, so if you've come from sea level, you might want to take it easy on your first day.

11 The **Iglesia de San Sebastián y Santa Prisca** has dominated Plaza Borda—one of the busiest and most colorful town squares in all Mexico—since the 18th century. Usually just called Santa Prisca, it was built by French silver magnate José de la Borda in thanks to the Almighty for his having literally stumbled upon a rich silver vein. According to legend, St. Prisca appeared to workers during a storm and prevented a wall of the church from tumbling to the ground. Soon after, the church was named in her honor. The style of the church—sort of Spanish Baroque meets rococo—is known as churrigueresque, and its pale pink exterior is a stunning surprise. This is one of Mexico's most beautiful colonial churches and Taxco's most important landmark, and its facade, naves, and *bovedas* (vaulted ceilings), as well as important paintings by Mex-

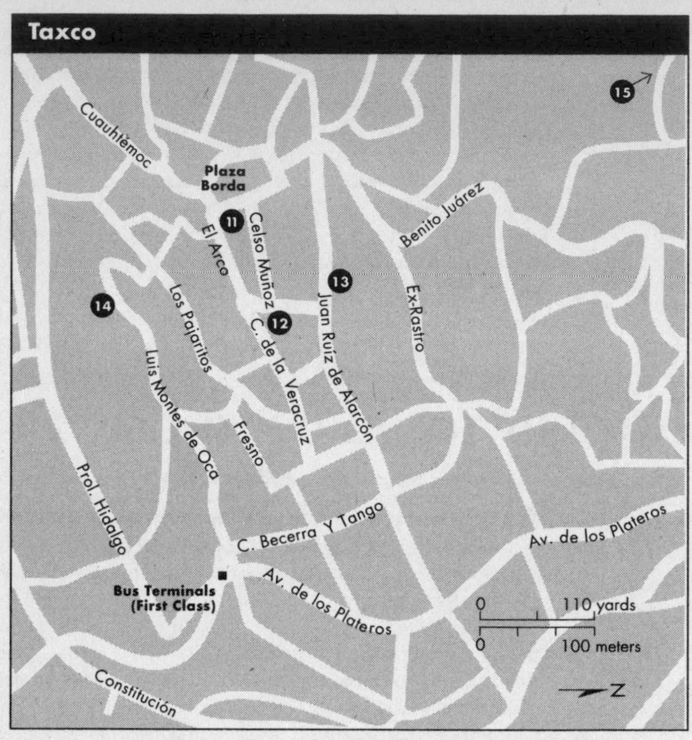

ican Juan Cabrera, are slowly being restored. ✉ *Southwest side of Plaza Borda,* ⏲ *Daily 6 AM–9 PM.*

NEED A BREAK? Around Plaza Borda are several *neverías* (ice cream stands) where you can treat yourself to ice cream in exotic flavors such as tequila, corn, avocado, or coconut. **Bar Paco,** directly across the street from Santa Prisca, is a Taxco institution; its terrace is the perfect vantage point for watching the comings and goings on the zócalo while sipping a margarita or a beer.

12 The former home of William G. Spratling houses the **Spratling Museum.** This small gallery explains the working of colonial mines and displays Spratling's collection of pre-Columbian artifacts. ✉ *Porfirio Delgado 1,* ☎ *744/622–1660.* 🎫 *$3.* ⏲ *Tues.–Sat. 9–6, Sun. 9–3.*

13 **Casa Humboldt** was named for the German adventurer Alexander von Humboldt, who stayed here in 1803. The Moorish-style 18th-century house has a finely detailed facade. It now houses a wonderful little museum of colonial art. ✉ *Calle Juan Ruíz de Alarcón 6,* ☎ *7/622–5501.* 🎫 *$2.25.* ⏲ *Tues.–Sat. 10–5, Sun. 10–3.*

14 If you want to experience a typical Mexican market, with everything from peanuts to electrical appliances, the **Mercado Municipal** is worth a visit. Saturday and Sunday mornings, when locals from surrounding towns come with their produce and crafts, the market spills out onto the surrounding streets. You'll find it directly down the hill from the Church of San Sebastián and Santa Prisca. Look for the market's chapel to the Virgin of Guadalupe.

15 The largest caverns in Mexico, the **Grutas de Cacahuamilpa** (Caves of Cacahuamilpa) are about 15 minutes northeast of Taxco. These 15 large chambers encompass 12 km (7½ mi) of geological formations. All the

caves are illuminated, and a tour takes around two hours. 🎫 *$3 (includes tour).*

Dining and Lodging

Gastronomes can find everything from tagliatelle to iguana in Taxco restaurants, and meals are much less expensive than in Acapulco. Dress is casual, but less so than at Acapulco resorts. There are several categories of hotel to choose from within Taxco's two types: the small inns nestled on the hills skirting the zócalo and the larger, more modern hotels on the outskirts of town.

$ ✕ **Cielito Lindo.** This charming restaurant has a Mexican-international menu. Give the Mexican specialties a try—for example, *pollo en pipian verde* (chicken simmered in a mild, pumpkin seed–based sauce). ✉ *Plaza Borda 14,* ☎ *7/622–0603. MC, V.*

$ ★ ✕ **Hostería el Adobe.** The lack of view (there are only two window tables) is more than made up for by the original decor—for example, hanging lamps made of a cluster of masks—and the excellent food. Favorites include garlic-and-egg soup and the *queso adobe,* fried cheese on a bed of potato skins, covered with a green tomatillo sauce. ✉ *Plazuela de San Juan 13,* ☎ *7/622–1416. MC, V.*

$ ★ ✕ **El Mural.** This is one of the nicest restaurants in town, with seating indoors or on a poolside terrace, where there's a view not only of a Juan O'Gorman mural but of the stunning Santa Prisca church. The chef prepares classic international favorites—filet mignon and surf and turf—and some delicious Mexican specialties, including cilantro soup, and huitlacoche crepes. The daily three-course fixed-price meal is $14. ✉ *Posada de la Misión, Cerro de la Misión 32,* ☎ *762/622–2198. AE, DC, MC, V.*

$ ★ ✕ **Pagaduría del Rey.** This restaurant has a long-standing reputation for international fare served in a colonial setting. ✉ *Calle H. Colegio Militar 8 (Col. Cerro de la Bermeja, south of town),* ☎ *7/622–3467. MC, V.*

$ ✕ **Santa Fe.** Mexican family-type cooking at its best is served in this simple place. Puebla-style mole, Cornish hen in garlic butter, and enchiladas in green or red chili sauce are among the tasty offerings. There's a daily *comida corrida* (fixed-price) meal for $5. ✉ *Hidalgo 2,* ☎ *762/622–1170. No credit cards.*

$ ✕ **Señor Costilla.** That's right, the name of this whimsical restaurant translates as "Mr. Ribs." The Taxco outpost of the zany Anderson chain serves barbecued ribs and chops in a restaurant with great balcony seating. ✉ *Plaza Borda 1,* ☎ *7/622–3215. MC, V.*

$ ✕ **Toni's.** Prime rib and lobster are the specialties at this eatery that features a great view and a romantic setting. ✉ *Monte Taxco Hotel,* ☎ *7/622–1300. AE, MC, V. Closed Sun. No lunch.*

$$$ ★ 🏨 **Posada de la Misión.** Laid out like a colonial-style village, this hotel is within walking distance of town. Rooms range from standard doubles to two-bedroom suites with kitchenettes, fireplaces, cable TV, hair dryers, and terraces. The pool area is adorned with a mural by noted Mexican artist Juan O'Gorman. Rates include taxes, breakfast, and dinner; two children under 12 can stay with their parents at no extra charge. ✉ *Apdo. 88, Cerro de la Misión 32, 40230,* ☎ *762/622–0063,* FAX *762/622–2198. 120 rooms, 30 suites. Restaurant, cable TV, pool, bar, dance club, free parking. AE, DC, MC, V.*

$$ 🏨 **De la Borda.** Long a Taxco favorite, De la Borda is a bit worn, but the large and comfortable rooms were painted in 2001 and the staff couldn't be more hospitable. Ask for a room overlooking town. There's a restaurant, and many bus tours stay here overnight. ✉ *Apdo. 6, Cerro del Pedregal 2, 40200,* ☎ *762/622–0025,* FAX *762/622–0617. 98 rooms,*

4 suites. Restaurant, pool, bar, laundry service, free parking; TV in Spanish only. AE, MC, V.

$$ **Monte Taxco.** A colonial style predominates at this hotel, which has a knockout view, a funicular, three restaurants, a disco, and nightly entertainment. It is a few miles from town, so plan to take taxis to get back and forth. ✉ *Apdo. 84, Lomas de Taxco, 40210,* ☎ *762/622–1300,* FAX *762/622–1428. 153 rooms, 6 suites, 32 villas. 3 restaurants, cable TV, 9-hole golf course, 3 tennis courts, horseback riding, dance club, laundry services. AE, DC, MC, V.*

$ **Agua Escondida.** Popular with some regular visitors to Taxco, this small hotel has simple rooms decorated with Mexican-style furnishings. ✉ *Guillermo Spratling 4, 40200,* ☎ *762/622–1166,* FAX *762/622–1306. 50 rooms. Restaurant, café, cable TV, pool, bar, free parking. MC, V.*

$ **Posada de los Castillo.** This in-town inn is straightforward, clean, and good for the price; however, there are no phones or TVs in rooms. The Emilia Castillo silver shop is off the lobby. ✉ *Juan Ruíz de Alarcón 7, 40200,* ☎ *762/622–1396. 14 rooms. No credit cards.*

$ ★ **Posada de San Javier.** Set somewhat haphazardly around a garden with a pool and a wishing well is this sprawling, very private establishment. In addition to the rooms, there are seven one-bedroom apartments with living rooms and kitchenettes (generally monopolized by wholesale silver buyers). ✉ *Estacas 32 or Exrastro 6, 40200,* ☎ *762/622–3177,* FAX *762/622–2351. 18 rooms, 7 apartments. Restaurant, cable TV, pool, bar. No credit cards.*

$ **Rancho Taxco-Victoria.** This hotel is under the same management as De la Borda. Like De la Borda, it is past its prime but exudes a certain charm. The rooms are always freshly painted, and the Mexican decor is simple but attractive. There's also the requisite splendid view. ✉ *Apdo. 83, Carlos J. Nibbi 5, 40200,* ☎ *762/622–0210,* FAX *762/622–0010. 60 rooms, 4 suites. Restaurant, cable TV, pool, bar. AE, MC, V.*

Nightlife and the Arts

FESTIVALS

Taxco's biggest single cultural event is the Jornadas Alarconianos in May. But it is also known for its abundance of fiestas, which are an integral part of the town's character. These fiestas provide an opportunity to honor almost every saint in heaven with music, dancing, marvelous fireworks (Taxco is Mexico's fireworks capital), and lots of fun. The people of Taxco demonstrate their pyrotechnic skills with set pieces—wondrous blazing "castles" made of bamboo. (Note: Expect high occupancy at local hotels and inns during fiestas.)

January 18–20, the feast of Santa Prisca and San Sebastián, the town's patron saints, is celebrated with music and fireworks.

Holy Week, from Palm Sunday to Easter Sunday, brings processions and events that blend Christian and Indian traditions; the dramas involve hundreds of participants, images of Christ, and, for one particular procession, brown-hooded penitents who flagellate themselves with boughs of thorns following a colonial custom. Most events are centered on Plaza Borda and the Santa Prisca Church. You must reserve a hotel months in advance for Easter week.

The **Jornadas Alarconianos,** during the third week of May, honors one of Mexico's greatest dramatists with theater, dance, and concerts.

September 29, Saint Michael's Day (Dia de San Miguel), is celebrated with regional dances and pilgrimages to the Chapel of Saint Michael the Archangel, on Calle José María Morelos.

In **early November,** on the Monday following the November 1–2 Day of the Dead celebrations, the entire town takes off to a nearby hill for the Fiesta de los Jumil. The *jumil* is a crawling insect, said to taste strongly of iodine, that is considered a great delicacy. Purists eat them alive, but others prefer them stewed, fried, or combined with chili in a hot sauce.

In **late November or early December,** the National Silver Fair (Feria Nacional de la Plata) draws hundreds of artisans from around the world for a variety of displays, concerts, exhibitions, and contests.

NIGHTLIFE

You should satisfy your appetite for fun after dark in Acapulco. Taxco has a few discos, a couple of bars, and some entertainment, but the range is limited. Still, you might enjoy spending an evening perched on a chair on a balcony or in one of the cafés surrounding the Plaza Borda. The **Bar Paco** (✉ Plaza Borda 12, ☎ 762/622–0064) is a traditional favorite. At **Bertha's** (✉ Plaza Borda 9, ☎ 762/622–0172), Taxco's oldest bar, a tequila, lime, and club soda concoction called a Bertha is the house specialty. It is supposedly the forerunner of today's margarita cocktail. In addition, some of the town's best restaurants have music on weekends.

Or immerse yourself in the thick of things, especially on Sunday evening, by settling in on a wrought-iron bench on the zócalo to watch the action and fellow people-watchers.

La Pachanga discotheque (✉ Cerro de la Misión 32, ☎ no phone) at Posada de la Misión is open Tuesday–Sunday and is popular with townsfolk and tourists. **Passagge** (✉ Av. de los Plateros s/n, ☎ 762/627–1177) is a popular disco. Much of Taxco's nighttime activity is at the Monte Taxco hotel's **Windows** discotheque (✉ Lomas de Taxco, ☎ 762/622–1300) on weekends. Or, on Saturday night, the hotel has a buffet and a terrific fireworks display.

Outdoor Activities and Sports

You can play golf or tennis, swim, and ride horses at a few hotels around Taxco. Call to see if the facilities are open to nonguests, because the policy seems to change from time to time. Bullfights are occasionally held in the small town of Acmixtla, 6 km (4 mi) from Taxco. Ask at your hotel about the schedule.

Shopping

CRAFTS

Lacquered gourds and boxes from the town of Olinalá and masks, bowls, straw baskets, bark paintings, and many other handcrafted items native to the state of Guerrero are available from strolling vendors and are displayed on the cobblestones at "sidewalk boutiques."

Arnoldo (✉ Palma 2, ☎ 762/622–1272) has an interesting collection of ceremonial masks; originals come with a certificate of authenticity as well as a written description of origin and use. For $100 per person, Arnoldo will take you on a tour of the villages where the dances using the masks are performed on February 2, May 15, and December 12.

D'Elsa (✉ Plazuela de San Juan 13, ☎ 762/622–1683), owned by Elsa Ruíz de Figueroa, carries a selection of native-inspired clothing for women, and a wide and well-chosen selection of arts and handicrafts.

Sunday is market day, which means that artisans from surrounding villages descend on the town, as do visitors from Mexico City. It can get crowded, but if you find a seat on a bench in **Plaza Borda,** you're set to watch the show and peruse the merchandise that will inevitably be brought to you.

SILVER

Most of the people who visit Taxco come with silver in mind. Many of the more than 2,000 silver shops carry almost identical merchandise, although a few are noted for their creativity. Three types are available: sterling, which is always stamped .925 (925 parts in 1,000) and is the most expensive (and desirable); plated silver; and the inexpensive alpaca, which is also known as German or nickel silver. Sterling pieces are usually priced by weight according to world silver prices. Fine workmanship will add to the cost. Work is also done with semiprecious stones and rosewood.

Bangles start at $4, and bracelets and necklaces range from $10 to $200 and higher, depending on where you buy them. William Spratling, Andrés Mejía, and Emilia Castillo, daughter of renowned silversmith Antonio Castillo, are some of the more famous design names. Designs range from traditional bulky necklaces (often inlaid with turquoise) to streamlined bangles and chunky earrings. Just about every hotel has an in-house silver shop or one next door, so you don't have to go far to shop.

Emilia Castillo (✉ Juan Ruíz de Alarcón 7, in the Posada de los Castillo hotel, ☎ 762/622–3471) is the most famous and decidedly one of the most exciting silver shops; it's especially renowned for innovative designs and for combining silver with porcelain (Neiman Marcus sells the wares in its U.S. stores).

The stunning pieces at **Galería de Arte en Plata Andrés** (✉ Av. de los Plateros 113A, near the Posada de la Misíon Hotel, ☎ 762/622–3778) are created by the talented Andrés Mejía. He showcases his own fine designs and copies those sent to him by Tiffany's, Elsa Piretti, and Paloma Picasso, which are then sold abroad.

Spratling Ranch (✉ south of town on the Taxco–Iguala Hwy, Km 177, ☎ 762/622–6108) is where the heirs of William Spratling turn out designs using his original molds. By appointment only.

Talleres de los Ballesteros (✉ Florida 14, ☎ 762/622–1076) and their branch, Joyería San Agustín (✉ Cuauhtémoc 4, ☎ 762/622–3416), carry a large collection of well-crafted silver jewelry and serving pieces. They have three additional branches in Mexico City and one in San Antonio, Texas.

Taxco A to Z

BUS TRAVEL TO AND FROM TAXCO

First-class Estrella de Oro buses leave Acapulco for Taxco five times a day from 7 AM to 6:40 PM from the Terminal Central de Autobuses de Primera Clase. The cost for the approximately 4½-hour ride is about $12 one-way for first-class service. Sistema Estrella Blanca buses depart Acapulco several times a day from the Terminal de Autobuses. Purchase your tickets at least one day in advance at the terminal. The one-way ticket is about $11 for first-class service. Buses depart from Taxco just about every hour starting at 6 AM.

➤ BUS INFORMATION: **Estrella de Oro** (✉ Av. Cuauhtémoc 158, ☎ 744/485–8705 or 7/622–0648; Taxco terminal: ✉ Av. de los Plateros 126, ☎ 762/485–8705 or 762/622–0648). **Sistema Estrella Blanca** (✉ Ejido 47, ☎ 744/469–2028; Taxco terminal: ✉ Av. de los Plateros 104, ☎ 762/622–0131).

CAR TRAVEL

It takes about three hours to drive to Taxco from Acapulco using the expensive (about $38) toll road. Overnight tours are common; check with your hotel for references and prices.

TAXIS

Minibuses travel along preset routes through Taxco and charge about 25¢, and Volkswagen "bugs" provide inexpensive (average $1.50) taxi transportation.

TELEPHONES

Taxco's area code, used when dialing a Taxco number from outside the city, is 762.

TRANSPORTATION AROUND TAXCO

Because of the byways, alleys, and tiny streets, maneuvering anything bigger than your two feet through Taxco will be difficult. Fortunately, almost everything of interest is within walking distance of the zócalo. Wear sensible shoes for negotiating the hilly streets.

VISITOR INFORMATION

The tourism office is open weekdays 9–2 and 5–8; Saturday 9–3.

➤ TOURIST INFORMATION: **Tourism Office** (✉ Av. de los Plateros 1, ☎ 762/622–6616).

ACAPULCO A TO Z

To research prices, get advice from other travelers, and book travel arrangements, visit www.fodors.com.

AIR TRAVEL

There are several airlines that fly directly to Acapulco from major United States cities. From New York via Dallas, the flying time to Acapulco is 4½ hours; from Chicago, 4¼ hours; from Los Angeles, 3½ hours.

CARRIERS

From the United States, American has nonstop flights from Dallas, with connecting service from Chicago and New York. Continental has nonstop service from Houston and winter and spring service nonstop from Newark. Delta's direct flights are from Los Angeles and Atlanta. Mexicana's flights from Chicago and Los Angeles stop in Mexico City before continuing on to Acapulco. Aeroméxico has nonstop service from Los Angeles; flights from New York stop in Mexico City except December 23–May 5. Aeroméxico also has one-stop or connecting service from Atlanta, Chicago, Houston, Miami, and Orlando. America West has a flight from Phoenix.

➤ AIRLINES AND CONTACTS: **Aeroméxico** (☎ 744/466–9109). **America West** (☎ 744/466–9257). **American** (☎ 744/466–9227). **Continental** (☎ 744/466–9063). **Delta** (☎ 01–800–902–2100). **Mexicana** (☎ 744/486–7586).

AIRPORTS AND TRANSFERS

The Juan N. Alvarez International Airport is located about 20 minutes east of the city.

➤ AIRPORT INFORMATION: **Juan N. Alvarez International Airport** (☎ 744/466–9434).

AIRPORT TRANSFERS

Private taxis aren't permitted to carry passengers from the airport to town, so most people rely on Transportes Aeropuerto, a special airport taxi service. The system looks confusing, but there are dozens of helpful English-speaking staff members to help you.

Look for the name of your hotel and its zone number on the overhead sign on the walkway in front of the terminal. Then go to the desk designated with that zone number and buy a ticket for an airport taxi. The ride from the airport to the hotel zone on the strip costs about $8 per person for the *colectivo* (shared minivan) and starts at $31 for a nonshared cab. The drivers are usually helpful and will often take you to hotels that aren't on their list. Tips are optional.

➤ TAXIS AND SHUTTLES: **Transportes Aeropuerto** (☎ 744/462–1095).

BOAT AND FERRY TRAVEL

Many cruises include Acapulco as part of their itinerary. Most originate from Los Angeles. Celebrity Cruises is popular with tourists. Crystal P&O is a reliable operator. Cunard Line also offers cruises that include Acapulco. Krystal Cruises plies the Riviera Mexicana, which includes Acapulco. Princess Cruises offers trips several times a year. Bookings are generally handled through a travel agent.

➤ BOAT AND FERRY INFORMATION: **Celebrity Cruises** (☎ 800/437–3111). **Crystal P&O** (☎ 310/785–9300). **Cunard Line** (☎ 800/528–6273). **Krystal Cruises** (☎ 800/446–6640). **Princess Cruises** (☎ 800/421–0522).

BUS TRAVEL TO AND FROM ACAPULCO

Bus service from Mexico City to Acapulco is excellent. First-class buses, which leave every hour on the hour from the Tasqueña station, are comfortable and in good condition. The trip takes 5½ hours, and a one-way ticket costs about $22. There is also deluxe service, called *Servicio Diamante,* with airplanelike reclining seats, refreshments, rest rooms, air-conditioning, movies, and hostess service. The deluxe buses leave four times a day, also from the Tasqueña station, and cost about $37. *Plus* service (regular reclining seats, air-conditioning, and a rest room) costs $25.

BUS TRAVEL WITHIN ACAPULCO

The buses tourists use the most are those that go from Puerto Marqués to Caleta and stop at the fairly conspicuous metal bus stops along the way. Yellow air-conditioned tourist buses, marked ACAPULCO, run about every 15 minutes along this route. If you want to go from the zócalo to the Costera, catch the bus that says LA BASE (the naval base near the Hyatt Regency). This bus detours through Old Acapulco and returns to the Costera just east of the Ritz Hotel. If you want to follow the Costera for the entire route, take the bus marked HORNOS. Buses to Pie de la Cuesta or Puerto Marqués say so on the front. The Puerto Marqués bus runs about every 10 minutes and is always crowded.

CAR RENTAL

Acapulco has franchises of major U.S. car rental companies, all of which have offices at the airport.

➤ MAJOR AGENCIES: **Avis** (☎ 744/466–9190). **Budget** (☎ 744/481–2433). **Dollar** (☎ 744/466–9493). **Hertz** (☎ 744/485–8947). **Quick** (☎ 744/486–3420).

CAR TRAVEL

The trip to Acapulco from Mexico City on the old road takes about six hours. A privately built and run four-lane toll road connecting Mexico City with Acapulco is expensive (about $48 one way) but well maintained, and it cuts driving time between the two cities to 4½ hours. Many people go via Taxco, which can be reached from either road.

If you plan to visit some of the more remote beaches or decide to visit Taxco on your own, renting a car is convenient but fairly expensive. Prices start at about $61 a day for a Volkswagen sedan without air-conditioning. Don't expect a full tank; your car will have just about enough gas to get you to the nearest Pemex station.

CONSULATES

➤ CONSULATE INFORMATION: **Canadian Consulate** (✉ Marbella Mall, Suite 23, Costera, ☎ 744/484–1305). **U.S. Consulate** (✉ Continental Plaza Hotel, Costera Miguel Alemán 121–14, Costera, ☎ 744/469–0556).

EMERGENCIES

Your hotel can locate an English-speaking doctor, but they don't come cheap—house calls are about $100. The U.S. consular representative has a list of doctors and dentists, but it's against the consulate's policy to recommend anyone in particular.

Call the police or the Red Cross in case of an emergency. The Hospital Privado Magallanes and the Hospital del Pacífico are reliable.
➤ CONTACTS: **Hospital del Pacífico** (✉ Fraile y Nao 4, Costera, ☎ 744/487–7180). **Hospital Privado Magallanes** (✉ Wilfrido Massieu 2, Costera, ☎ 744/485–6194). **Police** (☎ 744/485–0650). **Red Cross** (☎ 744/445–5912).

ENGLISH-LANGUAGE MEDIA

English-language books and periodicals can be found at **Sanborns,** a reputable American-style department-store chain, and at the newsstands in some of the larger hotels. Many small newsstands carry the Mexico City *News.*

HORSE CARRIAGE TRAVEL

Buggy rides up and down the Costera are available in the evenings. There are two routes: from Parque Papagayo to the zócalo and from Playa Condesa to the naval base. Each costs about $10 (be sure to agree on the price beforehand).

INTERNET

More and more Internet facilities are cropping up in Acapulco to keep you connected while traveling. Smart PCs is in a shopping arcade next to Carlos 'n' Charlie's restaurant. iNternet Cyber Café is near the Marbella Hotel on the Costera Miguel Alemán.
➤ INTERNET CAFÉS: **iNternet Cyber Café** (✉ Horacio Nelson 40–7A, Costera, ☎ 744/484–8254). **Smart PCs** (✉ Costera Miguel Alemán 112–4, Costera, ☎ 744/484–2877).

SIGHTSEEING TOURS

There are organized tours everywhere in Acapulco, from the red-light district to the lagoon. Tour operators have offices around town and desks in many of the large hotels. Contact Mexico Travel Advisors at La Torre de Acapulco for tours of Acapulco. Viajes Acuario is another reliable tour company.

BOAT TOURS

The famous cliff divers at La Quebrada give one performance in the afternoon and four performances every night. The *Bonanza*'s sunset cruise, with open bar and live and disco music, costs about $20. All boats leave from downtown near the zócalo at 4:30 and 10:30. Many hotels and shops sell tickets, as do the ticket sellers on the waterfront.
➤ FEES AND SCHEDULES: ***Bonanza*** (☎ 744/482–4947). **Mexico Travel Advisors** (✉ Costera Miguel Alemán 1252, Costera, ☎ 744/484–7400). **Viajes Acuario** (✉ Costera Miguel Alemán 186–3, Costera, ☎ 744/485–6100).

TAXIS

How much you pay depends on what type of taxi you get. Hotel taxis are the most expensive, the roomiest, and in the best condition. A price list that all drivers adhere to is posted in hotel lobbies. Fares in town are usually about $3 to $7; to go from downtown to the Princess Hotel is about $15; to go from the hotel zone to Playa Caleta is about $8.

Cabs that cruise the streets usually charge by zone, with a minimum charge of $2. Before you go anywhere by cab, find out what the price should be and agree with the driver on a fare. A normal fare is about $3 to go from the zócalo to the International Center. Rates are about 30% higher at night, and although tipping isn't expected, Mexicans usually leave small change.

You can also hire a taxi by the hour or the day. Prices vary from about $10 an hour for a hotel taxi to $8 an hour for a street taxi; always negotiate. Never let a taxi driver decide where you should eat or shop, since many get kickbacks from some of the smaller stores and restaurants.

TRANSPORTATION AROUND ACAPULCO

Getting around in Acapulco is quite simple. You can walk to many places, and the bus costs less than 50¢. Taxis cost less than they do in the United States.

TRAVEL AGENCIES

American Express offers tours of Acapulco. Viajes Wagon-Lits has a wide variety of excursions.

➤ LOCAL AGENT REFERRALS: **American Express** (✉ La Gran Plaza shopping center, Costera Miguel Alemán 1628, Suites 7–9, Costera, ☎ 744/469–1166). **Viajes Wagon-Lits** (✉ Carretera Escénica 5255, Las Brisas, ☎ 744/484–1650 Ext. 392).

VISITOR INFORMATION

Procuraduría del Turista, the State Attorney General's Tourist Office, is open 9 AM–11 PM daily. It's also the place to report a crime or voice a complaint.

➤ TOURIST INFORMATION: **Procuraduría del Turista** (✉ Acapulco International Center, Costera Miguel Alemán, Costera, ☎ 744/484–4416).

11 OAXACA

The geographic and ethnic diversity of Oaxaca has made the state a favorite of Mexico aficionados. In Oaxaca City and surrounding towns live the descendants of Zapotec and Mixtec peoples who centuries ago built Monte Albán and Mitla, now lying in fascinating ruin. Skilled artisans produce a wealth of folk art, and Oaxacan cuisine also is varied and unique. At the coast, the arts take a back seat to snorkeling, surfing a huge swell, or simply swinging in a hammock overlooking one of the lovely beaches or bays.

Updated by Jane Onstott

OAXACA (pronounced wah-*hah*-kah) is both a pre-Columbian and a colonial treasure. Characterized by a vast geographic and ethnic diversity, Oaxaca—together with neighboring Chiapas—has the largest Indian population in the country, which explains its richness and variety in arts and crafts, folklore, and culture. Two out of three Oaxaqueños descend from Zapotec or Mixtec Indians, whose villages dot the valleys, mountainsides, and coastal lowlands. They come from one of 17 distinct ethnic groups and speak 52 dialects. And although many people in the capital, Oaxaca City, are now fluent in English, in the villages and small hamlets, even Spanish is a second language.

Indigenous civilizations flourished in the area thousands of years ago, and the archaeological ruins of Monte Albán, Mitla, and Yagul are among the vivid remnants of their cities. Within a 40-km (25-mi) radius of the city of Oaxaca, the ruins bear witness to highly religious, artistic, and advanced cultures.

In the 15th century much of the state was conquered by the Aztecs, who gave Oaxaca its name: *Huaxyaca.* In the Nahuatl language it probably means "by the acacia grove," referring to the location of the Aztec military base. The next century witnessed the Spanish conquest of Mexico, for which the monarch Charles V rewarded Hernán Cortés with the title of *Marqués del Valle de Oaxaca* in 1528. Cortés lived elsewhere, but his descendants kept the property until Mexico's bloody Revolution, which began in 1910.

Oaxaca's legacy to Mexican politics came in the form of two presidents: Benito Juárez, the first full-blooded Indian to become chief of state, and Porfirio Díaz, a military dictator who declared himself president-for-life. Juárez, a Zapotec, was a sheepherder from San Pablo Guelatao, a settlement about 64 km (40 mi) north of Oaxaca. As a child he spoke only his native Zapotec tongue. Often referred to as Mexico's Abraham Lincoln, Juárez was trained for the clergy but later studied law and entered politics. He was elected governor of the state (1847), chief justice of the Supreme Court of Mexico (1857), and then president (1858–72). Juárez moved his capital to the north and used military resistance against the French after Napoleon III crowned Austria's Archduke Maximilian emperor of Mexico in 1864. Once the nascent French empire collapsed in 1867, however, Juárez returned to Mexico City, where he enjoyed reelection.

Juárez was reelected again in 1871, when he defeated Porfirio Díaz, one of his generals. Díaz was defeated a second time in 1876 but rose against his opponent and seized the presidency in his 1877 coup. He held office until he was kicked out in 1911 by a revolutionary movement spearheaded by Francisco I. Madero, who was elected president that year.

Oaxaca sits on the vast, fertile, 1½-km-high (1-mi-high) plateau of the Oaxaca Valley, encircled by the majestic Sierra Madre del Sur mountain range. Mexico's fifth-largest state, it lies in the southwest, bordered by the states of Chiapas to the east, Veracruz and Puebla to the north, and Guerrero—whose touristic claims to fame are Acapulco and Ixtapa—to the west. The south of Oaxaca state spans 509 km (316 mi) of lush tropical Pacific coast with magnificent beaches. Until the 1980s, these beaches remained relatively unexploited and unknown by tourism, except for the small fishing town and seaside hideaway of Puerto Escondido and the even smaller town of Puerto Ángel. But now Bahías de Huatulco (Huatulco Bays), 125 km (77 mi) east of Puerto Escondido, is on the map; the government is *still* trying to turn it into a world-class resort.

Note: Assaults and highway banditry still occur in Mexico. Among the most obvious targets are first-class buses, especially on the route between Juchitán, on the Oaxaca coast, and San Cristóbal de las Casas in Chiapas. Night buses are most vulnerable; you should travel by day whenever possible. Although the possibility of an attack is cause for concern, occurrences are infrequent.

Pleasures and Pastimes

Dining

One highlight of Oaxaca is its traditional cookery, one of the finest and most elaborate in all Mexico. Oaxaca is known as "the land of seven *moles*" because of its seven distinct kinds of multispiced mole sauces. One of the most popular, *mole negro* (black mole), has dozens of ingredients including chocolate, sesame seeds, nuts, chilies, and stale tortillas. Tamales, either sweet or stuffed with chicken or pork, are another treat. The home- and factory-made *mezcal,* an alcoholic drink derived from the maguey cactus, differs in flavor with each maker and can be as high as 80 proof. The cream variety, thick and sweet, is flavored with orange, lime, or other fruits or nuts.

Oaxacan cuisine—the cheeses, mole sauces, and meats that make dining in the capital memorable—is less evident along the coast, where seafood reigns. Restaurants in the seaside resort of Huatulco struggle for a consistent client base, and some of the best eateries there are found in the hotels. Despite its laid-back atmosphere, Puerto Escondido has quite a few interesting restaurants. Cuisine is varied, and competition keeps prices low. In Puerto Ángel and surrounding beach towns, expect the simplest of grilled fish dishes served with white rice and few frills. Dress is casual and reservations are unnecessary at all restaurants unless otherwise noted.

CATEGORY	COST*
$$$$	over $20
$$$	$12–$20
$$	$7–$12
$	under $7

**per person for a main course at dinner*

Lodging

Oaxaca City has few luxury resorts, but it does have some magnificently restored properties, including a 16th-century convent and dozens of smaller, moderately priced accommodations. During peak periods rooms should be booked six months to a year in advance. These periods include Day of the Dead celebrations (October 31–November 2), Easter week, and Christmas–New Year's vacations. July and August, although during the rainy season, are popular with Mexican and foreign families traveling during school vacations.

Hotel rates vary considerably in the coastal area. In Puerto Escondido and Puerto Ángel, most of the accommodations fall into the $$ or $ price range. Those in Huatulco, where you'll find luxury chains such as the Quinta Real, can cost as much as $300 per night for a standard double. The high season along the coast runs from mid-December through Holy Week; rates increase 20% or more during this time. Budget accommodations are scarce in Huatulco, but both inexpensive and moderately priced rooms can be found in the town of Crucecita, a short taxi ride from the beach, and on Santa Cruz Bay.

CATEGORY	COST*
$$$$	over $200
$$$	$100–$200
$$	$50–$100
$	under $50

**All prices are for a standard double room, including 17% tax.*

Shopping

Oaxaca City is a wonderful place to shop. Galleries exhibit the pottery, textiles, and fanciful wooden animals called *alebrijes*. In the villages surrounding Oaxaca City and throughout the city, artisans create truly fantastic folk art in a wide range of genres. The city is home to a sophisticated fine arts scene as well, and Oaxaca produces more than its share of painters of international renown. In addition, Oaxaca's marketplaces—while selling more practical items than crafts—make for fabulous outings. On market day both *mestizos* (people of mixed European and Indian descent) and indigenous people head to town to buy and sell, barter, and gossip. As large and lively now as it has been for centuries, Oaxaca City's Abastos Market attracted the attention of D. H. Lawrence, who wrote about it in *Mornings in Mexico* (1927). Expect hectic activity and bright colors; listen for the singsong, tonal Zapotec and Mixtec languages as you drift among the mountains of produce and stacks of dried herbs.

Surfing

Oaxaca's Puerto Escondido is a household name for serious surfers who migrate to this sunny port for surfing championships each year. The challenging waves have been attracting surfers from all parts of the globe since word first got out in the 1960s.

Exploring Oaxaca

Travelers tend to gravitate toward two parts of Oaxaca. Oaxaca City, the state capital, is tucked into a beautiful mountain valley and surrounded by tradition-minded towns and villages and fields of corn, beans, and alfalfa. Several rather narrow and potholed highways follow the tortuous curves of the Sierra de Oaxaca to Pacific surf spots and palm-lined beaches due south of the capital.

Numbers in the text correspond to numbers in the margin and on the Oaxaca City and Oaxaca Coast maps.

Great Itineraries

If you have only three days to spend in the state, choose between Oaxaca City and the coast. Oaxaca City is food for the soul for history and folk-art aficionados, with its magnificent colonial buildings, world-famous crafts, and the ruins of ancient temples just outside the city. If you opt to see the coast, go to Puerto Escondido or the even smaller surrounding beach towns for a casual, friendly, laid-back vacation among surfers and sun-worshipers. Or upgrade to Huatulco—still relatively unsophisticated by resort standards despite its smattering of luxury resorts. For a culture-beach combination, plan at least seven days—Oaxaca City and the coast merit at least three days each.

IF YOU HAVE 3 DAYS IN OAXACA CITY

Explore downtown to see the stunning colonial monuments that have been declared World Heritage structures by the United Nations. The first day, take in the **Catedral Metropolitana de Oaxaca** ④ and the adjoining ***zócalo*** ①, the **Museo de Arte Contemporáneo de Oaxaca** ⑤, the **Iglesia y Ex-Convento de Santo Domingo** ⑦, and the adjoining **Museo de las Culturas** ⑧. On Day 2, beat the crowds by catching a tour or bus right after breakfast for **Monte Albán,** the ruins of an ancient, mountaintop Zapotec capital. After returning to the city and a late lunch, enjoy coffee at the 16th-century **Ex-Convento de Santa Catalina** ⑥, now the Hotel Camino Real, and take in the patio garden with the stone tubs where the nuns washed clothes. Visit the **Museo de Arte Prehispánico Rufino Tamayo** ⑪, the **Centro Fotográfico Álvarez Bravo** ⑨, and the **Central de Abastos** on Day 3. Alternately, you might spend an entire day shopping for fine arts or regional crafts in the shops and fine arts galleries in the historic center. Watch the sun set over Oaxaca from the terrace bar of the **Hotel Victoria,** just above the city proper.

IF YOU HAVE 5 DAYS IN OAXACA CITY

Follow the three-day itinerary, and on Day 4 add a visit to the Mixtec ruins at **Mitla,** stopping on the way or back to see the 2,000-year-old *ahuehuete* cypress in Tulc and to experience a country market day in **Tlacolula** (especially grand on Sundays). Dine in one of the many restaurants on Calle Macedonio Alcalá, or in the zócalo. On Day 5, head to one of the other villages near Oaxaca City for market days or to purchase crafts direct from the artists. Back in the city, visit the **Basílica de Nuestra Señora de la Soledad** ⑫.

IF YOU HAVE 3 DAYS IN THE COASTAL BEACH RESORTS

Using **Bahías de Huatulco** ⑮–⑰ as your base, take a boat tour of the bays on the first day, followed by a sunset cocktail and evening meal at the Camino Real's Chez Binni restaurant. On Day 2, tour the small beaches and hidden bays between Huatulco and **Puerto Escondido** ⑬. On Day 3, laze on the beach and, in the late afternoon, taxi to **Crucecita** ⑱ for some strolling, followed by dining at one of the small restaurants on the main square.

IF YOU HAVE 5 DAYS IN THE COASTAL BEACH RESORTS

Follow the three-day itinerary, then sign up for bird-watching on the **Manialtepec Lagoon** on Day 4. On Day 5, head inland for a special lunch on the **coffee plantation tour.** If you choose laid-back **Puerto Escondido** ⑬ as your base, you might spend Day 4 touring the **Chacahua Lagoon,** and Day 5 riding horses on the beach in the morning, then relaxing with a soothing Temescal steam bath (a pre-Hispanic–style sauna) and massage in the afternoon.

IF YOU HAVE 7 DAYS OR MORE

You can immerse yourself in the cultural treasures of **Oaxaca City** ①–⑫ and **Monte Albán** before kicking back with some sea and sun. Spend Days 1–4 at the sights outlined in the first four days of the city itinerary. On Day 5, fly to **Bahías de Huatulco** ⑮–⑰ and, on arrival, sign up for a boat tour of the bays. On Days 6 and 7, head to the beach, go bird-watching, or explore **La Crucecita** ⑱. If you're staying longer, visit the beautiful beaches of Zipolite and Mazunte; at the latter you can also visit the **Museum of the Sea Turtle.**

When to Tour Oaxaca

Oaxaca celebrates Mexican holidays and state fiestas with an intensity of tradition, color, and enthusiasm that attracts hordes. *El Día de los Muertos* (Day of the Dead) begins with altar decorating in the city and nearby villages on October 31 and ends in the cemeteries on November 2, when families partake of the favorite food of those they are honoring. The most frequently visited village is Xoxo, but many others, including Atzompa and Xochimilco, also have colorful festivities.

December is full of fiestas, starting with the miraculous *Virgen de Juquila* on December 8 in the village of Juquila, and continuing with Mexico's patron saint, the Virgen de Guadalupe on December 12. The feast day of Oaxaca state's patron, *la Virgen de la Soledad,* is December 18, and regional and indigenous dances are traditionally performed

Close-Up

DÍA DE LOS MUERTOS

DÍA DE LOS MUERTOS, Day of the Dead, which actually takes place over three days (October 31–November 2), is one of Mexico's most passionately celebrated fiestas—equal to Christmas in terms of its sacred importance and ritual splendor.

The roots of the fiesta are a tangle of pre-Hispanic indigenous Mexican beliefs and post-Conquest Spanish Catholic influence. For the Aztecs, religion and art were inextricably bound together. A central component of their religion was ritual sacrifice of human beings and animals, and so death imagery abounds in their sculpture, painting, architecture, and poetry. They believed that a soul's destiny was determined not by the moral correctness of one's behavior while living, but rather by the cause of a person's death. People who died in battle, perished during childbirth, or were sacrificed to the gods went to a heaven called the Dwelling Place of the Sun. If they died of drowning, dropsy, gout, or lightning, they went to Tlalocan, a heaven ruled by the rain god Tlaloc. Infant souls went to a heaven called Chichihuacuauhco, where a wet-nurse tree fed them milk from its branches. Those unfortunate enough to die of natural causes went to a hell called Mictlán, where they underwent a series of trials that included trekking eight deserts and eight hills, and facing wild animals and obsidian-bladed winds. The dead were buried with goods—food and drink, clothing, toys, pottery, arrows—and sacrificed servants to take with them on their journey.

The Aztecs celebrated two major holidays in honor of the dead. The first, the Little Feast of the Dead, occurred in the ninth month and was dedicated to deceased children; the other, the Great Feast of the Dead, in honor of adults, took place in the tenth month. These festivals included music, dancing, and graveside offerings of flowers, tamales, and figurines of deities sculpted from a dough of amaranth seeds and human blood.

After the Spanish Conquest of 1521, 12 Franciscan friars were charged with the spiritual conversion of the Indians. The friars burned pagan icons, destroyed sacred shrines, and imprisoned the idolators' priests. Because the Aztec feasts for the dead somewhat mirrored the Catholic feast days honoring All Souls and All Saints, the friars merged these holidays to facilitate the conversion process. All Saints' Day, on November 1, honors all Christian saints and martyrs; All Souls' Day, on November 2, commemorates all the faithful departed. Although the Indians observed the new holidays, many of them secretly clung to their native religion. The result is the Day of the Dead, a creative fusion of Catholicism and indigenous beliefs.

The Day of the Dead festivities of the Purépecha Indians in Michoacán and the Zapotec Indians in Oaxaca are especially beautiful. Both at home and in cemeteries, families construct elaborate altars called *ofrendas* to honor their ancestors. They adorn these altars with fragrant marigold blossoms, candles, photos, favorite foods and belongings of the deceased, copal incense, and candy skulls. The vibrant mix of colors, smells, flavors, and potent nostalgia are meant to lure and guide the spirits back to Earth for a family reunion.

Families lovingly prepare, in abundance, the favorite foods of the deceased. Care is taken to make the food and drinks especially rich and spicy: souls absorb the essence of offerings rather than physically consuming them.

— Gina Hyams

outside the Basílica on Independencia and Galeana streets. On December 23, *Noche de Rábanos* (Night of the Radishes), the zócalo is packed with growers and artists displaying their hybrid radishes carved and arranged in tableaux that might depict anything from the Nativity to space travel. Other arrangements are made with *flores inmortales* ("eternal flowers"; small dried flowers) or *totomoxtl* (corn husks, pronounced to-to-*mosh*-tl). Be prepared to line up for a long time to enter the square (or better yet, come early, while the artists are still arranging their scenes). December 24 is *la Noche de Calendas* with street processions of bright papier-mâché figures.

Another of Oaxaca's major celebrations is the *Guelaguetza* (Zapotec for "offering" or "gift"), generally held on the last two Mondays in July. Dancers from all the mountain and coastal communities converge on the city bearing tropical fruits, coffee, and other regional products. They perform elaborate dances in authentic costumes from early morning until early afternoon at the Guelaguetza Auditorium, an open-air amphitheater in the hills just northwest of the city center.

Easter week and Independence Day (September 15 and 16) are also very busy. Keep in mind that if you plan to come for these celebrations, you'll need to book far in advance.

OAXACA CITY

Oaxaca City is traditionally Indian, and although cosmopolitan touches are everywhere, women and children still peddle everything from wooden combs to chili-seasoned grasshoppers, and men and boys offer shoe shines around the city's many parks. Underemployment and unemployment are severe problems and beggars are a ubiquitous part of the street scene. You'll see families playing accordions along the city streets for spare change, and men, women, and children selling pencils, sweets, ears of barbecued corn, and lots more in the parks and on street corners.

The city is officially called Oaxaca de Juárez, and it is decidedly the state's major attraction, with a population of about 260,000 and around a million visitors a year.

Exploring Oaxaca City

The colonial heart of Oaxaca is laid out in a simple grid, with all major attractions within walking distance of one another. Most of the streets in the city's core change names once they pass the zócalo.

A Good Walk

Begin your exploration of Oaxaca at the shady **zócalo** ①, the heart of the city and its pedestrian-only main square. On the south side of the square visit the **Palacio de Gobierno** ②—step inside and check out the mural by Arturo García Bustos stretching from the first to the second floor. Upon leaving the government palace, go to the northwest corner of the zócalo to reach **El Alameda** ③, a second square that abuts the central plaza. On the east side of the Alameda, you can't miss the **Catedral Metropolitana de Oaxaca** ④. After visiting the cathedral, turn right on Avenida Independencia and left at the next corner. This puts you on the pedestrian mall on Calle Macedonio Alcalá, where you'll see restored colonial mansions in a palate of pastels, and some of Oaxaca's best galleries, shops, museums, and restaurants. It's also lively and well lighted at night. After a short 1½ blocks you'll see the **Museo de Arte Contemporáneo de Oaxaca** ⑤ on your right. Continue north on Calle Macedonio Alcalá, turn right on Calle Murguía, and left on

El Alameda . . . 3
Basílica de Nuestra Señora de la Soledad 12
Catedral Metropolitana de Oaxaca . . 4
Centro Fotográfico Álvarez Bravo 9
Ex-Convento de Santa Catalina. 6
Iglesia y Ex-Convento de Santo Domingo 7
Museo Casa de Benito Juárez 10
Museo de Arte Contemporáneo de Oaxaca . . . 5
Museo de Arte Prehispánico Rufino Tamayo 11
Museo de las Culturas. . . 8
Palacio de Gobierno. . . . 2
Zócalo. 1

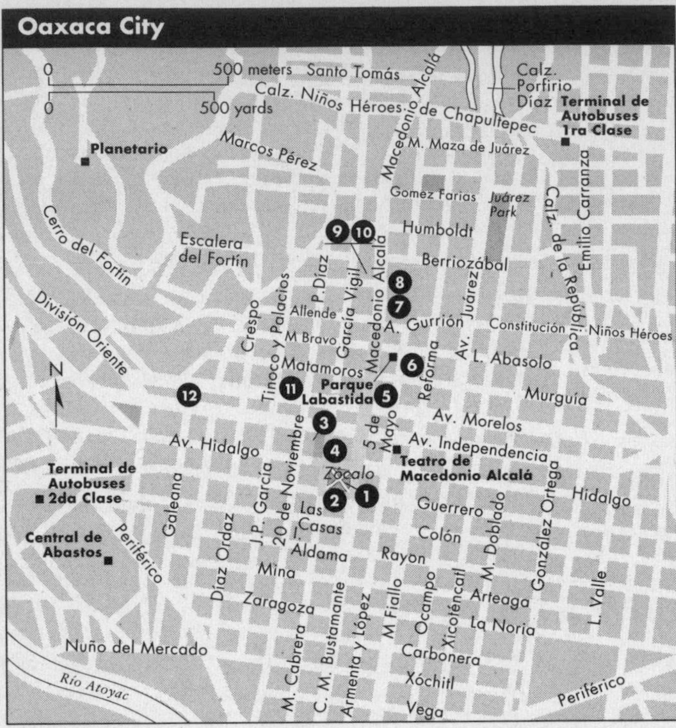

the first street, Calle 5 de Mayo. Taking up the entire block on the east side of the street is the **Ex-Convento de Santa Catalina** ⑥, now the Hotel Camino Real. Continue north until Calle 5 de Mayo ends at Calle Gurrión and the beautifully restored **Iglesia y Ex-Convento de Santo Domingo** ⑦. Adjacent to the church is the cavernous **Museo de las Culturas** ⑧, which contains priceless artifacts taken from Tomb 7 of Monte Albán, a library of antique books, and an informative ethnographic exhibit.

Walk east on Constitución, along the south side of Santo Domingo, to Av. Juárez. Turn right and walk two blocks to Murguía; turn right and walk half a block to the **Centro Fotográfico Álvarez Bravo** ⑨. After seeing the current photo exhibition, walk up the steps of La Plazuela del Carmen Alto, where Triqui women in red, beribboned *huipiles* (tunics) sell embroidered blouses, dresses, and crafts. Take a right on Calle García Vigil, and just a half block up, on the left side of the street, you'll find the **Museo Casa de Benito Juárez** ⑩, a museum honoring Oaxaca's most revered statesman. Upon leaving, return south on García Vigil 4½ blocks and turn right on Avenida Morelos. One and a half blocks up on the right, in a tranquil colonial home, is the **Museo de Arte Prehispánico Rufino Tamayo** ⑪. After seeing the museum's elegant presentation of pre-Hispanic art, continue west on Morelos 2½ blocks. Descend the steps and cross the large plaza to the massive **Basílica de Nuestra Señora de la Soledad** ⑫. On the left side of the church is a small museum housing items related to Oaxaca's patron saint. Go east on Avenida Independencia past the telegraph office and you'll be back at El Alameda and the zócalo, where you can stop and watch the daily parade of Oaxaqueños.

Sights to See

3 **El Alameda.** This shady square is home to the Catedral Metropolitana de Oaxaca and the post office. Locals gossip on wrought-iron benches

or read the newspaper while their kids chase pigeons or beg for giant balloons or snacks sold by itinerant vendors.

⓬ **Basílica de Nuestra Señora de la Soledad.** The Baroque basilica houses the statue of the Virgin of Solitude, Oaxaca's patron saint. According to legend, this statue was found in the pack of a mule that had mysteriously joined a mule train bound for Guatemala; when the mule perished at the site of the present church and the statue was discovered in its pack, the event was construed as a miracle, and the church was built in 1682 to commemorate it. The Virgin, who is believed to have supernatural healing powers, remains the object of fervent piety for the devout populace. Robbers in the 1980s removed her jewel-studded crown; she is now housed in a shrine surrounded by glass. A small museum at the side of the church displays devotional items left by the faithful over the years. ⊠ *Av. Independencia 107, Centro, at Calle Galeana,* ☎ *no phone.* ⏲ *Daily 7–7.*

❹ **Catedral Metropolitana de Oaxaca.** Begun in 1544, the cathedral was destroyed by earthquakes and fire and not finished until 1733. The church honors the Virgin of the Assumption, whose statue can be seen on the facade above the door. The chapel at the back of the church left of the altar houses the cruxifix of El Señor del Rayo (Our Lord of the Lightning Bolt). This revered statue was the only piece to survive a fire that started when lightning struck the thatch roof of the original structure. ⊠ *Av. Independencia 700, Centro,* ☎ *951/516–4401.* ⏲ *Daily 8 AM–9 PM.*

❾ **Centro Fotográfico Álvarez Bravo.** Famed Oaxaca painter and graphic artist Francisco Toledo inaugurated this photography museum in the mid-1990s. Also here is a large, free Braille library. ⊠ *Calle Murguía 302, Centro,* ☎ *951/516–4523.* 🎫 *Free.* ⏲ *Wed.–Mon. 9:30–8.*

❻ **Ex-Convento de Santa Catalina.** This building is now the Hotel Camino Real and, like many structures in downtown Oaxaca, is a National Heritage Site. Even if you're not staying here, it's worthwhile to explore the hotel's three courtyards. On a rear patio, check out the still-working font where the nuns washed the convent's laundry 400 years ago at 12 stone basins and tubs. ⊠ *Calle 5 de Mayo 300, Centro.*

★ ❼ **Iglesia y Ex-Convento de Santo Domingo.** Behold Oaxaca City's most brilliantly decorated church, whose 17th-century facade is framed by two domed bell towers. The interior is a profusion of white and gold—real gold leaf—typical of the energy with which Mexico seized on the Baroque style. Adjoining the temple, the former Dominican monastery was the object of an ambitious and costly renovation in the late 1990s. The botanical gardens are open for free Spanish-language tours at 1 and 5 PM (reserve in advance), and you can browse in the gift shop and the library of antiquarian books. Don't miss the beautifully augmented **Museo de las Culturas.** ⊠ *Calles Macedonio Alcalá and Gurrión, Centro,* ☎ *951/516–2991; 951/516–7915 for botanical garden reservations.* ⏲ *Church: daily 7 AM–1 PM and 5–8 PM; museum: Tues.–Sun. 10–7:45.*

❿ **Museo Casa de Benito Juárez.** Benito Juárez lived in this house as a servant during his youth. The museum re-creates a typical 19th-century house; none of the furnishings or memorabilia belonged to Juárez or his employer–benefactor. ⊠ *Calle García Vigil 609, Centro,* ☎ *951/516–1860.* 🎫 *$2.70, free Sun.* ⏲ *Tues.–Sat. 10–7, Sun. 10–5.*

★ ❺ **Museo de Arte Contemporáneo de Oaxaca.** This museum, also known as the MACO, is housed in an attractive colonial residence. As its name implies, the MACO houses changing exhibitions of contemporary art on its two floors. Be sure to check out what remains of the frescoes in the second-floor front gallery. ✉ *Calle Macedonio Alcalá 202, Centro,* ☎ *951/514–2228.* 🎫 *$1.* ⏲ *Wed.–Mon. 10:30–8.*

★ ⓫ **Museo de Arte Prehispánico Rufino Tamayo.** You'll find a beautifully displayed collection of pre-Hispanic pottery and sculpture at this carefully restored colonial mansion. Originally it was the private collection of the painter Rufino Tamayo, who presented it to his hometown in 1979. ✉ *Av. Morelos 503, Centro,* ☎ *951/516–4750.* 🎫 *$2.* ⏲ *Mon. and Wed.–Sat. 10–2 and 4–7, Sun. 10–3. Closed Tues.*

★ ❽ **Museo de las Culturas.** Laid out in a series of galleries around the cloister of the **Ex-Convento de Santo Domingo,** this museum, along with the entire monastery, has been completely refurbished. The ground floor now contains temporary galleries, a gift shop, the Francisco de Burgoa Library of antique books, and administrative offices. On the second floor you'll find 10 excellent thematic rooms, including those dedicated to Oaxacan music, medicine, indigenous languages, and pottery. More than a dozen other salons have been organized chronologically; here you'll find the treasure taken from the tombs at Monte Albán. The stunning gold jewelry from Tomb 7 was among the greatest archaeological finds of all time. Free Spanish-language tours of the botanical gardens (reserve in advance) are available Tuesday–Saturday at 1 and 5 PM. ✉ *Plaza Santa Domingo, Centro,* ☎ *951/516–2991.* 🎫 *$3.50, free Sun.* ⏲ *Tues.–Sun. 10–7:45.*

★ ❷ **Palacio de Gobierno.** The 19th-century neoclassical state capitol sits on the south side of the zócalo. Completed in 1988 and painted in fresco, the mural that wraps around the stairwell is a treasure: altars to the dead, painters of codices, fruit sellers, gods, and musicians crowd together to catalog the customs and legends of Oaxaca's indigenous people. The mural also bespeaks the conquest and the Revolution. At the top, on the left side of the mural, note the *apoala* tree, which according to Mixtec legend bore the flowers from which life sprang. ✉ *Portal del Palacio, Centro,* ☎ *951/516–0677.* ⏲ *Daily 9–8.*

★ ❶ **Zócalo.** During the day, everyone comes to Oaxaca's shady main plaza, with its green wrought-iron benches and matching bandstand. At night, mariachi and marimba bands play under colonial archways or in the bandstand. ✉ *Bounded by Portal de Clavería on the north, Portal del Palacio on the south, Portal de Flores on the west, and Portal de Mercaderes on the east, Centro.*

Dining and Lodging

The open-air cafés surrounding the zócalo are good for drinks, snacks, and people-watching, with the scene changing from serene early mornings to crowded parades with brass bands, floats, and *monos* (giant papier-mâché dolls) on holiday evenings. Most serve the economical *comida corrida* (midday set menu) after 1:30 PM. But you won't be very much out of pocket wherever you choose to dine.

Hotels here fill up quickly during Easter, July, the Day of the Dead, and December, so book as far ahead as possible if you'll be visiting during those times.

$$$ ✕ **El Asador Vasco.** Basque (*vasco*) cuisine is served in this distinguished restaurant, where diners can overlook the main square. Try the lamb or sumptuous gratiné of oysters in chipotle chili sauce. From 8 to 9 PM, serenading by *tunas* (traditionally dressed student minstrels, not singing fish) evokes medieval Spain. ✉ *Portal de Flores 10-A (west side of zócalo, upstairs), Centro,* ☎ *951/514–4755,* FAX *951/514–4762. AE, DC, MC, V.*

$$$ ✕ **Restaurant Casa Oaxaca.** Gifted young chef Alejandro creates his imaginative version of nouvelle Mexican cuisine with a light but sure touch. You'll dine in a small room by the kitchens or on the elegant patio of the eponymous hotel. Creative entrées may include squash blossom stuffed with fresh soft cheese and herbs; a superb main dish is pork with *manchamanteles* ("tablecloth-staining") mole. Alejandro also conjures up mouthwatering concoctions with fresh sea bass. ✉ *Calle García Vigil 407, Centro,* ☎ *951/514–4173,* FAX *951/516–4412. AE, MC, V. Reservations required.*

$$–$$$ ✕ **El Sagrario.** There's something for everyone at this multistory restaurant just a block from the zócalo. Mexican couples slide into Naugahyde booths during lunch before scurrying over to the popular salad bar. The cavernous upstairs dining room is one of Oaxaca's popular spots for pizza; pasta dishes are available and waiters prepare the traditional Caesar salad tableside. After 9 PM, *trova* or tropical tunes waft up to these dining areas from the basement-level bar. You can do your moves on the tiny dance floor until 2 AM. ✉ *Calle Valdivieso 120, Centro,* ☎ *951/514–0303. AE, MC, V.*

$$ ✕ **Catedral.** This elegant yet accessible local favorite graces the courtyard and first floor of a colonial house. Popular dishes include mushroom soup flavored with *epazote* (a pungent local herb), chicken in squash-blossom sauce, served with rice and a squash blossom stuffed with cheese, and the *lechón* (suckling pig). You can feast at the lavish Sunday lunch buffet, served 2–6, ending with some of Catedral's great strong coffee. There's dancing in the bar Thursday, Friday, and Saturday nights after 9:30. ✉ *Calle García Vigil 105, Centro, at Av. Morelos,* ☎ *951/516–3285. AE, MC, V.*

$$ ✕ **El Colibrí.** Favored by upscale Mexican families and beeper-toting businesspeople, El Colibrí is quiet and air-conditioned, with romantic background music, free refills of super hot coffee, and fresh rolls and butter on the table. The menu is extensive: in addition to Oaxacan specialties, there are 10 different salads and five spaghetti dishes, plenty of appetizers, and burgers with fries. ✉ *Calzada Niños Héroes de Chapultepec 903, Colonia Reforma,* ☎ *951/515–8087. AE, MC, V.*

$$ ✕ **La Escondida** For a special treat, head for this splendid Mexican lunch-only buffet (1:30–6 PM) just outside the city. The outdoor venue serves up more than 70 different dishes, including seafood soup, several different types of mole, meat fresh from the grill, and a lineup of unusual salads. When you arrive, waiters bring a welcome cocktail along with a typical appetizer, such as *memelas* or tacos. This is the place to linger before, during, and after your meal, so let the kids loose on the small playground while you listen to the wandering musicians. ✉ *Carretera a San Agustín Yatareni Km.7, San Agustín Yatareni,* ☎ *951/517–6655. AE, MC, V.*

$$ ✕ **El Naranjo.** A large, covered interior patio with soft music in the background welcomes diners to this popular place, which specializes in contemporary Mexican cuisine. Each of Oaxaca's seven moles is featured once a week, and there are many delicious variations of *chiles rellenos* (stuffed peppers)—from mild to hot. Try the poblano pepper stuffed with corn, squash blossom, and cheese in puff pastry with almond sauce. The bilingual owner, Iliana, occasionally gives cooking classes. ✉ *Calle Trujano 203, Centro,* ☎ *951/514–1878,* WEB *www.elnaranjo.com.mx. MC, V.*

$ ✕ **El Gecko.** The mustard-color courtyard of this tranquil coffeehouse is drenched in purple flowering vines. A variety of coffee drinks—including a fabulous iced cappuccino—are offered along with light food. You can use the Internet services at Axis, in the same plaza, as you sip your coffee. ✉ *Calle 5 de Mayo 412, Centro, in Plaza Gonzalo Lucero,* ☎ *951/514–8024. No credit cards. Closed Sun.*

$ ✕ **El Mesón.** Mesón's inviting, inexpensive buffet is right off the zócalo. Stop by for a snack or full meal from the paper menu, where you check off your choices. Tortillas are made fresh in the evenings, and there are a variety of tacos, as well as *pozole* (hominy soup) and other Mexican dishes. For a sugar fix, have a cup of rich Oaxacan chocolate and a slice of nut or cheese pie. ✉ *Av. Hidalgo 805, Centro, at Calle Valdivieso,* ☎ *951/516–2729. MC, V.*

$ ✕ **La Olla.** The strengths of this restaurant are the large, delicious salads, the health-conscious regional dishes, and the personal supervision of the kitchen by owner Pilar. Service tends to be slow, so you'll have time to admire the artwork of local artists that adorns the walls. By far the best deal is the fixed-price lunch menu, which includes soup or salad, a choice of main dish, a beverage, and dessert. ✉ *Calle Reforma 402, Centro,* ☎ *951/516–6668,* WEB *www.mexonline.com/laolla.htm. Closed Sun. AE, MC, V.*

$$$$ ★ ✕🏨 **Hotel Camino Real Oaxaca.** A monastic air lingers in the breezy patios and enclosed gardens of this beautifully restored 16th-century convent; Gregorian chants float softly through the hotel in the morning hours. The enormous buffets are the main draws at El Refectorio restaurant: the Saturday night spread is accompanied by mariachi music; the Sunday brunch is elaborate. If you missed the Guelaguetza dance festival in July, you can watch a miniversion here on Friday night. ✉ *Calle 5 de Mayo 300, Centro,* ☎ *951/516–0611,* FAX *951/516–0732,* WEB *www.caminoreal.com/oaxaca. 84 rooms, 7 suites. Restaurant, room service, in-room safes, minibars, pool, 2 bars, baby-sitting, laundry service, travel services. AE, DC, MC, V.*

$$$ ★ ✕🏨 **Casa Oaxaca.** A trio of eccentric Europeans poured their hearts and souls into creating this most unusual bed-and-breakfast. Their restored, 200-year-old downtown house combines colonial scale and traditional materials (adobe, cantera stone, etc.) with a distinctly contemporary minimalist sensibility. Treat yourself to a dip in the beautiful indigo-blue-tile pool or get purified in the shaman-sanctioned *temazcal* (pre-Hispanic-style sweat lodge). You can also take advantage of yoga and aromatherapy. Rooms have fresh flowers, 100% cotton sheets, marble bathrooms, and artwork of well-known local artists. Breakfast is included. ✉ *Calle García Vigil 407, Centro,* ☎ *951/514–4173,* FAX *951/516–4412. 5 rooms, 2 suites. Restaurant, room service, pool, massage, sauna, bar, laundry service. AE, MC, V.*

$$$ ✕🏨 **Hostal de la Noria.** The comfortable rooms in this restored colonial mansion two blocks off the zócalo are decorated with unique folkloric touches—some with carved wooden headboards, others with wrought-iron or hammered-tin ones. All have marble bathrooms, phones, and cable TV. Among the house favorites at the hotel's elegant Restaurante Asunción are chicken mole, and foil-wrapped fish fillets steamed in a mezcal sauce. ✉ *Av. Hidalgo 918, Centro, 68000,* ☎ *951/514–7844,* FAX *951/516–3992,* WEB *www.lanoria.com. 17 rooms, 33 suites. Restaurant, room service, bar, baby-sitting, laundry service, free parking. AE, MC, V.*

$$$$ 🏨 **Hacienda Los Laureles.** Surrounded by a quiet, green oasis about a 15-minute drive from Oaxaca's historical center, this resort hotel offers all modern amenities. The pool, hot tub, and spa, which includes temazcal steam baths and massage, help you regain your inner balance. If you can't leave your busy world behind, you can stay current via the Internet and business center and read English-language magazines in the library. The adventurous can try horseback, bicycle riding, or ecological tours to the nearby mountains. ✉ *Av. Hidalgo 21, San Felipe del Agua,* ☎ *951/501–5300,* FAX *951/520–0890,* WEB *www.hotelhaciendaloslaureles.com. 16 rooms, 9 suites. Restaurant, room ser-*

vice, pool, gym, massage, steam room, bar, baby-sitting, laundry service, free parking. AE, MC, V.

$$$ ★ **Hotel Victoria.** Surrounded by terraced grounds and well-kept gardens, this sprawling salmon-color complex is perched on a hill overlooking the city. Draw back your curtains at dawn and catch your breath at the view of Oaxaca awakening under the Sierra Madre. Rooms, bungalows, and suites are available; be sure to request one with a view. You can take a shuttle bus on the half hour to the city center, 10 minutes away. ✉ *Calle Lomas del Fortín 1, Lomas del Fortín,* ☎ *951/515–2633,* FAX *951/515–2411,* WEB *www.hotelvictoriaoax.com.mx. 59 rooms, 57 suites, 34 bungalows. Restaurant, room service, in-room safes, minibars, tennis court, pool, bar, baby-sitting, laundry service, travel services, free parking. AE, MC, V.*

$ **Las Azucenas.** This intimate hotel occupies a charmingly restored old home near La Soledad church downtown. Pluses are the fine bed linens, the helpful staff, and the rooftop patio where coffee, *pan dulce,* cheese, and fresh fruit are served each morning. On the downside, rooms are rather small, with no phones. Ask for a tiny *tele* at the reception desk if you can't bear to miss the evening news or the nightly Mexican soaps. ✉ *Calle Martiniano Aranda 203, 68000, at Matamoros,* ☎ *951/514–7918; 877/780–1156 in the U.S.,* FAX *951/514–9380,* WEB *www.hotelazucenas.com. 10 rooms. MC, V.*

$ ★ **Las Golondrinas.** Tastefully ablaze with color, this intimate hotel sustains a profusion of flowering plants whose blossoms stand out against pink, blue, mustard, and rust walls. Guests read or lounge around the blissfully tranquil patios. Simple yet cheerful rooms have red-tile floors and comfortable beds; none has TV or phone, but there's a TV in the common sitting room. Breakfast (not included in room rates) is served 8–10 AM. ✉ *Calle Tinoco y Palacios 411, Centro 68000,* ☎ *951/514–3298. 24 rooms. Laundry service. V.*

$ **Hotel Cazomalli.** Even the baked-earth floor tiles shine in this lovable hostelry, 15 minutes from downtown Oaxaca in the sleepy, cobblestone barrio of Jalatlaco. Clean, bright, quiet rooms have blond-pine furnishings and handwoven bedspreads and curtains. Rooms have no TVs—there's one in a small second-floor salon—but they do have phones. Owner Marina Flores and her family create a friendly ambience and serve breakfast 8–10 AM. ✉ *Calle El Salto 104, Jalatlaco, 68080, at Calle Aldama,* ☎ FAX *951/513–3513. 15 rooms. AE, MC, V.*

$ **Las Mariposas.** María Teresa, the owner of this well-stocked, cozy hotel, proudly shows prospective guests the bathroom amenities, pretty tin mirrors, and other special touches of her restored early-20th-century home. Guests share an outdoor kitchen, with sink, fridge, and cupboards and mingle on the open patio gladdened with laurel and lemon trees. Studios have kitchenettes with coffeemakers and other essentials. Continental breakfast is included. ✉ *Calle Pino Suárez 517, Centro 68000,* ☎ FAX *951/515–5854,* WEB *www.mexonline.com/mariposas.htm. 4 rooms, 6 studios. No credit cards.*

$ **Posada del Centro.** Simple but clean, with rustic-style Mexican wardrobes and night tables, comfortable mattresses, and locally made cotton bedspreads, this friendly, family-owned hotel sits smack-dab in the center of the old city. Europeans and Aussies converse at several groupings of tables and chairs on the front patio, lively with purple bougainvillea, red geraniums, and pink hibiscus. Rooms around this patio share a bath; rooms at the back patio (where breakfast is served 8–11 AM) have private bathrooms. ✉ *Av. Independencia 403, Centro 68000,* ☎ FAX *951/516–1874,* WEB *www.mexonline.com/posada.htm. 22 rooms. No credit cards.*

Nightlife and the Arts

Oaxaca has plenty of entertainment in the evening hours. On almost any night you'll find live marimba, Andean music, or nouveau flamenco in at least one of the open-air cafés surrounding the zócalo. Several discotheques play salsa, rock, or techno-pop, and Sunday at 12:30 PM the **Oaxaca State Band** sets up under the Indian laurel trees in the main square. See the monthly *Guía Cultural* ($1.50 at the MACO and Sedetur information booth on Av. Independencia), or the free *Oaxaca Times* for information on these and other events.

Dance to live salsa music every night at the longtime leading dance club, **Candela** (✉ Calle Murguía 413, at Calle Pino Suárez, ☎ 951/514–2010).

For the classic Mexican cantina experience, push aside the saloon-style swinging doors of **La Casa del Mezcal** (✉ Calle Flores Magón 209, ☎ no phone), near the Júrez market. The old-time atmosphere may be diminished by the presence of a large TV set (or two), but this casa is still a bastion of classic machismo and strong spirits.

Cinema Pochote (✉ Calle García Vigil 817, ☎ 951/513–2087) offers art films in various languages, often English, with Spanish subtitles. Dark Mondays.

Every Friday night—and Monday and Wednesday in busier seasons—the **Hotel Camino Real** (✉ Calle 5 de Mayo 300, Centro, ☎ 951/516–0611) hosts a regional dance show that's considered the town's best. The $30 admission includes a buffet dinner (beginning at 7 PM) and the show (8:30 PM) in the former convent's 16th-century chapel. Drinks aren't included; reservations are recommended.

The **Hotel Monte Albán** (✉ Alameda de León 1, Centro, ☎ 951/516–2330) presents nightly dance shows at 8:30 PM. Admission is about $5 and dinner and drinks are available.

El Sol y La Luna (✉ Calle Reforma 502, Centro, at Calle Constitución, ☎ 951/514–8069; closed Mon.) is the place to listen to live music, often jazz or jazzy Mexican and American ballads. You can sit over drinks or order dinner on the outside patio or inside at the residence-turned-restaurant. A cover is charged ($2–$4, depending on the band) when the music begins at 9–9:30 PM. Off-season, there's usually music Thursday–Saturday only.

Shopping

Prospective folk-art buyers in Oaxaca City and surrounding villages should heed one major caveat: be sure you have a receipt showing that you paid the 15% sales tax on all purchases. If you don't, you can still ship your purchases home from shops or shipping services, but you'll pay extra for them to provide the paperwork. Ask for receipts and for referrals to shipping agents if you plan to buy more than you can carry home. Also, check out the high-end shops on Calle Macedonio Alcalá first; then compare prices and quality with the items you find in the *mercados* (markets), smaller shops, or in the pueblos themselves, where artisans live and work.

Markets

Oaxaca's largest and oldest market is held at the functionally named **Central de Abastos** (Supply Center) on the southern edge of downtown. Saturday is the traditional market day, but the enormous covered market swarms daily with thousands of sellers and shoppers—from Oaxaca and the surrounding villages. For visitors, the Abastos market is more of a cultural experience than a shopping stop. Along with mounds of multicolored chilies and herbs, piles of tropical fruit, electronics, homemade tapes, and bright plasticware of every imaginable size and shape, you'll find straw baskets, fragile green and black pottery, and *rebozos* (shawls) of cotton and silk. If possible, don't burden yourself with lots of camera equipment or purses and bags; and keep an eye out for pickpockets and purse-slashers. Polite bargaining is expected.

The daily **Mercado Benito Juárez** (☒ south of the zócalo between Calles 20 de Noviembre and Miguel Cabrera at Las Calas, Centro) offers souvenirs, arts and crafts, leather sandals and bags, cheese, mole, chocolate, fruits, and much more.

Locals, budget travelers, and other adventurers eat regional food in the lively stalls of the daily **Mercado 20 de Noviembre** (☒ between Calles 20 de Noviembre and Miguel Cabrera at Calle Aldama, Centro), across the street from the Juárez market.

Each neighborhood has its own market day in an outdoor plaza or permanent structure, although these don't generally sell arts and crafts. If you're interested in seeing neighborhood markets, check out **Mercado de Conzatti** (☒ Calle Reforma at Calle Humboldt, Centro) Friday until 4 PM. Sunday is market day for the **Mercado de Merced** (☒ Calzada de la República at Calle Morelos, Centro).

Some of the best markets are found in the towns and villages surrounding Oaxaca. Wednesday is market day in **San Pablo Etla,** which is famous for its fresh white cheese. In addition to the standard cooked food, breads, groceries, and clothing, Thursday's market at **Zaachila** has an interesting animal market where farmers barter for spotted piglets and braying goats as well as larger animals. The animal market ends by noon, so plan to arrive early. Friday's *tianguis* (open-air market) is held at the pretty town of **Ocotlán,** where you can also admire the restored Dominican church and monastery of Santo Domingo. Sunday is market day in the Zapotec town of **Tlacolula.**

Shops and Galleries

Besides having a mother lode of markets, Oaxaca has some spectacular shops and galleries; some are closed Sunday and others close at midday, so plan your shopping days accordingly.

FINE ARTS

Galería Arte Mexicano (☒ Plaza Santo Domingo, Calle Macedonio Alcalá 407–16, Centro, ☎ 951/516–3255) displays local artists' work, and in adjoining rooms, folk art, antiques, and silver jewelry.

Galería Indigo (☒ Allende 104, Centro, ☎ 951/514–3889) is a lovely gallery in an enormous restored mansion. Ceramics, graphics, paintings, and other fine art from talented artists from Oaxaca and beyond are for sale.

Galería Quetzalli (☒ Calle Constitución 104, Centro, ☎ 951/514–2606) features both established and up-and-coming Oaxacan artists. Prices are high, but the work is excellent.

ARTS AND CRAFTS

ARIPO (☒ Calle García Vigil 809, Centro, ☎ 951/514–4030) is a government-run artist cooperative with competitive prices and exclusively Oaxacan work. It's one of the few craft stores open on Sunday.

Artesanías Chimalli (☒ Calle García Vigil 513-A, Centro, ☎ 951/514–2101) has an excellent selection of painted copal-wood animals with comical expressions and an assortment of quality crafts. Chimalli will ship what you buy here, or what you've bought elsewhere.

The **Fonart** store (✉ Crespo 114, Centro, ☎ 951/516–5764) has a representative selection of quality arts and crafts from elsewhere in Mexico.

Doing business since 1961, **Jarciería El Arte Oaxaqueño** (✉ Calle Mina 317, at J. P. García, ☎ 951/516–1581) has a good selection of stamped tin products, unique carved animals, and great prices.

La Mano Mágica (✉ Calle Macedonio Alcalá 203, Centro, ☎ 951/516–4275) is a crafts and fine-arts gallery with a large inventory of interesting pieces.

For textiles, don't miss **Mercado de Artesanías** (✉ Calle J. P. García near Calle Ignacio Zaragoza, Centro), a great place to shop for hand-woven and embroidered clothing from Oaxaca's seven regions. This is also the place to find the short velveteen *huipiles* worn in the Isthmus of Tehuantepec.

You'll support the women artists' co-op (open daily) by shopping at the huge warren of shops that makes up **Mujeres Artesanas de las Regiones de Oaxaca** (✉ Calle 5 de Mayo 204, Centro, ☎ 951/516–0670). The selection and quality are good, and prices are reasonable.

JEWELRY

The streets west of Mercado 20 de Noviembre between Trujano and Mina are crowded with jewelry shops; most offer 10- and 12-karat gold and modern and traditional styles.

A family business since 1963, **El Diamante** (✉ García Vigil 106-H, ☎ 951/516–3983) offers reliable workmanship and courteous service within a few blocks of El Alameda.

Oro de Monte Albán (✉ Calle Macedonio Alcalá 403, Centro, ☎ 951/514–3813) is one of several branches of this store, which sells gold and silver reproductions of pre-Columbian jewelry found in the tombs of royalty at Monte Albán (there's also a shop at the archaeological site).

Side Trips from Oaxaca City

Your trip to colonial Oaxaca isn't complete unless you head out to explore the region's ancient past and discover its influence on modern-day village life. Dramatic Zapotec and Mixtec ruins at Monte Albán, Mitla, and Yagul provide insight into ancient civilizations. Their golden era had passed when they were conquered by the Aztecs in the 15th century; shortly thereafter, the Spaniards arrived. Despite these conquests, indigenous languages are still extensively spoken in dozens of towns surrounding Oaxaca, where traditional lifestyles are slowly infused with modern trends and mores.

Many of the villages are known for the skill of artisans who create pottery, woven rugs, wood carvings, and other items. The visitor may see these pieces as charming, perhaps naive, folk art; for the artisans, however, the objects are likely utilitarian and probably embody generations of craftsmanship and unique family designs.

You can easily fill a week with tours to the following artisan towns, churches, pre-Hispanic ruins, and markets. Guided tours have the advantage of providing transportation; most agency tours stop at two or three venues. A car is helpful, especially for the Mitla route, which has half a dozen stops, some a kilometer or two off the highway. Buses, co-op taxis, and private taxis round out the options.

If you would like to experience life in the villages for yourself, consider taking advantage of the Tourist Yu'u project, developed by Sedetur, the state tourism board. You stay in basic, comfortable cabins that have semistocked kitchens or access to simple eateries nearby. Some venues have a tradition of arts and crafts to share with visitors. **Santa Ana del Valle** and **Teotitlán del Valle** are two Zapotec towns known for their rug making. At 28 km and 38 km (18 mi and 24 mi) from Oaxaca respectively, both also have community museums where demonstrations and outdoor activities may be arranged. Other villages have been selected because of their natural beauty. Visit the cold-water springs and fossilized waterfalls at **Hierve el Agua** or the valley-view village of **Benito Juárez,** surrounded by pines.

Even more isolated, **Santiago Apoala** is three hours from Oaxaca, with the last 42 km (26 mi) down a dirt road. Inexpensive packages to these cabins include breakfast, lunch, and a hike to the waterfall, the town's star attraction. Remember that these hostels and community museums are attended by villagers who are not paid for their services, and who sometimes have commitments to harvest or plant. Don't expect five-star services, and bring reading material, water, and a few provisions. Contact the tourism department for details and reservations.

Monte Albán

 *9 km (5½ mi) west of Oaxaca.*

The onetime holy city of more than 30,000 Zapotecs, Monte Albán is easily the most interesting and extensively excavated ruin in the state. Still, experts estimate that only about 10% of the site has been uncovered. Excavations take place whenever the budget permits, unearthing more hints about the fascinating culture of the Zapotec people who lived here.

Monte Albán overlooks the Oaxaca Valley from a flattened mountaintop 4,300 m (1,300 ft) high. Either Zapotecs or their predecessors leveled the site around 600 BC. The Zapotecs then constructed the existing buildings along a north–south axis, with the exception of one structure thought to have been an observatory; that one is more closely aligned with the stars than with the Earth's poles. The varying heights of the site follow the contours of distant mountain ranges. The oldest of the four temples is the **Dancers' Gallery,** so named for the elaborately carved stone figures that once covered the building—most of the originals are now in the site museum. Experts are unsure whether the figures, mostly male nudes, represent captives, medical cases, or warriors; the theory that they were dancers has been discarded.

Another major point of interest is the **Ball Court,** where one or more ball games were played. Hips, shoulders, knees, and elbows were probably used to hit a wooden or rubber ball. Although the exact outcome of these games is unknown, there's some speculation that the games were a means of solving disputes among factions or villages within the domain. The loser may have been sacrificed to the gods.

No one knows for sure whether the Zapotecs abandoned the site gradually or suddenly, but by AD 1000 they had vacated it. Until then, they had expanded the city over the centuries, influencing and being in turn influenced by the architecture, philosophy, and religious beliefs of the Maya and other ethnic groups. The Mixtecs, who took over the site years after the Zapotecs' departure, used Monte Albán as a lofty necropolis of lavish tombs. More than 200 tombs and 300 burial sites have been explored to date. The most fantastic of these, **Tomb 7,** yielded a treasure unequaled in North America. Inside were more than 500 priceless Mixtec objects, including gold breastplates; jade, pearl, ivory, and gold jewelry; and fans, masks, and belt buckles of precious stones and metals. Many of these treasures are now on view at the Museo de las Culturas in Oaxaca City. At Monte Albán proper, you'll find a

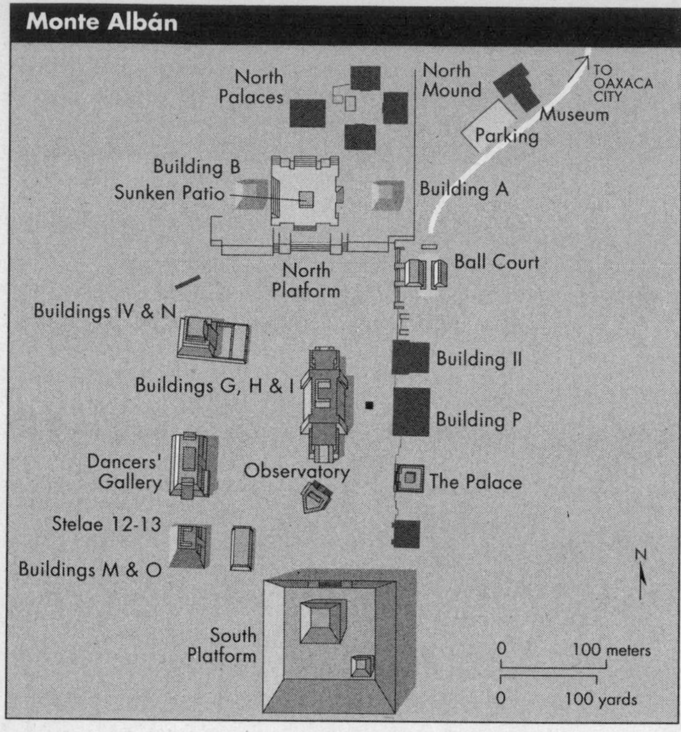

small **site museum** with a gift shop (☎ 951/516–1215). The cafeteria isn't half bad and has a great view of the valley of Oaxaca.

Direct buses serve Monte Albán from the Hotel Rivera del Ángel on the half hour from 8:30 to 3:30; the last bus back is at 6 PM. The round-trip fare is about $3; to stay longer than two hours you must pay a small surcharge. A taxi from the zócalo costs about $10. *$3.50, free Sun. and holidays.* *Daily 8–5.*

Southeast of Oaxaca City

A trip along Highway 190 (better known as "the road to Mitla") offers a full day of pleasant surprises. On Sunday it seems that all of Oaxaca takes this route, visiting the archaeological ruins of Mitla, the Tule Tree, and the market at Tlacolula.

Mitla expanded and grew in influence as Monte Albán declined. Like its precursor, Mitla is a complex of structures started by the Zapotecs and later taken over by the Mixtecs. Unlike Monte Alba, however, Mitla's charm lies not in the scale and number of buildings but in their unusual ornamentation. Mitla's striking architecture is almost without equal within Mexico thanks to the exquisite workmanship on the fine local quarry stone, which ranges in hue from pink to yellow. Unlike other ancient buildings in North America, there are no human figures or mythological events represented—only complex, repetitive abstract designs. The name, from the Aztec word *mictlan,* means "place of the dead." The journey takes about 50 minutes from Oaxaca. Catch a *colectivo* (collective taxi) at the side of Oaxaca City's second-class bus station or a bus from the terminal or along the road to Mitla. ✉ *40 km (25 mi) southeast of Oaxaca.* *$2.50, free Sun. and holidays.* *Archaeological zone daily 8–5.*

Along the road to Mitla, the small hamlet of **Santa María del Tule** is known for the huge *ahuehuete* cypress that towers over the pretty colonial-era church behind it. Thought to be more than 2,000 years old, it's one of the largest trees in the world, with roots buried more than 60 ft in the ground and its canopy arcing some 140 ft high. It has an estimated weight of nearly 640,000 tons; to embrace the trunk, 35 adults must stretch out their arms around it. ✉ *14 km (8½ mi) east of Oaxaca.* 🎫 *20¢.*

NEED A BREAK?

At an informal series of outdoor eateries in the Tule tree's shadow, local ladies tend large griddles, serving *atole* (a thick corn drink), hot chocolate, soups, and snacks.

Giant rug looms sit in the front rooms of many houses in **Teotitlán del Valle.** The small **Museo Comunitario** (closed Monday) on the main square focuses on the anthropology, crafts, and culture of the area. For tacos and other regional treats, head for **El Descanso** restaurant at Av. Juárez 51. ✉ *25 km (15½ mi) east of Oaxaca.*

The rug- and *sarape*-making town of **Santa Ana del Valle** is less well known than Teotitlán but equally worth visiting. ✉ *25 km (15½ mi) east of Oaxaca.*

Although most often visited during its bustling Sunday market, **Tlacolula** (30 km from Oaxaca) makes an interesting stop midweek to visit the Baroque Dominican church. ✉ *31 km (19 mi) east of Oaxaca.*

The ruins at **Yagul** are not nearly as elaborate as those at Monte Albán or Mitla, but they do stand handsomely atop a hill and are certainly worth a visit. This city was predominantly a fortress set slightly above a group of palaces and temples; it includes a ball court and more than 30 uncovered underground tombs. ✉ *36 km (22 mi) east of Oaxaca.* 🎫 *$2.50, free Sun. and holidays.* ⏲ *Archaeological zone daily 8–5.*

South of Oaxaca City

In the prosperous village of **Arrazola,** first- and second-generation artists carve angels, animals, and *alebrijes* (fanciful figures) of light, porous copal wood. These statues, from tiny to tremendous, are then painted and decorated with dots, squiggles, and other artful touches. This relatively new craft was developed by Arrazola's best-known and highest-paid artisan, don Manuel Jiménez. Not far beyond Arrazola you'll come to the ruined Dominican church and monastery at **Culiapan.** The long, roofless structure was the first church, begun in the 16th century but never finished. The adjoining church is often closed. ✉ *12 km (7½ mi) southwest of Oaxaca.*

Zaachila was an important center of Zapotec civic and religious authority at the time of the Spanish invasion. On Thursday, oxcarts loaded with alfalfa or hay head for the area's most authentic livestock market. The town also boasts a colorful church, a small archaeological zone with two underground tombs, and restaurants serving typical regional fare. ✉ *17 km (11 mi) southwest of Oaxaca.*

The Spanish-Nahuatl name of **San Bartolo Coyotepec** literally translates as "Saint Bartholomew, Place of the Coyotes." Across from the stately church is a multistall cooperative where you can purchase the fragile, glossy, unglazed black pottery for which the town is deservedly famous. ✉ *12 km (7½ mi) south of Oaxaca on Hwy. 175.*

In the small town of **Santo Tomás Jaliezam,** women produce belts, table runners, and other woven goods on small, back-strap looms. Prices in the co-op in the center of town are uniform and very reasonable, and there are usually a few items of worked leather for sale. ✉ *29 km (18 mi) south of Oaxaca, off a small road off Hwy. 175.*

San Martín Tilcajete is a town full of painted wooden animals as well as cute carved devils, stern saints, and multipiece tableaux of various village scenes. As in Arrazola, most homes double as workshops and invite shoppers to browse. ✉ *27 km (17 mi) south of Oaxaca on Hwy. 175.*

Friday's colorful market in **Ocotlán** is known for its handcrafted machetes and knives. The large town has a beautifully restored Dominican church and monastery on the attractive main plaza. At the entrance to town, the Aguilar family makes distinctive figures of clay, which they paint with bright acrylic paints. ✉ *32 km (20 mi) south of Oaxaca on Hwy. 175.*

North and West of Oaxaca City

Take some time to wander the few main streets of unimposing **Atzompa,** whose inhabitants produce fanciful clay pots and sculptures as well as the more traditional green-glazed plates, bowls, and cups. You can often visit the potters' simple home-workshops where the pieces are made. More convenient (although quality of work can be disappointing) is the *mercado artesanal,* open daily from 8 to 7. ✉ *8 km (5 mi) northwest of Oaxaca.*

OFF THE BEATEN PATH

North of Oaxaca, the road to Mexico City leads to several unmarked and untouristy villages worth visiting. **San Pablo Etla** is known for its high-quality white cheese, which you can purchase at the Wednesday market along with fresh buns. Just behind the market, the **La Fonda** (open for breakfast and lunch) has no sign, but at its simple indoor and outdoor tables, you're served excellent stuffed chilies, chicken soup, and other regional fare. Neighboring **San Agustín Etla** is known for its abundance of water. Ask locals to direct you to the papermaking co-op in the old hydroelectric plant (closed Sunday). A neighborhood of San Agustín, **Vistahermosa** has several sprawling outdoor bathing facilities where you can swim, lie in the sun, lunch in the shade, and sip a cool drink. One of the nicest facilities is **Balneario Vistahermosa** (✉ Calle Hidalgo 16, San Agustín Etla, ☎ 951/521–2049; 🎫 $2.50).

Oaxaca City A to Z

To research prices, get advice from other travelers, and book travel arrangements, visit www.fodors.com.

AIR TRAVEL

You can fly to Oaxaca City's Benito Juárez Airport, 8 km (5 mi) south of town, from several U.S. cities, always making a stop in Mexico City. There's also service for triangle flight itineraries, including the Oaxacan coastal resorts of Bahías de Huatulco or Puerto Escondido.

CARRIERS

Mexicana flies from various U.S. cities (including Chicago, Los Angeles, Miami, New York, and San Francisco) to Oaxaca City with a stop in Mexico City, as does Aeroméxico (from Chicago, Dallas–Fort Worth, Houston, Los Angeles, Miami, New York, and Phoenix). Domestic service to Oaxaca includes Aviacsa from Tuxtla Gutiérrez; Aero Vega for charters to and from Puerto Escondido; and Aerocaribe and Aerotucán from Puerto Escondido and Huatulco.

➤ AIRLINES AND CONTACTS: **Aerocaribe** (☎ 951/516–6088 or 951/516–2066 in Oaxaca; 958/582–2023 in Puerto Escondido; 958/587–

1220 in Huatulco). **Aeroméxico** (☎ 951/516–1066 or 800/237–6639). **Aerotucán** (☎ 951/501–0532). **Aero Vega** (☎ 951/516–4982 in Oaxaca; 958/582–0151 in Puerto Escondido). **Aviacsa** (☎ 951/514–5304). **Mexicana** (☎ 951/516–8414 or 951/516–7352).

AIRPORT TRANSFERS

At the airport, Transportes Aeropuerto will trundle you into the soonest available van and drop you off at your hotel for $5.50 (more if there are no other passengers). From town, buy a ticket ahead of time ($2 for city center; $5.50 beyond) for inexpensive airport transportation or hail a regular cab for about $8. The company is closed on Sunday; for Monday departures, purchase tickets by the preceding Saturday.
➤ TAXIS AND SHUTTLES: **Transportes Aeropuerto** (✉ Alameda de León, Centro, ☎ 951/514–4350).

BUS TRAVEL TO AND FROM OAXACA

Deluxe buses make the six-hour nonstop run from Mexico City to Oaxaca for about $23. Oaxaca City's first-class terminal is called the ADO, from which the ADO and Cristóbal Colón bus lines provide service. The second-class bus station, Central de Autobuses, serves intermediate towns within the state. Other lines have desks at one or both terminals.
➤ BUS INFORMATION: **ADO** (✉ Calzada Niños Héroes de Chapultepec 1036, at Calle Emilio Carranza, ADO, ☎ 951/515–1703). **Central de Autobuses** (✉ Prolongación de Trujano at the Periférico, Central de Abastos, ☎ 951/516–5824). **Cristóbal Colón** (☎ 951/513–0529).

CAR RENTAL

Cars are available for rent at the airport, in town, and through travel agencies at various hotels.
➤ MAJOR AGENCIES: **Alamo** (✉ 5 de Mayo 203, Centro, ☎ 951/514–8534). **Budget** (✉ Calle 5 de Mayo, across from the Camino Real Hotel, ☎ 951/516–4445). **Hertz** (✉ La Bastida 115–4, Centro, ☎ 951/516–2434, ☎ FAX 951/516–0009; ✉ Benito Juárez Airport, Aeropuerto, ☎ 951/511–5478).

CAR TRAVEL

From Mexico City, you can take Mexico 190 (Pan American Highway) south and east through Puebla and Izúcar de Matamoros to Oaxaca City—a distance of 546 km (338 mi) along a rather curvy road. This route takes six to seven hours. The toll road (*cuota*) that connects Mexico City to Oaxaca City via Tehuacán costs about $30 one way. It cuts driving time to four hours.

You won't need a car in Oaxaca City, which is fairly compact. Even outlying sights are easily accessible by taxi or on a tour. That said, a car is a great way for adventurous souls to see the countryside.

EMBASSIES

The Canadian Consulate is open weekdays 11–2. The U.S. Consulate is open weekdays 10–3.
➤ CANADA: **Canadian Consulate** (✉ Calle Pino Suarez 700, Local 11-B, Centro, ☎ 951/513–3777 or 951/515–2147).
➤ UNITED STATES: **U.S. Consulate** (✉ Calle Macedonio Alcalá 407, Int. 20, Centro, ☎ 951/514–2147, FAX 951/516–2701).

EMERGENCIES

Dial **060** locally for all emergencies, including police and hospital.
➤ CONTACTS: **Hospital–Red Cross** (☎ 951/516–4455). **Police** (☎ 951/516–0400).

INTERNET

There are several Internet cafés downtown. Axis, open weekdays 10–8 and Saturday 10–6, charges about $2 an hour.

➤ INTERNET CAFÉS: **Axis** (✉ Calle 5 de Mayo 412, Centro, ☎ 951/514–8024).

TAXIS

Taxis are plentiful, clearly marked, and reasonably priced. You can usually find them at any hour of the day cruising on downtown streets. There are also taxi stands on Avenida Independencia at Calle García Vigil, on the north side of Alameda Park, and on Calles Abasolo and 5 de Mayo, near the Hotel Camino Real. Cabs aren't metered. Determine the fare ahead of time (in town, usually $2–$3); for outlying destinations, ask the driver to show you the tariff card.

TELEPHONE CODES

In February 2002 Mexico switched to a 10-digit dial plan, according to which all phone numbers were revised and extended. The following three-digit regional codes now precede the old seven-digit numbers: 951 for Oaxaca City, 958 for Huatulco, and 954 for Puerto Escondido. If dialing Oaxaca City long-distance from within Mexico, dial 01-951 and the 7-digit telephone number.

Many people (and older printed materials) still refer to the five-digit phone numbers used prior to 1999; in that case, first dial the appropriate three-digit regional codes, then the two-digit extension (51 for Oaxaca City; 54 for Puerto Escondido; 58 for Huatulco), and then the old five-digit number.

TOURS

Unless you're on a strict budget, take advantage of the many tour companies that offer guided trips to the archaeological sites, colonial churches and monasteries, outlying towns (some of which have weekly market days), and folk-art centers. Prices start at $15. Licensed guides are available through travel agencies for approximately $5 per hour for a minimum of three people. Viajes Turísticos Mitla and Agencia Marqués del Valle are among the most established agencies. For expeditions a bit farther from the beaten tourist track contact Expediciones Sierra Norte or TierrAventura. Tierra Dentro specializes in bird-watching, and offers hiking, rock climbing, and mountain biking.

➤ TOUR OPERATOR RECOMMENDATIONS: **Agencia Marqués del Valle** (✉ Portal de Clavería s/n, Centro, ☎ 951/514–6970 or 951/514–6962, FAX 951/516–9961). **Expediciones Sierra Norte** (✉ Garcia Vigil 406, Centro, ☎ 951/514–8271, FAX 951/516–7745, WEB www.sierranorte.org.mx). **Tierra Dentro** (✉ Reforma 528–B, Centro, ☎ 951/514–9284, WEB www.tierradentro.com). **TierrAventura** (✉ Boca del Monte 110, Centro, ☎ 951/514–3843, WEB www.tierraventura.com). **Viajes Turísticos Mitla** (✉ Calle Mina 518, in the Hotel Rivera del Ángel, Centro, ☎ 951/516–6175, FAX 951/514–3152).

VISITOR INFORMATION

The Oficina de Turismo is open daily 9–8. The adjoining shop has fairly good quality regional crafts at low prices; money goes directly to the artisans. A branch of the tourism office is open daily 6 AM–8 PM in the Oaxaca airport.

➤ TOURIST INFORMATION: **Oficina de Turismo** (✉ Av. Independencia 607, at Calle García Vigil, Centro, ☎ 951/516–4828; 951/511–5040 airport booth, WEB www.oaxaca.gob.mx/sedetur).

THE OAXACA COAST

Oaxaca's 520-km (322-mi) coastline is mainland Mexico's last Pacific frontier. Huatulco, a project of Fonatur (the government's tourism developer), was launched in the early 1980s. Bahías de Huatulco, as the entire area is called, covers 51,900 acres, 40,000 acres of which is dedicated as a nature reserve. The focal point of the master-planned development is a string of nine sheltered bays that stretches across 35 km (22 mi) of some of the Pacific's prettiest coastline.

Huatulco's beauty is arguably best seen from a boat, even though some of the bays are accessible by road. Bahía Tangolunda is the site of the area's most exclusive hotels, whereas Santa Cruz has midrange hotels, a marina, and a small plaza. Development of Bahía Chahué has begun slowly, with one hotel already closed due to the owner's financial and legal problems. A new spa is almost ready to open there, and a parking lot makes the beach accessible. A Best Western and a few other small hotels are near this bay, but across the highway. The town of Crucecita, originally built to house the construction crews and workers building Huatulco, has come along nicely: it has the requisite Catholic church on the plaza as well as some budget and moderately priced hotels and plenty of restaurants.

Puerto Escondido has long been prime territory for international surfers. The town has the coast's first airport (not international) and has grown up to tourism in a much more natural way than Huatulco. The four-block pedestrian walkway—crowded with open-air seafood restaurants, shops, and café bars—is lively. But across the highway, the "real" town above, with its busy market and stores, provides a look at local life and a dazzling view of the coast. Midway between Puerto Escondido and Bahías de Huatulco, the tiny port town of Puerto Ángel has a limited selection of hotels and bungalows tucked into the hills. The growing number of accommodations in nearby beach villages such as Zipolite and Mazunte has seduced some of Puerto Ángel's previously faithful sun-lovers.

Puerto Escondido

⓭ *310 km (192 mi) south of Oaxaca City.*

A coffee-shipping port in the 1920s, Puerto Escondido is the first tourist town on the Oaxaca coast, southeast of Acapulco on Highway 200. The town market, **Mercado Benito Juárez,** is a long walk (but a short cab or bus ride) from most hotels, and it's worth checking out on market days: Saturday and Wednesday.

If you want a bit of pampering, cleanse body and soul according to ancient traditions at the **Temazcalli** (✉ Av. Infraganti 28, at Calle Temazcalli, ☎ FAX 958/582–1023), which claims to combine the energy of wood, fire, rock, and medicinal herbs. Choose an individual (for one or two) steam or a ritualistic group cleansing; the latter involves chants and prayers. Massages are also offered.

To explore Puerto's pretty coves and best swimming beaches, consider hiring a boatman from among the fishing skiffs for bay tours at Playa Marinero or Playa Zicatela. It's around $4.50 per person or $33 for your own boat to visit **Puerto Angelito** and **Carrizalillo** bays. (Both can also be accessed on foot or by car or taxi.) Fishing trips are a little steep at about $30 per hour. The Playa Principal and the **Laguna Agua Dulce** are at the south end of the tourist strip, followed by **Marinero Beach**, a sharp outcropping of rocks, and, finally, the most famous—and dangerous—beach of all, **Zicatela.**

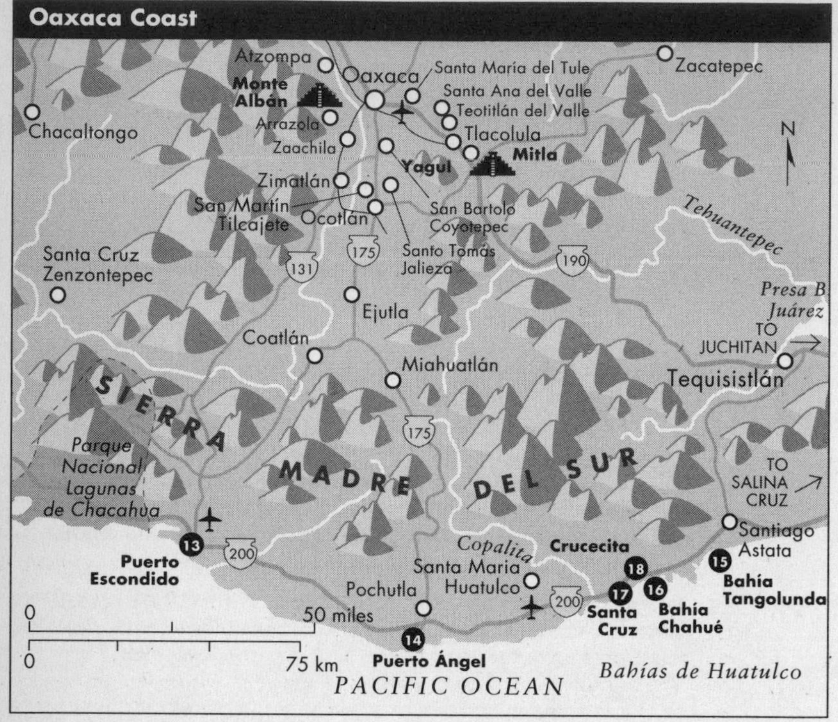

En Route If you're driving to Puerto Escondido via Sola de Vega (Highway 231), take a detour to see the miracle-working, diminutive **Virgen de Juquila,** in the town of Juquila. The saint's day, December 8, is preceded by nine days of prayers and festivities, including fireworks, carnival rides, dances, and general gaiety. Any time of year, however, is pleasant to visit the small town in the heart of coffee country. Due to the constant flow of pilgrims, inexpensive hotels line the hilly streets. Consider spending the night, or get an early start and stop in just for a short interview with the 12-inch icon. To reach Juquila from Oaxaca City, turn inland on a signed road just south of Sola de Vega on Route 131, about halfway (3 hours) between the capital and the coast.

The main intersection in Puerto Escondido is at Highway 200 (also called the *carretera costera,* or coast highway) and Avenida Pérez Gasga, which meanders south into the tourist zone. On the north side of the highway this street is called Avenida Oaxaca. Traveling down a steep hill, Avenida Gasga passes many of the tourist hotels; at the bottom, traffic is prohibited and the street becomes a four-block-long pedestrian mall (*el adoquín*) lined with shops, restaurants, and lodgings paralleling the main beach.

The airport is on the northern edge of town, as are the hotels favored by charter groups. **Playa Bacocho,** south of the airport, is an upscale housing-and-hotel development. The beach is generally not considered safe for swimming, as there are strong rip currents. Some inviting bars, discos, and restaurants have opened in this area, although most of the action still centers around the tourist zone to the south.

Beaches

One of the top 10 surfing beaches in the world, **Zicatela** is a long stretch of cream-colored sand battered by the Mexican Pipeline, as this stretch of mighty surf is called. In November international surfing championships are held here, and the town fills with sun-bleached aficionados of both sexes intent on serious surfing and hard partying. The water is only for expert swimmers, although it is slightly safer now that lifeguards are often on duty. None but the most confident should swim in these waters, even when they appear calm, as the undertows and rip currents can be deadly. If you have any doubts about your swimming prowess, settle for watching the surfers from the thatch-roof restaurant at the Arco Iris or Santa Fe hotels.

Of the seven beaches in Puerto Escondido, the safest for swimming and snorkeling are **Puerto Angelito** and **Carrizalillo;** both can be reached on foot from paths west of town, or by cab ($2) or by boat ($4.50 per person) from the playa principal.

Dining and Lodging

Understandably, coastal cuisine focuses on fresh seafood dishes, although some savvy townspeople and European transplants have introduced Italian and vegetarian food for variety. For such a small town, Puerto Escondido has more than its share of good restaurants.

$$ ★ ✕ **La Galería.** This art-filled restaurant on the tourist strip is deservedly popular for its range of meat and fish dishes, but the main draw are the homemade pastas and the wonderful pizzas (try the "Helena," with eggplant, garlic, mushrooms, and herbs). The delicious five-cheese ravioli is stuffed with Roquefort, Gouda, Parmesan, provolone, and string cheese. For dessert, order an espresso and a big slice of chocolate pie: dense and not too sweet. ✉ *Av. Pérez Gasga, west end,* ☎ *958/582–2039. No credit cards.*

$$ ✕ **La Perla.** Because it's in the "real" town uphill from the tourist zone, this seafood restaurant has some of the best prices in town. The cavernous dining room is prepared to serve multitudes; don't feel put off if you're the only one there. The restaurateurs have their own fishing fleet and even sell to other local restaurants. The octopus is wonderfully tender; excellent ceviche comes in a spicy cocktail sauce. ✉ *Calle 3a Poniente s/n, Sector Juárez,* ☎ *958/582–0461. No credit cards.*

$$ ✕ **Perla Flameante.** Fresh dorado, shark, tuna, and pompano come with teriyaki, Cajun, or garlic seasonings at this second-story bamboo restaurant, often to the tune of background reggae. The deep-fried onion rings and zucchini are terrific. "The Flaming Pearl" is open for dinner only, starting at 6:30 in low season, at 4 PM in high season (December–Easter). ✉ *Av. Pérez Gasga, near end of tourist zone,* ☎ *958/582–0167. MC, V.*

$ ★ ✕ **Cafecito.** A long-standing favorite for great coffee, whole-grain breads, and sinful pastries, this is the second coming of the original Carmen's Bakery, but with a better location. Start your day with good, strong coffee and a bowl of fresh fruit, yogurt, and homemade granola. Occupying side-by-side venues on Zicatela Beach, Cafecito is best for breakfast but serves a respectable lunch as well. ✉ *Calle del Morro s/n, Zicatela Beach,* ☎ *no phone. No credit cards. No dinner.*

$ ✕ **La Gota de Vida.** Surfers and health-conscious travelers love this vegetarian café and health-food store for its variety of *licuados* (shakes made with milk, water, or yogurt and fruit) as well as the large variety of fresh vegetable and fruit juices. They also make great bread, pastries, *tortas* (bread roll sandwiches), and chocolate mousse, all of which are generally better than the main dishes, which include tofu and tempeh dishes. ✉ *Calle del Morro s/n, Zicatela Beach,* ☎ *no phone. No credit cards.*

$$$ ★ ✕🏨 **Hotel Santa Fe.** Framed by exuberant tropical plants, this pretty hotel has colonial-style furnishings, and curtains and spreads of hand-loomed cloth. Some rooms have balconies overlooking the pools and

patios or the beach. Eight one-bedroom bungalows have well-stocked kitchenettes, cozy furnishings, and wide verandas. Even nonguests should treat themselves to at least one meal at the hotel restaurant. Traditional Mexican dishes are created using seafood but are otherwise meatless (try the tacos with potato, cheese, and mushrooms); tables overlooking the surf have wonderful views. ✉ *Calle del Morro s/n, 71980,* ☎ *958/582–0170 or 888/649–6407,* FAX *958/582–0260,* WEB *www.hotelsantafe.com.mx. 59 rooms, 2 suites, 8 bungalows. Restaurant, 2 pools, wading pool, bar, shops, laundry service, free parking. AE, MC, V.*

$ ★ ✕ **Flor de María.** Hand-painted birds, flowers, and tropical scenes adorn this bright, attractive hotel a half block up from Playa Marinero. Crisp sheets cover firm beds, and rooms are bright and immaculate, but have no TV or phone. In the outstanding restaurant, Canadian restaurateur Joanne brings Italian and Peruvian touches to the daily dinner specials, always with at least one vegetarian choice. Desserts are homemade delights. ✉ *Entrance to Playa Marinero s/n, 71980,* ☎ *958/582–0536* FAX *958/582–2617,* WEB *www.mexonline.com/flordemaria.htm. 24 rooms. Restaurant, fans, pool, bar, laundry service. MC, V. Restaurant closed Tues. May–Nov.*

$$–$$$ **Paraíso Escondido.** Hidden halfway up the steps of Calle Unión, this colonial-style hotel has the charm of a wealthy, eccentric, and somewhat dotty relative's house. No two rooms are alike, and all are furnished with a folkloric mixture of wood dressers, tin mirrors, and brightly colored curtains and spreads. Five third-floor suites have kitchenettes and private, ocean-view terraces. ✉ *Calle Unión 10, 71980,* ☎ *958/582–0444. 20 rooms, 5 suites. Restaurant, pool, bar. No credit cards.*

$$ **Hotel Aldea del Bazar.** This sparkling white hotel with perfectly manicured lawns sits on a bluff overlooking Playa Bacocho, just south of the airport. The restaurant has a view of the garden and pool; from some of the rooms you'll see the beach, which can be reached by a ramp. All the tastefully decorated rooms have small living rooms and satellite TVs. One of the hotel's best features is the pre-Hispanic–style eucalyptus sauna; the massages are just mediocre. ✉ *Av. Benito Juárez 7, Fracc. Bacocho, 71980,* ☎ FAX *958/582–0508. 47 rooms. Restaurant, pool, massage, spa, bar, travel services, free parking. AE, MC, V.*

$–$$ ★ **Studios Tabachín del Puerto.** Special touches such as clocks, vases, and shelves with books give these wonderfully furnished studio apartments a homey feel. Each of the six studios, behind the Hotel Santa Fe near Zicatela Beach, has a kitchenette stocked with necessities. Owner don Pablo also manages a small country inn, **Posada Nopala,** about two hours inland, open October 31 to April 30. This comfortable yet rustic lodge in the pine forests of the Oaxaca mountains is perfect for experiencing life in rural Mexico. ✉ *Calle de Morro s/n, Zicatela Beach, 71980,* ☎ FAX *958/582–1179,* WEB *www.tabachin.com.mx. 6 apartments. Restaurant. MC, V.*

$–$$ **Villa Belmar.** The variety of accommodation—from one-bedroom apartments to comfortable double rooms and spartan surfer huts—attracts a nice mix of people, despite paint splatters and shabby maintenance. Overlook the east end of Zicatela Beach from within an array of arches, domes, and cupolas done in Mediterranean white and blue. The pool is Olympic. You can rent by day in high season, by week or month other times. Dogs and cats are welcome. ✉ *Calle del Morro s/n, Zicatela Beach, 71980,* ☎ *958/582–0244,* FAX *958/582–0895,* WEB *www.villabelmar.com. 18 rooms, 15 suites, 5 apartments. Restaurant, pool, free parking. MC, V.*

$ **Cabañas de Playa Acali.** Although rooms are plain, with uninspired decor, this clutch of rooms has a large pool, a good location on Zicatela Beach, and variety of types of accommodation. The cheapest are the rustic cabañas; the most expensive are eight bungalows with small terraces and kitchens. This is a good choice for groups of four or six who are sharing expenses and preparing their own meals. ✉ *Calle del Morro s/n, 71980,* ☎ *958/582–0754,* FAX *958/582–0055. 8 cabañas, 6 bungalows. Kitchenettes, pool. No credit cards.*

$ ★ **Hotel Arco Iris.** This sprawling, three-story hotel on Zicatela Beach resembles a gracefully aging, old-fashioned guest house. The rooms are simple yet clean, with firm beds and worn but comfortable furnishings. Some rooms have kitchenettes; most have wide verandas (bring a hammock) that overlook the surfing beach just beyond. There's a large pool, a video salon, and a second-story restaurant with a wonderful ocean breeze. ✉ *Calle del Morro s/n, Zicatela Beach 71980,* ☎ FAX *958/582–0432 or 958/582–1494,* WEB *www.hotel-arcoiris.com. 32 rooms, 4 suites. Restaurant, pool, bar, laundry service, free parking. MC, V.*

Nightlife

CANTINAS

Beto, the affable host of **Los Flamingos** (✉ Ave. Hidalgo 607, Sector Reforma "A," ☎ 958/582–2902), serves up a different, free *botana* (appetizer) with every drink you order. He also concocts the best French onion soup in all of Puerto. You can easily make a meal of the delicious little appetizer plates. The cantina is open Monday to Saturday 1–6; it's cash only.

For spirited live entertainment, stop by **Son y La Rumba** (✉ a few steps behind the tourist information booth on the cobblestone path, next door and upstairs from the Tequila Discoteque, ☎ no phone). Owner Myka sings every night, but you never know who will drop in to jam with her—be it a classical violinist, a flamenco guitarist, or a European sax player. The bar is open from 10:30 PM until whenever they close, usually around 2 AM.

Outdoor Activities and Sports

LAGOON TOURS

About 74 km (46 mi) west of Puerto Escondido is a tropical park encompassing the **Chacahua Lagoon.** You can tour the lagoon in a small motor launch, watching the waterbirds that hunt among the mangroves. The bird population is most numerous during the winter months, when migratory species arrive from the frozen north. Most tours include a rather prosaic visit to a crocodile farm, and an hour or two on the beach at Cerro Hermoso, where you eat a simple meal of grilled fish or just play on the beach. Canadian ornothologist Michael Malone (*see* Bird-Watching Tours *under* Oaxaca Coast A to Z) leads tours in winter; otherwise, local guides usually speak enough English to make themselves understood.

WATER SPORTS

You can rent boogie boards and surfboards at **Bulldog** (✉ Calle del Morro s/n, ☎ 958/582–0919) for about $9 a day. You must pay a cash deposit, which will be refunded at the end of the day unless the equipment is damaged.

Puerto Ángel and Surrounding Beaches

⓮ *81 km (50 mi) southeast of Puerto Escondido.*

The leading seaport of the state 100 years ago, Puerto Ángel today is a tiny hamlet on a beautiful bay. Simply by being overlooked in favor of more accessible sites, it has managed to avoid the commercialization of Huatulco and the growth of Puerto Escondido. Puerto Ángel and the beaches of Zipolite and Mazunte appeal to those who prefer a rustic atmosphere and simple pleasures.

The navy has its installations on the central town beach. The most popular swimming-and-sunning territory is at **Playa Panteón,** past the oceanfront cemetery (*panteón* means "cemetery"). Other good (and less populated) swimming and snorkeling beaches are nearby.

Four km (2.5 mi) west of town is **Zipolite,** a long stretch of creamy sand known for its nude sunbathing. It's a favorite with surfers, wild young things, and travelers content with a hammock on the beach and little else in the way of creature comforts; it's not really a favorite with families. The undertow is extremely strong and riptides are unpredictable, and swimming here is not recommended.

West of Zipolite, **Playa San Agustanillo** is another long stretch of beach, equally pretty and somewhat less dangerous for swimming, although the current is still strong. Vendors roam the sand selling cool drinks and grilled fish on a stick.

About 13 km (8 mi) from Puerto Ángel, **Mazunte** is yet another stunning stretch of sand, which, like Zipolite and San Agustanillo, has its share of simple seafood restaurants and low-key wood and thatch accommodations.

Mazunte also has a legitimate sightseeing destination: the **Centro Mexicano de la Tortuga** (Museum of the Sea Turtle). It was born as a center of exploitation of the *golfina* (Olive Ridley) turtle and even had its own slaughterhouse for their meat. A 1990 government ban on turtle hunting has for the most part stopped the carnage, and Mazunte is now devoted to protecting the species. The name Mazunte derives from the Nahuatl *Maxonteita,* which means "please come and spawn" and indeed seven of the world's eight species of marine turtles come to spawn on Oaxaca's shores. A dozen aquariums are filled with turtle specimens that once again flourish in the nearby ocean. From Puerto Ángel, take Highway 200 toward San Pedro Pochutla; about 15 km (9 mi) past town, follow the turnoff marked SAN AGUSTÍN. A few kilometers later at the sign for PLAYA MAZUNTE, ask for directions to the *museo,* which is on the beach. ✉ *Playa Mazunte,* ☎ *no phone.* *$3.* ⏲ *Tues.–Sat. 10–4.*

Dining and Lodging

$ ✕ **Posada Cañon Devata.** Simple bungalows at this ecological hideaway in a wooded canyon offer private quarters; other rooms and buildings are scattered on the hillsides. At the top of the hill, the bar El Cielo (Heaven) is a good place to take in the sunset. Windows have screens; a drawback for some folks is the lack of hot water. The cool *palapa* (thatched roof) restaurant is a find for vegetarians; it's open to nonguests as well. Reserve ahead for the 7 PM dinner, which runs about $8. ✉ *Past the cemetery, off Blvd. Virgilio Uribe, 70902,* ☎ *958/584–3137. 16 rooms, 6 bungalows. Restaurant, bar. No credit cards.*

$ ✕ **La Buena Vista.** Some of the clean, simple accommodations here have balconies, some have terraces with hammocks, but none has hot water. The third-floor restaurant (which serves breakfast and dinner) has one of the most dependable kitchens in town, and rooms at the top level of the hotel have a great view as well as the best breezes. There are a lot of steps to negotiate here, and no elevator. ✉ *Calle la Buena Compañía, 70902,* WEB *www.labuenavista.com,* ☎ FAX *958/584–3104. 23 rooms. Restaurant. No credit cards.*

Bahías de Huatulco

277 km (172 mi) south of Oaxaca City, 111 km (69 mi) east of Puerto Escondido, 48 km (30 mi) east of Puerto Ángel.

Bahías de Huatulco continues to march slowly forward toward a completion date sometime in the early 21st century. Three of its nine bays have been developed to date, but only Bahía Tangolunda, with its golf course and five-star hotels, has the look of a real resort. Conejos Bay is next in line for hotels and restaurants; Cacaluta has been designated a national park. Huatulco's pristine bays encompass a total of 36 tropical beaches. Because of the fits and starts of its construction, Huatulco has an unfinished look, a lack of polish in comparison to Cancún and Ixtapa. Environmentalists may prefer it for being Mexico's only resort that does *not* pump sewage into the ocean. If you have a car at your disposal, you can drive to several bays that so far haven't been developed and play Robinson Crusoe to your heart's content.

Another popular option is to tour the bays by boat. Standard four- to eight-hour trips—depending on how many bays you visit—might include a lunch of freshly caught fish (which costs extra). Fishing, diving, and snorkeling tours visit the beaches or reefs most suitable for those activities.

15 The Huatulco of the future is most evident at **Bahía Tangolunda,** where the poshest hotels are in full swing and the sea is abob with sightseeing *lanchas* (small motorboats), kayaks, and small sailboats. The site was chosen by developers because of its five beautiful beaches. There's a challenging 18-hole golf course here, the **Campo de Golf Tangolunda** (☎ FAX 958/581–0059), designed by Mario Schetjnan. A small shopping-restaurant center is across from the entrance to the Barceló, but most of the shopping and dining take place in the towns of Santa Cruz and Crucecita, each about 10 minutes from the hotels by taxi, or, for the economy-minded, by buses or cooperative taxis.

16 **Bahía Chahué** is a pleasant place to spend a relaxing beach day. The beach parking lot includes a veranda lookout point. The club here charges $2 for use of the pool, restaurant, and palapas. The only hotel actually on the bay has already closed due to legal and financial woes; a spa is currently under construction.

17 **Santa Cruz,** on the bay of the same name, was the center of a 30-family fishing community until the development of the Huatulco bays forced everyone inland. Today the bay is the perfect spot for swimming, snorkeling, and boating. Arrange a sightseeing tour or a fishing expedition from the marina. A central zócalo with a wrought-iron gazebo has been built nearby; tourists and locals mingle in the little plaza, where you can sip a cool drink or cappuccino in the Café Huatulco, a showcase for the region's best Pluma coffee.

18 **Crucecita,** off Highway 200, is the only place in Huatulco that resembles—in a prefab way—a real Mexican town, with its central plaza and Catholic church whose inside walls are covered with naive frescoes. Restaurants and hotels frame the park on all sides, and—due to a distinct lack of competition—this is the place for dining, hanging out at sidewalk cafés and shopping in boutiques. The bus station, ice-cream shops, and Internet cafés are here, along with a smattering of smaller, less expensive, and more intimate hotels.

Dining and Lodging

$$$ ★ ✕ **Don Porfirio.** You can dine inside or out on the covered patio in this Tangolunda restaurant. There's a good variety of seafood and international dishes; try the grasshoppers fried with garlic, or the less exotic combination shish kebab sautéed in tequila, served on a bed of rice with steamed veggies and potato. There's no air-conditioning, and the outdoor patio is loud with street noise, but the food and service are good. ✉ *Zona Hotelera Tangolunda, Bahía Tangolunda, across from Hotel Gala,* ☎ *958/581–0001. AE, MC, V.*

$$$ ★ ✕ **Restaurant Ve El Mar.** The owner, Leonarda Liborio, has been here more than 20 years and can tell tales about the transformation of Huatulco. She converted her snack-by-the-sea place into this friendly restaurant where you can wiggle your toes in the soft sand by the water's edge. This is a good spot for a romantic candlelight dinner, a casual lunch, or a "morning after" ceviche. ✉ *Santa Cruz,* ☎ *958/587–0364. No credit cards.*

$$ ✕ **Restaurante María Sabina.** Strangely named for a Oaxaca medicine woman immortalized for her use of magic (hallucinogenic) mushrooms, this is a great place for watching locals and tourists mingle in Crucecita's pretty plaza. The specialty, grilled meats, are served with grilled onion, baked potato, and sour cream. A favorite is *reboso María Sabina,* steak with melted cheese, guacamole, and fresh salsa. ✉ *Calle Flamboyan 306, Crucecita,* ☎ *958/587–0219. MC, V.*

$–$$ ✕ **Oasis.** The varied menu and consistently good food makes Oasis the most popular spot in town. Choose California or Philadelphia rolls or Tepanyaki (meat or seafood grilled with veggies) from the Japanese menu, or have a burger and fries, shrimp cocktail, or chicken salad. You can sit on the patio overlooking the mostly pedestrian traffic near the square, or at the newer indoor venue across the street. ✉ *Calle Flamboyan 211, at Bugambilia,* ☎ *958/587–0045. AE, MC, V.*

$$$$ ★ 🏨 **Camino Real Zaashila.** This contemporary stucco Mexican-cum-Mediterranean palace overlooks a secluded lagoon with its own beach and a large, free-form pool with built-in lounge chairs around the rim. The resort has 27 landscaped acres of gardens, fountains, and waterfalls; going from one end of the hotel to the other is a dreamy nature walk. All rooms have ocean views; 10 luxurious suites and 41 rooms have small private pools. ✉ *Blvd. Benito Juárez 5, Bahía Tangolunda 70989,* ☎ *958/581–0460 or 800/722–6466,* FAX *958/581–0461,* WEB *www.caminoreal.com/zaashila. 120 rooms, 10 suites. 3 restaurants, in-room safes, minibars, tennis court, 2 pools, wading pool, gym, beach, 2 bars, baby-sitting, travel services. AE, DC, MC, V.*

$$$$ ★ 🏨 **Quinta Real.** This hilltop resort takes Huatulco luxury to exclusive—and almost excessive—heights. A combination of Moorish domes and palapas, the property's 27 tranquil suites are airy and plush, each with creamy white leather furnishings, exquisite Guatemalan tapestries, Jacuzzi tub, terrace, and spectacular ocean views. Nine suites have plunge pools on their corner patios, and a few are equipped with telescopes for dolphin- and star-gazing. Nonguests should pop in for breakfast. ✉ *Blvd. Benito Juárez 2, Bahía Tangolunda 70989,* ☎ *958/581–0428 or 800/457–4000,* FAX *958/581–0429,* WEB *www.quintareal.com. 28 suites. 2 restaurants, in-room safes, minibars, tennis court, 2 pools, wading pool, beach, bar, baby-sitting, laundry service, free parking. AE, DC, MC, V.*

$$$ ★ ✕🏨 **Barceló.** You will have a bay view from the balcony of any room in this cheerful resort hotel. Guests who choose the all-inclusive rate have free use of most watersports equipment, including kayaks and sailboats; dive masters are on hand with dive equipment. The Casa Real restaurant (dinner only) is one of the most glamorous dining options in Huatulco. The menu emphasizes northern Italian dishes, the pianist is superb, and flickering candles are set out as night falls. ✉ *Blvd. Benito Juárez, Bahía Tangolunda 70989,* ☎ *958/581–0055,* FAX *958/581–0335,* WEB *www.barcelo.com. 347 rooms, 9 suites. 3 restaurants, 4 tennis courts, 2 pools, wading pool, gym, massage, sauna, beach, dive shop, boating, 3 bars, shops, children's programs (ages 4 and up), travel services, free parking. AE, DC, MC, V.*

$$ ✕🏨 **Hotel Marlin.** Combining standard hotel anonymity with a certain level of intimacy, this three-story Santa Cruz Bay hotel has its own disco (open Thursday–Saturday). One of the nicest hotels on this bay, it's con-

venient to the marina and some good beachfront restaurants. Rooms have noisy but efficient air-conditioning, and wood furnishings, stamped tin mirrors, and cotton spreads and curtains. Hotel managers and other executives frequent the popular restaurant, which features specialty crêpes, homemade bread, and pizzas in addition to broiled shrimp and filet mignon. ✉ *Paseo Mitla 107, Santa Cruz Bay 70989,* ☎ *958/587–0055,* FAX *958/587–0546. 28 rooms. Restaurant, pool, bar, dance club.*

$$$ **Gala.** This all-inclusive resort caters to charter groups and Mexican families as well as lone travelers. The emphasis is on fun; there's a kids' club to entertain the tots and plenty of water toys for kids and adults. Rooms are spacious, colorful, and adorned with heavy pastel fabrics and light wooden furniture. Considering that the price per person ($165) includes all food, drinks, and access to most water and gym sports, this is a good deal if you want to do more than just work on your tan. ✉ *Blvd. Benito Juárez 4, Bahía Tangolunda 70989,* ☎ *958/581–0000 or 877/888–4252,* FAX *958/581–0220,* WEB *www.galaresorts.com. 290 rooms, 12 suites. 4 restaurants, in-room safes, 3 tennis courts, 4 pools, gym, beach, 7 bars, dance club, baby-sitting, children's programs (ages 2–15), car rental. AE, DC, MC, V.*

$$ **Misión de los Arcos.** Everything about this intimate hotel spells class and luxury, despite the moderate price. Each room is different, but all have adobe-style rounded walls, cream and beige appointments, comfortable beds, and both air-conditioning and ceiling fans. The delightful honeymoon suite has a huge garden patio filled with plants, a wrought-iron table and chairs, and a lovely fountain. ✉ *Gardenia 902, Crucecita,* ☎ *958/587–0165,* FAX *958/587–1904,* WEB *www.misiondelosarcos.com. 15 rooms. Gym, Internet. AE, MC, V.*

$ **Hotel Arrecife.** Popular with Mexicans and offering lots of special deals, this hotel has firm beds, ceiling fans, and cable TV, but no phone; a bit more money gets you air-conditioning. The hotel staff is courteous and helpful, and an informal restaurant sits aside the small patio pool. ✉ *Calle Colorín 510, La Crucecita 70989,* ☎ *958/587–1707,* FAX *958/587–1412. 28 rooms. Restaurant, pool. No credit cards.*

$ **Hotel Las Palmas.** Plain but acceptable furnishings and rock-bottom prices (for Huatulco) are what you'll find at this small second-story hotel just a block from the plaza in Crucecita. The cramped rooms have TVs, hot water, and both fans and air-conditioning. ✉ *Calle Guamuchil 206, Crucecita 70989,* ☎ *958/587–0060,* FAX *958/587–0057. 11 rooms. Restaurant, bar. AE, MC, V.*

Outdoor Activities and Sports

BICYCLING

Aventuras Huatulco (✉ Blvd. Guelaguetza, Lote C9, Crucecita, ☎ 958/587–1695) is recommended for guided or unguided mountain-bike tours, as well as bird-watching and rappelling. You can also rent mountain bikes from **Eco-Discover Tours Huatulco** (✉ Plaza las Conchas 6, Tangolunda Bay, ☎ 958/581–0002). **Jungle Tour** (✉ in the Hotel Gala, Blvd. Benito Juárez 4, Bahía Tangolunda 70989, ☎ 958/581–0000 Ext. 18) offers guided four-wheeler tours.

FISHING

Sportfishing for sailfish, tuna, dorado, marlin, and other fish can be arranged through **Sociedad Cooperative Tangolunda** (☎ 958/587–0081), the boat-owners' cooperative at the marina on Santa Cruz Bay. A second fleet is operated by **Ventures Huatulco** (☎ 958/587–1788).

HORSEBACK RIDING

Arturo Casillas of **Rancho Caballo de Mar** (☎ 958/587–0530) will collect you from your hotel. Rates are about $33 for a morning or afternoon ride.

WATER SPORTS

Most of the major hotels can arrange dive classes and excursions. The PADI-certified dive masters at **Hurricane Divers** (✉ Hotel Fiesta Mexicana, Blvd. Benito Juárez 2–3, Bahía Chahué, ☏ FAX 958/587–1107, WEB www.hurricanedivers.com) are recommended.

RIVER RAFTING

Rafting has become popular in recent years in the area. Try out your skills in this adventure sport or kayak with **Piraguas Aventuras.** (✉ Plaza Oaxaca 19, La Crucecita, ☏ 958/587–1333, FAX 958/587–1339, WEB www.piraguas.com).

Shopping

Crucecita's **Mercado Municipal** (municipal market; ✉ Calle Guanacaste at Bugambilias, Crucecita, ☏ no phone) is a fun place to shop; in addition to leather sandals, postcards, and other tourist items, you'll see mountains of fresh fruits and vegetables.

The **Museo de Artesanías Oaxaqueñas** (✉ Calle Flamboyan 216, Crucecita, ☏ 958/587–1513) is really a store, not a museum, and the artisans who create the fanciful wooden alebrijes, the woven tablecloths, typical pottery, painted tinware, and rugs from throughout the state are sometimes on hand to demonstrate how they make their traditional crafts. It's open daily; avoid going at lunchtime, when the artisans take a break.

Paradise boutique (✉ Calle Gardenia esq. Guarumbo, Crucecita, ☏ 958/587–0268), open daily, has an excellent selection of casual, stylish beach and resort wear, much of which comes from Bali and India. The Mexican crafts, including silver jewelry, coconut masks from Guerrero, and black pottery make great gifts.

Oaxaca City A to Z

To research prices, get advice from other travelers, and book travel arrangements, visit www.fodors.com.

AIR TRAVEL

You can fly into Puerto Escondido from Oaxaca, and into Huatulco from Oaxaca as well as several other Mexican and U.S. cities.

CARRIERS

Aero Vega has daily service to Puerto Escondido from Oaxaca's International Airport. Mexicana subsidiary AeroCaribe connects Puerto Escondido and Oaxaca City five times a week, with daily connections to Huatulco. Mexicana flies to Huatulco from Mexico City, Guadalajara, Cancún, Monterrey, and several other Mexican and U.S. gateways, all with connections in Mexico City. Aerotuc, based in Oaxaca City, offers regular and charter service to Huatulco and Puerto Escondido.

➤ AIRLINES AND CONTACTS: **AeroCaribe** (☏ 958/582–2023 in Puerto Escondido; 958/587–1220 in Huatulco). **Aerotucán** (☏ 958/582–1725 in Puerto Escondido). **Aero Vega** (☏ 958/582–0151 in Puerto Escondido). **Mexicana** (☏ 958/587–0223 in Huatulco).

AIRPORTS AND TRANSFERS

Aeropuerto Puerto Escondido is a 10-minute taxi ride from town on Highway 200. Aeropuerto Bahías de Huatulco is about 16 km (10 mi) from Tangolunda on Highway 200.

➤ AIRPORT INFORMATION: **Aeropuerto Bahías de Huatulco** (☏ 958/581–9008). **Aeropuerto Puerto Escondido** (✉ Carretera Costera Km 3, Puerto Escondido, ☏ 958/582–0492 or 958/582–0491).

BUS TRAVEL

Cristóbal Colón has several first-class buses per day leaving from Oaxaca's first-class bus terminal, frequently referred to as the ADO, as well as a luxury bus, *Servicio Plus,* leaving just before midnight to Huatulco (7½ hours; $16). There are also several first-class buses each day to Pochutla (six hours; $15), where you can connect to Puerto Ángel in collective or private taxis. Pochutla buses continue to Puerto Escondido, about another hour.

Direct service between Oaxaca City and Puerto Escondido is available on first-class Autotransportes Turísticos. Buses leave from Oaxaca City and Puerto Escondido twice a day.

Frequent, inexpensive second-class buses connect Puerto Escondido, Puerto Ángel, and Huatulco, but you must stop at Pochutla, off the highway near Puerto Ángel. These buses roar down the highway every 15 minutes or so, and each costs about $2. Avoid traveling at night whenever possible.

➤ BUS INFORMATION: **Autotransportes Turísticos** (✉ Calle Armenta y López 721, Oaxaca City, ☎ 951/514–0806 or 958/581–0288; ✉ Av. Hidalgo between 16 de Septiembre and 4a Nte., Puerto Escondido, ☎ 958/582–0050). **Cristóbal Colón** (✉ Booking office: Calle 20 de Noviembre 204A, Oaxaca City, ☎ 951/514–6655). **Huatulco bus stations** (✉ Calle Gardenias esq. Ocotillo, Crucecita, ☎ 958/587–0261). **Puerto Escondido bus station** (✉ Calle Primera Nte. 201, Puerto Escondido, ☎ 958/582–2919).

CAR RENTAL

Cars can be rented at the Huatulco airport, in Puerto Escondido, and in the Huatulco Bays area. International firms include Budget and Dollar. Rental cars are expensive, starting at $55 or more a day for a Volkswagen Beetle, for example, and there's an additional drop-off fee if you don't return the car where you picked it up. Nonaffiliated local firms often quote lower rates, but their vehicles may be in questionable condition.

➤ MAJOR AGENCIES: **Alamo** (✉ Av. Pérez Gasga 113, Puerto Escondido, ☎ 958/582–3003). **Budget** (✉ entrada Blvd. Benito Juárez, Puerto Escondido, ☎ 958/582–0312). **Dollar** (✉ Barceló Hotel, Blvd. Benito Juárez, Huatulco, ☎ 958/581–0055 Ext. 787 or 958/581–0480; ✉ Huatulco airport ☎ 958/581–0055 Ext. 787 or 958/581–9004).

CAR TRAVEL

The drive on Highway 175 from Oaxaca City to the coast at Pochutla is nerve-wracking, with plenty of sheer cliffs and hairpin turns. From Pochutla, motorists can head south to Puerto Ángel or Huatulco or west to Puerto Escondido. Highway 131, from Oaxaca City to Puerto Escondido via Sola de Vega, is theoretically the shorter route but frequent roadwork may add to travel time and frustration. Do *not* attempt any of these roads at night. Plan on taking about eight hours, and leave early enough to arrive before dark. Having a car allows you more freedom for exploring secluded beaches, although if you're not using it on a daily basis, hiring a taxi for day outings can be significantly less expensive in the long run.

EMERGENCIES

In case of an emergency call either the Red Cross or the police at the local number in Puerto Escondido or Huatulco.

➤ CONTACTS: **Red Cross** (☎ 958/587–1188 in Bahías de Huatulco; 954/582–0550 in Puerto Escondido). **Police** (☎ 958/587–0020 in Bahías de Huatulco; 958/582–0111 or 958/582–0498 in Puerto Escondido).

INTERNET

In Huatulco, Choco Latté is the most attractive place for a coffee and Internet use.

➤ INTERNET CAFÉS: **Choco Latté** (✉ Gardenia 902 at Tamarindo, Crucecita, ☎ 958/587–0165).

TELEPHONE CODES

For details about telephone changes in effect since 2002, see ☞ Oaxaca City A to Z.

TOURS

BIKING TOURS

Proximity to jungle flora and fauna is one of the appeals of a bicycle tour. Edgar Jiménez offers 10–35 km trips to the mountains on 21-gear aluminum bikes with Eco-Discover Tours Huatulco. Protective helmet, water, and an English-speaking guide are included in the price of around $18–$40, depending on length of trip and whether lunch is included.

BIRD-WATCHING TOURS

In Puerto Escondido the most exciting tours are run by ornithologist Michael Malone, who offers dawn and sunset excursions (December–April) into the Manialtepec Lagoon, a prime bird-watching area. Arrange tours (about $35 per person) through your hotel or through Viajes Ditmar, the most reliable and comprehensive agency in town.

COFFEE PLANTATION TOURS

Visiting the coffee plantations in the mountains is a popular activity in Huatulco; it's especially alluring when the heat and humidity soar. Prices average $60 per day, which includes lunch. Call Max Scherenberg (✉ Residencial Chahué, Casa 31, ☎ 958/587–0697) to join his eight-hour trip to Rio Copalitilla, 72 km (45 mi) from Huatulco at Finca La Gloria. This trip includes time for a visit to the Copalitillo waterfalls.

SIGHTSEEING TOURS

Bahías Plus, with offices in Crucecita, is one of the most comprehensive travel agencies in Huatulco; it has tours to Puerto Ángel and Puerto Escondido (van tours start at around $20 a person in a group of six), as well as plane tours to Oaxaca ($350 a person). Most major hotels also have travel agencies.

Paraíso Huatulco has all-day bay cruises for $30 a person, excluding food. It also offers eco- and fishing tours. Piraguas Tours has great kayak and river rafting tours on Class I to V rapids; prices are about $99 for a day trip. Combo packages are available for multiday treks. Jungle Tour offers three-hour four-wheeler tours of three bays (Santa Cruz, Cacvalata, and Organo) with time to swim. The cost is about $45 per person.

➤ TOUR OPERATOR RECOMMENDATIONS: **Bahías Plus** (✉ Calle Carrizal 704, Huatulco 70989, ☎ 958/587–0216 or 958/587–0932). **Eco-Discover Tours Huatulco** (✉ Plaza las Conchas, Tangolunda Bay, ☎ 958/581–0002, FAX 958–70678). **Jungle Tour** (✉ Blvd. Benito Juárez at Barceló Hotel, Tangolunda, Huatulco 70989, ☎ 958/581–0055 Ext. 787). **Paraíso Huatulco** (✉ Barceló Hotel, Blvd. Benito Juárez, Bahía Tangolunda, ☎ 958/581–0218, FAX 958/581–0200). **Piraguas Tours** (✉ Plaza Oaxaca 19, Crucecita, ☎ 958/587–1333, FAX 958/587–1339, WEB www.piraguas.com). **Viajes Ditmar** (✉ Av. Pérez Gasga 905, Puerto Escondido, ☎ 958/582–0734).

VISITOR INFORMATION

The Puerto Escondido tourism office is open weekdays 9–3 and 4–6, Saturday 10–1. Gina Machorro, who staffs the small information desk at the west end of the pedestrian walkway, is actually more helpful than the main tourism office staff. Her booth is open weekdays 10–2 and 4–6, Saturday 10–1. (Gina also leads interesting walking and market tours Wednesday and Saturday 8–10 AM.) In Huatulco, the Oficina de Convenciones y Visitantes offers friendly help in English from 9 to 6. The Huatulco state tourism office is open weekdays 8–5, Saturday 9–1. Sedetur is open Friday 9–5 and Saturday 9–1.

➤ TOURIST INFORMATION: **Oficina de Convenciones y Visitantes** (Convention and Visitor's Bureau: ✉ Plaza San Miguel 1B, Santa Cruz, ☏ FAX 958/587–1037, WEB www.baysofhuatulco.com.mx). **Puerto Escondido tourism office** (✉ Blvd. Benito Juárez, Puerto Escondido, about a block from Aldea del Bazar Hotel, Playa Bacocho, ☏ FAX 958/582–0175). **Sedetur** (✉ Blvd. Benito Juárez s/n, Bahía Tangolunda, in front of Restaurante Misión Fa-Sol, ☏ 958/581–0177, ☏ FAX 958/581–0176).

12 CHIAPAS AND TABASCO

The state of Chiapas is a study in contrasts, with the luxuriant tropical lowlands around Palenque—one of the country's most brilliant Mayan ruins—giving way to gorgeous valleys and finally the highlands, home to many of Mexico's most traditional indigenous peoples.

Updated by Michael de Zayas

KNOWN TO MANY foreigners only for the ruins of Palenque, the charming colonial town of San Cristóbal de las Casas, and the indigenous Zapatista movement, Chiapas and Tabasco have typically drawn trekkers and travelers rather than tourists. If you're looking for an outstanding travel experience, a well-planned trip to this area can be very satisfying, particularly if you come during a local festival. Unlike the country's popular beach resorts, Chiapas and Tabasco require transfers from Mexico City. Substantial ground transportation, either by bus or car, is usually part of the itinerary, although Tuxtla Gutiérrez and Villahermosa have busy airports, and Palenque and San Cristóbal de las Casas have national airports with limited routes. Tourist information can be more difficult to obtain in Tabasco than in Chiapas.

World attention was drawn to off-the-beaten-path Chiapas in the mid-1990s, when guerrillas staged a brief but potent rebellion, launching what has turned out to be a long-term struggle for equal rights for Mexico's indigenous groups. A bloody past of exploitation by and fierce confrontation with outsiders remains vividly present, as already impoverished indigenous communities in Chiapas are forced to compete for their lands with developers and new settlers. In fact, Chiapas has been at the margin of the nation's development and is one of the poorest states in Mexico. Land distribution is skewed as well: 1% of landowners holds 15% of the territory—about 50% of the arable land—keeping the colonial system nearly intact, and repression is rampant. It was the indifference of the Mexican government to their plight that helped bring the anger of the indigenous people to a boil in 1994, leading the Zapatista National Liberation Army (EZLN is the Spanish acronym) to an armed uprising. The government of President Vicente Fox succeeded in holding meaningful talks with EZLN, and the national and international interest sparked by the indigenous movement bodes well for further development in the region. The pipe-smoking Zapatista spokesperson, Subcomandante Marcos, has become a cult figure in Mexico, his ski-masked image appearing on everything from magazine covers to children's toys, and he puts his poetic communiqués on the Internet for worldwide consumption.

Nominally enriched a half century ago with the discovery of oil in the Gulf of Mexico on its northern border, Tabasco also has a bloody past. During the 1920s and 1930s, Tomás Garrido Canabal, a vehemently anticlerical governor, outlawed priests and had all the churches either torn down or converted to other uses. Riots, deportations, and property confiscations were common. That said, you won't find much evidence of Tabasco's turbulent past today; the spirit that prevails here is wholly different from that of Chiapas.

Although the Mexican economic crisis has delayed plans for a stronger tourism infrastructure, travel to Chiapas is getting a boost from a government promotion program—a segment of the Mundo Mayan travel circuit. The circuit showcases its Mayan ruins and colonial cities, all in the name of regional development and ecotourism. Yet this development has done little to help the environment or the indigenous groups in the region. The Lacandon jungle is disappearing, its Mayan inhabitants being driven to live in a smaller portion of their ancestral lands. Massive erosion and deforestation are taking their toll as new settlers, forced off communal farmlands in the highlands, try unsuccessfully to farm the rain forest with highland farming techniques: after a couple of years, the soil loses its nutrients and the settlers must clear fresh plots. The soil is further depleted by ranchers who move into the abandoned lands to raise their cattle.

When you set out along tortuous mountain roads—full of dramatic hairpin turns along the edges of mist-filled ravines—you'll still find remote clusters of huts and cornfields planted on near-vertical hillsides. You'll pass traditional women wrapped in deep-blue shawls and coarsely woven wool skirts, and Indian children selling fruit and flowers by the roadside. Chiapas has nine distinct linguistic groups, primarily the highland-dwelling Tzotzils and the Tzeltals, who live in both highland and lowland areas. In more isolated regions, many villagers speak only their native language, or a rudimentary Spanish necessary for interaction with the outside world.

Business travelers make up the majority of those who visit Villahermosa, Tabasco's capital. But the city has a superb museum of pre-Columbian archaeology at the CICOM complex and a collection of massive Olmec heads and altars at Parque Museo La Venta. Both provide a good introduction to the Indian heritage of Tabasco and Chiapas. Palenque, with its incredible Mayan ruins, is culturally and geographically linked with the lowlands in Tabasco. Geographically stunning, Tabasco has lakes, lagoons, caves, and wild rivers surging through the jungle.

Note: Although travel in the area is reasonably safe, at this writing the U.S. State Department was advising travelers to "exercise caution" in Chiapas because of the presence of armed rebels and armed civilian groups in some areas of the state. Check the State Department's Web site for updated information: travel.state.gov/mexico.html. Although sporadic confrontations haven't been near the main tourist destinations—and no tourist has ever been harmed—contact the State Department or any of the Mexican Government Tourist Offices in the United States for the current status before you go. Carry your visa and passport even on day trips throughout the region, as there may be military checkpoints along both main and secondary roads.

Pleasures and Pastimes

Archaeological Sites

Ruins of Mayan cities in mysterious, overgrown jungles are a big draw in this area. Unparalleled Palenque has the most appeal, and the lesser-known sites of Toniná, Bonampak, and Yaxchilán (pronounced yash-chee-*lan*) are attracting more attention than ever.

Dining

Chiapas has regional specialties but borrows heavily from Yucatán and Oaxaca. Culinary adventurers should try *atole* (a cornmeal drink), the many local variations of tamales, locally smoked pork called *cochito horneado,* candied fruit, and any dishes that contain the tasty Mexican herbs *chipilín* and *yerba santa* (or *mumu,* as locals call it). San Cristóbal's restaurants have a varied selection of Mexican and international cuisines, and most of them have added vegetarian dishes to their menus. Restaurants are generally not outstanding compared with those in other regions of Mexico.

Prices are quite reasonable: a filling dinner (helped out by tortillas in one of their myriad forms) usually won't cost more than $10 per person. There's no dress code to speak of in this part of Mexico, and reservations aren't necessary. San Cristóbal closes down early, so unlike in other parts of Mexico, it's a fairly common practice to eat dinner before 8 PM. As is the case throughout Mexico, lunch is the main meal of the day, served between 1 and 4 PM.

Tabasco saves some of its export beef for the Villahermosa restaurants, which also serve lots of fresh fish from the Gulf and freshwater lakes and rivers. Local specialties include *pejelagarto,* an ancient fish with the head of an alligator and a strong, sweet flavor. Also try *puchero,* beef stew with vegetables and plantains; river shrimp; *tostones* (fried plantain chips); baked bananas with cream; banana liqueur; and the region's fresh, white cheese.

Generally speaking, the food served in the town of Palenque is modest in both quality and price. Many restaurants are open-air, which is where you want to be in this hot, humid part of Mexico. You'll spend more in the higher-price hotels; most moderate and inexpensive restaurants don't bother to charge sales tax.

CATEGORY	COST*
$$$$	over $15
$$$	$10–$15
$$	$5–$10
$	under $5

**per person for a main course at dinner*

Lodging

Almost all the hotels in San Cristóbal are within walking distance of the major attractions. Most of those we list are colonial—historically and architecturally—in keeping with the rest of the town. In fact, few are the towns in the world with such a bounty of charming and affordable lodging. All rooms, unless otherwise stated, have showers; air-conditioning isn't necessary at this high altitude, and in fact, fireplaces are welcome.

Tuxtla Gutiérrez lodgings tend to be more functional than frilly; this town is the no-nonsense business and transportation hub of Chiapas. An exception to the rule is the Camino Real, which resembles a small palace perched on a hilltop.

Palenque is no longer the jungle outpost it used to be, fit only for those who consider rustic amenities colorful. This is a growing town with modern, comfortable hotels. The best and newest are strung along the Palenque-Pakalná highway that goes to the Palenque ruins just outside town; most have lush gardens, inviting pools, and air-conditioning or ceiling fans. There are quite a few *posadas* (guest houses) downtown and a couple of agreeable hotels and restaurants in the quiet neighborhood of La Cañada, between downtown and the highway.

Villahermosa's good hotels, which cater to the business interests of the oil industry, are expensive. These fancier hotels tend to be away from the city center, near the neighborhood called Tabasco 2000 and Parque La Venta; this area is sometimes called the hotel zone, or *zona hotelera.* But there are comfortable and economic hotels downtown, near the Grijalva River, or in the nearby, pedestrian-friendly Zona Luz (Light Zone).

Many hotels (especially budget and moderate lodgings) quote prices that already include the 15%–17% tax, which varies from county to county; others do not. Be sure to ask.

CATEGORY	COST*
$$$$	over $90
$$$	$60–$90
$$	$30–$60
$	under $30

**All prices are for a standard double room, excluding tax (15%–17%).*

Shopping

The artisans of Chiapas, especially in and around San Cristóbal, produce some of the most striking indigenous folk art of Mexico. Best are the embroidered blouses, *huipiles* (tunics), bedspreads and tablecloths, and leather goods. Lacandon bows and arrows and the beribboned ceremonial hats worn by local indigenous officials also make good souvenirs.

Chiapas is one of the few places in the world that has amber mines, so finely crafted jewelry made from this prehistoric resin is easy to find in San Cristóbal—as are plastic imitations sold by street vendors (stores usually sell amber and street vendors commonly have the fakes, although there is some crossover). San Cristóbal is also known for the wrought-iron crosses that bless its rooftops. Although many of the iron-working shops have closed, you can still find the crosses in crafts stores. Tuxtla Gutiérrez and Palenque, although not known for crafts, have a few shops selling quality arts and crafts from throughout the state.

Exploring Chiapas and Tabasco

The abode of the ancient Olmecs who gave Mexico its mother culture, Tabasco is lush, green, and pastoral; Chiapas is for the most part mountainous, its Mayan ruins and villages isolated from modern Mexico by sinuous roads and footpaths. The colonial city of San Cristóbal de las Casas once dominated both regions when the Spanish conquistadores held sway over the country. Modern Villahermosa is now the economic force in the two regions because of the petroleum industry.

The highlights of a trip to Chiapas and Tabasco are still the ruins of Palenque and the colonial town of San Cristóbal. These and all other major sights are accessible by road from either Tuxtla Gutiérrez or Villahermosa, the only cities with international airports. The once-isolated ruins of Yaxchilán and Bonampak are now more accessible—by paved roads or via bush planes that fly from the two internationally connected cities as well as from Palenque, Ocosingo, and Comitán. Palenque and San Cristóbal de las Casas have small airports that land small-body jets on a limited basis. If you're a first-time visitor, and especially if you don't speak Spanish, it's faster, more efficient, and more comfortable to take tours to the area's major attractions.

Numbers in the text correspond to numbers in the margin and on the Chiapas and Tabasco and San Cristóbal de las Casas maps.

Great Itineraries

The farther you wander into the region, the more you'll be fascinated with its natural diversity and its remnants of Mayan and Spanish-colonial cultures. A three-day trip gives only a superficial glance at what the region has to offer, but it will give you a chance to visit Palenque and San Cristóbal de las Casas, two of Mexico's outstanding attractions. Stays of five to eight or more days will allow you to get to the lesser-known wonders of Chiapas and Tabasco.

IF YOU HAVE 3 DAYS

Spend the first day and night at the Mayan ruins at **Palenque** ㉒, visiting the stunning jungle waterfalls at nearby **Misol-Há** ㉑ and **Agua Azul** ⑳. Tours from Palenque are the best way to pack it all into one day. The next day, drive south to **San Cristóbal de las Casas** ①–⑧, the oldest city in Chiapas. Spend at least two hours on a walking tour of town, starting at the centuries-old ***zócalo*** ① (town square). Overnight at San Cristóbal and, on Day 3, visit the Mayan villages of **San Juan Chamula** ⑭, known for its Catholic church where pre-Hispanic rituals are performed, and **Zinacantán** ⑮, famous for its handwoven tunics and pink shawls. Return to San Cristóbal to visit the market, shop for Indian crafts, and spend the night.

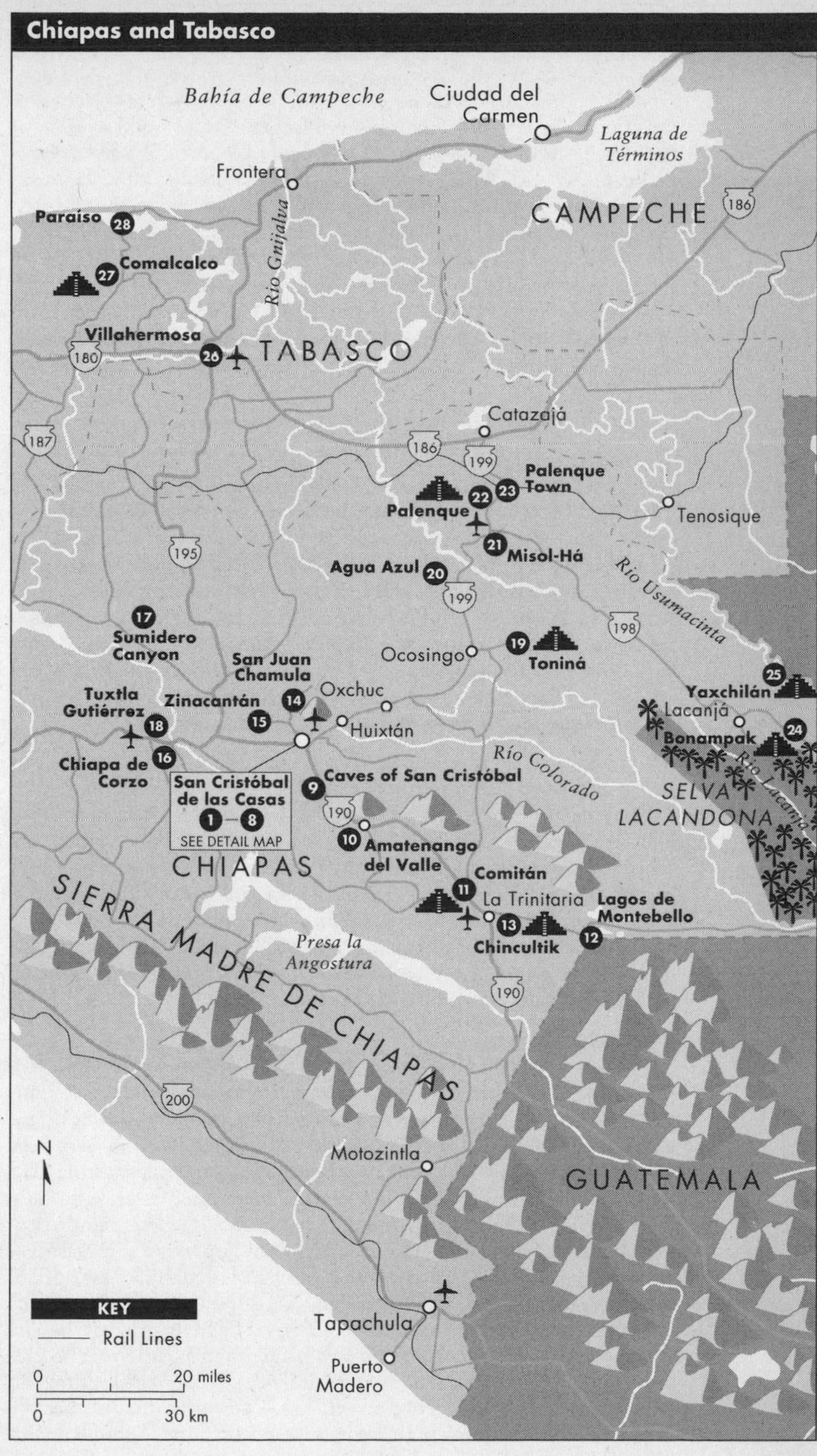
Chiapas and Tabasco
Bahía de Campeche
Ciudad del Carmen
Laguna de Términos
Frontera
CAMPECHE
186
Paraíso 28
Comalcalco 27
Río Grijalva
Villahermosa
180
26 TABASCO
Catazajá
187
186
199
Palenque Town 23
22
Palenque
Tenosique
195
21 Misol-Há
Agua Azul 20
199
Río Usumacinta
17
Sumidero Canyon
198
San Juan Chamula
Ocosingo
19 Toniná
Tuxtla Gutiérrez
Zinacantán
14
Oxchuc
25
Yaxchilán
Lacanjá
15
18
Huixtán
Bonampak 24
16
Chiapa de Corzo
San Cristóbal de las Casas
1–8
SEE DETAIL MAP
9 Caves of San Cristóbal
190
Río Colorado
SELVA LACANDONA
Río Lacanjá
10 Amatenango del Valle
CHIAPAS
Comitán
11
La Trinitaria
Lagos de Montebello
13
12
Chincultik
SIERRA MADRE DE CHIAPAS
Presa la Angostura
190
200
N
Motozintla
GUATEMALA
KEY
Rail Lines
Tapachula
Puerto Madero
0
20 miles
0
30 km

IF YOU HAVE 5 DAYS

Spend the first day and night in Villahermosa ㉖, exploring the giant Olmec heads, the river walkway, and the anthropology museum. On Day 2, drive to Palenque ㉒, visit the ruins, and stay overnight. On Day 3, drive to the waterfalls at **Misol-Há** ㉑ and **Agua Azul** ⑳, or the Mayan site of **Toniná** ⑲, near Ocosingo, en route to **San Cristóbal de las Casas** ①–⑧. On Day 4, see **San Juan Chamula** ⑭ and **Zinacantán** ⑮ in the morning and then return to San Cristóbal to shop for native crafts and spend another night. On Day 5, drive south on Highway 190 to see the **Lagos de Montebello** ⑫. After seeing the lakes, visit on the return trip as many of the following as your schedule permits: the small Mayan sites of **Chincultik** ⑬ and **Tenam Puente;** the charming town of **Comitán** ⑪; the pottery-producing town of **Amatenango del Valle** ⑩; and the stalactite- and stalagmite-graced **Caves of San Cristóbal** ⑨. For a less rushed visit, plan to spend the night in Comitán and return early the next morning for San Cristóbal or Tuxtla.

IF YOU HAVE 8 DAYS

Spend the first day and night in **Villahermosa** ㉖, as in the five-day itinerary, adding a visit to the unusual Mayan temples at **Comalcalco** ㉗. Spend the next four days as on Days 2–5 of the five-day itinerary—seeing **Palenque** ㉒, **Misol-Há** ㉑, **Agua Azul** ⑳, and **Toniná** ⑲ on the way to **San Cristóbal de las Casas** ①–⑧, from which you can take day trips north and southeast. On Day 7, head west, touring colonial **Chiapa de Corzo** ⑯ and the impressive **Sumidero Canyon** ⑰ by boat en route to **Tuxtla Gutiérrez** ⑱. Spend that night and the next in Tuxtla. On Day 8, visit Tuxtla's zoo, shop at the **Casa de las Artesanías,** and stroll in the **Parque Jardín de la Marimba** in the late afternoon.

If you want to go all out seeing Mayan sites, add a day trip to **Bonampak** ㉔ and **Yaxchilán** ㉕—the paved highway from Palenque makes for a good road trip (chartered planes to the ruins are also sometimes available from Tuxtla Gutiérrez). You can arrange to spend the night at the ecotourism site Escudo Jaguar, on the Usumacinta River near the boat launch for Yaxchilán, or in Palenque. From San Cristóbal, you can still squeeze in a long day trip to **Comitán** ⑪, the **Lagos de Montebello** ⑫, and **Chincultik** ⑬. A paved road connects Bonampak with the Lagos de Montebello, but check with the tourist office first before venturing out. Certain safety precautions may be advised.

When to Tour

Scheduling your visit to coincide with local festivals is worthwhile. Just make hotel reservations well in advance. Important holidays are January 15–23 for Chiapa de Corzo's San Sebastian festival (also held January 20–22 in Zinacantán); Carnival and Easter week in San Juan Chamula, where villagers walk over hot coals; every Friday during Lent in Zinacantán; June 22–24 for Chamula's San Juan festival; the July 24–25 festival of the patron saint of San Cristóbal, when brightly decorated trucks, buses, and taxis parade up a hilltop to the San Cristóbal Church; the August 6–11 celebration of San Lorenzo in Zinacantán; the November 1–2 Día de los Muertos (Day of the Dead) celebrations in Zinacantán, with spirited graveside festivals; and the feast of the Virgin of Guadalupe (celebrated for a week in Tuxtla Gutiérrez) on December 12. Several indigenous highland villages hold celebrations on December 31 to install new civil officials. Remember that it's beastly hot in the lowlands most of the year, but especially after February, with temperatures peaking in May and June.

SAN CRISTÓBAL DE LAS CASAS

★ San Cristóbal is a pretty town of about 150,000 in a valley of pine forests interspersed with maize fields and orchards—all at an altitude of 6,888 ft above sea level. It's the most touristic city of the Chiapas highlands; here indigenous women with babies tied tightly in colorful shawls share the plaza with starry-eyed backpackers. Travelers who come to San Cristóbal aren't put off by headlines about government troops and the EZLN—or are even intrigued by the political ramifications. In truth, the rival sides are more likely to snipe at each other via newspaper editorials or the Internet, than in hostile confrontations.

San Cristóbal is beautiful and inexpensive, the perfect hub for exploring some of the region's lakes, villages, and archaeological sites. Small enough to take in on foot in the course of a day, the town is also captivating enough to invite a stay of three days, a week, or even longer. In addition to viewing colonial monuments, consider planning an early morning visit to the *mercado* (market) to check out local culture and browse for crafts, or explore one of the traditional villages in the vicinity (Sunday is the best day for visiting village markets). Just soaking up the ambience in one of San Cristóbal's little cafés or unpretentious restaurants is a pleasure. Its lodgings are divine.

San Cristóbal is among the finest colonial towns in Mexico, and its cool climate is a refreshing change from the sweltering heat of the lower altitudes. On chilly evenings, smoke from chimney fires curls lazily over the red-tile roofs of small, brightly painted stucco houses and elegant colonial mansions. The mystical atmosphere here is intensified by the fog and low clouds that hover over the town and by the remarkable quality of the early morning and late-afternoon light.

The highlands were originally inhabited by the Maya, who, along with most of Mesoamerica, harvested maize and had no centralized government; they also resisted the Spanish conquest more forcefully than the indigenous groups of northern Mexico, who welcomed the conquistadors as either gods or allies in their opposition to the dominant Aztecs. In 1526 the Spaniards under Diego de Mazariegos finally defeated the Chiapan Indians at a battle outside town. Mazariegos founded the city, which was called Villareal de Chiapa de los Españoles, in 1528. For most of the viceroyalty, or colonial era, Chiapas, with its capital at San Cristóbal, was a province of Guatemala. Lacking the gold and silver of the north, it was of greater strategic than economic importance to the Spaniards.

Under Spanish rule the region's agricultural resources became entrenched in the *encomienda* system, in which wealthy Spanish landowners forced the locals to work as slaves. "In this life all men suffer," lamented a Spanish friar in 1691, "but the Indians suffer most of all." The situation improved only slightly through the efforts of Bartolomé de las Casas, the bishop of San Cristóbal, who in the mid-1500s protested the torture and massacre of the local people; these downtrodden protested in another way, murdering priests and other *ladinos* (Spaniards) in infamous uprisings.

Mexico, Guatemala, and the rest of New Spain declared independence in 1821. Chiapas remained part of Guatemala, until electing by plebescite to join Mexico on September 14, 1824—the date is still celebrated in San Cristóbal and all over Chiapas as the *día de la mexicanidad* (Day of Mexicanization) of Chiapas. In 1892, because of San Cristóbal's allegiance to the Royalists during the War of Independence, the capital was moved to Tuxtla Gutiérrez. With that shift went all hope that the town would keep pace with the rest of Mexico. It wasn't until the

Close-Up

THE ZAPATISTAS: A VOICE OF MANY VOICES

IN THE EARLY HOURS OF JANUARY 1, 1994, while most of Mexico was sleeping off the New Year's festivities, the Zapatista National Liberation Army (EZLN) took the world by surprise when it captured the colonial tourist center of San Cristóbal de las Casas and several surrounding towns, demanding land redistribution and equal rights for Chiapas's indigenous peoples.

The Zapatista military triumph was short-lived. The mostly Tzotzil and Tzeltal troops soon departed San Cristóbal, and on January 12, President Carlos Salinas de Gortari called for a unilateral cease fire. According to government figures, 145 lives were lost during the 12-day struggle. But hundreds have been killed in years of clashes between rebel supporters and paramilitary groups; thousands have been displaced. "We did not go to war on January 1 to kill or to have them kill us," declared Subcomandante Marcos, the EZLN's charismatic leader and spokesperson. "We went to make ourselves heard."

The social, economic, and political factors that led to the Zapatista uprising are many and complex. Centuries of land appropriation, first by the Spanish and then by the Mexican aristocracy, repeatedly uprooted Chiapas's Maya-descended indigenous groups. The North American Free Trade Agreement (NAFTA), which went into effect on January 1, 1994, symbolized Mexico's entry into the First World for its political and business elite. But, as the Zapatista movement forced Mexico to recognize, much of the nation, and much of Chiapas, remained mired in the developing world. Despite its natural resources—Chiapas provides nearly half of Mexico's electricity and has extensive oil and gas reserves—the state's indigenous residents suffer appallingly high rates of illiteracy, malnutrition, and infant mortality.

In 1995 President Ernesto Zedillo sent troops into the Lacandon jungle to capture the Zapatista leadership, including Marcos, whom the government identified as former Mexico City communications professor Rafael Sebastian Guillen. The ambush failed. The following year negotiations with the rebels resulted in the so-called San Andrés Accords, which called for a constitutional amendment recognizing indigenous cultural rights and limited autonomy. Yet President Zedillo refused to implement the accords and instead pursued a policy of low-intensity warfare—often in the name of "development" or "reforestation"—throughout the rest of his administration. The policy led to disastrous results, including the massacre of 45 unarmed Zapatista supporters at the hands of pro-government paramilitary forces in the village of Acteal, Chenalho, in December 1997.

During his presidential campaign, Vicente Fox insisted that he could resolve the Zapatista conflict in 15 minutes, an example of Foxspeak frequently chided by his critics. Nevertheless, during his inaugural address the president announced that he was ordering partial troop withdrawals and would submit legislation to Congress based on the San Andrés Accords. In turn, Subcomandante Marcos announced three conditions for the restoration of negotiations—further military withdrawals, the release of Zapatista prisoners, and implementation of the accords. The first two have been achieved; whether the third has is a matter of some debate. Fox continues to be engaged in a protracted media war with Marcos, who began to express doubts about the president's desire to pursue peace in Chiapas. In early 2001, a Zapatista caravan took to the streets, traveling through 12 Mexican states and into the capital to demand negotiations. More than 100,000 supporters gathered in the city's zócalo in a dramatic culmination of the two-week procession.

Fox, who welcomed the Zapatistas to the capital, has come under attack from members of the Institutional Revolutionary Party (PRI) as well as members of his own National Action Party (PAN), who have criticized the indigenous movement and indicated they would not support the president's legislation. The restoration of negotiations would be a triumph for Fox, but hardly a solution to centuries-old problems in southern Mexico.

1950s that the roads into town were paved and the first automobiles arrived. Modern times came late to San Cristóbal, for which many locals and visitors are thankful.

Because of the altitude, it gets cold here at night, and can be chilly during the day as well; pack a warm sweater and layer your clothing. When the sun does appear, it can get quite hot, but most restaurants keep doors open even during cold weather, and hotels are for the most part unheated. The cobblestone and flagstone streets are best suited to comfortable, flat shoes.

Exploring San Cristóbal de las Casas

San Cristóbal is laid out in a grid pattern centered on the zócalo, with street names changing on either side of the square. For example, Calle Francisco Madero to the east of the square becomes Diego de Mazariegos to the west.

The town was originally divided into several *barrios* (neighborhoods), which now blend together into a city center that is easily negotiated. In colonial times, Indian allies of the triumphant Spaniards were moved onto lands on the outskirts of the nascent city. Each barrio was dedicated to a different occupation. There were weavers, Tlaxcala fireworks manufacturers, and pig butchers from Cuxtitali. Although these divisions no longer exist, other customs have been kept alive. For example, each Saturday certain houses downtown will put out red lamps to indicate that fresh homemade tamales are for sale.

A Good Walk

Head for the heart of downtown, the Plaza 31 de Marzo, or **zócalo** ①, and take in the colonial buildings around the square, many of them homes of the Spanish conquistadors. Note the 16th-century **Casa de Diego de Mazariegos** ② on its southeast corner (now the Hotel Santa Clara). Continue in a northwesterly direction around the square to the neoclassical **Palacio Municipal** ③—which gets painted a different color according to the whim of each new governor—with its numerous arcades. **La Catedral** ④ (cathedral), on the north side of the zócalo, has a fascinating facade. Continue north five blocks along Avenida General Utrilla to the 16th-century **Templo de Santo Domingo** ⑤ with its ornamental Baroque facade; walk around the complex to its museum and famous textiles cooperative amid the Indian families selling goods in the large exterior courtyard. Head for Avenida General Utrilla again and walk north three blocks to the **mercado** ⑥ to visit the stalls filled with fruits, vegetables, candles, and other necessities. You can catch a cab, or walk the nine long blocks east on Comitán, to the **Museo Na Bolom** ⑦, a great local repository of Indian artifacts. As the museum is shown by tour only, you'll probably want to time your arrival for the 4:30 tour. To end the day, catch another taxi (or walk five blocks south on Av. Vicente Guerrero and eight blocks west on Calle Real de Guadalupe) back downtown to see the gorgeous regional costumes on display at the **Museo Sergio Castro** ⑧.

Sights to See

❷ **Casa de Diego de Mazariegos.** One of the most accessible pieces of colonial architecture in San Cristóbal is now the **Hotel Santa Clara**. The stone mermaid and lions outside it are typical of the period's plateresque style—as ornate and busy as the work of a silversmith. ✉ *Av. Insurgentes 1.*

NEED A BREAK? Cozy and relaxing, **La Galería Café** (✉ Calle Hidalgo 3, ½ block south of the zócalo, ☎ 967/678–1547) is the favorite haunt of local intellec-

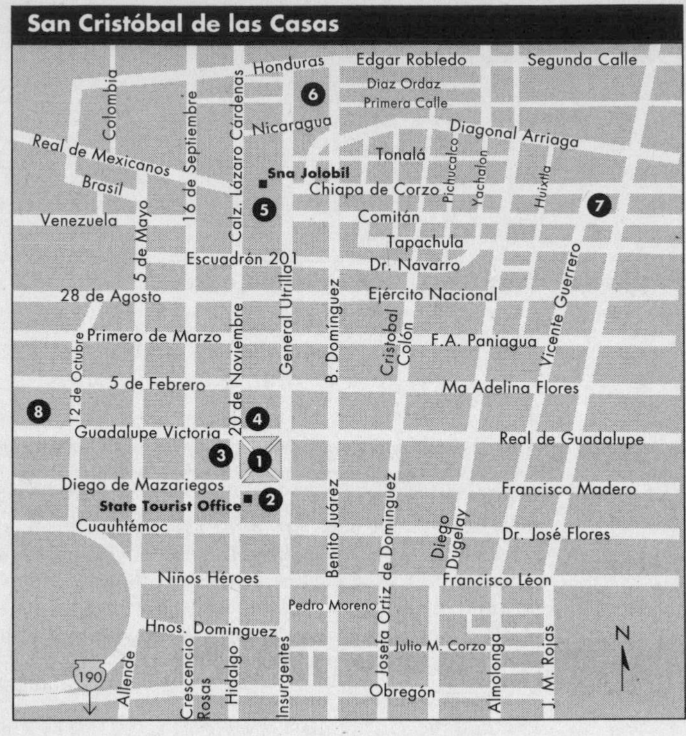

tuals and poets who quaff cappuccinos, espressos, or beers until midnight. Appetizers, pizza, and hard liquor are also served. You can enter through the excellent art gallery and craft store. Live music is played every day.

❹ **La Catedral.** Dedicated to San Cristóbal Mártir (St. Christopher the Martyr), the cathedral was built in 1528, then demolished, and rebuilt in 1693, with additions during the 18th and 19th centuries. Note the classic colonial traits on the wonderful ornate facade on the south wall—turned columns, arched windows, and doorways with miniature statues in niches. The floral embellishments in mauve, black, and white accents on the ochre background are unforgettable. Inside, don't miss the painting *Nuestra Señora de Dolores* (Our Lady of Sorrows) to the left of the altar, beside the gold-plated *retablo de los reyes* (Reredos of Kings), the Chapel of Guadalupe in the rear, and the gold-washed pulpit. ✉ *Calle Guadalupe Victoria at the zócalo; entrance on south side.* ⏲ *Daily 9–2 and 4–8, daily mass at 7* PM.

❻ **Mercado.** This municipal market occupies an eight-block area. Best visited early in the morning—especially on the busiest day, Saturday—the market is the social and commercial center for the Indians from surrounding villages. Stalls overflow with local produce, turkeys, medicinal herbs, flowers, firewood, and wool, as well as *huaraches* (sandals), grinding stones, candles, and candied fruit. Do not carry anything of value: robberies at the market are common. If you must bring your camera, be discreet, and, as always, ask permission before photographing people. ✉ *At Av. Gral. Utrilla, Nicaragua, Honduras, and Belisario Domínguez.*

★ ❼ **Museo Na Bolom.** Set aside an afternoon to tour this nonprofit organization, housed in a handsome 22-room neoclassical building built as a Christian seminary in 1891. Frans (a Danish archaeologist) and Gertrude (a Swiss social activist) Blom bought the house in 1950, and created the institute for ethnological and ecological advocacy, which is still carried on today. It got its name, Na Bolom (House of the Jaguar), from the Lacandon Maya with whom Trudi worked: Blom sounds like the Mayan word for jaguar. Both Frans and Trudi fought to preserve and publicize the disappearing Mayan cultures in the area.

Na Bolom showcases the Bloms' small collection of religious treasures, which had been hoarded in attics during the anticlerical 1920s and 1930s. Also on display are Frans Blom's findings from the Classic Mayan site of Moxviquil (pronounced mosh-vee-*keel*), found on the outskirts of San Cristóbal, and his personal effects. Trudi's bedroom contains her jewelry, shawls, canes, collection of indigenous crafts, and wondrous wardrobe of 95 embroidered dresses. Also on the premises is a room full of objects from the daily life of the Lacandon, whose traditions and way of life the Bloms documented. A library holds more than 10,000 volumes on Chiapas and the Maya.

The organization is dedicated to reforestation of the surrounding area, planting thousands of trees each year. Its own extensive nursery-garden is filled with firs, fruit trees, vegetables, and other flowering plants.

Across the street from the museum is Na Bolom's **Jaguar Garden,** which encompasses a central garden as well as a crafts and souvenir store. Look for the thatch hut, a replica of local Chiapan architecture. It consists of a mass of woven palm fronds tied to branches, with walls and windows of wooden slats, and high ceilings that allow the heat to rise. The gift shop sells Lacandon crafts such as flutes and bows and arrows, as well as black-and-white photos.

Revenue from Na Bolom's guest house, tours, restaurant, and gift shop goes to support the work of the institute. You can arrange for a meal at Na Bolom, even if you don't stay here. The facilities can also be used by groups as a base for special events or workshops, combining any permutation of accommodations, meals, and organized tours. Na Bolom's staff is well connected within San Cristóbal and can arrange tours to artisans' co-ops, villages, and nature reserves that are a bit off the beaten path. ✉ *Av. Vicente Guerrero 33, between Comitán and Chiapa de Corzo,* ☎ *967/678–1418.* 🎫 *Museum and tour $3.* ⏲ *Library weekdays 10–4, store daily 9:30–1:30 and 3–7. The only way to visit the museum is on a tour, conducted daily in English and Spanish at 11:30 and 4:30.*

8 **Museo Sergio Castro.** Sergio Castro, an agronomist from northern Mexico who has dedicated himself to building schools in the highlands of Chiapas, has spent a lifetime working with the Indians; many of the ceremonial costumes were given to him as payment for his work in the communities. There are around 1,000 pieces in the collection, including textiles, weavings, and carved wooden saints, musical instruments, and toys. Sergio gives tours and slide shows in English, Spanish, and French every evening, but you must make reservations in the morning. ✉ *Calle Guadalupe Victoria 61,* ☎ *967/678–4289.* 🎫 *$2.50, including tour and slide show. Donations toward educational and health projects for indigenous communities are also welcome.* ⏲ *Daily 5–9.*

3 **Palacio Municipal** (Municipal Palace). This two-story gray-and-white mansion off the zócalo was the seat of the state government until 1892, when Tuxtla Gutiérrez became the capital. It now houses municipal government offices. ✉ *Av. Hidalgo between Calles Diego de Mazariegos and Guadalupe Victoria.*

5 **Templo de Santo Domingo.** This three-block-long complex houses a church, former convent, regional history museum, and the **Templo de la Caridad** (Temple of the Sisters of Charity). A two-headed eagle—emblem of the Hapsburg dynasty that once ruled Spain and its American dominions—broods over the pediment of the church, which was built between 1547 and 1569. The pink stone facade (which needs a good cleaning) is carved in an intensely ornamental style known as Baroque Solomonic: saints' figures, angels, and grooved columns overlaid with vegetation motifs abound. The interior is dominated by lavish altarpieces, an exquisitely fashioned pulpit, a sculpture of the Holy Trinity, and wall panels of gilded, carved cedar—one of the precious woods of Chiapas that centuries later lured the woodsmen of Tabasco to the obscure highlands surrounding San Cristóbal. At the southeast corner of the church park lies the tiny and much more humble Templo de la Caridad, built in 1715 to honor the Immaculate Conception. Its highlight is the finely carved altarpiece. Indians from San Juan Chamula are often lighting candles and making offerings here. (Do *not* take photos of the Chamulas.)

The Ex-Convento de Santo Domingo, adjacent to the Santo Domingo church, now houses **Sna Jolobil,** an Indian cooperative selling an excellent selection of rather expensive local weavings, embroidered clothing, and colorful postcards. The shop is open Tuesday through Saturday 9–2 and 4–7. The small **Museo de los Altos** (Highlands Museum, ☎ 967/678–1609), also part of the complex, displays archaeological pieces and textiles and is open Tuesday–Sunday 10–5. Admission is $2, free Sunday. ✉ *20 de Noviembre s/n, near Real de Mexicanos.*

1 **Zócalo.** This main square around which the colonial city was built has in its center a gazebo used by musicians most evenings and weekend afternoons. You can have a coffee on the top or middle floor of the gazebo; expect small children and women selling bracelets and other wares. Surrounding the square are a number of 16th-century buildings, many former mansions of the conquistadors, with wood-beam ceilings and plant-filled central patios. Don't be afraid to go into buildings whose doors are open. ✉ *Between Avs. Gral. Utrilla and 20 de Noviembre and Calles Diego de Mazariegos and Guadalupe Victoria.*

Outside San Cristóbal. Surrounding San Cristóbal are many small and seldom-visited Indian villages celebrated for the exquisite colors and embroidery work of their inhabitants' costumes. Huixtán (hweesh-*tan*) and Oxchuc (osh-*chuc*) are about 28 km and 43 km (17 mi and 27 mi), respectively, on the road to Ocosingo. Neither village is known for its market, although they are visited during their town festivals; Huixtán venerates San Miguel (Saint Michael) on September 29, and Oxchuc celebrates patron San Tomás (Saint Thomas) on July 3. The Thursday market in Tenejapa, 27 km (17 mi) northeast of San Cristóbal, is worth seeing.

Dining

$$ ★ ✕ **Na Bolom.** Doña Bety, the late Trudi Blom's adopted daughter, heads the kitchen at this famous ethnological-ecological museum. Home-cooked meals emphasizing vegetarian and chicken dishes are the norm here. Overhung with sombrero light fixtures, the communal oak dining table is shared by international volunteers, Lacandon Indians, resident scholars, travelers, and artists in residence. Breakfast is served 7–11 and a five-course dinner at 7 (no lunch). If you're not staying at the institute, call at least an hour ahead for a reservation. ✉ *Av. Vicente Guerrero 33,* ☎ *967/678–1418. MC, V.*

$$ ★ ✕ **Paris-Mexico.** The cozy, laid-back atmosphere of these two bistros, each a couple of blocks from the zócalo, makes them local favorites for breakfast, lunch, and dinner. Attentive waiters who speak French and Spanish (but no English) serve a range of traditional Mexican and French entrées, soups, and desserts topped off with your choice of a fine French wine or a margarita. ✉ *Calle Madero 20 and Diego de Manzanares 19,* ☎ *967/678–0695. AE, MC, V.*

$$ ✕ **Restaurante Continental.** The large enclosed courtyard of this converted neoclassical colonial home, which is easy to miss off the street, is an ideal setting for this family-style restaurant. Every day between 2:30 and 4:30 live marimba music makes it a pleasant place to spend an hour or two after a long morning tour of the city. On Sunday, there's a buffet with regional dishes, and folkloric dancers perform from 2 to 4. Try the *trenzado Chamula* (strips of grilled beef and pork) and the guacamole served with tostadas. Craft shops surround the dining area. ✉ *Real de Guadalupe 24,* ☎ *967/678–4861. MC, V.*

$$ ★ ✕ **Restaurant L'Eden.** Local expats rave about the steaks and just about all other dishes at this intimate, chalet-style restaurant within the Hotel El Paraíso. The burnt-orange and cerulean interior has eight cozy candelit dining tables, piped-in classical music, a fireplace, Mexican ceramics, and friendly service. Start with margaritas, which are so big you'll laugh out loud when they come to your table. Swiss delights include classic raclette (melted cheese and potato) and fondue bourguinonne (beef with eight different sauces) for two. These dishes are simple, but perfect. ✉ *Av. 5 de Febrero 19,* ☎ *967/678–0085. AE, MC, V.*

$$ ✕ **Restaurante el Teatro.** Sunshine streams in the second-story windows here during the day, warming yellow walls decorated with European and local artwork. At night, candlelight presides. The French owner keeps the atmosphere unhurried and makes most everything himself, including the fresh pasta and chocolate mousse. The menu features primarily French and Italian dishes—including chateaubriand and crêpes. The wood-fired pizzas and shish kebab are also delicious; a few Mexican dishes are served. ✉ *Av. 1 de Marzo 8, at Av. 16 de Septiembre,* ☎ *967/678–3149. MC, V. Closed Mon.*

$–$$ ★ ✕ **La Casa del Pan.** Organically grown fruits, vegetables, and coffee get top billing at this vegetarian restaurant. The tasty tamales *chiapanecos* with a spicy cheese filling, hot bean soup, and the best salads in town draw return visits, and the four-course special of the day, which includes variations on traditional Mexican cooking, really shines. The bakery sells homemade breads, bagels, coffee, cookies, and fruit preserves. You can also buy Chiapan organic coffee and crafts here. Musical groups perform every night. ✉ *Dr. Navarro 10 at Av. Belisario Domínguez,* ☎ *967/678–5895. MC, V. Closed Mon.*

$ ✕ **Emiliano's Moustache.** Handmade tortillas with a wide variety of meat, chicken, and vegetarian fillings make this a popular spot among locals and tourists. The upstairs bar overlooks the nicely decorated restaurant named after Mexican peasant revolutionary hero Emiliano Zapata; photos and paintings bear his likeness. Live music plays Monday through Saturday 9–11:30; the food seems to noticeably lose its freshness near closing time. ✉ *Crescencio Rosas 7, at Diego de Mazariegos,* ☎ *967/678–7246. V.*

$ ✕ **La Selva Café.** This ecoconscious coffee shop has more than a dozen organic javas and assorted coffee-flavored concoctions. The menu features baguette sandwiches, salads and cold plates, with exceptions such as codfish pie, chopped-meat pie, and Chiapas tamales. A few tables are in the lush garden out back. A self-styled "culture café," La Selva promotes the indigenous values of Chiapas in its eight Mexico City branches. ✉ *Crescencio Rosas 9, at Calle Cuauhtémoc,* ☎ *967/678–7244. No credit cards.*

Lodging

$$$ **Hotel Casa Mexicana.** This beautifully designed hotel in a restored colonial mansion is colorful, clean, and friendly. Good beds, beam ceilings, and attractive artwork all help make this an outstanding hostelry. A lovely newer wing across the street, also in a colonial home with a collonaded and verdant courtyard, is quiet, with bigger rooms in light colors, wood furniture, and tasteful photographs of San Cristóbal. The restaurant, which surrounds a lovely, plant-filled courtyard with a bubbling fountain in the middle, serves international dishes, such as chicken in pistachio sauce and eggplant Parmesan. ✉ *28 de Agosto 1, 29200, at Av. Gral. Utrilla,* ☎ *967/678–0698, 967/678–0683, or 967/678–1348,* FAX *967/678–2627,* WEB *www.hotelcasamexicana.com. 52 rooms, 2 junior suites, 1 master suite. Restaurant, room service, cable TV, massage, sauna, bar, laundry service, free parking. AE, MC, V.*

$$$ **Hostal Flamboyant Español.** With its three lovely courtyards, archways, and lots of colorful Mexican tile, this refurbished mansion in the heart of the city retains its beautiful colonial style. The carved wooden furniture and other Mexican furnishings add charm to the three-story hotel, built in 1907. The traditionally decorated rooms all have tile baths, but ask for one of the charming, high-ceilinged rooms that surround the single-level front courtyard. ✉ *1 de marzo 15, 29200,* ☎ *967/678–0045,* FAX *967/678–0514,* WEB *www.flamboyant.com.mx. 82 rooms. Restaurant, room service, cable TV, gym, bar, laundry service, free parking. AE, MC, V.*

$$$ ★ **Posada Diego de Mazariegos.** This quaint hotel—really two perfectly preserved 18th-century colonial homes—has incredible interior courtyards with wooden arcades, beautiful gardens, and skylights throughout. Rooms have high ceilings and lovely tile bathrooms; some rooms have fireplaces the staff will light for you. Ask for one of the stunning rooms that number in the 300s—these are in an older wing and have high wood-beam ceilings with working carbon heaters. Inexpensive suites can sleep up to six people. The hotel's main bar, Tequila Zoo, stocks more than 115 brands of tequila. The restaurant serves three meals a day inside its warm wooden confines. ✉ *5 de Febrero 1, corner of Av. Gral. Utrilla, 29200,* ☎ *967/678–0833,* FAX *967/678–0827,* WEB *www.diegodemazariegos.com.mx. 70 rooms, 4 suites. Restaurant, cafeteria, room service, in-room data ports, cable TV, 2 bars, laundry service, car rental, travel services, free parking. AE, MC, V.*

$$ **Casavieja.** Three blocks east of the zócalo, this spectacular hotel maintains the architectural style of the original colonial house, built in 1740. Each comfortable room is charmingly decorated in Mexican furnishings and has large windows looking out onto one of the three interior courtyards. For a mountain view, ask for a room on the second floor of the open courtyard. Suites have hot tubs. The Espinosas, who run and own the hotel, are warm and knowledgeable hosts. ✉ *Ma. Adelina Flores 27, 29230,* ☎ *967/678–0385,* ☎ FAX *967/678–6868,* WEB *www.casavieja.com.mx. 38 rooms, 2 suites. Restaurant, cable TV, bar, free parking. AE, MC, V.*

$$ **Hotel Arecife de Coral.** Four blocks from the zócalo, this colonial-style hotel has a gorgeous interior courtyard presided over by resident peacocks and paradisiacal fruit trees, cypress, and bougainvillea. The manicured grounds add to the effect of the charming two-story units that are covered with climbing plants. The hotel gets its name (Coral Reef Hotel) from its owner, an avid diver. ✉ *Av. Crescencio Rosas 29, corner of Alvaro Obregón,* ☎ *967/678–2125,* FAX *967/678–2098. 50 rooms. Restaurant, cable TV, bar, laundry facilities, meeting rooms, free parking. MC, V.*

$$ 🏨 **Hotel El Paraíso.** High beam ceilings ennoble the 13 guest rooms in this charming late 19th-century colonial home that once served as a private hospital. Some of the rooms have lofts and carpeting; all vary in size. Comfortable leather-backed chairs in the guest lounge overlook a sunny, plant-filled, indoor-outdoor patio area with tables for breakfast. The bar and restaurant offer the personal attention of owners Daniel and Teresa Suter, who met as students in Switzerland. For more solitude, request one of two rooms in the exterior courtyard. ✉ *Av. 5 de Febrero 19, 29200,* ☎ *967/678–0085,* FAX *967/678–5168,* WEB *www.mexonline.com/hparaiso.htm. 13 rooms. Restaurant, cable TV, bar, laundry service. AE, MC, V.*

$$ 🏨 **Hotel Santa Clara.** Once the home of city founder Diego de Mazariegos, this rambling 16th-century mansion is now a hotel overlooking the action in the main plaza. It has a tangible air of past grandeur: beam ceilings, antique furnishings, and time-worn hardwood floors. Six of the nine extra-roomy units with balconies overlook the zócalo. There's a tiny round pool in the lovely courtyard. For entertainment, Bar Cocodrilos has live Latin rock and pop most nights. For location and charm, it's a great deal; because this is no secret, it tends to be noisier and busier than the other options. ✉ *Av. Insurgentes 1, 29200, at the zócalo,* ☎ *967/678–0871 or 967/678–1140,* FAX *967/678–1041,* WEB *www.hotelstaclara.com. 37 rooms, 2 suites. Restaurant, coffee shop, cable TV, pool, bar, travel services, free parking. AE, MC, V.*

$$ 🏨 **Mansión del Valle.** A few blocks from the zócalo, this 19th-century property has been converted into a modest yet comfortable hotel with Spanish-colonial design details. There's a rather plain sitting room for card-playing or socializing in the large inner atrium. Rooms on the first floor are dark; the seven second-story rooms with patios overlooking La Merced church across the street are nicer. ✉ *Calle Diego de Mazariegos 39, 29240, corner of Calle Guadalupe Victoria,* ☎ *967/678–2582 or 967/678–2583,* FAX *967/678–2581. 40 rooms, 7 suites. Restaurant, coffee shop, bar, meeting rooms, car rental, free parking. AE, MC, V.*

$$ ★ 🏨 **Na Bolom.** Each of the rustic but cozy rooms available at this center for the study and preservation of the Lacandon Maya and the rain forest is decorated with the accoutrements of a specific indigenous community—including crafts, photographs, and books. About half the rooms have bathtubs; all have fireplaces. Na Bolom may be a 10-minute walk from the center, but it does offer exquisite gardens and an environment that feels intellectually stimulating. Book well in advance, and ask for a garden view. ✉ *Av. Vicente Guerrero 33, 29200,* ☎ *967/678–1418,* FAX *967/678–5586,* WEB *www.ecosur.mx/nabolom. 13 rooms. Restaurant, library, shop, free parking. MC, V.*

$$ 🏨 **Rincón del Arco.** The touches at this hotel include a freestanding fireplace in each room. Since each of the rooms is different, ask to see several until you find the one you like best. Room 11 is secluded and has a pretty view of the garden. Rooms on the top floor share a wide balcony from which you can sit and enjoy the cityscape: a view of the Church of Guadalupe and ancient houses with red-tile roofs. The dining room has a fireplace and wrought-iron wagon-wheel chandeliers. You can also visit the textile workshop on the premises. ✉ *Calle Ejército Nacional 66, 29200,* ☎ *967/678–1313,* FAX *967/678–1568,* WEB *www.mundomaya.com.mx/hernanz. 48 rooms, 2 junior suites. Restaurant, bar, free parking. V.*

Nightlife and the Arts

The number of cultural offerings in San Cristóbal is on the rise. Ask at the tourist office, La Pared bookshop, and El Puente coffeehouse and cultural center about upcoming lectures or concerts.

Museo Na Bolom (✉ Av. Vicente Guerrero 33, between Comitán and Chiapa de Corzo, ☎ 967/678–1418) occasionally sponsors talks and film presentations. **El Puente** (✉ Real de Guadalupe 55, ☎ 967/678–3723), a casual, hip restaurant-cum-social-center, serves breakfast all day, shows videos most nights, offers Internet access, and hosts occasional art exhibitions. It's a good place to hear what's happening around town. The elegant **Teatro Hermanos Domínguez** (✉ Diagonal Hermanos Paniagua s/n, just outside the city limits, ☎ 967/678–3637) features programs such as folkloric dances from throughout Latin America.

Although nightlife hasn't traditionally been one of San Cristóbal's main draws, several clubs now host live music. **El A-Dove** (✉ Miguel Hidalgo 2, ☎ 967/678–6666) is the town's hippest club, with a fire-house design and DJ music until 4 Thursday through Sunday. **Bar Cocodrilos** (✉ Av. Insurgentes 1, ☎ 967/678–0871 or 967/678–1140), part of the Hotel Santa Clara, on the zócalo, has a mellow tavern feel and hosts live rock and salsa bands most nights from 9:30 to midnight. **Latinos** (✉ Francisco y Madero 23, corner of Benito Juárez, ☎ 967/678–2083) serves up live Latin jazz, salsa, or tropical music after 9:30 daily. Flamenco guitar players perform Thursday through Saturday 9–11 at **Restaurant Bar Margarita** (✉ Real de Guadalupe 34, ☎ 967/678–0957), followed by a small salsa band until 1. **Las Velas Danza-Bar** (✉ Francisco I. Madero 14, ☎ 967/678–0417) is a popular disco with live rock and reggae music, open daily 8 PM until 4 AM.

Outdoor Activities and Sports

A horseback ride into the neighboring indigenous villages is good exercise for mind and body. Most hotels can arrange rentals of horses. Guides working through some travel agencies can also hire horses and will accompany tourists. Five or six hours are needed to visit area villages or the nature reserve at Huitepec. Novices should be aware, however, that several hours on a horse can be, well, a pain in the rear. Many outfitters do *not* take experience into account when assigning mounts.

Shopping

The market in San Cristóbal, although picturesque, sells more produce than arts and crafts. The shops on Avenida Gral. Utrilla, south of the market, have a large selection of goods from Guatemala—but not always those of the highest quality. Guatemalan textiles often sell for less than Chiapan textiles, and the Mexican government is considering barring their import because of unfair competition with local producers. Nevertheless, make sure to bargain for these textiles to get a good price. Most Guatemalan cloth is dark-blue cotton with multicolor cotton needlepoint or trim.

Shops are generally open 9–2 and 4–8. Indian women and children will often approach you on the streets with their wares—mostly fake amber, woven bracelets, and small dolls—but their selections aren't as varied as those in the shops, and prices won't necessarily be better. On the other hand, you can be assured that the proceeds go directly to the craftspeople.

Among the smart shops clustered along Real de Guadalupe are two subsidiaries of **El Árbol de la Vida** (✉ Real de Guadalupe 27 and 28-A, ☎ 967/678–4085 or 967/678–5050), one block apart. They specialize in attractive designer amber jewelry mixed with silver and gold. There's a small museum inside the shop displaying the different types of amber found around the world. A video explains how this prehistoric resin is extracted from the mines and later transformed into this precious natural gem. Open daily 8:30–8:30.

Artesanías Chiapanecas (✉ Calle Real de Guadalupe 46C, at Diego Dugelay, ☎ no phone) has an excellent selection of embroidered blouses, huipiles, tablecloths, and bags. The government-run **Instituto de las Artesanías** (✉ Calle Niños Héroes and Av. Hidalgo, ☎ FAX 967/678–1180, ⏲ Mon.–Sat. 10–2, 4–8; Sun. 10–2) has wooden toys, ceramics, embroidered blouses, bags, and handwoven textiles from throughout the state, and a tiny ethnographic museum in back. Among its excellent selection of wares, **Sna Jolobil** (Weaver's House in Tzotzil; ✉ Ex-Convento de Santo Domingo, Calzada Lázaro Cárdenas 42, ☎ 967/678–7178), the regional crafts cooperative, sells hand-dyed woolen sweaters and tunics, embroidered pillow covers, and pre-Hispanic-design wall hangings. It's closed Sunday and lunchtime. **Taller Leñateros** (✉ Flavio A. Paniagua 54, ☎ 967/678–5174), a unique indigenous co-op in an old colonial San Cristóbal home, has original top-quality crafts as well as free informal tours to observe artisans at work. Run by expat Ambar Past, the co-op sells handmade books, boxes, postcards, and writing paper fashioned on the premises out of recycled flower petals, plants, and bark. At the Rincón del Arco Hotel, **Textiles Soriano** (✉ Calle Ejército Nacional 66, ☎ 967/678–1313, ⏲ Mon.–Sat. 10–2, 4–8) specializes in handwoven bedspreads and other cloth, which can be made to order in a few days.

SOUTH AND EAST OF SAN CRISTÓBAL

Southeast of San Cristóbal lies one of the least explored and most exotic regions of Chiapas: the Selva Lacandona, said to be the second-largest rain forest in the Western Hemisphere. Incursions of developers, settlers, controversial government development projects, and refugees from neighboring Guatemala are transforming Mexico's last frontier, which for centuries has been the homeland of the Lacandon, a small tribe descended from the Maya of Yucatán. Some of the people still maintain their ancient customs, living in huts and wearing long, plain tunics. Their custom of not marrying outside the tribe is causing serious problems, however, and their numbers, never large to begin with, have been reduced to about 350. The fabulous Caves of San Cristóbal (also known as Las Grutas de Rancho Nuevo) are in this region.

The Caves of San Cristóbal

❾ *13 km (8 mi) south of San Cristóbal off Rte. 190.*

Spectacular limestone stalactites and stalagmites are illuminated along a 2,475-ft concrete walkway inside these labyrinthine caves, which were discovered in 1960. But the caves were fully explored more recently, prompting the creation of the **San Cristóbal Recreational Park.** The Spanish-speaking gatekeeper (or his kids) is usually available to guide visitors for a small fee. The caves may be closed in inclement weather; if in doubt, check with the San Cristóbal tourist office first. You can rent horses ($3 per hour) for a ride around the surrounding pine forest, and there's a small restaurant and picnic area on the site. To get here, catch a Teopisca-bound microbus at Boulevard Juan Sabines Gutiérrez, across from the San Diego church. Make sure to tell the driver to let you off at the "grutas." Get off at the signed entrance, and walk about 1 km (½ mi) along the dirt road. Or, you can catch a taxi from town for about $4. For about twice that price, the driver will wait while you explore the caves. ☎ *No phone.* 🎫 *50¢.* ⏲ *Daily 9–5.*

Amatenango del Valle

10 *37 km (23 mi) southeast of San Cristóbal.*

Amatenango del Valle is a Tzeltal village known for the handsome, primitive pottery made principally by the town's women, whose distinctive red and yellow huipiles are also much remarked upon. On the road to Comitán, the village currently has no signage; watch closely for the ocher, black, and natural-clay flowerpots and animal figurines—primarily gray doves—sitting by the side of the road. You can stop at any of these roadside houses, or turn into the town; almost every household has wares to sell. If you go during the dry season, you might get to see some of the pots being fired over open flames (not stoves) outside, as long as rain isn't a threat. Spanish is definitely a second language here, and women negotiate without a lot of chitchat, or use younger children as interpreters.

Comitán

11 *55 km (34 mi) southeast of Amatenango del Valle.*

Comitán, whose Mayan name, Balún-Canán, means "nine stars" or "guardians," is a pleasant commercial center and agricultural town of about 120,000. It's also the base from which many visitors tour the Lagos de Montebello and the small archaeological sites nearby. Built by the Spaniards, the city flourished early on as a major center linking the lowland temperate plains to the edge of the Mayan empire on the Pacific. Even today it serves as the principal trading point for the Tzeltal Indians; such Guatemalan goods as sugarcane liquor and orchids come through here. One of the "Hundred Colonial Cities," Comitán was renovated with a federal government grant, and its pretty plaza and surrounding streets were all refurbished in colonial style.

Two notable churches are **Santo Domingo de Guzmán,** with architecture showing a Moorish influence, and **San Caralampio,** whose Spanish Baroque style reveals the influence of Guatemalan artisans.

The **Casa-Museo Dr. Belisario Domínguez,** the lovely former home of a martyr of the revolution, opened as a museum in 1985. It houses a fascinating collection of medical instruments, pharmaceuticals, and late-19th-century furnishings, as well as photographs, documents, and letters from the Mexican Revolution, during which the doctor was assassinated for his outspoken criticism of President Victoriano Huerta. ✉ *Av. Central Sur Dr. Belisario Domínguez 35,* ☎ *962/622–1300.* 🎫 *$1.* 🕒 *Tues.–Sun. 9–7.*

The centrally located **Museo de Arte Hermila Castellanos** shows work by modern Mexican artists, including master painters Rufino Tamayo and Francisco Toledo, both from Oaxaca (many of the painters represented here are Oaxaqueños). The subject matter deals largely with mestizo and indigenous people, most often in stylized, contemporary depictions. ✉ *Av. Central Sur Dr. Belisario Domínguez 51,* ☎ *962/622–2082.* 🎫 *$2.* 🕒 *Mon.–Sat. 10–6, Sun. 10–1.*

Some 7 km (4 mi) from Comitán, **Tenam Puente** is on a hill with a spectacular view of the valley. The Mayan site, primarily a ceremonial center, was built around the same time as Chincultik and occupied during the Classic and post-Classic period. Archaeologists Frans Blom and Oliver LeFarge discovered the site; during restoration in the 1990s a royal tomb was unearthed. There are three ball courts, apparently one each for the lower, middle, and upper classes. Most of the site has yet to be explored. 🎫 *Free.* 🕒 *Daily 9–4.*

Lagos de Montebello

12 *64 km (40 mi) southeast of Comitán.*

The 56 lakes and surrounding pine forest of the Lagos de Montebello (Lakes of the Beautiful Mountain) constitute a 2,437-acre park that is shared with Guatemala. A different color permeates each lake, whose waters glow with vivid emerald, turquoise, amethyst, azure, and steel-gray tints, produced by various oxides. The setting is serene and majestic, with clusters of oak, pine, and sweet gum. Practically the only denizens of the more accessible part of the forest are the clamorous goldfinches and mockingbirds. To the east roam puma, jaguar, deer, bear, and the rare quetzal bird.

At the park entrance, the paved road forks. The left fork leads to the Lagunas Coloradas (Colored Lakes). At Laguna Bosque Azul, the last lake along that road, there's a humble sit-down café in addition to the food and beverage stalls that crop up near every lake with a parking lot. Small boys will approach and offer a 45-minute horse-riding expedition to a cave and two cenotes (sinkholes) within the forest. You can also tour the lake in a rowboat for $4 (up to four people).

Back at the park entrance, the right fork leads past various groupings of lakes to Tziscao Lake and, just outside the park boundaries, a village of the same name. The restaurant has a spectacular view of the lake. A 30-minute boat ride costs $2.50 per person, and Tziscao and Montebello are the only lakes the tourist board recommends for swimming. Check with the Comitán tourist offices if you'd like to stay in the park; the remodeled Tziscao Lodge has several small cabins and a community hostel (about $5 per person).

You can pick up a helpful map of the lakes at the tourist office in Comitán. La Angostura (☎ 963/632–6000) and Transportes Cuxtepeque (☎ 963/632–1728) buses leave about every half hour from the Comitán bus station (✉ 2da Av. Pte. Sur 17-B, between 2a and 3a Calles Sur Pte.) to both Laguna Bosque Azul and Tziscao. If you take the bus, you can either walk or catch the same bus between lakes; check the map and time your forays to catch the bus on the half hour. To get to Tziscao from Laguna Bosque Azul you must go to the fork in the road, catch the Bosque Azul bus to the next fork in the road, and then board a Tziscao bus.

The tourist office recommends that you take a tour to save time and lots of walking. It's also safer. Tourists have been assaulted while walking from one lake to another. Police checkpoints are now dispersed throughout the area, but it's still best to be careful. If you travel on your own, stay on the paved roads. Don't wander off onto the dirt paths.

Chincultik

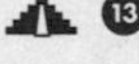

56 km (35 mi) southeast of Comitán.

You can visit the small, Late Classic Mayan site of Chincultik on the way to or from the Lagos de Montebello. It's a steep hike of about 10 or 15 minutes to the top of a restored pyramid (as well as a walk from the highway if you don't come by car). From the top you're rewarded with a fabulous view of the Montebello Lakes and the surrounding countryside. Since signage is poor, ask the guard to point you toward the Cenote Agua Azul, the large sinkhole on the site. The ruins, which are only partially restored, also include a ball court and stelae (inscribed slabs). *About $2, free Sun.* ⏲ *Tues.–Sun. 9–5.*

To get to Chincultik from Comitán, continue south 15 km (9 mi) on Route 190, and turn left at the sign LAGOS DE MONTEBELLO outside of La Trinitaria. After 39 km (24 mi), there's a road on the left leading to the ruins, which are 5 km (3 mi) off the highway. A bus runs from Comitán: you have to get off at the road that leads to the ruins and walk to the site.

Dining and Lodging

$$ ✕ **Museo Parador Santa María.** Built around the remains of a hacienda from the 1830s, this hotel has an excellent restaurant, six well-appointed rooms, and a small free museum showcasing 16th–19th-century religious art (open daily 10–6). Each hotel room is decorated with a different period of antiques—be it plateresque, Chiapas, or French—and some have lovely sunken-tile bathtubs and fireplaces. The regional food here is known throughout the state; top off your visit to the lakes or ruins with the fixed three-course meal. ✉ *Km 22 on the road to the Lagos de Montebello,* ☎ FAX *963/632–5116. 6 rooms, 2 suites. Restaurant, bar, laundry service. MC, V.*

NORTH AND WEST OF SAN CRISTÓBAL

San Juan Chamula and Zinacantán are traditional villages in the scenic western outskirts of San Cristóbal. The small colonial town of Chiapa de Corzo will be the first major town you come to when you drive west from San Cristóbal along Route 190. Tuxtla Gutiérrez, the modern state capital, is about 15 km (9 mi) beyond Chiapa de Corzo. The riverboat ride to view Sumidero Canyon begins south of Tuxtla in the town of Chiapa de Corzo; the farthest lookout point is 22 km (14 mi) from the capital.

San Juan Chamula

⓮ *12 km (7½ mi) northwest of San Cristóbal de las Casas.*

The spiritual and administrative center of the Chamula Indians is justly celebrated, as much for its rich past as for its turbulent present. The Chamula are a Tzotzil-speaking Mayan group of nearly 52,000 individuals (of a total 300,000 Tzotzils) who live in hamlets throughout the highlands; several thousand of them live in San Juan Chamula.

The Chamula are fiercely religious, a trait that has played an important role in their history. The Chamula uprising of 1869 started when some tribesmen were imprisoned for crucifying a boy in the belief that they should have their own Christ. Some 13,000 Chamula then rose up to demand their leaders' release and massacred scores of ladino villagers in the process. More recently, the infiltration of Protestant evangelists into the community led to the expulsion of the Indian converts by Chamula authorities. In the past 30 years, more than 30,000 have been forced to abandon their ancestral lands and now live on the outskirts of San Cristóbal de las Casas, dressing in conventional clothing and often selling crafts in San Cristóbal's street markets. The Human Rights Commission is trying to mediate their return to the Chamula community.

Physically and spiritually, life in San Juan Chamula revolves around the church, a white stucco building whose doorway is decorated with a flower motif. To enter the church, pay a token fee (about 50¢) at the tourist office on the main square. A pamphlet gives guidelines about how to conduct yourself in the church and the village.

Extreme discretion must be exercised inside the church. Taking photographs and videos is absolutely prohibited and strictly enforced. There are no pews, and the floor is strewn with fragrant pine needles.

The Chamula sit praying silently or chanting while facing colorfully attired statues of saints. For the most part, worshipers appear oblivious to intruders, continuing with their rituals: they burn candles of various colors, drink soft drinks, and may have a live chicken or eggs with them for healing the sick. They "pass" the illness to the chicken or egg, which then gets disposed of outside the church. The church is named after Saint John the Baptist, the main god of the universe, according to Chamulan belief; Jesus Christ is revered as his younger brother.

Outside the church there is no taboo against photography, but it is illegal to photograph Chamulan authorities, who wear black ponchos and carry a baton. Flocks of children will pester you to buy small trinkets and to photograph them for money (about 50¢ a shot). The best time to visit San Juan Chamula is on Sunday, when the market is in full swing and more formal religious rites are performed.

To get here from San Cristóbal, head west on Calle Guadalupe Victoria, which veers to the right onto Ramón Larrainzar. Continue 4 km (2½ mi) until you reach the entrance to the village. Most of these roads are paved. Because of the threat of robbery, walking between San Cristóbal, San Juan Chamula, and Zinacantán isn't recommended.

Zinacantán

⓯ *4 km (2½ mi) west of San Juan Chamula.*

The village of Zinacantán (Place of the Bats) is even smaller than San Juan Chamula and is reached via a paved road west just outside San Juan Chamula (from San Cristóbal, take the Tuxtla road about 8 km [5 mi] and look for the signed turnoff on your right). Here photography is totally forbidden, except for the row of village weavers on view along the main street. It's the scenery en route to Zinacantán—terraced hillsides with cornfields and orchards—that draws visitors. There isn't much to see in the village except on Sunday, when people gather from the surrounding parishes, or during religious festivals. The men wear bright pink tunics embroidered with flowers; the women cover themselves with bright pink *rebozos* (shawls). If you take a tour you'll visit the homes of back-strap loom weavers. Watch for the plethora of crosses around the springs and mountains on the way to Zinacantán: they mark a Christian Chamulan cemetery.

The **Museo Ik'al Ojov,** on the *calle principal* (main street) behind the church, is in a typical home and displays Zinacantán costumes through the ages. ☎ *No phone.* 🎫 *Donation encouraged.* ⏲ *Tues.–Sun. 9–5.*

Chiapa de Corzo and Sumidero Canyon

⓰ **Chiapa de Corzo** was founded in 1528 by Diego de Mazariegos, who one month later fled the mosquitoes and transported all the settlers to San Cristóbal (then called Chiapa de los Españoles, to distinguish it from Chiapa de los Indios, as Chiapa de Corzo was originally known). The mosquitoes are still here. ✉ *70 km (43 mi) northwest of San Cristóbal; 15 km (9 mi) east of Tuxtla Gutiérrez.*

Life in this small town on the banks of the Grijalva revolves, inevitably, around the **zócalo,** which is lorded over by *la pila,* a bizarre Mozarabic brick fountain built in 1562 in the shape of the crown of the Spanish monarchs Fernando and Isabella—the only of its kind in the Americas. The interior is decorated with stories of indigenous peoples. Several craft shops line the square, selling huaraches, ceramics, lacquerware, elaborately carved wooden Parachico masks (used in ceremonial dances), and regional costumes.

The **Centro Cultural Ex-Convento de Santo Domingo de Guzmán,** in front of the public market one block from the zócalo, has a permanent exhibition of Chiapa de Corzo engraver Franco Lázaro Gomez, who died in a tragic accident at 27 in 1949. The center also houses Chiapa's **Museo de la Laca** (lacquerware museum), which has a modest collection of delicately carved and painted *jícaras* (gourds). "The sky is no more than an immense blue jícara, the beloved firmament in the form of a cosmic jícara," according to the *Popul Vuh,* a 16th-century chronicle of the Quiché Maya. The lacquerware here is both local and imported—from Michoacán, Guerrero, Chiapas, Guatemala, and Asia. Free lacquerware workshops are held weekdays 4–7. ✉ *Calle Mexicanidad de Chiapas 10,* ☎ *961/616–0055.* *Free.* *Museum open Tues.–Sun. 10–5.*

★ 17 **Sumidero Canyon** came into being about 36 million years ago, with the help of the Grijalva River, which flows north along the canyon's floor. The fissure meanders for some 23 km (14 mi); its near-vertical walls, partly obscured by vegetation, rise 3,500 ft at the highest point. You can admire it from above, as there are five lookout points along the highway; one of them, La Atalaya, has a restaurant. ✉ *23 km (14 mi) north of Tuxtla Gutiérrez.*

Viajes Miramar (✉ Camino Real, Local 2, Tuxtla Gutiérrez, ☎ 961/617–7777 Ext. 7230) offers a five-hour minivan trip for about $7 a person. You can also take a taxi or bus to the Cahuaré dock, 10 minutes from Tuxtla, just before Chiapa de Corzo, and then a boat trip to the Chicoasen hydroelectric dam. The best time of day is 10–2, when you won't have to wait long for your boat to fill up. The trip there and back takes approximately two hours and costs about $7 a person (there's a 10-person minimum).

Boats also leave from Chiapa de Corzo dock between 8 AM and 4 PM daily. From the boat you can admire the canyon's steep, striated walls, some odd rock formations, and the animals—including crocodiles, ducks, pelicans, herons, raccoons, iguanas, and butterflies—that live inconspicuously at its base. As you visit the canyon, consider the fate of the Chiapa Indians, who in the 16th century jumped into it rather than face slavery at the hands of the Spaniards.

Dining

$ ✕ **Jardines de Chiapa.** Sample an excellent and inexpensive variety of regional cuisines in this lovely patio setting. Try the *tasajo* (sun-dried beef served with pumpkin-seed sauce) and the *chipilín con bolita* soup, made with balls of ground corn paste cooked in a creamy herbal sauce and topped with cheese. A marimba band enlivens afternoon meals Thursday to Sunday 2:30–5. The restaurant is open daily 9–7:30. ✉ *Av. Francisco I. Madero 395, Chiapa de Corzo,* ☎ *961/616–0198,* ☎ FAX *961/616–0070. AE, MC, V.*

Tuxtla Gutiérrez

18 *289 km (179 mi) southwest of Villahermosa, 15 km (9 mi) northwest of Chiapa de Corzo, 85 km (53 mi) northwest of San Cristóbal.*

Tuxtla Gutiérrez is the thriving capital city of the state of Chiapas. In 1939 Graham Greene characterized it as "not a place for foreigners—the new ugly capital of Chiapas, without attractions." The accuracy of that bleak description is slowly fading, but Tuxtla Gutiérrez is still a city most visitors will just pass through, even if it is of vital economic and political importance. It's the state's transportation hub, and it has what is probably the most innovative zoo in Mexico. It's also convenient for its proximity to Chiapa de Corzo and the Sumidero Canyon, where there is little in the way of accommodations.

Tuxtla's first name derives from the Nahuatl word *tochtlan,* meaning "abundance of rabbits." Its second name, Gutiérrez, honors Joaquín Miguel Gutiérrez, who fought for the state's independence from Spain and incorporation into newly independent Mexico.

The highway into town is endless. Tuxtla (population 550,000), the state capital since 1892, doesn't have many conveniences for tourists, but you can get your bearings best by staying on the main drag, which will run you smack into the zócalo, known locally as the *parque central* and fronted by huge government buildings.

All the species at the **Miguel Alvarez del Toro Zoo** (a.k.a. ZooMAT) are native Chiapans, and the more docile creatures roam free. The 100-plus species on display include jaguars, marsupials, iguanas, quetzal birds, boa constrictors and other snakes, tapirs, eagles, and monkeys. Nature videos are often shown Saturday at 11 AM, and you can visit the tiny museum and the well-stocked gift shop. Admission is free. The zoo reopens in November 2002 after a yearlong renovation. ✉ *Calzada Cerro Hueco s/n, southeast of town off Libramiento Sur,* ☎ *961/614–4701 or 961/614–4765.* *Free.* *Tues.–Sun. 9–5.*

Amateur archaeologists and botanists should head for **Parque Madero,** which includes the **Botanical Garden,** the free **Botanical Museum,** and the **Regional Museum of Chiapas.** The Regional Museum actually houses an excellent history museum, an ethnological museum, and a salon for revolving cultural exhibits. The botanical museum is unimpressive, but the garden is pleasant and has labels identifying the native plant species. ✉ *Northeast of downtown, between Av. Nte. 5a and Calle Ote. 11a,* ☎ *961/613–4479 or 961/613–4554.* *Regional Museum $3, free Sun. and holidays.* *Garden Tues.–Sun. 9–5, museums Tues.–Sun. 9–4.*

The government-run **Casa de Artesanías** has a fine small museum of indigenous Indian cultures in Chiapas, as well as a good selection of regional crafts for sale. Among the local specialties: amber fashioned into necklaces, earrings, and pendants; hand-embroidered and brocaded table mats, blouses, and huipiles; leather bags; gold filigree jewelry; and lacquerware. ✉ *Blvd. Dr. Belisario Domínguez 2035,* ☎ *961/612–2275.* *Free.* *Mon.–Sat. 10–3, 5–8.*

As its name suggests, the **Parque Jardín de la Marimba** (✉ Av. Central and 8 Pte.) hosts marimba bands, which play regional dancing music. You can grab a partner and join in—every evening 7–9.

Dining and Lodging

$$$$ ✕ **Montebello.** Prime rib and Mexican specialties headline the menu at this intimate restaurant at the Camino Real—where every roll, cake, dessert, and tortilla is made on the premises. Montebello is most romantic at night, when the city lights shimmer into view. The elegance of the earth-tone decor is set off by an unusual white mural of the Sumidero cliffs sculpted into a wall. Live, unobtrusive violin and piano music plays after 2 PM. ✉ *Blvd. Dr. Belisario Domínguez 1195,* ☎ *961/617–7777. AE, DC, MC, V. Closed Sun.*

$$$ ★ ✕ **El Asador Castellano** (The Castillian Grill). Mouthwatering Spanish dishes such as *calamares a la romana* (Roman calamari) and *poches estofadas con chistorra* (navy beans with sausage) as well as imported choice U.S. beef cuts can be paired with one of more than 50 imported wines difficult to find in Mexico City, let alone Chiapas. Service is very attentive and the presentation flawless. Weekend reservations are helpful. ✉ *Blvd. Dr. Belisario Domínguez 2320-A,* ☎ *961/602–9000. AE, MC, V. Closes at 6 PM Sun.*

$$$ ✕ **Restaurant Algarabia.** Choose from a wide array of savory seafood dishes—some prepared at your table—at this spacious *palapa* (thatch-roof restaurant). Try the *camarones en salsa de queso* (shrimp in cheese sauce) or any other of the Mexican-style shrimp dishes. Service is excellent, and a salsa band plays daily 3–5. Monday and Tuesday are buffet days and Wednesday all dishes are half price. ✉ *Av. Central 1440,* ☎ *961/614–7148. AE, MC, V.*

$$ ✕ **Las Pichanchas.** An outstanding variety of regional dishes, including tamales and *cochito horneado* (smoked pork), is available here, as well as live marimba music in the afternoon and evening, and folkloric dances 9–11 PM. The restaurant is a favorite among Mexican families. ✉ *Av. Central Ote. 837,* ☎ *961/612–5351. AE, MC, V.*

$ ✕ **La Carreta.** This handsome two-story open-air restaurant is a fine place to inexpensively fill up on *churrasco,* a tasty Argentine grilled steak, as well as tacos and salads. Portions are huge. Enjoy marimba Tuesday through Sunday afternoons and nights in the patio with stone arches and iron lanterns. A beautiful wooden staircase leads to second-floor seating. The restaurant was designed to resemble an eatery along the 19th-century Camino Real trade route, which led through Chiapas from San Cristóbal to Pichucali. ✉ *Blvd. Dr. Belisario Domínguez 703,* ☎ *961/612–5518. MC, V.*

$$$$ ★ **Camino Real.** This hilltop oasis of luxury sets a standard for accommodations in Chiapas. The interior spaces—set around a huge open-air lagoon-pool and bar area with exotic vegetation—are reminiscent of superior Caribbean resorts. The 24-hour Los Azulejos restaurant, enclosed in a sky-blue glass dome (the buffets are well worth the price) is complemented by the upscale Montebello. All rooms have views of the mountains and full bathroom amenities, including a tub with silky swagged curtains. This member of the Camino Real chain offers more services and amenities than others charging twice as much. ✉ *Blvd. Dr. Belisario Domínguez 1195, 29060,* ☎ *961/617–7777, 800/272–1107, or 800/722–6466,* FAX *961/617–7799,* WEB *www.caminoreal.com/tuxtla. 174 rooms, 36 suites. 2 restaurants, in-room data ports, in-room safes, minibars, cable TV, 2 tennis courts, pool, health club, hair salon, sauna, 3 bars, shop, concierge floor, business services, convention center, meeting rooms, car rental, travel services, no-smoking rooms. AE, DC, MC, V.*

$$$ **Hotel Arecas.** The Arecas is a haven of quiet gardens and tasteful colonial decor, with fruit trees, flowering plants, a secluded swimming pool, and bungalow-style junior suites. Both restaurants, the elegant Los Candiles for international cuisine and the more informal La Calabaza for regional dishes, offer relaxing environments and good service. All rooms have air-conditioning. The Arecas is 10 minutes by car from city center. ✉ *Blvd. Dr. Belisario Domínguez 1080, 29020,* ☎ *961/615–1122 or 961/615–1128,* FAX *961/615–1121,* WEB *www.hotelarecas.com.mx. 44 rooms, 16 suites. 2 restaurants, cable TV, pool, bar, dance club, Internet, meeting rooms, free parking. AE, DC, MC, V.*

$$$ **Hotel María Eugenia.** Although a touch sterile, this air-conditioned downtown hotel has clean rooms with floral spreads as well as a floral scent. There's cable TV and a nice pool surrounded by white wrought-iron furniture. ✉ *Av. Central Ote. 507, 29000,* ☎ *961/613–3767 or 961/613–3770,* FAX *961/613–2860,* WEB *www.mariaeugenia.com.mx. 83 rooms. Restaurant, pool, bar, meeting rooms, travel services, free parking. AE, MC, V.*

$$ **Hotel Flamboyant.** The rooms in this luxury hotel have a soothing atmosphere and Moorish touches. Twenty-four rooms face the large garden, and a dozen more are off a smaller, tranquil inner garden. Capacious is the byword here: the pool is huge and the public areas vast. The restaurant is light and airy, and the food is good, but the service

is poor; the bar is dark and tacky. A disadvantage is the location—a 10-minute drive west of the town center. ✉ *Blvd. Dr. Belisario Domínguez 1081, 29000,* ☎ *961/615–0888 or 961/615–0999,* FAX *961/615–0087,* WEB *www.flamboyant.com.mx. 120 rooms, 2 suites. Restaurant, coffee shop, cable TV, tennis court, pool, bar, Internet, travel services. AE, MC, V.*

THE ROAD TO PALENQUE AND BEYOND

The road from San Cristóbal to Palenque veers slightly east on Highway 190 upon leaving town, then links up to Highway 199, which heads north to Palenque. You'll pass Ocosingo and the turnoff to Toniná along the first half of the journey, then Agua Azul and Misol-Há before reaching the ruins. It's sierra country most of the way until the mild valleys around Ocosingo; the climate will get progressively hotter and more humid as you descend from the highland and approach Palenque. The vegetation will also change, from mountain pine to thick, green tropical foliage. To get to Villahermosa from Palenque, head north for 56 km (35 mi) on Highway 199, and then turn left onto Highway 186 at Catazajá for a leisurely drive on a fairly straight road. Frequent buses are available for all routes.

At **Rancho Esmeralda** (✉ Turnoff about 8 km [5 mi] along road from Ocosingo to Toniná ruins, Apdo. 68, ☎ no phone, FAX 967/673–0711, WEB www.ranchoesmeralda.net), resident cowboy Valentín can take you on a three- to four-hour horseback excursion ($20) through the beautiful Ocosingo Valley, where more than 50 species of exotic birds live year-round. The hosts of the same resort can help arrange an air excursion to the Bonampak and Yaxchilán ruins (about $100) and whitewater rafting trips on the Shumulja River (about $85 a day).

Toniná

98 km (61 mi) northeast of San Cristóbal; 118 km (73 mi) south and east of Palenque.

Between San Cristóbal and Palenque, on a paved road running along the Jataté River in the mild Ocosingo Valley, is the archaeological site of Toniná. The name means "house of stone" in Tzeltal. Excavations indicate that the vanquished rulers of Palenque and Yaxchilán were brought here as prisoners for execution. Several ball courts and the main pyramid platform (taller than those of Tikal and Teotihuacán) have been uncovered; a small, on-site museum exhibits many relics from the site. Toniná, with its monumental architecture and noteworthy sculptures, is thought to be the last major Mayan ceremonial center to flourish in this area. To get to the site, follow the road from Ocosingo, off Route 199. *$2.50. Daily 9:30–4.*

Lodging

$ ★ **Rancho Esmeralda.** This macadamia-nut farm has eight comfortable wooden cabins just a 15-minute walk from the ruins. The accommodations are rustic, with limited electricity and no phones; there are clean latrines and a common bathhouse from which you can savor the view as you soak in the extra-long claw-foot tub. The staff is friendly, and you could spend an afternoon just talking with the young barman in the thatch-roof, communal dining area. Delicious, filling meals are served at extra cost; the coffee is organic—grown, roasted, and ground on the premises. Tent camping is also permitted. ✉ *Turnoff about 8 km (5 mi) along road from Ocosingo to Toniná ruins, Apdo.*

Close-Up

THE ROUTE OF THE MAYA: A MESOAMERICAN GIZA

THE MAYA WERE OUTSTANDING architects, without compare in the Americas. They erected immense palaces and towering pyramids in less-than-hospitable climates without the aid of metal tools, the wheel, or beasts of burden. Their ancient cities still resound with the magnificence of their cultures, even though the civilizations have faded.

Río Usumacinta. Builders of pyramids of this style typically gave them additional height by placing them on hillsides or crests—as you'll see at the otherworldly Palenque—and the principal structures were covered with exquisite bas-reliefs carved in stone. The small one-story pyramid-top temples characteristically had vestibules and rooms adorned with vault ceilings. The wide, spacious chambers inside the pyramids had smaller, attached rooms filled with bas-relief carvings of important events that occurred during the reign of the ruler who built the pyramid. Río Usumacinta friezes slope inward, rather than standing perpendicular under the large roof combs. Finest examples: Palenque, Yaxchilán.

Río Bec. Influenced by Guatemala's Petén style, the pitch of these pyramids is rather steep, and the foundations elaborately decorated. The stairways on the outside of some pyramids were built for aesthetic rather than practical purposes, and were "false" (unclimbable). The principal structures were long, one-story affairs containing two or sometimes three tall towers. Each was capped by a large roof comb emboldened with a dramatic stucco facade. Río Bec is found only in what is now the state of Campeche. Finest examples: Calakmul, Xpuhil, Río Bec.

Chenes. Found mainly in Campeche, this style likewise had long, single-story structures. In this case they were divided into three distinct sections, each with its own doorway charmingly surrounded by a face of the rain god, Chaac, whose mouth is the entrance. Facades were smothered in serpentlike embellishments. Finest examples: Hochob, Chicanná.

Puuc. Uxmal is the most striking illustration of the beautifully proportioned Puuc style. Commonly found in the state of Yucatán, it of all styles looks like the "typical" Mayan style. The buildings were designed in a low-slung, quadrangle shape and had many, many rooms. Exterior walls were probably kept plain in order to show off the friezes above, which were lavishly embellished with stone-mosaic deities surrounded by geometric and serpentine motifs. The corners of buildings were characteristically lined with the curl-nosed Chaac. Pyramids here didn't have roof combs. Finest examples: Uxmal, Labná, Kabah, Sayil.

Northeast Plains. The fusion of two Mayan groups—the early Chichén Maya and later Itzá Maya—produced this Late Classic (AD 600–900) style famously exemplified by Chichén Itzá. Here new forms such as columns and grand colonnades were introduced. Palaces with row upon row of columns carved in the form of serpents looked over private patios, platforms were dedicated to the planet Venus, and pyramids were offered to Kukulcán (the plumed serpent god borrowed from the Toltecs, who called him Quetzalcóatl). Chichén Itzá is also famous for its temple-top, reclining, carved stone chacmool (a reclining figure with an offering tray carved in its middle)—another Itzá addition. Finest examples: Chichén Itzá, Mayapán.

Quintana Roo Coast. Although somewhat influenced by the Itzá Maya, a style entirely different eventually evolved here. The large, squat-looking, one-story buildings have interior columns, wood-beam-supported ceilings, and numerous figures of the descending or Upside Down god that began appearing in the Post-Classic era (900–1530). Friezes were distinctively decorated with small niches. Finest examples: Tulum, El Rey, San Gervasio.

— Patricia Alisau

68, ☎ *no phone,* FAX *967/673–0711,* WEB *www.ranchoesmeralda.net. 8 cabins. Restaurant, horseback riding, free parking. No credit cards.*

Agua Azul

★ 20 *68 km (42 mi) northwest of Toniná, 64 km (40 mi) southwest of Palenque.*

The series of waterfalls and crystalline blue pools at Agua Azul is breathtaking during the dry season—from about November through March (the water is murky in the rainy season). The site has lost its sense of isolation since the road was paved in the 1980s; food shacks and camping facilities sprang up, and the natural beauty has been somewhat marred. Still, it's a breathtaking spot, and you can swim in a series of interconnected pools—be sure to bring a bathing suit. The falls are surrounded by giant palm fronds and tropical flowers; monkeys and toucans frolic in the vicinity. Six-hour trips, which include a visit to Misol-Há, cost about $10 per person and include the entrance fees (50¢ per person or $2 per car); you can book with most travel agencies in Palenque. For about $7 a person (including the entrance fee), you can ride with Sociedad Cooperative Chambalum (✉ Calle Allende at Av. Juárez s/n, Palenque, ☎ no phone) to both sites. Their service runs every 30 minutes, 6–6.

Misol-Há

★ 21 *46 km (29 mi) northeast of Agua Azul, 18 km (11 mi) southwest of Palenque.*

If the single cascade at Misol-Há is smaller than those at Agua Azul, the area surrounding it is also less peopled with vendors and less littered with trash—and it's no less breathtaking at first sight. You can swim in the pool formed by the 100-ft cascade, or explore behind the falls, where a cave leads to another, subterranean pool (a guide, who will be happy with $1, leads the way with a flashlight). Surrounded by oversize tropical vegetation, the site has rustic rest rooms, restaurants, and campgrounds. Wear a bathing suit. *See* Agua Azul, *above,* for how to get there.

Palenque

★ 22 *191 km (118 mi) northeast of San Cristóbal de las Casas, 150 km (93 mi) southeast of Villahermosa.*

Of all the Mayan ruins, none is more sublime than Palenque—only Tikal in Guatemala is its equal. Teotihuacán might be more monumental and Chichén Itzá more expansive, but Palenque possesses a mesmerizing quality, in part because of the intimacy that the surrounding jungle creates. In early morning or late afternoon, sunlight illuminates the structures in a hazy, iridescent glow. Birds call shrilly, and the local descendants of the Maya wander about collecting banana leaves, oranges, and avocados. You may even see a spider monkey or two, or hear their wild cries.

Antonio de Solis, a Spanish priest, accidentally dug into a buried wall here in 1740 while he was trying to plant crops. In 1805 a royal Spanish expedition ventured here to follow up on the discovery. In 1832 an eccentric count, Jean-Frédéric Maximilien de Waldeck, set up house with his mistress for a year in a building known today as the Templo del Conde (Temple of the Count). Explorers John Lloyd Stephens and Frederick Catherwood lived briefly in the palace during their 1840 expedition. Serious excavations began in 1923, under the direction of Frans

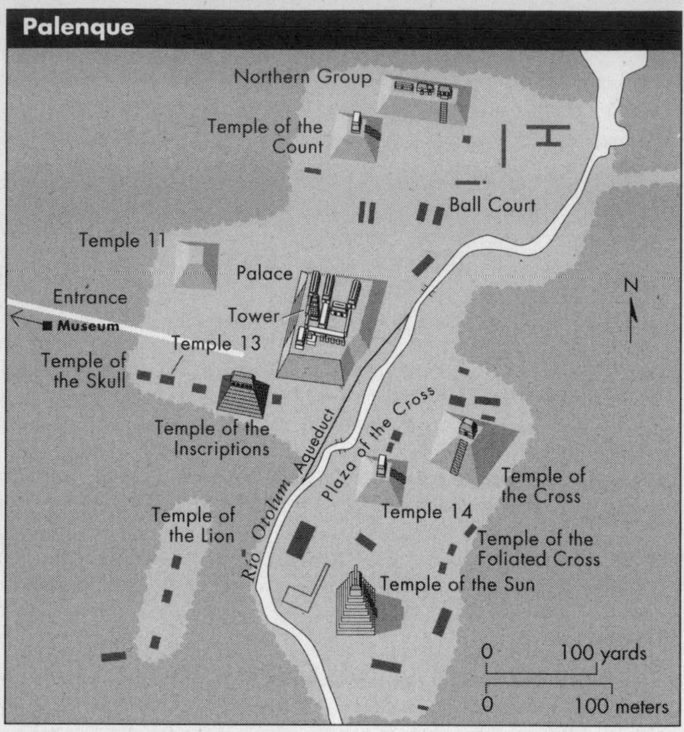

Blom, cofounder of the Na Bolom foundation in San Cristóbal. Work continued intermittently until 1952, when Alberto Ruz Lhuillier, a Mexican archaeologist, uncovered the tomb of the 7th-century ruler Pakal beneath the Temple of the Inscriptions. Since the early 1970s, groundbreaking work has been done on the Maya by archaeologists, linguists, and astronomers.

Palenque's elegance makes clear why archaeologist Sylvanus Morley called the Maya the "Greeks of the New World"—not only for their remarkable buildings, but also for the supple naturalism of the culture's art. The masters at work here shaped stone, stucco, and ceramics into ornate, lyrical designs. Artisans also took liberties here: relief sculpture of great expressiveness replaces the freestanding stelae of other Mayan cities.

The most important buildings of the site date from the Mid- to Late Classic period (AD 600–900), although Palenque was inhabited as early as 1500 BC. At its zenith, the city dominated the greater part of Tabasco and Chiapas. The site was abandoned around AD 800, making it one of the earliest Mayan sites to be deserted in what was a west-to-east pattern of abandonment. The reasons for the Mayas' departure are still in debate.

Palenque's graceful tower—one of the site's signature structures—sets it apart from other Mayan settlements. The Temple of the Inscriptions, a 75-ft pyramid, is another. It was dedicated to Pakal, who took Palenque to its most glorious heights during his 28- to 38-year reign. He died around AD 692, having become the ruler at age 12 and living into his 40s.

The ruling priest kings communicated life at Palenque in elaborate glyphs and reliefs on the temples. The deciphering of a good portion of Palenque's hieroglyphics in 1988 has revolutionized scholars' understanding of both the Maya and the bloody history of Palenque. Only 800 of the thousands of glyphs have been deciphered, but they have already revealed the complex history of the Palenque dynasties. Exciting finds by archaeologists from the University of Texas in 1998 introduced a new character, Uc-Pakal-Kinich, into the lineage of Palenque rulers. Other clues unearthed at Temple 19 point to a probable liaison between rulers of Palenque and of Copán, in what is now Honduras.

In its heyday, Palenque encompassed an astonishing 128-plus square km (49 square mi). Artificial terraces were built to support the temples, which surrounded plazas, a ball court, altars, and burial grounds. The temples had a complex array of corridors, narrow subterranean stairways, and galleries. And they served as fortresses in time of war. Only about 30% of the site has been excavated. Since late 1994, a huge portion of the ruins around the Temple of the Inscriptions has been reconstructed and is open. Explanations in Spanish, English, and Tzotzil have been placed at all major buildings.

As you enter the site, the first temple on your right is the reconstructed **Temple of the Skull,** which the Maya had painted red and blue in their time. A skull-shape stucco relief, presumed to be that of a rabbit, was found at the small entrance to the temple. It's now at the top of the stairs.

The **Temple of the Inscriptions** is just past Temple 13; its nine tiers correspond to the nine-level Mayan underworld. Atop this temple and the smaller ones around it are vestiges of roof combs—delicate vertical extensions that are among the features of southern Mayan cities. From the top, you'll get the best view of Palenque and an excellent orientation to its other buildings. Reaching the tomb inside involves a relatively easy, if slow, climb. Once at the summit, turn and take a long look back toward the once-mighty palace on the right. From the top of the Temple of Inscriptions, down the steep, damp flight of stairs 80 ft below is the **tomb of Pakal,** one of the first crypts found inside a Mexican pyramid. The tomb is no longer open to the public, but Pakal's remains along with his diadem and majestic jade, shell, and obsidian mask are on display at Mexico City's Museum of Anthropology. The intricately carved sarcophagus lid, weighing some 5 tons and measuring 10 by 7 ft, however, remains. A psychoduct—a stone tube in the shape of a snake through which Pakal's soul was thought to have passed to the netherworld—leads up to the temple. It can be difficult to make out the carvings on the slab, but they depict the ruler, prostrate beneath a sacred ceiba tree, which is still revered by the Maya today. The lords of the nine underworlds are carved into stucco reliefs on the walls around him.

In 1994, the small and unassuming **Temple 13,** attached to the Temple of the Inscriptions, revealed a royal tomb hidden in its depths. The tomb, which probably belonged to Pakal's mother or grandmother, is under investigation and isn't currently open to the public.

The patios, galleries, and other buildings that make up the **palace** are set on a 30-ft-high plinth. Stucco work adorns the pillars of the galleries and the inner courtyards. Inside are numerous friezes and masks, most of them depicting Pakal and his dynasty. Steam baths in the southwestern patio suggest that priests once dwelled in the adjoining cellars. The palace's iconic tower was built on three levels, representing the three levels of the universe as well as the movement of the stars.

To the east of the palace is the tiny Otulum River, which in ancient times was roofed over to form a 9-ft-high vaulted aqueduct. Cross the river and climb up 80 easy steps to arrive at the reconstructed **Plaza**

of the Cross, which contains the Temple of the Foliated Cross, Temple of the Sun, Temple 14, and the Temple of the Cross, the largest of the group. Inside Temple 14, there's an underworld scene in stucco relief, done 260 days after Pakal died. The most exquisite roof combs are found on these buildings, which are open to the public.

To reach the cluster called the **Northern Group,** walk north along the river, passing the palace and then the unexcavated ball court on your left. There are five buildings here in various states of disrepair; the largest and best preserved is the **Temple of the Count.**

A short hike northeast of the Northern Group lies **Group C,** an area containing remains of the homes of Mayan nobles and a few small temples shrouded in jungle. In order to maintain the natural setting in which the ruins were found, minimal restoration is being done. Human burials, funeral offerings of Jaina figurines, ceramics, and kitchen utensils have been found here as well as in the **Group B** area, which lies on the 20-minute "Ecological Path" hike through the jungle. On the way, you'll pass a small waterfall called El Baño de la Reina (The Queen's Bath). The path is poorly marked; be sure to veer left through the Group B ruins when you reach them.

The on-site **museum** has a remarkable collection of finely preserved heads of Mayan deities in elaborate zoomorphic headdresses, discovered in front of the Temple of the Foliated Cross. The group includes 13 figures of the sun god Kinich Ahau. Also noteworthy are the handsome, naturalistic stucco faces of Mayan men. Displays are labeled in English, Spanish, and Tzotzil. There's also a snack bar and an arts and crafts store with weavings, hand-embroidered fabrics, leather, ceramics, amber jewelry, hand-painted wooden crosses, and children's toys. The museum can be reached from the main road leading to the ruins.

Since explanatory signs inside the ruins are scant and in Spanish, you may want to hire a multilingual guide at the ticket booth. Guides charge about $35 for a group of up to seven people. *Ruins and museum $4. Ruins daily 8–4:45, museum Tues.–Sun. 9–3:45.*

Palenque Town

23 *8 km (5 mi) north of the ruins.*

Whereas cool highlander San Cristóbal has a polite but reserved exterior, Palenque Town wraps you in a warm tropical embrace. Its days as a sleepy cattle town are far behind, as the city swells with newcomers and longtime residents rush to turn family homes into rent-paying posadas. In only the past few years, thanks to tourism, upgraded services like e-mail servers have arrived; likewise ATMs and 24-hour long-distance phone service. Women and children from San Juan Chamula hawk crafts and souvenirs in front of restaurants and pharmacies along the principal downtown streets.

The dominant landmark in Palenque Town is the chalk-white "cabeza Maya," a giant sculpture of the head of a Mayan chieftain that graces the town's one traffic circle. West of downtown is the quiet neighborhood of La Cañada.

Dining and Lodging

$$$ ★ ✕ **Maya Cañada.** This round, thatch-roof restaurant in La Cañada is the baby sister to the aging but still popular (and less expensive) Maya downtown. Here, your Mexican dining experience is enlivened by an attractive blue color scheme and plentiful floral plantings. A romantic tiled terrace upstairs is lighted by iron lanterns and overlooks the back garden, where a few tables are set out for lunch. Mexican wines

are served, and there's a full bar. A trio plays music Thursday through Sunday 9–midnight. ✉ *Calle Merle Green s/n, La Cañada,* ☎ FAX *916/345–0216. AE, MC, V.*

$$ ✕ **El Arbolito.** On the main road to the ruins, this fun and funky restaurant is full of souvenirs of old ranch life. There's a wall full of hats, each inscribed with a different Mexican proverb. Other walls have mounted animal heads and pelts. It's no surprise that the house specialty is meat. Favorites include the spicy *consomé de borrego especial,* a broth with barbecued mutton, onions, and fresh cilantro. Beef tips in smoky chipotle sauce or other, mild chili sauces are served with beans, rice, garnish, and piping hot tortillas. ✉ *Carretera Palenque–Pakalná Km 1.5, across from Days Inn,* ☎ *916/345–0900. MC, V.*

$$ ✕ **Casa Grande.** This pleasant, art-filled café has an upstairs terrace overlooking Palenque's zócalo. Typical Mexican fare such as tacos and fried bananas complement the more exotic seafood dishes, which are expertly seasoned with Chiapan spices. This is the perfect place to perk up with an espresso or wind down with a glass of wine. ✉ *Av. Hidalgo 6, corner of Jiménez,* ☎ *916/345–0125. No credit cards.*

$$ ✕ **Pizzería Palenque.** This favorite spot of travelers has thin-crust pizzas (with a Mexican touch) that are so good, even Italians rave about them. You can also order pastas and sandwiches. It's not far from the downtown bus station, on the town's main road. ✉ *Av. Juárez 168,* ☎ *916/345–0332. No credit cards.*

$ ✕ **Maya.** Billed as Palenque's first restaurant, this 1958 original is where locals come for hearty, fresh, affordable fare. While the setting is humble, management runs this eatery with pride. Try the $3.50 set lunch menu, consisting of soup, a main dish, and dessert, or choose something from the extensive appetizer menu, which includes tacos and tostadas. À la carte dishes include New York and T-bone steaks, a tasty cordon bleu, and medallion of *robalo,* a local fish that comes fried or breaded. The coffees are the best in town. ✉ *Independencia at Av. Hidalgo, facing the zócalo,* ☎ *916/345–0042. AE, MC, V.*

$ ★ ✕ **La Selva.** Although a stop on the tour-group route, this spacious *palapa* (thatch-roof) restaurant is still popular with locals. The setting, surrounded by luxuriant jungle gardens, is superb, and so is the food, including the chips and salsa. There's a scrumptious Sunday brunch buffet after 1 PM for about $9. ✉ *Carretera Ruinas Km 5,* ☎ *916/345–0363. MC, V.*

$$$$ ★ **Chan Kah.** Four km (2½ mi) from the ruins in a paradisiacal jungle setting that's also a forest reserve, Chan Kah shouldn't be confused with the sister hotel of the same name in downtown Palenque. There's a stone-lined, lagoon-style pool, aromatic jasmine bushes, and a stream flowing around the back. The very comfortable bungalows have wide terraces, mahogany furnishings, and ceiling fans and/or air-conditioning. Bungalows 6–10 have views of the pool and stream. The emphasis here is on tranquility: there are no TVs in the rooms. ✉ *Carretera Ruinas Km 3.5, 29960,* ☎ FAX *916/345–1100 or 916/345–1134,* WEB *www.chan-kah.com. 76 bungalows. Restaurant, pool, bar, free parking; no room TVs. AE, MC, V.*

$$$$ **Misión Palenque.** Four blocks from the zócalo, this resort is Palenque's finest, with a staff of more than 100 and lovely 22-hectare grounds. Walk through the on-site jungle to a natural swimming well formed by two streams; a stone sauna and a mud bath are beside the well. The master suite has wide jungle views and large bedrooms with unique wood furniture. You can hop on the hotel's free shuttle bus to the ruins, and you can request a 4 PM check-out time. Tour groups are common. ✉ *Rancho San Martín de Porres, 29960,* ☎ *916/345–0499 or 800/448–8355,* FAX *916/345–0300,* WEB *www.hotelesmision.com.mx. 208 rooms, 2 suites. Restaurant, cable TV, 2 tennis courts, pool, hot tub, steam room,*

croquet, Ping-Pong, soccer, volleyball, bar, shops, laundry service, meeting rooms, travel services, free parking. AE, DC, MC, V.

$$$ **Ciudad Real Palenque.** This yellow-and-white colonial-style hotel sits amid glorious jungle gardens of the type possible only in Palenque. A small waterfall and creek run through the grounds. All rooms have balconies facing the gardens. ✉ *Carretera Pakal-Na Km 1.5, 29960,* ☎ FAX *916/345–1285, 916/345–1315, or 916/345–1343,* WEB *www.ciudadreal.com.mx. 69 rooms, 3 suites. Restaurant, cable TV, pool, bar, travel services, free parking. AE, MC, V.*

$$$ **Hotel Calinda Nututún Palenque.** A large natural pool forms from a bend in the Nututún River, which runs through the grounds of this hotel. The plain, ample rooms have tile floors; pay an additional $7 for a small, furnitureless terrace and a TV. Camping is permitted near the river for about $5.50 per person. ✉ *Carretera Palenque–Ocosingo Km 3.5, Apdo. 74, 29960,* ☎ *916/345–0100, 916/345–0161, or 800/221–2222,* FAX *916/345–0620,* WEB *www.reservhotel.com. 55 suites, 12 rooms. Restaurant, pool, bar, playground, free parking. AE, MC, V.*

$$$ **Maya Palenque.** This bright blue four-story Best Western affiliate, just behind the white head that marks the main intersection in Palenque town, is simple and reliable. Ask for a room facing the back pool and small but lush garden—the nicest feature of an otherwise plain but comfortable hotel. Rooms run cheaper ($60) in the off season (mid-Aug.–mid-July). ✉ *Merle Green at Av. Juarez,* ☎ *934/345–0780,* FAX *934/345–0907. 48 rooms, 3 junior suites. Restaurant, room service, cable TV, pool, shop, meeting rooms, free parking. AE, DC, MC, V.*

$$ **Casa Inn Tulijá.** You can't beat the price or location of this cheerful little hotel, which is about a 10-minute walk from downtown. It has the basics for a comfortable stay, although rooms are smallish. The 25-m-long pool is a great boon for swimmers. The tequila bar boasts more than 35 brands of the distilled agave liquor. ✉ *Apdo. 57, Carretera Ruinas Km 27.5, 29960,* ☎ *916/345–0104 or 800/900–1400,* FAX *916/345–0163,* WEB *www.tulija.mx. 48 rooms. Restaurant, cable TV, pool, billiards, bar, laundry service, meeting rooms, travel services, free parking. AE, MC, V.*

Bonampak

24 *183 km (113 mi) southeast of Palenque.*

Bonampak, which means "painted walls" in Mayan, is renowned for its courtly murals of ancient Mayan life. The settlement was built on the banks of the Lacanjá River during the 7th and 8th centuries and was uncovered again in 1946. Explorer Jacques Soustelle called it "a pictorial encyclopedia of a Mayan city." In remarkable ocher and faience colors, the scenes portrayed in the three rooms of the **Templo de las Pinturas** graphically recall subjects such as life at court and the prelude and aftermath of battle. It's open daily 8–5; admission is $2.50. For an extra $5 a Lacandon guide will join you near the park entrance. Segments of the murals are deteriorating because the high humidity in the area eats away at the colors, and thick white deposits of calcium from dripping water have covered some of the paintings completely. In 1984 Mexican experts devised a technique for cleaning and restoring the murals, and with the help of the National Geographic Society—and computerized, digital amplification techniques—remarkable details and color have come to light. The reproductions at the archaeological museums in Mexico City and Villahermosa are more legible than these on-site specimens.

Until recently, only the most devoted fans of the Maya attempted the trip to the ruins of Bonampak and Yaxchilán. Now, however, you can drive or take a three-hour bus ride from Palenque on the newly paved Highway 198 directly to Bonampak. If you drive, hook up with tour groups that meet around 6 AM in Palenque and travel together for added safety. Tour groups are escorted by a highway patrolman and a Green Angel truck that can assist you in case of a mechanical problem. Buses or tour vans will take you all the way to the ruins, or drop you at Lacanjá and let you hike the last 3 km (2 mi) into Bonampak, as was done before the road was built.

Getting to Yaxchilán still requires a one-hour jungle boat ride on the Usumacinta River; you must first drive or take a bus to the small town of Frontera Corozal, off Highway 198, where boats depart for the ruins and Guatemala. This is best arranged through travel agencies or state tourist offices in Mexico City, Palenque, or San Cristóbal de las Casas, which can also arrange for you to stay at the wonderful Tzeltal Indian cooperative Escudo Jaguar. Be sure to wear sturdy shoes, and bring insect repellent, good sunglasses, and a hat to protect yourself from mosquitoes, ticks, sand flies, undergrowth, and the jungle sun.

Yaxchilán

★ 25 *50 km (31 mi) northeast of Bonampak, 190 km (118 mi) southeast of Palenque.*

Excavations at Yaxchilán (yash-chee-*lan*), on the banks of Usumacinta River, have uncovered stunning temples and delicate carvings in an isolated jungle setting. Spider monkeys and toucans are, at this point, more prolific than tourists, and howler monkeys growl like lions from the towering *chico zapote* (fruit tree) and 100-year-old ceiba trees. Yaxchilán, which means "place of green stones," reached its cultural peak during the Late Classic period, from about AD 600 to 900. It's dominated by two acropolises containing a palace, temples with finely carved lintels, and great staircases. Until recently, the Lacandon, who live in the vicinity, made pilgrimages to this site in the heart of the jungle, leaving behind "god pots" (incense-filled ceramic bowls) in honor of ancient deities. They were particularly awed by the headless sculpture of Yaxachtun (ya-sha-*tun*) at the entrance to the temple (called Structure 33) and believed that the world would end when its head was replaced on its torso.

Yaxchilán was situated on the trade route between Palenque and Tikal, and the existence of a 600-ft bridge crossing the Usumacinta River to connect Yaxchilán to Guatemalan territory has been discovered. The engineering know-how of the people of Yaxchilán is still being deciphered by modern-day engineers. The site was once threatened with destruction by a huge dam to be built by Mexico and Guatemala. Thankfully, plans seem to have been put off indefinitely due to lack of funds. *Free. Daily 9–5.*

Lodging

$$ ★ **Escudo Jaguar.** This ecotourism project 144 km (89 mi) south of Palenque is run by the local Tzeltal people and is designed to bring people closer to the Mayan ruins of Bonampak and Yaxchilán. If you don't mind going a bit rustic, it's the ideal place to stay while you take in the jungle and both archaeological sites. Each of the 13 wooden cabins has a wide concrete veranda with two large, colorful hammocks for lounging. Inside, the thatch-roof cabins have screened windows, mosquito nets, and fans. The restaurant serves sandwiches and shakes in addition to full breakfasts, lunches, and dinners. It's best to book trips to Bonampak and Yaxchilán ahead of time, mentioning that you want to stay overnight at Escudo Jaguar. *Frontera Corozal, Ocosingo;*

reservations: Miditel operator, ☎ 961/612–9020. 13 cabins. Restaurant. No credit cards.

VILLAHERMOSA AND TABASCO

Graham Greene's succinct summation of Tabasco in *The Power and the Glory* as a "tropical state of river and swamp and banana grove" captures its essence. Although the state played an important role in the early history of Mexico, its past is rarely on view. Instead, it's Tabasco's modern-day status as a supplier of oil that defines it. Set on a humid coastal plain and crisscrossed by 1,930 km (1,197 mi) of rivers, low hills, and unexplored jungles, the land is still rich in banana and cacao plantations. Shantytowns and refineries are for the most part invisible to the visitor, who on bus trips passes small ranches with pastures of tall, green grass feeding horses and beef cattle. The capital city of Villahermosa epitomizes the mercurial development of Tabasco (the airplane was here before the automobile). Thanks to oil and urban renewal, the cramped and ugly neighborhoods in the mosquito-ridden town of the 1970s have been replaced by spacious boulevards, lush green parks, and cultural centers. Sandwiched between the Grijalva River and the historic downtown, the Zona Luz has been redone as a brick-paved pedestrian zone housing galleries and museums in addition to restaurants, ice cream shops, and a Howard Johnson hotel.

This is not to say that the rest of Tabasco has nothing to offer. There are beaches, lagoons, caves, and nature reserves, but the tourism infrastructure is minimal. The fired-brick Mayan ruins of Comalcalco attest to the influence of Palenque. Probably the most interesting region is the one to the south and east of Villahermosa, where rivers and canyons are home to jaguars, deer, and alligators.

Tabasco—specifically the mouth of the Grijalva River—runs along the route of the Spanish explorations of Mexico in 1518–19. At that time, the state's rivers and waterways, along which the Maya lived, served as a trade route between the peoples of the north and those of the south. When the Spaniards came to Tabasco, they had to bridge 50 rivers and contend with swarms of mosquitoes, beetles, and ants—as well as the almost unbearable heat. At the same time, the region was so lush that one early chronicler termed it a Garden of Eden.

The Spanish conquest was made easier by the extreme antipathy and tribal warfare between the Tabascans and their Aztec overlords. Among the 20 slave women turned over to the Spaniards upon their arrival in the Aztec capital was a Chiapan named Malintzín (or Malinche), who was singled out by the Spaniards for her ability to speak both the Mayan and the Nahuatl languages. Called Doña Marina by the Spaniards, she learned Spanish and became not only Cortés's mistress and the mother of his illegitimate son but also an interpreter of Indian customs. Malinche's cooperation helped the conquistador vanquish both Moctezuma and Cuauhtémoc, the last Aztec rulers. Even today, "La Malinche" is synonymous with "traitor" throughout Mexico.

Until the early 20th century, Tabasco slumbered. It didn't become a state until 1924. After the American Civil War, traders from the southern United States began operating in the region and on its rivers, hauling the precious mahogany trees upstream from Chiapas and shipping them north from the small port of Frontera. This was Tabasco's most prosperous era until the oil boom of the 1970s and 1980s.

Villahermosa

26 *821 km (509 mi) southeast of Mexico City, 632 km (392 mi) southwest of Mérida.*

There are a good many ways to spend your time in Tabasco's capital. The Zona Luz is a grid of pedestrian-only streets with restored colonial buildings, sidewalk cafés, galleries, and museums.

Most people make a beeline for the **Carlos Pellicer Museo Regional de Antropología** (Regional Museum of Anthropology). This museum on the right bank of the Grijalva is named after the man who donated many of its artifacts and who has been called the "poet laureate of Latin America." Pellicer (1897–1978) was deeply influenced by a love of his native Tabasco; his poems record the rhythms and visual intensity of the landscape. In his poem *Deseos* (Desires), he asks: "Tropics, why did you give me/These hands brimming with color?"

The museum is part of the huge CICOM cultural complex dedicated to research on the Olmec and Maya (which is what the Spanish acronym CICOM stands for). It provides one of the last tranquil vistas of Villahermosa as it might have looked in the mid-20th century. Note that all the explanations are in Spanish.

Much of the collection is devoted to Tabasco and the Olmec, or "inhabitants of the land of rubber," who flourished in Tabasco as early as 1200 to 1300 BC and disappeared around AD 800. The Olmecs have long been honored as inventors of the numerical and calendrical systems that spread throughout the region. The pyramid is also attributed to them. Some of the most interesting artifacts of the Olmec, apart from the remarkable stone sculptures and giant stone heads on view at Parque Museo La Venta, are the remnants of their jaguar cult displayed here. The jaguar symbolized the Earth fertilized by rain (i.e., procreation), and many Olmec sculptures portray half-human, half-jaguar figures, and jaguar babies. Other sculptures portray human heads emerging from the mouth of a jaguar, bat gods, bird-headed humans, and female fertility figurines.

Many of Mexico's ancient cultures are represented on the upper two floors, from the red-clay dogs of Colima and the nose rings of the Huichol Indians of Nayarit to the huge burial urns of the Chontal Maya, who built Comalcalco. The CICOM complex also houses a theater, restaurant, public library, and an arts and crafts shop. ✉ *Periféico Carlos Pellicer 511, an extension of the malecón (boardwalk),* ☎ *993/312–6344.* 🎫 *$1.* ⏲ *Tues.–Sun. 9–8.*

The giant stone heads and other figures carved by the Olmec were salvaged from the oil fields of La Venta, on the western edge of Tabasco ★ near the state of Veracruz. They are on display in the 8-hectare **Parque Museo La Venta,** in a tropical garden on the beautiful Lago de las Ilusiones (Lake of Illusions)—also founded by Carlos Pellicer, in 1958. The 6-ft-tall, bold-featured carved stone heads, wearing what look like helmets and weighing up to 20 tons, have sparked endless scholarly debate. It has been theorized that they depict ancient Phoenician slaves or space invaders. The latest and least outlandish (or offensive) theory is that the faces on the sculptures—very similar to today's Tabasco Maya—are actual portraits of successful Olmec athletes, war heroes, and other public figures. La Venta contains 33 sculptures, including jaguars, priests, monsters, stelae, and stone altars. Within the park is a zoo with creatures such as Tabascan river crocodiles, deer, jaguars, coatimundi, monkeys, and wild parrots. There's also a gift shop and several outdoor stands selling embroidered blouses, T-shirts, and souvenirs. ✉ *Blvd. Ruíz Cortines near Paseo Tabasco,* ☎ *993/314–1652.* 🎟 *$2.* ⏲ *Daily 8–5 (ticket booth closes at 4), zoo closed Mon.*

The small **Museo de la Historia Natural** (Natural History Museum) is just outside the entrance to the park. Of most interest are the displays of Tabasco's native plants and animals, many of which are now under government protection. Other rooms are dedicated to geology, evolution, and the solar system. ✉ *Blvd. Ruíz Cortines next to Parque Museo La Venta,* ☎ *no phone.* 🎟 *$1.* ⏲ *Tues.–Sun. 9–4:30.*

One of Villahermosa's most popular attractions is **Yumká,** which means "the spirit that looks after the forest" in Chontal Maya. It's a nature reserve spread over 250 acres of jungle, savannah, and wetlands. Half-hour guided walking tours take you over a hanging bridge and past free-roaming endangered or threatened species such as spider monkeys, red macaws, toucans, crocodiles, and native *tepezcuintles* (a giant rodent). Next comes a longer aerial tram ride past Asian and African species such as elephant and zebra. Optional $1.50 boat tours glide past birds wading or taking flight. ✉ *16 km (10 mi) from downtown, before the airport at Poblado Dos Montes,* ☎ *993/356–0115,* FAX *993/356–0107.* 🎟 *$3.* ⏲ *Daily 9–5 (ticket window closes at 4).*

Dining and Lodging

$$$$ ✕ **Bougainvillea.** Fresh roses, red carpets, oriental lanterns, and live jazz music by candlelight Wednesday through Saturday make the dozen tables here an intimate fine dining spot. Though one of the city's more expensive restaurants, the food and service are well worth the price. Try the carpaccio or breaded brie for starters, and filet mignon or duck à l'orange for the main course. The dessert tray includes such delights as raspberry and peach cobbler with ginger coconut ice cream. ✉ *In the Hyatt Regency, Av. Juárez 106,* ☎ *993/315–1234. AE, DC, MC, V. Closed Sun.*

$$$–$$$$ ✕ **El Mesón del Duende.** Standard meat and fish dishes are prepared with a regional accent in the "House of the Elf." Try the favorites, *filete en salsa de espinaca y queso* (beef fillet in a spinach and cheese sauce) and *la posta de robalo* (grilled snook). The modest decor is in keeping with the family-style atmosphere. ✉ *Gregorio Méndez 1703,* ☎ *993/315–1324. AE, MC, V.*

$$$–$$$$ ★ ✕ **Los Tulipanes.** Reputed to serve the city's best regional food, Los Tulipanes specializes in seafood and has a soothing river view. Try the regional appetizers, including stuffed tortillas and *empanadas* (turnovers stuffed with crab or shrimp), or the Tabasco specialty, *pejelagarto,* a succulent fish. The same owners run the Capitán Buelo, a small cruiser that runs 1½-hour dining trips on the Grijalva River Tuesday through Saturday at 3:30 and 9:30 PM, and Sunday at 1:30 and 3:30. ✉ *Periférico Carlos Pellicer 511, in the CICOM complex,* ☎ *993/312–9209,* FAX *993/312–9217. AE, MC, V.*

$$ ✕ **La Fontana Italiana Trattoria.** If you're tiring of Mexican cuisine, enjoy Italian fare (including pizza) at this air-conditioned restaurant near the Parque Museo La Venta. It's a favorite among locals. ✉ *Av. Ruíz Cortines 1410, Col. Lopez Mateos,* ☎ FAX *993/314–3283. AE, MC, V.*

$ ✕ **Don Marisco.** A block from the entrance to La Venta park is one of the town's most popular seafood restaurants. The nearly three-story thatched roof is an easy landmark. You'll stay cool beneath the high ceiling of this *palapa.* Breezes and ceiling fans keep things airy. Try the *filete de pescado villahermosa,* a local fish stuffed with *chaya,* a local spinach. ✉ *Corner of Paseo Tabasco and Av. Ruíz Cortines,* ☎ FAX *993/352–0690. MC, V.*

$$$$ **Calinda Viva & Spa Villahermosa.** Smack in the city's biggest intersection, the Calinda has the advantage of being across the street from La Venta park, but despite its attractive marble lobby and a big square pool surrounded by lounge chairs, the hotel is overpriced. All rooms have small balconies and coffeemakers, ironing boards, and irons. The restaurant serves many regional dishes, with a daily breakfast and lunch buffet. ✉ *Av. Ruíz Cortines at Paseo Tabasco, 86050,* ☎ *993/315–0000 or 800/711–5555,* FAX *993/315–3073. 239 rooms, 1 suite. Restaurant, cable TV, pool, gym, massage, sauna, steam room, 2 bars, dance club, laundry service, Internet, business services, travel services. AE, MC, V.*

$$$$ **Camino Real.** A full gamut of luxury amenities and excellent city views await you in this inviting 12-story resort. The rambling lobby, with rattan furniture in attractive niches, leads to the Tabasco 2000 mall, which has the largest number of upscale stores in Villahermosa. Shaded by bamboo curtains, the restaurant's floor-to-ceiling windows overlook a lovely garden; the hotel's pool is one of the largest in the state. There's live entertainment in the lobby lounge nightly. Continental breakfast and an appetizer hour are offered for those staying in the more capacious rooms on the executive floor. ✉ *Paseo Tabasco 1407, 86030,* ☎ *993/316–4400,* FAX *993/316–4569,* WEB *www.caminoreal.com/villahermosa. 180 rooms, 16 suites. Restaurant, coffee shop, room service, in-room data ports, in-room safes, minibars, cable TV, pool, gym, hair salon, laundry service, concierge floor, Internet, business services, convention center, meeting rooms, car rental, travel services, free parking, no-smoking rooms. AE, DC, MC, V.*

$$$$ **Cencali.** This two-story hotel, across from La Venta museum and park, sits on a lagoon and is surrounded by lush greenery, offering the best view in town. The big, cheerfully decorated rooms have large TVs and balconies; many overlook the lagoon, which has a lovely island filled with birds. Interior courtyards are filled with vines, and coconut-palm, mango, and cacao trees. Don't miss the fabulous lobby mural of pre-Columbian indigenous life (inspired by the *Popol Vuh*) by Tabascan master Daniel Montúy (1925–). The airy La Isla restaurant has a free daily breakfast buffet. ✉ *Av. Juárez and Paseo Tabasco, 86040,* ☎ FAX *993/315–1999,* WEB *www.cencali.com.mx. 104 rooms, 8 suites. Restaurant, cable TV, pool, bar, Internet, business services, meeting rooms, airport shuttle, car rental. AE, DC, MC, V.*

$$$$ **Hyatt Regency Villahermosa.** Although it's surprisingly plain on the outside, this American-style luxury hotel offers superior service, and excellent dining and reunion possibilities. Rooms have marble floors and polished wood furnishings. The La Ceiba Café has pleasing tropical decor and a superb daily breakfast buffet. Bougainvillea is one of the finest restaurants in the region. In the lobby, the El Plataforma video bar is decked out like the inside of an offshore oil platform; there's live music nightly at 8 in the El Flamboyan bar. An attractive pool area and tropical grounds are in the rear. ✉ *Av. Juárez 106, Zona Hotelera, 86050,* ☎ *993/315–1234 or 800/228–9000,* FAX *993/315–1235. 198 rooms, 9 suites. 2 restaurants, room service, in-room data ports, in-room safes, minibars, cable TV, 2 tennis courts, pool, bar, shop, playground, laundry service, concierge floor, Internet, business services, convention center, meeting rooms, car rental, travel services, no-smoking rooms. AE, DC, MC, V.*

$$$ **Howard Johnson.** This cheery five-story hotel is conveniently located in the pedestrian-only Zona Luz area, not far from the historic downtown and the malecón (boardwalk). It has lots of conveniences for its price range, including complimentary newspapers, irons, hair dryers, and an Internet café. Weekend rates offer a substantial discount (as in most business-oriented hotels here). The coffee shop's attentive wait-

ers serve mugs of hot coffee with real cream and refills. ✉ *Aldama 404, at 27 de Febrero, 86000,* ☎ FAX *993/314–4645 or 800/505–4900,* WEB *www.hojo.com.mx. 93 rooms, 6 suites. Coffee shop, room service, in-room data ports, in-room safes, cable TV, bar, Internet, meeting rooms, airport shuttle, free parking. AE, DC, MC, V.*

$$$ **Maya Tabasco Best Western.** A few blocks from the first-class (ADO) bus station—though neither downtown nor walking distance from La Venta park—the Maya Tabasco has comfortable rooms and an energetic staff. This hotel is outclassed by others of similar price range, but it will do if your first choices are booked. You can check out open-mike night in the Belle Epoque Trova Bar Café, smack in the middle of the swimming pool. ✉ *Av. Ruíz Cortines 907, 86000,* ☎ *993/312–1111 or 800/237–7700,* FAX *993/312–1097. 149 rooms, 3 suites. Restaurant, café, cable TV, pool, bar, dance club, Internet, business services, meeting rooms, airport shuttle, car rental, travel services. AE, MC, V.*

Comalcalco

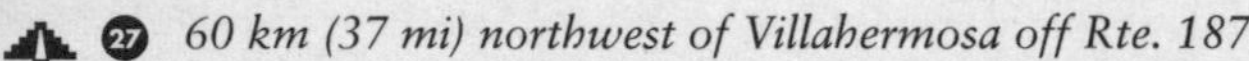

27 *60 km (37 mi) northwest of Villahermosa off Rte. 187.*

Comalcalco, which means "place of the clay griddles" (bricks) in Nahuatl, is the most important Mayan site in Tabasco. The abundant cacao trees in the region provided food and livelihood for a booming population during the Late Classic period (AD 600–900); it was founded approximately in the 1st century BC. The site marks the westernmost reach of the Maya, and descendants of its builders, the Chontal, still live in the vicinity. This site is unique among Mayan cities for its use of fired brick (made of sand, seashells, and clay), as the Tabasco swamplands lacked the stone for building that was found elsewhere in the empire. The bricks were inscribed and painted with figures of reptiles and birds, geometric figures, and drawings of hands and feet before being covered with stucco. The major pyramid on the Great Eastern Acropolis is decorated with large stucco masks of the sun god Kinich Ahau and carvings. The burial sites are another radical departure from Mayan custom: the dead were placed in cone-shaped clay urns, in a fetal position. Some have been left in situ, others are on display in the site **museum,** which houses many of the artifacts that were uncovered here. *About $2.50, free Sun.* ⌚ *Daily 10–4:30.*

Paraíso

28 *19 km (12 mi) north of Comalcalco.*

As you head toward the Gulf of Mexico coast and Paraíso, stop at one of the cacao plantations and chocolate factories. To visit **Hacienda Cholula,** about 2 km (1¼ mi) from Comalcalco, call ahead (☎ 933/334–3815) to arrange a free tour in English. You'll learn everything about cacao, from the plant to the chocolate stage. The cocoa bean was used as currency here in pre-Hispanic times.

From here, continue on to the coast, where you'll get a glimpse of small-town life. Climb nearby **Teodomiro Hill** for a spectacular view of Las Flores lagoon and coconut plantations. Small seafood restaurants and several small hotels dot the shore here; others are a few kilometers inland, in town. The small dark beaches here are unattractive; the best way to spend your time is in **Puerto Ceiba,** a fishing community whose inhabitants breed and harvest oysters, 15 km (8 mi) southeast of Paraíso. You can take a two-hour boat tour aboard the *Puerto Ceiba I* around a mangrove-lined Mecoacán Lagoon and the coastal rivers. Afterward, you can head to the **Puerto Ceiba Restaurant,** where you can board the $5 boat, or **La Posta** restaurant, where you can eat some of the freshest seafood you've ever tasted. The Villahermosa tourist office has information on the boat rides.

CHIAPAS AND TABASCO A TO Z

To research prices, get advice from other travelers, and book travel arrangements, visit www.fodors.com.

AIR TRAVEL

Villahermosa and Tuxtla Gutiérrez are the major airports of the region, though San Cristóbal Airport serves Mexico City daily on Aeromar. The closest major airport to San Cristóbal is in Tuxtla Gutiérrez, 85 km (53 mi) to the west. You can fly into Villahermosa, Tuxtla Gutiérrez, or San Cristóbal from Mexico City, or from smaller Mexican cities to Villahermosa and Tuxtla Gutiérrez.

CARRIERS

Aeroméxico has three daily nonstop flights to Villahermosa from Mexico City. Mexicana has five daily nonstop flights to Mexico City from Villahermosa. Both airlines have connecting flights to other Mexican cities. Aviacsa flies to Villahermosa nonstop to and from Mexico City three times a day. AeroCalifornia has one daily nonstop flight from Villahermosa to Mexico City. Aerocaribe, Mexicana's regional line, serves southwest Mexico, Palenque, Campeche, Merida, and Flores/Tikal from Villahermosa.

From Tuxtla Gutiérrez, Aerocaribe flies nonstop to Mexico City, Oaxaca, and Villahermosa; from Villahermosa, the flight continues on to Palenque. Aerocaribe also flies between Palenque and Flores, Guatemala (near the Tikal ruins), and Tuxtla Gutiérrez (with connections to Oaxaca and Mexico City). Aviacsa also has direct flights to Tuxtla Gutiérrez from Mexico City, Oaxaca, and Tapachula; from Cancún, Guadalajara, and other cities you have to connect through Mexico City.

➤ AIRLINES AND CONTACTS: **AeroCalifornia** (☎ 993/356–0170 at the Villahermosa airport, and 993/316–8000 for Villahermosa reservations). **Aerocaribe** (☎ 993/316–5046 at the Villahermosa airport, 993/316–5046 for Villahermosa reservations; 961/615–1530 at the Tuxtla airport; 961/612–1692 or 961/612–0020 for Tuxtla Gutiérrez reservations). **Aeromar** (☎ 961/614–3003 in Tuxtla Gutiérrez). **Aeroméxico** (☎ 993/356–0007 at Villahermosa airport; 993/312–1528 or 993/312–9554 for Villahermosa reservations). **Aviacsa** (☎ 993/356–0131 at Villahermosa airport; 993/316–5733 for Villahermosa reservations; 961/671–5225 at the Tuxtla Gutiérrez airport; 961/612–8081 and 961/611–2000 for Tuxtla Gutiérrez reservations). **Mexicana** (☎ 993/356–0101 at Villahermosa airport; 993/316–3132 or 993/316–3133 for Villahermosa reservations; 961/671–5120 at the Tuxtla Gutiérrez airport).

AIRPORTS AND TRANSFERS

Terán Airport, 8 km (5 mi) southwest of the city center, is Tuxtla Gutiérrez's major airport. The Capitan Carlos A. Rovirosa Airport, 15 km (9 mi) to the south, in Rancheria Dos Montes, serves Villahermosa. The San Cristóbal Airport has daily flights to Mexico City. None of the three airports receives direct flights from the United States or Canada.

➤ AIRPORT INFORMATION: **Capitan Carlos A. Rovirosa Airport** (☎ 993/356–0157 or 993/356–0156). **San Cristóbal Airport** (✉ Corazón de María Km 17, ☎ 967/674–3016). **Terán Airport** (☎ 961/615–0498 or 961/615–1437).

AIRPORT TRANSFERS

Taxis from Tuxtla Gutiérrez's Teran Airport cost 50 pesos ($5) into Tuxtla. Check as well for affordable *colectivo* (shared minivan) service to San Cristóbal from the airport.

You can catch a colectivo taxi from San Cristóbal to Tuxtla at the corner of Boulevard Juan Sabines Gutiérrez and Avenida Ignacio Allende, across from the second-class bus station. The taxi ($5 per person) will leave when it has four passengers.

The only transportation from Villahermosa's airport is via taxi. A trip to downtown Villahermosa costs $15 (150 pesos). Taxis can also drive you straight to Palenque for $75 (750 pesos).

BUS TRAVEL

From Palenque, first- and luxury-class service is available to Ocosingo (two hours), Villahermosa (2½ hours), San Cristóbal (four hours), Campeche (six hours), Tuxtla Gutiérrez (seven hours), Mérida (eight hours), Cancún (11 hours), and Mexico City (12 hours) on the first-class ADO and Cristóbal Colón. Buses leave from the ADO bus terminal. If you can't get a first-class bus, many of the same destinations can be reached on the second-class buses Omnibus de Chiapas and Express Plus, both a few doors away from the ADO bus terminal.

From San Cristóbal, Cristóbal Colón bus station has deluxe and first-class buses to major destinations in Chiapas and beyond. To avoid bus station lines and limited timetables, the best way to reach Tuxtla is from the bus station directly across the street on one of a fleet of 36 Chevy Suburban vans that belong to Tres Estrellas (no phone). Vans leave as soon as they fill up (about every 20 minutes) 5 AM–10 PM and cost less than $4 per person. Second-class service on Transportes Tuxtla Express Plus to Tuxtla, Palenque, and Comitán departs from the terminal at Avenida Ignacio Allende, ½ block from Boulevard Juan Sabines Gutiérrez, about four blocks to the west. You can purchase bus tickets without going to the bus terminal at Ticket Bus, a convenient service with an office in the center of San Cristóbal.

From Tuxtla Gutiérrez, Cristóbal Colón bus station offers deluxe and first-class service between Tuxtla and Oaxaca, Palenque, Villahermosa, Tapachula, Mérida, Mexico City, San Cristóbal, Cancún, Puerto Escondido, and Playa del Carmen. First- and second-class transportation within the state is available on Sociedad de Transportes Dr. Rodulfo Figueroa. You can get from Tuxtla to San Cristóbal by first-class bus, which leaves several times each day (two hours; about $3.50).

From Villahermosa, deluxe and first-class service to Campeche, Chetumal, Mérida, Mexico City, Palenque, San Cristóbal, Tapachula, Tuxtla Gutiérrez, Veracruz, and elsewhere is available from the ADO bus terminal, which is served by UNO and G. L. and Cristóbal Colón. There is frequent second-class service to the same cities from the Central Camionera de 2a Clase.

➤ BUS INFORMATION: **ADO bus terminal** (✉ Av. Juárez near Av. de la Vega, Palenque, ☎ 916/345–1344; ✉ Calle F. J. Mina 297, corner of Lino Merino, Villahermosa, ☎ 993/312–7692 or 993/312–1446). **Central Camionera de 2a Clase** (✉ Av. Ruíz Cortines s/n, Villahermosa, ☎ 993/312–2977 or 993/312–1091). **Cristóbal Colón** (☎ 993/312–2937; 993/312–8900 in Villahermosa). **Cristóbal Colón bus station** (✉ Av. Insurgentes and Blvd. Juan Sabines Gutiérrez, San Cristóbal, ☎ 967/678–0291; ✉ Av. 2a Nte. Pte. 268, Tuxtla Gutiérrez, ☎ 961/612–1639 or 961/612–2624). **Express Plus** (☎ 916/345–1012 in Palenque). **G. L.** (☎ 993/312–7692 in Villahermosa). **Omnibus de Chiapas** (☎ 916/345–1322). **Sociedad de Transportes Dr. Rodulfo Figueroa** (✉ 4a

Pte. Sur 1060, Tuxtla Gutiérrez, ☎ 961/613–6592 in Tuxtla Gutiérrez). **Ticket Bus** Av. Real de Guadalupe 5-E, San Cristóbal, ☎ 967/678–8503. **Transportes Tuxtla Express Plus** (☎ 967/678–4869 in San Cristóbal). **UNO** (☎ 993/312–7627 in Villahermosa).

CAR RENTAL

In San Cristóbal, Budget is inside the Mansión del Valle hotel. Excellent is near the zócalo.

Tuxtla's Teran Airport has four rental agencies: Alamo, Budget, Hertz, and National.

The Villahermosa airport has three rental agencies, each with one other downtown branch: Budget, Dollar, and Hertz.

➤ MAJOR AGENCIES: **Advantage** (☎ 993/315–5833 or 993/315–5048). **Budget** (✉ Calle Diego de Mazariegos 36, San Cristóbal, ☎ FAX 967/678–1871 or 967/678–3100; Teran Airport, Tuxtla Gutiérrez, ☎ 961/615–0672; Airport, Villahermosa, ☎ 993/356–0118; Av. 27 de Febrero 712, Villahermosa, ☎ 993/314–3790). **Dollar** (✉ Airport and Hyatt Regency, Av. Juárez 106, Villahermosa, ☎ 993/315–1234). **Hertz** (✉ Airport, Villahermosa, ☎ 993/356–0200; Hotel Camino Real, Paseo Tabasco 1407, Villahermosa, ☎ 993/316–0163). **National** (✉ Teran Airport, Tuxtla Gutiérrez, ☎ 961/614–6681).

➤ LOCAL AGENCIES: **Excellent** (✉ Real de Guadalupe 5-E, San Cristóbal, ☎ 967/678–7656).

CAR TRAVEL

From Tuxtla Gutiérrez, Highway 190 goes east through Chiapa de Corzo to San Cristóbal before continuing southeast to Comitán and the Guatemala border. Highway 199 to Highway 186 (the turnoff is at Catazajá) is the preferred route from San Cristóbal to Villahermosa; it'll take you via Toniná, Agua Azul, and Palenque. The drive from San Cristóbal to Palenque takes about five hours along a winding paved road, and it's another two hours from Palenque to Villahermosa along a fairly straight road.

On the map, Highway 195 may look like the most direct way to travel between San Cristóbal and Villahermosa, but it entails hours of hairpin curves—it's only for the stalwart and absolutely not to be traveled at night because of seasonal fog as well as a lack of reflectors, illumination, and other cars to help in case of emergency.

To get to Villahermosa from Coatzacoalcos and Veracruz, take Highway 180. In all cases, exercise caution during the rainy season (June through October), when roads are slick. Although expensive, car rentals are available at the Tuxtla and Villahermosa airports as well as in San Cristóbal.

EMERGENCIES

In larger cities such as Tuxtla Gutiérrez and Villahermosa, dial 060 for fire, theft, and medical emergencies. If you don't speak Spanish, it might be better to call hotel personnel or the tourist office (during open hours) and ask for an English-speaking representative.

For tourist-related problems in Palenque contact the Agencia del Ministerio Público at the tourist office. Travelers in Villahermosa are advised to call the state tourist office for all emergencies. Visit the Centro de Salud in Palenque, weekdays 7 AM–8 PM, for medical consultation. In an emergency, Hospital General, next door, is open 24 hours a day, as is Farmacia Lastra. In San Cristóbal, Farmacia Bios is open 7 AM–11 PM. In Tuxtla, Farmacia del Ahorro is open 24 hours and offers delivery services. Farmacia Unión in Villahermosa is open 24 hours.

➤ CONTACTS: **Cruz Roja** (Red Cross, ✉ Prolongación Ignacio Allende 55, San Cristóbal, ☎ 967/678–0772 or 967/678–6565). **Federal Highway Police** (✉ Blvd. Juan Sabines Gutiérrez, s/n, San Cristóbal, ☎ 967/678–6466). **Municipal police** (✉ Blvd. Juan Sabines Gutiérrez, s/n, near Unidad Deportiva, San Cristóbal, ☎ 967/678–0554).

➤ HOSPITALS AND CLINICS: **Centro de Salud** (✉ Prolongación Juárez s/n, Palenque, ☎ 916/345–0025). **Hospital General** (✉ Prolongación Juárez s/n, Palenque, ☎ 916/345–0733). **Hospital General** (✉ Av. Insurgentes 24, San Cristóbal, ☎ 967/678–0770). **Red Cross Hospital** (✉ Av. Sandino, s/n, Col. Primero de Mayo, Villahermosa, ☎ 993/315–5555 or 993/315–6263).

➤ PHARMACIES: **Farmacia del Ahorro** (✉ Av. Central Pte. 874, Tuxtla, ☎ 961/613–8818). **Farmacia Bios** (✉ Av. Hidalgo at Av. Cuauhtémoc, San Cristóbal, ☎ 967/678–1818). **Farmacia Lastra** (✉ Av. Juárez s/n at Abasolo, downtown, Palenque, ☎ 916/345–1119). **Farmacia Unión** (✉ Av. 27 de Febrero 1205, Villahermosa, ☎ 993/315–4717).

ENGLISH-LANGUAGE MEDIA

In San Cristóbal, Chilam Balam has the latest editions of travel, archaeology, and art books along with posters and maps of Mexico. There's a second store at Avenida Insurgentes 18. La Mercantil has the best selection of English- and Spanish-language periodicals.

➤ BOOKSTORES: **Chilam Balam** (✉ Casa Utrilla at Av. Gral. Utrilla 33 and Dr. Navarro, ☎ 967/678–0486). **La Mercantil** (✉ Calle Diego de Mazariegos 21).

INTERNET

Palenque Red Maya has a dozen fast computers on the main street in town. An hour costs $1.50. Red Maya is open daily 9 AM–10:30 PM.

San Cristóbal has at least one Internet café per block near the center of town. You can check e-mail while you eat and listen to music at the Cafetería del Centro ($1.50/hr), half a block from the zócalo. It's open daily 7 AM–10 PM. Next door, PoderNet C@fé has cheaper computers ($1) with less atmosphere. It's open Monday through Saturday 9 AM–11 PM and Sunday 11–9.

There's a great Internet café in Villahermosa at the coffee shop of the Howard Johnson's hotel, in the popular Zona Luz district. It's open weekdays 8 AM–10 PM, Saturday 8–8, and Sunday noon–8, and charges $2 an hour.

The CyberCafe is about 10 blocks from the Cristóbal Colón bus station, in Tuxtla Gutiérrez, but the price is right: $1.50 an hour for Internet access. It's open daily 9–9.

➤ INTERNET CAFÉS: **Cafetería del Centro** (✉ Real de Guadalupe 7, San Cristóbal, ☎ 967/678–3922). **CyberCafe** (✉ 3a Nte. Pte. 1346, Tuxtla Gutiérrez, ☎ 961/612–3900). **Howard Johnson's** (✉ Aldama 404, Villahermosa, ☎ 993/312–9659). **PoderNet C@fé** (✉ Real de Guadalupe 3, San Cristóbal, ☎ 967/678–7488). **Red Maya** (✉ Av. Juarez 133, Palenque, ☎ 916/345–0934).

TAXIS

In Palenque the local *sitio* (taxi stand) is at the town park. A ride to the ruins is $4, $5 if you call from your hotel. San Cristóbal has group taxi service to outlying villages, departing from and returning to the sitio at Blvd. Jaime Sabines and Insurgentes near the Cristóbal Colón bus station.

Within the city of Villahermosa itself, trips are fixed at 15 pesos in yellow *colectivo* taxis, and 20 pesos in the white *especial* taxis.

Within the city of Tuxtla Gutiérrez, taxis cost 15 to 20 pesos. You can take a taxi 10 minutes away to Chiapa de Corzo for 60 pesos ($6); and to San Cristóbal, about 1½ hours, for about $15. Many travel agencies in both cities provide private taxi service.

➤ TAXI COMPANIES: **Palenque taxi stand** (☎ 916/345–0379 or 916/348–2353). **Radio Taxis Uno Tuxtla** (☎ 961/612–5672). **San Cristóbal Taxis Jovel** (☎ 967/678–6899). **Villahermosa radio taxi** (☎ 993/315–8333 or 993/315–8433).

TOURS

From the town of Palenque, most tour operators offer half-day guided tours of Palenque ruins for about $6, which includes guide, entrance to the ruins, hotel pickup, and lunch. Also offered are six-hour tours to the waterfalls at Misol-Há and Agua Azul, at about $10 per person—a good deal as it includes entrance to both sites and transportation. Longer trips to San Cristóbal, Toniná, and the Sumidero Canyon are also available. Reliable, recommended tour operators include Turismo Quetzal and Kukulcán. Both have one- and two-day trips to Bonampak and Yaxchilán by land. A one-day trip costs $30–$40 via land and boat, including transportation, Spanish-speaking guide, and lunch. Two-day trips overnight in tents at the Lacandon village of Lacanjá cost about $60, including five meals, transportation, and guide services. Both companies can arrange river trips to the Mayan ruins at Tikal, in Guatemala, as well as day trips to Misol-Há and Agua Azul waterfalls near Palenque.

Ceiba Adventures has guided adventure tours throughout the Ruta Maya, including excursions to Palenque, Bonampak, Yaxchilán, and Tikal. Available are cave explorations and river rafting along several Chiapan waterways sunk deep in the jungle.

Pepe Santiago, a Lancandon native raised by Na Bolom founder Gertrude Blom, and his partner lead tours ($10) daily to San Juan Chamula and Zinacantán, leaving from Na Bolom at 10 AM and returning around 3:30. Pepe's name is a veritable ticket of acceptance in the more remote regions of Chiapas; he can set you up with insider tours anywhere in the state. Gabriela Gudiño, who has more than 20 years' experience as a guide specializing in history, archaeology, and ethnography of the Maya Route and southeast Mexico, can be reached at (☎ 967/678–6570). She charges about $11. Mercedes Hernández leaves from the zócalo at approximately 9 AM; look for her colorful umbrella. She charges about $5 per person. These guides speak English.

A.T.C., Viajes Pakal, Viajes "Chincultik," Posetur, and Viajes Navarra offer local tours around San Cristóbal and beyond, as well as tours of Bonampak, Yaxchilán, Palenque, Agua Azul, Lagos de Montebello, Amatenango, Chincultik, and Sumidero Canyon; some arrange transportation to Guatemala, the Yucatán, and Belize. Pronatura offers day trips to the tropical cloud forests of Reserva Huitepec; profits go to Chiapas conservation and reforestation programs. Most tour operators transport passengers in minibuses and can arrange hotel pickup. DANA offers low-impact four-day guided hiking tours to Laguna Miramar, the largest natural lake in southwestern Mexico, in the Lacandon rain forest. Here you'll experience camping, swimming, snorkeling, fishing, horseback riding, and visits to small area ruins and indigenous communities. A three-night stay (the minimum) costs about $180 if you go by land.

Viajes Lido and Viajes Miramar, run by the Castillo sisters, offer city tours of Tuxtla Gutiérrez, plus five-hour excursions to Chiapa de Corzo and Sumidero Canyon for $10.

In Villahermosa, Turismo Creativo (Creatur) runs ecotours in Tabasco and beyond. Expedición Ayin specializes in equipped cave tours and trips to the Panatanos de Centla Biosphere. Rutas del Usumasinta specializes in tours to Chiapas and Guatemala, including Bonampak and Yaxchilán. Agencia de Viajes Tabasco is a big travel agency, a good place to buy air tickets.

➤ Tour Operator Recommendations: **Agencia de Viajes Tabasco** (✉ Hyatt Regency, Av. Juárez 106, Zona Hotelera, Villahermosa, ☎ FAX 993/316–1058 or 993/316–4454; ✉ Galería Tabasco 2000, Local 173, Villahermosa, ☎ 993/315–1234, 993/315–5790, or 993/316–4088, FAX 993/316–4090). **A.T.C.** (✉ Av. 16 de Septiembre 11, San Cristóbal, ☎ 967/678–2550 or 967/678–2557, FAX 967/678–3145). **Ceiba Adventures** (✉ Box 2274, Flagstaff, AZ 86003, ☎ 520/527–0171, FAX 520/527–8127). **DANA** (✉ Calle de los Arcos 9, San Cristóbal, ☎ FAX 967/678–4307). **Expedición Ayin** (✉ Pedro Gil Cadena no. 11, Villahermosa, ☎ 993/351–2439). **Kukulcán** (✉ Av. Juárez s/n at Calle Allende, Palenque, ☎ 916/345–1506). **Posetur** (✉ 5 de Febrero 1, in the Posada Diego de Mazariegos hotel, San Cristóbal, ☎ 967/678–0833). **Pronatura** (✉ Av. Juárez 11-B, San Cristóbal, ☎ 967/678–5000). **Rutas del Usumasinta** (✉ Calle Remo 215, Residencial Cuidad Deportiva, Villahermosa, ☎ 993/351–0405, FAX 993/351–0535. **Turismo Creativo** (✉ Av. Paseo Tabasco 715, Villahermosa, ☎ 993/315–3999). **Turismo Quetzal** (✉ Av. Juárez 135, Palenque, ☎ 916/345–0601). **Viajes "Chincultik"** (✉ Real de Guadalupe 34, San Cristóbal, ☎ 967/678–0957, FAX 967/678–7832). **Viajes Lido** (✉ Av. Central Pte. 861-A, Tuxtla Gutiérrez, ☎ 961/613–6671, FAX 961/612–1130). **Viajes Miramar** (✉ Camino Real, Local 2, Tuxtla Gutiérrez, ☎ 961/617–7777 Ext. 7230, FAX 961/615–5925). **Viajes Navarra** (✉ Real de Guadalupe 15-D, San Cristóbal, ☎ 967/678–1143). **Viajes Pakal** (✉ Calle Cuauhtémoc 6A, San Cristóbal, ☎ FAX 967/678–2818).

TRANSPORTATION AROUND CHIAPAS AND TABASCO

A car or a tour arranged through a local travel agency is the easiest way to reach Palenque's surrounding attractions, although the ruins themselves can easily be reached via private taxi or inexpensive colectivo service from downtown (corner of Av. Hidalgo and Calle Allende) or from the ADO bus station. The downtown itself is small enough to traverse on foot.

As with many other colonial towns, the most enjoyable and thorough way to explore San Cristóbal is on foot. If you do come to town with a car, leave it in the hotel garage until you're ready to take an excursion outside San Cristóbal.

Of the three rivers surrounding it, Villahermosa is oriented toward the Grijalva River to the east, which is bordered by a malecón. The city is huge, and driving can be tricky. The main road through town, Ruíz Cortines, is almost a highway; exit ramps are about 1 km (½ mi) apart, and tourist destinations aren't clearly marked. Information about city buses can be difficult to find.

VISITOR INFORMATION

The state of Chiapas has a toll-free tourist information number, which can be dialed from anywhere in Mexico, but which isn't always answered. The most helpful Web site is the state-sponsored www.turismo.chiapas.gob.mx.

The people in the tourist office in Comitán are very knowledgeable and helpful. The office is open weekdays 9–4 and 6–9, weekends 9–2. (Both are open weekdays 8–8, Saturday 9–8, Sunday 9–2.)

The people at the municipal tourist office in San Cristóbal have some information about San Cristóbal proper. You can get more information about attractions throughout the city and state at the state tourist office. The municipal office is open Monday through Saturday 8–8; the state office is open weekdays 8–8, Saturday 9–8, Sunday 9–2.

The folks at the state tourist office in Tuxtla Gutiérrez are extremely helpful; they're there weekdays 9–9, Saturday 9–8, Sunday 9–3.

The state tourist office in Villahermosa, next to the municipal palace, is open weekdays 8–4. The auxiliary office at Parque Museo La Venta is open daily 9–4. The best Web site is the flashy www.naturalmentetabasco.com.mx, which provides an overview of the state's attractions, as well as lodging and dining options.

➤ TOURIST INFORMATION: **Chiapas tourist information hot line** (☎ 800/280–3500). **Palenque Tourist information** (✉ Av. Juárez and Abasolo, at Plaza de Artesanías, Palenque, ☎ 916/345–0365). **Municipal tourist office–San Cristóbal** (✉ Palacio Municipal [City Hall], ground floor, on the zócalo, San Cristóbal, ☎ 967/678–0665 or 967/678–0135). **State tourist office–San Cristóbal** (✉ Miguel Hidalgo 1-B, San Cristóbal, ½ block from zócalo, ☎ 967/678–6570). **State tourist office–Tuxtla** (✉ Edificio Plaza de las Instituciones, ground floor, Blvd. Dr. Belisario Domínguez 950, Tuxtla Gutiérrez, ☎ 961/602–8613 or 800/280–3500). **State tourist office–Villahermosa** (✉ Av. Los Ríos at Calle 13 s/n, Villahermosa, ☎ 993/316–3633 or 993/316–2889). **Tourist office–Comitán** (✉ ground floor of Municipal Palace, facing zócalo, Comitán, ☎ 963/632–4047).

13 VERACRUZ AND THE NORTHEAST

The superb but little-explored pyramids of El Tajín and the raffish, rhythmic charm of Veracruz, the first European city established on the North American mainland and Mexico's musical mecca, are among this country's indisputable highlights. Many Texans get their first taste of Mexico in the northeastern border towns of Nuevo Laredo, Reynosa, and Matamoros. Texan or otherwise, if you venture farther down to Monterrey, you'll find far more sophisticated dining, shopping, and cultural attractions.

Updated by Barbara Kastelein

THERE ARE PLENTY of reasons to make your way to the state of Veracruz: its culture, history, cuisine, and a characteristic laid-back friendliness. You can explore El Tajín—its Temple of the Niches is one of the most enchanting pre-Columbian buildings in Mexico. Or wander the venerable port of Veracruz, where the Spanish first landed in 1519; witness the fascinating aerial ritual of the *voladores* (flyers) of Papantla; and enjoy an archaeological museum second only to the one in Mexico City. You can also stroll the plazas of quaint mountain villages, laze on sandy beaches, and dine on some of the best seafood in Mexico.

The three cultural-hybrid border cities of Nuevo Laredo, Reynosa, and Matamoros are industrial areas that lure American day-trippers with moderate-price crafts and authentic Mexican dishes. Improved roads have led more people to take advantage of the opportunity to visit Monterrey, Mexico's third-largest city. With its cultural attractions, five-star hotels and restaurants, modern outlook, and, of course, shops, it's a highlight of the region. You can arrange horseback rides, mountain-biking excursions, and treks into the pine forests of the nearby Sierra Madre.

Pleasures and Pastimes

Dining

The state of Veracruz is home to some of Mexico's most accessible regional dishes. Many of the traditional specialties show the influence of the Spanish and African communities of nearby Cuba, including the state's signature dish, *huachinango à la veracruzana* (red snapper in the Veracruz style, covered in tomatoes, onions, garlic, green olives, and capers). Leaving without sampling this would be both a shame and a bit of a feat, as every chef has his own version, which he will insist you try. Although this dish recalls Mediterranean cuisine, it also incorporates New World ingredients like jalapeños and tomatoes. Other dishes reflect African ties in their use of beans, plantains, yucca, taro, white sweet potatoes, and especially peanuts, which appear in the classic *puerco encacahuatado* (pork in peanut sauce). You'll find peanut ice cream all over the state, along with another sweet-tooth tempter, *buñuelos Veracruzanos* (Veracruz beignets), golden doughnuts to be dipped in a sugar and cinnamon mixture or served with sticky *piloncillo* (brown loaf-sugar syrup).

In Veracruz, as befits a hot, breezy port town, the emphasis is on simple, fresh food, mostly *pescado* (fish) and *mariscos* (shellfish). Night or day, a stop at one of the town's cafés is de rigueur—the 19th-century Café del Portal is known internationally for its atmosphere and memorably strong coffee. Jalapa is considered to have the best restaurants in the state, with creative integration of beans, rice, cheese, and occasionally chilies (this is, after all, the hometown of the jalapeño) into main dishes of meat and river fish such as trout. Some of the best places to eat here are the small, family-run seafood *palapas* (thatch-roof huts) lining the beach as well as the river, as it makes its way to the gulf. Just ask for the *platillo del día* (daily dish).

The Northeast isn't renowned for the subtlety of its cuisine, but its cattle country ensures an abundance of good beef cuts, the most typical being *arrachera*. A prime regional treat is kid (*cabrito*), which, when well prepared, has a delicate lamblike flavor. If you'd like to try it, Monterrey is the place to give it a go; you cannot be in this city for long without seeing goat sizzling on the grill. Plunge ahead and order the back or kidneys, or, if you're a bit apprehensive, the leg or breast.

Very little in the state of Veracruz or the Northeast is truly formal, although in the cities of Veracruz and Monterrey reservations may be needed for popular restaurants. A jacket and tie would look out of place almost anywhere, apart from the business hub of Monterrey.

CATEGORY	COST*
$$$$	over $20
$$$	$15–$20
$$	$10–$15
$	under $10

**per person for a main course at dinner*

Fishing

Northeastern Mexico is a popular place for American anglers. You're likely to hook something at La Pesca—as the name would indicate—on the Tamaulipas coast between Matamoros and Tampico east of Ciudad Victoria and Soto La Marina.

Lodging

World-class hotels have started to arrive in the state of Veracruz. The port city also offers a number of inexpensive hotels with plenty of atmosphere, and both the moderately priced and more expensive places offer good value for your money—especially in comparison with their counterparts in areas of Mexico that see more foreign tourists.

Although there are plenty of clean, comfortable, and inexpensive options in downtown Jalapa, more upscale choices are limited. Some people choose to see El Tajín as a day trip from the more developed port town of Tuxpán, only passing through Papantla, where accommodation options are limited.

Catering mostly to business travelers and short-term tourists, accommodations in the border towns increasingly tend to fall into two camps: the chains of more standardized small hotels or the wilting individual establishments whose heyday has passed. Monterrey affords more choices in all price ranges, and new hotels keep popping up to keep pace with the increase in corporate travelers.

CATEGORY	COST*
$$$$	over $160
$$$	$90–$160
$$	$40–$90
$	under $40

**All prices are for a standard double room, excluding tax.*

Exploring Veracruz and the Northeast

The lively port city of Veracruz was of vital importance in the history of the Spanish conquest of Mexico. Raucous and sweaty, its Caribbean flavor, energetic music, and multiracial population give it a particular flair. The exuberance of *jarochos,* as the city's residents are known, does not falter even in the broiling midday heat or when faced with the strong *nortes* (brisk north winds).

The lush coastal state of Veracruz also harbors pockets of colonial history, as well as fine native ruins and some of Mexico's most outstanding adventure tourism routes. Jalapa, the state capital, is a university town and cultural hub, filled with pretty parks and stately government buildings.

Northeastern Mexico consists of a string of border towns across from the United States, the city of Monterrey, and some surrounding natural wonders. The border towns' charm is limited, aside from sampling Mexican cuisine and buying crafts. You might prefer to linger in Monterrey, a major city with elegant hotels, cutting-edge art at the Museum of Contemporary Art, a phenomenal 100-acre city square, and a variety of natural wonders in the surrounding areas, including Horsetail Falls.

Numbers in the text correspond to numbers in the margin and on the Veracruz and East Central Mexico, Veracruz, Northeastern Mexico, and Monterrey maps.

Great Itineraries

The state of Veracruz and Northeast Mexico are separate regions, which is how most travelers approach them when planning a trip. Veracruz is closer to Mexico City and is a popular domestic getaway. Northeast Mexico is closer to Texas and is more often frequented by Texans hopping across the border than by people using Mexico City as a gateway. Our approach to the northeast is therefore from Texas. The drive up the coast from Veracruz is possible, but the distances—502 km (311 mi) between Veracruz and Tampico and 1,005 km (623 mi) from Veracruz to Monterrey—may be daunting from behind the wheel.

IF YOU HAVE 3 DAYS

If you're flying, head straight for the port of **Veracruz** ①–⑤, the most Caribbean of the Gulf of Mexico cities. You'll have no problem spending two days here, enjoying the aquarium and museums, and visiting the beaches and seafood restaurants of **Boca del Río,** a small fishing village that has practically turned into a suburb of Veracruz. On Day 3, visit the village of **La Antigua** and the archaeological site of **Cempoala** ⑧, a major Totonac city.

If you're driving down from Texas, you could simply explore the area around **Monterrey** ⑯–㉓, the cultural and industrial giant of the northeast. Spend the first day walking around the Gran Plaza area, with its outstanding modern-art and history museums, and then drive to the **Cuauhtémoc Brewery** ㉑ on the outskirts of town. Devote the next two days to enjoying some of the region's natural attractions, including the **Barranca de la Huasteca** ㉔, an impressive gorge; the ancient **Grutas de García** ㉕; and the **Parque Nacional Cumbres de Monterrey** ㉖, with its spectacular waterfall.

IF YOU HAVE 6 DAYS

Start in **Veracruz** ①–⑤. On the third day drive out of the city to the cool hill towns of **Los Tuxtlas** ⑥, where you can consult a *curandero* (healer) for whatever ails you, and stay overnight by Catemaco Lake. On Day 5 make your way to the city of **Jalapa** ⑨ and visit the anthropology museum, staying overnight to enjoy the magnificent falls at **Xico.** On Day 6 head back down the coast to Veracruz, stopping on the way at **La Antigua** and **Cempoala** ⑧.

For six days in the northeast, add an excursion to **Tampico** ㉗, on the Gulf of Mexico, to the three-day jaunt. Check out sculptures of Tlazoltéotl, the pre-Hispanic Huastecan Goddess of Love, at the Museo de la Cultura Huasteca, and relax with picnicking Mexican families at Playa Miramar.

IF YOU HAVE 8 DAYS

In east central Mexico, follow the six-day itinerary above, but on Day 5 extend the trip to overnight in the picturesque colonial town of Coatepec after visiting **Xico.** The next day, go river rafting on the Río Pescados southeast of Jalapa. And on Day 7 go to **El Tajín** ⑩ ruins, overnighting in the nearby town of **Papantla de Oloarte** ⑪.

When to Tour

In Veracruz, the weather is balmy between November and April. The notorious *nortes*—chilly winds that blow in off the Gulf of Mexico—usually appear between October and February, and especially in December. Pack a sweater and light coat or jacket if you plan to travel during these months. In summer, both the temperature and humidity soar, but the frequent rains afford a respite from the heat.

A great time to visit Veracruz is the week before Ash Wednesday for the Mardi Gras *Carnaval,* Mexico's major pre-Lenten bash. It's glitzy, merry, and wild but retains a small-town ambience that keeps it saner and safer than the better-known celebrations in Río or New Orleans. The biggest problem at such times is finding a room (reserve well in advance). The same is true during Christmas as well as Easter week, when all of Mexico goes on vacation and heads for the beach. An Afro-Caribbean music and dance festival normally takes place for a week in June or July. Check in advance with tourist information or the Veracruz Cultural Center (IVEC).

The hottest months in the northeast are June through August. The cooling rains arrive in July and last through November. There are never any crowds at the border towns or in Monterrey except during major U.S. holidays, when Americans head south for a day or weekend.

THE STATE OF VERACRUZ

A long, slim crescent of land bordering the Gulf of Mexico, the state of Veracruz is often ignored by foreign travelers, many of whom do no more than glimpse it through the window of a bus barreling toward the Yucatán Peninsula. Although Veracruz's beaches don't comply with glossy magazine clichés, the state holds a romantic allure for those drawn to the sensuous joie de vivre of Veracruz city or the mysterious hill towns of the Sierra de Los Tuxtlas.

Descending from the volcanic Sierra, the Veracruz coast consists of flat lowlands that have their share of terrible heat and swamps and are pockmarked by noisome oil refineries. As you head inland—Veracruz is only 140 km (87 mi) across at its widest point—the land rises to meet the Sierra Madre Oriental range, with its stunning 6,100-m (20,130-ft) Pico de Orizaba (also called Citlaltépetl), Mexico's highest peak. In the foothills of this range, you'll find the university town and state capital Jalapa, where students share the colonial streets with local farmers marketing their crops. Jalapa is a favored place for foreigners to study Spanish, and the nearby town of Jalcomulco is a base for river-rafting explorations on the Río Pescados.

The state does have some good beaches along the coast, particularly around the northern city of Tuxpán, but the real reasons to come are the atmosphere, the history, and the people. All these are at their best in the musical, multicultural city of Veracruz, formerly the country's point of entry. Travelers arrived by ship, then boarded a train to Mexico City, often looking back wistfully. Today the fun-loving town lures domestic vacationers with its excellent seafood and lively nightlife. The city remains a working port and navy base with so many marimba bands in the *zócalo* (main square) on weekend evenings that they have to compete to be heard.

Olmec civilization thrived in Veracruz long before the rise of the Maya. The state's best-preserved ruins, at El Tajín near Papantla, are thought to have been the work of yet another (unidentified) civilization, which had its heyday later, between AD 550 and 1100. By the time Hernán

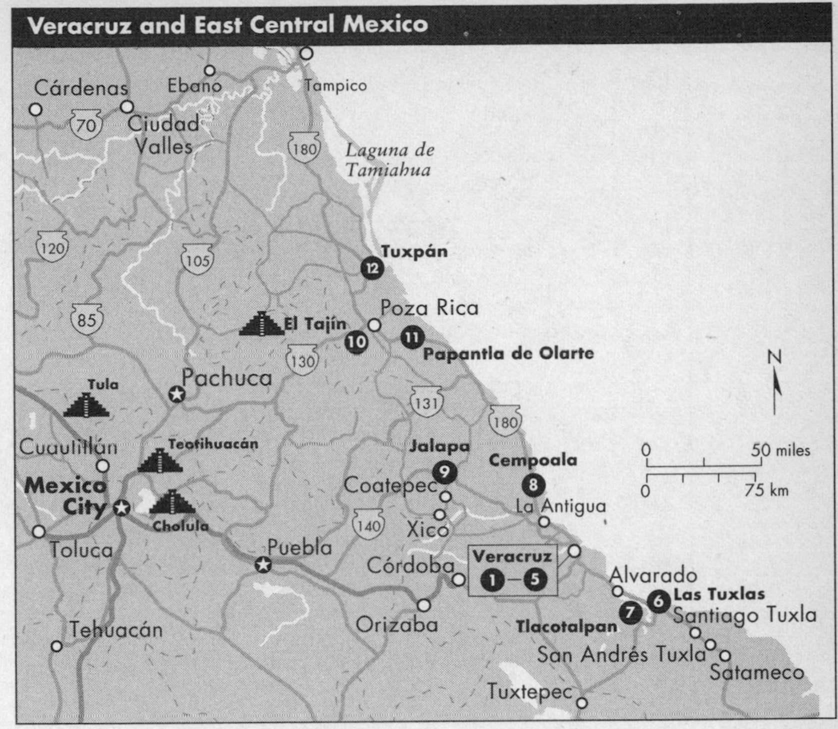

Cortés landed in Veracruz in 1519, the Aztecs held sway, but within a very short time the Indian population was decimated by war and European diseases.

The state of Veracruz played a pivotal role in Cortés's march to Tenochtitlán. A government-sponsored circuit called the Ruta de los Dioses (Route of the Gods) traces the Spanish conquistador's footsteps, from his Veracruz landing to his arrival in Mexico City, where he defeated the Aztec rulers. It's a mélange of soft adventure excursions, such as river rafting, combined with visits to colonial cities, old haciendas, and archaeological zones.

Veracruz

502 km (311 mi) south of Tampico, 345 km (214 mi) west of Mexico City.

In 1519 Cortés landed in La Antigua, a slip of a place nested in jungle, but it was Veracruz that became the major gateway for Spanish settlement of Mexico. Its name, which appears throughout Latin America, means "true cross." Pirates frequented the steamy coastal site, and their battles to intercept Spanish goods add a further swashbuckling edge to the history of the oldest port in the Americas. The Spanish brought thousands of African slaves to Veracruz; later, Cuban immigrants flooded the town. Today Veracruz city is still the most important port in Mexico, and you'll immediately sense its extroverted, open-minded character. Huge cargo ships, ocean liners, and fishing vessels crowd its harbor, and the *malecón* (paved boardwalk) is always abuzz with strollers and sailors.

Veracruz's diverse influences can be heard in its contagious music, swayed by African and Caribbean rhythms. The *Son Jarocho* is one of seven different regional variations of Mexican *sones* (musical forms) and can

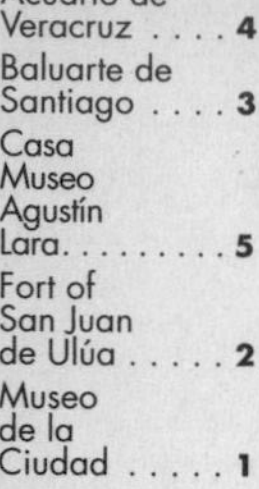

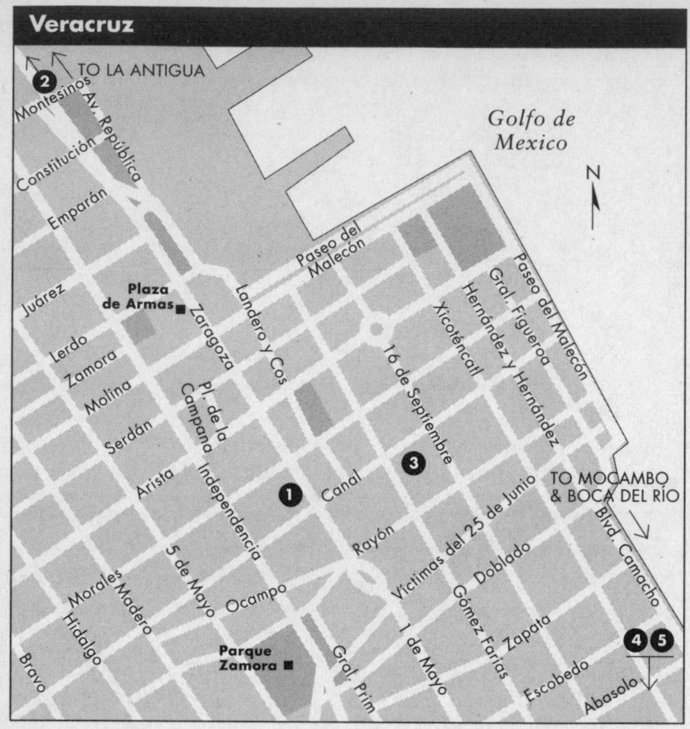

be in 4/6 or 4/4 time. Doubtless the best known is "La Bamba," which originated here and dates back to the 17th century. Traditionally, the *cantadores* (singers) create endless new *coplas* (verses); in addition to their vocal talents, they are talented wordsmiths, ad-libbing messages, jokes, and insults to the dancers or audience.

The music centers on strings and percussion, using *arpas* (harps), *jarana* (a 6–10-string small guitar), violins, *bocona* (a four-string bass), *panderos* (tambourines), and *requinto* (a small rhythm guitar). Musicians, dressed in white, will flock into restaurants to energize the atmosphere with their vigorous strumming. A young woman dancer often accompanies them, performing flamenco-like steps in a frilly frock; the *tarima* (wooden dance platform) where dancers pound out the rhythms becomes another essential instrument. In the evening at the zócalo, the famous Veracruz *marimba* adds to the throng. Bands compete for space and time, their songs often overlapping in a stirring riot of sound.

The *danzón,* a languorous two-person dance with lots of subtle hip movement, was brought to the city by refugees fleeing Cuba in 1879 following its Ten Years' War. Most ended up living outside the city walls (only Veracruz aristocrats were allowed to live inside), but the sons of the Mexican elite sneaked into the poor neighborhoods at night and eventually introduced the danzón to high society. Sensuous compared with the stiff and formal dance that had been the norm until this time, and perfectly designed for hot climates, the danzón was at first considered scandalous, but soon it won over its detractors and became the most popular dance in the city. It still fills dance halls throughout the republic, and inspired a nostalgic 1980s movie, "Danzón," with Mexican actress and politician María Rojo, largely set in the port of Veracruz. You can see people of all generations dance danzón in the Parque Zamora on Sunday evenings.

Sights to See

1 **Museo de la Ciudad.** This pristine museum is a good place to get oriented. The region's history is narrated through artifacts and displays, and scale models of the city help you get the lay of the land. Also exhibited are copies of pre-Columbian statues and contemporary art. Tours in English are available through the municipal tourism office. ✉ *Zaragoza at Morales,* ☎ *229/989–8872 or 229/989–8873.* *$2.50.* ⏲ *Wed.–Mon. 10–6.*

★ 2 **Fort of San Juan de Ulúa.** This fabulous, unique coral-stone fort has been witness to some of the most momentous events in Mexican history. During the viceregal era, Veracruz was the only east-coast port permitted to operate in New Spain and so was frequently attacked by pirates. The great island fort, the last territory in Mexico to be held by the Spanish Royalists, is a monument to that buccaneering era. A miniature city in itself, it is a maze of moats, ramparts, drawbridges, prison cells, and torture chambers, smack in the middle of the busy port area. Fortification began in 1535 under the direction of Antonio de Mendoza, the first viceroy of New Spain. A few centuries later, it was used as a prison, housing such prominent figures as Benito Juárez, who was held here by conservative dictator Santa Anna before being exiled to Louisiana in 1853. After independence, it was used in unsuccessful attempts to fight off first the invading French, the Americans, the French again, and, in 1914, the Americans yet again. The fort is under extensive renovation through at least 2005, but remains open to the public. There are no explanatory materials in place yet, but you can explore the former dungeons and store rooms, climb up on the ramparts, and wander across beautiful grassy patios. It's connected to the city center by a causeway; taking a taxi there should cost about $4. ✉ *Via causeway from downtown Veracruz,* ☎ *229/938–5151.* *$3, free Sun.* ⏲ *Tues.–Sun. 9–5.*

3 **Baluarte de Santiago.** The fortress and museum is all that's left of the old city walls; like the Fort of San Juan de Ulúa, the colonial bulwark was built as a defense against pirates, but some 100 years later, in 1635. The structure is impressively solid from the outside and romantically lighted at night. Inside is a tiny museum that has an exquisite permanent exhibition of gold pre-Hispanic jewelry—definitely Spanish plunder—which was discovered by a fisherman in the 1970s. ✉ *Francisco Canal, between Gómez Farías and 16 de Septiembre,* ☎ *229/931–1059.* *$3, free Sun.* ⏲ *Tues.–Sun. 10–4:30.*

★ 4 **Acuario de Veracruz.** Veracruz is home to one of the biggest and best aquariums in Latin America. In addition to its accessible public displays, the complex also houses a marine research center. The main exhibits include a tank with 2,000 species of marine life native to the Gulf of Mexico, including nurse sharks, manta rays, barracudas, sea turtles, and the prehistoric-looking *pejelagartos,* which resemble a combination of crocodile and fish. Check out the delicate lion fish, the various colorful and comical tropical species, and two gentle manatees—as well as the 18-ft-long outline on the far wall, above the caption THIS IS THE ACTUAL SIZE OF A GREAT WHITE SHARK CAUGHT OFF THE COAST OF TUXPÁN, VERACRUZ. ✉ *Plaza Acuario, Blvd. Manuel Avila Camacho s/n,* ☎ *229/932–7984 or 229/932–8006.* *$4.* ⏲ *Weekdays 10–7, Fri.–Sun. 10–7:30.*

5 **Casa Museo Agustín Lara.** Lara is one of Mexico's most beloved songwriters and singers. Among his occupations were piano player in a house of ill repute and bullfighter; he is also famous for marrying seven women, including Mexican screen goddess María Félix. He died in 1970 at age 73, having spent the last years of his life writing and recording

music in this house. Among his most famous songs are "María Bonita," which he dedicated to Félix, and "Granada." Newspaper clippings, caricatures, and a replica of the radio station where Lara went on the air nightly with "La Hora Azul" (The Blue Hour) are on view. ✉ *Adolfo Ruíz Cortines s/n, at Av. Manuel Avila Camacho, Boca del Río,* ☎ *229/937–0209 or 229/931–4078.* 🎫 *$3.* ⊙ *Tues.–Sat. 10–7, Sun. 10–5.*

OFF THE BEATEN PATH

LA ANTIGUA – This sleepy village, given its name by the Spaniards after they abandoned it, was the site of the first European landing in the New World and the conquistadors' capital for 75 years. The customhouse, which once had 22 rooms surrounding a huge courtyard, is worth seeing if only for its crumbling masonry, taken over by clinging vines and massive tree roots. La Antigua also has the first church of New Spain, Ermita del Rosario, a little white stucco structure that's been restored (and changed) many times over the years. Small seafood restaurants cater for weekend day-trippers when city dwellers come to swim in the river and take boat rides. La Antigua is 25 km (16 mi) northwest of Veracruz, off Highway 180 (toward Poza Rica). The turnoff is just past the toll booth. You can also take the "San Juan De Ulúa" bus from Av. República; it costs about $1.50.

Beaches

Veracruz City's beaches are not particularly inviting, being on the brownish side of gold, with polluted water. Decent beaches with paler, finer sand begin to the south in **Mocambo,** about 7 km (4½ mi) from downtown, and get better even farther down. About 4 km (2½ mi) south of Playa Mocambo is **Boca del Río,** a small fishing village at the mouth of the Río Jamapa, which is quickly getting sucked into Veracruz's orbit. A taxi from the city center costs about $4. **Mandinga** is a farther 8 km (5 mi) south and is less frequented by tourists.

Dining and Lodging

In addition to the restaurants in central Veracruz, you'll want to head to Mocambo and Boca del Río. Boca del Río holds a spot in the *Guinness Book of Records* for the largest fish fillet stuffed with shellfish—408 ft long and weighing almost 2 tons—prepared at Pardiño's restaurant. Many restaurants here are modest but serve some of the finest seafood in Mexico.

$$–$$$$ ✕ **El Gaucho Restaurante.** Since 1983, meat-lovers have packed this cavernous family-friendly ranch-style restaurant morning, noon, and night. The epic menu lists nearly 100 dishes—from spicy chorizo and Veracruz-style tongue to chicken fajitas. The house specialty drink, *jarra de clericot* (red wine with chewy bits of watermelon, pineapple, and cantaloupe), is delicious. ✉ *Bernal Díaz del Castillo 187, at Colón,* ☎ *229/935–0411. AE, MC, V.*

$$$ ✕ **Che Tango.** The smart atmosphere and soft-hued lights at this intimate Argentine steak house near the aquarium encourage guests to linger. If the sun and surf has gone to your head, try the refreshing house cocktail—*Rosita* (a blended anise cocktail)—guaranteed to cool throbbing temples. For starters, order any of the flaky empanadas topped with a secret-recipe *chimchuri* (sauce made with olive oil and parsley). Select your cut of rib eye, tenderloin, top sirloin, or strip steak from the chilled display plate brought to your table; all are charcoal grilled to order. ✉ *Calle 16 de Septiembre 1938, at Calle Enríquez, Col. Flores Magón,* ☎ *229/932–1745 or 229/932–1756. AE, MC, V.*

$$–$$$ ★ ✕ **Pardiño's.** This modest eatery, a local favorite, is a landmark among Boca del Río's many seafood restaurants and its branches have spread throughout the republic. Plain tables in a nondescript storefront belie the elegant preparation of such dishes as crabs *salpicón* (finely chopped with cilantro, onion, and lime), grilled sea bass, and a truly memorable huachinango à la veracruzana. ✉ *Zamora 40, Boca del Río,* ☎ *229/986–0135. AE, DC, MC, V.*

$–$$$ ★ ✕ **Mariscos Villa Rica Mocambo.** Tucked away on a small street that runs parallel to Playa Mocambo, this apparently casual open-air palapa eatery is one of the best seafood restaurants in the country. A firm favorite with locals, it has a large playground for children so the cream of jarocho society can spend weekends lunching at leisure within view of the waves. Specialties include mussels, grouper, crab claws, and octopus prepared as you wish. For those who relish spicy food, the *ostiones enchilpayados* (oysters in cream and chipotle chili) are sublime. Popular bands play Thursday through Sunday from 3 to 7, so you may need a reservation on these days. ✉ *Calz. Mocambo 527, near Mocambo, Boca del Río,* ☎ *229/922–2113 or 229/922–3743. AE, DC, MC, V.*

$–$$ ✕ **La Casita Blanca.** This elegant restaurant on the ground floor of the Agustín Lara Museum is decorated with colorful murals and photographs of the popular singer. The menu consists of seafood dishes and thick cuts of steak, and includes a wonderful rendition of a local favorite—*pampano huachinango* (red snapper topped with tomatoes, onions, and herbs). ✉ *Adolfo Ruíz Cortines s/n, at Av. Manuel Avila Camacho, Boca del Río,* ☎ *229/937–1338 or 229/937–1363. AE, MC, V.*

$–$$ ★ ✕ **Gran Café del Portal.** Opened by a Spanish immigrant in 1835 in a former monastery, this most famous of Veracruz's sidewalk cafés eventually grew to cover an entire city block. Formerly Gran Café de la Parroquia, it resumed its original name after a family feud in the mid-nineties. Every Mexican president since Benito Juárez has been here and it's lively from dawn to dusk. The menu has a wide selection of egg dishes, as well as soups, sandwiches, and yet another huachinango à la veracruzana. But the *café lechero* (coffee with hot milk)—made using well-guarded family secrets—is the real draw. ✉ *Independencia 1185, across from cathedral,* ☎ *229/931–2751. No credit cards.*

$–$$ ★ ✕ **El Rincón.** This elegant restaurant fulfills its aim to be a little European corner in Veracruz. Chef-owner José Alonso prepares delicately balanced Mediterranean dishes; the salmon fusilli with white wine and tarragon is exquisite, and the saffron shrimp is becoming a local favorite. The fresh salad bar is a rare treat in the area. Musicians perform on Friday and Saturday. ✉ *Calz. Mocambo 1, at Gaviotas, Playa de Oro, Boca del Río,* ☎ *229/921–6001. AE, DC, MC, V.*

$–$$ ✕ **Villa Marina Shrimp and Steak House.** You'll find this laid-back restaurant sitting on stilts above the water just off the *malecón* (boardwalk). Waiters bring platters of the day's catch to the table for you to choose from—fresh lobster, shrimp, clams, and sea bass. Then you get to ponder the 18 *al gusto* ways your selection can be cooked—breaded, grilled, sautéed in garlic, with cheese sauce, and so on. The menu also lists various beef cuts and pasta dishes. Enjoy live music Friday and Saturday, 3 PM to closing. ✉ *Av. Manuel Avila Camacho s/n,* ☎ *229/935–1034. MC, V.*

$$$$ **Fiesta Americana.** This splashy hotel on Playa Costa de Oro has the best business facilities in the state of Veracruz. It has seven floors and miles of marble corridors, all of which seem to lead to the giant serpentine pool and lush gardens facing the ocean. Rooms have terraces; voice mail; closet safes; and luxurious bathrooms with tubs, phones, audio systems, and hair dryers. Guests have access to a 9-hole golf course 20 minutes away. No-smoking rooms and wheelchair-accessible units are available. ✉ *Blvd. Manuel Avila Camacho at Boca del Rio, Fracc. Costa de Oro 94299,* ☎ *229/989–8989 or 800/343–7821,* FAX *229/989–8907,* WEB *www.fiestaamericana.com.mx. 211 rooms, 22 suites. 4* *restaurants, room service, in-room safes, tennis court, indoor-outdoor pool, 3 hot tubs, massage, dive shop, 2 bars, shops, baby-sitting, children's programs (ages 4 and up), business services, meeting rooms, free parking, no-smoking rooms. AE, DC, MC, V.*

$$$ ★ **Hotel Emporio.** The lobby of this large, elegant hotel on the malecón is a dramatic sweep of marble and potted palms. Some of the immaculate, light-filled rooms have superb harbor views and ample balconies; all have marble bathrooms with bathtubs (those in the suites are hot tubs), satellite TVs, and air-conditioning. Dine in the popular restaurant, which is decorated in neoclassical French style, or in the shade of an umbrella at any of the hotel's three pools (one is equipped with a waterfall, slides, and a miniature "ship" for kids). ✉ *Paseo del Malecón 244, 91700,* ☎ *229/932–2222, 229/932–0020, or 800/295–2000,* FAX *229/932–5752,* WEB *www.hotelemporio.onmex.com. 182 rooms, 23 suites. Restaurant, coffee shop, 3 pools, gym, sauna, bar, shops, playground, business center, meeting rooms, free parking. AE, MC, V.*

$$$ **Torremar.** The lobby in this deluxe high-rise resort on Playa Mocambo is adorned with glass sculptures and pastel oil paintings. Suites have small balconies with fantastic views of the Gulf of Mexico. An executive floor, with special concierge service and complimentary breakfast, is also available. The cascading poolside fountain and the organized activities in the play area make this a good bet for families traveling with young children. ✉ *Adolfo Ruíz Cortines 4300, Playa Mocambo, Boca del Río 94260,* ☎ *229/989–2100 or 800/712–9900,* FAX *229/989–2121,* WEB *www.torremar.com. 212 rooms, 18 suites. Restaurant, room service, 2 pools, gym, bar, baby-sitting, children's programs (ages 3–11), laundry service, concierge floor, car rental, free parking. AE, DC, MC, V.*

$$–$$$ **Hotel Lois.** For those with a sense of humor, this swanky Boca del Río hotel is an over-the-top mishmash of art deco, '50s kitsch, and riotous neon colors. The coffee shop alone has sparkling ceilings, lavender Naugahyde chairs, etched-glass windows, several random Roman columns, and lots of gleaming chrome. Guest rooms are more conventional, with a subdued pastel palette, rattan furniture, and cable TVs. ✉ *Adolfo Ruíz Cortines 10, Boca del Río 94249,* ☎ *229/937–8290 or 800/712–9136,* FAX *229/937–8089,* WEB *www.hotellois.com. 112 rooms, 17 suites. Restaurant, coffee shop, room service, in-room safes, minibars, pool, gym, hair salon, sauna, billiards, squash, 2 bars, baby-sitting, children's programs (ages 3–9), meeting room, car rental, free parking. AE, MC, V.*

$$ **Calinda Veracruz.** The rooftop patio (with a pool) at the Calinda has a fantastic view of the zócalo. Immaculate rooms have cool marble floors, bright-peach walls, cable TVs, and phones. Downstairs, Sanborns offers a variety of foreign magazines, candies, and toiletries. ✉ *Av. Independencia s/n, at the corner of Miguel Lerdo 91700,* ☎ *229/931–2233 or 800/290–0000,* FAX *229/931–5134. 116 rooms, 5 master suites, 5 junior suites. Restaurant, cafeteria, room service, pool, laundry service, free parking. AE, MC, V.*

$$ ★ **Hotel Hawaii.** This sweet hotel with a prime location on the malecón is one of the best deals in town, offering comfort, class, and personalized service at a reasonable price. Rooms are impeccably maintained and come with air-conditioning, phone, and cable TV. The staff is eager to please, and there's always a bowl of flowers at the check-in desk. You can have all the free coffee and ice cream you want at the snug ground-floor coffee shop; maps are available for the asking; and the management also sees to it that each guest receives a bag of Veracruz coffee to take home. ✉ *Paseo del Malecón 458, 91700,* ☎ *229/931–*

0427, FAX 229/932–5524. 32 rooms. Coffee shop, room service, in-room safes, indoor pool, laundry service, free parking. AE, MC, V.

$$ **Hotel Ruiz Millàn.** Although guest rooms in this multistory waterfront hotel are on the small side, they are clean, comfortable, and modern. (Ask for a newly remodeled one.) All have TVs (local stations only), phones, air-conditioning, balconies, ample closet space, and sizable bathrooms. The invitingly cool marble-floor lobby is usually crowded with Mexican businesspeople, and the hotel itself has the amenities of a more expensive establishment, including an indoor pool, a pleasant restaurant, and free covered parking. ✉ *Paseo del Malecón 432, 91700,* ☎ *229/932–6707. 69 rooms, 19 suites. Restaurant, room service, indoor pool, meeting room, free parking. AE, MC, V.*

$$ **Villa del Mar.** This unassuming hotel, across from one of the nicer sections of the downtown beach, is a good place to bring children. The standard, motel-style rooms are spacious and comfortable and surround a garden with a tennis court, pool, and small playground. Accommodations have TVs, phones, and air-conditioning. A number of bungalows (accommodating up to five people) are also available: they aren't air-conditioned and are a bit gloomy, but some have kitchenettes. Breakfast is included in the room rate. ✉ *Blvd. Avila Camacho at Bartolomé de las Casas, 91910,* ☎ *229/931–3366,* FAX *229/932–7135. 91 rooms, 14 bungalows. Restaurant, tennis court, pool, hot tub, bar, playground, laundry service, free parking. MC, V.*

$ **Hotel Concha Dorada.** The basically characterless Concha Dorada has the cheapest accommodations on the zócalo. Rooms are cramped but brightly painted, and all have cable TVs, phones, and air-conditioning. Ask for an inside room to avoid the marimba battles that last until the wee hours. The downstairs restaurant–sidewalk café serves simple fare and is especially popular (noisy) at lunchtime and on weekend nights. ✉ *Miguel Lerdo 77, near Zaragoza, 91700,* ☎ *229/931–2996 or 800/712–5342,* FAX *229/931–3246. 46 rooms, 2 suites. Restaurant, room service, bar, laundry service. AE, MC, V.*

Nightlife and the Arts

The **Plaza de Armas** (or *zócalo*) is a pulsing Babel of marimba, norteño music, hustling, and dating (to put it politely) every night, with plenty of kids and clowns in attendance, too. Every Tuesday, Friday, and Saturday night after 8, a local troupe, many elderly, dressed in white performs danzón on stage. On Sunday night, there's danzón at **Parque Zamora** from 6 to 9. The **Instituto Veracruzo de Cultura** (Veracruz Cultural Institute; ✉ Calles Canal and Zaragoza, ☎ 229/931–6967) offers danzón classes for a minimal fee.

For authentic Cuban music, head for the unpretentious **El Rincón de la Trova** (✉ Callejón de Lagunilla 59, ☎ no phone), where people of all ages gather Thursday through Saturday to dance to famous tropical bands until the wee hours; the floors are concrete and the ambience is fun and strictly local. El Rincón de la Trova's six-day Cuban music festival in November draws performers and fans from all over Mexico and the Caribbean.

Discos and video bars are plentiful along the waterfront. Most are packed Friday and Saturday nights with a young, largely local crowd. **Ocean** (✉ Adolfo Ruíz Cortines 8, at Avila Camacho, ☎ 229/935–2390) is a flashy, modern discotheque. **Carioca** (✉ Adolfo Ruíz Cortines 10, at Avila Camacho, ☎ 229/937–8290) is in the wildly decorated Hotel Lois and has salsa dancing and live music Thursday through Sunday starting at 9. **Blue Ocean** (✉ Avila Camacho 9, ☎ 229/922–0355) is a tropical-theme video bar open on Friday and Saturday, replete with rock sculptures, waterfalls, and a light show.

Outdoor Activities and Sports

Deep-sea fishing is popular in Veracruz. An annual **regatta** from the port of Galveston in Texas to the port of Veracruz takes place at the end of May. Check with the Mexican Government Tourist Office (☏ 713/780–3740 in Houston) for details.

Shopping

Stands lining the **malecón** sell a variety of ocean-related items: seashells and beauty creams and powders derived from them, black-coral jewelry, ships-in-a-bottle. You'll also find Coatepec coffee, T-shirts, bloody crucifixes, and tacky stuffed frogs, iguanas, and armadillos. The **Plaza de las Artesanías** market on the malecón purveys high-quality goods, including leather and jewelry—with high prices to match. For an authentic slice of Mexican daily life, head for the wildly vibrant and chaotic **Mercado Hidalgo** (✉ Bounded by Calles Cortés, Soto, Madero, and Hidalgo), where you'll find artful displays of strawberries and chilies beside heaps of mysterious medicinal herbs and platters of cow eyeballs and chicken feet. One of the more unusual shops in town is in the aquarium: **Fiora** (✉ Plaza Acuario, Blvd. Manuel Avila Camacho s/n, ☏ 229/932–9950) sells beautiful jewelry designed from miniature flowers grown in Veracruz.

Veracruzanos have adopted the fashion of neighboring Yucatán, and its famous embroidered guayabera shirts are as popular here as mariscos. For the best-quality guayabera shirts in the area, visit **Guayaberas Fina Cab** (✉ Av. Zaragoza 233, between Calles Arista and Serdán, ☏ 229/931–8427). This family-run shop has a great selection of hand-stitched shirts and dresses, with embroidery ranging from basic interlocking cables to elaborate floral designs. **El Mayab** (✉ Calle Zamora 78, at Av. Zaragoza, ☏ no phone) has machine-produced guayaberas, which go for less than the hand-embroidered variety.

With its sizable Cuban population, Veracruz does a brisk business in cigars. Around Plaza de Armas, there are plenty of streetside stands that specialize in both Mexican and Caribbean tobacco. For the largest variety of cigars, try the small kiosk on Avenida Independencia, in front of Gran Café del Portal; it sells Cuban Cohibas for less than a buck. Although Cuban smokes are the big draw for cigar-puffing tourists, keep in mind that Veracruz upholds its own proud tradition in the tobacco trade. **Cubahi** (✉ Av. Sarmiento 59, ☏ no phone) offers the finest local-tobacco products, and owner José Antonio Sarmiento is happy to make a house call to your hotel.

Los Tuxtlas

❻ *140 km (87 mi) south of Veracruz.*

Lush and mysterious, Los Tuxtlas is a hilly region where a small volcanic mountain range, the Sierra de Los Tuxtlas, meets the sea. Lakes, waterfalls, rivers, mineral springs, fishing villages, and quiet beaches make it a popular stopover for travelers heading east from Mexico City to the Yucatán. The region's three principal towns—**Santiago Tuxtla, San Andrés Tuxtla,** and **Catemaco**—are carved into the mountainsides some 600 ft above sea level, lending them a freshness even in summer that's the envy of the perspiring masses on the coastal plain. The cool, gray fog that slips over the mountains and lakes provides the perfect setting for Los Tuxtlas' most famous attraction: the *brujos* (witches), also called *curanderos* (healers). Conventional medicine failed to penetrate this jungle area until the 1940s, so the folk traditions have survived, making use of herbal remedies (typically using sweet basil, rosemary, and ingredients of doubtful origin), *limpias* (cleansings), and spells, both for good and for evil. Los Tuxtlas is also known for its cigars; the town of San Andrés Tuxtla makes a famous hand-rolled variety, which comes in several sizes. Tours of the cigar factories can be arranged just by showing up. **Te-Amo** (✉ Blvd. 5 de Febrero 10) is just outside San Andrés Tuxtla on the highway to Catemaco and Santa Clara, on the bypass road. All the factories have stores open to the public.

Although much of the architecture here in Los Tuxtlas is of the 1960s school of looming concrete, all three towns are laid out in the colonial style around a main plaza and a church and have a certain amount of charm, especially Santiago Tuxtla. The Olmec civilization, Mexico's oldest, flourished here between 900 and 600 BC, and Olmec artifacts and small ruins abound. A huge stone Olmec head dominates the zócalo at Santiago Tuxtla, and 21 km (13 mi) east are the ruins of **Tres Zapotes,** now unspectacular but once an important Olmec ceremonial center. The town's **Museo Regional Tuxteco** holds some valuable stone carvings and is worth a visit to learn about the region's indigenous heritage and contemporary local cultures. ✉ *Circuito Lic. Angel Carvajal s/n, opposite Parque Juárez,* ☎ *294/947–0196 or 294/947–6209.* *$2.* *Mon.–Sat. 9–6, Sun. 9–3.*

The largest of the three towns, and the only one with an ATM, is San Andrés, but Catemaco is by far the most picturesque and relaxing place to stay. Many lodgings are on the lake shore; others are grouped around the small square. Catemaco is popular among Mexicans as a summer and Christmas resort and is also the place to go for a *consulta* (consultation) with a brujo for a *limpia* (cleansing). This costs anywhere between $1 and $20, depending on your ailment, which may range from misfortune in love to financial woes to health problems, and the brujo's assessment of how much you are able to pay. Tours of Lake Catemaco, which was formed from the crater of a volcano and harbors a colorful colony of fish-eating baboons, can be arranged through most local hotels. Beyond Catemaco, a paved road continues over the hills and down to a lovely stretch of undeveloped coastline. Twenty kilometers (12½ mi) from Catemaco is the village of **Sontecomapan,** where you can take a *lancha* (launch) across the lagoon to a desolate beach. A bumpy dirt road follows the coast 19 km (12 mi) north of Sontecomapan to the sleepy fishing village of **Montepío,** which has a wide beach and a couple of inexpensive, basic hotels.

Lodging

$$ **Hotel Naciyaga.** These rustic, four-person cabins surrounded by jungle are among the most secluded and attractive accommodations on the shores of Lake Catemaco. Sheets are clean and, although there is no hot water, you can enjoy the warm, curative *temascal* steam baths on Saturdays. Lake trips by kayak, jungle tours, and limpias ($10) can be arranged. The restaurant's regional cuisine includes fish from the lake as well as the so-called *carne de chango* (monkey meat), which is actually smoked pork. ✉ *Km 7 Carretera Catemaco, 70410,* ☎ FAX *294/943–0199. 10 cabins. Restaurant. MC, V.*

Tlacotalpan

7 *90 km (56 mi) south of Veracruz.*

The name Tlacotalpan is of Nahuatl origin and means "in the middle of the earth" or "where the land is divided," referring to the settlement's location on what was then an island, between the banks of the river Paploapan and the lagoon. The old town is very pretty, with lovely streets, attractive churches and squares, and brightly painted houses, but the real attractions are the town's festivals, the most thrilling being that of

Tlacotalpan's patron saint, the Virgin de la Candelaria. Before the conquest, native inhabitants worshiped the goddess Chalchiutlicua, better known as *Encamisada de Verde* (gowned in green), who ruled bodies of water. With the arrival of the Spanish and the subsequent Catholic conversion, she was replaced by the Virgin of the Candelaria, patron saint of fishermen, whose saint's day is February 2. Tlacotalpan's fiesta begins January 31 with an equestrian parade involving hundreds of horses, followed by regattas and the famous running of the bulls through the streets. An image of the Virgin floats down the river with a candle, followed by a flotilla of little boats, and there are cockfights, musical competitions, horse races, and more parades. Other lively times to visit are Semana Santa, the week before Easter; *Carnaval,* held in May; and the fiesta of San Miguelito from September 27 to the 29. Tlacotalpan is 10 km (6 mi) south of Alvarado on Highway 180 on the dramatic road that heads inland toward Tuctepec.

Cempoala

 *42 km (26 mi) northwest of Veracruz.*

Cempoala (often spelled Zempoala) was the capital of the Totonac nation, whose influence spread throughout Veracruz in pre-Hispanic times. The name means "place of 20 waters," after the sophisticated irrigation system the Totonacs used. The site gained its role in history as the place where, in 1519, Cortés formed his first alliance with a native chief. The Totonac leader—dubbed Fat Chief by his own people because of his enormous girth—was an avowed enemy of the powerful Aztecs. At the time, the population of Cempoala was around 25,000; the alliance enlarged Cortés's paltry army of 200 men and encouraged the Spaniard to push on to Mexico City and defeat the Aztecs.

Cempoala was rediscovered by Francisco del Paso y Troncoso in 1891. Ten of the 60 to 90 structures at Cempoala have been excavated and can be visited. All are built of river stones, shells, sand, and "glue" made from the whites of turtle and bird eggs. As the story goes, when Cortés first sighted Cempoala at night, the buildings glowed white under a full moon and the conquistador thought he had discovered a city of silver.

Upon entering the ruins, you see **Circulo de los Gladiadores,** a small circle of waist-high walls to the right of center. This was the site of contests between captured prisoners of war and Totonac warriors: each prisoner was required to fight two armed warriors. One such prisoner, the son of a king from Tlaxcala, won the unfair match and became a national hero. His statue stands in a place of honor in Tlaxcala. Another small structure to the left of the circle marks the spot where an eternal flame was kept lighted during the sacred 52-year cycle of the Totonacs.

The **Templo Mayor,** the main pyramid, is the largest structure on the site. Follow the dirt path that lies straight ahead when you enter. Cortés, after gaining the allegiance of Fat Chief, placed a Christian cross atop this temple—the first gesture of this sort in New Spain—and had mass said by a Spanish priest in his company.

At the smaller **Templo de la Luna** (Temple of the Moon), to the far left of Templo Mayor, outstanding warriors were honored with the title "Eagle Knight" or "Tiger Knight" and awarded an obsidian nose ring to wear as a mark of their status. Just to the left of the Moon Temple is the **Templo del Sol** (Temple of the Sun), where the hearts and blood of sacrificial victims were placed.

Back toward the dirt road and across from it is the **Templo de la Diosa de la Muerte** (Temple of the Goddess of Death), where a statue of the pre-Hispanic deity was found along with 1,700 small idols.

There's a small on-site **museum** housed in a palapa. The voladores of Papantla usually give a performance on weekends. Well-trained guides are available, but tours are mainly in Spanish. ☎ *No phone,* WEB *www.cnca.gob.mx/cnca/inah/zonarq/zempoala.html or www.xalapa.gob.mx/zonarq/cempoala.html.* *$2, free Sun.* *Tues.–Sun. 10–5.*

Jalapa

9 *90 km (56 mi) northwest of Veracruz.*

Jalapa, which was a Totonac ceremonial center when Cortés arrived, perches on the side of a mountain between the coastal lowlands of Veracruz and the high central plateau. More than 4,000 ft above sea level, the city has a bizarre climate—sun, rain, and fog are all likely to show themselves in the course of a day. The state capital, Jalapa has been called "The Athens of Veracruz" for its thriving arts scene. The university guarantees a mixed population; wizened campesinos walking to work mix with earnest students and hippies sitting around in cafés. The town is also home to a state theater that attracts big-name performers.

Much of the city seems to have been built haphazardly, and that's the source of its charm. The hills here pose intriguing engineering problems, and major avenues tend to make 180-degree turns, following level surfaces rather than adhering to a strict grid system. In some places, the twisting cobblestone streets are bordered by 6-ft-high sidewalks to compensate for sudden sharp inclines. Locals refer to the city as a *plato roto* (broken dish) because of this scattered, logic-defying layout.

You'll often see the name of the city spelled Xalapa: Jalapa is the Hispanicized version of the original Nahuatl word. Residents of Jalapa call themselves *jalapeños.*

★ The town's prime cultural attraction is the **Museo de Antropología de Jalapa.** With 3,000 of 29,000 pieces on display, it is second only to Mexico City's archaeological museum. Its treasure trove of artifacts covers the three main pre-Hispanic cultures of Veracruz: Huasteca, Totonac, and most important, Olmec. Its three sections are filled with magnificent stone Olmec heads; carved stelae and offering bowls; terra-cotta jaguars and cross-eyed gods; cremation urns in the forms of bats and monkeys; lovely Totonac murals; and touching life-size sculptures of women who died in childbirth (the ancients elevated them to the status of goddesses). At a burial site, you can see ritually deformed skulls and ceremonial figurines. Tours by English-speaking students are available daily 11–4, but it's best to call in advance and make an appointment, as the tour schedule is unpredictable. ✉ *Av. Jalapa s/n,* ☎ *228/815–0920.* *$2.50, $15 for tour in English.* *Tues.–Sun. 9–5.*

Dining and Lodging

$–$$ ★ ✕ **La Casa de Mamá.** The dark, antique furnishings and lazy ceiling fan almost succeed in giving this popular restaurant the feel of a northern Mexican hacienda, but the incessant street noise reminds you that you're in a busy capital city. Never mind; you'll be focusing on the generous portions of charcoal-broiled steaks and the succulent shrimp and fish dishes, served with *frijoles charros* (black beans cooked in a spicy sauce) or Mexican rice. The place is known for its desserts, which include flan with caramel and bananas flambéed in brandy. ✉ *Avila Camacho 113,* ☎ *228/817–3144.* *AE, MC, V.*

$–$$ ★ **La Estancia de los Tecajetes.** For fine regional dishes with a dash of creativity, try this rustic, lodgelike restaurant overlooking the lushly tropical Parque los Tecajetes. (As it's tucked into a small strip mall, the restaurant can be a bit difficult to find.) Inside, it's cozy and relaxing, always buzzing with diners feasting on *cecina* (paper-thin beef fillet) with enchiladas, beans, and avocado and *crepa consentida* (crêpes filled with chicken and smothered in poblano chilies and cheese). Corn tortillas are made on the premises, and the walls are filled with charming sepia-tone photos of Jalapa's past. ✉ *Plaza Tecajetes, Avila Camacho 90–12,* ☎ *228/818–0732. MC, V.*

$ **La Casona del Beaterio.** In contrast to the cafeteria-style eateries along Avenida Zaragoza, La Casona dishes up fine local fare in a comfortable setting. The restaurant's two spacious rooms, surrounding a courtyard garden with a fountain, are set with sturdy wooden furniture, stained-glass windows, historical photos, and hanging plants. Breakfast specials are a steal, and the generous steak and seafood dinners, including the house specialty—*cazuela de mariscos* (stew of shrimp, octopus, and clams cooked with chipotle chilies)—draw crowds. This is java country, so the menu has a dozen different coffee and espresso concoctions. ✉ *Av. Zaragoza 20,* ☎ *228/818–2119. AE, MC, V.*

$ **La Fonda.** The entrance to this traditional breakfast-and-lunch restaurant is hidden on a small pedestrian walkway off busy Calle Enríquez, a block from Parque Juárez. Brightly colored streamers, baskets, flowers, and paintings of Jalapa churches adorn the walls, and the warm corn tortillas served with every meal are made before your eyes. The food is hearty northern Veracruzan fare: beef or chicken and beans, *nopales* (cactus strips), and/or chili are essential elements of almost every dish. ✉ *Callejón del Diamante 1, at Calle Enríquez,* ☎ *228/818–7282. No credit cards. Closed Sun. No dinner.*

$ **La Sopa.** Modest as it may look, this restaurant draws hearty eaters from all walks of life—politicians, students, and blue-collar workers—who make a beeline for the bargain *comida corrida* (fixed-price lunch). One of the best-kept secrets in town, La Sopa's four-course attraction might include carrot-and-potato soup, chicken with rice and fresh corn tortillas, and vanilla pudding served with coffee or tea. The menu features Mexican *antojitos* (appetizers) in the evening, including *chiles rellenos* (stuffed poblano chilies) and tamales. Live music fills the air Thursday (danzón), Friday (son Huasteca), and Saturday (arpa jarocho), about 7:30–11:30. ✉ *Antonio M. de Rivera 3-A, also known as Callejón del Diamante,* ☎ *228/817–8069. No credit cards. Closed Sun.*

$$$ **Fiesta Inn Xalapa.** This attractive chain hotel is a bit out of the way—in a primarily residential neighborhood 10 minutes by car from the center of town—but a good bet if you're looking for a comfortable, quiet, secure, and well-equipped base. The modern guest rooms in the two-story, colonial-style structure have satellite TVs, phones, air-conditioning, bathtubs, and plenty of morning sunlight. Airport transfers from the port of Veracruz are available for a fee. ✉ *Carretera Xalapa–Veracruz Km 2.5, Fracc. Las Animas 91000,* ☎ *228/812–7920 or 800/504–5000,* FAX *228/812–7946. 119 rooms, 3 suites. Restaurant, coffee shop, room service, in-room data ports, pool, gym, bar, free parking. AE, DC, MC, V.*

$$$ **Hotel Xalapa Finca Real.** Though its prices remain reasonable, this hotel is notably well equipped, with many of the amenities of more expensive establishments: phones, TVs, air-conditioning (in most units), bathtubs, free covered parking, and a disco. The 1960s institutional behemoth sits on a hill above Parque Los Tecajetes; though the building isn't particularly attractive, the rooms are large, sunny, and quiet. ✉ *Victoria at Bustamante, Zona Centro 91000,* ☎ *228/818–2222 or 228/*

817–7064, FAX 228/818–9424. 170 rooms, 28 suites, 2 villas. 2 restaurants, room service, pool, bar, dance club, baby-sitting, playground, laundry service, meeting rooms, car rental, free parking. AE, DC, MC, V.

$$$ ★ **Posada Coatepec.** Once the home of a coffee baron, the 19th-century Posada now specializes in fine food and caters to the elite with an exquisite private villa. It has regal guest rooms, each with original tile floors, satellite TV, and a heater for Coatepec's chilly, rainy winters; ask for one away from the murmur of street noise. The lobby and courtyard are splendidly decorated with a fine collection of antiques; a bar framed by lead-crystal windows is stylishly romantic, and the heated courtyard pool draped in flowering plants is delightful. The hotel is a 15-minute drive from Jalapa. True to its roots, it can arrange tours to nearby coffee plantations. ✉ *Hidalgo 9, Coatepec 91500,* ☎ *228/816–0544, FAX 228/816–0040. 7 rooms, 16 suites. Restaurant, room service, pool, bar, laundry service. AE, MC, V.*

$$ ★ **Mesón del Alférez.** A royal lieutenant of the Spanish viceroy lived in this colonial house some 200 years ago. Now it's a gem of a hotel, restored with earthenware tiles, rustic wood, and lime pigment washes on the walls in such luminous hues as lilac, sky blue, and magenta. Rooms surround three small bougainvillea-drenched courtyards and have lovely hand-carved wood headboards, Talavera lamps, and hand-loomed bedspreads, as well as phones and TVs (local channels only). ✉ *Sebastián Camacho 2, at Zaragoza, 91000,* ☎ *228/818–6351, 228/818–0113, or 800/715–5172, FAX 228/812–4703. 15 rooms, 6 suites. Restaurant, room service, laundry service, free parking. AE, MC, V.*

$ **Hotel Posada El Virrey.** This spiffy hotel is a short walk from Parque Juárez. The rooms are quiet, but on the small side, with phones and cable TVs. Bathrooms offer the basics, with showers. Internet service is available for an extra fee. ✉ *Dr. Lucio 142, Col. Centro 4, north of Parque Juárez, 91000,* ☎ *228/818–6100. 40 rooms. Restaurant, bar, laundry service, Internet, free parking. AE, MC, V.*

Nightlife and the Arts

The **Agora** (✉ Parque Juárez, ☎ 228/818–5730) cultural center has art exhibitions and the occasional folk-music performance and shows classic and avant-garde films in its cinema club. Stop by during the day to see what's planned; it's closed Monday. The **Teatro del Estado** (✉ Ignacio de la Llave s/n, ☎ 228/817–3110) is the big, modern state theater of Veracruz. The Orquesta Sinfónica de Jalapa performs here, often giving free concerts during the off-season (early June–mid-August). Check *Diario Xalapa* (the Jalapa city newspaper in Spanish, available at newsstands) for dates and times of performances, or stop by the Agora. You might find someone who speaks English.

La 7a Estacion (✉ 20 de Noviembre near Central Camionera, ☎ 228/817–3155) draws the disco crowds on Friday and Saturday nights. **Tempo Libero** (✉ Av. Camacho 101, ☎ no phone) is a video dance bar that attracts mostly university students with thumping house-music rhythms Tuesday through Sunday. The **Bar Lovento** (✉ 20 de Noviembre Ote. 641, ☎ 228/817–8334) heats up with a salsa beat for dancing Wednesday through Saturday night. A good mix of locals, tourists, and expats jams **Bar Boulevard 93** (✉ Av. Camacho 93, ☎ no phone), a tony, neon-lit all-night club across from Parque Los Tecajetes.

Outdoor Activities and Sports

RIVER RAFTING

With its access to six good rivers for white-water rafting, Veracruz is now an established mecca for the sport in Mexico. The rivers drain the steep slopes rising up to the flanks of 18,000-ft Pico de Orizaba and are the usual tropical-storm drains: wide valley floors with shoal-like rapids at every twist and turn. The rafting high season runs from August to November, when the water is high.

The Antigua has five runs, all classed at level IV or under. The nearby Actopan is a beautiful class III stream. But for pure whitewater fun Río Pescados is the best run in the area. In the rainy season, it has some rapids on the high side of class IV, but mostly the rapids are class III. Surfing is excellent and tight turns against the towering cliffs make for some great splatting.

Many of the operators who run these trips are trained in Canada and the United States, and are highly professional. Base camps with tents, rafting equipment, and dining facilities are near the river at Jalcomulco, 42 km (26 mi) southeast of Jalapa. **Expediciones Mexico Verde** (✉ Homero 526, Int. 801, Col. Polanco, Mexico, D.F. 11560, ☎ 55/5255–4400 or 01-800/362–8800, ☎ FAX 55/5255–4465) organizes one-day or overnight rafting trips to Río Pescados. **Quest Expeditions Inc.** (✉ Box 499, Benton, TN 37307, ☎ 800/277–4537, FAX 423/338–0283, WEB www.questexpeditions.com) leads multiday trips to Actopan and Río Pescados. On trips led by **RioAventura** (✉ Business Room 20 E, Las Americas Shopping Mall, Boca del Rio, Veracruz, ☎ 229/922–8640, FAX 229/922–8641, WEB www.rioaventura.com.mx), you can combine rafting with other sports.

Shopping

Mexico's finest export coffee is grown in this region, specifically in the highlands around the picturesque colonial towns of Coatepec and Xico, less than 10 km (6 mi) from Jalapa. Shops selling the prized *café de altura* (coffee of the highlands) abound in the main squares of both places. **Cafécali** (✉ Callejón del Diamante 2, 4, and 6, ☎ 228/818–1339) offers a wide selection of excellent coffee at competitive prices. **Café Colón** (✉ Calle Primo Verdad 15, between Avs. Zaragoza and Enríquez, ☎ 228/817–6097) in Jalapa sells 20 varieties of coffee for about $3 a pound.

Callejón del Diamante, also known as Antonio M. Rivera, is a charming pedestrian street with vendors hawking a variety of wares: cheap jewelry, keepsakes, books, and fleece-lined slippers among them.

The **Mercado Juareguí** (✉ Av. Revolución and Calle Altamirano), open daily, is a wild indoor bazaar with everything from jewelry, blankets, and fresh vegetables to some rather dubious-looking natural "healing" potions and supposedly aphrodisiacal body pastes.

Side Trip to Xico

19 km (12 mi) south of Jalapa on road to Coatepec.

If you close your eyes and try to imagine the ideal Mexican small town, it couldn't be any more perfect than Xico. Aside from the occasional passing automobile, this village seems untouched by time; donkeys hauling burlap sacks of fresh beans clip-clop along the quaint cobblestone streets, followed by coffee-picking locals, machetes tied to their waists with red sashes. Lying in coffee country at the base of the mist-filled Perote foothills, Xico is famous for its native cuisine (*mole xiqueno,* or simply *mole de xico,* a tasty mix that includes poblano chili and chocolate sauce) and its raucous summer festival (beginning July 22) celebrating the town's patron saint, Mary Magdalene.

But Xico is perhaps even better known for its natural wonders, notably the **Cascada de Texolo,** a majestic waterfall set in a deep gorge of tropical greenery. The setting for much of the 1984 film *Romanc-*

ing the Stone, this lush, scenic area is great for exploring; numerous paths lead off from the main falls through forests of banana trees to smaller cascades and crystal-blue pools, perfect for a refreshing swim. There's also a steep staircase that will take you from the observation deck to the base of the falls, a favorite spot for picnicking locals.

The falls are about 3 km (2 mi) from the center of town. To reach them, start from the red-and-white church where Calles Zaragosa and Matamoros meet and follow the cobblestone street downhill, bearing right when you reach the small roadside shrine to the Virgin Mary. Continue through the coffee plantations, following the signs for "La Cascada" until you reach the main observation deck, which includes a small restaurant (and a view of the nearby hydroelectric dam). Entry is free.

El Tajín

★ ⑩ *13 km (8 mi) west of Papantla.*

The extensive ruins of El Tajín—the Totonac word means "thunder"—express the highest degree of artistry of any ancient city in the coastal area. The city remained hidden until 1785, when a Spanish engineer came upon it. Early theories attributed the complex—believed to be a religious center—to a settlement of Maya-related Huasteca, one of the most important cultures of the Veracruz area. Because of its immense size and unique architecture, however, scholars now believe it may have been built by a distinct El Tajín tribe related to the Maya. Although much of the site has been restored, many structures are still hidden under thick jungle growth.

El Tajín is thought to have reached its peak between AD 600 and 1200. During this time, hundreds of structures of native sandstone were built here, including temples, double-storied palaces, ball courts, large retaining walls, and hundreds of houses. But El Tajín was already an important religious and administrative center during the first three centuries AD. Its influence is in part attributed to the fact that it had large reserves of cacao beans, used as money in pre-Hispanic times.

Evidence suggests that the southern half of the uncovered ruins—the area around the lower plaza—was reserved for ceremonial purposes. Its centerpiece is the 60-ft-high **Pyramid of the Niches,** surely one of the finest pre-Columbian buildings in Mexico. The finely wrought seven-level structure has 365 coffers—one for each day of the solar year—built-in around its seven friezes. The reliefs on the pyramid depict the ruler, 13-Rabbit—all the rulers' names were associated with sacred animals—and allude also to the El Tajín tribe's main god, the benign Quetzalcóatl. One panel on the pyramid tells the tale of heroic human sacrifice and of the soul's imminent descent to the underworld, where it is rewarded with the gift from the gods of sacred *pulque,* a milky alcoholic beverage made from cactus.

Just south of the pyramid is a series of 10 I-shape **ball courts**—more than at any other site in Mesoamerica—where the sacred pre-Columbian ball game was played. The walls are covered with relief sculpture. The game, played throughout Mesoamerica, is similar in some ways to soccer—players used a hard rubber ball that could not be touched with the hands, and suited up in knee pads and body protectors—but far more deadly. Intricate carvings at this and other complexes indicate that the games ended with human sacrifice. It's still a subject of debate whether the winner or loser of the match was the sacrificial victim. It is surmised that the players may have been high-standing members of the priest or warrior classes.

El Tajín Chico, to the north, is thought to have been the secular part of the city, administrative and residential. It was likely the location of the elite's living quarters. Floors and roofing were made with a pre-Columbian concrete of volcanic rock and limestone. The most important structure here is the Complejo de los Columnos (Complex of the Columns). The columns once held up the concrete ceilings, but early settlers in Papantla removed the ceiling stones to construct houses.

You can leave bags at the visitor's center at the entrance, which includes a restaurant and small museum that displays some pottery and sculpture and tells what little is known of the site. But because guided tours of El Tajín aren't available, the rest is left to your imagination. A *voladores* (Papantla flyers) show normally takes place at midday. The area outside is lined with covered stalls that sell inexpensive meals and tacky souvenirs. Start early to avoid the midday sun, and take water, hat, and sunblock. If you're prepared to work your way through the thick jungle, you can see some more recent finds along the dirt paths that lead over the nearby ridges. ☎ *No phone,* WEB *www.tourbymexico.com/veracruz/tajin/tajin.htm and www.coacade.uv.mx/turist/tajin.html (in Spanish).* *$3, free Sun.* ⏲ *Daily 9–5.*

Papantla de Olarte

⓫ *250 km (155 mi) northwest of Veracruz.*

Papantla de Olarte sits amid tropical hills, the center of a vanilla-producing region; vanilla products are sold in every corner store and restaurant. A distinctive mix of Spanish colonial and indigenous influence can be seen here: Totonac men in flowing white pants lead their donkeys through the crowded streets, and palm trees shade the traditional, tile zócalo. A good overnight base for visiting El Tajín, Papantla is also known for its voladores, who twirl off an 82-ft pole next to the town's ornate cathedral. This ritual was originally performed as a tribute to the god of sun and rain. The four voladores begin the dance on a platform at the top of the ceremonial pole, each facing one of the cardinal directions. They start their descent from the side of the platform facing east—where the sun rises and the world awakes—twisting left for 13 full rotations each. Between them, the four flyers circle the pole 52 times, representing the sacred 52-year cycle of the Totonacs (the Maya calendar had the same 52-year cycle). A fifth man, the prayer giver, sits atop the pole, playing a small flute while keeping rhythm on a drum as the flyers descend. Originally the ceremony was held on the vernal equinox, but now the voladores fly for the crowds every Saturday and Sunday at 12:45 PM and give special shows on Corpus Christi (late May) when the town bursts into life with parades and traditional dances.

Dining and Lodging

$$ ✕ **Plaza Pardo.** From the balcony of this colorful second-story café you can watch the happenings in the zócalo. Bright yellow tablecloths adorn the tables where house specialties—including *tampiqueña* (Tampico-style fillet of beef), *bocoles* (chicken- or cheese-stuffed gordita), and *rellenos al gusto* (green chilies stuffed with your choice of chicken, cheese, or beef)—are served. ✉ *Enríquez 105 Altos A,* ☎ *784/842–0059. No credit cards.*

$ ★ ✕ **Restaurante Sorrento.** With more than 200 items on the menu, this is the most popular restaurant in Papantla, crowded with locals who come to enjoy the cheap regional seafood and to catch a few minutes of the *telenovela* (soap opera) on the corner set. It's ideal for people-watching, as large picture windows overlook the zócalo and the voladores' ceremonial pole. ✉ *Enríquez 105,* ☎ *784/842–0067. No credit cards.*

$$ **Hotel Tajín.** The trick at the Tajín is getting the right room; be sure to ask for the "superior" rooms, which come with air-conditioning (and possibly a less lumpy bed). The phones don't always work, but the rooms are spotless and have cable TVs. The hillside perch makes for nice views, and there's usually an English-speaking staff member at the reception desk. ✉ *Nuñez y Domínguez 104, 93400,* ☎ *784/842–0121,* FAX *784/842–1062. 59 rooms. Hair salon. MC, V.*

$ **Hotel Premier.** Right on Papantla's zócalo, the Premier is not only the town's swankiest hotel, it's a real bargain to boot. The lobby is lined with mirrors and etched glass and furnished with small purple chairs. The rooms are spotless and good-sized, with tiny balconies overlooking the square. Amenities include tile bathrooms, air-conditioning, phones, and satellite TVs. ✉ *Enríquez 103, 93400,* ☎ *784/842–1645 or 784/842–4213,* FAX *784/842–4214. 16 rooms, 4 suites. Room service. MC, V.*

Shopping

A half block downhill from the zócalo, along Avenida 20 de Noviembre, is a teeming **street market** selling native Totonac costumes, carvings, woven baskets, handbags, cassettes, and food. The quality is not great, but if you poke around, you can find some good deals. The real draw is vanilla, the chief product of this region, which is sold in every conceivable form—beans and extract are common, but for a real souvenir, pick up a box of vanilla-flavored cigars.

Tuxpán

12 *193 km (120 mi) south of Tampico, 309 km (192 mi) northwest of Veracruz, 89 km (55 mi) north of Papantla.*

Tuxpán is a peaceful riverside town with graceful winding streets—and the Río Tuxpán is even clean enough to swim in. **Juárez,** the main street, running parallel to the river, is lined with diners, hotels, and shops. The **Parque Reforma** is the center of social activity in town, with more than 100 tables set around a hub of cafés and fruit stands. It has a memorial to Fausto Vega Santander, a member of the 201st Squadron of the Mexican Air Force and the first Mexican to be killed in combat during World War II. Launches shuttle passengers across the river to the **Casa de Fidel Castro,** where Castro lived for a time while planning the overthrow of Fulgencio Batista. A replica of the *Granma,* the ship that carried Fidel's men from Tuxpán to Cuba, molders outside. Inside, the casa is bare save some black-and-white photos of Fidel.

Beaches

Tuxpán's main appeal is the untouristed miles of beaches that begin 7 km (4½ mi) east of town. The first, and most accessible beach from Tuxpán, is **Playa Tuxpán.** The surf here isn't huge, but there's enough action to warrant breaking out your surf or boogie board. Of the palapas on Playa Tuxpán, the most established is Restaurant Miramar, which has an extensive menu and also provides umbrella-covered beach chairs for customers.

Dining and Lodging

$ ✕ **Antonio's.** Antonio's is a quiet, comparatively elegant restaurant with a varied menu. The cazuela de mariscos is excellent, as are the prawns, served grilled or in garlic sauce. Enjoy a cocktail from the full bar. ✉ *Av. Juárez 25, at Garizurieta,* ☎ *783/834–1602. AE, MC, V.*

$ ✕ **Berra de Mariscos.** Don't be fooled by the white plastic tables and the bare-bones decor: the quality of the seafood dishes here easily rivals fancier places in town. Hunker down with a cold beer and a plate of *pulpos* (octopus cooked with onions, butter, and garlic) or the house specialty, *camarones a la diabla* (a spicy concoction of grilled prawns and chilies). All meals are preceded by a generous serving of freshly made tortilla chips. ✉ *Av. Juárez 44, at Calle Mina,* ☎ *783/834–1061. No credit cards.*

$$ ★ **Hotel Florida.** Don't be deceived by the harsh fluorescent light in the lobby: this is the best hotel deal in downtown Tuxpán. The rooms, all with phones, cable TV, and air-conditioning, are decorated in soft pastels; most have ample light and space as well as immaculate bathrooms. Outer rooms have terraces and views of the cathedral and waterfront. The staff is remarkably friendly. ✉ *Av. Juárez 23, across from cathedral, 92800,* ☎ *783/834–0222 or 783/834–0602,* FAX *783/834–0650. 75 rooms. Restaurant, room service, bar, meeting room. DC, MC, V.*

$$ **Hotel May Palace.** The most luxurious lodgings in Tuxpán are at this hotel in the center of town, a modern five-story property geared to a business clientele. Rooms are swathed in pastels and set off by rattan furniture. All have phones, satellite TVs, and air-conditioning. Guest services include a small video bar, a restaurant specializing in seafood and regional dishes, a rooftop pool, and meeting salons. ✉ *Av. Juárez 44, facing Parque Reforma, 92800,* ☎ FAX *783/834–8882 or 783/834–4461. 68 rooms, 2 suites. Restaurant, room service, pool, gym, bar, laundry service, meeting room, free parking. AE, MC, V.*

$$ ★ **Hotel Plaza Palmas.** In a sleepy suburban neighborhood five minutes from the city center, this hostelry is a welcome respite from Tuxpán's riverfront bustle. And although the mounted stag heads overseeing the spare lobby give the Palmas a rather incongruous tropical-motel-cum-hunting-lodge quality, the quirkiness ends there. Two U-shape buildings surround a large palm-lined pool area with tables and a small seafood bar. The guest rooms are spacious, with air-conditioning, phone, and cable TV. ✉ *Galeana and Libramiento Carretera s/n, 92800,* ☎ *783/834–3529 or 783/834–3574,* FAX *783/834–3535. 98 rooms, 3 suites. Restaurant, room service, 2 tennis courts, pool, bar, playground, laundry service, meeting room. AE, MC, V.*

Outdoor Activities and Sports

WATER SPORTS

For scuba diving, head to **Tamiahua,** a small village just north of Tuxpán, where you can hire a fishing boat for the 45-minute journey to the prime diving around **Isla Lobos** (Wolf Island), a protected ecoreserve that shares its space with a military outpost and a lighthouse. In the shallow water offshore are a few shipwrecks and colorful reefs that host a large variety of sea life, including puffer fish, parrot fish, damselfish, and barracuda. Generally, the best time to dive is between May and August. **Aquasport** (☎ 783/837–0259), just west of Playa Tuxpán, arranges scuba-diving trips to Isla Lobos and also has deep-sea fishing excursions. Other outfits run trips to the island that include permits, scuba gear, lunch, and transportation.

VERACRUZ A TO Z

AIR TRAVEL TO AND FROM VERACRUZ

There are nonstop flights on Mexicana and Aeroméxico from Mexico City to Heriberto Jara International Airport about 8 km (5 mi) south of downtown Veracruz.

➤ AIRLINES AND CONTACTS: **Aeroméxico** (☎ 22/9935–0833 or 22/9935–0283, 55/5625–2622 in Mexico City; 01-800/021–2622; WEB www.aeromexico.com). **Mexicana** (☎ 22/9932–2242 or 22/9932–8699, WEB www.mexicana.com.mx).

AIRPORTS AND TRANSFERS

➤ Airport Information: **Heriberto Jara International Airport** (☎ 22/9934–5372 or 22/9934–9008).

TRANSFERS

A cab to the city center costs $8.50 and takes roughly half and hour. Taxis are readily available at the airport. No city bus serves the airport. An air-conditioned private car ($10) runs between the airport and the downtown office of Transavion.

➤ Taxis and Shuttles: **Transavion** (✉ Av. Diaz Miron 3008, ☎ 22/9937–8978).

BUS TRAVEL TO AND FROM VERACRUZ

Of Mexico City's four bus terminals, the one offering the most departures to Veracruz is the Tapo; buses leave daily about every 20 minutes. The trip takes about five hours, passing through Puebla and near the magnificent Pico de Orizaba. Veracruz's main bus terminal is about 4 km (2½ mi) south of the zócalo. The main bus company is ADO, with round-the-clock departures for Mexico City. ADO also offers first-class all-day service to Reynosa, on the Texas border. If you're headed north and east, the deluxe bus line UNO goes to Veracruz, Puebla, and Mexico City daily. Cristóbal Colón offers daily first-class service to Oaxaca. A toll free central reservations number, TicketBus, covers all lines and will take credit card bookings; you can pick up your tickets half an hour before departure.

➤ Bus Information: **Bus Terminal** (✉ Díaz Mirón 1698). **ADO** and **UNO** (☎ 22/9937–2922). **Cristóbal Colón** (☎ 22/9937–5744). **TicketBus** (☎ 01-800/702–8000).

BUS TRAVEL WITHIN VERACRUZ

ADO runs daily buses to Jalapa every 20 minutes from 6 AM to 11:30 PM. The deluxe bus line UNO also goes daily to Jalapa. Autobuses Unidos has daily second-class service to Los Tuxtlas. All buses run from Veracruz's main bus terminal.

➤ Information: **ADO** and **UNO** (☎ 22/9937–2922). **Autobuses Unidos** (☎ 22/9937–5732).

CAR RENTAL

Sun del Golfo is the only rental agency in Jalapa. Avis is the only service in the Herberto Jara International Airport, but Dollar and National are both close to the center of Veracruz. Hertz has service in Boca del Río.

➤ Major Agencies: **Avis** (✉ Heriberto Jara International Airport, ☎ 22/9932–1676). **Dollar** (✉ Víctimas del 5 y 6 de Julio 883, ☎ 22/9935–8807). **Hertz** (✉ Hotel Costa Verde, Avila Camacho 3797, Boca del Río, ☎ 22/9937–4776).

CAR TRAVEL

The city of Veracruz can be reached in about eight hours by traveling south from Tampico via Mexico 180, or in six hours from Mexico City via Mexico 150. The highways throughout the state, paved and kept up with oil money, are generally very good.

EMERGENCIES

Dial 060 in Veracruz for medical, fire, and theft emergencies. If you find yourself in a medical emergency situation, call the local Red Cross (Cruz Roja) for ambulance service. The local police can handle small incidences, but if you feel the situation could escalate, contact the Angeles Verdes (Green Angels), a highway patrol service coordinated by the tourism industry.

➤ HOSPITALS: **Hospital General de Veracruz** (✉ 20 de Noviembre s/n, Veracruz, ☎ 22/9931–7848).

➤ EMERGENCY SERVICES: **Angeles Verdes** (☎ 229/932–8498). **Jalapa Cruz Roja** (☎ 22/8817–8158). **Jalapa Police** (☎ 22/8818–7490 or 22/8818–7199). **Papantla Cruz Roja** (☎ 784/842–0126). **Papantla Police** (☎ 784/842–0075). **Tuxpán Cruz Roja** (☎ 783/834–0158). **Tuxpán Police** (☎ 783/834–0252). **Veracruz Cruz Roja** (☎ 22/9937–5500). **Veracruz Police** (✉ Playa Linda s/n, Veracruz, ☎ 22/9938–0664 or 22/9938–0693).

HEALTH

PHARMACIES

In Jalapa, Calle Enríquez is lined with pharmacies. For 24-hour service, the Farmacia Plus is your best option. Farmacia de Descuento, the largest pharmacy in Papantla, is open daily 7:30 AM–10 PM. In downtown Tuxpán, Farmacia El Fenix is open daily 8 AM–10 PM. In Veracruz, Farmacia del Ahorro is a big, convenient drugstore on the boardwalk with other branches all over town. It offers good prices and does home deliveries; it closes at 10:30 PM daily. For 24-hour home delivery in Veracruz, call Las Torres Pharmacy.

➤ PHARMACY INFORMATION: **Farmacia del Ahorro** (✉ Paseo del Malecón 342, at Calle Fariaz, Veracruz, ☎ 22/9937–3525). **Farmacia de Descuento** (✉ Gutiérrez Zamora 103, Papantla, ☎ 784/842–0640). **Farmacia El Fenix** (✉ Calle Morelos 1, at Av. Juárez, Tuxpán, ☎ 783/834–3023). **Farmacia El Fenix** (✉ Enrique 103, Zona Centro, Papantla, ☎ 784/842–0636). **Farmacia Plus** (✉ Revolución 173, Sayago, Jalapa, ☎ 22/8817–2797) **Las Torres Farmacia** (✉ Díaz Mirón 165, Veracruz, ☎ 22/9932–6363).

MAIL AND SHIPPING

Mail and fax services in Jalapa are available at the main post office. Caseta Telefonica has three computers for e-mail and Internet access, charges $1.50 an hour, and is open weekdays 7 AM–10 PM and weekends 8 AM–9 PM. Compupapel has eight computers; it's open daily 9–8:30 and charges $1.50 an hour.

Several blocks from the Papantla zócalo, PC's Palafox has 10 computers with Internet access for $1.80 an hour 8 AM–9 PM weekdays, 8–7 Saturday, and 8–5 Sunday.

The Tuxpán post office is a half block from Avenida Juárez. Internet cafés in the downtown area all charge about $1.50 an hour. Sesico, which has 10 computers, is open Monday–Saturday 9–8:30 and Sunday 10–3.

In Veracruz, the main post office is a five-block walk from the zócalo. For Internet access, Web Café has the fastest machines, for $1.80 an hour, with slightly cheaper rates for students. It's open 10–10 daily. Netcha Boys, open weekdays 9–9 and weekends noon–8, will run you $1.50 an hour for Internet access.

➤ POST OFFICES: **Jalapa post office** (✉ Av. Zamora 70, at Calle Diego Leno, Jalapa). **Tuxpán post office** (✉ Calle Morelos 12, Tuxpán). **Veracruz post office** (✉ Plaza República 213, Veracruz).

➤ INTERNET SERVICES: **Caseta Telefonica** (✉ Av. Enríquez 16, Jalapa, ☎ 22/8812–2462). **Compupapel** (✉ Calle Primo Verdad 23, at Av. Zaragoza, Jalapa, ☎ 22/8817–2322). **PC's Palafox** (✉ Aquiles Serdán 500, at Calle Galeana, Papantla, ☎ 784/842–1357). **NetchaBoys** (✉ Calle Miguel Lerdo 369, Veracruz, ☎ no phone). **Web Café** (✉ Calle Rayon 579-A, between Avs. Independencia and Zaragoza, Veracruz, ☎ no phone). **Sesico** (✉ Av. Juárez 52, off Parque Reforma, Tuxpán, ☎ 783/834–4505).

MONEY MATTERS

About seven blocks from Jalapa's Parque Juárez, Casa de Cambio Monendes Internacional has good rates; it's open 9–3 and 5–7:30 weekdays. You can also change money in the morning at several banks on Parque Juárez. Most have 24-hour ATMs.

There are plenty of banks surrounding the Papantla zócalo, most of which change money weekday mornings. Banamex changes both cash and traveler's checks weekdays 9–noon and has a 24-hour ATM that accepts Cirrus, Plus, Visa, and MasterCard.

The Tuxpán Banamex changes cash and traveler's checks 9–5 weekdays; it has a 24-hour ATM. Bancomer has a 24-hour ATM and changes cash and traveler's checks weekdays 8:30–2:30.

The best rates in Veracruz are at Bancomer, but money-changing hours are limited to 9–noon weekdays, so you'll have to arrive early to make it through the lines. The Casa de Cambio Puebla is open weekdays 9–6. Or use the ATMs that are readily available downtown.
➤ BANKS: **Banamex** (✉ Enríquez 102, Papantla, ☎ 784/842–0189; ✉ Av. Juárez at Calle Corregidora, Tuxpán, ☎ 783/834–7907). **Bancomer** (✉ Av. Juárez at Escuela Médico Militar, Tuxpán, ☎ 783/834–0009; ✉ Av. Juárez at Independencia, Veracruz, ☎ 22/9931–0095 or 22/9989–8000). **Casa de Cambio Monedas Internacionales** (✉ Elustres 48, Jalapa, ☎ 22/8817–2060). **Casa de Cambio Puebla** (✉ Av. Juárez 112, Veracruz, ☎ 22/9931–2450).

SIGHTSEEING TOURS

Expediciones Mexico Verde has river rafting along the Río Pescados near Jalapa. One-day or overnight excursions are available. All equipment, including life jackets, helmets, and oars, is provided. The outfit also runs 7- or 10-day trips on the Cortés Route, which includes Veracruz City, La Antigua, Cempoala, Jalapa, and Coatepec (in the state of Veracruz) and continues on to conquistador-related sites in the states of Tlaxcala, Puebla, and Mexico. English is spoken.

Boat tours of Veracruz's bay depart from the malecón daily 7–7. Boats leave whenever they're full, and the $2.50 half-hour ride includes a (Spanish-language) talk on Veracruz history. Longer trips to nearby Isla Verde (Green Island) and Isla de Enmedio (Middle Island) leave daily from the shack marked PASEO EN LANCHITA near Plaza Acuario. Boats wait until they're full to set off, so it's best to be in a group. The cost should be about $3–$5 per person, but feel free to bargain.

Martin Sandoval Tours has city tours of Veracruz as well as trips to El Tajín and Papantla, Los Tuxtlas, and Jalapa. Diving and fishing trips are available, too.

VIP Tours offers tours along the Route de los Dioses.
➤ FEES AND SCHEDULES: **Expediciones Mexico Verde** (✉ Homero 526, Int. 801, Col. Polanco, Mexico, D.F. 11560, ☎ 55/5255–4400 or 01-800/362–8800, ☎ FAX 55/5255–4465). **Martin Sandoval Tours** (✉ Balboa 327, between Washington and Martí, Veracruz, ☎ 22/9937–1984, ☎ FAX 22/9935–3172). **VIP Tours** (☎ 229/922–3315).

VISITOR INFORMATION

The Jalapa tourist office is in the large office building on the way out of town toward Veracruz (known as Torre Animas) and is open weekdays 9–9. There's also a Jalapa tourist information booth in front of the Palacio Municipal; it's open daily 9–9.

The Tuxpán tourist office is open daily 8–3 and 4–6.

The Veracruz Dirección Municipal de Turismo is open Monday–Saturday 9–9, Sunday 10–1.

The Instituto Veracruzo de Cultura can provide information on on exhibitions, festivals, and dance classes.

➤ TOURIST INFORMATION: **Instituto Veracruzo de Cultura** (✉ Calles Canal and Zaragoza, Veracruz, ☎ 229/931–6967). **Jalapa tourist information booth** (✉ Calle Enríquez 14, Jalapa, ☎ no phone). **Jalapa tourist office** (✉ Blvd. Cristóbal Colón 5, Jardines de las Animas, Jalapa, ☎ 22/8812–8500 Ext. 130, FAX 22/8812–5936). **Tuxpán tourist office** (✉ Av. Juárez 26, Tuxpán, ☎ 783/834–0177). **Veracruz Dirección Municipal de Turismo** (✉ Palacio Municipal on zócalo, Veracruz, ☎ 22/9922–2314, FAX 22/9932–7593).

THE NORTHEAST

Few travelers go out of their way to visit northeastern Mexico. The arid area is becoming increasingly industrial as multinational companies establish more *maquiladoras* (foreign-owned factories in duty-free zones) along the border, often creating grim living conditions for the maquila workers, who come from all over Mexico.

But day- and weekend-trippers from Texas enjoy the foreign color and cuisine of border towns such as Nuevo Laredo, Matamoros, and Reynosa. And only about three hours from the border is Monterrey, a fast-paced city that's home to Mexico's major brewery, some good museums, and one of Latin America's finest universities.

Nature-lovers can enjoy the Parque Nacional Cumbres de Monterrey, northwest of the city, with its impressive Cola de Caballo waterfall. Also near Monterrey is the dramatic cut of the Barranca de la Huasteca, as well as the Grutas de García, caves with an underground lake and a stalactite and stalagmite forest. Tampico is known both for its seaside appeal and its interesting architectural sights.

Nuevo Laredo

⓭ *1½ km (1 mi) south of Laredo, Texas.*

Of all the eastern border towns, Nuevo Laredo receives the largest onslaught of American souvenir-seekers. You'll find a warren of stalls and shops as well as a large crafts market concentrated on Avenida Guerrero in a seven-block stretch that extends from the International Bridge to the main plaza. Wander a few blocks off the main drag in any direction for better prices and smaller crowds.

Nuevo Laredo was founded after the Treaty of Guadalupe Hidalgo in 1848, which ended the Mexican-American War. The treaty established the Río Bravo (or Rio Grande) as the border between the two countries and forced Mexico to give up a substantial amount of territory. Many of Laredo's Mexican residents, who suddenly found themselves living in the United States, crossed the river and founded Nuevo Laredo on what had been the outskirts of town. Now, in addition to being a giant truck stop, the economy depends on gringos who head south for a few days of partying.

Dining and Lodging

$$$ ★ ✕ **Restaurant Victoria 3020.** Set back from the street and surrounded by a garden, the Victoria offers the swankiest dining in town with such rich creations as broiled New York steak topped with demiglace burgundy and marrow butter and rainbow trout in a sweet almond sauce.

The white-jacketed waiters won't let you get away without trying the *tunas borrachas victoria* (prickly pear and kiwi served with tequila and vanilla ice cream) for dessert. The candlelit courtyard in back is perfect for a quiet, romantic dinner. ✉ *Victoria 3020, at Matamoros,* ☏ *867/712–6900 or 867/713–3020. AE, MC, V.*

$$–$$$ ✕ **El Dorado.** Dating from the Prohibition era, this spot is a favorite with the Texas crowd—a hangout better known for its atmosphere than for its cuisine. Try the combination plate of grilled meat, which includes two selections of either goat, quail, or frogs' legs. ✉ *Ocampo at Calle Belden,* ☏ *867/712–0015. AE, MC, V.*

$–$$ ✕ **México Típico.** This establishment, decorated in murals from various Mexico cities, offers indoor and outdoor dining, with mariachis coming in from the street to entertain. The patio, partially covered, has a fountain. Specialties are carne asada and cabrito. True to its name, México Típico serves the typical Mexican plate of beef or chicken enchiladas with rice and refried beans. ✉ *Av. Guerrero 934,* ☏ *867/712–1525. MC, V.*

$$$ **Hotel Hacienda Real.** A carved wooden statue of San Judas and another of San Miguel guard the tiled lobby here. It's the small touches—the wrought-iron balconies, the European-style streetlamps along the walkways—that make the Hacienda Real well worth the 15-minute trip from the city center. The bright, immaculate rooms, overlooking a central garden and palm-lined pool area, all have hand-carved wooden furniture, embroidered bedspreads, large tile bathrooms, air-conditioning, and cable TV. ✉ *Av. Reforma 5530, 88280,* ☏ *867/717–0000 or 800/718–7470,* FAX *867/717–0420. 72 rooms, 2 suites. Restaurant, room service, tennis court, pool, hair salon, basketball, bar, meeting room. AE, MC, V.*

$$ **Hotel Reforma.** An older hotel a half block south of Plaza Hidalgo, Reforma has a restaurant, marble lobby, and secure parking. Rooms in the older section, although somewhat small and rather nondescript, are comfortable; the junior suites in the newer section are slightly bigger and have fresh carpets and curtains, although the hallways smell musty. All units come with shower, air-conditioning, cable TVs, and phones. ✉ *Av. Guerrero 822, 88000,* ☎ *867/712–6250,* FAX *867/712–6714. 45 rooms. Restaurant, room service, tennis court, bar. MC, V.*

Nightlife and the Arts

All of the popular dance clubs are on Avenida Guerrero in the heart of the shopping district. **Victoria's** (☎ 867/412–6900), three blocks from International Bridge 1, is a noisy favorite. The **El Dorado** (☎ 867/812–0015) is somewhat more sedate.

Shopping

On the stretch where International Bridge 1 leads into Avenida Guerrero, you'll find most of Nuevo Laredo's shops—classy and junky alike. Most stores stay open until 8 PM. **Granada** (✉ Av. Guerrero 504, ☎ 867/712–8644) has better-quality items than many of the other vendors, including lead crystal and serapes. Artisan shops selling lots of leather goods and ceramics are in the **Nuevo Mercado de la Reforma,** a market three blocks south of International Bridge 1, at Avenida Guerrero and Calle Belden. The **Maria Cristina** mall, at Avenida Guerrero 631, houses about three dozen curio outlets.

Reynosa

14 *16 km (10 mi) south of McAllen, Texas.*

Because of its manageable size and mellow attitude, Reynosa is one of the least unpleasant points of entry into Mexico. It's also a convenient starting point if you're bound for Mexico City, Monterrey, or Veracruz. That said, it has very limited charm, as it's driven economically by the petrochemicals industry. As you enter town, you'll see the **Zona Rosa** (Pink Zone) tourist district, with a few curio shops and a couple of bars and restaurants. The heart of the city, around **Plaza Principal,** is about five blocks from the International Bridge and is fairly tidy. After leaving downtown, Reynosa is a jumble of tacky border-town urban sprawl.

Plaza Principal is in many ways a typical Mexican town center, but its original colonial church has been joined like a Siamese twin to an ultramodern newer addition with arches and stained-glass windows, bordered on one side by a movie theater and on the other by a Nike outlet store. **Hidalgo Street,** a colorful pedestrian mall of shops and street vendors, leads off from the plaza. Many Texans save money by having their teeth fixed south of the Rio Grande—which explains the many dental offices you'll see in this area.

Dining and Lodging

$$$ ✕ **La Fogata.** Baby goat, stuffed goat intestines, lamb ribs, and a variety of beef cuts are all prepared on a smoky open grill at the back of this popular cabrito joint. The Herculean portions of slow-roasted meat are served in the classic northern style, with side dishes of guacamole, lime, jalapeños, and tortillas. ✉ *Matamoros 750, at Chapa,* ☎ *899/922–4772 or 899/922–8216. AE, MC, V.*

$$ ✕ **Sam's.** Wild game such as quail and dove (served November–January) and seafood are the reasons to come here. Desserts include ice cream, flan, and cheesecake. In winter, Sam's is frequented by Americans from the Rio Grande Valley and snowbirds from Minnesota. ✉ *Allende 1100,* ☎ *899/922–0034 or 899/922–3434. AE, MC, V.*

$ ✕ **Café Paris.** Grab a coffee and a pastry or the spicy *comida corrida* (lunch special) and watch the action in this boisterous café. Decorated in cool white-tile floors and equipped with strong air-conditioning, the Café Paris is an oasis from the heat; friends and lovers flock here for an afternoon of visiting amidst clanging silverware and walk-in music trios (which often include a harp). ✉ *Hidalgo 815,* ☎ *899/922–5535. No credit cards.*

$$$ **Hacienda.** Along the highway to Monterrey about 16 km (10 mi) from the U.S. border, this sparkling hotel is luxurious by Reynosa standards. Its tile lobby is decorated with colonial-style furniture and crafts, which carry over into the light-filled, cheerful rooms; all have cable TVs, air-conditioning, and direct-dial phones. ✉ *Blvd. Hidalgo 2013, 88650,* ☎ *899/924–6010,* FAX *899/923–5962. 20 rooms, 13 suites. Restaurant, room service, bar, meeting room. AE, MC, V.*

$$ **Astromundo.** Downtown and close to the market and the few good local restaurants, this popular hotel gets a lot of traffic from weekending Texans. Rooms are clean with strong air-conditioning units, and each floor is painted a different bright color. ✉ *Juárez 675, 88500,* ☎ *899/922–5625,* FAX *899/922–9888. 90 rooms, 6 suites. Restaurant, room service, bar. AE, MC, V.*

$$ **San Carlos.** This five-story hotel on the square has air-conditioned rooms with colonial-style furniture and satellite TVs. Business travelers and tourists appreciate its central location, close to the square and shopping center, and the friendly staff. ✉ *Hidalgo 970, 88500,* ☎ *899/922–1280,* ☎ FAX *899/922–4000. 66 rooms, 10 suites. Restaurant, room service, laundry service. MC, V.*

Nightlife and the Arts

The **Imperial** (✉ Av. Virreyes 1087, entrance at the back of gift shop, ☎ no phone) offers slow-dance music on weeknights and disco on weekends; don't get too close to the live chained monkey on the patio—he bites! The Zona Dorada (along Emilio Portés Gel) has the most popular discos, including **Frida's** (✉ Emilio Portés Gel 1410, ☎ 899/922–2233); it's decorated with Frida Kahlo memorabilia.

Shopping

Treviño's (✉ Av. Virreyes 1075, ☎ 899/922–1444) has a good selection of Mexican arts and crafts, sculpture, papier-mâché, perfumes, liquor, and clothing.

Matamoros

⓯ *1 km (about ½ mi) south of Brownsville, Texas.*

Matamoros, across from Brownsville, Texas, is the most historic of the border towns, dating from the 18th century. It actually is named H. Matamoros, or Heroic Matamoros, for one of the many rebellious priests who were executed by the Spanish during the War of Independence (1810–21). The first major battle of the Mexican-American War was fought here when guns in Matamoros began shelling Fort Brown on the north side of the Rio Grande. Shortly afterward, troops of Zachary Taylor occupied Matamoros and began their march south.

Today Matamoros is the commercial center of a rich agricultural area and a manufacturing center for multinational corporations. Of the three border towns, Avenida Alvaro Obregón makes the prettiest entryway. The town's best shops, restaurants, and accommodations are here.

The **Casa Mata Museum** is in the remains of Fort Mata, built in 1845 to defend the city against American invasion. The fortress wasn't completed in time, and Zachary Taylor's troops were able to capture Matamoros easily. Casa Mata now displays photos and artifacts, mostly from the Mexican Revolution. ✉ *Guatemala and Santos Degollado,* ☎ *868/813–5929.* *Free.* *Mon.–Sat. 9:30–5, Sun. 9:30–3.*

Dining and Lodging

$$–$$$$ ✕ **Garcia's.** Rebuilt and redecorated over its own parking garage, this is a romantic place for dancing and dining on lobster or steak and your choice of a dozen fine tequilas. An elevator from the garage takes you up to a gift shop with wares from all over Mexico as well as to the restaurant and a bar. ✉ *Av. Alvaro Obregón 82,* ☎ *868/812–3929 or 868/813–1833. AE, MC, V.*

$ ✕ **Los Norteños.** A goat slow-roasting over hot coals in the window is the not-so-subtle advertisement for the best cabrito in town. Don't let the mixed decor of rich wooden columns and tables beneath harsh fluorescent lights drive you away from a tender 12-ounce T-bone steak or Tampequeño Fajitas. All meals are served with a tasty black-bean soup and a heaping pile of tortillas. ✉ *Calle Matamoros between 8 and 9,* ☎ *868/813–0037. No credit cards.*

$$ ★ **Gran Hotel Residencial.** The best hotel in the city, this pleasant low-rise built along Spanish colonial lines is near the center of Matamoros. All rooms have terraces, two queen- or one king-size bed, and cable TVs. There's also a large pool and a children's play area in the lush garden. ✉ *Av. Alvaro Obregón 249, at Amapola, 87330,* ☎ *868/813–9811 or 800/718–8230,* FAX *868/813–2777. 109 rooms, 5 suites. Restaurant, room service, pool, bar, playground, meeting room, travel services, car rental. AE, MC, V.*

$$ **Hotel Plaza Matamoros.** This member of the Best Western chain has comfortable, clean rooms near the center of town. Rooms have heavy wooden furniture, thick burgundy carpeting, air-conditioning, phones, and cable TVs, and look out over a central indoor restaurant. ✉ *Calle 9 No. 1421, at Bravo, 87330,* ☎ *868/816–1696 or 868/816–1602,* FAX *868/816–1687. 40 rooms. Restaurant, room service, bar, shops, laundry service, meeting room. AE, MC, V.*

Nightlife and the Arts

The **Teatro Reforma** (✉ Calle 6 and Abasolo, ☎ 868/816–6207 or 868/812–5120), Matamoros's cultural hub, presents music and dance performances from around the country.

Garcia's offers live music in a dimly lit bar. The **Gran Hotel Residencial** is an elegant and relaxed place to stop for a drink. If you're looking for some dance action, head out to Avenida Alvaro Obregón toward the International Bridge, where you'll find several discos.

Shopping

The most appealing shops are on Avenida Alvaro Obregón, which leads from the border bridge to the center of town. The salmon-color building that houses **Garcia's** restaurant also contains a huge gift shop, where you can buy everything from big sombreros to quality tequila, silver, Oaxacan wedding dresses, and leather jackets. Across from Garcia's, **Aztlan** (✉ Av. Alvaro Obregón 75, ☎ 868/816–2947) has high-quality jewelry, pewter, clothes, some contemporary artwork, and wooden and stone carvings. **Barbara** (✉ Av. Alvaro Obregón 37, ☎ 868/816–5456) sells attractive craft items, home furnishings, good costume jewelry, and imported cosmetics. It's also the only store that prepares free margaritas for shoppers. The covered, block-long **Mercado Juárez** downtown, between Calle 9 and Matamoros, is the place to haggle for bargains on souvenirs and pottery.

Monterrey

16–23 *235 km (146 mi) southwest of Nuevo Laredo, 225 km (140 mi) west of Reynosa, 325 km (201 mi) west of Matamoros.*

Monterrey is a favorite with weekenders and "winter Texans" from the Rio Grande Valley (it's a three-hour drive from the border or a short flight from Dallas, Houston, or San Antonio). The top hotels are clustered downtown in the Zona Rosa or Barrio Antiguo (Old Quarter). Several streets, including Avenida Morelos—the main drag—are pedestrian malls.

Mexico's third-largest city and the capital of the state of Nuevo León, this industrial center is a brewer of beer and forger of steel, with nothing in the way of a laid-back lifestyle. Some of the country's most powerful captains of industry hold sway here—a fact that earned the city its nickname, the Sultan of the North. Monterrey also has the country's most sophisticated convention center, the high-tech facility called Cintermex, as well as a gigantic sports arena to host international events.

The 100-acre **Gran Plaza**—better known as Macroplaza—was part of a 1985 urban renewal project that included several grand fountains, curio shops, and museums. It extends from the modernistic Palacio Municipal (City Hall) several blocks past the newly painted cathedral, the old City Hall, and the Legislative Palace to the Palacio de Gobierno (Statehouse). It's also within walking distance of the downtown hotels.

16 Towering above the plaza, opposite the neoclassical **Palacio de Gobierno,** is a giant orange concrete slab topped by the Beacon of Commerce, a laser beam that flashes from 8 to 11 nightly. It was designed by Luis Barragán to commemorate the 100th anniversary of the founding of the city's Chamber of Commerce. The grandly lighted Palacio de Gobierno stays open all night, piping out soft classical music over a loudspeaker, and makes for a wonderful evening visit. ⊠ *Surrounded by 5 de Mayo, 15 de Mayo, and Avs. Zaragoza and Zuazua.*

★ 17 The opulent **Museo de Arte Contemporaneo** (Museum of Contemporary Art) is the principal sight on the Gran Plaza. Designed by renowned Mexican architect Ricardo Legorretta, it has 11 galleries that display cutting-edge art of Mexico and Latin America and sometimes other parts of the world. There's an outstanding collection of art books for sale at the gift shop. Listen to live music alongside a reflecting pool on the beautiful marble patio Wednesday evening (6–8) and watch the candlelit tables fill up with culture vultures sipping coffee and nibbling on pie. ⊠ *Gran Plaza at Av. Zuazua and Jardón,* ☎ *81/8342–4820,* WEB *www.mtyol.com/marco.* 🎟 *About $3, free Wed.* ⊙ *Tues. and Thurs.–Sun. 10–6, Wed. 10–8.*

18 The **Museo de Historia Mexicana** (Mexican History Museum) has a mini-riverwalk with cafés and a boat ride on its grounds. It displays the country's most complete history of its 1910–20 revolution. Period newsreels play in a multimedia show held inside a railroad car that served as a troop carrier for the insurgents. Life-size plaster-of-paris casts of the Villistas (soldiers under the command of Pancho Villa) sit shotgun on the roof of a car that has just been "liberated" from the Mexican army. Other exhibits include the first bottle-capping machine used by Coca-Cola, a history of Mexican cinema, and pre-Columbian Huasteca artifacts. Free guided tours are available in English (call ahead to confirm that an English-speaking guide is available). ⊠ *Dr. Coss 445 Sur,* ☎ *81/8345–9898.* 🎟 *$1, free Tues., 50¢ Sun.* ⊙ *Tues.–Thurs. 11–7, Fri.–Sun. 11–8.*

Monterrey

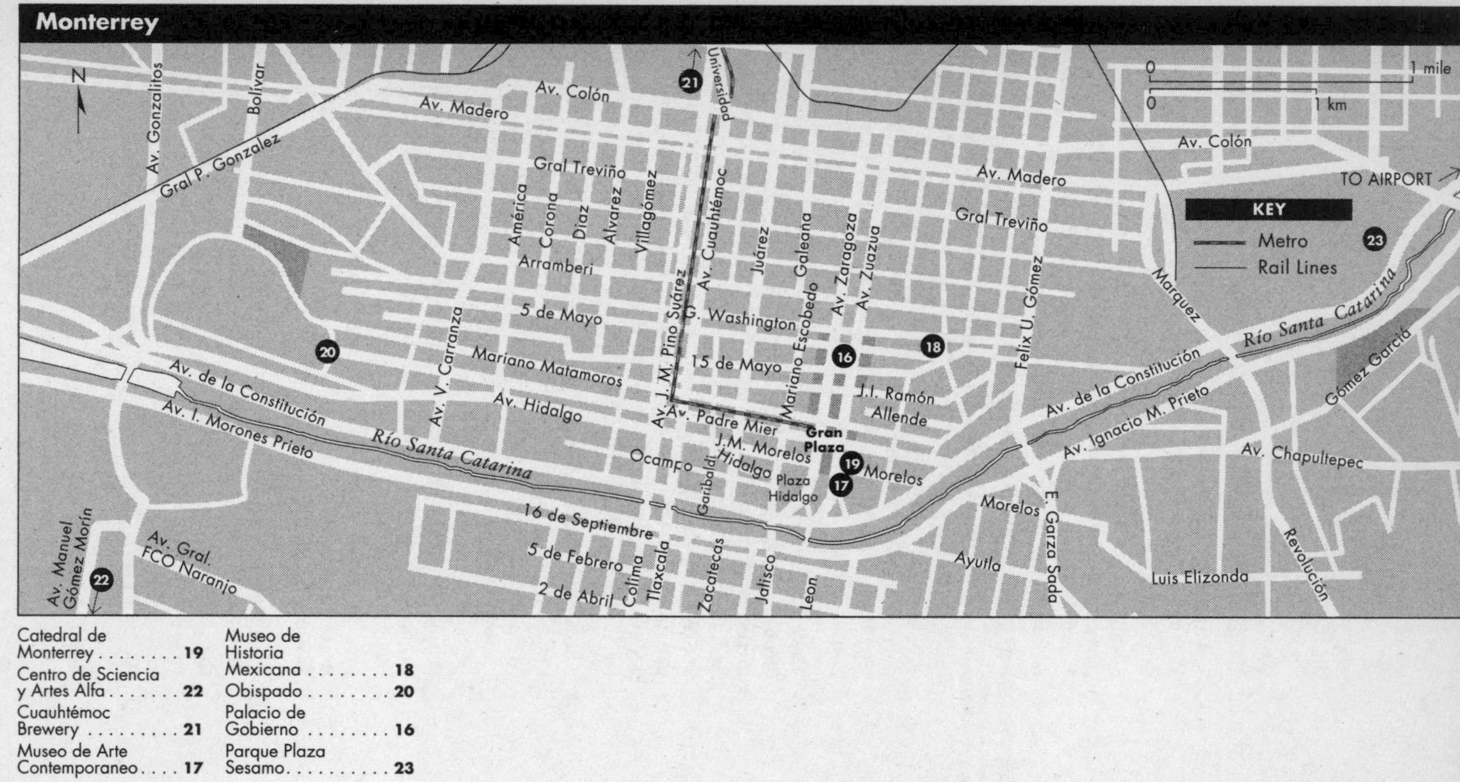

Catedral de Monterrey	19	Museo de Historia Mexicana	18
Centro de Sciencia y Artes Alfa	22	Obispado	20
Cuauhtémoc Brewery	21	Palacio de Gobierno	16
Museo de Arte Contemporaneo	17	Parque Plaza Sesamo	23

Monterrey's Spanish history began in 1596, and for its first couple of
19 centuries it was little more than an outpost. Construction of the **Catedral de Monterrey** began in 1600 but took some 250 years to finish. As a result, a Baroque facade is set off by neoclassical columns and two huge ornate plateresque medallions on the main door. Murals by local artists frame the main altar. ✉ *Gran Plaza at Av. Zuazua and Jardón.*

20 The **Obispado** (Bishop's House) is the only landmark to be completed in the colonial era (1788). Built on a hilltop as a home for retired prelates, it was used as a fort during the Mexican-American War (1847), the French Intervention (1862), and again during the Mexican Revolution (1915). Today it houses the **Museo Regional de Nuevo León El Obispado,** with exhibits that focus on the history of the entire area. From here you'll have a splendid view of Monterrey. ✉ *Far west end of Av. Padre Mier, at Rafael José Berger,* ☎ *81/8346–0404.* *$3.* *Tues.–Sun. 10–5.*

The explosion of the popularity of Mexican beer owes much to the
21 **Cuauhtémoc Brewery,** which opened a century ago. Named after a famous Aztec chief, the brewery is the heart of an industrial empire that produces Carta Blanca and Tecate beer. The brewery complex includes the Mexican Baseball Hall of Fame, and a beer garden with free beer—obviously the big draw. ✉ *Av. Alfonso Reyes 2202 Nte.,* ☎ *81/8328–5000; 81/8328–5355 for brewery tours; 81/8328–5745 for Hall of Fame,* WEB *www.femsa.com.mx.* *Free.* *Tues.–Fri. 9:30–5:45, weekends 10:30–6. Brewery tours by request, weekdays 9–1 and 3–6.*

The Cuauhtémoc Brewery spawned a glass factory for bottles, a steel mill for caps, a carton factory, and, eventually, several industrial con-
22 glomerates. One of the last, Alfa, gave Monterrey the **Centro de Sciencia y Artes Alfa** (Alfa Cultural Center), probably the best museum of science and technology in the country. The museum has many hands-on exhibits and an IMAX theater. Explanatory materials are in Spanish only. Free buses to the museum run from the downtown *alameda* (main square) hourly 3–8 daily. ✉ *Roberto Garza Sada 1000,* ☎ *81/8303–0002,* WEB *www.planetarioalfa.org.mx.* *$3, $6 for IMAX; 2 admissions for the price of 1 on Wed.* *Tues.–Fri. 3–8:30, Sat. 2–8:30, Sun. noon–8:30.*

23 The cleverly designed **Parque Plaza Sesamo** (Sesame Plaza Park) is an impressive recreational-educational play area for children. This sprawling theme park is built on the grounds of Parque Fundidora that also houses the city's Cintermex convention complex. There are three main areas. One has a world of water sports with 17 water toboggans, pint-size pools, interactive games, and minirivers. A second area has a computer center where children can plug into the Internet and play (nonviolent) video games. The last section is taken up by restaurants and theaters where the park's own personalities put on musical shows. Families can easily spend an entire day here. ✉ *Calle Agricola 3700–1 Ote., Col. Agricola in Parque Fundidora,* ☎ *81/8354–5400,* WEB *www.monterrey-mexico.com/ingles/parques/sesamo.html.* *$14; children under 90 cm free.* *June–Aug., daily 11–9:30; Sept.–May, daily 3–8.*

Dining and Lodging

$$–$$$ ★ ✕ **Luisiana.** Perhaps the most elegant dining room downtown, this is a taste of how New Orleans is imagined in Mexico. There are no Cajun specialties on the menu, but the deepwater crawfish are divine. Steak and seafood dishes are wonderfully prepared, the waiters wear tuxedos, and there's always soft piano music playing at dinnertime. ✉ *Av. Hidalgo Ote. 530,* ☎ *81/8340–3753 or 81/8343–1561. AE, MC, V.*

$-$$$ ★ ✕ **Vitrales.** Join the friendly staff at Vitrales for an elegant night of dining under a grand stained-glass ceiling. The sizeable smoked salmon appetizer is served with fresh herbs, Bermuda onions, and hard-boiled eggs. For an entrée, choose from a selection of freshly prepared pastas, *arrachera* steak, and the broiled salmon fillet served with rice and fresh steamed vegetables. Enjoy an after-dinner coffee and dessert while listening to live piano music. ✉ *Hidalgo 310 Ote., inside the Sheraton Ambassador,* ☎ *81/8380–7000. AE, DC, MC, V.*

$$ ✕ **El Rey de Cabrito.** The restaurant's name (King of Kid) is no lie: this is *the* place where everyone comes to try roast kid. (The owner keeps his own goat herds.) The hunting lodge–theme restaurant covers half a city block and has become so well known that it's constantly filling out-of-town orders. ✉ *Constitución 817, at Dr. Coss,* ☎ *81/8345–3232 or 81/8345–3292. MC, V.*

$ ✕ **Las Monjitas.** Cruise down tiled steps into the bustling dining room of the little nuns (waitresses are in full habits). Murals of peacefully cooking nuns adorn the walls of this hopping Mexican diner. Choose from three commida corridas, or for a casual dinner try "La Pecadora" (thinly sliced grilled chicken topped with melted asadero cheese, fried onions, and mushrooms and served with guacamole, refried beans and lettuce). ✉ *Escobedo 903 Sur,* ☎ *81/8344–6713. AE, MC, V.*

$$$ ★ ✕ **Residence.** A clubby meeting place for Monterrey's high-powered industrialists and executives, Residence has a menu featuring both Mexican specialties and Continental dishes such as prime rib. The "tasting menu" provides six small portions from some of the restaurant's best specialty dishes. ✉ *Degollado 605 Sur, at Matamoros,* ☎ *81/8342–7230, 81/8345–5040, or 81/8345–5478. AE, DC, MC, V.*

$$$$ ★ **Quinta Real.** This elegant all-suites business hotel holds sway among Monterrey's financial elite and exudes the aura of a prosperous hacienda of bygone days. The high-dome lobby is set with French furnishings in soothing colors, huge bowls of flowers, and carvings of classic Mexican crafts. Suites have either two double beds or one king, robes, TVs, and luxury bathroom soaps and lotions. The hotel's restaurant serves excellent French and Mexican cuisine and has built up quite a local following. ✉ *Av. Diego Rivera 500, Fracc. Valle Ote., San Pedro Garza García 66260,* ☎ *81/8368–1000 or 800/713–1966,* FAX *81/8368–1070,* WEB *www.quintareal.com. 165 suites. Restaurant, room service, minibars, gym, sauna, bar, baby-sitting, laundry service, concierge, car rental, travel services, free parking, no-smoking rooms. AE, DC, MC, V.*

$$$$ ★ **Radisson Plaza Gran Hotel Ancira.** Built in 1912, this hotel is reminiscent of the grand hotels of Europe: an elegant spiral staircase dominates an expansive art deco lobby accented by crystal chandeliers. Legend has it that Pancho Villa, taken with the place, settled in and stabled his horse in the lobby. All rooms have minibars, cable TVs, and large marble baths. The Plaza Club business-floor suites have impeccable concierge service. ✉ *Ocampo No. 443, Ote. Centro or Hidalgo at Escobedo, 64000,* ☎ *81/8150–7000 or 800/830–6000,* FAX *81/8344–5226. 236 rooms, 26 suites. Restaurant, minibars, pool, gym, hair salon, outdoor hot tub, sauna, 2 bars, shops, baby-sitting, laundry service, concierge floor, travel services, car rental, free parking, no-smoking rooms. AE, DC, MC, V.*

$$$$ ★ **Sheraton Ambassador.** This downtown landmark has spacious rooms decorated in burgundy and forest green and equipped with cable TVs, phones in the room and the bathroom, and feather pillows. The concierge floor has secretarial and fax service, and a comfortable executive lounge. A health club, a restaurant, and a piano bar with a stained-glass ceiling are among the other amenities. ✉ *Hidalgo 310 Ote., 64000,* ☎ *81/8380–7000 or 800/325–3535,* FAX *81/8345–1984,* WEB *www.sheraton.com. 223 rooms, 16 suites. Restaurant, room ser-*

vice, minibars, tennis court, pool, health club, massage, racquetball, bar, laundry service, concierge floor, meeting room, travel services, free parking, no-smoking rooms. AE, DC, MC, V.

$$$ 🏨 **Fiesta Americana Centro Monterrey.** In the center of the Zona Rosa, this spiffy pink sandstone building has a striking atrium lobby that is abuzz with business travelers. The light-filled units (all of them two-room suites) are tastefully decorated and have burgundy carpets. Each suite has cable TV and a fold-out sofa, and the bathroom is stocked with specialty lotions and soaps. Rooms facing the plaza have fabulous mountain views. ✉ *Privada Corregidora Ote. 519, Zona Rosa, 64000,* ☎ *81/8319–0900 or 800/504–5000,* FAX *81/8319–0980,* WEB *www.fiestaamericana.com.mx. 207 rooms. Restaurant, room service, minibars, indoor pool, gym, bar, baby-sitting, laundry service, concierge, parking (fee), no-smoking rooms. AE, DC, MC, V.*

$$$ 🏨 **Hotel Chipinque.** If you have a car, this hilltop resort overlooking the city on 700 acres of forest land is a tranquil choice. The view from the restaurant is extraordinary, especially at night. All rooms have either a king or two queen-size beds, satellite TVs, and phones; some have fireplaces. ✉ *Meseta de Chipinque 1000, San Pedro Garza García, 66297,* ☎ *81/8378–1100, 81/8378–6600, or 800/849–4681,* FAX *81/8378–6759. 58 rooms, 12 suites. Restaurant, room service, tennis court, pool, outdoor hot tub, billiards, bar, meeting room, free parking. AE, MC, V.*

Nightlife and the Arts

Fashionable residents and visitors flock to downtown hotels for after-dark action. The pianist at the **Sheraton Ambassador** (✉ Hidalgo 310 Ote., ☎ 81/8340–7000) performs soothing pieces that provide the perfect accompaniment to a restful cocktail. A talented jazz pianist performs in the lobby bar of the **Fiesta Americana Centro Monterrey** (✉ Av. Corregidora Ote. 519, ☎ 81/8319–0900). **Monasterio** (✉ Calle Escobedo 913, ☎ no phone), presents an eclectic mix of live music—from rock to romantic Mexican ballads—Tuesday through Saturday nights. **Vat–Kru,** (✉ Blvd. Constitución 3050 Pte., ☎ 81/8333–5241), bizarre name and all, is one of the hottest discos in town.

The charming Barrio Antiguo has a number of live music bars; a local favorite is **Fonda San Miguel** (✉ Morelos 924 Ote., ☎ 81/8342–6659), where you'll find an eclectic mix of locals and visitors.

Shopping

Top-quality shops center on Plaza Hidalgo, near the major hotels. Leather and cowboy boots are the local specialties. Owner Porfirio Sosa handpicks all the items he sells at the upscale **Carápan** (✉ Hidalgo 305 Ote., ☎ 81/8345–4422) and loves to talk about them. His array of Mexican antiques, hand-loomed rugs, shawls, clay figures from Michoacán, metal sculptures, and handblown glassware rivals that of stores anywhere in the country. **Sanborns** (✉ Escobedo 920, off Plaza Hidalgo, ☎ 81/8343–1834) offers a standard selection of silver, onyx, and other Mexican craft items. **Plaza Fiesta San Agustín** (✉ Av. Real de San Agustín at Lázaro Cárdenas, San Pedro Garza García) is an enormous mall where Monterrey socialites shop for evening gowns, precious gems, and imported perfumes. The **Mercado Indio** (✉ Bolivar Nte. 1150) is a typical Mexican market with dozens of stalls, although the selections are a little monotonous.

Outdoor Activities and Sports

ICE SKATING

Pista de Hielo San Pedro (✉ Plaza San Pedro Local 10, ☎ 81/8356–7293) is a popular ice-skating rink. It's open weekdays 10–3 and 4:30–8, weekends 10–8.

ROCK CLIMBING

Tierra Norte Tours (☏ 81/8134–8164) runs climbing and hiking tours to Canyon de la Huasteca and canyoning tours to Matacanes.

Canyon de la Huasteca (Huasteca Canyon)

24 *23 km (14 mi) southwest of Monterrey.*

The Canyon de la Huasteca, with its 1,000-ft-deep gorge, is spectacular for the striated grooves etched into its walls that make it resemble a giant piece of Lalique glassware. The trails are various and well-maintained, and the spectacular peaks—with evocative names like Devil's Tower and Cat's Walk—attract climbing enthusiasts. A children's play area has a miniature train ride and two pools. ✉ *From Monterrey, 20 km (12 mi) west on Hwy. 40 to Santa Catarina, then 3 km (2 mi) south on marked road to canyon,* ☏ *no phone.* *$1 per car and 10¢ per person.* ⏲ *Daily 9–6.*

Grutas de García (Garcia Caves)

25 *49 km (30 mi) northwest of Monterrey.*

The Grutas García are an estimated 50–60 million years old and at one time were submerged by an ocean. Petrified sea animals are visible in some of its walls. From the entrance, you can hike the steep 1 km (½ mi) to the caves or hop on a swaying funicular. Guides lead the way through a strenuous mile of underground grottoes and caverns. ✉ *From Monterrey, Hwy. 40 west for 40 km (25 mi) to Saltillo, then 9 km (5½ mi) on marked road to caves,* ☏ *81/8347–1599.* *$5 with funicular.* ⏲ *Daily 9–5.*

Parque Nacional Cumbres de Monterrey

26 *90 km (56 mi) northwest of Monterrey.*

One of the highlights of a trip to the Parque Nacional Cumbres de Monterrey, tucked into the Sierra Madre, is a view of **La Cascada Cola de Caballo** (Horsetail Falls), a dramatic 75-ft-high waterfall that tumbles down from the pine-forested heights. The waterfall is about 1 km (½ mi) from the park's entrance, up a cobblestone road. You can rent a docile horse or burro for about $3 an hour from the local kids who hang out by the ticket booth, or hop on a horse-drawn carriage for $2. ✉ *From Monterrey, Hwy. 85 northwest 90 km (56 mi) to falls,* ☏ *no phone.* *$1.50.* ⏲ *Daily 9–7.*

Tampico

27 *504 km (312 mi) south of Matamoros, 583 km (361 mi) southeast of Monterrey.*

Tampico is a picturesque port adjoining Ciudad Madero, now an oil-refining center. In 1828 the Spaniards attempted to reconquer then-independent Mexico by landing troops at Tampico, but they were soundly defeated. After later invasions by the Americans and the French, the port languished until oil was discovered in the region about a century ago. The British and Americans developed the industry until it was nationalized in 1938. Petroleum helped Tampico to prosper, but has hardly enhanced tourism. The Río Pánuco is so polluted that it no longer attracts tarpon fishermen, although the big ocean freighters are an impressive sight.

Because of its relative proximity to the border, Tampico gets a smattering of U.S. visitors. And it is a fascinating place to wander around for a spell—the old part of town has something of the feel of a rundown New Orleans French Quarter. **Plaza de la Libertad,** near the harbor, is surrounded by old colonial buildings. A block away is the regal **Plaza de Armas,** its majestic City Hall guarded by towering palms. The **cathedral** here, started in 1823, was completed with funds donated by Edward L. Doheny, an oil magnate implicated in the U.S.'s Teapot Dome scandal of the 1920s.

In Ciudad Madero (between Tampico and the coast), the small **Museo de la Cultura Huasteca** (Museum of Huasteca Culture) houses an exquisite collection of pre-Hispanic ceramics, shellwork, and costumes, and some pots dating as far back as 1100 BC. ✉ *Instituto Tecnológico, 1 de Mayo at Sor Juana Inés de la Cruz, Ciudad Madero,* ☏ *833/210–2217.* 🎫 *By donation.* ⏲ *Weekdays 10–6, Sat. 10–3.*

Beaches

Playa Miramar, about 5 km (3 mi) from town, is a favorite with locals. For a fee, lounge chairs, towels, and showers are available from the hotels and restaurants along the beach. Public transportation from Tampico consists of public buses marked "Playa," which cost about $1, and colectivos (the old bright-yellow cars and vans), which take groups for about $5 per person.

Dining and Lodging

$$ ✕ **Papa Cuervo Restaurant and Bar.** Enter an underwater fantasy world where the bar is a pirate ship equipped with sails, crates, and a monkey hanging off the stern (he doesn't bite) and each wall is a three-dimensional mural of the undersea world. Try the *pollo San Miguelito,* a rolled chicken breast stuffed with cheese, spinach, and mushrooms and drizzled with pecan sauce. Servings tend to be small but satisfying. Save some energy for live music and dancing on the weekends. ✉ *Morelos 779 Centro,* ☏ *833/222–0180. No credit cards.*

$–$$ ✕ **Restaurant La Troya.** Exceedingly rich meat and seafood dishes are the focus of this restaurant in one of Tampico's oldest buildings, the Hotel Posada del Rey. House specialties include *paella a la troya* (a saffron-flavored stew of chicken, pork, seafood, and vegetables) and *caldo gallego* (Spanish broth with pork, sausage, beans, potatoes, and chard). The best tables are out on the balcony, overlooking the Plaza de la Libertad. ✉ *Calle Madero 218 Ote., at Av. Juárez,* ☏ *833/214–1155. AE, MC, V.*

$ ✕ **Café y Nevería Elite.** This is a popular gathering spot for breakfast, coffee, and ice-cream treats. Don't be put off by the noise and the rather worn Formica tables; it's all part of the local color. ✉ *Av. Díaz Mirón 211 Ote.,* ☏ *833/212–0364. MC, V.*

$$$ 🏨 **Camino Real.** Attractively decorated, this low-rise property 20 minutes from the city center is a resort hotel—the best you'll find in Tampico (in spite of the name, it's not part of the Camino Real chain). Its rooms and bungalows surround a huge garden overflowing with tropical trees and flowers. Rooms contain Chippendale-style furniture, minibars, cable TVs, and direct-dial phones. Fishing excursions can be booked through the hotel's travel agency. ✉ *Hidalgo 2000, Col. Smith, 89140,* ☏ *833/213–8811 or 800/570–0000,* FAX *833/213–9226,* WEB *www.caminorealtampico.com. 100 rooms, 3 suites. Restaurant, room service, minibars, tennis court, pool, bar, laundry service, travel services, car rental. AE, DC, MC, V.*

$ 🏨 **Posada del Rey.** The art nouveau facade of this fourth-oldest building in Tampico faces the Plaza de la Libertad. Rooms are clean, air-conditioned, carpeted, and have TVs and phones; lighting is somewhat dim, but the effect is cozy and charming. ✉ *Francisco Madero 218 Ote.,*

Zona Centro 89000, ☎ 833/214–1155 or 833/214–1024, FAX 833/212–1077. 40 rooms. Restaurant, bar. AE, MC, V.

Nightlife and the Arts

Byblos (✉ Byblos 1, ☎ 833/213–0827) is a popular disco. The bar at the **Camino Real** hotel (✉ Hidalgo 2000, ☎ 833/213–8811) has evening piano music every night except Sunday. **Papa Cuervo Restaurant and Bar** (✉ Morelos 779 Centro, ☎ 833/222–0280) has live music and dancing on Friday and Saturday night 10–1 with a $4 cover charge.

Outdoor Activities and Sports

FISHING

Although the river is polluted, tarpon and snapper fishing is still popular at **Chairel Lagoon,** with boats and equipment available for rent (just don't plan to eat what you hook). You can arrange for a boat, guide, and equipment through the **Camino Real** hotel (✉ Av. Hidalgo 2000, ☎ 833/213–8811 or 800/570–0000).

GOLF

Lagunas de Miralta Country Club (☎ 833/224–0003) sells day passes at Centro Commercial Tres Arcos on Hidalgo for its 18-hole golf course at Km 26.1 on the Carretera Tampico–Altamira. Ask at your hotel about passes or special discounts at other local clubs.

THE NORTHEAST A TO Z

To research prices, get advice from other travelers, and book travel arrangements, visit www.fodors.com.

AIR TRAVEL

The airport in Monterrey is the only international one in the region, but you can fly to Tampico, Nuevo Laredo Matamoros, and Reynosa on various Mexican airlines.

CARRIERS

From Mexico City, Aeroméxico has service to Matamoros, Tampico, and Reynosa. Mexicana flies to Nuevo Laredo and Tampico from Mexico City. Aerolitoral has nonstop flights to Tampico from the capital.

From the United States, Mexicana has flights from Chicago, Denver, Los Angeles, New York, San Antonio, and San Francisco to Monterrey, via Mexico City. Aeroméxico has direct service to Houston and Los Angeles and flights to New York via Mexico City. Continental flies from Chicago, Las Vegas, Los Angeles, Miami, and New York, via Houston. American has six flights a day to Monterrey from Dallas. Aerolitoral has service from McAllen and San Antonio, Texas.

➤ AIRLINES AND CONTACTS: **Aerolitoral** (☎ 81/8221–1600 in Monterrey; 833/228–4197; 833/228–0857 in Tampico, WEB www.aerolitoral.com). **Aeroméxico** (☎ 868/812–2460 in Matamoros; 81/8343–5560 in Monterrey; 899/922–1115 in Reynosa; 833/213–9600 in Tampico, WEB www.aeromexico.com). **American** (☎ 81/8340–3031 in Monterrey, WEB www.aa.com). **Continental** (☎ 81/8348–4282 in Monterrey, WEB www.continental.com). **Mexicana** (☎ 81/8124–2500 in Monterrey; 867/712–2052 in Nuevo Laredo; 833/213–9600 in Tampico, WEB www.mexicana.com.mx).

AIRPORTS

Monterrey's Aeropuerto Internacional Mariano Escobedo has luggage storage ($4 a day) and a money-exchange booth and is 6 km (4 mi) northeast of downtown. The only way to get here is by taxi, which will cost about $14.

➤ AIRPORT INFORMATION: **Aeropuerto Internacional Mariano Escobedo** (☎ 81/8369–0753).

BUS TRAVEL TO AND FROM THE NORTHEAST

Northeastern Mexico is well connected by buses, which are becoming downright luxurious while maintaining low fares. Information on Mexican bus service is available from Transportes del Norte in Laredo, McAllen, and Brownsville. In conjunction with Greyhound, Transportes del Norte runs from San Antonio, Dallas, and Houston to Monterrey.
➤ BUS INFORMATION: **Transportes del Norte** (☎ 81/8318–3737 or FAX 81/8318–3738 in Monterrey; ☎ 956/723–4324 in Laredo, Valley Transit; 956/686–5479 in McAllen, Valley Transit; 956/546–7171 in Brownsville, Valley Transit).

BUS TRAVEL WITHIN THE NORTHEAST

Monterrey's Central de Autobuses (main bus terminal) is the hub of bus transportation in the northeast. Transportes del Norte buses cover the region quite thoroughly, with frequent, daily service from Monterrey to the border towns and Tampico. Omnibus de México sends one bus a day between Monterrey and Tampico and Monterrey and Nuevo Laredo; it also offers frequent daily service to Reynosa.
➤ BUS INFORMATION: **Central de Autobuses** (✉ Av. Colón, at Amado Nervo, Monterrey, ☎ 81/8374–1648 or 81/8375–3238). **Omnibus de México** (☎ 81/8375–7121 in Monterrey). **Transportes del Norte** (☎ 81/8318–3737 or FAX 81/8318–3738 in Monterrey; ☎ 956/723–4324 in Laredo, Valley Transit; 956/686–5479 in McAllen, Valley Transit; 956/546–7171 in Brownsville, Valley Transit).

CAR TRAVEL

Downtown Nuevo Laredo is reached by two bridges: International Bridge 1 in town, and the Columbia-Laredo Bridge (42 km, or 26 mi, northwest of Laredo). At both you can be cleared for travel to the interior of Mexico. (In Nuevo Laredo, use only parking lots with attendants on duty—there have been a number of reports of theft.)

The New Bridge is the best route from Brownsville to Matamoros. U.S. 281 leads down to Hidalgo, Texas, and the bridge into Reynosa. For brief excursions across the border, consider leaving your car in Texas and walking over. This eliminates the long wait—often a half hour or more—to bring a car back into the United States.

From Matamoros, Mexico 180 runs down the Gulf coast to Tampico, Veracruz, and beyond. Mexico 97 leads from Reynosa to Mexico 101/180. From Reynosa, you can drive the free routes Mexico 40 to Mexico 35 to Linares; here Mexico 58 will lead you across to San Roberto (and Mexico 57) via a spectacular road with a most unusual mural by Frederico Cantú chiseled out of the side of a mountain.

From Laredo, the old Pan-American Highway, Mexico 85 Libre (free), and the four-lane Mexico 85 Cuota (toll) both lead to Monterrey, some 242 km (150 mi) south. The latter road, which ends in Monterrey, is a much better one, although the toll is expensive (about $15). It's about the same price to take the toll road Mexico 40 to Monterrey from Reynosa. Although the Laredo route is more scenic, traversing some nice mountains, Laredo itself is more congested to get through than Reynosa. The Reynosa road, although flat and dull, is more convenient to downtown Monterrey.

The port of Tampico is roughly a seven-hour drive from Matamoros on Mexico 180, or eight hours from Monterrey via Mexico 85, which connects with Mexico 80.

Distances are deceiving in this part of Mexico because of mountainous driving in the Sierra Madre Oriente. It generally takes three hours to drive from the border to Monterrey. From Monterrey to Ciudad Victoria, it's another four hours.

A car trip is not without its red tape. Sanborn's Mexican Insurance can help you complete the paperwork in advance—free if you buy insurance there, otherwise for a fee.

➤ CONTACTS: **Sanborn's Mexican Insurance** (✉ 2009 S. 10th St., McAllen, TX 78503, ☎ 800/222–0158, FAX 956/686–0732, WEB www.sanbornsinsurance.com).

EMBASSIES

➤ CONSULATES: **Canadian Consulate (Monterrey)** (✉ Edificio Kalos, 108-A Calle Mariano Escobedo and Av. Constitución, Monterrey, ☎ 81/8344–3200, FAX 81/8344–3048, WEB www.canada.org.mx/consular/english/monterrey.asp). **U.S. Consulate (Matamoros)** (✉ Calle 1 No. 232, Matamoros, ☎ 868/812–4402). **U.S. Consulate (Monterrey)** (✉ Av. Constitución 411 Pte., Monterrey, ☎ 81/8343–7124 or 81/8345–2120, FAX 8/343–9399, WEB www.usembassy-mexico.gov/Monterrey.html).

EMERGENCIES

Dial **066** in Monterrey for medical, theft, and fire emergencies. Call the local Red Cross (Cruz Roja) for ambulance service.

➤ CONTACTS: **Hospital Santander in Reynosa** (✉ Fco. Madero and Ortiz Rubyo, Reynosa, ☎ 899/922–9622 or 899/922–9397). **Matamoros Cruz Roja Hospital** (✉ García and L. Caballero, Matamoros, ☎ 868/812–0044). **Matamoros Police** (✉ Pedro Cárdenas and Soledad, Matamoros, ☎ 868/817–2205). **Monterrey Cruz Roja** (✉ Av. Alfonso Reyes 2503, Monterrey, ☎ 81/8375–1212). **Monterrey Police** (✉ Gonzalitos 2300, at Lincoln, Monterrey, ☎ 81/8151–6000). **Nuevo Laredo Cruz Roja** (✉ Independencia 1619 and San Antonio, Nuevo Laredo, ☎ 867/712–0949 or 867/712–0989). **Nuevo Laredo Police** (✉ Maclovio Herréra and Ocampo, Nuevo Laredo, ☎ 867/712–3025). **Reynosa Cruz Roja** (☎ 899/922–1314 or 899/922–6250). **Reynosa Police** (✉ Morelos between Veracruz and Nayarit, ☎ 899/922–0008 or 899/22–0790). **Tampico Cruz Roja Hospital** (✉ Tamaulipas and Colegio Militar, Zona Centro, Tampico, ☎ 833/212–1333). **Tampico Police** (✉ Sor Juana Inés de la Cruz and Tamaulipas Tampico, ☎ 833/212–1032).

PHARMACIES

You will have no trouble locating pharmacies, many of them open until 8 or 10 PM. Fenix and Benavides are among the better-known chains.

➤ CONTACTS: **Farmacia Benavides** (✉ Morelos 499, at Escobedo, Monterrey, ☎ 81/8345–0257). **Farmacia Calderón** (✉ Guerrero 704, Nuevo Laredo, ☎ 867/712–5177). **Farmacia Droguería del Pueblo** (✉ Juárez 308 Sur, Tampico, ☎ 833/212–1542). **Farmacia El Fenix** (✉ Abosolo 806, Matamoros, ☎ 868/812–2909).

MAIL AND INTERNET

Monterrey's central post office is at the far northern end of Macro Plaza. Ships 2000, above the video arcade, offers the only Internet service in the Zona Rosa; the rates are steep at $3.50 an hour. It's open daily 10–10.

The Reynosa post office is on the corner of Díaz and Colón. Cyberspace Internet Café is generally open weekdays 9–9, weekends until 4, and charges about $1.50 per hour.

In Tampico, there's a post office just off the Plaza de la Libertad. Coffee Net has 10 computers with Internet access for $1.50 an hour; it's open Monday–Saturday 9–9.

➤ Post Offices and Internet Services: **Coffee Net** (✉ Carranza 106 Pte., Tampico, ☎ 833/214–1390). **Cyberspace Internet Café** (✉ Hidalgo and Allende, Reynosa, ☎ no phone). **Monterrey post office** (✉ Washington, between Zaragoza and Zuazua, Monterrey). **Ships 2000** (✉ Escobedo 819 Sur, Monterrey, ☎ 81/8343–2568). **Tampico post office** (✉ Madero 309 Ote., Tampico).

MONEY MATTERS

Some banks won't cash traveler's checks, but most have ATMs.

There are plenty of banks in downtown Matamoros, mostly around Plaza Hidalgo, that change money and traveler's checks. Money-changing hours at banks generally end at 3 PM weekdays.

Banks in Monterrey's Zona Rosa generally change money and traveler's checks weekdays 9–3. For later money-changing and traveler's check services, try Eurodivisas; it stays open until 8 PM Sunday through Friday, 9 PM Saturday.

In Reynosa, many casas de cambio line Avenida Alemán at the entrance to town via the International Bridge. Most banks change money only, but Citibank will change traveler's checks weekdays 9–2. The best exchange rates are closer to the city center, around Plaza Principál and along Calle Hidalgo.

Citibank in Tampico changes money and traveler's checks weekdays 9–3. Banamex changes money and traveler's checks until 5 PM. Casa de Cambio is open weekdays 9–6, Saturday 9–1:30.

➤ Exchange Services: **Banamex** (✉ Madero 403 Ote., Tampico, ☎ 833/214–0230). **Casa de Cambio** (✉ Juárez 215 Sur, Tampico, ☎ 833/212–9000). **Citibank** (✉ Av. Alemán 100, Reynosa, ☎ 899/922–5619 or 899/922–5660). **Citibank** (✉ Aduana 309 Sur, Tampico, ☎ 833/212–9240). **Eurodivisas** (✉ Morelos 359 Ote., Monterrey, ☎ 81/8340–1683).

TOURS AND PACKAGES

Various sightseeing excursions are available through Tours Gray Line, Osetur Tours, and Sanborn's Viva Tours, which run shopping and sightseeing excursions to border towns and the interior, including to El Tajín.

➤ Tour-Operator Recommendations: **Osetur Tours** (✉ Calle San Francisco 2,700, at Loma Grande, Monterrey, ☎ 81/8347–1599 or 81/8347–1614). **Sanborn's Viva Tours** (✉ 2015 S. 10th St., McAllen, TX 78503, ☎ 800/395–8482; 956/682–9872 in the U.S., WEB www.sanborns.com/tours.htm). **Tours Gray Line** (✉ Av. Eugenio Garza Sada 2256, Monterrey, ☎ 81/8369–6472 or 81/8369–6473).

TRANSPORTATION IN MONTERREY

METRO TRAVEL

The Monterrey metro, which runs along elevated tracks across the city, is modern and efficient. There are only two lines. Magnetic cards are used to enter the station. Buy them from station vending machines in units of one, three, or five rides. Each ride costs less than 50¢. The metro runs 6 AM–midnight daily. Maps are posted in the stations.

TAXIS

Taxis are pretty scarce and expensive in border towns but plentiful and moderately priced in Monterrey. In Monterrey, Metro Taxi provides reliable on-call service.

➤ Contact: **Metro Taxi** (☎ 81/8342–2069).

VISITOR INFORMATION

In the United States, the best information about this part of Mexico is found in Texas border towns, especially at places that sell the (mandatory) Mexican automobile insurance. The Brownsville Chamber of Commerce, one block from International Bridge, is open daily 9–5.

In Mexico, Matamoros Tours-Transport, a few blocks from International Bridge, is open daily 8–6. The Nuevo Laredo office is open daily 8–8, and the Reynosa office weekdays 7:30 AM–8 PM. Also near the International Bridge, cabdrivers and roving tourist-department representatives are glad to dispense free information to travelers. Monterrey Infotour is open Tuesday through Sunday 10–5. The Tampico office is open weekdays 9–7.

➤ TOURIST INFORMATION NORTH OF THE BORDER: **Bravo Insurance** (✉ 2212 Santa Ursula St., Laredo, TX 78040, ☎ 956/723–3657, FAX 956/723–0000, WEB www.mxins.com). **Brownsville Chamber of Commerce** (✉ 1600 E. Elizabeth St., Brownsville, TX 78520, ☎ 956/542–4341, WEB www.brownsvillechamber.com). **Johnny Ginn's Travel** (✉ 1845 Expressway 77, Brownsville, TX 78520, ☎ 956/542–5457, FAX 956/504–2919). **Sanborn's Mexican Insurance** (✉ 2009 S. 10th St., McAllen, TX 78503, ☎ 800/222–0158, FAX 956/686–0732, WEB www.sanbornsinsurance.com). **Sanborn's Viva Tours** (✉ 2015 S. 10th St., McAllen, TX 78503, ☎ 800/395–8482 or 956/682–9872, WEB www.sanborns.com/tours).

➤ TOURIST INFORMATION SOUTH OF THE BORDER: **Nuevo Laredo office** (✉ Calles Herrera and Juárez, ☎ 867/712–7397, WEB www.tamaulipas.gob.mx/sedeem/sectores/turismo). **Matamoros Tours-Transport** (✉ Tamaulipas and Av. Alvaro Obregón, ☎ 868/812–2118). **Monterrey Infotour** (✉ Hidalgo 441 Ote., ☎ 81/8345–0870 or 81/8345–0902, WEB www.monterrey-mexico.com/ingles). **Reynosa office** (✉ Puente Internacional/International Bridge, ☎ 899/922–1189 or 899/922–2449). **Tampico office** (✉ 20 de Noviembre 218 Ote., ☎ 833/212–2668 or 833/212–0007).

14 THE YUCATÁN PENINSULA

The Yucatán Peninsula is Mexico's perennial favorite for more reasons than you can count—the high-profile sparkle of Cancún, the laid-back beachcombing of Isla Mujeres, the spectacular seas around Cozumel, the fascinating Spanish-Maya mix of Mérida, and the evocative Maya ruins of Tulum, Chichén Itzá, and Uxmal. And if the heart of nature moves your blood, there are two huge coastal ecozones: Sian Ka'an Biosphere Reserve and Parque Natural Río Lagartos, migration stopovers for thousands of flamingos and other birds.

FOR MOST PEOPLE, Mexico's great appeal is its beaches and its ancient ruins. Cancún and the Yucatán have the best of both. Cancún is Mexico's most popular tourist mecca, and it rises against a backdrop of Maya culture—both ancient ruins and modern villages. Although much of the Yucatán Peninsula is vast, scrubby desert with a smattering of jungles and hills, its eastern coastline on the clear, turquoise waters of the Caribbean has superb natural features. In addition to a semitropical climate, the Caribbean coast has unbroken stretches of beach and the world's second-longest barrier reef, starting off the coast of Cancún and extending in its entirety down into South America. Isla Mujeres (Isle of Women) and Cozumel are also part of the Yucatán. And on the west side of the peninsula, Mérida, one of Mesoamerica's first Spanish cities, has colonial atmosphere rare in this part of Mexico.

In its entirety, the 113,000-square-km (43,600-square-mi) peninsula encompasses the Mexican states of Yucatán, Campeche, and Quintana Roo, as well as Belize and part of Guatemala. Within its bounds are tremendous bird-watching, water sports, archaeology, handicrafts, and savory Yucatecan cuisine. Above all, there are the friendly and open Yucatecos themselves.

As many activities as there are on the Yucatán, there is an equal range of accommodations, from the never-leave-the-site resorts of Cancún to more modest properties near the ruins and humble but adequate beach shacks. That means that you'll see a broad range of travelers: package-tour groups, backpackers, people tripping around in rental cars. International airports at Cancún and Cozumel provide nonstop service from several North American cities. The Mérida airport handles primarily domestic flights. Cruise ships call at Cozumel and Playa del Carmen.

Pleasures and Pastimes

Archaeological Sites

Amateur archaeologists will find heaven in Yucatán, where the ancient Maya most abundantly left their mark. Pick your period and your preference, whether for well-excavated sites or overgrown, out-of-the-way ruins barely touched by a scholar's shovel. The major Maya sites are Cobá and Tulum and Chichén Itzá and Uxmal, but smaller sites scattered throughout the peninsula are often equally fascinating.

Beaches

Cancún and the rest of Yucatán offer a wonderful variety of beaches. You'll find white sands, rocky coves and promontories, curvaceous bays, and murky lagoons. Resorty Playa Chacmool and Playa Tortugas are on the bay side of Cancún, which is calmer if less beautiful than the windward side. Go to the north end of Isla Mujeres to Playa Norte for great sunsets. Beaches on Cozumel's east coast—once used by buccaneers—are rocky, and the swimming is treacherous, but they offer privacy. On the relatively sheltered leeward side are the widest and best sand beaches. The Caribbean coast abounds with exquisite hidden beaches and coves, as well as not-so-hidden beaches. There are also long stretches of white sand, usually filled with sunbathers, at Puerto Morelos, Akumal, and especially Playa del Carmen. Around Campeche, the Gulf waters are deep green, shallow, and tranquil.

Bird-Watching

The Yucatán Peninsula is one of the finest areas for birding in Mexico. Habitats range from wildlife and bird sanctuaries to unmarked lagoons, estuaries, and mangrove swamps. Frigates, tanagers, warblers, and macaws inhabit Isla Contoy (off Isla Mujeres) and the Laguna Colombia on Cozumel; an even greater variety of species is to be found in the Sian Ka'an Biosphere Reserve on the Boca Paila peninsula south of Tulum. Along the north and west coasts of Yucatán—at Río Lagartos, Laguna Rosada, and Celestún—flamingos, herons, ibis, cormorants, pelicans, and peregrine falcons thrive.

Dining

The mystique of Yucatecan cooking has a lot to do with the generous doses of local spices and herbs, although generally the food tends not to be too spicy. In the early days, it was tremendously influenced by French, Cuban, and New Orleans cooking because of continual cultural contact. This multicultural approach resulted in such distinctive specialties as *pollo pibíl* (chicken marinated in a sour orange and annatto seed sauce and baked in banana leaves); *poc chuc* (Yucatecan pork marinated in a sour-orange sauce with pickled onions); *tikinchic* (fried fish prepared with sour orange); *panuchos* (fried tortillas filled with black beans and topped with diced turkey, chicken, or pork as well as pickled onions and avocado); *papadzules* (tortillas rolled up with hard-boiled eggs and drenched in a sauce of pumpkin seed and fried tomato); and *codzitos* (rolled tortillas in pumpkin-seed sauce). *Achiote* (annatto), cilantro (coriander), and the fiery *chile habañero* are zesty condiments. Along the Gulf coast, there's nothing finer than a dish of fresh blue crab, or baby shrimp.

CATEGORY	CANCÚN, ISLA MUJERES, COZUMEL, AND THE CARIBBEAN COAST	YUCATÁN AND CAMPECHE STATES
$$$$	over $30	over $15
$$$	$21–$30	$11–$15
$$	$10–$20	$6–$10
$	under $10	under $6

**per person for a main course at dinner*

Fishing

Sportfishing is popular in Cozumel and throughout the Caribbean coast. The rich waters of the Caribbean and the Gulf of Mexico support hundreds of species of tropical fish, making the Yucatán coastline and the outlying islands a paradise for deep-sea fishing, fly-fishing, and bonefishing. Particularly between the months of April and July, the waters off Cancún, Cozumel, and Isla Mujeres teem with sailfish, marlin, red snapper, tuna, barracuda, and wahoo, among other denizens of the deep. Bill fishing is so rich around Cozumel that it holds an annual tournament.

Farther south, along the Boca Paila peninsula, bonefishing for these feisty little critters and light-tackle saltwater fishing for banana fish, shad, permit, and sea bass are the hands-down favorites, and oysters, shrimp, and conch lie on the bottom of the Gulf of Mexico near Campeche and Isla del Carmen. At Progreso, on the north coast, sportsfishing for grouper, dogfish, and pompano is quite popular.

Lodging

You have a variety of accommodations to choose from if you plan to stay in Cancún or Cozumel. Here, luxurious and expensive internationally affiliated properties, with lots of restaurants, cafés, and bars, have the latest room amenities, boutiques, and sports facilities. These beach resorts also have more-modest accommodations—usually a short walk or a shuttle ride from the water. Of course, as you get into the less-populated and -visited areas of the Yucatán, accommodations tend to be simpler and more typically Mexican: inexpensive bungalows, campsites, and beachside places to hang a hammock. The lodgings and facilities we list are the cream of the crop in each price category. When pricing accommodations, always ask what's included and what costs extra.

CATEGORY	CANCÚN, ISLA MUJERES, COZUMEL, AND CAMPECHE STATE	CARIBBEAN COAST AND YUCATÁN STATE
$$$$	over $200	over $100
$$$	$120–$200	$70–$100
$$	$50–$120	$40–$70
$	under $50	under $40

**All prices are for a standard double room, excluding 12% tax.*

Scuba Diving and Snorkeling

Underwater enthusiasts come to Cozumel, Akumal, Xcalak, Xel-Há, and other parts of Mexico's Caribbean coast for the clear turquoise waters, the colorful and assorted tropical fish, and the exquisite coral formations along the Palancar reef system. Currents allow for drift diving, and both reefs and offshore wrecks lend themselves to dives, many of which are safe enough for neophytes. The peninsula's cenotes, or natural sinkholes, and underwater caverns provide an unusual dive experience. Individual chapters will direct you to the dive sites that will best suit you.

Exploring the Yucatán Peninsula

Numbers in the text correspond to numbers in the margin and on the Cancún, Isla Mujeres, Cozumel, North Caribbean Coast, State of Yucatán, Mérida, and Campeche City maps.

Great Itineraries

If you go to the major beach resorts of Cancún and Cozumel, you're likely to settle in for the entire stay, perhaps taking side trips to the ruins of Tulum or Chichén Itzá or the city of Mérida. As for beach experiences, Cancún has a higher profile and is more expensive. Isla Mujeres tends to be more relaxed. The following itineraries are designed to keep you on the move from a base either in one of the Caribbean Coast towns or in Mérida. The first is ideal for water sports, the others for steeping yourself in Maya civilization.

IF YOU HAVE 3 DAYS

If you want to base yourself on the Caribbean Coast, get a room in **Playa del Carmen** ⑲ and relax on the white-sand beach or go diving around the nearby reefs. Day 2, visit the ruins of the Maya city of **Tulum** ㉑. Afterward, climb down to the small beach alongside it for a dip in the ocean. Day 3, head for **Akumal** ⑳ for diving, deep-sea fishing, snorkeling, or swimming. Later in the day visit the tiny lagoon of **Yalkú,** which was around during the time of the Maya traders.

An alternative is to spend two days in **Mérida** ㉔–㉟, savoring the city's unique character as you make your way among its historic churches and mansions, and enjoy its parks and restaurants. You can easily devote a day to exploring the heart of downtown, including the ***zócalo*** (main square) ㉔ and its surrounding buildings. Take a second, more leisurely day to visit the Museum of Anthropology and History in the **Palacio Cantón** ㉟ and, perhaps, the **Museo de Arte Contemporáneo** ㉚. On Day 3, drive or take a tour to one of Yucatán's most famous Maya ruins—**Chichén Itzá** ㊱ or **Uxmal** ㊵. Each is within about two hours of Mérida.

IF YOU HAVE 7 DAYS

Again basing yourself in **Playa del Carmen** ⑲, spend Day 2 visiting **Tulum** ㉑. Day 3, tour the Maya ruins of **Cobá** ㉒. Day 4, head for **Akumal** ⑳ and its water sports. Day 5, sign up for a tour of the **Sian Ka'an Biosphere Reserve** ㉓. On Days 6 and 7, head west for the colonial city of **Mérida** ㉔–㉟. Spend one day in the city and the next out at **Chichén Itzá** ㊱ or **Uxmal** ㊵.

On a weeklong trip in and around Mérida, take in the city's sights first and then take two separate overnight excursions. First, head for Uxmal and overnight at one of the nearby archaeological hotels. The next day explore the Ruta Puuc, the series of lost cities south of Uxmal that includes **Kabah, Sayil,** and **Labná,** as well as the fascinating **Loltún Caves.** On the second excursion, to Chichén Itzá, allow as much as a full day en route to explore some of the present-day Maya villages along the way. An alternate side trip—go north of **Valladolid** ㊴ to see the flamingo nesting grounds at **Parque Natural Río Lagartos** ㊵.

IF YOU HAVE 9 DAYS

With even more time, consider continuing from **Mérida** ㉔–㉟ to **Campeche City** ㊷–㊿. After spending a day seeing the city's sights—almost all those of interest are within the compact historic district—head inland the next morning to **Edzná,** a magnificently restored ceremonial center an hour's drive from the city.

When to Tour the Yucatán Peninsula

Thousands of people swarm to Chichén Itzá for the vernal equinox on the first day of spring to see the astronomical phenomenon that makes a shadow resembling a snake—which represented the plumed serpent god Kukulcán—appear on the side of the main pyramid. The phenomenon also occurs on the first day of fall, but the rainy autumnal weather tends to discourage visitors. Both the capital and outlying villages of Campeche state celebrate the Day of the Dead (November 1–2) with special fervor because it corresponds to a similar observance in ancient Maya tradition.

High season in the states of Yucatán and Campeche generally corresponds to high season in the rest of Mexico: Christmastime, Easter week, and July and August. Rainfall is heaviest and—humidity most uncomfortable—from May to October or November. On the Caribbean Coast, including Cancún, Cozumel, and Isla Mujeres, the peak tourist times are mid-December through late March. In less visited towns, levels of service differ drastically between the high and low seasons (when staff and activities may be cut back), so be prepared for the trade-off. The rainy season isn't a bad time to visit if you don't mind the afternoon showers and the sometimes reduced tourist attentions. On the coast, hurricane season is September–October.

CANCÚN

Updated by Shelagh McNally

FLYING INTO CANCÚN, you see nothing but green treetops for miles. It's clear from the air that this resort was literally carved out of the jungle. When development began here in the early 1970s, the beaches were deserted except for birds and iguanas. Now luxury hotels, shopping malls, and restaurants line Cancún's oceanfront. More vacationers come here than to any other part of Mexico, and many come again and again for the white-sand beaches, crystalline turquoise waters, sizzling nightlife, numerous restaurants, and the proximity of Maya ruins throughout the Yucatán peninsula.

Cancún has two very different sides. On the mainland is the actual Ciudad Cancún (Cancún City), the commercial center that is also informally known as El Centro. The other half, the Zona Hotelera (Hotel Zone), is the tourist heart. The Zone is actually a 22½-km (14-mi) barrier island off the Yucatán Peninsula. A separate northern strip called **Punta Sam,** north of Puerto Juárez (where the ferries to Isla Mujeres depart), is sometimes considered part of the Zone and is unofficially referred to as the Northern Hotel Zone. Both areas have been designed to please average American tastes: most people speak English, and there are fast-food outlets, brand-name stores, and cable TV. Shopping, eating, and lounging in the year-round tropical warmth are the main activities. (The sun shines an average of 240 days a year, reputedly more than at almost any other Caribbean spot. Temperatures linger at about 80°F.) At night you can enjoy activities such as knocking back tequila slammers at a bar, listening to great music at clubs, watching folkloric dance performances, and sampling Yucatecan food.

But there is more to Cancún than plopping yourself down under a *palapa* (thatch roof). Downtown offers a more authentic glimpse into the sights and sounds of Mexico. For diving and snorkeling, the reefs off Cancún and nearby Cozumel, Puerto Morelos, and Isla Mujeres are among the best in the world. Cancún also makes a relaxing base for venturing to the stupendous ruins of Chichén Itzá, Tulum, and Cobá, remnants of the area's rich Maya heritage.

As for Cancún's history, not much was written about it before its birth as a resort. The Maya people did settle the area during the Late Preclassic era, around AD 200, and remained until the 14th or 15th century, but little is known about them. Other explorers seem to have overlooked the barrier island—it doesn't appear on early navigators' maps. It was never heavily populated, perhaps because its terrain of mangroves and marshes (and resulting swarms of mosquitoes) discouraged settlement. Some minor Maya ruins were discovered in the mid-19th century, but archaeologists didn't get around to studying them until the 1950s.

In 1967, the Mexican government, under the leadership of Luis Echeverría, commissioned a study to pinpoint the ideal place for an international Caribbean resort. The computer chose Cancún, and the Cinderella transformation began. At the time the area's only residents were the three caretakers of a coconut plantation. In 1972 work began on the first hotel, and the island and city grew from there.

But Cancún's success has not come without a price. Its lagoons and mangrove swamps have been polluted; a number of species, such as conch and lobster, are dwindling; and parts of the coral reef are dead. And although the beaches still appear pristine for the most part, an increased effort will have to be made in order to preserve the physical beauty that is the resort's prime appeal.

Exploring

Cancún is divided into two parts: the Hotel Zone, Zona Hotelera, a numeral 7–shaped island; and Cancún City or downtown Cancún, known as El Centro, 4 km (2½ mi) west of the Hotel Zone on the mainland. The Hotel Zone consists entirely of hotels, restaurants, shopping complexes, marinas, and time-share condominiums, with few residential areas. It's not the sort of place you can get to know by walking, although there is a bicycle/walking path that starts at the Convention Center, ending downtown.

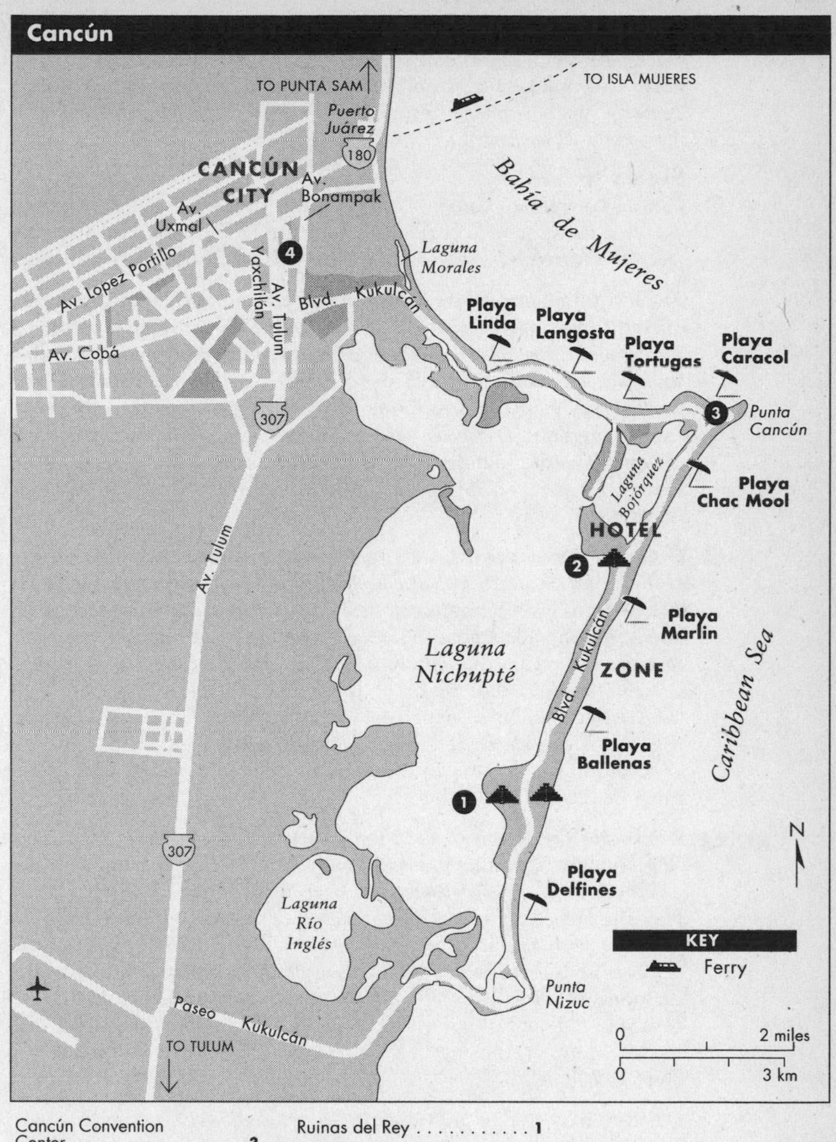

Cancún Convention Center **3**
El Centro **4**
Ruinas del Rey **1**
Yamil Lu'um **2**

A Good Tour

Cancún's scenery consists mostly of its beautiful beaches and crystal-clear waters, but there are also a few intriguing historical sites tucked away among the modern hotels. In addition to the attractions listed below, two modest vestiges of the ancient Maya civilization are worth a visit, but only for dedicated archaeology buffs. Neither is identified by name. On the 12th hole of Pok-Ta-Pok golf course (Boulevard Kukulcán, Km 6.5)—the name means "ball game" in Maya—stands a ruin consisting of two platforms and the remains of other ancient buildings. And the ruin of a tiny Maya shrine is cleverly incorporated into the architecture of the Hotel Camino Real, on the beach at Punta Cancún.

You don't need a car in Cancún, but if you've rented one to make extended trips, start in the Southern Hotel Zone at **Ruinas del Rey** ①. Drive north to **Yamil Lu'um** ②, and then stop in at the **Cancún Convention Center** ③, with its small anthropology and history museum, before heading west to **El Centro** ④.

Sights to See

3 **Cancún Convention Center.** This strikingly modern venue for cultural events is the jumping-off point for a 1-km (½-mi) string of shopping malls that extends west to the Presidente Inter-Continental Cancún.

The **Instituto Nacional de Antropología e Historia** (National Institute of Anthropology and History; ☎ 998/883–0305), a small museum on the ground floor of the convention center, traces Maya culture with a fascinating collection of 1,000- to 1,500-year-old artifacts collected throughout Quintana Roo. Looking through it is a great way to spend a rainy afternoon. Admission to the museum is about $3 (free Sunday); it's open Tuesday–Sunday 9–7. Guided tours are available in English, French, German, and Spanish. ✉ *Blvd. Kukulcán, Km 9, Hotel Zone,* ☎ *998/883–0199.*

4 **El Centro** (Downtown Cancún). Markets, instead of malls, offer a glimpse into a more provincial Mexico. The main street, **Avenida Tulum,** is easily recognizable for the huge seashell sculpture in the roundabout, which adds drama to the city when lit up at night. It has many restaurants and shops, including **Ki Huic,** the largest crafts market in Cancún. If you're looking for shopping bargains, however, the parallel **Avenida Yaxchilán** usually has better prices, particularly in the Mercado Veintiocho (Market 28). Just off Avenidas Yaxchilán and Sunyaxchén, this is the hub of downtown, filled with shops and restaurants frequented by locals.

1 **Ruinas del Rey** (Ruins of the King). Large signs on the Zone's lagoon side, roughly opposite the Playa de Oro and El Pueblito hotels, point out these small ruins, which have been incorporated into the Caesar Park Beach & Golf Resort complex. First entered into Western chronicles in a 16th-century travelogue, then sighted in 1842 by American explorer John Lloyd Stephens and his draftsman, Frederick Catherwood, the ruins were finally explored by archaeologists in 1910, though excavations did not begin until 1954. In 1975 archaeologists, along with the Mexican government, began the restoration of the Ruinas del Rey and San Miguelito.

Del Rey may not be particularly impressive when compared with major archaeological sites such as Tulum or Chichén Itzá, but it is the largest ruin in Cancún, and it's definitely worth a look. Dating from the 3rd to 2nd century BC, del Rey is notable for its unusual architecture: two main plazas bounded by two streets—most other Maya cities contained only one plaza. The pyramid here is topped by a platform, and inside its vault are paintings on stucco. Skeletons interred both at the apex and at the base indicate that the site may have been a royal burial ground. Originally named Kin Ich Ahau Bonil, Maya for "king of the solar countenance," the site was linked to astronomical practices in the ancient Maya culture. If you don't have time to visit the other major sites, this one will give you an idea of what the ancient Maya cities were like. ✉ *Blvd. Kukulcán, Km 17, Hotel Zone,* ☎ *no phone.* *About $3, free Sun.* *Daily 8–5.*

2 **Yamil Lu'um.** A small sign at the Sheraton directs you to a dirt path leading to this site, which stands on the highest point of Cancún—the name Yamil Lu'um means "hilly land." Although it comprises two structures—one probably a temple, the other probably a lighthouse—this

is the smallest of Cancún's ruins. Discovered in 1842 by John Lloyd Stephens, the remains date from the late 13th or early 14th century. ✉ *Blvd. Kukulcán, Km 12, Hotel Zone,* ☏ *no phone.* 🎟 *Free.*

Dining

With more than 1,200 restaurants in Cancún, finding the right dining spot might be the hardest work you do while on vacation. Both the Hotel Zone and downtown have plenty of great places to eat. There are some pitfalls: restaurants that line Avenida Tulum are often noisy and crowded with gas fumes, detracting from the romantic ambience of the outdoor cafés. In the Hotel Zone, restaurants often cater to what they assume is a tourist preference for bland food.

One key to eating well in Cancún is to find the local haunts, most of which are in the downtown area. Parque de las Palapas, just off Avenida Tulum, is where locals go for expertly prepared Yucatecan-style food. Farther into the city center, you can find the freshest seafood and other traditional Mexican fare at Mercado Veintiocho. Dozens of small restaurants there serve great food at reasonable prices. Unless otherwise stated, restaurants serve lunch and dinner daily.

Hotel Zone

Hotel Zone restaurants are located on the Cancún Hotel Zone Dining and Lodging map.

$$$$ ✕ **Club Grill.** The dining rooms of Cancún's Ritz-Carlton are the hands-down favorite for romantic dining. Everything is quietly elegant with rich wood, fresh flowers, crisp linens, and courtyard views. Classic dishes have been given a distinctly Mexican flavor. The sautéed foie gras with caramelized mango is a good starter, followed by the bean and lentil soup with habañero chili. The tasting menu offers a small selection of all the courses paired with wines followed by wickedly delicious desserts. Cynthia Davis, one of Cancún's top jazz vocalists, entertains nightly. ✉ *Blvd. Kukulcán (Retorno del Rey 36), Hotel Zone,* ☏ *998/885–0808. AE, MC, V. No lunch.*

$$$–$$$$ ★ ✕ **Côté Sud.** Dining is relaxed and stylish in the main restaurant at Le Meridien hotel. Decorated with fresh green-and-taupe plaids, white linen, and contemporary table settings, it offers dishes from France's Provence region with creative twists. Try the duck breast in a potato *galette* (buckwheat pancake) and lavender sauce or Moroccan-style rack of lamb. Fresh fish is grilled to perfection, and the wine list is extensive. "The Fifth Element"—a chocolate extravaganza designed to look like the planet Mars, dripping with strawberry sauce—should not be missed. ✉ *Le Meridien, Blvd. Kukulcán, Km 14 (Retorno del Rey 37), Hotel Zone,* ☏ *998/881–2260. AE, DC, MC, V.*

$$–$$$$ ✕ **Blue Bayou.** The first Cajun restaurant in Mexico, Blue Bayou was an immediate success and continues to be popular with locals and visitors alike. Five levels of intimate dining areas are decorated in wood, rattan, and bamboo against a backdrop of cascading waterfalls and a tropical garden. Specialties include Cancún jambalaya, blackened grouper, herb crawfish Louisiana, plantation duckling, and chicken Grand Bayou. There is live jazz every night and dancing on the weekends. ✉ *Hyatt Cancún Caribe, Blvd. Kukulcán, Km 10.5, Hotel Zone,* ☏ *998/883–0044. Reservations essential. AE, DC, MC, V. No lunch.*

$$–$$$ ★ ✕ **Gustino Italian Beachside Grill.** A dramatic staircase leading to a brick and wood entrance is only the beginning at this graceful restaurant. Walk past the open-air kitchen into the dining room with its leather furniture, sleek table settings, and artistic lighting, and enjoy the exquisitely presented, delicious food. The black-shells mussels in a white wine sauce is a good start followed by the pasta in sweet pepper sauce

Dining

Blue Bayou **9**
Cenacolo. **12**
Club Grill. **15**
Côté Sud **16**
La Destileria **13**
Gustino **17**
Iguana Wana. **4**
Maria Bonita **6**
100% Natural . . . **3, 14**
Pacal. **5**

Lodging

Baccará. **10**
Hilton Cancún Beach & Golf Resort **18**
Holiday Inn Express **8**
Hyatt Cancún Caribe Villas & Resort **9**
Le Meridien **16**
Oasis Playa **19**
Park Royal Pirámides Cancún **11**
Presidente Inter-Continental Cancún . . **2**
Ritz-Carlton Cancún **15**
Suites Sina. **7**
Villas Tacul. **1**

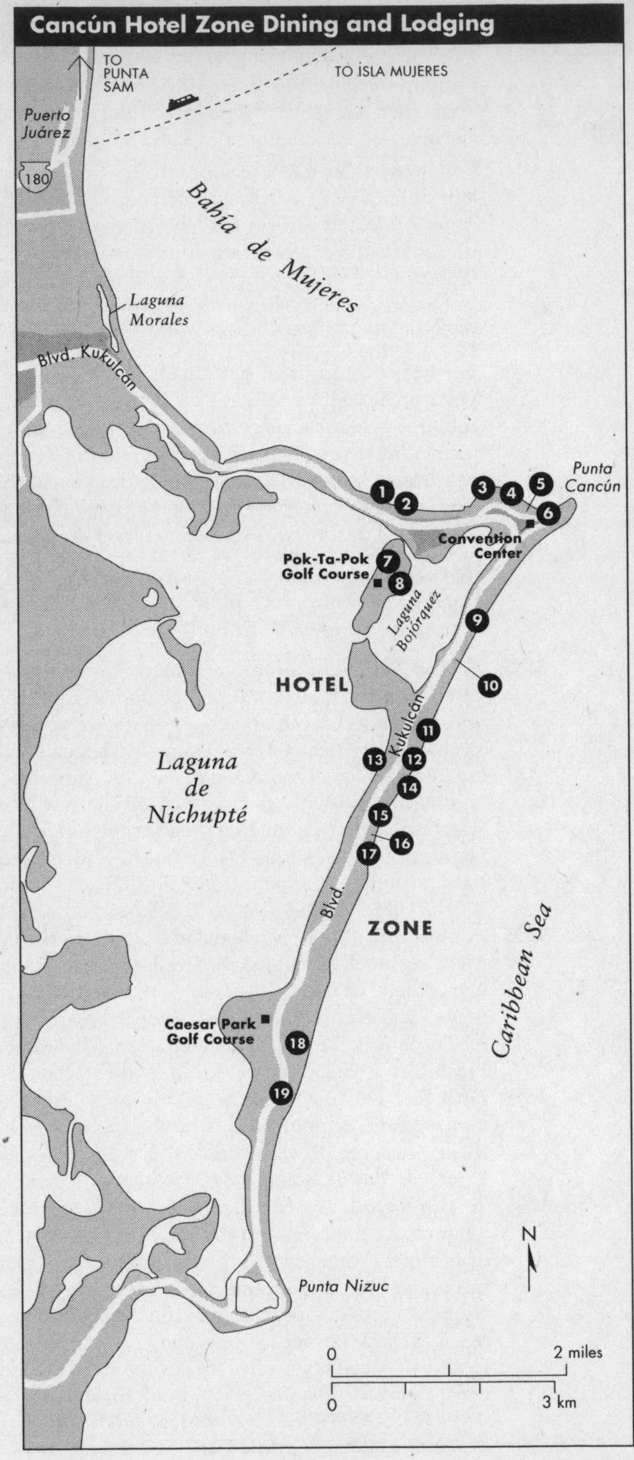

or the braised veal shank served with mushroom polenta. While dining, enjoy the panoramic views and romantic violin music. Reservations are recommended. ✉ *JW Marriott Resort, Blvd. Kukulcán, Km 14.5, Hotel Zone,* ☎ *998/848–9600 Ext. 6649. AE, MC, V.*

$–$$$ ★ ✕ **Maria Bonita.** Here is authentic Mexico in food, music, and atmosphere. This delightful restaurant is decorated as a Mexican hacienda with lots of green, red, and white tile work, ceramics, and paintings. The glass-enclosed patio with an ocean view is the perfect spot to enjoy the best of Mexican cuisine. Worth trying are the various mole dishes, such as chicken almond mole (with chocolate, almonds, and chilies) or any of the various Tex-Mex or grilled entrées. The menu explains the different chilies used by the kitchen. ✉ *Hotel Camino Real, Punta Cancún, Blvd. Kukulcán, Km 9, Hotel Zone,* ☎ *998/848–7000. AE, MC, V. No lunch.*

$$ ✕ **La Destileria.** Be prepared to have your perceptions about tequila changed forever at this combination restaurant–tequila museum decorated like an antique tequila distillery. Enjoy one of the 100 tequilas offered or their superb margaritas. (Cheap tequila drinks will never be the same.) The menu is traditional Mexican cuisine that includes shark *panuchos* (tortillas filled with fish) and *El Chiquihuite Maximiliano* (pastry filled with chicken and corn truffle). Afterward, you can drop by the tequila shop and pick up your favorite brand. ✉ *Blvd. Kukulcán, Km 12.65 (across from Kukulcán Plaza), Hotel Zone,* ☎ *998/883–1087. AE, MC, V.*

$–$$ ✕ **Cenacolo.** Italian art and stained glass fill the relaxed interior of this charming neighborhood restaurant, where musicians serenade you throughout your meal. Outside is a bustling, plant-filled patio overlooking Boulevard Kukulcán. The food is consistently good, especially the salad of mixed greens, the ricotta ravioli, the lasagna with béchamel, and the sliced filet mignon in balsamic vinegar. The staff spoils you completely. ✉ *Kukulcán Plaza, Blvd. Kukulcán, Km 13.5, Hotel Zone,* ☎ *998/885–3603. AE, MC, V.*

$–$$ ✕ **Pacal.** Try Pascal for sophisticated renditions of regional Maya cuisine. To match the food there is fine linen and silverware against a backdrop of Maya carvings and stelae. Start off with the Yucatecan lime soup followed by *Ya Hax* (duck in a fried peanut and green tomato base). Also on the menu are the classic *cochinita pibil* (pork baked in banana leaves) and *Tikin Xic* (fish in sour-orange sauce). ✉ *Blvd. Kukulcán, Km 8.5, next to Plaza Caracol, Hotel Zone,* ☎ *998/883–2184. AE, MC, V.*

$ ✕ **100% Natural.** Looking for something light and healthful? Head to one of these cheery open-air restaurants, done up with plenty of plants and modern Maya sculptures. The menus emphasize soups, fruit and veggie salads, fresh fruit drinks, and other nonmeat items, though egg dishes, sandwiches, grilled chicken and fish, and Mexican and Italian specialties are also available. *Hotel Zone:* ✉ *Kukulcán Shopping Plaza, Blvd. Kukulcán, Km 13.5, Hotel Zone,* ☎ *998/885–2903;* ✉ *Forum-by-the-Sea, Blvd. Kukulcán, Km 9.5, Hotel Zone,* ☎ *998/883–1180; Downtown:* ✉ *Av. Sunyaxchén 62, Sm 25,* ☎ *99/884–3617;* ✉ *Plaza las Américas, Av. Tulum, Super Manzana 4,* ☎ *no phone. MC, V.*

Downtown

Downtown restaurants are located on the Downtown Cancún Dining and Lodging map.

$$–$$$ ★ ✕ **Lacanda Paolo.** Southern Italian cuisine is brought to new heights of excellence in this sophisticated, innovative restaurant—considered by many to be the best Italian in Cancún. Don't even think of passing up the black pasta in calamari sauce or the penne with basil and tomato sauce. Also delicious are the steamed lobster in garlic sauce and

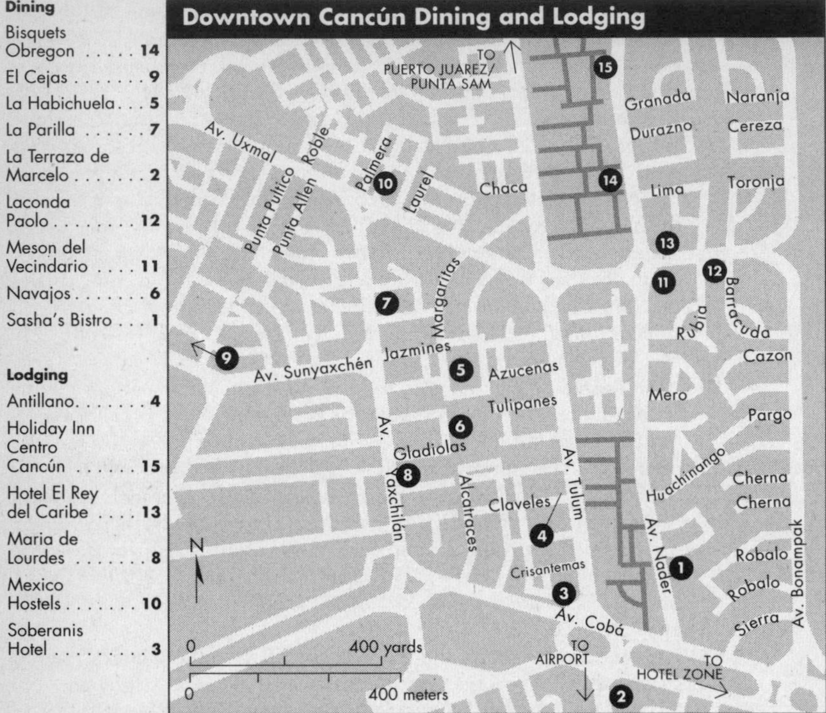

the lemon fish. Flowers, artwork on the walls, and attentive service give the restaurant a warmth without being fussy. ✉ *Av. Uxmal 35, Sm 3,* ☎ *998/887–2627. AE, DC, MC, V.*

$$–$$$ ✕ **La Parilla.** This Mexican grill is a favorite with locals and tourists alike. With its palapa roof, hacienda style, and energetic waiters, it remains a Cancún classic. Popular dishes are the mixed Mexican grill, which includes chicken, steak, shrimp, and lobster, or the grilled steak Tampiqueña style. Enjoy these and many other Mexican specialties along with a wide selection of tequila. ✉ *Av. Yaxchilán 51, Sm 24,* ☎ *998/887–6141. AE, MC, V.*

$$ ★ ✕ **La Habichuela** (The Green Bean). Once an elegant home, this much-loved restaurant is decorated with Maya sculpture among local trees and flowers. When lit up at night, the garden is especially enchanting. In the 24 years that the Pezzotti family has been running the restaurant there have been few complaints. Don't miss the famous *crema de habichuela* (a rich, cream-based seafood soup) or the *cocobichuela* (lobster and shrimp in a light curry sauce served inside a coconut). Finish off your meal with Xtabentun, a Maya liqueur made with honey and anise. ✉ *Av. Margaritas 25, Sm 22,* ☎ *998/884–3158. AE, DC, MC, V.*

$–$$ ★ ✕ **El Cejas.** In the heart of the bustling, lively Mercado Veintiocho, this is a neighborhood restaurant with an international reputation. The seafood is the freshest there is and it's cheaper than in the Hotel Zone. If you've had a wild night, try the *vuelva la vida,* or "return to life" (conch, oysters, shrimp, octopus, calamari, and fish with a hot tomato sauce). Equally wonderful is the ceviche and hot, spicy shrimp soup. ✉ *Mercado Veintiocho, Av. Sunyaxchén, Sm 26,* ☎ *998/887–1080. MC, V.*

$–$$ ✕ **Mesón del Vecindario.** This sweet little restaurant tucked away from the street resembles an A-frame house in the woods. The menu specializes in all kinds of cheese and beef fondues along with terrific salads, fresh pasta, and baked goods. Breakfasts are hearty and economical. It makes a pleasant change from the usual downtown fare. ✉ *Av. Uxmal 23, Sm 3,* ☎ *998/884–8900. AE.*

$–$$ ★ ✕ **Sasha's Bistro.** Dinner at this not-to-be-missed bistro is an experience you're not likely to forget. Owner Alexander (Sasha) Rudin, a Swiss master chef, knows how to play up the subtleties of his ingredients. He serves the most original and inspired menu along this coast—a fusion of Asian and European flavors—and the presentation is as artful as the food. The menu changes monthly so it's always fresh. Past masterpieces have included pork chops with a creamy porcini mushroom sauce. ✉ *Av. Nader 118, at Av. Mojarro, Sm 3,* ☎ *998/887–9105. MC, V. Closed Sun. and Mon. No lunch.*

$–$$ ✕ **La Terraza de Marcelo.** This is a perfect place for that quiet romantic dinner, with a terrace for dining under the stars. The menu combines the flavors of Mexico and Italy to produce dishes like cambray salad (artichoke and avocado in a vinaigrette dressing), the pork loin in tamarind sauce, and the Terrasaniz breast of chicken (stuffed with ham and spices). Finish off your meal with one of the rich desserts or a fine espresso. ✉ *Av. Labna 29, at Gacela, Sm 20,* ☎ *998/884–2056. AE, MC, V.*

$ ✕ **Bisquets Obregon.** With its cheery colors, two levels of tables, and sit-down luncheon counter, this cafeteria-style spot is *the* place to have breakfast downtown. Begin your day with hearty Mexican classics such as *huevos rancheros* (eggs sunny-side up on tortillas, covered with tomato sauce) and do try the *cafe con leche* (coffee with hot milk)—just watching the waiters pour it is impressive. The place opens early (7 AM). ✉ *Av. Nader 9, Sm 2,* ☎ *998/887–6876. MC, V.*

Lodging

You might find it bewildering to choose among the many hotels in Cancún. For luxury and amenities, the Hotel Zone is the place to stay. For the most part the downtown hotels don't offer anything near the luxury of the Hotel Zone properties. They will, however, give you the opportunity to stay in a popular resort without paying resort prices, and many places have free shuttle service to the beach. Downtown hotels are also closer to Ki Huic, Cancún's crafts market, and restaurants that are more authentic—and less costly—than those in the Zone.

Expect minibars, satellite TV, laundry and room service, private safes (check to see if there is an extra charge for safe use), and bathroom hair dryers in hotels in the $$$$ category; in addition, almost every major hotel has suites, rooms for people with disabilities, no-smoking rooms, an in-house travel agency and/or a car-rental concession, guest parking, water-sports facilities, hair salon and spa, fully equipped gymnasium, and a daily schedule of planned games and activities for guests. Unless otherwise noted, all hotels have private baths.

For most of the hotels, it's best to make reservations at least one month in advance and up to three months in advance for the Christmas season. Many of the larger chain hotels also offer special Internet deals, with room rates dropping considerably when reserved on-line.

Hotel Zone

Hotels in this section appear on the Cancún Hotel Zone Dining and Lodging map.

$$$$ ★ **Baccará.** Each suite of this gorgeous Yucatan Resorts property, a perfect example of a boutique hotel, is decorated differently, with Mexican art, furniture, and textiles. All have fully equipped kitchens, living and dining rooms, and private hot tubs that overlook either the ocean or the lagoon. Downstairs is a lobby and beach bar centered on an art-

fully designed pool area. The attentive staff adds to the hotel's warmth. ✉ *Blvd. Kukulcán, Km 11.5, 77500, Hotel Zone,* ☎ *998/883–2077 or 800/713–8170,* FAX *998/883–2173,* WEB *www.yucatanresorts.com. 34 rooms. 3 restaurants, in-room hot tubs, kitchens, pool, beach, 3 bars, car rental. AE, DC, MC, V.*

$$$$ ★ **Hilton Cancún Beach & Golf Resort.** This elegant hotel has rooms done up in bright yellows and greens that complement the terra-cotta floors and rattan furniture. All rooms have a balcony or terrace with an ocean view; some have views of the resort's championship 18-hole, par-72 golf course. Seven lavish, interconnecting pools wind through palm-dotted lawns, ending at the magnificent beach. For total luxury consider staying at the Beach Club, with its 80 oceanfront villas. In the evening enjoy incredible Asian fare at the romantic seaside restaurant, Sirenita. ✉ *Blvd. Kukulcán, Km 17 (Retorno Lacandones), 77500, Hotel Zone,* ☎ *998/881–8000,* FAX *998/881–8082,* WEB *www.hilton.com. 426 rooms, 4 suites. 3 restaurants, 18-hole golf course, 2 tennis courts, 7 pools, aerobics, gym, hair salon, hot tubs, sauna, beach, 3 bars, lobby lounge, shops, children's programs (ages 4–12), car rental. AE, DC, MC, V.*

$$$$ ★ **Le Meridien.** High on a hill, this refined yet relaxed hotel has an art deco style with subtle Maya influences; there's lots of wood, glass, and mirrors. Rooms have spectacular ocean views. The many thoughtful extras—such as different temperature in each swimming pool—make a stay here special. The Spa del Mar is the best in the area, offering the latest European techniques along with an outdoor hot tub and waterfall. It's open to the public, so you can visit even if you're not at the hotel. Gourmet dining can be found at the wonderful Côté Sud. ✉ *Blvd. Kukulcán, Km 14 (Retorno del Rey, Lote 37), 77500, Hotel Zone,* ☎ *998/881–2200 or 800/543–4300,* FAX *998/881–2201,* WEB *www.meridiencancun.com.mx. 213 rooms, 28 suites. 3 restaurants, 2 tennis courts, 3 pools, gym, hot tub, spa, beach, 2 bars, shops, children's programs (ages 4–12). AE, MC, V.*

$$$$ **Presidente Inter-Continental Cancún.** It's hard to miss the striking yellow entrance of this hotel, five minutes from Plaza Caracol. Inside, lavish marble with accents of Talavera pottery decorates the hotel throughout. It has a quiet beach and a waterfall in the shape of a Maya pyramid by the pool. Larger-than-average rooms have royal-blue or beige color schemes with light wicker furniture and area rugs on stone floors. Rooms on the first floor have patios and outdoor hot tubs. The suites offer contemporary furnishings, in-room video equipment, and spacious balconies. ✉ *Blvd. Kukulcán, Km 7.5, 77500, Hotel Zone,* ☎ *998/848–8700 or 800/327–0200,* FAX *998/883–2602,* WEB *www.interconti.com. 290 rooms, 6 suites. 2 restaurants, tennis court, 2 pools, gym, hair salon, hot tubs, beach, bar, shops. AE, MC, V.*

$$$$ ★ **Ritz-Carlton Cancún.** Ultraposh, ornate, and sumptuous, the Ritz exudes opulent charm. Its thick carpets, plush furniture, European antiques, and oil paintings may lead you to forget that you are in Mexico. Rooms are decorated in shades of teal, beige, and rose, with wall-to-wall carpeting and large balconies overlooking the Caribbean. Marble bathrooms are fitted with separate tubs and showers. In the evening enjoy fine dining at the Club Grill. ✉ *Blvd. Kukulcán, Km 14 (Retorno del Rey 36), 77500,* ☎ *998/881–0808 or 800/241–3333,* FAX *998/885–1048,* WEB *www.ritzcarlton.com. 365 rooms, 40 suites. 3 restaurants, 3 tennis courts, pro shop, 3 pools, health club, hot tub, spa, beach, 2 bars, shops. AE, DC, MC, V.*

$$$ ★ **Park Royal Pirámides Cancún.** This charming hotel with its twin pyramids has a compact but well-planned lobby done with cool beige furnishings. Rooms have sea and sunset colors with original artwork (some of it created with local sand). Standard suites have two double

beds and full baths; Ambassador suites have fully equipped kitchens, living-dining rooms, three double beds, and full baths. Selected suites also have private hot tubs and terraces. Some have views of the Maya ruin, Yamil Lu'um, next door. The property has two pools joined by a waterfall, a lovely beach, and a well-stocked, reasonably priced grocery store. ✉ *Blvd. Kukulcán, Km 12.5, 77500, Hotel Zone,* ☎ *998/885–1333,* FAX *998/885–0113,* WEB *www.piramidescancun.com.mx. 232 rooms, 54 suites. Restaurant, grocery, some kitchens, 2 pools, gym, beach, bar, shops, children's programs (ages 4–12), travel services. AE, MC, V.*

$$$ **Villas Tacul.** Originally built for traveling dignitaries, these 23 villas are a great place to set up home. The grounds are beautifully landscaped with well-trimmed lawns and gardens that lead down to a private beach. All villas have kitchens and from two to five bedrooms, making them ideal for families or couples traveling together. They have red-tile floors, authentic Mexican colonial–style furniture, wagon-wheel chandeliers, and tin-work mirrors. You can also have a housekeeper who cleans and serves breakfast. Less expensive rooms without kitchen facilities are also available. ✉ *Blvd. Kukulcán, Km 5.5, 77500, Hotel Zone,* ☎ *998/883–0000 or 800/842–0193,* FAX *998/883–0349,* WEB *www.cancun.com/hotels/villastacul. 23 villas. Restaurant, kitchens, 2 tennis courts, pool, beach, basketball, bar. AE, DC, MC, V.*

$$ **Holiday Inn Express.** Within easy walking distance of the Pok-Ta-Pok golf course, this pleasant hotel was built to resemble a Mexican hacienda—but with a pool instead of a courtyard at its center. Rooms are bright with blues and reds and modern furniture and have either patios or small balconies that overlook the pool and deck. Although not luxurious, it's perfect for families in which Dad wants to golf, Mom wants to shop, and the kids want to hit the beach. A complimentary shuttle bus takes you to the shops and beaches five minutes away; taxis are inexpensive alternatives. ✉ *Paseo Pok-Ta-Pok, 77500, Hotel Zone,* ☎ *998/883–2200,* FAX *998/883–2532,* WEB *www.holidayinncancun.com.mx. 119 rooms. Restaurant, pool. AE, MC, V.*

$$ **Suites Sina.** These economical suites are in the heart of the Hotel Zone in front of Laguna Nichupté and close to the golf course. Each suite is equipped with comfortable furniture, kitchenette, dining-living room with sofa bed, balcony or terrace, television, and double beds. Outside is a central pool and garden. Perhaps the best deal in the Hotel Zone, they are particularly affordable if you rent for a few weeks or share with someone. ✉ *Club de Golf, Calle Quetzal 33, 77500, Hotel Zone,* ☎ *998/883–1017 or 877/666–9837,* FAX *998/883–2459,* WEB *www.cancunsinasuites.com.mx. 33 suites. Kitchenettes, pool. AE, MC, V.*

Downtown

Downtown hotels appear on the Downtown Cancún Dining and Lodging map.

$$ ★ **Antillano.** On the main strip, this beautifully maintained hotel stands out from the others in its league. Each room is fitted with wood furnishings, one or two double beds, a sink area separate from the bath, red-tile floors, and a small television. There is a cozy little lobby bar and decent-size pool. The quietest rooms are those facing the interior—avoid the noisier rooms that face Avenida Tulum. ✉ *Av. Tulum at Calle Claveles, 77500, Sm 21,* ☎ *998/884–1532,* FAX *998/884–1878,* WEB *www.hotelantillano.com. 48 rooms. Pool, bar, shops, baby-sitting. AE, DC, MC, V.*

$$ ★ **Holiday Inn Centro Cancún.** This is the place to stay if you want to pay modest rates and be near the restaurants and shops but still have luxury hotel amenities. The attractive pink four-story building is reminiscent of a hacienda and has modern rooms with mauve and blue color

schemes and Mexican ceramics and textiles. All rooms overlook a large pool surrounded by tropical plants. Its sister hotel, Margaritas Cancún, at Avenida Yaxchilán 41 (☎ 9/884–9333), also downtown, has pretty rooms with balconies and the same amenities and is a little less expensive. ✉ *Av. Nader 1, 77500, Sm 2,* ☎ *998/887–4455 or 800/465–4329,* FAX *998/884–7954,* WEB *www.sixcontinentshotels.com/holiday-inn. 246 rooms. 2 restaurants, tennis court, pool, gym, hair salon, 2 bars, nightclub, laundry facilities, car rental, travel services. AE, DC, MC, V.*

$$ ★ **Hotel El Rey del Caribe.** A marvel in downtown Cancún, El Rey del Caribe has been designed to have zero impact on the environment, in part by using solar energy for electricity, a water recycling plan, and special composting toilets. And its luxuriant garden, which blocks the heat and noise of downtown, makes it an oasis. Hammocks hang poolside, and wrought-iron tables and chairs are placed throughout the grounds. Rooms are on the small side but are pleasant and have convenient kitchenettes. The hotel is within walking distance of all downtown shops and restaurants. ✉ *Avs. Uxmal and Nader, 77500, Sm 2,* ☎ *998/884–2028,* FAX *998/884–9857,* WEB *www.reycaribe.com. 26 rooms. Kitchenettes, pool, hot tub. AE, MC, V.*

$ ★ **Maria de Lourdes.** This budget hotel offers a lot of luxury at extremely reasonable rates. Basic rooms are furnished with two queen-size beds, television, and bath. A well-maintained, decent-size swimming pool is surrounded by tables, where guests gather to play cards and chat. The staff is as amiable as the surroundings. It's within walking distance of shops and restaurants along Tulum. ✉ *Av. Yaxchilán 31, 77500, Sm 22,* ☎ *998/884–4744,* FAX *998/884–1242. 50 rooms. Restaurant, pool, bar. MC, V.*

$ ★ **Mexico Hostels.** Four blocks from the main bus terminal and open 24 hours, this is absolutely *the* cheapest place to stay in Cancún. The pleasant space has four beds per room, private lockers, access to a full kitchen, a lounge area, and Internet access. Those who want to sleep outdoors can share a space with 20 others under a palapa roof. ✉ *Calle Palmera 30 (off Av. Uxmal, beside the BMW dealership), 77500, Sm 23,* ☎ *998/887–0191 or 212/699–3825 Ext. 7860,* FAX *425/962–8028,* WEB *www.mexicohostels.com. 50 beds. No credit cards.*

$ ★ **Soberanis Hotel.** This is both a hostel and a hotel. Rooms are elegant and uncluttered, with modern furniture and white-tile floors. Downtown banks, shops, and restaurants are within walking distance. The hostel section has four bunks to a room, each with its own locker, for $12 per night. A Continental breakfast is included in the price. This is one of the best deals in Cancún. ✉ *Av. Coba, Calle 5 y 7, 77500, Sm 22,* ☎ *998/884–4564,* FAX *998/884–5138,* WEB *www.soberanis.com.mx; 78 rooms. Restaurant, room service, cable TV, Internet, meeting room, free parking. MC, V.*

Nightlife and the Arts

The Arts

The **Casa de Cultura** (✉ Prolongación Av. Yaxchilán, Sm 26, ☎ 998/884–8364) hosts local cultural events, including art exhibits, dance performances, plays, and concerts, throughout the year.

FESTIVALS

Cancún's **Jazz Festival** is an annual weeklong event in late May that draws a huge international crowd from the United States, South America, and Europe. The Cancún Hotel Association (☎ 998/884–7083) can provide information about this popular gathering.

Each fall the city of Cancún hosts a festival of music and dance. Past events have included the **Caribbean Culture Festival** and the **Viva Mex-**

ico Festival. Artists and musicians from all over Mexico and the Caribbean come to participate in events that range from dance to music to poetry readings, and restaurants participate by offering special dishes. Consult your hotel for details.

PERFORMANCES

Every weeknight the **Teatro de Cancún** (✉ El Embarcadero, Blvd. Kukulcán, Km 4, Hotel Zone, ☎ 998/849–4848) presents two shows: *Voces y Danzas de Mexico* (*Voices and Dances of Mexico*), a colorful showcase of popular songs and dances from different cities in Mexico, as well as *Tradución del Caribe* (*Caribbean Tradition*), which highlights the rhythms, music, and dance of Cuba, Puerto Rico, and other Caribbean destinations. Tickets for each performance are $29. Dinner packages are also available.

Nightlife

Nightlife happens all over Cancún and in a variety of different settings. Many restaurants do double duty as party centers; discos offer music (sometimes taped, sometimes live) and light shows; and most nightclubs have live music and dancing. Sometimes the lines between the three get blurred.

DISCOS

Cancún wouldn't be Cancún without its glittering discos, which generally start jumping about 10:30. **La Boom** (✉ Blvd. Kukulcán, Km 3.5, Hotel Zone, ☎ 998/883–1152) is always the last place to close; it has a video bar with a light show and regular weekly events. The **Bull Dog Rock 'n Roll Cafe** (✉ Krystal Cancún hotel, Blvd. Kukulcán, Km 9, Lote 9, Hotel Zone, ☎ 998/883–1793) has an all-you-can-drink bar and the latest dance music with an impressive laser light show. **Dady'O** (✉ Blvd. Kukulcán, Km 9.5, Hotel Zone, ☎ 998/883–3333) has been around for a while but is still very "in" with the younger set. Next door to Dady'O, **Dady Rock** (✉ Blvd. Kukulcán, Km 9.5, Hotel Zone, ☎ 998/883–3333) draws a high-energy crowd with live music, a giant TV screen, contests, and food specials. **Fat Tuesday** (✉ Blvd. Kukulcán, Km 6.5, Hotel Zone, ☎ 998/849–7199), with its large daiquiri bar and live and taped disco music, is another place to go and dance the night away. **Ma'Ax'O** (✉ Blvd. Kukulcán, Km 1.5, Hotel Zone, ☎ 998/883–5599), in La Isla Shopping Village, is a club-bar with the latest music and a wild dance floor.

MUSIC

To mingle with locals and hear great music for free, head down to the **Parque de las Palapas** (✉ bordered by Avs. Tulum, Yaxchilán, Uxmal, and Cobá, Sm 22). Every Friday night at 7:30 there is live music that ranges from jazz to salsa to Caribbean.

Azucar (✉ Hotel Camino Real, Blvd. Kukulcán, Km 9, Hotel Zone, ☎ 998/883–7000) showcases the very best Latin American bands. Go just to watch the locals dance (the beautiful people don't turn up here until *really* late) and enjoy the hot salsa. Proper dress is required—no jeans or sneakers. **Batacha** (✉ Hotel Miramar Misión, Blvd. Kukulcán, Km 9.5, Hotel Zone, ☎ 998/883–1755) is a terrific, down-to-earth spot for Latin American and Mexican music, as well as a great place to practice your salsa moves. The **Blue Bayou Jazz Club** (✉ Hyatt Cancún Caribe, Blvd. Kukulcán, Km 10.5, Hotel Zone, ☎ 998/883–0044) has nightly jazz in the lobby bar. The classy downtown **Roots Bar** (✉ Av. Tulipanes 26, near Parque de las Palapas, Sm 22, ☎ 998/884–2437) is the place for jazz, fusion, flamenco, and blues.

Outdoor Activities and Sports

Golf

The main golf course is at **Pok-Ta-Pok** (✉ Blvd. Kukulcán, between Km 6 and Km 7, Hotel Zone, ☎ 998/883–1230), a club with fine views of both sea and lagoon; its 18 holes were designed by Robert Trent Jones, Sr. The club also has a practice green, a swimming pool, tennis courts, and a restaurant. The greens fees start at $80 ($45 after 2 PM); electric cart, $30; and caddies, $20. Playing hours are 6 AM–5 PM (last tee-off is at 4). There is an 18-hole championship golf course at the **Hilton Cancún Beach & Golf Resort** (✉ Blvd. Kukulcán, Km 17, Hotel Zone, ☎ 998/881–8016); greens fees are $100 ($65 for hotel guests), carts are included, and club rentals run from $20 to $30. The 13-hole executive course (par 53) at the **Hotel Meliá Cancún** (✉ Blvd. Kukulcán, Km 12, Hotel Zone, ☎ 998/885–1160) forms a semicircle around the property and shares its beautiful ocean views. The greens fee is about $20.

Water Sports

There are lots of ways to get your adrenaline going while getting wet in Cancún. You can find places to go parasailing (about $35 for eight minutes), waterskiing ($70 per hour), or jet-skiing ($70 per hour, or $60 for Wave Runners, double-seated Jet Skis). Paddleboats, kayaks, catamarans, and banana boats are readily available, too.

El Embarcadero (✉ Blvd. Kukulcán, Km 4, Hotel Zone), at Playa Linda, is the largest marina complex where most water tours depart. At the dock you can find the Garrafon Ferry, the Isla Mujeres Tour Boat, the *Capitán Hook* galleon, the Nautibus, the Aquabus, and HeliTours. Inside the complex are Xcaret ticket booths, a folkloric museum, an artists' flea market, two restaurants, a rotating scenic tower, and the Teatro Cancún, where there are nightly performances.

Aqua Fun (✉ Blvd. Kukulcán, Km 16.5, Hotel Zone, ☎ 998/885–2930) maintains a full-service marina with large fleets of water toys such as Wave Runners, Jet Skis, speedboats, kayaks, and windsurfers. **AquaWorld** (✉ Blvd. Kukulcán, Km 15.2, Hotel Zone, ☎ 998/848–8300), a full-service marina, rents boats and water toys to thousands of people a day. If you would like to swim with the dolphins or feed some sharks without leaving the Hotel Zone, head over to the **Interactive Aquarium** (✉ Blvd. Kukulcán, Km 12.5, Hotel Zone, ☎ 998/883–5725), at La Isla Shopping Village. Prices start at $65 for a half-hour dip with the dolphins, $29.95 sans dolphins. **Parque Nizuc** (✉ Blvd. Kukulcán, Km 25, Hotel Zone, ☎ 998/881–3030) is the area's newest marine park. Your entry fee gets you into the Wet 'n Wild water park and free snorkeling at Baxal-Há Snorkel area, where you will find gentle sharks and manta rays. There is an extra charge to swim or play with the dolphins at the Atlántida Aquarium. Visitors are asked not to bring food or beverages into the park.

FISHING/MARINAS

Some 500 species of tropical fish, including sailfish, wahoo, bluefin, marlin, barracuda, and red snapper, live in the waters adjacent to Cancún. Deep-sea fishing boats and gear may be chartered from outfitters starting at about $350 for four hours, $450 for six hours, and $550 for eight hours. Charters generally include a captain and first mate, gear, bait, and beverages. The following all have charter boats for deep-sea fishing at competitive prices: **Aqua Tours** (✉ Blvd. Kukulcán, Km 6, Hotel Zone, ☎ 998/849–4444); **Marina del Rey** (✉ Blvd. Kukulcán, Km 15.5, Hotel Zone, ☎ 998/885–0273); **Marina Punta del Este** (✉ Blvd. Kukulcán, Km. 10.3, Hotel Zone, ☎ 998/883–1210); **Mundo Marina** (✉ Blvd. Kukulcán, Km 5.5, Hotel Zone, ☎ 998/849–7257).

SNORKELING AND SCUBA DIVING

Snorkeling is best at Punta Nizuc, Punta Cancún, and Playa Tortugas, although you should be especially careful of the strong currents at the last. You can generally rent gear for $10 per day from many of the scuba-diving places, and most hotels and resorts have their own gear for rent. If you've brought your own snorkeling gear and want to save money, take a city bus down to Punta Nizuc.

Barracuda Marina (✉ Blvd. Kukulcán, Km 14, Hotel Zone, ☎ 998/885–3444) has a two-hour Wave Runner jungle tour through the mangroves, which ends with snorkeling at the Punta Nizuc coral reef. The $38.50 fee includes snorkeling equipment, life jackets, and refreshments.

Scuba diving has gained in popularity in Cancún. A word of caution about one-hour "resort" courses offered as freebies by the resorts: this does not prepare you to dive in the ocean, no matter what the high-pressure concession operators tell you. A one-hour lesson in a controlled environment such as a pool differs vastly from one in the open ocean. If you have caught the scuba bug, invest in a few more lessons and prepare yourself properly so you can enjoy the experience. Remember that scuba-diving accidents can be fatal.

The secret of a good scuba company is personal attention, which is more often found at the smaller companies. Ask to meet the dive master, and check out the company's equipment and certifications thoroughly. **Scuba Cancún** (✉ Blvd. Kukulcán, Km 5, Hotel Zone, ☎ 998/849–4736) specializes in diving trips and offers NAUI, CMAS, and PADI instruction. It's operated by Luis Hurtado, who has more than 35 years of experience. A two-tank dive starts at $60. **Solo Buceo** (✉ Blvd. Kukulcán, Km 9, Hotel Zone, ☎ 998/883–3979) charges $50 for two-tank dives, with NAUI, SSI, and PADI instruction. The outfit goes to Cozumel, Akumal, Xpu-ha, and Isla Mujeres. Extended diving trips are available from $180.

Shopping

Resort wear and handicrafts are the most popular purchases in Cancún, but the prices are higher than in other cities and the selection is limited. If your vacation includes visits to other Mexican locales, it's best to postpone your shopping spree until then. Still, it is possible to find Mexican specialties such as handwoven textiles, leather goods, and jewelry handcrafted from silver and local coral. Cancún is most noted for luxury items. Many stores are "duty-free," selling designer goods at reduced prices, sometimes as much as 30%–40% off the usual retail price.

A note of caution about tortoiseshell products: the turtles from which they're made are an endangered species, and it is illegal to bring tortoiseshell into the United States and several other countries. Simply refrain from buying anything made from tortoiseshell. Also be aware that there are some restrictions regarding black coral. You must purchase it from a recognized dealer.

In Cancún, shopping hours are generally weekdays 10–1 and 4–7, although more and more stores are staying open throughout the day rather than closing for siesta between 1 and 4. Many shops keep Saturday-morning hours, and some are now open on Sunday until 1. Shops in the malls tend to be open weekdays 9 AM or 10 AM–8 PM or 10 PM.

Downtown

There are large numbers of shops downtown along Avenida Tulum (between Avenidas Cobá and Uxmal). **Fama** (✉ Av. Tulum 105, Sm 21,

☎ 998/884–6586) is a department store that sells clothing, English books and magazines, sports gear, toiletries, liquor, and *latería* (crafts made of tin). The oldest and largest of Cancún's crafts markets is **Ki Huic** (✉ Av. Tulum 17, between Bancomer and Bital, Sm 3, ☎ 998/884–3347). It is open daily 9 AM–10 PM and houses about 100 vendors. **Ultrafemme** (✉ Av. Tulum and Calle Claveles, Sm 21, ☎ 998/885–1402) is a popular downtown store that carries duty-free perfume, cosmetics, and jewelry. It also has branches in the Hotel Zone at Plaza Caracol, Plaza Flamingo, Kukulcán Plaza, and La Isla Shopping Village.

Hotel Zone

There is only one open-air market in the Hotel Zone. **Coral Negro,** next to the convention center, is a collection of about 50 stalls selling crafts items. It's open daily until late evening. Everything here is overpriced, but bargaining does work.

Kukulcán Plaza (✉ Blvd. Kukulcán, Km 13, Hotel Zone, ☎ 998/885–2304) is a mall that never seems to end, with around 130 shops (including Benetton and Harley Davidson boutiques), 12 restaurants, a bar, a liquor store, a bank, bowling lanes, and a video arcade. The plaza is also notable for the many cultural events and shows that take place in the main public area.

Leading off Plaza Caracol is the oldest and most varied commercial center in the Zone, **Mayafair Plaza** (✉ Blvd. Kukulcán, Km 8.5, Hotel Zone, ☎ 998/883–0571). Mayafair has a large open-air center filled with shops, bars, and restaurants, including El Mexicano. An adjacent indoor shopping mall is decorated to resemble a rain forest, complete with replicas of Maya stelae.

Galleries

The **Huichol Collection** has three locations: Plaza Kukulcán (✉ Blvd. Kukulcán, Km 13, Hotel Zone, ☎ 998/883–6078), Plaza Caracol (✉ Blvd. Kukulcán, Km 8.5, Hotel Zone, ☎ 998/883–5059), and La Isla Shopping Village (✉ Blvd. Kukulcán, Km 12.5, Hotel Zone, ☎ 998/883–5025). Each store sells handcrafted beadwork and embroidery made by the Huichol Indians of the West Coast. You can also watch a visiting tribe member doing this amazing work. The **Modern Art Café** (✉ La Isla Shopping Village, Blvd. Kukulcán, Km 12.5, Hotel Zone, ☎ 998/883–4511) is decorated with a revolving exhibit of works by local and international artists, all for sale. The **Renato Dorfman Gallery** (✉ La Isla Shopping Village, Blvd. Kukulcán, Km 12.5, Hotel Zone, ☎ 998/883–5573, FAX 998/883–0359) carries Dorfman's original pieces as well as his hand-carved replicas of Maya art and stelae.

Cancún A to Z

To research prices, get advice from other travelers, and book travel arrangements, visit www.fodors.com.

ADDRESSES

In Cancún addresses, "Sm" stands for Super Manzana, literally a group of houses. All neighborhoods are classified with an Sm number (Sm 23, Sm 25, etc.). Each Sm has its own park or square, and the area streets are fashioned around the park.

AIR TRAVEL TO AND FROM CANCÚN

Aeroméxico flies nonstop to Cancún from Houston, Miami, and New York. American has nonstop service from Dallas and Miami. Continental offers daily direct service from Houston. Mexicana's nonstop flights are from Los Angeles, Miami, and New York. From Cancún,

Mexicana subsidiaries Aerocaribe and Aerocozumel fly to Cozumel, the ruins at Chichén Itzá, Mérida, and other Mexican cities. Aerocosta flies to cities, ruins and haciendas on the mainland. If you are coming from the Midwest or Canada, your flight will stop over in either Atlanta, Dallas, Miami or Houston.

➤ AIRLINES AND CONTACTS: **Aerocaribe/Aerocozumel** (☎ 998/884–2000 downtown; 998/886–0083 airport). **AeroCosta** (☎ 998/884–2000 downtown). **Aeroméxico** (☎ 998/884–1097 downtown; 998/886–0003 airport). **American** (☎ 998/883–4460 airport). **Continental** (☎ 998/886–0006 airport). **Mexicana** (☎ 998/887–4444 downtown; 998/886–0068 airport).

AIRPORTS AND TRANSFERS

Cancún International Airport is 16 km (9 mi) southwest of the heart of Cancún and 10 km (6 mi) from the southernmost point of the Hotel Zone. There are three terminals. The main terminal is the largest building and handles international departures as well as domestic arrivals and departures. Next door to the main terminal is a smaller building where all regular international flights arrive. A separate terminal, 1 km (½ mi) south of the main terminal, handles all international charter flights.

➤ AIRPORT INFORMATION: **Cancún International Airport** (✉ Cancún–Puerto Morelos Hwy./Hwy. 307, Km 9.5, ☎ 998/886–0073).

AIRPORT TRANSFER

The public-transport options are taxis or *colectivos* (vans); buses are not allowed into the airport due to an agreement with the taxi union. A counter at the airport exit sells colectivo and taxi tickets; prices range from $15 to $40, depending on the destination. Getting back to the airport for your departure is less expensive; taxi rates to the airport range from about $15 to $22. Hotels post current rates. Be sure to agree on a price before getting into the taxi.

BOAT AND FERRY TRAVEL

From Playa Linda, Plaza Caracol, and Playa Tortuga on Cancún, you can take a shuttle boat to the main dock at Isla Mujeres. Municipal ferries carry vehicles and passengers between Cancún's Punta Sam and Isla's dock. (*See* Chapter 3 for more information about boat travel to and from Isla Mujeres.)

Aquabus, a water-taxi service in the Hotel Zone, travels from the hotels to various restaurants and shops; a one-way fare is $3, a day pass is $15, and a week pass is $35.

➤ WATER-TAXI INFORMATION: **Aquabus** (☎ 998/883–3155 or 998/883–5649).

BUS TRAVEL TO AND FROM CANCÚN

First-class and second-class buses arrive at the downtown bus terminal from all over Mexico. ADO, Mayab, and Playa Express are the main companies servicing the coast. Buses leave every 20 minutes for Puerto Morelos and Playa del Carmen. Check the bus schedule for departure times for Tulum, Chetumal, Cobá, Valladolid, Chichén Itzá, and Mérida.

➤ BUS INFORMATION: **ADO** (☎ 998/884–5542). **Bus terminal** (✉ Avs. Tulum and Uxmal, Sm 23, ☎ 998/887–1149). **Playa Express** (☎ 998/884–0994).

BUS TRAVEL WITHIN CANCÚN

Public buses run between the Hotel Zone and downtown from 6 AM to midnight; the cost is 5 pesos. There are designated bus stops—look for blue signs with white buses in the middle—but you can also flag down drivers along Boulevard Kukulcán. The service is frequent and quite reliable. Take Ruta 8 (Route 8) to reach Puerto Juárez and Punta Sam for the ferries to Isla Mujeres. Take Ruta 1 (Route 1) to and from the Hotel Zone. Buses from the Zone do not go into downtown Cancún but will drop you off anywhere along Avenida Tulum, from where you can catch a connecting bus that takes you into the city. Taking the bus can save you a considerable amount of money on taxis, particularly if you are staying in the Hotel Zone.

CAR RENTAL

Cars are available at Cancún International Airport or from any of a dozen agencies in town. Most of the agencies have several locations in the area: Avis, Thrifty, and Localiza Rent a Car have five each; Hertz has nine; and National has seven. The telephone numbers given here are for the airport locations.

Most rental cars are standard-shift subcompacts and Jeeps; air-conditioned cars with automatic transmissions should be reserved in advance (though bear in mind that some smaller car-rental places have only standards). Rates average around $55 per day but can be as high as $75 daily if you haven't reserved a car; you can save a great deal on a rental by booking before you leave home, particularly over the Internet. It's also a good idea to shop around. In addition to the rental agencies, the Car Rental Association can help you arrange a rental.

➤ MAJOR AGENCIES: **Avis** (✉ Cancún International Airport, ☎ 998/886–0222). **Hertz** (✉ Cancún International Airport, ☎ 998/884–1326). **National** (✉ Cancún International Airport, ☎ 998/886–0152). **Thrifty** (✉ Cancún International Airport, ☎ 998/886–0333).

➤ LOCAL AGENCIES AND CONTACTS: **Car Rental Association** (☎ 998/887–3109 or 998/884–7569). **Econorent** (✉ Avs. Bonampak and Cobá, Sm 4, ☎ 998/887–6487). **Executive** (✉ Av. Yaxchilán 160, Sm 20, ☎ 998/884–2699). **Localiza Rent a Car** (✉ Av. La Costa 128, Sm 30, ☎ 998/887–3109). **Zipp Rental Cars** (✉ Baccará hotel, Blvd. Kukulcán, Km 11.5, Hotel Zone, ☎ 998/883–2077).

CAR TRAVEL

Driving any kind of vehicle in Cancún is not for the faint of heart. Traffic moves at a breakneck speed; adding to the danger are the many one-way streets, traffic circles (*glorietas*), sporadically working traffic lights, ill-placed *topes* (speed bumps), numerous pedestrians, and large potholes. Be sure to observe speed limits in the Hotel Zone and downtown. The traffic police are quite vigilant and eager to hand out tickets. In addition, car travel becomes expensive, as it entails tips for valet parking as well as gasoline and rather costly rental rates.

Although driving in Cancún is not recommended, you might want a car to explore the surrounding areas on the peninsula. The roads are excellent within a 100-km (62-mi) radius.

Route 180 runs from Matamoros at the Texas border through Campeche, Mérida, Valladolid, and into Cancún. The trip from Texas can take up to three days. Route 307 runs south from Cancún through Puerto Morelos, Tulum, and Chetumal, then into Belize. Gas stations are located only in the major cities and towns, so keep your tank full. Route 307 has three Pemex stations between Cancún and Playa del Carmen. When approaching any village, town, or city, watch out for the numerous speed bumps—hitting them at top speed can ruin your transmission and tires.

EMBASSIES AND CONSULATES

The consulates in Cancún operate with skeleton staffs, and for complicated problems you need to contact the offices in Mérida. The U.S.

Consulate, in the Hotel Zone, is open weekdays 9–1; the Mérida offices are open weekdays 7:30–4.

The Canadian Consulate is open daily 9–5. Should you have an emergency when the embassy is closed, contact the Canadian Embassy in Mexico City.

➤ CANADA: **Consulate** (✉ Plaza Caracol 11, 3rd floor, Hotel Zone, ☎ 998/883–3360, 800/706–2900 emergencies, FAX 998/883–3232).

➤ UNITED STATES: **Consulate** (✉ Plaza Caracol, 3rd floor, Hotel Zone, ☎ 998/883–0272, FAX 998/883–1372).

EMERGENCIES

In case of medical emergency, the safest bet is the American Medical Centre, run by Dr. Michael McFall with his wife, Lisa McFall, from the United States.

Cancún has a lot of pharmacies. Among those that offer delivery service are Canto, Farmacia Cancún, and Paris (all downtown) and, in the Hotel Zone, Roxsanna's. Paris delivers around the clock.

➤ DOCTORS AND DENTISTS: **American Medical Centre** (✉ Blvd. Kukulcán, Km 8, Hotel Zone, ☎ 998/883–1001, 998/883–0113, 998/887–1455 pager PIN 10844).

➤ EMERGENCY SERVICES: **Emergencies** (☎ 06). **Fire Department** (☎ 998/884–9480). **Highway Police** (☎ 998/884–1107). **Immigration Office** (☎ 998/884–1749). **Municipal Police** (☎ 998/887–3435). **Red Cross** (✉ Avs. Xcaret and Labná, Sm 21, ☎ 998/884–1616). **Traffic Police** (☎ 998/884–0710).

➤ PHARMACIES: **Farmacia Cancún** (✉ Av. Tulum 17, Sm 22, ☎ 998/884–1283). **Paris** (✉ Av. Yaxchilán 32, Sm 3, ☎ 998/884–3005). **Roxsanna's** (✉ Plaza Flamingo, Kukulcán Blvd., Km 11.5, Hotel Zone, ☎ 998/885–1351, 998/885–0860 delivery service).

MAIL AND SHIPPING

The post office (*correos*) is open weekdays 8–5 and Saturday 9–1; there's also a Western Union office in the building and a courier service. Bear in mind, however, that postal service to and from Mexico is extremely slow and may take four weeks or more. Avoid sending or receiving parcels—and never send checks or money through the mail. Invariably they are stolen.

You can receive mail at the post office if it's marked "Lista de Correos, Cancún, 77500, Quintana Roo, Mexico." If you have an American Express card, you can have mail sent to you at the American Express Cancún office for a small fee. The office is open weekdays 9–6 and Saturday 9–1.

➤ SERVICES: **American Express** (✉ Av. Tulum 208, at Calle Agua, Sm 4, ☎ 998/881–4020). **Post office** (✉ Av. Sunyaxchén at Av. Xel-há, Sm 26, ☎ 998/884–1418). **Western Union** (✉ Av. Sunyaxchén at Av. Xel-há, Sm 26 ☎ 998/884–1529).

MONEY MATTERS

Generally, banks in Cancún are open weekdays 9–5, with money-exchange desks open 9–1:30. Downtown locations are along Avenida Tulum; some of the larger banks have branches in the Hotel Zone as well. All have automatic teller machines that dispense Mexican money. The ATMs at the smaller banks are often out of order, but the larger banks generally have working machines. If your PIN (personal identification number) has more than four digits, you may have trouble using the ATMs. Also, don't delay in taking your card out of the machine. ATMs are quick to eat up cards, and it takes a visit to the bank and a number of forms to get them back. If your transactions require a teller, go early to avoid long lines.

Banamex and Bital both have offices downtown and in the Hotel Zone and can exchange or wire money. Other banks include Banca Serfin, Banco del Sureste, Bancomer, Scotiabank Inverlat, and Santander Mexicano.

➤ BANKS: **Banamex** (Downtown: ✉ Av. Tulum 19, next to City Hall, Sm 1, ☎ 998/884–6403; Hotel Zone: ✉ Plaza Terramar, Blvd. Kukulcán, Km 37, ☎ 998/883–3100). **Banca Serfin** (Downtown: ✉ Av. Cobá at Av. Tulum, Sm 3, ☎ 998/884–4850). **BBVA Bancomer** (Downtown: ✉ Av. Tulum 20, Sm 3, ☎ 998/884–3288; Hotel Zone: ✉ Plaza El Parián, Blvd. Kukulcán, Km 9.5, next to the convention center, ☎ 998/883–0802). **Banco del Sureste** (Downtown: ✉ Avs. Yaxchilán and Sunyaxchén, Sm 24, ☎ 998/881–4991). **Bital** (Downtown: ✉ Av. Tulum 15, Sm 4, ☎ 998/881–4103; Hotel Zone: ✉ Plaza Caracol, Blvd. Kukulcán, Km 8.5, ☎ 998/883–4652). **Santander Mexicano** (Downtown: ✉ Av. Tulum 173, Sm 3, ☎ 998/884–0629). **Scotiabank Inverlat** (Downtown: ✉ Av. Tulum 26, Sm 3, ☎ 998/884–1333).

TAXIS

Taxi rides within the Hotel Zone cost $5–$7; between the Hotel Zone and downtown, $8 and up; and to the ferries at Punta Sam or Puerto Juárez, $15–$20 or more. Prices depend on distance, your negotiating skills, and whether you pick up the taxi in front of a hotel or decide to save a few dollars by going onto the avenue to hail one yourself (look for green city cabs). Most hotels list rates at the door; confirm the price with your driver *before* you set out. If you lose something in a taxi or have questions or a complaint, call the Sindicato de Taxistas.

➤ INFORMATION: **Sindicato de Taxistas** (☎ 998/888–6985).

TELEPHONES

Most hotels charge the equivalent of between 50¢ and $1 for each local call you make from your room. In addition, there is usually a hefty service charge on long-distance calls, and it can add up quickly. In order to make a phone call—local or long distance—from any public phone, you must purchase a Ladatel phone card, sold in blocks of about $3, $5, $10, and $20. An alternative to the phone card is the *caseta de larga distancia*—the long-distance telephone office. There are casetas in Plaza Kukulcán, Plaza Mayafair, and Plaza Caracol and one at the downtown bus terminal. These places have specially designed booths where you take your call after the number has been dialed by a clerk. A service fee of $3.50–$5 is added on top of the steep long-distance charge. The booths do, however, offer more privacy and comfort than many public-phone booths.

LOCAL CALLS

For local calls, the 8 of Cancún's 998 area code must be dialed first.

TOURS

BOAT TOURS

Day cruises to Isla Mujeres are popular. They generally include snorkeling, shopping downtown, lunching at an open-bar buffet, and listening to music or lounging at Playa Norte. Plenty of tour operators offer such trips. Pirate's Night offers a trip to Treasure Island on Isla Mujeres aboard a sailboat that is decked out like a pirate ship. Prices start at $35. Capitán Hook also runs an Isla Mujeres day tour that departs at 10 AM from El Embarcadero Marina on Boulevard Kukulcán and returns at 5 PM; it costs about $55. Dolphin Discovery sails daily from

Playas Langosta and Tortugas to the company's dock on Isla Mujeres; its program includes an instruction video, a 30-minute swim session with the dolphins, and time to explore the island. Tickets start at $75. Turimex offers a three-day, two-night cruise from Cancún to Havana for $189.

➤ FEES AND SCHEDULES: **Capitán Hook** (✉ El Embarcadero, Blvd. Kukulcán, Km 4.5, Hotel Zone, ☎ 998/883–3736). **Dolphin Discovery** (✉ Playa Langosta, Local 16, Blvd. Kukulcán, Km 3, Hotel Zone ☎ 998/883–0779 or 998/883–0780). ***Pirate's Night*** (✉ Playa Langosta Dock, Blvd. Kukulcán, Km 5.5, Hotel Zone, ☎ 998/849–4621). **Turimex Travel** (✉ Plaza America, Av. Coba 5, Suite B-7, Sm 4, ☎ 998/887–4038, FAX 998/887–1936, WEB www.turimex.com/cuba.html).

ECOTOURS

Although many claim to have ecological tours, few outfits actually deliver truly ecological experiences in authentic jungle settings. An exception is Reserva Ecológica El Edén, established by one of Mexico's leading naturalists, Arturo Gómez-Pompa, and his nephew, Marco Lazcano-Barrero. The 500,000-acre reserve, 48 km (30 mi) northwest of Cancún, is dedicated to research for biological conservation in Mexico. It offers excursions for people interested in experiencing the reserve's wetlands, mangrove swamps, sand dunes, savannas, and tropical forests. "Eco-scientific" tours include bird-watching, animal-tracking, stargazing, crocodile ecology, and cenote and archaeological explorations. Prices include transportation between Cancún and the reserve, one to two nights' accommodation at La Savanna Research Station, meals, cocktails, guided nature walks, and all tours. Two-day, one-night excursions start at $235 per person, three-day, two-nights at $315.

➤ FEES AND SCHEDULES: **Reserva Ecológica El Edén** (✉ Box 770 Cancún, Quintana Roo 77500, ☎ FAX 998/880–5032, WEB www.ucr.edu/pril/peten/images/el_eden/Home.html).

PLANE TOURS

Promocaribe flies one-day tours between Cancún and Guatemala City, continuing on to Flores and the ruins at Tikal. A round-trip fare of $267 includes all ground transfers, departure taxes, entrance to ruins, a tour guide, and lunch.

➤ FEES AND SCHEDULES: **Promotora Caribena** (✉ Plaza Centro, Av. Nader 8, Sm 5, ☎ 998/884–9073, WEB www.promocaribe.com).

TRAVEL AGENCIES

Mayaland Tours, Intermar Caribe (IMC), and Olympus Tours all offer day trips. You can shop around for the best price or call the Travel Agency Association for further information.

➤ LOCAL AGENT REFERRALS: **Travel Agency Association** (✉ Plaza México, Av. Tulum 200, Suite 301, Sm 5, ☎ 998/887–1670, FAX 998/884–3738).

➤ LOCAL AGENTS: **Intermar Caribe** (✉ Av. Tulum at Av. Cobá, Sm 4, ☎ 998/884–0584). **Mayaland Tours** (✉ Av. Robalo 30, Sm 3, ☎ 998/988–0870). **Olympus Tours** (✉ Av. Bonampak 107, Sm 3, ☎ 998/887–2417).

VISITOR INFORMATION

➤ TOURIST INFORMATION: **State Tourism Information Center** (✉ Av. Tulum 26, Sm 5, ☎ 998/884–8073). **State Tourism Office—Quintana Roo** (SECTUR; ✉ Government Palace, Av. Tulum, Sm 1, ☎ 998/881–9000; 800/903–9200 toll free in Mexico).

ISLA MUJERES

Updated by Shelagh McNally

ISLA MUJERES (*ees*-lah moo-*hair*-ayce) has a magic of its own that seems to defy change. It makes this tiny, fish-shape island 8 km (5 mi) off Cancún a tranquil alternative to its bustling western neighbor. Only about 8 km (5 mi) long by 1 km (½ mi) wide, Isla has flat, sandy beaches on its northern end and steep, rocky bluffs to the south. The name means "Island of Women," although no one is exactly sure who dubbed it that. Many believe it was the ancient Maya, who used the island as a religious center for worshiping Ixchel (ee-*shell*), the Maya goddess of rainbows, the moon, and the sea, and the guardian of fertility and childbirth. Another popular legend has it that the Spanish conquistador Hernández de Córdoba named the island when he landed here in 1517 and found hundreds of female-shape clay idols dedicated to Ixchel and her daughters. Others say the name dates from the 17th century, when Isla was a haven for buccaneers and smugglers. Pirates would stash their women here before heading out to rob the high seas.

After its popularity waned with brigands, Isla settled into life as a quiet fishing village. In the 1950s it became a favorite vacation spot for Mexicans. Americans discovered it shortly afterward, and in the 1960s Isla became well known among hippies and backpackers. As Cancún grew so did Isla. During the late 1970s, the number of day-trippers coming over from the mainland increased, bringing Isla's hotel, restaurant, and shop owners more business than ever. Boatloads were streaming off the ferries for quick lunches followed by frenzied shopping, and thus the island became a small-scale tourist haven. Like the rest of the area, Isla is being developed, but it manages to keep its character as a peaceful retreat with its own local history and culture centered on the sea. And it continues to be a favorite of people who prefer such seaside pleasures as scuba diving, snorkeling, and relaxing on the beach to spending time in Cancún's fast-food joints and rollicking discos.

Exploring

To get your bearings, think of Isla Mujeres as an elongated fish, the head being the southeastern tip, the northwest prong the tail. The minute you step off the boat, you see how small Isla is. Directly in front of the ferry piers is the island's only town, known simply as El Pueblo. It extends the full width of Isla's northern "tail" and is sandwiched between sand and sea to the south, west, and northeast, with no high-rises to block the view.

A Good Tour

The best way to explore the entire island is to take a taxi or rent either a moped or golf cart. You can walk to Isla's historic **Cemeterio** ⑤ by going northwest from the ferry piers on Avenida López Mateos. Then head southeast (by car or other vehicle) along Avenida Rueda Medina past the piers to reach the Mexican naval base, where you can see the flag ceremonies at sunrise and sunset. Just don't take any photos—it's illegal to photograph any military sites in Mexico. Continue southeast out of town; 2½ km (1½ mi) farther down the road is **Laguna Makax** ⑥, on the right.

At the southeast end of the lagoon, a dirt road to the left leads to the remains of the **Hacienda Mundaca** ⑦. About a block southeast of the hacienda, turn right off the main road at the sign that says SAC BAJO to a smaller, unmarked side road, which loops back northwest. Approximately ½ km (¼ mi) farther on the left is the entrance to the **Tortugranja** ⑧.

Isla Mujeres

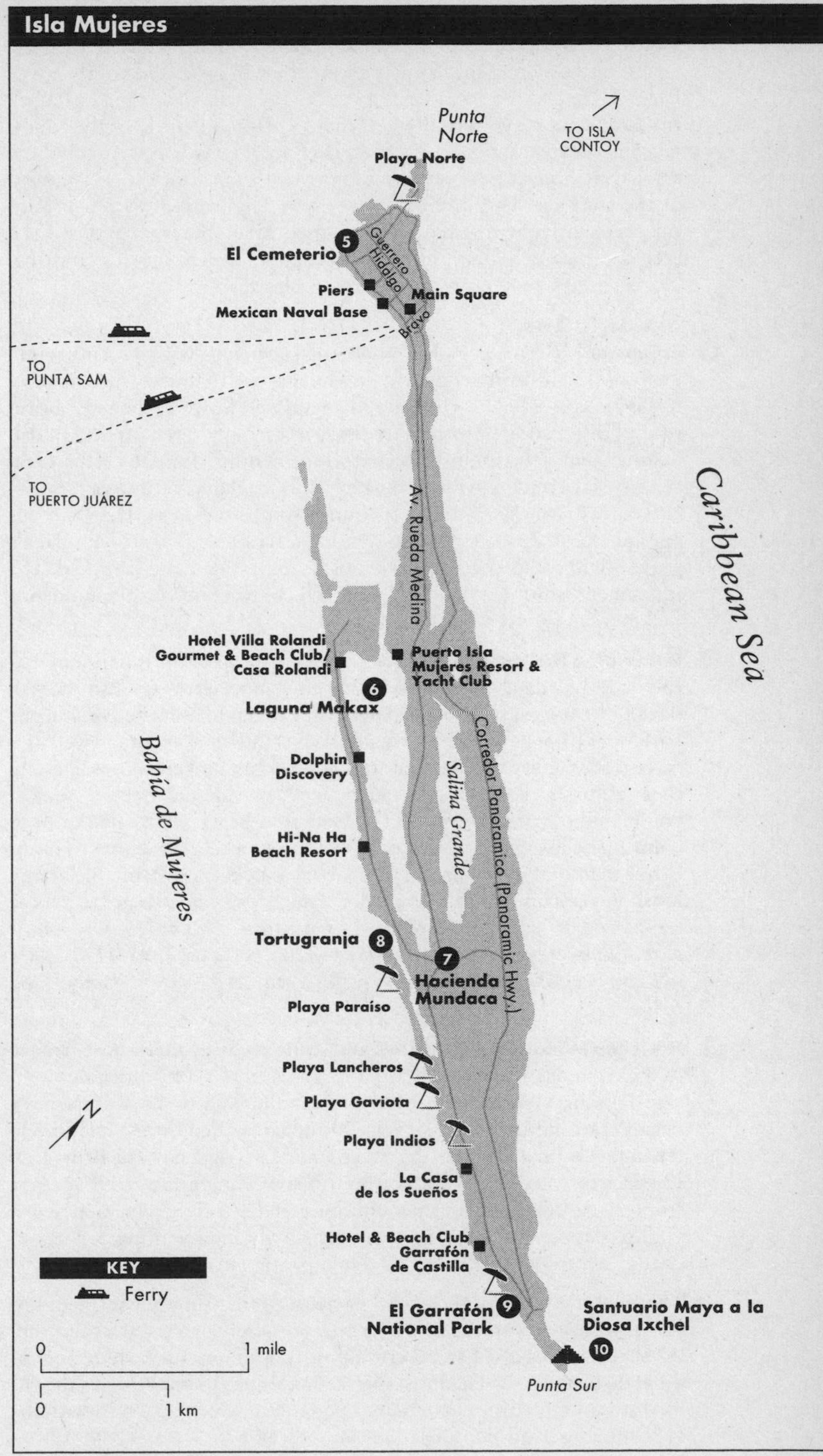

Punta Norte
TO ISLA CONTOY
Playa Norte
El Cemeterio
Guerrero
Hidalgo
Piers
Main Square
Mexican Naval Base
Bravo
TO PUNTA SAM
TO PUERTO JUÁREZ
Av. Rueda Medina
Caribbean Sea
Hotel Villa Rolandi Gourmet & Beach Club/ Casa Rolandi
Puerto Isla Mujeres Resort & Yacht Club
Laguna Makax
Corredor Panoramico (Panoramic Hwy.)
Salina Grande
Dolphin Discovery
Bahía de Mujeres
Hi-Na Ha Beach Resort
Tortugranja
Hacienda Mundaca
Playa Paraíso
Playa Lancheros
Playa Gaviota
Playa Indios
La Casa de los Sueños
Hotel & Beach Club Garrafón de Castilla
KEY
Ferry
El Garrafón National Park
Santuario Maya a la Diosa Ixchel
Punta Sur
0
1 mile
0
1 km
N

Return to Avenida Rueda Medina and continue southeast past Playa Lancheros to **El Garrafón National Park** ⑨. Slightly more than ½ km (¼ mi) farther along the same road, on the windward side of the tip of Isla Mujeres, sit the remains of a small Maya ruin dedicated to Ixchel, the **Santuario Maya a la Diosa Ixchel** ⑩. Although little of the ruin is left, the ocean and bay views from here are well worth seeing. Follow the paved eastern perimeter road northwest back into town. Known as the Corredor Panorámico (Panoramic Highway), this is a beautiful, scenic drive with a few pull-off areas along the way, perfect for a secluded picnic. Swimming is not recommended along this coast because of the strong currents and rocky shore.

Sights to See

5 **El Cemeterio** (Cemetery). Isla's unnamed cemetery, with its century-old gravestones, is on Avenida López Mateos, the road that runs parallel to Playa Norte. Filled with carved angels and flowers, the most beautiful of the decorated tombs are those in memory of children. Hidden among them is the tomb of the notorious Fermín Mundaca. This 19th-century slave trader—who's often billed more glamorously as a pirate—carved his own skull-and-crossbones tombstone with the ominous epitaph: AS YOU ARE, I ONCE WAS; AS I AM, SO SHALL YOU BE. Mundaca's grave is empty, however; his remains lie in Mérida, where he died. The monument is not easy to find—ask a local to point out the unidentified marker. ✉ *Av. López Mateos.*

9 **El Garrafón National Park.** Much of the coral reef at this national marine park has died—a result of too many snorkelers—and so the fish have to be bribed with food. There isn't much for snorkelers, but the park does have kayaks and ocean playground equipment, as well as a three-floor facility with restaurants, bathrooms, and gift shops. Despite these efforts to keep visitors entertained, you should bring a book if you intend to spend the day. (The Garrafón Beach Club, next door, is a much less expensive alternative and the snorkeling is equal to if not better than that in the park.) Marine-park tickets are available at any kiosk in Cancún and in Playa del Carmen; you can also get tickets at the park entrance. ✉ *Carretera El Garrafón, 2½ km (1½ mi) southeast of Playa Lancheros,* ☎ *998/883–3233 in Cancún, 984/473–2801 in Playa del Carmen,* WEB *www.garrafon.com.* 🎫 *$19.95.* ⏲ *Daily 8:30–6:30.*

7 **Hacienda Mundaca.** A dirt drive and stone archway mark the entrance to the remains of the mansion that 19th-century slave trader–cum–pirate Fermín Mundaca de Marechaja built. When the British navy began cracking down on slavers, Mundaca settled on the island. He fell in love with a local beauty nicknamed La Trigueña (The Brunette). In order to woo her, Mundaca built a sprawling estate with verdant tropical gardens. Apparently unimpressed, La Trigueña married a young islander—and Mundaca went slowly mad waiting for her to change her mind. He finally died in a brothel in Mérida.

There is little to see of the actual hacienda; it has simply vanished. Locals say the government tore it down, or merely neglected its upkeep. All that remains are a small crumbling guardhouse, a rusted cannon, an arch, and a well. The most interesting things to see here are the ruined stone archway and triangular pediment, which is carved with the following inscription: HUERTA DE LA HACIENDA DE VISTA ALEGRE MDCCCLXXVI (Orchard of the Happy View Hacienda 1876). The gardens are well kept, lush, and colorful with tropical flora. ✉ *East off Av. Rueda Medina (take main road southeast from town to S-curve at the end of Laguna Makax and turn left onto dirt road),* ☎ *no phone.* 🎫 *$1.50.* ⏲ *Daily 9 AM–dusk.*

6 **Laguna Makax.** Pirates are said to have anchored their ships in this lagoon as they lay in wait for the hapless vessels plying the Spanish Main (the geographical area in which Spanish treasure ships trafficked). These days the lagoon houses a local shipyard and is a safe harbor for boats during hurricane season. The lagoon is off of Avenida Rueda Medina about 2½ km (1½ mi) south of town, across the street from a Mexican naval base and some *salinas* (salt marshes).

10 **Santuario Maya a la Diosa Ixchel** (Sanctuary of the Goddess Ixchel). The sad vestiges of a Maya temple once dedicated to Ixchel are about 1 km (½ mi) southeast of El Garrafón National Park, at Isla's tip. Though Hurricane Gilbert walloped the ruin and succeeded in blowing most of it away in 1988, part of it has since been restored. A lovely walkway around the remains continues down to a natural arch underneath the ruin. The view from here, of the open ocean on one side and the Bahía de Mujeres (Bay of Women) on the other, is spectacular. Adjacent is a **lighthouse.** The official word is that climbing to the top is no longer allowed, but a small tip and your powers of persuasion may convince the keeper to let you up to see the incredible view. The ruin is at the point where the road turns northeast into the Corredor Panorámico.

8 **Tortugranja** (Turtle Farm). Run by an outfit called Eco Caribe, this facility is dedicated to the study and preservation of sea turtles. During hatching season (May–September) upward of 6,000 turtles hatch along the coast of Quintana Roo. Some are brought to the farm to be raised until they are large enough to survive at sea. You can view hatchlings and young turtles of various species in outdoor tanks, go on a tour led by one of the biologists, and watch feedings. A small but well-designed museum explains the various stages of turtle life and different parts of the coral reef. ✉ *Take Av. Rueda Medina south of town; about a block southeast of Hacienda Mundaca, take the right fork (the smaller road that loops back north); the entrance is about ½ km (¼ mi) farther, on the left,* ☎ *998/877–0595.* 🎫 *$2.* ⏲ *Daily 9–5.*

Beaches

The superb **Playa Norte,** known for its congenial atmosphere, is easy to find: simply head north on any of the north–south streets in town until you hit it. The turquoise sea is as calm as a lake, and you can wade out for 40 yards in waist-deep water.

The beaches between Laguna Makax and El Garrafón National Park, including **Playa Paraíso,** are good spots for having lunch or for shopping at the small stands that sell local handicrafts, souvenirs, and T-shirts. Some pet sea turtles and harmless *tiburones gatos* (nurse sharks) are housed in sea pens at **Playa Lancheros.** You can have your picture taken with one of the sharks. (These sharks are tamer than the *tintoreras,* or blue sharks, which live in the open seas. They have seven rows of teeth and weigh up to 1,100 lbs.)

Dining

As in the rest of Mexico, locals eat their main meal during siesta hours, between 1 and 4, and then have a light dinner in the evening. Unless otherwise stated, restaurants are open daily for lunch and dinner.

$$–$$$$ ★ ✕ **Casa Rolandi.** Part of the Rolandi family of restaurants, this Casa Rolandi has the Swiss–northern Italian menu that won high marks at its Cancún location. The carpaccio *di tonno alla Giorgio* (thin slices of fresh tuna with extra-virgin olive oil and lime juice) is particularly good, as are the pastas—including lasagna and shrimp-filled black ravi-

oli. The restaurant is part of the Hotel Villa Rolandi lobby and extends out to an open-air deck that juts out over the beach. The sunset views are spectacular. ✉ *Hotel Villa Rolandi Gourmet & Beach Club, Fracc. Laguna Mar Makax, Sm 7,* ☎ *998/877–0100. AE, MC, V.*

$–$$$ ★ ✕ **Lo Lo Lorena.** The innovative menu at this restaurant, one of the island's best, changes daily according to what's available. However, because of their popularity, a few of the dishes created by Lolo, the flamboyant chef-owner, have become permanent fixtures, including "Lover's Salad," with conch and ginger, and a fantastic tart Tatin. Lolo also puts on an entertaining show in the open kitchen. Wooden shutters, a wide porch, wicker furniture, and pastel colors give the old wooden house a lovely Caribbean flavor. ✉ *Av. Guerrero 7,* ☎ *no phone. MC, V. Closed Mon. No lunch.*

$–$$ ★ ✕ **Leopard Lounge.** Enjoy fresh sushi at this outdoor restaurant-bar, which combines the hip style of Hollywood's Rat Pack with a tropical island atmosphere. Pull up a stool at the palapa bar and order a cold martini. If your taste doesn't run to sushi, try the teriyaki beef and chicken instead, or the tempura vegetables. There is live music here until 1 AM. ✉ *Plaza Los Almendros, between Avs. Hidalgo and Guerrero at Av. Matamoros,* ☎ *998/877–0679. MC, V. Closed Sun. and Mon. No lunch.*

$–$$ ★ ✕ **Velazquez.** This family-owned restaurant on the beach is open until dusk and serves the freshest seafood on the island. You haven't eaten Yucatecan until you've tried the regional specialty *tikinchic*—fish marinated in a sour-orange sauce and achiote paste, wrapped in banana leaves, and cooked over an open flame. Feasting on a fantastic fish meal while you sit outside and watch the boats go by is the true Isla experience. ✉ *Av. Rueda Medina (2 blocks northwest of ferry docks),* ☎ *no phone. No credit cards.*

$ ✕ **All Natural Café.** This haven for vegetarians serves breakfast, lunch, and light dinners. Try the fresh juice mixes along with salads, soups, and veggie sandwiches served on baguettes. For dinner you can also try next door at the Nauti Pete Bistro, the sister restaurant to the café. ✉ *Centro Hidalgo, Plaza Karlita,* ☎ *998/877–0720. MC, V.*

$ ✕ **Café Cito.** Cito is one of the prettiest cafés on the island, done in bright blue and white, with simple watercolor paintings adorning the walls, shell-decorated tabletops, and wind chimes dangling from the rafters. Breakfast choices include fresh waffles, fruit-filled crêpes, and egg dishes, as well as great cappuccino and espresso. For lunch the chef whips up different daily specials. You can join the island's Harley Davidson Club here, or visit Sabrina next door for a tarot reading. ✉ *Avs. Juárez and Matamoros,* ☎ *998/877–0438. No credit cards.*

Lodging

Isla has plenty of hotels. Generally the older, more modest places are in town, and the newer, more expensive resorts tend to front the beach around Punta Norte or the peninsula near the lagoon. Most hotels have ceiling fans, and some have air-conditioning, but few have TVs or phones. Local travel agents can provide information about luxurious, self-contained time-share condominiums, which are another option.

$$$$ ★ 🏨 **La Casa de los Sueños.** Tucked away at Isla's south end, this dazzling residence-turned-bed-and-breakfast is honeymoon-perfect. A large interior courtyard leads to a sunken, open-air living room decorated in sunset colors, which extends to a terrace with a cliffside swimming pool overlooking the ocean. All rooms are individually decorated, with artwork and wooden furniture, and have ocean-view terraces. The

master bedroom also has a Jacuzzi with a sunset view. Note that two Great Danes live in the house and like to mingle with the guests. ✉ *Carretera El Garrafón, 77400,* ☎ *998/877–0651 or 800/551–2558,* FAX *998/877–0708,* WEB *www.lossuenos.com. 9 rooms. Dining room, fans, pool, beach, dock, snorkeling, boating, bicycles; no room phones, no kids, no smoking. AE, MC, V.*

$$$$ ★ **Hotel Villa Rolandi Gourmet & Beach Club.** This compact hotel is as posh as any Cancún property. A private yacht delivers you to the island, where 20 elegant suites await. Decorated in bright colors, all suites have ocean views, king-size beds, and a sitting area that leads to the balcony with its heated whirlpool bath. The showers have six adjustable heads and convert into a sauna. Both the Casa Rolandi restaurant and the lovely garden pool overlook the Bahía de Mujeres and lead down to an intimate beach. Room rates include Continental breakfast and lunch or dinner. ✉ *Fracc. Laguna Mar Makax, Sm 7, Mz 75, 77400,* ☎ *998/877–0100,* FAX *998/877–0700,* WEB *www.rolandi.com. 20 suites. Restaurant, in-room hot tubs, pool, gym, spa, beach, dock, boating; no smoking, no kids under 13. AE, MC, V.*

$$–$$$ ★ **Hotel Roca Mar.** The turquoise sea is the star here, as this is one of the few downtown hotels overlooking the water. You can see, smell, and hear the ocean as soon as you step into your room. The private balcony, the wooden slats on the windows, and the simple furnishings—all are designed to be inconspicuous. Of course, the lovely courtyard, which is filled with plants, birds, and strategically placed benches, overlooks the ocean, too. ✉ *Calle Nicolas Bravo, Zona Maritima, 77400,* ☎ FAX *998/877–0101,* WEB *www.mjmnet.net/HotelRocaMar/home.htm. 31 rooms. Restaurant, fans, pool, beach, snorkeling; no air-conditioning in some rooms, no room TVs, no room phones. AE, MC, V.*

$$ ★ **Playa Gaviota.** The real plus at this hilltop hotel sandwiched between a garden and the ocean is the private beach with its barbecue, palapas, coconut trees, white sand, and gorgeous sunset views. Each of the 10 suites, decorated in basic blue and white, has a fully equipped kitchenette, two queen-size beds, a small eating area, and a large terrace facing the ocean. Three smaller, older (but still comfortable) cabins on the beach are for rent as well. The owners, a quiet Mexican family, live on-site. ✉ *Carretera El Garrafón, Km 4.5, 77400,* ☎ FAX *998/877–0216,* WEB *http://playagaviotasuite.cjb.net. 10 suites, 3 cabins. Fans, kitchenettes, beach; no room phones. No credit cards.*

$ **Hi-Na-Ha Beach Resort.** This intimate and luxurious hotel faces the Bahía de Mujeres with the Laguna Makax at the back. Suites have queen-size beds and ocean-view balconies. Villas have two bedrooms, fully equipped kitchens, dining rooms, and balconies. Cable television is available upon request, at an additional charge. With a lovely garden, pool, restaurant, and dock, it's a perfect retreat for families. ✉ *Fracc. Laguna Mar Makax, Sm 7, Mz 75,* ☎ FAX *998/877–0615,* WEB *www.hinaha.com. 10 suites, 2 villas. Restaurant, fans, kitchenettes, massage, beach, boating, bar, Internet, travel services; no room phones. MC, V.*

Nightlife and the Arts

The Arts

The island celebrates many religious holidays and festivals in the main square, usually with live entertainment. Carnival is in February and is spectacular fun. Other popular events include the springtime regattas and fishing tournaments. Founding Day, August 17, marks the island's official founding by the Mexican government. During the **Isla Mujeres International Music Festival,** held the second week in October, the island fills with music and dancers from around the world.

Casa de la Cultura (✉ Av. Guerrero, ☎ 998/877–0639) has art, drama, yoga, and folkloric-dance classes year-round. It's open Monday–Saturday 9–1 and 4–8.

Nightlife

Plaza Isla Mujeres at Avenidas Hidalgo and Guerrero has become the official nightlife spot, with a number of bars and restaurants open until the wee hours. **Buho's** (✉ Cabañas María del Mar, Av. Arq. Carlos Lazo 1, ☎ 998/877–1479) remains the favorite restaurant on Playa Norte for a relaxing sunset drink. There is a small bar and a large television at **Chiles Loco** (✉ Plaza Isla Mujeres, Av. Hidalgo 81, Local A-4, ☎ no phone).

Outdoor Activities and Sports

For water sports, Playa Norte is the calmest beach.

Fishing

If you're interested in participating in the **Red Cross Billfish Tournament,** held in April, contact Michael Creamer (☎ FAX 998/877–0443, WEB www.mjmnet.net/redcross/fishing.htm).

Captain Anthony Mendillo Jr. (✉ Av. Arq. Carlos Lazo 1, ☎ 998/877–0213, FAX 998/877–0156) offers specialized fishing trips aboard his 29-ft vessel, the *Keen M*, starting at $600 a day. **Sea Hawk Divers** (✉ Av. Arq. Carlos Lazo, Playa Norte, ☎ 9/9877–0296) runs fishing trips—for barracuda, snapper, and smaller fish—that start at $150 for a half day. The **Sociedad Cooperativa Turistica** (☎ 998/877–0274) offers four hours of fishing close to shore for $100; eight hours farther out is $240.

Marinas

Puerto Isla Mujeres Resort & Yacht Club (✉ Puerto de Abrigo, Laguna Makax, ☎ 998/877–0093), the only place along the coast to get your boat repaired, has a full-service marina for vessels up to 170 ft. Daily mooring costs are $1.50 for vessels up to 89 ft and $2 for vessels 90 ft and over. The marina offers a full-service fuel station, a 150-ton lift, customs assistance, 110/220 V single and three-phase hookups, crew services, 24-hour security, and laundry, interior cleaning, and boatyard services. If you need to sleep over on land, the luxury resort is steps away from the docks.

Snorkeling and Scuba Diving

DIVE SITES

The famous coral reefs at **El Garrafón National Park** have suffered tremendously because of human negligence, boats' dropping anchors (now outlawed), and the effects of Hurricane Gilbert in 1988. Some good snorkeling can be had near Playa Norte on the north end.

Isla is a good place to learn how to dive, since the snorkeling is close to shore. Offshore, there's excellent diving and snorkeling at **Xlaches** (pronounced *ees*-lah-chayss) reef, due north on the way to Isla Contoy. One of Contoy's most alluring dives is the **Cave of the Sleeping Sharks,** east of the northern tip. The caves were discovered by an island fisherman known as Vulvula and extensively explored by Ramon Bravo, a local diver, cinematographer, and Mexico's foremost expert on sharks. It's a fascinating 150-ft dive for experienced divers only.

At the extreme southern end of the island on the leeward side lies **Los Manchones.** At 30 ft–40 ft deep and 3,300 ft off the southwestern coast, this coral reef is a good dive site. During the summer of 1994, an ecology group hoping to divert divers and snorkelers from El Garrafón commissioned the creation of a 1-ton, 9¾-ft bronze cross, which was sunk here. Named the Cruz de la Bahía (Cross of the Bay), it is a tribute to all the people who have died at sea. Most area dive spots are also described in detail in *Dive Mexico,* a colorful magazine readily available in local shops.

DIVE SHOPS

Coral Scuba Dive Center (✉ Av. Matamoros 13-A, ☎ 998/877–0371) offers two-tank dives for $39; shipwreck dives or photo dives for $59; and snorkel trips for $14. **Mundaca Divers** (✉ Av. Francisco Madero 10, ☎ 998/877–0607, FAX 998/877–0601) rents tanks starting at $45 along with snorkeling gear for $5 a day. **Sea Hawk Divers** (✉ Av. Arq. Carlos Lazo, Playa Norte, ☎ 998/877–0296) rents two tanks for $40; it also has dive gear and snorkeling equipment. It will also set up accommodations for divers in pleasant rooms starting at $35 per day.

Water Parks

Dolphin Discovery (☎ 998/883–0777 or 998/883–0779) offers humans the chance to play with the delightful sea mammals in a small, supervised group in a pool. There are four swims daily, at 9, 11, 1, and 3. Each session consists of a 30-minute instruction video and 30 minutes in the water. The cost is $134 and includes the boat ride from Cancún and an all-you-can-eat Mexican buffet.

Shopping

Shopping on Isla Mujeres is a mixture of stores selling T-shirts, suntan lotion, beer, and groceries and those that sell Mexican crafts, including silver and jewelry, folk art, textiles, and clothes. Most shops accept credit cards. Hours are generally Monday–Saturday 10–1 and 4–7, although quite a few stores stay open during siesta hours (1–4).

Many local artists display their works at the public **Artesanias Market** (✉ Av. Matamoros and Av. Arq. Carlos Lazo, ☎ no phone), which offers plenty of bargains. **Artesanias El Nopal** (✉ Av. Guerrero at Av. Matamoros, ☎ 998/877–0555) has an excellent selection of fine Mexican handicrafts from across the country, handpicked by the owner. **Casa Isleño II** (✉ Av. Guerrero Nte. 3-A, ☎ FAX 998/877–0265) offers hand-painted T-shirts in beautiful colors as well as a collection of shells and crafts.

Isla Mujeres A to Z

To research prices, get advice from other travelers, book travel arrangements, visit www.fodors.com.

BIKE AND MOPED TRAVEL

You can rent bicycles on Isla, but keep in mind that it's very hot here and the road conditions aren't great (especially those unexpected speed bumps). Don't ride at night; many roads don't have streetlights, so drivers have a hard time seeing you. Most of the moped rental places carry bicycles starting at about $5.50 an hour.

Mopeds are the most popular mode of transportation on Isla and are available at a number of rental agencies. Most places charge $22–$27 a day, or $5.50–$11 per hour, depending on the moped make and year. ➤ RENTALS: **Ciro's Motorent** (✉ Av. Guerrero Nte. 11, at Av. Matamoros, ☎ 998/877–0578). **P'pe's Rentadora** (✉ Av. Hidalgo 19, ☎ 998/877–0019). **El Sol** (✉ Av. Francisco Madero 5, ☎ 998/877–0068). **R Cardenas** (✉ Av. Guerrero 107, ☎ 998/877–0079).

BOAT AND FERRY TRAVEL

Speedboats and passenger ferries run between the main dock on Isla and Puerto Juárez on the mainland. Faster and more expensive shuttles to Isla's main dock leave from Cancún's Hotel Zone. Other departure points include Playa Linda, Plaza Caracol, and Playa Tortuga. Municipal ferries carry vehicles and passengers between Isla's dock and Cancún's Punta Sam.

The passenger ferries (*Sultana del Mar* and *Blanca Beatriz*) are the least expensive option. A one-way ticket is $1.60 and the trip takes at least 45 minutes. Delays and crowding aren't unknown, but often there is live music on board, which makes the trips festive.

The speedboats *Caribbean Savage* and *Caribbean Lady* are air-conditioned cruisers with bar service. A one-way ticket costs $4 and the crossing takes about 20 minutes.

Passenger ferries and speedboats leave every half hour from Cancún and Isla Mujeres 6:30 AM–8:30 PM, with a final ferry at 11 PM. Always check the times posted at the dock, as the schedule is subject to change, depending on the season and weather conditions. The ferry boats also leave early when they are full.

Shuttles from Cancún cost between $9.95 and $15 round-trip and take approximately 30 minutes, depending on weather conditions. Two shuttle services, *The Isla* and *Nauti Shuttle,* depart from El Embarcadero at Playa Tortugas. *Isla* leaves for the island at 9, 11, 1, and 3:45 and returns to Cancún at 10, 12:30, and 2:30. The *Nauti Shuttle* leaves Cancún at 9:30, 10:30, 11:45, 1:15, 2:30, and 5:45 and returns to Cancún at 10, 11, 2, 3:30, 5, and 6:30. The *Asterix Water Taxi* departs from Plaza Caracol at 9, 11, 1, and 3, returning at 10, noon, 2, and 5. Colon Tours has one ferry leaving Playa Linda at 9:30 and returning at 4 PM.

You don't need a car to get around on Isla, but you can bring one over on a municipal ferry. The ride takes about 45 minutes and the fare is $1.35 per person and about $27–$50 per vehicle, depending on the size of your car. From Punta Sam, the ferry leaves at 8, 11, 2:45, 5:30, and 8:15. Departures from Isla are at 6:30, 9:30, 12:45, 4:15, and 7:15. Again, check the schedule. Landlubbers' note: if you have a sensitive stomach, this ferry offers the smoothest ride when the sea is rough.

➤ BOAT AND FERRY INFORMATION: **Asterix Water Taxi, Colon Tours** (☎ 998/884–5333). ***Caribbean Lady, Caribbean Savage*** (☎ 998/877–0254 or 998/877–0253). **Isla Ferry office** (☎ 998/877–0065). **Isla Shuttle service** (☎ 998/883–3448). **Nauti Shuttle** (☎ 998/883–3646). ***Sultana del Mar, Blanca Beatriz*** (☎ 998/877–0065).

BUS TRAVEL

Municipal buses run at 20- to 30-minute intervals daily between 6 AM and 10 PM, generally following the ferry schedule. The route goes from the Posada del Mar hotel on Avenida Rueda Medina out to Colonia Salinas on the windward side. Service is slow because the buses make frequent stops. Fares are about 55¢.

➤ BUS INFORMATION: **Municipal buses** (☎ 998/877–0307 on Isla, 998/884–5542 in Cancún).

CAR TRAVEL

There is little reason to bring a car to Isla Mujeres. Taxis are inexpensive and the island is small. In addition, driving can be slow going.

EMERGENCIES

The Centro de Salud (Health Center) has a 24-hour emergency service and accepts regular visits 8 AM–8 PM. Isla also has an excellent Red Cross Clinic, which is run by a British doctor. Payment is by donation (the clinic doesn't receive government funding and operates on a shoestring budget). Your hotel can also help you find an English-speaking doctor.

A couple of pharmacies are open late: Farmacia Isla Mujeres, Monday–Saturday 9 AM–10 PM and Sunday 9–3, and Farmacia Lily, daily 8 –11 PM, with 24-hour service available.

➤ CONTACTS: **Centro de Salud** (✉ Av. Guerrero 5, on the plaza, ☎ 998/877–0117). **Police** (☎ 998/877–0082). **Port Captain** (☎ 998/877–0095). **Red Cross Clinic** (✉ Colonia La Gloria, south side of island, ☎ 998/877–0280, WEB www.mjmnet.net/redcross/home.htm).

➤ LATE-NIGHT PHARMACIES: **Farmacia Isla Mujeres** (✉ Av. Juárez 8, ☎ 998/877–0178). **Farmacia Lily** (✉ Av. Francisco Madero 17, ☎ 998/877–0116).

MAIL AND SHIPPING

The post office is open weekdays 8–7 and Saturday 9–1. You can have mail for you sent to "Lista de Correos, Isla Mujeres, Quintana Roo, Mexico"; the post office will hold it for 10 days, but it will take up to 12 weeks to arrive.

➤ POST OFFICE: ✉ Av. Guerrero at Av. López Mateos, ½ block from market, ☎ 998/877–0085.

MONEY MATTERS

Bital, the only bank on the island, is open weekdays 8:30–6 and Saturday 9–2. Its ATM often runs out of cash or has a long line, especially on Sunday, so be sure to save some money for the ferry ride back to the mainland.

Bital exchanges currency Monday–Saturday 10–noon. You can also exchange money at Cunex Money Exchange, which is open weekdays 8:30–7 and Saturday 9–2.

➤ BANKS: **Bital** (✉ Av. Rueda Medina 3, ☎ 998/877–0104 or 998/877–0005).

➤ EXCHANGE SERVICES: **Cunex Money Exchange** (✉ Av. Hidalgo at Av. Francisco Madero 12-A, ☎ 998/877–0421).

TAXIS

Taxis line up by the ferry dock around the clock. Fares run $1.65 to $3 from the ferry or downtown to the hotels on the north end, at Playa Norte. You can also hire a taxi for a private island tour at about $16.50 an hour.

➤ TAXI COMPANIES: **Sitio de Taxis** (Taxi Syndicates; ✉ Av. Rueda Medina, ☎ 998/877–0066).

TELEPHONES

Isla's area code is 998 and in order to dial local calls you must dial 98 followed by the 7-digit telephone number.

Isla has plenty of phones. Those that encourage you to "pick up and dial 0" charge ridiculously high prices. It's better to use the TELMEX phones that accept Ladatel phone cards. You can buy the cards from local stores in blocks equivalent to $3, $5, $10, and $20. Once connected, you can dial direct anywhere in the world.

To place a collect call, dial 090 for an international operator from any phone booth (no card is required) and ask for *para cobrar* (literally, "to charge").

TOURS

Cooperativa Lanchera runs four-hour trips to the submerged Virgin statue, the lighthouse, the turtles at Playa Lancheros, the coral reefs at Los Manchones, and El Garrafón, for about $28 including lunch. Cooperativa Isla Mujeres rents boats for a maximum of four hours and six people ($120). An island tour with lunch (minimum six people) costs $19 per person.

Sundreamers offers daytime and sunset tours around the island on its 52-ft catamaran. Prices start at $49 per person and include food and drinks.

Sociedad Cooperativa Isla Mujeres and La Isleña launch boats to Isla Contoy daily at 8:30 AM and return at 4 PM. Groups are a minimum of 6 and a maximum of 12 people, depending on the size of the boat. Captain Jaime Avila Canto, a local Isla Contoy expert, offers an excellent tour for large groups aboard his boat the *Anett.*

The trip to Isla Contoy takes about 45 minutes, depending on the weather and the boat; the cost is $38–$50. Sociedad Cooperativa Isla Mujeres tour operators provide a fruit breakfast on the boat and stop at Xlaches reef on the way to Isla Contoy for snorkeling (gear is included). The tour of Contoy's leeward side includes views from the water of Bird Beach and Puerto Viejo Lagoon. Along the way your crew trolls for the lunch it cooks on the beach—you may be in for anything from barracuda to snapper (beer and soda are also included). While the catch is being barbecued, you have time to explore the island, snorkel, check out the small museum and biological station, or just laze under a palapa.

➤ FEES AND SCHEDULES: **Captain Jaime Avila Canto** (✉ Av. Lic Jesús Martínez Ross 38, ☎ 998/877–0478). **Cooperativa Isla Mujeres** (✉ Av. Rueda Medina, ☎ 998/877–0274). **Cooperativa Lanchera** (✉ waterfront near dock, ☎ no phone). **La Isleña** (✉ corner of Avs. Morelos and Juárez, ½ block from pier, ☎ 998/877–0578). **Sociedad Cooperativa Isla Mujeres** (✉ pier, ☎ 998/877–0500). **Sonadoras del Sol** (Sundreamers; ✉ Av. Juárez 9, ☎ 998/877–0736, WEB www.sundreamers.com).

TRANSPORTATION AROUND ISLA MUJERES

Many places on Isla rent golf carts, a fun way to get around the island, especially when traveling with children. Ciro's Motorent and P'pe's Rentadora both have as low as $38 for 24 hours. Most island motorists are quite accommodating, but be prepared to move to the side of the road to let vehicles pass you.

➤ RENTALS: **Ciro's Motorent** (✉ Av. Guerrero Nte. 11, at Av. Matamoros, ☎ 998/877–0578). **P'pe's Rentadora** (✉ Av. Hidalgo 19, ☎ 998/877–0019). **El Sol** (✉ Av. Francisco Madero 5, entrance off Av. Guerrero and Playa Norte, ☎ 998/877–0068).

TRAVEL AGENCIES

Mundaca Travel sells plane and bus tickets, offers Federal Express services, and arranges airport transfers, tours, and house rentals.

➤ LOCAL AGENCIES: **Mundaca Travel** (✉ Av. Hidalgo, ☎ 998/877–0025, 998/877–0026, or 888/501–4952, FAX 998/877–0076).

VISITOR INFORMATION

The Isla Mujeres tourist office is open weekdays 9–2 and 7–9 and has general information about Isla Contoy and the island itself. The Isla Mujeres Hotel Association has information on various rentals.

➤ TOURIST INFORMATION: **Isla Mujeres Hotel Association** (☎ 998/877–0279). **Isla Mujeres tourist office** (✉ Plaza Isla Mujeres, Av. Rueda Medina 130, ☎ 998/877–0307, FAX 998/877–0307, WEB www.isla-mujeres.net).

COZUMEL

Updated by Maribeth Mellin

A **490-SQUARE-KM** (189-square-mi) island 19 km (12 mi) east of the Yucatán peninsula, Cozumel is mostly flat, with an interior covered by parched scrub, dense jungle, and marshy lagoons. White, sandy beaches with calm waters line the island's leeward (western) side, which is fringed by a spectacular reef system, while the windward (eastern) side, facing the Caribbean Sea, has powerful surf and rocky strands. A lot of Cozumel has been developed, but a good deal of the land and the shores has been set aside as national park; a few Maya ruins provide what limited sightseeing there is aside from the island's glorious natural attractions. San Miguel is the only town.

The island's name comes from the Maya word *Ah-Cuzamil-Peten*, which means "land of the swallows." For the Maya, Cozumel was the sacred site of the fertility goddess Ixchel, as well as a key center of trade and navigation. For the Spanish, it was useful as a naval base in the late 16th century. For pirates, its safe harbors and the catacombs and tunnels the Maya dug were ideal for their treasure-gathering and -storing needs. After cycles of settlement and abandonment that included an economic boom based on the island's abundant supply of zapote trees, which produce chicle, a chewing-gum industry staple, Jacques Cousteau discovered Cozumel's incredible reefs and diving opportunities in 1961, and the trajectory of its current life was set.

Despite the inevitable effects of cruise ships that dock here, the island's earthy charm remains largely intact, and the relaxing atmosphere remains typically Mexican—friendly and unpretentious. A mainstay of Cozumel's mood is the isleños, descendants of the Maya who have inhabited the island for centuries.

Exploring

Cozumel is 53 km (33 mi) long and 15 km (9 mi) wide and, aside from the road leading to Punta Molas, has excellent paved roads. Beware of flash flooding during the rainy season; the dirt roads can become difficult to navigate in minutes. Aside from the 15% of the island that has been developed, Cozumel is made up of expanses of sandy or rocky beaches, quiet little coves, palm groves, lagoons and swamps, scrubby jungle, and a few low hills. Several minor Maya ruins dot the eastern coast of the island. One of them, El Caracol, served as an ancient lighthouse. There are also a couple of minuscule ruins—El Mirador (The Balcony) and El Trono (The Throne)—identified by roadside markers.

A Good Tour

Taxis have become so costly on the island that it's worth renting a vehicle for a day or two to explore Cozumel. Be forewarned that most car-rental companies have a policy that voids your insurance when you leave the paved roads and journey to Punta Molas or other off-road points. Most dirt roads are not maintained, so proceed with great caution (if at all), especially after rain.

Head south from **San Miguel** ⑪ and in about 15 minutes you come to **Parque Chankanaab** ⑫. Continue past the park to reach the beaches: Playa Corona, Playa San Clemente, Playa San Francisco, and Playa Sol. If you stay on this road you eventually reach, on your left, the turnoff for the ruins of **El Cedral** ⑬. Look for the red arch alongside the road announcing the turnoff.

Cozumel

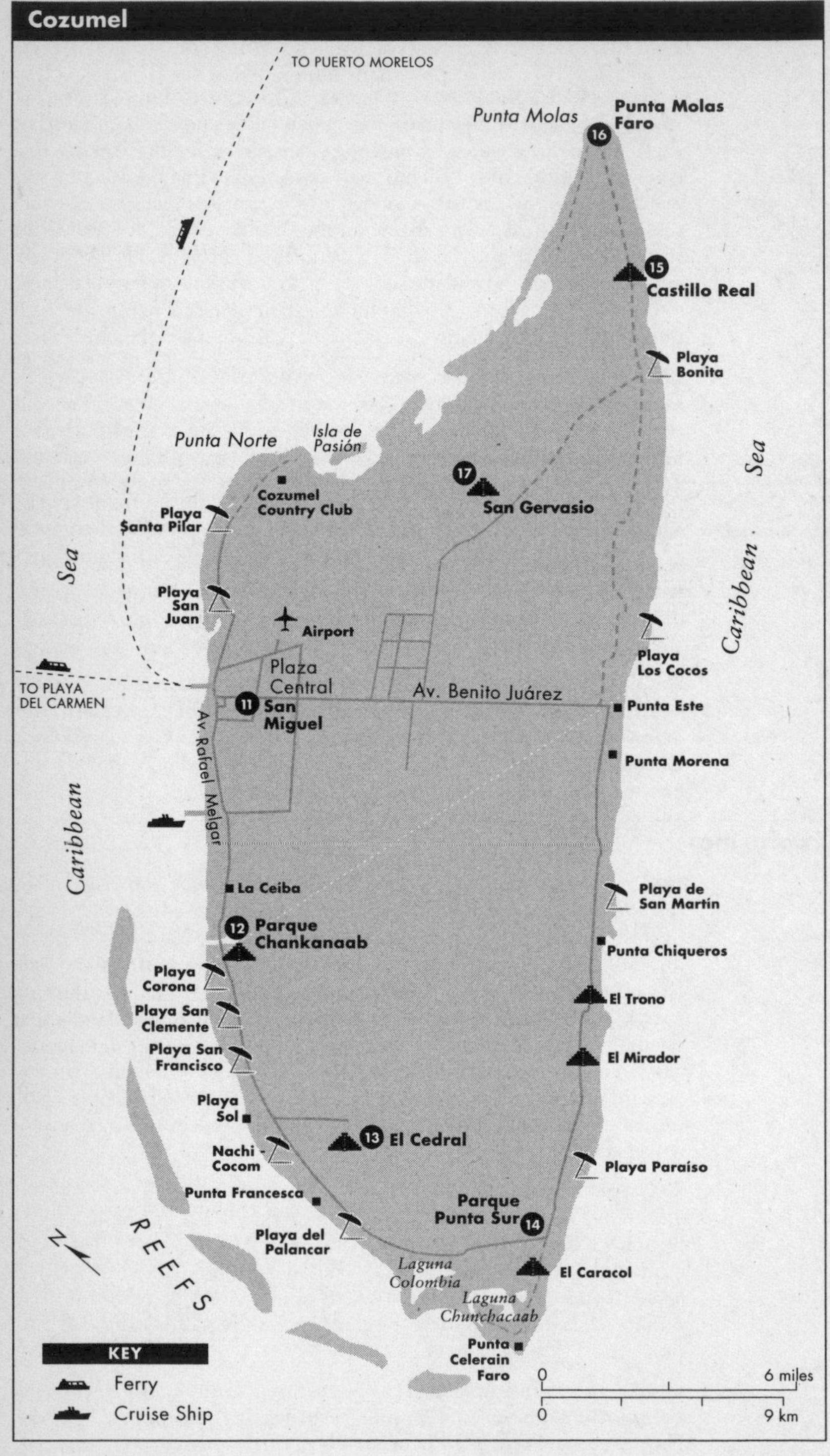

TO PUERTO MORELOS
Punta Molas
Punta Molas Faro
16
15
Castillo Real
Playa Bonita
Punta Norte
Isla de Pasión
17
San Gervasio
Cozumel Country Club
Playa Santa Pilar
Sea
Caribbean Sea
Playa San Juan
Airport
Playa Los Cocos
Plaza Central
TO PLAYA DEL CARMEN
11
San Miguel
Av. Benito Juárez
Punta Este
Av. Rafael Melgar
Punta Morena
Caribbean
La Ceiba
Playa de San Martín
12
Parque Chankanaab
Punta Chiqueros
Playa Corona
El Trono
Playa San Clemente
Playa San Francisco
El Mirador
Playa Sol
13
El Cedral
Nachi - Cocom
Playa Paraíso
Punta Francesca
Parque Punta Sur
14
Playa del Palancar
REEFS
N
Laguna Colombia
El Caracol
Laguna Chunchacaab
KEY
Ferry
Cruise Ship
Punta Celerain Faro
0
6 miles
0
9 km

Back on the main coast road, continue south until you reach the turnoff for Playa del Palancar, where the famous reef lies offshore. Continue to the point where the road swings north—the most southern point of the island—and you come to the **Parque Punta Sur** ⑭ entrance. The park encompasses Laguna Colombia and Laguna Chunchacaab as well as an ancient Maya lighthouse, El Caracol, and the modern lighthouse, Faro de Celarain. You have to leave your car at the gate and use either the bicycles or public bus provided by the park.

At Punta Sur the coast road turns north. Not far from the Parque Punta Sur entrance are the minuscule ruins of **El Mirador** and **El Trono.** This road also passes one beach after another: Playa Paraíso, Punta Chiqueros, Playa de San Martín, and Punta Morena. At Punta Este, the coast road intersects with Avenida Benito Juárez, which crosses the island to the opposite coast. You can take this road back into San Miguel or continue toward Punta Molas.

The road to Punta Molas is quite rough, and only half of it is accessible by car—you must walk the rest of the way. The beaches on this part of the island are marvelously deserted: Ixpal Barco, Los Cocos, Hanan Reef, Ixlapak, and then Playa Bonita, with the small **Castillo Real** ⑮, another Maya site. Farther north are a number of other minor ruins, including a lighthouse, **Punta Molas Faro** ⑯, at the island's northern tip.

If you take Avenida Benito Juárez from Punta Este, you come to the turnoff (just past the army airfield) for the ruins of **San Gervasio** ⑰. Turn right and follow this well-maintained road for 7 km (4½ mi) to get to the ruins. To return to San Miguel, return to Avenida Benito Juárez and continue driving west.

Sights to See

15 **Castillo Real** (Royal Castle). A Maya site on the coast near the northern tip of the island, the *castillo* (castle) includes a lookout tower, the base of a pyramid, and a temple with two chambers capped by a false arch. The waters here harbor several shipwrecks, and it's a fine spot for snorkeling, because there are few visitors to disturb the fish. Note, however, that the surf can get quite strong, so pick a time when the sea is tranquil.

13 **El Cedral.** Once the hub of Maya life on Cozumel, this was the first site found by Spanish explorers in 1518. It was also the island's first official city, founded in 1847. These days it's a quaint farming community with small houses and gardens that show little evidence of its past glory. Conquistadors tore down much of the temple, and the U.S. Army Corps of Engineers destroyed the rest during World War II to make way for the island's first airport. All that remains of the ruins is a small structure with an arch; be sure to look inside to see the faint traces of paint and stucco. Alongside is a green-and-white cinder-block church, decorated inside with crosses shrouded in embroidered lace where, reportedly, the first Mass in Mexico was celebrated. Every May there's a fair here, with dancing, music, bullfights, and a cattle show, celebrating the area's agricultural roots. Hidden in the surrounding jungle are other small ruins, but you need a guide to find them. Check with the locals near the ruins who offer excellent tours on horseback. ✉ *Turn at Km 17.5 off Carretera Sur or Av. Rafael E. Melgar, then drive 3 km (2 mi) inland to the site,* ☎ *no phone.* *Free.* *Daily dawn–dusk.*

12 **Parque Chankanaab** (Chankanaab Park). A 15-minute drive south of San Miguel, Chankanaab (the name means "small sea") is a lovely saltwater lagoon that the government has made into a national park with

an archaeological park, botanical garden, dolphin aquarium, and wildlife sanctuary.

Scattered throughout the archaeological park are 60 reproductions of Olmec, Toltec, Aztec, and Maya stone carvings from well-known sites in Mexico. Guides lead interesting, informative tours, explaining the history of the most significant pieces. Also on-site is a good example of a typical Maya house.

The botanical garden has more than 450 species of plants from the region. Enjoy a cool walk through pathways leading to the lagoon, where 60-odd species of marine life, including fish, coral, turtles, and various crustaceans, live. Unfortunately, swimming is no longer allowed in the lagoon; the area's ecosystem has become quite fragile since the collapse of the underwater tunnels linking the lagoon to the sea. But you can swim, scuba dive, or snorkel at the beach. There's plenty to see under the sea: a sunken ship, crusty old cannons and anchors, a Maya Chacmool (the revered rain god), and a beautiful sculpture of the Virgin del Mar (Virgin of the Sea). In addition, hordes of brilliant fish swim around the coral reef. To maintain the health of the reef ecosystem, park rules forbid the feeding of fish and touching the coral reef.

A small but worthwhile museum near the beach has photographs illustrating the history of the park, coral and shell exhibits, and some sculptures. There's also a sea-lion park, where children can enjoy watching the sea lions perform at one of their daily shows. Come early, as the park fills up fast, particularly on the days when cruise ships dock. ✉ *Carretera Sur, Km 9,* ☎ *987/872–2940 for park, 987/872–6606 for dolphin reservations.* 🎫 *$7.* ⏲ *Daily 7–6.*

14 **Parque Punta Sur.** The 247-acre national preserve, at Cozumel's southernmost tip, has numerous birds and animals, including crocodiles, flamingos, foxes, egrets, and herons. Cars aren't allowed on the premises, so you must use park transportation: bicycles or public buses. From observation towers you can spot crocodiles and birds in **Laguna Colombia** or **Laguna Chunchacaab.** Or visit the ancient Maya lighthouse, **El Caracol,** constructed to whistle when the wind blows in a certain direction. At the southernmost point of the park (and the island) is the **Faro de Celarain** (Celarain Lighthouse), now a navigational museum outlining the history of seamanship in the area. You can climb the 134 steps to the top of the lighthouse; it's a steamy effort, but the views are incredible. The beaches here are deserted and wide, and there's great snorkeling offshore. Snorkeling equipment is available for rent, as are kayaks. The park also has an excellent restaurant, information center, small souvenir shop, and rest rooms. If you don't rent a vehicle to get here, a round-trip taxi ride from San Miguel costs close to $40. You are not allowed to bring in food or drinks. ✉ *Southernmost point in Punta Sur Park and the coastal road,* ☎ *987/872–2940 or 987/872–0914.* 🎫 *$15.* ⏲ *Daily 7–4.*

16 **Punta Molas Faro** (Molas Point Lighthouse). At the northernmost point of Cozumel, the lighthouse is an excellent spot for sunbathing and birding. The jagged shoreline and the open sea offer magnificent views, making it well worth the time-consuming and somewhat difficult trip. Be prepared to walk some of the way. Area car-rental companies actively discourage visitors from driving here. Access is easier by boat, or you may prefer to take a guided tour.

17 **San Gervasio.** Standing in a lovely forest, these remarkable ruins make up the largest existing Maya and Toltec site on Cozumel. San Gervasio was once the island's capital and ceremonial center, dedicated to the fertility goddess Ixchel. The Classic- and Postclassic-style buildings

were continuously occupied from AD 300 to AD 1500. Typical architectural features include limestone plazas and arches atop stepped platforms, as well as stelae and bas-reliefs. Be sure to see the "hands" temple, which has red hand imprints all over its altar. Plaques clearly identify each of the ruins in Maya, Spanish, and English. At the entrance there's a snack bar and some gift shops. If you want a rugged hike, take the 15-km (9-mi) dirt road that travels north to the coast and Castillo Real. ✉ *From San Miguel, take Av. Benito Juárez east to San Gervasio access road; turn left and follow road for 7 km (4½ mi).* *Access to road $1, ruins $3.50.* ⏲ *Nov.–Sept., daily 8–5.*

11 **San Miguel.** Although highly commercialized and packed with tourists, Cozumel's only town has retained some of the flavor of a Mexican village. Stroll along the malecón and take in the ocean breeze. The main square is where townspeople and visitors hang out, particularly on Sunday night, when musical groups join the assortment of food and souvenir vendors.

Beaches

Cozumel's beaches vary from long, treeless, sandy stretches to isolated coves and rocky shores. Most development is on the leeward (western) side, where the coast is relatively sheltered by the proximity of the mainland 19 km (12 mi) to the west. The best sand beaches lie along 5 km (3 mi) of the southern half of Cozumel's leeward side—from **Playa Corona** south to **Punta Celerain.** In between them are **Playa San Clemente,** which has wide, sandy beaches and shallow waters, **Playa San Francisco,** considered one of the longest and finest on Cozumel, and **Playa del Palancar,** which has kept its prices down in order to keep drawing divers to its famous Palancar Reef.

Reaching beaches on the windward (eastern) side is more difficult and requires transportation, but you'll be rewarded with solitude. Near El Mirador is **Playa Paradiso** (also known as Playa Bosh), the southernmost of the windward beaches. North of Playa Paradiso, **Punta Chiqueros** is a moon-shape cove sheltered from the sea by an offshore reef. Where the paved road toward Punta Molas Faro ends lies a long stretch of deserted beaches, including **Playa Bonita,** which extends to Punta Molas at the island's northern tip. It's unspoiled and quite beautiful—perfect for sunbathing and communing with nature.

Dining

Dining options on Cozumel reflect the nature of the place as a whole: breezy and relaxed with the occasional harmless pretensions. The downtown core has more than 80 restaurants, so you can choose among fast food, great regional dishes, and fresh seafood. Many restaurants accept credit cards; café-type places generally don't. A dining tip: don't follow the suggestions of cabdrivers, who may be paid to recommend restaurants.

$–$$$ ★ ✕ **La Veranda.** This charming wooden Caribbean house with comfortable rattan furniture, soft lighting, and good music oozes romance. You can sit and enjoy the evening on the outside terrace, or inside. Choices include poblano chilies stuffed with goat cheese, cilantro ravioli with jalapeño pesto, and coconut shrimp; the flambé desserts are sensational. ✉ *Calle 4 Nte. 140, between Avs. 5 and 10 Nte.,* ☎ *987/872–4132. AE, MC, V. No lunch.*

$–$$ ✕ **La Choza.** Purely Mexican in design and cuisine, this family-owned restaurant is a favorite for *mole rojo* (a spicy sauce with cinnamon and chilies), *chiles rellenos,* and *cochinita pibíl* (marinated pork baked in banana leaves). Leave room for the chilled chocolate pie, or go for the avocado pie if you're feeling adventurous. ✉ *Calle Adolfo Rosado Salas 198, at Av. 10,* ☎ *987/872–0958. MC, V.*

$–$$ ★ ✕ **Chen Río Restaurant.** The best fish on Cozumel is served here, on the east side of the island at Playa de San Martín. The restaurant is run by a Maya family whose sons go out in the morning to catch the fish they serve for lunch. Relax under the coconut trees, watch the surf, or go for a swim while you wait for your meal to arrive. The combo plate—with shrimp, lobster, fish, rice, and vegetables—is a phenomenal bargain. ✉ *East-coast road, Km 28,* ☎ *no phone. No credit cards.*

$–$$ ★ ✕ **La Cocay.** The name is Maya for "firefly," and like its namesake, this place is a bit magical. The chef creates a menu every four to five weeks; dishes might include spiced-nut-crusted chicken breast, pumpkin-stuffed *medialunas* (half-moon pasta) with sage and Parmesan butter sauce, and rack of lamb with a red-onion sauce. The sophisticated restaurant has wood tables, wrought-iron chairs, soft lighting, and an open-air kitchen that lets you watch the staff do its magic. Desserts are fantastic, and the wine list has a nice selection. ✉ *Av. 17 Sur 1000, at Av. 25,* ☎ *987/872–5533. No credit cards. Closed Sun. and Oct. No lunch.*

$–$$ ★ ✕ **Prima.** The pastas are wonderful, salads exemplary, and the steaks juicy and tender at this breezy second-floor terrace restaurant. Try the salad with blue cheese, pasta with pesto, shrimp stuffed with crab, or an Angus steak. Coffee and key lime pie are the perfect end to a perfect meal. There can be lines during the busy season (even if you have a reservation), but you can wait for your table downstairs in the cigar–sports bar. ✉ *Calle Adolfo Rosado Salas 109-A,* ☎ *987/872–6567. AE, MC, V. No lunch.*

$ ✕ **Plaza Leza.** The best fajitas and ceviche in town are served in this unpretentious Mexican sidewalk café. You can let the hours slip away while enjoying the great food and watching the action in the square. For more privacy, go indoors to the somewhat secluded, cozy inner patio for everything from *poc chuc* (pork chops grilled Yucatecan-style with hot spices), enchiladas, and lime soup to chicken sandwiches and coconut ice cream. You can get breakfast here, too. ✉ *Calle 1 Sur, south side of Plaza Central,* ☎ *987/872–1041. AE, MC, V.*

$ ★ ✕ **Rock 'n Java Caribbean Café.** Healthful is the key word here. The extensive breakfast menu offers such delights as whole-wheat French toast and cheese blintzes. For lunch or dinner, consider the vegetarian tacos or linguini with clam sauce, or choose from the selection of more than a dozen salads. To balance things out there are scrumptious pies, cakes, and pastries baked daily on the premises. Enjoy your healthful meal or sinful snack while sitting on the wrought-iron studio chairs. ✉ *Av. Rafael E. Melgar 602-6,* ☎ *987/872–4405. No credit cards. Closed Sun.*

$ ★ ✕ **El Turix.** Off the beaten track, about 10 minutes by cab from downtown, this simple place is worth the trip for a chance to experience true Yucatecan cuisine served by the amiable owners, Rafael and Maruca. Don't miss the pollo pibíl or the poc chuc. There are also daily specials, and paella on request (call 24 hours ahead). ✉ *Av. 20 Sur, between Calles 17 and 19,* ☎ *987/872–5234. No credit cards. No lunch.*

Lodging

All of Cozumel's hotels are on the leeward (west) and south sides of the island. Hotels north and south of San Miguel tend to be the larger resorts, and less expensive places are in town. Because of the proximity of the reefs, divers and snorkelers tend to congregate at the southern properties, whereas swimmers prefer the hotels to the north, where the beaches are better.

North Hotel Zone

$$$–$$$$ ★ **Paradisus Cozumel.** A long white-sand beach with clear, shallow water fronts this all-inclusive gem at the far end of the north coast, right across the street from the golf course. The spacious rooms are cool and comfortable and have ocean-view balconies. Families congregate around the kid's club and pool; there's also a gym, water-sports center, and horseback riding. The meals are very good and the staff extremely helpful. Up to two children under 12 stay and eat free with their parents. ✉ *Carretera Costera Norte, Km 5.8, 77600,* ☎ *987/872–0411 or 800/336–3542,* FAX *987/872–1599,* WEB *www.solmelia.com. 150 rooms. 2 restaurants, snack bar, 2 pools, 2 tennis courts, gym, dive shop, windsurfing, kayaking, 4 bars, car rental. AE, MC, V.*

$$$ ★ **Playa Azul Hotel.** This boutique hotel filled with artistic touches is the perfect place for romantic getaways. The bright, airy rooms face the ocean or tropical gardens and have wicker furnishings and sun-filled terraces. Master suites have private hot tubs. Small palapas are shade lounge chairs on the perfect beach, and Carlos Scuba offers snorkeling, and diving trips from Playa Azul's own dock. The Palma Azul restaurant serves delicious Continental meals. Greens fees at the Cozumel Country Club are included in the room rate. ✉ *Carretera Costera Norte, Km 4, 77600,* ☎ *987/872–0199,* FAX *987/872–0110,* WEB *www.playa-azul.com. 34 rooms, 16 suites. Restaurant, pool, some in-room hot tubs, massage, dive shop, dock, snorkeling, fishing, billiards, 2 bars, car rental. AE, MC, V.*

South Hotel Zone

$$$$ ★ **Presidente Inter-Continental Cozumel.** Luxury, comfort, service, and privacy are hallmarks of the Presidente. The stylish rooms are done in bright, contemporary colors with white cedar furnishings and private terraces; a majority of the rooms overlook the ocean. Mature landscaping adds to the exotic, tropical feel. The pool is modest, but the beach is the nicest on the island and has great snorkeling: fish swim in the waters a few feet off the beach. There's a dive and water-sports center, tennis courts, and a serene botanical garden. The restaurants are highly recommended. ✉ *Carretera Chankanaab, Km 6.5, 77600,* ☎ *987/872–0322 or 800/327–0200,* FAX *987/872–1360,* WEB *www.interconti.com. 253 rooms. 2 restaurants, 2 tennis courts, pool, gym, hot tub, dive shop, 3 bars, shops, children's programs (ages 4–12), meeting rooms, car rental. AE, DC, MC, V.*

$$$ **Fiesta Americana Cozumel Dive Resort.** Well situated for divers, this hotel sits across the road from the water; a pedestrian walkway over the road provides easy access to the dive shop, dock, beach, pool, and restaurant. Standard rooms are large, with light-wood furnishings; all have oceanfront balconies. The 56 casitas set along jungle paths have balconies with hammocks and outdoor lockers for dive gear. This is an excellent choice for those spending lots of time in the water. ✉ *Carretera Chankanaab, Km 7.5, 77600,* ☎ *987/872–2622 or 800/343–7821,* FAX *987/872–2666,* WEB *www.fiestamexico.com. 172 rooms, 56 villas. 3 restaurants, 2 tennis courts, 2 pools, dive shop, dock, 3 bars, car rental, travel services. AE, MC, V.*

$$$ **Iberostar.** This all-inclusive resort at the southernmost point of Cozumel has managed to keep the local flora and fauna intact in a jungle setting. Rooms are small but pleasantly decorated with wrought iron and have either a king-size bed or two queen-size beds; all have terraces or patios. There isn't much privacy, since paths through the resort wind around the rooms. There are plenty of activities to keep the whole family busy. ✉ *Carretera Chankanaab, Km 17, 77600 (past El Cedral turnoff),* ☎ *987/872–9900,* FAX *987/872–9909,* WEB *www.iberostar.com. 300 rooms. 3 restaurants, 2 tennis courts, 2 pools, hair*

salon, gym, dive shop, dock, boating, 3 bars, theater, children's programs (ages 4–12), car rental. AE, MC, V.

$$ ★ **Villablanca Garden Beach Hotel.** Beautiful architecture carries through from the hotel's white facade into the rooms, which have archways separating sleeping and living areas. Suites have refrigerators, sunken bathtubs, and private terraces. La Veranda, the restaurant, is very accommodating and can prepare special meals for those with dietary restrictions. The hotel has a beach club, pool, tennis courts, and a huge garden. Excellent dive packages are available at bargain prices. ✉ *Carretera Chankanaab, Km 3, 77600,* ☎ *987/872–0730,* FAX *987/872–0865,* WEB *www.villablanca.net. 25 rooms, 25 suites. Restaurant, refrigerators (some), tennis court, pool, dock. AE, MC, V.*

Downtown Hotels

$$ **Casa Martillo Condos.** At this luxurious condo complex all units face the pool and have full kitchens, dining-living areas, sofa beds, and balconies or patios. There's a minimum three-night stay, and many guests stay a week or more. The staff is wonderful and pays a lot of attention to details while keeping the place spotless. If you share, these condos are a great bargain. ✉ *Calle 19 Sur and Av. 15 Sur, 77600,* ☎ *987/872–3139 or 877/627–8455,* FAX *530/623–2671,* WEB *www.casamartillo.com. 6 condos. Kitchens, pool, laundry facilities. MC, V.*

$ **Tamarindo Bed & Breakfast.** The owners of this five-room charmer have created a place that combines the flavor of Mexico with the elegance of France. Rooms are gracefully decorated with individual touches. Breakfast consists of fresh breads, fruits in season, homemade yogurt, and French-pressed coffee. The staff arranges diving expeditions, and there's a rinse tank and gear storage facility on the premises. ✉ *Calle 4 Nte. 421, between Avs. 20 and 25, 77600,* ☎ FAX *987/872–3614,* WEB *www.cozumel.net/bb/tamarind. 5 rooms. Fans, massage, bicycles, baby-sitting, laundry service. MC, V.*

$ ★ **Charrita's.** This charming bed-and-breakfast is a delightful change from standard hotels. Its quiet location in a residential neighborhood 11 blocks from the beach gives you a chance to experience the real Mexico. Each of the five rooms is extremely comfortable, with individual decorations and private bath. Upstairs there's a terrace for sunbathing or taking in sunsets. Guests rave about the huge Mexican breakfast included in the rate. ✉ *Calle 11 at Av. 55 Bis, 77600,* ☎ *987/872–4760,* WEB *www.cozumelbandb.com. 5 rooms. No credit cards.*

Nightlife and the Arts

The arts scene on Cozumel tends to focus on the local culture; every Thursday during high season there's a folkloric dance performance at the **Fiesta Americana** (☎ 987/872–2622). The whole island explodes with music, costumes, dancing, parades, and parties for Carnival, which takes place just before the start of Lent. Visitors from around the world are encouraged to dress up and catch the fever.

Bars

Cactus (✉ Av. Rafael E. Melgar 145, ☎ 987/872–5799) has a disco, live music, and a bar that stays open until 5 AM. Sports fiends can catch all the news on ESPN at **Sports Page Video Bar and Restaurant** (✉ Av. 5 Nte. and Calle 2, ☎ 987/872–1199).

Discos

The oldest disco on the island, **Neptune Dance Club** (✉ Av. Rafael E. Melgar at Av. 11, ☎ 987/872–1537) still lets you boogie into the night. **Viva Mexico** (✉ Av. Rafael E. Melgar, ☎ 987/872–0799) has a DJ who spins dance music until the wee hours. There's also an extensive snack menu.

Live Music

Cafe Salsa (✉ Av. 10, ☎ no phone) has live tropical music nightly at 10:30 and is the best place in town for Latin dancing. For sophisticated jazz, smart cocktails, and great cigars, check out the **Havana Club** (✉ Av. Rafael E. Melgar, between Calles 6 and 8, second floor, ☎ 987/872–1268). Beware of ordering imported liquors such as vodka and scotch, as the drink prices are very high. The food isn't the draw at **Joe's Lobster House** (✉ Av. 10 Sur 229, between Calles Adolfo Rosada Salas and 3 Sur, ☎ 987/872–3275), but the reggae and salsa bring in the crowds nightly, from 10:30 until dawn. Sunday evenings 8–10, locals head for the *zócalo,* or *la plaza* (the plaza), to hear mariachis and island musicians playing tropical tunes.

Outdoor Activities and Sports

Most people come to Cozumel for the water sports—scuba diving, snorkeling, and fishing are particularly popular. Services and equipment rentals are available throughout the island, especially through major hotels and water-sports centers such as **Scuba Du** (✉ at the Presidente Inter-Continental and El Cozumeleño hotels, ☎ 987/872–0050).

Fishing

Regulations forbid commercial fishing, sportfishing, spear fishing, and collecting any marine life in certain areas around Cozumel. It's illegal to kill certain species within marine reserves, including billfish, so be prepared to return prize catches back to the sea. (Regular participants in the annual billfish tournament have seen some of the same fish caught over and over again.) U.S. Customs allows you to bring up to 30 pounds of fish back into the country.

CHARTERS

You can charter high-speed fishing boats for $400 for a half day or $500 for a full day (maximum six people). **Albatros Deep Sea Fishing** (☎ 987/872–2390 or 888/333–4643) is a local outfit specializing in fishing trips. **Marathon Fishing & Leisure Charters** (☎ 987/872–1986) is popular with fishermen. Full-day rates for both places include the boat and crew, tackle and bait, and lunch with beer and soda. Your hotel can help you arrange daily charters—some hotels have special deals, with boats leaving from their own dock.

Golf

The long-awaited **Cozumel Country Club** (✉ Carretera Costera Norte, Km 5.8, ☎ 987/872–9670, WEB www.cozumelcountryclub.com.mx) is home to the island's first championship golf course. The gorgeous fairways set amid mangroves and a lagoon are the work of the Nicklaus Design Group. The greens fees is $110, including golf cart; many hotels are offering golf packages.

Scuba Diving

The options for divers in Cozumel include deep dives, drift dives, shore dives, wall dives, and night dives, as well as theme dives focusing on ecology, archaeology, sunken ships, and photography. With so many shops to choose from (there are now more than 100), divers should look for high safety standards and documented credentials. The best places are those that offer small groups and individual attention. Next to your equipment, your dive master is the most important aspect of your dive, particularly if you're new to diving.

There's a reputable recompression chamber at the **Buceo Medico Mexicano** (✉ Calle 9 Sur 21-B, ☎ 987/872–2387, 987/872–1430 24-hr hot line). The **Cozumel Recompression Chamber** (✉ San Miguel Clinic, Calle 6 between Avs. 5 and 10, ☎ 987/872–3070, 987/872–2387, or 987/872–

1848) is a fully equipped recompression center. These chambers, which aim for a 35-minute response time from reef to chamber, treat decompression sickness, commonly known as "the bends," which occurs when you surface too quickly and nitrogen is absorbed into the bloodstream. Recompression chambers are also used to treat nitrogen narcosis, collapsed lungs, and overexposure to the cold. Consider getting DAN (Divers Alert Network) insurance, which covers dive accidents.

When diving, stay at least 3 ft above the reef, not just because the coral can sting or cut you but also because coral is easily damaged and grows very slowly: it has taken 2,000 years for it to reach its present size.

DIVE SHOPS AND TOUR OPERATORS

Most dive shops can provide you with all the incidentals you'll need. Equipment rental is relatively inexpensive, ranging from $6 for tanks or a lamp to about $8–$10 for a regulator and BC; underwater-camera rentals can cost as much as $35, video-camera rentals run about $75, and professionally shot and edited videos of your own dive are priced at about $160. You can choose from two-tank boat trips and specialty dives ranging from $45 to $60. Most companies also offer one-tank afternoon and night dives for $30–$35. The dive shops handle more than 1,000 divers per day; naturally, many of them run what are called "cattle boats," carrying lots of divers and gear. It's worth the extra money to go out with a smaller group on a fast boat, especially if you're an experienced diver.

Because dive shops tend to be competitive, it's well worth your while to shop around. Many hotels have their own on-site operations, and there are dozens of dive shops in town. **ANOAAT** (Aquatic Sports Operators Association; ☎ 987/872–5955, WEB www.anoaat.com) has listings of affiliated dive operations. Before signing on, ask some experienced divers about the place, check credentials, and look over the boats and equipment.

Aqua Safari (✉ Av. Rafael E. Melgar 429, between Calles 5 and 7 Sur, ☎ 987/872–0101). **Blue Bubble** (✉ Av. 5 Sur at Calle 3 Sur, ☎ 987/872–1865). **Carlo Scuba** (✉ Carretera Costera Norte, Km 4.5, ☎ 987/872–0199). **Del Mar Aquatics** (✉ Costera Sur, Km 4, ☎ 987/872–5949). **Dive Cozumel** (✉ Calle Adolfo Rosado Salas 72, at Av. 5 Sur, ☎ 987/872–4167). **Dive Paradise** (✉ Avs. Chichén and Pamuul, ☎ 987/872–5735). **Michelle's Dive Shop** (✉ Av. 5 Sur 201, at Calle Adolfo Rosado Salas, ☎ 987/872–0947). **Pepe Scuba** (✉ Carretera Costera Norte, Km 2.5, ☎ 987/872–3200). **Yucatech Expeditions** (✉ Av. 15 Sur 144, ☎ 987/872–5659).

Snorkeling

Snorkeling equipment is available at nearly all hotels and beach clubs as well as at Chankanaab Bay, Playa San Francisco, and Parque Sur. Gear rents for less than $10 a day.

One option is to contact the dive shops to see if you can tag along when they go out to a suitable snorkeling reef. Official snorkeling tours run from $25 to $50, depending on the duration, and take in the shallow reefs off Palancar, Colombia, and Yucab. **Fiesta Cozumel** (✉ Calle 11 Sur 598, between Avs. 25 and 30, ☎ 987/872–0725, FAX 987/872–1389) runs snorkeling tours from the 45-ft catamarans *El Zorro* and *Fury*. Rates begin at about $50 per day and include equipment, a guide, soft drinks and beer, and a box lunch. Sunset cruises aboard *El Zorro* are also available; they include unlimited drinks and live entertainment and cost about $35.

Shopping

Cozumel's main shopping area is **downtown** on the waterfront along Avenida Rafael E. Melgar and on some of the side streets around the plaza (there are more than 150 shops in this area alone). There's a **crafts market** (✉ Calle 1 Sur, behind the plaza) in town, which sells a respectable assortment of Mexican wares. In addition, small clusters of shops can be found at **Plaza del Sol** (on the east side of the main plaza), **Villa Mar** (on the north side of the main plaza), and **Plaza Confetti** (on the south side of the main plaza). The major jewelry, electronics, and fashion shops are in **Punta Langosta** (✉ Av. Melgar 551 at Calle 7). As a general rule, the newer, trendier shops line the waterfront, while the area around Avenida 5a houses the better crafts shops. The crafts market **Puerto Maya,** where the cruise ships dock, has some crafts at good prices. Bargains are best after the ships have departed.

Specialty Stores

CLOTHING

Several trendy sportswear stores line Avenida Rafael E. Melgar between Calles 2 and 6. **Exotica** (✉ Av. Benito Juárez at the plaza, ☎ 987/872–5880) has high-quality sportswear and shirts with nature-theme designs. **Poco Loco** (✉ Av. Rafael E. Melgar 18 and Av. Benito Juárez 2-A, ☎ 987/872–5499) sells casual wear and beach bags.

JEWELRY

The opening of the Punta Langosta mall will surely change the lineup of ultra-expensive jewelry shops along Avenida Rafael E. Melgar. Jewelry on Cozumel is pricey, but it tends to be of higher quality than what you'll find in many other Yucatán towns. **Diamond Creations** (✉ Av. Rafael E. Melgar Sur 131, ☎ 987/872–5330) lets you custom-design a piece of jewelry from its collection of loose diamonds, emeralds, rubies, sapphires, or tanzanite. You'll find silver, gold, and coral jewelry—bracelets and earrings especially—at **Joyería Palancar** (✉ Av. Rafael E. Melgar Nte. 15, ☎ 987/872–1468). Quality gemstones and striking designs are the strong points at **Rachat & Romero** (✉ Av. Rafael E. Melgar 101, ☎ 987/872–0571).

MEXICAN CRAFTS

Bugambilias (✉ Av. 10 Sur, between Calles Adolfo Rosado Salas and 1 Sur, ☎ 987/872–6282) sells handmade Mexican linens. **Talavera** (✉ Av. 5 Sur 349, ☎ 987/872–0171) carries beautiful ceramics from all over Mexico, including tiles from the Yucatán, masks from Guerrero, brightly painted wooden animals from Oaxaca, and carved chests from Guadalajara.

Cozumel A to Z

To research prices, get advice from other travelers, and book travel arrangements, visit www.fodors.com.

AIR TRAVEL

CARRIERS

Continental flies nonstop from Houston to Cozumel; US Airways flies nonstop on weekends from Charlotte, NC, to Cozumel. Mexicana has nonstop service from Mexico City. AeroMéxico flies nonstop from Atlanta to Cozumel. Mexicana subsidiaries Aerocaribe and Aerocozumel fly between Cozumel and Cancún and other destinations in Mexico, including Chichén Itzá, Chetumal, Mérida, and Playa del Carmen.

➤ AIRLINES AND CONTACTS: **Aerocaribe** (☎ 987/872–0503). **Aerocozumel** (☎ 987/872–3456). **Continental** (☎ 987/872–0487). **Mexicana** (☎ 987/872–2945). **U.S. Airways** (☎ 800/622–1015 toll free in the U.S.).

AIRPORTS

The Cozumel airport is 3 km (2 mi) north of San Miguel.

➤ AIRPORT INFORMATION: **Cozumel airport** (☎ 987/872–0928).

AIRPORT TRANSFER

Because of an agreement between the taxi drivers' and bus drivers' unions, there is taxi service *to* the airport but not *from* the airport. The *colectivo,* a van that seats up to eight, takes arriving passengers to their hotels; the fare is about $7. If you want to avoid waiting for the van to fill or for other passengers to be dropped off, you can hire an *especial*—an individual van. A trip via an individual van to one of the hotel zones costs about $15; a trip to the city runs about $10. Taxis to the airport cost between $8 and $25 from the hotel zones and approximately $5 from downtown.

BOAT AND FERRY TRAVEL

Passenger-only ferries to Playa del Carmen leave Cozumel's main pier (☎ 987/872–1508) approximately every hour on the hour from 4 AM to 10 PM (no ferries at 5 and 11 AM, 1, 7, and 9 PM). They leave Playa del Carmen's dock also about every hour on the hour, from 5 AM to 11 PM (no service at 6 AM, noon, 2, and 8 PM). The trip takes 45 minutes. Call to verify the times. Bad weather often prompts cancellations.

There is a car ferry from Puerto Morelos, but travelers don't need a car on the island. The trip takes three to four hours, the ferry is infrequent, the departure times aren't convenient, and the fare is about $70 for small cars (more for larger vehicles) and $6 per passenger.

➤ BOAT AND FERRY INFORMATION: **Playa del Carmen dock** (☎ 987/873–0067).

BUS TRAVEL

Because of a union agreement with taxi drivers, public buses cannot operate in the North and South Hotel zones; local bus service runs mainly within the town of San Miguel, although there is a route from town to the airport. Service is irregular but inexpensive.

CAR RENTAL

A rental car is a great way to get around the island, particularly as taxi prices are high here. A vehicle with four-wheel-drive (check to make sure that it hasn't been disconnected) is a must if you want to get to the more secluded beaches and ruins.

All the large hotels have rental offices, and most of the major car-rental companies have a location at the airport. Rental rates start at about $40 a day. Insurance doesn't cover trips off the main roads. Many of the smaller companies carry only standard transmission cars, so request an automatic in advance.

➤ MAJOR AGENCIES: **Avis** (☎ 987/872–0099 airport). **Hertz** (☎ 987/872–3888 airport).

➤ LOCAL AGENCIES: **Aguila Rentals** (✉ Calle 11 No. 101, ☎ 987/872–0729). **Cocodrilos Car Rental** (✉ Av. Rafael E. Melgar 601, ☎ 987/872–5030). **Rentadora Islena** (✉ Calle 7 No. 49, ☎ 987/872–0788).

EMERGENCIES

Both the Centro Medico de Cozumel (Cozumel Medical Center) and the Medical Specialties Center offer 24-hour air-ambulance service and a 24-hour pharmacy. The Centro de Salud (Health Center) offers round-the-clock emergency care.

Farmacia Dori is open daily 7 AM–midnight and offers hotel delivery service; Farmacia Joaquin is open Monday–Saturday 8 AM–10 PM and Sunday 9–1 and 5–9. Farmacias Canto, open 24 hours, delivers to hotels.

➤ CONTACTS: **Air Ambulance** (☎ 987/872–4070). **Centro Medico de Cozumel** (Cozumel Medical Center; ✉ 1A Sur 101, corner of Av. 50, ☎ 987/872–3545 or 987/872–5370). **Centro de Salud** (✉ Av. 20 Sur at Calle 11, ☎ 987/872–0140). The **Chiropractic Center** (✉ Av. 5 Sur 24-A, between Calles 3 and 5, ☎ 987/872–5099). **Medical Specialties Center** (✉ Av. 20 Nte. 425, ☎ 987/872–1419 or 987/872–2919). **Police** (✉ Anexo del Palacio Municipal, ☎ 987/872–0409). **Recompression Chamber** (✉ Calle 5 Sur 21-B, between Avs. Rafael E. Melgar and 5 Sur, ☎ 987/872–2387). **Red Cross** (✉ Calle Adolfo Rosada Salas at Av. 20 Sur, ☎ 987/872–1058).
➤ LATE-NIGHT PHARMACIES: **Farmacias Canto** (☎ 987/872–5377). **Farmacia Dori** (✉ Calle Adolfo Rosada Salas, between Avs. 15 and 20 Sur, ☎ 987/872–0559). **Farmacia Joaquin** (✉ north side of plaza, ☎ 987/872–2520).

MAIL AND SHIPPING

The local post office (*correos*), six blocks south of the plaza, is open weekdays 8–8, Saturday 9–5, and Sunday 9–1. Holders of American Express cards can receive mail at Fiesta Cozumel Holidays/American Express, which is open weekdays 8–1 and 5–8, Saturday 8–5.
➤ SERVICES: **Fiesta Cozumel Holidays/American Express** (✉ Calle 11 Sur 598, between Avs. 25 and 30, ☎ 987/872–0725 or 987/ 872–0925). **Post office** (✉ Calle 7 Sur at Av. Rafael E. Melgar, ☎ 987/872–0106).

MONEY MATTERS

Most of the banks are in the main square and are open weekdays 9–4 or 5. Many change currency all day.
➤ BANKS: **Banamex** (✉ Av. 5 Nte., at the plaza, ☎ 987/872–3411). **Bancomer** (✉ Av. 5 Nte., at the plaza, ☎ 987/872–0550). **Banco Serfín** (✉ Calle 1 Sur, between Avs. 5 and 10 Sur, ☎ 987/872–0930). **Bancrecer** (✉ Calle 1 Sur, between Avs. 5 and 10, ☎ 987/872–4750). **Bital** (✉ Av. Rafael E. Melgar 11, ☎ 987/872–0142).

CURRENCY EXCHANGE

After banking hours, you can exchange money at Promotora Cambiaria del Centro, open Monday–Saturday 8 AM–9 PM.
➤ EXCHANGE SERVICES: **Promotora Cambiaria del Centro** (✉ Av. 5 Sur between Calles 1 Sur and Adolfo Rosada Salas, ☎ no phone).

TAXIS

You can hail taxis on the street, and cabs wait at all the major hotels. The fixed rates (at press time but subject to change) run about $1.50 within town; $5–$8 between town and either hotel zone; $10 from most hotels to the airport; and about $20–$40 from the northern hotels or town to Parque Chankanaab or Playa San Francisco. The cost from the cruise-ship terminal to San Miguel is about $6. Prices quoted by the drivers should be in pesos. Tipping isn't necessary, as most drivers own their vehicles. Despite the established taxi fares, many of the younger and quite aggressive cab drivers have begun charging double or even triple these rates. If you have to take a taxi, be firm on a price before getting into the car.

TELEPHONES

In order to accommodate a growing number of telephone lines, all phone numbers have been changed. Phone numbers now have a three-digit area code (987) and seven-digit local number. Some of the printed material on Cozumel does not reflect this change.

The least expensive way to make an international call is to buy a Ladatel phone card (sold in blocks of $3, $5, $10, and $20) and use the TELMEX public phones. The TELMEX phones can be hard to find, as they are being replaced with private services' blue and red phones that urge you to "pick up and dial zero" and have very high rates. However, you can make local calls from these phones using peso coins. Local calls start at the equivalent of about 10¢. An alternative to the phone card is the *caseta de larga distancia*—the long-distance telephone office. There's an office on Calle 1, on the south side of the plaza; it's open 8–1 and 4–9. These offices have specially designed booths where you take your call after the number has been dialed by a clerk.

More expensive than the TELMEX phones but handier is the Calling Station, at Avenida Rafael E. Melgar 27 and Calle 3 Sur. It also offers video and cell-phone rentals, currency exchange, and Internet access and is open 8 AM–11 PM daily during high season.

TOURS

BOAT AND SUBMARINE TOURS

Atlantis Submarine runs 1½-hour submarine rides that explore the Chankanaab Reef and surrounding area; tickets for the tours are $72 for adults, $36 for children.

➤ FEES AND SCHEDULES: **Atlantis Submarines** (✉ Carretera Chankanaab, Km 4, across from Hotel Casa del Mar, ☎ 987/872–5671, WEB www.goatlantis.com). **Fiesta Cozumel Holidays/American Express** (✉ Calle 11 Sur 598, between Avs. 25 and 30, ☎ 987/872–0725).

HORSEBACK TOURS

Aventuras Naturales offers two-hour guided horseback tours. They start at $40 and visit Maya ruins and the beach. Rancho Buenavista offers four-hour horseback rides through the jungle starting at $65 per person.

➤ FEES AND SCHEDULES: **Aventuras Naturales** (✉ Av. 35 No. 1081, ☎ 987/872–1628, WEB www.aventurasnaturales.com). **Rancho Buenavista** (✉ Av. Rafael Melgar & Calle 11 Sur, ☎ 987/872–1537).

ORIENTATION

Tours of the island's sights, including the San Gervasio ruins, El Cedral, Parque Chankanaab, and the Museo de la Isla de Cozumel, cost about $45 a person and can be arranged through travel agencies. Fiesta Cozumel Holidays, which has representatives in most major hotels, and Caribe Tours sell a number of similar tours. Another option is to take a private tour of the island via taxi, which costs about $50 to $70 for the day, depending on which parts of the island you visit.

➤ FEES AND SCHEDULES: **Caribe Tours** (✉ Av. Rafael E. Melgar at Calle 5 Sur, ☎ 987/872–3100). **Fiesta Cozumel Holidays/American Express** (main office: ✉ Calle 11 Sur 598, between Avs. 25 and 30, ☎ 987/872–0725).

TRAVEL AGENCIES

A number of local travel agencies offer tours. Fiesta Cozumel Holidays and Turismo Aviomar are represented in the lobbies of several hotels.

➤ LOCAL AGENTS: **Caribe Tours** (✉ Av. Rafael E. Melgar at Calle 5 Sur, ☎ 987/872–3100). **Fiesta Cozumel Holidays/American Express** (✉ Calle 11 Sur 598, between Avs. 25 and 30, ☎ 987/872–0725). **IMC** (✉ Calle 2 Nte. 101–8, ☎ 987/872–1535). **Turismo Aviomar** (✉ Av. 5 Nte. 8, between Calles 2 and 4, ☎ 987/872–0588).

VISITOR INFORMATION

The island's official Web site is www.islacozumel.com.mx. The state tourism office is open weekdays 9–2:30. The Cozumel Island Hotel Association offers information on affiliated hotels and tour operators.

➤ TOURIST INFORMATION: **Cozumel Island Hotel Association** (✉ Calle 2 Nte. at Av. 15, ☎ 987/872–3132, FAX 987/872–2809). **Fidecomiso** (tourism office: ✉ upstairs at Plaza del Sol, at east end of main square, ☎ FAX 987/872–0972).

THE NORTH CARIBBEAN COAST

Updated by Patricia Alisau

SOUTH OF CANCÚN, the coast of the Yucatán Peninsula runs the gamut of tropical possibilities. Whereas Puerto Morelos retains the relaxed atmosphere of a Mexican fishing village, the once laid-back town of Playa del Carmen now has resorts as glitzy as those in Cancún and Cozumel. The beaches are beloved by scuba divers, snorkelers, birders, and beachcombers, and there are accommodations to suit every budget, from campsites and bungalows to condos and luxury hotels. Rustic but comfortable fishing and scuba-diving lodges on the even more secluded Boca Paila in the Sian Ka'an Biosphere Reserve and on the Xcalak Peninsula have a well-deserved reputation for excellent bonefishing and superb diving on virgin reefs. At the same time this coast is one of the most threatened by development, and concerned environmentalists are supporting the rise of ecotourism programs such as the ones at Xcacel that get visitors involved in helping to save the threatened sea-turtle population.

Against this backdrop is the Maya culture. The modern Maya live in the cities and villages along the coast; the legacy of the ancient inhabits the ruins. The dramatic remains of Tulum stand on a bluff overlooking the Caribbean. A short distance inland, at Cobá, there are towering jungle-shrouded pyramids, a testament to the site's importance as a leading center of commerce in the ancient Maya world.

The coast is divided into two areas: Puerto Morelos to Tulum, which has the most ancient sites and places to lodge; and south of Tulum to Chetumal, where civilization thins out quite a bit. We detail the coast as far as the Sian Ka'an Biosphere Reserve just south of Tulum. If you want to venture farther, you'll be rewarded with remote beaches, coves, inlets, lagoons, and tropical landscapes.

Puerto Morelos

18 *8 km (5 mi) south of Punta Tanchacté on Hwy. 307, 36 km (22 mi) south of Cancún.*

For years, Puerto Morelos was known as the small, relaxed coastal town where the car ferry left for Cozumel. This lack of regard actually helped it avoid the development that engulfed other communities, though now the construction of massive all-inclusive resorts nearby (640 rooms in total) may spoil the fishing-village atmosphere. Still, more and more people are discovering that Morelos, exactly halfway between Cancún and Playa del Carmen, makes a great base for exploring the region.

In ancient times this was a point of departure for pregnant Maya women making pilgrimages by canoe to Cozumel, the sacred isle of the fertility goddess, Ixchel. Remnants of Maya ruins exist along the coast here, but nothing has been restored. The town itself is small but colorful, with a central plaza surrounded by shops and restaurants; its trademark is a leaning lighthouse. Puerto Morelos's greatest appeal lies out at sea: the superb coral reef only 1,800 ft offshore, which provides excellent grounds for snorkeling and scuba diving. The proximity of the reef creates an exceptionally calm and safe beach, though it isn't as pretty as others, as it isn't cleared of seaweed on a regular basis. Still, you can walk for miles here and see only a few people. In addition, the mangroves in back of town are home to 36 species of birds, making it a great place for birders.

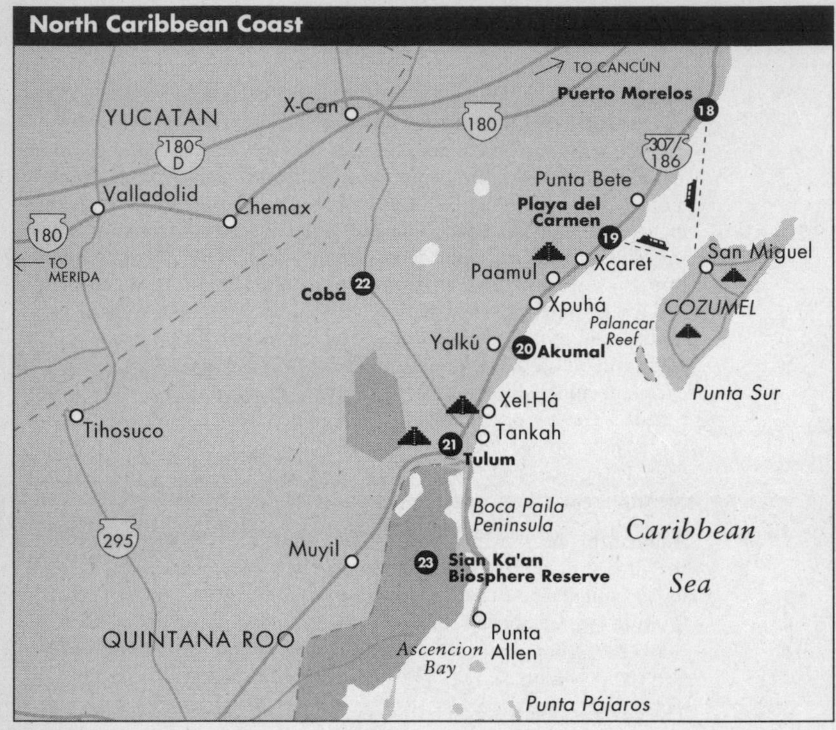

Dining and Lodging

$–$$ ★ **Che Carlito's.** Some of the best food in town is at this lovely restaurant run by Carlito and his family, in the Casita del Mar hotel. Choices include delicious empanadas, chicken fajitas, fresh salads, pastas, and incredible steaks that rival anything at the larger steak houses in Cancún (and for half the price). The restaurant has an outdoor terrace with a palapa bar that leads down to the beach. ✉ *Casita del Mar, Calle Heriberto Frias 6,* ☏ *998/871–0522. MC, V.*

$$ ★ **Casa Caribe.** This small, pretty hotel sits a few blocks from the town center and five minutes from the beach. The breezy rooms have king-size beds and roomy tile baths. Terraces have hammocks and views of the ocean or the mangroves. A large kitchen, huge terrace, and lounge area are available for guests' use. The grounds include a walled courtyard and a fragrant tropical garden. Children under 10 stay free. ✉ *Av. Javier Rojo Gómez and Ejercito Mexicano, 3 blocks north of town,* ☏ *998/871–0049, 763/441–7630 in the U.S.,* WEB *www.us-webmasters.com/Casa-Caribe. 6 rooms. Refrigerators; no air-conditioning, no room phones, no room TVs. No credit cards.*

Outdoor Activities and Sports

WATER SPORTS

Enrique at **Almost Heaven Adventures** (☏ 998/871–0230), in the main square by the currency exchange, can set up snorkeling and fishing trips. **Brecko's** (✉ Casita del Mar, Calle Heriberto Frias 6, ☏ 998/871–0301) offers snorkeling and deep-sea fishing in a 25-ft boat. Snorkeling trips start at $15–$20 and fishing trips at $200.

Playa del Carmen

19 *10 km (6 mi) south of Punta Bete, 68 km (42 mi) south of Cancún.*

Once upon a time, Playa del Carmen was a fishing village with a ravishing, deserted beach. The villagers fished and raised coconut palms to produce copra, and the only foreigners who ventured here were society dropouts and beach bums. These days, however, it's the fastest-growing city in Mexico, with a population of more than 30,000 and a pace almost as hectic as Cancún's. The beach is still delightful—alabaster-white sand, turquoise-blue waters—it's just not deserted. For the past few years a construction boom has been continually transforming the city every few months. Hotels, restaurants, and shops multiply faster than you can say "Kukulcán."

Dining and Lodging

Playa has scores of hotels, and more are opening. Playa's most luxurious rooms are at the 880-acre Playacar development; the more modest rooms are farther north. Competition among the smaller hotels is fierce, so most ask for a deposit (usually the price of one night) before taking your reservation. As for the dining scene, mediocrity reigns supreme, though most restaurants have great decor.

$$–$$$$ ★ ✕ **Yaxche.** This is the best restaurant along the Riviera Maya. The decor includes hand-carved stelae from famous ruins and ceiling and wall murals of Maya gods and kings, but the real knockout is the food. Dishes such as *halach winic* (chicken in a spicy four-pepper sauce) and *tikinchic* (fish in a sour orange–onion sauce with annatto-seed spice) bring Maya cuisine to gourmet levels. Finish your meal with a "Maya Kiss" (Kahlúa and Xtabentun, a local liqueur flavored with anise and honey). ✉ *Calle 8 at Avs. 5 and 10,* ☎ *984/873–2502. AE, MC, V.*

$–$$ ✕ **Media Luna.** The Canadian couple that runs this stylish restaurant, formerly called Zas, has combined vegetarian dishes with the best of Toronto's cuisine, then spiced them both with Mexican flavors. Owner-chef Carla creates dishes such as curried root-vegetable puree with cilantro cream and black-crusted fish with steamed rice. A fixed-price lunch for $5 and dinner for $8 are featured daily. ✉ *Av. 5 at Calles 12 and 14,* ☎ *no phone. No credit cards.*

$ ✕ **Sabor.** The prices have gone up and beer and wine are now on the menu, but the savory salads, sandwiches, and baked goods are still tasty and the location is great. Seats at breakfast and lunch are hard to find; avoid breakfasting here if you don't like rap music. ✉ *Av. 5, between Calles 2 and 3,* ☎ *no phone. No credit cards.*

$$$$ ★ 🏨 **Royal Hideaway.** On a breathtaking stretch of beach, this 13-acre, ultraluxurious adults-only resort offers exceptional amenities and superior service. The two- and three-story villas are a fusion of Spanish-Mexican colonial architecture and are surrounded by winding rivers, waterfalls, and fountains. Each villa has its own concierge to take care of your needs. Deluxe rooms have two queen beds, sitting areas, and ocean-view terraces. The lobby area features a medley of art and artifacts from around the world. Meals are à la carte, and the resort is wheelchair accessible. ✉ *Fracc. Playacar, Lote 6, Playacar,* ☎ *984/873–4500; 877/284–0935 in the U.S.,* FAX *984/873–4506,* WEB *www.allegroresorts.com. 192 rooms, 8 suites. 5 restaurants, in-room data ports, cable TV, 2 tennis courts, 2 pools, exercise equipment, spa, beach, snorkeling, windsurfing, bicycles, 3 bars, library, recreation room, theater, shops, laundry service, concierge, meeting rooms, travel services, free parking; no kids. AE, MC, V.*

$$$–$$$$ ★ 🏨 **Lunata.** This small but classy inn has Spanish tile floors, hand-tooled furniture, and an elegant, high-ceilinged entrance. Rooms are decorated with dark hardwood furnishings and high-quality crafts and have sitting areas and terraces, some with hammocks. Phones are in the process of being installed. A Continental breakfast is laid out in the lush tropical garden each morning for guests. Service is personal and gracious. ✉ *Av. 5 between Calles 6 and 8,* ☎ *984/873–0884,* FAX *984/873–1240,* WEB *www.lunata.com. 10 rooms. Cable TV, laundry service. AE, MC, V.*

$$$ ★ **Itzaes.** This modern, colonial-style hotel is business-traveler friendly, with modem hookups in rooms, concierge, car rental, and minibars. Huge guest rooms have two double beds, dark-wood furniture, a desk area, tiled floors, and full bathroom amenities including a hair dryer. Divers like to stay here, as it's two blocks from the beach. Rates include Continental breakfast. ✉ *Av. 10 and Calle 6,* ☏ *984/873–2397,* FAX *984/873–2373,* WEB *www.itzaes.com. 16 rooms. In-room data ports, minibars, cable TV, pool, concierge, car rental. MC, V.*

$$$ **Mosquito Blue.** At once casual, exotic, and elegant, the rooms and lobby of this beautiful adults-only hotel have lovely mahogany furniture, Indonesian decor, and soft lighting. King-size beds and great views round out the rooms. A cloistered courtyard has a garden, pool, and open-air bar. Children under age 16 are not allowed. ✉ *Calle 12 between Avs. 5 and 10,* ☏ FAX *984/873–1335,* WEB *www.mosquitoblue.com. 46 rooms, 1 suite. Restaurant, cable TV, 2 pools, gym, massage, 2 bars, laundry service; no kids under 16. AE, MC, V.*

$$–$$$ ★ **Baal Nah Kah.** True to its name, which means "home hidden among the gum trees" in Maya, this small hotel is quite homey. Guests have the use of a large kitchen, common sitting room, and barbecue pit. The five bedrooms and one studio are on different levels, affording complete privacy. Two rooms have spacious balconies with panoramic views of the ocean; all have tile baths, fans, double or king-size beds, and Mexican decor. A small café next door serves breakfast, snacks, and light meals. The beach is a block away. ✉ *Calle 12 near Av. 5,* ☏ *984/873–0110,* FAX *984/873–0050,* WEB *www.cancunsouth.com/baalnahkah. 5 rooms, 1 studio. Fans; no air-conditioning. No credit cards.*

$$ ★ **Posada Mariposa.** One of the best hotels in Playa, this impeccable Italian-style property in the quiet north section of town is comfortable and well priced. Rooms center on a tropical garden filled with plants, flowers, trees, and a small fountain. All have ocean views, luxurious bathrooms, and shared patios and are furnished with queen-size beds and wall murals. Suites have full kitchens. Sunset on the rooftop is quite spectacular, and the beach is five minutes away. ✉ *Av. 5 No. 314, between Calles 24 and 26,* ☏ *984/873–3886,* FAX *984/873–1054,* WEB *www.posadamariposa.com. 18 rooms, 6 apartments. Car rental, free parking; no air-conditioning, no room phones. No credit cards.*

$–$$ **Posada Freud.** This quirky little hotel on the main strip has a European flavor. Each room is decorated differently, with Mexican textiles and wall murals. The bigger rooms have refrigerators and coffeemakers. The inner courtyard and garden do a remarkable job of keeping out the Avenida 5 noise. Guests get a discount on food at a local restaurant. ✉ *Av. 5 between Calles 8 and 10,* ☏ *984/873–0601. 12 rooms. Some refrigerators; no air-conditioning in some rooms. No credit cards.*

Nightlife and the Arts

Most of Playa closes down around 11 PM, but a growing number of bars and discos stay open until the wee hours. Unfortunately, Playa's drug culture sometimes surfaces in the clubs. Resist the temptation to indulge, not only because it can land you in jail but because you may get robbed during drug transactions.

The **Blue Parrot** (✉ Calle 12 at Av. 1, ☏ 984/873–0083) has live music every night until midnight; the bar sometimes stays open until 3 AM. **Babaloo** (✉ Av. 5 between Calles 8 and 10, ☏ 984/980–0444–0186) has a popular terraced bar, which gets extra lively at night til 3 AM. **Capitán Tutix** (✉ Calle 4 Nte., ☏ no phone) is a beach bar designed to resemble a ship. Good drink prices and live jazz keep the crowd dancing until dawn.

Outdoor Activities and Sports

DIVING

Playa del Carmen's scuba scene has grown considerably in the past few years. Most dive shops offer similar services, but the quality of the equipment and dive instructors varies; it's best to shop around. The **Abyss** (☎ 984/873–2164) offers training courses in addition to dive trips. The oldest shop in town, **Tank-Ha Dive Shop** (☎ FAX 984/873–5037) has PADI-certified teachers and runs diving and snorkeling trips to the reefs and caverns. **Yucatek Divers** (☎ 984/873–0283) specializes in cenote dives and diving packages and works with divers who have disabilities.

Shopping

Avenida 5 between Calles 4 and 10 is the best place to shop along the coast. Unique shops and boutiques sell folk art and textiles from around Mexico, and clothing stores carry original designs created from hand-painted Indonesian batiks. Shops usually are open from about 10 in the morning to 9 or 10 at night.

Amber Museum Shop (✉ Av. 5 between Calles 4 and 6, ☎ FAX 984/873–0446) has elegantly crafted amber jewelry by a local designer who imports the amber from Chiapas; there is also a small jewelry-making workshop for children. **Telart** (✉ Av. Juárez 10, ☎ 984/873–0066) carries textiles from all over Mexico.

Akumal

20 *37 km (23 mi) south of Playa del Carmen, 102 km (63 mi) south of Cancún.*

The Maya name means "place of the turtle," and for hundreds of years this beach has been a nesting ground for turtles (the season is June–August and the best place to see them is on Half Moon Bay). The place first attracted international attention in 1926, when explorers discovered the *Mantanceros,* a Spanish galleon that sank in 1741. In 1958, Pablo Bush Romero, a wealthy businessman who loved diving these pristine waters, created the first resort, which became the headquarters for the club he formed—the Mexican Underwater Expeditions Club (CEDAM). Akumal soon became a gathering spot for wealthy underwater adventurers who flew in on private planes and searched the waters for sunken treasures, some of which you can see at the Museo CEDAM in Puerto Aventuras.

These days Akumal is probably the most Americanized community on the coast. Akumal consists of three distinct areas: Half Moon Bay, with some pretty beaches, the best snorkeling around, and the greatest concentration of rentals; Akumal Proper, a large resort with a market, grocery stores, laundry facilities, a pharmacy, and, farther up across the highway, the original Maya community; and Akumal Aventuras, to the south, with more condos and homes.

Devoted snorkelers may want to walk to **Yalkú,** a couple of miles north of Akumal in Half Moon Bay, along an unmarked dirt road. A series of small lagoons that gradually reach the ocean, Yalkú is home to schools of parrot fish in superbly clear water with visibility to 160 ft. It's now an eco-park, which means it has a toilet, a small parking lot, and an entrance fee of about $6.

Dining and Lodging

$–$$ ✕ **Que Onda.** A Swiss Italian couple created this northern Italian restaurant at the end of Half Moon Bay. Served under a charming open-air palapa, dishes include great homemade pastas, shrimp flambéed in cognac with a touch of saffron, and vegetarian lasagna made with spinach. Que Onda also has an intimate six-room hotel next to the restaurant, which is creatively furnished with native Mexican and Guatemalan handicrafts. ✉ *Caleta Yalkú lots 97–99, enter through Club Akumal Caribe and turn left, or go north to very end of road at Half Moon Bay,* ☎ *984/875–9101. MC, V. Closed Tues.*

$ ✕ **Restaurante Oscar y Lalo.** A couple of miles outside of Akumal, at Bahías de Punta Soliman, is this wonderful restaurant run by a local Maya couple. The seafood is excellent and the pizza divine. If you're inspired to sleep on the beach, campgrounds and RV hookups are available. ✉ *Hwy. 307 north of Akumal (look for faded white sign),* ☎ *no phone. No credit cards.*

$$$$ ★ **Club Akumal Caribe & Villas Maya.** This beachfront resort was founded by Pablo Bush Romero in the 1960s to host his diving buddies and still offers congenial accommodations and staff. Rooms have rattan furniture; large, comfortable beds; lovely tile work; and ocean views. The quaint but rustic bungalows are surrounded by a tropical garden and have lots of beautiful Mexican tile. More secluded options are the one-, two-, and three-bedroom condominiums called Villas Flamingo, on Half Moon Bay, with kitchenettes and a separate beach and pools. Dive and meal-plan packages available. ✉ *Hwy. 307, Km 104,* ☎ *984/875–9012; 800/351–1622 in the U.S. and Canada; 800/343–1440 in Canada;* WEB *www.hotelakumalcaribe.com. 21 rooms, 40 bungalows, 4 villas, 1 condo. Restaurant, some kitchenettes, pool, beach, 2 dive shops, bar, children's programs (ages 5–14), baby-sitting; no room phones. AE, MC, V.*

$$$ **Vista Del Mar.** Each smallish room has an ocean view, king-size bed, small refrigerator, and colorful decor with Guatemalan-Mexican accents. Next door are more expensive condos with Spanish colonial decor. The spacious one-, two-, and three-bedroom units have full kitchens, living and dining rooms, and oceanfront balconies. They are a great bargain off-season. ✉ *South end of Half Moon Bay,* ☎ *984/875–9060; 800/925–6325 Ext. 15 in the U.S.,* WEB *www.akumalinfo.com. 15 rooms, 8 condos. Restaurant, grocery, some kitchenettes, cable TV with movies, pool, beach, dive shop; no air-conditioning in some rooms. AE, MC, V.*

Outdoor Activities and Sports

SCUBA DIVING

Akumal Dive Center (✉ about 10 mins north of Club Akumal Caribe, ☎ 984/875–9025) is the oldest and most experienced dive operation, offering reef or cenote diving, fishing, and snorkeling.

Tulum

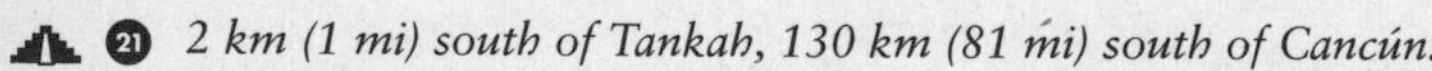

21 *2 km (1 mi) south of Tankah, 130 km (81 mi) south of Cancún.*

One of the Caribbean coast's biggest attractions, Tulum is the Yucatán Peninsula's most-visited Maya ruin, attracting more than 2 million people annually. Unfortunately, this means you have to share the site with roughly half of the tourist population of Quintana Roo on any given day, even if you arrive early. Though most of the architecture here is of unremarkable Postclassic (AD 900–1541) style, the amount of attention that Tulum receives is not entirely undeserved. Its location by the blue-green waters of the Caribbean is indeed breathtaking.

At the entrance to the ruins you can hire a guide, but keep in mind that some of their information is more entertaining than historically accurate. (Disregard that stuff about virgin sacrifices atop the altars.) Because you are not allowed to climb or enter the fragile structures—only three really merit close inspection anyway—you can take in the

Tulum

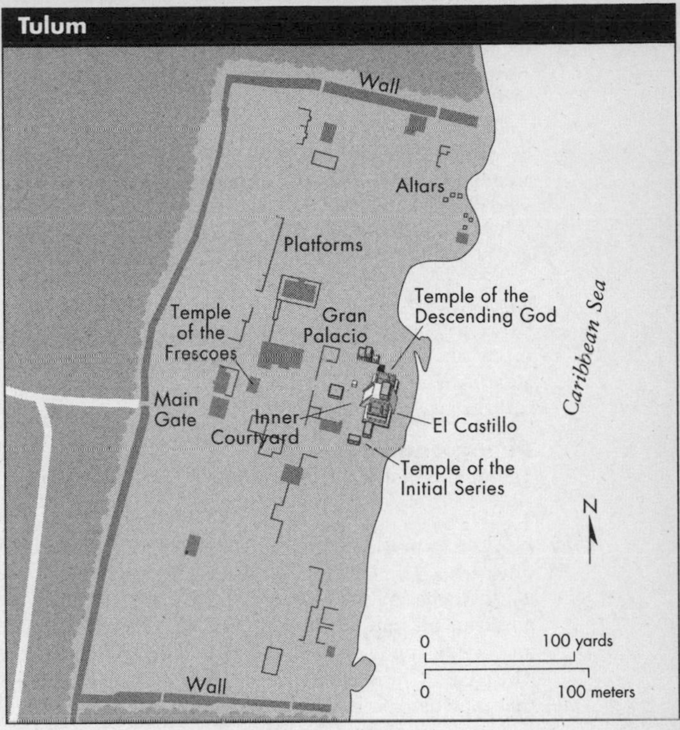

ruins in two hours. You might, however, want to allow extra time for a swim or a stroll on the beach.

Tulum is one of the few Maya cities known to have been inhabited when the conquistadors arrived in 1518. In the 16th century, Tulum functioned as a safe harbor for trade goods from rival Maya factions; it was considered neutral territory where merchandise could be stored and traded in peace. The city reached its height when traders, made wealthy through the exchange of goods, for the first time outranked Maya priests in authority and power. When the Spaniards arrived, they forbade the Maya traders to sail the seas, and commerce among the Maya died.

Tulum has long held special significance for the Maya. A key city in the League of Mayapán (AD 987–1194), it was never conquered by the Spaniards, although it was abandoned about 75 years after the conquest. For 300 years thereafter, it symbolized the defiance of an otherwise subjugated people; it was one of the last outposts of the Maya during their insurrection against Mexican rule in the War of the Castes, which began in 1846. Uprisings continued intermittently until 1935, when the Maya ceded Tulum to the government.

The first significant structure is the two-story **Temple of the Frescoes,** to the left of the entryway. The temple's vault roof and corbel arch are examples of classic Maya architecture. Faint traces of blue-green frescoes outlined in black on the inner and outer walls refer to ancient Maya beliefs (the clearest frescoes are hidden from sight now that you can't walk into the temple). Reminiscent of the Mixtec style, the frescoes depict the three worlds of the Maya and their major deities and are decorated with stellar and serpentine patterns, rosettes, and ears of maize and other offerings to the gods. One scene portrays the rain god seated on a four-legged animal—probably a reference to the Spaniards on their horses.

The largest and most famous building, the **Castillo** (castle), looms at the edge of a 40-ft limestone cliff just past the Temple of the Frescoes. Atop the castle, at the end of a broad stairway, sits a temple with stucco ornamentation on the outside and traces of fine frescoes inside the two chambers. (The stairway has been roped off, so the top temple is inaccessible.) The front wall of the Castillo has faint carvings of the Descending God and columns depicting the plumed serpent god, Kukulcán, who was introduced to the Maya by the Toltecs. To the left of the Castillo is the **Temple of the Descending God**—so called for the carving of a winged god plummeting to earth over the doorway.

The tiny cove to the left of the Castillo and Temple of the Descending God is a good spot for a cooling swim, but there are no changing rooms. A few small altars sit atop a hill at the north side of the cove and have a good view of the Castillo and the sea. *$8, free Sun.; use of video camera extra. Daily 8–5.*

Dining and Lodging

Tulum's official Web page for hotels and cabanas is www.hotelstulum.com.

$$$$ ★ **Las Ranitas.** Both stylish and ecologically correct, Las Ranitas ("the little frogs") creates its own power through wind-generated electricity, solar energy, and recycled water. Each chic room is decorated with gorgeous tile and fabric from Oaxaca. Terraces overlook the gardens and ocean, and jungle walkways lead down to the breathtaking beach. The pièce de résistance is the French chef, who creates incredible food that matches the hotel's magic (in the $$ price range). ✉ *Carretera Tulum–Boca Paila, Km 9 (last hotel before Sian Ka'an Biosphere Reserve),* ☎ FAX *984/877–8554,* WEB *www.lasranitas.com. 17 rooms. Restaurant, tennis court, pool, beach, snorkeling. No credit cards. Closed mid-Sept.–mid-Nov.*

$$$ **Zamas.** Set on the wild and isolated Punta de Piedra (Rock Point), with ocean views as far as the eye can see, this spectacular, kick-back-and-groove hotel draws a lot of the U.S. business-suit crowd. The romantically rustic cabanas—with bare-bulb lighting, mosquito nets over the spartan beds, big tile bathrooms, and gay Mexican colors—are nicely distanced from one another, offering privacy and space. The restaurant ($–$$) is one of the best on the coast, with an eclectic Italian-Mexican-Yucatecan menu and fresh fish that comes from the first catch of the day. ✉ *Carretera Tulum–Boca Paila, Km 5,* ☎ *984/871–2067; 415/387–9806 in the U.S.;* WEB *www.zamas.com. 15 cabanas. Restaurant, beach, bar; no air-conditioning, no room phones. No credit cards.*

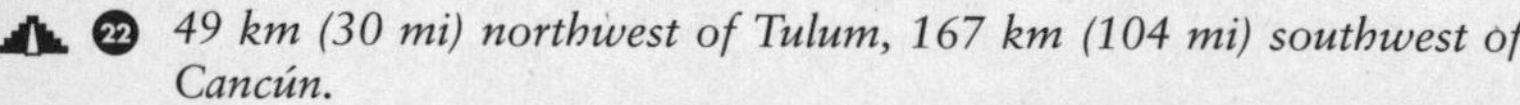

Cobá

22 *49 km (30 mi) northwest of Tulum, 167 km (104 mi) southwest of Cancún.*

Cobá, Maya for "water stirred by the wind," flourished from AD 800 to AD 1100, with a population of as many as 55,000. Now it stands in solitude, with the jungle having taken many of its buildings. Cobá exudes a certain stillness, the silence broken by the occasional shriek of a spider monkey or the call of a bird. Processions of huge army ants cross the footpaths as the sun slips through openings between the tall hardwood trees, ferns, and giant palms.

Situated on five lakes between coastal watchtowers and inland cities, Cobá exercised economic control over the region through a network of at least 16 *sacbéob* (white stone roads), one of which measures 100 km (62 mi) and is the longest in the Maya world. The city once covered 70 square km (27 square mi), making it a noteworthy sister state to Tikal in northern Guatemala, with which it had close cultural and commercial ties. It is noted for its massive temple-pyramids, one of which is 138 ft tall, the largest and highest in northern Yucatán. The main groupings of ruins are separated by several miles of dense tropical vegetation, so the best way to get a sense of the immensity of the city is to scale one of the pyramids. It's easy to get lost here, so stay on the main road and don't be tempted by the narrow paths that lead into the jungle unless you have a qualified guide with you.

The first major cluster of structures, off the main path to your right as you enter the ruins, is the **Cobá Group,** whose pyramids are built around a sunken patio. At the near end of the group, facing a large plaza, is the 79-ft-high Iglesia (church), where some Maya people still place offerings and light candles in hopes of improving their harvests. Around the rear to the left is a restored ball court, where a sacred ball game was once played to petition the gods for rain, fertility, and other boons. Farther along the main path to your left is the **Chumuc Mul Group,** little of which has been excavated. The principal pyramid here is covered with the remains of vibrantly painted stucco motifs (*chumuc mul* means "stucco pyramid"). A kilometer (½ mile) past this site is the **Nohoch Mul Group** (Large Hill Group), the highlight of which is the pyramid of the same name, the tallest at Cobá. The pyramid, which has 120 steps—equivalent to 12 stories—shares a plaza with **Temple 10.** The Descending God (also seen at Tulum) is depicted on a facade of the temple atop Nohoch Mul, from which the view is excellent.

Beyond the Nohoch Mul Group is the **Castillo,** with nine chambers that are reached by a stairway. To the south are the remains of a ball court, including the stone ring through which the ball was hurled. From the main route follow the sign to **Las Pinturas Group,** named for the still-discernible polychrome friezes on the inner and outer walls of its large, patioed pyramid. An enormous stela here depicts a man standing with his feet on two prone captives. Take the minor path for 1 km (½ mi) to the **Macanxoc Group,** not far from the lake of the same name. The main pyramid at Macanxoc is accessible by a stairway.

Cobá is a 35-minute drive northwest of Tulum along a pothole-filled road that leads straight through the jungle. You can comfortably make your way around Cobá in a half day, but spending the night in town is highly advised, as doing so will allow you to visit the ruins in solitude when they open at 8 AM. Even on a day trip, consider taking time out for lunch to escape the intense heat and mosquito-heavy humidity of the ruins. Buses depart from Cobá for Playa del Carmen and Tulum at least twice daily. Taxis to Tulum are still reasonable (about $14). *$4, free Sun.; use of video camera $6. Daily 8–5.*

Lodging

$$ **El Bocadito.** The warmth of the family who owns and operates this hotel makes up for the lack of luxury. Each of the extremely basic rooms has two double beds, a ceiling fan, toilet, and, if you are lucky, hot water. The ruins are a 10-minute walk away. Rooms fill up quickly—if you're thinking of spending the night, stop here before visiting the ruins. The restaurant next door serves simple but tasty meals. ✉ *On road to ruins,* ☎ *987/42087. 10 rooms. No air-conditioning, no room phones. AE, V.*

$$ **Uolis Nah.** This small thatch-roof complex has extra large, quiet rooms with kitchenettes and basics such as high ceilings, two beds, fans, and tile floors. You're less than a mile from the Tulum highway but away from the noise. An extra person in a double room costs $11 more. ✉ *Km. 2 on road to Cobá,* ☎ *9/879–5013. 6 rooms. Fans, kitchenettes; no air-conditioning, no room phones. No credit cards.*

Sian Ka'an and the Boca Paila Peninsula

23 *15 km (9 mi) south of Tulum to the Punta Allen turnoff, located within Sian Ka'an; 137 km (85 mi) south of Cancún.*

Sian Ka'an ("where the sky is born") was first settled by the Maya in the 5th century AD. In 1986 the Mexican government established the 1.3-million-acre **Sian Ka'an Biosphere Reserve** as an internationally protected area. The next year, it was named a World Heritage Site by the United Nations Educational, Scientific, and Cultural Organization (UNESCO); later, it was extended by 200,000 acres. The Riviera Maya and Costa Maya split the Biosphere Reserve; Punta Allen and north belong to the Riviera Maya, and everything south of Punta Allen is part of the Costa Maya.

The Sian Ka'an reserve constitutes 10% of the land in Quintana Roo and covers 100 km (62 mi) of coast. Freshwater and coastal lagoons, mangrove swamps, watery cays, savannas, tropical forests, a barrier reef, hundreds of species of local and migratory birds, fish, other animals and plants, and fewer than 1,000 local residents (primarily Maya) share this area. There are approximately 27 ruins (none excavated) linked by a unique canal system—one of the few of its kind in the Maya world in Mexico. This is one of the last undeveloped stretches of coastline in North America.

Many species of the once-flourishing wildlife have fallen into the endangered category, but the waters here still teem with rooster fish, bonefish, mojarra, snapper, shad, permit, sea bass, and crocodiles. Fishing the flats for wily bonefish is especially popular, and the peninsula's few lodges also run deep-sea fishing trips.

In order to see the sites you must take a guided tour offered by one of the private, nonprofit organizations, such as **Amigos de Sian Ka'an** (✉ Crepúsculo 18, at Amanecer, Sm 44, Mz 13, Cancún, Quintana Roo 77506, ☎ 998/848–1618, 9/848–2136, or 998/880–6024, FAX 998/887–3080). The four-hour boat tour includes bird-watching, a visit to the Maya ruins of Xlapak (where you can jump into one of the channels and float downstream), and a tour of the mangroves. Tour groups depart from Cabañas Ana y José in Tulum every Wednesday and Saturday morning; the fee includes a bilingual guide and binoculars.

Lodging

$$$$ ★ ✕☏ **Boca Paila Fishing Lodge.** Home of the "grand slam" (fishing lingo for catching three different kinds of fish at once), this charming lodge has nine spacious cottages, each with two double beds, couches, large bathrooms, and screened-in sitting areas. Boats and guides for fly-fishing and bonefishing are provided; tackle is for rent at the lodge. Meals, included in the room rate, are excellent, ranging from fresh fish to Maya specialties. During the high season, a 50% prepayment is required and the minimum stay is one week (three nights the rest of the year). ✉ *Boca Paila Peninsula (reservations: Frontiers, Box 959, Wexford, PA 15090, ☎ 724/935–1577 or 800/245–1950). 9 cottages. Restaurant, beach, snorkeling, fishing, bar, laundry service, airport shuttle; no air-conditioning in some rooms, no room phones. No credit cards unless arranged with Frontiers.*

$$$$ ★ ✕☏ **Casa Blanca Lodge.** This American-managed, all-inclusive lodge is set on a rocky outcrop on remote Punta Pájaros island—reputed to be one of the best places in the world for light-tackle saltwater fishing. Ten large, modern guest rooms have tile and mahogany bathrooms and provide a pleasant tropical respite at dusk. An open-air thatch-roof bar welcomes anglers with drinks, fresh fish dishes, fruit, and vegetables at the start and end of the day. Only weeklong packages can

be booked March–June. Rates include charter flight from Cancun, all meals, a boat, and a guide; nonfishing packages are cheaper. ✉ *Punta Pájaros (reservations: Frontiers, Box 959, Wexford, PA 15090,* ☎ *724/935–1577; 800/245–1950 for Frontiers;* ☎ *800/533–7299 for Outdoor Travel). 10 rooms. Restaurant, bar; no air-conditioning, no room phones. MC, V.*

The North Caribbean Coast A to Z

To research prices, get advice from other travelers, and book travel arrangements, visit www.fodors.com.

AIR TRAVEL

Almost everyone who arrives by air into this region flies into Cancún. In Chetumal, however, there is an airport on the southwestern edge of town, along Avenida Alvaro Obregón where it turns into Route 186. In Playa del Carmen, there's an air strip across from Plaza Antigua.

➤ AIRPORT INFORMATION: **Chetumal airport** (✉ Rte. 186, Chetumal, ☎ no phone).

BOAT AND FERRY TRAVEL

Passenger-only ferries and two large speedboats depart from the dock at Playa del Carmen for the 45-minute trip to the main pier in Cozumel. They leave approximately every hour on the hour 5 AM–11 PM, with no ferries at noon, 2, 8, or 10. Return service to Playa runs every hour on the hour 4 AM–10 PM, with no ferries at 5, 11 AM, 1, 7, or 9 PM. Call ahead, as the schedule changes often.

➤ BOAT AND FERRY INFORMATION: **Playa del Carmen passenger ferry** (☎ 984/872–1508, 984/872–0588, or 984/872–0477).

BUS TRAVEL

Playa del Carmen has two bus stops. Buses arriving from south of Playa and continuing north to Cancún drop people off at the terminal on the highway. All other buses leave from downtown. All the major bus lines run express, first-class, and second-class buses to major destination points. Service to Cancún is every 10–20 minutes, and buses to Chetumal leave twice daily. It's always best to check the times at the main bus terminal (Avenida Juárez at Avenida 5). The scheduled times change frequently.

➤ BUS INFORMATION: **ADO** (☎ 984/832–9877). **Caribe Express** (☎ 984/832–7889).

CAR RENTAL

Most first-class hotels in Puerto Aventuras, Akumal, and Chetumal also rent cars. In Puerto Morelos you are better off renting from Cancún, as there aren't many bargains in town. In Playa del Carmen, it's best to stick with the bigger rental agencies: Hertz, Budget, and Thrifty. If you want air-conditioning or automatic transmission, reserve your car at least one day in advance.

➤ MAJOR AGENCIES: **Budget** (✉ Continental Plaza, Playa del Carmen, ☎ 984/873–0100). **Hertz** (✉ Plaza Marina, Loc. 40, Playa del Carmen, ☎ 984/873–0702). **Thrifty** (✉ Calle 8 between Avs. 5 and 10, Playa del Carmen, ☎ 984/873–0119).

CAR TRAVEL

The entire coast from Punta Sam near Cancún to the main border crossing to Belize at Chetumal is traversable on Highway 307. This straight road is entirely paved and has been widened into four lanes south to Xcaret. Drive with caution—there are lots of speed demons on this highway. Puerto Morelos, Playa del Carmen, Tulum, and Felipe Carrillo Puerto have gas stations.

Good roads that run into Highway 307 from the west are Route 180 (from Mérida and Valladolid), Route 295 (from Valladolid), Route 184 (from central Yucatán), and Route 186 (from Villahermosa and, via Route 261, from Mérida and Campeche). There is an entrance to the *autopista* toll highway between Cancún and Mérida off Highway 307 just south of Cancún. Approximate driving times are as follows: Cancún to Felipe Carrillo Puerto, 4 hours; Cancún to Mérida, 4½ hours (3½ hours on the *autopista* toll road, $27); Carrillo Puerto to Chetumal, 2 hours; Carrillo Puerto to Mérida, about 4½ hours; Chetumal to Campeche, 6½ hours.

If you drive south of Tulum, keep an eye out for military and immigration checkpoints. Have your passport handy, be friendly and cooperative, and don't carry any items, such as firearms or drugs, that might land you in jail.

ECOTOURISM

You can visit the ruins of Cobá and the Maya village of Pac-Chen, located deep in the jungle, with Alltournative Expeditions. The group offers a variety of other ecotours as well.

ATV Explorer offers two-hour rides through the jungle on all-terrain vehicles; explore caves, see ruins, and snorkel in a cenote. Tours start at $38.50.

➤ CONTACTS: **Alltournative Expeditions** (✉ Av. 10 No. 1, Plaza Antigua, Playa del Carmen, ☎ 984/873–2036, WEB www.alltournative.com). **ATV Explorer** (✉ Hwy. 307, 1 km [½ mi] north of Xcaret, ☎ 984/873–1626).

EMERGENCIES

In Puerto Morelos, there are two drugstores in town on either side of the gas station on Highway 307.

In Playa del Carmen, there's a pharmacy at the Plaza Marina shopping mall; several others are on Avenida 5 between Calles 4 and 8. There are two pharmacies on Avenida Juárez between Avenidas 20 and 25.

➤ CHETUMAL: **Chetumal Hospital General** (✉ Av. Andres Quintana Roo, ☎ 983/832–1932). **Farmacia Social Mechaca** (✉ Av. Independencia 134-C, ☎ 983/832–0044). **Police** (✉ Av. Insurgentes and Av. Belice, ☎ 983/832–1500). **Red Cross** (✉ Av. Héroes 279, ☎ 983/832–0571).

➤ PLAYA DEL CARMEN: **Centro de Salud** (✉ Av. Juárez at Av. 15, ☎ 984/872–1230 Ext. 147). **Police** (✉ Av. Juárez between Avs. 15 and 20, ☎ 984/873–0291). **Red Cross** (✉ Av. Juárez at Av. 25, ☎ 984/873–1233).

LODGING

Puerto Aventuras has a large community of condo owners who rent out their properties. Caribbean Realty has price lists and availability information.

Mary Lowers of Mayansites Bookings can help you arrange house and apartment rentals in other areas along the coast.

➤ CONTACTS: **Caribbean Realty** (Sally Wood Evans; ✉ Centro Commercial Marina, Puerto Aventuras, ☎ 984/873–5098, FAX 984/873–5158, WEB www.caribbean-realty.com). **Mayansites Bookings** (☎ 877/620–8715 in the U.S., WEB www.mayansites.com).

MAIL AND SHIPPING

The Chetumal post office is open weekdays 8–7 and Saturday 8–noon. The Playa del Carmen post office is open weekdays 8–7.

➤ POST OFFICES: **Chetumal** (✉ Calle Plutarco Elias 2, ☎ 983/832–2578). **Playa del Carmen** (✉ Av. Juárez, next to the police station, ☎ 983/873–0300).

MONEY MATTERS

Local banks in Playa del Carmen include Bital, Bancomer, Banamex, Inverlat, and Bancrecer. In Chetumal, Bital and Bancomer offer banking services, including currency exchange.

➤ BANKS: **Banamex** (✉ Av. Juárez between Avs. 20 and 25, Playa del Carmen, ☎ 984/873–0825). **Bancomer** (✉ Av. Juárez between Calles 25 and 30, Playa del Carmen, ☎ 984/873–0356; ✉ Av. Alvaro Obregón 222, at Av. Juárez, Chetumal, ☎ 9/832–5300). **Bancrecer** (✉ Av. 5 by the bus station, Playa del Carmen, ☎ 984/873–1561). **Bital** (✉ Av. Juárez between Avs. 10 and 15, Playa del Carmen, ☎ 984/873–0272; ✉ Av. 30 between Avs. 4 and 6, Playa del Carmen, ☎ 984/873–0238; ✉ Av. Héroes 37, Chetumal, ☎ 984/832–2776). **Scotiabank Inverlat** (✉ Av. 5 between Av. Juárez and Av. 2, Playa del Carmen, ☎ 984/873–1488).

TELEPHONES

You can find TELMEX phones that use phone cards in every town up and down the coast (buy the cards in gift shops and grocery stores). There are several long-distance calling stations in Playa del Carmen on Avenida 5 as well as in front of the post office on Avenida Juárez and at the corner of Avenidas Juárez and 5.

TOURS

Although some guided tours are available in this area, the roads are quite good for the most part, so renting a car is an efficient and enjoyable alternative. Most of the sights you see along this stretch are natural, and you can hire a guide at the ruins. If you would like someone else to do the planning and driving for you, contact Maya Sites Travel Services, which offers inexpensive tours and the chance to create your own travel itinerary.

MAYA SITES

Based in Playa del Carmen, Tierra Maya Tours runs trips to the ruins of Chichén Itzá, Uxmal, Palenque, and Tikal. It can also help you with transfers, tickets, and hotel reservations. Many first-class hotels in Playa del Carmen and Puerto Aventuras can arrange day tours to Tulum, Chichén Itzá, and Cobá.

In Chetumal, Turistica Maya de Quintana Roo offers tours to Kohunlich, Dzibanché, the Laguna de Bacalar, and Fuerte de San Felipe.

➤ TOUR-OPERATOR RECOMMENDATIONS: **Maya Sites Travel Services** (☎ 719/256–5186; 877/620–8715 in the U.S.; WEB www.mayasites.com). **Tierra Maya Tours** (✉ Av. 5 at Calle 6, Playa del Carmen, ☎ 984/873–1385, FAX 984/873–1386). **Turistica Maya de Quintana Roo** (✉ Av. Héroes 165-A, Chetumal, ☎ 983/832–0555, FAX 983/832–9711).

TRANSPORTATION AROUND THE CARIBBEAN COAST

You can hire taxis in Cancún to go as far as Playa del Carmen, Tulum, or Akumal, but the price is steep unless you have many passengers. Fares run about $65 or more to Playa alone; between Playa and Tulum or Akumal, expect to pay at least another $25. It's much cheaper from Playa to Cancún, with taxi fare running about $30; negotiate before you hop into the cab. Getting a taxi along Highway 307 can take a while. Ask your hotel to call one for you.

TRAVEL AGENCIES

There are more major travel agencies and tour operators along the coast than ever, and first-class hotels in Playa del Carmen, Puerto Aventuras, and Akumal usually have their own in-house travel services.

➤ LOCAL AGENT REFERRALS: **Alltournative Expeditions** (✉ Av. 10 No. 1, Plaza Antigua, Playa del Carmen, ☎ 984/873–2036). **IMC** (✉ Plaza Antigua, Playa del Carmen, ☎ 984/873–1439, FAX 984/873–1439, WEB www.imcplay.com). **Turistica Maya de Quintana Roo** (✉ Holiday Inn Puerta Maya, Chetumal, ☎ 984/832–0555 or 9/832–2058, FAX 984/832–9711).

VISITOR INFORMATION

The Tourist Information Booth in Chetumal is open weekdays 8:30–2:30 and 6–9. In Playa del Carmen it's open Monday–Saturday 8 AM–9 PM.

➤ TOURIST INFORMATION: **Chetumal** (✉ Av. Héroes opposite Av. Efraín Aguilar, ☎ 983/832–3663). **Playa del Carmen** (✉ Av. Juárez by the police station, ☎ 983/873–2804).

THE STATE OF YUCATÁN

Updated by Jane Onstott

CULTURALLY, THE YUCATÁN is one of the richest parts of Mexico. It is the heart of a fascinating juxtaposition of two powerful civilizations—that of the Maya and that of transplanted Europeans. Vestiges of the past are evident in this land of oval thatch-roof huts and stately old mission churches, and in its people—particularly the women who still dress in traditional garb. Mysterious "lost cities" lie hidden in the forests. Small fishing villages dot beaches that are so far unjaded by the tourist industry. In the midst of this exotic landscape stands the elegant city of Mérida, for centuries the main stronghold of Spanish colonialism in the land of the Maya.

It is, of course, the celebrated Maya cities—including Chichén Itzá, Uxmal, and a spate of smaller sites—that bring most people to the state of Yucatán. Indeed, the Puuc hills south of Mérida have more archaeological sites per square mile than any other place in the hemisphere.

Mérida

Travelers to Mérida are a loyal bunch, content to return again and again to favorite restaurants, neighborhoods, and museums. The city's traffic, complete with diesel fumes and noise, is frustrating, particularly after a peaceful stay on the coast or at one of the archaeological sites, but the city's merits far outweigh its flaws. Mérida is the cultural and intellectual center of the peninsula, with museums and attractions that can greatly enhance your insights into the history and character of Yucatán. Indeed, the quality and number of its offerings make it one of Mexico's leading cultural centers. Consider making it one of the first stops in your travels, and make sure your visit includes a Sunday, when traffic is light and the city seems to revert to a more gracious era.

A Good Walk

Start at the **zócalo** ㉔: see the **Casa de Montejo** ㉕ (now a Banamex bank), on the south side; the **Palacio Municipal** ㉖ and the **Centro Cultural de Mérida Olimpo** ㉗, on the west side; the **Palacio del Gobierno** ㉘, on the northeast corner, and, catercorner, the **Catedral de San Ildefonso** ㉙; and the **Museo de Arte Contemporáneo** ㉚ on the east side. Step out on Calle 60 from the cathedral and walk north to Parque Hidalgo and the **Iglesia de la Tercera Orden de Jesús** ㉛, which is across Calle 59. Continue north along Calle 60 for a short block to the **Teatro Peón Contreras** ㉜, which lies on the east side of the street; the entrance to the **Universidad Autónoma de Yucatán** ㉝ is on the west side of Calle 60 at Calle 57. A block farther north on the west side of Calle 60 is the Parque Santa Lucía. From the park, walk north four blocks and

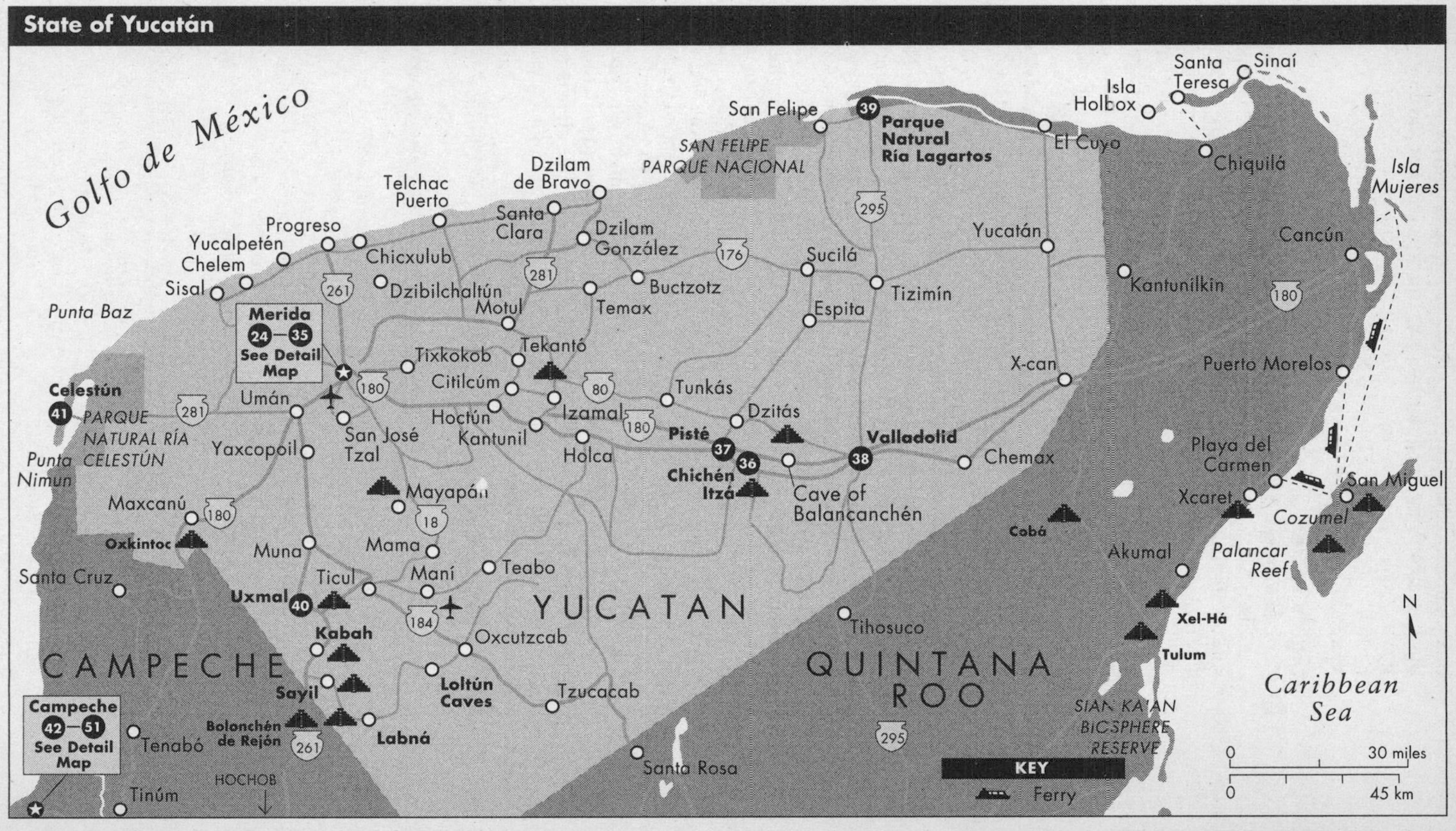
State of Yucatán
Golfo de México
San Felipe
39
Parque Natural Ría Lagartos
SAN FELIPE PARQUE NACIONAL
Isla Holbox
Santa Teresa
Sinaí
El Cuyo
Chiquilá
Isla Mujeres
Cancún
Kantunilkin
180
Dzilam de Bravo
Telchac Puerto
Santa Clara
Dzilam González
Progreso
Yucalpetén
Chelem
Chicxulub
Sisal
261
Dzibilchaltún
281
Buctzotz
176
Sucilá
Tizimín
Yucatán
295
Punta Baz
Merida
24—35
See Detail Map
Motul
Temax
Espita
Tekantó
Tixkokob
Citilcúm
180
80
Tunkás
X-can
Puerto Morelos
Celestún
41
PARQUE NATURAL RÍA CELESTÚN
Umán
281
Hoctún
Izamal
Kantunil
Pisté
Dzitás
Valladolid
37
36
38
Chemax
Playa del Carmen
San José Tzal
Holca
Chichén Itzá
Cave of Balancanchén
Punta Nimun
Yaxcopoil
Mayapán
Xcaret
San Miguel
Cozumel
Maxcanú
18
Cobá
Oxkintoc
Muna
Mama
Akumal
Palancar Reef
Santa Cruz
Ticul
Maní
Teabo
Uxmal
40
184
YUCATAN
Tihosuco
Xel-Há
Kabah
Oxcutzcab
Tulum
CAMPECHE
QUINTANA ROO
Sayil
Loltún Caves
Tzucacab
Caribbean Sea
Campeche
42—51
See Detail Map
Bolonchén de Rejón
Labná
SIAN KA'AN BIOSPHERE RESERVE
Tenabó
261
295
Santa Rosa
HOCHOB
KEY
Ferry
Tinúm
N
0
30 miles
0
45 km

turn right on Calle 47 for two blocks to **Paseo Montejo** (34). Once on this street, continue north for two long blocks to the **Palacio Cantón** (35). From here look either for a *calesa* (horse-drawn carriage) or cabs parked outside the museum to take you back past the zócalo to the Mercado Municipal—or walk if you're up to it.

Sights to See

25 **Casa de Montejo.** This stately palace sits on the south side of the plaza, on Calle 63. Francisco de Montejo—father and son—conquered the peninsula and founded Mérida in 1542; they built their "casa" 10 years later. The property remained with the family until the late 1970s, when it was restored by banker Agustín Legorreta and converted to a bank. Built in the French style, it represents the city's finest—and oldest—example of colonial plateresque architecture, which typically has elaborate ornamentation. A bas-relief on the doorway—the facade is all that remains of the original house—depicts Francisco de Montejo the younger, his wife, and daughter as well as Spanish soldiers standing on the heads of the vanquished Maya. Even if you have no banking to do, step into the building weekdays between 9 and 5 to glimpse the leafy inner patio.

29 **Catedral de San Ildefonso** (St. Ildefonse Cathedral). Begun in 1561, this is the oldest cathedral in Mexico and the second-oldest on the North American mainland. It sits on the east side of the plaza. It took several hundred Maya laborers, working with stones from the pyramids of the ravaged Maya city, 36 years to complete it. Designed in the somber Renaissance style by an architect who had worked on the Escorial in Madrid, its facade is stark and unadorned, with gunnery slits instead of windows, and faintly Moorish spires. Inside, the black **Cristo de las Ampollas** (Christ of the Blisters) occupies a side altar to the left of the main one. The statue is a replica of the original, which was destroyed during the revolution (this was also when most of the gold that typically burnished Mexican cathedrals was carried off). According to one of many legends, the Christ figure burned all night yet appeared the next morning unscathed—except that it was covered with the blisters for which it is named. The crucifix above the side altar is reputedly the second-largest in the world. ✉ *Calle 60 at Calle 61, centro,* ☎ *no phone.* ⏲ *Daily 7–11:30 and 4:30–8.*

27 **Centro Cultural de Mérida Olimpo** (Mérida Olimpo Cultural Center). Referred to as just Olimpo, this is the best venue for free cultural events in the city. The beautiful, porticoed cultural center was built adjacent to City Hall in late 1999, occupying what used to be a parking lot. The marble interior is a showcase for top international art exhibits, classical-music concerts, conferences, and theater and dance presentations. Next door, a movie house renovated to its 1950s look shows art films most nights: classics by such directors as Buñuel, Fellini, and Kazan. The complex also includes a Librería Dante bookstore and cybercafé. ✉ *Calle 62 between Calles 61 and 63, centro,* ☎ *999/928–2020.* 🎫 *Free.* ⏲ *Tues.–Sun. 10–10.*

31 **Iglesia de la Tercera Orden de Jesús** (Church of the Third Order of Jesus or Church of the Jesuits). To the north of Parque Hidalgo is one of Mérida's oldest buildings and the first Jesuit church in the Yucatán. The church was built in 1618 of limestone from a Maya temple that had stood on the site, and faint outlines of ancient carvings are still visible on the stonework of the west wall. Although it is a favorite place for society weddings because of its antiquity, the church interior is not very ornate. The former convent rooms in the rear of the building now host the small **Pinoteca Juan Gamboa Guzmán** (State Repository of Paintings). ✉ *Calle 59 between Calles 58 and 60, centro,* ☎ *no phone.* 🎫 *$1, free Sun.* ⏲ *Tues.–Sat. 8–8, Sun. 8–2.*

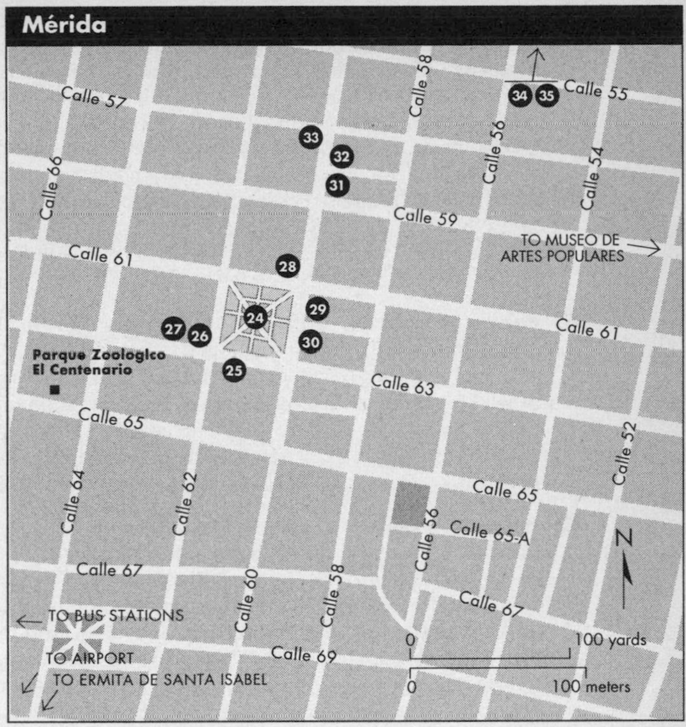

30 **Museo de Arte Contemporáneo** (Museum of Contemporary Art). Originally designed as an art school but used until 1915 as a seminary, this enormous two-story building is full of light, just perfect for an art museum. It showcases the works of Yucatecan artists such as Gabriel Ramírez Aznar and Fernando García Ponce and has excellent international art exhibits in the second-floor galleries. These make up for the halfhearted reproductions of some of the world's masterpieces in the World History of Art room. There's also a bookstore (closed Sunday). ✉ *Pasaje de la Revolución 1907, between Calles 58 and 60 (on main square), centro,* ☎ *999/928–3258 or 999/928–3236.* 🎫 *$2.20, free Sun.* ⏲ *Wed.–Mon. 10–6.*

35 **Palacio Cantón.** The most compelling of the mansions on ☞ **Paseo Montejo,** the pale-peach palacio presently houses the air-conditioned **Museo de Antropología e Historia** (Museum of Anthropology and History). Designed by Enrique Deserti, who also did the blueprints for the Teatro Peón Contreras, the building has grandiose airs that seem more characteristic of a mausoleum than a home, but in fact it was built for a general between 1909 and 1911. There is marble everywhere, likewise Doric and Ionic columns and other Italianate Beaux Arts flourishes. From 1958 to 1967 the mansion served as the residence of the state governor. In 1977 it became a museum dedicated to the culture and history of the Maya. Although it's not as impressive as its counterparts in other Mexican cities, it can serve as an introduction to ancient Maya culture before you visit nearby Maya sites. Exhibits explain the Maya practice of dental mutilation and incrustation. A case of "sick bones" shows how the Maya suffered from osteoarthritis, nutritional maladies, and congenital syphilis. The museum also has conch shells, stones, and quetzal feathers that were used for trading. There is a bookstore on the premises; it's not open on Sunday. ✉ *Calle 43 and Paseo Montejo, Paseo Montejo,* ☎ *999/923–0557.* 🎫 *$3.50, free Sun.* ⏲ *Tues.–Sat. 8–8, Sun. 8–2.*

28 **Palacio del Gobierno** (Statehouse). Occupying the northeast corner of the main square is this structure, built in 1885 on the site of the Casa Real (Royal House). The upper floor of the Statehouse contains Fernando Castro Pacheco's vivid murals of the bloody history of the conquest of the Yucatán, painted in 1978. On the main balcony (visible from outside on the plaza) stands a reproduction of the **Bell of Dolores Hidalgo,** on which Mexican independence rang out on the night of September 15, 1810, in the town of Dolores Hidalgo in Guanajuato. On the anniversary of the event, the state governor tolls the bell to commemorate the occasion. ⊠ *Calle 61 between Calles 60 and 62, centro.* 🎫 *Free.* ⏲ *Daily 8 AM or 9 AM–9 PM.*

26 **Palacio Municipal** (City Hall). The west side of the main square is occupied by this 17th-century building, which is painted pale yellow and trimmed with white arcades, balustrades, and the national coat of arms. Originally erected on the ruins of the last surviving Maya structure, it was rebuilt in 1735 and then completely reconstructed along colonial lines in 1928. It remains the headquarters of the local government. ⊠ *Calle 62 between Calles 61 and 63, centro.* ⏲ *Daily 9–8.*

34 **Paseo Montejo.** North of downtown, this 10-block-long street was *the* place to reside in the late 19th century, when wealthy plantation owners sought to outdo each other in the opulence of their elegant mansions. Inside, the owners typically displayed imported Carrara marble and antiques, opting for the decorative and social standards of New Orleans, Cuba, and Paris over styles that were popular in Mexico City. (At the time there was more traffic by sea via the Gulf of Mexico and the Caribbean than there was overland across the lawless interior.) The broad boulevard, although still lined with tamarinds and laurels, has lost most of its former panache, however, and many of the once-stunning mansions have fallen into disrepair. Others are being restored as part of a citywide beautification program bolstered by private investment.

32 **Teatro Peón Contreras.** This 1908 Italianate theater was built along the lines of the grand turn-of-the-20th-century European theaters and opera houses. In the early 1980s the marble staircase and the dome and frescoes were restored. Today, in addition to performing arts, the theater also houses the main **Centro de Información Turística,** to the right of the lobby, as well as the occasional art exhibit. The information center distributes maps and brochures and can provide details about attractions in the city and state. A café serving cappuccino and other coffees, plus light snacks and some meals, spills out to a patio from inside the theater to the right of the information center. ⊠ *Calle 60 between Calles 57 and 59, centro,* ☎ *999/923–7354; 999/924–9290 tourist-information center.* ⏲ *Theater daily 7 AM–1 AM, tourist-information center daily 8 AM–9 PM.*

33 **Universidad Autónoma de Yucatán.** The arabesque university plays a major role in the city's cultural and intellectual life. The folkloric ballet performs on the patio of the main building Friday at 9 PM ($4). A Jesuit college built in 1618 previously occupied the site; the present building, which dates from 1711, has crenellated Moorish ramparts and archways. Bulletin boards just inside the entrance announce upcoming cultural events. ⊠ *Calle 60 between Calles 57 and 59, centro,* ☎ *999/924–8000.*

24 **Zócalo** (main square). Meridanos also traditionally call this the Plaza Principal and Plaza de la Independencia, and it's a good spot from which to begin any tour of the city. Ancient, geometrically pruned laurel trees and *confidenciales* (S-shape benches designed for tête-à-têtes) in-

vite lingering. The plaza was laid out in 1542 on the ruins of T'hó, the Maya city demolished to make way for Mérida, and is still the focal point around which the most important public buildings cluster. Lampposts keep the park beautifully illuminated at night. ✉ *Bordered by Calles 60, 62, 61, and 63, centro.*

Dining and Lodging

$$$–$$$$ ★ ✕ **Habichuela.** Both the food and service at this quietly elegant spot are excellent. Custom-made hardwood furniture, marble floors, and lots of leaded-glass accents lead local businessmen here for power lunches; at night, it's filled with families and couples. For starters, sample seafood crêpes or salmon pâté. Meat, fish, and fowl are prepared with flair; try the chicken Veronica stuffed with serrano ham; also delicious are butterflied shrimp with ginger, tamarind, or fruit sauce. The chocolate-mousse cake is the star of the dessert menu. ✉ *Calle 21 No. 416, at Calle 8 (about 20 mins by car from main square), Col. México Oriente,* ☎ *999/926–3626. AE, MC, V. No breakfast.*

$$–$$$$ ✕ **Alberto's Continental Patio.** This romantic restaurant in a 1727 building is adorned with mosaic floors from Cuba. The two dining rooms are fitted with handsome antiques and stone sculptures, and candles glow in glass lanterns. A lovely courtyard surrounded by rubber trees is ideal for starlit dining. There's lots of Lebanese food: shish kebab, fried *kibi* (meatballs of ground beef, wheat germ, and spices), cabbage rolls, hummus, eggplant dip, and tabbouleh; don't forget the pita bread, almond pie, and Turkish coffee. There are Mexican dishes and meatless options for vegetarians. ✉ *Calle 64 No. 482, at Calle 57, centro,* ☎ *999/928–5367. AE, MC, V.*

$ ★ ✕ **Café La Habana.** Old-fashioned ceiling fans and a gleaming wood bar contribute to the Old Havana nostalgia at this overwhelmingly popular café. The aroma of fresh-ground coffee fills the air at this busy 24-hour place with a nonsmoking section sometimes closed due to lack of interest. Sixteen javas are offered, including Irish, frappé, espresso, and Arab. The menu has light snacks such as lime soup, as well as some entrées, including spaghetti, fajitas, and breaded shrimp. The waiters are friendly and service is brisk. ✉ *Corner of Calles 59 and 62, centro,* ☎ *999/928–6502. No credit cards.*

$$$$ ★ ✕🏨 **Hacienda Katanchel.** This romantic, rambling 17th-century henequen hacienda was brought back to its original splendor by Anibal Gonzalez and his wife, Monica Hernandez. Rooms and suites in spacious pavilions line a winding garden walkway; they have overhead fans, hammocks, huge tile bathrooms, and plunge pools. The double beds look like pieces of modern sculpture. The gorgeous restaurant serves contemporary Yucatecan cuisine, making liberal use of the hacienda's organically grown fruits and vegetables. Offerings include cream of beet soup, chicken in pumpkin seed and pistachio sauce, and desserts such as vanilla ice cream with tangy sour-orange sauce. Massages using herbs and floral essences bring pampering to a new level. Expensive excursions by plane or private car can be arranged. ✉ *25 km (15 mi) east of Mérida on Hwy. 180 (toward Cancún),* ☎ *999/923–4020 or 800/223–6510;* FAX *888/882–9470 from the U.S; 999/923–4000;* WEB *www.hacienda-katanchel.com. 25 rooms, 13 suites. Restaurant, pool, massage, bar, car rental, travel services. AE, MC, V.*

$$$$ ★ ✕🏨 **Hacienda Teya.** The draw at this beautiful henequen-era hacienda 8 mi from the city is the fabulous regional food; reservations for Sunday lunch or dinner are essential. After a typical lunch of cochinita pibíl or baked chicken, you can stroll in the orchard or surrounding gardens, or swim in the huge rectangular pool. The 10 guest rooms have handmade rustic furniture, TV, and a whirlpool bath; rates include Continental breakfast. ✉ *13 km (8 mi) east of Mérida on Hwy. 180,*

Kanasín, ☎ *999/924–3800; 999/924–3880 in Mérida;* FAX *999/924–5853;* WEB *www.haciendateya.com. 10 rooms. Restaurant, in-room hot tubs, pool, bar, free parking. AE, MC, V.*

$$$$ ★ **Fiesta Americana Mérida.** This posh hotel and shopping-business center caters to business travelers, conventions, and high-end travelers, its lovely facade echoing Paseo Montejo mansions on an epic scale. The colonial accents carry into the spacious lobby, with gleaming marble and a 300-ft-high stained-glass atrium. Floral prints and slightly larger-than-life proportions maintain the theme of bygone elegance in the guest rooms, which nonetheless have all the modern conveniences, including remote-control TV and three phones. Guests on the business floor have access to the Fiesta Club for morning breakfast or afternoon appetizers. ✉ *Av. Colón 451, at Paseo Montejo, Paseo Montejo,* ☎ *999/942–1111 or 800/343–7821,* FAX *999/942–1122,* WEB *www.fiestaamericana.com. 323 rooms, 27 suites. 2 restaurants, in-room data ports, pool, health club, 2 bars, shops, business services, car rental, travel services, free parking, no-smoking rooms. AE, MC, V.*

$$$ ★ **Casa del Balam.** This pleasant hotel two blocks from the zócalo is still owned by the Barbachanos, pioneers of Yucatán tourism. Rocking chairs in the hallways impart a colonial feeling, as do the carved cedar doors and other lovely touches. The rooms are well maintained, with painted sinks, refrigerators, hair dryers, and double-pane windows. Meals are served around the splashing fountain on the open courtyard or inside the restaurant. Guests have access to a golf and tennis club about 15 minutes (by car) away. ✉ *Calle 60 No. 488, centro,* ☎ *999/924–8844; 800/624–8451 in the U.S.;* FAX *999/924–5011. 51 rooms, 3 suites. Restaurant, room service, minibars, pool, bars, car rental, travel services, free parking, no-smoking rooms. AE, DC, MC, V.*

$$$ **Casa Mexilio.** Four blocks from the main square is this eclectic B&B run by partners Jorge and Roger. Middle Eastern wall hangings, French tapestries, and colorful tile floors crowd the public spaces; individually decorated rooms have tile sinks and folk-art furniture. Casa Mexilio lacks the amenities of the larger hotels; some find it private and romantic, although for others it's a bit too intimate. ✉ *Calle 68 No. 495, between Calles 57 and 59, centro, 97000,* ☎ FAX *999/928–2505;* ☎ *800/538–6802 in the U.S.;* WEB *www.mexicoholiday.com. 8 rooms. Restaurant, pool. MC, V.*

$$ ★ **Dolores Alba.** This comfortable, friendly star at the low end of the $$ range is sister to the equally engaging hotel-restaurant in Pisté, near Chichén Itzá. The newer wing has spiffy rooms with quiet yet strong air-conditioning, fans, and telephones, TVs, and comfortable beds; rooms in the older section, with no air-conditioning or TV, are less expensive. The big, rectangular pool is surrounded by lounge chairs and shaded by giant trees, and there's a comfortable restaurant and bar at the front of the property. ✉ *Calle 63 No. 464, between Calles 52 and 54, centro,* ☎ *999/928–5650,* FAX *999/928–3163,* WEB *www.doloresalba.com. 95 rooms. Restaurant, fans, pool, bar, free parking; no air-conditioning in some rooms. No credit cards.*

$$ **Residencial.** Location is the major draw at this classy bright-pink hotel, a replica of a 19th-century French colonial mansion. It sits on Calle 59, the main entrance to town, and has gated parking. Its elegant dining room is more recommended for its silk drapes and fine linen tablecloths than for the food itself. Rooms have powerful showers, comfortable beds, remote-control cable TV, and spacious closets. The small swimming pool in the central courtyard is pleasant for reconnoitering but far from private. ✉ *Calle 59 No. 589, at Calle 76, centro,* ☎ *999/924–3899 or 999/924–3099,* FAX *999/924–0266,* WEB *hotelresidencial.com.mx. 64 rooms, 2 suites. Restaurant, room service, pool, bar, free parking. AE, MC, V.*

Nightlife and the Arts

Mérida has an unusually active and diverse cultural life, including free government-sponsored music and dance performances many evenings, as well as sidewalk art shows in local parks. On Saturday check out the **Noche Mexicana,** a free, outdoor spectacle of music, dance, comedy, and regional handicrafts that draws more locals than tourists. It happens 8 PM–11 PM at the foot of Paseo Montejo at Calle 47. On Sunday, when six blocks around the zócalo are closed off to traffic, you can hear live music at Plaza Santa Lucía and Parque Hidalgo: mariachis, marimbas, folkloric dance, and other treats at the main plaza. For more information on these and other performances, consult the tourist office, the local newspapers, or the billboards and posters at the **Teatro Peón Contreras,** Calle 60 at Calle 57; the **Universidad Autónoma de Yucatán,** Calle 57 at Calle 60; the recently renovated **Teatro Mérida,** Calle 60 at Calle between Calles 59 and 61; or **Centro Cultural Olimpo,** on the northwest corner of the main plaza.

DANCING

Dancing sometimes erupts spontaneously at **La Planta Alta** (✉ Paseo Montejo 444, at Calle 56-A, ☎ 999/927–9847), open daily from 5:30 PM until about 1 AM, but most people are content to converse (i.e., shout), listen to music, sip drinks, and watch large-screen music videos. **Pancho's** (✉ Calle 59 No. 509, between Calles 60 and 62, centro, ☎ 999/923–0942), open daily 6 PM–2:30 AM, has a lively bar as well as a restaurant and dance floor.

FOLKLORIC SHOWS

Paseo Montejo hotels such as the Fiesta Americana, Hyatt Regency, and Holiday Inn stage dinner shows with folkloric dances; check with concierges for schedules. The **Folkloric Ballet of the University of Yucatán** presents a combination of music, dance, and theater, every Friday at 9 PM (every other Friday in off-seasons) at the Universidad Autónoma de Yucatán (✉ Calle 57 at Calle 60, centro, ☎ 999/924–7260); tickets are $3. This includes the "University Serenade," with music, folkloric dance, and poetry. (There are no shows from August 1 to September 22 and during the last two weeks of December.)

Outdoor Activities and Sports

GOLF

The 18-hole championship golf course at **Club de Golf La Ceiba** (✉ Carretera Mérida–Progreso, Km 14.5, ☎ 999/922–0053) is open to the public. It is about 16 km (10 mi) north of Mérida on the road to Progreso; greens fees are about $50, and it's closed Monday.

Shopping

MARKETS

The **Mercado Municipal** (✉ Calle 56 at Calle 67, centro) has crafts, food, flowers, and live birds, among other items. If you are interested strictly in handicrafts, visit the government-run **Casa de Artesanías** (✉ Calle 63 No. 503, between Calles 64 and 66, La Mejorada, ☎ 999/923–5392). It sells folk art from throughout Mexico, including hand-painted wooden mythical animals from Oaxaca, handmade beeswax candles and leather bags from Mérida, and hand-embroidered vests, shawls, blouses, and place mats from Chiapas. The **Bazar García Rejón** (✉ Calle 65 at Calle 62, centro) has rather sterile rows of indoor stalls with leather items, palm hats, and handmade guitars, among other things.

SPECIALTY STORES

Clothing. Mexicanísimo (✉ Calle 60 No. 496, at Calle 61, Parque Hidalgo, ☎ 999/923–8132) sells expensive designer cotton clothing inspired by regional dress. You might not wear a guayabera to a business meeting as some men in Mexico do, but the shirts are cool, comfortable, and attractive; for a good selection, try **Camisería Canul** (✉ Calle 62 No. 484, between Calles 57 and 59, centro, ☎ 999/923–0158). Pick up a *jipi* (or order one custom made) at **El Becaleño** (✉ Calle 65 No. 483, between Calles 56 and 58, centro, ☎ 999/985–0581); the famous hats are made at Becal in Campeche by the González family.

The Scenic Route to Chichén Itzá

Although you can get to Chichén Itzá (120 km [74 mi] east of Mérida) along the shorter Route 180, it's far more scenic to follow Route 80 until it ends at Tekantó, then head south to Citilcúm, east to Dzitas, and south again to Pisté. These roads have no signs but are the only paved roads going in these directions.

Chichén Itzá

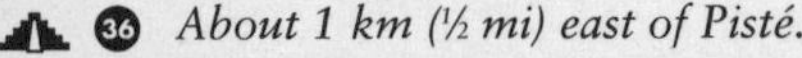

About 1 km (½ mi) east of Pisté.

One of the four most magnificent Maya ruins—along with Palenque in Chiapas in Mexico, Tikal in Guatemala, and Cobá in Honduras—Chichén Itzá was the most important city in Yucatán from the 10th through the 12th century. Its architectural mélange covers pre-Hispanic Mesoamerican history and shows the influence of several different Maya groups. Because epigraphers have been able to read 85% of the Chichén inscriptions, the site's history has become clearer to archaeologists. At one time it was believed that Chichén Itzá was dominated by the Toltecs from present-day central Mexico; now historians believe that the city was indeed influenced by trade with the north, not, however, by conquest. Chichén *was* altered by successive waves of inhabitants, and archaeologists are able to date the arrival of these waves by the changes in the architecture and information contained in inscriptions. That said, they have yet to explain the long gaps of time when the buildings seem to have been uninhabited. The site is believed to have been first settled in AD 432, abandoned for an unknown period of time, then rediscovered in 868 by the Maya-speaking Itzás, who migrated north from the region of the Petén rain forest around Tikal (in what is now northern Guatemala). The latest data point to the city's having been refounded by not only the Itzás but also by two other foreign groups—one from the Valley of Mexico (near present-day Mexico City) and another from Ek Balam. The trio formed a ruling triumvirate. The Itzás may have also abandoned the site, but they were the dominant group until 1224, when the city appears to have been abandoned for all time.

Chichén Itzá means "the mouth of the well of the Itzás." The enormity and gracefulness of this site are unforgettable. Chichén Itzá encompasses approximately 6 square km (2½ square mi), though only 30 to 40 structures and buildings of the several hundred at the site have been fully explored. It's divided into two parts, called Old and New, although architectural motifs from the Classic period are found in both sections. A more convenient distinction is topographical, since there are two major complexes of buildings separated by a dirt path.

The martial, imperial architecture of the Itzás and the more cerebral architecture and astronomical expertise of the earlier Maya are married in the 98-ft-tall pyramid called **El Castillo** (the Castle), which dominates the site and rises above all the other buildings. Atop the Castillo is a temple dedicated to Kukulcán/Quetzalcoatl, the legendary Toltec priest-king from Tula in the Valley of Mexico who was held to be an incarnation of the mystical plumed serpent. An open-jawed plumed ser-

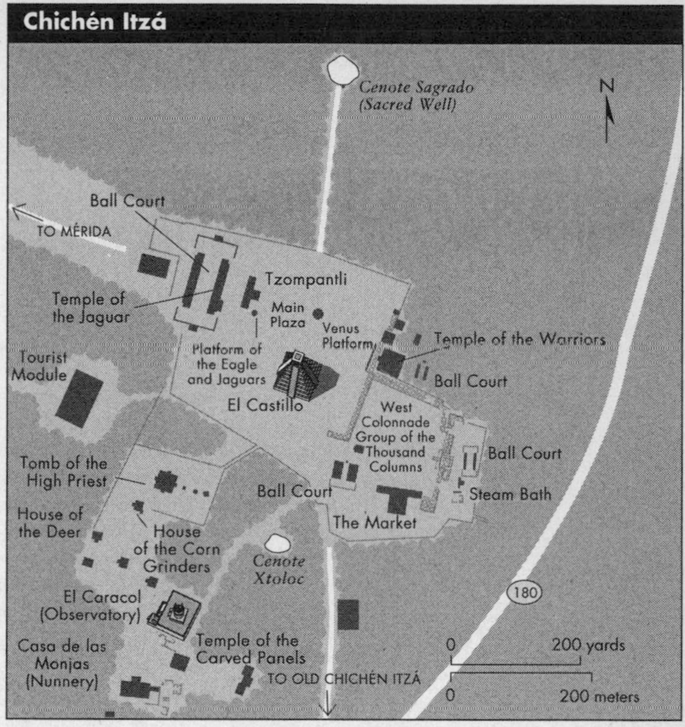

pent rests on the balustrade of each stairway, and serpents reappear at the top of the temple as sculptured columns. At thc spring and fall equinoxes, the afternoon light strikes one of these balustrades in such a way as to form a shadow representation of Kukulcán undulating out of his temple and down the pyramid to bless the fertile earth. Each evening there's a sound-and-light show that highlights the architectural details in El Castillo and other buildings with a clarity the eye doesn't see in daylight, though its accompanying narration has inaccuracies.

The temple rests on a massive trapezoidal square, on the west side of which is Chichén Itzá's largest **ball court,** one of seven on the site. Its two parallel walls are each 272 ft long, with two stone rings on each side, and 99 ft apart. The game played here was something like soccer (no hands were used), but it had a strictly religious significance. Bas-relief carvings at the court depict a player being decapitated, the blood spurting from his neck fertilizing the earth. Other bas-reliefs show two teams of opposing players pitted against each other during the ball game.

Between the ball court and El Castillo stands a **Tzompantli,** or stone platform, carved with rows of human skulls. In ancient times such walls were made of real skulls: the heads of enemies impaled on stakes. Legend has it that the **Sacred Well,** a cenote 65 yards in diameter that sits 1 km (½ mi) north of El Castillo at the end of a *sacbé,* was used for human sacrifices; another cenote at the site supplied drinking water. Many archaeologists believe that nonhuman sacrifices were carried out by local chiefs hundreds of years after Chichén Itzá was abandoned. Thousands of artifacts made of gold, jade, and other precious materials, most of them not of local provenance, have been recovered from the brackish depths of the cenote.

East of El Castillo is the **Group of the Thousand Columns** with the famous **Temple of the Warriors,** a masterful example of the Itzá influence at Chichén Itzá. The temple was used as a meeting place for the high lords of the council that ruled Chichén Itzá. The temple-top sculpture of the reclining Chacmool—its head turned to the side, the offertory dish carved into its middle—is probably the most photographed symbol of the Maya. Murals of everyday village life and scenes of war can be viewed here, and an artistic representation of the defeat of one of the Itzás' Maya enemies can be found on the interior murals of the **Temple of the Jaguar,** west of the Temple of the Warriors at the ball court.

To get to the less visited cluster of structures at **New Chichén Itzá**—often confused with Old Chichén Itzá—take the main path south from the Temple of the Jaguar past El Castillo and turn right onto a small path opposite the ball court on your left. Archaeologists have been restoring several buildings in this area, including the Tomb of the High Priest, where several tombs with skeletons and jade offerings were found, and the northern part of the site, which was used for military training and barracks for the army. The most impressive structure within this area is the astronomical observatory called El Caracol. The name, meaning "snail," refers to the spiral staircase at the building's core. Built in several stages, El Caracol is one of the few round buildings constructed by the Maya. Judging by the tiny windows oriented toward the four cardinal points, and the structure's alignment with the planet Venus, it was used for observing the heavens. Since astronomy was the province of priests and used to determine rituals and predict the future, the building undoubtedly served a religious function as well. After leaving El Caracol, continue south several hundred yards to the beautiful **La Casa de las Monjas** ("the nunnery") and its annex, which have long carved panels.

At so-called **Old Chichén Itzá,** south of the remains of Thompson's hacienda, the architecture shows less outside influence: a combination of Puuc and Chenes Maya styles—with playful latticework, Chaac masks, and gargoylelike serpents on the cornices—dominates. Highlights include the Date Group, so named because of its complete series of hieroglyphic dates; the House of the Phalli; and the Temple of the Three Lintels. Maya guides will lead you down the path by an old narrow-gauge railroad track to even more ruins, barely unearthed, if you ask. A fairly good restaurant and a great ice cream stand are in the entrance building, as is a gift shop where you can purchase film, bus tickets, postcards, and books. A small museum includes information on the migration patterns of the ancient Maya inhabitants and some small sculptures recovered from the site. 🎫 *$8.50 (includes museum and sound-and-light show), free Sun.; parking $2; use of video camera $7.* ⏲ *Daily 8–5; sound-and-light show Apr.–Oct., daily at 8 PM, Nov.–Mar., daily at 7 PM.*

Lodging

$$$$ ★ 🏨 **Mayaland.** The hotel closest to the ruins, this charming 1920s lodging is set in a large garden on the 100-acre site. You can actually see part of Old Chichén from the grounds, and the hotel has its own entrance to the ruins. Colonial-style guest rooms have decorative tiles, air-conditioning, and cable TV. The 24 bungalows at the rear of the hotel are the quietest and prettiest accommodations, with hammocks on the wide verandas, bathtubs, and thatch roofs. Snacks served poolside are a better choice than the expensive meals in the dining room. ✉ *Carretera Mérida–Puerto Juárez, Km 120,* ☎ *999/924–2099; 800/235–4079 in the U.S.;* FAX *999/924–6290,* ☎ FAX *985/851–0129;* WEB

www.mayaland.com. 24 bungalows, 67 rooms, 10 suites. 4 restaurants, room service, minibars, tennis court, 3 pools, volleyball, 2 bars, travel services, free parking. AE, DC, MC, V.

$$$ ★ **Hacienda Chichén.** A converted 16th-century hacienda with its own entrance to the ruins, this hotel once served as the headquarters for the Carnegie expedition to Chichén Itzá. The rustic-chic cottages have handwoven bedspreads, dehumidifiers, and air-conditioning. All rooms, which are simply but beautifully furnished in colonial Yucatecan style, have verandas but no phone or TV. There's a satellite TV in the library. An enormous old pool as well as a chapel now used for weddings grace the landscaped gardens. Meals are served on the patio overlooking the grounds or in the air-conditioned restaurant. ✉ *Carretera Mérida–Puerto Juárez, Km 120,* ☎ *985/851–0045, 999/924–2150; 800/624–8451 in the U.S.;* ☎ FAX *999/924–5011. 24 rooms, 4 suites. Restaurant, pool, bar, free parking; no room phones. AE, DC, MC, V.*

Pisté

37 *116 km (72 mi) southeast of Mérida.*

The town of Pisté serves mainly as a base camp for travelers to Chichén Itzá. Hotels, campgrounds, restaurants, and handicrafts shops tend to be less expensive here than those at the ruins. At the west end of town is a Pemex gas station, but the town has no bank, so bring all the cash you'll need. On the outskirts of Pisté and a short walk from Chichén Itzá is **Pueblo Maya,** a pseudo-Maya village with a shopping and dining center for tour groups. The restaurant serves a bountiful buffet at lunch ($12). Across from the Dolores Alba hotel, in town, is the **Parque Ik Kil** ("place of the winds"). The park is built around a lovely cenote where you can swim between 8 AM and 6 PM for $3. The park includes the Restaurant el Jardín, which serves Mexican and international fare; a swimming pool; bungalows inspired by Maya dwellings; and a row of shops where artisans demonstrate their crafts. ✉ *Carretera Mérida–Puerto Juárez, Km 112,* ☎ *985/851–0000.*

Lodging

$$ **Dolores Alba.** The best low-budget choice near the ruins is this family-run hotel, a longtime favorite in the area south of Pisté. Rooms have colonial-style furniture and air-conditioning. Hammocks hang by one of the two pools, and breakfast and dinner are served family-style in the main building. Free transportation to Chichén Itzá is provided, and there is a covered, guarded parking lot. ✉ *Carretera Mérida–Cancún, Km 122, 3 km (2 mi) south of Chichén Itzá,* ☎ *999/928–5650,* FAX *999/928–3163,* WEB *www.doloresalba.com. 40 rooms. Restaurant, 2 pools, free parking. No credit cards.*

Valladolid

38 *44½ km (28 mi) east of Chichén Itzá.*

The second-largest city in the state of Yucatán, Valladolid is a picturesque provincial town, much smaller than Mérida. It has been enjoying growing popularity among travelers en route to or from Chichén Itzá or Río Lagartos who want a change from the more touristy places. Montejo founded Valladolid in 1543 on the site of the Maya town of Sisal. The city suffered during the War of the Castes—when the Maya in revolt killed nearly all Spanish residents—and again during the Mexican Revolution.

Today, however, placidity reigns in this agricultural market town. The center is mostly colonial, although it has many 19th-century structures. The main sights are the colonial churches, principally the large **Cate-**

dral de San Servacio (San Servace Cathedral) on the central square and the 16th-century **Convento y Iglesia de San Bernadino** (San Bernardino Church and Monastery) three blocks southwest. Both were pillaged during the War of the Castes. A briny but pretty cenote in the center of town draws lots of local boys busily showing off for each other; if you're not up for a dip, visit the adjacent **ethnographic museum.** West of the main square and on the old highway to Chichén Itzá, you can swim with the catfish in lovely, mysterious **Cenote Dzitnup,** in a cave lit by a small natural skylight; admission is $2.50.

Valladolid is renowned for its cuisine, particularly its sausages; try one of the restaurants within a block of the central square. You can find good buys on sandals, baskets, and the local liqueur, Xtabentún, flavored with honey and anise.

Dining and Lodging

$$ ✕ **El Mesón del Marqués.** On the north side of the main square is this well-preserved, very old hacienda, which was built around a lovely courtyard. All rooms have air-conditioning, phones, and cable TV and are attractively furnished with rustic and colonial touches. The 25 junior suites have large bathrooms with bathtubs. The charming restaurant, set under porticos surrounding the courtyard, serves Yucatecan specialties such as pollo pibíl and local sausage served in different ways. It's open 7 AM–11 PM. ✉ *Calle 39 No. 203, 97780,* ☎ *985/856–2073 or 985/856–3042,* FAX *985/856–2280. 58 rooms, 25 suites. Restaurant, pool, bar. AE.*

$$ **Ecotel Quinta Real.** This attractive salmon-color hotel is a mix of colonial Mexican and modern. Near a leafy park five blocks from downtown, the pretty rooms have cool tile floors, cable TV, air-conditioning, and spacious balconies. Wander the tree-filled garden; visit the pool, palapa bar, tennis court, or duck pond; or head to the game room for Ping-Pong or billiards. Continental breakfast is included in room rate. ✉ *Calle 40 No. 160-A, at Calle 27, 97780,* ☎ *985/856–3472 or 985/856–3473,* FAX *985/856–2422,* WEB *www.ecotelquintareal.com.mx. 48 rooms. Restaurant, tennis court, pool, bar, car rental, travel services, free parking. MC, V.*

Parque Natural Ría Lagartos

★ 39 *52 km (32 mi) north of Tizimín.*

If the thought of a phenomenal flamingo spectacle appeals, don't miss Parque Natural Ría Lagartos. Flamingos can be seen year-round here but are particularly abundant from April through June. Actually encompassing a long estuary, the park was developed with ecotourism in mind, though most of the alligators for which it and the village were named have long since been hunted into extinction. In addition to seeing flamingos, birders also can spot snowy and red egrets, white ibis, great white herons, cormorants, pelicans, and even peregrine falcons flying over the murky waters. Fishing is good, too, and the protected hawksbill and green turtles lay their eggs on the beach at night.

To get here, you can drive or take a bus or a tour out of Mérida or elsewhere. Buses leave Mérida and Valladolid regularly from the second-class bus terminals to either Río Lagartos or, 10 km (6 mi) west of the park, San Felipe. A boat tour to see the flamingos is available from either point. About ½ km (¼ mi) from the entrance to Río Lagartos is an information station. The helpful people who work here can contact a guide with a boat for you. The boat glides up the estuary east of the dock and in 10 minutes is deep into mangrove forests; another hour and the boat is at the flamingo feeding grounds. For a bilingual birding guide ($10–$15 an hour), you must make arrangements at least three days in advance with the reserve office in Tizimín (☎ 996/863–4390).

Uxmal, the Ruta Puuc, and the Coast

Passing through the large Maya town of Umán on Mérida's southern outskirts, you enter one of the least populated areas of the Yucatán. The highway to Uxmal and Kabah is a fairly traffic-free route through uncultivated woodlands. The forest seems to become more dense beyond Uxmal, which was connected to a number of smaller ceremonial centers in ancient times by *caminos blancos* (white roads). Several of these satellite sites, including **Kabah,** with its 250 Chaac masks; **Sayil,** with its majestic, three-story palace; and **Labná,** with its iconic, vaulted *Puerta* (gateway), are open to the public along a side road known as the Ruta Puuc, which winds its way eastward and eventually joins busy Highway 184, a major highway. Along this route you'll also find the **Loltún Caves,** the largest known cave system in the Yucatán, containing wall paintings and stone artifacts from Maya and pre-Maya times. You can make a loop to all of these sites, ending the loop in the little town of **Plaza,** which produces much of the pottery you'll see around the peninsula. **Ticul** is a convenient alternative to spending the night at the hotels just outside the Uxmal ruins, and the reasonable **Plaza** hotel (☎ 997/20026), a block from the town square, is a suitable place to stay.

Uxmal

78 km (48 mi) south of Mérida on Rte. 261.

If Chichén Itzá is the most impressive Maya ruin in Yucatán, Uxmal is arguably the most beautiful. Where the former has a Maya Itzá grandeur, the latter seems more understated and elegant—pure Maya. The architecture reflects the Late Classical renaissance of the 7th–9th centuries and is contemporary with that of Palenque and Tikal, among other great Maya metropolises of the southern highlands.

The site is considered the finest and largest example of Puuc architecture, which embraces such details as ornate stone mosaics and friezes on the upper walls, intricate cornices with curled noses, rows of columns, and soaring vaulted arches. Lines are clean and uncluttered, with the horizontal—especially the parallelogram—preferred to the vertical. Although most of Uxmal hasn't been restored, three buildings in particular merit attention:

At 125 ft high, the **Pyramid of the Magician** is the tallest and most prominent structure at the site. Unlike most other Maya pyramids, which are stepped and angular, it has a strangely round-corner design. It was built five times at 52-year sequences to coincide with the ceremony of the new fire, each time over the previous structure. The pyramid has a stairway on its western side that leads through a giant open-mouthed mask of Chaac to two temples at the summit.

West of the pyramid lies the **Quadrangle of the Nuns,** considered by some to be the finest part of Uxmal. The name was given to it by the Spanish conquistadors because it reminded them of a convent building in Old Spain. According to research, what is called the **Nunnery** was actually the palace and living quarters of a high lord of Uxmal by the name of Chaan Chak, which means "abundance of rain." You may enter the four buildings; each comprises a series of low, gracefully repetitive chambers that look onto a central patio. Elaborate decoration—masks, geometric patterns, coiling snakes, and some phallic figures—blankets the upper facades.

Continue walking south; you pass the ball court before reaching the **Palace of the Governor,** which archaeologist Victor von Hagen considered the most magnificent building ever erected in the Americas. Interestingly, the palace faces east, whereas the rest of Uxmal faces west. Archaeologists believe this is because the palace was used to sight the planet Venus. Covering 5 acres and rising over an immense acropolis, the palace lies at the heart of what must have been Uxmal's administrative center.

Today a sound-and-light show recounts Maya legends. The artificial colored light brings out details of carvings and mosaics that are easy to miss when the sun is shining. The show is performed nightly in Spanish; earphones provide an English translation. *Site, museum, and sound-and-light show $8.50; free Sun. (English-translation of sound-and-light show, $3); parking $2; use of video camera $8. Daily 8–5; sound-and-light show Apr.–Oct., nightly at 8 PM; Nov.–Mar., nightly at 7 PM.*

Dining and Lodging

$$$$ **Hacienda Uxmal.** Just across the road from the ruins, and the oldest hotel at the site, this pleasant colonial-style building has lovely floor tiles, ceramics, and iron grillwork. The rooms—all with ceiling fans, satellite TV, and air-conditioning—are fronted with wide, furnished verandas; the courtyard contains two pools surrounded by gardens. Ask about packages that include free or low-cost car rentals, or comfortable minivans traveling to Mérida, Chichén, or Cancún. ✉ *Carretera Merida-Campeche, Km 78,* ☎ *997/976–2012; 998/884–4510 in Cancún; 800/235–4079 in the U.S.;* FAX *997/976–2011; 998/884–4510 in Cancún;* WEB *www.mayaland.com. 80 rooms, 2 suites. 2 restaurants, room service, 2 pools, billiards, Ping-Pong, bar, free parking. AE, MC, V.*

$$$$ **Lodge at Uxmal.** Classy materials (glossy red-tile floors, carved and polished hardwood doors and rocking chairs, and local weavings) are combined with luxury amenities in a sprinkling of rustic-looking, two-story thatch-roof buildings. All have bathtubs, cable TV, and minibars, as well as fans, screened windows, plus air-conditioning. Suites have king-size beds and jet baths. The effect is suitably comfortable yet luxuriant. ✉ *Carretera Uxmal, Km 78,* ☎ *998/884–4510 in Cancún; 800/235–4079 in the U.S.;* FAX *998/884–4510 in Cancún;* WEB *www.mayaland.com. 30 rooms, 10 suites. 2 restaurants, some in-room hot tubs, minibars, 2 pools, bar, free parking. AE, MC, V.*

$$ **Villas Arqueológicas Uxmal.** Rooms in this pretty two-story Club Med property are small and functional, with wooden furniture that fits the niches nicely, and quiet air conditioners. Half of the rooms have garden views. The French and Continental food served in the restaurant—including niçoise salad, pâté, and filet mignon—can be a delightful change from regional fare. Meal plans are available and reasonable for Club Med guests. ✉ *Carretera Uxmal, Km 76,* ☎ *997/976–2018 or 800/258–2633,* FAX *997/976–2020. 40 rooms, 3 suites. Restaurant, pool, billiards, bar, library, free parking. AE, MC, V.*

Celestún

41 *90 km (56 mi) west of Mérida.*

This tranquil fishing village, with its air of unpretentiousness and Gulf-coast flavor, sits at the end of a spit of land separating the Celestún estuary from the Gulf on the western hump of the Yucatán. Celestún is the only point of entry to the **Parque Natural Ría Celestún,** a 100,000-acre wildlife reserve with extensive mangrove forests and salt flats and one of the largest colonies of flamingos in North America. The best months for seeing them in abundance—as many as 500 flamingos at a time—are April through June. This is also the fourth-largest wintering ground for ducks of the Gulf-coast region, with more than 300 other species of birds and a large sea-turtle population.

Celestún Expeditions (✉ Calle 10 No. 97, between Calles 9 and 11, ☎ 988/916–2049) is a small company run by two natives of Celestún. In addition to the standard flamingo tours, they offer three-hour guided bike tours, jungle walks (day or night), crocodile tours at night, bird-watching excursions, and trips to the Maya ruins and haciendas. Tours range from $20 per person for the bike jaunt to $75 per person for the bird-watching outing.

Dining and Lodging

$–$$ ✕ **La Palapa.** A conch-shell facade decorates the most popular seafood place in town, famous for its *camarones a la palapa* (fried shrimp smothered in a garlic and cream sauce). Unless it's windy or rainy, most guests dine on the beachfront terrace. Choose fresh fish (including sea bass and red snapper), plus crab, squid, or the most expensive plate: lobster tail and moro crab. Usually open 11 AM–7 PM, La Palapa sometimes closes early in low season. ✉ *Calle 12 No. 105, between Calles 11 and 13,* ☎ *988/916–2063. MC, V.*

$$$$ **Hotel Eco Paraíso Xixim.** On an old coconut plantation outside town, this hotel offers classy comfort in thatch-roof bungalows right on a long, seashell-strewn beach. Each suite has two comfortable queen beds, tile floors, and attractive wicker, cedar, and pine furniture. There's no air-conditioning, TVs, or phones, but the extra-large porch has twin hammocks and comfortable chairs. Bring strong insect repellent, as mosquitoes can be vicious. Room rates include ample breakfasts and dinners. Biking tours as well as those to old haciendas or archaeological sites can be arranged; kayaks are available for rent. Breakfast and dinner are included in the price. ✉ *Camino Viejo a Sisal, Km 10,* ☎ *981/916–2100; 888/264–5792 in the U.S.;* FAX *999/916–2111;* WEB *www.ecoparaiso.com. 15 cabanas. Restaurant, fans, in-room safes, pool, beach, billiards, bar, library; no air-conditioning, no room phones, no room TVs. AE, MC, V.*

$ **Hotel Sol y Mar.** Gerardo Vasquez, the friendly owner of this small hotel, also owns the local paint store next door and chose a tasteful combination of gray and rose for the walls and curtains of these cool, spacious units. Across the street from the town beach, this hotel has sparsely furnished rooms with two double beds, small table and chairs, and tile bathrooms. The more expensive rooms, downstairs, have air-conditioning, TV, and tiny refrigerators. There's no restaurant, but the recommended La Palapa restaurant is across the street. ✉ *Calle 12 No. 104, at Calle 10,* ☎ *988/916–2166. 15 rooms. Air-conditioning in some rooms, fans, some refrigerators. No credit cards.*

The State of Yucatán A to Z

To research prices, get advice from other travelers, and book travel arrangements, visit www.fodors.com.

AIR TRAVEL

Aerocaribe, a subsidiary of Mexicana, has flights from Cancún, Chetumal, Cozumel, Oaxaca City, Tuxtla Gutiérrez, Palenque, and Villahermosa, with additional service to Central America. It also flies from Cozumel and Cancún to Chichén Itzá. Aeroméxico flies direct to Mérida from Miami with a stop (but no plane change) in Cancún. Aviacsa flies nonstop from Mérida to Guadalajara, Mexico City, and Tijuana and makes connections to Cancún, Villahermosa, Tuxtla Gutiérrez, Tapachula, Oaxaca, Chetumal, and Mexico City. Mexicana has a connecting flight from Newark via Cancún and a number of other connecting flights from the United States via Mexico City.

➤ AIRLINES AND CONTACTS: **Aerocaribe** (☎ 999/928–6790). **Aeroméxico** (☎ 800/021–4000). **Aviacsa** (☎ 999/926–9087 or 999/925–6890). **Mexicana** (☎ 999/946–1332).

AIRPORTS

The Mérida airport, Aeropuerto Manuel Crescencio Rejón, is 7 km (4½ mi) west of the city on Avenida Itzaes, a 20- to 30-minute cab ride.

A private taxi from the airport costs $9 or $10. Bus 79 goes from the airport to downtown—very inexpensive, but a hassle if you've got more than a day pack or small suitcase. If you're driving into town, take the airport exit road, make a right at the four-lane Avenida Itzaes (the continuation of Route 180), and follow it to the one-way Calle 59, just past Parque Zoológico El Centenario. Turn right on Calle 59 and go straight until you reach Calle 62, where you turn right and drive a block to the main square. (Parking is difficult here.)

➤ AIRPORT INFORMATION: **Aeropuerto Manuel Crescencio Rejón** (☎ 999/946–1300).

BUS TRAVEL

Mérida's municipal buses run daily 5 AM–midnight, but service is somewhat confusing until you master the system. In the downtown area buses go east on Calle 59 and west on Calle 61, north on Calle 60 and south on Calle 62. You can catch a bus heading north to Progreso on Calle 56. There is no direct bus service from the hotels around the plaza to the long-distance bus station; however, taxis are reasonably priced.

There are several first-class bus stations offering deluxe buses with high-powered air-conditioning and spacious seats. The most frequently used is CAME (Camionera Mérida; Calle 70 No. 555, at Calle 71). From here you can take the major bus lines: ADO, UNO, and Clase Elite to Akumal, Cancún, Chichén Itzá, Playa del Carmen, Tulum, Uxmal, Valladolid, and other major Mexican cities. ADO, UNO, and Super Expresso have direct buses to Cancún from their terminal at the Fiesta Americana hotel, on Paseo Montejo.

There are other smaller lines in addition to these. If you're not sure which line to take, or are heading to a more out-of-the-way destination, look for the free magazine *Yucatán Today,* which often lists all of Mérida's bus stations and their locations and the destinations. Otherwise, check with the tourist office.

➤ BUS LINES AND STATIONS: **ADO/Super Expresso/UNO** (✉ Paseo Montejo at Av. Colón, ☎ 999/924–7868 or 999/924–8391; 999/925–0910 in Fiesta Americana). **Autotransportes del Sureste** (ATS; ☎ 999/923–2287). **Camionera Mérida** (CAME; ✉ Calle 70 No. 555, at Calle 71, ☎ 999/924–8391 or 999/924–4440). **Elite/Nuevos Horizontes** (☎ 999/923–9913). **Terminal de Autobuses del Noreste** (✉ Calle 50 No. 527-A, between Calles 65 and 67, ☎ 999/923–4602 or 999/324–6355). **Terminal de Autobuses (2da clase)** (✉ Calle 69 No. 544, between Calles 68 and 70, ☎ 999/923–2287 or 999/923–4440). **Terminal del Autobuses a Progreso** (Progreso station; ✉ Calle 62 No. 557, between Calles 65 and 67, ☎ 999/928–3965).

CAR RENTAL

Mérida has almost 20 car-rental agencies, including Budget, Hertz, National, and Thrifty outlets. Prices are sometimes lower if you arrange your rental in advance of your visit.

➤ MAJOR AGENCIES: ✉ **Advantage** (✉ Fiesta Americana, ☎ 999/920–1920). **Budget** (✉ Hotel Misión Mérida, Calle 60 No. 491, near Calle

57, ☎ 999/928–6759; ✉ Holiday Inn, Av. Colón 498 and Calle 60, ☎ 999/925–6877 Ext. 516; ✉ airport, ☎ 999/946–1323). **Hertz** (✉ Fiesta Americana, ☎ 999/925–7595; ✉ Calle 60 between Calles 55 and 57, ☎ 999/924–2834 or 999/984–0028; ✉ airport, ☎ 999/946–1355). **National** (✉ Fiesta Americana, ☎ 999/925–7524; ✉ airport, ☎ 999/946–1394).

CAR TRAVEL

Driving in Mérida can be frustrating because of the one-way streets (many of which are in effect one-lane because of the parked cars) and because of dense traffic. But having your own wheels is the best way to take excursions from the city. For more relaxed sightseeing, consider hiring a cab for short excursions. Most charge approximately 120 pesos per hour. Route 180, the main road along the Gulf coast from the Texas border, passes through Mérida en route to Cancún. Mexico City lies 1,550 km (961 mi) west, Cancún 320 km (198 mi) due east.

The *autopista* is a four-lane toll highway between Mérida and Cancún. Beginning at the town of Kantuníl, 55 km (34 mi) southeast of Mérida, it runs somewhat parallel to Route 180. The toll road cuts driving time between Mérida and Cancún—around 4½ hours on Route 180—by about an hour and bypasses about four dozen villages. Access to the toll highway is off old Highway 180 and is clearly marked. The highway has exits for Valladolid and Pisté (Chichén Itzá), as well as rest stops and gas stations. Tolls between Mérida and Cancún total about $25.

CONSULATES

➤ CONTACTS: **United Kingdom** (✉ Calle 53 No. 498, at Calle 58, ☎ 999/928–6152). **United States** (✉ Paseo Montejo 453, at Av. Colón, ☎ 999/925–5011; 999/845–4364 after-hours emergencies).

EMERGENCIES

➤ DOCTORS AND HOSPITALS: **Centro Médico de las Américas** (✉ Calle 54 No. 365 between Calle 33-A and Av. Pérez Ponce, ☎ 999/927–3199). **Red Cross Hospital** (✉ Calle 68 No. 533, between Calles 65 and 67, ☎ 999/928–5391).

➤ EMERGENCY SERVICES: **Fire, police, Red Cross,** and **general emergency** (☎ 060).

➤ PHARMACIES: **Farmacia de Ahorros** (San Fernando branch: ✉ Calle 60 at Av. Colón, ☎ 999/925–8126; Central branch: ✉ Calle 60 at Calle 63, ☎ 999/928–5027). **Farmacia Yza** (☎ 999/926–6666 information and delivery).

MAIL AND SHIPPING

Mérida has only one post office, open weekdays 8–3 and Saturday 9–1. However, you can buy postage stamps at handicrafts shops in town. If you must send mail from Mexico, the Mex Post service can speed delivery a bit, even internationally, for a higher fee than regular mail.

➤ POST OFFICE: (✉ Calle 65 at Calle 56, ☎ 999/928–5404 or 999/924–3590).

MONEY MATTERS

Most banks throughout Mérida are open weekdays 9–5. Banamex has its main offices, open weekdays 9–5 and Saturday 9–1:30, in the handsome Casa de Montejo, on the south side of the main square, with branches at the airport and the Fiesta Americana hotel. All have automatic teller machines that can be accessed with Cirrus, Plus, MasterCard, and Visa bank cards. Several other banks can be found on Calle 65, between Calles 62 and 60, and on Paseo Montejo, and most have the same automatic teller service.

CURRENCY EXCHANGE

There are several exchange houses in Mérida, including Casa de Cambio del Sureste, open weekdays 9–5 and Saturday 9–1; Centro Cambriano Canto, open weekdays 9–1 and 4–7; and two on the ground level of the Fiesta Americana hotel, open weekdays 9–5.
➤ EXCHANGE SERVICES: **Centro Cambriano Canto** (✉ Calle 61 No. 468, between Calles 52 and 54, ☎ 999/928–0458).

TAXIS

Taxis charge beach-resort prices, which makes them a little expensive for this region of Mexico. They don't normally cruise the streets for passengers but are available at 13 taxi stands (*sitios*) around the city, or in front of the Hyatt Regency, Holiday Inn, Fiesta Americana, or other major hotels. The minimum fare is $3. Taxis operate around the clock.
➤ TAXI COMPANIES: **Sitio Mejorada** (☎ 999/928–5589). **Sitio Parque de la Madre** (☎ 999/928–5322).

TELEPHONES

Mérida's new area code is 999; the new area code needn't be used unless you are dialing Mérida from outside the city.

Mérida has many Ladatel phone booths: at the airport and bus stations, in the main plaza, at Avenidas Reforma and Colón, and throughout the city. You can make both local and international direct calls at these public phones. Coin-operated phones are history—these take only Ladatel cards, electronic phone cards you can buy at newsstands and pharmacies.

TOURS

Mérida has more than 50 tour operators, who generally go to the same places. What differs is the mode of transportation—and whether or not the vehicle is air-conditioned and insured. Beware the *piratas* (street vendors) who stand outside the offices of reputable tour operators and offer to sell you a cheaper trip. They have been known to take your money and not show up; they also do not carry liability insurance.

A two- to three-hour group tour of the city, including museums, parks, public buildings, and monuments, costs $20 to $55 per person. Or you can pick up an open-air sightseeing bus at Parque de Santa Lucía for $8 (departures are Monday–Saturday at 10, 1, 4, and 7 and Sunday at 10 and 1).

A day trip to Chichén Itzá, with guide, entrance fee, and lunch, costs approximately $53. For about the same price you can see the ruins of Uxmal and Kabah in the Puuc region; for a few more dollars you can add the neighboring sites of Sayil, Labná, and the Loltún Caves. Early afternoon departures to Uxmal allow you to take in the sound-and-light show at the ruins and return by 11 PM, for $56 (including dinner). Another option is a tour of Chichén Itzá followed by a drop-off in Cancún, for about $80. Most tour operators take credit cards.

Diego Nuñez is an outstanding guide who conducts boat tours of Río Lagartos. He charges $42 for a 2½-hour tour, which accommodates five or six people. He usually can be found at the restaurant called Isla Contoy, which he runs.

Ecoturismo Yucatán is recommended for its kayaking trips along the northwest coast, as well as birding and biking adventures. Its specialty is arranging custom trips to suit the needs and abilities of its clients.
➤ TOUR OPERATORS: **American Express** (✉ Calle 56 No. 494, between

Calles 41 and 43, ☎ 999/942–8200 or 999/924–4326, FAX 999/942–8270). **Amigo Travel** (✉ Av. Colón 508-C, Col. García Ginerés, ☎ 999/920–0101 or 999/920–0107). **Carmen Travel Service** (✉ Hotel María del Carmen, Calle 63 No. 550, at Calle 68, ☎ 999/924–1212, FAX 999/924–1288). **Diego Núñez** (c/o Restaurant Isla Contoy, ✉ Calle 19 No. 12, Tizimín, ☎ 998/862–0000). **Ecoturismo Yucatán** (✉ Calle 3 No. 235, between Calles 32-A and 34, Col. Pensiones, ☎ 999/920–2772 or 999/925–2187, FAX 999/925–9047). **Felgueres Tours** (✉ Holiday Inn, Av. Colón 498, at Calle 60, ☎ 999/920–4477 or 999/920–3444, FAX 999/925–6389). **Mayaland Tours** (✉ Calle 57 between Calles 58 and 61, ☎ 999/924–2099 or 800/235–4079; ✉ Fiesta Americana, Calles Colón and 60, ☎ FAX 999/924–6290); request a Mayaland guide rather than a guide subcontractor. **Yucatán Trails** (✉ Calle 62 No. 502, between Calles 57 and 59, ☎ 999/928–2582, FAX 999/924–1928).

VISITOR INFORMATION

Mérida has an information kiosk at the airport that's open daily 8–8. The City Tourist Information Center and the kiosk at Calle 39 and Paso de Montejo are open weekdays 8–2 and 5–7. The state tourist center is open daily 8–8.

➤ MÉRIDA: **City Tourist Information Center** (✉ Calle 59 between Calles 62 and 64, ☎ 999/928–6547). **State Tourist Information Center** (✉ Teatro Peón Contreras, Calle 60 between Calles 57 and 59, ☎ 999/924–9290 or 999/924–9389).

THE STATE OF CAMPECHE

Updated by Jane Onstott

CAMPECHE, THE LEAST VISITED and most underrated corner of the Yucatán, is the perfect place for adventure. The people here are friendly and welcoming, the colonial cities and towns retain an air of innocence, and protected biospheres, farmland, and jungle traverse the remaining expanse. The forts of Campeche City have 300-year-old cannons pointing across the Gulf of Mexico, relics from pirate days that give the city an aura of romance and history. Beyond its walls, the pyramids and ornate temples of ancient Maya kingdoms—some of the most important discoveries in the Maya empire to date—lie waiting in tropical forests. The terrain of the state of Campeche varies, from the northeastern flatlands to the rolling hills of the south. More than 60% of the territory is covered by jungle, which is filled with precious mahogany and cedar. The Gulf Stream keeps temperatures at about 26°C (78°F) year-round; the humid, tropical climate feels hotter, though it is eased by evening breezes.

Campeche City

The city of Campeche has a time-weathered and lovely feel to it—no contrived, ultramodern tourist glitz here, just a friendly city by the sea (population 240,000) that is proud of its heritage and welcomes all to share in it. This good-humored, open-minded attitude is described as *campechano,* an adjective that means "easygoing and cheerful."

Because it has been walled (though not successfully fortified) since 1686, most of the historic downtown is neatly contained in an area measuring just five blocks by nine blocks. The city is easily navigable—on foot, that is. With its narrow cobblestone roads and lack of parking spaces, navigating a car can be a frustrating exercise. On strategic corners surrounding the old city, or Viejo Campeche, stand the seven remaining *baluartes* (bastions) in various stages of disrepair. These were once con-

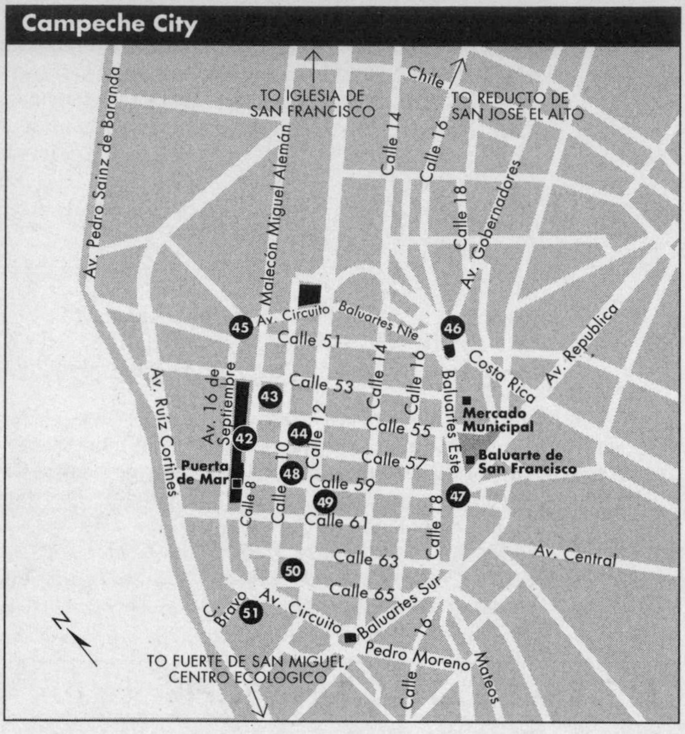

nected by a 3-km (2-mi) wall in a hexagonal fortification that was built to safeguard the city against the pirates who continually ransacked it. Only bits of the wall still stand, and two stone archways—one facing the sea, the other the land—are all that remain of the four gates that once provided the only means of access to Campeche.

A Good Walk

The Ciudad Viejo, the old city center, is the best place to start a walking tour, beginning with the **Baluarte de la Soledad** ㊷, which has a small Maya stelae museum. At the nearby Parque Principal, the city's central plaza, view some of the Yucatán Peninsula's most stately Spanish colonial architecture, including the **Catedral** ㊸ and, on the opposite side of the street, the **Casa Seis** ㊹. On Calle 10 between Calles 51 and 53 is the Mansión Carvajal; **Baluarte de Santiago** ㊺ is about one block to the north. Head south on Calle 51 several blocks to the small, well-fortified **Baluarte de San Pedro** ㊻, at Circuito Baluartes Norte and Avenida Gobernadores. Walk west along Calle 18 to **Puerta de Tierra** ㊼ and the Baluarte San Francisco; then take **Calle 59** ㊽ past the beautiful **Iglesia de San Francisquito** ㊾. Turn down Calle 10 to reach the **Ex-Templo de San José** ㊿ and then the **Iglesia de San Román** (51). Both are considered masterpieces of colonial religious architecture. Proceed north along Calle 8 for a look at the contrasting, modernistic designs of the Congreso del Estado and the Palacio del Gobierno. Finish the walk along the beachfront malecón.

Sights to See

★ ㊷ **Baluarte de la Soledad.** Originally built to protect the Puerta de Mar (sea door), one of the four city gates through which all seafarers were forced to pass, this bastion is on the west side of Parque Principal. Because it stands alone, without any wall to shore it up, it resembles a Roman triumphal arch. The largest of the bastions, this one has comparatively complete parapets and embrasures that offer a sweeping view of the cathedral, municipal buildings, and the 16th- to 19th-century houses along Calle 8. Inside, the **Museo de las Estelas** (Stelae Museum) has artifacts that include a well-preserved sculpture of a man wearing an owl mask, columns from Edzná and Isla Jaina, and at least a dozen well-proportioned Maya stelae from ruins throughout Campeche. ✉ *Calles 8 and 57, centro,* ☎ *no phone.* 🎫 *$2.* ⏲ *Mon. 8–noon, Tues.–Sun. 8–7:30.*

46 **Baluarte de San Pedro.** Built in 1686 to protect the city from land attacks by pirates, this bastion's thick walls, flanked by watchtowers, now house a handicrafts and souvenir shop and a satellite office for the Secretary of Tourism, where you can book an English-speaking tour guide. Many of the tours to ruins such as Calakmul and Edzná leave from this point. ✉ *Av. Gobernadores and Circuito Baluartes, centro,* ☎ *no phone.* 🎫 *Free.* ⏲ *Mon.–Sat. 9–9.*

45 **Baluarte de Santiago.** The last of the bastions to be built (1704) has been transformed into the **X'much Haltún Botanical Gardens.** More than 200 plant species from the region are housed here, including the huge, beautiful *ceiba* tree, which had spiritual importance to the Maya, symbolizing a link between heaven, earth, and the underworld. Although the original bastion was demolished at the turn of the 20th century, and then rebuilt in the 1950s, architecturally the fort looks much the same as the others in Campeche—a stone fortress with thick walls, watchtowers, and gunnery slits. Extensive changes planned for 2002 include adding specimens of medicinal, botanical, and ornamental plants used by the Maya, and videos in English and Spanish explaining their use. ✉ *Calles 8 and 59, Circuito Baluartes, centro,* ☎ *no phone.* 🎫 *Free.* ⏲ *Daily 9–6.*

48 **Calle 59.** On this city street, between Calles 8 and 18, once stood some of Campeche's finest homes, most of them two stories high, with the ground floors serving as warehouses and the upper floors as residences. The richest inhabitants built as close to the sea as possible, in case escape became necessary. (Legend has it that beneath the city a network of tunnels crisscrossed, linking the eight bastions and providing temporary refuge from pirates. The tunnel network has never been found, although rumors of its existence persist.) These days, behind the delicate grillwork and lace curtains, you can glimpse genteel scenes of Campeche life, with faded lithographs on the dun-color walls and plenty of antique furniture and gilded mirrors. To see the oldest houses in Campeche, walk south along Calle 10 past Circuito Baluartes to where it meets the malecón in the San Román neighborhood.

★ 44 **Casa Seis** (House No. 6). One of the first colonial homes built in Campeche, this is now the city's Cultural Center. It has been beautifully restored—the rooms are furnished with original antiques and a few reproductions to create a replica of a typical 19th-century colonial house. The original frescoes bordering the tops of the walls remain, some dating from 1500. The courtyard has Moorish architecture offset by lovely 18th-century stained-glass windows; it's used as an area for exhibits, lectures, and performances. The small restaurant off the original kitchen area serves excellent local specialties daily, from 9 to 2 and 6 to 10. ✉ *Calle 57, across from main plaza, centro,* ☎ *981/816–1782.* 🎫 *Free.* ⏲ *Daily 9–9.*

★ 43 **Catedral de la Inmaculada Concepción** (Cathedral of the Immaculate Conception). It took two centuries (from 1650 to 1850) to finish this grand temple, and as a result, it incorporates both neoclassical and Renaissance elements. The present cathedral occupies the site of Montejo's original church, which was built in 1540 on what is now Calle

55, between Calles 8 and 10. The simple exterior is capped with two bulbous towers rising on each side of the gracefully curved stone entrances, the fluted pilasters echoing those of the towers. Sculptures of saints in niches recall French Gothic cathedrals. The interior is no less impressive, with a single limestone nave, supported by Doric columns set with Corinthian capitals, arching toward the huge octagonal dome above a black-and-white marble floor. The pièce de résistance, however, is the magnificent Holy Sepulchre, carved from ebony and decorated with a multitude of stamped silver angels. ✉ *East side of the Plaza Principal, centro.* ⏲ *Daily 6–noon and 5:30–7.*

50 **Ex-Templo de San José** (Former Church of Saint Joseph). The Jesuits built this fine Baroque structure in 1756, and today it is one of the most beautiful of the city's churches. It has a block-long facade and a portal that is completely covered with blue-and-yellow Talavera tiles and crowned with seven narrow stone finials that resemble both the roof combs on many Maya temples and the combs Spanish women used to wear as part of their elaborate hairdos. The former convent school next door is now the **Instituto Campechano** (Campeche Institute), used for cultural events and art exhibitions. Campeche's first lighthouse, built in 1864, now sits atop the right tower. Although it's currently not open to the public, the guard at the Instituto Campechano will let you in to see the church interior. Cultural events are held here Tuesday evening starting at 7. ✉ *Calle 10 at Calle 65, centro.*

Fuerte de San Miguel (Saint Michael's Fort). The scenic Avenida Ruíz Cortínez near the west end of the city winds its way to a hilltop, where this fort commands one of the grandest views overlooking the city and the Gulf of Mexico. Built between 1686 and 1704, the fort was positioned to bombard enemy ships with its long-range cannons. But as soon as it was completed, pirates stopped attacking the city. Its impressive cannons were fired only once, in 1842, when General Santa Anna used Fuerte de San Miguel to put down a revolt by Yucatecan separatists seeking independence from Mexico. The fort houses the **Museo de la Cultura Maya** (Museum of Mayan Culture), which has some world-class exhibits that include Maya mummies and funeral masks, as well as jewelry and pottery found at various tombs in the Calakmul ruins. Also noteworthy are funeral vessels, masks, many wonderfully expressive figurines from Isla Jaina, stelae and stucco masks from the Río Bec ruins, and an excellent pottery collection. The gift shop sells replicas of artifacts. The "El Guapo" tram ($2.20 round-trip) makes the trip daily at 10 AM, 6 PM, and 7 PM, leaving from the east side of the main plaza, across from Los Portales; visitors are given about 10 minutes to see the fort before the tram returns them to the plaza. ✉ *Av. Francisco Morazán s/n, west of town center, Fuerte de San Miguel,* ☎ *no phone.* 🎫 *$2.50.* ⏲ *Tues.–Sun. 8:30–8.*

49 **Iglesia de San Francisquito (Iglesia de San Roque)** (Church of Little Saint Frances). With its elaborately carved altars, Baroque columns adorned with gold leaf, and carved, wooden pews and créches with statues of San Francisco, this long, narrow church—built as a convent in 1565—adds to historic Calle 59's old-fashioned beauty. The church was originally called Iglesia de San Francisco, but now some know it only as Iglesia de San Roque—a name derived from the neighborhood in which it lies. ✉ *Calle 12 at Calle 59, San Roque.* ⏲ *Daily 8:30–noon and 5–7.*

51 **Iglesia de San Román** (Church of Saint Roman). Just outside the intramural boundary in the barrio of the same name, at Calles 10 and Bravo, San Román, with its bulbous bell tower typical of other Yu-

catán churches, was built to house the *naboríos* (Indians brought by the Spaniards to aid in the conquest and later used as household servants). The barrio, like other neighborhoods, grew up around the church. Built in the early part of the 16th century, the church became central to the lives of the Indians when an ebony image of Christ, the "Black Christ," was brought from Italy in about 1575. The Indians had been skeptical about Christianity, but this Christ figure came to be associated with miracles. The legend goes that a ship that refused to carry the tradesman and his precious statue was wrecked, but the ship that did take him on board reached Campeche in record time. To this day, the Feast of San Román—when the black-wood Christ mounted on a silver filigree cross is carried through the streets as part of a colorful and somber procession—is the biggest celebration of its kind in Campeche. ✉ *Calles 10 y Bravo, San Román.* ⏲ *Daily 7–1 and 3–7.*

★ 47 **Puerta de Tierra** (Land Gate). Old Campeche ends here, at the only one of the four city gates with its basic structure intact. (The walls, arches, and gates were refurbished in 1987.) The stone arch intercepts a stretch of the partially crenulated wall, 26 ft high and 10 ft thick, that once encircled the city. You can walk along the full length of the wall to the **Baluarte San Juan**, where there are some excellent views of both the old and new cities. The staircase leads down to an old well, underground storage area, and dungeon. There is a two-hour light show (🎟 $2.20) offered at Puerta de Tierra in Spanish (with French and English subtitles), Tuesday, Friday, and Saturday at 8:30 PM, daily during spring, summer, and Christmas vacation periods. The spectacle is performed by local musicians and dancers and gives an excellent historical overview of Campeche. ✉ *Calles 18 and 59, centro.* ⏲ *Daily 8–5.*

Reducto de San José el Alto. This lofty redoubt, or stronghold, at the opposite end of town from Fuerte de San Miguel, is home to the **Museo de Armas y Barcos** (Museum of Arms and Boats). The displays focus on 18th-century weapons of siege and defense used in the many wars fought against the pirates. Also look for scale ships-in-a-bottle, manuscripts, and religious art. The view is terrific from the top of the ramparts, which were used to spot invading ships. The "El Guapo" tram ($2.20 round-trip) makes the trip daily at 9 AM, 11 AM, and 5 PM, leaving from the east side of the main plaza, across from Los Portales; visitors are given about 10 minutes to see the museum before the tram returns to the main plaza. ✉ *Av. Escénica s/n, south of downtown, Reducto de San José,* ☎ *no phone.* 🎟 *$2.50.* ⏲ *Tues.–Sun. 8–8.*

Dining and Lodging

$$–$$$ ★ ✕ **La Pigua.** A favorite with local professionals lingering over long lunches, La Pigua is arguably the best seafood restaurant in town, with the most pleasant ambience. The restaurant's two long glass walls form a terrarium of trees and plants. A truly ambitious lunch would start with a seafood cocktail, plate of cold crab claws, or *camarones al cocado* (coconut-encrusted shrimp), followed by fresh local fish in a myriad of presentations, and, for dessert, local peaches drenched in sweet liqueurs. ✉ *Av. Miguel Alemán 179-A, Guadalupe,* ☎ *981/811–3365. MC, V. No breakfast or dinner.*

$–$$$ ★ ✕ **Marganzo.** Traditional Campeche cuisine is served by a traditionally attired waitstaff at this colorful and rustic restaurant a half block south of the plaza. Recommended is the *pompano en escabeche* (grilled fish with chilies and orange juice), as well as the fresh shrimp dishes. ✉ *Calle 8 No. 267, between Calles 57 and 59, centro,* ☎ *981/811–3898. AE, MC, V.*

$–$$ ✕ **Casa Vieja.** Look for the hidden stairway on the east side of the plaza next to the Modatela store, and climb to this fabulous nightspot overlooking Campeche's main plaza. Dinner outside on the balcony is a perfect way to enjoy one of the city's savviest eateries. The Cuban owner has created an international menu of pastas, salads, and regional food, and even the music (occasionally live) is modern and international. Delicious desserts are prepared daily. ✉ *Calle 10 No. 319 (altos), between Calles 57 and 55, centro,* ☎ *981/811–1311. No credit cards. No breakfast or lunch.*

$–$$ ★ ✕ **Chez Fernando.** This café-style eatery may have moved to a new location, but it still offers Mediterranean, Italian, French, and Mexican food, including fresh pastas, salads, fish, chicken, and steak. The lasagna Florentine, pollo Dijon, and fettuccine gambetti are all excellent. The chocolate mousse is the best in the state. ✉ *Av. Resurgimiento s/n, Jardín Coca Cola,* ☎ *981/816–2125. No credit cards. No lunch.*

$$$ ★ **Del Mar Hotel.** Formerly the Ramada Inn, this is the fanciest hotel in town, even if by international standards it is quite average. Rooms are fairly large, with tasteful drapes and floor tiles, rattan furniture, cable TV, and balconies that overlook the pool or the bay across the street. The lobby coffee shop, El Poquito, serves standard but tasty fare, and Lafitte's, the bar-restaurant, offers room service until 2 AM. ✉ *Av. Ruíz Cortínez 51 (on the waterfront), 24000, centro,* ☎ *981/816–2233,* FAX *981/811–4124. 138 rooms, 11 suites. Restaurant, coffee shop, room service, pool, travel services, free parking. AE, MC, V.*

$$ **Hotel América.** A converted colonial home, this hotel has three levels of rooms that open onto large corridors with dramatic black-and-white checked floors, offsetting the white Moorish arches. The rooms all have two double beds, ceiling fans, local television, and bamboo furniture. Rooms facing the street have balconies but are noisier. This is one of the few hotels in the center with parking. ✉ *Calle 10 No. 252, 24000, centro,* ☎ *981/816–4588,* FAX *981/816–4576. 52 rooms. Fans, parking (fee). AE, MC, V.*

$ ★ **Colonial.** This romantic building dates to 1812 but was converted into a hotel in the 1940s, when its colorful tiles were added. All rooms are delightfully different, with cool cotton bedding, good mattresses, tile bathrooms, and window screens. Most rooms still have the original telephones and antique plumbing (which works quite well). Rooms 16, 18, 27, and 28 have wonderful views of the cathedral and city at night. Public areas include two leafy patios, a small sun roof, and a second-floor sitting room. ✉ *Calle 14 No. 122, between Calles 55 and 57, 24000, centro,* ☎ *981/816–2222. 30 rooms. Fans; no air-conditioning in some rooms, no room TVs. No credit cards.*

Nightlife and the Arts

If you're in the mood to dance, try Campeche's discos. **KY8** (✉ Calle 8 between Calles 59 and 61, centro, ☎ no phone), open Friday and Saturday only, plays dance music popular with locals. The high-tech **Jaxx** (✉ Av. Resurgimiento 112, Carretera a Lerma, ☎ 981/818–4555), formerly the Millennium club, offers laser shows and dance music on Friday and Saturday. North of the city, **Plataforma 21** (✉ Privada Loma Azul 2 at Av. López Portillo, ☎ 981/812–6178 or 981/812–7193) is open Wednesday–Saturday. You need to take a taxi to get here.

Outdoor Activities and Sports

Hunting, fishing, and birding are popular throughout the state of Campeche. Contact **Don José Sansores** at the Snook Inn in Champotón (✉ Calle 30 No. 1, centro, ☎ FAX 981/828–0018) to arrange sportfishing or wildlife photo excursions in the Champotón area. **Francisco Javier Hernandez Romero** (✉ La Pigua restaurant, Av. Miguel Alemán 179–

A, centro, ☎ 981/811–3365) can arrange boat or fishing trips to the Peténes Ecological Reserve.

Shopping

Because Campeche is a seaport, ships-in-a-bottle, tacky statues made of seashells, and mother-of-pearl and black coral jewelry are everywhere. Note that buying black coral is environmentally incorrect, since the harvesting of the coral destroys reef that takes thousands of years to grow.

In a lovely old mansion, the government-run **Casa de Artesanía Tukulna** (✉ Calle 10 No. 333, between Calles 59 and 61, centro, ☎ 981/816–9088) sells well-made embroidered dresses, blouses, pillow coverings, regional dress for men and women, hammocks, Campeche's famous Panama hats, posters, books on Campeche ecology in Spanish, jewelry, baskets, and stucco reproductions of Maya motifs. The shop is open Monday–Saturday 9–8 and Sunday 10–2.

From Campeche City to Mérida on Highway 261

This is the longer way to reach the Yucatán capital of Mérida, passing by the Chenes ruins of eastern Campeche. Chenes-style temples are recognized by their elaborate stucco facades decorated with geometric designs, giant masks of jaguars, and birds. Also characteristic of the style are doorways shaped like the open mouth of a monster. It is a scenic route, leading through green hills with tall dark forests and valleys covered by low scrub, cornfields, and citrus orchards.

Edzná

55 km (34 mi) southeast of Campeche City.

The Maya ruin of Edzná deserves more fame than it has. Archaeologists consider it one of the peninsula's most important ruins because of the crucial transitional role it played among several architectural styles. Occupied from around 300 BC to AD 1450, Edzná reached its pinnacle between AD 600 and AD 900. Over the course of several hundred years, Edzná grew from a humble agricultural settlement into a major political-religious center. The city served as a trading center of sorts, situated at a "crossroads" between the cities of the Petén region of Guatemala and the lowlands of northern Yucatán. The region's agricultural products were traded for hand-carved ritual objects and adornments from Guatemala.

Commanding center stage in the **Gran Acrópolis** (Great Acropolis) is the **Pirámide de los Cinco Pisos** (Five-Story Pyramid), which rises 102 ft. The structure consists of five levels, each narrower than the one below it, terminating in a tiny temple crowned by a roof comb. Hieroglyphs were carved into the vertical face of the 15 steps between each level, and numerous stelae depict the opulent attire and adornment of the ruling class—quetzal feathers, jade pectorals, and skirts of jaguar skin. Near the temple's base, the **Templo de la Luna** (Temple of the Moon), **Templo del Sureste** (Southwest Temple), **Templo del Norte** (North Temple), and **Temezcal** (steam bath) surround a small plaza. West of the acropolis, the Puuc-style **Plataforma de las Navajas** (Platform of the Knives) was so-named by a 1970 archaeological exploration that found a number of flint knives inside. In 1992 Campeche archaeologist Antonio Benavides discovered that the Five-Story Pyramid was so constructed that, during certain dates of the year, the setting sun would illuminate the mask of the creator god, Itzamná, inside one of the pyramid's rooms. This happens annually on May 1, 2, and 3, the beginning of the planting season for the Maya—then and now—when they invoke the god to bring rain. It also occurs on August 7, 8, and 9, the days of harvesting and thanking the god for his help. South of the Great Acropolis lies the **Small Acropolis,** whose four buildings each face a cardinal point in the compass. Carved into the **Temple of the Masks (Building 414),** adjacent to the Small Acropolis, are some masks of the sun god with huge protruding eyes, filed teeth, and oversize tongues.

If you're not driving, consider taking one of the inexpensive day trips offered by most travel agencies in Campeche; this is far easier than trying to get to Edzná by municipal buses. **Servicios Turísticos Picazh** (✉ Calle 16 No. 348, between Calles 57 and 59, ☎ 981/816–4426) offers transportation only or guided service to Edzná at reasonable prices. ✉ *Rte. 261 east from Campeche City for 44 km (27 mi) to Cayal, then Rte. 188 southeast for 18 km (11 mi),* ☎ *no phone.* *$3.30, free Sun.* ⏲ *Daily 8–5.*

The State of Campeche A to Z

To research prices, get advice from other travelers, and book travel arrangements, visit www.fodors.com.

AIR TRAVEL

Aeroméxico has two flights daily from Mexico City to Campeche City. Aerocaribe flies to Veracruz, Villahermosa, Mérida, and Cancun.
➤ AIRLINES AND CONTACTS: **Aeroméxico** (☎ 800/021–4000). **Aerocaribe** (☎ 981/816–9074).

BUS TRAVEL

ADO, a first-class line, runs buses from Campeche City to Mérida, Villahermosa, and Ciudad del Carmen almost every hour, with less frequent departures for Cancun, Chetumal, Oaxaca, and other destinations. Adjacent to the ADO station, the second-class bus station has service on Unión de Camioneros to intermediate points throughout the Yucatán Peninsula, as well as less desirable service to Chetumal, Ciudad del Carmen, Escárcega, Mérida, Palenque, Tuxtla Gutiérrez, and Villahermosa. A half block from the ADO station is the office of the Elite Nuevos Horizontes bus company, which offers first-class service at least once a day to Mérida, Ciudad del Carmen, Mexico City, Veracruz, Cancún, Playa del Carmen, Jalapa, and Villahermosa. Try to avoid an extended stopover in Escárcega, along Route 261. Though the government has beefed up security—Escárcega was an unsafe spot for tourists, with bus passengers the targets of robberies and assaults—and things have calmed down quite a bit, it is still not a place to linger, for safety as well as aesthetics.

Within Campeche City, buses run along Avenida Ruíz Cortínez and cost the equivalent of about 30¢.
➤ BUS INFORMATION: **ADO** (✉ Av. Gobernadores 289, at Calle 45, along Rte. 261 to Mérida, ☎ 981/816–3445). **Elite Nuevos Horizontes** (✉ Av. Gobernadores 575, between Calles 15 and 17, ☎ 981/811–0261). **Unión de Camioneros** (✉ Calle Chile, at Av. Gobernadores, ☎ no phone).

CAR RENTAL

Reliable rental agencies are AutoRent—which charges $45 a day including insurance and allows 200 km (120 mi) per day—and the slightly more expensive Maya Rent a Car, which rents small Chevys for $59 a day, including insurance and unlimited mileage.
➤ MAJOR AGENCIES: **AutoRent** (✉ Hotel del Paseo, Calle 8 No. 215, ☎ 981/811–0100). **Maya Rent a Car** (✉ Del Mar Hotel, Av. Ruíz Cortínez, at Calle 59, ☎ 981/816–2233, FAX 981/811–1618).

CAR TRAVEL

Campeche City is about two hours from Mérida along the 160-km (99-mi) *via corta* (short way), Route 180. The alternative route, the 250-km (155-mi) *via larga* (long way), Route 261, takes about three to four hours but passes the major Maya ruins of Uxmal, Kabah, and Sayil. From Chetumal, take Route 186 west to Escárcega, where you pick up Route 261 north; the drive takes about seven hours. Villahermosa is about six hours away if you drive inland via the town of Escárcega but longer if you hug the Gulf and cross the bridge at Ciudad del Carmen.

EMERGENCIES

Las Ángeles Verdes (the Green Angels), an organization funded by the government, patrols the highways on a regular basis and offers emergency roadside assistance. Medical care is available at the government-funded Social Security Clinic or the Hospital General de Campeche.
➤ DOCTORS: **Hospital General de Campeche** (✉ Av. Central at Circuito Baluarte, ☎ 981/816–0920). **Social Security Clinic** (✉ Av. López Mateos and Av. Talamantes, ☎ 981/816–1855 or 981/816–5202).
➤ EMERGENCY SERVICES: **Emergencies** (☎ 060). **Police** (✉ Av. Resurgimiento 77, Col. Lazareto, ☎ 981/816–2309). **Red Cross** (✉ Av. Las Palmas, at Ah-Kim-Pech s/n, Campeche City, ☎ 981/815–2411).
➤ HOSPITALS: **Hospital General** (✉ Av. Central at Circuito Baluartes, ☎ 981/816–0920).
➤ 24-HOUR PHARMACIES: **Clínica Campeche** (✉ Av. Central 65, near the Social Security Clinic, Campeche City, ☎ 981/816–5612).

MAIL AND SHIPPING

The post office (*correos*) in Campeche City is open weekdays 8–8, Saturday 9–1.
➤ SERVICES: **Post office** (✉ Av. 16 de Septiembre, between Calles 53 and 55, ☎ 981/816–2134).

MONEY MATTERS

Campeche City banks will change traveler's checks weekdays 9–4. Two large chains are Banamex and Bancomer.
➤ BANKS: **Banamex** (✉ Calle 53 No. 15, at Calle 10, ☎ 981/816–5251). **Bancomer** (✉ Av. 16 de Septiembre 120, ☎ 981/6–6622).

TAXIS

Taxis can be hailed on the street in Campeche City or from the stands by the bus stations, cathedral, and market. Because of the scarcity of taxis, it's quite common to share them with other people headed in the same direction—rarely will you have a cab to yourself, and drivers will not ask your permission to pick up another fare. To get picked up, just wait for one to slow down near you. A shared cab ride costs under $1. If you have one to yourself, it's $1.50–$3.
➤ TAXI COMPANIES: **Radio Taxis** (☎ 981/816–1113 or 981/816–6666).

TELEPHONES

LONG-DISTANCE CALLS

TELMEX phones that take the electronic Ladatel cards are found throughout the city. Intertel also has long-distance phone and fax service. Another *larga distancia* (long-distance) store can be found at the corner of Calle 10 and Calle 59.
➤ SERVICES: **Intertel** (✉ Calle 57 No. 1, ☎ 981/816–6863, FAX 981/816–7334).

TOURS

Trolley tours of Campeche City leave from the Plaza Principal several times on the half hour in the morning, and generally in the evening at

6 and 8. The one-hour tour costs about $2. You can buy tickets on board the trolley, or ahead of time in the municipal tourist office right next to the cathedral, also on the plaza.

TRAVEL AGENCIES

➤ LOCAL AGENTS: **American Express/VIPs** (✉ Prolongación Calle 59, Edificio Belmar, Depto. 5, ☏ 981/811–1010 or 981/811–1000, FAX 981/816–8333). **Destinos Maya** (✉ Av. Miguel Alemán 162 [altos], Loc. 106, ☏ 981/811–0934; 713/440–0291 in the U.S., FAX 981/811–0934). **Viajes Programados** (✉ Calle 59 between Av. 16 de Septiembre and Av. Ruíz Cortínes, ☏ 981/811–1010).

VISITOR INFORMATION

The Secretaría de Turismo (Tourism Office) is open daily 9–3 and 6–9. The *oficina de turismo de municipio* (municipal tourism office) is open daily 8–2:30 and 4–8. The staff speaks very little English, but you can pick up a map. City trolley tours are booked here.

➤ TOURIST INFORMATION: **Oficina de turismo de municipio** (✉ Calle 55, west of the cathedral, ☏ 981/811–3989 or 981/811–3990). **Secretaría de Turismo** (✉ Av. Ruíz Cortínez s/n, Plaza Moch Couoh, across from Palacio del Gobierno, ☏ 981/816–9229, ☏ FAX 981/816–6767).

15 PORTRAITS OF MEXICO

Life Behind the Headlines

Chronology

Further Reading

LIFE BEHIND THE HEADLINES

MEXICO OFFICIALLY ENTERED the 21st century as a new democracy, finally booting out the party that had lorded over Mexican politics for 71 years. The PRI, or Institutional Revolutionary Party, grew out of the 1910 Mexican Revolution, and kept its hold on power through a combination of political maneuvering, co-optation, and outright electoral fraud. In July 2000, however, Mexican voters—armed with new electoral laws and fed up with official corruption and economic hardship—dethroned the PRI. With 43 percent of the vote (compared with the PRI's 36 percent), the swashbuckling businessman Vicente Fox, from the center-right National Action Party (PAN), became the first opposition president of modern Mexico. The new president stands tall (six-foot-five) and in striking contrast to those who came before him: he talks colloquially instead of using the stiff speech of traditional *políticos,* he dons cowboy boots and a giant silver belt buckle that reads F-O-X, he entered office a divorced man, then made his presidential campaign adviser the First Lady. He pledges to run the country much like he used to run Coca-Cola de México. The changes President Fox promised during his campaign, however, have been excruciatingly slow in coming. Nonetheless, he has taken some important steps toward modernizing the country's economy, battling corruption, and strengthening relations with the United States.

Mexico, for all its ancient history, is a young country. About a third of the population is between 15 and 29 years old. Many of these young people were raised on economic and political turmoil. Mexicans today are tired of seeing themselves as downtrodden. Many prefer to look for inspiration to actress Salma Hayek—a Veracruz native—or to the successful young Harvard Business School entrepreneur Miguel Angel Davila, who started the Cinemex movie chain. Signs of modern Mexico are everywhere: cash machines even in some small towns, *People en Español,* and the proliferation of cell phones. But as ever, modernity does not come all at once. In much of Mexico, a brand new VW Beetle may share the road with a burro. Mexico's struggle with progress is like a Latin dance: two steps forward, one step back.

As the country has opened economically over the past two decades, a slow push for political opening followed. Those growing up now are often dubbed the NAFTA generation, after the free-trade agreement: they are more outward looking, more free-enterprise savvy, and more cynical about the old one-party system. That old system failed them when the bottom fell out of the economy just after the 1994 presidential election, and the memory of what Mexicans simply call *la crisis* is very much alive. People are still shy of bank accounts, credit cards, and home loans, which have been practically nonexistent since the peso crashed. Wages remain below what they were before the crisis, full-time jobs are always in short supply, and the new government has tightened the belt even further. Much of Mexico, however, is booming. Exports—driven by the free-trade agreement with the United States—are thriving. Investors have returned, betting on the perennial comeback. The economy is still vulnerable to global recession, but it is much more stable than it was before la crisis.

Emphasizing his experience as a former CEO of Coca-Cola in Mexico, Fox promised to improve Mexico's economy by running the country more like a business. He even announced he'd improve efficiency by placing the government on a "matrix-style management plan." At press time, however, most of Fox's efforts to create jobs and jump-start the economy had been frustrated by the U.S. economic recession. During 2001, Fox met an unprecedented number of times with his newly elected U.S. counterpart, lobbying both George W. Bush and the U.S. Congress for a major liberalization of immigration laws between the two countries. Mexico's 2,000-mile border with the United States, which serves as a pressure valve during hard times, has always made for tricky politics between the two nations. Although the U.S. Congress at first seemed receptive to the fiery new president's proposals, the Sept. 11, 2001 terrorist attacks effectively ended all talk of loosening immigration laws.

Although change may seem painstakingly slow, it seems clear the 2000 political opening is pervasive. In state and local politics, the PRI has lost considerable ground in recent years. Fox's conservative PAN has won the governorships in nine of Mexico's 31 states, whereas the liberal Revolution Democratic Party (PRD) controls four states and Mexico City. In the small Pacific Coast state of Nayarit, the diametrically opposed PAN and PRD formed an alliance in order to unseat the PRI governor in 1999. Opposition parties have also achieved real power in Congress for the first time in modern Mexican history. Congressmen used to be called *levantadedos* (finger lifters) because all they did was vote the president's bidding. Today, there is competition—even the occasional fistfight—on the House floor.

Democratic reform has also brought an end to the extreme formality of Mexican politics. No one used to look the Mexican president in the eye—such was his power. Today, some political commentators use the informal *tu* (you) when addressing President Fox, a tradition that began with Fox's PRI predecessor, former President Ernesto Zedillo. Fox is pilloried regularly in political cartoons. The press have angered Fox by poking fun at everything from his cowboy boots, his occasional mispronunciation of words, and the lavish charity benefits thrown by First Lady Martha Sahagun.

Much of the credit for Mexico's new democracy is owed to former President Zedillo (1994–2000), who paved the way for his own party's fall from power. Zedillo was often dubbed the "accidental candidate" because he stepped into the presidential race at the last minute after front-runner Luis Donaldo Colosio was assassinated in 1994, a tragedy from which Mexico has never fully recovered. But during his *sexenio* (six-year term), Zedillo proved himself more of an accidental reformer. By not playing the role of ironclad president, he opened the door to the opposition. He expanded political funding for all parties, returned some power and money to the country's 31 states, and relinquished his traditional right to name his successor. This PRI tradition of handpicking the next president, called the *dedazo* (literally "the finger-pointing"), existed from the time the PRI took power in 1929 until 1999, when the party held its first-ever primaries to choose its presidential candidate.

But the PRI's continued power and influence in the new political landscape should not be underestimated. During its seven decades of power, the party showed an uncanny ability to learn from its mistakes and to remake itself to fit the national mood. Many older Mexicans yearn for the security the party once provided. In some states, the PRI seems to be gaining popularity by moving away from its technocrats—the term refers to the cocky young reformers epitomized by former president Carlos Salinas (1988–94). The "Harvard-trained economist," as he was invariably described, brought Mexico free trade, privatization, and all the promises of neoliberalism.

Salinas also brought discredit on his party and his country. Not only did his dream of First World membership die with the peso crisis, but his administration is now considered one of the most corrupt in Mexican history. Salinas lives in self-imposed exile in Dublin, Ireland, but he is still called Mexico's favorite villain. Street vendors sell masks of his face with his inimitable big ears. Bankers who cashed in under Salinas's privatizations have gone on the lam. And Salinas's older brother, Raúl, has been sentenced to 27 years for allegedly masterminding the murder of a former PRI leader. Meanwhile, Swiss investigators seized $114 million from Raúl's Swiss bank accounts in 1998, claiming that the money was proceeds from protecting drug traffickers. Now Mexico is investigating drug ties in the Salinas administration.

There has been a kind of don't-ask-don't-tell attitude about drug-trafficking in Mexico for years. Since Mexico became the main transportation route for Colombian cocaine growers in the 1980s, drug cartels have insinuated themselves into Mexican life, and Mexican cartels are now every bit as powerful as their Colombian counterparts. Drug use is up, and drug culture, touching everything from clothing to music, is spreading. People wink and nudge each other about the gaudy hotels and new shopping complexes, especially along the U.S. border, that they assume were built with drug money. But they shrug it off. And although both the Mexican and U.S. governments are working together to fight traffickers, it may be too little too late. Drug violence hasn't hurt the average citizen enough (except in border cities such as Juárez and Tijuana) for Mexicans to get really angry about it. But increased crime—driven by corruption, and not poverty—has. Most Mexicans' biggest concern, they'll tell you, is public safety. Although crime is still no worse than in many big U.S. cities, poor policing and weak courts make it seem that way.

As in much of Latin America, hard-liners are making a comeback. Some Mexicans are beginning to clamor for the death penalty, something almost unheard of in Catholic countries. The army has been called in to help fight street crime, drugs, and guerillas. And the human-rights situation, especially in states considered guerilla-friendly, is bleak. In December 1997, paramilitary forces massacred 45 peasants thought sympathetic to the Zapatista rebels in Acteal in the southern state of Chiapas. Digna Ochoa, a leading human rights attorney who had defended Zapatista sympathizers and environmentalists, was murdered in 2001 in her Mexico City office; her murderers left a note warning her colleagues to stop their work. Peace talks with the Zapatistas, who sprang up in 1995, are stalled even though the cease-fire holds. The Zapatistas, or EZLN, are only the most publicity-savvy of a few small guerilla groups. They—with their charismatic spokesman Subcomandante Marcos—are still a leftist cause célèbre. At first, Mexicans had a brief romance with the pipe-smoking Marcos because he seemed to speak for the downtrodden. Now, they say they are mostly weary of the violence. President Fox boasted during his campaign that he could solve the Zapatista conflict in 15 minutes. He had not, however, been able to bring the guerrillas to the negotiating table after a year and a half in office (by press time).

One thing is certain, however. The opening represented by the 2000 presidential elections, along with the growth of nonprofit and civic organizations, has had a tremendous impact on Mexican politics, economics, and culture. There is greater debate from the ballot box to the board rooms to the kitchen tables every day. From the scathing editorials in the growing free press to the customer-service hot lines at once indifferent monopolies, Mexico is going through a transition made all the more dramatic in part because it does not always make the nightly news.

— Martha Brandt and Paige Bierma

MEXICO AT A GLANCE

Pre-Columbian Mexico

ca. 50,000 BC Asian nomads cross land bridge over the Bering Strait to North America, gradually migrate south.

ca. 5000–2000 BC Archaic period, which marked the beginnings of agriculture and village life.

ca. 2000–200 BC Formative or pre-Classic period: development of pottery, incipient political structures.

ca. 1500–900 BC The powerful and sophisticated Olmec civilization develops along the Gulf of Mexico in the present-day states of Veracruz and Tabasco. Olmec culture, the "mother culture" of Mexico, flourishes along Gulf coast.

ca. 200 BC–AD 900 Classic period: height of pre-Columbian culture. Three centers at Teotihuacán (near Mexico City), Monte Albán (Oaxaca), and Maya civilization in the Yucatán. Priest-run city-states produce impressive art and architecture.

650–900 Decline of Classic cultures: fall of Teotihuacán ca. 650 leads to competition among other city-states, exacerbated by migrations of northern tribes.

ca. 900–1521 Post-Classic period: rule passes to military; war and war gods gain prominence.

ca. 900–1150 Toltecs, a northern tribe, establish a flourishing culture at their capital of Tula under the legendary monarch Topiltzin-Quetzalcóatl.

ca. 1200 Rise of Mixtec culture at Zapotec sites of Monte Albán and Mitla; notable for production of picture codices, which include historical narratives.

ca. 1000–1450 Maya culture, declining in south, emerges in the Yucatán; under Toltec rule, Chichén Itzá dominates the peninsula.

1111 Aztecs migrate to mainland from island home off the Nayarit coast. They are not welcomed by the peoples of central Mexico.

1150–1350 Following the fall of Tula, first the Chichimecs, then the Tepanecs assert hegemony over central Mexico. The Tepanec tyrant Tezozómoc (1320–1426), like his contemporaries in Renaissance Italy, establishes his power with murder and treachery.

1376 Tezozómoc grants autonomy to the Aztec city of Tenochtitlán, built in the middle of Lake Texcoco.

1420–1500 Aztecs extend their rule to much of central and southern Mexico. A warrior society, they build a great city at Tenochtitlán.

1502 Moctezuma II (1466–1520) assumes throne at the height of Aztec culture and political power.

1517 Spanish expedition under Francisco Hernandez de Córdoba (1475–1526) lands on Yucatán coast.

1519 Hernán Cortés (1485–1547) lands in Cozumel, founds Veracruz, and determines to conquer. Steel weapons, horses, and smallpox, combined with a belief that Cortés was the resurrected Topiltzin-Quetzalcóatl, minimize Aztec resistance. Cortés enters Tenochtitlán and captures Moctezuma.

The Colonial Period

1520–21 Moctezuma is killed; Tenochtitlán falls to Cortés. The last Aztec emperor, Cuauhtémoc, is executed.

1528 Juan de Zumarraga (1468–1548) arrives as bishop of Mexico City, gains title "Protector of the Indians"; conversion to Catholicism begins.

1535 First Spanish viceroy arrives in Mexico.

1537 Pope Paul III issues a bull declaring that native Mexicans are indeed human and not beasts. First printing press arrives in Mexico City.

1546–48 Silver deposits discovered at Zacatecas.

1547 Spanish conquest of Aztec Empire—now known as "New Spain"—completed, at enormous cost to native peoples.

1553 Royal and Pontifical University of Mexico, first university in the New World, opens.

1571 The Spanish Inquisition established in New Spain; it is not abolished until 1820.

1609 Northern capital of New Spain established at Santa Fe (New Mexico).

1651 Birth of Sor (Sister) Juana Inés de la Cruz, greatest poet of colonial Mexico (d. 1695).

1718 Franciscan missionaries settle in Texas, which becomes part of New Spain.

1765 Charles III of Spain (1716–88) sends José de Galvez to tour New Spain and propose reforms.

1769 Franciscan Junípero Serra establishes missions in California, extending Spanish hegemony.

1788 Death of Charles III; his reforms improved administration, but also raised social and political expectations among the colonial population, which were not fulfilled.

1808 Napoléon invades Spain, leaving a power vacuum in New Spain.

The War of Independence

1810 September 16: Father Miguel Hidalgo y Costilla (1753–1811) preaches his *Grito de Dolores,* sparking rebellion.

1811 Hidalgo is captured and executed; leadership of the movement passes to Father José Maria Morelos y Pavón (1765–1815).

1813 Morelos calls a congress at Chilpancingo, which drafts a Declaration of Independence.

1815 Morelos is captured and executed.

The Early National Period

1821 Vicente Guerrero, a rebel leader, and Agustín de Iturbide (1783–1824), a Spanish colonel converted to the rebel cause, rejuvenate the Independence movement. Spain recognizes Mexican independence with the Treaty of Córdoba.

1822 Iturbide is named Emperor of Mexico, which stretches from California through Central America.

1823 After 10 months in office, Emperor Agustín is turned out.

1824 A new constitution creates a federal republic, the Estados Unidos

Mexicanos; modeled on the U.S. Constitution, the Mexican version retains the privileges of the Catholic Church and gives the president extraordinary "emergency" powers.

1829 President Vicente Guerrero abolishes slavery. A Spanish attempt at reconquest is halted by General Antonio López de Santa Anna (1794–1876), already a hero for his role in the overthrow of Emperor Agustín.

1833 Santa Anna is elected president by a huge majority; he holds the office for 11 of its 36 changes of hands by 1855.

1836 Although voted in as a liberal, Santa Anna abolishes the 1824 constitution. Already dismayed at the abolition of slavery, Texas—whose population is largely American—declares its independence. Santa Anna successfully besieges the Texans at the Alamo. But a month later he is captured by Sam Houston following the Battle of San Jacinto. Texas gains its independence as the Lone Star Republic.

1846 The U.S. decision to annex Texas leads to war.

1848 The treaty of Guadalupe Hidalgo reduces Mexico's territory by half, ceding present-day Texas, New Mexico, Arizona, California, Nevada, Utah, and part of Colorado to the United States.

1853 Santa Anna agrees to the Gadsden Purchase, ceding a further 48,000 square km (30,000 square mi) to the United States.

The Reform and French Intervention

1855 The Revolution of Ayutla topples Santa Anna and leads to the period of The Reform.

1857 The liberal Constitution of 1857 disestablishes the Catholic Church, among other measures.

1858–61 The Civil War of the Reform ends in liberal victory. Benito Juárez (1806–72) is elected president. France, Spain, and Britain agree jointly to occupy the customhouse at Veracruz to force payment of Mexico's huge foreign debt.

1862 Spain and Britain withdraw their forces; the French, seeking empire, march inland. On May 5, General Porfirio Díaz repulses the French at Puebla.

1863 Strengthened with reinforcements, the French occupy Mexico City. Napoléon III of France appoints Archduke Ferdinand Maximilian of Austria (1832–67) as Emperor of Mexico.

1864 Maximilian and his empress Charlotte, known as Carlotta, land at Veracruz.

1867 With U.S. assistance, Juárez overthrows Mexico's second empire. Maximilian is executed; Carlotta, pleading his case in France, goes mad.

1872 Juárez dies in office. The Mexico City–Veracruz railway is completed, symbol of the new progressivist mood.

The Porfiriato

1876 Porfirio Díaz (1830–1915) comes to power in the revolution of Tuxtepec; he holds office nearly continuously until 1911. With his advisers, the *cientificos,* he forces modernization and balances the budget for the first time in Mexican history. But the social cost is high.

1886 Birth of Diego Rivera (d. 1957).

1890 José Schneider, who is of German ancestry, founds the Cerveceria Cuauhtémoc, brewer of Carta Blanca.

1900 Jesús, Enrique, and Ricardo Flores Magón publish the anti-Díaz newspaper *La Regeneración.* Suppressed, the brothers move their campaign to the United States, first to San Antonio, then to St. Louis.

1906 The Flores Magón group publish their Liberal Plan, a proposal for reform. Industrial unrest spreads.

The Second Revolution

1907 Birth of Frida Kahlo (d. 1954).

1910 On the centennial of the Revolution, Díaz wins yet another rigged election. Revolt breaks out.

1911 Rebels under Pascual Orozco and Francisco (Pancho) Villa (1878–1923) capture Ciudad Juárez; Díaz resigns. Francisco Madero is elected president; calling for land reform, Emiliano Zapata (1879–1919) rejects the new regime. Violence continues.

1913 Military coup: Madero is deposed and murdered. In one day Mexico has three presidents, the last being General Victoriano Huerta (1854–1916). Civil war rages.

1914 American intervention leads to dictator Huerta's overthrow. Villa and Zapata briefly join forces at the Convention of Aguascalientes, but the revolution goes on. Birth of poet-critic Octavio Paz.

1916 Villa's border raids lead to an American punitive expedition under Pershing. Villa eludes capture.

1917 Under a new constitution, Venuziano Carranza, head of the Constitutionalist Army, is elected president. Zapata continues his rebellion, which is brutally suppressed.

1918 CROM, the national labor union, is founded.

1919 On order of Carranza, Zapata is assassinated.

1920 Carranza is assassinated; Alvaro Obregón (1880–1928), who helped overthrow dictator Huerta in 1914, is elected president, beginning a period of reform and reconstruction. Schools are built and land is redistributed. In the next two decades, revolutionary culture finds expression in the art of Diego Rivera and José Clemente Orozco (1883–1949), the novels of Martin Luis Guzmán and Gregorio Lopez y Fuentes, and the music of Carlos Chavez (1899–1978).

1923 Pancho Villa is assassinated. The United States finally recognizes the Obregón regime.

1926–28 Catholics react to government anticlericalism in the Cristero Rebellion.

1934–40 The presidency of Lázaro Cárdenas (1895–1970) leads to the fullest implementation of revolutionary reforms.

1938 Cárdenas nationalizes the oil companies, removing them from foreign control.

1940 On August 20, exiled former Soviet leader Leon Trotsky murdered in his Mexico City home.

Post-Revolutionary Mexico

1951 Mexico's segment of the Pan-American Highway is completed, confirming the industrial growth and prosperity of post-war

Mexico. Culture is increasingly Americanized; writers such as Octavio Paz and Carlos Fuentes express disillusionment with the post-revolution world.

1968 The Summer Olympics in Mexico City showcase Mexican prosperity, but massive demonstrations indicate underlying social unrest.

1981–82 Recession and a drop in oil prices severely damage Mexico's economy. The peso is devalued.

1985 Thousands die in the Mexico City earthquake.

1988 American-educated economist Carlos Salinas de Gortari is elected president; for the first time since 1940, support for the PRI, the national political party, seems to be slipping.

1993 North American Free Trade Agreement (NAFTA) is signed with United States and Canada.

1994 Uprising by the indigenous peoples of Chiapas, led by the Zapatistas and their charismatic ski-masked leader, Subcomandante Marcos; election reforms promised as a result.

Popular PRI presidential candidate Luis Donaldo Colosio assassinated while campaigning in Tijuana. Ernesto Zedillo, generally thought to be more of a technocrat and "old boy" PRI politician, replaces him and wins the election.

Zedillo, blaming the economic policies of his predecessor, devalues the peso in December.

1995 Recession sets in as a result of the peso devaluation. The former administration is rocked by scandals surrounding the assassinations of Colosio and another high-ranking government official; ex-President Carlos Salinas de Gortari moves to the United States.

1996 Mexico's economy, bolstered by a $28 billion bailout program led by the United States, turns upward, but the recovery is fragile. The opposition National Action Party (PAN), which is committed to conservative economic policies, gains strength. New details of scandals of the former administration continue to emerge.

1997 Mexico's top antidrug official is arrested on bribery charges. Nonetheless, the United States recertifies Mexico as a partner in the war on drugs. The Zedillo administration faces midterm party elections.

1998 Death of Octavio Paz.

1999 Raúl Salinas, brother of the former president Carlos Salinas de Gortari (in exile in Ireland), sentenced for the alleged murder of a PRI leader.

2000 Spurning long-ruling PRI, Mexicans elect opposition candidate Vicente Fox president.

2001 U.S.-Mexico relations take on increased importance as Fox meets repeatedly with George W. Bush to discuss immigration reform and economic programs.

President Fox frees imprisoned Zapatista rebel sympathizers and signs into law a controversial Indian rights bill in hopes of bringing peace to southern Chiapas state; however, peace talks remain stalled.

FURTHER READING

Considering how little most U.S. citizens know about Mexico, there is a world of reading available with which to educate yourself about the country. Fiction written both in and outside of Mexico is a great place to start. The best nonfiction on Mexico blends history, culture, commentary, and travel description. Some may be out of print and available only in libraries.

Pre-Columbian and Colonial Works and Histories

If the pre-Columbian way of thinking has any appeal to you, Dennis Tedlock's superb translation of the Maya creation myth, *Popol Vuh,* is essential reading.

Good general reference works that can deepen your understanding of Mexico's indigenous peoples (and enrich your trips to the many marvelous archaeological sites in Mexico) include *The Conquest of the Yucatán* by celebrated ethnographer and champion of indigenous cultural survival Frans Blom; *A Rain of Darts: The Mexican Aztecs,* by Burr Cartwright Brundage; *In the Land of the Aztec* and *The Maya and Mexico,* by Michael D. Coe; *The Toltec Heritage,* by Nigel Davies; *The Last Lords of Palenque: The Lacandon Mayas of the Mexican Rain Forest,* by Victor Perera and Robert D. Bruce; *The Blood of Kings: Dynasty & Ritual in Maya Art,* by Linda Schele and Mary Ellen Miller; and the colorful *Ancient Mexico,* by Maria Longhena. Mary Miller has also collaborated with Karl Taube to produce a useful glossary-style handbook called *The Gods and Symbols of Ancient Mexico and the Maya.*

A number of fascinating firsthand accounts of the colonial period by some of its most important figures have been translated and published. Of these, the most compelling may be *Letters from Mexico,* by conquistador Hernán Cortés, and *Tears of the Indians,* an unsparing account of Spanish brutality toward the native population by the outspoken Catholic priest Bartolomé de las Casas. Although no 19th-century history of the conquest of Mexico could be reconciled with our contemporary view of the conquistadors' barbarism, Prescott's *The Conquest of Mexico* is no less intriguing for its dated conceits.

For decades, the standard texts written by scholars for popular audiences have been *A History of Mexico,* by Henry B. Parkes; *Many Mexicos,* by Lesley Byrd Simpson; and *A Compact History of Mexico,* an anthology published by the Colegio de México. Michael C. Meyer and William L. Sherman's *The Course of Mexican History* and Eric Wolf's *Sons of the Shaking Earth* are also good survey works.

Contemporary Histories

Most people's understanding of Mexico is such that an absorbing history of the country is the best reading to start with. Enrique Kraus's ambitious *Mexico: Biography of Power* begins its romantic sweep with the Insurgent priests of the early 1800s. Jorge Castañeda's 1995 *The Mexican Shock* is an important study of the financial and political crisis in Mexico and its ramifications for United States–Mexico relations. His previous works, *Utopia Unarmed* and, with American political scientist Robert A. Pastor, *Limits to Friendship: The United States and Mexico,* are also excellent resources.

A number of journalists have made important contributions to the literature on historical and contemporary Mexico. Pulitzer Prize-winning *Miami Herald* Latin American correspondent Andres Oppenheimer's *Bordering on Chaos: Mexico's Roller-Coaster Journey to Prosperity* (1996) chronicles two of the most tumultuous years in recent Mexican history. The book investigates the country's descent into turmoil following the 1994 Zapatista uprising, two shocking 1994 political assassinations, the 1994 elections, and the 1995 peso crisis. William Langewiesche's *Cutting for Sign* examines life along the 1,951-mi-long Mexican–U.S. border; his book *La Capital: The Biography of Mexico City* is also notable. *Los Angeles Times* correspondent Sam Quiñones' *True Tales from Another Mexico: The Lynch Mob, the Popsicle Kings, Chalino, and the Bronx* (2001) recounts engaging stories about everyday Mexican people that manage to reveal the complexities and peculiarities of Mexico's social, economic, and political situations. And Alan Riding's *Distant Neighbors: A Portrait of the Mexicans* and Jonathan Kandell's *La Capital: The Biography of Mexico City* are both notable. Elena Poniatowska, better known in the English-speaking world for her fiction, is one of Mexico's most highly respected journalists. *Massacre in Mexico,* her account of government repression of a demonstration in Mexico City in 1968, is an enlightening and disturbing work. Bill Weinberg writes of oppression and rebellion in one of Mexico's poorest states in *Homage to Chiapas.* Setting Chiapas's indigenous movement of resistance in a broad historical context, it's also an education in Mexican politics, economics, and traditional culture. More academic works on Mexico's modern history include Hector Aguila Camín's *In the Shadow of the Mexican Revolution,* Roderic A. Camp's *Politics in Mexico,* and Merilee Grindle's *Bureaucrats, Politicians and Peasants in Mexico.*

Culture/Ethnography

Excellent ethnographies include Oscar Lewis's classic works on the culture of poverty *The Children of Sanchez* and *Five Families*; *Juan the Chamula,* by Ricardo Pozas, about a small village in Chiapas; *Mexico South: The Isthmus of Tehuantepec,* by Miguel Covarrubias, which discusses Indian life in the early 20th century; Gertrude Blom's *Bearing Witness,* on the Lacandones of Chiapas; and *Maria Sabina: Her Life and Chants,* an autobiography of a shaman in the state of Oaxaca.

Food

Perhaps one of the most unusual and delightful books published on Mexican cookery in recent years is *Recipe of Memory: Five Generations of Mexican Cuisine* (New Press, 1995). Written by Pulitzer Prize–winning food journalist Victor Valle and his wife, Mary Lau Valle, this book reproduces recipes the couple found in an antique chest passed down through the Valle family and in the process weaves an intriguing family and social history. Two lushly photographed cookbooks capturing the culinary history and culture of Mexico are Patricia Quintana's *The Taste of Mexico* (Stewart, Tabori & Chang, 1993) and *Mexico the Beautiful Cookbook* (HarperCollins, 1991). Diane Kennedy's culinary works are also popular, including her classic *The Art of Mexican Cooking* (1989) and her most recent compilation work of more than 300 recipes, *The Essential Cuisines of Mexico* (2000). Marita Adair's *The Hungry Traveler Mexico,* with descriptions of Mexican foods and their origins, goes beyond the typical food list. *Frida'sFiestas: Recipes and Reminiscences of Life with Frida Kahlo* is a cookbook memoir by the artist's stepdaughter, Guadalupe Rivera Marin. It assembles photos, a personal account of important events in Kahlo's life, and recipes for over 100 dishes Kahlo used to serve to family and friends.

Travelogues

Two of the more straightforward accounts from the early 19th century are the letters of Frances Calderón de la Barca (*Life in Mexico*) and John Lloyd Stephens's *Incidents of Travel in Central America, Chiapas and Yucatán.* Foreign journalists have described life in Mexico during and after the revolution: John Reed (*Insurgent Mexico*); John Kenneth Turner (*Barbarous Mexico*); Aldous Huxley (*Beyond the Mexique Bay*); and Graham Greene (*The Lawless Roads,* a superbly written narrative about Tabasco and Chiapas, which served as the basis for *The Power and the Glory*). In much the same vein, but more contemporary, are works by Patrick Marnham (*So Far from God*), about Central America and Mexico, and Hugh Fleetwood, whose *A Dangerous Place* is informative despite its cantankerousness. Alice Adams's 1991 *Mexico: Some Travels and Some Travelers There,* which includes an introduction by Jan Morris, is available in paperback; James A. Michener's 1992 novel, *Mexico,* captures the history of the land and the personality of the people. Probably the finest travelogue-cum-guidebook is Kate Simon's *Mexico: Places and Pleasures. Into a Desert Place* chronicles Graham Mackintosh's trek along the Baja coast. So entranced by San Miguel de Allende that he decided to stay, Tony Cohen recounts a gringo's daily life there in *On Mexican Time.* James O'Reilly and Larry Habegger have edited a diverse collection of articles and essays by contemporary authors in *Travelers' Tales Mexico.*

Contemporary Literature

The late poet-philosopher Octavio Paz was the dean of Mexican intellectuals. His best works are *Labyrinth of Solitude,* a thoughtful, far-reaching dissection of Mexican culture, and the biography of Sor Juana Inés de la Cruz, a 17th-century nun and poet. For more on Sor Juana, including her own writings, see Alan Trueblood's *A Sor Juana Anthology.* Other top authors include Carlos Fuentes (*The Death of Artemio Cruz* and *The Old Gringo* are among his most popular novels), Juan Rulfo (his classic is *Pedro Páramo*), Jorge Ibarguengoitia, Elena Poniatowska (*Dear Diego* and *Fleur de Lis,* among others), Rosario Castellanos (*The Nine Guardians* and *City of Kings*), Elena Garros (*Recollections of Things to Come*), Gregorio López y Fuentes (*El Indio*), Angeles Mastretta (*Mexican Bolero*), and José Emilio Pacheco (*Battles in the Desert and Other Stories*).

Recent biographies of the artist couple Frida Kahlo and Diego Rivera (by Hayden Herrera and Bertram D. Wolfe, respectively) provide glimpses into the Mexican intellectual and political life of the '20s and '30s. Laura Esquivel's novel-cum-cookbook, *Like Water for Chocolate,* captures the passions and palates of Mexico during the revolution. Edited by Juana Ponce de Léon, *Our Word Is Our Weapon* contains writings by the articulate Subcomandante Insurgente Marcos. They range from communiqués made on behalf of the Zapatista movement to Marcos's own stories and poetry.

English Literature

D. H. Lawrence's *The Plumed Serpent* is probably the best-known foreign novel about Mexico, although its noble savage theme is quite offensive. Lawrence recorded his travels in Oaxaca in *Mornings in Mexico.* A far greater piece of literature is Malcolm Lowry's *Under the Volcano.* The mysterious recluse B. Traven, whose fame rests largely on his *Treasure of the Sierra Madre,* wrote brilliantly and passionately about Mexico in *Rebellion of the Hanged* and *The Bridge in the Jungle.* Also noteworthy is John Steinbeck's *The Log from the Sea of Cortez. The Reader's Companion to Mexico,* edited by Alan Ryan, includes material by Langston Hughes, D. H. Lawrence, and Paul Theroux.

INDEX

Icons and Symbols

★ Our special recommendations
✕ Restaurant
Lodging establishment
Lodging establishment whose restaurant warrants a special trip
Archaeological site
Good for kids (rubber duck)
☞ Sends you to another section of the guide for more information
✉ Address
☎ Telephone number
Opening and closing times
Admission prices

Numbers in white and black circles ③ ❸ that appear on the maps, in the margins, and within the tours correspond to one another.

A

B

D

Q

R

NOTES

NOTES

Fodor's Key to the Guides

America's guidebook leader publishes guides for every kind of traveler. Check out our many series and find your perfect match.

Fodor's Gold Guides
America's favorite travel-guide series offers the most detailed insider reviews of hotels, restaurants, and attractions in all price ranges, plus great background information, smart tips, and useful maps.

Fodor's Road Guide USA
Big guides for a big country—the most comprehensive guides to America's roads, packed with places to stay, eat, and play across the U.S.A. Just right for road warriors, family vacationers, and cross-country trekkers.

COMPASS AMERICAN GUIDES
Stunning guides from top local writers and photographers, with gorgeous photos, literary excerpts, and colorful anecdotes. A must-have for culture mavens, history buffs, and new residents.

Fodor's CITYPACKS
Concise city coverage with a foldout map. The right choice for urban travelers who want everything under one cover.

Fodor's EXPLORING GUIDES
Hundreds of color photos bring your destination to life. Lively stories lend insight into the culture, history, and people.

Fodor's POCKET GUIDES
For travelers who need only the essentials. The best of Fodor's in pocket-size packages for just $9.95.

Fodor's To Go
Credit-card–size, magnetized color microguides that fit in the palm of your hand—perfect for "stealth" travelers or as gifts.

Fodor's FLASHMAPS
Every resident's map guide. 60 easy-to-follow maps of public transit, parks, museums, zip codes, and more.

Fodor's CITYGUIDES
Sourcebooks for living in the city: Thousands of in-the-know listings for restaurants, shops, sports, nightlife, and other city resources.

Fodor's AROUND THE CITY WITH KIDS
68 great ideas for family days, recommended by resident parents. Perfect for exploring in your own backyard or on the road.

Fodor's ESCAPES
Fill your trip with once-in-a-lifetime experiences, from ballooning in Chianti to overnighting in the Moroccan desert. These full-color dream books point the way.

Fodor's FYI
Get tips from the pros on planning the perfect trip. Learn how to pack, fly hassle-free, plan a honeymoon or cruise, stay healthy on the road, and travel with your baby.

Fodor's Languages for Travelers
Practice the local language before hitting the road. Available in phrase books, cassette sets, and CD sets.

Karen Brown's Guides
Engaging guides to the most charming inns and B&Bs in the U.S.A. and Europe, with easy-to-follow inn-to-inn itineraries.

***Baedeker's* Guides**
Comprehensive guides, trusted since 1829, packed with A–Z reviews and star ratings.

At bookstores everywhere. www.fodors.com/books

NOTES